Social Work Treatment

Social Work Treatment

Interlocking Theoretical Approaches

Fifth Edition

Edited by

Francis J. Turner

OXFORD

UNIVERSITY PRESS

OXFORD

UNIVERSITY PRESS

Oxford University Press, Inc., publishes works that further
Oxford University's objective of excellence
in research, scholarship, and education.

Oxford   New York
Auckland   Cape Town   Dar es Salaam   Hong Kong   Karachi
Kuala Lumpur   Madrid   Melbourne   Mexico City   Nairobi
New Delhi   Shanghai   Taipei   Toronto

With offices in
Argentina   Austria   Brazil   Chile   Czech Republic   France   Greece
Guatemala   Hungary   Italy   Japan   Poland   Portugal   Singapore
South Korea   Switzerland   Thailand   Turkey   Ukraine   Vietnam

Published by Oxford University Press, Inc.
198 Madison Avenue, New York, New York 10016

www.oup.com

Oxford is a registered trademark of Oxford University Press

Library of Congress Cataloging-in-Publication Data

Social work treatment : interlocking theoretical approaches / edited by
Francis J. Turner.—5th   ed.
     p. cm.
  Includes bibliographical references and index.
  ISBN 978-0-19-539465-8 (hardback)
  1. Social service. I. Turner, Francis J. (Francis Joseph)
  HV37.S579 2011
  361.3—dc22   2010038980

5 7 9 8 6

Printed in the United States of America
on acid-free paper

To Florence Hollis and Helen Harris Perlman,
two mentors who moved us forward down
the path of inquiry.

Preface

I am pleased that another edition of this book has come to fruition. At the time of the last edition in 1996 it appeared that the process of the development of further theories for our profession had probably come to an end. I anticipated that rather than developing new theories the thrust would be towards a further development of existing theories, marked by a melding of theories, as common ground between the various approaches was found.

But this is not what has happened; rather, the contrary has occurred! The emergence of new theories has continued. In this edition, 36 theories are addressed, an addition of 9 from the last edition. In the first edition 14 theories were addressed, in the second 19, in the third 22, and in the fourth 27. At this point there is no indication that this process is slowing down.

Does this trend speak to a growing understanding of the multifaceted expansion of our knowledge of the complexity of the reality we attempt to understand in assisting a diverse spectrum of clients in their bio-psycho-social realities? This in a highly complex world of economic, political and environmental change—often in situations of great oppression. I think it does! We are becoming increasingly aware of the complexity of our clients and of the labyrinthine quality of their lives and of the diverse ways in which problems are addressed and solved.

The foreword to the first edition was written by Dame Eileen Younghusband the then honorary President of International Schools of Social Work. I mention this because much of what she wrote then is still relevant to today's theoretical challenges. Her admonitions to us are still timely. The range of challenges that she set out for us some 35 years ago are the same ones we face today. At that time she urged us to rigorously test our theories and our practice.

She foresaw our contemporary rallying cry to "evidence based" practice of today. She warned of the risks that a lack of discipline might bring by recalling the 19th century "social observer" who noted that men who wore top hats did not die of starvation and a society to distribute top hats was almost launched until wiser heads prevailed.

The need for rigor in testing new theories remains a critical challenge for us. As we move to the second decade of this new century we are expanding not only the range of theories but what was often missed in the past: the competences and tools to test our theories and modify or discard them if they do not stand being challenged. Testing of what we offer as explanations and conclusions of how we help is essential.

Students at all levels have found the book useful, for their overall professional education and practice, as well as in preparation for licensing or certification exams. Researchers have also used it to compare and contrast concepts between and among theories. From a sociopolitical perspective the book has helped to inform others of the differential theoretical bases from which we teach and practice. Finally professors have drawn on the book as a resource in various theory and practice courses.

Over the past few years I have received strong encouragement that the time has come for a new edition, this both to update material to reflect development in theories and to add theories that were not included in the last edition. To all of these colleagues, I am appreciative.

It is my earnest wish that this, the fifth edition of *Social Work Treatment,* will continue to assist our profession wherever it is practiced, in our ongoing commitment to understanding and finding ways to assist individuals, groups, and systems in an effective, ethical, culturally responsive manner.

Using the Theory Chart

This textbook covers the principal theoretical approaches most commonly used by social work practitioners. In this new edition we are pleased to introduce a feature to help students digest this information: an illustrated chart that graphically depicts all 36 theories. In the legend below, readers will find five important variables that we use to describe each theory.

Principal Time Orientation

All theories have to help clients look at past, present, and future issues depending on their life situation, but does the theory have a primary orientation? For example, in Psychoanalysis, clients are asked to reflect upon their life stories principally from the past.

Human Nature

Does the theory view people as being inherently good, flawed, or as some combination of both? A differential view of human nature can affect how clients view the world, and that informs the practitioner on what kind of approach would most suit their value sets. A positive impression of human nature is a critical aspect of Strengths Perspective; Chaos Theory's examination of complexity takes this predictability away.

Importance of Diversity

This variable looks at the level of attention that needs to be given to various aspects of diversity such as race, ethnicity, gender, culture, etc. Another way of looking at this is whether diversity is considered essential in every situation—which is inherent in the General Systems approach—or in only specified cases, as with Crisis Theory. It is understood, of course, that we always have to be sensitive to diversity issues.

Risk

When improperly used, theories can do harm to clients. Indeed, at times an improperly used theory could have life and death implications, when a practitioner fails to understand who the client is, what the client needs and wants, and what the client is capable of doing. Some theories can be effectively learned, understood, and used much more easily than others; some require highly skilled assessment and diagnostic skills, as well as special training and supervision. We want to be sure that students using this book will not oversimplify how to make use of the conceptual bases of these 36 theories in a manner that could be highly inappropriate. Hypnosis is a good example of an approach that requires great caution.

Empirical Strength

The amount of contemporary research-based data that are available for an approach helps to indicate the degree of confidence a trained practitioner would have in employing an established theory such as Cognitive Behavior. "Emerging" is included as a variable value to describe theories that, while they might not have the weight of publications yet, are very much theories that are undergoing active assessment. While historically rooted, Self Efficacy is a topical example of an emerging approach.

Using the chart located on the back of the dust jacket, readers will be able to quickly take in the most important qualities of each approach, and even begin to compare and contrast between them. Each of these approaches should be taken as a potential tool to use in your kit. Please note that each approach is labeled with both the chapter number and theory name for quick reference. For a more complete treatment, refer to the associated chapter. A slightly expanded version of each "theory bubble" is also featured on the first page of each chapter.

Principal Time Orientation

Present Past Future

Human Nature

Good Flawed Neutral

Importance of Diversity

Minimal Moderate Essential

Risk

Minimal Low Moderate

Empirical Strength

Emerging Minimal Strong Extensive

Acknowledgments

On each occasion that I engage in the process of writing the traditional paragraph of acknowledgments I am humbled by an awareness of the many persons who have assisted in the multiple tasks of bringing the book to fruition. I suspect that this network is much broader than one is aware of. Over the years the family has been consistently supportive of my publishing activities, albeit from the distances that their lives have taken them. Joanne has played a much more direct role in recent projects.

I am most pleased that Oxford University Press has recognized the need for a fifth edition, and they have been most helpful throughout the editing process. The support of Maura Roessner at the Press has been especially helpful.

Finding and assembling the group of contributors was a challenging process, and the collegial help of the group as it developed served to make the process manageable and functional. Throughout, my research assistant Carlos Pereira played a major role in planning and implementing the required and constantly changing strategy that eventually brought the book to fruition. To him and to all, I am grateful.

Toronto, February 2010

Contents

Contributors

Dan Andreae, PhD, University of Waterloo and University of Guelph-Humber.

G. Brent Angell, PhD, School of Social Work, University of Windsor.

Suzanne Brown, MSW, Mandel School of Applied Social Sciences, Case Western Reserve University.

Sandy Loucks Campbell, PhD, Department of Social Work, Renison College, University of Waterloo.

Donald E. Carpenter, PhD, Department of Social Work, University of Minnesota-Duluth.

Pranab Chatterjee, PhD, Mandel School of Applied Social Sciences, Case Western Reserve University.

Elaine P. Congress, MA, Graduate School of Social Service, Fordham University.

Au-Deane Shepherd Cowley, PhD, College of Social Work, University of Utah.

Elizabeth Ann Danto, PhD, Human Behavior in the Social Environment at the Hunter College School of Social Work, City University of New York.

David S. Derezotes, PhD, College of Social Work and Peace and Conflict Studies Program, University of Utah.

Katie M. Dunlap, PhD, School of Social Work, University of North Carolina at Chapel Hill.

Kathleen J. Farkas, PhD, Mandel School of Applied Social Sciences, Case Western Reserve University.

Anne E. (Ricky) Fortune, PhD, School of Social Welfare, The University at Albany, State University of New York.

Alex Gitterman, EdD, School of Social Work University of Connecticut.

Eda Goldstein, DSW, Silver School of Social Work New York University.

Gilbert J. Greene, PhD, College of Social Work, Ohio State University.

Rhonda E. Hudson, PhD, School of Social Work, Union University.

Carol Kaplan, PhD, Graduate School of Social Service, Fordham University.

Thomas Keefe, DSW, Department of Social Work, University of Northern Iowa.

Patricia Kelley, PhD, School of Social Work, University of Iowa.

Dennis Kimberley, PhD, MSW, School of Social Work, Memorial University.

Donald Krill, MSW, Graduate School of Social Work, University of Denver.

Judith A. B. Lee, DSW, Dmin, School of Social Work, University of Connecticut.

Mo Yee Lee, PhD, College of Social Work, Ohio State University.

Robert MacFadden, PhD, Factor-Inwentash Faculty of Social Work, University of Toronto.

Anne Marie Mawhiney, PhD, School of Social Work, Laurentian University.

Dennis Miehls, PhD, School for Social Work, Smith College.

Annie E. Wenger-Nabigon, MSW, "Raising the Spirit" Mental Wellness Team, Sudbury, Ontario.

Herb Nabigon, MSW, School of Native Human Services, Laurentian University.

Louise Osmond, MSW, School of Social Work, Memorial University.

Timothy Page, PhD, School of Social Work, Louisiana State University.

Cheryl Regehr, PhD, Factor-Inwentash Faculty of Social Work, University of Toronto.

Susan P. Robbins, PhD, Graduate College of Social Work, University of Houston.

Howard Robinson, DSW, Graduate School of Social Service, Fordham University.

William Rowe, DSW, School of Social Work, University of South Florida.

Dennis Saleebey, DSW, School of Social Welfare, University of Kansas.

Michael L. Shier, Faculty of Social Work, University of Calgary.

Bruce A. Thyer, PhD, MSW, College of Social Work, Florida State University.

Barbara Thomlison, PhD, School of Social Work, Institute for Children and Families at Risk, Florida International University.

Ray J. Thomlison, PhD, School of Social Work, College of Public Health and Social Work, Florida International University.

Elizabeth M. Tracy, PhD, Mandel School of Applied Social Sciences, Case Western Reserve University.

Francis J. Turner, DSW, Faculty of Social Work, Wilfrid Laurier University.

Mary Valentich, PhD, Faculty of Social Work, University of Calgary.

Dan Wulff, PhD, Faculty of Social Work, University of Calgary.

Social Work Treatment

1

Theory and Social Work Treatment

Francis J. Turner

"Everybody has won and all must have prizes."
I am certain that Lewis B. Carroll was not think-
ing of social work and social work theories when
he penned these words from "Alice in Wonderland"
in Oxford many years ago. However, their theme
reflects accurately my viewpoint as I continue to
wrestle with the ever-expanding reality of our pro-
fession's rich theory base. For me each of our sev-
eral theories stands as an important contribution
to the field if it gives us a better way of helping
even one client. And whether or not one or another
of these theories fits our individual view of the
world and how we believe our practice is to be
conducted each deserves a prize and each needs to
be a part of our practice treasury.

The above paragraph is the same one that
began Chapter 1 in the previous edition of this
book. Instead of casting it differently. I decided
to use it just as it was written some 12 years ago.
This is because it reflects for me where we are as
a profession and where I find myself after some
50 years of watching and pondering the highly
diversified development of theories for social
work practice.

In the previous edition I had presumed that
the process of our highly diversified theory base
development would be slowing down and moving
to a greater integration, perhaps even to the prospect of a general theory of social work. Rather,
the reverse is happening. Instead of fewer, better
integrated theories, we have more with less integration. Whether this is an aid to our practice or
not is a moot question and undoubtedly will be
the basis of many academic debates.

The Goals

As in earlier editions, the aim of this book is to provide colleagues with a readily available overview of the principal theories currently extant in social work practice around the world. It seeks to serve a broad spectrum of audiences, including at least the inquiring student, the conscientious practitioner, the searching professor, and the harried administrator.

It aspires to achieve this goal based on the assumption that to fully appreciate and make effective and ethical use of these theories, they must be understood both as individual conceptual constructs and also as bodies of thought that are inter-influencing, interconnecting, and interlocking.

Underlying these objectives is a strongly held assumption that theory and practice, to be effective, must be inexorably interconnected. Even though we argue strongly that theory is critical to practice, it is often difficult to demonstrate that these two factors are closely intertwined in our practice. The challenge now is how to gather and evaluate evidence to demonstrate that we are doing so.

In addressing this challenge we can certainly no longer decry a paucity of theory. We know we have a well-established richness of old and new theories, as well as theories in the making and theories in development. Accompanying this reality is a growing acceptance of interest in, and indeed excitement about, the implications and challenges of this diversity for practice.

This diversity has been and is an exciting step forward. It is a position that strengthens our understanding of the importance of tested ethical theory. Further, it helps us add precision to the growing complexities of our practice by providing us with tools to better understand its scope, dimensions, and effects.

However, to tap the potential of the differential use of specific theories, each of us must be familiar with all of them, whether we subscribe to them or not. This is a strong statement but an important one. Many theories exist in contemporary social work. Others continue to emerge. All have an impact on some components of practice.

We begin from the assumption that what we do in practice is closely connected to what we know. As yet, though, we still have difficulty in

demonstrating the validity of this concept. This does not mean that practitioners function irresponsibly or ineffectively. Our challenge is to build a rigorous conceptual base to make practice even more effective and accountable (Howard, Perron, & Vaughan, 2009).

To take a further step in this direction, an overview of each of the major theories currently affecting practice will be presented by a colleague knowledgeable about it.

What is Theory?

One of the difficulties in clarifying the meaning of the word *theory* in a social-work-practitioner–oriented text stems from the various ways in which this term is used in our day-to-day exchanges. Most of us can recall from our research courses that the more precise meaning of this term describes a model of reality appropriate to a particular discipline and includes terms such as *concepts*, *facts*, *hypotheses*, and *principles*. Such a model helps to understand what is, what is possible, and how to achieve the possible for the discipline (Hearn, 1958; Siporin, 1989; Unrau, Gabor, & Grinnell, 2006).

Clearly this is a highly summarized and stylized description of the involved and ongoing efforts of all disciplines, including our own, to develop bodies of tested facts in a manner that helps us understand and predict some aspect of the reality with which we deal and so provide us with guidelines for effective action. Hence, the development of any theory, especially in all of the helping professions, is an ongoing process. We can never say that a theory is fully developed.

What Constitutes a New Theory?

This, then, raises the complex and oft-debated question of when an evolving body of concepts can be designated as a theory, and who should say that this has occurred. When are we talking about some interesting new ideas from which a theory may or may not develop? When are we talking about a developing theory? When are we talking about a body of thought that is sufficiently well developed to be called a theory? Debates about these questions go on in all professions.

However, since in this volume decisions have been made about which theories to include or to exclude, it is important to set out the criteria that were used for the selection of topics; indeed, it is a question that has been frequently put to me (Goldstein, 1990). More often I have been queried as to why some particular body of thought was omitted or included.

Overall I have leaned to inclusivity rather than exclusivity, aware that some would not view a particular body or bodies of thought to have achieved the rank of theory. But even discussions as to when a particular thought system has achieved the status of theory is a way of advancing the theory. The answer as to when a thought system becomes a theory has been and will continue to be a highly pragmatic practitioner-based one, where there will be and needs to be ongoing differences of viewpoint.

It is my position that we have a new or continuing theory in practice when the following 10 criteria are met:

1. The ideas are new and are not restatements of earlier knowledge using only new terminology.
2. The ideas generated by the system give us new insights into an important aspect of the human condition or a significant group of clients or into some aspect of relevant and environmental or societal systems.
3. There is a beginning body of tested knowledge that supports the new ideas.
4. The system has been found to be demonstrably useful by a significant component of the profession.
5. The interventions emerging from the theory are ethical.
6. The interventions and concepts can be learned, understood, and utilized by a significant component of the profession.
7. The system addresses a broad spectrum of practice and methodologies.
8. The system has some beginning acceptance by the profession.
9. The system is generally within the value system of the profession.
10. The system has not been formally rejected by the profession.

Obviously there is a range of judgments involved in this paradigm. Since theory is an evolving dynamic process, there will probably never be (nor should there be) full consensus on the point of a system's development at which it can be said that it is now a theory. For example, a chapter on meditation included in the second edition of this book raised criticism by some segments of the profession. Now there is a much broader acceptance and understanding of its relevance to social work, and meditation is viewed by many as an important therapeutic resource. Also in the previous edition we included a chapter on hypnotism, which also raised some colleagues' eyebrows but is also now accepted on a much wider base—although some would not consider it a theory.

Theory in Social Work History

As befits any responsible profession, the search for a strong theoretical base has been a continuing theme throughout the history of social work. At least 13 such approaches can be identified in the literature. Their presentation in the list that follows is not to imply that they arose sequentially; rather, many of them continue to be employed simultaneously and independently.

1. The first approach describes what is best described at the pre-theory period in our theoretical development, when our early colleagues were attempting to conceptualize practice, to formulate definitions, and to classify interventive procedures and methods. Examples of these efforts are found in Mary Richmond's *Social Diagnosis* and Gordon Hamilton's classic *Theory and Practice of Social Casework*, a book that for a long time was the basic text for clinicians (Hamilton, 1951; Richmond, 1917). Despite the word *theory* in the title, Hamilton rarely uses the word and makes little reference to the process of theory building and the place of research in the process. Rather than discussing concepts and tested hypotheses she refers to "basic assumptions which cannot be proved" and uses such terms as *axioms, values, attitudes,* and *exhortations.* She speaks authoritatively and comfortably from her knowledge of and competence in practice. Her writing is more prescriptive than theory-based. These early writings are not to be disparaged: they were the essential first steps in bringing together

the practice wisdom of the profession, from which theory evolved.

2. A second approach to theory building can be found reflected in an important but largely unknown book by Frank J. Bruno, *The Theory of Social Work* (Bruno, 1936). In spite of its title, it is not about social work theory. Rather, it is about various theoretical bodies of thought from which social work practice of the time drew upon. The author argues strongly against a search for an uni-theory for the profession, stating that any answer that pretends to explain social events in a single formula must be viewed with strong suspicion (p. 85). In criticizing the search for a single theory, he gives particular attention to the strong influence of Freudian thinking on the practice of the day. He is challenged by the complexity of social work's mandate and reviews the bodies of knowledge from which, in his view, social work needs to draw. Interestingly, in addition to emphasizing the need to understand the physical bases of some of the problems we encounter, he discusses the importance of psychoanalysis, functionalism, gestalt, Adlerian thinking, and Jungian thought, as well as the work of Marx. He quotes Tennyson: "Our little systems have their day: They have their day and cease to be." By this quote he warns of the dangers of faddism but anticipates the reality of a multitheory base for the profession.

3. A third approach to theory building is seen in the rich cluster of writings by social workers, based on a particular body of theory on which some elements of the profession were drawing. These authors build their works on a strong adherence to one or another school of thought and then postulate the implications of the relevant concepts for social work practice. Two influential examples of this are Howard Parad's two books, *Ego Psychology and Dynamic Casework*, and *Ego-Oriented Casework*, co-authored with Roger Miller (Parad, 1958b; Parad & Miller, 1963). These writings do not attempt to develop a new or different theory for social work but rather apply existing theory to practice.

4. A fourth approach to theory building is found in the work of authors who begin to formulate a distinct theory base for social work practice again drawing on their own experience and that of others with whom they have practiced. In most instances, the theory that evolves in these situations is not totally unique but builds on other thought systems, to which is added a conceptual framework that represents a new understanding of practice. Florence Hollis's "Psychosocial System" and Helen Harris Perlman's "Problem Solving Process" are well-known examples (Hollis, 1964; Perlman, 1957; Woods & Hollis, 1990), and Konopka's work represents this approach (Konopka, 1963).

Both Hollis and Konopka state the conceptual base of their approach, while Perlman presents a set of axioms or principles that underlie each of their approaches to a theory of practice. These systems are based on well-thought-out conceptual systems unique to social work and each contains the foundation for the further development of a theory. These were and remain major contributions to our profession, albeit often underestimated in our current commitment to modernity. One consequence of the emergence of different theories for social work was the tendency to take an either/or position: if you were drawn to one system, you were expected to reject the other. This of course was the situation during the diagnostic/functional schism of an earlier day, and the division was similar, although not as intense, between the positions of Hollis and Perlman.

5. A fifth approach to theory building is seen in the early custom of dividing practice and the emerging theories of practice along method lines. This was done initially with casework and group work, but later family therapy was also separated out. The historical reasons for this separation are complex and related to the way in which these different methodologies emerged. The tendency to these method-oriented theories helped foster the perception that our practice needed a pluralistic theoretical base, one for each method. It has only been in the past four or five decades that attention has been drawn to theoretical commonalities across methods and hence the possibility and indeed the necessity of multimethod and multi-theory practitioners.

6. Prior to the 1950s the majority of clinical theoretical writing was based on some form of psychodynamic thinking or small group theory. In the early 1960s we began to see a growing acceptance of theoretical plurality, which led to a series of important social work writings based on a range of other theoretical systems. Hence we find Perlman writing a book from a role theory perspective, Parad editing a work on crisis theory, Harold Werner publishing a book on cognitive theory, and Derek Jehu and Edwin Thomas each producing major writings from a learning theory and behavioral approach (Jehu, 1967; Parad, 1958a; Perlman, 1968; Thomas, 1967; Werner, 1965). Similarly, there were writings related to systems theory by Werner Lutz and Gordon Hearn, among others (Hearn, 1958; Lutz, 1956). Later, we saw a number of important writings from both feminist and constructive perspectives. The exciting aspect of the pluralistic development is the awareness and acceptance that there are many sources from which theory develops.

7. The next identifiable approach to theory building is seen in the search for interconnectedness between systems, both old and new. As practice began to develop a diverse theoretical base, the question arose as to how these various approaches did or did not fit together. The concept of separate methodologies remained the general model of practice, so these comparisons of theories for the most part were made along methodological lines. In this way Joan Stein and her associates compared the various emerging theories related to family therapy (Stein, 1969). Roberts and Nee and later Strean wrote about diverse theories of casework (Roberts & Nee, 1970; Strean, 1971). Hollis and later Hollis and Woods showed how some of these theories could be incorporated into the psychosocial approach (Hollis & Woods, 1981, Strean, 1971; Woods & Hollis, 1990). In the group treatment field we find Schwartz and Zalba doing a similar study of the differential theoretical bases of group practice (Schwartz & Zalba, 1971). Although there was a strong hope being expressed that by comparing the various systems a unified theory of social would emerge, this did not take place.

8. The next observable component of theory development flowed from the growing acceptance of, and enthusiasm for, the potential of plurality. Once some segments of the profession had broken away from the tradition of staying too close to one or two theories, there was a growing interest in searching widely for new ideas and less concern about their interconnections. In this way we moved rapidly from the 6 systems described in the Roberts and Nee book to the 14 addressed in the first edition of this work, to 19 in the second edition, 22 in the third, 27 in the fourth, and 36 in this, the fifth edition (Roberts & Nee, 1970, Turner, 1976; Turner, 1979; Turner, 1986b;).

Under this umbrella colleagues began to look at such things as Transactional Analysis and gestalt, to wonder about the potential utility of other systems such as meditation and existentialism, and to develop systems of our own, such as Task-Centered and the Life Model. This trend was declared by some to be a confounding outcome of faddism, while others saw it as a mature and commendable way of better responding to the diversity of client needs.

9. With the rapid growth in the number of theories and the return to a close identification with the interests and disciplines of the social sciences, more attention was being given to the process of formal theory building and the nature and characteristics of theory (Merton, 1957). Examples include the work of Lutz, Hearn, and Paley (Hearn, 1958; Lutz, 1956; Paley, 1987). Much of this early work was influenced by systems theory and the wish to understand how theoretical systems and practice systems interfaced (Nugent, 1987) Although this process did not demonstrably lead to the enrichment of practice, it did lead us to reexamine the concept of theory and to be more precise in the use of theoretical terminology.

10. A further theory-building activity is related to the very essence of theory—that is, the testing of concepts through research. As theory almost became equivalent to dogma for many colleagues, who then followed

a particular theory unquestioningly, and as the risks of this trend were recognized, there developed increasing interest in, and commitment to, empirical testing of various components of the theories being practiced. That is a growing demand for tested theory.

This is an area that is never finished and must continue on an ongoing basis. In this mode various concepts from different theories are operationally defined and tested through the formulation of hypotheses and the publication of the resultant data. The amount of practice-based research has expanded greatly. This is exemplified in the richness of material published in our many excellent refereed journals.

11. A contemporary approach to the plurality of practice theories that is frequently employed and that has much potential to strengthen practice theory is eclecticism (Koglevzon & Maykrznz, 1982). In this approach, concepts are adopted from various theories and an amalgam is formed, which is used as the basis of practice.

There appear to be two forms of eclecticism. In the first, choices are made based on the preferences of the particular practitioner or the nature of the practice setting. This strategy appears to be strongly influenced by the person's own value base and his or her perception of practice, rather than on an analysis of all theories from which a conceptual framework might be developed (Latting, 1990).

A second form of eclecticism is best explicated by Dr. Joel Fischer, who postulates that only those elements of a theory that have been demonstrated to be effective should be used (Fischer, 1978). Our knowledge base thus should be built on the findings of research, not on preference—that is, on evidence. This approach fosters a process in which theory is developed in an ongoing selective and incremental manner.

12. A more recent approach to theory building is reflected in the increasing number of articles in the professional literature that address highly discrete components of selected theories. Rather than attempting to address a

system in its entirety and its application in practice, these authors are more targeted. In some instances, they are looking at a specific application of a theory, such as the use of crisis theory in a particular practice situation such as physical assault. In other instances, they are concerned with practice applications of a discrete concept, such as the concept of homeostasis in work with couples (Turner, 1986a). Both of these strategies reflect the growing appreciation that progress in the more precise use of theoretical concepts will take place in a step-by-step manner rather than efforts to test an entire theory or a major component of it.

13. A more contemporary approach to theory building is reflected in the strong interest in evidence-based practice. It is an approach that stresses that we need to build practice on known outcomes of practice, which when positive gives us the basis for theory development. In many ways this approach reflects the admonishment of Leonardo da Vinci to his colleagues: "When it is impossible to make a good theory it is better to get along without one" (Santilanna, 1956). What this growing emphasis does not always demand is that some aspect of theory is being tested; it does demand that what we do in particular practice situations results in positive outcomes that can be replicated in similar situations. It is these kinds of studies, of course, which lead us to seek explanations of outcomes, and this is the way in which theory is advanced.

There are undoubtedly other approaches to theory building that can be identified in our history. This range has been presented not to be exhaustive or definitive but to help us understand that our commitment to theory has always been viewed as an essential commitment of our profession, a commitment that has been multifaceted in its fulfillment.

These various approaches demonstrate that we have always been committed to the search for a strong theoretical base. Just as our theoretical base is diverse, so too are the various strategies we have used to foster our commitment. But always these seekers emanate from the work of concerned colleagues. Hence, all theories and all responsible approaches to theory building should be seen as being important in themselves and as having differential value only in their proper or improper use. Sigmund Freud underscored this position in speaking of the validity of a pluralistic theory base: "There are many ways and means of practicing psychotherapy. All are good that lead to health" (Freud, 1905).

As we continue our search for strong and selectively effective theories to cope with the demands of our complex practice, the long-standing academic/clinical and theoretical/practical dichotomies will, we hope, continue to blur. We are beginning to better understand the close connection between practice and theory building. We understand that the process of assessment and diagnosis is very much akin to the process of hypothesis formulation and testing, which is the heart of theory building. Harold Lewis (1982) described this well some 30 years ago:

Every practitioner should know that her observations are not simply casual scannings; they involve a conceptually ordered search for evidence. Her eyes and ears are trained to help her select evidence related to some framework that will permit inferences to be drawn, order revealed, meanings surmised, and an exploratory guide for action planned. Their organizing frameworks are theories. (p. 6).

Theory in Social Work Practice

The principal thesis of this work is that responsible, ethical practice needs to be built on strong theory, based on relevant evidence. But what are the functions of theory for the practitioner? Why is it so important?

Clearly the most important function of theory is its ability to explain and hence predict phenomena. The answers to two questions are sought in practice: What will happen if I do nothing in this situation? And what will happen if I respond in a particular way or ways? Theory helps us to recognize patterns, relationships, and significant variables that assist in bringing order to the complexities of contemporary practice.

In consciously formulating a treatment plan based on assessment and diagnosis, a practitioner is involved in either a theory-building or a theory-testing activity. A treatment plan presumes sufficient understanding of a situation

that actions can be taken with predictable outcomes. Without such an understanding, practice remains in the realm of guesswork and impressionistic response and artful use of techniques.

Theory aids in anticipating outcomes and speculating about unanticipated relationships between variables—that is, theory helps us to recognize, understand, and explain new situations. If we understand sufficiently well the phenomena with which we are dealing and their interrelationships, we should have the conceptual tools for dealing with unexpected or unanticipated behaviors. To the extent that our theory is sound, we should meet with fewer surprises in our practice and be better able to solve problems.

Theory also helps us carry knowledge from one situation to the next by helping us recognize what is similar or different in our ongoing practice experiences. Rather than distracting us from our commitment to individuality or self-determination, theory can enhance these by helping us see not only how the client or situation resembles other clients and situations, but how each is unique.

Theory helps us to expand our horizons as we follow the implications of some observation that does not appear to fit what we know or have experienced before. In these situations we are led to speculate about other ways of viewing reality. This, in turn, can lead to an enriched perspective on clients and situations.

A sound and logically consistent theoretical structure and mindset permit us to explain our activity to others. This allows us to transfer our knowledge and skills in a testable and demonstrable way and to have our activities scrutinized and evaluated by others. If we have sound theories, others can profit by our experience by applying those theories on the basis of how action was being taken in particular situations.

Further, theory helps us to recognize when we encounter new situations that indicate gaps in our knowledge. For example, when the application of a theoretical concept does not have the expected outcome, we have either misunderstood or our knowledge is not sufficient to deal with the situation at hand. After meeting with a difficult or new practice situation, practitioners frequently blame themselves, assuming that if they had been more aware they would have coped more effectively. In fact, there may have been no available theoretical construct to explain the presenting phenomenon. It is just as important to know what is not known as it is to know what is.

Theory also provides the practitioner with assurance. We have all experienced the awesome responsibility of practice and endured the loneliness that it can bring. Theory will never completely dispel these feelings. However, a firm theoretical orientation gives us a base to organize what we do not know. A set of anchoring concepts can help us avoid the aimless wandering with the client that can occur when we do not know what we are doing (Pilalls, 1986).

Theory brings order to our practice by helping to put into perspective the mass of facts, impressions, and suppositions developed in the process of our therapeutic contact with an individual, dyad, family, group, or community. A cynic might even suggest that theory, whether sound or not, gives a sense of security to the therapist, thus increasing effectiveness, even when the theory has little to do with the treatment employed.

In addition, knowledge of one theory permits us to assess other theories. If we are clear about which of our concepts are empirically verifiable and connected, we are in a much better position to evaluate emerging ideas in light of what we know. There can often be several theoretical explanations for a single phenomenon. Determining which of these is most useful requires constant testing and seeking for evidence. Theoretical explanations different from our own help us to better understand and modify our own theoretical stance.

Finally, a strong and inquiring theoretical mindset helps us look at new ideas and emerging developments and to find a middle way between the dismissiveness of the cynic who has "heard it all before" and the overeagerness of those who leap on every bandwagon that passes by.

Other Roles of Theory

It is also important to understand the role that theory plays in the dynamics, sociology, and politics of our profession and its interaction with other professions.

The increased interest in theory has strengthened our commitment to research, which in turn has raised our profile with scholars in other disciplines. Implied in the very nature of theory is an essential commitment to testing, experimentation, and conceptual and empirical development. Following the era in which theory was treated by many almost as dogma, the essential role of research came to be accepted. Thus, in addition to the great expansion of research activities, we have seen the establishment of research centers; the rapid expansion of quantity and quality of professional journals, whose primary interest is the dissemination of research; the strengthening of the research component of the curricula; and an enriched perspective of the essential interface between research, practice and theory. These have greatly enhanced the status of and respect for the profession on many fronts.

Thus, there is now within the profession a very strong commitment to the essential place of theory. However, this commitment is far from total: there is still a strong perception among many that the development of theory is something to be carried out by academics and graduate students, and by professional researchers at research centers. We still do not seem to have built a sufficiently strong practice–theory link, and hence there is still an unfortunate chasm between these two essential components of any professional endeavor.

Another interesting phenomenon related to our plurality of theories is that each is recognized and prized to different degrees at different times in different parts of the profession and at different stages in the lives of colleagues. Since theories are strongly value-driven, they are respected, rejected, or ignored, depending on the values of the practitioner.

As the status of a theory increases it acquires a corresponding power base, which influences position and recognition. Political correctness influences the popularity of theories to ebb and flow, and can in turn have an impact on what knowledge is available to clients. This is a serious problem with serious ethical implications.

Changing preferences or viewed importance for particular theories also create challenges in the design and implementation of curricula at schools and faculties of social work at all levels. In the face of an expanded diversity of theories, the challenges of what to teach and how to teach theory are numerous. The pedagogical challenge becomes even more complex given the changing status of different theories. It is not being suggested that every theory needs to be taught in the same manner and afforded the same emphasis, but students do need to be taught to respect each theory and to be given the tools with which to learn and incorporate each into their theoretical base of available therapeutic resources.

But Can Theory also be Harmful?

There are several ways in which theory can be a detriment to practice and harmful to clients. This can happen when we define clients' help based only on the dictates of a particular theory rather than responding on a personalized, ad hoc basis. When theory becomes overly cerebral and mechanistic, stressing labeling and classifying rather than the individuality of each client and situation, it can become an end in itself. Then the ability to predict, explain, and even control can become the goal, rather than the optimizing of human potential and the facilitating of growth. Here the client can become an interesting subject for study rather than a fellow human coexisting with us on life's journey.

Theory can also become self-fulfilling, especially if we become overly attached to a particular system and begin to see the world only from our chosen theoretical perspective. Here we tend to interpret all phenomena in a way that fits that conceptual framework. This can be very limiting, preventing us from taking into account alternative and perhaps more accurate explanations of situations.

Similarly, theory that takes the form of dogma ceases to be living, self-examining, and dynamic. This often happens when a particular system is identified with a charismatic founder, group, movement, or ideology. When this occurs, the theory tends to be used to close out other explanations and to dismiss those who offer them as quasi-heretics.

At times theory can acquire a form of political power. When a particular theory gains power or ascendancy within professional circles, agencies or practitioners can be granted or deprived of status depending on their adherence to the "official truth." This can have a powerful influence on what kinds of client goals are served,

what services are offered, what problems are addressed, and who is considered competent to act in the prescribed therapeutic role.

Finally, some suggest that the search for a theory for social work is a futile one and should be eschewed. They argue that the subjects of our professional practice are so complex, individualized, and mobile that they cannot be understood or influenced in terms of any theory, and efforts to do so only diminish the uniqueness of the individual client. Clearly we will never fully understand everything about our profession's areas of interest, but the history of humankind has made it abundantly clear that the quest to do so can only help us to become more effective. Dr. Bruce Thyer discusses this question of the potential negative effects of theory in a thorough manner in a recent paper (Thyer, 2008). Because theories can be harmful, it doesn't follow that we should ignore them, only that we need to be very cautious in our use of them. We cannot live without them as a responsible profession.

The Classification of Theory

One of the challenges presented by each edition of this book is how to order the spectrum of theories addressed. Since a major premise of the work is that these theories need to both stand alone as well as interlock and inter-influence each other, it is important to consider different organizational methods of classification and their implications.

For example, theories could be ranged along various continua, from the most abstract to the most concrete; from the most particular to the most general; or from the most individualistic to the most socially oriented. It is important to note that no one of these is better or more correct than any of the others. Each is useful and could lead to a better understanding of the various theories, how they interface, or what they add to each other and to our pool of knowledge. In this era of evidence-based practice, another approach would be to order the theories on the basis of their research strength.

Theories could also be organized into clusters, such as foundation theories that provide a general orientation and practice theories that are more action-specific. Or they could be clustered into three groups: highly general, midrange-specific, and highly focused. Siporin's suggestion is that theories could be clustered according to those that are assessment-oriented by nature and those that are intervention-oriented. In his view, there are theories that help us understand phenomena but do not provide much help in knowing what to do, while others are more action-oriented than conceptual (Siporin, 1975).

Golan calls some theories "transitional" and suggests that this is a basis for clustering theories into those that can be connected with other theories and those that can stand alone (Turner, 1986b). Another way of clustering is according to value base. For example, some theories are more individualistically oriented, some more group-oriented, some more family-oriented, and some more community-focused.

Many other approaches to clustering could be considered as well (Fischer, 1971). Each in its own way will and does help us to understand theories in themselves as well as how theories are interconnected and interlocking, and like the theories, contributes to the ongoing development of our body of knowledge.

One thing we noticed in preparing this volume was that authors devoted more time than in earlier editions to commenting on other theories with which the one about which they were writing connected. This could lead to a further way of classifying chapters, by focusing in on clusters of theories that have some similarity with each other.

Undoubtedly there are many other ways of classifying theory. Each comes from a different perspective. But to make this book generally useful, any effort at classifying has been avoided. We choose to let each person use it as he or she will. Thus, as in earlier editions, an alphabetical format has been chosen. (This too probably has a bias that holds they are all equal.)

Summary

Certainly from our earliest days we have been cognizant of the nature and critical importance of tested theory as the hallmark of all professions. As our understanding of the requisite of theory has expanded, so too has our awareness that the term *theory* is a complex one, dynamic and changing in nature, that not only gives us a basis for ethical and evidence-based practice but also plays a spectrum of roles in the politics and sociology of all professions. In particular we have learned that our profession has no unitary theory but a plurality of theories, each of which changes and activates and inter-influences each other. To best understand this interlocking factor it is important that we seek to understand the specificity of each, aware that the concept of a "theory for social work" is a naïve one and a sign of our maturity is our growing comfort with the discomfort of plurality.

In the final chapter, we will discuss some of the interlocking perspectives of the range of approaches, discuss some of our research challenges, and speculate on possible further developments for their building in the decade ahead.

References

Bloom, M., Fisher, J., & Orme, J. G. (2006). *Evaluating practice: Guidelines for the accountable professional*, 5th ed. Boston: Allyn & Bacon.

Borden, W. (2009). Comparative theories. In A. J. Roberts (Ed.), *Social worker's desk reference* (pp. 359–364). New York: Oxford Press.

Bruno, F. J. (1936). *The theory of social work*. New York: D. C. Heath and Co.

Carew, R. (1979). The place of knowledge in social work activity. *British Journal of Social Work, 9*, 349–364.

Fischer, J. (1971). A framework for the analysis and comparison of clinical theories of induced change. *Social Service Review, 45*(4), 440–454.

Fischer, J. (1978). *Effective casework practice: An eclectic approach*. New York: McGraw-Hill.

Freud, S. (1905). *On psychotherapy: The standard edition of the complete psychological works of Sigmund Freud*, Vol VII. Chapter I.

Gambrill, E. (2000). Evidence-based versus authority-based social work practice. *Families in Society: The Journal of Contemporary Human Services, 80*(4), 341–350.

Gibbs, L. (2009). How social workers can do more good than harm. In A. J. Roberts (Ed.), *Social worker's desk reference* (pp. 168–174). New York: Oxford Press.

Goldstein, H (1990). The knowledge base of social work practice: theory, wisdom, analogue, craft? *Families in Society, 71*(1), 32–43.

Hamilton, G. (1951). *Theory and practice of social casework* (2nd ed.). New York: Columbia University Press.

Hearn, G. (1958). *Theory building in social work.* Toronto: University of Toronto Press.

Hollis, F. (1964). *Casework: a psychosocial therapy.* New York: Random House.

Hollis, F. (1972). *Casework: a psychosocial therapy* (2nd ed.). New York: Random House.

Hollis, F., & Woods, M. (1981). *Casework: a psychosocial therapy* (3rd ed.). New York: Random House.

Howard, M. O., Perron, B. E., & Vaughan, M. G. (2009). In A. J. Roberts (Ed.), *Social worker's desk reference* (pp. 1157–1162). New York: Oxford Press.

Jehu, D. (1967). *Learning theory and social work.* London: Routledge.

Koglevzon, M., & Maykrznz, J. (1982). Theoretical orientation and clinical practice: uniformity versus eclecticism. *Social Service Review,* 56(1), 120–129.

Konopka, G. (1963). *Social group work: a helping process.* Englewood Cliffs, NJ: Prentice Hall.

Latting, J. K. (1990). Identifying the "isms": enabling social work students to confront their biases. *Journal of Social Work Education,* 26(1), 36–44.

Lewis, H. (1982). *The intellectual base of social work practice.* New York: Haworth Press.

Lutz, W. (1956). *Concepts and principles underlying casework practice.* Washington DC: National Association of Social Workers.

Merton, R. K. (1957). *Social theory and social structure.* Glencoe, IL: Free Press.

Nugent, W. R. (1987). Use and evaluation of theories. *Social Work Research and Abstracts,* 23(1), 14–19.

Paley, J. (1987). Social work and the sociology of knowledge. *British Journal of Social Work,* 17(2), 169–186.

Parad, H. J. (ed.) (1958a). *Crisis intervention: selected readings.* New York: Family Service Association of America.

Parad, H. J. (ed.) (1958b). *Ego psychology and dynamic casework.* New York: Family Service Association of America.

Parad, H. J., & Miller, R. (eds.). (1963). *Ego-oriented casework: problems and perspectives.* New York: Family Service Association of America.

Perlman, H. H. (1957). *Social casework: a problem solving process.* Chicago: University of Chicago Press.

Perlman, H. H. (1968). *Persona: social role and responsibility.* Chicago: University of Chicago Press.

Pilalls, J. (1986). The integration of theory and function: a reexamination of a paradoxical expectation. *British Journal of Social Work,* 16(1), 79–96.

Reid, W. J., & Hanrahn, P. (1982). Recent evaluations of social work: grounds for optimism. *Social Work,* 27(4), 328–340.

Richmond, M. (1917). *Social diagnosis.* New York: Russell Sage Foundation.

Ripple, L., Alexander, E., & Polemis, B. (1964). *Motivation, capacity and opportunity.* Social Service Monographs. Chicago: University of Chicago Press.

Roberts, R. W., & Nee, R. H. (1970). *Theories of social casework.* Chicago: University of Chicago Press.

Rubin, A. (1985). Practice effectiveness: more grounds for optimism. *Social Work,* 30, 469–476.

Santilanna, G. de (1956). *The physics of De Vinci.* In Sabastiano Tempanaro. New York: Reynal & Co.

Schwartz, W., & Zalba, S. R. (1971). *The practice of group work.* New York: Columbia University Press.

Siporin, M. (1975). *Introduction to social work practice.* New York: Macmillan.

Siporin, M. (1979). Practice theory for clinical social work. *Clinical Social Work Journal,* 7(1), 75–89.

Siporin, M. (1989). Metamodels, models and basics: an essay review. *Social Service Review,* 63(3), 474–480.

Specht, H. (1990). Social work and the popular psychotherapies. *Social Service Review,* 64(3), 345–357.

Stein, J. W. (1969). *The family as a unit of study and treatment.* Seattle: Regional Rehabilitation Research Institute, University of Washington School of Social Work.

Strean, H. F. (ed.). (1971). *Social casework: theories in action.* Metuchen, NJ: Scarecrow Press.

Stricker, G., & Gold, J. Integrative approaches to psychotherapy. In A. Gurman & S. Messer (Eds.), *Essential psychotherapies* (pp. 317–349). New York: Guilford.

Thomas, E. J. (1967). *Behavioral science for social workers.* New York: Free Press.

Thomlison, R. J. (1967). Something works: evidence from practice effectiveness studies. *Social Work,* 29 (Jan.-Feb), 51–56.

Thyer, B. A. (2008). The potentially harmful effects of theory in social work. In: B. A. Thyer (Ed.), Comprehensive handbook of social work and social welfare; Volume II: Human behavior in the social environment (pp. 519–541). New York: Wiley.

Thyer, B. A. (2001). The role of theory in research on social work practice. *Journal of Social Work Education,* 37, 9–25.

Thyer, B. A. (2009). Evidence based practice, science and social work: an overview. In A. J. Roberts (Ed.), Social worker's desk reference (pp. 1115–1119). New York: Oxford Press.

Timms, N. (1970). *Social work.* London: Routledge.

Turner, F. J. (1976) Interlocking theoretical approaches to clinical practice: some pedagogical perspectives. *Canadian Journal of Social Work Education,* 2(2), 6–14.

Turner, F. J. (ed.) (1979). *Social work treatment: interlocking theoretical perspectives* (2nd ed.). New York: Free Press.

Turner, F. J. (ed.) (1986a). *Differential diagnosis and treatment* (3rd ed.). New York: Free Press.

Turner, F. J. (ed.) (1986b). *Social work treatment: interlocking theoretical perspectives* (3rd ed.). New York: Free Press.

Unrau, Y. A., Gabor, P. A., & Grinnell, R. M. (2006). *Evaluation in social work. The art and science of practice* (4th ed.). New York: Oxford University Press.

Werner, H. (1965). *A rational approach to social casework*. New York: Association Press.

Woods, M. E., & Hollis, F. (1990). *Casework: a psychosocial therapy* (4th ed.). New York: McGraw-Hill.

This centuries-old body of wisdom builds on the wisdom of an elder, and the knowing affinity with natural creative agents, to guide the client in achieving balance

Aboriginal Theory: A Cree Medicine Wheel Guide for Healing First Nations

Herb Nabigon and Anne-Marie Mawhiney

Introduction

In this chapter, the authors introduce an aboriginal approach to healing individuals, groups, and communities. The approach is a holistic one based on Cree traditional teachings[1] in existence in North America for many centuries. It is only recently that First Nations ways of helping people have become visible to those working from a Western worldview. However, aboriginal people all over the world have been practicing their traditional ways of healing for many years before contact with Westerners. In this chapter only one of many such traditional aboriginal approaches is described, using the ancient Cree oral teachings of the medicine wheel, the four directions, and the hub. These teachings help describe ways of healing and growing spiritually by interpreting symbols. The Cree teachings provide a spiritual map to heal people and help them maintain balance.

For many First Nations and other aboriginal social workers, this chapter will provide a summary of concepts and traditional practices with which they may already be familiar. For others working with traditional healing practices, it will provide an interesting point of comparison with their own traditional healing methods. For non-aboriginal social workers, the chapter can provide an introduction to a holistic First Nations approach to helping others that is successful with many First Nations individuals, families, and communities. While this introduction cannot provide sufficient detail to develop skills in the application of the approach, interested and motivated social workers may choose to engage in a long-term learning process guided by an elder or a traditional teacher. For other social workers, this chapter will provide enough of an overview that they can learn to understand, respect, and support the use of the approach by others, especially First Nations colleagues and clients. For still others, this chapter will present some basic concepts and practices, such as the hub, that can be incorporated into their day-to-day practice. In all these cases, the hope is that this chapter will help build a bridge between First Nations and those with other worldviews, and show that while the healing paths may be different, the intent is the same: to recreate harmony and oneness with ourselves and our surroundings.

Overview of the Approach

Aboriginal teachings from North America provide a way to frame our experiences.[2] Its simple analogies and natural-world symbolism are a means to connect all creation. Life itself is sacred and a Great Mystery, but these teachings help us to accept the interrelation of all parts of creation. Traditionally, First Nations people did not see nature as being apart from us, but rather as an extension of our being. The natural world was not something separate from our emotional and mental life, and so could not be dominated or mastered (Colorado & Collins, 1987). Nature was part of us and we were a part of the natural world. Unlike Westerners, who see themselves as dominating other parts of nature, First Nations people viewed our relationship with nature as an equal; humility is to know ourselves as a sacred part of Creation, no better and no worse than other parts.

The teachings assume that all humans can exist in balance with themselves, their families, communities, and their natural surroundings. Where alcoholism, violence, abuse, or any kind of dysfunction exist there is imbalance: the dark side dominates. When the dark side dominates, people who act out of rage, anger, or any strong emotion in destructive ways are out of harmony within themselves—a form of spiritual disease. What is needed is for these people to find their way back to a balance. In other words, problems occur when people focus or act out of the dark side. A person who is functioning well feels balanced, in touch with self and others, including

nature; the person is in touch with reality. The dark and light sides are in balance.

The Cree teachings, which include the medicine wheel, the hub, and the four directions, provide a map to restore an individual's spiritual balance. Symptoms such as greed, materialism, low self-esteem, and other kinds of problems can be healed by incorporating Native teachings into our way of thinking and living.

Path into Social Work

The spiritual masters say it is time to share our teachings with the world, because of the pain and environmental damage that exist in the world today. The teachings from the five colors and the dark sides provide a method for healing the pain and the environment. An old grandmother, Elizabeth (now deceased), always said, "The sun shines for everyone, not just for Indians, and we all need sun for our survival." This teaching applies to all of Creation.

There is only one race of people, but four colors of people are represented: red, yellow, white, and black, and there are only four blood types among humans. For that reason we can reproduce, and we are all part of the human family. Spiritual knowledge helps to diminish racism and we strive to build healthier communities. The elders also say that the time to revisit the teachings has arrived again, and we need the spiritual teachings to improve our social and environmental conditions.

At the same time that elders are empowering younger First Nations people to share traditional teachings, some social work educators have started to look beyond Western worldviews for alternate ways of helping. In Canada, schools of social work at the University of Regina, Laurentian University, the University of Victoria, and Dalhousie University initiated social work education for Native students in the mid-1980s. While each of these programs, as well as the ones that followed, was established and taught in different ways, all were guided by the ideas of local First Nations people. As some schools started to hire First Nations professors, teaching, research, and program structures started to reflect these new professors' worldviews, and some students and faculty have started to be heavily influenced by these ways of thinking.

Social Work Literature

First Nations traditional teachings exist in many forms, many oral, some written, many kept hidden from outsiders to maintain their sacredness. The first written forms of the traditions and ways of living were descriptions by early visitors to North America, including explorers, missionaries, and early anthropologists (see, for example, Jameson, 1990; Spence, 1914). Some of these writings have been interpreted more recently by academics and others (Anderson, 1985; Milloy, 1983; Nazar, 1987; Tobias, 1983) in order to regain some of the traditional knowledge that was lost as a result of colonialism and eurocentrism. Most literature of immediate relevance to social work focuses on social policy (Mawhiney, 1994; McKenzie & Hudson, 1985; Weaver, 1981), including the history of relations between First Nations and the government of Canada, self-government, and self-determinations (Boldt & Long, 1985; Penner, 1983). Many of these were written by non-aboriginal authors, and as a first generation of materials for teaching about First Nations and social work have been useful. Since 1985, the literature has started to expand to include writing by aboriginal authors and co-authors on themes related to social work and helping (Antone et al., 1986; Brown et al., 1995; McKenzie & Morrisette, 1993; Mussel et al., 1993; Nabigon, 1993).

Basic Assumptions

Presuppositions of the Cree Map

Traditionally, First Nations teachings suggest that all humans need healing and that the means to grow spiritually are incorporated into every aspect of life. Healing is a lifelong journey and individuals strive constantly to create and recreate balance and harmony. Spiritual life is not separate from everyday life. Every aspect of existence is spiritual. Emphasis is on *being* rather than *doing*. Our traditional teachings tell us that all things *are* related. There is no sense of object and subject; all is one. Mind, body, emotions, and spirit are not separate, and humans are not separate from the earth and everything on and in it.

The First Nations philosophy of life helps people to understand the relationship among all things. Understanding necessitates acceptance and putting into practice a way of life that promotes healing. Healing reconnects us with our innermost self and our surroundings. This, in turn, shapes our surroundings. All aspects of life may be improved, whether we are seeking help because of dysfunction, change, or a desire for a greater awareness of life and self.

Cree ways of helping offer us ways to balance our inner selves by listening to ourselves, our surroundings, and others. When we listen to our self, we get in touch with our inner spiritual fire. Facing the pain and understanding takes courage. Most people do not consciously start a journey of personal growth unless the pain of not growing is greater than the pain of growing. However, once the journey is started, it is virtually impossible to return to the old ways of relating, and the journey is a constant, ongoing process of change.

Nature of Personality

There are two parts of life that each person needs to pay attention to or risk imbalance: the external self and the inner self. The external self is the image we project to the outside world in our day-to-day interactions. We cultivate our external self to fit into the current culture and times. This takes many forms, including our dress, language, education, and likes and dislikes. We take care of our inner life by personal reflection. Personal reflection can make use of the hub, medicine wheel, sweet grass, and the sacred pipe. Through reflection we change and grow spiritually.

A way to present the Cree understanding of the personality is by using the conceptual device called the hub (Fig. 2.1). The hub consists of three circles, one inside the other. The outer circle represents the negative or dark side of life. The second circle represents the positive or light side, and the center represents the spiritual fire at the core of one's being. The center circle has light and dark sides, also. Balance of the three parts is the ideal to strive for. The circles are divided into four directions: north, south, east, and west. All aspects of a person's psychological and emotional life can be placed on the hub, which provides a means of understanding problems. The hub and the medicine wheel are the basic components in the Cree approach to healing.

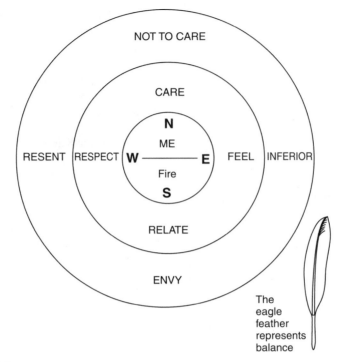

Figure 2.1. The Hub.

The inner circle represents positive values, while the outer circle represents negative values. Native people who walk the red road attempt to balance their lives between positive and negative cycles of life.

Outer Circle East. Feelings of inferiority and shame are represented on the outer circle, in the east. A person who feels inferior does not feel equal to the next person. This often starts when children, who are small, feel that big people have all the power. Unless children are allowed to feel they have some power of choice over their own lives as they grow up, they are likely to feel they are victims, or at the very least, they will fear people they perceive as having authority over them. This perception is often carried over into adulthood and can lead to a sense of powerlessness, feelings of being trapped, depression, and other psychological problems. Let us not forget that we co-create our lives with our souls (minds), and so we must learn how to empower ourselves so that we can create the kind of life we really want.

Feelings of inferiority and shame very often lead to the pretense that we are better than we feel. Western families, schools, and religion often teach this to children. The competitive nature of our society causes people to compare themselves to others, contributing to this condition. On the other hand, feelings of inferiority and shame are broken as we begin to shed our inner pain in the face of unconditional acceptance and love. Denial becomes more and more difficult when we see ourselves in so many others.

Outer Circle South. Elders explain that when a person feels inferior, he or she begins to envy other people. Envy is represented on the outer circle of the hub in the south. Envy is simply wanting what other people have but not wanting to do the work necessary to get it. Envy can range from the material to the spiritual.

Envy can reinforce feelings of inferiority by providing evidence that one does not have what it takes in comparison with others. Envy promotes discontent, unhappiness, and greed. Envious thoughts produce nothing but feelings of helplessness, which in turn prevent action. However, many who feel envy do not know how to change. It is when the techniques for change are known and are not used that laziness also results. Envy may also serve to prod us into looking for methods to change.

We are often taught to compare ourselves to others by competitive values throughout society. However, success should be defined only by the individual, in relation to her or his personal goals and journey's path. Cree teachings promote self-empowerment and responsibility for ourselves and our actions.

Outer Circle West. An envious person more often than not harbours resentment. Resentment means refeeling unexpressed negative or dark feelings from the past. In other words, the emotion was not expressed at the time and was held in the body. These build up and cause a sickness called resentment that permeates a person's attitude. Repression of positive feelings can also lead to resentment. This can be seen in unemotional people. They usually go around with stony faces that are unlined, impenetrable masks. A resentful person can only focus on the dark side and is unable to look twice at her or his personal dilemma.

Outer Circle North. The attitude of uncaring is represented in the north. Apathy and disregard for our well-being signify an attitude of uncaring. Many misunderstand this concept. Many will say they care. They go out of their way to help family, friends and neighbors, and do not think twice about themselves and their needs. They do this in the belief that they are being selfless, good, and kind. They forget that real caring starts with self; no one can really care about another until she or he has learned to care about self. Conversely, we cannot receive caring from another unless we already care about ourselves.

Center Circle. There is no doubt that a person who feels inferior, envious, resentful, and uncaring harbors jealousies as well. Jealousy is represented as the negative side of the center circle. A jealous person does not know how to listen to self and cannot share self. This often leads to possessiveness and unfulfillment.

The inability to listen to self, to be quiet long enough to listen for feelings and let them be useful guides to action, can in extreme cases lead to suicide. Elders say that people who commit suicide did not listen. At the very least, not listening will cause a person to be out of touch with feelings and therefore not know what to pay attention to. Listening to our bodies is also very important. Many illnesses could be treated sooner if the patient listened to his or her body before the symptoms got really serious.

Middle Circle East. The middle circle represents the positive side. A number of positive aspects are represented in the east, such as good feelings, food, and vision in the sense of representing the mind. To have a clear mind and feelings of well-being, one needs good food. Both physical and spiritual food are represented here, and both are essential. Appropriate sharing of feelings, not minimizing them or exaggerating them no matter what they are, is very important because when we choose not to share our feelings, those old inferiority feelings come up again. Sometimes it helps to just tell a trusted friend who can keep calm.

Sharing of positive feelings is also necessary for mental health. Sharing laughter with friends and family has extraordinary healing value. Awareness of the language of feeling is essential to spiritual growth, for how does one know who one is without feeling? Appropriate expression of feeling provides energy and reduces stress.

Middle Circle South. A good feeling from within usually leads to good relationships with self and others. The ability to relate is represented in the south on the hub. Here it means to relate to self, which is closely connected to listening to self. If we do not listen to ourselves we feel alienated from ourselves. When this happens, people refer to feeling lost or to having lost their way. Relationship with self and others requires an inner quietness and an inner peace that are gained by listening.

Developing relationships with ourselves is always a lifelong journey. Time is a dimension of our reality, and we often wish to hurry it along so that we can be there sooner. However, taking the time to prepare properly, experience nuances, and savor the present moment often requires patience. The hub and medicine wheel show us what is. We cannot be other than we are at the present moment, so what is the rush? Where are we going that we have to get there so fast? And where is "there," anyway?

Middle Circle West. Respect is represented in the west on the middle circle. The literal meaning of respect is to look twice. Developing a good relationship with ourselves eventually leads to self-respect. Nonjudgmental attitudes are also important in developing self-respect *and* respect for others. The power of reason is placed in the west door. With reasoning power we can think twice before thinking inappropriate thoughts or saying something that might be harmful to ourselves and others. Respect has to do with honoring ourselves by allowing appropriate expression of feeling. Integrity comes with honoring ourselves.

Middle Circle North. Caring is represented at the north door on the middle circle. Caring is more than a feeling. It is action. It is important to remember the reasons for caring as well. Taking risks on behalf of ourselves, being willing to change, and keeping the focus on ourselves rather than what others do are the keys to action and are all important aspects to caring. This always involves persistence.

Some cultures say it is selfish to think of ourselves first. This is a misunderstanding of the dynamics involved. Providing space to care about ourselves allows others the space to start caring for themselves without being overly dependent.

Center Circle (Light Side). Cree elders teach that spiritual fire is symbolized in the center circle, opposite the dark side of not listening. The mystery of life, the spark of energy that gives life, is situated at the core of being. It is the core of being that must be contacted to live a happy, successful, productive life. It is also the place from which intuitive knowledge and understanding spring. Compassion flows freely from the spiritual fire if all is in balance because love flows through one's whole nature.

Process of Change

The tools, or conceptual frameworks, that guide the healing process are very different from Western approaches. The hub and medicine wheel are used in healing circles and sweat lodge ceremonies. The hub can be applied to one's inner life and used orally, guided by an elder as in the Cree tradition, or used introspectively on one's own. It is used to guide our thoughts about ourselves and how we understand the world as we are experiencing it. The healing journey starts with looking inward and dealing with internal conflicts. No one is an island, however. The immediate environment of family, friends, and community influences a person, as does the greater environment—the earth. We, as individuals and collectively, influence these things, too. In fact, we cannot be separated from them, nor can we be separated from our ancestors, as we see time as a spiral connecting our past through our present to our future not only as individuals but also as people.

There are many paths to growth, and although everyone has different experiences along the way, there are commonalities in human spirituality that make it possible to create methods that many can use. The ancients developed some tools that are as applicable today as they were before Caucasians came to the shores of North America.

The relationship between those seeking help and the helper is not so different from that in many of the Western helping approaches. A person—or people—unable to deal with his or her own concerns or pain seeks help from someone who has some wisdom or knowledge that might help in improving the situation. In the case of healing using Cree approaches, the guide or helper is most often an elder or elderly teacher. In approaching the teacher or elder, we are asking for help in a process that integrates our mind, body, and spirit through traditional ceremonies and healing practices.

The hub is used to sort out confusion and decipher the aspects of human thought, feeling, and behavior. The hub shows how the parts can relate to each other in a coherent format that is easy to understand. It is a simple, concrete map that helps people decipher parts of their being and points the way to healing of the mind, body, and spirit. This, in turn, helps people to live more wholesome, balanced lives.

The process starts with taking a look at one's inner self and changing that before going on to look at one's environment. In fact, there is a ripple effect that starts at the center of our being and flows outward to make a difference in all aspects of our lives. The medicine wheel is used to guide the healing process.

Sweet grass, sage, cedar, and tobacco are traditional sacred plants. Each has spiritual properties and is used for specific purposes. Sweet grass, sage, and cedar are used for smudging, among other things, and tobacco is well known as an offering during prayer. The elders braid sweet grass and ignite the end, allowing it to smolder. The smoke smells pleasant and sweet. They use the smoke of the burning sweet grass to clean the mind, body, and spirit by smudging the body with it. The ritual of cleansing through sweet grass smoke represents simple honesty and simple kindness, the kind of honesty and kindness we have as children. When we burn sweet grass we are smudging our minds, body, and spirit to remind ourselves of the importance of honesty and kindness, to wash away the darkness, to cleanse our inner self.

Importance of the External World

The Cree approach is used with individuals, groups (including families), and communities. However, it is impossible to separate one of these elements from the other; we cannot separate any person from his or her context, nor can we separate a community from the people who live in it. The hub is useful in showing the interconnectedness of people and their external world, which includes ancestors, families, friends, the community, and the natural environment. Traditional healing, at times, has meant that those who have done harm to others, and therefore to their community and natural environment, are part of the healing process for those affected.

In addition to those aspects of our lives that we can observe, we also consider our spiritual world, including our grandfathers, as being an extension of the external world. The grandfathers can be understood in terms of universal spirit guides who possess all the knowledge of the universe. They are available to everyone. Sometimes they may plant thoughts in our minds to give us direction and guidance. These thoughts always make the utmost sense in light of their purpose, which is to help us in our

spiritual evolution. The term "grandfather" was coined eons ago when the traditions were being laid down, because it was a word people connected with wisdom.

Value Base of the Cree Approach

We see time as a spiral, where everything that went before is behind us, leading us through the present towards the future (Dumont, 1989). The past time includes that of our ancestors and all they did to set us on our present path, as individuals and as peoples. As we live in the present, we need to be constantly mindful not only of the immediate results of our actions but also the consequences for future generations; our teachings tell us that everything we do today will have an impact on the next seven generations.

We use sweet grass to put us in touch with our past, present, and future to reintroduce traditional Cree concepts to those who are interested in re-examining traditional values that are treasured by all peoples of the world. Honesty and kindness are central to all cultures and religions. However, the traditional native culture expresses these values in a unique way. All of our values are expressed through nature, and nature teaches us how to behave and how to conduct our lives. The trick is to learn how to read and understand nature. It takes a long time to get close to nature. The Teachings of the Seven Grandfathers show the traditional values that shape the healing process. These are wisdom, love, respect, bravery, honesty, humility, and truth (Benton-Benai, 1988).

The tree is the symbol of honesty in our traditions. If you take a walk in the forest you will notice there are many kinds of trees: white trees, yellow trees, black trees, red trees, and many shades in between. Trees symbolize the four races of the world. The different shades symbolize the products of intermarriage among the races. Also, if you walk in the bush, you will see trees of different shapes, different sizes: some are tall, some are crooked, and some are twisted. They represent all the people of the world. Walking the sweet grass road helps me be tall and straight like a tall, straight tree. Long straight trees symbolize honesty.

The Cree also believe that the rock and the tree have a spirit. Grass and animals have a spirit too; all the living things the Creator made in our garden have a spirit. This is what the elders teach.

Animals teach affection. A little house dog is a very affectionate animal. If you call him, he will always come to you wagging his tail. He will rub his body against your legs. If you get angry with him, a few seconds later he will forgive you. Animals teach us not to abuse sex. For instance, loons mate for life. They are loyal to each other. Animals teach us many things if we have the courage to admit our weaknesses. The elders teach that animals are equal to us and can teach us if we know how to observe and understand their behavior. Animals can also teach us companionship. Their companionship is a model of how we should relate to companions and friends. Finally, animals can teach about sacrifice. Our collective relationship with animals is such that they die so we can live. The animal makes the ultimate sacrifice and teaches us that we, also, should sacrifice. In this way, animals are key to our survival. We need to maintain the well-being of animals for our own well-being; this is a basic teaching of our elders.

The Cree map has been used for many generations of Crees. It has the most direct importance for the Cree and other First Nations.

Treatment

Principal Therapeutic Goal

The goal of treatment is to promote balance and harmony within individuals and groups of people, including communities, and to assist in taking action to relieve pain in the communities and nations of the world.

Practice Model

In our Native culture, we relate to and learn much by observing nature over a long period of time. The First Nations worldview is divided into the four sacred directions. These directions are used to search for harmony and peace from within. The Cree and other North American aboriginal cultures use the medicine wheel to heal individuals, communities, and nations. The medicine wheel uses the compass points of the four directions to help each person to rediscover

and find the way back to his or her path (Fig. 2.2). In Cree teachings, the healer starts the helping process in the east.

East. It is believed that the Creator began life in the east, symbolized by the color red. In the spring, when the east wind blows a soft breeze the earth, our mother begins to get warmer. Plants, especially the roots and the alder shoots, turn reddish brown. Spring is symbolized by the color red because the roots are renewing themselves as the earth renews herself. The earth cleans herself every spring like a woman's womb is cleansed once a month. Spring is a healing season. Everything is healed and all life is reborn during the spring months. New life and new feeling come to all living things in the springtime.

Aboriginal people are represented in the east, and the Creator bestowed the gifts of food, feelings, and vision on the people. In the spring, the animals have their young and we use those animals for food. In the Ojibwa culture, the symbols for food are the moose and the whitefish. Historically, the moose provided us with meat, clothes, and tools. The moose and fish were great providers. Without food we do not live very long. Food is medicine; it doctors us and heals us. There is a strong relationship between food and feelings. Good food brings us good feelings. When we feel good about ourselves, we enjoy vision. In this sense, vision means purpose and direction. Feelings of inferiority also come from this direction. Today many people experience inferior feelings and strong anger comes from the east. Anger from the east can be translated into many of our domestic problems, which are signs of inappropriately expressed anger. Traditional teachings from this direction bring a message of peace and harmony into our communities. The turtle clan and the fish clan are also represented in the east. Traditionally, these clans were poets and orators.

In the east door, elders and traditional teachers help the person to look at her or his aspirations; the person reflects on where she or he is heading and what is to be accomplished.

South. The color yellow is a symbol of summer, time, relationships, and the sun. At midday, the sun is facing south. The heat of summer teaches us patience because it is too hot to move very

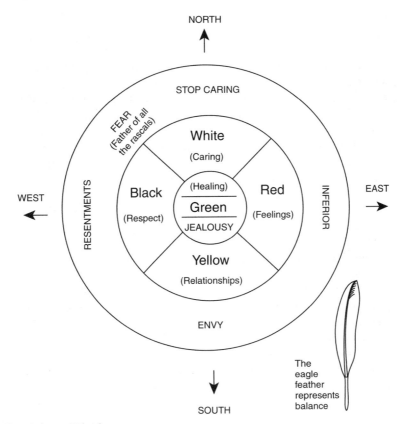

Figure 2.2. The Medicine Wheel.

quickly. Patience helps us in our relationships with others and with ourselves. When we sit quietly, we become aware of our feelings, thoughts, and spiritual ways; we become aware of our mind, body, and spirit; there is power in silence.

We are helped to understand self through our relationships with family, extended family, friends, and community. It takes time to understand our identity as human beings. We learn and understand ourselves by interacting with peers, and values are transmitted through our parents and institutions like school and church.

Puberty is a time of change for all young people. Adolescence is often a time of crisis. For young Natives, it is a time to define their Nativeness. The process of defining cultural heritage takes precedence over all activities, including education. It is during this period of self-exploration that a young person's academic grades may begin to decline. Educators and some parents forget to take this factor into consideration

when there is a crisis at school. Elders and traditional teachers can help to understand and defuse the crisis.

The opposite of a good relationship is envy. Envy can be defined as wanting what someone else has, but not being willing to work for it. Envy needs to be diffused in sacred healing circles. Late in the summer the leaves start to turn yellow. Yellow reminds us of patience, which is essential to any relationship. Oriental people, represented in the south, bring the gifts of time, patience, and relationships because these are so highly valued in their cultures.

The *Ginoo* (golden eagle) is represented in the south. The eagle is a very sacred bird, traditionally. Because the eagle flies so high in the sky it is considered to be able to deliver messages for the Great Mystery. An eagle's feather is held in great respect.

In the south door, the person reflects on his or her relationship to family and community, seeking to build on existing strengths and overcoming barriers and problems.

West. The color black is a symbol of respect, reason, water, and fall. When the west wind comes, fall is around the corner. In the fall, everything turns black. Leaves and other living things, especially green things, turn black. The quality of our inner life is enhanced when we understand and implement the word *respect*. If a person thinks twice before making a decision or taking some action, her or his reasoning is good.

Many adolescents have a difficult time reviewing their inner life because of change and crisis. Native spiritual leaders have an intimate understanding of adolescence and healing ceremonies are made available. There are times when dysfunctional families overburden their older children with the responsibility for taking care of younger siblings. This practice creates hostility and resentment. Elders and traditional teachers conduct sacred ceremonies to diffuse resentment, which destroys any self-respect we may have.

Black in the fall also reminds us of the black people, who understand humility. Humility is the recognition of our place within nature. We have much to learn about respect.

Black clouds appear in the spring and they bring rain showers and the thunderbirds. The thunderbirds' purpose is to shed light on our inner life. Water, brought by rain showers, is a very important source of energy for every being. Water is used in many different ways. But, like everything else, we can have too much water: we can bloat up, or drown in a lake.

In the west door, the person reflects on intimate relationships and her or his own behavior. Showing respect for others and for one's self is central to balance in relationships with others.

North. White is the symbol of winter, caring, movement, and air. Caring can be defined by our level of interaction with family, school, community, and nation. Isolation usually indicates that problems exist and they need to be dealt with accordingly. "All human beings are capable of using common sense," said a grandmother a long time ago. For her it was common sense to care. Care is as important as the air we breathe. Infants die if they are not cared for or touched in a caring way. If we are not taught to care for ourselves we will always be dependent, compulsively needing others to nurture us. Our belief is that caring is given to us in the north.

When the strong north wind blows, everything turns white and we have the season of winter. The north wind is a great mover. It is a master of movement: it can move trees, houses, almost anything that gets in its way. So air moves everything on our planet, Mother Earth. This is a reminder that every action has a consequence, either a caring one or one that promotes fear. Also, everyone makes a difference, either in a caring way or an uncaring way. Some methods of natural healing are yelling, laughing, sweating, crying, yawning, and shaking. These can help a person move through fear.

White also symbolizes the white race. Caring is being moved. Have you noticed how the white race has moved, or spread, all over the world? When caring was not considered during their movement, many peoples of other races were displaced.

In the north door, the person builds on his or her understanding of the ways that his or her behavior affects the family and community.

Center. Green is a healing color and is the symbol of Mother Earth, which is at the center of all things. The earth nurtures the four races of humankind and all living things. Thus, green and Mother Earth are in the center circle on the medicine wheel. When we are in balance we are in touch with our inner spiritual fire. Green is a symbol of balance and listening. Spiritual leaders emphasize that we should listen and pay attention to the dark side of life so that we can learn and heal. The dark side can be denied by the five little rascals of inferiority feelings: envy, resentment, not caring, and jealousy. The dark side of green means we stop listening. The first step towards healing is to learn how to listen to the dark side. Listening helps to make the appropriate changes from negative to positive behavior. The underlying assumption at the center of the wheel is that the ability to listen is needed in the healing process.

The four sacred directions help people to balance themselves and to know their place in the world. The importance of a balanced diet cannot be overemphasized. Food is one of the sacred gifts. A long time ago, a grandmother said that the earth is our garden—the Creator made this garden for us and it was up to us to live in harmony with it. When we take from Mother Earth to feed ourselves, we should always thank Mother Earth and the animals and put something back. The principle that whenever you take, you must also give was what our grandmother was teaching.

The white race has improved technology for harvesting food from nature, which makes it easier for us. But we should always remember that without nature, human beings are nothing. Our dependency on nature should never be forgotten. Nature's diversity—the different colors and smells of nature, the sound of animals—are very good things. They remind us of our dependency on nature. They also remind us of the gifts that the creator has provided for us to live on this earth.

Another tool that is used in helping people regain inner balance and well-being is fasting in natural surroundings. Fasting is a purification ritual or vision quest that facilitates one's spiritual growth. It is very sacred within the Anishinabe context. We abstain from food and water while living in the forest for four days and nights. Food is a symbol of the animals and the east door. We use animals for food. Anishinabe honors that relationship and we are grateful for that life support. Red is a symbol for the aboriginal people of renewal. Fasting is a time of renewal. Just as life begins in the east, we experience a time of renewal during the fast. When we honor the spirits in this way, they honor us by giving us the power of understanding.

Basic Assessment Questions

The following questions can be used as guides in using the medicine wheel to help people develop a basic understanding of their own behavior, their environment, and the ways in which they are influenced by and influence this environment.[3]

East Door—Aspirations

1. Why do you think you were sent here?
2. What is your understanding of your problems?
3. Where do you hope to be one year from now?
4. What do you want to be doing for the rest of your teen years?
5. What do you want to be doing when you are an adult?

South Door—Relationships and Time

1. Describe your relationship with your family or caregiver.
2. Have you been with your family since birth?
3. Are there happy times in your family?
4. Describe what you like most about your family.
5. Describe what you like least about your family.
6. Do you have a girlfriend/boyfriend? (Further questions may be necessary; for example, Are you sexually active?)

West Door—Respect and Reason

1. What would you say is positive about your community?
2. Is there any alcohol, drug abuse, or sniffing in your family?
3. Describe the good parts of your family.
4. Describe what happens when there is alcohol or drug abuse or a party in your family.
5. Do you personally drink alcohol, use drugs, or sniff?
6. Did anyone ever touch you in a way that made you feel uncomfortable?

North Door—Behavior

1. How would you describe your own behavior in your family?
2. What do you like most about yourself?
3. Is there something you don't like about yourself?
4. Would you describe your behavior in your family as gentle or harsh?
5. Describe your interaction with family when you seek to relieve pain or hurt. (Further questions may be needed; for instance, about withdrawing behavior.)

Center Healing Strategies

1. How important is listening to you?
2. Why is listening important?

3. Do you believe listening teaches us how to be good? Give some examples.
4. What are some things you must do to heal yourself from pain?
5. Is there someone you can talk to regarding your pain?

Original Teachings

According to teachings, the sacred sweat lodge was given to us by the Creator through a little boy. The Creator took the boy into his home and taught him the meaning of the lodge.

The sweat lodge is a purification ceremony, and within the lodge there are four sacred doors we use to heal ourselves. The actual ceremony provides an inner body experience that helps individuals to understand the spirit realm. The lodge is built in the form of a mother's womb, and inside it is totally dark. We return to the womb in order to remind ourselves of our humble beginnings; we all come from her womb. The powerful and the poor are equal in the eyes of the Creator.

According to the spiritual masters, life begins in the east. At sunrise, the sky turns red. Dawn signifies a new beginning. The gifts from the east are vision, animals, and feelings. In the beginning, tobacco was given by the creator. We offer tobacco when we pray for strength and guidance. Animals, including the bear, wolf, moose, fish, and waterfowl, are born in the spring and sit in the east. We use animals for food, and when we eat properly, our feelings and vision improve. In our society, we often eat poorly and our vision and feelings suffer as a result. We develop inferior feelings and poor vision.

Our Children and Families

The Creator gave the animals instructions on the proper ways to use sex. For example, the loon mates for life, and there is no physical or sexual abuse among the loons. Perhaps we can take some lessons from loons on how to behave when it comes to taking care of our families.

The sun moves from left to right across the sky and at midday the sun faces the south. The south represents the summer, the color yellow, time, relationships, and patience. Everything takes time. For example, it takes time to understand the mysteries of life. Yellow people remind us how important it is to practice patience in our relationships. Patience is very important to maintain and sustain relationships. Time is given by the Creator without condition, and how we use time in our lifetime is our own choice to make. The golden eagle, in Ojibwa called *Ginoo*, delivers all our thoughts and prayers to the Creator. The eagle has powerful eyesight and her invisible helpers will visit our lodges: they come in from the blue lights and the sound of flapping wings. The lodge is the home of the Creator and the grandfathers.

The west is the door of reflection. It is a door we use to heal pain from yesterday. The spiritual master says you must look back in order to move forward. Denial plays a major role in this door; so many people refuse to look back, and they block their feelings. The color in the west is black or blue, depending on the First Nation. Some people use the hub in the west door as a method of looking inward, and it is used to heal inner life. The grandfather who sits in the west is the thunderbird. The thunderbird brings us water in early spring; clean water is a strong medicine.

The north wind represents the north. When it is cold in winter a white blanket covers up our part of Turtle Island (Earth). Many people find peace by taking a walk in the bush during the winter. For our people, white represents peace. Air is a life-giver. Without air nothing moves; air is the master of movement. The white people through their technology move things around. For example, you can travel anywhere and find soda cans. The red, yellow, or black races did not make or move the cans to remote places, it was the white race with its commerce and technology. We say that the white race is the master of movement. Harmful technology is destroying our Mother Earth and the human race. The white race needs to build technology to support life, not destroy it.

The grandfather who sits in the north is the bear. We see the bear as a healer. Unlike all other animals, the bear is a meat-eater and a vegetarian; she carries all these good medicines and all the other animals go to her for healing. She also represents peace. We pray to the grandfathers to send us messengers of peace like Mother Teresa, who knew the sacredness of life and for that reason fed the poor in India. In many ways, she represents what is good about our white sisters and brothers.

According to our traditional teachings, there are four levels of knowledge that help us understand the natural laws of balance. The first level is understanding self; without this knowledge there can be no balance. The second level is understanding others through our understanding of self. The third level is understanding and appreciating the Creator. The fourth level provides us with a deep understanding of balance. When we integrate all four levels of knowledge we are in balance not only within ourselves but also with those around us and with our environment. When we miss one or more levels of understanding, we and those around us are not in balance. To those of us from the east door, many people from the north door seem to be missing this balance because they do not integrate all four levels of knowledge. As we look at the world around us, this sense of imbalance is shown by the ways that Mother Earth has been exploited for the benefit of a few people. By regaining understanding and balance in all things, we can start to improve our natural environment.

The four directions form a sacred circle and invite the four colors of women and men to join us and build a strong sacred circle of life. To make the invitation possible, the spiritual masters say we must empty our hearts of all our credentials and material possessions and make room for the spirit. We must make room in our hearts and enter the world of the sacred. The north door in the lodge has enormous responsibilities from promoting peace and building technologies that support life instead of destroying it.

Vignettes

Loon. A long time ago a loon was badly hurt. He lived on a lake of firewater. He, and many other loons who lived there with him, drank the water of this lake, which made them all very sick. The loon's spirit was broken, and his mind and body were confused because he drank too much firewater. The lake was polluted and the surroundings of the lake were ugly to look at because all the loons that lived on the lake drank too much.

One day the loon met two other loons from a different lake. The confused loon, the one with the broken spirit, began to talk with the visiting loons. The two loons called Eddy and Michael took time to talk to the loon. They talked and walked the sweet grass road. They told him that only through simple honesty and simple kindness are we able to build our fire. If we cannot build this fire we eventually die. Imagine dying on this lake, alone and forlorn, never knowing love. The two loons said that love embraces everything. Love does not exclude everything, or anyone. If we cannot accept love ourselves, they told him, then we can never experience loving someone else.

"How can I love when there is so much cruelty and injustice?" said the loon with the broken spirit. He felt self-pity, which is not good because it leaves no room for healing due to narrowing of vision. The loon did not feel he had the strength to follow the sweet grass road. He did try for many months, however, but he kept stumbling and falling down.

Then one winter he met another loon called John. John showed the broken-spirited loon what the two other loons had been telling him. The wise old loon took him and showed him how to pray in a native way. So the three strong loons—Eddy, Michael, and John—taught the loon with the broken spirit how to pray the native way.

Gradually, the loon with the broken spirit began to feel his fire and he left the lake of confusion, pain, and violence. He didn't want any more water from this lake, the lake that was full of poison. The three strong loons carried the loon with the broken spirit on their backs and they flew through the sky until they found a quiet spot on the ground and they taught him the old ways. The loon with the broken spirit slowly began to feel good about himself. He no longer desired to take a drink of poison. The compulsion left him entirely. He did not want to drink anymore. He never wanted to touch that firewater again.

Sue White Sue is an Anishinabekwe (an Ojibwa woman) living in Manitou Reserve in Northern Ontario. She has three children, aged 4, 7, and 16. Her husband was killed in a car accident three years ago. Manitou Reserve is an isolated First Nation accessible by plane or, in the summer months only, by an old lumber road. Sue spends her winters going out to her trap line and fishing to support her family, including her mother and a sister, who has one child. Her 7-year-old son, Adam, goes to school in the community, and her 16-year-old daughter, Brenda, is living with a cousin in an urban community 300 miles away and attending a high school there. Her cousin has called, concerned about Brenda's social activities on the weekends, which include drinking with her friends and staying out late at parties. Brenda has done very well in school but her grades have recently been dropping. Sue is very concerned but doesn't have the money to pay for a trip to visit Brenda, nor can she take the time away from the trap line. Brenda may be implicated in an incident in which a group of students were drinking and driving. Brenda's education counselor has said that Brenda may be suspended because of this incident.

Summary

The Cree medicine wheel, as it is described here, presents an overview of one First Nations healing process. Training to become an elder is a very long process, one that is not undertaken lightly and one that elders do not confer on just anyone. It is our intention in presenting this overview to guide the reader through an initial journey in order to promote respect for an alternative treatment approach—one that is from a worldview different from those found in the rest of this book.

Notes

1. The authors acknowledge the teachings of Eddy Bellrose, Michael Thrasher, Rebecca Martel (*Kakgee Sikaw Wapestak*, "Keeper of the Dawn"), the late Abe Burnstick, and one other senior elder who prefers to remain anonymous. Their teachings have guided and shaped this chapter.
2. The authors have chosen to refer to First Nations people in the first person plural to highlight that this chapter focuses on a worldview that is separate from the dominant one. The senior author is Anishinabe from Northern Ontario.
3. This section is based on an assessment framework developed by Herb Nabigon and Barbara Waterfall (1995) for adolescents seeking help from within Weechi-it-te-win Family Services in Fort Francis, Ontario. The questions were pretested for 6 months

and then changed to better fit the language and ways of thinking of this adolescent client group. Used with permission of Weechi-ti-te-win.

References

Anderson, K. (1985). Commodity, exchange and subordination: Montagnais and Huron women 1600 to 1650. *Signs: Journal of Women in Culture and Society*, 48–62.

Antone, R., Miller, D., & Meyers, B. (1986). *The power within people*. Desoronto, Ont.: Peace Trees Technologies Inc.

Benton-Banai, E. O. (1988) *The Mishomis book*. Hayword, WI: Indian Country Comm and Company.

Boldt, M., & Long, J. A. (1985). *The quest for justice: Aboriginal peoples and aboriginal rights*. Toronto: University of Toronto Press.

Boudreau, F., & Nabigon, H. (2000). Se rapproprier l'esprit: l'autonomie gouvernementale, le paradigme culturel et l'intervention sociale. *Reflets*, 6(1), 108–127.

Brown, L., Jamieson, C., & Kovach, M. (1995). Feminism and First Nations: Conflict or concert? *Canadian Review of Social Policy*, 35, 68–78.

Carrière, R., Kauppi, C., & Nabigon, H. (2001). Sondage auprès des diplômées et diplômés de l'École de service social de l'Université Laurentienne. *Reflets*, 7(7), 192–204.

Colorado, P., & Collins, D. (1987). Western scientific colonialism and the re-emergence of native science. *Practice: The Journal of Politics, Economics, Psychology, Sociology and Culture*, V(3, Winter), 50–65.

Dumont, J. (1989). *Culture, behaviour and the identity of the native person*. Course manual for NATI 2105 EZ. Sudbury: Centre for Continuing Education, Laurentian University.

Duran, E. (2006). *Healing the soul wound*. New York: Teachers College Press.

Fixico, D. L. (2003). *The American Indian mind in a linear world: American Indian studies and Traditional knowledge*. New York and London: Routledge.

Freeman, B., & Lee, B. (2007). Towards an aboriginal model of community healing. *Native Social Work Journal—Resistance and Resiliency: Addressing Historical Trauma of Aboriginal Peoples*, 6, 97–120.

Hart, M. A. (2002). *Seeking mino-pimatisiwin: An aboriginal approach to helping*. Black Point, Nova Scotia & Winnipeg, Manitoba: Fernwood Publishing.

Hill, G., & Coady, N. (2003). Comparing Euro-Western counseling and aboriginal healing methods: An argument for the effectiveness of aboriginal approaches to healing. *Native Social Work Journal–*

Articulating Aboriginal Paradigms: Implications for Aboriginal Social Work Practice, 5, 44–63.

Jameson, A. (1990). Winter studies and summer rambles in Canada (1838). Toronto: McLellan Stewart.

Koerner, J. (2003). *Mother, heal my self: An intergenerational healing journey between two worlds.* California: Crestport Press.

Kuokkanen, R. (2007). *Reshaping the university: Responsibility, indigenous epistemes, and the logic of the gift.* Vancouver-Toronto, Canada: UBC Press.

Mawhiney, A. (1994). *Towards aboriginal self-government.* New York: Garland Publishing.

McKenzie, B., & Hudson, P. (1985). Native Children, child welfare and the colonization of Native people. In K. L. Levitt & B. Wharf (Eds.), *The challenge of child welfare.* Vancouver: University of British Columbia Press.

McKenzie, B., & Morrisette, L. (1993). Cultural empowerment and healing for aboriginal youth in Winnipeg. In A. Mawhiney (Ed.), *Rebirth.* Toronto: Dundurn Press.

Milloy, J. (1983). The early Indian acts: Developmental strategy and constitutional change. In I. A. L. Getty & A. S. Lussier (Eds.), *As long as the sun shines and water flows.* Toronto: University of Toronto Press.

Mussel, W., Nicholls, W., & Adler, M. (1993). *Making meaning of mental health: Challenge in First Nations.* Chiliwack, British Columbia: Salt'shan Institute.

Nabigon, H. (1993). Reclaiming the spirit for First Nations self-government. In A. Mawhiney (Ed.), *Rebirth.* Toronto: Dundurn Press.

Nabigon, H. (Associate editor) (1997). *Native Social Work Journal, Nishnaabe Kinoomaadwin Naadmaadwin,* 1.

Nabigon, H. (Associate editor) (2000). Special Edition, HIV/AIDS, Issues Within Aboriginal Populations. *Native Social Work Journal, Nishnaabe Kinoomaadwin Naadmaadwin,* 3.

Nabigon, H. (2003). Inclusivity and diversity at the macro level: Aboriginal self-Government. *Native Social Work Journal, Nishnaabe Kinoomadwin Naadmaadwin,* 5.

Nabigon, H. (2006). *The hollow tree: Fighting addiction with traditional native healing.* McGill-Queens University Press, 2006.

Nabigon, H., & Waterfall, B. (1995). An assessment tool for First Nations individuals and families. Used with the permission of Weech-it-te-win Family Services, Training and Learning Centre, Fort Francis, Ontario. Unpublished.

Nabigon, H., Hagey, R., Webster, S., & MacKay, R. (1999). The learning circle as a research method: The trickster and windigo in research. *Native Social Work Journal, Nishnaabe Kinoomaadwin Naadmaadwin,* 1.

Nazar, D. (1987). *The Jesuits and Wikwemikong, 1840–1880.* Unpublished manuscript.

Penner, K. (1983). *Report of the Special Committee on Indian Self-Government.* Ottawa: Ministry of Supply and Services.

Rice, B. (2005). *Seeing the world with aboriginal eyes: A four directional perspective on human and non-human values, cultures and relationships on Turtle Island.* Winnipeg: Aboriginal Issues Press.

Spence, L. (1914). *Myths and legends of the North American Indians.* London: George G. Harrap.

Tobias, J. L. (1983). Protection, civilization, and assimilation: an outline history of Canada's Indian policy. In I. A. L. Getty & A. S. Lussier (Eds.), *As long as the sun shines and water flows.* Toronto: University of Toronto Press.

Waldram, J. B. (2004). *Revenge of the Windigo: The construction of the mind and mental health of North American aboriginal peoples.* Toronto: University of Toronto Press.

Weaver, S. (1981). *Making Canadian Indian policy: The hidden agenda.* Toronto: University of Toronto Press.

This foundation theory, developed by John Bowlby, focuses on the form, quality, and strength of human attachments made in early life and their effect on development and pro-social behaviors

Attachment Theory and Social Work Treatment

Timothy Page

History and Development of the Theory

Origins

Attachment theory was created in the mid-20th century by the British psychiatrist John Bowlby, Director of the Department for Children and Parents at the Tavistock Clinic in London. The first public presentation of attachment theory occurred in three seminal lectures Bowlby gave to the British Psychoanalytical Society in London, one each year from 1957 to 1959 (Bretherton, 1992). His audience was the child psychiatry establishment of that era, including such notable figures as Anna Freud, Melanie Klein, and Donald Winnicott, and their view of human development and psychotherapy was firmly rooted in Freudian psychoanalytic theory.

The classical psychoanalytic model of human development was based on a concept of psychosexual drive energy as its primary motivating force (Greenberg & Mitchell, 1983). In the Freudian view, the process of buildup and discharge of psychosexual drive energy creates internal fantasies that ultimately are responsible for the emergence of personality, social relationships, and virtually every other aspect of human development. This so-called hydraulic model of motivational drive was based on ideas taken from 19th-century physics concerning the process of accumulation and discharge of energy within closed systems, the goal of which is a state of relative quiescence. In the classical Freudian theories of development and psychoanalytic treatment, internally created fantasies are even more important to the course of human growth and development than the child's actual experience.

Bowlby's attachment theory diverged from Freudian theory in many important ways, none more so than his emphasis on the importance of actual experience to human development (Bowlby, 1982). In Bowlby's view, the quality of interactions between infant and caregiver(s), beginning at birth, motivated specifically by the child's needs for safety and protection, are central to lifespan development. Reaction from the Psychoanalytical Society, including his own mentors, to his attachment papers was immediately condemnatory because of his explicit rejection of core tenets of Freudian theory. Although he remained a member of the Society for the rest of his life, he never formally presented a paper there again (Bretherton, 1992).

A New Model of Instinct

In attachment theory, Bowlby replaced the Freudian notion of instinct as psychosexual drive, and the hydraulic model's relative emphasis on internally derived motivation, with a model conceptualizing instinct as an interaction of organism and environment. Taking language primarily from the field of cybernetics, and adapting this to studies in ethology and human development, Bowlby saw instinctive behavior in terms of "control systems." The expression of an intrinsic need is thought of as goal-directed behavior in a relational context. Modification of the behavior occurs through feedback from the environment, especially the quality of response from the relational partner involved, a process he referred to as "goal-correction." Bowlby integrated the control systems model with the term "behavioral system," which he borrowed from ethology, to explain the basic processes governing instinct-based social behavior in humans (Stevenson-Hinde, 2007). He discussed the hunting behavior of a falcon in flight and a frightened infant's seeking of his caregiver in essentially the same terms as the way in which the power steering mechanism works on a car (Bowlby, 1982). In each of these cases, there is a goal to which the object is directed, and behavior is modified or corrected as information is fed back about its progress toward the goal, be it the hunt, the turning of the wheel, or the comfort-seeking of the infant. By conceptualizing instinct as an interaction of inherited predispositions

and environmental response, he laid an important theoretical foundation: What we consider to be the "normative" parameters of human experience must include considerable diversity and variation.

Bowlby's influence from the field of ethology is reflected in the comprehensive analyses and syntheses of scores of diverse studies, particularly primate studies, he used to establish attachment theory within the larger theory of Darwinian evolution. Attachment theory has been called a "major middle level" evolutionary theory (Simpson & Belsky, 2008), because of its foundation in and refinement of Darwinian theory. Evolution theory became increasingly established as the dominant paradigm of the natural sciences in the 20th century, though it had not, until Bowlby, had a significant place in our understanding of human psychosocial development. One of the great achievements, therefore, of Bowlby's attachment theory is that it represents the first time that a major theory of human psychosocial development became integrated into the dominant paradigm of modern biological sciences.

Attachment Behavior

Among the ethological researchers of his time, Bowlby was profoundly influenced by the now-classic studies of Konrad Lorenz (1935) on imprinting in ducks and geese and Harry Harlow (1958) on infant rhesus monkey behavior toward wire adult models. This and other ethological research inspired Bowlby to see that the formation of social bonds in these species was not dependent on feeding, an insight he then applied to human development. In doing so, he explicitly rejected the views of Freudian and behavioral theories alike, which posited that the formation of social bonds between human children and their caregivers is secondary to the oral gratification associated with feeding. If social bonds form independently of feeding and not secondary to pleasure, he had to explain what their larger purpose was.

Bowlby's main interest was the formation, beginning in infancy, of the behaviors that collectively compose the attachment behavioral system. He saw in the development of attachment behavior powerful relational themes influencing the entire life course. Similar to the way in which the neonate responds to tactile stimulation of the lips and hard palate with grasping and sucking, Bowlby proposed that the infant responds to conditions of vulnerability such as fear, pain, cold, hunger, fatigue, and illness with an array of behaviors that result in the maintenance of *proximity* to the caregiver. Around the age of 6 months, the early behaviors of crying, clinging, smiling, visually following the caregiver, signaling, and, later, movement toward the caregiver become increasingly organized into the attachment behavioral system (Bowlby, 1982). The attachment system becomes activated in conditions of vulnerability, including distance and separations from caregivers. The caregiver's response to the infant's activated attachment behavior amounts to, in control systems terminology, the feeding back of information to the infant and produces, under favorable conditions, calming and a growing sense of security. Proximity-seeking directed to a specific caregiver is the fundamental component of attachment behavior, the proximate purpose of which is to calm feelings of insecurity and the ultimate, evolutionary function of which is to ensure the survival of the infant and species (Bowlby, 1982).

The term "attachment figure" is applied to the specific caregivers to whom children direct attachment behavior by virtue of their protective role for the child. Attachment relationships typically involve parents, and may include other relatives such as grandparents, aunts, uncles, and older siblings, or close relationships with non-family members. Attachments, the internalized bonds that form in attachment relationships, reflect specific dyadic qualities, interactive histories, yet are considered characteristics of the child. An attachment bond involves, is indeed defined by, the child's affective tie to a specific attachment figure, not the attachment figure's bond to the child. The term "attachment" is therefore not used in the colloquial sense of "connection," and specifically refers to an emotional bond experienced by a relatively more vulnerable person in relation to a relatively stronger one. Most children, fortunately, have multiple attachment bonds, each specific to the relational history with the individual attachment figure. Bowlby (1982) believed that, despite the presence of multiple attachments, children organize attachment relationships in some form of hierarchy, with one preferred attachment figure, usually the mother, above others, a principle he referred to as the "monotropy" of attachment bonds.

Attachment, Fear, and Exploration

The attachment behavioral system functions directly in relation to two other major behavioral systems within the child (Bowlby, 1982), the fear/wariness and exploratory behavioral systems, representing, respectively, the instinct to withdraw from frightening circumstances and the instinct to explore novel situations. Bowlby proposed that the attachment and fear/wariness behavioral systems operate in close, but not absolute, synchrony. Very frequently, but not always, Bowlby argued, attachment behavior is activated by fear-inducing conditions that simultaneously activate withdrawal from the feared object. Attachment behavior may also be activated, however, according to Bowlby, in conditions not directly associated with an instinct to withdraw, such as fatigue and illness. The exploratory behavioral system, in contrast to the fear/wariness system, plays a role fully equal in importance to the attachment system in determining how attachment behavior ultimately becomes expressed and, thus, how the attachment bond is formed. A natural, instinctive desire to explore the social and physical environment is normally activated in conditions where the child is relatively stress-free. Through this process, the child learns about the world, taking in new information and developing perceptual, analytic, and motor skills that provide opportunities for the child's development of mastery and autonomy.

Inevitably, however, the child experiences depletion in energy or becomes distressed by encounters with unfamiliar objects or events, or from the separation from an attachment figure, all of which produce felt vulnerability, activating the attachment behavioral system. In this way, exploratory and attachment systems are regarded as polar dimensions of a larger process, whereby the activation of one normally involves the relative deactivation of the other. In order for the child to be able to explore the world with confidence, he or she must be able to trust in the availability of the "secure base" of the attachment relationship, as described by Ainsworth (Ainsworth & Bowlby, 1991), from which the child ventures outward, and to which the child can return, as a "safe haven," for care and protection when needed. The way in which the attachment figure accurately perceives and responds to the child's alternating needs for exploration and attachment will determine the nature of the attachment bond that the child will form with the attachment figure. As Ainsworth (1989) later demonstrated, the transactions associated with exploration and proximity-seeking provide the infant with opportunities to learn an array of communication and social skills that become a foundation for social relatedness in ever-widening social spheres as the infant matures into childhood. Essential relational styles involving the communication of needs, and the expectations of others' responses to expressions of need, are therefore first learned in infancy in the first attachment relationships.

Bowlby's emphasis on predictable functions of behavioral systems led some critics in the Psychoanalytical Society to label him a "behaviorist" (Bretherton, 1992), referring to the mechanistic competing theory of the day, behaviorism, or social learning theory. Although to a great extent attachment theory is compatible with and can subsume important tenets of behaviorism, it is profoundly different from it in several ways. First, as discussed above, attachment theory contains a theory of instinctive motivation for safety and protection. Behaviorism, in contrast, has no theory of instinctive motivation beyond the pursuit of pleasure. Ainsworth and Bowlby repeatedly emphasized the dangers of employing a behaviorist model to understand children's distress when in need of their caregivers. According to behaviorism, children's expressed distress is presumed to be learned behavior. Learning theory predicts that when parents respond to fussy or distressed behavior with comfort, the behavior will be reinforced and thus likely to continue, and the child is thereby endangered with "dependency" or insufficient autonomy. The risk to children of this approach is that it ignores their intrinsic needs for safety, comfort, and protection, and that to withhold comfort risks creating longstanding anxiety and emotional insecurity. Autonomy, from the attachment viewpoint, is enabled not through withholding comfort, but through security-enhancing behavior, including ample provision of comfort when needed.

Cognition and Development

Bowlby's interest in the development of attachment in children led him to theorize that the attachment behavioral system had to operate as part of central nervous system circuitry, in which memory systems play a crucial role. Through repeated experiences with an attachment figure in times of distress, the child learns, and begins to make generalizations, about the responsiveness and reliability of the caregiving environment. These early experiences become increasingly organized in memory in structures Bowlby (1973, 1982) referred to as "internal working models," a term first used by the philosopher and cognitive psychologist Kenneth Craik. Bowlby preferred this term over more static representations of cognitive structures, because it communicates a sense of patterned responses to the social environment and, at the same time, the capacity for ongoing revision, based on learning from new social experiences. Internal working models, thus, can account for continuity of individual development as well as individual change. Internal working models become increasingly established and resistant to major revisions as the child grows, however. (The conceptualization of stability and change in cognition is one of several areas where Bowlby [1973] acknowledged the influence of Piaget on his thinking.) According to Bowlby, the primary adaptive function of internal working models is to provide the developing child with the capacity to predict the likely responses of potentially protective figures in situations where the child experiences vulnerability. Expectations of responsive care from others derive from and further promote emotional security, an attribute that can facilitate the building of positive relationships, and provide a buffer against future negative interpersonal experiences (Bretherton, 2005).

The process of organization of internal working models of attachment relationships is theorized to begin at the approximate age at which the formation of "object permanence," in the

Piagetian sense, begins for most children. The cognitive capacity of object permanence is, thus, thought to have a functional role in the development of internal working models (Bowlby, 1980). From this initial period of approximately age 6 months until approximately the age of 18 months, Bowlby viewed the child's development of internal working models as embryonic. At this latter age the child, under favorable conditions, is able to apply the representation of attachment figure in a new capacity. From the approximate age of 18 months to 3 years, the child's internal working model of attachment figure becomes increasingly available for the purpose of executing increasingly complex behavioral plans, especially those that involve venturing farther away from the proximity of the caregiver. The child is now able to *use* the internal representation of the caregiver to make predictions concerning his or her availability (Bowlby, 1980). As most children approach the end of the third year, the internal representation of the caregiver begins to carry with it the security-providing functions that, for the infant, were previously associated only with the actual presence of the attachment figure.

While an approximate developmental chronology is useful for tracking these changes, it is important to note that Bowlby disliked the use of "watershed"-type age markers. He saw the development of internal working models as a gradual life process, which changes qualitatively over time and is susceptible to revision. At the same time, however, according to theory, it is the formation of internal working models in infancy that accounts for the enduring quality of early attachment relationships throughout life (Bowlby, 1982).

Internal Working Models, Adversity, and Defensive Processes

In optimal conditions, attachment figures respond adequately and consistently to children's experiences of vulnerability. A child forms internal working models of attachment figures as reliable and trustworthy when these conditions are present. When a child consistently encounters behavior on the part of an attachment figure that does not adequately address conditions of vulnerability, however, the child is likely to form conflicting internal working models of the same attachment figure: a conscious one that preserves a sense of the parent as trustworthy, and one that is defensively excluded from consciousness containing the information regarding the parent's inadequacy (Bowlby, 1973). If the mental representations of the untrustworthy parent were integrated into the child's conscious internal working model, according to Bowlby, the resultant experience of threat and persistent insecurity would be overwhelming to the child. In order to preserve some sense of safety and security, therefore, the child maintains an illusory mental model of a reliable and responsive parent.

The formation of the internal working model of self reflects an appraisal process: A small child makes appraisals of himself or herself inferred from the nature of responses received from attachment figures. Internal working models of self and attachment figures are, thus, likely to be *complementary* (Bowlby, 1973). In non-optimal circumstances, where an attachment figure has not consistently responded to the child in reassuring ways, the internal working model of self is likely to take on qualities of inadequacy. An unloved child will appraise himself or herself as unlovable.

Effects of Prolonged Separations from Caregivers

One central, organizing idea of attachment theory that propelled much of Bowlby's work, and set him apart from most psychoanalysts of his day, is that children's intense reactions to prolonged separations from or loss of their primary caregivers provide direct and observable evidence for the existence of attachment bonds (Bowlby, 1982). Classical psychoanalytic theory discounted the experience of mourning in young children as a result of its emphasis on internal versus actual experience. Prolonged separations from or loss of attachment figures during the critical period for the formation of attachment, 6 to 36 months, and the quality of subsequent care children receive, may have profound developmental effects across the lifespan.

Bowlby incorporated a stage theory of children's reactions to prolonged separations, first developed by social worker James Robertson, a colleague of Bowlby's at Tavistock. Robertson proposed, based on filmed observations he made of children separated from their parents in hospitals (1952), as well as observations he and his wife, Joyce, made of their foster children, that young children normally react to prolonged separations from their attachment figures in phases characterized by protest, despair, and (if the separation is not addressed) detachment. In the first stage, the child exhibits a high level of anger, uncooperative behavior, searching, and anxiety, the function of which was, according to Bowlby, to challenge and eliminate interpersonal barriers standing in the way of reunion with the attachment figure. The protest of this stage is thus connected to the activation of attachment behavior, the expression of which may take different affective forms; it is designed to accomplish proximity to the missing attachment figure.

The next stage, despair, begins after the young child's protest at the separation has gone unanswered by the attachment figure. Depending on circumstances, this stage may begin after a period of days or weeks following the separation. At this stage, sadness and withdrawal are common features, though typically still intermingled with anxiety and/or anger.

In the final stage, if the attachment figure has failed to appear for the child and no substitutes are available, a virtual shutdown of the systems responsible for the child's attachment behavior begins and the child detaches emotionally from significant others. The longer that separation from the attachment figure continues, under circumstances where no substitute caregivers are available, the greater the risk for a progression into detachment and despair.

Bowlby's theory of grief and mourning, influenced by the work of Colin Murray Parkes (Bowlby, 1960, 1980), involves a normative progression through four major phases of adjustment: (a) numbing and shock; (b) yearning and searching, accompanied by anger and disbelief; (c) disorganization and despair, including the dismantling of internal working models of the relationships; and (d) reorganization and redefinition. This theory proved to be very influential on the work of others in the field, including that of Kubler-Ross (1969).

Conditions in the grieving child's life may or may not promote the child's successful reorganization of internal equilibrium. Often, the most important variable affecting this process is the way in which significant adults in the child's life react to the loss themselves and how they appraise and respond to the child's needs at this time. According to Bowlby, the most basic and, perhaps, single most helpful thing a significant adult in the child's life can do to promote the child's successful grieving of a lost figure is to permit and encourage the child to express, uncensored, the emotions associated with the loss (Bowlby, 1980). In this way, the risk to the child of developing a rigid defensive exclusion of the emotions associated with the loss and with the actual relationship with the lost figure is minimized. The ability of significant adults to provide a child with opportunities for grieving necessarily depends on their own capacity to accept and express the range of emotions associated with the loss.

When conditions do not favor a person's successful resolution of loss, characteristics of "disordered mourning" are likely to appear. Among the manifestations of disordered mourning discussed by Bowlby are (a) chronic mourning, when the resolution of the loss is not effected and the person remains "stuck" in earlier phases of searching/yearning or disorganization/despair, and (b) the absence of grief, when the experience of the loss is largely defensively excluded from conscious awareness. Bowlby describes several types of symptoms associated with children's reactions to loss, which fall generally under these two major rubrics, including the following: fear that a surviving parent will die; fear of the child's own death; hopes for death as a way to be reunited with the lost figure (this is especially likely for children who do not perceive death as irreversible); persisting blame, of self or of others, or guilt; aggression and destructive outbursts (Bowlby believed that virtually all children who react in this way have a hidden sense of guilt for the loss); compulsive caregiving; compulsive self-reliance; euphoria and depersonalization; and the development of symptoms similar to those the lost person had (Bowlby, 1980).

In Bowlby's view, psychological defense, separation anxiety/reaction, and grief and mourning are interrelated processes, functioning as part of one larger process involving initial activation and subsequent deactivation of attachment behavior for a missing, lost, or unresponsive attachment figure; thus the meaning and function of these processes were recast as expressions of attachment behavior (1973). He also emphasized that the course taken in childhood in reaction to separation or loss may well affect a person throughout the entire lifespan, depending to a great extent on the way in which attachment behavior was expressed in the relationship and the nature of response received from the caregiving environment.

The Contributions to Attachment Theory of Mary Ainsworth and Colleagues

Bowlby's crowning achievement was the construction of an elegant, new developmental framework. In contrast, he participated less in empirical research. The application of attachment theory to empirical research was left by and large to his colleagues and followers, beginning, most notably, with Mary Ainsworth, an American developmental psychologist and colleague of Bowlby's at the Tavistock Clinic. Ainsworth conducted the first major empirical studies of attachment, beginning with work she did in rural Uganda (Ainsworth, 1963) and later in Baltimore (Ainsworth, Blehar, Waters, & Wall, 1978). Her interest in children's emotional security went back to her days as a doctoral student in Toronto, where her dissertation, completed in 1940, incorporated the "security theory" of her mentor, William Blatz (Ainsworth & Marvin, 1995).

Ainsworth's research utilized primarily observations of mother–child interactions, which became a major part of her enduring legacy, the inspiration for which she credited Robertson's observations of children in hospital settings. In their Baltimore study, Ainsworth and colleagues created a major innovation in observational research methods, the Strange Situation Procedure, a laboratory assessment containing several progressive steps designed to observe firsthand how infants react to separations from their mothers. Significant associations were found between home observations of the quality of mother–child interactions and attachment patterns observed in the Strange Situation, suggesting that the laboratory observations were

valid indicators of interactive behavioral patterns between mother and child, and likely represented enduring dyadic relationship qualities.

In brief, the Strange Situation consists of the following seven episodes: (1) the mother and infant enter a small room containing several toys, and the infant is allowed to play and explore as desired; (2) a female "stranger"/assistant enters the room and sits quietly; (3) mother leaves the room, leaving the infant alone with the assistant, who freely interacts with the child; (4) the mother returns and the assistant leaves the room; (5) the mother departs, leaving the infant alone; (6) the stranger returns to the room; (7) the mother returns to the room, and the assistant leaves. Each of the major episodes lasts 3 minutes, unless curtailed because of infant distress.

In her Baltimore study, Ainsworth's subjects (N = 106) were collected over four separate projects; all were white and middle-class. Observations of the infants' responses to absences from and, especially, reunions with the mother were recorded by scoring numerous types of infant behavior in interaction with their mothers. On the basis of these observations, Ainsworth created three main categories (composed of eight subgroups) of attachment security: insecure-avoidant (A); secure (B); and insecure-ambivalent (resistant) (C). Avoidant babies tended to display little attachment behavior and little emotion, in general, toward their mothers. They typically avoided their mother upon her return by turning their backs or snubbing maternal overtures toward them. Secure babies showed clear distress and attachment behavior toward their mothers during separations. When reunited with their mothers, they approached and sought contact, and after a period of comforting, returned to exploration. These babies were distinguished from the other groups by their abilities to regain emotional equilibrium and regulation after reassuring contact with the mother. Ambivalent babies tended to approach their mothers upon her return but remained dissatisfied and angry, not soothed by her presence.

Ainsworth's findings supported and elucidated several important aspects of Bowlby's theory of attachment, especially the notion that attachment behavior will look different for children depending on their life experiences. Consistent with theory, the three main categories of attachment security were primarily distinguished by patterned activation or deactivation of attachment behavior, and qualities of synchronous interaction of parent and child. In Bowlby's original terms, the attachment relationship provides the infant with an interpersonal system of regulation, which eventually leads to the child's own physiological regulatory capacities development (Bowlby, 1982). Ainsworth's classification system identified specific variations in how this goal is accomplished. Parents of securely attached babies, in contrast to those of insecurely attached children, were notable for their *sensitivity* and *responsiveness* toward their children. They were expert at understanding their children's needs for them, with great insight into the child's point of view, and had the necessary personal resources to be able to respond to them according to their needs.

The Strange Situation was important first because it provided a standard behavioral measure of attachment for infants up to approximately 2 years of age (it is typically used for infants between the ages of 12 and 18 months). (Two of Ainsworth's students, Jude Cassidy and Robert Marvin, adapted the original Strange Situation Procedure for use with preschool children up to age 5 [Cassidy & Marvin, 1992]). It also came to be viewed as, essentially, a shortcut in the assessment of parent and child interaction that normally would be done in the naturalistic setting of the home (Ainsworth & Marvin, 1995). Assessment in the Strange Situation, then, has become a standard against which other measures of attachment, especially those taking place later in childhood, are compared. In some ways, Ainsworth regretted that the classifications derived from Strange Situation assessments had become essentially synonymous with attachment, and presumed by many to be sufficient for understanding attachment behavior in parent–child dyads. She advocated all her life for behavioral scientists to study children by observing them in their natural environments, especially their homes (Ainsworth & Marvin, 1995), which she regarded as essential to capturing a full understanding of attachment relationships.

As researchers around the world began to use the Strange Situation, providing validation in varied settings, it became apparent to many that a significant minority of children were difficult to classify according to the Ainsworth tripartite system, especially for high-risk samples. Mary Main, another of Ainsworth's former students, and colleagues ultimately discovered consistencies in behavioral profiles for many of these children, resulting in a fourth category of attachment behavior, the disorganized/disoriented category (Main & Solomon, 1990). Characteristics observed in the Strange Situation reunion behavior of children assigned to this group are immobilization and disorientation upon the mother's return, contradiction in physical movement, and, inferred from the contradictory physical movements, contradictions in intended, or planned, behavior. The disorganized/disoriented attachment pattern is considered a more severe adaptation to inadequate caregiving circumstances, distinguished by the absence of any coherent strategy for engagement and interaction. As such, it is considered a "non-organized" attachment strategy, compared to the original three categories identified by Ainsworth. Even though the avoidant and ambivalent patterns are insecure attachment strategies, they are at least organized strategies—that is, predictable patterns of interaction that function to maintain contact with attachment figures, however limited. In contrast, the young child with disorganized attachment is disoriented, without a predictable means of engagement with attachment figures. Disorganized attachment has been shown to be prevalent among maltreated children (as high as 82% reported in Carlson, Cicchetti, Barnett, & Braunwald, 1989). As the child matures, however, many do develop patterned interactions with their caregivers, but not in the sense of reliance on them. By the age of 6, role-reversed, controlling interactive patterns, of punitive or caretaking dimensions, have been observed among many children classified in infancy as insecure-disorganized (Main & Cassidy, 1988). These behavioral adaptations, of course, are not oriented to the child's needs, and they are not typically stable or predictable, since they tend to occur in the context of a maltreating relationship.

Ainsworth stressed the importance of recognizing secure and insecure attachments as variations, or individual patterns, of attachment bonds and not, except in relatively rare circumstances, equivalent to the presence or absence of attachments per se. Insecure children by and large have attachments to their caregivers that are equal in intensity to secure children. Child welfare workers and foster parents see this every day of their professional lives, in the protest and activated attachment behavior in children who have been seriously maltreated. When such behavior is not seen for what it is, the anxious, insecure child who has been separated from a parent will often be misunderstood and perceived simply as having a behavior problem.

Another major innovation in the development of attachment theory and research was marked with the publication of a seminal paper by Main, Kaplan, and Cassidy (1985), which brought attention to the study of the *representational* dimension of attachment. Following Bowlby's theory of internal working models, Main, Kaplan, and Cassidy argued that attachment organization could be assessed beyond infancy with evidence of organized memories, the internally represented dimension, of attachment relevant experience. This approach to measurement is critical for the study of attachment in older children and adults, since attachment behavior becomes attenuated as the child matures and observational measures lose their utility.

A major innovation to arise from this line of research was created by Mary Main and colleagues, the Adult Attachment Interview (AAI), to which Main applied her background in psycholinguistics with her knowledge of attachment in infancy gained from her years in Ainsworth's infant laboratory (Main, 1999a). The major innovation of the AAI was the discovery that the assessment of attachment organization in adulthood could be accomplished primarily on the basis of nonverbal discourse qualities, particularly the *coherence* of discourse, moderation in affective expression, and sense of objectivity regarding important events. Coherence of discourse involves qualities such as consistency, flow, truthfulness, and richness of supporting memories offered in responses, as well as the succinctness, completion, relevancy, and clarity of responses (Hesse, 2008). The AAI interview questions focus on the respondent's history of care received as a child, especially major events relevant to safety and protection. Attachment classifications are identified based on the discourse qualities revealed in the telling of this personal narrative. Four main adult attachment classifications are used, reflecting the four similar classifications used for infants: secure/autonomous; dismissing (avoidant); preoccupied (ambivalent); and unresolved/disorganized.

The process of recall in the interview activates feelings associated with early attachment-related events, as well as the respondent's characteristic style of making sense of and coping with these. The degree to which the respondent has access to the memory systems involved is an important indicator of the extent of past emotional pain and defenses employed to address this. Dismissing adults tend to have difficulties accessing the often-intense affect associated with these memories, coping to a great extent by relying on emotional distance. Preoccupied adults tend towards the reverse, with relatively greater access to affectively charged memories, to the point of being overwhelmed with intense and unfocused emotion, with relatively weak abilities to use synthesized memories to gain a more dispassionate and balanced perception of past events. The unresolved/disorganized classification is characterized by evidence of lack of resolution of past trauma or major loss (Hesse, 2008).

Numerous studies over the past 20-plus years have attested to the reliability and validity of the AAI as a measure of attachment organization in adulthood (see Hesse, 2008, for a review).

Concurrent linkages between infant Strange Situation classifications and parents' AAI classifications have been found in several studies, with moderately strong effect sizes. Hesse (2008) reports 4 U.S. samples, involving a total of over 200 subjects, where high, though not absolute, concordances between Strange Situation and AAI classifications have been found for individuals longitudinally, across their lifespans. The AAI has also been used, most impressively, to prospectively predict attachment security in dyads. AAI classifications of mothers assessed in their third trimester of pregnancy have been found to predict their infants' attachment classification to them when the children were 12 months old. (Fonagy, Steele, & Steele, 1991). The AAI has led to a new understanding of the significance of discourse qualities in speech and has spawned a new generation of interview protocols that reflect these insights (Koren-Karie,

Oppenheim, Dolev, Sher, & Etzion-Carasso, 2002; Zeanah & Benoit, 1995).

Current Research

Since the publication of the first volume of Bowlby's *Attachment and Loss* trilogy in 1969, attachment research has grown exponentially. A cursory search of indexed databases shows applications of attachment theory in all major areas of human development and therapeutic intervention, and across all major related disciplines. Attachment theory is regarded, according to the eminent developmental scholar Michael Rutter, as the leading theory of the development of early social behavior in childhood (Rutter & Rutter, 1993).

The body of evidence, including major longitudinal studies of attachment in different countries, has confirmed the major tenets of Bowlby's theory: that it is universal, transmitted across generations, relatively enduring, predictive of major developmental sequelae, yet subject to environmental influence across the lifespan. Due to space limitations, a sampling of selected topics, with perhaps particular relevance to social workers, is presented here.

Attachment Across the Lifespan

Several longitudinal studies have now shown strong consistencies in attachment security from infancy, into childhood, and adulthood. Many developmentally relevant correlates of secure attachment have been discovered across the lifespan. Among this very large body of research, attachment security assessed in infancy has been shown to predict supportive social networks, including peer relationships, ego resilience, emotion regulation, positive self-concept, conscience development and pro-social behavior, emotion understanding, and empathic responsiveness in childhood (see Thompson, 2008, for a review). In short, secure attachment is regarded as an essential developmental foundation that is the basis for the acquisition of critical social skills that determine social and emotional functioning beyond infancy and across the lifespan.

Developments in representational assessments have enabled researchers to advance the study of attachment into early and middle childhood. Among these, the Attachment Story Completion Task (ASCT; Bretherton, Ridgeway, & Cassidy, 1990) is based on Bowlby's theory that attachment experience becomes organized, and increasingly relied upon, via internal working models. Children aged 4 to 7 are presented with short story stems depicting everyday stressors (e.g., the parents go away for an overnight trip and the grandmother babysits), enacted with basic family doll figures and props. In response, the children create spontaneous narratives, which researchers videotape and code for themes of interest, such as enactments of caregiving, conflict, attachment behavior, and coherence. A growing body of story completion task literature has demonstrated that children's story-stem responses are significantly correlated with indices of attachment security, including infant Strange Situation classifications and mothers' AAI classifications (Bretherton, 2005), and a variety of other measures of social and emotional well-being, including pro-social behavior with peers, anxiety, maltreatment history, and mothers' depression (Emde, Wolf, & Oppenheim, 2003; Page, 2001). Story-stem responses have also been used as a dependent variable following a parenting intervention, showing change in children's perceptions of their parents (Toth, Maughan, Todd Manly, Spagnola, & Cicchetti, 2002), as well as a measure of perceptions of mother–child interactive qualities associated with observed behavior in the home (Dubois-Comtois & Moss, 2008).

Attachment has also been increasingly studied beyond childhood, into adolescence and adulthood, a subject that Ainsworth was particularly interested in and wrote about in the latter part of her career (1989). This emerging empirical literature began with Hazan and Shaver's (1987) discovery of attachment-oriented interactive styles in romantically involved young adults that were conceptually consistent with Ainsworth's original attachment categories. Subsequent findings from two prospective longitudinal studies have found that attachment security in infancy indirectly predicts the quality of romantic relationships in early adulthood, via a developmental pathway through childhood peer relationships (Berlin, Cassidy, & Appleyard, 2008).

Social Ecology/Social Systems

Attachment theory is an ecological theory, taking into account biology and individual, micro-system interdependence, as well as larger system influences, external to the family, on the development of emotional security in children (see Belsky, 2005). At its core, attachment is a dynamic concept. The behavioral systems governing its operation are in constant interaction, in states of relative activation and deactivation, with overarching system goals of balance and regulation characterizing their optimal functioning. The infant develops within a dyadic, mutually regulatory, interactive system that promotes and eventually leads to the achievement of more internalized management of regulatory capacities (Bowlby, 1982).

Attachment patterns tend to be transmitted intergenerationally, though not absolutely; that is, children tend to develop the same basic attachment type as their attachment figures (Bretherton & Munholland, 2008), but various forces operating in the social ecology affect this process. Attachment type thus represents a learned coping strategy. Since attachment type is specific to a given dyadic relationship, a child may have different attachments within the family, depending on the attachment figure. How children synthesize their attachment experiences into a dominant attachment interpersonal style is likely influenced by their primary attachment figure, though as yet little is known about this process.

Attachment and Developmental Psychopathology

Attachment theory has proved to be useful in understanding the developmental consequences of risk, resilience, and trauma on children, including the emergence of psychopathology. Bowlby (1973) adapted the concept of the "developmental pathway" from the biological sciences to explain how early events, especially those affecting attachment security, can come to influence later development, not necessarily linearly, but in interaction with various other events and circumstances the growing child encounters in the environment over the years.

Attachment insecurity has been shown to be associated with specific forms of psychopathology, but these relationships are complex and determined by other risks encountered in the child's social ecology, including child characteristics (primarily biologically inherited characteristics), insensitive parental practices, and family-level risks (DeKlyen & Greenberg, 2008), among which poverty has a dominating influence. The evidence thus far is consistent with theory: Organized insecure attachments (avoidance and ambivalence) are moderate risk factors for the development of some forms of psychopathology (e.g., affective disorders, conduct disorders; DeKlyen & Greenberg, 2008), whereas disorganized/disoriented attachment presents significantly stronger risks, in particular for conduct, affective, self-injurious, and dissociative disorders (Sroufe, 2005).

Attachment theory has contributed to significant innovation in thinking about the needs of maltreated children in foster care systems, and children who are exposed to chronic extreme distress, such as family violence. Seen from an attachment perspective, traumatic events are damaging to children first and foremost because they threaten a child's sense of safety and protection. A child whose attachment figure inflicts abuse and trauma faces an unresolvable dilemma: Attachment behavior is instinctively activated toward the very source of distress, a desire for proximity with the person who presents the most immediate threat. This dilemma is the heart of disorganized attachment, and its confused and contradictory behavioral strategies are familiar to every child welfare worker and foster parent, as well as many adult victims of domestic violence, and are a powerful influence in the emergence of the psychopathology associated with disorganized attachment.

Recovery from trauma must begin with the reestablishment of confidence in the safety and protection of the caregiving environment. Attachment theory has been instrumental in demonstrating that children need to have protective adults, including adoptive and foster parents, make emotional investments in them, as opposed to guarding against emotional commitment as a way to protect the child (and themselves) from the pain of potential or eventual separation (Dozier & Rutter, 2008).

Reactive Attachment Disorder

The psychiatric literature has been influenced by attachment theory, as reflected in the diagnostic disorder known as Reactive Attachment Disorder. Critics of this diagnosis point out, however, that its criteria are more relevant to maltreatment, broadly construed, and focus on problematic social behavior of the child, as opposed to specific qualities of attachment relationships (Deklyen & Greenberg, 2008). Alternative attachment disorder typologies have been put forward that emphasize specific relational dynamics and types of attachment disorders (i.e., non-attachment, extreme distortions in secure base behavior, and attachment disruptions due to extreme circumstances involving loss). Attachment disorders, thus, are not simply insecure attachments, and must be thought of as extreme disruptions or deprivations in attachment, associated with the most profound of developmental risks.

Pseudoscience

It is important to note, finally, that attachment theory has been seriously misapplied, at the expense of children's lives, by some proponents of so-called "attachment therapies." In perhaps the most notorious of these cases, a 10-year-old girl was smothered to death by ersatz "therapists" practicing "holding therapy" (Mercer, Sarner, & Rosa, 2003), a dangerous treatment without evidentiary base that does not derive in any logical way from attachment theory (O'Connor & Zeanah, 2003). It is imperative that social workers and other human services professionals have accurate information about what attachment is and is not, and that their practice is consistent with developmental knowledge and evidence-based approaches.

Current Status and Relevance in the Social Work Profession

Attachment scholarship has been the province primarily of developmental psychologists, ever since Mary Ainsworth's pioneering studies in the 1960s. Social work has been comparatively late in integrating attachment theory into its research and practice, especially in the United States, but this is changing quickly. This chapter, in fact, marks the first time that attachment theory has been included in *Social Work Treatment*. Contributions by social work scholars toward integrating attachment theory into social work

practice now appear across a wide range of topics, including theory development (McMillen, 1992; Sable, 1979); practice roles (Howe, 1995); clinical supervision (Bennett, 2008); assessment and intervention with foster children and/or foster parents (Schofield & Beek, 2005); parental visitation in child welfare (Haight, Kagle, & Black, 2003); adoption (Howe, 2001); narrative assessments with young children (Page, 2001); child-bearing motivations (Warren, Sable, & Csizmadia, 2008); risk for disruptive behavior problems in childhood (Keller, Spieker, & Gilchrist, 2005); treatment for reactive attachment disorder (Drisko & Zilberstein, 2008); eating disorders (Barth, 2008); parenting assessments (Farnfield, 2008; Koren-Karie, Oppenheim, Dolev, Sher, & Etzion-Carasso, 2002; Lewis, 1999; Rosenblum, Zeanah, McDonough, & Muzik, 2004); and intervention with couples (Solomon, 2009) and parents (Page & Cain, 2009), among others. Special issues of the *Clinical Social Work Journal* and *Child and Adolescent Social Work Journal* have recently been dedicated to addressing applications of attachment theory to clinical practice (in 2008 and 2009, respectively). Haight and Taylor's 2007 text for social work courses on human behavior in the social environment was the first to use attachment theory as a major organizing framework, and stands in marked contrast to the cursory treatment attachment theory gets, if it is mentioned at all, in most other HBSE texts. New edited volumes on attachment theory and social work practice with children and adults are in press as of this writing.

Assessment and Intervention

Attachment theory holds important implications for psychotherapeutic practice, a topic that was of special concern to Bowlby (1988). According to his guidelines, a therapist should be sensitive to the primacy of safety and protection in the developmental experience of the client. Interpretations and analysis of the client's relational experience, including within the therapeutic relationship, should be based on an understanding of the centrality of the expression of attachment behavior in social experience and with regard to the creation of personal identity. Psychotherapy from an attachment perspective involves the "reappraisal of inadequate, outdated working models of self in relation to attachment figures" (Bretherton, 1992, p. 768), focusing on heightened understanding of the characteristic ways in which needs for safety and protection are expressed in current relationships, including defensive strategies, and the extent to which these behaviors represent attempts to cope with unresponsive attachment figures, learned early in life. Discussions of clients' perceptions of the therapeutic relationship should include sensitivity to the client's regard for the therapist as an attachment figure, and the actual limitations of this role.

There is a particular imperative for social workers, including social work educators, to be thoroughly grounded in attachment theory and research. As a profession, we have a unique responsibility to provide services to the most vulnerable of our society's children in our child welfare systems. Making the best-informed decisions about the well-being of these children requires thorough knowledge of the processes through which children form attachments to their caregivers. Unless we understand these issues in depth, reflecting the current state of knowledge in the field, we are neither honoring our professional responsibilities nor practicing ethically.

Case Example

This case involves Jerri, a 21-year-old mother, who was reported to child protective services for inadequate supervision of her son, Brian (both names are pseudonyms). At age 2, Brian was found wandering alone along a busy highway, the latest of several incidents when he had been found wandering outside unsupervised, necessitating police involvement. After a brief stay in kinship foster care, Brian was returned to Jerri's custody, and Jerri was referred for parenting services. Jerri worked an afternoon/night shift as a nursing home attendant, often up to 16 hours, and child care was inconsistently provided. At the time of this intervention, Jerri had been a client of the child welfare system for 2 years. In childhood, she had been severely emotionally and sexually abused by her father. She had attained a ninth-grade education (she dropped out in 10th grade) and had been diagnosed with dyslexia.

The parenting service provided was the Circle of Security® (Hoffman, Marvin, Cooper, & Powell, 2006; Marvin, Cooper, Hoffman, & Powell, 2002; Page & Cain, 2009), a small-group intervention for six to eight

participants based on attachment principles. Children's interactions with caregivers are presented as representing the two principal behavioral systems discussed by Bowlby, attachment and exploration, integrated as continuous and alternating dimensions of one interactive circle. Empathic understanding and responsiveness toward children's alternating needs for exploration and attachment are taught primarily through videotape review sessions where participants watch themselves in interaction with their children. The video segments are selected from pre-intervention assessments by group leaders to illustrate key relationship qualities as identified in treatment plans. Each participant receives three review sessions.

Assessments included attachment ratings for child and mother provided by the Strange Situation Procedure (parent attachment was assessed with Marvin's Caregiver Behavior Scales, rated by the author, Robert Marvin [Britner, Marvin, & Pianta, 2005]; child attachment classifications were also provided by Robert Marvin). Parent insightfulness ("the parent's capacity to invoke motives that underlie the child's behavior"; Oppenheim & Koren-Karie, 2002) was also assessed using an attachment-inspired interview, the Insightfulness Assessment (rated by the authors, David Oppenheim and Nina Koren-Karie). All assessments were rated independently. Jerri and Brian were assessed at the pretest observation with disorganized attachment, and Jerri was assessed with the most problematic of three classes of insightfulness, corresponding to disorganized attachment (Oppenheim & Koren-Karie, 2002). The intervention was led by this author.

The following dialogue was taken from Jerri's second tape-review session. Second tape-review sessions are designed to focus on the most profound problems in the relationship, conceptualized as the parent's difficulties in responding to the child's expressions of exploration or attachment, or both. For Jerri, as for other dyads rated with disorganized attachment, the major relationship difficulties typically involve inconsistent responsiveness to *both* the child's exploration and attachment. In the following excerpt, we see Jerri's frustration and irritation for Brian's anxiety and need for her, which were often activated when she came home from work feeling emotionally and physically depleted. The therapeutic challenge was to reframe Brian's behavior so Jerri could understand it as activated attachment behavior.

Jerri: You know, when I work, he is usually up at 6 o'clock in the morning waiting for me to get home . . . He is very demanding in the morning time. He is like, "I don't want to go to school, I want to stay home with you," and I am like, "You can't stay here, you have to go to school, so we are going to sit here and watch TV."…It is very aggravating at times, only from exhaustion, because you know I am so exhausted sometimes…

Later in this session, a short video clip was shown to Jerri of her interaction with Brian in the Strange Situation Procedure, showing her reunion with him after a brief separation, to illustrate and explain Brian's attachment behavior, directed toward her:

Group Leader 1: So this first clip, you have been out of the room, and we are looking at how he is responding to you when you return. What are we seeing?

Jerri: Going back to his mom.

Group Leader 2: He made a beeline for you.

Jerri: Yeah, he does that all the time. It's like he can smell me when I walk in the door, whether he sees me or not, he knows when I walk in the door. Sometimes I try to sneak, he's in his room, so I try to shower before he comes out, and he's like, "Mama, let me in." He knows, he knows.

Group Leader1: This kind of behavior has been studied a lot. That behavior has been identified in every mammal in the planet. When there has been a separation, you see the exact same thing. I am imagining that it can kind of feel aggravating at times, but it is also important to see that it's normal.

Jerri: Oh yeah, as much as it aggravates me when he runs up to me, my back is killing me and he goes, "Hold me," there is nothing I like better than when he runs up to me and hugs me and kisses me and holds me and I don't want to let go.

Group Leader 1: Right. He just wants to be near you…

Later, Jerri reflected on her conflict over wanting Brian to be more autonomous and for her to have more emotional "space," yet at the same time fearing separation from him, the loss of his love, and her own abandonment.

Jerri [discussion turned to anticipation of Brian's visits with his father]: I am so jealous. I want him to be all mine. I don't like to have to share him. I had him by myself this whole while, so I don't want to share him with anybody. I don't want to know that he could love somebody else more than he loves me…Man, they grow up so fast. You want them to be able to do their own little thing, but once they do it, it sucks. The older they get, the less they act like they need you to be there.

Later in this session, Jerri reflected further:

Jerri: Most of my [anxiety] comes on when I feel that threat that he is going to be taken away from me or he is going to love someone more than me. I guess my mother did this to me, she was the same way. If we ever acted like we had more fun at my father's, she would be like, "You had more fun with him than you did with me."

Group Leader 1: You put your finger on the idea that… you feel anxious about being separated. It is important to look at where that leaves him. He gets a little confused. Keep in mind, when you are in that situation, "Is he feeling like he needs to soothe me or am I being the 'bigger, stronger, wiser, and kind' person?" *[a phrase used in the intervention to refer to the authoritative role]*

Jerri: I think it is good for your children to feel like they help you as much as you help them. I think it is good for him to feel needed. Even though I hate when I feel that way, it only takes a second of his wonderful personality to make me better…as soon as I notice that he notices that I feel that way and he is like, "Give me a hug, let's lay down, mama," I automatically perk up and smile and everything is okay. He doesn't realize that I am dying inside.

In this passage, we see tendencies toward role-reversal, indicating Jerri's strong unmet needs for her own nurture, a characteristic commonly associated with disorganized attachment and child maltreatment. Jerri's primary treatment goal was to become more empathic in recognizing and responding to Brian's need for proximity to and comfort from her and, in the process, to maintain a nurturing and authoritative parental role. At the same time, she had to learn to cope with her own anxiety about his normally developing autonomy and separateness from her. The intervention thus focused on challenges she faced in responding to "both sides" of the attachment–exploration circle.

Several sessions later, during her third and final tape review, Jerri reflected on how her discomfort at Brian's expressions of attachment typically evoked a circular set of responses, wherein she became irritated and withdrew, which elicited stronger attachment behavior and frustration for him. This sort of interchange typically involved hostility and coercion.

Jerri: He does that. He knows right when I am at the boiling point, I am just right there, don't mess with me, then he is like, he likes to go a couple feet over the edge there.

Group Leader 1: What might that be about?

Jerri: Testing.

Group Leader 1: What might a child be needing when you are almost going to boil over?

Jerri: I think he is just, because when I am to the point where I have just had enough, I am distant…Sometimes when you are distant, a lot of children experience this, it doesn't, sometimes doesn't matter good or bad, they want attention.

By conceptualizing Jerri's struggles with her son in terms of an integrated circle of expression of exploration and attachment needs, Jerri was able to reframe Brian's neediness for her, and she was able to respond empathically to his need. This facilitated her growing capacities to reflect on and cope with her own anxieties about separation and abandonment, and her occupation of the authoritative parental role. She very obviously and deliberately began to change her behavior toward Brian to be more nurturing when she perceived him to be anxious and needing her, and more supportive when she perceived him to need autonomy.

At the post-test assessments, approximately 6 months after the pre-test, Jerri and Brian were rated with secure attachment, and Jerri's Insightfulness Assessment revealed a Positively Insightful rating, which corresponds to secure attachment. Anecdotal follow-up with them in subsequent years has shown that they continue to do well, and Jerri consistently regards the Circle of Security intervention as having provided a positive turning point in her relationship with her son.

Research Challenges Still Lying Ahead

Growth in the field of attachment research has given rise to many new questions about its applicability across many dimensions of the human experience (see Main, 1999b, for a discussion of research challenges). A sampling of these issues is presented here.

Cultural Variation

Several cross-cultural studies have shown that attachment is a universal human phenomenon (van Ijzendoorn & Sagi-Schwartz, 2008), but that frequencies within attachment patterns appear to vary with culture. Larger numbers of people have been identified, for example, as insecure-ambivalent in Mediterranean countries compared to U.S. and northern European samples.

The extent to which attachment patterns are shaped by culture, and the mechanisms through which this occurs, are as yet not well understood.

Instinctive Inheritance and the Brain

Attachment theory locates attachment behavior among other instinctive behaviors, the functions of which ultimately promote species survival. It is as yet unclear how other instinct-based behavioral systems such as, for example, social dominance hierarchies and mating behavior may interact and influence or be influenced by the attachment behavioral system. Much more study is needed of the brain functions responsible for these behaviors.

Measurement

The best-known systems for measuring attachment quality are the categorical systems derived from Strange Situation classifications: secure, insecure-avoidant, insecure-ambivalent, insecure-disorganized. Other approaches to the measurement of attachment quality have used dimensional systems, placing variations on a continuum or continua of dimensions of central characteristics, such as security versus insecurity. It is not yet known what the "best" way for conceptualizing differences in attachment quality will prove to be.

Research Applications to Social Work Practice

The needs for new knowledge concerning applications of attachment theory to social work practice are too numerous to include here, spanning virtually every practice area. Little is yet known, for example, about how children who have been exposed to extreme adversity in their caregiving environments form healthy attachments later in childhood, so-called second attachments, as in the case of placement in foster homes. Other important practice areas in need of more research include assessments with children, especially adapting representational measures to clinical settings; adult interviewing, using the insights of research with the AAI on the significance of discourse qualities to attachment organization; the use of videotape, using technical achievements from the history of observational attachment research; and education for parents and foster parents, applying our developmental knowledge about the significance of attachment to development to problems in parenting. Opportunities abound for social work researchers interested in furthering these fields of inquiry.

Attachment scholarship, beginning with Bowlby over 40 years ago, has profoundly changed our understanding of the human needs for care and protection in close relationships. Although the field of social work has been relatively late in understanding and integrating this new knowledge, we are now being transformed by it, in many different areas of practice. This is a very promising development: The quality of social work services, especially for children and families, depends on our mastery of the most current scientific knowledge of human behavior, among which attachment theory must be regarded as a foundational pillar.

Acknowledgment

Significant portions of this chapter appeared in Page, T., & Norwood, R. (2007). Attachment theory and the social work curriculum. *Advances in Social Work*, 8(1), 30–48.

References

Ainsworth, M. D. S. (1963). The development of infant-mother interaction among the Ganda. In B. M. Foss (Ed.), *Determinants of infant behavior* (pp. 67–104). New York: Wiley.

Ainsworth, M. D. S. (1989). Attachments beyond infancy. *American Psychologist, 44*, 709–716.

Ainsworth, M. D. S., Blehar, M. C., Waters, E., & Wall, S. (1978). *Patterns of attachment: A psychological study of the strange situation*. Hillsdale, N.J.: Erlbaum Associates.

Ainsworth, M. D. S., & Bowlby, J. (1991). An ethological approach to personality development. *American Psychologist, 46*(4), 333–341.

Ainsworth, M. D. S., & Marvin, R. S. (1995). On the shaping of attachment theory and research: An interview with Mary D. S. Ainsworth. *Monographs of the Society for Research in Child Development, 60*(2-3): *Caregiving, Cultural, and Cognitive Perspectives on Secure-Base Behavior and Working Models: New Growing Points of Attachment Theory and Research*, pp. 3–21.

Barth, D. F. (2008). Hidden eating disorders: Attachment and affect regulation in the therapeutic relationship. *Clinical Social Work Journal, 36*(4), 355–365.

Belsky, J. (2005). Attachment theory and research in ecological perspective: Insights from the Pennsylvania Infant Family Development Project and the NICHD Study of Early Child Care. In K. E. Grossmann, K. Grossmann, & E. Waters (Eds.), *Attachment from infancy to adulthood: The major longitudinal studies* (pp. 71–97). New York: The Guilford Press.

Bennett, S. (2008). The interface of attachment, transference, and countertransference: Implications for the clinical supervisory relationship. *Smith College Studies in Social Work, 78*(2-3), 301–320.

Berlin, L. J., Cassidy, J., & Appleyard, K. (2008). The influence of early attachments on other relationships. In J. Cassidy & P. R. Shaver (Eds.), *Handbook of attachment: Theory, research, and clinical applications* (2nd ed.) (pp. 333–347). New York: The Guilford Press.

Bowlby, J. (1960). Grief and mourning in infancy and early childhood. *Psychoanalytic Study of the Child, 15*, 9–52.

Bowlby, J. (1973). *Attachment and loss, Vol. II: Separation: Anxiety and anger*. New York: Basic Books.

Bowlby, J. (1980). *Attachment and loss, Vol. III: Loss: Sadness and depression*. New York: Basic Books.

Bowlby, J. (1982). *Attachment and loss, Vol. I: Attachment* (2nd ed.). New York: Basic Books.

Bowlby, J. (1988). Attachment, communication, and the therapeutic process. In J. Bowlby, *A secure base* (pp. 137–157). New York: Basic Books.

Bretherton, I. (1992). The origins of attachment theory: John Bowlby and Mary Ainsworth. *Developmental Psychology, 28*(5), 759–775.

Bretherton, I. (2005). In pursuit of the internal working model construct and its relevance to attachment relationships. In K. E. Grossmann, K. Grossmann, & E. Waters (Eds.), *Attachment from infancy to adulthood: The major longitudinal studies* (pp. 13–47). New York: The Guilford Press.

Bretherton, I., & Munholland, K. A. (2008). Internal working models in attachment relationships: Elaborating a central construct in attachment theory. In J. Cassidy & P. R. Shaver (Eds.), *Handbook of attachment: Theory, research, and clinical applications* (2nd ed.) (pp. 102–127). New York: The Guilford Press.

Bretherton, I., Ridgeway, D., & Cassidy, J. (1990). Assessing the internal working models of the attachment relationship: An attachment story completion task for 3-year-olds. In M. T. Greenberg,

D. Cicchetti, & E. M. Cummings (Eds.), *Attachment in the preschool years: Theory, research, and intervention* (pp. 273–308). Chicago: University of Chicago Press.

Britner, P. A., Marvin, R. S., & Pianta, R. C. (2005). Development and preliminary validation of the caregiving behavior system: Association with child attachment classification in the preschool Strange Situation. *Attachment & Human Development, 7*(1), 83–102.

Carlson, V., Cicchetti, D., Barnett, D., & Braunwald, K. (1989). Disorganized/disoriented attachment relationships in maltreated infants. *Developmental Psychology, 25*, 525–531.

Cassidy, J., & Marvin, R. S. (1992). Attachment organization in preschool children: Procedures and coding manual (5th ed.). Unpublished manuscript, MacArthur Working Group on Attachment, Seattle, WA.

DeKlyen, M., & Greenberg, M. T. (2008). Attachment and psychopathology in childhood. In J. Cassidy & P. R. Shaver (Eds.), *Handbook of attachment: Theory, research, and clinical applications* (2nd ed.) (pp. 637–665). New York: The Guilford Press.

Dozier, M., & Rutter, M. (2008). Challenges to the development of attachment relationships faced by young children in foster and adoptive care. In J. Cassidy & P. R. Shaver (Eds.), *Handbook of attachment: Theory, research, and clinical applications* (2nd ed.) (pp. 698–717). New York: The Guilford Press.

Drisko, J. W., & Zilberstein, K. (2008). What works in treating reactive attachment disorder: Parents' perspectives. *Families in Society, 89*(3), 476–486.

Dubois-Comtois, K., & Moss, E. (2008). Beyond the dyad: Do family interactions influence children's attachment representations in middle childhood? *Attachment & Human Development, 10*(4), 415–431.

Emde, R. N., Wolf, D. P., & Oppenheim, D. (Eds.) (2003). *Revealing the inner worlds of young children: The MacArthur story stem battery and parent-child narratives.* New York: Oxford University Press.

Farnfield, S. (2008). A theoretical model for the comprehensive assessment of parenting. *British Journal of Social Work, 38*, 1076–1099.

Fonagy, P., Steele, H., & Steele, M. (1991). Maternal representation of attachment during pregnancy predict the organization of infant-mother attachment at one year of age. *Child Development, 62*, 891–905.

Greenberg, J. R., & Mitchell, S. A. (1983). *Object relations in psychoanalytic theory.* Cambridge, MA: Harvard University Press.

Haight, W. L., Kagle, J. D., & Black, J. E. (2003). Understanding and supporting parent-child relationships during foster care visits: Attachment theory and research. *Social Work, 48*(2), 195–207.

Haight, W. L., & Taylor, E. H. (2007). *Human behavior for social work practice: A developmental-ecological framework.* Chicago: Lyceum Books.

Harlow, H. F. (1958). The nature of love. *American Psychologist, 13*(12), 673–685.

Hazan, C., & Shaver, P. R. (1987). Romantic love conceptualized as an attachment process. *Journal of Personality and Social Psychology, 52*, 511–524.

Hesse, E. (2008). The Adult Attachment Interview: Protocol, method of analysis, and empirical studies. In J. Cassidy & P. R. Shaver (Eds.), *Handbook of attachment: Theory, research, and clinical applications* (2nd ed.) (pp. 552–598). New York: The Guilford Press.

Hoffman, K. T., Marvin, R. S., Cooper, G., & Powell, B. (2006). Changing toddlers' and preschoolers' attachment classifications: The Circle of Security intervention. *Journal of Consulting and Clinical Psychology, 74*(6), 1017–1026.

Howe, D. (1995). *Attachment theory for social work practice.* London: MacMillan.

Howe, D. (2001). Age at placement, adoption experience and adult adopted people's contact with their adoptive and birth mothers: An attachment perspective. *Attachment & Human Development, 3*, 222–237.

Keller, T. E., Spieker, S. J., & Gilchrist, L. (2005). Patterns of risk and trajectories of preschool problem behaviors: A person-oriented analysis of attachment in context. *Development and Psychopathology, 17*(2), 349–384.

Koren-Karie, N., Oppenheim, D., Dolev, S., Sher, E., & Etzion-Carasso, A. (2002). Mothers' empathic understanding of their infants' internal experience: Relations with maternal sensitivity and infant attachment. *Developmental Psychology, 38*, 534–542.

Kubler-Ross, E. (1969). *On death and dying.* New York: MacMillan Press.

Lewis, M. (1999). Hair combing interactions: A new paradigm for research with African-American mothers. *American Journal of Orthopsychiatry, 69*(4), 504–514.

Lorenz, K. Z. (1935). Der Kumpan in der Umwelt des Vogels [The companion in the bird's world]. *Journal fuer Ornithologie, 83,* 137–213. (Abbreviated English translation published 1937 in *Auk, 54,* 245–273.)

Main, M. (1999a). Mary D. Salter Ainsworth: Tribute and portrait. *Psychoanalytic Inquiry, 19,* 682–776.

Main, M. (1999b). Attachment theory: Eighteen points with suggestions for future studies. In J. Cassidy & P. Shaver (Eds.), *Handbook of attachment: Theory, research, and clinical applications* (pp. 845–887). New York: Guilford Press.

Main, M., & Cassidy, J. (1988). Categories of response to reunion with the parent at age 6: Predictable from infant attachment classifications and stable over a1-month period. *Developmental Psychology*, 24(3), 415–426.

Main, M., Kaplan, N., & Cassidy, J. (1985). Security in infancy, childhood, and adulthood: A move to the level of representation. *Monographs of the Society for Research in Child Development*, 50(1–2), 66–104.

Main, M., & Solomon, J. (1990). Procedures for identifying infants as disorganized/disoriented during the Ainsworth Strange Situation. In M. T. Greenberg, D. Cicchetti, & E. M. Cummings (Eds.), *Attachment in the preschool years: Theory, research, and intervention* (pp. 121–160). Chicago: University of Chicago Press.

Marvin, R., Cooper, G., Hoffman, K., & Powell, B. (2002). The Circle of Security project: Attachment-based intervention with caregiver-preschool child dyads. *Attachment & Human Development*, 4(1), 107–124.

McMillen, C. J. (1992). Attachment theory and clinical social work. *Clinical Social Work Journal*, 20(2), 205–218.

Mercer, J., Sarner, L., & Rosa, L. (2003). *Attachment therapy on trial: The torture and death of Candace Newmaker*. Westport, CT: Praeger.

O'Connor, T. G., & Zeanah, C. H. (2003). Attachment disorders: Assessment strategies and treatment approaches. *Attachment & Human Development*, 5(3), 223–244.

Oppenheim, D., & Koren-Karie, N. (2002). Mothers' insightfulness regarding their children's internal worlds: The capacity underlying secure child-mother relationships. *Infant Mental Health Journal*, 23(6), 593–605.

Page, T. (2001). The social meaning of children's narratives: A review of the attachment-based narrative story stem technique. *Child and Adolescent Social Work Journal*, 18(3), 171–187.

Page, T., & Cain, D. S. (2009). "Why don't you just tell me how you feel?": A case study of a young mother in an attachment-based group intervention. *Child and Adolescent Social Work Journal*, 26(4), 333–350.

Robertson, J. (1952). *A two-year-old goes to hospital: A scientific film record* [Film]. Concord Media: Ipswich, U.K.

Rosenblum, K. L., Zeanah, C., McDonough, S. C, & Muzik, M. (2004). Video-taped coding of working model of the child interviews: A viable and useful alternative to verbatim transcripts? *Infant Behavior and Development*, 27(4), 544–549.

Rutter, M., & Rutter, M. (1993). *Developing minds: Challenge and continuity across the life span*. New York: Basic Books.

Sable, P. (1979). Differentiating between attachment and dependency in theory and practice. *Social Casework*, 60(3), 138–144.

Schofield, G., & Beek, M. (2005). Providing a secure base: Parenting children in long-term foster family care. *Attachment & Human Development*, 7(1), 3–25.

Simpson, J. A., & Belsky, J. (2008). Attachment theory within a modern evolutionary framework. In J. Cassidy & P. R. Shaver (Eds.), *Handbook of attachment: Theory, research, and clinical applications* (2nd ed.) (pp. 131–157). New York: The Guilford Press.

Solomon, M. (2009). Attachment repair in couples therapy: A prototype for treatment of intimate relationships. *Clinical Social Work Journal*, 37(3), 214–223.

Sroufe, L. A. (2005). Attachment and development: A prospective, longitudinal study from birth to adulthood. *Attachment & Human Development*, 7(4), 349–367.

Stevenson-Hinde, J. (2007). Attachment theory and John Bowlby: Some reflections. *Attachment & Human Development*, 9(4), 337–342.

Thompson, R. A. (2008). Early attachment and later development: Familiar questions, new answers. In J. Cassidy & P. Shaver (Eds.), *Handbook of attachment: Theory, research, and clinical applications* (2nd ed.) (pp. 348–365). New York: Guilford Press.

Toth, S. L., Maughan, A., Todd Manly, J., Spagnola, M., & Cicchetti, D. (2002). The relative efficacy of two interventions in altering maltreated preschool children's representational models: Implications for attachment theory. *Development and Psychopathology*, 14, 877–908.

van Ijzendoorn, M. H., & Sagi-Schwartz, A. (2008). Cross-cultural patterns of attachment: Universal and contextual dimensions. In J. Cassidy & P. Shaver (Eds.), *Handbook of attachment: Theory, research, and clinical applications* (2nd ed.) (pp. 880–905). New York: Guilford Press.

Warren, W. B., Sable, M. R., & Csizmadia, A. (2008). Pregnancy wantedness and child attachment security: Is there a relationship? *Maternal and Child Health Journal*, 12, 478–487.

Zeanah, C. H., & Benoit, D. (1995). Clinical applications of a parent perception interview. *Child and Adolescent Psychiatric Clinics of North America*, 4(3), 539–553.

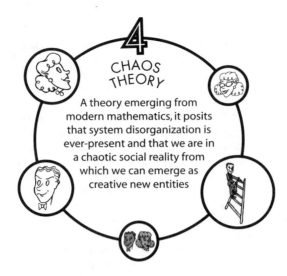

CHAOS THEORY

A theory emerging from modern mathematics, it posits that system disorganization is ever-present and that we are in a chaotic social reality from which we can emerge as creative new entities

Chaos Theory and Social Work Treatment

Sandra Loucks Campbell

Who could argue that chaos exists in our new world? Nowhere is this as true as in the settings where social workers find themselves. Multilayered client contexts are chaotic, and when the levels of complexity increase, the pressure is also increased on workers already grappling with increasing numbers of people with overlapping needs, new management models, and declining government dollars. In this world, the old ways of working in traditional hierarchies are not working, and social and health service networks are reaching the boiling point. Social workers are finding it increasingly difficult to cope with the new demands and heavier workload imposed by these advancements. The people served by social workers suffer as a result.

Despite our search for order and control in all facets of our lives, unpredictability remains (Tarnas, 1991). And it is out of that unpredictability that chaos theory, sometimes called complexity theory, has emerged. As a species, we both create and exist in a state of disequilibrium and unpredictability—chaos. The theory of chaos presents an interesting contradiction, not only to our human tendency to seek control but also to the work of Newton (1729) and of Max Weber (1947). This relatively new theory suggests a novel lens for social workers as they work with individuals, families, groups, organizations, and communities—a challenge to social workers. In this chapter, I will describe chaos theory and its origins, and present ideas for the applications it evokes for social workers in the 21st century.

Background of Chaos Theory

Chaos theory developed in an era ripe for change and new ideas. It was time for movement away from the absolutes of the industrial and modern age.

In 1687, Isaac Newton developed and described the Laws of Thermodynamics in his *Principia*, a publication acclaimed by scientists for generations. In this important touchstone to the science of the natural world, Newton postulated that energy is neither created nor destroyed and that disorder does not decrease. In other words, he believed that entropy, a measure of disorganization in a system, was ever-increasing in the natural world (Barber, 2001). His assertion that disorder could be predicted to be ever-present and on the rise served to impose order on the natural world. The world could be seen as predictable.

We might claim similarity between this Newtonian thinking and the work of Max Weber wherein he described bureaucracy as an "organization of offices" (1947, p. 331) hierarchically developed by the assignment of precise roles and sanctions. During the industrial age, from 1830 to 1970, the metaphor of the machine dominated. Humans understood a whole by learning about its parts and sought order through enhanced knowledge of a hierarchy of parts or functions, and we accepted that, over time, most matter moves toward deterioration. Both the laws of the natural world (Newton, 1729; Kuhn, 1962) and the principles of Weber's bureaucracy in 1947 define and value similar principles: determinism, stability, orderliness, uniformity, and equilibrium (Prigogine & Stengers, 1984).

But that predictable world has changed. Taken together, the computer age, financial crises and cutbacks, organizational restructuring, and the ongoing quest for information propel all of us, with astonishing speed, into a new social reality (Greenwood & Lachman, 1996; Peters, 1987). As we move away from the certainty of modernity, chaos theorists present an alternate view, an idea that might be called a contradiction of Newton's work. Chaos theory suggests we take a further look at our quest for the precision, balance, and control, lauded in Newton's natural world and in the organizational world of Weber. A new metaphor might be useful for social workers during such immense change.

Developers

Chaos theory, primarily a theory of physics and mathematics, originated with Prigogine and Stengers (1984) and was augmented by Mandelbrot (1983) and Lorenz (1963). This relatively new theory hypothesizes that creative new entities emerge from chaos (Gleick, 1987; Prigogine & Stengers, 1984). Chaos makes space for complex systems, allowing for the simultaneous existence of order and disorder, complexity and simplicity, and other dualities. Theorists describe a flow of energy through a system that is "self organizing" (Zimmerman, 1996). As creators describe the theory's essential premise, that creativity emerges from chaos, they also point to the initial development of chaos itself. Readers are asked to consider an evolving, erratic, and incredibly complex situation. Far from the homeostasis and balance suggested by traditional systems theory, a vibrant tension exists—at the margin of chaos. It is at the margins, at this point of division, of "bifurcation," that chaos is set into full motion and creativity surfaces—a new entity emerges. Out of tension comes a new beginning (Gleick, 1987; Prigogine & Stengers, 1984).

Within chaos theory we have access to two supplementary but fascinating ideas. The first one, the butterfly effect, was described by Lorenz (1963) while studying weather patterns. He noticed that even a small change in initial computerized weather conditions could create huge weather change over time (Gleick, 1987). This challenging idea allows us to pose the question "can the breeze from the flap of a butterfly's wing in Brazil cause a tornado in Texas?" (Lorenz, 1972, as cited in Hudson, 2000). He began to discuss this "butterfly effect" as the "sensitive dependence on initial conditions" (as quoted in Gleick, 1987, p. 23).

The second supplementary concept, also closely related to chaos theory, was developed and given shape by Mandelbrot (1983)—the fractal. Mandelbrot's contribution, demonstrated in his famous Mandelbrot Set, gives a pictorial representation of an interesting phenomenon. Here he defined and gave structure to the fractal. This complex, irregular, and almost mathematical form, said to "give form to chaos," is similarly variable and random on all scales. Repeating their random forms at macro and micro levels, fractals have been described as "exposing the geometric nature of chaos" (Mandelbrot, 1983). The "butterfly" and the "fractal" will be discussed in relation to social work later in the chapter.

The principles of Weber's bureaucracy and Newton's laws of the natural world identify and value similar principles noted earlier, including stability, uniformity, predictability, and balance (Kuhn, 1962; Prigogine & Stengers, 1984; Weber, 1947). The chaotic system's basic elements, as defined by its creators (nonlinearity, numerous parts with no causal relationship, a network of feedback loops, unpredictability, a flow of energy toward self-organization, an openness of the system to the environment), offer us a new vision of reality (Gleick, 1987; Prigogine & Stengers, 1984).

Why Chaos Theory with Social Work?

Certainly, in the scientific world of Newton, the concepts of chaos theory hold fast. This thinking may lead to a more complete understanding of science, itself an open system embedded in society, with feedback loops of learning and expanding knowledge. In his classic book *The Structure of Scientific Revolutions*, Thomas Kuhn identified that "anomalous experiences..., by evoking crisis, prepare the way for a new theory" (Kuhn, 1962, p. 146). But can this theory be applied to social work and the settings in which we work?

Since its conceptual origin in the 1980s, chaos theory has found its way into social work literature and practice. With the potential to provide a new frame for practice, chaos expands our expertise with systems theory and builds on our experience as agents of change (Hudson, 2000; Woehle, 2007). Although some social work authors attempt to integrate mathematical and physical origins of chaos theory with social work, this chapter takes a big-picture view. Here, we apply the overarching ideas and the metaphor of chaos to human systems and social work practice.

Most human beings know intuitively that chaos is a part of being human. When we compare our nature and that of human organizations, we can see "the systems through which we administer ourselves, have become estranged from the social relations by which we define

ourselves" (Sossin, 1994, p. 367). The seeming compatibility between the central tenets of chaos theory and the nature of humans and the contexts in which we live builds on our understanding of systems theory. Human beings may actually thrive in chaotic situations and settings. In our complex world, fast-paced social changes, disorder and nonlinear relationships coexist with our search for control—in street gangs, in large corporations, and in health and social service organizations. Chaos theory offers help in understanding human relationships and organizations, but it also demands that we abandon our obsession with control. Our new ability to see the boundary between the control that exists prior to the "bifurcation" point and the creativity that can be released when we abandon that control offers the key.

Yet, the organizations of today's social work practice resemble the bureaucracies defined by Weber in 1947. As with the machine metaphor of the industrial age, we try to understand the entirety by understanding component parts. We have sought order and control through a hierarchy of functions or roles, and we have been on the alert for deterioration (Prigogine & Stengers, 1984). Ever-watchful internal and external agents assess for risk, ready to move to control when disorder erupts.

Like the impact of a butterfly wing, a small change will lead to creativity only as we accept and learn to live with chaos. In the 20th century we have built a myriad of mechanisms of control into our interpersonal relationships and our organizations. In families, we seek to ensure a family structure that is healthy, not dysfunctional (as defined by the perhaps white, professional social worker). We structure groups according to our own educated stance, built through our enmeshment in the Western educational and professional systems of which we are a part. In organizations we present the idea that the goals of strategic 5-year plans are attainable, even in a chaotic world. We bureaucratize our health and social services in an attempt, as predicted by Weber, to ensure control at each and every level. We might ask whether these strategies actually reach the intended goals. This machine-like control described and applied from Newton's time to today might be questioned. Chaos theory presents an interesting counter-thesis to our previously held views about gaining control in chaotic families, in interpersonal relationships, and through our bureaucratization of social and health services.

As we practice social work in this new century, technological advances, rapid intensified change, and globalization have catapulted the natural world, its people, and its human organizations into a new reality. Here, cutbacks, restructuring, the ongoing quest for information at breakneck speed, and the ever-occurring crises and change have become the norm (Greenwood & Lachman, 1996; Peters, 1987).

Against this backdrop of change, chaos theory's fundamental premise that creative new entities or ideas arise from chaos (Gleick, 1987) is a direct contradiction of the stability and order held as fundamental conditions essential to the machine metaphor, to Newton's natural laws, and to the built bureaucracy proposed by Weber. The creators of this new theory have described its *non–machine-like* elements: nonlinearity, multiple components, a labyrinth of feedback spirals, an energy that organizes itself, and openness to the environment. And likewise, social work principles engage and reflect nonlinear thinking, complex systems, communication feedback systems, the environment, human systems, a vision of both sides of an issue, and an openness to change. This theory seems ideally suited to social work.

Authors

Since the genesis of chaos theory, social work and other authors have analyzed and applied the ideas of chaos in many forums. Some claim that chaos theory validates what social workers have always known intuitively, that "things are not that simple or deterministic" (Bolland & Atherton, 1999, p. 370). Stating that "the human mind is naturally creative," Lee (2008) argues for social workers to build an environment that will foster creativity. As an example, he (2008) outlined a model to foster creativity and growth that involved changing perspectives of transition, of developing meaningful goals, of doing something new to see what happens, and of modifying thoughts and actions based on the actual outcome. Bolland and Atherton (1999), in their writing about practice and research, also target

chaos theory as a useful frame of reference for thinking about complexities.

Several social work authors have discussed change in relation to chaos. Some use chaos thinking to frame social work counseling, itself a change process, to build on general systems theory and to present a new perspective on change (Halmi, 2003; Hudson, 2000; Woehle, 2007). Bussolari and Goodell (2009), discussing the applicability of chaos theory to life transitions counseling, contend that instability and lack of control are normal experiences during a life transition and argue that incorporating postmodern thought, specifically teaching clients to construct new stories to fit within a context of growth rather than disorder, would be helpful. Woehle (2007) provided detail about the relationship between change and chaos by comparing four processes of change: (1) an entropic/equilibric process, (2) a homeostatic/equilibric process, (3) a complex change process at the edge of chaos, and (4) a chaotic change process. His findings suggest that chaos theory extends entropic and homeostatic processes beyond ecosystems theory while providing a new view of client outcomes. Other authors build on the relationship between change and chaos while applying the theory to social work practice in very specific ways. Halmi, for example (2003), contends that this new understanding of change could lead to the development of specific interventions at the micro level of practice, noting that brief therapists, for example, hold assumptions and beliefs consistent with ideas basic to chaos theory.

Stevens and Hassett (2007) and Stevens and Cox (2008) discussed the application of chaos theory, sometimes called complexity, in child protection practice specifically. Stevens and Cox asserted that current applications of linear thinking and processes, which tend to be static and narrow, may oversimplify assessment, hypothesis building, and intervention, leaving service providers with a false sense of security about their accuracy. In their study of child welfare Stevens and Cox suggested that social workers develop assessments that incorporate a systemic view. This broad view could point to the use of techniques and interventions that would enhance workers' understanding of complex adaptive systems in child protection, including their own professional involvement in the system, and account for unanticipated events. Stephens and Hassett used chaos theory to frame risk and risk assessment in child welfare. They argued that a linear approach of cause and effect can lead to cause and blame explanations for harm to children (i.e., too few visits by the social worker). They suggest a complexity-based model using a nonlinear spatial analysis approach, to focus on processes and interactions of systems at macro levels rather than on procedures and tasks. This model seeks to identify the boundaries of instability in an effort to provide effective interventions.

Other authors have applied chaos theory to group processes. In describing a participatory action research project, Traver reported that the "act of centralizing empowerment of multicultural groups becomes a process that moves towards complexity" (2005, p. 3) and is best understood through a chaos lens. She used chaos theory to frame the characteristic uncertainty in the lives of immigrants and refugees in her meso/macro-level qualitative study. The concept of bifurcation led Traver to better understand and explain crisis points in the lives and interaction of researchers with study participants and helped demonstrate complexity and uncertainty in the system. "This project, in a state of constant change, seemed to be an embodiment of the participants' unpredictable lives" (2005, p. 16). In their study of turn-taking in a youth group therapy session, the use of chaos thinking and nonlinear dynamics led Pincus and Guastello (2005) to see strong correlations between turn-taking in groups and control, closeness, and conflict in groups. They found the existence of coherent yet complex patterns of interaction, consistent with their other studies and with the fractals of chaos.

Bolland and Atherton (1999) argued the chaos theory framework provides not only an alternative to cause-and-effect thinking but also a basis on which social workers can clarify their understanding of how people are connected with the environment as well as to better understand the complexities of client's varying perceptions of reality. Ramsay (2003) compared 11 traditional and transformative concepts of social work in an effort to modernize the working definition of social work for the next century. He suggested that use of the idea of equilibrium

(balance and stability) to indicate healthy social functioning should be replaced with the postmodern understanding, based on Prigogine's discoveries, that far-from-equilibrium states are ideal for one's health and well-being as they permit flexibility and adaptation to change in one's environment.

Brenda Zimmerman (1994) and others applied chaos theory to organizational dynamics (Nonaka, 1988; Tetenbaum, 1998). She proposed that the chaos lens enhances understanding of organizational change in this time of unparalleled societal change and postulated that although an organization may appear disorganized, there may be an order, not always visible, beneath the surface (Zimmerman, 1996). She recommended that executive officers view management in an evolving system, or set of systems, not as managing change, but as managing "changeability" (Zimmerman, 1996, p. 16).

Several authors have commented on the limitations of chaos theory as currently applied in social work venues. Hudson (2000) observed that for the application of the theory to social work to move beyond conceptual aspects, additional research and skill development will be needed. He asserted that the theory does not offer exclusively good news to the field of social work, suggesting that in accepting the existence of chaotic processes within social systems, the theory makes it difficult to predict therapeutic or other outcomes. However, since chaos theory is helpful in predicting overall trends, processes, and change in a client's life, it can be used to plan interventions. Woehle (2007) also recommended that the field of social work could benefit from additional research to understand and apply chaos theory at the levels possible.

Application Concepts

Chaos theory pushes us as social workers to advance our work in a number of ways. We are challenged to stretch our imagination as we look at the systems we work in, and at the systems in which our clients live. We are drawn to notice flourishing interactions with coworkers and with clients as we work together in thriving networks of communication feedback loops. These somewhat covert challenges to our profession ensure an ongoing emergence of novel social work interventions from this new theory, chaos. However, if we truly engage with chaos, the future outcomes may be unpredictable. In fact, our need to control, even if only to satisfy the naysayers, may be our undoing in this venture. If we are truly to accept chaos theory and its basic premise, we will need to resist the temptation to seize control. We may be asked to consider the impact of randomness, the consequences of giving up control, and the true meaning of creativity in social work practice. This section of the chapter provides a few basic examples as a starting point for readers who wish to "think chaos" in their practice.

Micro Practice

As we listen to an individual's story, how do we respond? Do we look at the client's complex, perhaps chaotic world, through a lens of acceptance? Do we ask ourselves if this client will find the creativity, the new way of being, that will emerge from the edge of his or her chaotic world? Or are we intent on working with our clients to control chaos and build predictable systems into their world? Rather than imposing the order and calmness that could activate a move toward entropy, we might look for indicators that foreshadow an emerging novel approach in the individual's life. Can the social worker help the client move toward a new creative reality?

Consider this example. You meet with a young woman who tells a story of her life bouncing around the country as her parents change locations through her childhood. She reports attending 12 different schools through her childhood. Now she finds herself unable to settle into a consistent life, wandering around from one home to another, from one job to another, and from one friend to another. She reports that her friends and family suggest she is a failure because she is not building solid roots from which to grow. You might find yourself wishing to assist her in settling into a friendly neighborhood and a solid job so she can find some peace. Yet, as you trace her history with her, listening without imposing your own life goals and priorities, you may discover an excitement in her as she moves from place to place, finding different parts of herself in each location and job. Perhaps you could support her in her movement—perhaps rephrasing

the pattern as a treasure hunt, an adventure. As she moves and grows she may find the treasure, she may find her future. And her future may emerge from her scattered early years, capturing a positive essence from each experience. She may need a worker with a chaos lens, a worker who can see the energy bursting forth, the creative potential, that could emerge from her chaotic experiences.

Fractal: Social workers often observe and analyze patterns in the lives of their clients. Fractals allow us to build our expertise in this kind of analysis. In the previous example we can see fractals in the foreground of the story, between the lines of the case, the "same degree of irregularity on all scales" (Gleick, 1987, p. 98; Mandelbrot, 1983) in the life of this young woman. Her relationships, homes, schools, and jobs share the same patterns, irregular but similarly irregular. Perhaps in the future, these degrees of irregularity will merge into colorful, repeating patterns of rich experience. That experience may give this client exactly what she needs to build a life of creativity and richness.

Butterfly: In the example we can see the butterfly rising as the young woman, emerging from her first meeting with the liberating social worker, feels, perhaps for the first time in many years, accepted and supported in her chaotic life. She begins to wonder if there might be some hope for her to retain the lifestyle she has secretly enjoyed, where she may finally find her treasure. The small change, the support of a social worker, could lead to a transformational shift in her life.

Meso Practice

During an era of lawsuits and demands for accountability in a world of flourishing technology and burgeoning information, health care teams are increasingly influenced by the governing policies and standards under which they function. In fact, government and insurance regulations, demands for efficiency (Stein, 2001), and concerns about liabilities can easily slip onto center stage, taking the spotlight off quality care.

The chaotic environment of a layered bureaucracy is complicated further by its interdisciplinary nature and increasing costs. When cuts to available funds lead to lower staff levels, workers are stressed to the limit. Managers seek control through high-level planning, restructuring, smaller staff teams, through streamlined meetings and processes, enhanced documentation requirements, and demands for uniformity. Social workers are further stressed as fewer team members do more work to serve more people. Staff shortages can also lead to essential interdisciplinary team meetings being cancelled or shortened, or conversely, team meetings may be held with some disciplines unable to attend due to workload. In a setting where teamwork has been determined to be vital to the overall success, cancelled meetings can pose a problem (Wituk et al., 2002).

Interdisciplinary groups, with members often wearing their discipline on their sleeve, can slide into a situation of restrained conflict, where some members seek control of the agenda, primarily to gain control of their own mandate and workload. When meetings are cut and team members each work in isolation, there can be an atmosphere that encourages individual workers to hunker down, do the work, go home, recover, return to work, and hunker down again…and on it goes. Efforts by managers to impose control may actually backfire. Some might claim this pattern of work leads not to a controlled environment, but to chaos.

Weber's bureaucracy and Newton's linear thinking, along with the temptation to control, are easily spotted in health care settings. Here, uniformity, black-and-white choices, and controlled risk are sought; variability, changeability, creativity, and chaos are to be avoided. In a complex environment where managers find it difficult to impose control, chaos thinkers might question whether the current model is, indeed, the best path to success in interdisciplinary health care.

Workers comfortable with change, who can manage and work through challenges, may have skills to work through chaos rather than trying to block it. We might question what would happen if teams worked together—interdisciplinary teams flying in evolving formation through the chaos together (Zimmerman, 1996). A team member thinking about chaos may propose the enhancement of interdisciplinarity rather than its diminishment. This social worker could wonder whether creative solutions would surface from teams meeting more often, not less

often. Chaos thinking suggests that a novel approach might develop, not in sporadic small-team meetings, but rather from meeting together more often, sometimes spontaneously, brainstorming new solutions and enhancing team support of each other in the work.

Rather than isolated workers hunkering down and doing the work, consider the image of workers spending time together, providing mutual support, helping each other, having breakfast together, and watching the edge of chaos. This unified team, riding the wave and welcoming change, using trial-and-error strategies, brainstorming for new creative ideas might learn to manage and work through ongoing "changeability" (Zimmerman, 1996, p. 16). Teams might move from cutting meeting times and numbers of staff to natural and unstructured, but joint, decision-making about programs, client needs, staffing, and budgets. Instead of isolating themselves from each other, team members will come closer together. Members of cohesive teams in an organization with open budget documents may offer, for example, to take a week off without pay so someone else can earn more. True team members could build solid cross-disciplinary relationships, having each other's back, like a family pulls together when faced with adversity. Managers need only to trust the creativity and competence of the team.

Fractal: Social workers often identify and use parallel processes in their work with clients where their therapeutic relationship with a client bears similar qualities to the client's relationships with others in his or her life *or* when the social worker's relationship with the client bears similarities to the social worker's relationship with his or her own supervisor. In clinical practice I have observed similarities, and perhaps parallel processes, arise at different levels between client and worker, client and family, and worker and environment. One day, working in a long-term care health care setting, while listening to nurses talking about their bosses, I was surprised to hear the nurses using the same words about their bosses as I had heard their patients use about their nurses. This observation led, finally, to the development of a research project using the fractals of chaos as a base metaphor of analysis of layers of parallel levels of decision-making power in a long-term care facility (Campbell, 2003).

Butterfly: Perhaps one unit's small interdisciplinary team can develop competencies riding the crest of change while keeping the rigidities of the larger bureaucratic system at bay. The principle of the butterfly effect would suggest that this small area of competency could grow and develop to surprising levels. Perhaps individual workers or teams could build transforming change in a second team, rotating through the facility, spreading and teaching a new chaotic way to think about the work.

Macro Practice

Consider the implications of replacing the firm bounds of a traditional organization with the more flexible boundaries suggested by chaos. In such a system, managers would need to trust that a more open process would unfold to produce something better, through employee creativity. Such an evolution would be maintained by manager and worker commitment rather than by the power of those in charge (Helgesen, 1990). Supervisors would encourage staff to take responsibility for the organization's credibility. Traditional management methods (re-engineering, quality control, strategic planning, and others) impose control and view equilibrium and stability as a sign of success (Zimmerman, 1996). Chaotic management strategies make trust, not control, the essential element.

In traditional organizations, management has sought order from the top down. Management by objectives, strategic planning, and hierarchical flow charts have often been the result in these ordered and machine-like, non-chaotic systems. But they may quash creative potential along the way. Chaos theory, on the other hand, fits with and explains some of the uncertainty and randomness of organizations (Zimmerman, 1996). In "chaotic" organizations, the valued worker learns quickly and is comfortable with ambiguity and chaos (Tetenbaum, 1998). Work becomes de-bureaucratized (Peters, 1987). Though the system with fewer barriers of control is much less predictable, many more options become possible (Peters, 1987; Zimmerman, 1994). As we begin to see the connecting relationships and the suppressed energy, we will be free to let go of control and release creativity. Like fractals, the assets of the organization (employee creativity,

adaptability, and novel ideas) will exist at all levels (Zimmerman, 1996).

If the true state of our natural and human world does allow for coexistence of order and disorder, irregularity and stability, simplicity and complexity, closed systems and open systems, perhaps organizations can accommodate a similar duality. During crises, when decisions to downsize and make rapid change are questioned, bureaucratic managers often try to regain control through rational processes and planning. Managers who follow chaos principles, on the other hand, would manage through the crisis, giving staff autonomy, freedom, and the power to develop their potential (Prigogine & Stengers, 1984; Tetenbaum, 1998; Zimmerman, 1996). While organizational boundaries may appear rigid and closed, there are few truly closed systems, even in the scientific world. Most organizations are, underneath all the mechanisms of control, open and creative. They exchange energy with the environment—compatible with the systems described by chaos theorists. The chaotic terms "edge of chaos," "far from equilibrium," and its point of dynamic tension could well apply to a social or health system undergoing change (Prigogine & Stengers, 1984, p. 178, p. 231).

Fractal: While working in long-term care, I began to wonder about power, particularly about the flow of power through the organization. Here we have some of the most powerful people, titled scientists and top-level bureaucrats, working in one of the largest organizations in Canadian government. These powerful people provide service to some of the most powerless service recipients—frail elders living with cognitive impairment. I wondered whether the power I could see was held at the top, or whether the power at the top actually emanated from the powerlessness at the bottom. In a related study, I used chaos theory and fractals to define a research question about parallel processes of decision-making power in long-term care organizations. I found that similar levels of perceived decision-making power, or lack of decision-making power, existed at all organizational levels: care recipients, front-line workers, middle managers, senior managers, and the chief executive officer. None of these groups or individuals believed they had any decision-making power. I began to see that, like fractals, the power in human relationships and organizations at one level might be parallel to the processes and relationships at other levels (Campbell, 2003).

Butterfly: You can see the butterfly emerge in organizations with "the impact of a simple memo as it flows through an organization, demonstrating Lorenz's butterfly effect" (Campbell, 2003, p. 53) as the note moves from desk to desk with escalating impact. A carefully worded memo can sometimes create the transformational shift of the butterfly.

Future Possibilities

The opportunities for social workers to develop our profession from a base of chaos are virtually limitless. Social work authors have applied this theory to change. Social workers are change agents. It is here, where client meets context and where change happens, that social workers do their best work. When we consider our professional goals, to intervene and advocate for clients in an atmosphere of respect, chaos theory can play a central role. To maximize the possibilities for our profession we will need to engage in further research, develop chaos-based interventions at the micro, meso, and macro levels, and find ways to prove their worth, despite the unpredictability essential to chaos.

Conclusion

Chaos theory provides space for an open interrelated world where randomness happens, where disorder and order coexist, and where in the midst of disorder we can find creative new entities. The pressure defined at the borders of disorder or chaos, the creativity that is thought to follow that pressure, and the subsequent settling back into equilibrium all can be related to human beings and their relationships. As a fluttering memo creates hushed conversation at water coolers and as stressed, overworked workers try to help their clients, chaos is everywhere. Social workers work for change in and with systems, where the individual meets the context (Gray & Webb, 2009). Chaos theory, a theory based in concepts of change, is ideally suited for our profession.

Social work has long been thought to be part science and part art (Martinez-Brawley & Zorita,

1998). Chaos theory, with its emphasis on non-linearity, creativity, and unrestrained human capacity, takes us, with renewed energy, to the "art" of social work. Here, we can find our way back to fundamental social work principles and processes. We can revisit the relationship between multiple parts of a system in an open environment. We can call for "feedback loops" of communication in our work. And we can look beyond modernity and postulate new ideas about parallel processes metaphorically pictured in the fractals of Mandelbrot. The unbridled energy in the client system and the possibility of working simultaneously with dualities at all levels of practice opens the doors of social workers who want to develop the "art" of social work.

Here we can question whether the idea of an "edge of chaos" (Gleick, 1987; Prigogine & Stengers, 1984) may be a useful way to challenge conventional views of individuals, families, groups, and organizations. We can consider whether the "butterfly effect" might help the social worker leap from his or her traditional social work role in an ineffective system to a changed role working to create the broad impact, the transformation, imagined by Lorenz (1963). We can visualize new connections in the social work milieu of overlapping relationships, perhaps parallels or "fractals," for use in this world of contradiction and complexity—the 21st century.

Chaos thinking will help us understand and adapt as we take a broad view of multiple intersection points between person and context. It calls us to expand our already well-developed understanding of layers of contextual reality exponentially and invites us to consider that all doors are open. In a profession that prides itself on being contextually competent, chaos theory may call our bluff.

References

Barber, K. (Ed.). (2001). *Canadian Oxford Dictionary*. Canada: Oxford University Press.

Bolland, K. A., & Atherton, C. R. (1999). Chaos theory: An alternative approach to social work practice and research. *Families in Society: The Journal of Contemporary Human Services, 80*(4), 367–373.

Bussolari, C. J., & Goodell, J. A. (2009). Chaos theory as a model for life transitions counseling: Nonlinear dynamics and life's changes. *Journal of Counseling and Development*, 87, (winter), 98–107.

Campbell, S. L. (2003). Chaotic patterns of restraining power: The dynamics of personal decision making in a long-term care facility. *Dissertation Abstracts International, A: The Humanities and Social Sciences*, 64(1), 286–A.

Gleick, J. (1987). *Chaos: Making a new science*. Middlesex: Penguin Books.

Gray, M., & Webb, S. (2009). The return of the political in social work. *International Journal of Social Welfare*, 18(1), 111–115.

Greenwood, R., & Lachman, R. (1996). Change as an underlying theme in professional service organizations: An introduction. *Organizational Studies*, 17(4), 563–572.

Halmi, A. (2003). Chaos and non-linear dynamics: New methodological approaches in the social sciences and social work practice. *International Social Work*, 46(1), 83–101.

Helgesen, S. (1990). *Female advantage*. New York: Doubleday.

Hudson, C. G. (2000). At the edge of chaos: A new paradigm for social work. *Journal of Social Work Education*, 36(2), 215–230.

Kuhn, T. (1962). *The structure of scientific revolutions*. Chicago: University of Chicago Press.

Lee, M. Y. (2008). A small act of creativity: Fostering creativity in clinical social work practice. *Families in Society: The Journal of Contemporary Social Services*, 89(1), 19–31.

Lorenz, E. (1963). The mechanics of vacillation. *Journal of Atmospheric Sciences*, 20(5), 448–464.

Lorenz, E. N. (1969). Atmospheric predictability as revealed by naturally occurring analogues. *Journal of Atmospheric Sciences*, 26(4), 636–646.

Mandelbrot, B. (1975). Stochastic models for the Earth's relief, the shape and the fractal dimension of the coastlines, and the number-area role for islands. *Proceedings of the National Academy of Sciences of the United States of America*, 72(10), 3825–3828.

Mandelbrot, B. B. (1983). *The fractal geometry of nature*. New York: W. H. Freeman.

Martinez-Brawley, E., & Zorita, P. (1998). At the edge of the frame: Beyond science and art in social work. *British Journal of Social Work*, 28, 197–212.

Newton, I. (1729). *Principia* (Motte, A., Trans.). Original work published 1687.

Nonaka, I. (1988). Creating organizational order out of chaos: Self-renewal in Japanese firms. *California Management Review*, Spring, 57–71.

Peters, T. (1987). *Thriving on chaos*. New York: Alfred A. Knopf.

Prigogine, I., & Stengers, I. (1984). *Order out of chaos*. New York: Bantam Books.

Puncus, D., & Guastello, S. J. (2005). Nonlinear dynamics and interpersonal correlates of verbal turn-taking patterns in a group therapy session. *Small Group Research*, 36 (6), 635–677.

Ramsay, R. (2003). Transforming the working definition of social work into the 21st century. *Research on Social Work Practice*, 13(3), 324–339.

Sherer, M. (1998). Organizational position: Influences on perceived organizational properties. *Journal of Sociology and Social Welfare*, 25(4), 3–18.

Sossin, L. (1994). The politics of discretion: Toward a critical theory of public administration. *Canadian Public Administration*, 36(3), 364–391.

Stein, J. G. (2001). *The cult of efficiency*. Toronto: Anansi Press Ltd.

Stevens, I., & Cox, P. (2008). Complexity theory: Developing new understandings of child protection in field settings and in residential child care. *British Journal of Social Work*, 38, 1320–1336.

Stevens, I., & Hassett, P. (2007). Applying complexity theory to risk in child protection practice. *Childhood*, 14, 128–144.

Tarnas, R. (1991). *The passion of the Western mind*. New York: Ballantine Books.

Tetenbaum, T. (1998). Shifting paradigms: From Newton to chaos. *Organizational Dynamics*, Spring, 21–32.

Traver, E. (2005). A chaotic dance of cultural competence: A participatory oral history project with immigrants and refugees. *Social Work with Groups*, 27(2), 3–21.

Weber, M. (1947). *The theory of social and economic organization*. London: Collier-Macmillan Limited.

Wituk, S., Shepherd, M., Warren, M., & Meissen, G. (2002). Factors contributing to the survival of self-help groups. *American Journal of Community Psychology*, 30(3), 349–366.

Woehle, R. (2007). Complexity theory, nonlinear dynamics and change: Augmenting systems theory. *Advances in Social Work*, 8(1), 141–151.

Zimmerman, B. (1993). Chaos and nonequilibrium: The flip side of strategic processes. *Organizational Development Journal*, 11(1), 31–38.

Zimmerman, B. (1994). *Tension through suspension: Systemic barriers to changeability* (Working Paper). Faculty of Administrative Studies Working Paper Series.

Zimmerman, B. (1996). *The art, science of managing changeability: Lessons from chaos and complexity theories*. Keynote Presentation at the Order and Chaos conference, Grenfeld College, Memorial University, Newfoundland, Canada.

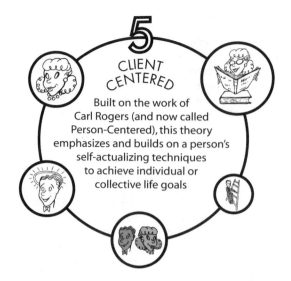

CLIENT CENTERED

Built on the work of Carl Rogers (and now called Person-Centered), this theory emphasizes and builds on a person's self-actualizing techniques to achieve individual or collective life goals

Client-Centered Theory: The Enduring Principles of a Person-Centered Approach

William Rowe

Introduction

I had mentioned in the fourth edition of *Social Work Treatment* that the term "client-centered" had been primarily replaced with the term "person-centered," and that the two had become for most purposes interchangeable. The principles underlying Carl Rogers' client-centered theory and person-centered approach continue to have an enduring nature. Even if they are not directly attributed to this body of work they provide a major contribution to the helping professions today. Silberschatz and George (2007) noted that many of the ideas are pertinent to current intensely debated issues such as the role of techniques in therapy, therapeutic relationship, therapeutic alliance, and empirical research in psychotherapy. LaCombe (2008) cited a 2006 survey asking counselors, "over the last 25 years which figures have most influenced your practice?" Of the 2,598 who responded, they overwhelmingly said Carl Rogers.

Rogers passed away in 1987 after a rich and varied life that saw the development, expansion, and globalization of his theories. Prior to his death, he had continued to test and develop his theories by applying them to some of the more complex social dilemmas and exploring areas of convergence with other significant thinkers in psychology and human behavior (Rogers, 1986). Even though the parallels with social work thinking and social work activity remain constant, the vast majority of literature in person-centered theory is now developed and expanded outside of social work and indeed, for the most part, outside of the United States.

Many of the tenets of client-centered theory have been hallmarks of the social work profession since its beginnings. The term "client" as opposed to "patient" was in popular use by social workers long before the field of psychology embraced client-centered theories. In addition, the values espoused by client-centered theorists were established and accepted by the earliest of workers, including Octavia Hill and Mary Richmond (1917). Today the principles of client-centered theory can be seen in patient-centered medical practice, student-centered learning, and even customer-centered business practices.

The fact that most of the theory and research in the client-centered approach has developed outside of the social work profession is somewhat of a historical anomaly. Carl Rogers developed many of the original principles of client-centered theory via the influence and observation of social work practitioners (Rogers, 1980). The following pages present the historical origins and basic principles of client-centered theory, explore its confluence with and divergence from social work practice, and reflect on new developments in and uses for person-centered theory.

Historical Origins

Client-centered theory and Carl Rogers have been all but synonymous for over four decades. When an individual is so central to a thought system, biographical data tend to illuminate the theory as well as the person (Seeman, 1990). What is unique about Rogers's influence on client-centered theory is that even though he was its parent and chief proponent, his force was derived more from the integration and organization of existing concepts than from the generation of new ideas. This may account for the lack of authoritative rigidity and dogma that is characteristic of client-centered theory.

Therefore, the persons and ideas that shaped Rogers's early development also influenced the formulation of client-centered theory. Rogers's ideas were both an expression of and a reaction to the suburban, upper-middle-class Protestant family to which he was born in 1902. His experience on the family farm, to which they moved when he was 14, led to an interest in agriculture and to scientific methodology and empiricism,

which later became an important feature of client-centered theory (Rogers, 1961b). However, after studying agriculture at the University of Wisconsin, Rogers decided to pursue a career in the ministry and attended Union Theological Seminary in New York.

Rogers later applied the liberal religious outlook that he found at UTS to client-centered theory by stressing the importance of individuality, trust in feeling and intuition, and nonauthoritarian relationships (Sollod, 1978). Even though Rogers was at UTS for a short time, he helped organize a study group that was reminiscent of later encounter groups.

After deciding that the ministry was too constrictive for his own professional growth and development, Rogers elected to pursue an M.A. in education and psychology at Columbia University. It was here that Rogers was significantly influenced by the pragmatic philosophy of John Dewey and the educational wisdom of William Kilpatrick. Kilpatrick, as a leader of the progressive education movement, stressed learner-focused education and redefined education as a process of continuous growth (Kilpatrick, 1926). The connection between Kilpatrick's ideas and what was later articulated as client-centered theory is by no means coincidental.

Rogers began his professional career as a psychologist at the Rochester Child Guidance Clinic while continuing to work on his doctorate at Columbia. The academic and professional isolation he experienced in Rochester allowed him to develop his approach to working with clients in a relatively unencumbered manner. In this pragmatic creative environment, Rogers first became interested in effective therapeutic methods as opposed to psychological ideologies. After attending a two-day seminar led by Otto Rank, he found that his practice was similar to that of the Rankians. Rogers learned even more about Rank's theories from a social worker at the Rochester Clinic who had been trained at the Philadelphia School of Social Work (Rogers, 1980).

In 1939, Rogers published *The Clinical Treatment of the Problem Child*, a book that drew heavily on the work of Jessie Taft and relationship therapy. Many aspects of Rankian-based relationship therapy, as expressed in this book, show up later as tenets of client-centered theory. Among these are an emphasis on present experiences and circumstances, a positive valuation of the expression of feelings, a focus on individual growth and will, and a devaluation of the authority relationship in therapy. Relationship therapy continued to be developed in psychology by Rank, Taft, and Patterson and in social work by the functional school led by Taft, Virginia Robinson, and Ruth Smalley (1967). In "relationship therapy," Rogers found the practical affirmation of the progressive educational concepts that he had embraced earlier. There can be no mistaking the similarity between client-centered theory and the following description of therapist attitude by Taft (1951):

It is not so easy as it sounds to learn to ignore content and to go through it to the fundamental attitude and emotions behind it, but it is possible, if one has no need for the patient to be or feel one thing rather than another and then is free to perceive and accept what is happening even if it means rejection of the therapeutic goal. The analyst in this view has no goal, has no right to one. He is passive in the sense that he tries to keep his own ends out of the situation to the extent of being willing to leave even the "cure" so-called, to the will of the patient.

Rogers's definition and articulation of the essential elements of the counseling and psychotherapy he had practiced for a decade began at Ohio State University, where he received an appointment in 1940. In the same year he attended a symposium at Teachers College at Columbia that was presided over by Goodwin Watson, who at the time was attempting to discover the essential elements of effective therapy. The model of therapy articulated by Watson at this time was similar to the nondirective model that was to be the basis for Rogers's ideas in *Counseling and Psychotherapy*. Rogers identified this as an emerging viewpoint for which there was a "sizable core of agreement" (1942).

During his tenure at Ohio State University, Rogers reaffirmed his earlier commitment to empiricism. In his own work and the work he did with his graduate students, he attempted to operationalize and study the process of psychotherapy. The recording and analysis of interviews and outcome research were significant innovations for the time. Those activities brought Rogers's ideas into the mainstream of psychology.

In 1945, Rogers accepted an invitation to head a new counseling center at the University of Chicago. The 12 years he spent there resulted in his wide recognition as a leading therapist, theorist, teacher, and researcher. This period also signaled the shift from the theoretical period described as nondirective to the period described as reflective or client-centered. It was during this period that interest in Rogers's ideas developed in an ever-widening circle. As Rogers described it later, "To me, as I try to understand the phenomenon, it seems that without knowing it I had expressed an idea whose time had come. It is as though a pond had become utterly still so that a pebble dropped into it sent ripples out farther and farther and farther having an influence that could not be understood by looking at the pebble" (1980, p. 49). Theoreticians and practitioners from various fields, who gravitated to the principles that Rogers espoused, advanced client-centered theories in their own disciplines. Rogers's flexibility and nonauthoritarian stance helped characterize him as the benign parent of client-centered theory in a variety of areas to be described later in this chapter.

In 1957, Rogers moved to the University of Wisconsin, where he helped bridge the gap between psychology and psychiatry through the completion of his work on schizophrenics and the loosening of the psychiatric monopoly on the practice of psychotherapy.

In 1964, Rogers moved to California, where he was able to fully develop the work with encounter groups that he had begun in Chicago. In 1968, Rogers and several staff members left to found the Center for Studies of the Person at La Jolla, California. Through the center, Rogers was able to apply the person-centered approach to perplexing problems in Northern Ireland, South Africa, Warsaw, Venezuela, and many other areas. With the publication of *Carl Rogers on Personal Power* (1977) and *A Way of Being* (1980), Rogers moved person-centered theory into the realm of politics and philosophy.

Rogers continued to be an extraordinary philosopher and scientist up to his passing in 1987. He attended the Evolution of Psychotherapy conference at Phoenix in 1986, where he presented a paper that compared his person-centered theory with the work of Kohut and Erikson (Rogers, 1986). This author was fortunate to take part in some "conversation" and "demonstration" sessions that illustrated Rogers's personification of the theories he developed and espoused. In his eighties, Rogers retained the clarity, honesty, personal warmth, and therapeutic effectiveness that had set the standard for an entire field of psychology. Even after Rogers's passing, person-centered theories continue to be debated and advanced in the literature, in terms of both fundamental theory (Moreira, 1993; Purton, 1989) and practical application (Lambert, 1986; Quinn, 1993; Silberschatz & George, 2007).

Principal Proponents of Client-Centered Theory

Counseling and Clinical Psychology

By far, client-centered theory has had its greatest impact on the field of counseling and clinical psychology. From the outset, it was clear that this approach represented a third force in American psychology. Many therapists embraced it as a desirable alternative to orthodox analysis or rigid behaviorism. The term "client," as opposed to "patient" or "subject," suggested the person's active, voluntary, and responsible participation.

The process, or "how to," of psychotherapy was described for the first time, allowing students to study and become proficient in observable counseling skills. A second attractive feature for counselors was the attention to the expression of positive humanistic values in a pragmatic approach to therapy. Finally, the continuing concern with effectiveness and outcome in the client-centered approach added to the credibility of the worker.

Many of the individuals who were influenced by Rogers and client-centered theory developed orientations of their own. Eugene Gendlin (1978) furthered the concept of "focusing" as a significant tool for change. Robert Carkhuff (1969), along with Bernard Berenson (Carkhuff & Berenson, 1977), and C. B. Truax (Truax, 1967), advanced the client-centered principles in greater depth and with greater precision. Greenberg, Rice, and Elliot (1993) and Rice and Greenberg (1984) also advanced the notion of "process-experiential," which remains closely aligned with the person-centered approach. Numerous others have incorporated the essential elements of client-centered theory, which will likely ensure that it will continue to be a major component of the theory base of both counseling and clinical psychology.

Psychiatry

Rogers was for some time engaged in a struggle to get the field of psychiatry to recognize the value of client-centered theory to psychotherapy. Psychiatry to that point had retained a virtual stranglehold on the practice of psychotherapy. It was not until the results of his work with schizophrenics were published that psychiatry as a whole began to recognize the value of his approach (Gendlin, 1962; Rogers 1961a). Currently, client-centered theory is an accepted, if not widely practiced, orientation in psychiatry. Even though recent studies have reaffirmed the effectiveness of Rogerian counseling with patients diagnosed as paranoid schizophrenic (Gerwood, 1993), the approach does not appear to have been developed or expanded in psychiatry. After Rogers turned his attention to working with "nonpathological" clients in nontraditional or nonstructured settings, psychiatry as a whole appeared to lose interest in this form of counseling.

Some encounter group principles are still utilized in psychiatric settings in group psychotherapy and therapeutic communities. But as psychiatry has increased its concern with the organic etiology of the more severe psychological impairments, there has been a diminishing interest in client-centered theory and much greater emphasis on psychopharmacology.

Coincidently, a body of literature has surfaced in family medicine and general practice that is referred to as patient-centered (Stewart, Weston, Brown, McWhinney, McWilliam & Freeman, 1995). The parallels are obvious and physicians appear to be embracing the concepts as they are increasingly faced with a diverse patient body that is informed, empowered, and demanding of a more equal helping relationship.

Administration and Leadership

The whole field of administration and leadership training has been noticeably affected by client-centered theory. Client-centered principles found easy application in conflict resolution, organizational behavior, and employer–employee relations. Many of the practices were utilized and expanded by those involved with the National Training Laboratories in Bethel, Maine, and the numerous T-groups and sensitivity training sessions that were organized to help groups work more effectively and meaningfully (Lewin, 1951; Maslow, 1971). Helen MacGregor's "Y theory" and Abraham Maslow's "Z theory" of management are both clearly reflective of the application of client-centered principles to this area (Maslow, 1971).

These ideas have lost some of their allure in today's highly competitive workplace, which is increasingly less concerned with the person as an entity in favor of a set of skills that serve the corporate purpose and can be discarded when necessary. As people adapt to the modern workplace, their need for personal fulfillment, interrelatedness, and community building will likely be expressed in a different form. Hence, there may be an even greater role for person-centered theory in the workplace of the future.

Social Work

Client-centered theory was highly acceptable to social workers from its inception. This is partly due to the fact that in its infancy, client-centered theory was more or less a conceptualization of many of the practices of relationship therapy, which was the central force of the functional school of social casework. Many of the values that are expressed in client-centered theory are fundamental to social work practice.

Rogers found himself closely aligned with the social work profession in the early part of his career, and in fact held offices in social work organizations at both the local and national levels while in Rochester (Rogers, 1961b). In the 1940s, Rogers and client-centered theory became identified with the field of psychology. Since social work had become entangled in the debate between the diagnostic and functional schools of casework, client-centered theory as a separate entity received less attention. Many of the principles of client-centered theory continued to be applied by social workers, but relatively little of this was reported or researched.

In the 1950s and 1960s, the profession turned its attention to the development of a unified theory of social work based on the person–environment continuum. Client-centered theory to this point had appeared too person-centered to be of much use in this effort. Barrett-Lennard's description of client-centered theory and its usefulness in social work practice theory was the first major reference in social work literature to Rogers's contribution (Barrett-Lennard, 1979).

In the 1970s, an increased concern with effectiveness and accountability sent theorists and investigators in search of methods that could be demonstrated and evaluated. As a result, there was a resurgence of interest in client-centered theory and its utility in social work, since it was one of the few demonstrably effective treatment approaches. It was followed up by investigations into the value of client-centered principles in training social workers (Keefe, 1976; Larsen, 1975; Rowe, 1981; Wallman, 1980). Today, most interpersonal skills training takes place in the undergraduate curriculum, and it is increasingly difficult to discern client-centered principles from good basic interviewing skills. At this point, practice skills texts utilize client-centered theory and practice, but as part of a set of generic or eclectic skills that are framed in a social work context. Recent contributions to the literature by Greene (2008), Shulman (1979), and Brodley (2006) have demonstrated the practical utility and generally positive application of person-centered approaches. Social work educators continue to incorporate some of the person-centered ideas related to complex social and political problems into the macro and international spheres of the curriculum.

Theoretical Perspectives and Basic Concepts

Theory Building

As noted earlier, Rogers was more a coordinator than a generator of the principles that are associated with person-centered theory. Because he essentially followed a deductive reasoning process in his early investigations, his personality theory emerged ex post facto.

Epistemologically, his work is best described by the term "humanistic phenomenology" (Nye, 1975). Rogers's "humanism" is related to his belief that humans are essentially growth-oriented, forward-moving, and concerned with fulfilling their basic potentialities. He assumes that basic human nature is positive, and that if individuals are not forced into socially constructed molds but are accepted for what they are, they will turn out "good" and live in ways that enhance both themselves and society.

Phenomenology is concerned with the individual's perceptions in determining reality. Rogers believes that knowledge of these perceptions of reality can help to explain human behavior. Objective reality is less important than our perception of reality, which is the main determinant of our behavior. The phenomenological approach guided Rogers's approach to both therapy and research as he struggled with the difficulty of perceiving reality through another person's eyes.

As a scientist, Rogers sees determinism as "the very foundation stone of science" (Rogers, 1969), and hence he is committed to objective study and evolution. He sees this approach as incomplete in fostering an understanding of the "inner human experience," and embraces freedom as critical to effective personal and interpersonal functioning.

Basic (Key) Concepts

Rogers gave a detailed presentation of his theories of therapy, personality, and interpersonal relationships in volume three of *Psychology: A Study of a Science* (1959). The following are nine propositions that outline the personality theory underlying this approach:

1. "All individuals exist in a continually changing world of experience of which they are the center." The "phenomenal field," as it is sometimes called, includes all that the individual experiences. Only the individual can completely and genuinely perceive his experience of the world.
2. "Individuals react to their phenomenal field as they experience and perceive it." The perceptual field is reality for the individual. Individuals will react to reality as they perceive it, rather than as it may be perceived by others.
3. "The organism has one basic tendency and striving to actualize, maintain and enhance the experiencing organism." Rogers suggests that all organic and psychological needs may

be described as partial aspects of this one fundamental need.
4. "Behavior is basically the goal-directed attempt of individuals to satisfy their needs as experienced in their phenomenal field as perceived." Reality for any given individual is that individual's perception of reality, whether or not it has been confirmed. There is no absolute reality that takes precedence over an individual's perceptions.
5. "The best vantage point for understanding behavior is from the internal frame of reference of the individual." This includes the full range of sensations, perceptions, meanings, and memories available to the conscious mind. Accurate empathy is required to achieve this understanding.
6. "Most ways of behaving adopted by the individual are consistent with the individual's concept of self." The concept of self is basic to client-centered theory. Self-concept is an organized internal view consisting of the individual's perceptions of himself alone, himself in relation to others, and himself in relation to his environment and to the values attached to these perceptions. Self-concept is seen as an ever-evolving entity.
7. "The incongruence that often occurs between an individual's conscious wishes and his behaviour is the result of a split between the individual's self-concept and his experiences." As the individual gains an awareness of self, he develops a need for positive regard and positive self-regard. When the individual feels loved or not loved by significant others, he develops positive or negative self-regard.
8. "When there is incongruence between the individual's self-concept and experiences with others, a state of anxiety results." This anxiety is often the result of the incongruence between the ideal and real self. To lower an individual's anxiety, the self-concept must become more congruent with the individual's actual experiences.
9. "The fully functioning individual is open to all experiences, exhibiting no defensiveness." Such a person fully accepts himself and can exhibit unconditional positive regard for others. The self-concept is congruent with the experiences and the individual is able to assert his basic actualizing tendency.

With regard to motivation, Rogers believed the organism to be active initiator that exhibits a directional tendency (Rogers, 1977). He agreed with White's description of motivation as more than simple stasis: "Even when its primary needs are satisfied and its homeostatic chores are done, an organism is alive, active and up to something" (White, 1959). Rogers affirmed that there is a central source of energy in the organism that is concerned with enhancement as well as maintenance (Rogers, 1977).

The following are some of the most significant assumptions of Rogers's personality theory from the perspective of therapy:

We behave in accordance with our perception of reality. In light of this, in order to understand the client's problem, we must fully understand how she perceives it.

We are motivated by an innate primary drive to self-actualization. The individual will automatically develop her potential under favorable conditions. These conditions can be established in therapy and the stance of the therapist must, as a result, be nondirective.

The individual has a basic need for love and acceptance. This translates into a focus on relationship and the communication of empathy, respect, and authenticity by the therapist.

The individual's self-concept is dependent upon the nature of the acceptance and respect she experiences from others. The client's self-concept can be changed by her experiencing unconditional positive regard in therapy.

Values

The valuing process has been discussed at some length in client-centered theory. Rogers hypothesized that "there is an organismic commonality of value directions" and that "these common value directions are of such kinds as to enhance the development of the individual himself or others in his community and to make for the survival and evolution of his species" (Rogers, 1964). This positive and hopeful view of human beings is by and large acceptable to a profession like social work that is dedicated to the enhancement of social relationships and functioning.

In addition to being concerned with the "organismic valuing process," client-centered theory professes both general and specific attitudinal values. In its early stages, client-centered theory was essentially neutral regarding values. Over the years, it has progressed to the point where person-centered or humanistic values are asserted (Carkhuff & Berenson, 1967). These include the following (Boy & Pine, 1982; Rogers, 1964, 1977):

1. The counselor who intends to be of service to a client must value the client's integral worth as a person.
2. Responsible action occurs within the context of respect for the dignity and worth of others.
3. The counselor who values the client has a fundamental respect for the client's freedom to know, shape, and determine personal attitudes and behavior.
4. The client possesses free will; she can be the determiner of a personal destiny.
5. A person's free functioning not only tends toward development of the self, but also includes a responsibility to other persons.
6. The client enhances the self by fulfilling obligations to herself and others.
7. The client begins to relate to others with a sense of personal responsibility and ethical behavior.
8. Love and peace are basic strivings and must be advanced during one's lifetime.

These values are universally expressed and professed in social work. A belief in the fundamental dignity and worth of an individual is similar to 1 and 2. Social work's commitment to self-determination is captured in 3 and 4. The importance of social responsibility and reciprocity has also become a more broadly accepted value (Compton & Gallaway, 1979; Siporin, 1975) and is reflected in 5, 6, and 7. Number 8 (a commitment to the advancement of love and peace) is a value that few social workers would reject, although it is not articulated and asserted by the mainstream in the profession as yet.

The major values of the person-centered approach appear to be closely aligned with those expressed in social work. This is partly because of the similarity of historical roots, but it is also due to the cross-cultural, time-tested effectiveness of these values. In other words, they appear to be functional as well as philosophical.

Sociocultural Sensitivity

Person-centered theory, especially that characterized by Rogers's early work, has come under criticism for placing too much emphasis on individualism and independence, although dependency on family, friends, and authority figures is considered appropriate and necessary in many cultures (Usher, 1989). Rogers recognized the importance of a client's natural support systems and traditional healing methods in his later writings, and others have managed to find significant points of convergence in cross-cultural settings (Hayashi et al., 1992). It is notable that person-centered theory has received more attention and generated more interest in multicultural settings outside of North America in the past decade than in its historical stronghold.

Treatment

The basic goal of client-centered therapy is to release an already existing capacity for self-actualization in a potentially competent individual. The underlying assumptions are as follows:

1. The individual has the capacity to guide, regulate, direct, and control himself providing certain conditions exist.
2. The individual has the potential to understand what is in his life that is related to his distress and anxiety.
3. The individual has the potential to reorganize himself in such a way as not only to eliminate his distress and anxiety, but also to experience self-fulfillment and happiness.

In 1957, Rogers postulated the following elements that he believed were necessary and sufficient for a positive outcome in therapy:

1. The therapist is genuine and congruent in the relationship.
2. The therapist experiences unconditional positive regard toward the client.

3. The therapist experiences empathic understanding of the client's internal frame of reference.
4. The client perceives these conditions at least to a minimal degree.

These core conditions, as they came to be known, have been linked with positive outcomes in therapy for a wide variety of clients in various settings (Carkhuff, 1971; Carkhuff & Berenson, 1967; Truax & Mitchell, 1971). Additional dimensions of the therapist, such as concreteness, confrontation, self-disclosure, and immediacy, have been recognized as important (Carkhuff, 1969). Quinn (1993) has argued for an expansion of the concept of genuineness to include a developmental-interactional component, and Natiello (1987) has suggested that the therapist's personal power is so crucial that it should be treated as a fourth condition. The process of therapy and counseling in the client-centered approach is basically the following:

1. The therapist and client establish a mutual counseling contract.
2. The therapist presents an attitude in the relationship characterized by the core conditions.
3. The client's greatest capacity for problem solving is released because he is free from the anxiety and doubts that were blocking his potential.

It is difficult to make a comprehensive statement about person-centered therapy because, true to its basic philosophy, it has been changing, evolving, and actualizing since its inception. Table 5.1, adapted from David Cole (1982) and J. T. Hart (1970), illustrates some of the major points associated with those changes over the past 40 years.

The person-centered developments referred to in the table are more indicative of Rogers's orientation since 1970. Some proponents of person-centered theory have continued to develop and refine the microlevel counseling aspects. Carkhuff and his associates have developed specific training programs in which the novice counselor first learns how to discriminate between high-level responses (understanding and direction) and low-level responses (little understanding or direction). Second, the student

Table 5-1. The Development of Client-Centered Therapy

Therapy	Therapist Goals	Therapist Roles
Nondirective cognitive orientation (insight) 1940–1950	1. Create an atmosphere of permission and acceptance 2. Help client clarify thoughts and feelings rather than interpret for him 3. Help client increase knowledge of self	1. Passive, nonjudgmental listening 2. Empathic 3. Nonconfronting 4. Nonsharing of self 5. Feedback objective, rephrasing, repeating, clarifying
Client-centered or reflective emotional orientation (self-concept) 1950–1957	1. Develop the conditions necessary and sufficient for constructive personality change 2. Communicate to client: • empathy • unconditional positive regard • genuineness	1. Active listening 2. Accurate, emphatic 3. Nonconfronting 4. Sharing of self 5. Noninterpretive 6. Feedback, subjective indicating how therapist believes client feels
Experimental existential/ encounter orientation (humanistic) 1957–1970	1. Establishing therapeutic relationship 2. Reflecting client experiencing 3. Expressing therapist experiencing 4. Client as a unique individual and as a group member	1. Active listening 2. Accurate empathy 3. Confronting 4. Sharing an authentic friendship 5. Interpreting, if appropriate 6. Feedback is subjective prizing, loving, caring
Person-centered • Community • Institution • Political orientation (militant humanism) 1970 to present	Humanize and facilitate the actualization of communities, institutions, and political systems	1. Apply effective components of person-centered approach to such organizations 2. Assert humanistic values 3. Quiet revolutionary

counselor learns how to communicate high levels of accurate empathy, authenticity, and positive regard. The following dialogue exemplifies this process:

Client: I don't know if I'm right or wrong feeling the way I do, but I find myself withdrawing from people. I don't seem to socialize and play their stupid little games any more.

Counselor's response (Low level): Friendships like this are precarious at best.

(Medium level): You're really down because they won't let you be yourself.

(High level): You feel really bad because you can't be yourself and you want to be. The first thing you might do is spend a little time exploring who you are without them.

Client: Sometimes I question my adequacy raising three boys, especially the baby. Well, I call him the baby because he's the last. I can't have any more, so I

know I kept him a baby longer than the others. He won't let anyone else do things for him. Only Mommy!

Counselor's response (Low level): Could you tell me, have you talked with your husband about this?

(Medium level): You feel concern because your son is so demanding.

(High level): You're disappointed in yourself because you haven't helped him develop fully and you really want to. Now a first step might be to design a little program for you and for him (Carkhuff, 1976).

Person-centered theory can no longer be described or evaluated in a singular fashion. So many individuals and groups have embraced the approach that the underlying philosophy and principles are evident even in approaches that are not specifically identified as client-centered. For the beginning counselor or therapist, person-centered theory still appears to offer a comprehensive approach. In a refinement of this approach, Angelo Boy and Gerald Pine offered the following reasons for utilizing person-centered theory in counseling (Boy & Pine, 1982):

Possesses a positive philosophy of the person

Articulates propositions regarding human personality and behavior

Possesses achievable human goals for the client

Possesses a definition of the counselor's role within the counseling relationship

Has research evidence supporting its effectiveness

Is comprehensive and can be applied beyond the one-to-one counseling relationship

Is clear and precise regarding application

Has an expansive intellectual and attitudinal substance

Focuses on the client as a person rather than on the client's problem

Focuses on the attitudes of the counselor rather than on techniques

Provides the counselor with a systematic response pattern

Provides flexibility for the counselor to go beyond reflection of feelings

Can be individualized to the particular needs of a client

Enables client behavior to change in a natural sequence of events

Can draw from the process components of other theories of counseling and human development

Not surprisingly, person-centered theory is most often identified with the person end of the person–environment continuum. The concept of self is so important to Rogers's view of personality that it is often referred to as self-psychology or self-theory.

Rogers viewed human nature as growth-oriented and positive and believed that maladaptation is generally more a problem in the environment than in the person. In most cases, client-centered therapy is predicated on the belief that the client's innate self-actualizing tendencies will flourish if the conditions are right. This view recognizes the importance of the environment and places the locus of change in that area. Essentially, the environment should

be altered or adjusted to suit humans, rather than the reverse.

This view has received limited acceptance in social work. Most social work approaches afford equal importance to both aspects of the person–environment continuum, at least in theory. In practice, a great deal of social work activity is directed toward helping the individual adjust to society. Person-centered theory is at odds with both of these.

Social Work with Individuals

Person-centered theory has found both acceptance and expression in social work with individuals, or "social casework." Person-centered theory is most closely aligned with the functional approach to social casework, although there are areas of convergence with and divergence from the other major approaches. This is understandable given Rogers's involvement with social work and the functional school in the 1930s.

Psychosocial History. The place of a psychosocial history in casework, firmly established by Mary Richmond (1917), for the most part has been broadly accepted by the profession. Person-centered theory has historically placed little emphasis on this aspect of the helping process. In applying the person-centered approach narrowly, workers would concern themselves with history-taking only to the degree the client was willing. A broader interpretation of person-centered theory would also promote history-taking, since a full appreciation and credible acceptance of the client can be better realized when the worker is cognizant of both the past and the present. History-taking is one of the areas that has become more acceptable to person-centered therapists in its more eclectic form.

Diagnosis. Another area of traditional divergence has been the place of diagnosis in casework. Person-centered theory has been fundamentally opposed to diagnostic classification. This theory's belief in the uniqueness of the person disallows the categorization, classification, and dehumanized labeling of individuals. Diagnosis has been and continues to be an important concept in social casework (Hollis, 1972; Turner,

1968, 1976), where it is generally viewed as a dynamic and functional process. Smalley's approach, in which the worker and client are both fully considered in the diagnosis, is most reminiscent of the person-centered approach.

Rogers and others have demonstrated that the person-centered approach is effective with a variety of diagnostic categories, including schizophrenics and psychotics (Gerwood, 1993; Rogers, 1980; Rogers et al., 1967). This research, coupled with the person-centered philosophy, has established some of the rationale for rejecting the concept of diagnosis. The person-centered approach in social work need not reject this concept wholly, and may indeed discover that person-centered theory applied within the diagnostic framework can increase its effectiveness. This latter approach would undoubtedly be more acceptable to social caseworkers.

The Helping Interview. By far the greatest contribution person-centered theory has made to social casework has been the helping interview. Most approaches to social casework recognize the utility of the "core conditions of helping." These conditions of communicating accurate empathy, authenticity, and positive regard in the helping interview have been demonstrated as effective by Truax, Carkhuff, and Mitchell. In the 1970s, social work educators introduced training in the core conditions to the social work curriculum (Fischer, 1978; Hammond et al., 1978; Wells, 1975). Silberschatz and George (2007) further suggest that these necessary and sufficient conditions of therapeutic personality change are still pertinent to many of the major techniques commonly used in counseling. Clearly the core conditions appear to be a good base from which to begin skill development in the helping interview. In order to be more broadly useful and acceptable to social caseworkers, they need to be expanded and adapted to fit the wide variety of situations and circumstances.

Case Example

Brian is a client who has reportedly suffered from low self-esteem and feelings of anxiety for several years. According to Brian, these issues have intensified recently and he's not sure why.

Brian: "Today has been an awful day. I have always felt like less of a person compared to everyone else, but recently it seems as though things have gotten worse and I don't know why."

Therapist: "I understand that you feel bad. This is a very difficult time for you and I wonder if it feels a little scary to be unsure of what is wrong."

Brian: "It is scary, because I don't like to feel as if I'm not in control of myself. Also, sometimes I feel like there is no one around me who understands how I feel, or they just think my feelings are wrong. I mean my family gets mad that I don't talk to them enough, but how can I open up to them when they won't understand me?"

Therapist: "Currently, things seem so overwhelming to you and you feel that you have no one in your personal life who understands what you're going through, so you can't see the point of sharing your feelings with them."

Brian: "Yes, they just don't get it. Maybe I'm just not worth the trouble of listening to."

Therapist: "Well, I believe that you are worth listening to. I am glad to see you when you come for sessions and share your thoughts and feelings. I also believe that you are able to make your own decisions about who you want to speak to and when."

Brian: "You are confident in my ability to make my own decisions. I am afraid that I will ruin my life, but you aren't afraid of that for me."

Therapist: "You are a competent person who is capable of determining the correct choices for your life."

Brian: "Well, I think if I try to look at my life more positively than negatively I will be better off. If I think more positively, then I will start to speak and act in more positive ways, which will lead to a much happier and more positive life. That's all I want, and now I believe that I actually deserve it and can achieve it."

Therapist: "I feel so proud of you and the bravery you have shown while in therapy. I am honored to have shared in your personal journey and growth."

Using a client-centered therapy approach provided the ability for Brian to decide what to talk about and when, without direction, judgment, or interpretation by his therapist. The therapist's unconditional positive regard, empathy, and congruence allowed Brian to feel more comfortable expressing himself without any worries. This gave him the opportunity for plenty of self-exploration and personal growth. His therapist's confidence in him empowered Brian to take back the control in his life that he felt he was losing and to be more open in his personal relationships.

Social Work with Families

Person-centered principles have had a wide impact on the whole area of work with children and families. Rogers (1939), in his doctoral dissertation and his first book, focused on therapy with children and found it necessary to include the entire family.

A few years after Rogers published *Counseling and Psychotherapy* (1942), Virginia Axline (1947) presented a work that drew from his nondirective principles and from the relationship therapy orientation of Taft (1951) and Allen (1942). Axline's approach to nondirective play therapy included the basic principles of acceptance, relationship, freedom of expression, and freedom of behavior. Others, like Clark Moustakas (1953), expanded and developed these principles to help make the person-centered approach a significant force in child therapy.

By the late 1950s, therapists were increasingly including parents and family members in the counseling context and applying person-centered principles to work with families. Guerney described a process of filial therapy in which parents were taught person-centered skills so they could deal with their children themselves (Guerney, 1964; Guerney & Andronico, 1970). Some explored the development of self-concept in families (Van der Veen et al., 1964), while others used person-centered principles in working with couples (Rogers, 1972a).

While the person-centered approach to working with families has by and large been found useful and philosophically acceptable by social workers, it has essentially been overshadowed by concurrent developments in the application of systems theory to both family work and social work. These two schools of thought appear to be fundamentally divergent in terms of basic assumptions, but some have attempted to establish a dialogue between the two. For example, O'Leary (1989) has written: "Family members need to be received as subjects while being encouraged to face their reality as part of a system with patterns not entirely in their consciousness or control. They need to be acknowledged as mysteries as well as confronted with the limits and unacknowledged potential in their interpersonal living."

Social Work with Groups

Group work in the person-centered tradition has received sporadic acceptance in social work circles. Social work had a rich history in group work long before person-centered principles were applied to this area. The major application of person-centered principles to group work has been in the form of the encounter group or T-group, as developed by Rogers (1970). The encounter group began in the 1940s at the University of Chicago with Rogers, and in Bethel, Maine, with Kurt Lewin. Rogers viewed the intensive group experience as an important vehicle for therapeutic growth and attitudinal change, whereas Lewin focused on the improvement of human relations and interpersonal interaction.

Rogers (1970) noted the following as central to the process of change in intensive group experience:

Climate of safety
Expression of immediate feelings and reactions
Mutual trust
Change in attitudes and behavior
Understanding and openness
Feedback
Innovation, change, and risk
Transfer of learning to other situations

Many of the above are seen as essential elements of mutual aid in social group work (Shulman, 1979). Also, the following description of the goals of the therapist leader (Beck, 1974) are not incompatible with the orientation of many social group workers:

1. The facilitation of group members to take responsibility for themselves in whatever way is realistically possible
2. The clarification and solution of problems and conflicts by a process of self-understanding and the development of an empathic understanding of others
3. Recognition of the client as she is and recognition of her reality as she sees it
4. Attempts to offer an attitude that is nonjudgmental in order to facilitate exploratory and self-reflective behavior in the client

5. Recognition of the significance of maintaining as high a degree as possible of clarity about the leader's own views, feelings, and reactions while he is in the therapeutic relationship.

The expression of the core conditions by group leaders has been shown to have a positive impact on increasing client self-exploration (O'Hare, 1979).

Given the therapeutic aim of encounter groups and their focus on the individual in group, they are most readily identified with the remedial model of social group work. However, many of the underlying principles and some of the techniques are more reminiscent of the reciprocal model of social group work. Some aspects, such as adherence to democratic principles, are aligned with social group work in general. Recently, some researchers have argued that there may be points of compatibility between structuring group process and nondirectiveness (Coughlan & McIlduff, 1990). This opens the door for a much wider use of person-centered group work with, for example, low-functioning or involuntary clients (Foreman, 1988; Patterson, 1990).

Social Work with Communities

The more recent developments in person-centered theory have included an interest and involvement in the concept of community. Rogers applied the fundamental principles of person-centered theory to both community concerns and community development.

Much of this was initiated at the Center for Studies of the Person in workshops and learning laboratories. Some concurrent efforts continued at the University of Chicago, where Gendlin and others established a therapeutic community called Changes, which was based on person-centered principles (Rogers, 1980). The experiments in community have included work with a wide variety of neighborhoods, cultures, religions, and political situations.

In the tradition of the person-centered orientation, writers have first concerned themselves with establishing propositions that describe the basic assumptions concerning communities. Barrett-Lennard (1979) has postulated that "a well functioning community would be an open system in interface with other systems … continually in process … and characterized by an organismic egalitarianism." William Rogers (1974) suggests that, from the person-centered viewpoint, "individuals seek a community of belonging, understanding and mutual support that will enhance the actualization of life," and that "persons within a community are potentially better able to understand and articulate the identity and hopes of that community than are persons from outside." William Rogers moves to the next phase by considering the necessary steps in the process of social change. Some of the person-centered principles contained in his approach are:

The importance of listening deeply to the needs and concerns of individuals and groups within the constituent communities

The facilitation of community self-perception

The recognition and encouragement of indigenous leadership

The facilitation of the communication among divergent groups

The identification of community goals

In work with communities, person-centered theory is most clearly aligned with the principles of locality development. The person-centered approach to community development articulated by William Rogers is both astute and pragmatic. As such, it is generally more acceptable to social workers than the more esoteric, unstructured offerings developed at such places as the Center for Studies of the Person and Changes. Many community workers in social work find the community-building techniques developed and experimented with in the person-centered approach to be useful in conjunction with their own theories. To this end, the person-centered approach affords an important laboratory for exploring different aspects of community building. Curiously, it is possible that the person-centered approach as it has evolved may be too value-laden and prescriptive for most social work community organizers to embrace.

Social Work Administration

For many years, Rogers viewed the tenets of person-centered theory as applicable to all human interaction. In *Carl Rogers on Personal Power* (1977), he described how these features have been successfully applied to agencies and organizations. Rogers provided examples of how person-centered approaches resulted in greater productivity, as well as greater career and personal satisfaction. In this approach, leadership is characterized by influence and impact, rather than power and control. The person-centered administrator, where possible, gives autonomy to persons and groups, stimulates independence, facilitates learning, delegates responsibility, encourages self-evaluation, and finds rewards in the development and achievements of others (Rogers, 1977).

Person-centered theories of administration did not originate with Rogers, but were articulated in administration circles since the early part of this century (Schatz, 1970). The major contribution of Rogers has once again been the operationalization and application of the concepts within an organized framework.

Social workers have found many aspects of person-centered administration to be compatible with their values. There has been a great deal of interest in and experimentation with participatory management approaches (McMahon, 1981; Schatz, 1970) and equality-based supervisory practices (Mandell, 1973). Rogers's approach to administration, with its antiauthoritarianism, is limited in its broad application in social work. As they are applied and refined, however, the principles may mature into an acceptable, coherent, and functional administrative orientation.

Empirical Base

Investigators received a new impetus from the study of client-centered theory. Rogers's personal commitment to empiricism and to outcome-and-evaluation research opened new avenues in research that had previously not been considered. Rogers's objective observations of the subjective experience of counselors and clients through hypothesizing and testing were clearly innovative. While his initial interest was in the systematic description of the process of psychotherapy, his attention later turned to effectiveness and outcome measures, and finally, to attempts to substantiate his theoretical postulates.

John Shlien and Fred Zimring (1970) identified four stages in the development of research

methods and directives in client-centered theory. In stage 1, the emphasis was on the client in the context of therapy. In stage 2, the emphasis expanded to cover the phenomenological aspects of perception and personality. In stage 3, the emphasis shifted to the study of the therapist, and in stage 4, all three elements merged into a process conception of psychotherapy. An extraordinary number of studies have been generated in all of these areas. Although many support the original claims, some challenge both the original assumptions and the external validity of some of the findings. Investigators such as Charles B. Truax and Robert Carkhuff further refined, expanded, and substantiated the basic principles of client-centered theory.

The research on the core conditions of therapy is especially notable. There is considerable agreement across a number of professions, including psychology, psychiatry, social work, and nursing, that the core conditions are demonstrably linked with effective counseling practices. As such, the core conditions remain one of the only substantive elements of effective counseling, and are supported by numerous studies.

With the possible exception of behavior therapy, no other approach has had such an intensive research orientation. This is in part attributable to the fact that, unlike most schools of therapy, client-centered theory was developed primarily in the university setting. As Rogers (1960) remarked, "Client-centered therapy will at least be remembered for its willingness to take a square look at the facts," and this emphasis has been embraced by most of those associated with the client-centered orientation. The methods employed in client-centered research appear to be particularly adaptable to the needs of social work research. The stages of development in client-centered research are closely aligned with social work concerns.

The first level of development in client-centered research was the recording of cases, the definition of concepts, the development of objective measures of the concepts, the application of the concepts, and the establishment of relationships among the concepts. This is similar to attempts in social work research to quantify and evaluate practice, as in Larry Shulman's study on casework skill (1978). It is widely acknowledged that much of what is considered to be practice wisdom in social work would be better understood and utilized if it were sub-jected to this kind of rigor (Siporin, 1975).

Another stage of research in client-centered theory that is directly useful to social work is outcomes research. Numerous effectiveness and outcome studies have been done using creative investigative techniques such as the Q-sort. Social work researchers are increasingly concerned with the same issues in light of increased demands for accountability. As social workers become better able to define and opera-tionalize their objectives, these research tech-niques have proven useful.

In the past decade, social work research has increased significantly and social workers have expanded their repertoire of research methods. Heuristic models and qualitative research meth-ods are finding increasing use in social work, and their congruence with the empirical base in per-son-centered theory is clear (Barrineau & Bozarth, 1989). As direct practice becomes more eclectic in nature, the challenge is to establish how per-son-centered approaches are more or less useful, under what conditions, and with what particular disorders or needs (Lambert, 1986). A good example of this is seen in a recent work by Joseph (2004) where he looks at the practical applica-tions of client-centered therapy for posttraumatic stress disorder (PTSD) and posttraumatic growth. While most of the major texts on PTSD make no reference whatsoever to client-centered therapy, Joseph suggests that PTSD symptoms may simply be another way of talking about what Rogers described as the breakdown and disorganization of the self-structure. He points out that the per-son-centered approach forces us view recovery from PTSD in terms of positive movement toward posttraumatic growth.

Prospectus

There are numerous areas of convergence and compatibility between person-centered theory and social work practice. Given the similarities in philosophy and practice, it is in some ways curious that person-centered theory is not more accepted by the profession. For example, not long ago, Howard Goldstein (1983) published an article, "Starting Where the Client Is," in which he competently articulated the value of his long-standing social work adage. It is odd that he made only passing reference to Rogers and

person-centered theory, considering the amount of theory and research available to support his thesis. Rogers presents what many believe is a naive and one-sided view of human nature.

Many social workers support this positive view of humanity in theory, but decades of practice with some of the more disturbing problems in society (poverty, child abuse and neglect, family violence) diminish enthusiasm for such beliefs. Much of person-centered theory was developed in controlled university settings, whereas the social worker's practice environ-ment is often far more unpredictable. Much of the work done in the past decade has advanced the use of person-centered methods with difficult-to-serve clients (Gerwood, 1993; Patterson, 1990) and should help to bridge this gap. Those who have advanced the work of Martin Luther King Jr. and use his ideas and methods to work with both perpetrators and victims of terror, gang violence, and even geno-cide readily trace their techniques and approaches to Rogerian values and philosophy.

Most of the research validating the concepts takes the expressions of the clients at face value and gives little attention to unconscious proc-esses. Many social workers firmly believe in the importance of understanding unconscious moti-vations and have experienced the usefulness of this understanding in both assessment and inter-vention. Some of the theory-bridging begun by Rogers (1986) and furthered by others (Purton, 1989; Quinn, 1993) will allow for more conver-gence on these issues in the future.

Another area of divergence between person-centered theory and social work pertains to the concept of authority. Rogers took an extreme position against authority and saw it as an essen-tially destructive component of relationships. While many social workers deemphasize author-ity, the major concern is more often how to make positive use of it, as opposed to simply denying its existence. Not all person-centered therapists are as adamant about this issue as Rogers was, and some of the more recent contributors have included rather than rejected the concept of authority relationships (Boy & Pine, 1982; Coughlan & McIlduff, 1990; O'Leary, 1989).

The development of person-centered theory in many ways has been a microcosm of the development of the social work profession. Both began with the worker–client interaction and progressed to include groups, families, organizations, communities, and political systems. Person-centered theory has matured along with social work theory to the point where Orlov (1990) made reference to "person-centered politics," a concept that would have been unthinkable a short time ago. Soloman (1990), in a work entitled "Carl Rogers's Efforts for World Peace," demonstrated advances in the application of person-centered theory that have significant ramifications for international work.

Many social work students, upon their introduction to person-centered concepts, dismiss them as simplistic and unsophisticated. It is only when workers have had significant experience that they are in a position to rediscover person-centered theory, with its many layers of depth and meaning. Miriam Polster (1987) captured this well when she referred to Rogers's work as "informed simplicity," not unlike a Picasso painting (Zeig, 1987, p. 198).

The term "person-centered" is highly appropriate for both theory and practice in a profession that has traditionally attempted to encompass both science and compassion. In essence, both the emphasis on the person and the research practices of person-centered theory are valuable to social work. In the past few years evidence-based practice has taken a central role in social work practice and social work education. At first glance it may appear that the ordered protocols inherent in evidence-based practice appear to be at odds with many of the fundamental tenets of client-centered theory as articulated by Rogers and as practiced by Rogerians. Actually, virtually all of Rogers's early work was based on observation and experimentation at a time when others were using mostly post-report information often gathered from the therapists themselves. Client-centered theory might better be described at this point as value-based, evidence-supported practice. Overall it is essential that, as professional boundaries become less distinct and multidisciplinary practice becomes more the norm, we re-embrace person-centered theory and all that it has to offer in its old and new forms.

References

Allen, F. H. (1942). *Psychotherapy with children*. New York: Norton.

Axline, V. M. (1947). *Play therapy*. Boston: Houghton Mifflin.

Barrett-Lennard, G. T. (1979). The person-centered system unfolding. In F. J. Turner (Ed.), *Social work treatment* (2nd ed.). New York: Free Press.

Barrineau, P., & Bozarth, J. (1989). A person-centered research model. *Person-Centered Review,* 4(4), 465–474.

Beck, A. M. (1974). Phases in the development of structure in therapy and encounter groups. In D. A. Wexler & L. M. Rice (Eds.), *Innovations in person-centered therapy*. New York: Wiley.

Boy, A.V., & Pine, G. J. (1982). *Person-centered counseling: A renewal*. Boston: Allyn and Bacon.

Brodley, B. T. (2006). Client-initiated homework in client-centered therapy. *Journal of Psychotherapy Integration,* 16(2), 140–161.

Brown, G. A. (2008). An F. for graphic exploration of psychological treatment and training psychiatric hospital. Doctoral dissertation, University of South Africa.

Carkhuff, R. R. (1969). *Helping and human relations*. Vol. 1 and 2. New York: Holt, Rinehart and Winston.

Carkhuff, R. R. (1971). *The development of human resources*. New York: Holt, Rinehart and Winston.

Carkhuff, R. R. (1976). *Counselor-counselee and audio-tape handbook*. Amherst, MA: Human Resource Development Press.

Carkhuff, R. R., & Berenson, B.G. (1967). *Beyond counseling and therapy*. New York: Holt, Rinehart and Winston.

Carkhuff, R. R., & Berenson, B.G. (1976). *Teaching as treatment*. Amherst, MA: Human Resource Development Press.

Carkhuff, R. R., & Berenson, B.G. (1977). *Beyond counseling and therapy* (2nd ed.). New York: Holt, Rinehart and Winston.

Cole, D. R. (1982). *Helping*. Toronto: Butterworth.

Compton, B., & Gallaway, B. (1979). *Social work processes* (rev. ed.). Homewood, IL: Dorsey Press.

Coughlan, D., & McIlduff, E. (1990). Structuring and nondirectiveness in group facilitation. *Person-Centered Review,* 5(1), 13–29.

Fischer, J. (1974). Training for effective therapeutic practice. *Psychotherapy: Theory, Research, and Practice,* 12, 118–123.

Fischer, J. (1978). *Effective casework practice*. New York: McGraw-Hill.

Foreman, J. (1988). Use of person-centered theory with parents of handicapped children. *Texas Association for Counseling and Development Journal,* 16(2), 115–118.

Gendlin, E. T. (1962). Person-centered developments and work with schizophrenics. *Journal of Counseling Psychology,* 9(3), 205–211.

Gendlin, E. T. (1978). *Focusing.* New York: Everest House.

Gerwood, J. (1993). Nondirective counseling interventions with schizophrenics. *Psychological Reports,* 73, 1147–1151.

Goldstein, H. (1983). Starting where the client is. *Social Casework* 64 (May), 267–275.

Gordon, T. (1970). *Parent Effectiveness Training.* New York: Vyden.

Greene, R. R. (2008). Carl Rogers and the person-centered approach. In R. Greene (Ed.), *Human behavior theory and social work practice* (3rd ed.). New Brunswick: Transaction.

Greene, R. R., & Burch, N. (1974). *T.E.T. Teacher Effectiveness Training.* New York: Wyden.

Guerney, B. G. (1964). Filial therapy: description and rationale. *Journal of Consulting Psychology,* 28, 304–310.

Guerney, B. G., Guerney, L. P., & Andronico, M. P. (1970). Filial therapy. In J. T. Hart & T. M. Tomlinson (Eds.), *New directions in person-centered therapy.* Boston: Houghton Mifflin, 372–386.

Hammond, D. C., Hepworth, D. H., & Smith, V. G. (1978). *Improving therapeutic communication.* San Francisco: Jossey-Bass.

Hart, J. T. (1970). The development of person-centered therapy. In J. T. Hart & T. M. Tomlinson (Eds.), *New directions in person-centered therapy.* Boston: Houghton Mifflin.

Hayashi, S., Kuno, T., Osawa, M., Shimizu, M., & Suetake, Y. (1992). The client-centered therapy and person-centered approach in Japan. *Journal of Humanistic Psychology,* 32(2), 115–136.

Hollis, (1972). *Casework: A psychosocial therapy* (2nd ed.). New York: Random House.

Holosko, M. J., Skinner, J., & Robinson, R. S. (2008). Person-centered theory. In B. A. Thyer (Vol. Ed.), *Comprehensive handbook of social work and social welfare, vol. 2* (pp. 297–326). Hoboken, NJ: Wiley.

Joseph, S. (2004). Client-centred therapy, post-traumatic stress disorder and post-traumatic growth: Theoretical perspectives and practical implications. *Psychology & Psychotherapy: Theory, Research & Practice,* 77(1), 101–119.

Keefe, T. (1976). Empathy: the critical skill. *Social Work,* 21, 10–14.

Kirschenbaum, H., & Jourdan, A. (2005). The current status of Carl Rogers and the person-centered approach. *Psychotherapy: Theory, Research, Practice, Training,* 42(1), 37–51.

Kilpatrick, W. H. (1926). *Foundation of method.* New York: Macmillan.

LaCombe, S. (2008). Carl Rogers *"Could 2598 therapists be wrong?"* Retreived March 25, 2009, from

http://www.myshrink.com/counseling-theory.php?t_id=87

Lambert, M. (1986). Future directions for research in client-centered psychotherapy. *Person-Centered Review,* 1(2), 185–200.

Larsen, J. A. (1975). *A comparative study of traditional and competency-based methods of teaching interpersonal skills in social work education.* Doctoral dissertation. University of Utah.

Lewin, K. (1951). *Field theory in social science.* New York: Harper.

Mandell, B. (1973). The equality revolution and supervision. *Journal of Education for Social Work* (Winter).

Maslow, A. (1971). *The farther reaches of human nature.* New York: Viking.

McMahon, P. C. (1981). *Management by objectives in the social services.* Ottawa: Canadian Association of Social Workers.

Moreira, V. (1993). Beyond the person: Marleau-Penty's concept of "flesh" as (re)defining Carl Rogers' person-centered theory. *The Humanistic Psychologist,* 21(2), 138–157.

Moustakas, C. E. (1953). *Children in play therapy.* New York: McGraw-Hill.

Natiello, P. (1987). The person-centered approach. *Person-Centered Review,* 2(2), 203–216.

Nye, R. D. (1975). *Three views of man.* Monterey, CA: Brooks/Cole Publishing.

O'Hare, C. (1979). Counseling group process: Relationship between counselor and client behaviours in the helping process. *Journal for Specialists in Group Work.*

O'Leary, C. (1989). The person-centered approach and family therapy. *Person-Centered Review,* 4(3), 308–323.

Orlov, A. (1990). Carl Rogers and contemporary humanism. (Karl Rodzhers i sovremennyi gumanizm). Vestn. Mosk, un-ta., Ser. 14, Psikhologiia, (2), 55–58.

Patterson, C. (1990). Involuntary clients. *Person-Centered Review,* 5(3), 316–320.

Pfeiffer, J., & Jones, J.A. (1971). *Handbook of structured experiences for human relations training.* Iowa City, IA: University Assoc.

Purton, C. (1989). The person-centered Jungian. *Person-Centered Review,* 4(4), 403–419.

Quinn, R. (1993). Confronting Carl Rogers: A developmental-interactional approach to person-centered therapy. *Journal of Humanistic Psychology,* 33(1), 6–23.

Richmond, M. E. (1917). *Social diagnosis.* New York: Russell Sage Foundation.

Rogers, C. R. (1939). *The clinical treatment of the problem child.* Boston: Houghton Mifflin.

Rogers, C. R. (1942). *Counseling and psychotherapy.* Boston: Houghton Mifflin.

Rogers, C. R. (1957). The necessary and sufficient conditions of therapeutic personality change. *Journal of Counseling Psychology,* 21, 95–103.

Rogers, C. R. (1959). A theory of therapy, personality and interpersonal relationships, as developed in the person-centered framework. In S. Koch (Ed.), *Psychology: A study of science.* Vol. 3. New York: McGraw-Hill, 184–256.

Rogers, C. R. (1960). Significant trends in the person-centered orientation. *Progress in Clinical Psychology,* 4, 85–99.

Rogers, C. R. (1961a). A theory of psychotherapy with schizophrenics and a proposal for its empirical investigation. In J. G. Dawson, H. K. Stone, & N. P. Dellis (Eds.), *Psychotherapy with schizophrenics.* Baton Rouge: Louisiana State University Press, 3–19.

Rogers, C. R. (1961b). *On becoming a person.* Boston: Houghton Mifflin.

Rogers, C. R. (1964). Toward a modern approach to values: the valuing process in the mature person. *Journal of Abnormal and Social Psychology,* 68(2), 160–167.

Rogers, C. R. (Ed.). (1967). *The therapeutic relationship and its impact: A study of psychotherapy with schizophrenics.* Madison: University of Wisconsin Press.

Rogers, C. R. (1969). *Freedom to learn.* Columbus, OH: Merrill.

Rogers, C. R. (1970). *Carl Rogers on encounter groups.* New York: Harper and Row.

Rogers, C. R. (1972a). *Becoming partners: Marriage and its alternatives.* New York: Delacorte.

Rogers, C. R. (1972b). My personal growth. In Arthur Burton et al. (Eds.), *Twelve therapists.* San Francisco: Jossey-Bass, 28–77.

Rogers, C. R. (1974). Person-centered and symbolic perspectives on social change: A schematic model. In D. A. Wexler & L. M. Rice (Eds.), *Innovations in person-centered therapy.* New York: Wiley.

Rogers, C. R. (1977). *Carl Rogers on personal power.* New York: Dell.

Rogers, C. R. (1980). *A way of being.* Boston: Houghton Mifflin.

Rogers, C. R. (1986). Rogers, Kohut and Erikson. *Person-Centered Review,* 1(2), 125–140.

Rogers, C. R., Gendlin, E. J., Kiesler, D. J., & Truax, C. B. (Eds.). (1967). *The therapeutic relationship and its impact: A study of psychotherapy with schizophrenics.* Madison: University of Wisconsin Press.

Rogers, C. R., & Stevens, D. (1975). *Person to person.* New York: Pocket Books.

Rogers, W. R. (1974). Person-centered and symbolic perspectives on social change: A schematic model. In D. A. Wexler & L. N. Rice (Eds.), *Innovations in person-centered therapy.* New York: Wiley.

Rowe, W. (1981). Laboratory training in the baccalaureate curriculum. *Canadian Journal of Social Work Education,* 7(3), 93–104.

Rowe, W. (1983). An integrated skills laboratory. *Review,* 83, 161–169.

Schatz, H. A. (1970). Staff involvement in agency administration. In H. A. Schatz (Ed.), *Social work administration.* New York: Council on Social Work Education.

Seeman, J. (1990). Theory as autobiography. *Person-Centered Review,* 5(4), 373–386.

Shlien, J. M., & Zimring, F. M. (1970). Research directives and methods in person-centered therapy. In J. T. Hart & T. M. Tomlinson (Eds.), *New directions in person-centered therapy.* Boston: Houghton Mifflin.

Shulman, L. (1978). A study of practice skills. *Social Work,* 23(4), 274–281.

Shulman, L. (1979). *The skills of helping.* Itasca, IL: Peacock.

Silberschatz, & George. (2007). Comments on "The necessary and sufficient conditions of therapeutic personality change." *Psychotherapy: Theory, Research, Practice, Training,* 44(3), 265–267.

Siporin, M. (1975). *Introduction to social work practice.* New York: Macmillan.

Smalley, R. E. (1967). *Theory for social work practice.* New York: Columbia University Press.

Sollod, R. N. (1978). Carl Rogers and the origins of person-centered therapy. *Professional Psychology,* 4(1), 93–104.

Solomon, L. (1990). Carl Rogers's efforts for world peace. *Person-Centered Review,* 5(1), 39–56.

Stewart, M. A., Weston, W. W., Brown, J. B., McWhinney, I. E., McWilliam, C., & Freeman, T. R. (1995). *Patient-centered medicine.* Thousand Oaks, CA: Sage Publications.

Taft, J. (1951). *The dynamics of therapy in a controlled relationship.* New York: Harper.

Truax, C. B., & Carkhuff, R. R. (1967). *Toward effective counseling and psychotherapy: Training and practice.* Chicago: Aldine.

Truax, C. B., & Mitchell, K. J. (1971). Research on certain therapist interpersonal skills in relation to process and outcome. In A. E. Bergin & S. L. Garfield (Eds.), *Handbook of psychotherapy and behavior change: An empirical analysis.* New York: Wiley, 299–344.

Turner, F. J. (1968). *Differential diagnosis and treatment in social work.* New York: Free Press.

Turner, F. J. (Ed.) (1974). *Social work treatment.* New York: Free Press.

Turner, F. J. (Ed.) (1979). *Social work treatment* (2nd ed.). New York: Free Press.

Usher, C. (1989). Recognizing cultural bias in counseling theory and practice: The case of Rogers.

Journal of Multicultural Counseling and Development, 17(2), 62–71.

Van der Veen, F., et al. (1964). Relationships between the parents' concept of the family and family adjustment. *American Journal of Orthopsychiatry*, 34 (January), 45–55.

Wallman, G. (1980). *The impact of the first year of social work education on student skill in communication of empathy and discrimination of effective responses*. Doctoral dissertation. Adelphi University, New York.

Wells, R. A. (1975). Training in facilitative skills. *Social Work*, 20, 242–243.

Wexler, D. A., & Rice, L. M. (Eds.). (1974). *Innovations in person-centered therapy*. New York: Wiley.

White, R. W. (1959). Motivation reconsidered: The concept of competence. *Psychological Review*, 66, 315.

Zeig, J. K. (Ed.). (1987). *The evolution of psychology*. New York: Brunner/Mazel.

Annotated Listing of Key References

Boy, Angelo v., & Pine, Gerald J. (1982). *Person-centered counseling: A renewal*. Boston: Allyn and Bacon. The authors focus on the current application of person-centered theory to individual and group counseling. Boy and Pine recognize the shift of most person-centered authors to applications in teaching, administration, community building, race relations, and conflict resolution. They offer a refinement of the original person-centered counseling principles and renewed possibilities for individual and group application. In addition, Boy and Pine critically discuss the counseling concerns of personality theory, values, accountability, evaluation, and counselor education.

Carkhuff, Robert R., & Berenson, Bernard G. (1977). *Beyond counseling and therapy* (2nd ed.). New York: Holt, Rinehart and Winston. Carkhuff and Berenson have significantly advanced person-centered theory through both clinical and research efforts. This book supplies a comprehensive statement of the research and clinical observations that support their view of the person-centered model of helping.

The authors compare the person-centered approach with other major helping theories and show the rationale for their particular beliefs. In addition, the philosophy, values, and content of a training approach for counselors are outlined.

Fischer, J. (1978). *Effective casework practice*. New York: McGraw-Hill. Fischer presents an approach to casework that bridges the gap between research and practice. He describes an eclectic approach that consists of empirically validated helping models. Fischer's "integrative model" includes components of behavior modification, cognitive procedures, and the core conditions of helping. A model for training and learning the core conditions is presented. Fisher's book represents one of the few significant references to person-centered theory in social work literature.

Greenberg, L. S., Rice, L., & Elliot, R. (1993). *Facilitating emotional change: The moment-by-moment process*. New York: Guilford Press.

Rice, L. & Greenberg, L. (Eds.) (1984). *Patterns of change: An intensive analysis of psychotherapeutic process*. New York: Guilford Press.

Rogers, Carl R. (1961). *On becoming a person*. Boston: Houghton Mifflin. This is a classic work that helped establish Rogers and person-centered theory as a major force in American psychology. Rogers articulates the culmination of three decades of theory development, clinical practice, and clinical research as a cohesive approach to helping and personal growth. As such, it is an excellent first reading for individuals interested in the person-centered approach.

Rogers, Carl R. (1977). *Carl Rogers on Personal Power*. New York: Dell. Rogers describes the impact of the person-centered approach on relationships, education, administration, and political systems. He reiterates the theoretical foundation of this approach and shows how it translates into a base for political activity and what he terms the "quiet revolution." Rogers details the principles of the person-centered approach and describes a number of examples of these principles in practice, in the workplace, and in the political arena. In conclusion, Rogers offers some humanistic alternatives to polarized conflict and entrenched political structures.

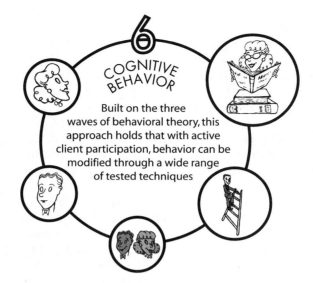

Cognitive Behavior Theory and Social Work Treatment

Ray J. Thomlison and Barbara Thomlison

The treatment of social, emotional, and behavioral problems of children, adolescents, and adults has developed remarkably in the past decades. Reviews of the evidence have consistently found that cognitive behavioral treatments produce lasting favorable changes for many problems. The purpose of this chapter on cognitive behavior therapy (CBT) is to provide the reader with an overview of this approach to social work practice. This overview is placed within the context of the development of CBT upon the base of the late-1960s clinical approach known as behavior modification. Since the earlier editions of this book (Turner, 1996), considerable change has occurred in the evolution of behavior modification to behavior therapy to the current concept of CBT. In large part, this has been driven by advances in research, practice, and training, and by the importance of increased accountability.

These transitions reflect, to some degree, the movement from the early emphasis by the behaviorists on the need for client and clinician to focus on observable behavior. While this principle served to discipline the clinicians and provide a systematic basis for the early clinical research models, it gave way to pressures to broaden and unify various contributing elements of the impact on behavior of cognitive and affective factors. Essentially, behavior modification, behavior therapy, and CBT are similar in that they share an emphasis on client behavior as the focus for therapy. CBT, however, refers to the inclusion of thoughts and beliefs in the determination of clients' problems and their alleviation. The idea behind CBT is that if you can change the way you think, you can change the way you feel.

A second purpose of this chapter is provide a brief overview of the history of CBT. Numerous researchers and clinicians have influenced the development of CBT. To have a basic knowledge of this history is essential in that it provides the clinician with a necessary understanding of the rationale for why this approach has departed from the more traditional psychotherapy approaches. In essence, CBT emerged from a commitment to the empirical study of human behavior and, specifically, conditions under which problem behaviors or maladaptive behaviors and responses are maintained, and then altered or changed. Learning new, more adaptive behaviors will lead to more rewarding behaviors. There is no single definition of CBT: it encompasses a broad array of techniques that are based in the behavioral conditioning theories, learning theory, and cognitive theory. One factor does separate CBT from the earlier traditional psychotherapies: the focus of clinical treatment is on the present. In terms of intervention, therefore, the conditions for change are viewed as being actions taken by the clients themselves and where possible by persons in the client's environment.

A third purpose of this chapter is to illustrate some common applications of behavior modification, behavior therapy, and CBT. The authors also hope to demonstrate the compatibility and applicability of CBT to social work treatment and to inspire social workers to integrate these approaches into their treatment model.

Development of Cognitive Behavior Therapy

The development of behavior therapy over the past decades has been referred to as the Three Waves of Behavior Therapy (Moran, 2008). Briefly, these "waves" or groupings are divided into the early behavior modification therapies, including the contingency management, stimulus control, exposure, and modeling approaches. The second "wave" reflects the major influences of cognitive theories of Aaron Beck (1976), Albert Ellis (1989), and Donald Meichenbaum (1977). Specifically, this second "wave" includes the cognitive approaches of rational emotive therapy, cognitive therapy, problem solving, thought stopping, and stress inoculation. The third wave, which remains somewhat controversial and challenging to the very roots of behavior therapy, comprises the three more recent therapies identified as acceptance and commitment therapy, dialectical behavior therapy, and mindfulness-based cognitive therapy. These three therapies, as the name suggests, share an emphasis on focusing less on painful thoughts, feelings, and experiences, accepting the discomfort, and living life by committing to important values and alternative ways of achieving life goals. Acceptance and mindfulness are important elements in Buddhism, in respect to the experiencing of the life situation without judgment and evaluation.

In the recent fifth edition of their book *Contemporary Behavior Therapy,* Spiegler and Guevremont (2010) offer a succinct description of the third wave or generation of behavior therapies:

Acceptance and commitment therapy (ACT) posits that psychological inflexibility—a narrowing of options for behaving—is at the core of psychological suffering and is maintained by six interrelated processes: (1) cognitive fusion (taking thoughts literally rather than seeing them as just thoughts), (2) attachment to the conceptualized self (how we view ourselves), (3) experiential avoidance (escape from or avoidance of unpleasant thoughts and feelings), (4) disconnection from the present moment, (5) unclear personal values, and (6) inaction with respect to values (failure to act in accord with what is personally important). These six sources of psychological inflexibility are treated in ACT to foster psychological flexibility. (p. 415)

Included in this third wave of behavior therapy is dialectical behavior therapy, developed by Marsha Linehan (1993). This therapy mode involves a relatively structured form of both individual and group therapy, and consistent with ACT, it merges the core conditions of acceptance and change with acceptance. This approach was developed for the treatment of borderline personality disorders. The approach evolved in her work with suicidal patients, whom she concluded were overwhelmed by change expectations but who also felt their problems to be ignored by acceptance theory. The synthesis of both a structured skills training approach and acceptance of the self provided a more effective outcome to therapy.

Behavior therapy[1] refers to the systematic application of techniques intended to facilitate behavioral changes that are based principally, but not exclusively, on the conditioning theories of learning. It is more appropriate to refer to the behavior therapies plural rather than to imply that a single method of behavior therapy exists. Behavior therapy is, however, characterized by multiple theories and techniques in the same way as other therapies such as psychotherapy, marital therapy, and family therapy.

Behavioral practice can trace its beginnings to the first quarter of the 20th century in the works of Ivan Pavlov (respondent or classical conditioning); Thorndike, Hull, Watson, and B. F. Skinner (operant conditioning); and Bandura (social learning theory) (Franks, Wilson, Kendall, & Foreyt, 1990). The contributions of Pavlov and Skinner are well documented in both the behavioral and social work literature and we need only mention here that these two individuals studied two distinct behavioral processes.

Pavlov's studies of the salivation reflex of dogs are familiar to most students of human behavior. The basic experimental procedure for the learning process involved placing food within the view of the dog. Salivation was elicited and the relationship between the unconditioned stimulus (food) and the unconditioned response (salivation) was established. An arbitrary event (stimulus), for example a bell, was then established to occur at the same time as the presentation of the food. Over a number of such pairings, the bell (the conditioned stimulus) took on the power to elicit the response of salivation (the conditioned response). This behavioral learning process is referred to as respondent conditioning and remains a foundational theoretical explanation for a variety of anxiety and phobic disorders in contemporary behavior therapy (Thomlison, 1984b).

Skinner's contribution to behavior therapy was initially motivated by a different set of objectives than those of Pavlov. Skinner was dedicated to the objective of the scientific study of human behavior. While he did not deny the possibilities of the internal mechanisms postulated by other theorists, he argued that human behavior could be empirically investigated only through the measurement of observable behavior. Underlying his approach was the belief that if we are to use the methods of science in the field of human affairs, we assume that behavior is lawful and

determined. We expect to discover that what an individual does is the result of specifiable conditions and that once these conditions have been discovered, we can anticipate and to some extent determine one's actions (Skinner, 1953, p. 6). It is necessary to understand that this commitment to science set relatively stringent requirements on the pursuit of knowledge within the behavioral school, not the least of which was the need to develop techniques of measurement compatible with the exploration of human behavior.

True to his commitment, Skinner evolved one of the most empirically based theories of human behavior and set the foundation for contemporary behavior therapy. At the heart of this Skinnerian theory was the concept of reinforcement. The frequency of operant behavior (voluntary behavior) emitted by an individual could be increased if such behavior was positively or negatively reinforced. Alternatively, its frequency could be decreased by either administering punishment or withholding reinforcement, this latter process being referred to as extinction. In other words, the essence of the Skinnerian or operant model of conceptualizing human behavior relied heavily upon an understanding of the environmental (behavioral) events that preceded and/or followed the behavior(s) under scrutiny. This theoretical explanation of human behavior acquisition has been refined and elaborated as a result of clinical experience and research. Importantly, however, the interaction of behavior, its prior and consequent events, remains the foundation of most contemporary behavior therapy.

In addition, cognitive behavioral approaches are also regarded as part of the behavioral paradigm and are illustrated by the contributions of Beck (1976), Ellis (1989), and Meichenbaum (1977). Cognitive approaches developed directly from behavior theory but are considered as distinct ideas and will therefore be discussed in Chapter 7.

It was not until the late 1960s that behaviorial approaches appeared in social work, at the same time that psychodynamic theories were under attack. Much of the impetus and contemporary development of behavior therapy to social work is represented by the practice and research contributions of Bruce Thyer (1987a; 1988; 1989; 1990; 1991; 1992). Other significant initial social work contributors are Ray Thomlison (1972; 1981; 1982; 1984a; 1984b) for the applications of behavior theory to marital problems and phobic disorders, and effectiveness for clinical social work practice; Richard Stuart (1971; 1977) in the development of behavior theory for delinquency, marital problems, and weight management; Sheldon Rose (1981) for behavior therapy conducted in groups; and Eileen Gambrill (1977; 1983; 1994) for her work with clinical problems.

Criticisms of the Cognitive Behavioral Approach

Before proceeding with an overview of the cognitive behavioral approach and its application to problematic conditions and behaviors, several comments are in order regarding critiques levied by some clinicians about the model. There has always been some question raised about behavioral therapy, both within and outside the behavioral schools of thought, regarding the place of human psychological or cognitive processes. Given recognition of the increased interest in the role of cognition in shaping behavior, the debate regarding the place of cognitions in behavior therapy has centered on several assertions by traditional behaviorists. Some theorists, such as Skinner (1988) and Wolpe (1989), argued that behavior therapy was sidetracked through the inclusion of cognitively based techniques and principles. They proposed that a reliance on cognitions in behavior therapy led to a general abandonment of individualized behavior analysis in favor of treating classes of problems. Behaviorism is based upon the idea that behavior is measurable and that behavior can be changed through the application of various behavioral principles such as classical and operant conditioning. It was thought that the empirical nature of behavior therapy was eroded through the inclusion of feelings and thoughts, which were inaccessible to direct, external observation. Furthermore, some argue that analyses of research data comparing behavior therapy outcomes to those of cognitive and/or cognitive behavioral therapy indicate that, in general, outcomes have not been improved through the addition of cognitive components to behavior therapy (Sweet & Loizeaux, 1991; Wolpe, 1989). For example, Sweet and Loizeaux (1991) reported that 83% of

the 40 clinical outcome studies used in their analysis demonstrated "no more beneficial outcome was achieved by adding therapy modules that specifically attended to cognitive-semantic variables" (p. 176). However, the efficacy of treatment methods tended to vary according to type of problem. When follow-up versus immediate post-treatment results were considered, cognitive behavior interventions seemed to offer longer-lasting results. The acceptance of CBT by so many clinicians is also due to the shorter-term treatment over other therapies. In CBT, clients see their therapist for an average of 10 to 16 sessions. In today's managed-care world, time is money.

Another criticism concerns the focus of CBT. CBT focuses on changing flawed thought processes, as well as the behavior caused by these thoughts. If you change the way you think, then you will behave differently. It is "based on the assumption that a re-organization of one's self-statements will result in a corresponding re-organization of one's behavior" (Corey, 2009, p. 275). On the surface it may sound simple, but simply being told that a view doesn't accurately reflect reality doesn't actually make individuals feel any better, and they may continue to worry and behave in the same way. But to suggest that a cognitive behavioral therapist merely tells the client something is wrong is to unfairly undermine the approach.

In CBT, active client participation is essential. The client and therapist, through the relationship, work together to identify faulty thought processes and goals and then help their clients attain a more positive and healthy way of thinking about these things. Some criticize the therapist as assuming an authority role, which for many clients is not helpful. From this perspective some people may also feel that therapists can be "leading" in their questioning and somewhat directive in terms of their recommendations. For clients who are comfortable with introspection and self-exploration, the basic theoretical approach of cognitive therapy may not be a good match. Clients who are less comfortable with any of these approaches, or whose distress is of a more general interpersonal nature—such that it cannot easily be framed in terms of interplay between thoughts, emotions, and behaviors within a given environment—may be less well served by cognitive therapy. Currently, cognitive and cognitive behavioral therapy is the most investigated treatment for clients suffering from depression, anxiety, panic, and obsessive-compulsive disorder. Whatever the final resolution of this debate, there is no doubt that a cognitively based behavior therapy has developed, one that is quite compatible with social work practice.

Areas of Well-Developed Cognitive Behavioral Practice

Social work clinicians need to take a close look at the support for the efficacy of CBT. An impressive and extensive research base exists for CBT that includes over 120 randomized controlled clinical trials between 1986 and 1993 (Hollon & Beck, 1994) and 325 outcome studies on cognitive behavioral interventions for numerous disorders and problem behavior (Butler, Chapman, Forman, & Beck, 2006). In 16 high-quality meta-analyses of a review of CBT for different disorders, CBT was identified as effective and the results strongly suggested that across many disorders the effects are maintained for substantial periods beyond treatment termination (Butler, Chapman, Forman, & Beck, 2006).

Much of the social work literature supporting the relative success of various therapies depends on anecdotal material from the case reports of social workers. Many of these accounts are unidimensional and relatively few are based on empirical findings, with before and after measures, with clear relationships being established between the therapeutic intervention and client change. The cognitive behavior therapies have, on the other hand, a built-in opportunity for data collection by both social workers and clients. Behavioral procedures involve the systematic application of specific techniques intended to facilitate observable behavior change. Measurement of change is therefore an integral part of CBT. This emphasis on problem assessment and concrete indicators of progress has lead to the extensive development and use of standardized measures. One example of a widely utilized behavioral measure is the Achenbach Child Behavior Checklist (Achenbach, 1991). Behavior therapy has championed the use of single-system research design (Gambrill, 1994; Hersen, 1990; Thyer & Thyer, 1992) as well as

studies in group outcome research (Barrios, 1990; Kazdin, 1989).

Individual CBT for Problems

Many cognitive behavioral interventions have been developed and are available to clinicians as a treatment manual with children and adults. This is a highly desirable opportunity for improving social work clinical practice. Treatment manuals in which interventions are illustrated on a step-by-step basis are standardized treatments that have been empirically validated for use with precisely defined populations and problems under clearly defined conditions. Social workers can find cognitive behavior interventions in the *Handbook of Child and Adolescent Treatment Manuals* (LeCroy, 2007), *Handbook of Prevention and Intervention Programs for Adolescent Girls* (LeCroy & Mann, 2007), and *Cognitive-Behavioral Methods for Social Workers: A Workbook* (Corcoran, 2006). This maturity and richness in empirical literature is the result of decades of clinical application of cognitive behavioral interventions and rigorous research. For example, large effect sizes have been found for CBT for unipolar depression, generalized anxiety disorder, panic disorder with or without agoraphobia, posttraumatic stress disorder and childhood depressive and anxiety disorders, and internalizing and externalizing behaviors (Butler, Chapman, Forman, & Beck, 2006). Moderate effect sizes were found using CBT for marital distress, anger, childhood somatic disorders, and chronic pain (Butler, Chapman, Forman, & Beck, 2006). These findings are consistent across reviews of CBT.

The development of cognitive behavioral interventions as applied to a wider, more specific spectrum of disorders, and challenging and problematic behaviors is needed. For example, CBT applications to substance abuse, bipolar disorder, personality disorders, and anorexia nervosa are receiving recent empirical attention. Evaluation of the long-term effects of CBT and the continuous evaluation of the effects of CBT as compared to alternative treatments is needed. It is noted that for some problems, behavior therapy is routinely and effectively used in conjunction with pharmacotherapy (e.g., adult depression, attention-deficit/hyperactivity disorder, obsessive-compulsive disorder). Table 6.1 shows selected problems and research studies identifying evidence-based practices for CBT in producing individual change with a wide range of problems.

Couple CBT for Problems

Couple counseling is another area where social workers frequently utilize a behavioral approach. Jacobson (1992) asserts that cognitive behavioral interventions are the most effective in reducing marital distress. Communication, conflict-management, and problem-solving skills building are the most common behavioral interventions used. Behavioral procedures have been demonstrated to be effective with a multitude of problems and circumstances, with diverse populations and settings. Indeed, behavioral social work treatments have been found to be superior to other treatment modalities (Shadish & Baldwin, 2005).

Group CBT for Problems

Cognitive behavior approaches to group work have a recognized place in social work, primarily due to the excellent research of Rose (2004; 1981), Gambrill (1983), Tolman and Molidor (1994), and others (Gambrill, 1983), who have used the behavioral approach successfully with a variety of groups, including adults and children (Finkelhor, Ormrod, Turner, & Hamby, 2005; Gamble, Elder, & Lashley, 1989; Tallant, Rose, & Tolman, 1989; Thyer, 1987b; Van Der Ploeg-Stapert & Van Der Ploeg, 1986). Group work often focuses on teaching assertive behaviors and other interpersonal skills. It has been utilized extensively in the treatment of depression, eating disorders, parent and child skills training, and addictions. Tolman and Molidor (1994) reviewed group work within social work practice throughout the 1980s. They noted that 69% of the articles reviewed had a cognitive behavioral orientation. Child social skills training and other behavior problems of children and adolescents were the most frequently targeted fields of social work practice research reviewed that utilized cognitive behavioral group work (Jenson & Howard, 1990; LeCroy, 2007; Zimpfer, 1992).

Community Behavioral Practice

Finally, applications of behavior therapy principles to community practice have been somewhat more limited but have not been ignored. Importantly, however, numerous examples of community projects based on behavioral principles are reported in the literature (Mattaini, 1993; Mattaini & McGuire, 2006; O'Donnell & Tharpe, 1990; Rothman & Thyer, 1984). Areas such as community violence or natural disasters are stressful conditions that may result in posttraumatic stress disorder. The behavioral interventions employed are the same as those utilized for individual change (for example, modeling, feedback, contingency management). Some of the problem areas addressed through behavioral community practice have been increasing the level and quality of community participation and decreasing undesirable and increasing prosocial community practices (Guide to Community Preventive Services, 2009; Mattaini & McGuire, 2006).

The current evidence overall shows CBT as efficacious for many problems compared to other treatments and approaches with a wide variety of mental health disorders and behavioral problems. Clearly more research is needed comparing CBT with other forms of therapy. Several gaps in knowledge and research are noted in the literature, such as the maintenance and generalization of the behavioral changes. Maintenance refers to the durability of the behavioral change over time; generalization refers to behavioral change in contexts different from the one in which the intervention took place. Strategies to enhance both maintenance and generalization need to become part of any behavioral change program and need to be validated through empirical research (Gambrill, 1994; Kendall, 1989; Whisman, 1990). Identifying critical variables that predict which clients will benefit from which intervention procedures can be advanced not only by looking at those clients for whom a specific behavioral procedure is effective but also by considering those clients who fail to improve from the treatment (Goldfried & Castonguay, 1993; Steketee & Chambless, 1992). The quality of efficacy and prediction research will improve if a number of common methodological problems are addressed, particularly if limitations of

Table 6-1. Empirically Supported Behavioral Treatment Problems

Problem Area	Empirical Research[*]
Addictions	Acierno, Donohue, & Kogan, 1994; Goldapple & Montgomery, 1993; Hall, Hall, & Ginsberg, 1990; Lipsey & Wilson, 1993; Peyrot, Yen, & Baldassano, 1994; Polansky & Horan, 1993; Sobell, Sobell, & Nirenberg, 1988
Anxiety disorders	Acierno, Hersen, & Van Hasselt, 1993; Beck & Zebb, 1994; Butler, Chapman, Forman, & Beck, 2006; Emmelkamp & Gerlsma, 1994; Lipsey & Wilson, 1993; Mitte, 2005a, 2005b; Rachmann, 1993; Van Oppen, De Haan, Van Balkom, Spinhoven, Hoogdin, & Van Dyck, 1995
Attention disorders	Fabiano, Pelham, Coles, Chronis-Tuscano, O'Connor, & Gnagy, 2009
Autism	Celiberti & Harris, 1993; Ducharme, Lucas, & Pontes, 1994; McEachin, Smith, & Lovaas, 1993; Reichow & Wolery, 2009; Scheibman, Koegel, Charlop, & Egel, 1990
Child maltreatment	Centers for Disease Control and Prevention, 2009; Gambrill 1983; Finkelhor & Berliner, 1995; Gaudin, 1993; Lundahl, Nimer, & Parsons, 2006; Meadowcroft, Thomlison, & Chamberlain, 1994; Wekerle & Wolfe, 1993; Wolfe, 1990; Wolfe & Wekerle, 1993
Conduct disorders	Bramlett, Wodarski, & Thyer, 1991; Christophersen & Finney, 1993; Dumas, 1989; Kazdin, 1990; Lochman & Lenhart, 1993; Maag & Kotlash, 1994; Magen & Rose, 1994; Raines & Foy, 1994
Couple problems	Granvold, 1994; Epstein, Baucom, & Rankin, 1993; Halford, Sanders, & Behrens, 1994; Hahlweg & Markman, 1988; Lipsey & Wilson, 1993; Montang & Wilson, 1992; O'Farrell, 1994; Thomlison, 1984a
Depression	Beach, Whisman, & O'Leary, 1994; Didden, Korzilius, Van Oorsouvv, Sturmey, 2006; Frame & Cooper, 1993; Hoberman & Clarke, 1993; Norman & Lowry, 1995; Rohde, Lewinsohn, & Seeley, 1994
Developmental disabilities	Butler, Chapman, Forman, & Beck, 2006; Feldman, 1994; Hile & Derochers, 1993; Kirkham, 1993; Nixon & Singer, 1993; Thomlison, 1981; Underwood & Thyer, 1990
Eating disorders	Garner & Rosen, 1990; Isreal, 1990; Kennedy, Katz, Neitzert, Ralevski, & Mendlowitz, 1995; Lipsey & Wilson, 1993; Morin, Winter, Besalel, & Azrin, 1987; Saunders & Saunders, 1993; Smith, Marcus, & Eldridge, 1994; Wilson, 1994
Family violence	Edleson & Syers, 1990; 1991; Faulkner, Stoltenberg, Cogen, Nolder, & Shooter, 1992; Peled & Edleson, 1992; Tolman & Bennett, 1990
Gerontology	Fisher & Carstensen, 1990; Hersen & Van Hasselt, 1992; Nicholson & Blanchard, 1993; Widner & Zeichner, 1993
Juvenile delinquency	Bank, Marlowe, Reid, Patterson, & Weinrott, 1991; Hagan & King, 1992; Hawkins, Jensen, Catalano, & Wells, 1991; Lipsey & Wilson, 1993; Meadowcroft, Thomlison, & Chamberlain, 1994; Zimpfer, 1992
Obsessive-compulsive disorder	Abramowitz, Whiteside, & Deacon, 2005; Watson & Rees, 2008
Pain management	Biederman & Schefft, 1994; Gamsa, 1994; Holroyd & Penzien, 1994; Lipsey & Wilson, 1993; Subramanian, 1991; 1994
Phobic disorders	Donohue, Van Hasselt, & Hersen, 1994; King, 1993; Mersch, 1995; Newman, Hofman, Trabert, Roth, & Taylor, 1994; Turner, Beidel, & Cooley-Quille, 1995
Posttraumatic stress	Butler, Chapman, Forman, & Beck, 2006; Caddell & Drabman, 1993; Corrigan, 1991; Foy, Resnick, & Lipovosky, 1993; Mitte, 2005a, 2005b; Richards, Lovell, & Marks, 1994; Roberts, Kitchiner, Kenardy, & Bisson, 2009; Saigh, 1992
Psychosis	Liberman, Kopelowicz, & Young, 1994; Lipsey & Wilson, 1993; Morrison & Sayers, 1993; Scotti, McMorrow, & Trawitzki, 1993; Tarrier, Beckett, Harwood, Baker, Yusupoff, & Ugarteburu, 1993
Sexual deviance	Camp & Thyer, 1993; Hanson, Steffy, & Gauthier, 1993; Marshall, Jones, Ward, Johnston, & Barbaree, 1991; Kaplan, Morales, & Becker, 1993; Marques, Day, Nelson, & West, 1994
Sleep disturbances	Lichstein & Riedel, 1994; Minde, Popiel, Leos, & Falkner, 1993
Stress management	Dubbert, 1995; Lipsey & Wilson, 1993
Substance abuse	Dutra, Stathopoulou, Basden, Leyro, Powers, & Ottow, 2008; Powers, Vedel, & Emmelkamp, 2008

[*]When possible, review articles and research directly applicable to social work practice were selected.

the meta-analytic approach are considered in the statistical analyses of the randomized clinical studies (Chambless, 2002).

Central Premises of CBT

CBT is grounded on several interrelated theoretical perspectives and underlying assumptions. First, behavioral approaches to change are based on the general view that problems can be understood within a behavioral context, and that all behaviors can be changed. Therefore, problem behaviors can be replaced with more positive adaptive behaviors, as well as by improving communication and problem-solving skills. Second, cognitions (i.e., beliefs and attitudes) play a significant role in shaping behaviors. Hence, behavioral changes need to be accompanied by cognitive shifts that support long-term, adaptive change. Finally, effecting positive, meaningful behavioral and cognitive changes requires a systematic approach. Effective cognitive behavioral treatments are contingent on accurate assessment and planned intervention strategies tailored to the specific individual, with systematic, ongoing evaluation of change. The following assumptions are central to cognitive behavioral interventions.

Assumption 1: Problem Behaviors can be Identified and Changed

All behavior is assumed to be learned and can be both defined and changed. It is first important to identify the problem targeted for intervention. The problem is formulated as the undesirable behavior, which can be understood through systematic exploration and modified through specific behavioral techniques. Thus, personal and social problems are translated into behavior that is *observable*, *measurable*, and *changeable*. Understanding the mechanisms that reinforce behaviors is an essential early step in assessing the problem. These *contingencies of reinforcement* are identified as targets of intervention. Change occurs through rearranging contingencies of reinforcement—that is, by altering what happens before and after the specified behavior. Behaviorists believe that behavioral change is brought about through changes in reinforcement by significant others in the person's environment,

or environmental transactions, as well as the enhanced perception of self that comes from acquiring new behavior. CBT acknowledges that a large number of *reinforcing and aversive events* can be operative in any given behavioral exchange. Identifying current and alternative stimuli is essential. By changing the contingencies of reinforcement, the behavior that needs to be changed can be extinguished or other behavior can be conditioned to replace it. The learning and changing of behavior can be understood using social learning theory. Specific approaches to using social learning theory are described later in the chapter.

Assumption 2: Cognitions Shape Behaviors

In its broadest definition, cognition incorporates many of the elements of human thought processes characteristically of concern to social work. Such a broad definition would include the processes by which information (input) from the environment is translated, considered, integrated, stored, retrieved, and eventually produced as some form of personal activity (output). Simply stated, how people think about their experiences shapes their experiences. Therefore, the process of examining one's attitudes, beliefs, and values is relevant for the practitioner to understand—not only how the client views his or her own behaviors and environment, but also potential deterrents and/or motivators for change. Cognitive behavioral practitioners have selected and explored certain cognitive elements in behavior change. The following elements of cognitive theory are used in modifying behavior:

1. *Information processing*: the acquisition, storage, and utilization of information, encompassing attention, perception, language, and memory
2. *Beliefs and belief systems*: ideas, attitudes, and expectations about self, others, and experience
3. *Self statements*: private monologues that influence behavior and feelings
4. *Problem solving and coping*: conceptual and symbolic processes involved in arriving at effective responses to deal with problematic situations (Schwartz, 1982, p. 269).

CBT incorporates both the behavior and cognition in the assessment and targeted intervention of cognitive processes to effect long-term behavioral change.

Assumption 3: Affecting Behavioral Change Requires a Systematic Approach

Behavioral approaches to assessment, intervention, implementation, and evaluation share a number of characteristics with the basic social work problem-solving process. Foremost, the plan for change includes a systematic process of intervention that begins with a thorough assessment of the problem and ongoing assessment of the effectiveness of the intervention. In general, the goals of cognitive behavioral social work treatment are increasing desirable behaviors and reducing undesirable behaviors so that those affected by the circumstances can improve their day-to-day and moment-to-moment functioning. As with all social work practice, relationship skills form the foundation to work with client systems. The basic behavioral assessment method is used to analyze the client's problem and assist in a plan of change through development of appropriate behavioral change goals. The selection of a specific intervention is based on the assessment process, during which presenting problems are translated into observable behaviors. Then, the behavior techniques and strategies to be followed are detailed in a treatment contract to address the client's problems and circumstances.

Conducting a behavioral assessment requires a focus on the here and now of the problem, as well as current environmental factors related to the problem behavior. Also, a clear description of the intervention is provided, along with concrete ways to measure progress. Building on client strengths while developing new skills and increasing the client's knowledge base is another characteristic of behavioral intervention. Generally, the etiology of the behavior is not investigated, and a diagnostic label is not pursued. Both of these factors are deemed stigmatizing and uninformative when considering behavioral change. Nevertheless, much of the behavioral research literature does use diagnostic labels (for example, agoraphobia, attention-deficit disorder, and posttraumatic stress syndrome) in the description of the problem behavior under investigation. This has resulted from the integration of behavior assessment methods with traditional psychiatric diagnostic classifications. This practice has been criticized as neglecting differences between clients (Gambrill, 1994; Wolpe, 1989) and potentially masking outcome differences between types of interventions (Eifert, Evans, & McKendrick, 1990).

Social Learning Theory and the A-B-C Paradigm

A classic perspective of behavioral change is the A-B-C paradigm, which is based on social learning theory. This assumes that behavior is learned within social contexts and thus is changed within the social environment. Social learning theory identifies three major elements: target behaviors, antecedents, and consequences (Bandura, 1976):

1. *Target behaviors* are the focus of the behavioral analysis. These are often identified during the period of assessment as undesirable, problematic, or the behavior that needs to be changed.
2. *Antecedents and consequences* are those incidents, behaviors, or environmental events that precede or follow the problematic or target behaviors, respectively. They are often identified as the controlling or maintaining conditions for the problem behaviors. For instance, an antecedent may incite a behavior to occur, while a consequence may deter the behavior from occurring again.

These events serve as the focus of the behavioral assessment. The interaction of these three elements is described as the A-B-C behavior therapy paradigm (Figure 6.1).

This paradigm serves to label one exchange in an ongoing sequence of exchanges between individuals. For the social worker to determine the antecedents and consequences, a decision as to the problem or target behavior is first made. With this target behavior in mind, the social worker then identifies the events or behaviors that precede or follow the target behavior. This identification process is usually done by direct observation by the social worker or by client self-report. This process, known as *behavioral*

Figure 6.1. The A-B-C Behavior Therapy Paradigm.

analysis, is considered essential to effective behavior therapy.

To illustrate the application of this social learning paradigm in behavior therapy assessment and change program, a common parent–child behavioral exchange is presented. Mr. S complains that his son, Josh, will "never do what he is told." One of the concerns is that Josh will not come to the dinner table when he is called. The presenting situation, as explained by Mr. S, is shown in Table 6.2.

To assess the behavior further, it is generally necessary to examine the nature of the consequences that might be provided for Josh. Behavioral consequences differ in terms of quality and purpose. Some are of a positive (pleasing) nature, while others are of a negative (displeasing) variety. The former, referred to as *positive consequences,* are employed to increase the occurrence of a behavior. The latter, usually referred to as *punishment,* is frequently observed when a parent attempts to prevent the recur-

rence of an undesired behavior by spanking the child; that is, physical punishment. While the use of physical punishment as a consequence is acknowledged as a means of decreasing the frequency of a behavior, it is viewed among behavioral social workers as an unacceptable means of altering behavior. In addition to humanitarian reasons, physical punishment is generally considered unacceptable because in many instances it suppresses a behavior without providing an alternative, more desirable behavior. Behavior therapy requires that any agreed behavioral change is defined in terms that are recognized to be desirable and to be increased in frequency by the participants. This requires that all parties to a behavioral change contract define what behaviors are desired, not simply what is undesired. This is often a difficult requirement, as it is almost always easier to tell someone to stop doing something that is undesirable as opposed to asking him or her to engage in a desired behavioral alternative. The use of positive consequences to

Table 6-2. Application of A-B-C Paradigm

	Antecedents (A)	Behavior (B)	Consequences (C)
Behavioral Analysis of Presenting Situation	Mr. S calls Josh several times to the table. There is an escalation of threats and yelling when Josh does not immediately respond.	Josh ignores his father's first requests but eventually presents himself angrily at the table and begins to eat.	Father is silent and appears angry.
Behavior Change Contract	Mr. S makes one verbal request in a pleasant tone for Josh to come to the table.	Josh comes to the table when called.	When Josh arrives at the table as requested, Mr. S verbally praises Josh and places a checkmark on Josh's tally sheet. If Josh chooses not to respond to his father's request, Mr. S will begin eating alone, ignoring Josh's absence. Josh will forego the opportunity for his father's praise and tangible, positive acknowledgment for this dinner time.

increase desirable behavior is the strength of the social learning approach to behavior therapy. The research strongly supports the use of positive consequences as a means of facilitating desired behavior. However, it is not always easy to put this principle into practice.

For example, Mr. S may feel that if Josh would do what he was told, then all would be okay, but until Josh changes, Mr. S feels he cannot give Josh any positive messages or praise. Unfortunately, Josh and his father have reached a stalemate wherein even if they agree that change is desirable, it is difficult because they are into a *coercive exchange* (Patterson & Reid, 1970).

Attempting to control another person's behavior by command and threat is familiar to most of us. In many instances, however, it has the effect demonstrated by Josh and his father. The commands and threats escalate until finally the child complies in order to terminate the threats and/or yelling. By the time the child obeys the parent's command, the parent has become agitated enough to lose any motivation to acknowledge, in positive terms, the child's compliance. This coercive process, then, can be conceptualized using Skinner's notion of a *negative reinforcement process* (the termination of a behavior [threats] upon occurrence of the desired behavior [compliance]), an *extinction process* (the withholding of a positive reinforcer upon the occurrence of the desired behavior [compliance]), and a *positive reinforcement process* (Mr. S achieves what he set out to get [compliance]).

In other words, when Josh cooperated by, for example, sitting down at the table, his father chose to ignore his compliant behavior. On the other hand, Mr. S achieved his objective and to some degree was positively reinforced, except for the feelings of frustration and anger. The difficulty is that one person (Josh) is being negatively reinforced and the other (Mr. S) is being positively reinforced. This behavioral exchange will therefore be strengthened and can be predicted to increase in frequency unless an alternative exchange can be identified and practiced by both.

To help Josh and his father alter their undesirable interaction, the social worker will need to help by devising a program in which the father can give a clear cue or instruction to Josh and positive consequences to Josh if he complies by arriving at the dinner table at the desired time. Intervention requires that a target behavior for desired change be clearly identified. In this case such a target might be labeled as "Josh coming to the table when called." New antecedents or instructions would be identified, as well as new consequences for this new target behavior. An agreement to change might well be formalized as a contractual statement detailing the new behavioral target, its antecedents, and its consequences.

This brief example illustrates the basic procedures of assessment and intervention in accordance with the A-B-C paradigm. While the overall behavior therapy program would require a more detailed assessment and a more comprehensive intervention strategy, behavior, and its controlling antecedents and consequences, remains the focus of this approach.

Behavioral Social Work Practice

The most common behavior therapy techniques social workers use include:

1. Cognitive behavioral procedures such as cognitive restructuring, self-instructional training, thought stopping, and stress inoculation training
2. Assertiveness training, which improves communication skills in personal, work, and other relations in how to express rights, requests, opinion, and feelings, honestly and directly through body language and self-awareness
3. Systematic desensitization and variants of this procedure such as eye movement desensitization, procedures involving strong anxiety evocation (e.g., flooding, paradoxical intention), operant-conditioning methods (e.g., extinction, positive or negative reinforcement)
4. Aversion therapy: inducing dislike to the problem behavior. This method is less respected, although it was historically used in addiction and paraphilias.

Each of these approaches requires a more extensive discussion that is not possible here. Books on behavior theory and practice will provide descriptions of the application of these procedures and their effectiveness (Corcoran,

2006; Franks, Wilson, Kendall, & Foreyt, 1990; Granvold, 1994; LeCroy, 2007; Sundel & Sundel, 1993; Thomlison, 1984b, 1986; Thyer, 1992; Wolpe, 1990). The choice of a specific intervention method is based on a careful assessment of client need and the empirically determined effectiveness of a procedure to meet that need (see Table 6.1).

Cognitive Behavioral Assessment and Intervention

Behavior therapy provides a planned, systematic approach to social work intervention. Indeed, there are specific stages through which all behavior therapy proceeds. While there are a range of activities that are specific to each of the different behavior therapy approaches, there is also a basic set of general procedures that serve as a framework. This framework is essentially a summary of a behavior therapy approach and is based primarily on the social learning paradigm. The procedural outline is based on the authors' practice and research with married couples, children, and families. Since much of clinical social work practice is carried out within the context of the family, the outline is presented as an approach to working with the family system.

Beyond the procedural steps identified here, it is important to emphasize that behavioral social workers bring a strong sense of importance to building a positive therapeutic relationship early in the contact with the client system and actively involve the client as much as possible in each step of the assessment and intervention. The importance of this relationship building is not to be underestimated as it establishes trust, rapport, and the necessary support to the analysis and management of problem behavior. Once the client system is engaged through the relationship, behavioral procedures can occur. A behavioral assessment to determine the client's problems is the next step.

Assessment

Social workers use the following procedures during a behavioral assessment in order to define as clearly as possible the problems or events for change and the desired outcome:

1. *Compilation of the problematic behavior inventory*
   a. Begin by asking for one member of the family group to identify the perception of the problems that have resulted in the meeting.
   b. Clarify these perceived problems by asking for behaviorally specific examples. Most perceived problems can be translated into statements of who does what to whom within what context.
   c. As each family member offers his or her perception of the problem, there is a high probability that the ensuing discussion will stimulate disagreements among family members. It is important to observe who disagrees with whom, and over what behavioral statements. These interchanges are allowed to occur, but they can become counterproductive to the objective of the assessment. When this occurs, the social worker will intervene, requesting the family members to terminate the debate yet acknowledging that differences of opinion are expected. Assure all family members that their perceptions of the problems are important and that each member will have an opportunity to present his or her personal views.
2. *Identify priority behavioral problems and their maintaining conditions.*
   a. Attempt to identify the antecedent events of at least those behaviors that arouse the highest level of intensity of feeling among family members. Antecedent events are those conditions that exist immediately prior to the occurrence of the target behavior—for instance, what other members of the family are doing or not doing prior to the occurrence of an undesired behavior.
   b. Identify the consequences of those problem behaviors that elicit the more intense family feelings. Identify the consequences of those events that occur after a target behavior—for instance, what other family members do after one of the problem behaviors has occurred.
3. *Identify the contingencies existent for the provision of consequences.* What rules appear to

govern the conditions under which these consequences are provided? For example, when is a child reprimanded versus when is he not? When are privileges withdrawn versus when are they not?

4. *Observe and record behavioral exchanges.* Identify recurrent behavior patterns in the exchanges among the family members. These behaviors will include coercive exchanges, shouting, avoidance responses, excessive demands, etc.

5. *Secure a commitment from each member of the family system, ensuring that he or she wishes to work toward change.* This commitment then clearly explicates that the clients: (a) will work as a unit on these family problems and (b) will work as individuals toward behavioral change. At this point in the assessment procedures, the social worker will be able to demonstrate to the family the interconnections of their individual behaviors in that when one individual behaves a certain way, all family members necessarily will respond in the same manner; that is, behaviors do not occur in isolation. For example, when the adolescent girl repeatedly violates her curfew, the resultant parent–youth conflict affects all members of the family.

6. *Begin to identify possible behavior targets for change.* The target behaviors will be desirable behaviors with the objective of increased frequency of occurrence. This identification is often assisted by asking each family member to answer two questions: How could you behave differently to make this a happier family? How would you like to see others behave to make this a happier family? These questions may be given as homework assignments, with each family member asked to provide as many answers as possible to each question. The social worker ought to point out to the family members that this assignment is a challenge as it requires the identification of desired behaviors, and individuals are more often accustomed to identifying what behaviors they do not like to see, as opposed to those they prefer. Homework is used to reinforce new thinking and behaviors that are introduced during the session.

7. On the basis of the family's homework assignment, discuss possible appropriate behavioral targets for change.
   a. Select behaviors that are to be accelerated in frequency in order to maximize the opportunities for positive consequences.
   b. Select behaviors that appear to be most relevant to enhancing this family's definition of its own happiness.
   c. Strive to select behaviors that are incompatible with the occurrence of undesirable (problematic) behaviors.
   d. For each child, select at least one behavior that is low risk for change. A *low-risk behavioral target* is one that can be easily attained by the child and one that, if performed by the child without positive reinforcement (a violation of the change contract), will not jeopardize the growing trust of the child. An example of a child's low-risk target behavior change might be combing her hair in the morning, or cleaning up after dinner each evening.
   e. Attempt to select behaviors that are commonly identified among family members (e.g., mealtime behavior, family get-together, tidying up cooperation, play time with siblings or peers).
   f. Keep in mind that a behavior needs to be *observable* to all, so it is necessary to explicate the indicators of some behaviors in order to minimize debates over whether the behavior has actually occurred. For many parents, the behavior "cleaning up your room" is a desired behavior change objective. Interestingly, what appears to be a very clear behavior has a great deal of opportunity for individual interpretation. It is therefore necessary to pinpoint such behaviors as picking up clothes, placing them in the appropriate locations, making the bed, placing trash in appropriate containers, etc.

8. *Commitment for change.* Allow time for all family members to present their concerns and their support for the target behaviors. Certain behavior choices will elicit strong feelings from some family members. *Negotiation* takes place before selected behaviors are settled upon and should

always take place within the spirit of the agreement, acceptance, or commitment for change. If one or more family member wishes to re-evaluate this commitment in light of the selected targets for change, then this request is honored. Such re-evaluation may have to take place within the context of the consequences of no change; that is, all persons have a right not to be required to change. There are, however, certain consequences for not changing. What are they for the individual and the family?

9. *Record baseline data/information.* When target behaviors have been agreed upon, set the conditions for a baseline measure.
   a. Before instructing the family to change, request that the parents monitor the frequency of occurrence of the target behaviors. This will allow for some "before" or baseline behavior frequency measures. These measures are recorded and can be used at a later date to assess the ongoing behavioral change within the family.
   b. Appoint the parents as the monitors of the behavior targets. Give the parents a tally sheet and instructions to record the frequency of occurrence of each target behavior.

10. *Behavioral intervention is compatible with the assessment in progress.* Throughout the assessment phase, the social worker may identify problems with an individual or the couple that require specific attention. On occasion, the assessment period indicates that the change process needs to be focused on the couple rather than on the child. With the couple's agreement, the intervention may be temporarily suspended in light of the recognized need to concentrate on the couple's problems.

Intervention

The intervention or implementation phase of a behavioral therapy program is marked by the identification of new contingencies between identified behaviors and their consequences. To this point the focus has been on the appropriate targeting of behaviors for change. At the time a program for change is to be implemented, a *contingency contract* might be formulated in order to facilitate a systematic, cooperative effort on the part of the family in facilitating change.

1. Clearly identify the target behaviors that have been agreed upon as the focus for change.
2. Establish new antecedent events for each of these target behaviors.
3. Establish new consequences that are to be provided for each occurrence or non-occurrence of a target behavior.
4. Write a contract specifying the following conditions:
   a. The target behaviors for change and their pinpointed elements
   b. New antecedents. If these are to be instructions, then specify by whom these instructions are to be given.
   c. New positive consequences: these might include checkmarks and/or tokens provided when the behavior occurs, as well a social reinforcer such as affection and praise.
   d. Specify what is to happen if there is a violation of the contract. If a behavior does not occur or if an undesired behavior occurs, then be clear as to what others in the family are to do. For example, if a target behavior focuses on "good dinnertime behavior" and one or more of the children violate this agreement, then all family members will be clear as to what is to happen.
   e. Specify those positive consequences that are to act as bonus reinforcers, particularly when certain behavioral objectives are accomplished. For example, it is often helpful to include special privileges, such as family outings, as bonus reinforcers for a designated behavioral achievement—say, if a target behavior occurs at the desired level for a period of one week or more.
   f. Specify those persons in the family unit who are to be responsible for recording the frequency of behavioral occurrences. This is usually one or both of the parents. These tally records are important in communicating to the family members the degree and intensity of change.

g. Contracts are written in a variety of ways, but they all contain the condition: Who does what to whom under what conditions. Spiegler and Guevremont (2010) provide different contract examples, such as with classroom behaviors, school attendance, homework, setting learning goals, social behaviors, sibling cooperation, studying, physical exercise, smoking, undereating, problem drinking, and marital discord.

5. After a program has been implemented, follow up with a series of telephone calls to ensure that the program is implemented. These telephone calls also provide the opportunity for members of the family, particularly the parents, to ask any questions that might have arisen as a result of implementing the program for change. These calls need not take long and must be limited to the pragmatics of the program implementation. Any conflict among family members reported at this time is then directed back to the family for resolution. If resolution is not possible, the person in charge of recording makes note of the nature of the conflict and the context in which it occurs. This will be dealt with at the next meeting with the social worker.

6. Difficulties in implementing the program are inevitable. These problems usually pertain to such things as tally recording, differences in target behavior definitions, and lack of cooperation on the part of certain family members. To deal with these problems, the social worker will refer to the contract as the reference point. Once agreed to, all problems arising with the behavioral changes must relate to the original document. Changes in the contract are negotiated by all members of the family. Essentially all problems related to the implementation of and adherence to a contract for family interactional modification may eventually have to be related back to the original commitment for change agreed to by the family during the assessment period.

7. Each interview with the family after implementation begins with an examination of the tally recording provided by the family members. Where change is evident in these data, the social worker then provides positive reinforcement by acknowledging the change and the hard work of all family members.

8. Discussion then shifts to focusing on problems arising between sessions. These discussions may flow to more general aspects of the family's functioning, and special techniques such as role-playing, modeling, and behavioral rehearsal may be introduced in an effort to assist the family in dealing with these problems.

9. Since much of the family's energy goes into problem-solving activity and conflict resolution, the social worker will spend time on these areas of family life. One of the advantages of having required the family to negotiate a contingency contract is that they have experienced a process of successful problem solving and negotiation. Examples derived from that process can be used in the ongoing problem-solving and conflict-resolution training.

10. If the monitoring of change has indicated that little if any change is taking place, it is necessary to examine certain aspects of the program design. Depending on the area in which the program is failing, it will be necessary to consider changes in target behavior, consequences, and violations in the contract. It is often necessary to assess whether people are in fact following through on the requirements of the contract. For example, it might be that a parent has agreed to read a bedtime story for successful achievement of a behavioral objective during the day, but fails to deliver.

11. When target behaviors have been achieved at the desired level of frequency, the social worker can identify new behaviors for change, or move toward termination of the behavioral therapy program.

Evaluation for Maintenance of Change

1. Together with the family system, evaluate the progress in relation to the objectives of the contract.

2. If the decision is made to terminate, then set the conditions for behavioral maintenance.

3. Behavioral maintenance requires the social worker to review with the family the basic learning principles identified during the modification of the target behaviors (e.g., positive consequences versus punishment).

4. Instruct the family to continue the tally recording over the next 4 weeks but without the regularly scheduled appointments.

5. Set up an appointment for 4 weeks from the last interview for the purposes of termination and follow-up.

Follow-up

The follow-up interview will be an assessment interview related to whether the behavioral changes have been maintained. If these changes have not been maintained at a level consistent with the expectations of the social worker and/or the family, it will be necessary to reinstitute the program structure. If, on the other hand, the social worker and family think that the behavioral changes have been maintained within desired parameters, then termination may take place. Termination, of course, does allow for the family members to contact the social worker at any point in the future where they feel the necessity.

From the perspective of clinical evaluation, it is important that the social worker analyze the results of the behavioral change program. Further, it is helpful for the social worker to assess the maintenance of change by contacting the family members 3 and 6 months later to ascertain the degree to which the behavioral changes have been maintained.

Implementation Considerations in Cognitive Behavioral Interventions

It is widely acknowledged that CBT reliably produces desirable effects, but does it work with everyone? Examples of designated evidence-based CBT interventions include applications to anxiety (Butler, Chapman, Forman, & Beck, 2006; Mitte, 2005a, 2005b), attention-deficit/hyperactivity disorder (Fabiano, Pelham, Coles, Chronis-Tuscano, O'Connor, & Gnagy, 2009), depression (Butler, et al. 2006), substance abuse (Powers, Vedel, & Emmelkamp, 2008), obsessive-compulsive disorder (Watson & Rees, 2008),

schizophrenia (Zimmerman, Favrod, Trieu, & Pomini, 2005), phobias (Mitte, 2005a, 2005b); issues between couples (Shadish & Baldwin, 2005), and others. For a more complete review see Dobson and Dobson (2009).

During the past two decades, one of the most important areas of behavioral practice to emerge has been that of dealing with parenting, parent training, and child management and skill acquisition. Using the basic A-B-C paradigm, many childhood problems have been reconceptualized as behavioral problems resulting from interactional exchanges between children and parents. By systematically altering these exchanges in the context of behavior therapy, it has repeatedly been demonstrated that both parental and child behavior can be altered toward their desired objectives (Dangel, Yu, Slot, & Fashimpar, 1994; Graziano & Diament, 1992; Sundel & Sundel, 1993). Typical child problems addressed using behavioral techniques include noncompliance, chore completion, enuresis, eating disorders, interrupting, fire setting, sleep problems and bedtime anxieties, and hyperactivity (Butterfield & Cobb, 1994). Conduct disorders or antisocial behaviors in children have received considerable clinical and research attention in the past decade. Behavioral techniques have been demonstrated as effective in changing these behaviors (Christophersen & Finney, 1993; Doren, 1993; Jenson & Howard, 1990; Kazdin, 1990). It has been estimated that 3% to 5% of school-age children have attention-deficit/hyperactivity disorder, which has been identified as a risk factor in conduct disturbance and antisocial behavior (DuPaul, Guevremont, & Barkley, 1991). Social workers encounter these children and adolescents within the program contexts of child welfare, treatment, foster care, juvenile incarceration, therapeutic day programs, and residential and school-based programs (CDC, 2009; Meadowcroft, Thomlison, & Chamberlain, 1994).

Home-based interventions with families and children are preferred for many child and parent-related problems (CDC, 2009). The focus is on family interaction supported by the social learning model. Maltreatment or risk of maltreatment of children by primary caretakers has become a focus of in-home intervention. Problem-solving and skills training for parents usually includes child management skills, anger management, and addressing parent issues involving substance abuse, communication difficulties, and social isolation (CDC, 2009; Gambrill, 1994; Hodges, 1994; Kaminski, Valle, Filene, & Boyle, 2008).

Since the late 1950s the treatment of choice for many professionals working with clients with anxiety and phobias has been Joseph Wolpe's (1990) systematic desensitization. Clients suffering the inhibitory effects of phobic disorders have been the subjects of a great deal of effective intervention by behavioral social workers. Combined with the basic systematic desensitization, new cognitive behavioral approaches are promising even more effective outcomes. In fact, today a social worker would be hard pressed to make an argument for an alternate treatment method for any of the phobic disorders.

At the same time, there is a serious problem concerning the slow and incomplete transfer of these evidence-based findings into day-to-day social work clinical practice (Fixsen, Blase, Naoom, & Wallace, 2009). Examining the quantity of behavioral articles in social work journals and books, behavioral social work has been characterized as a "major school of practice" (Thyer, 1991, p. 1). In a survey of clinical social workers, one third of the practitioners who participated in the study preferred a behavioral approach to their practice (Thyer, 1987a). Social workers reported that behavioral interventions were most influential when applied to disorders such as anxiety, depression, phobias, addictions, sexual dysfunction, and relationship distress. Nevertheless, a number of misconceptions about behavior therapy persist and may account for why more social workers do not employ evidence-based behavioral strategies in practice.

Education and Training

Training for behavior therapy occurs in a variety of educational contexts. The content, format, and objectives of behavior training vary widely (Alberts & Edelstein, 1990). A social work curriculum generally provides an overview of behavioral change principles and techniques but not detailed training (Thyer & Maddox, 1988).

More intensive training may be offered in organizations or treatment settings to social workers, foster parents, and teachers at child and family centers and schools. Given the emphasis on evidence-based processes, the efficacy of behavioral methods, and the extensive application to problems identified in clinical practice, an argument can be made for including CBT as part of the core curriculum in social work education. As evidence-based practice, it works!

Culturally Responsive Behavioral Practice

Concern for the needs of culturally different groups has received attention among behavior therapists as the population has increasingly become more diverse. Behavior theory, like many practice theories, emerged from Western cultural values, assumptions, and philosophy. In reality, both clients and behavioral social workers are racially and ethnically diverse. Efforts to offer ethnically sensitive social work practice are very much affected by the political, social, and economic power and status of each group and setting. Disparities are well documented and barriers exist in terms of the accessibility of and participation in social work intervention. Barriers include philosophical and value differences, language, and individual and organizational structures associated with Western helping systems (Corcoran & Vandiver, 1996).

Working with culturally diverse individuals involves recognizing diversity in both the context and behavior of individuals. Each cultural group develops its own coping strategies for problems and, like any identified group, cultural groups are not homogeneous in character. This originates out of the group's cultural values, history, rituals, religion, migration experiences, organization and family systems, and class values and norms (Devore & Schlesinger, 1996). The social worker should pay attention to the levels of assimilation and factors such as language, religion, lifestyle, expectations, and attitudes toward helping (Thomlison, 2010). Many of the techniques used by Western-trained behavioral social workers may run counter to the values, beliefs, and family traditions of the cultural group. For example, an understanding of time is critical to the concept of shaping, reinforcement schedules, and extinction, but this concept may have a different understanding by those who measure time by activities. Also, what constitutes problematic behavior, help-seeking behavior, and inappropriate behaviors is based on a Western culture perspective of the person, and what behaviors, thoughts, and feelings make up the person.

Many behavioral social workers argue, however, that on a theoretical basis the principles underlying behavior cross the boundaries of culture. The main concern actually rests with the fact that the assumptions beneath principles of learning are not universally accepted. For example, a positive reinforcer, operationally defined as an event that increases behavior frequency, would not be culturally determined—although a specific positive reinforcer, such as TV watching, that works in one culture may not work in another.

It is therefore very important for behavioral social workers at the beginning of assessment to understand how the concepts of family and the individuals who constitute family are defined in a given culture and to recognize that individuals make different choices based on their culture (Thomlison, 2010). If social workers mislabel behavioral interactions, then interventions can compound rather than resolve parenting dilemmas or other problematic behaviors. Therefore, interventions must be carefully sculpted to fit the client's cultural orientations and preferences. Existing interventions and understandings of behavior may need to be modified so that behaviors are grounded in local contexts for understanding (Landrine & Klonoff, 1995).

Organizations that serve ethnic and diverse communities should ensure that diversity is represented in the social work staff and that staff have a high level of self-awareness and openness. Behavioral social workers need to consider that individuals develop problem-solving styles that fit their culture and values, and therefore solutions fit the cultural attributes of diverse populations. In summary, current research of the relationship between cultural competencies, behavior theory, and outcomes requires further study.

Conclusions

This chapter has taken the reader through the evidence-based world of CBT and has discussed how to proceed with assessment and intervention in social work practice. Evidence has accumulated for the efficacy of a variety of treatments for mental health and behavioral problems, and cognitive behavioral practices can be applied to real-world clinical practices. As for final thoughts we conclude with the following summary:

1. CBT is action-oriented and leans heavily on an educative focus for client change. For those who want insight or a talking psychotherapy, this approach is not appropriate.
2. The focus is on behavior and/or cognitive change, or both, and generally requires a structured approach to change by both client and therapist.
3. Some nonprofessionals and professionals misunderstand or misrepresent the approach, seeing it as very simple and as "a quick fix" for complex problems. Such misunderstanding is probably most often illustrated by inappropriately designed child-management programs that rely on aversive methods of punishment for undesired behavior, often coupled with the unsystematic use of rewards for compliant behavior. Such interventions are devoid of the elements of behavior analysis and the systematic use of behavioral techniques essential for successful behavioral change.
4. The behavior therapies are often thought to be derived from a homogeneous theory, when in fact they are made up of numerous theories of behavior with an array of interventions, strategies, and techniques. Many social workers fail to understand that different approaches are often available for specific problems, identified through the process of behavioral assessment. Matching technique to problem is essential. Different applications relate to the problem and are guided by the behavioral analysis of the conditions under which the problem behavior occurs.
5. Cognitive behavioral techniques depend on relationship development, and sensitivity to the client's needs.

6. Because CBT has been applied to clients who have severely debilitating or difficult-to-treat conditions, ethical considerations play a prominent role in behavior therapy. Many programs have established protective mechanisms, such as treatment review processes, to address the issues of utilizing aversive procedures, determining appropriate individualized assessment and intervention, as well as keeping written records and assessment checklists and questionnaires (Sundel & Sundel, 1993).

To summarize, then, CBT, as it has been presented here, comprises a variety of distinctly different approaches to facilitating behavioral and in some cases cognitive changes. It has been developed from a strong commitment to planned and systematic assessment, a distinct strength over other therapeutic models of change. Intervention strategies evolve from the prescriptive approach to assessment, within a context of empirical inquiry, utilizing nominal and ratio levels of measurement to establish the frequency and duration of problems. Its impact on social work practice continues to be felt both directly in clinical practice and indirectly in practice areas such as task-centered approaches, as well as single-system designs in research, and evidence-based processes. Behavior therapy has been demonstrated to be effective in most areas of social work practice. Behavior theory as an effective therapeutic intervention is well established, and it can be argued that behavior theory is the most advisable therapeutic option. CBT will be invaluable to social workers in every practice situation.

Notes

1. Some argue that the concepts of behavior therapy and behavior modification are differentially applied (Franks, Wilson, Kendall, & Foreyt, 1990). For the purposes of this chapter we prefer "behavior therapy," but the concepts will be used synonymously.

References

Abramowitz, J. S., Whiteside, S. P., & Deacon, B. J. (2008). Meta-analysis of randomized, controlled treatment trials for pediatric obsessive-compulsive disorder. *Journal of Child Psychology and Psychiatry,* 49(5), 489–498.

Achenbach, T. M. (1991). *Manual for the child behavior checklist/4-18 and 1991 profile.* Burlington, VT: Department of Psychiatry, University of Vermont.

Acierno, R., Donohue, B., & Kogan, E. (1994). Psychological interventions for drug abuse: A critique and summation of controlled studies. *Clinical Psychology Review,* 14, 417–440.

Acierno, R., Hersen, M., & Van Hasselt, V. (1993). Interventions for panic disorder: A critical review of the literature. *Clinical Psychology Review,* 13, 561–578.

Acierno, R., Hersen, M., Van Hasselt, V., & Ammerman, R. (1994). Remedying the Achilles heel of behavior research and therapy: Prescriptive matching of intervention and psychopathology. *Journal of Behavior Therapy and Experimental Psychiatry,* 25, 179–188.

Alberts, G. M., & Edelstein, B. A. (1990). Training in behavior therapy. In A. Bellack, M. Hersen, & A. Kazdin (Eds.), *International handbook of behavior modification and therapy* (pp. 213–226). New York: Plenum Press.

Ammerman, R. T., & Hersen, M. (Eds.) (1993). *Handbook of behavior therapy with children and adults: A developmental and longitudinal perspective.* Boston: Allyn and Bacon.

Bandura, A. (1976). *Social learning theory.* Englewood Cliffs, NJ: Prentice-Hall.

Bank, L., Marlowe, J. H., Reid, J. B., Patterson, G. R., & Weinrott, M. R. (1991). A comparative evaluation of parent-training interventions for families of chronic delinquents. *Journal of Abnormal Child Psychology,* 19, 15–33.

Barrios, B. (1990). Experimental design in group outcome research. In A. Bellack, M. Hersen, & A. Kazdin (Eds.), *International handbook of behavior modification and therapy* (pp. 151–174). New York: Plenum Press.

Beach, S. R., Whisman, M. A., & O'Leary, K. D. (1994). Marital therapy for depression: Theoretical foundation, current status, and future directions. *Behavior Therapy,* 25, 345–372.

Beck, A. (1976). *Cognitive therapy and the emotional disorders.* New York: International Universities Press.

Beck, J. G., & Zebb, B. J. (1994). Behavioral assessment and treatment of panic disorder: Current status, future directions. *Behavior Therapy,* 25, 581–612.

Bell, A. C., & D'Zurilla, T. J. (2009). Problem-solving therapy for depression: A meta-analysis. *Clinical Psychology Review,* 29, 348–353.

Biederman, J. J., & Schefft, B. K. (1994). Behavioral, physiological, and self-evaluative effects of anxiety on the self-control of pain. *Behavior Modification,* 18, 89–105.

Bogels, S., & Phares, V. (2008). Fathers' role in the etiology, prevention, and treatment of child anxiety: A review and new model. *Clinical Psychology Review,* 28, 539–558.

Bramlett, R., Wodarski, J. S., & Thyer, B. A. (1991). Social work practice with antisocial children: A review of current issues. *Journal of Applied Social sciences,* 15, 169–182.

Butler, A. C., Chapman, J. E., Forman, E. M., & Beck, A. T. (2006). The empirical status of cognitive-behavioral therapy: A review of meta-analyses. *Clinical Psychology Review,* 26(1), 17–31.

Butterfield, W. H., & Cobb, N. H. (1994). Cognitive-behavioral treatment of children and adolescents. In D. K. Granvold (Ed.), *Cognitive and behavioral treatment: Methods and applications* (pp. 63–89). Pacific Grove, CA: Brooks/Cole Publishing Company.

Caddell, J. M., & Drabman, R. S. (1993). Post-traumatic stress disorder in children. In R. Ammerman & M. Hersen (Eds.), *Handbook of behavior therapy with children and adults: A developmental and longitudinal perspective* (pp. 219–235). Boston: Allyn and Bacon.

Camp, B. H., & Thyer, B. A. (1993). Treatment of adolescent sex offenders: A review of empirical research. *Journal of Applied Social Sciences,* 17, 191–206.

Celiberti, D. A., & Harris, S. L. (1993). Behavioral interventions for siblings of children with autism: A focus on skills to enhance play. *Behavior Therapy,* 24, 573–599.

Centers for Disease Control and Prevention (CDC). (2009). *Parent training programs: Insight for practitioners.* Atlanta, GA: Centers for Disease Control.

Chambless, D. L. (2002). Beware the dodo bird: The dangers of overgeneralization. *Clinical Psychology: Science & Practice,* 9, 13–16.

Christophersen, E. R., & Finney, J. W. (1993). Conduct disorder. In R. Ammerman & M. Hersen (Eds.), *Handbook of behavior therapy with children and adults: A developmental and longitudinal perspective* (pp. 251–262). Boston: Allyn and Bacon.

Coleman, D. (2008). Identifying evidence-based practices for mental health. In B. Thomlison & K. Corcoran (Eds.). *The evidence-based internship. A field manual.* New York: Oxford University Press.

Corcoran, J. (2006). *Cognitive-behavioral methods for social workers: A workbook.* Boston: Allyn & Bacon.

Corcoran, K., & Vandiver, V. (1996). *Maneuvering the maze of managed care.* New York: Free Press.

Corrigan, P. W. (1991). Social skills training in adult psychiatric populations: A meta-analysis. *Journal of Behavior Therapy and Experimental Psychiatry,* 22, 203–210.

Corey, G. (2009). *Theory and practice of counseling and psychotherapy* (8th ed.). Belmont, CA: Brooks/ Cole Cengage Learning.

Dangel, R. F., Yu, M., Slot, N. W., & Fashimpar, G. (1994). Behavioral parent training. In D. K. Granvold (Ed.), *Cognitive and behavioral treatment: Methods and applications* (pp. 108–122). Pacific Grove, CA: Brooks/Cole Publishing Company.

Dobson, D., & Dobson, K. (2009). *Evidence-based practice of cognitive-behavioral therapy.* New York: The Guilford Press.

Dobson, K. S., Beamish, M., & Taylor, J. (1992). Advances in behavior therapy: The changing face of AABT conventions. *Behavior Therapy,* 23, 483–491.

Donohue, B. C., Van Hasselt, V. B., & Hersen, M. (1994). Behavioral assessment and treatment of social phobia: An evaluative review. *Behavior Modification,* 18, 262–288.

Doren, D. M. (1993). Antisocial personality disorder. In R. Ammerman & M. Hersen (Eds.), *Handbook of behavior therapy with children and adults: A developmental and longitudinal perspective* (pp. 263–276). Boston: Allyn and Bacon.

Devore, W., & Schlesinger, E. G. (1996). *Ethnic-sensitive social work practice.* Boston, MA: Allyn and Bacon.

Didden, R., Korzilius, H., Van Oorsouw, W., & Sturmey, P. (2006). Behavioral treatment of challenging behaviors in individuals with mild mental retardation: Meta-analysis of single-subject research. *American Journal on Mental Retardation,* 111(4), 290–298.

Dubbert, P. M. (1995). Behavioral (lifestyle) modification in the prevention of hypertension. *Clinical Psychology Review,* 15, 187–216.

Dumas, J. E. (1989). Treating antisocial behavior in children: Child and family approaches. *Clinical Psychology Review,* 9, 197–222.

Ducharme, J. M., Lucas, H., & Pontes, E. (1994). Errorless embedding in the reduction of severe maladaptive behavior during interactive and learning tasks. *Behavior Therapy,* 25, 489–502.

DuPaul, G. J., Guevremont, D. C., & Barkley, R. A. (1991). Attention deficit-hyperactivity disorder in adolescence: Critical assessment parameters. *Clinical Psychology Review,* 11, 231–245.

Edleson, J. L., & Syers, M. (1990). Relative effectiveness of group treatments for men who batter. *Social Work Research and Abstracts,* 26, 10–17.

Edleson, J. L., & Syers, M. (1991). The effects of group treatment for men who batter: An 18-month follow-up study. *Research on Social Work Practice, 1*, 227–243.

Eifert, G. H., Evans, I. M., & McKendrick, V. G. (1990). Matching treatments to client problems not diagnostic labels: A case for paradigmatic behavior therapy. *Journal of Behavior Therapy and Experimental Psychiatry, 21*, 163–172.

Ellis, A. (1962). *Reason and emotion in psychotherapy.* New York: Zyle Stuart.

Ellis, A. (1970). *The essence of rational psychotherapy: A comprehensive approach in treatment.* New York: Institute for Rational Living.

Ellis, A. (1989). *Overview of the clinical theory of rational-emotive therapy.* In R. Grieger & J. Boyd (Eds.). *Rational-emotive therapy: A skills-based approach.* New York: Van Nostrand Reinhold.

Embry, D. D. (2004). Community-based prevention using simple, low-cost, evidence-based kernels and behavior vaccines. *Journal of Community Psychology, 32*, 575–591.

Emmelkamp, P. M., & Gerlsma, C. (1994). Marital functioning and the anxiety disorders. *Behavior Therapy, 25*, 407–430.

Epstein, N., Baucom, D. H., & Rankin, L. A. (1993). Treatment of marital conflict: A cognitive-behavioral approach. *Clinical Psychology Review, 13*, 45–57.

Fabiano, G. A., Pelham, W. E., Coles, E. K., Chronis-Tuscano, A., O'Connor, B. C., & Gnagy, E. M. (2009). A meta-analysis of behavioral treatments for attention-deficit/hyperactivity disorder. *Clinical Psychology Review, 29*(2), 129–140.

Faulkner, K., Stoltenberg, C. D., Cogen, R., Nolder, M., & Shooter, E. (1992). Cognitive-behavioral group treatment for male spouse abusers. *Journal of Family Violence, 7*, 37–55.

Feldman, M. A. (1994). Parenting education for parents with intellectual disabilities: A review of outcome studies. *Research in Developmental Disabilities, 15*, 299–302.

Finkelhor, D., & Berliner, L. (1995). Research on the treatment of sexually abused children: A review and recommendations. *Journal of the American Academy of Child and Adolescent Psychiatry, 34*, 1–16.

Finkelhor, C., Ormrod, R., Turner, H., & Hamby, S. (2005). The victimization of children and youth: A comprehensive, national survey. *Child Maltreatment, 10*(1), 5–25.

Fisher, J. E., & Carstensen, L. L. (1990). Behavior management of the dementias. *Clinical Psychology Review, 10*, 611–629.

Fixsen, D. L., Blase, K. A., Naoom, S. F., & Wallace, F. (2009). Core implementation components. *Research on Social Work Practice, 19*, 531–541.

Foy, D. W., Resnick, H. S., & Lipovsky, J. A. (1993). Post-traumatic stress disorder in adults. In R. Ammerman & M. Hersen (Eds.), *Handbook of behavior therapy with children and adults: A developmental and longitudinal perspective* (pp. 236–248). Boston: Allyn and Bacon.

Frame, C. L., & Cooper, D. K. (1993). Major depression in children. In R. Ammerman & M. Hersen (Eds.), *Handbook of behavior therapy with children and adults: A developmental and longitudinal perspective* (pp. 57–72). Boston: Allyn and Bacon.

Franks, C. M., Wilson, G. T., Kendall, P. C., & Foreyt, J. P. (1990). *Review of behavior therapy: Theory and practice* (Vol. 12). New York: The Guilford Press.

Gamble, E. H., Elder, S. T., & Lashley, J. K. (1989). Group behavior therapy: a selective review of the literature. *Medical Psychotherapy An International Journal, 2*, 193–204.

Gambrill, E. D. (1983). Behavioral intervention with child abuse and neglect. In M. Hersen, R. Eisler, & P. Miller (Eds.), *Progress in behavior modification* (pp. 1–56). New York: Academic Press.

Gambrill, E. D. (1977). *Behavior modification: A handbook of assessment, intervention, and evaluation.* San Francisco: Jossey-Bass.

Gambrill, E. D. (1994). Concepts and methods of behavioral treatment. In D. K. Granvold (Ed.), *Cognitive and behavioral treatment: Methods and applications* (pp. 32–62). Pacific Grove, CA: Brooks/Cole Publishing Company.

Gamsa, A. (1994). The role of psychological factors in chronic pain. I. A half century of study. *Pain, 57*, 5–15.

Garner, D. M., & Rosen, L. W. (1990). Anorexia nervosa and bulimia nervosa. In A. Bellack, M. Hersen, & A. Kazdin (Eds.), *International handbook of behavior modification and therapy* (pp. 805–817). New York: Plenum Press.

Gaudin, J. M. Jr. (1993). Effective interventions with neglectful families. *Criminal Justice and Behavior, 20*, 66–89.

Goldapple, G. C., & Montgomery, D. (1993). Evaluating a behaviorally based intervention to improve client retention in therapeutic community treatment for drug dependency. *Research on Social Work Practice, 3*, 21–39.

Goldfried, M. R., & Castonguay, L. G. (1993). Behavior therapy: Redefining strengths and limitations. *Behavior Therapy, 24*, 505–526.

Granvold, D. K. (1994), (Ed.), *Cognitive and behavioral treatment: Methods and applications.* Pacific Grove, CA: Brooks/Cole Publishing Company.

Graziano, A. M., & Diament, D. M. (1992). Parent behavioral training: An examination of the paradigm. *Behavior Modification, 16*, 3–38.

Guide to Community Preventive Services. (Fall 2009). Violence prevention. Retrieved from http://www.thecommunityguide.org/violence/traumaticevents/index.html

Hagan, M., & King, R. P. (1992). Recidivism rates of youth completing an intensive treatment program in a juvenile correctional facility. *International Journal of Offender Therapy and Comparative Criminology, 36,* 349–358.

Hahlweg, K., & Markman, H. J. (1988). Effectiveness of behavioral marital therapy: Empirical status of behavioral techniques in preventing and alleviating marital distress. *Journal of Consulting and Clinical Psychology, 56,* 440–447.

Halford, K. K., Sanders, M. R., & Behrens, B. C. (1994). Self-regulation in behavioral couples' therapy. *Behavior Therapy, 25,* 431–452.

Hall, S. M., Hall, R. G., & Ginsberg, D. (1990). Cigarette dependence. In A. Bellack, M. Hersen, & A. Kazdin (Eds.), *International handbook of behavior modification and therapy* (pp. 437–448). New York: Plenum Press.

Hanson, R. K., Steffy, R. A., & Gauthier, R. (1993). Long-term recidivism of child molesters. *Journal of Consulting and Clinical Psychology, 61,* 646–652.

Hawkins, J. D., Jenson, J. M., Catalano, R. F., & Wells, E. A. (1991). Effects of a skill training intervention with juvenile delinquents. *Research on Social Work Practice, 1,* 107–121.

Hersen, M. (1990). Single-case experimental designs. In A. Bellack, M. Hersen, & A. Kazdin (Eds.), *International handbook of behavior modification and therapy* (pp. 175–212). New York: Plenum Press.

Hersen, M., & Van Hasselt, V. B. (1992). Behavioral assessment and treatment of anxiety in the elderly. *Clinical Psychology Review, 12,* 619–640.

Hile, M. G., & Derochers, M. N. (1993). The relationship between functional assessment and treatment selection for aggressive behavior. *Research in Developmental Disabilities, 14,* 265–274.

Hoberman, H. M., & Clarke, G. N. (1993). Major depression in adults. In R. Ammerman & M. Hersen (Eds.), *Handbook of behavior therapy with children and adults: A developmental and longitudinal perspective* (pp. 73–90). Boston: Allyn and Bacon.

Hodges, V. G. (1994). Home-based behavioral interventions with children and families. In D. K. Granvold (Ed.), *Cognitive and behavioral treatment: Methods and applications* (pp. 90–107). Pacific Grove, CA: Brooks/Cole Publishing Company.

Holroyd, K. A., & Penzien, D. B. (1994). Psychosocial interventions in the management of recurrent headache disorders: I. Overview and effectiveness. *Behavioral Medicine, 20,* 53–63.

Hollon, S. D., & Beck, A. T. (1994). Cognitive and cognitive-behavioral therapies. In A. E. Bergin & S. L. Garfield (Eds.), *Handbook of psychotherapy and behavior change* (4th ed.) (pp. 428–466).

Isreal, A. C. (1990). Childhood obesity. In A. Bellack, M. Hersen, & A. Kazdin (Eds.), *International handbook of behavior modification and therapy* (pp. 819–830). New York: Plenum Press.

Jacobson, N. S. (1992). Behavioral couple therapy: A new beginning. *Behavior Therapy, 23,* 493–506.

Jenson, J. M., & Howard, M. O. (1990). Skills deficits, skills training, and delinquency. *Children and Youth Services Review, 12,* 213–228.

Jordan, C., & Franklin, C. (1995). *Clinical assessment for social workers. Quantitative and qualitative methods.* Chicago, IL: Lyceum.

Kaminski, J. W., Valle, L. A., Filene, J. H., & Boyle, C. L. (2008). A meta-analytic review of components associated with parent training program effectiveness. *Journal of Abnormal Child Psychology, 26,* 567–589.

Kaplan, M. S., Morales, M., & Becker, J. V. (1993). The impact of verbal satiation of adolescent sex offenders: A preliminary report. *Journal of Child Sexual Abuse, 2,* 81–88.

Kazdin, A. E. (1989). *Behavior modification in applied settings* (4th ed.). Homewood, IL: Dorsey.

Kazdin, A. E. (1990). Conduct disorders. In A. Bellack, M. Hersen, & A. Kazdin (Eds.), *International handbook of behavior modification and therapy* (pp. 669–706). New York: Plenum Press.

Kendall, P. C. (1989). The generalization and maintenance of behavior change: Comments, considerations, and the "no-cure" criticism. *Behavior Therapy, 20,* 357–364.

Kennedy, S. H., Katz, R., Neitzert, C. S., Ralevski, E., & Mendlowitz, S. (1995). Exposure with response treatment of anorexia nervosa-bulimic subtype and bulimia nervosa. *Behavior Research and Therapy, 33,* 685–689.

King, N. J. (1993). Simple and social phobias. *Advances in Clinical Child Psychology, 15,* 305–341.

Kirkham, M. A. (1993). Two-year follow-up of skills training with mothers of children with disabilities. *American Journal on Mental Retardation, 97,* 509–520.

Landrine, H., & Klonoff, E. (1995). Cultural diversity and the silence of behavior therapy. *The Behavior Therapist, 18*(10), 187–189.

Leahy, R. (2009). *Anxiety free: Unravel your fears before they unravel you.* New York: HayHouse Inc.

LeCroy, C. W. (2007). *Handbook of child and adolescent treatment manuals.* New York: Oxford University Press.

LeCroy, C. W., & Mann, J. E. (Eds.) (2007). *Handbook of prevention and intervention programs for adolescent girls*. New York: Wiley.

Liberman, R. P., Kopelowicz, A., & Young, A. S. (1994). Biobehavioral treatment and rehabilitation of schizophrenia. *Behavior Therapy, 25,* 89–107.

Lichstein, K. L., & Riedel, B. W. (1994). Behavioral assessment and treatment of insomnia: A review with an emphasis on clinical applications. *Behavior Therapy, 25,* 659–588.

Linehan, M. H. (1993). *Cognitive behavioral treatment of borderline personality disorder*. New York: Guilford.

Lipsey, M. W., & Wilson, D. B. (1993). The efficacy of psychological, educational, and behavioral treatment. *American Psychologist, 48,* 1181–1209.

Lochman, J. E., & Lenhart, L. A. (1993). Anger coping intervention for aggressive children: Conceptual models and outcome effects. *Clinical Psychology Review, 13,* 785–805.

Lundahl, B. W., Nimer, J., & Parsons, B. (2006). Preventing child abuse: A meta-analysis of parent training programs. *Research on Social Work Practice,* 16, 251–262.

Maag, J. W., & Kotlash, J. (1994). Review of stress inoculation training with children and adolescents. *Behavior Modification, 18,* 443–469.

Magen, R. H., & Rose, S. D. (1994). Parents in groups: Problem solving versus behavioral skills training. *Research on Social Work Practice, 4,* 172–191.

Marshall, W. L., Jones, R., Ward, T., Johnston, P., & Barbaree, H. E. (1991). Treatment outcome with sex offenders. *Clinical Psychology Review, 11,* 465–485.

Marques, J. K., Day, D. M., Nelson, C., & West, M. A. (1994). Effects of cognitive-behavioral treatment on sex offender recidivism: Preliminary results of a longitudinal study. Special Issue: The assessment and treatment of sex offenders. *Criminal Justice and Behavior, 21,* 28–54.

Mattaini, M. A. (1993). Behavior analysis and community practice: A review. *Research on Social Work Practice, 3,* 420–447.

Mattaini, M. A., & McGuire, M. S. (2006). Behavioral strategies for constructing nonviolent cultures with youth: A review. *Behavior Modification, 30,* 184–224.

McEachin, J. J., Smith, T., & Lovaas, O. I. (1993). Long-term outcome for children with autism who receive early intensive behavioral treatment. *American Journal on Mental Retardation, 97,* 359–372.

Meadowcroft, P., Thomlison, B., & Chamberlain, P. (1994). A research agenda for treatment foster family care. *Child Welfare (Special issue),* (73)5, 565–581.

Meichenbaum, D. (1977). *Cognitive behavior modification*. New York: Plenum.

Mersh, P. A. (1995). The treatment of social phobia: The differential effectiveness of exposure in vivo and the integration of exposure in vivo, rational emotive therapy and social skills training. *Behavioral Research and Therapy, 33,* 259–269.

Minde, K., Popiel, K., Leos, N., & Falkner, S. (1993). The evaluation and treatment of sleep disturbances in young children. *Journal of Child Psychology and Psychiatry and Allied Disciplines, 34,* 521–533.

Mitte, K. (2005a). A meta-analysis of the efficacy of psycho- and pharmacotherapy in panic disorder with and without agoraphobia. *Journal of Affective Disorders, 88*(1), 27–45.

Mitte, K. (2005b). Meta-analysis of cognitive behavioral treatments for generalized anxiety disorder. A comparison with pharmacotherapy. *Psychological Bulletin, 131*(5), 785–795.

Morin, C. M., Winter, B., Besalel, V. A., & Azrin, N. H. (1987). Bulimia: A case illustration of the superiority of behavioral over cognitive treatment. *Journal of Behavior Therapy and Experimental Psychiatry, 18,* 165–169.

Montang, K. R., & Wilson, G. L. (1992). An empirical evaluation of behavioral and cognitive-behavioral group marital treatments with discordant couples. *Journal of Sex and Marital Therapy, 18,* 255–272.

Moran, D. J. (2008). The three waves of behaviour therapy: Course corrections or navigation errors? *The Behavior Therapist,* Special Issue, Winter, 147–157.

Morrison, R. L., & Sayers, S. (1993). Schizophrenia in adults. In R. Ammerman & M. Hersen (Eds.), *Handbook of behavior therapy with children and adults: A developmental and longitudinal perspective* (pp. 295–310). Boston: Allyn and Bacon.

Nathan, P. E., & Gorman, J. M. (Eds.) (2007). *A guide to treatments that work* (3rd ed.). New York: Oxford University Press.

Newman, M. G., Hofman, S. G., Trabert, W., Roth, W. T., & Taylor, C. B. (1994). Does behavioral treatment of social phobia lead to cognitive changes? *Behavior Therapy, 25,* 503–517.

Nicholson, N. L., & Blanchard, E. B. (1993). A controlled evaluation of behavioral treatment of chronic headache in the elderly. *Behavioral Therapy, 24,* 395–408.

Nixon, C. D., & Singer, G. H. (1993). Group cognitive-behavioral treatment for excessive parental self-blame and guilt. *American Journal on Mental Retardation, 97,* 665–672.

Norman, J., & Lowry, C. E. (1995). Evaluating inpatient treatment for women with clinical depression. *Research on Social Work Practice, 5,* 10–19.

O'Donnell, C., & Tharpe, R. (1990). Community intervention guided by theoretical development. In A. Bellack, M. Hersen, & A. Kazdin (Eds.), *International handbook of behavior modification and therapy* (pp. 251–266). New York: Plenum Press.

O'Farrell, T. J. (1994). Marital therapy and spouse-involved treatment with alcoholic patient. *Behavior Therapy, 25,* 391–406.

Patterson, G., & Reid, J. (1970). Reciprocity and coercion: Two facets of social systems. In C. Neuringer & J. Michael (eds.), *Behavior modification in clinical psychology* (pp. 133–177). New York: Appleton-Century-Crofts.

Peled, E., & Edleson, J. L. (1992). Multiple perspectives on group work with children of battered women. *Violence and Victims, 7,* 327–346.

Peyrot, M., Yen, S., & Baldassano, C. A. (1994). Short-term substance abuse prevention in jail: A cognitive behavioral approach. *Journal of Drug Education, 24,* 33–47.

Phillips, E. L., Phillips, E. A., Fixsen, D. L., & Wolf, M. M. (1974). *The teaching-family handbook* (2nd ed.). Lawrence, KS: University Press of Kansas.

Polansky, J., & Horan, J. J. (1993). Psychoactive substance abuse in adolescents. In R. Ammerman & M. Hersen (Eds.), *Handbook of behavior therapy with children and adults: A developmental and longitudinal perspective* (pp. 351–360). Boston: Allyn and Bacon.

Powers, M. B., Vedel, E., & Emmelkamp, P. M. (2008). Behavioral couples therapy (BCT) for alcohol and drug use disorders: A meta-analysis. *Clinical Psychology Review, 28,* 952–962.

Rachmann, S. (1993). A critique of cognitive therapy for anxiety disorders. *Journal of Behavior therapy and Experimental Psychiatry, 24,* 279–288.

Raines, J. C., & Foy, C. W. (1994). Extinguishing the fires within: Treating juvenile firesetters. *Families in Society, 75,* 595–607.

Reichow, B., & Wolery, M. (2009). Comprehensive synthesis of early intensive behavioral interventions for young children with autism based on the UCLA Young Autism Project model. *Journal of Autism and Developmental Disorders, 39*(1), 23–41.

Richards, D. A., Lovell, K., & Marks, I. M. (1994). Evaluation of a behavioral treatment program. *Journal of Traumatic Stress, 7,* 669–680.

Roberts, N. P., Kitchiner, N. J., Kenardy, J., & Bisson, J. I. (2009). Systematic review and meta-analysis of multiple-session early interventions following traumatic events. *American Journal of Psychiatry, 166*(3), 293–301.

Rohde, P., Lewinsohn, P. M., & Seeley, J. R. (1994). Response of depressed adolescents to cognitive-behavioral treatment: Do differences in initial severity clarify the comparison of treatments? *Journal of Consulting and Clinical Psychology, 62,* 851–854.

Rone, T., & Freeman, A. (Eds.). (2007). *Cognitive behavior therapy in social work practice.* New York: Springer.

Rose, S. (1981). Cognitive behavioral modification in groups. *International Journal of Behavioral Social Work and Abstracts, 1*(1), 27–38.

Rose, S. D. (2004). Cognitive-behavioral group work. In C. Garvin, L. M. Gutierrez, & M. J. Galinsky (Eds.), *Handbook of social work with groups* (pp. 111–136). New York: Guilford.

Rothman, J., & Thyer, B. A. (1984). Behavioral social work in community and organizational settings. *Journal of Sociology and Social Welfare, 11,* 294–326.

Saigh, P. A. (1992). The behavioral treatment of child and adolescent posttraumatic stress disorder. *Advances in Behavior Research and Therapy, 14,* 247–275.

Saunders, R. I., & Saunders, D. N. (1993). Social work practice with a bulimic population: A comparative evaluation of purgers and nonpurgers. *Research on Social Work Practice, 3,* 123–136.

Scheibman, L., Koegel, R. L., Charlop, M. H., & Egel, A. L. (1990). Infantile autism. In A. Bellack, M. Hersen, & A. Kazdin (Eds.), *International handbook of behavior modification and therapy* (pp. 763–789). New York: Plenum Press.

Schwartz, R. (1982). Cognitive-behavior modification: A conceptual review. *Clinical Psychology Review, 2,* 267–293.

Scotti, J. R., McMorrow, M. J., & Trawitzki, A. L. (1993). Behavioral treatment of chronic psychiatric disorders: Publication trends and future directions. *Behavior Therapy, 24,* 527–550.

Sevier, M., Eldridge, K., Jones, J., Doss, B., & Christensen, A. (2008). Observed communication and associations with satisfaction during traditional and integrative behavioral couple therapy. *Behavior Therapy, 39,* 137–150.

Skinner, B. F. (1953). *Science and human behavior.* New York: Macmillan.

Skinner, B. F. (1988). The operant side of behavior therapy. *Journal of Behavior Therapy and Experimental Psychiatry, 19,* 171–179.

Shadish, W. R., & Baldwin, S. A. (2005). Effects of behavioral marital therapy: A meta-analysis of randomized controlled trials. *Journal of Consulting and Clinical Psychology, 73*(1), 6–14.

Smith, D. E., Marcus, M. D., & Eldredge, K. L. (1994). Binge eating syndromes: A review of assessment and treatment with an emphasis on clinical application. *Behavior Therapy, 25,* 635–658.

Sobell, L. C., Sobell, M. B., & Nirenberg, T. D. (1988). Behavioral assessment and treatment planning with alcohol and drug abusers: A review with an emphasis on clinical application. *Clinical Psychology Review,* 8, 19–54.

Spiegler, M. D., & Guevremont, D. C. (2010). *Contemporary behavior therapy* (5th ed.). Belmont, CA: Wadsworth.

Steketee, G., & Chambless, D. L. (1992). Methodological issues in prediction of treatment outcome. *Clinical Psychology Review,* 12, 387–400.

Stuart, R. B. (1971). Behavioral contracting with families of delinquents. *Journal of Behavior Therapy and Experimental Psychiatry,* 2, 1–11.

Stuart, R. B. (Ed.) (1977). *Behavioral self management: Strategies, techniques, and outcomes.* New York: Brunner/Mazel.

Subramanian, K. (1991). Structured group work for the management of chronic pain: An experimental investigation. *Research on Social Work Practice,* 1, 32–45.

Subramanian, K. (1994). Long-term follow-up of a structured group treatment for the management of chronic pain. *Research on Social Work Practice,* 4, 208–223.

Sundel, S., & Sundel, M. (1993). *Behavior modification in the human services* (3rd ed.). Newbury Park CA: Sage.

Sweet, A. A., & Loizeaux, A. L. (1991). Behavioral and cognitive treatment methods: A critical comparative review. *Journal of Behavior Therapy and Experimental Psychiatry,* 22, 159–185.

Tallant, S., Rose, S. D., & Tolman, R. M. (1989). New evidence for the effectiveness of stress management training in groups. Special Issue: Empirical research in behavioral social work. *Behavior Modification,* 13, 431–446.

Tarrier, N. Beckett, R., Harwood, S., Baker, A., Yusupoff, L., & Ugarteburu, I. (1993). A trial of two cognitive-behavioral methods of treating drug-resistant residual psychotic symptoms in schizophrenic patients: I. Outcome. *British Journal of Psychiatry,* 162, 524–532.

Thomlison, B. (2010*). Family assessment handbook: An introduction and practical guide to family assessment and intervention* (3rd ed.). Belmont, CA: Brooks/Cole Wadsworth.

Thomlison, R. J. (1981). Behavioral family intervention with the family of a mentally handicapped child. In D. Freeman & B. Trute (Eds.). *Treating families with special needs* (pp. 15–42). Ottawa: Canadian Association of Social Workers.

Thomlison, R. J. (1972). *A behavioral model for social work intervention with the marital dyad.* Unpublished doctoral dissertation. Toronto, ONT: University of Toronto.

Thomlison, R. J. (1982). Ethical issues in the use of behavior modification in social work practice. In S. Yelaja (Ed.), *Ethical issues in social work.* Springfield, IL: Charles B. Thomas.

Thomlison, R. J. (1984a). Something works: Evidence from practice effectiveness studies. *Social Work,* 29, 51–56.

Thomlison, R. J. (1986). Behavior therapy in social work practice. In F. Turner (Ed.), *Social Work Treatment: Interlocking theoretical approaches* (pp. 131–155). New York: Free Press.

Thomlison, R. J. (1984b). Phobic disorders. In F. Turner (Ed.), *Adult psychopathology: A social work perspective* (pp. 280–315). New York: Free Press.

Thyer, B. A. (1987a). Behavioral social work: An overview. *Behavior Therapist,* 10, 131–134.

Thyer, B. A. (1987b). Community-based self-help groups for the treatment of agoraphobia. *Journal of Sociology and Social Welfare,* 14, 135–141.

Thyer, B. A. (1988). Radical behaviorism and clinical social work. In R. Dorfman (Ed.), *Paradigms of clinical social work* (pp. 123–148). New York: Guilford.

Thyer, B. A. (1989). Introduction to the special issue. *Behavior Modification,* 13(4), 411–414.

Thyer, B. A. (1990). Single-system research designs and social work practice. In L. Sherman & W. J. Reid (Eds.), *Advances in clinical social work research* (pp. 33–37). Silver Spring, MD: National Association of Social Workers Press.

Thyer, B. A. (1991). Behavioral social work: It is not what you think. *Arete,* 16, 1–9.

Thyer, B. A. (1992). Behavior therapies for persons with phobias. In K. Corcoran (Ed.), *Structuring change. Effective practice for common client problems* (pp. 31–71). Chicago, IL: Lyceum.

Thyer, B. A., & Thyer, K. B. (1992). Single-system research designs in social work practice: A bibliography from 1965 to 1990. *Research on Social Work Practice,* 2, 99–116.

Thyer, B. A., & Maddox, M. K. (1988). Behavioral social work: Results of a national survey on graduate curricula. *Psychological Reports,* 63, 239–242.

Tolman, R. M., & Bennett, L. W. (1990). A review of quantitative research on men who batter. *Journal of Interpersonal Violence,* 5, 87–118.

Tolman, R. M., & Molidor, C. E. (1994). A decade of social work group work research: Trends in methodology, theory, and program development. *Research on Social Work Practice,* 4, 142–159.

Turner, F. J. (1996). Social work treatment: Interlocking theoretical perspectives (4th ed.). New York: The Free Press.

Turner, S. M., Beidel, D. C., & Cooley-Quille, M. R. (1995). Two-year follow-up of social phobics with social effectiveness therapy. *Behavior Research and Therapy,* 33, 553–555.

Underwood, L., & Thyer, B. A. (1990). Social work practice with the mentally retarded: Reducing self-injurious behaviors using non-aversive methods. *Arete,* 15, 14–23.

Van Der Ploeg-Stapert, J. D., & Van Der Ploeg, H. M. (1986). Behavioral group treatment of test anxiety: An evaluation study. *Journal of Behavior Therapy and Experimental Psychiatry,* 17, 255–259.

Van Oppen, P., De Haan, E., Van Balkom, A., Spinhoven, P., Hoogduin, K., & Van Dyck, R. (1995). Cognitive therapy and expose in vivo in the treatment of obsessive compulsive disorder. *Behavior Research and Therapy,* 33, 379–390.

Watson, H. J., & Rees, C. S. (2008). Meta-analysis of randomized, controlled treatment trials for pediatric obsessive compulsive disorder. *Journal of Child Psychology and Psychiatry,* 49(5), 489–496.

Wekerle, C., & Wolfe, D. A. (1993). Prevention of child physical abuse and neglect: Promising new directions. *Clinical Psychology Review,* 13, 501–540.

Whisman, M. A. (1990). The efficacy of booster maintenance sessions in behavior therapy: Review and methodological critique. *Clinical Psychology Review,* 10, 155–170.

Widner, S., & Zeichner, A. (1993). Psychologic interventions for elderly chronic patients. *Clinical Gerontologist,* 13, 3–18.

Wilson, G. T. (1994). Behavioral treatment of obesity: Thirty years and counting. *Advances in Behavior Research and Therapy,* 16, 31–75.

Wolf, M., Philips, E., Fixsen, D., Braukmann, C., Kirigin, K., Willner, A., & Schumaker, J. (1976). Achievement Place: The teaching family model. *Child Care Quarterly,* 5, 92–103.

Wolfe, D. A., & Wekerle, C. (1993). Treatment strategies for child physical abuse and neglect: a critical progress report. *Clinical Psychology Review,* 13, 473–500.

Wolfe, V. V. (1990). Sexual abuse of children. In A. Bellack, M. Hersen, & A. Kazdin (Eds.), *International handbook of behavior modification and therapy* (pp. 707–730). New York: Plenum Press.

Wolitzky-Taylor, Horowitz, J. D., Powers, M. B., & Telch, M. J. (2008). Psychological approaches in the treatment of specific phobias: A meta-analysis. *Clinical Psychology Review,* 28, 1021–1037.

Wolpe, J. (1989). The derailment of behavior therapy: A tale of conceptual misdirection. *Journal of Behavior Therapy and Experimental Psychiatry,* 20, 3–15.

Wolpe, J. (1990). *The practice of behavior therapy* (4th ed.). New York: Pergamon Press.

Zimmermann, G., Favrod, J., Trieu, V. H., & Pomini, V. (2005). The effect of cognitive behavioral treatment on the positive symptoms of schizophrenia spectrum disorders: A meta-analysis. *Schizophrenia Research,* 77(1), 1–9.

Zimpfer, D. G. (1992). Group work with juvenile delinquents. *Journal for Specialists in Group Work,* 17, 116–126.

Zlonke, K., & Davis, III, T. E. (2008). One-session treatment of specific phobias: A detailed description and review of treatment efficacy. *Behavior Therapy,* 39, 207–223.

7

COGNITIVE THEORY

Emerging from sociology, this theory helps us to understand how an individual, group, family, community, or organization thinks about a social reality and how such thoughts influence behavior

Cognitive Theory and Social Work Treatment

Pranab Chatterjee and Suzanne Brown

The famous French philosopher René Descartes (1596–1650) made a statement that has become well known in the annals of intellectual history: "I think, therefore I am." This statement guides one to the area of human thought, ways of organizing and classifying human thought, and the various forms of behavior that are then influenced by it. It is this study of human thought and consequent behavior that has come to be known in modern social sciences as cognitive theory. Social workers and those in other helping professions use this theory for interventions with individuals, families, groups, communities, and organizations.

A dictionary definition of the word "cognition" is "the process of knowing, or the capacity for it" (Merriam & Merriam, 1957, p. 160). The term *cognitive theory* has come to mean the art and science of understanding how humans perceive, think, and process various forms of situations and then respond to them. It has emerged as a discipline in psychology, sociology, sociobiology, anthropology, philosophy, and social work. It engages in the study of how humans make judgments and decisions, reason, and engage in problem solving. It includes how the human mind forms concepts that help organize various forms of information.

The development of cognitive theory has been significantly influenced by the fields of computer and information technology, with their interest in information processing and memory. Alternative forms of intelligence, logic, and memory were applied by theorists to the human mind and the processes of memory, cognition, and cognitive structure in humans. In the social sciences, the rise in popularity of Logical Positivism, with its focus on phenomena that are empirically verifiable, also contributed significantly to the development of cognitive theory and interventions. In the social sciences, Logical Positivism encouraged movement away from a belief in internal drives and unconscious forces as causes for human behavior, toward more observable and measurable phenomena such as environmental events and internal identifiable cognitions. The Personal Construct Theory of George Kelly (1958), with its focus on interpretation and reasoning, further influenced the development of cognitive theory and interventions (Walsh, 2006). Of special importance here is Kelly's notion of "personal constructs" (1955), referring to how individuals learn, create, and use important ideas to understand social realities.

Kelly (1955) identified three primary construct types, or frames through which individuals interpret the world: preemptive constructs, constellatory constructs, and propositional constructs. The preemptive constructs prevent the re-examination or reintegration of new information and allow individuals and events to be placed only in one realm (Hjelle & Ziegler, 1976). Once an opinion has been made, new information is not utilized to change or modify that opinion; once a label is applied to a person or event, that label remains fixed. Rigid or fundamentalist belief systems may be considered to be preemptive constructs. In psychological terms, the concept of learned helplessness may be considered a preemptive construct. Individuals with learned helplessness have learned over time that their actions are always ineffective, leading to hopelessness and a sense of helplessness in the face of problems. For these individuals, the preemptive construct of helplessness preempts their ability to consider alternative actions and to generate effective solutions to problems.

Similar to preemptive constructs, Kelly's (1955) constellatory constructs also encourage fixed assignment of individuals or events to one group. However, unlike preemptive constructs, constellatory constructs allow more flexible thinking, as individuals and events may be assigned to multiple groups at one time (Hjelle & Ziegler, 1976). Stereotypes are exemplars of constellatory constructs; an individual who belongs to a certain ethnic group is also assumed to reflect the stereotypes assigned to that group.

A propositional construct allows individuals to change their opinions based on new information and maintains room for the examination of new information and the reinterpretation of events (Hjelle & Ziegler, 1976). Kelly (1958) also identified lesser constructs that were comprehensive constructs, incidental constructs, core constructs, and peripheral constructs. An extension from the idea of personal constructs are constructs developed and used by groups, communities, and organizations, variously known as collective cognition, groupthink, definition of the situation by a group, or social construction of reality.

Disciplines and Political Correctness

Cognitive theory may be used to understand how the individual client or patient thinks about a social reality and how such thought, in turn, influences his or her behavior. It follows that this client can be a group, a family, a community, or an organization, and a helping process defines or guides ways of assessing and altering the client's thought and behavior. However, this very process can be turned around to ask: how does the help-provider, meaning the social worker, organize his or her thoughts about the client or the patient? Often an academic or professional discipline may get caught in the appropriateness or political correctness of a word, a concept, a linguistic usage, and ideas to understand clients or patients, and then some pathways to intervention become politically correct while others are seen as politically not correct. Before one ventures into how clients or patients and their cognition should be understood to guide intervention, it is important to review how the cognition of the help-provider is often immersed in the norms of political correctness of a professional culture.

The first of such political correctness emerges from the professional help provider's notion of functional or dysfunctional thought and behavior. Within a modern society, the United States for example, disciplines of clinical psychology and clinical social work often define an individual or a family as functional or dysfunctional within its environment. Such a way of defining an individual or a family is often politically correct and is supported by a medicalized (meaning using the traditions, rituals, and vocabulary of the medical profession) culture. However, it is sometimes not politically correct to define a group or a community culture as functional or dysfunctional, since such a way of defining a group culture is not seen as politically correct. For example, the marginalization of the male role in certain minority cultures in the United States is something that is known to professionals, but it is not appropriate to see such a minority culture as a dysfunctional community culture. In the discipline of social work, it is this norm of not seeing a community culture as dysfunctional that has contributed to what is known as "the strengths model" (Saleeby, 2005), or deliberately not focusing on the "deficits" of a group or a community.

Comparable to the concepts of functional and dysfunctional are those of adaptation and maladaptation, normalcy and deviance, normal and pathological, and wellness and illness. All of these concepts are used by academic disciplines and the helping professions to define an individual client, a family, a group, a community, or an organization. These constructs, when seen as cognition and consequent behavior in a given environment, however, may still be useful, because they guide social workers in setting goals and in identifying what kind of thoughts or behaviors need to be changed. The profession of social work has long used the term *person-in-environment* (and by derivation a family in an environment, a group in an environment, a community in an environment, or an organization in an environment), and use of this paradigm clarifies how clients are functional or dysfunctional, adaptive or not adaptive, normal or deviant, well or ill, and normal or pathological within one or more social environments.

Goffman's (1974) concepts of "frame" and frame analysis are also helpful to our understanding of how social workers conceptualize problems with individuals, groups, and communities. Frame analysis is a method of social inquiry that analyzes the cognitive schemas influencing the interpretation of events by individuals and groups. In Goffman's own words regarding frames, the "definition of a situation is built up in accordance with principles of organization which govern events . . . .; frame is the word I use to refer to these basic elements" (Goffman, 1974, p. 10). An example of the use of frames is our interpretation of popular rap music lyrics such as Eminem's "Now I don't wanna hit no women when this chick's got it coming. Someone better get this b—ch before she gets kicked in the stomach." Our interpretation of such music either as empowering creativity and expression for young, urban, poor, primarily black men, or as oppressive misogyny for young women, is ultimately determined by the frame we use to analyze and define this situation.

Origins in Sociology

The classic work of Chicago sociologist W. I. Thomas (1923) introduced a phrase, "definition of the situation," which meant how any given situation can be seen, interpreted, and acted upon differently by different individuals from different backgrounds. His axiom was then used in the classic study of Polish peasants in Europe and America (Thomas & Znaniecki, 1918). The Polish immigrant in American society, for example, viewed a situation very differently than did a peasant as a member of Polish society. Since the work of Thomas (1923), the axiom "definition of the situation" has become an important way of understanding how different individuals see and react to the same situation differently. Since the work of Thomas, Talcott Parsons (1951) has added the idea of "pattern variables," which suggests that there are about five ways one can view and respond to a given situation. One of these five ways is a definition of the situation either prompted from affectivity or from affect-neutrality. A tragic accident may create serious wounds to a given person, and an onlooker may define this situation with affect and start screaming. A medic or an emergency room physician is likely to respond to the same situation from affect-neutrality, since the response is prompted by years of medical and technical training that mandates a calm and problem-solving demeanor.

A further development of the ideas of Thomas and Parsons can be found in the treatise by Berger and Luckman (1966), where they introduce the idea that "reality" is socially constructed.

An example of this way of thinking can be found in the story of Teresa of Avila during the Spanish Inquisition. In this story, about 14 nuns were found to be communicating with spirits and other beings that most people could not see or hear. Some professionals in clinical social work today would label this behavior as hallucinations and delusions. The church fathers of the time, however, defined this behavior as "evil," and called for tying them to a stake and burning them. At this point, Teresa is supposed to have said that the nuns should be treated as *cosas enfermas*, meaning that they should be treated *as if sick* (Bates, 1977, p. 9). In this example, the first construction of reality was done by the church fathers when they defined the situation as "evil." Then, the second construction of reality was done by Teresa of Avila, when she defined that the nuns should not be treated as "evil," but as "sick." The definition of the situation by the church fathers called for burning the women, whereas that by Teresa called for putting the nuns in the custody of persons qualified to provide treatment.

Many individuals past and present believe that the experiences of Teresa of Avila were genuine experiences of God's actual presence, through which Teresa gained the wisdom and strength to establish convents and monasteries throughout Spain. Furthermore, Teresa's visions are presumed to have led her to a deeper, more reflective spiritual practice and the dissemination of her spiritual understanding through inspirational writings. For individuals with more mystical religious beliefs, a situation may be defined as a significant religious or spiritual experience. Walsh (2008) reminds us of the importance of incorporating this understanding into the social work assessment process.

The concept of the definition of the situation has seen important usages in current studies of managers in industry (Trompenaars & Hampden-Turner, 1997), who point out that managers in industry learn how to think and solve problems using their own personal, organizational, and other backgrounds. The study of organizational culture today, in order to understand management behavior (Schein, 2004) and make management effective and efficient, evolves from these contributions by sociological theorists.

Origins in Anthropology

How humans think and react to a situation was the subject of elaborate study by the anthropologist Malinowski (1955). The variety of ways in which different cultures appraise a situation was the focus of his study. For example, the finality of death is a universal experience in all human groups. However, how to give meaning to death, by the funeral procedures that vary from culture to culture, means varying definitions of the same situation.

A controversial paradigm emerged in anthropology when Lucien Lévy-Bruhl (1926) introduced the idea of cognitive relativism. This work suggested that all human groups develop a cultural style of adaptation to its environment. This cultural style, in turn, teaches its members how to think. Within the different styles of thought, some are more functional (that is, they help in the group's adaptation to its environment better) than others. The implication of this is that certain cognitive styles adopted by some cultures may be "superior" to that of others. The contemporaries of Lévy-Bruhl saw this theory of cognitive relativism as somewhat ethnocentric. However, even to date the idea of functional versus dysfunctional cognition at the individual level is very much accepted, and current psychologists and clinical social workers engaged in cognitive behavioral intervention use the idea of functional versus dysfunctional cognition (that is, an individual client or patient's way of thinking is either adaptive or maladaptive) in their professional practice. The controversy begins when one suggests that the cognitive style taught by one culture is "more functional" than that of another.

Origins in Sociobiology

An important pioneer in sociobiology is Edward O. Wilson (1978), who argued that human cognition and behavior cannot be well explained by the ideas of individual development, social environment, or cultural context, and should be understood as having emerged from an evolutionary sequence. This means that human cognition and behavior originate not exclusively from individual development (as many psychologists suggest) or from group or community culture (as sociologists, anthropologists, and social workers suggest), but from genetic and biological adaptation. This position created a controversy and was hotly disputed by many social scientists, who argued that it was close to the ideas suggested by Social Darwinism and eugenics during the latter part of the 19th and early part of the 20th centuries. This idea in sociobiology is especially unpopular in social work, since it leads to a position that many forms of human cognition and behavior are biological in origin, and subsequently not subject to social intervention.

Origins in Psychology

The work of Swiss psychologist Jean Piaget is usually thought of as a formal beginning of cognitive theory in the discipline of psychology. Piaget was the first to propose the concept that schemata form the basic structures of the mind that allow individuals to organize information and intellectually develop (Piaget, 1932; Robbins, Chatterjee, & Canda, 2006). He further proposed that humans maintain two biologically inherent cognitive functions: organization, which refers to the "tendency to blend and coordinate physical or mental structures into higher order structures" (Robbins et al, 2006, p. 261), and adaptation, which refers to the ways in which the mind changes and structure develops in order to accommodate the external environment. According to Piaget, important processes in cognitive development include three areas: (1) assimilation, meaning the ways in which new information is assimilated into existing mental schemata; (2) accommodation, which is the development of new schemata through assimilation; and (3) memory, which is the ability to learn and maintain new learning over time.

Piaget (1951) proposed a linear and stage-based model of cognitive development in which each stage builds upon the previous one. Stages are associated with a specific childhood age, and in each stage the child is expected to master specific sensory-motor and cognitive tasks. Stage 1, the sensorimotor stage, occurs between birth and age 2, during which children develop goal-directed behavior, gain a sense of objects and permanence, and develop the capacity for symbolic thought and for mentally representing objects (Robbins et al., 2006). Stage 2, the preoperational period,

occurs between ages 2 and 7 and involves the development of language, increased use of symbolization and mental representations, and increased skill in understanding interrelationships between objects. In stage 3, concrete operations, which occurs between ages 7 and 11, children learn the cognitive functions of reversibility and compensation. They become capable of focusing on more than one perception at once (compensation) and of undoing or redoing an action in their minds (reversibility). Stage 4, formal operations, occurs between ages 11 and 15 and includes the development of reasoning and increased capacity for abstraction.

While Piaget also proposed a theory of moral development that included a premoral stage, moral realism, and moral relativism, it was Kohlberg (1969) who proposed a more complex theory of moral development in children. Kohlberg's is a six-stage theory divided into three levels (Robbins et al., 2006). The first level, the preconventional level, includes the obedience and punishment stage and the egoistic orientation stage. This level is distinguished by its focus on rules, punishment, and rewards as motivators for moral behavior. The second level, the conventional level, includes the stages of the good boy/nice girl orientation and authority-maintaining morality. The focus at this level is on approval from authority figures and the avoidance of social disapproval. In the final level, the postconventional, which occurs from age 16 into adulthood, social contract and individual principled conscience are the stages. At this level "emphasis is placed on democratically accepted law and consensus as well as an understanding of the greater good and the potential to modify an unjust social contract" (Robbins et al., 2006, p. 276). Kohlberg believed that this third level was rarely achieved by most individuals.

A simple extrapolation from Kohlberg's theory of moral development, however, can be used to return to the matter of cognitive relativism of Lévy-Bruhl (1926). This extrapolation may be framed in the following manner. Kohlberg proposes (1969) that formal education can be an important contributor to the development of postconventional morality. This may mean that the more the formal education, the more the probability of attaining a moral frame that can be considered postconventional. Formal education is also often used as a measure of social class (Beeghley, 2007; Hollingshead, 1975)—that is, the more the formal education one has, the higher the likelihood of one's placement in a higher social class. Does that mean that persons placed in a higher social class are more likely to attain postconventional morality? This very awkward (and perhaps politically incorrect) position was raised by Kanjirathinkal (1990). Since his work, this politically incorrect question has not been pursued in subsequent research in the social sciences.

An example may be important here. Preserving the environment is a moral position adopted by many individuals. Is this a postconventional morality? Is it more common among the members of the upper classes than among the members of the poverty classes? Do the members of the upper classes have more investment in preserving the environment than those from the bottom end of the socioeconomic ladder? It is questions like this that return to the idea of cognitive relativism, and the political correctness of questions like this remains unsettled.

Biology and Cognitive Theory

The past decade has seen an increase in interest and research on the biological basis of cognition. Biological and neurological research has examined the ways in which neural systems mediate the relationships between cognition and the social environment, leading to increased understanding of disorders such as autism (Nurius, 2008). Technological methods for examining and measuring neuronal activity related to cognitive functioning such as positron emission typography (PET), which measures cerebral blood flow, and functional magnetic resonance imaging (fMRI), which measures brain activation, have been widely used over the past 10 years. It is assumed that better understanding of the neurological components of cognition will allow researchers to understand the effects of different types of neuronal activity on information coding, processing, and interpretation (Morris, Tarassenko, & Kenward, 2006). While some researchers have high hopes that neurobiological research will help in the treatment of individuals with cognitive disorders, such developments may be controversial for social work.

As biologically driven interventions are utilized, some may be concerned that they could make social work interventions obsolete.

Language Use and Cognitive Theory

Recently Begley (2009, p. 31) has summarized several research findings suggesting that language usage may shape cognition. An example given by her is that a very tall bridge in the south of France, Viaduct de Millau, is seen as feminine by German speakers. In French, it is seen as masculine. German speakers see it as a form of beauty, whereas French speakers see it as a powerful structure with an impressive presence. Begley then goes on to suggest that each language is embedded in a culture, and even though she does not use the term "cognitive relativism," she concludes that each and every language defines a situation in a unique way that is different when seen in comparison with other languages. Thus, within a language, words chosen to define a situation may vary from person to person, from group to group, and from profession to profession. Further, between languages, as shown in the example cited above, a situation may be defined in one given way in one language and in another way in another language.

Another example of linguistic construction of reality comes from how "madness" is defined in English-speaking cultures (Bates, 1977) and how its translation in Bengali (called "paglami") is defined in Bengali-speaking cultures. In English-speaking cultures, "madness" essentially has two definitions, and at times they can be overlapping. The first leads to defining a person who is not in contact with reality as the larger society knows it, and the person is seen as having hallucinations or delusions. This definition often leads to seeing the person as "sick," as was done by Avila (discussed above) during the Spanish Inquisition. This definition often calls for appointing members of medical and psychological professions as custodians of the situation. A second definition also exists in English-speaking cultures, and this leads to defining a person as "deviant" according to the norms of larger society, and requires ostracizing or incarcerating the person. In the latter case, members of the justice system are seen as appropriate custodians of the situation. Thus, one can suggest that English-speaking cultures, for the most part, maintain two definitions arising from the use of the word "madness."

In Bengali-speaking cultures, the two above-mentioned situations also prevail. In addition, the behavior of a person who gives up living as an everyday householder and pursues the meaning of life by deep introspection, or persons who go from village to village engaged in wanderlust and support themselves by begging and singing, may often be framed as additional forms of madness or "paglami" (Bhattacharya, 1984; Chatterjee, 2009). The act of begging is not seen as a stigma in Bengali culture. However, the same act in Europe and America, as done by the Hare Krishna groups (and the ideology of the Hare Krishna group was imported from Bengal to Europe and America) is seen as an annoying form of mild deviance that calls for both expressions of disapproval and, at times, forced removal from public spaces by law-enforcement authorities. The implication of this position is that language used by a therapist, a clinical psychologist, or a clinical social worker may guide the cognition of a patient or the ways in which a client thinks and acts. Thus, a therapist's choice of words may influence the outcome of therapy.

Social Work Treatment with Individuals and Families: Current Ideas

The focus of cognitive theory and intervention is on the conscious thought processes, which are considered the basis for all behavior and emotion (Walsh, 2008). The underlying assumptions of this theory are that behavior is affected by thoughts or cognitions, that these cognitions may be modified, and that behavior change may occur through the modification of these cognitions (Dobson, 2001). Albert Ellis, the developer of rational-emotive therapy (Ellis & Bernard, 1985), is considered to be one of the fathers of cognitive theory in the field of psychology. Trained in psychoanalytic methods, Ellis decided to pursue more active treatment methods. Ellis developed what has come to be known as the A-B-C model for assessing symptoms. This model maintains that an activating event (A) is followed by an individual's cognition or belief about the event (B), which leads to an individual's symptoms or consequences (C). This A-B-C model remains central to assessment in cognitive therapy. Ellis further maintained that individuals are irrational, and he identified 12 common beliefs or cognitive distortions to which individuals are vulnerable (Dobson, 2001). This concept is also central to current cognitive theory, which emphasizes the identification of cognitive distortions in assessment and intervention.

During the 1970s Aaron Beck made significant strides in the use of cognitive theory to develop interventions for the treatment of individuals with depression and anxiety (Beck, 1976; Beck et al., 1979). Beck developed his cognitive theory initially for the treatment of depression. Trained as a psychoanalyst, Beck attempted to embrace psychoanalytic theories of depression, but eventually concluded that depression was maintained by negative cognitions and negative schemas. These negative schemas were composed primarily of "personal ineffectiveness, personal degradation, and the world as an essentially unpleasant place" (Walsh, 2006). Beck's most significant contribution to cognitive theory was the importance of identifying automatic thoughts and challenging them (Leahy & Dowd, 2002). As Beck continued to develop cognitive theory and interventions, he extended the technique to include treatment for anxiety, phobias, and personality disorders.

Glasser (1988) further extended cognitive theory in his development of Choice Theory, which informed his approach to intervention: Reality Therapy. Choice Theory maintains that humans, rather than being externally motivated, have five intrinsic motivating needs: survival, love and belonging, power, freedom, and fun (Corey, 2009). Glasser's theory is based on the assumptions that individuals choose their behaviors and that the only thing individuals have control over is their own behavior (Glasser, 2001). Furthermore, an individual's behavior is based on his or her thoughts, feelings, physiology, and prior experience (Austad, 2009). Emerging from this theory, Reality Therapy encourages individuals to take responsibility for their choices, maintains a present focus in treatment, and rejects focusing on symptoms (Corey, 2009).

Recently, cognitive theory has led to the development of treatment for a variety of individual and relational problems. These include treatments for posttraumatic stress disorder (Foa, Keane, & Friedman, 2000), eating disorders (Fairburn, 2008), anxiety (Beck, 1976), stress and coping (Meichenbaum, 1996), depression (Beck, 1976; Ellis, 2006), obsessive-compulsive disorder (Steketee, 2006), schizophrenia (Kingdon & Turkington, 2004), personality disorders (Linehan, 1993), and relational concerns (Datilio & Padesky, 1990). Emery, Hollon, and Bedrosian (1981) extended the use of cognitive theory in the treatment of the elderly, individuals with sexual dysfunction, and individuals with alcohol dependence. Granvold (1994) added the dimension of constructivism to his discussion of cognitive theory, highlighting the individual's responsibility in forming his or her own reality. This line of cognitive-constructivist thought eventually developed into narrative theory and the narrative approach to counseling and psychotherapy (White & Epstein, 1990).

In the field of social work, at the level of what was called casework practice and case management practice, the use of cognitive theory became popular in the late 1970s (Chatterjee, 1984; Goldstein, 1982). Goldstein (1982) identified the development of psychoanalytic therapy as the impetus for the use of cognitive theory in social work: "Caseworkers at that time were admonished not to dabble in the psychoanalyst's domain of the unconscious. . . . (therefore) social workers assumed guardianship of the more conscious and cognitive realms of their clients' lives" (p. 546). Werner (1982) underscored the humanistic underpinnings of cognitive theory as a theory focused on the human capacities of thought, reasoning, and learning. His book *A Rational Approach to Social Casework* (1965) marked the beginning of the purposive use of cognitive therapy in the field of social work (Goldstein, 1982). Recently, Sharon Berlin has modified established principles of cognitive therapy to propose a cognitive-integrative perspective. While relying on established cognitive interventions, this model also focuses on the social causes of meaning in a client's cognitions and utilizes other therapeutic approaches, such as advocacy or case management, for intervening in the client's environment (Berlin, 2002).

The task-centered methods used in social work practice are also derived from cognitive theory. The task-centered model is usually time-limited and focused on the client's problem as defined by the client. In this model, the individual's beliefs, or views of himself or herself and the world, are considered to be the motivation for action (Reid, 1978). Emotions are the product of an individual's beliefs and the distance between what the person wants and their evaluation of their capacity to attain the desired outcome. Values underlying this model include client self-determination, a present-future focus, time-limited intervention, contracting (an agreement between client and social worker regarding the work to be done), and empirical orientation (Fortune, 1985). Many of the underlying values and assumptions of this model are similar to the values and assumptions of cognitive theory.

Assessment, as informed by cognitive theory, includes the identification of cognitive distortions through Socratic questioning. Cognitive distortions include overgeneralizing, negative scanning, personalization, catastrophizing, dichotomous thinking, emotional reasoning, magnifying, minimizing, personalizing, and selective abstraction (Gambrill, 2006; Walsh, 2006). Socratic questioning is done with the purpose of assisting people in identifying the distorted aspects of their thinking. Such questioning allows client and worker to understand the client's core beliefs about a situation and to examine the evidence both supporting and refuting those core beliefs. Cognitive therapy interventions include cognitive restructuring, where the worker assists the client in changing his or her perception of a problem and generating alternative interpretations of it. The task then is to develop and use coping skills; this entails learning new behaviors and thought processes such as problem-solving techniques and communication (Walsh, 2006).

Case Example

Martha is a 34-year-old married mother of three young children. She has been referred to treatment by her primary care physician, who noticed her depressed mood and irritability during her most recent doctor's visit. When questioned, Martha revealed that she has been feeling "overwhelmed" recently, irritable with her children, and discouraged by what she considers their "bad behavior." She also complained of marital concerns and a deteriorating relationship with her husband. Martha was referred by her physician to the area outpatient mental health center and was seen by a social worker. During the initial assessment, Martha described herself as depressed and anxious. She has three children under the age of 6, and she described her husband as "withdrawn" and "unhappy."

Assessment: After gathering a complete family, psychiatric, and medical history from this client, the social worker began to monitor the cognitive distortions evident in Martha's thinking. These included overgeneralizations such as thinking "I am a horrible mother" and "My children hate me." Magnifying and catastrophizing occurred frequently with Martha. When her eldest child was sent to the principal's office at school for talking during class, Martha immediately had thoughts such as "my child is heading for trouble" and "I have failed as a mother and my children are failing." The social worker then utilized Socratic questioning to challenge the rationality of Martha's thought process. The social worker also used an example presented by Martha that described a common and repetitive interaction between Martha and one of her children. Using the client's own example, the social worker identified the A-B-C's in this scenario: the activating event, belief about the event, and Martha's response of hopelessness and depression.

Intervention: The social worker worked with Martha on cognitive restructuring. Using a typical event, her child spilling his milk at the dinner table, Martha was made to identify her belief that her child was "purposely trying to get my goat" and the anger and resentment that resulted. This event was usually followed by Martha yelling at this child. Her son would then tell her he hated her (activating event), leading to Martha's thought that she was a bad mother (core belief) and the resulting hopelessness and depressed mood (emotional consequence).

Following an exploration of the A-B-C process in Martha's scenario, the social worker encouraged her to consider other thoughts and interpretations with which to replace the identified distortions. The social worker asked Martha to generate and consider other reasons why her son might spill his milk at the dinner table. He asked her: "Can you imagine how you would feel if you thought that David's behavior was simply an accident or that he was tired from a long day at school? How might you react differently if these were your thoughts?"

In this way, Martha was able to consider alternative interpretations to events and generate different emotional responses within herself. The social worker attempted to challenge Martha's irrational beliefs by setting up tasks for her to try in her daily life in order to test the veracity of her distortions. The social worker encouraged Martha to try an experiment at home: "When David spills his milk this week, calmly give him a towel with which to clean up the mess. Then notice the ways in which the outcome of this event changes." Martha was also instructed in the use of self-instruction training (Meichenbaum, 1996) or positive self-talk. The social worker helped Martha create statements that she could say to herself when she became upset with her children during difficult parenting moments: "My children are doing the best that they can," "Everyone makes mistakes and this one isn't the end of the world," and "All in all I am an adequate mother."

Given that Martha's depressed mood was also related to marital discord, the social worker recommended couples treatment for Martha and her husband Mark. Following three months of work with Martha individually, the social worker invited Martha's husband Mark in to engage in couples treatment. Cognitive restructuring, communication skills training, and training in problem solving were utilized with Martha and Mark. Both were able to identify distorted core beliefs that affected their interactions with one another. Using Beck's (1976) model the social worker helped Martha to identify the event, Mark's withdrawal from her; her automatic thought, "he refuses to help me with the house and kids"; her core belief, "I am unappreciated"; and her emotional reaction of depression and resentment toward Mark. Mark identified his automatic thought in response to Martha's resentment: "she's unhappy with me and I don't know why." His core belief was "I am inadequate," leading to his withdrawal from the relationship. Over time the social worker helped Mark and Martha use "I" statements in communicating with each other, to reflect back to each other the thoughts and feelings expressed by the other, and to make clear requests of each other.

Social Work Intervention with Groups: Current Ideas

At times, the use of the "treatment" metaphor may give an impression (or define the situation) that cognitive theory is more often applicable to social work intervention with individuals and families in clinical social work. This is not true, because cognitive theory is also useful in social work intervention with groups, and such interventions can be done for attaining ends of primary socialization (as in school social work and in neighborhood-based community centers), resocialization (as in prisons and other settings where juveniles and adults are incarcerated), and treatment (as in purposive group work with patients and substance abusers). Cognitive theory can also be used to accomplish what is called consciousness raising. For example, it can be a useful tool in working with groups of victims of domestic violence, child abuse, or elder abuse. The purpose of such intervention using the method of group work is to change the cognition of the group members from a definition of the situation of "I am a victim" to "I am capable of overcoming a victim role."

The legacy of Grace Coyle (1937) can be suggested as an intellectual journey that had its foundations in cognitive theory. Even though not formally referred to as an intervention based on cognitive theory (it was called a paradigm based on theories of socialization), the practice goals of this paradigm were focused on helping a group (like adolescent peer groups, and other types of human groups) change its cognitive style. Thus, for example, a group worker working with working-class adolescents would struggle to teach this group that the pursuit of success in schools and developing a career is more functional than the pursuit of gang violence.

Social work practice with groups has evolved into multiple areas of practice since the pioneering work of Coyle. Today, it can be used in health care settings to teach groups about cognitions and behaviors that contribute to wellness, avoiding addictions, and engaging in prevention of illness. It can be used in prisons and juvenile incarceration settings so that inmates in these settings learn how to become productive members of society. It can be used to bolster support groups for victims of domestic violence or child abuse. Groups that develop as "cults" or "new religions" often use a new form of cognition to indoctrinate their members. Thus, for example, Nation of Islam may teach cognitive styles to its members that are different from those offered in Christianity or Judaism. The same holds true for groups like Unification Church, Scientology, or

Hare Krishna groups. Depending on one's social position, one may identify these groups as "cults," or as "new religions." Also, there have been interventions developed in psychology and social work about how to engage in deprogramming persons who have become indoctrinated by one or more of these groups.

Case Example

Jamal Bana is the third Somali-American from the city of Minneapolis to head for Somalia and die there. He is one of more than a dozen missing Somali-Americans whose families believe have gone back to fight. "Someone must have put something in his mind," said Omar Jamal of the Minneapolis Social Justice Advocacy Center. "He must have been somewhat disillusioned and indoctrinated because he didn't have any clue about Somalia at all" (CNN.com/world, 2009).

Interpretation: Viewed from the discipline of sociology, this is a case of ideological indoctrination of a young American man to join al Qaeda and become a part of the Islamic fundamentalist war call. Viewed from the discipline of psychology, this is a case of a cognitive structuring of a Somali-American young man to join a call to war by a terrorist group. This was a case that, viewed from a psychological perspective, called for a cognitive restructuring. Such a restructuring would have deprogrammed Jamal Bana from thinking of al Qaeda as a noble organization to recognizing it as a very destructive and deviant group. Here, cognitive structuring is undertaken by two groups: the first are the recruiting agents of al Qaeda programming Jamal to go and fight in Somalia, and the second are the psychologists and clinical social workers who might engage in deprogramming Jamal to help him reject ideas to engage in terrorist causes. In this case, the act of deprogramming never happened.

Social Work Intervention with Communities: Current Ideas

Just like "truth," "justice," and "morality" are culturally constructed (cf. Geertz, 1973), so are "domestic violence," "child abuse," "elder abuse," and "setting up and utilizing mental health services." For example, violence in a family may be defined by one group as a situation requiring intervention, and by another group as a private matter in a family that should be ignored. Similarly, child abuse, elder abuse, or not seeking help for personal problems may be seen by one group as problems requiring intervention, and by another group as private matters that should be left alone. Working with community groups may necessitate developing awareness at the community level that these social problems require solutions at the community, regional, and national levels. Community organization and community development efforts can be established toward the pursuit of these ends. A special example of such efforts is in the works of Paolo Freire (1970), who taught that members of a community can be taught to see the inherent contradictions within a community culture, and such an education can create a new form of cognition in a disadvantaged community. This form of change in the cognitive structures of the disadvantaged was called *conscientization*.

Two other traditions that contribute to the study of cognitive structures at the community level and generate ideas for social work practice with communities are the semiotic tradition and the tradition that explores how the use of authority is socially constructed in a community culture. The semiotic tradition focuses on the study of meaning that a given behavior, ritual, art form, or procedure has for a given community (Danesi & Perron, 1999). In fact, the term "semiotics" means the study of semantic or linguistic structure. The common method for doing such studies is to develop narratives of these behaviors, rituals, art forms, or procedures in a way that the cognitive foundation and meaning inherent in them emerge by themselves. The discipline of cultural or social anthropology has pioneered this tradition, though the discipline of cultural sociology has also contributed to such efforts. This tradition can be used to develop narratives about an entire community culture, or about some important parts of a community culture, like how justice, morality, adolescence, or providing and utilizing mental health services is viewed in this culture.

Yet another tradition in community-based work may be called explorations in different forms and sources of authority. This tradition focuses on the study of different types of authority and their legitimacy in different sociocultural situations. Often this tradition is seen as having started with the work of Weber (1999), his influence on modernization theorists (Jaffee, 1998)

and on the works in economic sociology (Swedberg, 1990, 2003), and the work in the social construction of reality by Berger (1977) and Berger and Luckman (1966). The method used here is the tracing of events that show the bedrock of the authority structure in a given social setting, assessing whether that authority is based on tradition or modernity, and implying that authority and methods of production and governance based on modern knowledge are more likely to produce social and economic development.

Social Work Intervention with Organizations: Current Ideas

While the classic work of Weber (1999) can be seen as a formal beginning of the study of organizations, a current development influencing how organizations should be seen is emerging from the ideas of Schein (2004). At least two types of organizations are important in social work practice: social agencies, which are the means of social service delivery (where the personnel are mostly social workers), and organizations built for empowerment of community members (where the members of the organization often are community residents and are clients of social workers). Schein's work informs us that in order for organizations of both types to be effective (is this organization capable of attaining the goals it has set for itself?) and efficient (is this organization cable of pursuing its goals with efficient use of its resources, or is it caught in efforts that are not always cost-conscious?), it is important to learn how the cognitive scaffolding of an organization may have developed; this scaffolding is sustained by the culture of that organization, and it is capable of making an organization effective and efficient or caught in its "trained incapacity" (a term coined by Veblen, 1997).

Summary and Conclusions

Many disciplines have contributed to the ways in which cognitive theory is used to understand human thought and its consequent behavior, and have fed the development of cognitive interventions in the field of social work. The early developments of computer processing and logic, the anthropological and sociological examinations of culture and society, and the psychological understanding of cognitive development and intervention have all contributed to social work's person-in-environment perspective, encouraging the use of cognitive theory at multiple levels. Cognitive theory is a very useful tool in social work practice, community organizing, social casework, and nonprofit management, as well as clinical social work. While it has emerged as a popular form of intervention at the level of social work practice with individuals and families, it also has immense potential for social work practice with groups, communities, and organizations.

References

Austad, C. S. (2009). *Counseling and psychotherapy today: Theory, practice and research.* New York: McGraw Hill.

Bates, E. (1977). *Models of madness.* St. Lucia, Queensland: University of Queensland Press.

Beck, A. T. (1976). *Cognitive therapy and the emotional disorders.* New York: International Universities Press.

Beck, A. T., Rush, A. J., Shaw, B. F., & Emery, G. (1979). *Cognitive therapy of depression.* New York: The Guilford Press.

Beck, A. T., Emery, G., & Greenberg, R. L. (1985). *Anxiety disorders and phobias: A cognitive perspective.* New York: The Guilford Press.

Beeghley, L. (2007). *The structure of social stratification in the U.S.* Boston: Allyn & Bacon.

Begley, S. (2009). What's in a word? Language may shape our thoughts. *Newsweek,* July 20, p. 31.

Berger, P. L. (1977). *Facing up to modernity.* New York: Basic Books.

Berger, P. L., & Luckman, J. (1966). *The social construction of reality: a treatise in the sociology of knowledge.* Garden City, NY: Doubleday.

Berlin, S. B. (2002). *Clinical social work practice: A cognitive-integrative perspective.* New York: Oxford University Press.

Berlin, S. B., & Barden, J. E. (2000). Thinking differently: The cognitive-integrative approach to changing the mind. In P. Allen-Meares & C. Garvin (Eds.), *The handbook of social work direct practice.* London: Sage Publications.

Bhattacharya, D. (1984). *Paglami.* Bloomington, IN: Indiana University.

Chatterjee, P. (1984). Cognitive theories and social work practice. *Social Service Review,* March, 63–79.

Chatterjee, P. (2009). *A story of ambivalent modernization in Bangladesh and West Bengal: The rise and fall of Bengali elitism in South Asia.* New York: Peter Lang.

CNN.com/world. (2009, July 13). *Somali-American's family: Who sent son to die?* Retrieved from www.cnn.com/2009/WORLD/africa/07/13/somalia.american.killed/index.html.

Corcoran, J. (2006). *Cognitive-behavioral methods for social workers: A workbook.* Boston: Allyn & Bacon.

Corey, G. (2009). *Theory and practice of counseling and psychotherapy.* CA: Thompson Brooks/Cole.

Coyle, G. L. (1937). *Studies in group behavior.* New York: Harper and Brothers.

Danesi, M., & Perron, P. (1999). *Analyzing cultures.* Bloomington, IN: Indiana University Press.

Datilio, F. M., & Padesky, C. A. (1990). *Cognitive therapy with couples.* FL: Professional Resource Exchange.

Dobson, K. S. (2001). *Handbook of cognitive-behavioral therapies.* New York: The Guilford Press.

Ellis, A., & Bernard, M. E. (1985). *Clinical applications of rational-emotive therapy.* New York: Plenum Press.

Ellis, T. E. (2006). *Cognition and suicide: Theory, research and therapy.* American Psychological Association.

Emery, G., Hollon, S. D., & Bedrosian, R. C. (1981). *New directions in cognitive therapy.* New York: The Guilford Press.

Epstein, L., & Brown, L. B. (2002). *Brief treatment and a new look at the task-centered approach.* Boston: Allyn & Bacon.

Epstein, N. B., & Baucom, D. H. (2002). *Enhanced cognitive-behavioral therapy for couples.* American Psychological Association Press.

Fairburn, C. G. (2008). *Cognitive behavior therapy and eating disorders.* New York: Guilford Press.

Foa, E., Keane, T. M., & Friedman, M. J. (2000). *Effective treatments for PTSD.* New York: The Guilford Press.

Freire, P. (1970). *Pedagogy of the oppressed.* New York: Seabury Press.

Fortune, A. E. (1985). *Task-centered practice with families and groups.* New York: Springer Publishing Company.

Gambrill, E. (2006). *Social work practice: A critical thinker's guide* (2nd ed.). Oxford University Press.

Geertz, C. (1973). *The interpretation of cultures.* New York: Basic Books.

Glasser, W. (1988). *Using reality therapy.* New York: Harper & Row.

Glasser, W. (2001). *Counseling with choice theory.* New York: Harper & Row.

Goffman, E. (1974). *Frame analysis: An essay on the organization of experience.* New York: Harper & Row.

Goldstein, H. (1965). *A rational approach to social casework.* New York: Association Press.

Goldstein, H. (1982). Cognitive approaches to direct practice. *Social Service Review,* 539–555.

Granvold, D. K. (1994). Concepts and methods of cognitive treatment. In D. K. Granvold (Ed.), *Cognitive and behavioral treatment: Methods and applications.* Pacific Grove, CA: Brooks/Cole.

Hays, P. A., & Iwamasa, G. Y. (2006). *Culturally responsive cognitive-behavioral therapy.* American Psychological Association Press.

Hjelle, L. A., & Ziegler, D. J. (1976). *Personality theories: Basic assumptions, research, and applications.* New York: McGraw-Hill Book Company.

Hollingshead, A. (1975). *Four factor index of social structure.* Unpublished manuscript, Yale University, New Haven, CT.

Jaffee, D. (1998). *Levels of socio-economic development theory* (2nd ed.). New York: Praeger Publishers.

Kanjirathinkal, M. (1990). *A sociological critique of theories of cognitive development: The limitations of Piaget and Kohlberg.* Lewistown, NY: Edwin Mellen Press.

Kelly, G. (1955). *The psychology of personal constructs.* New York: Norton & Co.

Kelly, G. (1958). Man's construction of his alternatives. In G. Lindzey (Ed.), *Assessment of human motives.* New York: Holt, Rinehart & Winston.

Kingdon, D. G., & Turkington, D. (2004). *Cognitive therapy of schizophrenia.* New York: The Guilford Press.

Kohlberg, L. (1969). *Stages in the development of moral thought and action.* New York: Holt.

Lantz, J. (1996). Cognitive theory and social work treatment. In F. Turner (Ed.), *Social work treatment.* New York: The Free Press.

Leahy, R. L. (2004). *Contemporary cognitive therapy: Theory, research and practice.* New York: The Guilford Press.

Leahy, R. L., & Dowd, T.E . (2002). *Clinical advances in cognitive psychotherapy.* New York: Springer Publishing Company.

Lévy-Bruhl, L. (1926). *How natives think.* London: Allen & Unwin.

Linehan, M. (1993). *Cognitive behavioral treatment of borderline personality disorder.* New York: Guilford Press.

Malinowski, B. (1955). *Magic, science and religion and other essays.* New York: Doubleday & Co.

Meichenbaum, D. (1996). Stress inoculation training for coping with stressors. *The Clinical Psychologist, 49,* 4–7.

Merriam, G., & Merriam, C. (1957). Webster's New Collegiate Dictionary. Springfield, MA: G. & C. Merriam.

Morris, R., Tarassenko, L., & Kenward, M. (2006). *Cognitive systems: Information processing meets brain science.* New York: Elsevier Academic Press.

Nurius, P. S. (2008). Cognition and social cognitive theory. In T. Mizrahi & L. E. Davis (Eds.), *Encyclopedia of social work* (20th ed.). Washington, DC: NASW Press.

Parsons, T. (1951). *The social system.* Glencoe, IL: The Free Press.

Piaget, J. (1932). *The moral judgment of the child.* London: Routledge and Kegan Paul.

Piaget, J. (1951). *The child's perception of the world.* Baltimore, MD: Rowman & Littlefield Publishers.

Reid, W. J. (1978). *The task-centered system.* New York: Columbia University Press.

Robbins, S. P., Chatterjee, P., & Canda, E. R. (2006). *Contemporary human behavior theory* (2nd ed.). Boston: Pearson Publishers.

Rothbaum, B. O., Meadows, E.A., Resick, P., & Foy, D. W. (2000). Cognitive-behavioral therapy. In E. B. Foa, T. M. Keane, & M. J. Friedman (Eds.). *Effective treatments for PTSD.* New York: The Guilford Press.

Saleeby, D. (2005). *Strengths perspective in social work practice.* New York: Allyn & Bacon, Inc.

Schein, E. (2004). *Organizational culture and leadership.* San Francisco, CA: Jossey-Bass.

Steketee, G. (2006). *Cognitive therapy for obsessive-compulsive disorder.* New York: New Harbinger.

Swedberg, R. (1990). *Economics and sociology: Redefining their boundaries.* Princeton, NJ: Princeton University Press.

Swedberg, R. (2003). *Principles of economic sociology.* Princeton, NJ: Princeton University Press.

Thomas, W. I. (1923). *The unadjusted girl.* Boston: Little, Brown.

Thomas, W. I., & Znaniecki, F. (1918). *The Polish peasant in Europe and America.* Boston: R. G. Badger.

Trompenaars, F., & Hampden-Turner, C. (1997). *Riding the waves of culture: Understanding cultural diversity in business.* London: Nicholas Brealey Publishing.

Veblen, T. (1997). *Essays in our changing order.* New York: Transaction Publishers.

Walsh, J. (2006). *Theories for direct social work practice.* UK: Thomson Brooks/Cole.

Walsh, J. (2008). Cognitive therapy. In: *Encyclopedia of social work* (20th ed., vol. 1). New York: Oxford University Press.

Weber, M. (1999). *Essays in economic sociology.* Edited by R. Swedberg. Princeton, NJ: Princeton University Press.

Wenzel, A., Brown, G. K., & Beck, A. T. (2009). *Cognitive therapy for suicidal patients: Scientific and clinical applications.* American Psychological Association Publishers.

Werner, H. D. (1982). *Cognitive therapy: A humanistic approach.* New York: The Free Press.

White, M., & Epstein, D. (1990). *Narrative means to therapeutic ends.* New York: Norton.

Wilson, E. O. (1978). *On human nature.* Boston: Harvard University Press.

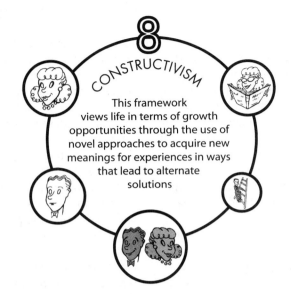

This framework views life in terms of growth opportunities through the use of novel approaches to acquire new meanings for experiences in ways that lead to alternate solutions

Constructivism: A Conceptual Framework for Social Work Treatment

Donald E. Carpenter

Introduction

Constructivism as a conceptual framework for social work practice is relatively new. While various practice perspectives and treatment approaches in social work have historically reflected constructivist concepts and principles, only recently have these been recognized as such. Constructivist ideas, however, have a long history in human thought, having found expression in such diverse fields as art, mathematics, literary criticism, philosophy, the social and behavioral sciences, and related helping professions. Any exhaustive examination of constructivism for its relevance to human behavior alone would lead to the complex deliberations of philosophers on metaphysics, epistemology, and ontology as well as the studies of psychologists on the nature of perception, cognition, and learning,

and more recently an exploration of the burgeoning field of neuroscience would need to be included. While an investigation of this scale is obviously beyond the scope of this chapter, aspects of these fields of inquiry will be visited in formulating a constructivist conceptual framework for social work practice.

In classifying the various theory development approaches taken by social work, Turner (1986) identified one of these as the introduction of "new thought systems" (e.g., role theory, ego psychology, and systems theory) (p. 8). Constructivism, as will be shown in this chapter, is indeed a new system of thought for social work and is specifically identified here as a philosophical-behavioral-methodological thought system. Philosophically, constructivism is concerned with the nature of reality and being (metaphysics and ontology) and the nature and acquisition of human knowledge (epistemology). The behavioral aspect pertains to certain understandings of human perception and cognition, personal and interpersonal dynamics, and the nature and execution of change. From the philosophical and behavioral components, methodological implications emerge for social work practice. It will also be shown that constructivism as a postmodern relativist theory can be deployed as a meta-theory for attaining a deeper understanding of the nature of modern or realist theories.

It should be clarified at the outset that constructivism is not a practice theory but a conceptual framework that can inform given practice theories, in the sense that ecological-systems theory informs the Life Model of practice, as one example. While general practice guidelines can be inferred from constructivist concepts and principles, some of which will be identified later in this chapter, specific and detailed practice guidelines reflecting constructivism as a conceptual framework can be found in a number of practice theories (e.g., Narrative and Solution-Focused theories) described elsewhere in this volume.

Historical Foundations

Historical Context

Constructivism as a thought system is best understood when placed in a context of major historical ideas about reality (ontology) and how human knowledge develops (epistemology). Three historical periods can be identified in the evolution of major human belief systems—premodern, modern, and postmodern—each characterized by certain approaches to understanding ourselves as humans, the world, and indeed the universe. These understandings become reflected in the nature of the theories that we devise for helping people with psychosocial problems. Following is an overview of human belief systems based on Sexton (1997), adapted from Mahoney (1991).

During the premodern period (the sixth century BC through the Middle Ages), idealism, religion, and faith mixed with rationalism were the primary mechanisms employed for understanding the major questions raised about human life. During the modern era (from the

Renaissance to the end of the 19th century), the predominate approaches for understanding the world were empiricism (sense experience is the only true source of knowledge), logical positivism (observation is the prime means of accessing truth), and scientific methodology (a highly rational approach to objective truths, primarily through testing hypotheses of deductive theories).

Whereas the premodern and modern periods stressed the discovery of objective knowledge and fixed truths, the postmodern/constructivist era stresses the creation of knowledge and relativity of truth. The proposition that knowledge is constructed, not discovered, is a major contribution of constructivism to social work practice theory, the implications of which will be discussed in a subsequent section of this chapter.

During this postmodern/constructivist era (the current era) there is less emphasis on the validity of knowledge (characteristic of an emphasis in "scientific research" of the modern era) but rather an emphasis on the viability of knowledge and increasing concern with how we know what we think we know (Sexton, 1997, pp. 4–6).

Early Beginnings of Constructivism

While constructivism has gained visibility in the social and behavioral sciences only recently in historical terms, the deepest roots of constructivism as a general theory lie in the soil of antiquity (i.e., the premodern era). The Greek Sophist Protagoras of Abdera (c. 490–c. 420 BC) maintained that "humans are the measure of all things—of things that are, that they are, of things that are not, that they are not." For Protagoras there was no "objective" world and no perception any truer than another, although some were more useful and should be followed (Ide, 1995, p. 752). Emanuel Kant (1724–1804) in his *Critique of Pure Reason* (1781/1938) argued that the human mind has an inherent structure that it imposes on both thought and experience and that a priori knowledge (knowledge independent of or prior to experience) is possible and in fact occurs. Kant maintained that the mind is not a passive slate upon which experience is written but a proactive organ-molding experience. The Kantian epistemological tradition concerning the nature and acquisition of knowledge, frequently cited as a major foundation block of constructivism, maintained that human knowledge is ultimately a function of the interaction of the world of experience (empirical) and the basic nature (a priori state) of the human mind.

Another major constructivist, Hans Vaihinger (1852–1933) emphasized the importance of cognitive processes in determining behavior. Vaihinger formulated the philosophy of "as if," which postulates that we hold concepts and beliefs as if they were true because of their utility (Mahoney, 1991, pp. 97–99). Vaihinger's "as if" concept is related, though not identical, to the postmodern/constructivist concept of viability: an idea or action is viable if it works relative to a stated purpose and need not represent some assumed fixed quality or truth, as a state of validity is presumed to establish.

The epistemological position of philosophers such as Protagoras and Kant is in direct opposition to that of the Lockean empiricists. John Locke (1632–1704) maintained that knowledge is imparted to the human mind from an external objective world by way of the senses and that, contrary to what Kant had maintained, a priori knowledge is not possible (Wolterstorff, 1995, pp. 437–440).

More Recent Contributions

In more recent times, the developmental psychologist Jean Piaget (1886–1980), from his studies in child development, formulated a theory of developmental epistemology. Piaget concluded that the newborn comes equipped with mental regulatory mechanisms (evolutionary in origin), which in interaction with the child's environment result in the development of intelligence (1929, 1950, 1970). The cognitive psychologist George Kelly has contributed significantly to constructivism with his theory of personal constructs, which are the means by which an individual construes, perceives, interprets, understands, predicts, and controls his or her world (Kelly, 1955). For Kelly, mental constructs are imposed on the world, not imposed by the world on the mind. Another psychologist, Paul Watzlawick (1976, 1984, 1990), must also be cited as a major contributor to modern constructivist theory, especially to constructivist epistemology, in his examination of our assumed

"realness" of an "objective" world and of the possibility of constructing more desirable individual worlds. Two other theoreticians, Ernst von Glaserfeld (1984) and Heinz von Foerster (1984), must be credited for significant contributions to constructivism. Each has accomplished important formulations of that aspect of constructivist epistemology concerned with the nature of reality as observer-dependent.

Two Chilean neurobiologists, Humberto Maturana and Francisco Varela, have exerted perhaps the most basic influence on present-day constructivist thought in the biological and behavioral sciences, and this influence has most recently found its way into the behavioral helping professions. From their experimentation with animals have come some rather astounding conclusions about the basic organization of living systems and the nature of the influence of perception on behavior (Maturana, 1980; Maturana & Varela, 1987). According to Maturana and Varela, living systems are *autopoietic* or self-organizing. The behaviors of organisms are not directly influenced by their mediums (environments) but are determined by their structure—that is, their neurophysiological makeup (Maturana & Varela, 1987, pp. 95–97). The neurobiological contributions of Maturana and Varela to constructivist theory are seen to hold important implications for social work practice theory and will be drawn on throughout the formulation here of a constructivist framework for social work practice.

Path into Social Work

Constructivism has been making its way quietly along the path into social work theory for some time, but only recently has been recognized as such. All theoretical frameworks that stress the importance of the individual's internal processes, especially perception and cognition, for understanding human behavior have kinship with constructivism. Some of these will be discussed in a later section of this chapter comparing constructivism with other theories that actually have constructivist elements that have traditionally gone unrecognized.

Examples of contributions to the application of constructivism to social work are Fisher (1991), Laird (1993), Carpenter (1996), and

Granvold (2001). Other specific case applications are Dean and Fenby (1989), Hartman (1991), Dean and Fleck-Henderson (1992), Greene and Lee (2002), and Tijerina (2009).

Variants of Constructivism

While the general theory of constructivism is clearly rooted in philosophical relativism, two major varieties of the theory can be identified. Mahoney (1991) makes a clear distinction between the two:

Radical constructivism is on the idealist end of the spectrum and has been differentially endorsed and expressed by Heinz von Foerster, Ernst von Glaserfeld, Humberto Maturana, Francisco Varela, and Paul Watzlawick. This perspective is most elegantly expressed in theory and research on the concept of *autopoiesis* (self-organizing systems). ... In its most extreme expressions, radical constructivism comes close to the classical position of ontological idealism, arguing that there is no (even hypothetical) reality beyond our personal experience.

Critical constructivists, on the other hand, do not deny the existence and influence of an unknowable but inescapable real world. They are, instead, critical or hypothetical realists, admitting that the universe is populated with entities we call "objects" but denying that we that we can ever "directly" know them. Representatives of modern critical constructivism include Guidano, Hayek, Kelly, myself (Mahoney) Piaget, and Weimer. For critical constructivists, the individual is not a self-sufficient, sole producer of his or her own experience. Rather, the individual is conceived as a "co-creator" or "co-constructor" of personal realities, with the prefix *co* emphasizing an interactive interdependence with their social and physical environments. (p. 111)

The radical variety of constructivism is so termed because of its assumptions about the nature of reality. It questions certain basic beliefs, the validity of which most take for granted. For example, it questions our "common-sense" notion that reality is obviously what all competent observers know is "real" or "true" about the world in which we live. It maintains that instead of there being only one reality, as might seem to be the case, there are as many "realities" as there are perceivers of reality (Goodman, 1972, pp. 31–32; Watzlawick, 1990, pp. 131–151). Common sense would have us believe with Gertrude Stein, for instance, that "a

rose is a rose is a rose" because all competent observers agree that a certain kind of flower *is* a rose and not an elephant. Radical constructivists would maintain, however, that greater accuracy is achieved by saying there are as many "rose realities" as there are individuals who experience the things we call roses. Each individual will experience "a rose" in some different way and derive a somewhat different meaning from the experience than all other individuals, but each will still call it a rose. By the same token, a therapist in her office with a mother, father, and three children is not in the presence of *a* family but as *many* families as there are family observers (the family members plus the therapist). For the radical constructivist, the roses and families that we ordinarily refer to are products of our nervous system. Radical constructivism moves sharply away from the Newtonian-Cartesian certainty of a single reality and a knowable objective world.

In contrast to radical constructivism, critical constructivism, which is frequently referred to in the literature as "social constructivism," does not deny the existence of an objective external world to which we all react. It does maintain, however, that we cannot "know" this world directly but only indirectly through the filtering mechanisms of perception, cognition, affect, belief systems, and language.

Presuppositions of Constructivism

Philosophical Relativism

The philosophical component of constructivism reflects the basic conceptions of a school of thought in Western philosophy known as *epistemological relativism*. This position holds that nothing is universally true and that the world cannot be attributed intrinsic characteristics; there are only different ways of interpreting it (Pojman, 1995, p. 690). Cognitive (epistemological) relativism is the view that truth and logic are always formulated in the framework of, and are relative to, a given thought-world with its own language (Elkana, 1978, p. 312). The relativist position denies certainties, absolutes, and permanence. In this vein, the philosopher Nelson Goodman (1972), a proponent of philosophical relativism, writes:

There are very many different equally true descriptions of the world and their truth is the only standard of their faithfulness. And when we say of them that they all involve conventionalizations, we are saying that no one of these different descriptions is *exclusively* true, since the others are also true. None of them tells us *the* way the world is, but each of them tells us *a* way the world is. (pp. 30–31)

In opposition to the position of relativism lies that of *philosophical realism*, which maintains essentially opposite notions about the "realness" and "objective" existence of the world:

Reality is a singular, stable order of events and objects external to and independent of mind and mental processes … the senses and other technical methods of observation are said to reveal, albeit imperfectly, regularities and principles of reality. (Mahoney, 1991, p. 36)

While realists hold the position of an ontologically existing world that is not observer-dependent for its reality, relativists contend that such a world, while seeming to exist, is actually observer-dependent relative to the nature of the perceptual and cognitive apparatus of human beings, which reveal not *a* world, but, as Goodman says, *versions* of a world (Goodman, 1984, pp. 29–34). It is the relativist position that is the philosophical bedrock of constructivism.

Constructivist Epistemology

An age-old problem for philosophers pertains to what is knowable by humans and the means by which knowledge is acquired. In constructivist epistemology, knowledge is not composed of impressions of an objective world or "reality" existing independently of knowers but instead is the creation of individual knowers, resulting in as many worlds or "realities" as there are world/reality observers. If this is so, how then do individuals seem to experience a common objective world? Constructivists maintain that what we refer to as common human experiences are based on a consensual world of language, thought, and experience. Boiled down to its essence, *reality is what we agree on.* The "we" can refer to a unit as small as a dyad or as large as a society. For example, during the premodern era of history, a common understanding was that the earth was flat and the sun circled around it. That was our "reality," upon which our beliefs and actions were

based. World explorers carefully plotted their routes across the seas so as not to sail off the edge of the earth. We thought (agreed) this was the "truth" of earth geography. At this present point in history, however, based on the scientific knowledge of geographers and astronomers, we say this understanding was not true. The earth is spherical, and orbits the sun; "we" (most people) now believe this to be true. However, to further illustrate the constructivist concept that truth is agreement, there are a few individuals who still believe what most people of the premodern era believed about the shape of the earth and the danger of going over the "edge." This small number of individuals constitutes another "we," and they tell each other that "we believe the earth is flat": this is their "truth" and their "reality." (Interested readers can check "flat earth beliefs" on the Internet.)

A practice-related example of the constructivist conception of "true" and "real" is provided by Cottone (2007):

What becomes real, for instance, about drugs to teenagers in a drug culture may be quite different than what is "real" to a parental system linked to a drug prohibitionist culture; therefore, whether drugs can be labeled as "good" or "bad" is defined in the communities of understanding within which a teenager or a parent is imbedded. And of course, a counselor, being imbedded in the sociolegal system, is limited when defining acceptable behavior related to use of illegal substances. So, in effect, social constructivism appears to form a triangle with objectivism and subjectivism, in a position outside the objectivism-subjectivism continuum and representing a different view about how things are known to be "true" i.e., truth derives from consensualizing [agreement]. (Social Constructivism Movement section, para. 4)

To appreciate the constructivist view of the nature of human knowledge and its acquisition requires a willingness to set aside some very basic prevalent beliefs about the phenomenon we have called "knowledge." It requires suspending notions of certainty, realness, objectivity, and externality and the belief that these are indeed the anchors of human experience:

… the phenomenon of knowing cannot be taken as though there were 'facts' or objects out there that we grasp and store in our head. The experience of anything out there is validated in a special way by the human structure, which makes possible 'the thing' that arises in the description ... *every act of knowing brings forth a world.* (Maturana & Varela, 1987, pp. 25–26)

The major contributions to epistemological theory have traditionally come from philosophy and psychology. Constructivist epistemology, however, has acquired foundation contributions from the experimental work and theoretical formulations of the two biologists noted earlier, Umberto Maturana and Francisco Varela. Much of what they have contributed runs counter to traditional realist views. The following, pertaining to the nature of the functional relationship between the brain and the environment, is an example:

The nervous system does not "pick up information" from the environment, as we often hear. On the contrary, it brings forth a world by specifying what patterns of the environment are perturbations (stimuli) and what changes trigger them in the organism. The popular metaphor of calling the brain an "information-processing device" is not only ambiguous but patently wrong. (Maturana & Varela, 1987, p. 169)

The central importance of constructivist epistemology for practice is that people behave and lead their lives based on what *they* believe to be true and real, and this is where the practitioner must initially meet his or her clients if effective help is to be given. An case example is provided in a subsequent section of this chapter.

Conceptual Framework

Structure Determinism

The conceptual framework for constructivism as formulated here draws primarily on the neuro-biological conceptions of Maturana, Varela, and associates. In gathering evidence in support of their concept of organisms as closed systems, they conducted several biological experiments. One of these, cited by Bell (1985), is representative of the nature and general outcome of the experiments:

[Maturana] demonstrated that no correlation could be established between colors (as defined by spectral energies and the relations of activity of retinal ganglion cells of either pigeons or human beings) (Maturana, Urbe, & Frenk, 1968). Instead, he found that the nervous system demonstrated its own *internal* correlations: the relations of activity of retinal ganglion

cells correlated with color-naming behavior of the organism (but did not correlate with the actual colors as defined by spectral energies). The implication of this finding is that the nervous system functions as a closed, internally consistent system and does *not* contain representations or coded transforms of the environment. (p. 6)

Efran, Lukens, and Lukens (1990) elaborate on this radically different conception of the relationship between the neurophysiological makeup of the individual and the environment:

People are brought up to believe they perceive the outside world. The visual system, for example, appears to provide direct and immediate access to our surroundings. The eyes are said to be our windows of the world. However, although the eyelids open, the neurons of the retina do not. Energy waves bump up against the retinal surface ... but outside light cannot get in ... Obviously, experiences we attribute to light—as well as all our other experiences—are created entirely within our own system ... This is evident in dreams, in response to sharp blows (when we "see" stars), when neurons are directly touched with electrical probes, and when chemical substances are ingested. At a fireworks display, there may be a lot going on outside, but nevertheless the sparkling colors we see are internal creations. That we are fooled into believing that we "see" the world outside dramatizes how well coupled we are with our environment. (pp. 67–68)

Based on this conception, what one actually "sees" in a visual experience is not an "outside" world but the nervous system itself, a counterintuitive conception indeed.

An important consequence of the structure-determined state of organisms is immunity to the reception of "information." Contrary to prevalent views in communications and systems theories, Maturana and Varela hold that structure determined systems are informationally closed. What Maturana and Varela call instructive interaction, which is the direct influence of one person on another, is held to be impossible. Mahoney (1991) explains:

The ongoing structural changes (and exchanges) that living systems undergo are the result of "perturbations," which can arise from interactions with their medium (environment) or, recursively, with themselves. These perturbations "trigger" structural changes in the organism but do not automatically convey information about the nature or properties of the perturbing entity. They are not, in other words, "instructive" in the traditional sense of that term. Perturbations do not "cause" changes in the organism by putting something into it (like "information"), they simply trigger changes of state that are structure-determined by the organism. From this perspective, "information" is not something transferred or processed. Instead, "information" is literally, translated from its Latin origin: *in formare*, "that which is formed from within." (p. 392)

Another important aspect of structure determinism pertains, again, to neurobiological considerations and distinguishes *feedback* (information processing) from the constructivist concept of *feedforward* (information creating). Mahoney (1991) provides an example of feedforward:

On the assumption that visual experience is highly correlated with neurochemical activity in the visual cortex, only about 20% of that activity can be attributed to impulses from the retina ... impulses from the retina can influence—but do not specify—activity in the visual cortex. On the average, as much as 80% of what we "see" may be a tacit construction "fed forward" from the superior colliculus, the hypothalamus, the reticular formation, and the visual cortex itself. (p. 101)

In other words, the elements that finally result in a visual experience point to an "inside-in" process (feedforward) rather than an "outside-in" process as in feedback. Structure determinism, and autopoiesis, to be discussed in the following section, form the cornerstones of constructivist theory as formulated by Maturana and Varela.

Autopoiesis

Because they are structure-determined and organizationally closed, living systems are said to be *autopoietic* or self-organizing entities. Autopoietic entities are autonomous in the sense that they survive, prosper, or perish under the "self-law" of their own makeup (Mahoney, 1991, p. 393). In contrast to a state of autopoiesis is that of *allopoiesis*, which is the essential principle of systems theory. A number of parts interrelate among themselves to produce a specified outcome. An example is an automobile. It is composed of a number of interrelated parts that work in unison to propel it down the road, but it has no capacity to produce and maintain itself as an autopoietic system does:

Autopoietic entities, because of the way they are structurally organized, are engaged in the process of producing more of themselves. This process is manifest at every level of organization, from the cell to the colony. Cells grow and split, forming additional like-structured cells. Parents have offspring, perpetuating the family line ... Living, from the ingestion of food to the excretion of waste, consists of cycles of self-production. For a living system there is a unity between product and process: In other words, the major line of work for a living system is creating more of itself (Efran et al., 1990, p. 47)

Structural Coupling

It is the constructivist principle of *structural coupling* that explains how autopoietic individuals interact with entities other than themselves and their own nervous systems. The principle of structural coupling also allows constructivist theory to avoid the epistemological pitfall of solipsism or a state of complete self-reference. Structural coupling corresponds roughly to the more traditional concept of "interpersonal interaction" that takes place in a "relationship" between individuals but with the important difference that the interaction is seen to be between closed, not open systems:

... Maturana and Varela assert that the interactions of living systems with their medium [environment] are "structure determined," meaning that changes in either are "triggered" (as contrasted with "produced") by their interaction. Thus, learning does not consist of being "instructed" by external agents or environments. Maturana and Varela have also asserted that learning cannot consist of the "pick-up" of prepackaged information from outside the living system, nor can it be understood as the acquisition of internalized "representations" of its medium. The changes exhibited by an organism in the course of its "structural coupling" with its medium reflect the organization and structure of the organism. They do not offer information about the medium itself (Mahoney, 1991, p. 391)

Episodes of interactions between individuals and their environments are instigated through mutual perturbations or triggering stimuli. These perturbations form the basis for changes in each (person and environment) but do not determine the changes, which are instead brought about by the nature of their respective structures. One person does not "cause" another person to do anything; this would be *instructive interaction*, or direct influence, which, according to Maturana and Varela, is not possible because of the closed nature of each person as a system.

Based on its epistemology, which blurs subject–object distinctions and questions notions of objectivity and reality, constructivism shift us to a "many worlds" frame of reference and away from normative views of truth and falsehood, right and wrong, functional and dysfunctional. Significant practice implications arise from the "many worlds" constructivist way of thinking about human behavior and experience.

Implications for Assessment, Diagnosis, and Treatment

Implications for Assessment

The case assessment process involves the knottiest of all problems in understanding human behavior—that of causality. Positivist causal explanations have assumed that a great deal of both individual and aggregate behavior is the direct result of identifiable "external" influences. Constructivist causal assumptions, however, are based on a view of the nature of the human nervous system and its relationship to the environment. This view maintains that the nervous system can only be perturbed or "bumped up against" but not "entered" by external stimuli, indicating a closed system. What, then, are some constructivist implications for assessment if the individual is viewed as a structure-determined closed system?

In constructivist theory, the individual is the only unit of attention seen to have ontological existence. Aggregate units such as family, group, and community are reifications existing only in language and thought and are devoid of ontological existence. While the term "system" is used in constructivist-based practice theories, it is only a convenient term referring to two or more individuals in relation to each other or to an individual made up of various biopsychological components. The constructivist practitioner may think in terms of working with systems but keeps in mind that there are as many "systems" involved in a case as there are system observers (i.e., clients and others). A major implication of this for assessment is that the practitioner must bring to each client case a "many worlds" mindset and from within this mindset must dedicate himself or herself to learning as much as possible about each individual client's ongoing views, understandings, and intentions toward self and others concerning problems being discussed. It is the client's sensing that the practitioner's main concern is to learn about him or her as a unique individual that conveys to the client a sense of high respect from the practitioner. This sense of being valued and respected helps free the client to develop alternative views or "stories" of problems and to reconstrue or reframe his or her problematic life situation. In this sense, constructivist theory supports the time-honored assessment principle in social work of starting (and staying) where the client is.

On the clinical level, essentially what is assessed in a constructivist-based approach is the client's frame of reference (constructions) pertaining to the problems being discussed, and the nature of reciprocal perturbations between the client and relevant aspects of his or her medium (environment). This is a process representing close collaboration between practitioner and client in which the client is made to feel that it is the practitioner who is learning and he or she who is teaching.

Implications for Diagnosis

Diagnosis, in the sense that it has been used in the so-called medical model by the behavioral helping professions, is not supported by constructivist theory. "What's wrong" is not seen as an entity in the same sense that the physician views a fractured leg or as inflamed appendix as entities having ontological existence. The principle of structure determinism negates the validity of externally imposed predetermined categories and labels. In the approach represented by the *Diagnostic and Statistical Manual of Mental Disorders*, for example, the diagnostic task in a case falls to the practitioner and his or her skill in use of the classification system applied to a particular client's "symptoms." The client's role becomes that of passive recipient of the practitioner's expertise. A constructivist-based approach to developing ideas about the nature of problems stresses the need for practitioner–client collaboration and mutuality, with the expert role of the practitioner being redefined from its usual meaning. The practitioner's expertise is in assuming a learning stance with the client by approaching each case assuming he or she knows nothing about the client. A case example in the next section illustrates this stance.

Treatment Implications

While radical and critical constructivism were previously discussed as the two major varieties of constructivism, considerations for treatment as discussed here will refer predominately to the assumptions of critical constructivism, generally referred to in the social work literature as *social constructivism* (see, for example, Cottone, 2007). Social constructivism assumes the existence of an objective reality but one that is knowable only through perception, language, and mentation. In the social constructivism view, the "reality" of structural and psychosocial social problems is fully acknowledged.

In more traditional practice approaches, especially psychodynamic ones, uncovering the "real problem" in a case has been seen as an essential job for the practitioner. The "real problem" concept implies that there is an objective pathological/dysfunctional condition of the client and/or his or her situation that can be discovered through the clinical skills of the practitioner, as when the physician finds malignant cells and diagnoses cancer—the "real" problem underlying the patient's pain and other symptoms. In constructivist-based assessment and treatment, however, no "real" problem is assumed to exist in the sense that there is an underlying problem with objective consequence not yet glimpsed by the client but that the practitioner will help him or her discover. This should not be misconstrued to mean that in the constructivist view no problem exists. Through the lens of critical constructivism (social constructivism) clients are seen as co-constructing their personal realities through interdependence with their social and physical environment. Contrary to a widespread practice among practitioners in the behavioral helping professions, the practitioner using a constructivist-based treatment methodology (e.g., narrative therapy) would not attempt to get the client to "own his problem" but to cognitively divest himself or herself of it instead.

For some cases dealt with in a narrative approach to treatment, separating the problem from the person is seen to be essential. A technique called "externalizing the problem" is frequently used, often with dramatic positive results (see, for example, White, 1989; O'Hanlon, 1994, p. 24). It is believed that externalizing the problem (essentially a process of giving it a name as apart from the client) helps free the client to view the problem as an adversary outside instead of inside of self, thus freeing him or her to develop alternative problem versions and solutions. This is thought to be especially helpful in cases where the client has seemed to incorporate the problem with his or her identity, for example as in anorexia.

Client Self-Determination. The observance of client self-determination has been held as a major intervention mandate in social work from the beginnings of the profession. Constructivism views self-determination not only as a treatment mandate to be followed but as a natural state of the person based on the individual's structure-determined, autopoietic nature. If the responses of individuals are structure-determined, they are by definition self-determining. The practitioner has no option of respecting or not respecting this as a practice principle. A practitioner could believe that he or she was executing a "controlling" technique of some kind (e.g., giving a client paradoxical instructions); however, the client's response would not be determined by the paradoxical instructions, but only selected by them— that is, they would "trigger" some response but would not determine what response, which would be brought about by the individual's neurophysiological structure and psychological makeup. However, acknowledging the client's self-determining nature does not mean accepting everything the client might want to do. "While accepting that there are multiple versions of reality, we may choose not to accept versions that are congruent with the perpetuation of racism, domestic violence, school dropouts, runaway teenagers, and other destructive behaviors. We may still try to change uglier versions of reality" (Colapinto, 1985, p. 30).

Practitioner Demands. Because of the counterintuitive flavor of constructivist theory, a certain tolerance for ambiguity is required on the part of practitioners—this making it possible to embrace the "many worlds" perspective of constructivism to accommodate the subjective (constructive) variability among their various clients while at the same time staying attuned to a presumed normative world to which they and their clients must respond. Some may feel uncomfortable with such a paradoxical-sounding professional mindset, while others will have no difficulty.

CASE EXAMPLE

Perhaps one of the most difficult aspects of constructivism to comprehend pertains to its epistemology, which de-emphasizes traditional normative perceptions and understandings of an "objective" world and stresses instead the importance of the individual's subjective idiosyncratic world as the primary basis for behavior. For those who may think constructivism is too philosophical to be practical, a case example may help clarify. The following case vignette, described by Harlene Anderson as cited by Sykes Wylie (1992), illustrates a practice implication of the constructivist epistemological stance.

A family came to therapy after the children had been removed from their home and the mother had gone to a shelter because the father had so severely beat them. The mother came in looking disheveled, wearing house slippers and missing several teeth. The father—a huge man, barefoot, weighing probably 300 pounds and wearing denim, bib-front overalls with no shirt on underneath—began shouting as soon as he was in the room that he was poor, white trash, he'd never be anything, but he would not be told what to do by anybody, he would handle his family the way he saw fit and the only reason he was there was because "the fuckers downtown" had made him come. He also announced, rather mysteriously, that he "hated niggers."

At that point, says Anderson, "everyone behind the mirror instinctively moved their chairs back," except Harriet Roberts, a consultant to the clinic, and a black woman. She got up, walked into the therapy session, calmly introduced herself and with apparently complete sincerity said she wanted to learn more about what he was saying and why he disliked blacks.

Roberts continued the therapy, seeing both husband and wife separately and together (the wife had gone back to live with him, as she always had in the past),

bringing in the man's mother, and the staff from the shelter where the woman had stayed, and consulting with the child protective agency. Gradually, as he became more human in therapy, his behavior outside improved; after the first session, he stopped beating his wife, and when his children were eventually returned, he did not beat them again, either. (p. 28)

A practice principle applied here, derived from constructivist epistemology, was in evidence from the therapist's assumption of the role of learner with the client—a client who at the moment was potentially dangerous to her and had proven himself dangerous to his family:

According to Anderson, the therapists [referring to other therapists subsequently involved] entered therapy with an attitude that they did not know, objectively, better than the man or his wife or the children or any of the other people involved in the case, what constituted universal truths about good and bad families, emotional pathology and health. They did not feel that their professional expertise allowed them to "write the story" for the family. Instead, they believed that in conversation, all these participants together could come up with a better, more humane story that locked nobody out of the process of creating it.

What seems to have happened is that a man who has felt ignored, ostracized and generally loathed for most of his life, meets a therapist who is unafraid of his hostility, uninsulted by his bigotry and unoffended by his repulsive persona. ... He says that for the first time in his life he feels he has been listened to and understood. (pp. 28–29)

By walking calmly into the client's presence saying she wanted to understand more about why he disliked blacks, the consultant demonstrated her respect and unconditional positive regard for him in the face of his anger and implied threats, making it possible for him to reconstrue his constructive world. Through her actions, the consultant recognized the client's structure-determined nature as reflected in his insistence that he would handle his family as he wanted and that he had the right to hate black people. In acknowledging the very being of this man as the only person he could be at the moment, he then became free to reconstrue his meanings closer to those of his medium (environment).

This case analysis reflects narrative intervention concepts (e.g., helping the family rewrite their story to a less destructive one). For more extensive discussion on narrative intervention as a constructivist-based approach see Chapter 20. A case example of treating depression using the narrative approach can be found in Neimeyer (2009, pp. 97–100).

Convergence with Neuroscience

From its birth in antiquity as a philosophical framework, constructivism has evolved in importance from the utility of its various applications. From the structure determinism and autopoiesis formulations of Maturana and Valera, constructivism can now be related to the burgeoning field of neuroscience. While various definitions of neuroscience can be found in the literature, depending on the particular focus of concern, it can be defined appropriately here for relating it to constructivism as the field of study pertaining to the structure and function of the brain and nervous system as related to various aspects of subjective experience and behavior. While an extensive examination of relevant aspects of neuroscience for the further understanding and development of constructivism is beyond the scope of this chapter, the topic is being flagged here for its potential significance. Toomey, Brian, and Ecker (2007) have written about the convergence of constructivism and neuroscience:

Psychological constructivism's central insistence on the active role of the individual in shaping experiential reality receives extensive corroboration from findings on how the brain functions … the neuroscientific community appears to be converging to a consensus regarding the capabilities of individual neurons and neural networks to actively shape and define what is experienced as reality. The emerging paradigm, which has been referred to as *neural constructivism* (Quartz & Sejnowsky, 1997), aligns well with psychological constructivism. (p. 205)

This view points to the influence that specific realist ("objective") entities (i.e., neurons and neuronal networks) exert on our experience of "reality." While constructivists have maintained all along that the human experience of reality is subjective, Toomey et al. now cite specific brain structures responsible. These authors further state: "Not only are neural networks constructivist in their organizing and model of reality, but the way the brain forms and organizes [constructs] those neuronal networks is itself a significantly experience dependent constructivist process" (p. 209).

Developments in both constructivism and neuroscience would seem to warrant further investigation of the ways in which they converge, potentially providing constructivism with a foot in science to help balance its more philosophical aspects. One avenue of investigation that would seem to be productive relating to practice concerns is the nature of the client's subjective experience (psychological constructions) related to specific brain structures thought to be the ground of subjective experiences. Following is an example of a therapist attending to these considerations:

When this author first began reflecting on the possibility of viewing psychotherapy through the lenses of neuroscience, there was a fear that increasing consideration of brain function would lead to coldness and estrangement in the psychotherapy process. It has been surprising that the opposite has been the case. For example, empathy with a client being overwhelmed by flashbacks of previous trauma has seemed stronger when this author has reflected on the implications of research indicating that visual cortex used to encode current information is also required for recall of memories of previously established visual images; while being used during visual memory of a traumatic event, visual cortex is unlikely to be available for processing of current experience. How frightening it must be not to be able to see the therapist even though the client can hear the therapist's voice "in the distance" during a flashback. Clients have seemed remarkably reassured when their inability to see the therapist is explained in terms of possible brain mechanisms for such an experience; the apparently "crazy" experience of not being able to see someone sitting in front of them now makes sense. (Folensbee, 2007, p. 2)

The constructivist element here is the practitioner's acknowledging the "realness" of the client's intense subjective experience (his constructed world harboring a flashback) while staying in touch with another "reality," which was his knowledge and utilization of brain science—an example of a therapist observing the constructivist "many worlds" conception and the relative nature of "truth" and "realness."

In addition to increasing the efficacy of psychotherapy by utilizing knowledge of brain science, Folensbee also sees an additional importance:

Assessment, conceptualization, intervention, and communication in therapy all seem likely to improve when the underlying nature of brain functioning as currently understood is kept in mind during the implementation of psychotherapy. Consideration of psychotherapy in terms of the framework of brain function offers the potential for integrating and coordinating various traditional treatment modalities within a structure that can facilitate communication between proponents of various schools of treatment, and can support collaborative rather than competitive interventions. (p. 186)

While social workers in their formal training typically receive minimal exposure to the topics of neuroscience, rapid advances in behavioral neuroscience with implications for various psychosocial problems dealt with by social workers may bring about increased attention to this area in schools of social work, particularly on master and doctoral levels. Examples for further reading in neuroscience related to psychotherapy can be found in Badenoch (2008), Pliszka (2003), Cozolino (2002), and Gabbard (1992).

Empirical Base

Attitude Toward the Empirical Stance

The constructivist view of positivistic science as a component of constructivist theory and the use of empirical evidence as data in its approach to research has evolved over time. Cole (1992) wrote that "Constructivists do not believe that empirical evidence plays a significant role in evaluation, and therefore the question of whether their position can be empirically supported would be taken by them only as evidence of naïveté" (p. 252). This clearly put constructivism at odds with empiricism, maintaining that it can't be evaluated by something it dismisses as an invalid instrument. While some constructivists would still agree with Cole, a competing stance has gained prominence. Morris (2006) provides a clear statement of and basis for this competing stance in the constructivist approach to research:

The Oxford dictionary defines research as "careful search or inquiry after or for or into; endeavor to discover new or collate old facts, etc., by scientific study of a subject, course of critical investigation." This definition rests on facts and science. It does not state that only variables measured quantitatively are facts, or that science is positivism. Constructivists argue that subjective constructions are facts and that the constructivist approach is science. A subjective description

of living with HIV-AIDS is something that is known to have occurred or be true; it is precise, its existence cannot be ignored, and it is real. All these are criteria for deciding whether something is a fact according to the same Oxford dictionary. The constructivist approach develops knowledge that is systematic, deduced from self-evident truths, and follows consistent principles. Constructivist research thus builds a legitimate body of knowledge using a methodology that is scientific. (p. 196)

In this view of constructivism's relationship to the science paradigm (of which empiricism is the hallmark), which is very different from its earlier stance, we see the manifestation of a basic tenant of constructivism applied to the theory itself—that is, change and variation are inevitable for progress.

Connections to Other Theories

A cursory examination reveals a number of theories that are compatible with constructivism. The phenomenological/humanistic-based theories such as client-centered and existential approaches place heavy emphasis on the client's perceptions, feelings, and attitudes. Other notable examples are the psychodynamic approaches that emphasize the importance of perception, meaning making, and idiosyncratic subjective experience (e.g., the psychosocial model and psychoanalytically oriented approaches). There are, of course, clear connections with approaches based in cognitive theory, with its emphasis on the "knowing" processes and mentation. Agreements are also to be found between the feminist perspective and constructivism. Both maintain that realty is socially constructed and that each person has his or her own reality of equal worth with all others. Both emphasize the oppressive influence that certain sociocultural norms can exert on individuals, families, groups, and organizations and the contribution of these toxic norms to the development of psychosocial problems on all levels. Theoretical perspectives that emphasize the individual's subjective experience and autonomous functioning will find compatibility with constructivism. Theories that may be trapped in an echo chamber hearing only their own voices saying they have found *the* truth will find lesser kinship with the constructivist perspective.

Another observation is being made here concerning constructivism's relation to major value positions and goals of the profession. While constructivism draws attention primarily to the autopoietic nature of the individual (structure-determined, organizationally closed), it should be emphasized that there is no implication of blaming the victim or negating social work's concerns with problems of social justice, discrimination, oppression, domestic violence, or other psychosocial or structural problems of concern to the profession. It does, however, require a *constructed* ever-changing view of reality from client case to client case. Granvold (2001) has written about the compatibility of constructivist approaches with the profession's more traditional ones:

Constructivist treatment is highly compatible with a generalist-eclectic social work practice perspective. Constructivism emphasizes the client's strengths and possibilities (Saleebey, 1992). A collaborative relationship is sought with the client in which the therapist assumes a nonauthoritarian, albeit knowledgeable, stance. Although the primary focus of constructivist assessment and intervention is on the meaning-making process (internal dispositions), in the social work tradition, environmental conditions and social factors are considered in the promotion of the client's immediate goals and ultimate personal development. (p. 315)

The profession's distinctive focus on person-in-situation and the interdependence between people and their environments remains intact with constructivism in the social work theory arena.

Constructivism as Meta-Theory

Constructivism can be seen to connect with other theories on various levels. One of these, which has received little attention in the literature to date, utilizes constructivism as a meta-theory for understanding the deeper nature of theories that have traditionally been classified primarily in the realist/objectivist tradition. Hanson (2007) has argued that a seemingly paradoxical situation, which he calls "epistemic contradiction," is present in many theories used by the counseling professions. As an example, referring to Freud's famous case of Little Hans diagnosed with a displaced Oedipal complex, Hansen writes:

When evaluated from an epistemological perspective, the archeological metaphor is simultaneously constructivist and objectivist. It is constructivist in the sense that psychic artifacts determine individual perception, as Hans's image of horses was internally constructed by ancient, psychically buried conflicts. The counselor (i.e., archeologist), using a psychoanalytic shovel, can dig through the psyche, thereby bringing to light the ancient relics in their pristine form. In this latter sense, the archeological metaphor is objectivist, because the counselor is deemed able to discover the essential nature of the buried conflict, as Freud discovered Hans's Oedipal conflict. Clearly, then, constructivist and objectivist epistemic assumptions are each present in the archeological metaphor. (Epistemic Contradictions in Counseling Theories section, para. 3)

Hansen maintains that this oscillation between subjectivity and objectivity in counseling theories reflects an essential part of human experience that is not simply subjective or objective but both. He further contends that cognitive, humanistic, and even behaviorist theories all have elements of constructivism, although presumably built on foundations of objectivist assumptions. Examining other theories, then, for this epistemic subjective–objective oscillation reveals that not only postmodern theories have constructivist elements in their very architecture (Epistemic Contradictions in Counseling Theories section. para. 8). As stated at the beginning of this chapter, constructivist elements have been around in theories used by social work for some time but not specifically recognized.

Training for Constructivist-Based Practice

Constructivist ideas are beginning to find their way into the HBSE curriculum, practice theory courses, field instruction, and research courses in most schools of social work. To help ensure a thorough grounding in the principles of constructivism as formulated in this chapter, students should have course work pertaining to all three aspects of constructivism as a thought system—philosophical, behavioral, and methodological. For the philosophical aspect, students should have an introductory exposure to the basics of epistemology in order to compare realist and constructivist epistemologies. Study of the behavioral aspect of constructivism should expose students to topics in psychology such as sensation, perception, and cognition presented on a level directly related to basic constructivist concepts such as structure determinism, autopoiesis, and structural coupling. If there is further development of the convergence of constructivism with neuroscience as presented in this chapter, topics in basic behavioral aspects of brain science would be in order. For the methodology aspect, the basic concepts and postulates of constructivism would be translated into assessment/treatment principles, techniques, and strategies, with opportunities provided for students to learn practice applications in their field experiences.

Some of the study topics mentioned above are highly technical and specific to disciplines other than social work, and interdepartmental cooperation might be necessary in providing some of these study areas. This, however, should not deter social work educators. The virtual explosion of findings from the life sciences taking place makes it essential for social work educators to move in the direction of incorporating highly technical/scientific material in course work if social work is to remain a highly credible discipline among related professions such as psychology and psychiatry. For an excellent source of information on some of the ways constructivist ideas have been incorporated into social work curricula, see Laird (1993), *Revisioning Social Work Education: A Social Constructionist Approach*. Although this is a 1993 publication, the material remains sound in terms of its presentation of the theory of constructivism and strategies for training students to incorporate constructivist concept and principles in their practice. Articles by Grossman (1993) and Greene and Lee (2002) also provide sound guidelines for the application of constructivist concepts to practice.

Limitations and Problems

As is always the case with any new theory (and old ones too), controversies and various concerns have arisen about constructivism and its implications for human behavior and change. On the conceptual side, it can be difficult to know if there are substantive differences with nonconstructivist concepts that are seemingly essentially similar. For example, Bell (1985) has questioned the validity of Maturana's view of interpersonal causation:

When Maturana says that causality is impossible, he means, for example, that the professor's lecture did not determine the response of his students (that would be instructive interaction). The professor's lecture *selected* the students' responses, but their structure *determined* their responses ... Maturana is claiming that our everyday use of the word "cause" always implies or threatens to imply a determining in the sense of instructive interaction—whereas "causation" is always only a selecting. Thus, he says causality is impossible. (p. 8)

Other concerns about conceptual and practical aspects of constructivism have been expressed by Mahoney (1991):

Beyond the heuristic abstractions of "structure determination," "organizational closure," and "structural coupling," what is it that determines an organism's adaptations to/of its environment? What are the parameters of "congruence" between the structures of a living system and its medium? Why are some systems capable of much wider ranges of self-restructuring than others, and what are the explicit implications for parent, education, and psychological services?

Another way of expressing this reservation is to say that ... current autopoietic theory pays too little attention to the world in which the living system lives, not to mention the mentation involved and the processes by which that system learns, changes, or develops. ... As many cognitive therapists have learned over the last two decades, psychotherapy clients can be urged to "restructure" their perceptions and beliefs about self and world, but the self-perpetuating aspects of that self and the everyday constraints imposed by that world are not always conducive to that undertaking. (p. 396)

It should be noted in relation to Mahoney's concern about the lack of an adequate concept in constructivist theory to account for the individual's adaptation to the environment that Mahoney, as a psychologist, is not taking into account, nor would he be expected to, the role of constructivism as only one member in the family of theories employed by social workers. Systems and ecological theories have long been effectively incorporated by social workers in their practice for understanding how the individual adapts to the environment (see chapters in this volume on the Life Model [Chapter 18] and Systems Theory [Chapter 15]). Mahoney's observation, however, about the need for further development of the abstract concepts in constructivism toward the operational level remains valid.

Conclusions

The selective use of an ever-expanding body of knowledge and theory in social work becomes increasingly important in order to meet the challenges of the increasing complexity of social work practice demands. Constructivism as a conceptual framework for social work practice has recently added to the profession's available technology. The future for constructivism in the profession will most likely unfold according to the extent to which it is found to be compatible with social work values, its usefulness to practitioners, and its effectiveness with clients. Payne (1991) wrote what is still true today:

New ideas within social work theory arise in various ways and go through a process of naturalization by which they become adjusted to the conventional framework of social work. Some theories have not fully naturalized, because they do not deal well with some of the important features of social work within the period in which they become important. Theories which do naturalize affect the common features of social work. (p. 7)

Cole (1992) has distinguished between "core" knowledge in a discipline and "frontier" knowledge. The core knowledge, including a relatively small number of theories, is the "given" or "starting point" for that discipline. The frontier component is composed of the knowledge that is in the early stages of being developed and about which substantial consensus is still lacking (p. 15). Constructivism as a framework for social work treatment fits into the frontier category at this point. Further use by practitioners and testing of constructivist-based practice approaches by researchers will be necessary for constructivism to arrive at a point where it may slip over into the core of social work knowledge, and it is making progress in that direction.

It has been shown in this chapter how some of the basic postulates of constructivism are not only compatible with major social work practice principles but also provide them with additional support. Constructivist-based practice clearly addresses current major concerns of the profession such as the need to empower clients; the rights of racial, cultural, ethnic, gender, and age

groups to be self-determining; and the need to enhance the degree of dignity and respect accorded to all people.

The formulation of constructivism set forth in this chapter as a conceptual framework for social work treatment has drawn substantially on the conceptions of Maturana and Varela. These conceptions are rooted in neurobiology, in contrast to the social and behavioral sciences that social work has traditionally drawn on for foundational theory. In closing this chapter, a statement of what might be viewed as the essence of the neurobiological constructivism of Maturana and Varela provided in their own words would seem appropriate:

Every human being, as an autopoietic system, stands alone. Yet let us not lament that we must exist in a subject-dependent reality. Life is more interesting like this, because the only transcendence of our individual loneliness that we can experience arises through the consensual reality that we create with others, that is, through love. (1978, p. 63)

From this constructivist duality of the individual standing alone in a subject-dependent reality, a central mandate arises for the practitioner, which is to carefully and persistently respect the individuality of clients as self-determining beings and by following this mandate increase the likelihood of clients being able to deal more effectively with the requirements of a normative world while broadening their vision to catch sight of more satisfying ways to conduct their lives (see the case example in this chapter).

References

Badenoch, B. (2008). *Being a brain-wise therapist: A practical guide to interpersonal neurobiology*. New York: W. W. Norton and Company.

Bell, P. (1985). Understanding Batten and Maturana: Towards a biological foundation for the social sciences. *Journal of Marital and Family Therapy*, 11(1).

Carpenter, D. (1996). Constructivism and social work treatment. In F. Turner (Ed.), *Social work treatment: Interlocking theoretical approaches* (4th ed.). New York: The Free Press.

Colapinto, J. (1985). Maturana and the ideology of conformity. *The Family Therapy Networker*, May-June.

Cozolino, L. (2002). *The neuroscience of psychotherapy: Building and rebuilding the human brain*. New York: W. W. Norton.

Cole, S. (1992). *Making science: Between nature and society.* Cambridge, MA: Harvard University Press.

Cottone, R. (2007). Paradigms of counseling and psychotherapy, revisited. *Journal of Mental Health Counseling,* 29, 189–203.

Dean, R., & Fenby, D. (1989). Exploring epistemologies: Social work action as a reflection of philosophical assumptions. *Journal of Social Work Education,* 25(1), 46–54.

Dean, R., & Fleck-Henderson, A. (1992). Teaching clinical theory and practice through a constructivist lens. *Journal of Teaching in Social Work,* 6(1), 3–20.

Efran, J., & Lukens, M., (1985). The world according to Humberto Maturana. *The Family Therapy Networker,* May-June.

Efran, J., Lukens, M., & Lukens, R. (1990). *Language, structure and change: Frameworks of meaning in psychotherapy.* New York: W. W. Norton.

Elkana, Y. (1978). Two-tier thinking: philosophical realism and historical relativism. *Social Studies of Science,* 8, 309–326.

Fisher, D. (1991). *An Introduction to constructivism for social workers.* New York: Praeger.

Folensbee, S. (2007).*The neuroscience of psychological therapies.* New York: Cambridge University Press.

Gabbard, G. O. (1992). Psychodynamic psychiatry in the "decade of the brain." *American Journal of Psychiatry,* 149, 991–998.

Goodman, N. (1972). The way the world is. In *Problems and projects* (pp. 30–31). New York: Bobbs Merrill.

Goodman, N. (1984). *Of mind and other matters.* Cambridge, MA: Harvard University Press.

Granvold, D. (2001) Constructivist theory. In *Theoretical perspectives for direct social work practice: A generalist-eclectic approach.* New York: Springer Publishing Company.

Grossman, D. R. (1993). Teaching a constructivist approach to clinical practice. *Journal of Teaching in Social Work,* 8(1/2), 55–75.

Greene, G., & Lee, M. (2002). Using social constructivism in social work practice. In A. R. Roberts & G. J. Greene (Eds.), *Social workers' desk reference* (pp. 143–149). New York: Oxford University Press.

Hansen, J. T. (2007). Epistemic contradictions in counseling theories: Implications for the structure of human experience and counseling. *Practice Counseling and Values,* 51(2).

Hartman, A. (1991). Words create worlds. *Social Work,* 36(1), 275–276.

Ide, H. (1995) Sophists. In R. Audi (Ed.), *The Cambridge dictionary of philosophy.* New York: Cambridge University Press.

Kant, I. (1938). *The critique of pure reason.* (Translated by N. K. Smith, originally written 1781). New York: Macmillan.

Kelly, G. (1955). *The psychology of personal constructs* (2 vols). New York: W. W. Norton.

Laird, J. (Ed.). (1993). *Revisioning social work education: A social constructionist approach.* New York: Haworth Press.

Mahoney, M. (1991). *Human change processes: The scientific foundations of psychotherapy.* New York: Basic Books.

Maturana, H. (1975). The organization of the living: A theory of the living organization. *The International Journal of Man-Machine Studies,* 7, 313–332.

Maturana, H. (1978). Biology of language: The epistemology of reality. In G. A. Miller & E. Lenneberg (Eds.), *Psychology and biology of language and thought.* New York: Academic Press.

Maturana, H. (1980). Biology of cognition. In H. Maturana & F. Varela (Eds.), *Autopoiesis and cognition: The realization of the living.* Boston: Reidel.

Maturana, H., Uribe, G., & Frenk, S. (1968). A biological theory of relativistic color coding in the primate retina. *Arch. Biologica y Med. Exp.,* Supplemonto No. 1, 1–30.

Maturana, H., & Varela, F. J. (1987). *The tree of knowledge: The biological roots of human understanding.* Boston: Shambhala Publications.

Morris, T. (2006) *Social work research methods: Four alternative paradigms.* Thousand Oaks, CA: Sage Publications.

Neimeyer, R. (2009). *Constructivist psychotherapy.* New York: Routledge.

O'Hanlon, B. (1994). The third wave. *The Family Therapy Networker,* 18(6).

Payne, M. (1991). *Modern social work theory: A critical introduction.* Chicago: Lyceum Books.

Piaget, J. (1929). *The child's conception of the world.* New York: Harcourt, Brace.

Piaget, J. (1950). *The psychology of intelligence.* New York: Harcourt, Brace.

Piaget, J. (1970). *Towards a theory of knowledge.* New York: Viking.

Pliszka, S. (2003). *Neuroscience for mental health clinicians.* New York: The Guilford Press.

Pojman, L. (1995). Relativism. In R. Audi (Ed.), *The Cambridge dictionary of philosophy.* New York: Cambridge University Press.

Quartz, S. R.; Sejnowski, T. J. (1997). The neural basis of cognitive development: a constructivist manifesto, *Behavioral and Brain Sciences,* 20(4), 537–596.

Saleebey, D. (Ed.). (1992). *The strengths perspective in social work practice*. New York: Longman.

Sexton, T. L., & Griffin, B. L. (1997). *Constructivist thinking in counseling, practice, research, and training*. New York: Teachers College Press.

Sykes Wylie, M. (1992). The evolution of a revolution. *The Family Therapy Networker*, 18(6).

Tijerina, M. (2009). Mexican American women's adherence to hemodialysis treatment: A social constructivist perspective. *Social Work,* 54(3).

Toomey, B., & Ecker, B. (2007). Of neurons and knowings: Constructivism, coherence psychology, and their neurodynamic substrates. *Journal of Constructivist Psychology*, 20(3), 201–245.

Turner, F. J. (1986). Theory in social work practice. In F. J. Turner (Ed.), *Social work treatment: Interlocking theoretical approaches* (3rd ed.). New York: Free Press.

von Foerster, H. (1984). On constructing a reality. In P. Watzlawick (Ed.), *The invented reality*. New York: W. W. Norton.

von Glaserfeld, E. (1984). An introduction to radical constructivism. In P. Watzlawick (Ed.), *The invented reality*. New York: W. W. Norton.

Watzlawick, P. (1976). *How real is real?* New York: Random House.

Watzlawick, P. (Ed.). (1984). *The invented reality*. New York: W. W. Norton.

Watzlawick, P. (1990). *Munchhausen's pigtail or psychotherapy and reality*. New York: W. W. Norton.

White, M. (1989). The externalizing of the problem and the re-authoring of lives and relationships. *Dulwich Centre Newsletter,* Summer, pp. 5–12.

Wolterstorff, N. (1995). Locke, John. In R. Audi (Ed.), *The Cambridge dictionary of philosophy*. New York: Cambridge University Press.

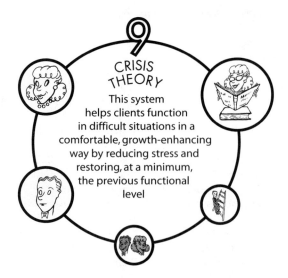

CRISIS THEORY
This system helps clients function in difficult situations in a comfortable, growth-enhancing way by reducing stress and restoring, at a minimum, the previous functional level

Crisis Theory and Social Work Treatment

Cheryl Regehr

A crisis is "a period of psychological disequilibrium, experienced as a result of a hazardous event or situation that constitutes a significant problem that cannot be remedied by using familiar coping strategies. A crisis occurs when a person faces an obstacle to important life goals that generally seems insurmountable through the use of customary habits and coping patterns" (Roberts, 2000, p. 7). The inability of normal coping strategies to manage the situation leads to a number of consequences, including (1) emotional distress, (2) impaired sense of personal self-worth, (3) inability to enjoy interpersonal contacts, and (4) impaired task performance, all of which result in the experience of a crisis state (Pearlin & Schooler, 1978). As a result of exposure to crisis-producing events, people may feel a sense of disorganization, confusion, anxiety, shock, disbelief, or helplessness, which may increase as attempts to resolve the situation prove to be ineffective.

Crisis intervention is a short-term intervention technique that is grounded in crisis theory. The central tenant of crisis intervention is that "a little help, rationally directed and purposefully focused at a strategic time is more effective than more extensive help given at a time of less emotional accessibility" (Rapoport, 1967, p. 38). This model has been applied to interventions with individuals, with groups who have experienced a shared crisis such as a critical event in the workplace, and with communities that have been exposed to disaster.

History of Crisis Theory

Crisis theory has had an interesting history in that it has been incorporated into social work,

134

psychiatry, psychology, and the community volunteer movement. Crisis theory is credited to have begun with the work of Erich Lindemann in the early 1940s. On November 28, 1942, a fire killed 492 people at the Cocoanut Grove Night Club in Boston. As the Cocoanut Grove was originally an illegal bar during Prohibition, several of its doors were bricked up or bolted shut, and the only exit at the front was a revolving door. One thousand people filled the club on the night of the tragedy, although it was licensed to hold only 500. Paper palm trees and coconuts quickly ignited the building, and the exit was blocked as people attempted to push the revolving door from both directions. Lindemann (1944) and his colleagues at the Massachusetts General Hospital observed and documented the reactions of the survivors, which included somatic responses, behavioral changes, and emotional responses such as grief and guilt.

Caplan (1964) built on the work of Lindemann from the perspective of preventive psychiatry and gave prominence to the community's role in supporting health and recovery. Caplan conceptualized that people generally live their lives in a steady state of homeostasis. Events occur throughout life that challenge the homeostasis, and the individual mobilizes resources (physical, psychological, emotional, intellectual, and social) to restore balance. When that balance is not quickly restored or a solution to the challenge is not evident, the experience of crisis can occur. Caplan also identified that crises emerge not only from unexpected events such as the Cocoanut Grove fire, but also from normal developmental crises that occur throughout life, such as the birth of the first child to a couple, an adolescent testing limits, the final child leaving home, or the death of a parent. In 1959, Caplan challenged social workers, as specialists in assessing environmental phenomena, to use their unique abilities and focus to contribute to the development of crisis theory and the practice of crisis intervention.

Several social workers answered the challenge. Martin Strickler (1965; Strickler & Bonnefil, 1974) identified similarities between crisis intervention and social casework, including a focus on the current problem, attention to social relationships, and targeting social dysfunction for intervention. He further identified central crisis theory concepts, including the presence of precipitating events and the setting of time-limited, focused goals that engage the client at the conscious level, which in his opinion required social workers to modify certain practices of social casework. For instance, in crisis intervention there is no separation between the assessment phase and the intervention phase; rather, a dynamic process must occur between the two. In addition, in crisis intervention the social worker must engage with the client on a cognitive level to quickly work to solve the problem rather than explore unconscious issues from a psychodynamic perspective. Naomi Golan and colleagues (1969) described the implementation of a crisis intervention model by psychiatric social workers in a mental health center. In this model, social workers assessed all walk-ins to the emergency service and discussed alternatives to hospitalization using a crisis intervention approach. This model is remarkably similar to current practices of social workers in emergency settings. Howard Parad and Gerald Caplan (1960) developed a framework for working with families in crisis.

Very early in its implementation, social workers began exploring the evidentiary basis for crisis interventions. Parad and Parad (G. Parad & H. Parad, 1968; H. Parad & G. Parad, 1968) examined the use of crisis intervention in 54 family and 44 child guidance clinics and determined that while the model was deemed effective, it was used in only a relatively small proportion of cases. Similarly, Duckworth (1967) tested the effectiveness of crisis intervention over a 24-week period in a social service agency and determined that crisis intervention was accessible to more people (particularly those at lower income levels), resolved problems in a shorter period of time, and was favorably reviewed by clients. Morris (1968) reviewed 50 cases in which crisis intervention had been used in a public welfare agency in addition to the provision of financial support. She determined that 24 clients responded positively, 14 dropped out of treatment, 7 did not respond to the offer of treatment, and 5 received help from other sources. She reported that when the crisis intervention model (accelerated casework) was used, the presenting problem was resolved within 3 months in half the cases.

In the 1970s crisis intervention became widely used with a large variety of populations by practitioners in all fields of mental health. Greenbaum and colleagues (1977) described the use of the model with Israeli Defense Forces before, during, and after the 1973 Yom Kippur War. Others identified use of crisis intervention with families in child psychiatry (Berlin, 1970); with survivors of earthquake (Blaufarb & Levine, 1972); with families of firesetters (Eisler, 1972); in community-based drug treatment (Spivack & Troupe, 1973); and in correctional centers (Kennedy, 1975), to name just a few target populations. Auerbach and Kilmann (1977) reviewed the outcome research regarding the use of crisis intervention in suicide prevention programs and psychiatric settings and with surgical patients. While a surprising number of outcome studies were found and reviewed, their conclusions are echoed in more current research on the evidentiary basis for psychosocial interventions—that is, definitional problems and outcome measures belie the ability to determine the effectiveness of crisis intervention models.

An Overview of Crisis Theory

As implied in the history presented above, two primary types of events can result in a crisis response: situational and developmental. *Situational crises* were first described and documented in 1944 by Lindemann following the Cocoanut Grove fire. Situational crises are now understood to span a wide range of events, including diagnosis of a life-threatening or serious illness, job loss, or divorce and separation. *Developmental crises* such as the birth or adoption of a child, adolescence, marriage, and retirement were identified by Caplan (1964). He suggested that the adaptation required by even expected events can tax an individual's coping resources and lead to a crisis response.

Nevertheless, whether an event results in a crisis response is highly individualized. The precipitating event is only one factor that can lead to a crisis. A second factor, as mentioned earlier, is the individual's crisis-meeting resources, which include both personal resources and social and community supports. A third factor is other stressors that are concurrently presenting challenges, such as ill health or other recent losses. Thus, an event that could have been coped with at another time may seem beyond coping due to being perceived as "the final straw." A final factor contributing to a crisis is the meaning attributed to the stressful event—that is, in order for a crisis to occur, the person must perceive the event to be a threat. This can be a threat to the person's needs or autonomy, it can be a loss of ability or self-esteem, or it can be a challenge to survival, growth, or mastery. In equation form: Crisis = the event + the individual's crisis-meeting resources + other concurrent stressors + the individual's perception of the event.

Crises are commonly viewed to have a number of characteristics (Regehr & Bober, 2005):

- *They are perceived as sudden.* Even if one anticipates a particular developmental event, when it arrives, the changes that accompany it are perceived as sudden. For instance, although one anticipates the birth of a baby, the changes in sleeping schedules, lifestyle, and relationships within the family feel sudden and unexpected.
- *The individual is not adequately prepared to handle the event and normal coping methods fail.* An event does not become a crisis if the individual has coping strategies that match the situation. The loss of a job can be a crisis for some and an opportunity for others who had been planning to start a small business for some time.
- *Crises are time-limited, lasting 1 day to 4 to 6 weeks.* In general, it is thought that people cannot function at a heightened level of arousal for prolonged periods of time. Thus, individuals work hard to adapt their coping strategies to match the situation and mobilize social supports to assist. Those who are unable to adapt may develop other more serious mental health or emotional problems.
- *Crises have the potential to produce dangerous, self-destructive or socially unacceptable behavior.* In times of disequilibrium, people may be so distressed that they feel suicidal. Others may express their distress by lashing out at others and undermining social support networks.
- *There is a feeling of psychological vulnerability, which can potentially be an opportunity for*

growth. Crises are said to offer both danger and opportunity. Frequently people emerge from a crisis situation with a greater confidence in their own strengths and abilities and new strategies for life.

The crisis response is viewed to occur in stages. The first stage is the *pre-crisis or equilibrium stage* where a person is unaware that the crisis is about to occur and is functioning in his or her customary manner. Stage 2, the *impact phase,* is when the event actually occurs. Stage 3, the *crisis phase,* is the point at which the person is aware of the event and perceives it as a threat in some way. This phase has two elements: (a) confusion and disorganization, during which functional level declines and the person experiences symptoms of anxiety, fear, and helplessness, and (b) trial-and-error reorganization, during which the person attempts various strategies to improve the situation and manage. Some of these strategies work and some do not. During stage 4, the *resolution phase*, the person regains control over his or her emotions and works toward a solution. In stage 5, the *post-crisis phase*, the crisis situation has been managed and the person resumes what is now to be his or her equilibrium. This new equilibrium may be at the same level of functioning that the person had prior to the crisis. However, the crisis may have also resulted in new learning and new insights and result in a higher level of functioning, or the person may have become depleted and now be at a lower level of functioning. This variable outcome has lead to the common statement that the Chinese symbol for crisis is made up of two symbols representing challenge and opportunity (although linguists dispute this colloquial belief; Regehr & Glancy, 2009).

危
機

Crisis theory and crisis intervention models have been useful in understanding and supporting people who are in the process of learning new adaptive skills to overcome an adversity. The short-term nature of response implied by this theory, however, does not fully account for the responses people have to life-threatening and horrifying events. In these cases, other longer-term models of treatment specifically designed to address post traumatic stress disorder (PTSD) will need to be considered (Regehr & Glancy, 2009).

Crisis Intervention with Individuals and Families

Crisis intervention is a brief treatment approach that is based on the premise that support, education, and guidance provided in a timely manner can assist individuals to mobilize their inherent strengths and resources for the purposes of moving toward a speedy resolution of the distress caused by a particular occurrence. Crisis intervention focuses on the resolution of an immediate problem. The goal is to prevent further deterioration and return to a least a pre-crisis level of functioning. Roberts (2000) defined seven stages of crisis intervention:

1. *Planning and conducting a thorough assessment*, including any acute risk of harm to self or others.
2. Rapidly *establishing rapport*, demonstrating respect, acceptance, and a nonjudgmental attitude. Rapport is established very quickly in a crisis situation through the demonstration of concern for the problems that are being experienced by the person in distress and a desire to assist with basic needs.
3. *Identifying various dimensions of the current problem*, including the "last straw" or precipitating events. The social worker attempts to quickly identify the biopsychosocial domains of the current problem. What are the underlying struggles that this person encounters? What has led up to the current crisis? In general, the social worker should be prepared for the fact that the client in crisis will present a wide range of problems, including those that have been continuing for sometime and those that are new. The social worker needs to be careful not to become

overwhelmed and rather begin to organize the problems in his or her own mind as the assessment interview continues.

4. Active listening while *exploring* and describing previous *coping strategies* and *successes and resources* available. The social worker using a crisis intervention approach seeks to discover the strengths that clients have within themselves and within their social network. Who could help them if they needed help? How have they coped in the past? If clients describe positive coping, the social worker reinforces their abilities and celebrates their successes.

5. Generating and exploring *alternative strategies* for managing the problem. Once the client has laid out the problems he or she is encountering, the social worker summarizes the issues for the client. The social worker then suggests that some of the issues can't be dealt with right now, but that a referral for future counseling is certainly possible. However, it does seem that together the client and the social worker might be able to come up with some ideas to manage the most recent problems over the next couple of days. At this point the social worker searches for possible solutions by gently exploring alternatives with the client. At any point, the social worker has to be prepared to change tactics and move from a community-based approach to other measures such as hospitalization if the client does not appear to be able to engage in problem solving and the risk, for instance of suicide, remains high.

6. Developing and formulating an *action plan* with the client. Once alternatives have been explored, the social worker and the client move to an immediate action plan. Generally both the client and the social worker have some responsibilities in the plan. For instance, the social worker may undertake to contact a parent, friend, or other support person who can assist the person. The social worker may also undertake to do some advocacy work to reduce some systemic pressures on the client. The client also agrees to undertake some tasks such as discussing his or her concerns with a particular person or following through on a task that he or she has been avoiding. In formulating the action plan, the social worker

will often provide notes to the client with necessary phone numbers or steps to be followed.

7. Establishing *follow-up* plans. Follow-up plans tend to be short term in crisis intervention. For instance, a client can agree to visit or phone the social worker the next day. Follow-up plans can also be longer term in nature, although it is important to note that quite commonly clients who attend crisis services do not follow through with referrals to longer-term services (Regehr & Glancy, 2009).

The efficacy of crisis intervention continues to be unclear from the perspective of evidence-based reviews. In large part this is due to the same challenges identified by Auerbach and Kilmann in 1977. One meta-analysis does provide some support for crisis models (Roberts & Everly, 2006). However, this review combines a number of types of interventions under the heading of crisis intervention, so it remains unclear what specific models are most effective. Irving and colleagues (2006) conducted a Cochrane review of crisis intervention in home-based care of people with psychiatric disorders and concluded, "Home care crisis treatment, coupled with an ongoing home care package, is a viable and acceptable way of treating people with serious mental illnesses." However, if this approach is to be widely implemented, more evaluative studies are still needed. Stapleton and colleagues (2006) conducted a meta-analysis of crisis intervention in the treatment of anxiety, depression, and posttraumatic stress. They concluded that crisis intervention conducted over multiple sessions with trained therapists is effective. However, concerns have been raised about the inclusion criteria for studies included in that review. Nevertheless, despite the absence of compelling research evidence, the crisis intervention model is nonintrusive and focuses on client needs and wishes and so is unlikely to cause harm.

Crisis Intervention with Groups

Beginning in the late 1980s and early 1990s, the crisis intervention model was adapted to focus on group interventions initially with emergency responders who encountered traumatic events in the workplace. These events included institutional fires where a number of patients were killed, terrorist events such as the Oklahoma City bombing by Timothy McVeigh, and the line-of-duty death of an emergency responder. The theoretical foundation supporting the use of crisis debriefings for emergency workers suggests that these individuals have the required coping mechanisms to manage most aspects of the job, even those the general public would find gruesome or disturbing. Nevertheless, on occasion a tragic event occurs such as a mass tragedy or the loss of a colleague in the line of duty for which normal mechanisms are inadequate. The emotional, physical, and cognitive aftermath of these events can affect an individual worker's ability to function effectively both on the job and in interpersonal relationships (Regehr & Bober, 2005). The model was then expanded to other groups, including victims of large-scale disasters such as floods and tornados and in organizations such as schools where a shooting has occurred; this practice has raised a great deal of controversy.

In the original model proposed by Mitchell and Everly (1993), the crisis debriefing was aimed at (1) helping the participant to understand the relationship between the event and his or her reactions, (2) providing an opportunity for cathartic release of feelings, thoughts, and emotions, (3) identifying successful coping strategies, and (4) promoting utilization of various support systems. A several-stage model was manualized and taught to a wide range of mental health and emergency professionals. The debriefing was not intended to be an intervention that stands on its own, but rather was considered to be one component of a comprehensive, integrated crisis response program (Mitchell & Everly, 1993). Other aspects of the program may include preventive education, informal group opportunities to discuss the event (defusings), individual defusings, family outreach, and follow-up counseling (Regehr & Bober, 2005). Nevertheless, in practice, it was often employed as a single-session group with no other follow-up.

Several variations of crisis debriefings are described in the literature, including psychological debriefings (Dyregrov, 1989; Raphael, 1986); critical incident stress debriefings (Mitchell & Bray, 1990); community crisis response teams (Young, 1991); and the multiple stressor debriefing model

(Armstrong, O'Callahan, & Marmar, 1991). Each of the crisis debriefing models involves a psychoeducational group meeting. The debriefer utilizes clinical skills in order to establish rapport, encourage discussion, and manage the group process. During the groups, a structured procedure is followed in order to allow individuals to process the tragic event and its aftermath. The first stage is to review the event. This includes describing the sights, sounds, and smells associated with the event, discussing each individual's involvement and the final outcome. Next, people are invited to discuss their reactions to the event, including the emotional and behavioral consequences both for themselves and their family life. Following this, the debriefer provides educational information designed to normalize reactions and reinforce coping skills. In addition, suggestions are made regarding specific stress management techniques. As the session draws to a conclusion, participants are invited to discuss their accomplishments and reinforce one another's efforts. Finally, participants are encouraged to provide mutual aid as required, and opportunities for professional follow-up are presented. The debriefer monitors the level of emotional intensity within the group to ensure that it remains manageable and does not become overwhelming. Members who are experiencing acute distress are offered individual assistance.

Recent reviews of the research, however, have questioned the conclusion that crisis debriefing groups reduce traumatic stress reactions and have expressed concern that debriefing may in fact exacerbate symptoms (Arendt & Elklit, 2001; Bisson, McFarlane, & Rose, 2000; Rose, Bisson, & Wesley, 2003; Raphael, Meldrum, & McFarlane, 1995; van Emmerik, Kamphuis, Huisbosch, & Emmelkamp, 2002). While most practitioners working in this area are quick to point out that the crisis debriefings are only one part of a comprehensive program aimed at reducing the impact of exposure to traumatic events in the workplace, the group debriefings have nevertheless often become a central part of the training and intervention programs.

Regehr (2001) examined conflicting research data in this area. This review, as others, concluded that there is no evidence to support the notion that single-session group debriefings prevent significant distress, such as the development of PTSD symptoms. Further, the evidence suggests that single-session debriefing groups may actually increase PTSD symptoms, in particular intrusion symptoms. On the other hand, anecdotal data and subjective ratings by participants in debriefings suggest that they do offer some clear benefits. The two primary components of crisis debriefing that have some empirical support are the provision and enhancement of social support and the psychoeducational components, specifically the use of cognitive behavioral strategies for symptom management. Other aspects of the model, such as reviewing in graphic detail the nature of the events experienced by various participants, are not empirically supported and indeed are likely to increase intrusive symptoms such as nightmares, flashbacks, and repetitive thoughts. Consequently, most practitioners have modified the original model of crisis debriefing groups to avoid graphic descriptions of the event and focus instead on the beneficial aspects of building supports and augmenting coping strategies.

Crisis Intervention with Communities

Disasters have occurred throughout the world since the beginning of time. However, the advent of large-scale disaster in North America, most notably with the terrorist attacks on the World Trade Center and Hurricane Katrina that devastated New Orleans, have made us more acutely aware of disaster and its human consequences. Mental health professionals have become increasingly aware of their role in ameliorating the impact of disaster and have begun to develop models for systematizing interventions.

Disaster challenges the equilibrium of individuals and communities. Interventions following disaster are clearly grounded in crisis theory. In general, these interventions focus on (1) assessing the needs of the affected population; (2) matching resources to those needs; (3) preventing further adverse effects; and (4) evaluating the effectiveness of strategies and improving contingency plans for the future (Noji, 2000). Reyes and Elhai (2004) emphasize the fit between crisis intervention and disaster response, the primary goals of which are ensuring the safety of the client and then assisting the client to obtain an adequate level of autonomous functioning. This is accomplished by developing a supportive relationship, assessing and securing resources, articulating alternative means for achieving goals, and embarking on a plan of recovery. They identify the need for a pragmatic approach with relatively humble goals and the achievement of a series of small successes.

A further disaster relief model that has emerged from the crisis intervention approach has been named psychological first aid (Ruzek et al., 2007; Vernberg et al., 2008). This model includes the following elements: (1) contact and engagement; (2) safety and comfort; (3) stabilization; (4) information gathering; (5) practical assistance; (6) connections with social supports; (7) linkages with services; and (8) psychoeducation.

Roberts (2006) proposed the Triple ABCD Model, which provides a systematic approach to crisis management in disaster situations. The model is based on a crisis intervention approach that focuses on immediate and short-term interventions aimed at enhancing the adaptive capacity of the affected individuals or community. As stated by Gerald Caplan (1964), "A relatively minor force, acting for a relatively short time, can switch the balance to one side or another, to the side of mental health or the side of mental ill health" (p. 293). The Triple ABCD Model integrates several assessment and triage protocols with the latest and most frequently used crisis-oriented intervention strategies and protocols. The Triple ABCD Model has four stages, each with three possible components (Regehr, Roberts, & Bober, 2008):

1. Arrival of emergency responders, Appraisal of risks, hazards, and needs; and Assessment of functioning
2. Build communication network and rapport; Briefly identify triggering incidents; and Boil down the problem
3. Crisis intervention; Cognitive restructuring; and Connecting to others and/or support groups
4. Develop a disaster and crisis resolution aftercare plan; Deal with trauma symptoms; and Discuss follow-up and booster sessions.

Social work crisis responses in the wake of disaster require both clinical and community organization skills. Applying the crisis intervention model, social workers quickly assess the nature of the problem and establish rapport. In the community context, social workers must work directly with the affected citizens and communities who best understand their strengths and needs. Establishing partnerships and relationships with community members forms the basis on which continuity of care and resources can be planned and implemented is critical to this process. An important component is encouraging local leadership and community building, thus enhancing natural social supports. Norris (2002) reviews substantial evidence related to factors that lead to increased distress after disaster and concludes that the social functioning of the collective is a critical factor in recovery from disaster. Temporary communities established in highly populated areas are unlikely to reflect predisaster neighborhood patterns as people are moved en masse to stadiums and community centers, as evidenced in the recent hurricane disaster in New Orleans. Such relocation and disruption of community serves to increase distress (Kilic et al., 2006; Najarian et al., 2001). Thus, community-based solutions that keep neighbors together are vital.

The securing of resources through joint problem solving and advocacy is a central component of recovery. When resources are perceived as inadequate, distress at both the individual and community level is intensified, also as evidenced in the aftermath of Hurricane Katrina (Cuddy, Rock, & Norton, 2007). Preexisting conditions of poverty, unemployment, or poorly coordinated health networks can serve as roadblocks to timely recovery (Norris et al., 2002), and social workers may need to advocate for those who have been disenfranchised.

Case Example

A tornado hits a small community 2 hours north of a large urban area. The town is not particularly prosperous. Many inhabitants live in trailer homes or wooden houses and drive to a nearby resort area where they work in a variety of service jobs. The tornado arrives suddenly and cuts a relatively narrow path: it tears the roofs off two houses, overturns trailer homes and a few vehicles, uproots trees, and disperses belongings. The tornado hits with little warning and children from the local school are caught off guard on a hike through the woods. One child in the group is killed. In this event, all three types of crisis responses are required.

Individual and Family Level: A family arrives at the hospital to learn that their child has died. Crisis intervention must focus on assisting them during the period of initial shock and grief as they attempt to absorb the news, supporting them in making decisions about whom to call and how to arrange the funeral, helping them mobilize their social supports during this time of terrible loss.

Family and Community Level: Other families must deal with the loss of their homes. Community supports must mobilized to provide immediate shelter, food, bedding, and clothing as necessary. Families may need assistance in contacting banks, insurance companies, and employers and in making decisions about how to manage in the days and weeks ahead as they rebuild or relocate. Longer-term community strategies will involve removal of refuse and rebuilding in the area that was affected. Building codes and community safety policies may or may not require review and community consultation.

Group Level: Group-level interventions may occur in the school as staff and students deal with the aftermath of the event. First, opportunities may be made available for those in attendance to talk about their experiences either individually or together. School administrators may need assistance in developing a plan to recognize the death of the child who was lost.

Summary

Crisis theory has emerged from individual and collective responses to significant challenges in life, both those that occur unexpectedly and those that are part of the life cycle. It integrates concepts of stress, resource availability, coping strategies, and the cognitive framing or meanings associated with a particular challenge. Crisis intervention that is based on crisis theory is an approach that has a longstanding history in social work as well as the other mental health disciplines. It focuses on short-term solutions to immediate problems that fully engage the client or client group in seeking solutions and mobilizing resources. Many social work positions, such as those in emergency departments, child welfare intake units, and adolescent and adult shelters, use crisis intervention as a primary strategy in their work. However, whether a social worker focuses his or her career in crisis services or not, at some point each social worker will be working with clients in crisis. As a result, this model should be a component of each social worker's therapeutic repertoire.

References

Arendt, M., & Elklit, A. (2001). Effectiveness of psychological debriefing. *Acta Psychiatrica Scandinavica*, 104, 423–437.

Armstrong, K., O'Callahan, W., & Marmar, C. (1991). Debriefing Red Cross disaster personnel: the multiple stressor debriefing model. *Journal of Traumatic Stress*, 4(4), 581–593.

Auerback, S., & Kilmann, P. (1977). Crisis intervention: A review of outcome research. *Psychological Bulletin*, 84(6) 1189–2117.

Berlin, I. (1970). Crisis intervention and short-term therapy: An approach in child-psychiatric clinic. *Journal of the American Academy of Child Psychiatry*, 9(4), 595–606.

Bisson, J., McFarlane, A., & Rose, S. (2000). Psychological debriefings. In E. Foa, T. Keane, & M. Friedman (Eds.), *Effective treatments for PTSD: Practice guidelines from the International Society for Traumatic Stress Studies* (pp. 317–319). New York: Guildford Press.

Blaufarb, H., & Levine, J. (1972). Crisis intervention in an earthquake. *Social Work*, 17(4), 16–19.

Caplan, G. (1959) The role of the social worker in preventative psychiatry for mothers and children. In *Concepts of mental health* (pp 247–257). Washington, DC: Government Printing Office.

Caplan, G. (1964). *Principles of preventive psychiatry*. New York: Basic Books.

Cuddy, A., Rock, M., & Norton, M. (2007). Aid in the aftermath of Hurricane Katrina: Inferences of secondary emotion and intergroup helping. *Group Processes and Intergroup Relations*, 10(1), 107–118.

Duckworth, G. (1967). A project in crisis intervention. *Social Casework*, 48(4), 227–231.

Dyregrov, A. (1989). Caring for the helpers in disaster situations: Psychological debriefing. *Disaster Management*, 2, 25–30.

Eisler, R. (1972). Crisis intervention in the family of a firesetter. *Psychotherapy: Theory and Practice*, 9(1), 76–79.

Golan, N., Carey, H., & Hyttinen, E. (1969). The emerging role of the social worker in the psychiatric emergency service. *Community Mental Health Journal*, 5(1), 55–61.

Greenbaum, C., Rogovsky, I., & Shalit, B. (1977). The military psychologist during wartime: A model based on action research and crisis intervention. *Journal of Applied Behavioral Science*, 13(1), 7–21.

Irving, C. B., Adams, C. E., & Rice, K. (2006). Crisis intervention for people with severe mental illnesses. *Cochrane Database of Systematic Reviews* Issue 4. Art. No.: CD001087. DOI: 10.1002/14651858. CD001087.pub3.

Kennedy, D. (1975). Crisis intervention in a correctional center. *Journal of Community Psychology*, 3(1), 93–94.

Kilic, C., Aydin, I., Taskintuna, N., Ozcurumez, G., Kurt, G., Eren, E., Lale, T., Ozel, S., & Zileli, L. (2006). Predictors of psychological distress in survivors of the 1999 earthquakes in Turkey: Effects of relocation after the disaster. *Acta Psychatrica Scandinavica*, 114, 194–202.

Lindemann, E. (1944) Symptomatology and management of acute grief. *American Journal of Psychiatry*, 101, 141–148.

Mitchell, J., & Bray, G. (1990). *Emergency services stress: Guidelines for preserving the health and careers of emergency services personnel*. Englewood Cliffs, NJ: Brady.

Mitchell, J., & Everly, G. (1993). Critical incident stress debriefing. Ellicot City, MD: Chevron Publishing.

Morris, B. (1968). Crisis intervention in a public welfare agency. *Social Casework*, 49(10), 612–617.

Najarian, L., Goenjian, A., Pelcovitz, D., Mandel, F., & Najarian, B. (2002). The effect of relocation after natural disaster. *Journal of Traumatic Stress*, 14(3), 511–526.

Noji, E. (2000). The public health consequences of disasters. *Prehospital and Disaster Medicine*, 15(4), 207–260.

Norris, F. (2002). Disasters in the urban context. *Journal of Urban Health*, 79(3), 308–314.

Norris, F., Friedman, M., Watson, P., Byrne, C., Diaz, E., & Kaniasty, K. (2002). 60,000 disaster victims speak: Part 1. An empirical review of the empirical literature. *Psychiatry*, 65(3), 207–239.

Parad, G., & Parad, H. (1968). A study of crisis-oriented planned short-term treatment: II. *Social Casework*, 49(7), 418–426.

Parad, H., & Caplan, G. (1960). A framework for studying families in crisis. *Social Work*, 5(3), 3–15.

Parad, H., & Parad, G. (1968). A study of crisis-oriented planned short-term treatment: I. *Social Casework*, 49(6), 346–355.

Pearlin, L., & Schooler, C. (1978). The structure of coping. *Journal of Health and Social Behavior*, 19, 2–21.

Raphael, B. (1986). *When disaster strikes: A handbook for caring professionals*. London: Unwin Hyman.

Raphael, B., Meldrum, L., & McFarlane, A. (1995). Does debriefing after psychological trauma work? *British Medical Journal*, 310, 1479–1480.

Rapoport, L. (1967) Crisis-oriented short-term case-work. *Social Service Review,* 41, 31–43.

Regehr, C., & Bober, T. (2005). *In the line of fire: Trauma in the emergency services.* New York: Oxford University Press.

Regehr, C., & Glancy, G. (2009). *Mental health social work in Canada.* Toronto: Oxford University Press.

Regehr, C. (2001). Crisis debriefings for emergency responders: Reviewing the evidence. *Journal of Brief Treatments and Crisis Intervention,* 1(2), 87–100.

Regehr, C., Roberts, A., & Bober, T. (2008) On the brink of disaster: A model for reducing the social and psychological impact. *Journal of Social Service Research,* 34(3), 5–14.

Reyes, G., & Elhai, J. (2004). Psychosocial interventions in the early phases of disasters. *Psychotherapy: Theory, Research, Practice and Training,* 41(4), 399–411.

Roberts, A., & Everly, G. (2006). A meta-anaysis of 36 crisis intervention studies. *Brief Treatments and Crisis Intervention,* 6(1), 10–21.

Roberts, A. R (Ed.) (2000). *Crisis intervention handbook: Assessment, treatment, and research.* New York: Oxford University Press.

Rose, S., Bisson, J., & Wessley, S. (2003). Psychological debriefing for preventing post-traumatic stress disorder (PTSD). The Cochrane Library. Retrieved June 5, 2003, from http://www.update-software.com.

Ruzek, J., Brymer, M., Jacobs, A., Layne, C., Vernberg, E., & Watson, P. (2007). Psychological first aid. *Journal of Mental Health Counseling,* 29, 17–49.

Spivack, J., & Troupe, C. (1973). The brotherhood of man: A community-based drug education and crisis intervention center. *Journal of Drug Education,* 3(2), 165–174.

Stapleton, A. B., Lating, J., Kirkhart, M., & Everly, G. S. (2006). Effects of medical crisis intervention on anxiety, depression, and posttraumatic stress symptoms: a meta-analysis. *Psychiatric Quarterly,* 77(3), 231–238.

Strickler, M., & Bonnefil, M. (1974). Crisis intervention and social casework: Similarities and differences in problem-solving. *Clinical Social Work Journal,* 2(1), 36–44.

Strickler, M. (1965). Applying crisis theory in a community clinic. *Social Casework,* 46, 150–154.

Van Emmerik, A., Kamphuis, J., Huisbosch, A., & Emmelkamp, P. (2002). Single-session debriefing after psychological trauma: A meta-analysis. *Lancet,* 360, 766–742.

Vernberg, E., Steinberg, A., Jacobs, A., Brymer, M., Watson, P., Osofsky, J. Layne, C., Pynoos, R., & Ruzek, J. (2008). Innovations in disaster mental health. *Professional Psychology: Research and Practice,* 39(4), 381–388.

Young, M. (1991). *Community crisis response team training manual.* Washington, DC: NOVA.

EGO
PSYCHOLOGY

This theory emphasizes the personality's executive function and its relationship to other personality components, assuming an optimistic view of human potential, respect for strengths, and lifelong growth capacity

Ego Psychology and Social Work Treatment

Eda Goldstein

General Overview

Ego psychological theory gained recognition in the United States in the late 1930s and 1940s. It emphasized the executive arm of the personality—the ego—and its relationship to other aspects of the personality and to the external environment. Although it initially developed as an extension of Freud's structural theory (1923), ego psychology differed significantly from his views in the following ways: (1) it was more optimistic about human potential; (2) it showed respect for people's strengths and resilience; (3) it drew attention to the more adaptive, rational, autonomous ego functions, defenses, problem-solving capacities, and other coping mechanisms of the person; (5) it described the lifelong nature of personality growth and development; and (6) it gave an important role to interpersonal relationships, the

environment, the society, and the culture in shaping human behavior (Goldstein, 1995). The prominent theorists who were associated with the early development of ego psychology included Anna Freud (1936), who focused on the adaptiveness of defense; Heinz Hartmann (1939), who initiated the concept of the ego's conflict-free sphere and its autonomous functions; Erik Erikson (1950, 1959), who described the eight stages of the life cycle and the interplay of psychological and social factors in development; and Robert White (1959, 1963), who attributed a drive for competence and mastery to the individual personality; and later, Rubin and Gertrude Blanck (1974), who elaborated on the treatment implications of ego psychological theory. Following these contributions, others began to study the constitutional and environmental factors that contribute to ego strength, coping capacity, and vulnerability (Escalona, 1968; Murphy & Moriarity, 1976), and expanded ego psychological thinking by delineating the influence of the child's earliest caretaking experiences and connections to others on personality development (Ainsworth, 1973; Bowlby, 1958; Jacobson, 1964; Mahler, 1968; Mahler, Pine, & Bergman, 1975; Spitz, 1945, 1965).

Ego psychology has evolved since its inception, and ego psychology's view of development has been refined and extended significantly. For example, originally ego psychology viewed object relations or the quality of interpersonal relationships as one of many ego functions. When theorists and researchers began to investigate the impact of the caretaking environment on the child, they delineated the complex processes by which the infant and small child attaches to and separates from the caretaker and takes the outside world inside (internalize it). Likewise, John Bowlby's (1969, 1973, 1980) work and Mary Ainsworth's (1973) studies on attachment, separation, and loss showed the nature of the complex interplay of caretaker and child during development. Members of the British school of object relations, which comprises the work of Melanie Klein (1948), W. R. D. Fairbairn (1952), D. W. Winnicott (1965), Harry Guntrip (1969, 1973), and others, also made important contributions. The writings of Otto Kernberg (1975, 1976)) reflected an attempt to integrate many concepts from the British school into American ego psychology.

Object relations theorists viewed the infant as innately object-seeking from birth. They described the interpersonal field as exerting an influence all through life, although they thought that children develop their unique or separate selves and acquire basic attitudes toward the self and others that affect all subsequent interpersonal relationships early in life (Goldstein, 2001). There has been a renaissance of interest in attachment theory recently, particularly as it sheds light on how early attachment styles influence interpersonal relationships and problems in adulthood (Biringen, 1994; Brandell & Ringel, 2007; Fish, 1996; McMillen, 1992; Sable, 1995).

Although reflecting different assumptions about personality development, cognitive theory has an important link to ego psychology. For example, Jean Piaget's (1951, 1952) theory of intelligence, Lawrence Kohlberg's (1966) theory of moral development, and other cognitive theorists shed new light on the ego's capacities and role in personality. Likewise, the study of how the ego copes with various types of biological, psychological, and environmental stress and crises enriched ego psychology (Grinker & Spiegel, 1945; Hill, 1958; Lazarus, 1966; Lindemann, 1944; Selye, 1956).

One of the early criticisms of ego psychology was that it reflected a male gender bias and showed a lack of knowledge regarding the developmental and life-cycle issues faced by gays and lesbians, people of color, and culturally diverse populations. As will be discussed later in this chapter, ego psychologists have integrated newer perspectives and knowledge about diversity. Increased understanding has illuminated the strengths and coping capacities of these groups and the special challenges that they face throughout the developmental process. More importantly, they have redefined behavior that has been viewed as pathological in more normal terms and generated different kinds of interventions (Drescher, 1998; Goldstein & Horowitz, 2003; Guttierez, 1990; Berzoff, Flanagan, & Hertz, 2007).

Basic Theoretical Principles

The following six propositions characterize ego psychology's view of human functioning (Goldstein, 1995):

1. Ego psychology views people as born with an innate capacity to function adaptively. Individuals engage in a lifelong biopsychosocial developmental process in which the ego is an active, dynamic force for coping with, adapting to, and shaping the external environment.
2. The ego is considered to be a mental structure of the personality that is responsible for negotiating between the internal needs of the individual and the outside world. Ego functions are innate and develop through maturation and the interaction among biopsychosocial factors.
3. Ego development occurs sequentially as a result of constitutional factors, the meeting of basic needs, identification with others, interpersonal relationships, learning, mastery of developmental tasks, effective problem solving, and successful coping.

4. The ego not only mediates between the individual and the environment but also mediates internal conflict among various aspects of the personality. It can elicit defenses that protect the individual from anxiety and conflict and that serve adaptive or maladaptive purposes.

5. The social environment shapes the personality and provides the conditions that foster or obstruct successful coping. Cultural factors, racial, ethnic, and religious diversity, gender, age, sexual orientation, and the presence or absence of physical challenges affect ego development.

6. Problems in social functioning must be viewed in relation both to possible ego deficits and to the fit between needs and capacities and environmental conditions and resources.

Ego psychology contains six main sets of concepts: ego functions; defenses; ego mastery, coping, and adaptation; life cycle stages; object relations; and attachment.

Ego Functions

Ego functions are the means by which the individual copes with and adapts to the world. Bellak and his colleagues (1973) identified the major ego functions:

1. Reality testing: involves the accurate perception of the external environment, of one's internal world, and of the differences between them.

2. Judgment: entails the capacity to identify certain possible courses of action and to anticipate and weigh the consequences of behavior in order to take action in order to bring about desired goals with minimal negative consequences.

3. Sense of reality of the world and of the self: the ability to feel or to be aware of the world and one's connection to it as real, to experience one's own body as intact and belonging to oneself, to feel a sense of self, and to perceive the boundaries between self and others.

4. Regulation and control of drives, affects, and impulses: involves the ability to modulate, delay, inhibit, or control the expression of impulses and affects (feelings) in accord with reality. It also entails the ability to tolerate anxiety, frustration, and unpleasant emotions such as anger and depression without becoming overwhelmed, impulsive, or symptomatic.

5. Object (or interpersonal) relations: refers to the quality of interpersonal relationships and the level of development of one's internalized sense of self and others.

6. Thought processes: refers to the shift from primary process thinking to secondary process thinking. The former follows the pleasure principle, which is characterized by wish-fulfilling fantasies and the need for immediate instinctual discharge irrespective of its appropriateness. In contrast, secondary process thinking follows the reality principle, which is characterized by the ability to postpone instinctual gratification or discharge until reality conditions are appropriate and available. Secondary process thinking is goal-directed, organized, and oriented to reality.

7. Adaptive regression in the service of the ego: ability to permit oneself to relax the hold on and relationship to reality; to experience aspects of the self that are ordinarily inaccessible when one is engaged in concentrated attention to reality; and to emerge with increased adaptive capacity as a result of creative integrations.

8. Stimulus barrier: involves a mechanism that regulates the amount of stimulation received so that it is optimal, neither too little nor too great.

9. Autonomous functions: refers to certain ego functions such as attention, concentration, memory, learning, perception, motor functions, and intentions that have a primary autonomy from the drives and thus are conflict-free—that is, they do not arise in response to frustration and conflict.

10. Mastery-competence: involves the individual's experiences of pleasure through exercising autonomous ego apparatuses in the service of adaptation.

11. Synthetic/integrative function: capacity to bind or fit together all the disparate aspects of the personality into a unified structure that acts upon the external world.

The assessment of these ego functions gives a measure of an individual's "ego strength," a composite picture of the internal psychological equipment or capacities that an individual brings to his or her interactions with others and with the social environment. Within the same individual certain ego functions may be better developed than others and may show more stability. In other words, they tend to fluctuate less from situation to situation, or over time, and are less prone to regression or disorganization under stress. Even in individuals who manifest ego strength, regression in selected areas of ego functioning may be normal in certain types of situations (for example, illness, social upheavals, crises, and role transitions), and this does not necessarily imply ego deficiencies. It is important to note that it is possible for the same individual to have highly variable ego functioning, although in cases of the most severe psychopathology ego functions may be impaired generally.

Defenses

All people use defenses, but their exact type and extent vary from individual to individual. Defenses are part of the ego's repertoire of mechanisms for protecting the individual from anxiety by keeping intolerable or unacceptable impulses or threats from conscious awareness. Defenses also may be used to help individuals adapt to their environment. The following are common defenses (Laughlin, 1979):

Repression: keeping unwanted thoughts and feelings out of awareness, or unconscious

Reaction formation: keeping certain impulses out of awareness

Projection: an individual attributes to others unacceptable thoughts and feelings that the person himself or herself has but that are not conscious

Isolation: sometimes referred to as isolation of affect; repression of the feelings associated with particular content or of the ideas connected with certain affects

Undoing: nullifying or voiding symbolically an unacceptable or guilt-provoking act, thought, or feeling

Regression: return to an earlier developmental phase, level of functioning, or type of

behavior in order to avoid the anxieties of the present

Introjection: taking another person into the self, psychologically speaking, in order to avoid the direct expression of powerful emotions such as love and hate

Reversal: alteration of a feeling, attitude, trait, relation, direction, or what have you, into its opposite

Sublimation: a high-level capacity; conversion of an impulse from a socially objectionable aim to a socially acceptable one while still retaining the original goal of the impulse

Intellectualization: warding off unacceptable affects and impulses by thinking about them rather than experiencing them directly

Rationalization: use of convincing reasons to justify certain ideas, feelings, or actions so as to avoid recognizing their true underlying motive, which is unacceptable

Displacement: shifting feelings or conflicts about one person or situation onto another

Denial: negation or nonacceptance of important aspects of reality or of one's own experience that one may actually perceive

Somatization: conversion of intolerable impulses or conflicts into physical symptoms

Idealization: overvaluing of another person, place, family, or activity beyond what is realistic

Compensation: attempt to make up for what one perceives as deficits or deficiencies

Asceticism: moral renunciation of certain pleasure in order to avoid the anxiety and conflict associated with impulse gratification

Altruism: obtaining satisfaction through self-sacrifice to others or through participating in causes as a way of dealing with unacceptable feelings and conflicts

Splitting: keeping apart two contradictory ego states such as love and hate so that contradictory aspects of feelings or characteristics of self and others cannot be integrated.

Since defenses operate unconsciously, the person is not aware that he or she is using a particular defense. Defenses may be adaptive or maladaptive. All defenses falsify or distort reality to some extent, but when a person uses defenses in a flexible rather than rigid fashion with minimal distortion of reality and the person is able to function well without undue anxiety, the defenses are said to be adaptive. A defense, however, can severely limit a person's ability to perceive reality or to cope effectively and thus may be maladaptive. A person does not deliberately seek to maintain his or her defenses, but because they serve a protective function, individuals usually resist efforts directed at modifying their defenses. This resistance, however, creates obstacles to achieving the very changes that the person would like. Although it may seem desirable to try to lessen or modify certain maladaptive defenses in a given individual because they interfere with effective coping, any effort of this sort will arouse considerable anxiety. In many instances, however, when defenses are adaptive, they should be respected, approached with caution, and at times strengthened.

Under acute or unremitting stress, illness, or fatigue, the ego's defenses, along with the other ego functions, may fail. When there is a massive defensive failure the person becomes flooded with anxiety. This can result in a severe and rapid deterioration of ego functioning, and in some cases the personality becomes fragmented and chaotic, just as in a psychotic episode. When defenses are rigid, an individual may appear exceedingly brittle, taut, and driven; his or her behavior may seem increasingly mechanical, withdrawn, or peculiar.

Ego Mastery, Coping, and Adaptation

A mastery drive or instinct (Hendrick, 1942; White, 1959, 1963) has been postulated by authors who believe there is an inborn, active striving toward interaction with the environment leading to the individual's experiencing a sense of competence or effectiveness. White described the ego as having independent energies that propelled the individual to gain pleasure through manipulating, exploring, and acting upon the environment. He called these energies effectance and suggested that feelings of efficacy are the pleasure derived from each interaction with the environment. In White's view, ego identity results from the degree to which one's effectance and feelings of efficacy have been nurtured.

These qualities affect present and future behavior, because they contribute to basic attitudes, such as one's self-esteem, self-confidence, trust in one's own judgment, and belief in one's decision-making capacities.

In the process of adaptation, human beings find ways of managing their internal states and negotiating the external environment. Some coping mechanisms go beyond what ego functions and defenses do. Such qualities as humor, perseverance, and conscious efforts to distract oneself from stressful circumstances can be thought of as aiding a person to deal with the vicissitudes of life.

Life Cycle Stages

Erik Erikson (1950, 1959) viewed optimal ego development as a result of the mastery of stage-specific developmental tasks and crises. He argued that the successful resolution of each crisis from birth to death leads to a sense of ego identity and may be said to constitute the core of one's sense of self. Erikson viewed later stages as dependent on earlier ones. The use of the term "crisis" reflects the idea that there is a state of tension or disequilibrium at the beginning of each new stage. The resolution of each stage is described in terms of the achievement of positive and negative solutions. In any individual, however, the resolution of the core developmental crisis posed by each stage may lie anywhere on a continuum from best to worst outcome. According to Erikson, resolution of each successive life cycle stage depends as much on those with whom the individual interacts as on his or her own innate capacities. Similarly, crisis resolution is dependent upon the impact of culture and environment as it shapes child-rearing practices and provides opportunities or obstacles to optimal adaptation.

Erikson was among the first theorists to suggest that adulthood is a dynamic rather than a static time and that ego development continues throughout adulthood. There is mounting interest in, and evidence for, the idea that personality change occurs in adult life. Adulthood is seen to contain elements of the past as well as dynamic processes, which lead to such changes. Benedek (1970), Butler (1963), Colarusso and Nemiroff (1981), Goldstein

(2005), Gould (1978), Levinson (1978), Neugarten (1964, 1968), and Vaillant (1977) are among the authors who have made seminal contributions to understanding adult developmental processes.

Recent Theoretical Developments

Newer perspectives on and knowledge about women, gays and lesbians, and culturally diverse populations can be integrated with ego psychology. For example, early members of the Stone Center for Developmental Studies, which included Jean Baker Miller, Judith Jordan, Alexandra Kaplan, Irene Stiver, and Janet Surrey (Jordan et al., 1991) as well as another prominent female theorist, Jessica Benjamin (1988), were among those who made major contributions to the study of women. The Stone Center group regarded women's self-development as evolving in the context of relatedness, believing that enhanced connection rather than increased self-object differentiation and separateness is women's major goal. Further, they contended that women grow optimally and change when they experience an interactive process in which mutual engagement, empathy, and empowerment with significant others occurs. Nonresponsive relationships and disconnection rather than problems in separation–individuation per se result in pathology. Benjamin stressed the balance between oneness and separateness, merging and differentiation. In Benjamin's view, true independence involves self-assertion and mutuality, separateness and sharing, and the individual's inability to reconcile dependence and independence leads to patterns of domination and submission.

More affirmative views of gay and lesbian development have been put forth and have helped to make ego psychology more attuned to these populations (Drescher, 1998; Glassgold & Iasenza, 1995; Goldstein & Horowitz, 2003; Gonsiorek, 1982; Weille, 1993). Recent research supports the view that lesbian object relations and self-development arise as a variant of positive developmental experiences, in contrast to the traditional belief that they reflect arrested, immature, narcissistic, and undifferentiated object relations. For example, in Spaulding's (1993) study of 24 college-educated lesbians who had positive

identities and achieved high scores on measures of psychological stability, the women showed "evidence of highly evolved, differentiated and integrated level of object and reality relatedness" (p. 17). Further, their views of their parents did not correspond to common stereotypes in that lesbians saw both their mothers and fathers as strong, positive role models, who were nurturing, successful, and warm (p. 19).

Finally, greater attention to culturally diverse populations also has enriched ego psychology. Increasing knowledge of the unique coping capacities and needs of people of color and other ethnic minorities has reshaped the treatment process and led to more respectful and empowering interventive approaches (Berzoff, Flanagan, & Hertz, 2007; de la Cancela, 1986, pp. 291–296; Guttierez, 1990; Pinderhughes, 1983, pp. 331–338; Ryan, 1985, 330–340; Wilson, 1989, pp. 380–385).

Impact on Social Work Practice

Ego psychology had a dramatic impact on social work practice beginning in the years of the Great Depression and then in the post-World War II period. As Gordon Hamilton (1958) so aptly observed, ego psychology's more optimistic view of human potential at a time when the world was "crumbling to pieces … was part of the vision of man's strength and sturdiness under adversity" (p. 22). Social workers who played an important role in applying ego psychological concepts to social work practice were Lucille Austin (1948), Louise Bandler (1963), Eleanor Cockerill and colleagues (1953), Annette Garrett (1958), Gordon Hamilton (1940, 1958), Florence Hollis (1949, 1964, 1972), Howard J. Parad (1958), Isabell Stamm (1959), and Charlotte Towle (1949).

The use of ego psychology in social work practice led to a shortening and refocusing of the study and assessment process. It emphasized (1) the client's person–environment transactions in the here and now, particularly the degree to which he or she is coping effectively with major life roles and tasks; (2) the client's adaptive, autonomous, and conflict-free areas of ego functioning as well as his or her ego deficits and maladaptive defenses and patterns; (3) the key developmental issues affecting the client's current reactions; and (4) the ways in which the stresses of the external environment or a lack of resources and environmental supports are creating obstacles to successful coping (Goldstein, 1995).

Ego psychology transformed the casework process from a never-ending, unfocused exploration of personality difficulties to a more deliberate and focused use of the client's strengths and underscored the importance of the client's self-determination and involvement in guiding intervention. In addition to the use of psychological techniques, it developed a repertoire of techniques for working with the social environment (Goldstein, 1995).

Ego-oriented treatment was categorized as supportive and modifying (Hollis, 1972). Ego-supportive intervention aims at restoring, maintaining, and enhancing clients' ego functions and coping capacities. It centers on improving clients' here-and-now functioning, uses the real aspects of the client–worker relationship as a positive and corrective force in the interventive process, and promotes ego mastery and problem solving. Ego-modifying intervention aims at understanding and changing a individual's maladaptive behavior and patterns of relating to others and in this respect is more focused on pathology. It employs more reflective and interpretive techniques, working with the person's past experiences as well as present circumstances, and deals with the more transferential rather than real aspects of the client–worker relationship. In an ego-modifying approach, greater understanding of the nature of maladaptive defenses and behavior and basic attitudes toward the self and others and new relationship experiences that help to repair, strengthen, and expand clients' inner capacities are important to the change process (Goldstein, 1995).

Ego-oriented treatment approaches can be utilized with a broad range of clients whose ego functioning is disrupted by current stresses or who show severe and chronic problems in coping, including moderate to severe emotional disorders. Although ego psychological intervention often has been associated with long-term psychotherapy, it can be used in crisis and short-term intervention. The use of brief treatment requires somewhat different skills than does extended treatment, since faster assessments and more active and focused interventions are necessary.

Efforts to incorporate ego psychology into social work practice also led to a distinctive problem-solving casework model developed by Helen Perlman (1957), who attempted to bridge the lingering dispute between diagnostic (psychoanalytic) and functional (Rankian) caseworkers as well as to offer correctives for practices that she viewed as dysfunctional for the client. It also contributed to the generation of crisis and more ecologically oriented models (Germain & Gitterman, 1980; Golan, 1978).

Changing Views and New Directions

Beginning in the 1960s and throughout the 1970s, despite its psychosocial framework, ego psychology often was criticized by a certain segment of the social work profession for its focus on the inner life of the individual, emphasis on psychopathology, and use of psychotherapeutic techniques rather than environmental interventions. At this time concern mounted regarding clients who were "harder to reach" and presented "multi-problems." Additionally, the push toward equality, social justice, and freedom from oppression on the part of people of color, women, and gays and lesbians contributed to a challenge of psychodynamic theory and individual treatment, which were associated with the general distrust of the medical model and its view that people who were different were deviant. Followers of ego psychology were criticized for blaming the victim rather than the effects of oppression, poverty, and trauma and for "pathologizing" the behavior of women, gays and lesbians, and those who are culturally diverse rather than respecting their unique characteristics and strengths. Moreover, because the concepts and associated practices stemming from ego psychology were not operationalized and studied, there was insufficient evidence supporting the efficacy of ego-oriented treatment.

In the 1960s, when social work embraced alternative theories and interventive models and emphasized social change or "macro-systems" intervention rather than direct practice or "micro-systems" intervention, ego psychology's prominent position in social work's knowledge base waned. When direct practice reasserted its importance during the 1970s and 1980s, however, ego psychology enjoyed a renaissance of interest. Almost 50 years after ego psychology's emergence, the results of a survey of the 1982 NASW Register of Clinical Social Workers (Mackey, Urek, & Charkoudian, 1987) showed that 51% "identified ego psychology as being the most instrumental to their approach" (p. 368).

Many of those who criticized ego psychology did not take into account its integration of newer theoretical developments and research and its openness to change. As a theory of personality, it has expanded to encompass new perspectives on attachment and interpersonal relationships, trauma, women's development and roles, the unique characteristics of and issues faced by culturally and ethnically diverse groups, people of color, and other oppressed populations, such as gays, lesbians, and transgendered persons. As an interventive model, ego-oriented intervention has been applied to diverse problems and populations and its proponents have attempted to integrate many of the ideas and principles that have been suggested by more culturally sensitive, affirmative, and empowering interventive approaches. Moreover, there is increasing evidence for the utility of ego psychological concepts and interventions. Changes in society and in the clients needing help have focused greater attention on the application of ego-oriented intervention to many client problems and populations: AIDS (Dane & Miller, 1992; Lopez & Getzel, 1984); rape and other forms of violent assault (Abarbanel & Richman, 1990; Lee & Rosenthal, 1983); child abuse (Brekke, 1990); domestic violence (Bowker, 1983); substance abuse (Chernus, 1985; Straussner, 1993); borderline and other types of character pathology (Goldstein, 1990); homelessness and chronic mental illness (Belcher & Ephross, 1989; Harris & Bergman, 1984); and the effects of childhood sexual abuse on adults (Courtois, 1988; Faria & Belohlavek, 1986). Likewise, ego psychology addresses the special needs of culturally diverse and oppressed populations (Berzoff, Flanagan, & Hertz, 2007).

Despite its person-in-situation focus, its broad application, and its continuing evolution, however, the criticism has lingered within some segments of the social work profession that intervention based on ego psychological principles and techniques is too psychotherapeutic and is intended for addressing the concerns of the "worried well" rather than clients presenting with difficult problems (Specht & Courtney, 1994). No doubt, this criticism has been fueled over the past two decades, in part, by the increasing numbers of social workers who entered private practice and the number of students entering social work educational programs who wanted to become therapists, even on a part-time basis. Nevertheless, most social work practitioners remain in agency practice, where they deal with a broad range of clients and client problems. Moreover, the view that psychotherapy is aimed only at self-understanding or self-actualization rather than helping clients cope more effectively with their life circumstances represents a serious misunderstanding of the treatment process.

Several other important factors have contributed to the decline of ego psychology's popularity in social work. There are many competing interventive models and approaches available to practitioners (Turner, 1996), some of which are presented as offering quick remedies to clients' difficulties. In the present climate of managed care and cutbacks in service delivery, there has been a resultant emphasis on very brief and seemingly solution-focused interventions, a minimization of the importance of the client–worker relationship as a force in treatment, and a disregard for psychodynamic thinking and interventive principles. Further, an emphasis on the use of evidence-based interventions has tended to favor the employment of cognitive behavioral interventions, which have been subjected to more systematic research than have ego psychological interventions. In this climate, most schools of social work in the United States have reduced the amount of content allotted to psychodynamic and ego psychological content and clinical practice principles. Yet these concepts continue to be popular among social work trainees and practitioners, as evidenced by their actively enrolling in electives or seeking out courses in other programs that address this content once they graduate.

Finally, as psychoanalysis has generated new theoretical paradigms and clinical frameworks, clinically oriented practitioners have expanded their knowledge base. For example, self-psychology (Kohut, 1971, 1977, 1984), which offers an alternative framework for understanding human behavior and psychopathology, appealed to many social work clinicians. More recently, contemporary relational thinking (Aron & Harris, 2005; Mitchell, 1988; Stolorow, Atwood, & Brandchaft, 1994; Stolorow, Brandchaft, & Atwood, 1987), which incorporates postmodern ideas, has gathered adherents. Although early self-psychology and relational theorists moved away from the "drive-structural model" of classical Freudian theory (Greenberg & Mitchell 1983), their formulations reflected what has been termed a "one-person" psychology that views development as an "individual" activity that is aided by the presence of a caregiving other. A second group of more contemporary theorists have put forth concepts that are broadly referred to as "two-person" psychologies that emphasize mutuality, openness, genuineness, collaboration, dialogue, and intersubjectivity in the therapeutic process. There is a rich relational tradition within social work historically, and both self-psychology and current relational ideas are very compatible with social work values and practices (Goldstein, Miehls, & Ringel, 2009).

Evidence-Based Foundations

Over the years greater sophistication in research methodology and design and more willingness on the part of theorists to subject their ideas to investigation have led to more systematic study of child and adult development and the ways in which people cope with stress, crisis, and various types of life demands and events. Tools for assessing normal and pathological ego functioning and adaptive functioning also have evolved. In contrast to these developments, intervention research has lagged considerably.

When social casework and its ego psychological base came under attack in the 1960s, studies of social work intervention that were based largely on the psychosocial model of practice and its ego psychological underpinnings were disheartening (Mullen et al., 1972). Upon closer analysis, however, the goals, processes, and outcomes studied were not well selected in the research design (Perlman, 1972). Since these studies, outcome research on social work practice has yielded more positive results (Rubin, 1985; Thomlison, 1984). Moreover, the study of

psychotherapy process and outcome, which also draws on ego psychological principles and techniques, has increased (Lambert & Hill, 1994.)

An important thrust of process-oriented studies has been the investigation of common factors that are associated with positive outcomes across different therapeutic models. Lambert and Bergin (1994, p. 163) list 33 such features. Perhaps the two most important foci in these studies have been on the therapeutic alliance and therapist characteristics such as accurate empathy, positive regard, nonpossessive warmth, and congruence or genuineness.

Although a review of outcome studies based on psychodynamic psychotherapy has shown many positive results (Fonagy, Roth, & Higgitt, 2005), isolating the specific factors that are associated with effectiveness has been more difficult, and the task of operationally defining psychosocial variables, interventions, and outcomes remains a difficult task. Consequently, there is a dearth of evidence for psychosocial interventions in comparison to cognitive behavioral approaches.

In the decades since the 1970s, much of what is referred to as evidence-based practice has been based on cognitive behavioral approaches that lend themselves to measurement and intervention (Linehan, 1993). Manuals of techniques that target specific disorders have been utilized and there has been a tendency to study more highly controlled rather than real-life clinical conditions. Nevertheless, there still appears to be a gap between the evidence that has been generated and the impact that it has had on practitioners (Nathan, Stuart, & Dolan, 2000). Concurrently, there is a good deal of evidence for the use of ego-oriented interventions that are not often integrated into courses on evidence-based practice.

It is critical that the rich knowledge base for social work practice provided by ego psychology and the interventive models that flow from this body of thought receive more research attention from social work practitioners. Although experimental designs are important, there is a need to use more diverse research strategies that are suited to psychosocial intervention and to real-life clinical situations. To produce clinical research findings that are relevant in today's practice, it will be necessary to encourage more collaborative partnerships between clinicians and researchers and to train social work clinician researchers.

References

Abarbanel, G., & Richman, G. (1990). The rape victim. In H. J. Parad & L. G. Parad (Eds.), *Crisis intervention book 2: The practitioner's sourcebook for brief therapy* (pp. 93–118). Milwaukee, WI: Family Service Association of America.

Ainsworth, M. D. S (1973). The development of mother-infant attachment. In B. Caldwell & H. Ricciuti (Eds.), *Review of child development research*, Vol. 3 (pp. 1–94). Chicago: University of Chicago Press.

Aron, L., & Harris, A (2005). Introduction. In L. Aron & A. Harris (Eds.), *Relational psychoanalysis*, Vol. 2, (pp. xiii–xxi). Hillsdale, NJ: Analytic Press.

Austin, L (1948). Trends in differential treatment in social casework. *Social Casework*, 29, 203–211.

Bandler, L (1963). Some aspects of ego growth through sublimation. In H. J. Parad & R. Miller (Eds.), *Ego-oriented casework* (pp. 27–44). New York: Family Service Association of America.

Belcher, J. R., & Ephross, P. H (1989). Toward an effective practice model for the homeless mentally ill. *Social Casework: Journal of Contemporary Social Work*, 70, 421–427.

Bellak, L., Hurvich, M., & Gediman, H (1973). *Ego functions in schizophrenics, neurotics, and normals.* New York: John Wiley & Sons.

Benedek, T (1970). Parenthood during the life cycle. In J. Anthony & T. Benedek (Eds.), *Parenthood: Its psychology and psychopathology* (pp. 185–208). Boston: Little, Brown.

Benjamin, J (1988). *The bonds of love: Psychoanalysis, feminism, and the problem of domination.* New York: Pantheon.

Berzoff, J. L., Flanagan, & Hertz, P (Eds.). (2007). *Inside out and outside in. Psychodynamic theories and practice in multicultural contexts* (2nd ed.) Lanham, MD: Roman and Littlefield Press.

Biringen, Z (1994). Attachment theory and research: Application to clinical practice. *American Journal of Orthopsychiatry*, 64, 404–420.

Blanck, G., & Blanck, R (1974). *Ego psychology in theory and practice.* New York: Columbia University Press.

Bowlby, J (1958). The nature of the child's tie to the mother. *International Journal of Psychoanalysis*, 39, 350–373.

Bowlby, J (1969). *Attachment and loss. Vol. I. Attachment.* New York: Basic Books.

Bowlby, J (1973). *Attachment and loss. Vol. II. Separation.* New York: Basic Books.

Bowlby, J (1980). *Attachment and loss. Vol. III. Loss.* London: Hogarth Press.

Bowker, L. H (1983). Marital rape: A distinct syndrome. *Social Casework: The Journal of Contemporary Social Work*, 64, 347–352.

Brandell, J. R., & Ringel, S. (2007). *Attachment theory and dynamic social work practice.* New York: Columbia University Press.

Brekke, J (1990). Crisis intervention with victims and perpetrators of spouse abuse. In H. J. Parad & L. G. Parad (Eds.), *Crisis intervention book 2: The practitioner's sourcebook for brief therapy* (pp. 161–178). Milwaukee, WI: Family Service Association of America.

Butler, R. N (1963). The life review: An interpretation of reminiscence in the aged. *Psychiatry*, 26, 65–76.

Chernus, L. A (1985). Clinical issues in alcoholism treatment. *Social Casework*, 66, 67–75.

Chodorow, N (1978). *The reproduction of mothering.* Berkeley: University of California Press.

Cockerill, E., et al (1953). *A conceptual framework of social casework.* Pittsburgh: University of Pittsburgh Press.

Colarusso, C., & Nemiroff, R. A (1981). *Adult development.* New York: Plenum Press.

Courtois, C. A (1988). *Healing the incest wound: Adult survivors in therapy.* New York: W. W. Norton.

Dane, B. O., & Miller, S. O (1992). *AIDS: Intervening with hidden grievers.* Westport, CT: Auburn House.

de la Cancela, V (1986). A critical analysis of Puerto Rican machismo: Implications for clinical practice. *Psychotherapy*, 23, 291–296.

Drescher, J (1998). *Psychoanalytic therapy and the gay man.* Hillsdale, NJ: The Analytic Press.

Erikson, E (1950). *Childhood and society.* New York: Norton.

Erikson, E (1959). Identity and the life cycle. *Psychological Issues*, 1, 50–100.

Escalona, S. K (1968). *The roots of individuality: Normal patterns of development in infancy.* Chicago: Aldine.

Fairbairn, W. R. D (1952). *Psychoanalytic studies of the personality.* London: Routledge & Kegan Paul.

Faria, G., & Belohlavek, N (1984). Treating female adult survivors of childhood incest. *Social Casework: The Journal of Contemporary Social Work*, 65, 465–471.

Fish, B (1996). Clinical implications of attachment narratives. *Clinical Social Work Journal*, 24, 239–254.

Fonagy, P., Roth, A., & Higgitt, A (2005). Psychodynamic psychotherapies: Evidence-based practice and clinical wisdom. *Bulletin of the Menninger Clinic*, 69, 1–58.

Freud, A (1936). *The ego and the mechanisms of defense*. New York: International Universities Press.

Freud, S (1923). The ego and the id. In J. Strachey (Ed.), *The standard edition of the complete psychological works of Sigmund Freud*, vol. 19. London: Hogarth, 1961.

Garrett, A (1958). Modern casework: The contributions of ego psychology. In H. J. Parad (Ed.), *Ego psychology and dynamic casework* (pp. 38–52). New York: Family Service Association of America.

Germain, C. B., & Gitterman, A (1980). *The life model of social work practice*. New York: Columbia University Press.

Gilligan, C (1982). *In a different voice: Psychological theory and women's development*. Cambridge, MA: Harvard University Press.

Golan, N (1978). *Treatment in crisis situations*. New York: The Free Press.

Glassgold, J. M., & Iasenza, S. (Eds.). (1995). *Lesbians and psychoanalysis: Revolutions in theory and practice*. New York: The Free Press.

Goldstein, E. G (1990). *Borderline disorders: Clinical models and techniques*. New York: Guilford Press.

Goldstein, E. G (1995). *Ego psychology and social work practice* (2nd ed.). New York: The Free Press.

Goldstein, E. G (2001). *Object relations theory and self psychology in social work*. New York: The Free Press.

Goldstein, E. G (2005). *When the bubble bursts: Clinical perspectives on mid-life issues*. Hillsdale, NJ: The Analytic Press.

Goldstein, E. G., & Horowitz, L. G (2003). *Lesbian identity and contemporary psychotherapy: A framework for practice*. Hillsdale, NJ: The Analytic Press.

Goldstein, E. G., Miehls, D., & Ringel, S (2009). *Advanced clinical social work practice: Relational principles and techniques*. New York: Columbia University Press.

Gonsiorek, J. C. (Ed.). (1982). *Homosexuality and psychotherapy: A practitioner's handbook of affirmative models*. New York: Haworth Press.

Gould, R. L (1978). *Transformations: Growth and change in adult life*. New York: Simon & Schuster.

Greenberg, J., & Mitchell, S (1983). *Object relations in psychoanalytic theory*. Cambridge, MA: Harvard University Press.

Grinker, R. R., & Spiegel, J. D (1945). *Men under stress*. Philadelphia: Blakiston.

Guntrip, H (1969). *Schizoid phenomena, object relations, and the self*. New York: International Universities Press.

Guntrip, H (1973). *Psychoanalytic theory, therapy, and the self*. New York: Basic Books (Harper Torchbooks).

Gutierrez, L. M (1990). Working with women of color: An empowerment perspective. *Social Work*, 35, 149–154.

Hamilton, G (1940). *Theory and practice of social casework*. New York: Columbia University Press.

Hamilton, G (1958). A theory of personality: Freud's contribution to social casework. In H. J. Parad (Ed.), *Ego psychology and dynamic casework* (pp. 11–37). New York: Family Service Association of America.

Harris, M., & Bergman, H. C (1986). Case management with the chronically mentally ill: A clinical perspective. *American Journal of Orthopsychiatry*, 56, 296–302.

Hartmann, H (1939). *Ego psychology and the problem of adaptation*. New York: International Universities Press.

Hendrick, I (1942). Instinct and the ego during infancy. *Psychoanalytic Quarterly*, II, 33–58.

Hill, R (1958). Generic features of families under stress. *Social Casework*, 39, 139–150.

Hollis, F (1949). The techniques of casework. *Journal of Social Casework*, 30, 235–244.

Hollis, F (1964). *Casework: A psychosocial therapy*. New York: Random House.

Hollis, F (1972). *Casework: A psychosocial therapy* (2nd ed.). New York: Random House.

Jacobson, E (1964). *The self and the object world*. New York: International Universities Press.

Jordan, J. V., Kaplan, A. G., Miller, J. B., Stiver, I. P., & Surrey, J. L (Eds.). (1991). *Women's growth in connection*. New York: Guilford Press.

Kernberg, O. F (1975). *Borderline conditions and pathological narcissism*. New York: Jason Aronson.

Kernberg, O. F (1976). *Object relations theory and clinical psychoanalysis*. New York: Jason Aronson.

Klein, M (1948). *Contributions to psychoanalysis: 1921–1945*. London: Hogarth Press.

Kohlberg, L (1966). A cognitive-developmental analysis of children's sex-role concepts and attitudes. In E. E. Macoby (Ed.), *The development of sex-differences*. Stanford, CA: Stanford University Press.

Kohut, H (1971). *The analysis of the self*. New York: International Universities Press.

Kohut, H (1977). *The restoration of the self*. New York: International Universities Press.

Kohut, H (1984). *How does analysis cure?* (A. Goldberg & P. Stephansky, eds.). Chicago: University of Chicago Press.

Lambert, M. J., & Bergin, A (1994). Psychodynamic approaches. In A. Bergin & S. L. Garfield, (Eds.), *Handbook of psychotherapy and behavioral change*

(4th ed., pp. 467–508). New York: John Wiley & Sons.

Lambert, M. J., & Hill, C. E (1994). Assessing psychotherapy outcomes and process. In A. Bergin & S. L. Garfield, (eds.), *Handbook of psychotherapy and behavioral change* (4th ed., pp. 72–113). New York: John Wiley & Sons.

Laughlin, H. P (1979). *The ego and its defenses* (2nd ed.). New York: Jason Aronson.

Lazarus, R. S (1966). *Psychological stress and the coping process.* New York: McGraw-Hill.

Lee, J. A. B., & Rosenthal, S. J (1983). Working with victims of violent assault. *Social Casework: The Journal of Contemporary Social Work,* 64, 593–601.

Levinson, D. J (1978). *The seasons of a man's life.* New York: Knopf.

Lindemann, E (1944). Symptomatology and management of acute grief. *American Journal of Psychiatry.*

Linehan, M. M (1993). *Cognitive-behavioral treatment of borderline personality disorder.* New York: Guilford Press.

Lopez, D., & Getzel, G. S (1984). Helping gay AIDS patients in crisis. *Social Casework: The Journal of Contemporary Social Work,* 65, 387–394.

Mackey, R. A., Urek, M. B., & Charkoudian, S (1987). The relationship of theory to clinical practice. *Clinical Social Work Journal,* 15, 368–383.

Mahler, M. S (1968). *On human symbiosis and the vicissitudes of individuation.* New York: International Universities Press.

Mahler, M. S., Pine, F., & Bergman, A (1975). *The psychological birth of the human infant.* New York: Basic Books.

McMillen, J. C (1992). Attachment theory and clinical social work. *Clinical Social Work Journal,* 20, 205–218.

Mitchell, S (1988). *Relational concepts in psychoanalysis.* Cambridge: Harvard University Press.

Mullen, E. J., Dumpson, J. R., et al. (Eds.). (1972). *Evaluation of social intervention.* San Francisco: Jossey-Bass.

Murphy, L. B., & Moriarity, A. E (1976). *Vulnerability, coping and growth from infancy to adolescence.* New Haven, CT: Yale University Press.

Nathan, P., Stuart, S. P., & Dolan A. L (2000). Research on psychotherapy efficacy and effectiveness. *Psychological Bulletin,* 126, 964–981.

Neugarten, B. L (1968). Adult personality: Toward a psychology of the life cycle. In W. E. Vinacke (Ed.), *Readings in general psychology* (pp. 332–343). New York: American Book.

Neugarten, B. L., et al. (Eds.) (1964). *Personality in middle and late life.* New York: Atherton Press.

Parad, H. J (Ed.). (1958). *Ego psychology and dynamic casework.* New York: Family Service Association of America.

Perlman, H. H (1957). *Social casework: A problem-solving process.* Chicago: University of Chicago Press.

Perlman, H. H (1972). Once more with feeling. In E. J. Mullen, J. R. Dumpson, et al. (Eds.), *Evaluation of social intervention* (pp. 191–209). San Francisco: Jossey-Bass.

Piaget, J (1951). *The child's conception of the world.* London: Routledge & Kegan Paul.

Piaget, J (1952). *The origins of intelligence in children.* New York: International Universities Press.

Pinderhughes, E. B (1983). Empowerment for our clients and for ourselves. *Social Casework: The Journal of Contemporary Social Work,* 64, 331–338.

Rubin, A (1985). Practice effectiveness: More grounds for optimism. *Social Work,* 30, 469–476.

Ryan, A. S (1985). Cultural factors in casework with Chinese Americans. *Social Casework: The Journal of Contemporary Social Work,* 66, 333–340.

Sable, P (1995). Attachment theory and post-traumatic stess disorder. *Journal of Analytic Social Work,* 2, 89–109.

Selye, H (1956). *The stress of life.* New York: McGraw-Hill.

Spaulding, E. C (1993). The inner world of objects and lesbian development. *Journal of Analytic Social Work,* 1, 5–31.

Specht, H., & Courtney, M (1994). *Unfaithful angels.* New York: The Free Press.

Spitz, R (1945). Hospitalism: An inquiry into the genesis of psychiatric conditions in early childhood. *Psychoanalytic Study of the Child,* 2, 313–342.

Spitz, R (1965). *The first year of life: A psychoanalytic study of normal and deviant development of object relations.* New York: International Universities Press.

Stamm, I (1959). Ego psychology in the emerging theoretical base of social work. In A. J. Kahn (Ed.), *Issues in American social work* (pp. 80–109). New York: Columbia University Press.

Stolorow, R., Atwood, G., & Brandchaft, B (1994). *The intersubjective perspective.* Northvale, NJ: Jason Aronson.

Stolorow, R., Brandchaft, B., & Atwood, G (1987). *Psychoanalytic treatment: An intersubjective approach.* Hillsdale, NJ: Jason Aronson.

Straussner, S. L. A (1993). Assessment and treatment of clients with alcohol and other drug abuse problems: An overview. In S. L. A. Straussner (Ed.), *Clinical work with substance-abusing clients* (pp. 3–32). New York: The Guilford Press.

Thomlison, R. J (1984). Something works: Evidence from practice effectiveness studies. *Social Work*, 29, 51–56.

Towle, C (1949). Helping the client to use his capacities and resources. *Proceedings of the National Conference of Social Work, 1948* (pp. 259–279). New York: Columbia University Press.

Vaillant, G. E (1977). *Adaptation in life*. Boston: Little, Brown.

Weille, K. L. H (1993). Reworking developmental theory: The case of lesbian identity formation. *Clinical Social Work Journal*, 21, 151–160.

White, R. F (1959). Motivation reconsidered: The concept of competence. *Psychological Review*, 66, 297–233.

White, R. F (1963). Ego and reality in psychoanalytic theory. *Psychological Issues*, Vol. 2. New York: International Universities Press.

Wilson, M. N (1989). Child development in the context of the black extended family. *American Psychologist*, 44, 380–385.

Winnicott, D. W (1965). *Maturational processes and the facilitating environment*. New York: International Universities Press.

EMPOWERMENT

This approach deals with empowering people, across the life span as individuals, families, groups, and communities, to develop potential and assets to change environments and make them more just

Empowerment Approach to Social Work Practice

Judith A. B. Lee and Rhonda E. Hudson

Overview

The second decade in the new millennium heralds many changes since the 1996 printing of this chapter, but sadly it is also witness to the many things that have remained the same. The Poverty described above has remained a constant over the years, well known by those who continue to live at the margins, and those, including social workers, who stand by them. Such unyielding poverty takes its toll on individuals, families, and communities, draining them physically, emotionally and spiritually. Those who are economically and socially disadvantaged often feel powerless against natural, social, economic, and political forces that overwhelm them like the waves that breached the levee in New Orleans.

Although there is disagreement as to when it will end, we face massive economic recession and unemployment on national and global fronts (Aversa, 2009; Elliot, 2009; Hopkins, 2009; Revkin, 2009; Roubini, 2009). The ranks of the new poor are growing dramatically, as many lose jobs, health coverage, economic security, and housing. Both authors of this chapter practice with the hungry and homeless in their communities and have seen the numbers swell in the past year. Additionally, the realities of terrorism, war, and natural disasters, including the effects of global warming, present challenging realities demanding our attention. These realities are the context in which current social work practice takes place. The empowerment approach is a response to living in the postmodern context. Adams (2008) notes that "in the postmodern era, empowerment has the potential to become either a unifying or a divisive theme of social work" (p. 22), depending on the response of agencies to empowered users of service, and, we add, depending on the response of educators, social workers, and agency administrators to the dictates of managed care, should it continue as it now is. Here, we affirm that empowerment on all interconnected levels of living (personal, interpersonal, communal, spiritual, and political) is needed as never before, and the empowerment approach to social work practice discussed here (Lee, 1994, 2001) and a variety of related empowerment-oriented conceptualizations (Adams, 2008; Hudson, 2009; Miley, O'Melia, & Dubois, 2009; Shera & Wells, 1999; Gutierrez & Lewis, 1999; Walton, Sandau-Beckler, & Mannes, 2001; Eamon, 2008; and others noted in this chapter) are just what is needed at this juncture in postmodern history.

British social work theorist Robert Adams (2008) reminds us that not all social work practice is empowering. Many mandated services are in fact delivered in disempowering ways. They may follow guidelines that are not responsive to empowerment-oriented principles or to the exigencies of the people served. The authenticity of empowerment should derive from and be rooted in the circumstances of those who use the services, not those who commission, manage, and deliver them, or those who research, write, and teach about them. Adams notes that an empowerment approach must be enacted on multiple levels, often simultaneously. He says: "To attempt to work at one level and separate it from the others is to risk tokenism at best and, at worst, failure" (p. 3). Further, empowerment practice must take into account global awareness and interdependence and apply in developing countries. He notes that Lee (2001) advances an empowerment approach that does this.

Lee's (2001) second edition of *The Empowerment Approach: Building the Beloved Community* deals with empowering people across the lifespan individually and in families, groups, and communities to develop their capabilities and assets and change noxious environments. Building the beloved community where justice reigns is both the process and the hoped-for outcome of individual and political empowerment. It is where we are going and how we will get there. Case

examples throughout the book illustrate how users of services in relational systems of all sizes are empowering themselves. This includes attention to those with special struggles, including the mentally ill, developmentally disabled, and a range of special populations. There are international examples throughout the book, culminating in a final chapter on empowerment in a global perspective that describes empowerment practice in developing countries.

This nation watched in horror at the plight of the inner-city poor in New Orleans after the time-worn and cracked levee broke and demolished lives, homes, and land to an extent not seen before in modern times in the United States of America. Yet, in their social commentaries Obama (2006) and Brokaw (2007) agree that the human compassion and concern evoked by the disaster quickly faded away.

The United States has experienced several defining events in the past decade that have challenged us to acknowledge that community and individualism are at least equally important, and that local and global interdependence are imperative. September 11, 2001 was a major tragedy that forced us to acknowledge our position in world politics, and our vulnerability and dependence upon one another for survival. Many social work articles describe the heroic, caring, and skillful responses of friends, family, neighbors, and strangers, as well as professionals, in the wake of the trauma caused by the tragedy and massive crisis. Ultimately, we were challenged to empower ourselves and one another back to "normalcy," health, confidence, security, and ope, personally, socially, and economically. The public exposure of "the realities of poverty and race in America" (Brokaw, 2007, p. 295) secondary to Hurricane Katrina in 2005 gave America still another wake-up call. Once again, social workers responded to the crisis with knowledge and skill, yet resources continued to be lacking.

At the same time, the era of managed care placed a stranglehold on health and mental health care and all but dictated the kinds of social work practice that would be valued in this era: that which is simply and easily measured as "successful" in short periods of time. Fewer and fewer Americans could afford to have any health care coverage at all. In 2008, there were 46.3 million Americans without any health care insurance or coverage, 15.4% of the population (U. S. Census Bureau, 2009). The number continues to grow and children, women, minorities of color, the working poor, and the elderly are particularly vulnerable in this regard.

The word "empowerment" took on new meaning as the election of the first African-American President of the United States, Barack Obama, in November 2008 ushered in a new age of hope. The "Yes, we can" mentality enlivened a wide range of new and first-time voters, including young people and minorities of color. Women also saw in Hillary Clinton's strong campaign the real possibility of a woman attaining the presidency. Dreams that were seeds in the 1950s and 1960s came to fruition for many. The challenge is now to move beyond expectations of magic cures and do the hard work to finally make some of the reforms and changes, including health care reform, actually happen. Remarkably, to achieve the Obama victory, supportive and organizational skills were utilized by a range of people committed to change from the grassroots level up. These same skills and others will be needed to bring about the desired reforms. Ultimately, matters fell into the hands of the people who empowered themselves to take action. Frances Fox Piven (2008) suggests that a people's movement protesting for the changes still needed would, in fact, empower a president (and Congress) to deliver what people need to survive and thrive. Making such change is, fortunately, not in the hands of social workers or any one profession or group of people alone, but our knowledge base, values, and empowerment-oriented skills superbly fit us to be helpful in the pursuit of distributive justice in the form of health care, income, services, and a range of resources for those who have been left out of the mainstream. If we fail to act at such a time in history, the relevance of the profession is sorely in question.

The lives of the many people of poverty, of color, and of difference that we have known through our social work practice, ministry, and teaching and our own life experiences convince us of the need for an approach to social work practice that addresses both personal and political empowerment, especially in working with oppressed groups. It is tragic that little has changed for the poor and outcast of the world except that the ranks of the poor are swelling. In 2008,

almost 40 million (39.8 million) Americans lived in poverty (U. S. Census Bureau, 2009). Almost one fifth (19%) of all American children live below the poverty level, 41% of American children live in low-income homes, and the poverty rate of Black and Hispanic children is now over 60% (NCCP, 2009). The elderly and children still compete for survival resources (Ozawa, 1989). Goodman (2009) notes that the October 2009 unemployment rate edged up to 9.8%: "We have a truly massive crisis of long term unemployment" (pp. 1, 2). For poor and working-class Americans, and many of the middle class, these are the hardest times since the Great Depression.

The empowerment approach to social work practice enables practitioners to co-investigate reality and challenge obstacles with people who are poor, the working poor, people of color, women, and those who are oppressed by virtue of sexual orientation, physical or mental challenges, youth, or age. Standing with people who are pushed to the edge of American or global society necessitates a joining with and validation of that experience and a dual focus on people's potentials and political/structural change. The synthesis of a wide range of theories and skills is needed for effective empowerment practice. The empowerment approach provides an overarching conceptualization that links the personal and political levels of empowerment.[1]

Now-classic theorist William Schwartz (1994b) elaborated on C. Wright Mills' notion that the "personal troubles of milieu and public issues of structure must be stated in terms of the other, and of the interaction between the two... There can be no choice or even a division of labor between serving individual needs and social problems..." (p. 390). Integrating these in theory and practice is the dual focus of the empowerment approach. Despite polarization in the profession throughout history, a focus on dual simultaneous concern for people and environments can guide social work past falsely dichotomizing individual growth and social change (Germain & Gitterman, 1996; Schwartz, 1994a, 1994b). But even this dual view of function needs an additional component: that people/clients themselves actively work to change the oppressive environment and mitigate the effects of internalized oppression. A side-by-side stance of worker and client is needed. As bell hooks (1990), the African-American feminist writer, notes: "Radical post modernism calls attention to those shared sensibilities which cross the boundaries of class, gender, race, etc., that could be fertile ground for the construction of empathy—ties that would promote recognition of common commitments and serve as a base for solidarity and coalition" (pp. 26–27). Such empathy is the *sine qua non* of the empowerment process. It enables bridges to be made and crossed so client and worker can stand together to confront personal blocks to empowerment and injustice.

Empowerment Concepts

The empowerment approach makes connections between social and economic injustice and individual pain and suffering. Utilizing empowerment theory as a unifying framework, it presents an integrative, holistic approach to meeting the needs of members of oppressed groups. As Adams (2008) notes: "Empowerment is holistic and non-hierarchical. Empowerment is about taking control, achieving self-direction, seeking inclusiveness rooted in connectedness with the experiences of other people. It concerns individual achievement and social action. One aspect feeds another" (p. 18).

This approach adapts an ecological perspective, as advanced by classic theorist Carel Germain, which helps us to see the interdependence and connection of all living and nonliving systems and the transactional nature of relationships (Germain, 1979, 1987, 1991). Yet it does not deny the possibility of conflict as one of the means to releasing the potentialities of people and environments (Germain, 1979, 1991; Germain & Gitterman, 1980). Potentialities are the power bases that are developed in all of us when there is a "goodness of fit" between people and environments. By definition, poor people and oppressed groups seldom have this "fit," as injustice stifles human potential. To change this unfavorable equation, people must examine the forces of oppression, name them, face them, and join together to challenge them as they have been internalized and encountered in external power structures. The greatest potentiality to tap is the power of collectivity, people joining together to act, reflect, and act again in the process of praxis. This process is fueled by mutual caring and support.

Multifocal Vision

Multiple perspectives are used to develop an empowerment practice framework. This "multifocal vision" also determines the view of the client: the historical perspective (learning a group's history of oppression, including a critical-historical analysis of related social policy); an ecological perspective (including a stress-coping paradigm and other concepts related to coping [a transactional view of ego functioning that takes oppression into account, problem solving, and cognitive restructuring of the false beliefs engendered with internalized oppression]; ethclass and feminist perspectives, which appreciate the ceilings and lowering floors imposed by class and race and gender, the concept that power may be developed and the unity of the personal and political; a critical perspective (analyzing the status quo); and cultural and global perspectives.

Imagine a pair of glasses with several lenses seamlessly ground in. Our vision is sharpened in particular areas, yet clearly focused. In addition to this multifocal perspective, the empowerment approach is based on values, principles, processes, and skills that are integrated into an overall conceptual framework to be discussed in this chapter. Helping processes include supporting strengths and ego functioning, challenging false beliefs, challenging external obstacles and unjust systems, developing pride in peoplehood, posing and solving problems, raising consciousness, conducting dialogues, and building collectivity. These are used with individuals, families, small groups, and the wider community, including the political arena. The group, in particular the "empowerment group," is the heart of empowerment practice. The uniqueness of this approach is the integration of the personal/clinical and the political in a direct practice approach relevant to poor and oppressed people.

Empowerment's Path into Social Work: Historical and Contemporary Precedents

Jane Addams—Settlement Movement

The most important historical precedents of empowerment practice in social work history are the settlement movement, particularly the work of Jane Addams and her colleagues; the generally unrecognized women's club and social reform work of 19th-century African-Americans and other minority groups with self-help approaches; early group work theorists, particularly Grace Coyle, who worked with a progressive group called the Inquiry; and the work of Bertha C. Reynolds, the radical psychoanalytic social caseworker.

The great women who are the predecessors of an empowerment approach did not have the right to vote, to live alone or unmarried without scandal, to attend universities of their choice, or to freely enter the professions as they built the profession of social work. Through Jane Addams and her colleagues, the empowerment tradition in social work also inherits a passion for social equality, social justice, and social reform; a respect for difference and the richness of diverse cultures; and a sense of world consciousness and responsibility (Addams, 1922, 1930; Lee, 2009; Pottick, 1989; Simon, 1994). At Hull House, outstanding and ordinary women and men gave their lives to living and working side by side with oppressed groups so that "reciprocity and a fair share of resources might flow between the classes" (Addams, 1910). Group work methodology, discussion and dialogue, and global and local action are the building blocks for an empowerment approach.

African-American Women's Clubs

African-Americans were forced to develop their own helping institutions due to rigid segregation laws (Solomon, 1976). Robenia and Lawrence Gary (1975) have documented the social welfare leadership of 56 black women. Nothing that the black church and mutual aid and fraternal organizations were the major social welfare institutions of the black community, they emphasize that black women played important roles in these organizations. Some black women's clubs also worked cooperatively with white women, including Jane Addams, who was dedicated to racial justice.

By the turn of the century, African-Americans were included in a separate and unequal service system (Solomon, 1976). Most settlement houses were segregated, as were the communities they served. Blacks entering white communities

usually met with violence and sometimes death (Berman-Rossi & Miller, 1992; Katz, 1986). Hull House also served large numbers of Mexican-Americans, despite negative neighborhood sentiment (Addams, 1930).

Many black women activists were instrumental in promoting social reform. Some spoke out at rallies, in political events, and through journalism, like Ida Bell Wells-Barnett. African-American women founded local organizations such as neighborhood improvement clubs, women's clubs, houses for the aged, and children's homes (Gary & Gary, 1975). Leading black social reformers who, among their many leadership roles, also developed women's clubs and settlement houses during the Progressive Era were Janie Porter-Barrett, Sarah A. Collins-Fernandis, Mary Eliza Church Terrell, and Ida Bell Wells-Barnett (Lee, 2001). The legacy of the settlement house movement and the Black Women's Clubs is a legacy of social action (Addams, 1910, 1930; Lee, 2001).

Grace Coyle translated 1920s–1930s progressive thinking for social group workers. She saw groups as "fermenting centers of potential change…In them are brewing the social movements of the future" (Coyle, 1930, p. 227), as "tapping the great molten stream of social discontent and social injustice underlying present conditions," and as providing direct education on social questions and social action (Shapiro, 1991, p. 11).

By the 1940s, this legacy of passion for democracy was transmuted into a concern for "social responsibility" and the development of methodology that displaced social action as the central concern of group work (Shapiro, 1991). The 1960s saw a short-lived revival of social action groups (Weiner, 1964) and was the heyday of grassroots community organizing (Lewis, 1991).

Bertha Capen Reynolds: A Radical Caseworker Who Stood Between Client and Community

A turning point in the American social welfare system was the period of the Great Depression and the New Deal, which provided a small measure of social security for working Americans. Yet few social workers made connections between major socioeconomic events and social work. Bertha C. Reynolds (1885–1978) was an exception. She was strongly influenced by her teaching experience with Dr. W. E. B. DuBois at Atlanta University in 1910. She graduated in 1918 from Smith College School of Social Work (where she served as associate director from 1925 to 1938) and combined the day's psychoanalytically oriented casework practice with a progressive, democratic socialist, and social action world view, which gave her unparalleled depth and an integrated perspective (Reynolds, 1934).

Reynolds asserted that social work had a mandate to work with "the plain people," to be "ever and always a go-between profession" (Reynolds, 1964, p.17). She saw social work as a "mediating function." Politically, her vision included the highest ideals of democracy, full citizen participation, and equity in the distribution of resources more common to socialism. The vision placed social work in the arena where people work and live. She emphasized: "Our practice is in the world of social living, whether we like it or not, and whether or not our theories correspond with it" (Reynolds, 1951, p. ix). Reynolds urged social work to cooperate with existing progressive forces. Empowered people themselves are the builders; we are fellow workers, and neighbors with special expertise in the struggle for social living and social justice.

Current Influences

Currently, political science, psychology, sociology, economics, religion (especially liberation theology), and spirituality have contributed to the synthesis of empowerment theory in social work practice (Lee, 1994; Simon, 1994). For some, the concept "liberation" more accurately describes the processes and objectives of empowerment. Social workers can assist people in empowering themselves to work toward liberation (Germain, 1991). There are two strong streams that feed into empowerment theory for social work practice: social/political/economic movements and human development/clinical theories from the helping professions related to releasing human potentialities. The empowerment approach seeks to channel the two streams into one mighty flow.

Personal and political power are interrelated. Barbara Bryant Solomon (1976) was the first major social work thinker who developed the concept of empowerment for the profession. Solomon identified direct and indirect blocks to power. Indirect power blocks represent internalized negative valuations (of the oppressor) that are "incorporated into the developmental experiences of the individual as mediated by significant others." Direct power blocks "are applied directly by some agent of society's major social institutions" (Solomon, 1976). Powerlessness is based on several factors, including economic insecurity, absence of experience in the political arena, absence of access to information, lack of training in critical and abstract thought, physical and emotional stress, learned helplessness, and the aspects of a person's emotional or intellectual makeup that prevent him or her from actualizing the possibilities that do exist (Cox, 1989). The actual and perceived ability to use resources that are available contributes to a sense of power, and this is directly connected to self-esteem (Parsons, 1989). Society "blames the victim" for power deficits even as power is withheld and abused by dominant groups (Ryan, 1971). Victim blaming can be blatant or subtle, as in the popular concept of codependency (Pence, 1987).

William Schwartz's interactionist approach builds on Reynolds's mediating function idea and appreciates that the oneness of private troubles and public issues is a foundation for the empowerment approach (Schwartz, 1994a, 1994b; Shulman, 2008). Radical casework approaches (Galper, 1980) seek to unite the personal and political and are an important forerunner of empowerment thinking. Tully (2000) adapted Lee's (1994) conceptual framework as a model for using the empowerment approach with gay and lesbian people. Gutierrez and Lewis (1999) applied an empowerment perspective to social work practice with women of color, while Yip (2004) applied an empowerment model to the Chinese culture, and Letendre (1999) applied it to school social work. Andrews, Guadalupe, and Bolden (2003) applied empowerment concepts to women in poverty, while Johnson and Lee (1994) applied them to homeless women, and Bay-Cheng, Lewis, Stewart, and Malley (2006) discussed empowerment in a feminist mentoring program. Chadiha, Adams, Phorano,

Ong, and Byers (2003) explored African-American caregivers' stories of empowerment. The uniqueness of the empowerment approach is that it weaves clinical and political thinking into one fabric.

Empowerment Defined

Empowerment "deals with a particular kind of block to problem-solving: that imposed by the external society by virtue of a stigmatized collective identity" (Solomon, 1976, p. 21). Merriam-Webster's (2009) definition of the word *empower* ("to give power or authority to; to give ability to, enable, permit") implies that power can be given to another. This is rarely so. Staples sees empowerment as the process of gaining power, developing power, taking or seizing power, or facilitating or enabling power (Staples, 1994). Barbara Simon (1994), who documented the empowerment tradition in social work practice, stressed, "Empowerment is a reflexive activity, a process capable of being initiated and sustained only by (those) who seek power or self-determination. Others can only aid and abet in this empowerment process" (Simon, 1990, p. 32).

The empowerment process resides in the person, not the helper. Narayan (2002), speaking from a global economic point of view, defined empowerment as "the expansion of assets and capabilities of poor people to participate in, negotiate with, influence, control and hold accountable institutions that affect their lives." Assets are "physical and financial while capabilities are inherent in people and enable them to use their assets in different ways to increase their wellbeing" (p. 11). Assets and capabilities are social and political, individual or collective. These may include good health (physical and mental), education, production, belonging, leadership, relations of trust, a sense of identity, the capacity to organize, and values that give meaning to life. It is clear that empowerment-oriented social workers may assist people in developing their capabilities so they can increase their assets.

There are three interlocking dimensions of empowerment: (1) the development of a more positive and potent sense of self; (2) the construction of knowledge and capacity for more critical comprehension of the web of social and political realities of one's environment; and (3) the cultivation of resources and strategies, or more functional competence, for attainment of personal and collective social goals, or liberation. In his classic work, Beck (1983) noted that as we partialize and operationalize the concept of empowerment, it is a keystone concept of social work.

The life model of social work practice (Germain & Gitterman, 1980, 1996; Gitterman & Germain, 2008) fits well with an empowerment approach, as it allows multilevel examinations and interventions that may be clinical or political; it is almost by definition a praxis model; and the empowerment perspective gives direction to life model practice (Mancoske & Hunzeker, 1989). The specialized assessment and interventive methods used in the empowerment approach (Lee, 2001) build on the categories and the spirit of the life model.

Critical consciousness and knowledge of oppression is power. Power also comes from healthy personality development in the face of oppression, which fuels the ability to influence others. This includes self-esteem/identity, self-direction, competence, and relatedness (Germain, 1991). Clinical and political interventions must challenge the external and internal obstacles to the development of these attributes. Transformation, or throwing off oppression in personal and community life, occurs as people are empowered through consciousness raising to see and reach for alternatives (Harris, 1993). It requires anger at injustice and the dehumanization of poverty, negative valuations, and the culture of personal greed (Mancoske & Hunzeker, 1989). The strengths perspective of Saleebey (2008) and the structural approach of Wood-Goldberg and Middleman (1989) are also compatible with the empowerment approach. Carol Swenson's development of the concept of justice as a meta-practice principle in social work practice (Swenson, 1998) is foundational in empowerment-oriented social work.

Social work practice with the oppressed builds on community and not on self-interest and broadens the possibility of the imaginable as it goes beyond immediate problem solving to the promulgation of hope (Mancoske & Hunzeker, 1989).

Empowerment practice addresses direct and indirect power blocks; individual, family, and organizational resource problems (multiple dimensions of poverty); problems of asymmetrical exchange relationships; problems of powerlessness; problems of constraining, inhibiting, or hindering power structures; and problems related to arbitrary social criteria or values (Staub-Bernasconi, 1992). Powerlessness is low social attractiveness due to poor resources (material and emotional resources and knowledge). To help empower, we must first learn to speak openly about power with clients, and then engage in examination of power bases stemming from personal resources and articulation power; symbolic power; value power; positional power or authority; and organizational power. Unfair social stratification and unfair distribution of goods is the most difficult question facing world society. Critical education and guaranteed basic incomes are imperative. International social work can help link different groups/cultures together to claim a fair share of power resources and resist domination (Staub-Bernasconi, 1992).

Paulo Freire

A major contributor to empowerment thinking in social work is Brazilian educator Paulo Freire (1973, 1990, 1994). It is the translation of Freire's critical thinking into social work theory that marks the uniqueness of this empowerment approach.

The "radical pedagogy" and "dialogic process" of Freire (1973) is clearly a relevant method for empowerment in social work (Breton, 1989; Freire, 1990; Gutiérrez, 1990; Lee, 1989, 1991; Mancoske & Hunzeker, 1989; Narayan, 2000; Parsons, 1989, Pence, 1987). "Every human being is capable of looking critically at (the) world in a dialogical encounter with others…in this process… Each wins back (his/her) own right to say (his/her) own word, to name the world" (Freire, 1973, pp. 11–13).

Freire's group- and community-oriented methods of dialogue promote critical thinking and action. Liberation theology, with its notions of base communities as units of social and political change and use of consciousness raising, is particularly pertinent to social work thinking (Breton, 1992; Evans, 1992; Germain, 1991; Lee, 1994, 2001; Lewis, 1991; Mancoske & Hunzeker, 1989). Freire defines conscientization

as "learning to perceive social, political and economic contradictions and to take action against the oppressive elements of reality" (1973, p. 20). Critical consciousness raising and dialogue are the key methods that help people to think, see, talk, and act for themselves (Freire, 1973).

Lorraine Gutiérrez cites consciousness raising as goal, process, and outcome in empowerment work (Gutiérrez, 1989, 1990). She notes, "It is not sufficient to focus only on developing a sense of personal power or developing skills or working toward social change….these three elements combined are the goal of empowerment in social work practice" (Gutiérrez, 1989).

Gutiérrez sees developing critical consciousness; reducing self-blame; assuming personal responsibility for change; and enhancing self-efficacy as critical to empowerment (Gutiérrez, 1989). She sees group work as central to empowerment-based practice (Gutiérrez & Ortega, 1989).

Empowerment Theory and Groups

Empowerment theory applied to group work was introduced in 1983 by Ruby Pernell at the Fifth Annual Symposium of the Association for the Advancement of Social Work with Groups. She noted that group work is a natural vehicle for empowerment, as its historic goals include "growth towards social ends" (Pernell, 1986).

Noting that black Americans have borne the lion's share of power insufficiency and inequities, Pernell emphasized that empowerment practice cannot remain politically neutral:

Empowerment as a goal is a political position, as it challenges the status quo and attempts to change existing power relationships…It goes beyond "enabling." It requires of the worker the ability to analyze social processes and interpersonal behavior in terms of power and powerlessness…and…to enable group members to…develop skills in using their influence effectively (Pernell, 1986, p. 111).

The skills of working with indigenous leadership, knowing resources (where the power lies and how to get it), and enabling the group members to "do for themselves" are important in attaining empowerment.

Margot Breton (1994) and Elizabeth Lewis (1983) have been major contributors in integrating humanism, liberation theology, and community group work into empowerment practice. Groups that seek change in the environment are empowering to the degree that group members (not organizers) have actually brought about and reflected upon the change.

The Interactionist Approach and the Mutual Aid Group

The Interactionist approach of William Schwartz (1994a) is a stepping stone to an empowerment approach. The group is a microcosm of social interaction. The worker's role is to mediate the processes through which individuals and their systems reach out to each other, particularly "when the ties are almost severed." This approach appreciates reciprocity and the strength of the group itself as a mutual aid and self-empowering system (Berman-Rossi, 1994). Papell and Rothman's (1980) conceptualization of the "mainstream model" of social work with groups draws on the interactionist approach. Formed or natural groups can encompass a variety of empowerment purposes. A blending of critical education and conscientization group methods with the interactionist and mainstream models form a foundation for the empowerment group (Lee, 1994, 2001).

Ruth Parsons (1989) emphasized the importance of the group in empowering low-income girls. Empowerment is an outcome and a process that comes initially through validation of peers and a perception of commonality. Groups may have consciousness raising, help to individuals, social action, social support, and the development of skills and competence as their overlapping foci in order to help members facing oppression gain equality and justice (Garvin, 1987). Reed and Garvin made important contributions regarding the empowerment of women through groups (Reed & Garvin, 1983), while Tully (2000) discussed the empowerment of gay, lesbian, bisexual, and transgendered people. Mullender and Ward (1991), major British theorists, stressed that empowerment group work must be a self-directed (not worker-directed) process. Parsons (1989, 1991) identified empowerment as a developmental process that begins with individual growth and may culminate in social change; a psychological state marked by heightened feelings of self-esteem, efficacy, and

control; and liberation. The conceptual framework presented here integrates these three kinds of empowerment into a unified approach.

Basic Assumptions

A basic assumption of the empowerment approach is that oppression is a structurally based phenomenon with far-reaching effects on individuals and communities. These effects range from physical death due to infant or child mortality; the death of adolescents and young adults due to gang violence, drugs, other forms of homicide, and suicide; to incarceration and the death of hope. Hopelessness leads to the destruction of the self and others, despair, apathy, internalized rage, and false beliefs about the worth of the self (Harris, 1993). When the effects of oppression become internalized, the maintenance of oppression may become a transactional phenomenon. Two societal institutions mitigate against the individual succumbing to or internalizing the oppressor's view of the self: a strong family unit and a strong community (Chestang, 1976). Hence, strong support networks and good human relatedness and connection are essential to developing a positive sense of identity and self-direction. The assumption is that self is found in community with others (Swenson, 1992). Building pride in "peoplehood" and community is both a preventive and a remedial measure. The problems caused by oppression almost always necessitate a dual focus on changing the environment and strengthening the self.

The assumption about people in this approach is that they are fully capable of solving immediate problems and moving beyond them to analyze institutionalized oppression and the structures that maintain it, as well as its effects upon themselves. They are able to strengthen their internal resources, to work collaboratively in their families, groups, and communities to change, and to empower themselves in order to challenge the very conditions that oppress. The basic principle of this approach is that "people empower themselves" through individual empowerment work, empowerment-oriented group work, community action, and political knowledge and skill. The approach sees people as capable of praxis: action-reflection and action, action-in-reflection, and dialogue.

A unitary conception of person-in-environment prevents us from blaming the victim on the one hand and naïveté regarding the panacea of environmental change on the other. It leads toward developing helping "technologies" (strategies, methods, knowledge, and skills) that are both clinical and political. Feminist social work theory, another forerunner of empowerment in social work, necessitates "both/and" conceptualizations of practice (Bricker-Jenkins & Hooyman, 1986; Bricker-Jenkins, Hooyman, & Gottleib 1991; Valentich, 1996; VanDenBergh & Cooper, 1986). People can and must take themselves and their environments in hand to attain empowerment. To envision social change that comes about without the full efforts of oppressed people is to envision a Machiavellian utopia. To envision oppressed people making this effort without changing themselves—to refuse oppression, to actualize potentialities, and to actively struggle to obtain resources—is to negate the effects of oppression in the lives of the oppressed. Both changed societies and changed people who will work toward this are the nature of the sought-for change. The goals are collective more than individual, and yet these two are inseparable. The assumption here is that both the oppressor and the oppressed, as well as those who seemingly stand by or pass by on the other side, are damaged by oppression and need liberation.

This view seeks unity and harmony among oppressed groups, yet it does not shy away from nonviolent confrontation and conflict, which may be a necessary part of liberation.

Value Base of the Empowerment Approach

Most practice models or approaches that serve "all people" neglect to pay adequate attention to women and people who are poor, of color, or oppressed (Lum, 1986). The NASW Code of Ethics and the ethical principle of impartiality entreats us to cultivate our knowledge and skill to reach out to clients who face bias and discrimination and to act (with them) to challenge oppression. Attempts at equanimity minimize central aspects of people's lives that necessitate exceptional coping abilities. Color, class, gender, stigma, or difference "blindness" is not useful to clients (Lum, 1986). Empowerment means that people (both workers and clients) draw strength from working through the meaning of these different statuses in their lives, which enables them to be the fullness of who they are, persons with a rich heritage. The value base and the conceptual framework that underpins this empowerment approach is summarized in Box 11.1.

Box 11.1 A Conceptual Framework: The Empowerment Approach to Social Work Practice

Professional Purpose: Based on a dual simultaneous concern for people and environments: to assist people who experience poverty and oppression in their efforts to empower themselves to enhance their adaptive potentials and to work toward changing environmental and structural arrangements that are oppressive.

The Value Base: Preference for working with people who are poor, oppressed, and stigmatized to strengthen individual adaptive potentials and promote environmental/structural change through individual and collective action; preference for social policies and programs that create a just society where equality of opportunity and access to resources exists.

Knowledge Base and Theoretical Foundations: Theory and concepts about person: environment transactions in situations of oppression. This includes multifocal vision: the history of oppression; ecological, ethclass, cultural, feminist, critical theory, and global perspectives, knowledge about individual adaptive potentialities, unique personhood, and the ways people cope—ego functioning, social and cognitive behavioral learning and problem solving in the face of oppression; empowering individual, family, group, and community helping processes; and larger systems and structural change processes in order that we may assist people in empowering themselves on the personal, interpersonal, and political levels.

Method—Principles, Processes, and Skills: The empowerment method rests on empowerment values and purposes and the eight principles that undergird the approach. The method may be used in one-to-one, group, or community relational systems. It depends on a collaborative relationship that encompasses mutuality, reciprocity, shared power, and shared human struggle; the use of empowerment groups to identify and work on direct and indirect power blocks towards the ends of personal, interpersonal, and political power; and collective activity that reflects a raised consciousness regarding oppression. The method uses specific skills in operationalizing the practice principles to address and promote action on all levels of living.

The Roles, Processes, and Skills of the Empowerment Approach

Processes and Skills to Promote Coping and Adaptation/Social Change

In an empowerment approach, the worker promotes reflection, thinking, and problem solving on person-in-environment transactions, including the client's role in them and the experience of oppression. Along with the client's self-defined problem focus, oppressive conditions and proposed solutions are the content of reflective procedures. The difficult work of empowerment is made possible by sustaining skills, particularly the use of well-attuned empathy borne of multifocal vision and listening (Germain & Gitterman, 1996). The worker also assesses ego functioning and provides ego-supportive intervention to bolster clients' strengths (Goldstein, 1994, 1996; Lee, 1994). Client and worker together then seek to change oppressive conditions using a range of skills.

According to Carel Germain (1984), people must develop certain attributes in order to cope and adapt. The attributes achieved by good-enough person-in-environment transactions are (1) motivation, which corresponds to the incentives and rewards provided by the environment; (2) problem-solving skills, which corresponds to the strengths and efficacy of society's socializing institutions (including the family and schools); (3) maintaining psychic comfort (including managing feelings) and (4) maintaining a favorable level of self-esteem, both of which correspond to the kind and degree of emotional and other support in the environment; and (5) self-direction, which corresponds to the provision of information, choices, and adequate time and space (Germain, 1984, 1991).

Empowering Skills to Bolster Motivation

Motivation can be sustained only if basic needs for housing, food, clothing, and support (financial and emotional) are met. As these needs are met by client and worker through gaining resources and opportunities and attending to presenting problems, the worker can help to keep hope alive. In Lee's current work with the homeless in Fort Myers, she employs an outdoor feeding program on Friday nights in a local park and a "Tuesday clubhouse" approach, where people enjoy lunch and socializing indoors as they wait for group and individual services. A strong community has formed where people serve one another. Since this city has few options for shelter and affordable housing, a strong focus of this practice is to help people obtain basic financial and housing resources even as individual and social change issues are worked on. Last year, 20 people moved from homelessness into permanent affordable housing as a result of the hard work of this helping community. Encouraging the client's own words about the problems and his or her life and accepting the client's problem definition also provide motivation. The worker can also reach for and convey understanding of feelings of difference, isolation, alienation, and being misunderstood, as well as experiences of discrimination at the hands of systems needed to sustain life and growth.

Lanetta, a white woman, age 48, with a long history of bipolar illness and homelessness, wrote a story about a "throwaway dog" that identified her feelings about herself and her struggle. Easily agitated, she had literally been thrown out of every program in Fort Myers and slept in the woods and on the streets before she came to live in our Joshua House Residence for 6 months. The worker empathically conveyed understanding of "being thrown away." Lanetta then worked hard individually and in groups and with a local mental health team to get stabilized on her medications and internalize her self-worth and turn her life around. She left Joshua House with a new sense of the intelligent, creative, witty, and capable person she was, and she was reconciled with her daughter and grandchild as well. Her disability benefits were in place, and she was able to rent her own small home. She continues to be a part of our "beloved community."

By partializing the stressful demands into workable segments with the client, the social worker also encourages the client to share how he or she has dealt before with similar problems. The skill of having the client name and own his or her strengths also provides motivation to continue. Hope of changing the oppressive systems must also be offered through the worker's skills of lending a vision and beginning to enlist the client's energy in this thinking. The worker may also use skills of appropriate self-disclosure about dealing with oppressive conditions to build bridges to the client's experiences and to offer further hope of change. The worker should also use skills of systems negotiation with the client so that the client gains expertise in this area.

To Maintain Psychic Comfort and Self-Esteem

In helping the client to maintain psychic comfort, manage feelings, and attain an optimal level of self-esteem, the worker has the additional tasks of externalizing the sources of oppression to reduce self-blame and to foster pride in "people-hood." Here the social worker has the role of co-teacher and critical educator as he or she helps the client identify and "own" his or her group's achievements and heighten awareness and appreciation of the client's own culture.

The worker would use family and group skills to help members share and validate each others' experiences with oppression (Wood-Goldberg & Middleman, 1989). As members discover they share a common experience, self-deprecatory feelings may diminish. Here also the worker co-teaches about the oppressed group's achieve-ments against the odds, which builds communal esteem and self-esteem. Giving information helps clients gain familiarity with how systems work, diminishes fear, and adds to feelings of competence. The worker also helps to mobilize natural helping networks and structures and focuses on changing systemic inequities that promote the clients' discomforts and anxiety.

To Enhance Problem Solving and Promote Self-Direction

The skills of problem solving are especially impor-tant in an empowerment approach. Ultimately the aim is to help people to think differently and act differently, not only in solving personal prob-lems but in dealing with the ever-connected problems of oppression. Berlin (1983) suggests a nine-step cognitive behavioral problem-solving process that moves from awareness of the prob-lem to taking action. Eamon (2008) discusses a cognitive behavioral approach that is empower-ing as the goals are the client's, not the worker's. Germain (1984) adds the dimensions of teaching

the skills needed for achieving the solutions by providing group experiences for such learning and working with the environment to offer the options and services needed.

The skills needed to solve problems in an empowerment approach include consciousness raising, praxis, and critical education. Skills of maintaining equality in the problem-solving process are critical. This includes observing the rules of symmetry and parity in communication. The worker who is directive and lectures or fili-busters or interprets frequently in the process is not providing the conditions necessary for empowerment. Lee's agency was gifted with a second-year social work student, Lucy Conley, from Flinders University in Australia. A particu-larly helpful skill that she used was to ask mem-bers of our feeding program and Tuesday "club" to share their expertise about homelessness in Fort Myers and how they coped with it. A corol-lary question was what she might do to make herself available to people who are homeless. One of our "elders" told her to watch and listen before she spoke so she could learn who the people are by what they do as much as by what they say. Another told her to "lead with her love," not her knowledge. Even as she empowered them in the role of expert, they empowered her as a growing practitioner.

Consciousness raising is a process of develop-ing a heightened awareness and knowledge base about situations of oppression that leads to new ways of thinking about the social order. As with all skills and processes discussed here, it may be done on the one-to-one or, family, group, or community levels. This is a tall order. The four attributes (motivation, psychic comfort, problem solving, and self-direction) are interdependent and must be sustained throughout the helping process. A raised consciousness provides moti-vation, but motivation and psychic comfort are necessary to raise consciousness because ulti-mately it means change in thinking and doing. To view the world differently may be initially both a frightening and a freeing experience. The worker's skill of working with feelings will include hearing, naming, staying with, validat-ing, and helping the client to express the pain, anger, and sadness that comes with consciously realizing that he or she has been oppressed and victimized socially and economically. The use of "codes" developed by the clients and of their own experiences (for example, using books, art, music, poetry, and other ways of reaching people's level of conscious awareness) can be extremely helpful.

The skills of gently sharing information in the co-teaching role are critical here as well. Knowledge is power; to be kept from knowledge is oppression. The skills of cognitive restructuring (Berlin, 1983) are needed to raise consciousness about being oppressed. The worker helps clients to identify thinking patterns, revise false beliefs, devise more adaptive ways of dealing with internalized and external oppression, and talk and think in a healthier way about themselves, their group, and their situation. The worker then encourages clients to rename and recreate their own reality using their own words.

The worker's skills of guiding in the process of praxis are extremely important. As noted, praxis: action-reflection and return to action, involves sometimes painful unpeeling of awareness and feeling that takes time. The ability to promote competence and action is critical. This is also a good time for the worker to share his or her own struggles in challenging such obstacles.

It is equally important to be a "problem poser" as it is to facilitate problem solving. The skills of critical education are central to the empowerment process. This includes the skill of posing critical questions that help people think about the oppressive situation in new ways. This is combined with the skills of information giving noted above—for example, the social worker can use recent newspaper articles or discuss a local news item.

As noted, Freire's method of critical education (Freire, 1973; Mancoske & Hunzeker, 1989; Pence, 1987) is an important set of processes and skills social workers can learn and utilize. It has five steps, which are taken with a team of representative persons called a culture circle. First, a survey is conducted. The team listens to what is on people's minds, assessing what people talk about and what emotions are linked to. This work must include emotionally cathected concerns. Second, a theme is chosen and problems are posed in question form. Themes broaden the base of an issue. For example, a theme in Pence's battered women's groups was, "What is the effect of abusive behavior on women?" (Pence, 1987). Third, the problem is analyzed

from three perspectives: the personal, the institutional, and the cultural. Questions are asked about each perspective. Fourth, a code is developed; a code is chosen to focus the work when a theme generates work on all three levels. Finally, options for action are generated on all three levels. When actions are taken, a process of praxis is used to consolidate and deepen the work of developing critical understanding and a vision of social change. Ultimately, work that promotes motivation, problem solving, and psychic comfort contributes to a client's self-direction and empowerment.

Skills to Promote Social Change

Beyond the gains to the self, empowering work can empower communities. Group- and community-centered skills are essential. Much of the above-noted work is done most effectively in small groups, which then may build coalitions with other groups and forces in the community to effect social change (Breton, 1991). Empowerment group skills include making a clear mutual contract that bridges the personal and the political and includes a social change focus (Lee, 1991); establishing the common ground and common cause among members; challenging the obstacles to the group's work; lending a vision; and reaching for each member's fullest possible participation in the process. These are a variation on Schwartz's skills and tasks of the group worker (Schwartz, 1994a). The worker will also skillfully pose critical questions and develop codes to focus the group's work, as discussed above (Freire, 1973). Combined, these become "empowerment group" method. "Community skills" incorporates these group skills but includes coalition building and the skills of task-oriented action. Here the social worker wants to help members choose initial tasks at which they can achieve success. Wider political skills include lobbying and testifying at legislative hearings as well as organizing meetings and protest and nonviolent resistance activities. These are skills for workers and clients to develop together (Lee, 1994; Richan, 1991; Staples, 1984).

Roles and Stance of the Worker

Above all, the worker in the empowerment approach is a real person who has awareness of his or her own experiences of oppression and/or membership in the oppressor group. This awareness begins with self-awareness, including issues of countertransference, but goes beyond this to having a raised consciousness about oppression itself and an ability to share this in the helping process through appropriate self-disclosure. There is no mysticism about the helper or the helping process. The stance is "side by side" and an authentic, transparent presentation of self. The helping process itself is shared with the client initially and as the process unfolds.

Assessment is important in this approach. The worker must gain an understanding of who the client is and what tolls oppression has taken on the his or her well-being, currently or in past history. In individual and family work and empowerment group work, it is helpful to make an assessment based on the client's story. The concept of "the client's story" includes the presenting problem as primary but often goes beyond it to the client's view of historical material that is relevant to the problem at hand. This is both a narrative and oral history approach, which also seeks to unearth the strengths of individuals and their people over historical time (Martin, 1995). While principles of good clinical assessment are utilized, two important differences of this assessment process from "purely" clinical approaches are the level of mutuality of the process, as the worker shares his or her thinking openly while seeking to comprehend how the client makes sense of the situation; and the explicit inclusion of ethclass, race, gender, and other areas where oppression and power shortages or power deficits may have been experienced by the client. Hence, the assessment is of the client in transaction with oppression and of the oppressive environment, not of the client as if he or she exists in a vacuum. For a detailed outline for an empowerment assessment, content and process, please see Lee (2001, pp. 216–218).

The contract or mutually derived working agreement then also explicitly includes looking at the experience of oppression as one of the foci of the work. Of course, as in any approach, immediate and material problems have priority. The client may choose, after being made aware of his or her options, to focus only on immediate problem solving. This approach assumes that poor people and other oppressed groups already

have a point of view on their oppression and the ability to reflect on, challenge, and take action to rid themselves and their cohorts of oppression. Many clients already have a raised consciousness and may in fact be surprised that a social worker shares this consciousness. Some, however, have become so accustomed to living in oppression that the anger or despair at victimization and discrimination has been unconsciously repressed. This illuminates another level of the term consciousness raising.

The length of intervention may vary, but extremely brief treatment focused on only the immediate problem is not the goal in empowerment practice. Whatever time it takes to both solve the issue(s) at hand and raise consciousness in order to challenge immobilizing oppression is the optimal time frame. However, this work is not open-ended and "forever"; at some point in the process, the client feels empowered enough to continue the work without the worker. The worker, in effect, does himself or herself out of a job as empowered people stand ready with awareness, resources, and knowledge to pursue their own goals.

Worker Training Within the Empowerment Approach

Workers need both clinical and political knowledge and expertise to do the job. They need to be what Armando Morales called "generalist-specialists," both broad and deep (1977). They need to be individual and family clinicians, group workers, and community workers and know how to use political process to effect change. Some master's and bachelor's programs with integrated curricula already aim at this kind of a graduate. Others are overspecialized in one end or the other of the spectrum of roles. It may take some shifting of curricula as well as postgraduate training and supportive supervision to develop this kind of a social worker. Team approaches may also help practitioners to deliver the breadth of empowerment-oriented services. This kind of work may begin in agencies that are constrained by managed care guidelines, but probably must come to fruition where there is greater flexibility in the way workers may approach services. Empowerment work is appropriate for anyone facing issues of oppression.

The vocabulary of empowerment work includes a few new words that we have defined in this chapter, such as consciousness raising, praxis, dialogue, and codes. The usual vocabulary of the clinically and politically astute practitioner has been used and explained as well throughout this chapter. As in all empowerment, as we use different words to describe our thoughts we begin to think differently. The tried-and-true approaches to personal/clinical work and to group, community, and political work and the newer strategies of empowerment are grafted in an approach that is therefore both old and new. Hence, the practitioner is empowered with a new yet not unfamiliar level of knowledge to share in working with oppressed groups.

We will conclude this chapter with practice vignettes exemplifying empowerment practice and the discussion of its status in the professional lexicon of approaches.

Practice Examples

Lee's work with homeless women in New York City (Lee, 1986, 1990, 1994); Hartford, Connecticut; Guyana, South America; and now with homeless women and men in Fort Myers, Florida, grounded the empowerment approach in practice reality (Lee, 1991, 1994, 2001). All of these individuals, and especially Judith Beaumont (1987), the executive director of a four-tiered agency serving the homeless in Hartford, Connecticut, and a co-worker in 20 years of empowerment work with people, along with social workers and staff, initially "co-authored" the empowerment approach.

1. The "Successful Women's Group"

Membership in an empowerment group is a matter of personal choice based on knowledge of the experience. A "try it and see" philosophy helps members who share common ground understand what it is like to be in such a group. In forming an empowerment group for women who had "graduated" from the services of the women's shelter, the co-workers began by inviting large groups of "alumnae" to six evening get-togethers. This approximated Freire's culture circle. The codes and themes for the empowerment work would emerge from these six

meetings, as would a nucleus of women interested in pursuing empowerment together. The format of the evening, which took place in the homey atmosphere of the shelter, included a dinner, where introductions and an informal style of sharing mutual concerns could take place, and then a formal period of group discussion when empowerment notions were introduced. Many attended national and local protest activities regarding affordable housing, which coincided with these meetings. Seven African-American women, ages 22 to 34, decided to become the "Alumnae Empowerment Group."

The co-workers started off as more central to the process in helping the group develop a structure and maintain a focus on issues of empowerment, but they soon took on a more advisory role. Within 4 months the group developed a club-style structure, with a president who called the meetings and maintained the work focus. They chose the meeting nights, time, frequency (biweekly), outreach to new members, and content of the meetings. The workers bolstered the leadership structure and continued to contribute information and to assist in guiding praxis and reflecting on feelings and facts to deepen the work. The group existed for 2 years, though some of the members continue to be activists and to be there for each other to the time of this writing (2009). This is an excerpt from a meeting 9 months into the life of the group in which they name themselves. Tracey, the president, said, "'Alumnae' just don't get it."

"Who are we?" asked Vesalie.
"We are successful women," said Tracey.
"Yeah," said Latoya, "The Successful Women's Group."
"No," said Vesalie, "We can't call ourselves that."
"Why?" Shandra asked.
Vesalie strongly replied, "It implies too much power, that we are powerful."
The worker asked if they felt powerful.
Vesalie said, "Yes, we are more powerful now. We've got good jobs, we're good mothers, we help others who are homeless, we are meeting our goals, but we haven't gotten there yet." The worker asked, "When you get there, then you have power?"
Tracey replied, "But that's just it: we need that power to get there, and we're on our way. Let's convey that we are powerful women we are successful women. Let's take that name and make it ours. We deserve to walk with that name!"

The others strongly agreed. Vesalie thoughtfully accepted this, and the name Successful Women was enthusiastically adopted.

Names mean a great deal. The worker's questions here are consciousness-raising questions. This renaming after 9 months of meeting represents a 360-degree turn in self-esteem, group pride, and conscientization. The use of codes helped the group achieve this new image.

In the Successful Women's Group two themes were codified: "barriers to success" and "African-American womanhood." On the first theme the worker asked the group members to define success. It was defined as personal achievement and "people-centered" accomplishments (giving back to the community). The Wall of Barriers was the code.

The members were asked to imagine and dramatically act out climbing and pulling bricks down from a wall, which represented barriers. The worker posed the question: What are the barriers to young African-American women getting over the wall to success for themselves and their people? Amika was first to try to dramatize it. She said, "The wall is over there, I'm going toward it."

"OOPS!" she said, as she slipped and fell with a great thud. "They greased the ground! I can't even get to the wall. Forget it!"

Everyone roared as Amika, a large heavily built woman, dramatized falling down in disarray.

Tracey said, "It isn't really funny. Amika is right: some of us can't even get to the wall. The grease is prejudice and racism."

"And sexism," Ves added, "Don't forget that."

Shandra said, "Yeah, but determination makes you try and you reach the wall. Like you finish high school and you think you're somewhere, but you didn't take the right courses to go to college so you got to start all over again."

Tracey said, "I was angry too when I found out my diploma meant so little."

Shandra got up and started using a hammer and a chisel, saying, "And this one you got to strike at: it's prejudice on the job. You get the job, but they treat you like you're stupid just because you're black."

She told of how she was treated by a nurse she worked with. She unwedged the brick and threw it down hard. Everyone applauded.

Ves said, "OK, watch out! I'm driving this bulldozer right into the wall. Later for brick by brick, or climbing; the whole thing is coming down. Slam! Crash!"

Everyone cheered her on. "Wait," said Latoya. "A brick hit me. I'm hurt."

She wiped imagined blood from her head. "It's the brick of hating myself because I believed 'if you're black, stand back' and I stood back and didn't go for even what you all went for, a real job and all. But I survived and stand here to tell it. I'm going to get me some too!" Everyone encouraged her.

The use of humor by African-Americans and other oppressed groups is an adaptive mechanism, but no one should mistake the seriousness of the meanings in this dramatic enactment and decoding, which was at once therapeutic and political, leading to a variety of actions.

Their next codification on African-American womanhood was the reading together of Ntozake Shange's Choreopoem *FOR COLORED GIRLS WHO HAVE CONSIDERED SUICIDE WHEN THE RAINBOW IS ENUF* (1977).

After several readings of selected poems and their discussion, Tracey, who had committed some to memory, concluded, "These are our lives. It could have gone either way for us: we too could have died, or chosen paths that lead to death of our spirits and our bodies. But we didn't because we found other women who was feeling what we were feeling and living what we was living. I will always see myself in Shandra. I will always be there for her. We found true Shelter and we found each other, and we found God in ourselves, like the poem says."

"Yes," said Ves, "and we found the truth about our struggles too. And we are free, no turning back."

Remarkably, at this 2009 writing, Tracey and Shandra continue to support each other and their families and continue to be activists for the homeless and others in the greater Hartford community. For Shandra's story and a summation of the empowerment work with her, including the tools of empowerment-oriented assessment and the skills of the work phase, please see Lee (2001, pp. 218–249).

2. Brenda: The Personal/Political Empowerment of a Woman with Mental Illness

Brenda Gary, a 29-year-old African-American woman with multiple physical problems and chronic paranoid schizophrenia, experienced periods of intermittent homelessness for 5 years. Leaving her children with relatives, she moved cyclically from the streets to the hospital to several shelters. Then she entered a residential support program that set her up in her own apartment and offered daily support and empowerment services. For the first time since the onset of her illness, Brenda experienced inner peace. Brenda's appearance is marred by skin eruptions but she radiates a quiet joy. She is not spontaneous, but when she is called on, her good intellect is revealed. Brenda volunteered to testify at public hearings on proposed state cutbacks of mental health programs. This is an excerpt:

We need our programs to keep us aware of life's possibilities. No matter what you want to be it's possible. These programs kept me on track and looking forward to life. If the State cuts these programs, the State also cuts the good that they do…We have a women's group every week. We talk about what goes on in our lives—the problems we experience and solutions to them—by getting feedback from each other.

To get Brenda and her peers to this point, the worker, Gail Bourdon, prepared the empowerment group to understand the issues and the process of testifying before asking for their participation. First, she shared specific details of the proposed cuts and elicited the group member's reactions. She proposed that they might want to learn how to testify at the hearings and speak up for themselves. Then, when interest was high, she took two volunteers (Brenda and Vicky) and the staff to a workshop on the legislative process. Two weeks later, during an empowerment meeting, a summary of the legislative process was given to the group by the worker and the members who went to the workshop. Brenda volunteered to speak and composed her testimony that night.

Early the next evening we went to testify. Brenda patiently waited 2 hours in line and an additional 2-1/2 hours before testifying. The testimony was presented in the Hall of the House of Representatives. Brenda and I presented our testimony. It was a striking image to see Brenda, in her woolen hat, speaking so well from the seat of the "Minority Leader." One Senator thanked Brenda for her testimony. Brenda was clearly the group leader that night.

The group then reflected on their actions in the next meeting. The worker invited praxis, the members' reflections on the process of testifying and going to the legislative hearing.

Group members read the entire newspaper article to each other. I asked what the women thought and felt about attending the hearings. Brenda smiled and proudly stated she felt good about having spoken. I asked Vicky how she felt about attending the hearing. Vicky said, I was happy. It was one of the happiest times in my life. I saw and heard things I never thought I'd even learn about. The entire group cheered…I asked Brenda if she thought her message was heard. Brenda said she thought so because they did not ask her unfriendly questions. They accepted her word and even thanked her. I asked the group members who went how it was for them and each replied affirmatively. Vicky added, I feel like I could do that sometime…I feel the strength. The entire group agreed, noting that they had a voice and were heard. Ida said that those who simply sat there also brought support and power in numbers, so they had a presence as well as a voice…Brenda added, it's good to know that I can accomplish things even with a mental illness. Sometimes people think you can't do things because you have a mental illness. I live with the illness, but this does not mean I am not able to take care of business. The other members thoughtfully agreed.

The careful preparation of the members paid off in the group members' confident action. The skills of guiding praxis helped the members own their gains and expand their understanding and political skill as well as their self-esteem and self-direction.

Use of Groups and Research As Empowering Process

At the invitation of a Guyanese social work educator, Lecturer Stella Odie-Ali, the senior author worked in collaboration with the Social Work Department at the University of Guyana in South America and the Guyanese Association of Professional Social Workers over a 3-year period as a resource person and consultant on empowerment and homelessness. This mutually empowering experience included several workshops, conferences, and research projects, as well as direct practice with Guyanese social workers. Lee describes the process of crossing cultural bridges to do mutually empowering work on women's issues with the use of empowerment groups (1999). A group of Guyanese social work students also visited Professor Lee in Fort Myers, Florida, to see empowerment practice in a North American context. The findings of four research studies, using qualitative and quantitative methods, were shared with the appropriate minister in the government, and this precipitated some changes in services to the homeless of Guyana. Reports of these studies of the mentally ill, street children, and the total homeless population include Lee, Odie-Ali, and Botsko, 2000; Lee and Odie-Ali, 2000; and Lee, Cudjoe, Odie-Ali, and Botsko, 2002. In each study, we hear the voices of those who have not been heard before, who were empowered to say their own words. In all of these examples, one can see that personal and political empowerment are part of the same process and outcome.

Status in the Profession

Empowerment practice has gained in momentum as the oppression of many groups, especially those who are poor, escalated in the reactionary political climate of the George H. W. Bush years. Many contemporary thinkers are researching and conceptualizing empowerment-oriented practice. Hence, there is a growing empirical base to anchor empowerment in the professional lexicon of social work approaches. Yet it is difficult to study and measure a concept that is transactionally based and both clinical and political. Perhaps in some ways such measurement is a moot point, for the power that people develop on the personal, interpersonal, and political levels ultimately makes up a whole that may defy quantification and oversimplification. At best, the separate aspects of the approach will be empirically documented. The empowerment approach is grounded in practice and conceptualized from qualitative data, which, I believe, is a prerequisite to quantification of such complex ideas (Lee, 1991, 1994, 2001). Further grounding in such qualitative data would be helpful.

The empowerment approach provides a conceptual framework for empowerment-oriented social work practice. It brings social work into the discourse between sociology, political science, progressive change, and religion. It is relevant in education, ministry, community work, and a range of helping professions. It is both old and new, both clinical and political. It is also a paradigm for international social work practice as it offers social workers a way to challenge oppression and build capabilities with people throughout the world.

Notes

1. This chapter includes some paraphrases and excerpts of record material from *The Empowerment Approach to Social Work Practice: Building the Beloved Community* by Dr. Judith A. B. Lee. Copyright © 2001 by Columbia University Press. Reprinted with permission.

References

Adams, R. (2008). *Empowerment, participation and social work*. Hampshire, England: Palgrave Macmillan.

Addams, J. (1910). *Twenty years at Hull House*. New York: Macmillan. Reprint, 1961.

Addams, J. (1922). *Peace and bread in time of war*. New York: Macmillan.

Addams, J. (1930). *The second twenty years at Hull House*. New York: Macmillan.

Andrews, A. B., Guadalupe, J. L., & Bolden, E. (2003). Faith, hope and mutual support: Paths to Empowerment as perceived by women in poverty. *Journal of Social Work Research and Evaluation*, 4(1), 5–18.

Aversa, J. (2009). Bernacke says recession "very likely over." Yahoo! News. Retrieved October 7, 2009, from http://finance.yahoo.com/news/Bernanke-says-recession-very-apf-912326394.html?x=0&.v=4

Bay-Cheng, L. Y., Lewis, A. E., Stewart, A. J., & Malley, J. E. (2006). Discipling "girl talk": The paradox of empowerment in a feminist mentorship program. *Journal of Human Behavior in the Social Environment*, 13(2), 73–92.

Beaumont, J. A. (1987). Prison witness: Exposing the injustice. In A. J. Laffin & A. Montgomery (Eds.), *Swords into plowshares: Nonviolent direct action for disarmament* (pp. 80–85). New York: Harper and Row.

Beck, B. M. (1959). Shaping America's social welfare policy. In A. J. Kahn (Ed.), *Issues in American social work* (pp. 191–218). New York: Columbia University Press.

Berlin, S. (1983). Cognitive behavioral approaches. In A. Rosenblatt & D. Waldfogel (Eds.), *The handbook of clinical social work* (pp. 1095–1119). San Francisco: Jossey Bass.

Berman-Rossi, T. (Ed.) (1994). *Social work: The collected writings of William Schwartz*. Belmont, CA: F. E. Peacock Publishers.

Berman-Rossi, T., & Miller, I. (1992). *Racism and the Settlement movement*. Paper presented at the 14th Annual Symposium for the Advancement of Social Work with Groups, Atlanta, Georgia.

Breton, M. (1989). The need for mutual aid groups in a drop-in for homeless women: The Sistering case. In J. A. B. Lee (Ed.), *Group work with the poor and oppressed* (pp. 47–59). New York: Haworth.

Breton, M. (1991). Toward a model of social group work: Practice with marginalized populations. *Groupwork*, 4(1), 31–47.

Breton, M. (1992). Liberation theology, group work, and the right of the poor and oppressed to participate in the life of the community. In J. A. Garland (Ed.), *Group work reaching out: People, places, and power* (pp. 257–270). New York: Haworth.

Breton, M. (1994). On the meaning of empowerment and empowerment-oriented social work practice. *Social Work with Groups*, 17(3), 23–37.

Bricker-Jenkins, M., & Hooyman, N. (1986). *Not for women only: Social work practice for a feminist future.* Silver Spring, MD: National Association of Social Workers.

Bricker-Jenkins, M., Hooyman N., & Gottleib, N. (Eds.). (1991). *Feminist social work practice in clinical settings.* Newbury Park, CA: SAGE.

Brokaw, T. (2007). *Boom! Voices of the sixties. Personal reflections on the 60s and today.* New York: Random House.

Chadiha, L. A., Adams, P., Phorano, O., Ong, S. L., & Byers, L. (2003). Stories told and lessons learned from African American female caregivers' vignettes for empowerment practice. *Journal of Gerontological Social Work*, 40(1), 135–144.

Chestang, L. (1976). Environmental influences on social functioning: The Black experience. In P. S. J. Cafferty & L. Chestang (Eds.), *The diverse society: Implications for sopial Policy* (pp. 59–74). Washington, DC: National Association of Social Workers.

Cox, E. O. (1989). Empowerment of the low-income elderly through group work. In J. A. B. Lee (Ed.), *Group work with the poor and oppressed* (pp. 111–125). New York: Haworth.

Coyle, G. L. (1930). *Social process in organized groups.* Hebron, CT: Practitioner's Press. Reprint, 1979.

Eamon, M. K. (2008). *Empowering vulnerable populations: Cognitive behavioral interventions.* Chicago, IL: Lyceum Books, Inc.

Elliot, L. (2009). Get ready for the dawning of the age of austerity. *The Guardian.* Retrieved on October 7, 2009, from http://www.guardian.co.uk/business/2009/aug/24/government-borrowing-economics-recession.

Evans, E. N. (1992). Liberation theology, empowerment theory and social work practice with the oppressed. *International Social Work*, 35, 3–15.

Freire, P. (1973). *Pedagogy of the oppressed.* New York: Seabury.

Freire, P. (1990). A critical understanding of social work. *Journal of Progress Human Services*, 1(1), 3–9.

Freire, P. (1994). *Pedagogy of hope: Reliving pedagogy of the oppressed.* New York: The Continuum Publishing Co.

Galper, J. H. (1980). *Social work practice: A radical perspective.* Englewood Cliffs, NJ: Prentice-Hall.

Garvin, C. (1987). *Contemporary group work* (2nd ed.). Englewood Cliffs, NJ: Prentice-Hall.

Gary, R. B., & Gary, L. E. (1975). Profile of black female social welfare leaders during the 1920s. National Institutes of Mental Health. Grant MH-25551-02, pp. 9–13.

Germain, C. B. (1979). Introduction: Ecology and social work In C. Germain (Ed.), *Social work practice: People and environments* (pp. 1–22). New York: Columbia University Press.

Germain, C. B. (1984). *Social work practice in health care.* New York: The Free Press.

Germain, C. B. (1987). Ecological perspective. In A. Minahan (Ed.)., *Encyclopedia of social work* (18th Ed., pp. 488–499). Silver Spring, MD: National Association of Social Workers.

Germain, C. B. (1991). *Human behavior in the social environment.* New York: Columbia University Press.

Germain, C. B., & Gitterman, A. (1980). *The life model of social work practice.* New York: Columbia University Press.

Germain, C. B., & Gitterman, A. (1996). *The life model of social work practice* (2nd ed.). New York: Columbia University Press.

Gitterman, A., & Germain, C. B. (2008). *The life model of social work practice: Advances in knowledge and practice* (3rd ed.). New York: Columbia University Press.

Goldstein, E. (1994). *Ego psychology and social work practice* (2nd ed.). New York: The Free Press.

Goldstein, E. (1996). Ego psychology theory. In F. Turner (Ed.), *Social work treatment* (4th Ed., pp. 168–190). New York: The Free Press.

Goodman, P. S. (2009). Jobs report highlights shaky US recovery. *The New York Times.* Retrieved October 7, 2009, from http://www.nytimes.com/2009/10/03/business/economy/03jobs.html

Guttiérez, L. (1989). *Empowerment in social work practice: Considerations for practice and education.* Paper presented at the annual meeting of the Council on Social Work Education, Chicago, IL.

Guttiérez, L. (1990). Working with women of color: An empowerment perspective. *Social Work*, 35, 149–155.

Guttiérez, L., & Lewis, E. (1999). *Empowering women of color.* New York: Columbia University Press.

Gutierrez, L., & Ortega, R, (1989). Using group work to empower Latinos: A preliminary analysis.

Proceedings of the Eleventh Annual Symposium of the Association for the Advancement of Social Work with Groups.

Harris, F. E., Sr. (1993). *Ministry for social crisis: Theology and praxis in the black church tradition.* Macon, GA: Mercer University Press.

hooks, b. (1990). *Yearning: Race, gender and cultural politics.* Boston: South End Press.

Hopkins, K. (2009). Recession over by Christmas, says CBI. *The Guardian.* Retrieved October 7, 2009, from http://www.guardian.co.uk/business/2009/sep/23/cbi-forecast-recession-over

Hudson, R. E. (2009). The empowerment approach. In A. Gitterman & R. Salmon (Eds.), *Encyclopedia of social work with groups* (pp. 47–50). New York: Routledge Taylor & Francis Group.

Johnson, A. K., & Lee, J. A. B. (1994). Empowerment work with homeless women. In M. P. Mirkin (Ed.), *Women in context: Toward a feminist reconstruction of psychotherapy* (pp. 408–432). New York: Guilford Press.

Katz, M. B. (1986). *In the shadow of the poorhouse: A social history of welfare in America.* New York: Basic Books.

Lee, J. A. B. (1986). No place to go: Homeless women. In A. Gitterman & L. Shulman (Eds.), *Mutual aid groups and the life cycle* (pp. 245–262). Itasca, IL: F.E. Peacock; 2nd edition, 1994, New York: Columbia University Press, pp. 297–234).

Lee, J. A. B. (Ed.). (1989). *Group work with the poor and oppressed.* New York: Haworth Press.

Lee, J. A. B. (1990). When I was well, I was a sister: Social work with homeless women. *The Jewish Social Work Forum,* 26, 22–30.

Lee, J. A. B. (1991). Empowerment through mutual aid groups: A practice grounded conceptual framework. *Groupwork,* 4(1), 5–21.

Lee, J. A. B. (1994). *The empowerment approach to social work practice.* New York: Columbia University Press.

Lee, J. A. B. (1999). Crossing bridges: Groupwork in Guyana. *Groupwork,* 11(1):6–23.

Lee, J. A. B. (2001). *The empowerment approach to social work practice: Building the beloved community.* New York: Columbia University Press.

Lee, J. A. B. (2009). Jane Addams. In A. Gitterman & R. Salmon R. (Eds.), *Encyclopedia of social work with groups* (pp. 13–16). New York: Routledge Taylor & Francis Group.

Lee, J. A. B., Odie-Ali, S., & Botsko, M. (2000) The invisible visible: A study of the needs of the homeless and mentally ill in Guyana. *International Social Work,* 43(2), 163–178.

Lee, J. A. B., & Odie-Ali, S. (2000). Carry me home: A collaborative study of street children in Georgetown, Guyana. *Journal of Research and Evaluation: An International Publication,* 1(2), 185–196.

Lee, J. A. B., Cudjoe, J., Odie-Ali, S., & Botsko, M. (2002). I'm trying but I'm dying: A two year collaborative study of homelessness in Guyana. *Journal of Research and Evaluation: An International Publication,* 3(1), 61–74.

Letendre, J. A. (1999). A group empowerment model with alienated, middle class eighth boys. *Journal of Child and Adolescent Group Therapy,* 9(3), 113–127.

Lewis, E. (1983). Social group work in community life: Group characteristics and worker role. *Social Work with Groups,* 6(2), 3–18.

Lewis, E. (1991). Social change and citizen action: A philosophical explanation for modern social group work. In A. Vinik & M. Levin (Eds.), *Social action in group work* (pp. 23–34). New York: Haworth.

Lum, D. (1986). *Social work practice and people of color.* Monterey, CA: Brooks/Cole.

Mancoske, R. J., & Hunzeker, J. M. (1989) *Empowerment-based generalist practice: Direct services with individuals.* New York: Cummings and Hathaway.

Martin, R. R. (1995). *Oral history in social work: Research, assessment, and intervention.* Thousand Oaks, CA: Sage.

Merriam-Webster. (2009). Definition of "empowerment." Retrieved October 18, 2009, from http://www.merriam-webster.com/dictionary/empowerment

Miley, K., O'Melia, M., & Dubois, B. (2009). *Generalist social work practice: An empowering approach* (4th Ed.). Boston: Allyn & Bacon.

Morales, A. (1977). Beyond traditional conceptual frameworks. In *Social work: A profession of many faces* (3rd Ed.). Boston: Allyn & Bacon.

Mullender, A., & Ward, D. (1991). *Self-directed group work: Users take action for empowerment.* London: Whiting and Birch.

Narayan, L. (2000). Freire and Ghandi: Their relevance for social work education. *International Social Work,* 43(2), 193–204.

Narayan, D. (2002). *Empowerment and poverty reduction: A sourcebook.* Washington, DC: PREM Worldbank. Retrieved October 9, 2009, from http://siteresources.worldbank.org/INTEMPOWERMENT/Resources/486312-1095094954594/draft.pdf

NCCP (2009). "Child Poverty." National Center For Children in Poverty: Mailman School of Public Health Columbia University. Retrieved October 9, 2009, from http://www.nccp.org/topics/childpoverty.html.

Obama, B. (2006). *The audacity of hope: Thoughts on reclaiming the American dream.* New York: Crown Publishers.

Ozawa, M. N. (1989). Nonwhites and the demographic imperative in social welfare spending. In I. C. Colby (Ed.), *Social welfare policy* (pp. 437–454). Chicago, IL.: The Dorsey Press.

Papell, C. P., & Rothman, B. (1980). Relating the mainstream model of social work with groups to group psychotherapy and the structural group approach. *Social Work With Groups, 3,* 5–22.

Parsons, R. J. (1989). Empowerment for role alternatives for low-income minority girls: A group work approach. In J. A. B. Lee (Ed.), *Group work with the poor and oppressed* (pp. 27–46). New York: The Haworth Press.

Parsons, R. J. (1991). Empowerment: purpose and practice principles in social work. *Social Work with Groups,* 14(2), 7–21.

Pence, E. (1987). *In our best interests: A process for personal and social change.* Duluth, MN.

Pernell, R. B. (1986). Empowerment and social group work. In M. Parnes (Ed.), *Innovations in social group work* (pp. 107–118). New York: Haworth Press.

Piven, F. F. (2008). Welfare reform and the economic and cultural reconstruction of low-wage labor markets. *City & Society,* 10(1), 21–36.

Pottick, K. (1989). Jane Addams revisited: Practice theory and social economics. In J. A. B. Lee, (Ed.), *Group work with the poor and oppressed* (pp. 11–26). New York: Haworth Press.

Reed, B. G., & Garvin, C. D. (Eds.) (1983). Group work with women/group work with men: An overview of gender issues in social group work practice. *Social Work with Groups, Special Issue,* 6 (3/4), 5–18.

Roubini, N. (2009). *A global breakdown of the recession in 2009.* Retrieved October 7, 2009, from http://www.forbes.com/2009/01/14/global-recession-2009-oped-cx_nr_0115roubini.html

Reynolds, B. C. (1934). *Between client and community: A study in responsibility in social casework.* Reissued in 1973. New York: Oriole Editions, Inc.

Reynolds, B. C. (1951). *Social work and social living explorations in philosophy and practice.* First National Association of Social Workers Classics Edition (1975). Silver Springs, MD: National Association of Social Workers.

Reynolds, B. C. (1964). *An uncharted journey: Fifty years of growth in social work.* Hebron, CT: Practitioner's Press.

Revkin, A. C. (2009). The greenhouse effect and the bathtub effect. New York Times: Dot Earth Blog-NY (January 28). Retrieved October 7, 2009, from http://dotearth.blogs.nytimes.com/2009/01/28/the-greenhouse-effect

Richan, W. C. (1991). *Lobbying for social change.* New York: The Haworth Press.

Ryan, W. (1971). *Blaming the victims.* New York: Vintage.

Saleebey, D. (2008). *The strengths perspective in social work practice.* New York: Allyn & Bacon.

Schwartz, W. (1994a). The social worker in the group. In T. Berman-Rossi (Ed.), *Social work: The collected writings of William Schwartz* (pp. 257–276). Itasca, IL: The Peacock Press.

Schwartz, W. (1994b). Private troubles and public issues: One social work job or two? In T. Berman-Rossi (Ed.), *Social work: The collected writings of William Schwartz* (pp. 377–394). Itasca, IL: The Peacock Press.

Shange, N. (1977). *For colored girls who have considered suicide when the rainbow is enuf.* New York: Macmillan Publishing Co.

Shapiro, B-Z. (1991). Social action, the group and society. *Social Work with Groups,* 14(3/4), 7–22.

Shera, W., & Wells, L. M. (Eds.) (1999). *Empowerment practice in social work: Developing richer conceptual frameworks.* Toronto: Canadian Scholars' Press.

Shulman, L. (2008), *The skills of helping individuals, families and groups.* New York: Cengage Learning.

Simon, B. L. (1990). Rethinking empowerment. *Journal of Progressive Human Services,* 1(1), 29.

Simon, B. (1994). *The empowerment tradition in American social work.* New York: Columbia University Press.

Solomon, B. B. (1976). *Black empowerment: Social work in oppressed communities.* New York: Columbia University Press.

Staples, L. (1984). *Roots to power.* New York: Praeger Publishers.

Staub-Bernasconi, S. (1992). Social action, empowerment, and social work: An integrating theoretical framework. *Social Work with Groups,* 14(3/4), 35–52.

Swenson, C. (1992). Clinical practice and the decline of community. Paper Presented at the Council on Social Work Education Conference, March 1992, Kansas City, Missouri.

Swenson, C. (1998). Clinical social work's contribution to a social justice perspective.(Special Centennial Issue). *Social Work,* 43(6), 527–537.

Tully, C. T. (2000). *Lesbians, gays and the empowerment perspective.* New York: Columbia University Press.

U.S. Census Bureau (2009). *Income, poverty, and health insurance coverage in the United States: 2008.* (Publication P60-236(RV)) Retrieved October 7, 2009, from http://www.census.gov/prod/2009pubs/p60-236.pdf

Van Den Bergh, N., & Cooper, L. B. (Eds.) (1986). *Feminist visions for social work*. Silver Springs, MD: National Association of Social Workers.

Walton, E., Sandau-Beckler, P., & Mannes, M. (2001). *Balancing family-centered services and child wellbeing*. New York: Columbia University Press.

Weiner, H. J. (1964). Social change and group work practice. *Social Work*, 9(3), 106–112.

Wood-Goldberg, G., & Middleman, R. R. (1989). *The structural approach to direct practice in social work*. New York: Columbia University Press.

Valentich, (1996). Feminist theory and social work practice. In F. Turner (Ed.), *Social work treatment: Interlocking theoretical approaches* (pp. 282–318). New York: The Free Press.

Yip, K-S. (2004). The empowerment model: A critical reflection of empowerment in Chinese culture. *Social Work,* 49(3), 479–487.

EXISTENTIAL

Born again in the disillusionment of recent decades, this worldview argues for more effective, flexible treatment of the poor and minorities from an enhanced, humanizing perspective

Existential Social Work

Donald Krill

The impact of existential philosophy upon the social work profession remains unclear. The first article on the subject appeared in social work literature in 1962, and three books by social workers delineated existential perspectives in 1969, 1970, and 1978. The topic of existentialism has seldom appeared at the National Conference of Social Workers.

On the other hand, those social workers familiar with the existential viewpoint emphasize that this perspective speaks to the profession's most pressing needs: for more effective treatment of the poor and minorities; for more present-focused, experiential, task-oriented work with families and individuals; for a more flexible and eclectic use of varied treatment techniques; for a lessening of categorization of people and of paternalistic efforts by therapists to adjust the values of clients to those of their families or

those of the established society. The existential perspective is even seen as providing an important humanizing effect to social workers' present experimentation with social change.

The failure of the existentialist viewpoint to attract major attention among social work professionals may be twofold. In the first place, writings of this type by philosophers, psychologists, theologians, and social workers tend to present a terminology that seems foreign to the average practitioner (Being, Nothingness, the Absurd, Dread, I-Thou, Bad Faith, etc.). Social workers tend to be "doers" rather than theoreticians, and even the theorists tend to be pragmatic rather than philosophical. Second, existential social work writers have proposed a more philosophical perspective rather than specific working techniques. This is primarily because there does not really seem to be an existential psychotherapy per se. To be more accurate, one might say there is an existential philosophical viewpoint of how one sees oneself and one's client system and what can happen between them. Various theoretical approaches may then be used to provide techniques compatible with this philosophical perspective.

The Existential Stance

Modern existentialism was born in the ruins, chaos, and atmosphere of disillusionment in Europe during and following World War II. Earlier existential writers, such as Kierkegaard and Dostoevsky, reacted against what they believed to be false hopes for the salvation of humanity and the world through a philosophy and politics of rationalism in their times. In the United States, with its boundless faith in achieving the good life through continued growth in economic productivity and scientific advancement, the interest in existentialism has been slower in coming.

The disillusioning events of the 1960s (assassinations, generation gap, protest movements, Vietnam War) continued into the early 1970s (Watergate, economic instability, mounting divorce and crime rates, failures of psychotherapy hopes). These troubling occurrences opened the minds of many Americans to the existential themes that had previously been the interest of beatniks, artists, and a scattering of intellectuals.

Existentialism has been termed a "philosophy of despair," partially because it seems to emerge from disillusionment. But we may view this emergence as the origin and rooting of existentialism and a turning away from a primary allegiance to those idols and values that have fallen. Where it goes beyond this point depends upon which particular writer, theologian, philosopher, or film director one chooses to follow.

In most of the philosophical literature on existentialism, four themes seem to recur: the stress upon individual freedom and the related fundamental value of the uniqueness of the person; the recognition of suffering as a necessary part of the ongoing process of life—for human growth and the realization of meaning; the emphasis upon one's involvement in the immediate moment at hand as the most genuine way of discovering one's identity and what life is

about (not in any finalized sense but, rather, in an ongoing, open way); and the sense of commitment that seeks to maintain a life of both discipline and spontaneity, of contemplation and action, of egolessness and an emerging care for others. In all of these there is an obvious emphasis upon an inward turning in contrast to the "organizational" or "outer-directed" man of the 1950s.

The existentialists disagree with those who hold human beings to be either essentially impulse-driven animals or social animals of learned conditioning. Both of these ideas deny the individual what is, for the existentialists, his or her source of dignity: the absolute value of his or her individual uniqueness. A person discovers his or her uniqueness through the way he or she relates to his or her own objective experience of life. Sartre points out that this subjectivity is a person's freedom; it is something that is there; it cannot be escaped from or avoided; one can only deny one's own responsibility for choices made within this freedom. From the existential view, psychoanalytic theory is sometimes misused by encouraging the individual's denial of responsibility on the basis of impulsiveness forces; similarly, sociological and learning theory may be misused by excusing a person on the basis of totally determining social forces.

Characters from fiction, drama, mythology, and philosophical tradition have portrayed the existential posture. Stoicism, courage, and individualism are common attributes. Existentialist heroes are often characterized as living on the edge of the traditions, values, and enticements of their society, prizing the preservation of their own uniqueness and authenticity above all else. They commonly suspect the motives of others, bordering on the cynical, and therefore avoid complete identity with any group espousing a "good cause." They are tough-minded in holding to their own code, evaluating it and preserving its integrity. They refuse to be "put down" by dehumanizing social forces through conformity or by selling themselves out to their rewards. They are against systemic efforts to suppress the individuality of others in society. Their values are concrete and inseparable from situations: certain arising social or political issues, loyalty to friends, unfolding creative potentials, honesty and sincerity in relationships. They live forever with a clear awareness of life's limits, the absurd, the tragic, yet they maintain a committed faith in their groundings of freedom—the springboard for unique assertion. Their interactions with life define who they are rather than the acceptance of some definition of themselves imposed by an outside authority, such as family, church, or economic system. The rhythm of responsive life-swinging-in-situation is their sole guide.

Existentialism is rejected by many as a narcissistic withdrawal from life when disappointments arise. At first glance, this might appear true, as we hear existentialists proclaim their own consciousness, subjectivity, and uniqueness as the sole absolute: "truth is subjectivity," said Kierkegaard. Existentialists do reject the world, in one sense, in their new commitment to their own deepest self. What they reject, however, is not life—its conditions, limits, joys, and possibilities—but the mistaken hopes and expectations they had held about life, which, under closer examination, failed to fit with the reality of their life.

What is real does shatter cherished yearnings in us all—about love, about divine protection, about our own abilities and goodness. Yet in surveying the landscape of rubble from broken aspirations and beliefs, we find that we still have a choice of how to relate to these realities. We can allow ourselves to be driven to despair, or to choose new illusional hopes, or we can accept the reality and go from there.

The Hemingway hero is a portrayal of this. We might expect him to say, "We lose in the end, of course, but what we have is the knowledge that we were going great." One's manhood, the sense of realistic pride, comes from the engagement with and assertion of one's own uniqueness. Each must discern what is right for him in terms of talent and skill, what is of value, and what is enjoyable. This becomes his own private personal perspective for which he alone is responsible. It changes throughout life, but it remains always his own, and hence truly unique.

The black concept of "soul" has been defined as "the force which radiates from a sense of selfhood, a sense of knowing where you have been and what it means. Soul is a way of life—but it is always the hard way. Its essence is ingrained in those who suffer and endure to laugh about it later." Soul is the beauty of self-expression, of self-in-rhythm. One swings from inside and in response to what is outside as well. Soul is mind operating free of calculation. It is humor and spontaneity and endurance. This concept of soul is consistent with the existential aim of authenticity. Here we have a shifted view of spirituality emphasizing personal integration arising from direct life engagement. This is not a remote God, but rather God found at the heart of our daily experience in our interchange with others, ourselves, and nature.

Subjectivity

What is this subjectivity, this freedom, that holds the devotion and loyalty of a person? To Sartre, freedom is "nothingness." For Kierkegaard, it is the human encounter with the Transcendent—one's moment before God. Buber sees this as the "I" meeting the "Thou" of life. Kazantzakis speaks of the cry from deep within the human personality. To respond to it is our sole possibility of freedom.

Yet this subjectivity, while termed by some as an encounter with the transcendent, should not be mistaken for a direct expression of the Divine. Each of us is all too soon aware of the finite nature of subjectivity. It is not all-knowing, and subjectivity is different in each person and constantly in the process of change within the same person. Subjectivity exists as a unique responsive relation to the world. Its primary activity is the conveyance of meaning through thought and feeling, intuition and sensation, and the assertion of this unique perspective through creative acts. Some would term this the activity of spirit, a divine possibility available to human beings. Yet divine and human remain intertwined.

It is this relationship between one's own subjectivity and the outside world that is the basis for responsible freedom instead of narcissistic caprice. One's inner objectivity encounters other reality again and again in the form of limits set up by life that challenge certain beliefs and meanings one has concluded about oneself. One experiences failures, misjudgments, hurt of others, neglect of self, conflict, and guilt. There is inevitable death, uncertainty, and suffering. These limiting situations, this suffering, becomes a revealing, guiding force of one's life. In a similar way, one realizes one's potentials. We sense that the world wants and needs some response from us. We feel called upon to choose, to act, to give, and to imprint ourselves on the world. This awareness of both limits and potentials is the foundation upon which we can judge our own unique perspective and readjust it when necessary. The ongoing encounter between subjectivity and the outside world may be looked upon as a continuing dialogue, dance, responsive process of inner and outer reality, continually affecting and being affected by the uniqueness of all forms involved.

Each of us must assume the burden of responsibility for our own freely chosen perspective and the associated consequences of our actions. To be a person is to assert our intelligence, knowing that we do not have an absolute knowledge of truth and that we may hurt others or ourselves; our efforts will often end in mistakes or failure. We must assert this uniqueness again and again—choosing courage or cowardice and knowing that suffering is often inevitable as our perspective conflicts with the limits of life.

We fail, finally, in our resurging hopes, the existentialist might say, but then we are a brotherhood in this—not only with others, but with all of nature. For there is a striving everywhere, a fight, and, in the end, only the remnants of our struggles—and a little later there are no longer even the remnants. Our loyalty is to the thrust behind this struggle in all things. What is this thrust? A mystery! A meaningful silence! Can we be sure it is meaningful? Who is to know? The questions of salvation or an afterlife must be held in abeyance. They can no longer be certainties. For many, these very uncertainties become the springboard to religious faith.

The mystical flavor of life is shared by both existential believers and nonbelievers alike. It affirms life as meaningful, not because it has been clearly revealed as such through science or Scripture, but rather because one has sensed a deeper or clearer experience of reality in certain moments. These moments are not dismissed lightly, but are preserved as precious and illuminating even though the full meaning of their revelation may be unclear. Such experiences as love, beauty, creative work, rhythm, awe, and psychic phenomena suggest seeing "through a glass darkly." Those followers of religious faiths may find a "rebirth," an adult reorientation to the message of revelation in religious writings. Yet the revelation of ultimate significance must be made personal.

The Bond with Others

If subjectivity and its uniqueness, development, and expression is valued in oneself, it must be valued in others as well. Since there is no absolute subjective perspective, each person's unique view and contribution contains an intrinsic value. Existentialists feel a bond with others and are responsive to their needs and to friendship, for they respect their subjectivity as being as valid as their own. They also know that the assertion of courage is difficult and often impossible without occasional affirmation from others. Human love is the effort to understand, share, and participate in the uniqueness of others. It is validating in others that which we also value within ourselves. Love is sometimes an act of helping, at other times a passive compassion. At times it reaches a total merging that takes one beyond the fundamental awareness of isolation.

The existentialists realize, too, the dangers in human relationships. Just as we guard against self-deceptions that tempt us toward a narcissistic idolization of ourselves, so we remain on guard in relation to the institutions of society. The assertion of individual uniqueness is often a threat to others and to a smoothly functioning social group. This is because such assertion will frequently defy those rules, patterns, habits, and values that are sources of defined security for others, or a group. Thus society and subgroups within a society will again and again attempt to suppress arising individual uniqueness out of a sense of threat or an inability to comprehend. Conformity is urged. It happens with family, friends, neighborhoods, and church, professional, and political groups. Existentialists often finds themselves estranged from others because of their own creativity and authenticity. Even when there is a relationship of mutual respect, with moments of unity through love, there will also come the moments of threat and misunderstanding because of the impossibility of one person's subjectivity fully comprehending that of another.

Yet conflict and threat in relationships do not move existentialists into a schizoid withdrawal.

They may display a touch of cynicism as they hear others identify themselves wholly with some group effort or as they proclaim the hope of humanity to be in their sensitive and loving interchange with their fellow man. But existentialists know that their own growth depends upon both affirmation from others and their occasional disagreement with them. The same interchanges are true for their growth. Existentialists believe in the beauty and warmth of love even though it is momentary. They know that people must stand together in respecting and validating the uniqueness of one another and resisting the forces of those who believe themselves to be blessed with an absolute truth that justifies their using other people as things instead of as valued, unique personalities.

The philosophical position described has stressed both faith and commitment to a perspective of life deemed valid as a result of one's direct and sensitive involvement in the life process. It is in opposition to establishing a life perspective by accepting some theoretical explanation of life as defined by some outside authority—whether parental, religious, scientific, or political. The subjective involvement of the whole person is essential to the life perspective that we finally concludes is our reality. This perspective is also in opposition to those who use fragmented life experiences as the ground for a total life perspective (as is sometimes found in the superficial assessments of the meaning of a weekend sensitivity group experience, or the realization of the "rightness" of a cause by a budding social activist). Human life is highly complex, and we must seek an openness to its totality of experiences if our search is to be legitimate. This sort of array should not neglect an opening up of oneself to the meaning of experience as described by others as well.

What becomes apparent is a movement in personal awareness—from egotistical striving to self-understanding; then to I-thou relationships with one's immediate surroundings; and finally, in the incorporation of some overall principle where humanity and universe are joined. Both discipline and spontaneity are societal elements on this road of increasing awareness. Disillusionment, freedom, suffering, joy, and dialogue are all important happenings along the way. The end of this process does not really arrive

until death. It is a continuing way that requires again and again the reaffirmation of that personal perspective called "truth." A transcendent view of existential freedom might be that of an illuminating light seeking understanding, compassion, and sometimes protective action in the surrounding world. This luminosity may also recognize that this very awareness is shared by all other humans, whether they know and validate it or not.

Professional Contributions

These ideas can be found in philosophical and religious writings as well as in motion pictures, plays, novels, and poetry labeled "existential." One of the earliest examples of existential literature is the Book of Ecclesiastes in the Old Testament. From the Orient, Zen Buddhism is also often compared with Western existential thinking.

Existential philosophy as we know it today had its initial comprehensive presentation by Soren Kierkegaard (1813–1855), whose writings were a passionate reaction to the all-embracing system of Hegelian philosophy. Later developments included the thought of Friedrich Nietzsche and Henri Bergson. Modern-day existential philosophers include Martin Heidegger, Jean-Paul Sartre, Albert Camus, Simone de Beauvoir, Miguel de Unamuno, Ortega y Gasset, Nicholas Berdyaev, Martin Buber, Gabriel Marcel, and Paul Tillich. This array of names suggests the widespread interest in existentialism among several European countries.

Much of existential psychology had its ideological rooting among the phenomenologists, most notably Edmund Husserl. Two European analysts, Ludwig Binswanger and Medard Boss, were constructing an existential psychology during Freud's lifetime.

Viktor Frankl, a Viennese psychiatrist, developed his "logotherapy" following his imprisonment in a German concentration camp during World War II. Logotherapy is based upon existential philosophy, and Frankl remains one of the most lucid writers in conveying existential thinking to members of the helping professions.

Rollo May's monumental work *Existence* (May et al., 1958) represented the first major impact of existential psychology upon American psychiatry and psychology. May presented the translations of existential psychologists and psychiatrists from Europe, where such thinking had become popular and in many places had replaced psychoanalytic thought. There was a readiness in America for existential thinking, and it quickly became part of the third force or humanistic psychology movement. This group included people such as Karen Horney, Carl Jung, Clark Moustakas, Carl Rogers, Abraham Maslow, Gordon Allport, Andras Angyal, and Prescott Lecky. Two journals devoted specifically to existential psychology and psychotherapy began quarterly publication in the United States in the early 1960s.

Existential thought was related to Gestalt therapy (Frederick Perls), the encounter movement (Carl Rogers and Arthur Burton), rational-emotive psychotherapy (Albert Ellis), and R. D. Laing's provocative "antipsychiatry" writings. Thomas Szasz pursued a similar attack upon psychiatry, particularly in relation to the "therapeutic state," the insanity plea, and the dehumanizing use of clinical diagnostic categories. Ernest Becker and Irvin Yalom presented challenging reappraisals of psychoanalytic thinking from existential postures. Perhaps the most intense descriptions of the existential therapists' use of self are found in the works of Thomas Hora and William Offman.

Perhaps the earliest social work writings with a decided existential flavor were by Jessie Taft of the functional school, which had its roots in the psychology of Otto Rank. In his Pulitzer prize-winning book *The Denial of Death*, Becker produced a monumental integration of the thought of Rank and Freud (Becker, 1958). Social workers, who once avidly debated the "dynamic" versus the "functional" schools of social work theory, appear to have totally ignored Becker's incisive thought as to how these two systems of thought could be effectively wedded. A welcome scholarly exception to this is Robert Kramer's work, which links Rank with Carl Rogers and Rollo May. (Kramer, 1995).

In 1962, David Weiss's article appeared in *The Social Worker* (1962) and Gerald Rubin's paper in *Social Work* (1962). Andrew Curry was publishing articles in the existential psychiatry journals. In the late 1960s, several articles appeared in various social work journals written by John Stretch, Robert Sinsheimer, David Weiss,

Margery Frohberg, and myself. These papers were specifically related to the application of existential philosophy in social work thought and practice.

There were also several social work papers published during this period that did not specifically emphasize existentialism but were related to similar concerns of the existential social work group. These writers included Elizabeth Salomon, Mary Gyarfas, and Roberta Wells Imre.

The first book on the subject of existentialism in social work was published in 1969 by Exposition Press. It was Kirk Bradford's *Existentialism and Casework* (1969). Its subtitle expresses its intent: *The Relationship Between Social Casework and the Philosophy and Psychotherapy of Existentialism*. It should be considered an introductory and integrative work rather than a comprehensive or prophetic book. In 1970, Alan Klein related existential thinking to social group work in his book *Social Work Through Group Process* (1970). A second book was published in 1975 by Dawson College Press of Montreal authored by David Weiss and titled *Existential Human Relations*. This was a more comprehensive work applying existential thought to various aspects of social work practice. In 1974, James Whittaker's book *Social Treatment* (1994) legitimized existential thinking as one of the four major theories contributing to social work practice. An effort to clarify both spiritual and systemic ideas for social workers appeared in *Existential Social Work* (Krill, 1968) by myself. Two of my subsequent books in practical application were *The Beat Worker* (1986) and *Practice Wisdom* (1990). The former focused upon psychotherapy and the latter upon teaching the integration of self-awareness, philosophical thinking, and the therapeutic relationship to graduate students. Other social work writers related the existential view to child abuse (Brown, 1980), to social work education (Swaine & Baird, 1977), and to cross-cultural counseling (Vontress, 1979).

While there appears to be a rising, if somewhat limited, interest in existential philosophy in social work literature, it would seem that the interest is far more widespread among social work students and younger professionals. Many of the newer therapeutic approaches being performed by social workers are closely akin to the existential view of the therapeutic process. Such points of emphasis as choice and action, here-and-now problem orientation, dispensing with the use of diagnostic categories, stressing the expression of the worker as a vital, human person, and recognizing the connection of personal identity with the quality of significant other relationships all have their existential linkages.

Therapeutic Concepts

The philosophical perspective discussed earlier suggests five organizing concepts of existential thought: disillusionment, freedom of choice, meaning in suffering, the necessity of dialogue, and a stance of responsible commitment. These same concepts can provide a way of viewing the therapeutic process (Krill, 1969).

Disillusionment

In existential thinking, one can move from a life of "bad faith" to one of authenticity. To do this one must risk the pain of disillusionment. Similarly, in psychotherapy, change can be viewed as a result of giving up those very defensive beliefs, judgments, symptoms, or manipulations that interfere with the natural growth process. This growth process would be seen as the emergence of unique personhood through responsive acts in relation to one's surroundings. Realistic needs and potentials begin to be the source of choice and action instead of neurotic, self-deceptive security needs.

An important therapeutic task, then, is to help clients experience disillusionment with those various security efforts that block their own growth. Disillusionment will seldom result from a rational exploration of one's past with the hope of realizing causal factors of present defensive behavior. It is rare that one gives up security patterns because they are viewed as irrational, immature, or no longer applicable. Disillusionment occurs through the pain of loneliness and impotence. On the far side of such despair arise the possibilities of new values and beliefs. It is the therapist's concern that these be more human values than those abandoned. The therapist acts as a midwife for the release of the natural growth energies within personality so that what is wholly and individually unique may emerge.

Any tampering with this natural direction, once begun, is likely to do more harm than good.

Freedom of Choice

Sartre characterizes consciousness as "no-thing-ness," for it is an awareness of oneself that transcends or goes beyond any fixed identity one might have concluded about oneself. Personality is always emerging. To view it as static or secured is our act of self-deception (bad faith). This conception of consciousness as freedom is a break with conceptions of personality as being totally ruled by "unconscious" or by early learned behavior.

Despite our past, despite any diagnostic label pinned upon us, we always have the capacity to change ourselves. We can choose new values or a new lifestyle. This does not always necessitate years or months of "working something through"; it may occur within days or weeks.

Choice is for action and differs from intellectual meandering or good intentions. Chosen actions occur in the present. Therapy is, therefore, present-focused and task or action-oriented. People learn from experience, not from reason alone, although the very process of understanding how one's current belief and value system operates (and its consequences) can itself lead to new choices.

The critical ingredient for change is the client's wish to do so. Therapy must, therefore, be designed to clarify quickly the nature of change sought by the client, and the therapist must be able to work within this framework rather than seeking to convince or seduce the client into redefining his or her problems and aiming for some type of change goal that pleases the therapist but is only vaguely understood by the client.

A therapist's belief in the client's capacity for change is a message of positive affirmation conveyed throughout treatment. There is no question but that a therapist's focus upon unraveling the intricacies of past relationships conveys a deterministic message that is a commentary upon the weakness and helplessness of a client.

Meaning in Suffering

Just as existentialists see suffering as an inherent part of a life of authenticity based upon responsibility and freedom, so, too, existential therapists do not seek to discredit or eliminate anxiety and guilt in their clients. Instead, they affirm such suffering as both necessary and directional for a person. They will help reveal what real anxiety and guilt may lie disguised behind neurotic (unrealistic) anxiety and guilt. But they would not seek to minimize or eradicate realistic anxiety and guilt. Such efforts would themselves be dehumanizing, unless used to prevent decompensation. In many cases the normalizing of pain or a problem as a natural consequence of one's valued conclusions about adjusting to life can enhance one's sense of responsibility and the potential for changing one's orientation.

Necessity in Dialogue

People do not grow from within themselves alone. Their emergence happens in responsive relation to their surroundings. They create their own meaning in response to situations, and these meanings become the basis for choices and actions. However, their own meanings are no more absolute than those of any other person. Their own growth has to do with the continued reassessment of personal meanings, and they depend upon feedback from their environment (particularly human responses) for this reassessment activity. In order to gain honest feedback, one must allow others to be honest and free in their own expression. In therapy, therefore, it is critical to help clients open themselves to relationships with others wherein they give up their manipulative or "game" efforts in order to invite free responses from others. In doing this they not only allow themselves experiences of intimacy, but they also realize that their own emerging sense of self requires such honest transactions with others.

Commitment

Clients' recognition of and commitment to their own inner emerging unique lifestyle is a hope of the existential therapist. Clients realize this commitment through their experience of the therapist's own affirmation of their worldview. This unique worldview is affirmed from the beginning in the therapist's acceptance of how clients perceive their symptoms, problems, conflicts—how

they perceive change and what they want changed. The client's uniqueness is also affirmed during treatment by the way a therapist relates to "where a client is" in each interview. The theme of a session comes as an emerging force from the client, rather than as a rationally predicted starting point made in advance by the therapist. Both the goal-setting process and the activity of entering upon and working with an interview theme are therefore client-centered rather than therapist-centered. This in no way crimps the therapist's operation as a skilled professional with expertise, but the therapist acts out of this expertise rather than displaying it in a manner that will inhibit the process of therapy. A useful axiom here is the idea that it is who one is, as a person, rather than the amount of knowledge one has, theoretically, that is most important in helping people.

Clients' awareness of and respect for their own unique lifestyle might be described as a turn away from self-pity and impotence. Rather than complaining about their lot in life, they discover that they are intricately involved in the life process itself. They learn to listen to what life says to them and find meaning in the response that is unique to themselves. This is what is meant by the existential concept of dialogue and commitment.

Related Therapeutic Approaches

As suggested earlier, there are obvious differences among those therapists claiming the existential label. This becomes more understandable if we consider the above therapeutic principles and note how they may be activated in a number of differing ways. A consideration of the ranging techniques that may fit with the principles outlined will also clarify how other treatment theories tend to be compatible with the existential view. Existentialism claims no technique system of its own and needs none. Its affirmation of the uniqueness of each client results in a perspective of each treatment situation being also unique. Whatever techniques can be used, from whatever treatment theory, become the tools toward accomplishment of the unique goal chosen. In this sense, existentialism is thoroughly eclectic. Techniques are always placed secondary to the uniqueness of clients and the puzzle they present to the therapist.

Several therapeutic systems are compatible with existential thinking. Some are not, and these will be considered later. The reality-oriented therapists (Glasser, Ellis, O. Hobart Mowrer, and Frankl) all stress choice and specific behavior change. William Reid, Laura Epstein, and Harold Werner have described similar cognitive-oriented approaches in social work literature. They are present-focused and commonly propose specific tasks for clients wherein the client is expected to put into immediate practice a decision for change. They tend to use reason to aid the decision for change, but then stress action. The action is usually expected to occur outside of the therapy interview (often as homework assignments), but its results are brought back for further discussion. Reality therapists focuses upon the disillusionment process by clearly identifying "faulty or irrational beliefs" that are responsible for problematic behavior. They affirm the client's freedom to choose and encourage a value shift through action.

Gestalt therapy, psychodrama, client-centered therapy, and provocative therapy techniques all stress a heightening of a client's awareness through action in the here and now. They seek the immediacy of experience as a thrust for change rather than a rational process of analyzing causal connections. They differ from the reality therapies in that the stress is upon choice and action that is more immediate; it is to occur in the here and now of the therapy meeting itself. Whether clients seek to make use of this experience in their outside daily life is usually left up to them. There is less effort to deal rationally with the disillusionment process of beliefs and manipulations. These are dealt with experientially as group members are encouraged to give direct and open feedback to the attitudes and behavior expressed by others. The activity of dialogue is stressed.

Family systems approaches, like those of Virginia Satir, Salvador Minuchin, and Murray Bowen, combine awareness heightening with choices and tasks yet add the ingredient of activating the significant other system in the helping process. Here the dimension of dialogue and intimacy is at last addressed within its daily living context. Bowen and Satir emphasize individuation, while Minuchin focuses more upon action tasks.

There are a few therapists to whom the term "existential" fits more accurately than any other: Carl Whittaker, Frank Farrelly, Lester Havens, William Offman, Walter Kempler, Irvin Yalom, Sydney Jourard, and Thomas Hora. Their common attribute is an intense, often surprising use of their personal self-expression combined with a general disdain for conceptualization about clients from theory. Here the subjective emphasis of existentialism reaches its height of therapeutic expression. When these therapists are paradoxical in their actions, it is seldom as a result of planned strategy. Paradox results from their intuitive response to the client and often expresses the paradoxical life stance of the therapist himself.

From the foregoing comparisons of therapeutic approaches, as they relate to existential thought, several areas of existential theory become more clear-cut. We shall look at these in more detail, considering the therapeutic relationship, nature of personality, concept of change, use of historical data and diagnosis, and treatment methods.

The Therapeutic Relationship

One might conclude that all psychotherapies value theory, techniques, and the therapeutic relationship, but the priority of importance varies. Ego psychology clearly elaborates theory in its maze of complexities. Behaviorism delineates a vast variety of techniques, matched to specific symptoms. Humanistic psychology, and especially the existential worker, stresses the relationship itself, its transparency, spontaneity, and intensity. The therapist's use of self and the type of relationship he or she seeks to foster with a client will be considered from two vantage points. First, the attitude of the therapist toward the client and the client's problems; and second, the behavior of the therapist as he or she interacts with the client—his use of self as a unique person in his or her own right.

There is a critical difference between a therapist who sees the client as a complex of defenses or learned behaviors that are dysfunctional and a therapist who views the client as a unique, irreplaceable worldview that is in the process of growth, emergence, and expansion. The latter is an existential position. It views the problems and symptoms of clients as their own efforts to deal with the growth forces within themselves and the risks these pose to them in relation to their self-image, relationship with significant others in their life, and their role in society.

The writings of R. D. Laing are aimed at clarifying the critical differences between the two types of therapists (1967). He points out that therapists who see the client as a mass of complexes, defenses, and dysfunctional learnings see themselves as "the authority." Their task is to diagnose the nature of these "dynamics" and convey these insights to the client either through verbal commentary or through specific behavioral tasks given to the client. But in doing so, the therapist also acts as another societal force that seeks to adjust the client to someone's definition of the functional personality. Such a therapist tends to support the view that the client's symptoms and problems identify him or her as ill (even "dysfunctional" implies the client is out of step with his or her surroundings). The therapist often becomes another dehumanizing force in the client's life in the sense of urging the "patient" to adjust to his or her family, instincts, needs, society's needs, etc. In contrast, existential therapists have no prescriptions of how the client should live. They sees their task as that of a midwife, an agent who has knowledge and skills to aid in the unblocking process that will allow the client to resume his or her own unique growth and emergence—whether or not this puts him or her in further conflict with family, friends, and society. The therapist may point out the potential risks and consequences of an emerging lifestyle but will not negate its potential value.

The existential therapist's attitude affirms the inherent value of the client as a unique person with a very special worldview or lifestyle that is his or hers alone to charter. The client is also aware that the therapist sees in him or her the power of free choice. Instead of being helplessly at the mercy of forces beyond his or her consciousness, clients can see the significant choices in their present life situation and have the power to decide which way they will proceed in shaping their life.

In one sense existential therapists do stand for a particular lifestyle, but it is one based upon their belief in the nature of humanness rather than a cultural viewpoint of how a person should pursue his or her role in family or society. The values conveyed by the existential therapist are these: human beings have the capacity for free choice; they are of fundamental worth in their own unique perspective of life and their assertion of this perspective; they require an open interaction with their surroundings in order to grow—emergence is a responsive and interactive process; suffering is an inevitable part of the growth process, for emergence involves risks and unknowns; and self-deception is a potent force.

These values are in opposition to several values supported by society at large: that an individual is a helpless creature both at the mercy of an unknown unconscious and of utter insignificance in the complex mechanisms called society; that one can and should find happiness through avoidance of suffering and pain and by means of the distractions and pleasures offered at every turn; that a person is what he is, so he should fulfill his role in his family or social system as best he can and be satisfied with his already finished identity; and that since there are groups of humans considered ultimately wise in politics, in universities, at the executive level of business and the military, in churches, and in medical buildings, Mr. or Ms. Citizen should essentially consider a conforming obedience to what these soothsayers say is best for him or her.

The existential value perspective of the worker also differ significantly from "value life models" all too often conveyed by "therapist gurus." These models have been described by the author in three forms: the hope of enlightening reason, the hope of flowering actualization, and the hope of satisfying mediocrity (Krill, 1986). The therapist-guru enjoys a priestly role of telling people how to attain happiness, enlightenment, or maturity. While existential workers sometimes address value issues, as they relate to the presenting problems, they are unwilling to represent a value life model, or ideal, to the client. They prefer that the client seek such ultimate definitions and commitments through his or her own significant others and/or support groups. Counseling is neither a truth search (guru model) nor an exercise in symptom alleviation (technician model). Problems are addressed in such a manner as to invite the client to consider the relationship of his or her current value framework and lifestyle as possibly problem-related. Problems are not merely annoyances to be discarded, but may be signposts for self-examination. There is an exception to the discussion of value life models: a worker who shares the same religious or philosophical belief system as the client may freely discuss belief understandings as a peer (not as an expert).

The behavior of the existential therapist reflects his or her philosophical-psychological attitudes toward the client. Another useful axiom regarding the therapeutic relationship is this: what facilitates change in people most powerfully are the values of the worker, not spoken but demonstrated in his or her response to the client's concerns. If the worker is not the authority with the answers, what is he or she? Existential therapists do see themselves as experts, but their expertise has to do with their skills and talents of empathy; understanding; appreciation of and compassion for individual human beings and their struggles; experience in the process of self-deception, having struggled with growth-defensive process within themselves; and affirmation of the value of the unique soul, having themselves been disillusioned with all the society-made authorities who offer solutions, happiness, etc.; and an open honesty that offers the client the possibility of genuine dialogue, if the client seeks to engage in such. Existential workers, then, seek to normalize the problems of the client by reference to the struggles of the human situation. They avoid paternalistic conclusions about the client, viewing both problem and person exploration as a mutual process. Another way in which the worker avoids paternalism is by being honest and clear, rather than hidden and deceptive, in relation to strategies utilized.

Existential workers may exhibit a type of detachment, but this detachment is not the cool aloofness of the objective mechanist who is dissecting and reforming the patient. The detachment of existential therapists is an expression of their profound belief in the freedom of the client. The client has a right to his or her own lifestyle. If the client chooses not to follow a direction of personal growth but chooses to maintain his or her defensive posture for security or other reasons, so be it. The therapist's sense of worth is not in the client's hands but within himself or herself. His or her detachment is from results, even though his or her actual activity in the helping process will be quite open and involved.

Detachment must not impair vitality and therefore cannot take the form of intellectual aloofness, analyzing the client from afar. Vital engagement through spontaneity, surprise, and unsettling responses is one of the valued methods of the existential worker. Genuine dialogue calls for an immediacy of feedback in many cases, and considered responses in others. Habitual mindsets and communication patterns of clients require interruption and jostling, on occasion, in order for the new, the creative, to be brought to awareness. The use of vitality, lightness, spontaneity, and humor will often unbalance a client's defensive posturing. The client becomes engaged emotionally and released from a fixed role or value position. At such moments he or she is freer to experiment with new possibilities.

The relationship between therapist and client is seen by many existential writers as the essential ingredient of change. The concepts of individual growth and genuine encounter with others are interdependent in the thought of Martin Buber. David Weiss emphasizes this same connectedness in his discussion of healing and revealing (1970). This I-thou relation need not be seen as mystical. Carl Rogers's description of this activity suggests that the therapist provides an atmosphere for growth by means of a nonthreatening, affirming, understanding responsiveness (1961). But this does not mean therapists remain passive. On the contrary, Rogers emphasizes the importance of therapists being themselves in the expression of important arising feelings. To offer a dialogue is at least to present one side of it in an open, honest fashion. Therapists reveal themselves in another manner at times. They share some of their own struggles, disillusionment, and experiences wherein they, too, sought growth in the face of pain. In both these examples of the therapist's openness, we see that the therapist sees his or her own unique world view as an important experience to share with the client—not in a "go and do likewise" spirit, but rather showing himself or herself as a fellow traveler on the rocky road of human existence.

Human Personality

Freudian theory proposed the ego as a balancing, organizing, controlling, harmonizing agent among the demands of the superego, the pressures of the "outside world," and the cravings of the id. Behavior theory suggests a passive psyche that is primarily molded by outside forces. What one learns from others is what one is. Both roles render the individual practically helpless to resist the many forces that work upon him or her.

Two key concepts differentiate the existential view from those above. The first is the idea of an integrating, creative force for growth at the core of the personality. The second is the belief that all individuals have the capacity to shift their style of life radically at any moment.

In terms of the human dynamo, the existentialists would not disagree with Freud's formulation of the id as a composite of Eros and Thanatos, or life and death instincts. To this is added, however, the notion of a force that moves one toward meaning and toward relations with one's surroundings on the basis of meanings concluded. There is an integrative, unifying, creative force within people that synthesizes their own experiences, potentials, and opportunities and provides them with clues for their own direction of growth. No matter how emotionally disturbed patients may seem, there is this integrative core within them that prompts them in the direction of experiencing and expressing their own uniqueness (realistic needs and potentials). They may shut themselves off from such integrative promptings; they may refuse to listen or mislabel such messages as dangerous. But they are with the patient always.

The existential idea of a core integration and creation suggests a conflict-free portion of personality that survives and transcends any dysfunctioning that may possess a person.

Such a force toward integration and meaning need not be considered separate from id. It is an expression of id activity. Teilhard de Chardin posits such a force as existing in all forms of existence: animals, plants, and even inanimate matter. Chardin sees in humans the fruition of this drive toward complexity, and it is experienced in the human need for meaning and for love. Martin Buber, too, suggests a force in humans that permits them to enter the realm of relation with nature, ideas, other humans, and God. This is a force that transcends what otherwise appears to be a person's limited, finite, individual self. This thinking helps distinguish the existential view of the creative force in humans

from what the ego psychologists have attempted to add to basic Freudian theory to explain creative functioning through certain basic powers of the ego.

The second major distinction has to do with the power of free choice possessed by every person. Even the most disturbed individuals are not solely at the mercy of chaotic, irrational, destructive forces—an id gone wild. Nor are they at the total mercy of environmental forces that seek to identify, coerce, dehumanize, conform, or destroy them. The individual personality is always in the process of change and emergence. Sartre defined human consciousness as a "nothingness." Since it is always in the process of becoming, it is never fixed and completed. This no-thing-ness is an openness to the new, the unknown; it is forever moving beyond whatever identity one has concluded about oneself. Sartre sees this as an essential human construct. One may deny one's freedom and find ways of avoiding responsibility for this very process of change and emergence, but the process itself goes on. Pathology is not the arrestment of growth but the self-chosen distortion of growth (Barnes, 1959).

Human consciousness is itself freedom—for it is a force that moves forever beyond whatever one has become as a fulfilled identity. As such, it is the power within humans to change, to alter their lifestyle, their direction, and their sense of identity. It is an ever-present potential for a conversion experience. "To find one's self, one must lose one's self."

If one has the capacity for free choice and also some awareness of integrative promptings toward growth from the very core of the psyche, then why should one choose dysfunctioning, defensive symptomatology, or madness?

Freud's concept of the superego and his view of defense mechanisms and pathological symptomatology are seen by the existentialist in a more holistic manner. The existential idea of bad faith is a person's activity of denying his or her nature of freedom and emergence for the sake of a sense of security and identity. Such people deceive themselves by a set of beliefs that define specifically who they are and what they can expect from others. This belief system contains both positive and negative judgments about oneself and suggests how one must relate to other people. It is the center of one's defensive control efforts, of one's symptomatology, of one's manipulations of relationships, and of one's fostering myths about who one is. These people choose to believe certain notions about themselves when they are quite young and undergoing the socialization process with parents, teachers, peers, etc. The beliefs they hold to are used to maintain a sense of secured identity. They are tempted somehow to reassure themselves of the solidity of their identity whenever they feel threatened. This they can do through manipulations of others, physical or psychological symptomatology, and reassuring beliefs about themselves. The belief pattern may change over the years, so that ideas implanted by parents may become more personalized beliefs, but it is the rigidity and response to threat that characterize this person's security image rather than the nature of the beliefs themselves.

This defensive belief system, or security image configuration, has its values, too. It helps the young, developing ego with limited experience and judgment conclude a manner of survival in a family constellation. The beliefs concluded about self and others provide habit patterns that furnish a sense of security so that one can use one's energy for other achievements as well. Even the adult ego is occasionally on the verge of exhaustion and needs to resort to the security image patterns of reassuring contentment. One will at times choose security image behavior, even when one knows it to be irrational and defensive, simply as a means of enduring and managing under considerable stress.

Security image patterns take the form of outer identifications, as well as inner passions. Outer identification includes all ways by which people use others to conclude who they are as a fixed identity—using their parents, spouse, children, friends, employer, profession, politics, church, race, social norms, etc. Inner passions have to do with feeling responses to life's situations that also fulfill a sense of identity, so that certain feelings become fanned into possessing passions. For the self identified as "Top Dog," irritation can become rage. For the self identified "Don Juan," sensual excitement can become lust. For some people, competition becomes greed. For others, pride becomes a quest for power. In the outer identifications, one identifies with beliefs and roles; in the inner passions, one identifies with specific feelings. In either case, the sense of self is experienced as fixed, solidified, and defined rather than flowing, free, and emerging.

The defensive belief system or security image configuration is sometimes referred to as one's world design, composed of self-concluded value positions. These are seldom the idealized values thought to be one's "ego ideal" but rather the everyday pragmatic values related to security-based hopes and fears. Such values are easily discerned by attending to the "self-chatter" of thinking at times of troubling stress.

The Process of Change

If you want to know who you are, don't conceptualize upon it: look at your actions, your behavior, your choices. Existentialism is a philosophy rooted in personal experience. "Truth is subjectivity," Kierkegaard's slogan, and "existence precedes essence," Sartre's assertion, are both ways of rooting identity in personal experience—one's active and unique response in a situation. Being-in-the-world is a concept of Heidegger's that asserts the same notion.

There are two components commonly accepted as necessary for the change process, one rational and the other experiential. Almost every form of psychotherapy includes both these components, despite their occasional assertions to the contrary.

The experiential component has to do with clients experiencing themselves in a new and different way. They may discover that they are being dealt with differently by a significant other person in their life. They may also find new kinds of feelings or symptoms arising within themselves. The rational component has to do with self-understanding through the process of reflecting and conceptualizing about themselves—the cause–effect relationships in their background, evaluating how they handled recent situations, considering the meaning to them of a new way they have experienced themselves, etc.

The existentialists see values in both components of change—one reinforces the other when both occur. The existentialists, however, are particularly wary of the common self-deception of intellectualizing about oneself—of dwelling on self-evaluation and introspection in a manner that negates any action or choice in the here and now. The self-understanding of importance is that of one's world design, its orienting values, and the negative consequences that naturally accompany this. William Offman (1976) stresses that an emphasis upon change agrees with the client's self-criticism (get rid of my problem), whereas a normalizing of the problem as an expression of the client's world design affirms the client while at the same time stressing his or her personal responsibility for the problem. There are no problem-free value positions, so the client may simply accept the problems as inevitable consequences or consider some alternate value position.

Here are some therapeutic activities that promote both clarified self-understanding and emotion-inducing experiences:

1. The attitude of the therapist toward the client can present a new type of affirmation by a significant other person that the client has never experienced.

2. The therapist's skill with empathy may provide the client an experience of being understood more intensely than by others in his or her life.

3. The openness of the therapist about himself or herself as a revealing, engaging person provides an invitation for the client to the dialogical experience. It can also offer an experience of an authority figure as human and of equal status. Such openness by a therapist may constructively take the form of provocative, negative feedback to the client about his or her appearance, attitudes, feelings, and behavior. Here the client experiences a candid honesty that may be otherwise denied to him or her in the everyday world of interactions.

4. Techniques designed for here-and-now heightening of awareness, such as in Gestalt, psychodrama, and encounter groups or the dealing with "transference" interactions between therapist and client, are obviously aimed primarily at the experiential component of change. Similarly, efforts to vitalize new interactions between group or family members quickly stir new areas of individual awareness.

5. Action tasks for the client to perform outside of therapy sessions provide new behavioral experiences.

Compatible with the existential therapist's emphasis upon experiential change is his lack of interest in historical data. Some history may be of value in the early interviews to help the therapist see the client in a more human, better rounded perspective, so that the therapist is less inclined to make superficial judgments about the client in response to the stereotype the client usually presents to other people. But the therapist often does not even need this aid. It is far more important to understand the dynamics of clients' present struggles, and what their symptoms or complaints reveal about their efforts to grow and meet their own needs (the present beliefs and activities of their defensive belief systems).

If client themselves bring up historical material, the existential therapist will often seek to make it immediately relevant. The therapist may do this by relating the past experience to present choices, or else (using Gestalt techniques) by asking the client to bring the early parent figure into the present interview session by role-playing the past interaction that the client is describing.

The existential therapist is in agreement with Glasser's position that an intent focus upon early historical material plays into the client's feelings of helplessness and/or efforts to rationalize his or her own impotence.

History sometimes serves a useful purpose in relation to understanding a client's world design. When clients are able to recall patterns of thinking, feeling, and behavior that have recurred time and again, the power of their determining value positions, or conclusions, becomes more poignant.

World Design and Diagnosis

Clinical diagnosis has its value as a shorthand way of communicating to peers about clients, in terms of areas of conflict and types of defenses. Other than this, it is of questionable value in the eyes of the existential therapist and commonly results in more harm than good. The danger of diagnosis is the categorization of a client, so as to provide therapists some "objective" way of defining prognosis, goals, the role therapists must play as they interact with the client, and their decision about termination. Such "objective" efforts based upon generalizations about clients with a similar history/symptomatology/mental status constellation miss what is unique about a particular client. A further danger described by Laing is that diagnosis is often used as a way of agreeing with the family that this client is "sick" and in need of readjustment to the demands and expectations of the family.

This depreciation of the value of clinical diagnosis, however, does not suggest a disregard for understanding the nature of a client's present struggles, conflicts, strivings, and fears. World design understanding remains of key importance. Here existentialists differ with behavioral modifiers who relate themselves only to a specific symptom without regard for its meaning and the client's present lifestyle.

It is critical to understand the unique world view of the client. This consists of patterns of relating to meaningful others and expectations of them. It also includes beliefs about oneself, both positive and negative judgments, and assumptions about oneself and how these affect the way one meets one's own needs and handles one's frustrations of need satisfaction. It is important to see how clients are interfering with their own growth, and this includes both the beliefs they hold about the sort of person they are and the notions they have about how they must deal with the significant people in their life. It may even include how they evaluate forces of society that play upon them and attempt to conform their behavior into some stereotype that is useful to society's needs (employers, church, racial attitudes, etc.). Normalization in the assessment phase conveys this message: given your special way of viewing the world and your patterns of affecting it and responding to it, your problem is perfectly understandable—it is a natural expression of you. This is not to say that the client created the problem; nor, on the other hand, is he or she a total victim of it.

This type of self-understanding in relation to orienting value conclusions stresses the here-and-now lifestyle—the client's present being-in-the-world. How the client gets this way is of questionable significance. The values of identity formulations are twofold. First, they provide the therapist with an understanding of each unique client and how the client's present symptoms are ways of handling a particular stress or conflict area. Second, world design gives therapists somewhat of a guideline to assess their own work

with the client, particularly when they discover that their therapeutic efforts are bringing no results.

The world design understanding of an existential social worker will often emphasize family dynamics (interactions, scapegoating, alliances, etc.). These usually make up the most significant area of the client's lifestyle functioning. Intervention efforts will frequently involve other family members for the same reason. The existential understanding of the person as "being-in-the-world" is wholly compatible with the dual focus model of social work. The personal, unique truth of the individual is known best through his or her relations with others and forces beyond his or her own ego—usually social but at times, perhaps, transcendental in nature.

Even when the problem is not set forth as family or marital in nature, the therapist will tend to see the presenting symptom as a means of dealing with significant others in the client's life. An interpersonal appraisal of symptoms is attuned to the absence, loss, breakdown, or dysfunctioning of important human relationships in the person's life. Therapeutic work will commonly be addressed to the creation, the restoration, or the improvement of such relationships. This interpersonal focus upon symptomatology need not neglect the individual's subjective experience of attitudes, values, and feelings; the two are obviously interdependent. However, the existential therapist sees catharsis and self-understanding as a vehicle for altering the person's world of human relationships, which is the fundamental goal. This interpersonal emphasis distinguishes the existential social worker from most existential psychiatrists and psychologists.

Treatment Methods

It is difficult to talk of treatment methods without first considering the types of clients and problems for which the methods are used. In one sense, the existential perspective is loyal to no particular treatment system. It is eclectic and uses whatever techniques will best meet the needs of a particular client. In another sense, the existential therapist may be considered best equipped to work with clients whose problem involves a loss of direction, a value confusion, a shaken identity in a swirling world of anomie.

For these clients, certain techniques have been developed to focus precisely on such difficulties. However, it should be clearly understood that the existentialist works out of his or her unique philosophical perspective with all clients and should not be viewed only as a specialist with clients experiencing personal alienation.

There are three principles of treatment that clarify the therapeutic approach of the existentialist:

1. A client-centered orientation
2. An experiential change emphasis
3. A concern with values and philosophical or religious perspectives.

Client-Centered Orientation

The client-centered focus has already become apparent in our introductory comments on the existentialist's antiauthoritarian stance. Client centeredness was also the major issue in the discussion on diagnosis and world design formulation. Two other areas exemplify client centeredness: goal formulations and work with an emerging theme in any given interview.

Goal formulation involves the therapist and client working out a mutual agreement in the early interviews as to the purpose of future treatment. What must be guarded against here is the type of therapeutic dogmatism that seeks to convince the client as to the "true implications" of his or her symptoms or problem, so that he or she will work in the manner the therapist wishes. The most important initial step in treatment, following the age-old social work principle, is to "start where the client is." This adage refers to focusing on how the client is experiencing the problem, what it is the client wants changed, and other ideas as to the type of help the client is seeking.

Elsewhere, I enumerated a framework of possible goals from which social workers may proceed with treatment (Krill, 1968). These are provocative contact; sustaining relationship; specific behavior (symptom) change; environmental change; relationship change; directional change; and combinations of the above.

The type of goal left off this list is the extensive insightful analysis that a client who enters psychoanalysis may be seeking. Whether or not the client ends up with any more significant change through insightful analysis than in some of the above-mentioned goals is highly questionable at this point in time, considering research efforts into the effects of treatment.

The above-stated goals can be briefly differentiated by considering the client's view of change in each category:

Provocative Contact. The client seeks neither change nor help of any kind. The caseworker assertively seeks to provoke a client into wanting change. This occurs often in protective services, in residential treatment centers for children, and in the "back wards" of psychiatric hospitals and institutions for the developmentally delayed. It is also common with the "hard-to-reach" families who present various problems to the community via the schools and police departments. Just how far caseworkers should go in their provocative efforts is itself an ethical decision related to the right of a client to his or her own unique lifestyle. Nevertheless, provocative efforts are often justified insofar as they provide an outreach effort and offer an opportunity that the client might otherwise never consider.

Sustaining Relationship. Here the client seeks help, in that he or she is lonely and wants an affirmative, interested contact in his or her life, but the client has no hope for changing his or her lifestyle in any way and will resist any such efforts. The client's need is for an affirming relationship without expectations of changed behavior. Change will commonly occur anyway as the client's self-esteem is boosted through a caring, nondemanding relationship.

Specific Behavior (Symptom) Change. The client is distressed with a particular troublesome behavior but has no interest in widening the problem area by seeing how this particular symptom is related to his or her past or present lifestyle and system of relationships. The client's motivation is restricted to symptom alleviation.

Environmental Change. The client sees his or her difficulty in relation to the environment beyond his or her family. The problem may have to do with employment, education, social contacts, or community forces that he or she experiences as dehumanizing. The client does not see himself or herself as part of the problem. The client seeks help in dealing with social institutions and systems.

Relationship Change. Here the client experiences difficulties in relationships with significant others in his or her life—spouse, children, parents, relatives, friends. The client realizes his or her own involvement and wants to alter a relationship pattern.

Directional Change. The client's sense of identity, of values, of personal direction is confused. He or she has difficulty in making choices and feels impotent in relation to the immediate future. The conflict is experienced as within himself or herself.

The mode of therapy used (individual, couple, group, family) or the types of techniques (reality, behavioral modification, encounter, psychoanalytic ego, Gestalt, etc.) will vary, of course, in accordance with the interest of the client, the skills of the therapist, and the nature of the treatment setting itself. However, certain techniques are obviously more appropriate for certain goals. Behavior modification would be particularly useful with the goals of provocative contact and specific behavior (symptom) change. The core conditions elaborated by Carl Rogers will be most useful in providing a sustaining relationship for a client. Social work literature provides many useful approaches to accomplishing the goal of environmental change. The goal of relationship change can be dealt with using communications theory (Satir, Haley, Jackson) and other family and marital therapy models. Directional change can be effected by techniques described by Rogers, Farrelly, the Gestaltists, reality therapy, cognitive therapy, task-centered casework, and psychoanalytic psychotherapy. The critical point here is that the therapeutic approach must fit the unique goal and needs of a client rather than fitting clients into some pet system of psychotherapy and dismissing the misfits as "unmotivated."

What is important to understand in this goal framework is that it provides a starting point for treatment in a manner that recognizes the unique experience of the client as valid. The goal may change during treatment as the client begins to experience his or her problems in some other light. The goal must also be tested out in early interviews so as to ascertain whether the goal agreed upon is merely a verbalized goal of the client, or whether it is indeed the way in which the client experiences the need for help and hope for change. With this framework, the therapist engages the client in a manner by which they can both "talk the same language" and have similar expectations for what is to follow.

There would appear to be a contradiction between some of the above-mentioned goals and what has previously been described as the existential focus upon disillusionment, freedom of choice, finding meaning and suffering, discovering the growth value of dialogue, and coming to a sense of personal commitment in relation to one's future. Such a focus seems most applicable to the goal category of directional change. The existential therapist, however, is not bound to pursue such a focus if it does not seem appropriate. Existentialist therapists' concern with client-centered treatment and an emphasis upon experiential change enable them to assert their philosophical perspective to a degree in all goal categories described.

The other client-centered activity deals with the interview theme of any given session. The client is not a problem to be solved, a puzzle to be completed; the client is a person who is undergoing constant change from week to week, day to day. Change occurs in the client's life for both the good and the bad apart from what happens during therapy sessions. For the therapist to pre-plan an interview, picking up where the last one ended or getting into what the therapist considers to be an area of increasing importance, is often presumptuous.

The interview begins and the therapist listens to both verbal and nonverbal expressions of the client, staying alert to possible inconsistencies among what the client says and the client's feeling state and behavior. The therapist's most important listening tool is his or her capacity for empathy. In the initial stages of the interview, therapists must free themselves of preconceptions about the client and preoccupations with themselves in order to open themselves to the whole person before them.

How the theme is made known and how it is dealt with are related to the goal of therapy (thinking in terms of the goal framework described earlier) and what particular therapeutic approach a therapist favors for work on such a goal. The therapist and client work together from the point of theme clarity.

An Experiential Change Emphasis

The experiential emphasis has already been discussed. The activities encouraging experiential change include attitude of therapist, empathy, therapist's openness or transparency, heightening of here-and-now awareness, tasks for choice, and action. In the earlier discussion of how various theories of therapy reflected existential points of emphasis, it was apparent that techniques could be tapped from many theoretical sources.

It is clear by now that the existentialist is radically concerned with the here-and-now encounter between a person and the person's world. For it is in this moment of responsiveness, of being-in-the-world, that one experiences freedom of choice and meaning making. Who the person is stems from what he or she does—the choice he or she activates—not from the intellectual conceptualization he or she holds about the self, nor from any dogmas or groups to which he or she holds allegiance in exchange for some bestowed identity.

A Concern With Values and Philosophical or Religious Perspectives

The concern with pinpointing, challenging, and clarifying values and philosophy or religious perspectives is also dealt with by various writers. There are strong similarities between the rational-emotive psychotherapy of Albert Ellis and the Morita therapy of Japan. Both pinpoint "irrational" or "unrealistic" beliefs and specifically propose other, more realistic and human beliefs in substitution for the dysfunctional beliefs. Hobart Mowrer's integrity therapy follows a similar course, where the emphasis is upon helping client see their guilt as a contradiction between the values they hold in common with their "significant others" and their behavior or actual lifestyle. Frankl has developed two techniques, deflection and paradoxical intention, that are designed to help clients re-examine

and alter their philosophical perspective so as to affirm a new way of viewing themselves in relation to their symptoms, choices, and life direction.

These "reality-oriented" approaches include four common ingredients:

1. Pinpointing specific values (attitudes, beliefs, and judgments about self and others) manifested by the client's lifestyle
2. Clarifying how these very values may be interfering with the client's own growth and intimacy needs or efforts
3. Helping the client consider more realistic, human values and beliefs for the dysfunctional ones so the client's realistic growth and intimacy needs might achieve more direct satisfaction
4. Encouraging decisions, choices, and actions (often as homework assignments) in order to activate the new values concluded to be more valid.

Thomas Hora (1977) discusses values by distinguishing between two versions of reality: "the way it seems" and "the way it is." The first of these describes the distorted and limited views the client has about his or her lifestyle and its related value perspectives. The second view of reality is that expanded by the therapist as he or she highlights other values in the client's lifestyle that are being ignored or minimized. Like Offman, Hora will also clarify negative consequences in relation to some of the client's value positions and pose alternative possibilities for the client's considerations. Hora emphasizes the personal stance of the therapist to be one of a "benevolent presence" through which the therapist may convey peace, assurance, gratitude and love as important human realities.

This therapeutic emphasis upon values and a philosophical perspective is designed for certain types of clients—those whose working goal is directional change. There is a growing recognition of the effects of anomie in modern culture with resulting personal alienation from the roots of human needs and human strivings. Jung reported this phenomenon 40 years ago and existential novelists, philosophers, and psychologists have been emphasizing the extent of alienation ever since.

In relation to religion and spirituality the existential teacher would strongly endorse a recent development in graduate social work programs across the country. Related to the emphasis on diversity, schools are developing courses on religion and spirituality in order for students to address their own prejudices and appreciate the varied religious resources in the lives of their clients.

The American culture has finally felt the same impact of alienation that shook Europe during and after World War II. In America, this awareness was helped along by the revolt of the youth, minority groups, and poor people. At this point, it is unclear whether alienation is a problem of a particular client population or whether it is really at the root of all emotional distress. The writings of Laing, Becker, and, recently, Irvin Yalom are certainly weighted toward the latter view.

Considering the three therapeutic principles discussed (the client-centered orientation, focus upon experiential change, and concern for values and philosophical perspectives), it becomes clear that existential caseworkers seek to work with all types of clients and human problems and that they could function with any kind of social agency or therapeutic setting, provided they were given the administrative approval to work as they wished. It is also clear that the existential position is in opposition to those therapeutic practices that seek to adjust clients to family and social norms or to those prognostic norms stemming from the rigid use of diagnostic categories. The authoritative misuse of behavior modification and psychoanalytic theory is a major concern of the existential social worker.

The existential social worker is also concerned with how monetary preoccupations of insurance companies and funding sources of agencies are dictating therapeutic approaches. The popular emphasis on short-term, symptom-relief therapies ignores the existentialist's view that a presenting problem is commonly a warning sign of more troubling value issues of the client's lifestyles. This Band-Aid, patchwork approach simply reinforces the inclination of many clients to view themselves in a superficial manner.

Considering the eclectic use of treatment approaches suggested by the existential perspective, it is also apparent that social workers can make more creative and varied use of the existential perspective than can psychiatrists, psychologists, ministers, or nurses. This is because of the wide-ranging problem activities that engage the efforts of social workers, necessitating a manner of work that includes multiple skills.

The modes of therapy (individual, couple, family, and group) are all effective ways of conducting an existential-oriented treatment. Application to individual counseling has been elaborated upon, particularly by Rogers, Farrelly, May, Frankl, and Perls. Work with groups with an existential perspective has been described by Helen Durkin, Carl Rogers, Arthur Burton, and Irvin Yalom. Social work writer Alan Klein relates the group work approach to existential thinking. Family therapists whose approaches are highly compatible with the existential perspective include Jay Haley, Virginia Satir, John Bell, and Carl Whittaker.

The existential approach fulfills two major needs of modern social work practice. First, it is the only social work approach that emphasizes value issues related to the client's problem. With the apparent increase of alienation and anomie, social work may require methods of response to value questions. Second, the emphasis upon the human ingredients of the therapeutic relationship, coupled with an "atheoretical" understanding of the client as a person, results in a restoration of humanitarian helping. Self-aware workers are better able to appreciate all clients as more like themselves and less as objects for diagnostic categorization and manipulation.

Case Example

The following could be considered an example of the existential social work approach. The case described is short-term casework with an individual from the goal framework of specific behavior change. It should be clear from the previous discussion about differing goals and the eclectic use of treatment techniques that other case examples would take much different forms from the one described. The three existential principles of client-centered focus, experiential change, and value focus are illustrated in this case.

A Latin-American woman, aged 34, came to me complaining of a severely inhibiting depression. In the course of the evaluation, it appeared that she had little interest or sensitivity for seeing any connection of her symptoms to her past or present living situation. She was somewhat troubled over her recent divorce, which happened only a year ago. There was also a problem with her mother (living across the street) who tried to dominate her and provoke her guilt, and who often took care of her two teenage daughters. Some rebellion in the older teenage daughter was apparent. She also believed herself "hexed" by her mother-in-law. These were areas of complaints, yet she saw no prospects for changing them. Her concerns for change were very concrete: she could not do her housework or cook the meals or discipline the children, for she would usually go to bed soon after she returned from work. In bed, she would either sleep or fantasize about how badly off she was, and the running of the house was left to the children, particularly the rebellious older one. She feared losing her job as a nurse's aide at the local hospital and had already missed several days of work because of feeling too tired. She had given up on going out with her boyfriend and felt extremely alone and worthless.

Within ten interviews, seen on an alternate week basis, the depression had lifted. She managed her housework well; disciplined the children—the older one was much less rebellious; she could stand up to her mother on a realistic basis; she was dating again; and she was taking a training course to become a practical nurse. The goal was specific behavioral change although its successful accomplishment resulted in a broadening of this woman's constructive activity in several areas of her life.

My techniques dealt primarily with the symptoms of depression and helplessness. In the second interview, I emphasized what I sensed to be her inhibited potential: I said that she could make herself get out of bed (or refuse to enter it) by performing the tasks of her housework and by going to her hospital work every day, no matter how tired she felt. I recognized that feelings of depression were strong within her, but pointed out that they represented a part of herself that seemed to be trying to convince her that she was no good. She could go on believing this or she could challenge this idea. In the third interview, I dealt actively with another belief, challenging its power and questioning her need to be dominated by it. She thought the depression resulted from being "hexed." I told her that I had doubts about the magic of hexing and if there was anything to it, it probably had to do with her own reaction to the notion that she had been "hexed." I linked this belief with the part of her that was trying to convince her that she was helplessly useless and inadequate.

As sessions went on, she did bring up material about her mother, husband, children, job, and relatives, but this was more from the standpoint of content for discussion in what she felt to be a positive, affirming

relationship. The actual therapeutic effort, in terms of pinpointing her problem and a way of dealing with it, was primarily in relation to the depressive symptom described. The techniques used were my ways of responding to her area of concern and view of change. We could communicate through the goal of specific behavior change. She was able to see the depression as being a self-defeating part of her. This freed her from the belief that the depressive symptom was a condemnation and failure of her whole personality, which had been implied in her notion of "being hexed."

While this was a limited shift in the belief system of this woman, it could still be a significant one. Furthermore, her resumption of responsibility in the family had its rewarding feedback responses from the children, as well as from her own mother who was closely involved with her family.

Note the three principles involved: a client-centered focus in terms of goal selection and interview management; emphasis upon experiential change through use of task assignment as well as through the attitude of the therapist regarding the client's potential strengths; and finally, an effort to deal with the woman's value system, specifically suggesting that she did have some capacity for free choice and need not identify herself completely with her symptoms (feelings of fated helplessness).

This case raises an interesting cultural issue in relation to the client's view of the change process and how she views change as possibly occurring. An alternative approach might have been a referral of this woman to a *curandera* to handle the "hexed" issue. Had she been unresponsive to my rational efforts to deal with her belief about "being hexed," I would have considered such a referral. Since she had sought out my help, I chose to deal with this belief issue in this more personal, challenging way. I felt free to share my personal view of most hexing experiences after sensing that she wanted to differentiate herself from her mother, who had been emphasizing the power of hexing. If she had deeply held to the hexing belief herself, I would have referred her to a *curandera*.

Existentialism and Community

Existentialism is sometimes criticized as an individualistic philosophy lacking a social ethic. This is a misnomer. Philosophers such as Camus, Berdyaev, Tillich, and Buber have written extensively on the application of existential thinking to social issues. Members of the helping professions have also related existential philosophy to social concerns. Edward Tiryakian, a sociologist, compares existential thought with that of Durkheim. Lionel Rubinoff's critique of modern philosophical, psychological, and sociological thought on the subject of the individual and his relationship to society. Rubinoff's basic premises are existential. R. D. Laing also uses an existential framework in his critique of society and of the helping professions as dehumanizing extensions of society's values.

Beginning with the existential belief that truth is not found in an objective fashion, within a doctrine or within a group of people, we find some implications for a view of society and social change. In the first place, the existentialist stands against tyranny in any form—not only by politically conservative, status-quo-oriented leaders, but also by the rational social engineers who would seek to establish the utopian society necessitating many controls and committed to adjustment of individuals to a "properly functioning" society. The existentialists are a prime opponent of Skinner in his appeal for a society that meets humanity's needs by limiting freedom and nonconformity.

The existentialists know that power corrupts and that much of the evil perpetrated is unpredictable at the moment of its inception. If, on the other hand, there is an effort to decondition evil-producing behavior, this effort itself, if successful, would result in the most profound evil of all: the dehumanization of people by depriving individuals of freedom—the only valid source of their sense of personal meaning and dignity.

On the other hand, an appeal for a completely free and open society, such as proposed by Charles Reich's *Greening of America* (1970), is again a naive position founded upon a disregard for the self-defeating, the aggressive, and the evil-producing behavior of people. Spontaneous "doing one's own thing" is too simple a commitment. We can be defeated by our own instincts and self-deceptions as easily as by our efforts to organize and construct the happy state.

Power itself results in an increased effort toward solidification and self-perpetuation. Society must be a dynamic, growing system, just as an individual is a being of responsive emergence. The healthy society is one attuned to the creative ideas and efforts of individuals and groups within its structure that propose change and new ideas. A participatory democracy is an expression of the existential affirmation of the unique perspective of each individual. In a participatory democracy, groups are seen to possess their own truths, which will differ from the attitudes and values of others who have not had the same life experiences.

The direction for a society's emergence stems from the sufferings and potentials of its people, and not from an elite group of rebels or social organizers. Eric Hoffer was right in saying that the most creative and innovative shifts in a society stem from its outcasts, nonconformists, and those who experience the failures of its present functioning. The existential model for social change would be one wherein the very people who suffer from dehumanizing social forces would be the indicators of what sorts of changes are needed. The community organization social worker would have a facilitating, clarifying, enabling role here, perhaps, and once a direction is clear he or she may use his or her knowledge of power structure and change tactics in order to mobilize the social change effort.

The "antiexistential" community organizer would be one who decides for himself or herself what change other people really need and then uses his or her knowledge and skills to "educate," seduce, and pressure a disadvantaged group into deciding what their problems are and the change indicated. The worker's basic notions of change, here, come either from his or her own needs, or his or her rational, analytical conclusions of what this group or community lacks in comparison with some ideal he or she holds about how people should live. The impetus for change is worker-oriented rather than community-oriented.

The opposite extreme, also antiexistential, is sometimes seen in community mental health clinics. Although such clinics are committed, by their very purpose (and federal funding), to a community outreach stance, there is little genuine effort at dialogue with those needy members of the community who do not enter the portals of the clinic itself requesting some specific help. In contrast, the genuinely committed community mental health clinic is actively seeking contact with those groups in its community who are known through police, welfare, and schools to have problems but who are not availing themselves of any helping services. Primary prevention at times of family or neighborhood crisis becomes a major way of help, and this most often takes the form of consultation with police, welfare workers, teachers, nurses, ministers, and physicians.

As discussed earlier, the existentialists see many of the forces of society as being in opposition to the individual's effort at an authentic lifestyle, establishing his or her unique direction out of an awareness of his or her own freedom, responsibility, and what he or she learns through personal suffering. Modern society encourages anomie and personal alienation by its forces of seduction and oppression. Insofar as the economic-political system uses people as objects in order to preserve its own efficient functioning, it may be said to be dehumanizing. Various social institutions combine their efforts to achieve this goal. Certain roles in the system are rewarded with status, financial remuneration, and prestige while others are ignored. Happiness is defined in such a way as to keep the public at large an active consumer of economic goods. An attunement to personal suffering is discouraged through the various tranquilization forms of drugs, alcohol, treadmill activities, and a work ethic that implies a solution to all of one's problems with the purchase of the next automobile, house, or packaged vacation plan. Such writers as Erich Fromm (1955) and Henry Winthrop (1967) have elaborated upon the multiple forms of social dehumanization, which are too numerous and complex to mention here.

Helping professionals are faced with a critical choice in relation to social dehumanization. They can become a part of this system that is a purveyor of anomie by the very way they perform their helping role. Or, on the other hand, they can be members of a vanguard actively in touch with many of society's victims, who can help bring individuals and groups to an active awareness of themselves as free and responsible beings despite the negative forces bestowed upon them by society. Beyond such awareness, such workers will help them toward personal direction and action that affirms human dignity in the face of tyrannical and dehumanizing social forces.

The institutions of society can and do provide constructive, affirming forces for individuals and groups, of course, through education, employment, protection, health and welfare care, as well as valued traditions, a sense of history, and a national spirit that affirms a set of values that is generally accepted and may be quite compatible with the freedom, responsibility, and valuing of uniqueness and personal dignity that characterize existentialism. The existential helping professional realizes, however, that the constructive forces of society cannot in themselves bring an individual to authenticity. The matter of personal choice and acceptance of responsibility for one's own world view and lifestyle remain essential. The existentialist is, therefore, cynical in response to social utopians who seek to construct a society of needs-met, happy people.

Research and Knowledge Gaps

The existential approach eludes research. Its lack of a specific theory of personality, its emphasis upon subjectivity and uniqueness, its eclectic use of varied techniques, and its concern about values are all factors that make structured studies difficult. On the other hand, the existential perspective extends the hand of gratitude to the numerous research studies that have clearly unseated dogmatic-authoritative assumptions proselytized by "sophisticated" adherents to the varied theories of personality. When it comes to practice, the existential worker tends to agree with the behaviorist: we should utilize what was proven effective in practice to avoid forcing clients to submit to our favored (though ineffective) methods. Research indicates that effective treatment can occur with the following conditions: client and worker who like one another; use of the "placebo" effect in structuring the treatment process; core conditions (warmth, genuineness, empathy) when combined with attitude change; attitude change when accompanied with emotional change as well as task assignments; and the use of significant others in the assessment and treatment process wherever possible (Krill, 1986).

Another important conclusion from practice research has been that no theory of treatment has proven itself superior to any other model. The existentialist sees this as a crucial statement about the place of theory in practice. Theory does not seem to be the important ingredient in helping people and is therefore considered of secondary (informative) value. While it is not clear what, then, is the magic ingredient, the existential worker would suggest it to be human sensitivity as developed over time through both self-awareness and learning from many experiences with clients. The better one comes to know oneself, the more clearly is one able to see oneself within the client's experiences as well. This is a most important area for future research study.

How are social work education programs preparing students for present practice? Do they foster those ingredients that may eventually result in a wise practitioner, given a few years of additional experience? Here the existentialist has serious concerns. An educational tradition has existed for many years in social work that has emphasized the pragmatic, diagnostic, rational-authoritarian approach. Teachers have often viewed students in this categorical manner and have in turn urged students to view their clients in a similar manner. This has been the phony guise of "scientism" that has sought to identify social workers as "scientific" when in fact the "objective nature" of most of their knowledge would be scoffed at by physical scientists. Many students, in their insecurity, seek comfort in categorizing clients according to the knowledge system taught them. Other students, rebelling against what feels like a rigid authoritarianism, will completely abandon diagnostic understanding of any type and naively seek to provide "Band-Aid" answers to problems posed by clients. It would appear that students need to be somehow "humanized" rather than "objectified." Self-awareness has been a goal of social work education, but it would seem that new educational approaches need to be devised to achieve this goal more effectively. Only by appreciating one's own personal complexity can one begin seriously to understand the complexities of others.

Human sensitivity is a bed-partner of humility. Humility results from personal disillusionment, or humiliation, providing the student is warned against too quickly attaching oneself to the notion that one has now achieved some "sophisticated maturity" as a result of personal insights. Humility can be also the springboard toward creativity. As one realizes one's personal blind spots, gaps in awareness, and withdrawal from knowledge and situations posing threat, students find a personalized direction for their reading and openness to new experience. They

sense, too, that their search for expanding truth will enable them to understand and help more clients.

I have found the classroom situation a useful "experimental lab" for generating human sensitivity among students. Assessment of clients is dealt with simultaneously with students' self-exploration. Personal exercises to promote such examination are used in class as well as through homework assignments. Peer sharing in small groups engenders honesty, spontaneity, and supportive feedback in relation to results of exercises (Krill, 1990). Exercises explore dimensions of the interplay between personal problems, emotions, attitudes, and values; of roles with family and significant others; and of trouble spots in personal response to certain clients. Reading of theory is encouraged, then, as the student's means of building upon and expanding self-knowledge in the directions necessary to handle areas of confusion, insufficient self or client understanding, and intrigue with new ideas. Values need to be clarified by both the instructor and students in terms of how they are used constructively with clients. Vitality and spontaneous engagement with clients are demonstrated and practiced in role-plays of common client–worker situations.

In conclusion, the existential stance provides a philosophical perspective that can be related to the many avenues of social work practice. One does not need a profound acquaintance with existential philosophy in order to benefit from the perspective. One might, instead, view the existentialists as emphasizing a sense or direction and a style of working that are primarily concerned with a greater humanization of the social work profession. From their emphasis upon the value of the uniqueness of the individual there comes an affirmation of a client-centered focus and an awareness of the dangers of anomie in a mechanistic society. From their view of growth through choice and action there comes a primary effort aimed at experiential change with clients. From their model of humans as meaning-making beings there comes a recognition of the importance of values, philosophy, and religion as ingredients of the casework process. From their emphasis upon dialogue there comes the concern for therapist transparency and authenticity as well as the valuing of a participatory democracy.

And from their appreciation of the powers of self-deception at work with human beings, there comes an emphasis upon personal commitment in the face of suffering and uncertainty, as well as a suspicion about any authority that establishes itself as knowing how other people should live their lives.

References

Allport, G. (1965). *Letters from Jenny*. New York: Harcourt, Brace and World.

Angyal, A. (1965). *Neurosis and treatment*. New York: Wiley.

Barnes, H. (1959). *The literature of possibility: A study of humanistic existentialism*. Lincoln: University of Nebraska Press.

Barret, W. (1958). *Irrational man*. New York: Doubleday.

Becker, E. (1958). *The denial of death*. New York: Free Press.

Berdyaev, N. (1944). *Slavery and freedom*. New York: Scribner.

Binswanger, L. (1963). *Begin in the world*. New York: Basic Books.

Borowitz, E. (1966). *A layman's guide to religious existentialism*. New York: Delta.

Boss, M. (1963). *Psychoanalysis and daseinsanalysis*. New York: Basic Books.

Bradford, K. A. (1969). *Existentialism and casework*. Jericho, NY: Exposition Press.

Brown, J. A. (1980). Child abuse: An existential process. *Clinical Social Work Journal*, 8(2), 108–111.

Buber, M. (1955). *Between man and man*. Boston: Beacon Press.

Buber, M. (1965). *The knowledge of man*. New York: Harper & Row.

Burton, A. (Ed.) (1969). *Encounter*. San Francisco: Jossey-Bass.

Camus, A. (1969). *The rebel*. New York: Knopf.

Curry, A. (1967). Toward a phenomenological study of the family. *Existential Psychiatry*, 6(27), 35–44.

Dorfman, R. A. (1988). *Paradigns of clinical social work*. New York: Branner/Mazel.

Durkin, H. (1964). *The group in depth*. New York: International Universities Press.

Edwards, D. (1982). *Existential psychotherapy*. New York: Gardner Press.

Ellis, A. (1962). *Reason and emotion in psychotherapy*. New York: Stuart.

Farber, L. (1966). *The ways of the will*. New York: Harper Colophon Books.

Farrelly, F. (1974). *Provocative therapy*. Madison, WI: Family, Social & Psychotherapy Services.

Ford, D., & Urban, H. (1964). *Systems of psychotherapy* (Chapter 12). New York: Wiley.

Frankl, V. E. (1962). *Man's search for meaning: An introduction to logotherapy*. Boston: Beacon Press.

Frankl, V. E. (1965). *The doctor and the soul: From psychotherapy to logotherapy*. New York: Knopf.

Frankl, V. E. (1967). *Psychotherapy and existentialism: Selected papers on logotherapy*. New York: Simon and Schuster.

Frohberg, M. (1967). Existentialism: An introduction to the contemporary conscience. *Perceptions*, 1(1), School of Social Work, San Diego State College, 24–32.

Fromm, E. (1955). *The sane society*. New York: Rinehart.

Glasser, W. (1965). *Reality therapy*. New York: Harper & Row.

Gyarfas, M. (1969). Social science, technology and social work: A caseworker's view. *Social Service Review*, 43(3), 259–273.

Haley, J. (1963). *Strategies of psychotherapy*. New York: Crune and Stratton.

Haley, J. (1976). *Problem-solving therapy*. San Francisco: Jossey-Bass.

Heinecken, M. J. (1956). *The moment before God*. Philadelphia: Muhlenberg Press.

Hora, T. (1977). *Existential metapsychiatry*. New York: Searbury Press.

Hoffer, E. (1951). *The true believer*. New York: Harper.

Imre, R. W. (1971). A theological view of social casework. *Social Casework*, 52(9), 578–585.

James, M., & Jongeward, D. (1971). *Born to win: Transactional analysis with Gestalt experiments*. Reading, MA: Addison-Wesley.

Jourard, S. (1964). *The transparent self*. Princeton, NJ: Van Nostrand.

Jung, C. G. (1933). *Modern man in search of a soul*. New York: Harcourt-Brace.

Katz, R. (1963). *Empathy*. New York: Free Press.

Kazantzakis, N. (1960). *The saviors of God*. New York: Simon & Schuster.

Klein, A.F. (1970). *Social work through group process*. Albany, NY: School of Social Welfare, State University of New York.

Kramer, R. (1995). Carl Rogers meets Otto Rank: The discovery of relationship. In T. Pauchant (Ed.), *In search of meaning: Managing the health of our organizations, our communities and the natural world* (pp. 197–223). San Francisco: Jossey-Bass.

Krill, D. F. (1965). Psychoanalysis, Mowrer and the existentialists. *Pastoral Psychology*, 16, 27–36.

Krill, D. F. (1966). Existentialism: A philosophy for our current revolutions. *Social Service Review*, 40(3), 289–301.

Krill, D. F. (1968). A framework for determining client modifiability. *Social Casework*, 49(10), 602–611.

Krill, D. F. (1969). Existential psychotherapy and the problem of anomie. *Social Work*, 14(2), 33–49.

Krill, D. F. (1978). *Existential social work*. New York: The Free Press.

Krill, D. F. (1986). *The beat worker*. Lanham, MD: University Press of America.

Krill, D. F. (1990). *Practice wisdom*. Newbury Park, CA: Sage.

Kuckelmans, J. J. (1967). *Phenomenology: The philosophy of Edmund Husserl and its interpretation*. New York: Doubleday.

Laing, R. D. (1964). *The divided self*. Baltimore: Penguin.

Laing, R. D. (1967). *The politics of experience*. Baltimore: Penguin.

Maslow, A. H. (1962). *Toward a psychology of being*. Princeton, NJ: Van Nostrand.

May, R., Angel, E., & Ellenberger, H. F. (Eds.). (1958). *Existence: A new dimension in psychiatry and psychology*. New York: Basic Books.

May, R. (Ed.) (1961). *Existential psychology*. New York: Random House.

May, R. (1967). *Psychology and the human dilemma*. Princeton, NJ: Van Nostrand.

Moustakas, C. (Ed.) (1956). *The self: Explorations in personal growth*. New York: Harper & Row.

Mowrer, O. H. (1961). *The crisis in psychiatry and religion*. Princeton, NJ: Van Nostrand.

Nuttin, J. (1962). *Psychoanalysis and personality*. New York: Mentor-Omega.

Offman, W. V. (1976). *Affirmation and reality*. CA: Western Psychological Services.

Perls, F. S. (1969). *Gestalt therapy verbatim*. Lafayette, CA: Real People Press.

Picardie, M. (1980). Dreadful moments: Existential thoughts on doing social work. *British Journal of Social Work*, 10, 483–490.

Reich, C. (1970). *The greening of America*. New York: Random House.

Reid, W. (1979). *The task-centered system*. New York: Columbia University Press.

Reinhardt, K. F. (1952). *The existentialist revolt*. New York: Unger.

Reynolds, D. (1984). *Playing ball on running water*. New York: Quill.

Rogers, C. (1961). *On becoming a person*. Boston: Houghton-Mifflin.

Rogers, C. (1969). The group comes of age. *Psychology Today*, 3(7), 29.

Rubin, G. K. (1962). Helping a clinic patient modify self-destructive thinking. *Social Work*, 7(1), 76–80.

Rubinoff, L. (1969). *The pornography of power*. New York: Ballantine.

Ruesch, J., & Bateson, G. (1968). *Communication: The social matrix of psychiatry*. New York: Norton.

Salomon, E. (1967). Humanistic values and social casework. *Social Casework*, 48(1), 26–32.

Satir, V. (1964). *Conjoint family therapy*. Palo Alto, CA: Science and Behavior Books.

Sinsheimer, R. (1969). The existential casework relationship. *Social Casework*, 50(2), 67–73.

Skinner, B. F. (1971). *Beyond freedom and dignity*. New York: Knopf.

Stretch, J. (1967). Existentialism: A proposed philosophical orientation for social work. *Social Work*, 12(4), 97–102.

Sutherland, R. (1962). Choosing as therapeutic aim, method, and philosophy. *Journal of Existential Psychiatry*, 2(8), 371–392.

Swaine, R. L., & Baird, V. (1977). An existentially based approach to teaching social work practice. *Journal of Education for Social Work*, 13(3), 99–106.

Szasz, T. (1984). *The therapeutic state*. New York: Prometheus Books.

Taft, J. (1950). A conception of the growth underlying social casework practice. *Social Casework*, 21(5), 311–316.

Teilhard de Chardin, P. (1959). *The phenomenon of man*. New York: Harper & Row.

Tillich, P. (1952). *The courage to be*. New Haven, CT: Yale Press.

Tillich, P. (1960). *Love, power and justice*. New York: Oxford.

Tiryakian, E. A. (1962). *Sociologism and existentialism*. Englewood Cliffs, NJ: Prentice-Hall.

Vontress, C. E. (1979). Cross-cultural counselling: An existential approach. *Personnel and Guidance Journal*, 58(2), 117–122.

Watzlawick, P., Weakland, J., & Fisch, R. (1974). *Change: Principles of problem formation and problem resolution*. New York: Norton.

Weiss, D. (1962). Ontological dimension—Social casework. *Social Worker*.

Weiss, D. (1967). The existential approach to social work. *Viewpoints*.

Weiss, D. (1968). Social work as authentication. *Social Worker*.

Weiss, D. (1969). Self-determination in social work—An existential dialogue. *Social Worker*.

Weiss, D. (1970). Social work as encountering. *Journal of Jewish Communal Service*.

Weiss, D. (1970). Social work as healing and revealing. *Intervention*, 50.

Weiss, D. (1971). The existential approach to fields of practice. *Intervention*, 55.

Weiss, D. (1972). The living language of encountering: Homage to Martin Buber, 1878–1965. Intervention, 57.

Wheelis, A. (1958). *The quest for identity*. New York: Norton.

Wilber, K. (1981). *No boundary*. Boulder, CO: Shambhala.

Winthrop, H. (1967). Culture, mass society, and the American metropolis; high culture and middle-brow culture: An existential view. *Journal of Existentialism*, 8(27), 371.

Whittaker, J. (1994). Social treatment.

Yalom, I. (1980). *Existential psychotherapy*. New York: Basic Books.

Annotated Listing of Key References

Bradford, K. A. (1969). Existentialism and casework. Jericho, NY: Exposition Press. A short review of existential thought in terms of its philosophical development and its entry into the field of psychology. A comparison and integration of existential psychology and social casework concepts.

Buber, M. (1965). *The knowledge of man*. New York: Harper & Row. Articles relating Buber's philosophy of dialogue to the psychotherapeutic relationship.

Curry, A. (1967). Toward a phenomenological study of the family. *Existential Psychiatry*, 6(27), 35–44. The effects of existential despair upon family life, described as a "web of unrelatedness."

Frankl, V. E. (1965). *The doctor and the soul from psychotherapy to logotherapy*. New York: Knopf. A very readable development of existential psychology in comparison with other psychologies and its application in therapeutic practice.

Krill, D. F. (1978). *Existential social work*. New York: Free Press. A delineation of existential and related thought to both theory and practice in social work. An eclectic-interpersonal perspective is emphasized.

Sinsheimer, R. (1969). The existential casework relationship. *Social Casework*, 50(2), 6–73. Concepts from existential psychology are related to the casework relationship in terms of the I-thou dialogue and encounter.

Stretch, J. (1967). Existentialism: A proppsed philosophical orientation for social work. *Social Work*, 12(4), 97–102. Existentialism provides a view of life that accepts the perennial crises of people as opposed to utopian hopes of a secured society.

Sutherland, R. (1968). Choosing as therapeutic aim, method and philosophy. *Existential Psychiatry*, 2(8), 371–392. The applicability of the concept of freedom of choice in specific techniques of psychotherapy.

Weiss, D. (1970). Social work as healing and revealing. *Intervention*, 50. Development of Buber's philosophy of dialogue according to the concepts of Being, Becoming, Belonging and Sympathy, Empathy, and Compathy.

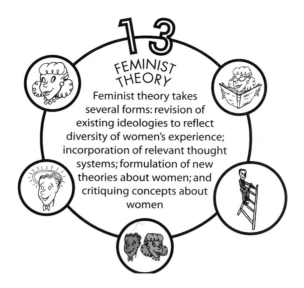

FEMINIST THEORY

Feminist theory takes several forms: revision of existing ideologies to reflect diversity of women's experience; incorporation of relevant thought systems; formulation of new theories about women; and critiquing concepts about women

Feminist Theory and Social Work Practice

Mary Valentich

Introduction

Chasing after developments in feminist theory and feminist social work practice is a recurring phenomenon in my professional life (Valentich, 1986, 1996). For a detailed picture of the emergence of feminist social work practice in Canada and the United States and how it bloomed from the mid-1980s to the mid-1990s, please consult my earlier chapters. In 2005, I stated that there had been societal backlash to feminism and a trend to social conservatism, resulting in feminist theory and practice standing at a threshold: "while established securely within social work, its further development remains in the hands of increasingly overburdened and politically constrained social workers and social work educators" (Valentich, 2005, p. 148).

In this chapter I will consider historical developments in feminist social work practice as well as recent sociopolitical and social work contexts within which feminist social workers, primarily in Canada and the United States, practice. I will identify major feminist theories used in social work practice as well as evolving models of practice. I will outline areas of practice where feminist theory and approaches are most evident and conclude by commenting on issues and future directions.

Historical Review of Feminist Social Work Practice

For many women in Canada and the United States, the 1960s and 1970s were times of awakening, turbulence, and flight to new realms of experience and possibilities. The second wave of the Women's Movement had emerged and there were sufficient members to challenge how institutions of health, education, organized religion, government, and the world of work treated women. Patriarchy was seen as embedded institutionally and in daily relations of women and men, with dire emotional and social consequences for women. Sexism reigned; women and some like-minded men prepared to remove its chains, even within the social work profession itself (Gripton, 1974).

Social workers and members of other helping professions listened to women, often in consciousness-raising groups, tell their stories of oppression within the confines of marriage and family life, on the street, at work, and in medical encounters. The "personal is the political" became the anchoring point for these practitioners who identified themselves as feminist counselors and therapists. By questioning the appropriateness of psychoanalytic and psychodynamic theories that tended to pathologize women, these practitioners began to place women's stories within sociopolitical contexts. Drawing primarily on liberal, socialist, and radical feminist perspectives, women in the early 1970s, some of whom were professional social workers, began to found shelters for battered women and rape (later sexual assault) crisis centers where women could receive assistance from other women who initially viewed them as victims, later as survivors.

Advocacy and social action characterized the practice of these social workers as well as collaborative ways of helping that entailed women listening to women, not judging them, offering a social or structural analysis and diminished power differences within a helping relationship that tended to be short term (Levine, 1976; Russell, 1984). Theorists and practitioners developed treatment models for practice with individuals, couples, and groups with opportunities for engagement in political action in later stages when the crisis had been addressed and if clients so chose (Bricker-Jenkins & Hooyman, 1986; Bricker-Jenkins, Hooyman, & Gottlieb, 1991). Services for abused women and children were developed as well as a Women's Health Movement to enable women to take charge of their physical and emotional well-being. Legislation was promoted to ensure women's rights with respect to property, pay equity, aboriginal status, sexual assault, and reproduction.

Sociopsychological and sociologically oriented perspectives were prominent, with key concepts of social role and gender central to most feminist theories. The distinction between sex and gender, with the latter seen as socially constructed, became well known. Other key concepts, still prominent, included gender identity, gender role stereotyping, norms, values, socialization, oppression, and power. One currently hears little about victimization, learned helplessness, self-actualization, and androgyny. All theories focused on eliminating inequities that kept women in a secondary status, not entitled to various human rights. By the mid-1990s, empowerment became a central concept, guiding various approaches to practice.

New ways of understanding women (Gilligan, 1982; Miller, 1986), based on women's capacity for connection, derived from a group of women psychotherapists working at the Stone Center. The original Self-in-Relation Model was renamed the Relational/Cultural Model by the late 1990s to include perspectives of women with diverse backgrounds (Jordan, n.d.; Marecek, 2000). Women's "ways of knowing" (Belenky et al., 1986) also received much attention. Social workers opted for perspectives congruent with the profession's longstanding person-in-environment stance and some explored the viability of feminist perspectives for work with men (McKechnie & Valentich, 1989; Milliken, 1985).

Saulnier (1996) identified liberal, radical, socialist, lesbian, womanism, global feminism, as well as cultural and ecofeminism and postmodernism, as major branches of feminist theory, all having implications for practice. In the United States and the United Kingdom, black feminism had gained prominence, as well as Hispanic feminism in the United States. Technological advances in communication connected women around the globe in addressing issues related to war, genocide, hunger, poverty, genital mutilation, and HIV/AIDS. White, well-educated, and relatively affluent women were no longer the primary leaders of the increasingly diverse women's movement. Multiculturalism and diversity became the new watchwords, as well as antiracist, anti-oppressive, and culturally competent social work.

Increasingly visible during the 1990s, postmodernism (Chambon & Irving, 1994; Sands & Nuccio, 1992; Van Den Bergh, 1995) challenged feminist perspectives with respect to their "essentialist" position of treating women homogeneously. Both poststructuralism and postmodernism, two distinct but related bodies of theories (Weedon, 2005), influenced feminist social work practice by challenging assumptions about commonalities; however, they have not become a prominent feature of feminist practice models, largely because their relativistic emphasis did not foster consensus regarding "societal wrongs" (Valentich, 1996).

By the mid-1990s social workers in diverse fields of practice were aided by the growth of qualitative research that elicited women's own voices. Practitioners facilitated access to resources and helped women heal, women's centers thrived in many cities, and egalitarian ideals were espoused by institutions that previously had been quite traditional in their perspective on gender. Feminist practitioners did not hesitate to identify themselves as such. Social work programs included courses in feminist social work practice and even more "feminisms" began to emerge. Yet forces beyond feminism strengthened their grip on Western economies and had a significant impact on the development of feminist theories and models of feminist social work practice.

Sociopolitical Contextual Considerations: Mid-1990s to 2009

One perspective on theory building is that it emanates from what social workers actually do; since feminist social workers are found in many countries, one could argue that feminist theorizing is widespread and even thriving. But some contexts may be more conducive to the evolution of feminist theory and practice. Gibelman's (1999) position is that social work is defined by its place in the larger social environment at any given time and that external economic, social, and political forces have been more influential in shaping the nature of practice than intraprofessional choices (p. 298). Thus, Reisch and Jarman-Rohde (2000) identify six major developments in the United States that have shaped social work practice and education: economic globalization, with an increase in social and economic inequality; a changing political climate; the growing use of technology; demographic shifts and their impact on cities; the changing nature of social service agencies; and changes in universities.

The increasing conservatism of various governments has tended to stifle feminist social work practice. Conservatism has resulted in cutbacks in various social services and benefits; the dismantling of previously funded organizations and programs; and legislative changes increasing the financial and social vulnerability of women. Women may be living longer than in earlier periods, but do they have access to needed financial and health resources? Increased military spending, especially in the United States, and the worldwide downturn in the economy have contributed to the ongoing "feminization of poverty," with elderly and poor women particularly vulnerable, and no bailouts available to them (Abramovitz, 2009). Social workers working for government agencies have next to no voice in advocating for women, homeless persons, those with disabilities and the transgendered; those somewhat outside the bureaucracies can question governments' increased reliance on food banks, church basements as shelters for homeless families, and gaming monies to support charities providing persons with basic needs (Valentich, 2002). Canadian tax regulations have even limited the extent of social action by women's centers (Valentich, 2000).

When there are widespread economic troubles and a dominant conservative ideology, feminist voices advocating for social change and justice are readily dismissed by those calling for tougher laws and penalties to deal with street crime, drug trafficking, and urban gangs. The election of Barack Obama and implementation of his change-oriented mission may, however, prompt a resurgence of socially focused change.

Feminism itself has greatly changed since the early 1990s. Following considerable backlash (Faludi, 1991), the media often questioned whether feminism was dead. Leaders of the second wave in Canada and the United States were heard less often: "The ideals of feminism now are much more diffuse and controversial ... There is a real dearth of charismatic feminist leaders right now, at least in the US and UK" (Gillis & Munford, 2004, p. 61). Occasionally there are outpourings of support for feminist ventures such as *The Vagina Monologues* (Ensler, 1998). But some have assumed that, given women's greater freedom, there is no further need for a Women's Movement. Conservative spokespersons such as Camille Paglia gained prominence. Feminists like Levy (2005) have asserted that second-wave feminism had failed younger women, who were now choosing to become sexual objects. Diversity and racism edged women/gender issues off center stage.

Second-wave feminism appeared to be faltering and not the wellspring for feminist theorizing that once was the case. This is not to disparage the voices of feminist environmentalists such as Vandana Shiva (Hanson, 2000), human rights activist Charlotte Bunch (Miles, 2000), and others who have made global feminism a defining feature of contemporary feminism. Issues such as genital mutilation, rape for purposes of genocide, sex trafficking, international adoptions, and the plight of refugee women have engaged persons concerned with justice all around the world. The significance of wearing the burka, so-called honor killings of women by family members for women's allegedly shameful activities, death penalties for women who have been raped—these have become familiar to feminists everywhere and have prompted action by radically oriented feminists. Yet, "anti-feminists" deride feminists for not doing more to address these horrific situations and/or focusing on seemingly less important local issues (Lakritz, 2009a, 2009b; Valentich, 2009).

Younger, newer voices, known as the third wave and encompassing a wide body of both popular and academic works (Starr, 2000), have emerged during the 1990s. Focusing on adolescent girls and young women, Baumgardner and Richards (2000) produced a 13-point "manifesta" that drew attention to freedom from sexual harassment, becoming a visible movement, the right to reproductive choice, removal of a double standard in sex and sexual health, equal access to health care, and making the workplace responsive to individuals (pp. 278–281). Miles, Rezai-Rashti, and Rundle (2001) identified three major areas addressed by third wave feminism: antiracism, global feminism, and younger feminists organizing, despite their feminism-defying "rigid definitions and clear prescriptions" (p. 15) and emphasizing multiplicity and reaching "across class, sex, and race lines to include many previously marginalized people within feminist movements (men, transgendered people, sex workers, and many others)" (p. 16). Georg (2009) sees the defiant stance of young feminists as based in the

1990s' "underground punk Riot Grrl movement." She notes their current issues as follow:

Today their causes reflect those of the global social justice movement, like peace and the environment. They advocate for the disability community and the GLBTQ (gay-lesbian-bisexual-transgender-queer) cause. They protest against racism. They work with men. (p. 34)

Before considering feminist theories deriving from second- and third-wave feminisms, I will consider the changing context of social work practice since the 1990s with respect to its influence on feminist practice.

The Changing Social Work Context

In 2001 the International Federation of Social Workers and the International Association of Schools of Social Work jointly agreed to a definition of the social work profession as promoting "social change, problem-solving in human relationships and the empowerment and liberation of people to enhance well-being" (IASSW, 2001). This inclusive definition clearly embraces feminist social work practice, though it may vary in relation to the particular set of historical and current circumstances within a country. It may be illuminating to identify significant contextual features in a few countries where feminist social work practice is strongly rooted.

Primary government ideologies from the 1990s onward have been neoliberalism and neoconservatism (Green, 2000), with the former advocating an economic arena free of government participation in the marketplace via public ownership and a retreat from the welfare state's commitment to social justice through the provision of a range of social services. Neoconservatism promotes a more traditional society based on patriarchal gender role arrangements that are explicitly anti-feminist and anti-egalitarian. These ideologies have been implemented as follows:

Recent efforts in Washington to decentralize the government, balance the budget, slash health care expenditures, and distribute funds to states via block grants are among the latest efforts in the 15-year trend to reduce government funding for social programs and contain costs. Further changing the nature and organization of human services are welfare and health care reform, an increasingly de-professionalized public sector, and the growth of service reimbursement, credentialing, private practice, and for-profit service delivery systems. (Jarman-Rohde, McFall, Kolar, & Strom, 1997, p. 2)

Managed care, a system where financial and clinical aspects of a client's care are controlled (Strom-Gottfried, 1997), has given rise to services that are rapid, outcome-oriented, profitable, and reimbursable, with agencies operating like businesses. Social workers in managed care are constrained by various limits on their services (Gibelman & Schervish, 1996), although their clients may have "complex and long-standing difficulties that are intricately related to environmental conditions, oppression, and poverty" (Strom-Gottfried, 1997, p. 6). Feminist social work practice is unlikely to flourish under conditions of managed care.

Canada does not have managed care, but similar cost-cutting measures have occurred. Homelessness and unemployment are on the rise and many people have difficulty meeting basic needs. Under such survival scenarios, a feminist goal of empowerment may seem far-fetched to clients and funders. Similarly, in the United Kingdom, where social work practice has been organized as social care and largely delivered through complex state bureaucracies (White, 2006), the outlook for feminist social work practice is gloomy. Dominelli (2009) wrote: "Social work is constantly being restructured by the state and emerging in different forms while retaining its core tasks of caring for people and regulating behavior" (p. 15). White (2006) concluded that the context of state social work seemed "to run counter to the development of the forms of practice advocated in the feminist practice literature" (p. 55).

On the other hand, in Canada and the United States, there are developments in social work that may foster the growth of feminist social work practice. Johnson (1999) lauded indirect work as follows: "I wish to include radical social work approaches because they have not only influenced the profession's current incorporation of feminist and culturally sensitive approaches, but recommend indirect action on the political front" (p. 329). An analysis of advanced clinical practitioners' theoretical frameworks (Timberlake, Sabatino,

& Martin, 1997) revealed considerable use of a structural perspective involving cognitive, behavioral, stress, crisis, and role theories as well as a basic person-in-society view of practice, all theories that can be utilized within a feminist framework. Advocates of the person-in-environment (P-I-E) classification system have argued for its promise as a mechanism for testing the efficacy of diverse theories, including feminist social work models (Karls, Lowery, Mattaini, & Wandrei, 1997). Private practice has become an increasingly popular choice for social workers in Canada and the United States; some practitioners might once again become frontrunners for reaching creative solutions to evolving social and personal issues (Valentich, 1986).

Finally, there have been numerous calls for social work to remain true to its commitment to social justice (Galambos, 2008; Linhorst, 2002; Valentich, 2009) and social change and activism (Abramovitz, 1998; Curry-Stevens, Lee, Hill, & Edwards, 2008; Murdach, 2006) as central pillars of professional practice. Clearly, feminist theorizing (Figueria-McDonough, Netting, & Nichols-Casebolt, 2001) can thrive if the profession heeds these calls and continues to give prominence to gender equality (CASW, 2009), multicultural perspectives (Fellin, 2000), diversity issues (Lusk & Mayadas, 1997) and culturally competent practice (Crisp & Van Den Bergh, 2004). Kreuger's (1997) predictions regarding the demise of social work in the next 100 years due to new hyper-technologies, the elimination of grand narratives, radical dislocations in societies, and the loss of public sector accountability may come to serve as warnings rather than a death knell.

Feminist Theories

In 1996, I wrote that feminist theory development takes several forms: the revision of existing ideological frameworks to reflect the diversity of women's experience; incorporation of relevant thought systems; formulation of new theories about women; and the critique of concepts and traditional theories about women (Valentich, 1996, p. 285). This statement still provides an outline for consideration of the conceptual bases for practice.

Feminist Frameworks

Jagger and Rothenberg's (1993) delineation of feminist frameworks remains relevant in contemporary feminist social work practice:

They identify women's subordination through the lens of sex as conservatism; gender as liberalism; through class as classical Marxism; through sex/gender and sexuality as radical feminism; and through sex/gender, sexuality and class as socialist feminism. To reflect changes in theory ... they offer two new frameworks: multicultural feminism, which views women's subordination through the lens of sex/gender, sexuality, class and race; and global feminism, which incorporates all social forces that divide women such as race, class, sexuality, colonialism, poverty, religion, and nationality. (p. 285)

Eliot and Mandell (2001) offer the roots of each perspective, its contemporary manifestation, and critiques, as well as antiracist/standpoint feminism and psychoanalytic feminism. The former identified race as a major category of oppression and criticized other perspectives for excluding visible minority women and not understanding women's lives from their own vantage points. Antiracist feminist critiques gained widespread circulation during the second wave (1970–1990), but only in the third wave of feminism in Canada (1990–present) did critiques relating to welfare, housing, First Nations, immigrant women, the poor, and the disabled begin to alter state policies and practices (Eliot & Mandell, 2001, p. 36). Psychoanalytic feminism has never been widely favored by feminist practitioners, but it has contributed to theoretical development by examining unconscious levels of functioning related to gender.

Saulnier (2008) reviewed those theories most likely to be useful to direct service social work practitioners:

Liberal feminism because of its wide use more than its potential for serving the needs of social and economic justice; socialist and lesbian feminist theories because of their power to challenge fundamental beliefs about issues that are often discussed but seldom addressed in American social work (i.e., economic class and sexual orientation hierarchies as two foundations upon which our culture is built); and radical feminist and womanist theories because they best synthesize

the interaction of psychological and sociological phenomena. (p. 343)

Lesbian feminism was prominent during the late 1960s and early 1970s as a grassroots movement challenging heterosexuality and calling for the elimination of the patriarchy and women's identification with men (Hoagland, 2000). Criticized as exclusionary and politically inept, it still retains viability, perhaps because lesbianism remains a threat for some. Saulnier noted that "the invisibility and active suppression of lesbianism is seen as a gauge of how threatening lesbianism is to the ideology of gender assignments, male superiority, and female dependence" (p. 349).

Womanism as a division of feminist theory originated with African American writers (Saulnier, 2008) or black feminists (Dominelli, 2002), some of whom reject this name and call themselves "womanists." Saulnier (2008) detailed this perspective as follows:

Womanism ... centers on a complex matrix of oppressions. Womanists argue that additive models of oppression—in which oppressive systems are seen as parallel and only occasionally intersecting—hide from view, and therefore from change interlocking systems ... Working from an assumption of interlocking systems is a paradigmatic shift away from focusing on separate, interacting systems. (pp. 350–351)

In their presentation of feminist frameworks, Nelson and Robinson (2002) include cultural feminism, also known as integrative, relational, and difference feminism, all of which "identify the suppression of distinctive or different female qualities, experiences, and values as the primary cause of women's subordination" (p. 94). Their depiction of inclusive feminism is similar to multicultural feminism.

Dominelli (2002) expressed her difficulty with such categorizations, finding them inadequate as they "fail to address the overlaps between them and the multiplicity of positions that any individual feminist or group may adopt" (p. 23). Third-wave feminism in the United States has given rise to even more qualifiers (Baumgardner & Richards, 2000, p. 50), with at least 17 prominent feminisms based on identity, including American Indian, Arab-American, Asian-American, Jewish, Latina, lesbian, Marxist, Puerto Rican, and working class (p. 57). Yet these feminist frameworks persist as relevant sets of ideas identifying an individual's theoretical/political stance, with the more prominent ones forming the theoretical bases for social change and direct service activities (Valentich & Gripton, 1984).

New Paradigms and Theories

Theorizing about the interlocking nature of oppressions has resulted in the development of intersectional feminist frameworks (IFFs; Canadian Research Institute for the Advancement of Women [CRIAW], 2006). While gender-based analysis became prominent during the second wave, the realization that a "gender-only" lens did not do justice to the complexity of women's lives was apparent by 1996, when I noted that more attention was being given to "complex conceptualizations of sex, gender, race and class" (Valentich, 1996, p. 286). CRIAW described IFFs as follows:

IFFs attempt to understand how multiple forces work together and interact to reinforce conditions of inequality and social exclusion. IFFs examine how factors including socio-economic status, race, class, gender, sexualities, ability, geographic location, refugee and immigrant status combine with broader historical and current systems of discrimination such as colonialism and globalization to simultaneously determine inequalities among individuals and groups. (p. 5)

The focus on the intersection of multiple forms of discrimination has become central in feminist theorizing and action to end oppression (Martinez & Phillips, 2008).

Incorporation of Theory

Psychologists Worell and Remer (2003) advocate incorporating compatible theories at both theoretical and applied levels. They argue that a theory is gender or culturally biased if its content is androcentric, gendercentric, ethnocentric, heterosexist, intrapsychic, or deterministic (p. 89). They provide four criteria for evaluating a theory for compatibility—(a) gender-balanced, (b) flexible/multicultural, (c) interactionist, and (d) lifespan (p. 94)—and demonstrate how many aspects of cognitive behavioral theory are well suited to their Empowerment

Feminist Theory, especially if they relabel pathologizing concepts, focus on feelings, and integrate social role theory.

Formulation of New Theory

Self-in-Relation theory, while not "new," did evolve into Relational/Cultural theory during the 1990s and continues to gain adherents. It has now formed the basis for a feminist social work practice model (Freedberg, 2009) that focuses on relationships.

Key Concepts

Theorizing about gender has not, however, ceased (Bradley, 2007). Nelson and Robinson (2002) extensively review key concepts related to sex and gender that are fundamental in feminist theories as well as social work practice. They present a gender perspective that argues "that apparent sex and gender differences are the product of ongoing multilevel social construction and reconstruction processes that occur at the sociocultural, institutional, interactional, individual and global levels" (p. 71).

Social workers have also called for renewed attention to gender for integrating knowledge about women into social work curricula (Nichols-Casebolt, Figueira-McDonough, & Netting, 2000) and for re-gendering the curriculum (McPhail, 2008). The latter would occur by including relational/cultural theory (Jordan, n.d.); reassessing the human stress response; considering women's sexuality in terms of research and theory about women, relational aggression by girls, and shame as underlying many client problems; theory and research about men and masculinities; and the significance of transgender issues for our understanding of gender (Burdge, 2007).

Critique of Concepts and Theories

Feminist theorists have generally been critical of traditional theoretical perspectives—in particular, psychoanalysis and behaviorism. Worell and Remer (2003) have defined a traditional theory as one that neglected to integrate all aspects of diversity into its constructs and assumptions, omitted the impact of external oppression, and embraced values of the dominant culture to the exclusion of alternative value systems.

Poststructuralism and postmodernism, two distinct but related bodies of ideas, have criticized feminist theories by questioning fundamental assumptions of the Enlightenment tradition in the West, namely the belief in rational human progress, universal standards and values, and singular truth (Weedon, 2000). East (1998) portrayed postmodern feminism as including the rejection of a single truth, replaced by multiple realities; the presence of power in the formation of knowledge; the centering of marginalized voices; and an understanding that the self was socially constructed in the context of narratives created by the society and the self. Deconstruction was identified as a primary postmodern strategy "for exposing supposed truths and grand systems of belief by unraveling a text to reveal its assumptions, contradictions, or inconsistencies" (p. 275).

The next section examines more recent feminist social work practice models by identification of principal authors.

Feminist Social Work Practice Models

A number of practice models outlined in my previous two chapters still form the foundation for feminist social work practice (Bricker-Jenkins & Hooyman, 1986, Levine, 1976; Russell, 1984; Van Den Bergh, 1995). All these models focused on liberating women from socially induced oppression and providing them with help through individual, couple, family, and group work as well as opportunities for social action. Saulnier (2008) stressed the commonalities across applications of feminist theory: engagement, data collection and assessment, planning/contracting, and intervention followed by evaluation and termination.

Lena Dominelli

Dominelli (2002) defined feminist social work as practice that takes women's experience of the world as its starting point and addresses women's needs in a holistic manner, "dealing with the complexities of their lives—including the numerous tensions and diverse forms of oppression" (p. 7). She outlined crucial features that differentiate feminist social work from other forms of social work, including assessing and dealing with the impact of patriarchy on all persons and their relationships, reconceptualizing dependency, avoiding equality traps when building egalitarian relationships, celebrating differences as well as women's strengths and abilities, valuing caring work, deconstructing community, "unpacking" motherhood, challenging notions of "the family," considering the social construction of gender, separating the needs of women, children, and men, working as an insider/outsider, mediating the power of the state, and understanding agency and the capacity of the powerless to resist oppression.

Vicky White

Drawing on Dominelli's work, White (2006) examined feminist social work within the United Kingdom, where the state, through "managerialism," is very powerful in determining what social workers can do. The evolution of many feminisms resulted in an eclectic approach. Social workers were urged to foster "woman to woman egalitarian relationships between service users and social workers with the goal of empowerment" (p. 30). But the state placed many restrictions on practice, which White detailed in her assessment of anti-oppressive and antidiscriminatory practice by women practitioners whom she interviewed. Most spoke of frustrations in dealing with organizational rules, masculinist language, closing down of practice possibilities with regard to collective work, preventive work and counseling, and loss of discretion. Few of the women in White's sample used the term "feminist" to describe their practice. White concluded by questioning whether there is a case for retaining the term "feminist social work" and its ideals with reference to state social work (p. 139). White's analysis demonstrates that simply appealing to the rhetoric and/or incorporating elements of feminist practice does not necessarily translate into full-fledged feminist practice.

Judith Worell and Pamela Remer

Worell and Remer (2003) do, however, present a forthrightly feminist model, empowerment feminist therapy, for work with diverse women.

Their model integrates feminist and multicultural perspectives and applies them to emergent client populations due to family role changes, greater societal awareness of violence toward women, the focus on women's body image, and women with diverse identities. Their principles of practice include attention to the diversity of women's personal and social identities, a consciousness-raising approach, an egalitarian relationship between client and therapist, and a woman-valuing and self-validating process. Their goal of empowerment enables individuals, families, and communities to exert influence over the personal, interpersonal, and institutional factors that affect their health and well-being, with the overall goals of personal and social empowerment emphasizing "client strengths and resilience in coping with past, current, and future trauma and stress" (p. 24). Their approach attends to strengths and the social environment, thereby making it congruent with social work perspectives as well as social work's considerable reliance on cognitive behavioral approaches.

Marsha P. Mirkin, Karen L. Suyemoto, and Barbara F. Okun

A psychotherapy model that focuses on diversity and the intersection of women's key identities is offered by Mirkin, Suyemoto, and Okun (2005). They highlight practice that integrates culture, race, ethnicity, class, gender, sexual orientation, and religion with the daily realities women experience throughout their lives. Social workers have contributed chapters on dealing with one's own privilege, low-wage-earning women, and Native American women.

Sharon Freedberg

Freedberg (2009) presents a different slant on practice based on relational theory, deriving from the Relational/Cultural Model. Connection and affiliation are seen as crucial to the development of the self, with the concept of mutual empathy given centrality in the relationship between worker and client as well as self-disclosure, relational authenticity, a perspective on transference and countertransference, boundaries as a place of meeting, and worker respect

for the dependency needs of the client. Freedberg states that the approach is congruent with an ecological systems perspective and social work's longstanding emphasis on relationship.

Barbara Fawcett, Brid Featherstone, Jan Fook, and Amy Rossiter

Engagement with postmodern feminism has resulted in these authors' *Practice and Research in Social Work* (2000), with social work contributors from Australia, Canada, South Africa, and the United Kingdom. The authors primarily address research, with practice touched on only indirectly. East (1998) offers this view on the implications of a postmodern approach to practice:

The tasks of postmodern feminist social workers are to provide feminist perspectives on society and culture as a way of exposing grand systems of belief, analyzing how power and knowledge affect women in the social world and how women think about themselves, and bringing the voices of marginalized women to the center. (p 275)

The next section will examine applications of these models within social work.

Applications Of Feminist Theories/ Feminist Practice Models

Feminist theories continue to influence practice at all levels of intervention: individual, couple, family (Avis, 2005; Pewewardy, 2004), group (Gagerman, 2004), and community (Dominelli, 2006), as well as policy development and research. Feminist social workers may also be found in almost any practice setting, but in some fields feminism is strongly featured, whereas the term is rarely heard in others. Feminist social work is pronounced in women's centers offering women a range of services and in agencies that serve women who have experienced any form of violence. Feminist models vie with other perspectives, in particular medical models, in practice in mental health, sexual problems, substance abuse, and other health issues. Further, there are numerous areas of practice that focus on women and their roles as mothers, wives, welfare recipients, caregivers, and workers, but do not explicitly identify their model or services as feminist. One could categorize literature and practice domains relating to women as self-identifiably feminist; somewhat feminist in that they contained some feminist content or used a gender lens or critique; and those not feminist (Baretti, 2001).

Violence Against Women

Intimate Partner Violence. Second-wave feminists brought the issue of woman battering to the forefront in the early 1970s in Canada and the United States, with social workers sometimes seen as contributing to battered women's revictimization (Danis, 2003a). A radical theoretical perspective is still prominent: women's lesser power within the society has made women vulnerable in relation to men as a group, with dire consequences for women's physical, emotional, and social well-being. However, a review of social work abstracts from 1985 to 2000 (Pyles & Postmus, 2004) revealed scant theorizing about the sexist origins of the problem. Concerns about the overutilization of the criminal justice system in the United States (Danis, 2003b), greater reliance by shelter workers on psychological perspectives rather than radical feminism (Hammons, 2004), and popularity of the term "domestic violence," which hides the condition of women being abused, have more recently led to intense theorizing.

McPhail, Busch, Kulkarni, and Rice (2007) present an integrative feminist model that looks at the intersections between gender and other systems of oppression, thereby retaining the feminist sociocultural framework but also including psychological, sociological, and neurobiological models that offer more specific explanations for intimate partner violence, namely:

… physiological and neurological factors, evolutionary psychology, substance abuse, childhood experiences of violence, intergenerational transmission of violence, shame and humiliation, attachment disorders, lack of anger control, psychopathology and difficult personality traits, general communication and coping skills deficit, personal inadequacy, and violence as a tool for constructing masculinity. (p. 833)

In a related vein, Damant, Lapierre, Kouraga, Fortin, Hamelin-Brabant, Lavergne, and Lessard (2008) critique a postmodern feminist approach as tending toward individualism and relativism

and rarely providing the basis for collective political actions. They argue for an intersectional feminist understanding of domestic abuse that takes into account child abuse and mothering. Through a qualitative study, Morgraine (2009) investigates whether a human rights perspective might gain credibility in this field and concludes that, at least in the United States, there are significant barriers. Advancement of both theory and practice requires the kind of collaborative approach by researchers, practitioners, and the community exemplified by a tri-provincial institute RESOLVE in conjunction with the University of Calgary's Brenda Strafford Chair in the Prevention of Domestic Violence (Tutty, 2006; Tutty & Goard, 2002).

Sexual Violence. Sexual violence against women is another area of practice where radical feminist models remain strong, with individual, group, and crisis counseling as major modalities (Galat, 2009) and political actions such as Take Back the Night marches. McMahon (2007) gives attention to myths and Verberg, Wood, Desmarais, and Senn (2000) discuss perceptions of date rape. Van Wormer (2009) promotes feminist theoretical development by using feminist standpoint theory (Code, 2000) to examine restorative justice models for victims of physical and sexual abuse. A participatory research approach for group work with rape survivors (Mason & Clemans, 2008) offers a unique type of feminist practice, and Murphy, Moynihan, and Banyard (2009) report on the meanings of surviving sexual assault to better inform social workers who may be advocates, therapists, hotline responders, managers, supervisors, policymakers, legislators, and researchers.

Other problematic behaviors involving violence against women include stalking viewed from a "post-modern, feminist, critical standpoint framework" (Cox & Speziale, 2009, p. 5); sexual harassment (Gould, 2000), with a focus on youth (Fineran, 2002; Fineran & Bennett, 1998); physical and sexual abuse of disabled women (Gilson, Cramer, & DePoy, 2001); sexual exploitation by psychotherapists (Sloan, Edmond, Rubin, & Doughty, 1998) and priests (van Wormer & Berns, 2004); and nonsexual boundary behavior (Gripton & Valentich, 2003, 2004).

Child Sexual Abuse. Child sexual abuse, brought to the fore by second-wave feminists, has been relatively quiescent with respect to feminist theorizing, with many researchers remaining gender-neutral in their work. Further, the enormous rifts within this area of practice related to accusations of false memory have resulted in "well-known and respected scientists with impressive credentials disagree[ing] about almost every important issue related to child sexual abuse" (Mildred, 2003, p. 493).

Cox, Kershaw, and Trotter (2000) do, however, specifically address the exclusion of feminist perspectives in this area and offer a framework for understanding child sexual assault from a feminist perspective as well as taking action. They argue that feminist analyses of male sexuality have shown the relationship between men's violence and sexuality, which is rooted in the unequal power relationships between men and women and men and children. Similarly, Bolen (2003) recommends prevention programs for reducing offender behavior that focus on healthy relationships and the social definition of the male sex role. Cyberspace is another domain where "feminist theorizing about gender, power, and violence" (Harrison, 2006, p. 376) along with the voices of survivors can break the silence about child sexual abuse and inform social work practice. Social workers are also being asked to use feminist perspectives in working with women who have sexually offended (Hovey, 2005).

Violence in War. War-related violence against women and children has been highly destructive of women's mental and physical health (Drumm, Pittman, & Perry, 2001; Jansen, 2006; Valentich, 2000), family functioning, and community survival. Feminists have long viewed rape as a war tactic (Milillo, 2006), with more recent theorizing on the intersections of gender, patriarchy, militarism, and ethnic, religious, and political identities (Farwell, 2004; Snyder, Gabbard, May, & Zulcic, 2006). Intervention is promoted on all levels, locally and globally, and with men, masculinities, and militarism.

Finally, it is important to remember that the various types of violence against women are not unrelated. Stout and McPhail (1998) capture this reality in their continuum model of various forms of sexism and different types of violence toward particular populations of women. The continuum includes institutional status, psychological wounding, gendered communication, economic assaults, controlling women's bodies, pornography and prostitution, sexual harassment, sexual assault, and femicide. Theory building of this type is an effective response to those who dismiss so-called minor issues that offend women and may result in more refined practice models.

Practice in Sexual Problems

Feminist perspectives have not been very evident in practice in sexual problems (Young, 2007), although *The Canadian Journal of Human Sexuality* (1996) published a special issue devoted to female sexuality, with a social work contribution to one article on relationship satisfaction (Apt, Hurlbert, Pierce, & White, 1996). A study of four U.S.-based sexological journals (Winton, 2001) revealed increasing medicalization, especially of women's sexual functioning, during the period 1990–2000. However, a feminist movement, the "New View Campaign" initiated by psychologist Leonore Tiefer in 2000, has challenged the medical model of sexual problems and pharmaceutical companies for promoting their products to enhance women's sexual satisfaction (The Working Group, n.d.).

Two social workers and a psychologist (Foley, Kope, & Sugrue, 2002) have written what has become a standard text for use by practitioners and clients: *Sex Matters for Women.* Feminist perspectives in couple sex therapy have received attention (Daniels, Zimmerman, & Bowling, 2002; Hurlburt, Apt, & Rombough, 1996; Young, 2007). Valentich and Ursacki-Bryant (in press) have identified issues facing transgendered persons in the workplace; Ayala and Luhtanen (2009) explore the service needs of GLBT persons, a group that has only had sporadic attention in the social work literature (Voorhis & Wagner, 2002). With the Obama administration (Guttmacher Institute, 2009) proclaiming a new day in sexual and reproductive health policy, there may be more applications of feminism in this area.

Prostitution/Sex Trafficking

Social work has not typically offered social services specifically to women who have been trafficked and/or have engaged in prostitution, but many social work clients have been sex workers. Sloan and Wahab (2000) detail the profession's long history of debate on sex work as violence and exploitation, with consideration of Marxist feminism, domination theory (related to radical feminism), black feminism, liberal feminism, and radical sexual pluralist theory (critical of all restrictions on sexual behavior). They argue that despite the disparate ideological and theoretical debates between prostitutes' rights groups and those who wish to abolish prostitution, there is agreement that sex workers are often victims of exploitation and should not be prosecuted for their work. They believe that social work should destigmatize and depathologize sex workers, supporting those who want to leave sex work and those who do not, thereby hearing and validating the voices of women who work or have worked as sex workers. This perspective has been embodied in recent work in Calgary whereby social workers enabled sex trade workers to tell their own stories via photography and subsequent exhibitions ("Do you know").

Valandra (2007) offers an Afrocentric approach to recovery from prostitution, and Boxill and Richardson (2007) present a community organizing approach to ending sex trafficking of children in Atlanta with outcomes of police intervention with pimps, legislative changes, and the purchase of a secure treatment facility. Examination of human trafficking, of which sex trafficking of women and children is the major component (Hodge, 2008; Hodge & Lietz, 2007), shows that this phenomenon has local/national/transnational dimensions and that an ecological perspective operating on macro, mezzo, and micro levels will enable social workers to advocate on behalf of "some of the most vulnerable and oppressed people in the global community" (p. 143).

Women and Health

Given the prominence of the women's Health Movement during the 1980s and 1990s and the many social workers working in health, it would be surprising not to find feminist perspectives within this broad domain. Morrow, Hankivsy, and Varcoe (2007) review the Canadian/international scene by locating women's health issues with respect to research, policy, and practice concerns as well as to the intersection of all three within the biological, social, political, environmental, and economic contexts of women's lives. Gender-based analysis remains in the forefront, but in conjunction with intersectional approaches on topics such as dis/ability, sexuality, transhealth, medicalization of menopause, media reporting on hormone replacement therapy, the ideology of health systems, and the barriers individuals face in managing their own health care.

Mental Health. Smith, Cox, and Saradjiam (1999) of the United Kingdom consider how women's self-mutilation may be understood with reference to gender, race, disability, and dynamics of power abuse as well as an etiology of sexual abuse, physical abuse, and neglect. Kokaliari and Berzoff (2008) examine nonsuicidal self-injury among nonclinical college women, focusing on women's internalized oppression. Berg (2002) considers liberal, radical, and socialist perspectives in relation to posttraumatic stress disorder, recognizing commonality among the perspectives in their emphasis on sexual and physical violence as causing much of the psychological suffering of women, a viewpoint that challenges traditional psychiatry. Chonody and Siebert (2008) detail the integration of two theories to explain the higher prevalence of depression among women: a general theory of gender stratification that uses a Marxist viewpoint and a theory of gender and power to explain how gender is organized within society. They believe that a synthesis of these two theories would challenge the prominence of the medical model, help avoid quick treatment fixes, and ultimately promote policy reform and social change.

Substance Abuse. Substance abuse by women of varying backgrounds engages many social workers, but feminist perspectives are not very evident, even in a major review of issues experienced by substance-abusing women in the child welfare system (Carlson, 2006). There were a few calls for gender-sensitive approaches to enable women to have different programs than men

(Carter, 1997, 2002; Kauffman, Silver, & Poulin, 1997). Zelvin (1999) also proposed a gender-specific approach that applied relational theory to the treatment of women's addictions by building on women's relationship strengths rather than devaluing their ability to connect. The relationship between partner abuse and women's substance abuse (Bennett, 1995; Call, 2007) receives attention, but the concept of codependence is now considered as pathologizing women (Stout & McPhail, 1998, pp. 54–55) and is rarely seen.

Research on stereotypes about lesbians and drug use revealed that the only significant difference within a sample of lesbian/bisexual and heterosexual women was a higher frequency of marijuana use by lesbian and bisexual women (Saulnier & Miller, 1997). Feminist social workers practice in problems related to fetal alcohol syndrome, but application of feminist perspectives appears limited (M. Munoz, personal communication, August 18, 2009). Sun (2009) offers a review of research on treatment effectiveness and gender-specific programs for six substance-abusing vulnerable groups: pregnant women, adolescent girls, older women, homeless women, street prostitutes, and lesbians. A more psychiatrically oriented work on gender differences in substance abuse focuses on women and addiction and details "how sex and gender likely moderate all aspects of the addiction process" (Brady, Back, & Greenfield, 2009, p. xi).

Other Health Issues. Lesbian health issues continue to get a modest degree of attention (Hunter, 2005; Saulnier, 2002; Saulnier & Wheeler, 2000). Feminist practice approaches are also employed in group work with women with HIV/AIDS (Emlet, Tangenberg, & Siverson, 2002;), with attention to psychodynamic issues, cultural diversity, socioeconomic status, and gender-based institutional inequalities. More typically HIV and STD risk behaviors are considered through a systems or ecological perspective.

Other Areas of Practice

Feminist theory and practice has become fundamental since the mid-1990s in homelessness (Boes & Van Wormer, 1997; Gross, 1997; Growing Home, 2009; Johnson, 1999; Kisor &

Kendal-Wilson, 2002) with intersectional/strengths perspectives often employed to depathologize women's behavior. Poverty provides the context for many of women's troubles, and social workers have endorsed feminist perspectives (Dinerman & Faulkner, 2000; Fitzpatrick & Gomez, 1997; Orleck & Jetter, 2007; Pearce, 2000). Research in this area promotes women's own voices altering social work practice to modify policies, increase financial support for further education and career support, improve worker–client relationships, and screen clients for interpersonal violence and mental health issues (Altman, 2007; Laakso & Drevdahl, 2006).

Child welfare practice, both in the United Kingdom (Scourfield, 2006) and the United States (Risley-Curtiss & Heffernan, 2003), according to these authors, remains rife with gender bias in research and practice, despite less mother-blaming and including fathers in parenting. In 1998, Gross indicated that feminist social workers had not focused on mothering (Gross, 1998). In Canada, the Association for Research on Mothering (ARM) (1998) has, however, fostered considerable interest. Feminist social work has addressed mothering in relation to women and battering (Buchbinder, 2004; Krane & Davies, 2007) and women's own sexual abuse histories (Saltzberg, 2000). Other foci have included death of mothers of adult daughters (Foote, Valentich, & Gavel, 1996), pregnancy (Sun, 2004), reproductive loss (Cacciatore & Bushfield, 2008; Price, 2008), and assisted reproductive technologies (Hammons, 2008; Shapiro, 2009).

Special Populations

There are numerous articles pertaining to women in most social work journals, but many do not identify their theoretical base as feminist. Others do cite Self-in-Relation theory, intersectional theory, empowerment, and quite often a strengths perspective. It is likely that feminist influences have played a part in identifying issues relating to black, Hispanic, Latina, Mexican, rural Alaskan Native, and American Indian women in the United States and First Nations, Aboriginal, South Asian, and Salvadorian women in Canada. One may also assume that feminist social workers are engaged in work with caregivers, immigrants, students, low-income women, incarcerated women, and lesbians, and women with HIV/AIDS, histories of being battered, and various disabilities.

Some literature very explicitly draws on feminist perspectives. Feminist family therapy was identified as an important force for working with lesbian couples, addressing resilience (Connolly, 2006) and intimate violence (Speziale & Ring, 2006). Parish, Magana, and Cassiman (2008) detailed the severe deprivation and multilayered hardships experienced by low-income mothers with disabilities. Wilson (2003) identified feminist principles of collaboration, mutual support, nurturance, and self-empowerment in the prevention of developmental disabilities as well as community organizing that included community education, legislative advocacy, mentoring of emerging leaders, and organizing community partnerships and social change. Pulleybank (2000) argued for feminist community development work to address the developmental needs of girls and women in rural communities. Wilson and Anderson (1997) stressed the importance of using short-term, goal-directed, and task-centered empowerment approaches with female offenders as well as promoting changes in educational and economic institutions.

Global Feminist Social Work

Increasingly, social workers have been drawn to global issues related to women (Dinerman, 2003; Ross-Sheriff, 2007) and have made connections between issues occurring locally and in distant regions, despite variations in social work practice around the world (Weis, 2005). Affirmation of women's rights to sexual and reproductive freedom (Alzate, 2009) is a universal anchoring point for feminist social work practice. Proclamations of human rights are fundamentally aligned with social work values (Steen, 2006). Feminist social workers work at macro, mezzo, and micro levels and, by virtue of their theoretical perspectives, recognize the intertwining of the personal and the political.

Issues and Future Directions

Despite the conservatism of the past two decades and the backlash toward feminism, the resilience

of second-wave and the development of third-wave and numerous identity feminisms have resulted in feminist frameworks of increasing complexity that have enabled practitioners to better understand the multiplicity of factors that affect women's functioning. Although some areas of practice remain "feminist-free," feminist practice models have been applied to diverse groups of women and problems. The richness of numerous feminisms may result in some "rising to the top" and providing a more comprehensive and integrated set of ideas to guide research and practice. Social workers do still organize around problematic situations involving oppression of women; feminist frameworks need not "essentialize" women, but can provide direction for therapy and social change. Research and practice must continue to address intersecting realities.

While the emergence of gender-sensitive practice in the early 1990s may have prompted feminist social workers to apply their perspectives to work with men (Valentich, 1992), contemporary feminist social work generally focuses on women and/or women and family members. Men are no longer a taboo topic: this is particularly evident in work with intimate partner violence. However, only a few social workers in the recent past have given attention to how and where men may be situated with respect to feminist social work practice (Dominelli, 2002; Stout & McPhail, 1998). Given the calls for gender gaining more prominence in social work practice and education, I envision a more comprehensive integration of theory and research relating to women and men within feminist perspectives. This would result in a clearer articulation of how feminist social work practice models could incorporate working with women and men.

If feminist social work is to be more inclusive, it must consider whether and how its theory and practice could relate more adequately to the situation of aboriginal women and men. Recognizing the limitations of my own research for this chapter, I still am surprised by the minimal attention these populations have received.

Research into the nature of women's oppression and ways of helping women has become a noticeable feature of feminist social work. Many of the articles cited are based on research that has been conducted, often using qualitative methods with considerable use of focus groups and/or in-depth interviewing using a grounded theory approach. This development is a very positive feature of the past period and bodes well for the future.

The other development that I believe will foster greater strength and viability over the next decade with respect to feminist social work is global feminism. Social workers are increasingly aware that we are all connected, and that one woman's pain due to societal oppression is cause for all persons to unite in efforts to seek remedies and social justice. My sense is that social work's traditional adherence to a liberal feminist framework may give way to greater radicalism because both second-wave and third-wave feminists are increasingly impatient and angry over injustice. All of us are inspired by those who will not give up on "Gender Equality: the single most important struggle on the planet" (Stephen Lewis, 2009).

References

Abramovitz, M. (1998). Social work and social reform: An arena of struggle. *Social Work,* 43(6), 512–526.

Abramovitz, M. (2009). Wall Street takes welfare it begrudges to women. [Electronic version]. *Affilia,* 24, 105–106.

Altman, J. C. (2007). Normative versus felt needs of women in the era of welfare reform. *Affilia,* 27(1), 71–83.

Alzate, M. M. (2009). The role of sexual and reproductive rights in social work practice. *Affilia,* 24(2), 108–119.

Apt, C., Hurlbert, D. F., Pierce, A. P., & White, L. C. (1996). *The Canadian Journal of Human Sexuality,* 5(3), 195–210.

ARM, Association for Research in Mothering. Retrieved August 11, 2009, from http://www.yorku.ca/arm/aboutarm.html.

Avis, J. M. (2005). Narratives from the field. *Journal of Feminist Family Therapy,* 17(1), 1–16.

Ayala, J., & Luhtanen, M. (September 2009). Is there still a need for GLBT services? Exploring the needs of GLBT persons. Paper presented at Canadian Sex Research Forum, Halifax, Nova Scotia.

Baretti, M. (2001). Social work, women, and feminism: A review of social work journals, 1988–1997. *Affilia,* 16(3), 266–294.

Baumgardner, J., & Richards, A. (2000). *ManifestA.* New York: Farrar, Straus & Giroux.

Belenky, M. F., Clinchy, B. M., Goldberger, N. R., & Tarule, J. M. (1986). *Women's ways of knowing: The development of self, voice and mind.* New York: Basic Books.

Bennett, L. W. (1995). Substance abuse and the domestic assault of women. *Social Work,* 40, 760–771.

Berg, S. H. (2002). The PTSD diagnosis: Is it good for women? *Affilia,* 17(1), 55–68.

Boes, M., & van Wormer, K. (1997). Social work with homeless women in emergency rooms: a strengths-feminist perspective. *Affilia,* 12(4), 408–426.

Bolen, R. M. (2003). Child sexual abuse: Prevention of promotion. *Social Work,* 48(2), 174–185.

Boxill, N. A., & Richardson, D. J. (2007). Ending sex trafficking of children in Atlanta. *Affilia,* 22(2), 138–149.

Bradley, H. (2007). *Gender.* Cambridge: Polity Press.

Brady, K. T., Back, S. E., & Greenfield, S. F. (Eds.). (2009). *Women and addiction.* New York: Guilford Press.

Bricker-Jenkins, M., & Hooyman, N. R. (Eds.) (1986). *Not for women only.* Silver Spring, MD: National Association of Social Workers.

Bricker-Jenkins, M., Hooyman, N. R., & Gottlieb, N. (Eds.). (1991). *Feminist social work practice in clinical settings.* Silver Spring, MD: National Association of Social Workers.

Buchbinder, E. (2004). Motherhood of battered women: The struggle for repairing the past. *Clinical Social Work Journal,* 32(3), 307–326.

Burdge, B. J. (2007). Bending gender, ending gender: Theoretical foundations for social work practice with the transgender community. *Social Work,* 52(3), 243–250.

Cacciatore, J., & Bushfield, S. (2008). Stillbirth: A sociopolitical issue. *Affilia,* 23(4), 378–387.

Call, C. R. (2007). Partner abuse and women's substance abuse problems. *Affilia,* 22(4), 334–346.

Carlson, B. E. (2006). Best practices in the treatment of substance-abusing women in the child welfare system. *Journal of Social Work Practice in Addictions,* 6(3), 97–115.

Carter, C. S. (1997). Ladies don't: A historical perspective on attitudes toward alcoholic women. *Affilia,* 12(4), 471–485.

Carter, C. S. (2002). Prenatal care for women who are addicted: Implications for gender-sensitive practice. *Affilia,* 17(3), 299–313.

CASW calls for equality for all women. (2009, March). *CASW Reporter,* 1.

Chambon, A. S., & Irving, A. (Eds.) (1994). *Essays on postmodernism and social work.* Toronto: Canadian Scholars' Press.

Chonody, J. M., & Siebert, D. C. (2008). Gender differences in depression: A theoretical explanation of power. *Affilia,* 23(4), 338–348.

Connolly, C. M. (2006). A feminist perspective of resilience in lesbian couples. *Journal of Feminist Family Therapy,* 18(1/2), 137–162.

Cox, L., & Speziale, B. (2009). Survivors of stalking. *Affilia*, 24(1), 5–18.

CRIAW-ICREF (2006). *An emerging vision*. (Available from Canadian Research Institute for the Advancement of Women, 151 Slater St., Suite 408, Ottawa, ON K1P 5H3; or www.criaw-icref.ca

Crisp, C., & Van Den Bergh, N. (2004). Defining culturally competent practice with sexual minorities: implications for social work education and practice. [Electronic version]. *Journal of Social Work Education*, 40(2), 221–238.

Curry-Stevens, A., Lee, C., Datta, J., Hill, E., & Edwards, V. (2008). Activist formation in a neoliberal era: A journey with multiple dimensions. *Affilia*, 232(3), 290–298.

Damant, D., Lapierre, S., Kouraga, A., Fortin, A., Hamelin-Brabant, L., Lavergne, C., & Lessard, G. (2008). Taking child abuse and mothering into account: Intersectional feminism as an alternative for the study of domestic violence. *Affilia*, 23(2), 123–133.

Daniels, K. C., Zimmerman, T. S., & Bowling, S. W. (2002). Barriers in the bedroom: A feminist application for working with couples. *Journal of Feminist Family Therapy*, 14(2), 21–50.

Danis, F. S. (2003a). Social work response to domestic violence: Encouraging news from a new look. *Affilia*, 18(2), 177–191.

Danis, F. S. (2003b). The criminalization of domestic violence: What social workers need to know. *Affilia*, 48(2), 237–246.

Dinerman, M. (2003). Globalization as a women's issue. *Affilia*, 18(2), 114–117.

Dinerman, M., & Faulkner, A. O. (2000). Guest editorial. *Affilia*, 15(2), 125–132.

Dominelli, L. (2002). *Feminist social work theory and practice*. New York: Palgrave Press.

Dominelli, L. (2009). *Introducing social work*. Malden, MA: Polity Press.

Dominelli, L. (2006). *Women and community action*. Bristol: Policy Press.

"Do you know what I mean? The lived experiences of sex trade workers." (n.d.). Retrieved August 7, 2009, from http://www.doyouknowwhatimean.ca

Drumm, R., Pittman, S., & Perry, S. (2001). Women of war: Emotional needs of ethnic Albanians in refugee camps. *Affilia*, 16(4), 467–487.

East, J. F. (1998). In-dependence: a feminist postmodern deconstruction [Electronic Version]. *Affilia*, 13(3), 273–288.

Emlet, C. A., Tangenberg, K., & Siverson, C. (2002). A feminist approach to practice in working with midlife and older women with HIV/AIDS. *Affilia*, 17(2), 229–251.

Ensler, E. (1998). *The vagina monologues*. New York: Villard.

Faludi, S. (1991). *Backlash*. New York: Crown.

Farwell, N. (2004). War rape: New conceptualizations and responses. *Affilia*, 19(4), 389–403.

Favorini, A. (1995). Concept of codependency: Blaming the victim or pathway to recovery. *Social Work*, 40(6), 827-.

Fellin, P. (2000). Revisiting multiculturalism in social work. *Journal of Social Work Education*, 36(2), 261–278.

Figueira-McDonough, J., Netting, F. E., & Nichols-Casebolt, A. (2001). *Affilia*, 16(4), 411–431.

Fineran, S. (2002). Sexual harassment between same-sex peers: Intersection of mental health, homophobia, and sexual violence in schools. *Social Work*, 47(1), 65–74.

Fineran, S., & Bennett, L. (1998). Teenage peer sexual harassment: Implications for social work practice in education. *Social Work*, 43(1), 55–64.

Fitzpatrick, J. A., & Gomez, T. R. (1997). Still caught in a trap: The continued povertization of women. *Affilia*, 12(3), 318–341.

Foley, S., Kope, S. A., & Sugrue, D. P. (2002). *Sex matters for women*. New York: The Guilford Press.

Foote, C., Valentich, M., & Gavel, L. (1996). When mothers of adult daughters die: A new area of feminist practice. *Affilia*, 11(2), 145–163.

Freedberg, S. (2009). *Relational theory for social work practice*. New York: Routledge.

Gagerman, J. R. (2004). The search for fuller mutuality and self experiences in a women's psychotherapy group. *Clinical Social Work Journal*, 32(3), 285–306.

Galambos, C. (2008). From the editor: A dialogue on social justice [Electronic version]. *Journal of Social Work Education*, 44(2), 1–6.

Galat, J. M. (2009). "Just listen" Elizabeth Olorenshaw. *The Advocate*, 34(1), 20–21.

Georg, A. (March 2009). The feminist evolution. *Fast Forward Weekly*, p. 34.

Gibelman, M. (1999). The search for identity: Defining social work—past, present, future. *Social Work*, 44(4), 298–310.

Gibelman, M., & Schervish, P. H. (1996). The private practice of social work: current trends and projected scenarios in a managed care environment. *Clinical Social Work Journal*, 24(3), 323–338.

Gillis, S., & Munford, R (2004). Interview with Elaine Showalter. In S. Gillis, G. Howie, & R. Munford (Eds.), *Third wave feminism* (pp. 60–64). New York: Palgrave Macmillan.

Gilson, S. F., Cramer, E. P., & DePoy, E., (2001). Redefining abuse of women with dis-abilities: A paradox of limitation and expansion. *Affilia*, 16(20), 220–235.

Gould, K. (2000). Beyond Jones v. Clinton: Sexual harassment law and social work. *Social Work*, 45(3), 237–248.

Gilligan, C. (1982). *In a different voice.* Cambridge, MA: Harvard University Press.

Green, J. (2000). Neoliberalism/neoconservatism. In L. Code (Ed.), *Encyclopedia of feminist theories* (p. 364). New York: Routledge.

Gripton, J. (1974). Sexism in social work: Male takeover of a female profession. *Social Worker,* 42(2), 78–89.

Gripton, J., & Valentich, M. (2003). Making decisions about non-sexual boundary behavior. *Canadian Social Work,* 5(1), 108–125.

Gripton, J., & Valentich, M. (2004). Dealing with non-sexual professional-client dual/multiple relationships in rural communities. *Rural Social Work,* 9, 216–225.

Gross, E. (Ed.) (1998). Motherhood in feminist theory. *Affilia,* 13(3), 269–272.

Gross, E. (Ed.) (1997). What is feminist about homelessness? *Affilia,* 12(4), 389–390.

Growing home/Housing and Homelessness in Canada. (February 2009). 2nd National Conference, Faculty of Social Work, University of Calgary, Calgary, AB. Retrieved August 11, 2009, from nhc2009.ca/en/conference_findings.html.

Guttmacher Institute (2009). *A new day: the Obama administration and U.S. sexual and reproductive health policy.* Retrieved August 6, 2009, from http://www.guttmacher.org/media/nr/2009/03/04/index.html.

Hammons, S. A. (2008). Assisted reproductive technologies: Changing conceptions of motherhood? *Affilia,* 23(3), 270–280.

Hammons, S. A. (2004). "Family violence": The language of legitimacy. *Affilia,* 19(3), 273–288.

Hanson, M. (2000). Vandana Shiva, b.1952. In L. Code (Ed.), *Encyclopedia of feminist theories.* New York: Routledge.

Harrison, C. (2006). Cyberspace and child abuse images: A feminist perspective. *Affilia,* 21(4). 365–379.

Hodge, D. R. (2008). Sexual trafficking in the United States: A domestic problem with transnational dimensions. *Social Work,* 53(2), 143–152.

Hodge, D. R., & Lietz, C. A. (2007). The international sexual trafficking of women and children: A review of the literature. *Affilia,* 22(2), 163–174.

Hovey, A. (2005). Feminism as a context for understanding and responding to female sexual offending. *Canadian Social Work Review,* 22(1), 89–102.

Hunter, S. (2005). *Midlife and older LGBT adults: Knowledge and affirmative practice for the social services.* New York: Routledge.

Hurlbert, D. F., Apt, C., & Rombough, S. (1996). The female experience of sexual desire as a function of sexual compatibility in an intimate relationship. *The Canadian Journal of Human Sexuality,* 5(1), 7–14.

IASSW (2001). Definition of social work. Retrieved July 31, 2009, from http://www.iassw-aiets.org/index.php?option=com_content&task=blogcategory&id=26&It

Jagger, A. M., & Rothenberg, P. S. (Eds.) (1993). *Feminist frameworks.* New York: McGraw-Hill.

Jansen, G. G. (2006). Gender and war. *Affilia,* 21(2), 134–145.

Jarman-Rohde, L., McFall, J., Kolar, P., & Strom, G. (1997). The changing context of social work practice: Implications and recommendations for social work educators [Electronic version]. *Journal of Social Work Education,* 33(1), 29–47.

Johnson, Y. M. (1999). Indirect work: Social work's uncelebrated strength. *Social Work,* 44(4), 323–334.

Jordan, J. V. (nd.). The development of relational-cultural theory. Retrieved August 14, 2009, from http://www.wellesley.edu/JBMTI/pdf/developingRCT.pdf

Karls, J. M., Lowery, C. T., Mattaini, M. A., & Wandrei, K. E. (1997). The use of the PIE (Person-in-Environment) system in social work [Electronic version]. *Journal of Social Work Education,* 33(1), 49–58.

Kauffman, S. E., Silver, P., & Poulin, J. (1997). Gender differences in attitudes toward alcohol, tobacco, and other drugs. *Social Work,* 42(3), 231–241.

Kikaliari, E., & Berzoff, J. (2008). Nonsuicidal self-injury among nonclinical college women: Lessons from Foucault. *Affilia,* 23(3), 259–269.

Kisor, A. J., & Kendal-Wilson, L. (2002). Older homeless women: Reframing the stereotype of the bag lady. *Affilia,* 17(3), 354–370.

Krane, J., & Davies, L. (2007). Mothering under difficult circumstances: Challenges to working with battered women. *Affilia,* 22(1), 23–38.

Kreuger, L. (1997). The end of social work [Electronic version]. *Journal of Social Work Education,* 33(1), 19–27.

Laakso, J. H., & Drevdahl, D. J. (2006). Women, abuse, and the welfare bureaucracy. *Affilia,* 21(1), 84–96.

Lakritz, N. (2009a, April 3). Shock and shame greet new Afghan law. *Calgary Herald,* p. A20.

Lakritz, N. (2009b, July 29). Sisterhood's silence over honour killings deafening. *Calgary Herald,* p. A14.

Levine, H. (1976). Feminist counseling: A look at new possibilities. Special Issue of *The Social Worker,* 12–15.

Levy, A. (2005). *Female chauvinist pigs.* New York: Free Press.

Linhorst, D. M. (2002). Federalism and social justice: Implications for social work. *Social Work,* 47(3), 201–208.

Lusk, M. W., & Mayadas, N. S. (1997). Should social work celebrate unity or diversity? [Electronic version]. *Journal of Social Work Education, 33*(2), 229–234.

McMahon, Sarah. Understanding Community-Specific Rape Myths: Exploring Student Athlete Culture. Affilia Winter 2007 22: 357-370,

Marecek, J. (2000). Miller, Jean Baker (b. 1927). In L. Code (Ed.), *Encyclopedia of feminist theories* (pp. 344–345). New York: Routledge.

Martinez, A., & Phillips, K. P. (2008). Challenging ethno-cultural and sexual inequities: An intersectional feminist analysis of teachers, health partners and university students' views on adolescent sexual and reproductive health rights. *Journal of Human Sexuality, 17*(3), 141–159.

Mason, S. E., & Clemans, S. E. (2008). Participatory research for rape survivor groups: A model for practice. *Affilia, 23*(1), 66–76.

McKechnie, R., & Valentich, M. (1989). Male-focused clinical social work practice. *Arete, 14*(1), 10–21.

McPhail, B. A. (2008). Re-gendering the social work curriculum: New realities and complexities. *Journal of Social Work Education, 44*(2), 33–52.

McPhail, B. A., Busch, N. B., Kulkarni, S., & Rice, G. (2007). Violence against women. *Affilia, 13*(8), 817–841.

Miles, A. (2000). Bunch, Charlotte, b. 1942. In L. Code (Ed.), *Encyclopedia of feminist theories* (p. 68). New York: Routledge.

Miles, A., Rezai-Rashti, & Rundle, L.B. (2001). Third wave feminism: Antiracists, trans-nationalists, and young feminists speak out. In N. Mandell (Ed.), *Feminist issues* (pp. 1–22). Toronto: Prentice Hall.

Milillo, D. (2006). Rape as a tactic of war. *Affilia, 21*(2), 196–206.

Miller, J. B. (1986). *Toward a new psychology of women* (2nd ed.). Boston: Beacon.

Milliken, E. (1985). *New directions in social work: Feminist counseling with male clients.* Unpublished master's project, University of Calgary, Calgary, AB.

Mirkin, M. P., Suyemoto, K. L., & Okun, B. F. (Eds.) (2005). *Psychotherapy with women.* New York: Guilford.

Morgraine, K. (2009). "You can't bite the hand … ": Domestic violence and human rights. *Affilia, 24*(1), 31–43.

Morrow, M., Hankivsky, O., & Varcoe, C. (Eds.). (2007). *Women's health in Canada: Critical perspectives on theory and practice.* Toronto: University of Toronto Press.

Murdach, A. (2006). Social work in the movies: Another look. *Social Work, 51*(3), 269–272.

Murphy, S. B., Moynihan, M. M., & Banyard, V. L. (2009). Moving within the spiral. *Affilia, 24*(2), 152–164.

Nelson, A., & Robinson, B. W.(2002). *Gender in Canada.* Toronto: Prentice Hall.

Nichols-Casebolt, A., Figueira-McDonough, J., & Netting, F. E. (2000). *Journal of Social Work Education, 36*(1), 65–78.

Orleck, A., & Jetter, A. (2007). What if poor women ran their own antipoverty programs? *Affilia, 22*(1), 116–119.

Parish, S. L., Magana, S., & Cassiman, S. A. (2008). It's just that much harder. *Affilia, 23*(1), 51–65.

Pearce, D. (2000). Rights and wrongs of welfare reform: A feminist approach. *Affilia, 15*(2), 133–152.

Pewewardy, N. (2004). The political is the personal: The essential obligation of white feminist family therapists to deconstruct white privilege. *Journal of Feminist Family Therapy, 16*(1), 53–67.

Price, S. K. (2008). Women and reproductive loss: Client–worker dialogues designed to break the silence. *Social Work, 53*(4), 367–376.

Prospero, M. (2007). Young adolescent boys and dating violence; The beginning of patriarchal terrorism? *Affilia, 22*(3), 271–280.

Pulleybank, E. (2000). Nobody tells you who you are: First notes on a community project for girls and women in rural Massachusetts. *Journal of Feminist Family Therapy, 11*(4), 47–63.

Pyles, L., & Postmus, J. L. (2004). Addressing the problem of domestic violence: How far have we come? *Affilia, 19*(4), 376–388.

Reisch, M., & Jarman-Rohde, L. (2000). The future of social work in the United States: implications for field education [Electronic version]. *Journal of Social Work Education, 36*(2), 201–214.

Risley-Curtiss, C., & Heffernan, K. (2003). Gender biases in child welfare. *Affilia, 18*(4), 395–410.

Ross-Sheriff, F. (2007). Globalization as a women's issue revisited. *Affilia, 22*(2), 133–137.

Russell, M. (1984). *Skills in counseling women: The feminist approach.* Springfield, IL: Charles C Thomas.

Saltzberg, M. (2000). Parenting challenges for women with abuse histories. *Journal of Feminist Family Therapy, 12*(1), 45–58.

Sands, R. G., & Nuccio, K. (1992). Postmodern feminist theory and social work. *Social Work, 37*(6), 489–494.

Saulnier, C. F. (2002). Deciding who to see: Lesbians discuss their preferences in health and mental health care providers. *Social Work, 47*(4), 355–365.

Saulnier, C. F. (2008). Feminist theories. In N. Coady & P. Lehmann (Eds.), *Theoretical perspectives for direct social work practice* (pp. 343–366). New York: Springer.

Saulnier, C. F. (1996). *Feminist theories and social work: Approaches and applications.* Binghamton, NY: Haworth Press.

Saulnier, C. F., & Miller, B. A. (1997). Drug and alcohol problems: Heterosexual compared to lesbian and bisexual women. *Canadian Journal of Human Sexuality*, 6(3), 221–231.

Saulnier, C. F., & Wheeler, E. (2000). Social action research: Influencing providers and recipients of health and mental health care for lesbians. *Affilia*, 15(3), 409–433.

Scourfield, J. (2006). Gendered organizational culture in child protection social work. *Social Work*, 51(1), 80–82.

Shapiro, C. H. (2009). Therapy with infertile heterosexual couples: It's not about gender—or is it? *Clinical Social Work Journal*, 37, 140–149.

Sloan, L., Edmond, T., Rubin, A., & Doughty, M. (1998). Social workers' knowledge of and experience with sexual exploitation by psychotherapists. *Social Work*, 43(1), 43–53.

Sloan, L., & Wahab, S. (2000). Feminist voices on sex work: Implications for social work. *Affilia*, 15(4), 457–479.

Smith, G., Cox, D., & Saradjiam, J. (1999). *Women and self-harm: Understanding, coping, and healing from self-mutilation.* New York: Routledge.

Snyder, C. S., Gabbard, W. J., May, J. D., & Zulcic, N. (2006). On the battleground of women's bodies. *Affilia*, 21(2), 184–195.

Steen, J. A. (2006). The roots of human rights advocacy and a call for action. *Social Work*, 51(2), 101–105.

Speziale, B., & Ring, C. (2006). Intimate violence among lesbian couples: Emerging data and critical needs. *Journal of Feminist Family Therapy*, 18(1/2), 85–96.

Starr, L. (2000). Third wave feminism. In L. Code (Ed.). *Encyclopedia of feminist theories* (pp. 474–475). New York: Routledge.

Stout, K. D., & McPhail, B. (1998). *Confronting sexism and violence against women: A challenge for social work.* New York: Longman.

Stephen Lewis to speak during Shaw lecture series. (February 2009). *The Globe and Mail*, p. R3.

Strom-Gottfried, K. (1997). The implications of managed care for social work education [Electronic version]. *Journal of Social Work Education*, 33 (1), 7–18.

Sun, A-P. (2009). *Helping substance-abusing women of vulnerable populations.* New York: Columbia University Press.

Sun, A-P. (2004). Principles for practice with substance-abusing pregnant women: A framework based the five social work intervention roles. *Social Work*, 49(3), 383–394.

The Working Group on a New View of Women's Sexual Problems (n.d.). *The New View Manifesto.* Retrieved on August 6, 2009 from http://www.fsd-alert.org/manifesto4.asp

Timberlake, E. M., Sabatino, C. A., & Martin, J. A. (1997). Advanced practitioners in clinical social work: A profile [Electronic version]. *Social Work*, 42(4), 374–385.

Tutty, L. (2006). There but for fortune: How women experience abuse by intimate partners. In M. Hampton & N. Gerrard (Eds.), *Intimate partner violence: Reflections on experience, theory and policy* (pp. 9–32). Toronto: Cormorant Books.

Tutty, L., & Goard, C. (Eds.). (2002). *Reclaiming self.* Halifax, Nova Scotia: Fernwood Publishing and Winnepeg, Manitoba: RESOLVE.

Valandra. (2007). Reclaiming their lives and breaking free: An Afrocentric approach to recovery from prostitution. *Affilia*, 22(2), 195–208.

Valentich, M. (2009). Calgary's resistance to changing from "Alderman" to "Councillor." *Theory in Action*, 2(1), 66–85.

Valentich, M. (1986). Feminism and social work practice. In F. J. Turner (Ed.), *Social work treatment* (pp. 564–589). New York: Free Press.

Valentich, M. (1996). Feminist theory and social work practice. In F. J. Turner (Ed.), *Social work treatment* (pp. 282–318). New York: Free Press.

Valentich, M. (2005). Feminist theory. In F. J. Turner (Ed.), *Encyclopedia of Canadian social work* (pp. 146–148). Waterloo, ON: Wilfrid Laurier Press.

Valentich, M. (2009). One man's pursuit of social justice: James Macpherson Gripton's social work career. Submitted for review.

Valentich, M. (2000). Reflections on charitable status. In N. Simpson (Ed.), *Centred.* Calgary, AB: The Women's Centre.

Valentich, M. (2002). The activist scholar: Contradictions and challenges. *Let it be known*, (Spring), 14–18.

Valentich, M. (2000). They stayed behind: Voices of Croatian women in the Karlovac area during the Serbian occupation—1991–1995. *Canadian Woman Studies*, 19(4), 127–131.

Valentich, M. (1992). Toward gender-sensitive clinical social work practice. *Areté*, 17(1), 1–12.

Valentich, M., & Gripton, J. (1984). Ideological perspectives on the sexual assault of women. *Social Service Review*, 58(3), 448–461.

Van Den Bergh, N. (Ed.) (1995). *Feminist practice in the 21st century.* Washington, DC: National Association of Social Workers.

Van Voorhis, R., & Wagner, M. (2002). Among the missing: Content on lesbian and gay people in social work journals. *Social Work*, 47(4), 345–354.

Van Wormer, K. (2009). Restorative justice as social justice for victims of gendered violence: A standpoint feminist perspective. *Social Work*, 54(2), 107–116.

Van Wormer, K., & Berns, L. (2004). The impact of sexual abuse: Female survivors' narratives. *Affilia*, 19(1), 53–67.

Weedon, C. (2000). Poststructuralism/postmodernism. In L.Code (Ed.), *Encyclopedia of feminist theories* (pp. 397–399). New York: Routledge.

Weis, I. (2005). Is there a common core to social work? A cross-national comparative study of BSW graduate students. *Social Work,* 30(2), 101–110.

Wilson, M., & Anderson, S. C. (1997). Empowering female offenders: Removing barriers to community-based practice. *Affilia,* 12(3), 342–358.

Winton, M. (2001). Paradigm change and female sexual dysfunction: An analysis of sexology journals. *Canadian Journal of Human Sexuality,* 10(1–2). 19–24.

White, V. (2006). *The state of feminist social work.* New York: Routledge.

Worell, J., & Remer, P. (2003). *Feminist perspectives in therapy.* Hoboken, NJ: John Wiley & Sons.

Young, T. L. (2007). The F.A.S.T. Model: Feminist assessment for use in sex therapy. *Journal of Feminist Family Therapy,* 19(2), 1–23.

Zelvin, E. (1999). Applying relational theory to the treatment of women's addictions. *Affilia,* 14(1), 9–23.

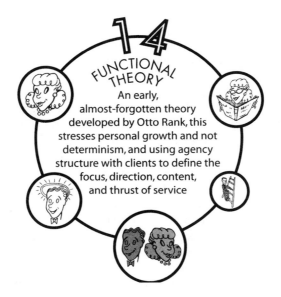

FUNCTIONAL THEORY An early, almost-forgotten theory developed by Otto Rank, this stresses personal growth and not determinism, and using agency structure with clients to define the focus, direction, content, and thrust of service

Functional Theory and Social Work Practice

Katherine M. Dunlap

Introduction

In a dramatic saga that is now mostly forgotten, early-20th-century social work leaders hotly argued over which practice method the profession should adopt. Most followed the medical profession and advocated for the psychoanalytic principles developed by Sigmund Freud. A smaller group embraced the functional principles promulgated by German psychoanalyst Otto Rank. The emotional climate was so charged that at least one national convention was disrupted by shouting (Dr. Alan Keith-Lucas, personal communication, circa 1984). In the short run, the psychoanalytic school prevailed; however, the principles of functional social work have survived and now underpin many current methods of practice. Functional theories have had a

dramatic impact on contemporary social work, yet most educators and practitioners have had limited exposure to the functional roots of modern methods. This chapter recapitulates the historical conditions from which the functional school emerged, explains major tenets, reviews applications, and examines the future of a once-powerful approach to social work practice.

The principles of functional theory were first developed by Otto Rank, a German psychoanalyst and erstwhile student of Sigmund Freud. Functional theory was subsequently adapted for social work practice by Jessie Taft and the faculty of School of Social Work at the University of Pennsylvania. Although only a few schools and agencies adopted this approach, functional methods were applied to individual, group, and community practice as well as to supervision, administration, research, and social work education, particularly on the east coast of the United States.

Functional social work is a therapeutic approach derived from psychoanalytic theory. Three characteristics differentiate functional social work from the Freudian or diagnostic school, which was the only other clearly formulated approach extant in the early 1920s (Smalley, 1971). First, functional theory was predicated on a psychology of growth, not determinism. To this end, the functional school replaced the concept of *treating* patients with that of *helping* clients. Second, functional theory assumed the structure of the agency defines the focus, direction, content, and duration of service. Third, functional theory stressed the concept of *process*, not diagnosis. Within the functional therapeutic relationship, the client and clinician work together to discover what can be done with the help that is offered.

Historical Antecedents

Functional theory was incorporated into social work practice in the United States during the turbulent 1920s and 1930s, but its roots must be traced to three antecedents: the emergence of the field of psychiatry during the first decades of the 20th century; concomitant changes in scientific thought; and the influence of Otto Rank, a disciple of Freud in Germany before the First World War. The following sections summarize the contributions of Freud, review scientific changes, and explore the life and work of Rank.

Psychoanalytic Theory

Sigmund Freud revolutionized the study of human behavior by developing the first systematic, scientific theory of personality. Today, Freud's contributions are well known. When first proposed, however, psychoanalytic theory was considered radical and controversial. Freudian methods were initially rejected by some; however, this theory offered hope to others seeking effective treatment for troubled people.

Freud's work was based on principles of scientific determinism. He and his disciples assumed that present behavior has meaning and can be understood through intense examination of past events. To garner meaning, they focused on the inner world of the self—thoughts, feelings, impulses, and fantasies.

Using case study methods, Freud and his followers engaged in a process of diagnosis. Their primary goal was to discover the cause of present difficulties. They assumed that by removing cause, they could remove symptoms, as in medical practice.

One of the keystones of Freud's personality structure was the concept of the unconscious mind, which he claimed to have discovered through his experiments in hypnosis and the study of dreams. To produce "unconscious" material without hypnosis, Freud proposed the technique he called "free association." To elicit material, the analyst was instructed to maintain an attitude of dynamic passivity. Freud declared that these techniques would enable the analyst to uncover the underlying motives that prompt behavior. Tentative hypotheses were confirmed by interpretation, a process through which the analyst shared insights gained "through the careful weighing of evidence and critical comparison" (Aptekar, 1955, p. 9). By analyzing the progress of people treated with these new methods, Freud identified several patterns of predictable responses, including resistance, blocking, and transference. The goal of psychoanalysis was understanding, not change. Freud maintained that rational people who understood their motives could make necessary changes independently of the analyst.

A number of Freud's theories have gained wide exposure, including the epigenetic process of psychosexual development; the organization of personality into three structures that together govern knowledge, emotion, and behavior; the creation and maintenance of defense mechanisms; and the presence of instinctive drives toward pleasure and death. As the following sections indicate, these theories were embraced by the diagnostic school of social work.

A Scientific Revolution

As Freudian theory reached maturity in the early decades of the 20th century, the entire arena of scientific thought experienced what Kuhn (1970) would call a paradigm shift. Drucker (1959) explains that there was a "philosophical shift from the Cartesian universe of mechanical cause to the new universe of pattern, purpose, and process" (p. XI). Scientists abandoned the deterministic search for irreversible causes as they faced the realization that the only thing predictable is unpredictability itself. Researchers in diverse fields began to explore the concept of growth as an orderly process with a universally recognizable purpose (Corner, 1944; Sinnott, 1950). Yelaja (1986) summarized four assumptions first articulated during this period: (1) the goal-directed whole of an organism transcends the sum of its parts; (2) despite common patterns, each being is unique; (3) the observer affects the observed; and (4) will and freedom exist and impel individual growth. These presumptions had profound implications, particularly for theorists in the field of human services (Mead, 1936).

Innovations of Otto Rank

Freud was surrounded by an inquisitive, dedicated circle of disciples who worked with him to elaborate and refine psychoanalytic theory, as the new school of thought came to be called. One of the most dedicated and brilliant of this circle was Otto Rank, and it was Rank who devised the concepts that led to functional social work. Since Rank is less well known that Freud, his life and work are recapitulated here.

Otto Rank was born Otto Rosenfeld in 1884, the third child of an alcoholic jeweler. According to Rudnytsky (1991), the family was economically and emotionally deprived. Rank's older brother Paul received academic training and a law degree, but Otto Rank was forced to attend trade school and work long hours in a machine shop. He still found time to attend the theater, and he read voraciously (Taft, 1958). Rank charted his own intellectual development in diaries and daybooks containing quotations, references, cryptic scribbles, personal notes, and theories. His ambition was to live fully and creatively (Lieberman, 1985).

When Rank was 21, Alfred Adler introduced him to Sigmund Freud. This was a dream come true for Rank (Rudnytsky, 1984). Freud readily accepted Rank into his circle of disciples, for Rank enriched the medical group with his discerning understanding of history and culture.

Freud brought Rank to the center of the group by making him secretary, and for many years Rank prepared the minutes of the weekly meetings of the Vienna Psychoanalytic Society (Klein, 1981).

Recognizing Rank's creative capacities, Freud helped him publish his first book, *Der Künstler (The Artist)*, in 1907 (Rank, 1925). Freud also financed Rank's studies at the University of Vienna, where Rank obtained his doctorate in 1912 for his dissertation on the Lohengrin legend. Rank was the first to employ psychoanalytic methodology in a doctoral dissertation, and he was also the first in psychodynamic literature to explore death symbolism and relate it to birth symbolism (Lieberman, 1985).

This was a period of great productivity for Rank. Under Freud's guidance and with his support, Rank engaged in theoretical research, edited journals, wrote monographs, organized the psychoanalytic movement, and practiced lay analysis for two decades (Progoff, 1956). However, as psychoanalysis began to harden into a standardized procedure, Rank reassessed and rejected many of Freud's notions and continued to experiment with innovative ideas of his own (Karpf, 1953).

Rank was surprised by the storm of controversy generated by the publication of *Trauma of Birth* in 1924 (Rank, 1924). Although the book was dedicated to Freud, it posited new, innovative concepts and was not well received by Freud or his followers.

The criticisms of the Vienna circle were sharp and bitter. With his subsequent departure for Paris, Rank dissociated himself from the official psychoanalytical group and continued to formulate his own theory and approach. His physical move to the United States was followed by an emotional breach with Freud that was never repaired. What began as a theoretical disagreement between colleagues grew into a vendetta that persisted for decades (Menaker, 1982). The two met for the last time in April 1926 to say goodbye. Rank was 42 and Freud was nearing 70.

In *Art and Artist* (Rank, 1932), Rank explained his view of the human condition. Rank was not a feminist, but he respected women's freedom of choice, and he recognized the significant power in the mother–child bond (Sward, 1980-81).

Using the metaphor that "life is a loan, death the repayment," Rank presented life as a series of separations beginning with a painful birth. He focused on the importance of living fully—with creativity, humor, and joy—in the limited time between beginnings and endings.

Rank believed that people oscillate between their need to merge with a larger entity and their desire for separation. To achieve a unique identity and live an abundant life, the individual must exercise personal will (Menaker, 1984).

The concept of will is elaborated in *Will Therapy* and *Truth and Reality*, written in 1928 (Rank, 1928) and 1929 respectively, and translated by Jessie Taft into English in 1936 (Rank, 1936). Rank explains will as a complex, organizing element that delineates the total personality of the person, including creative ideas, feelings, and the energy of action. Will arises from counter-will, or the oppositional stance of "not wanting to," a condition readily observed in young children. Rank maintains that people appropriately use will to adapt situations to their own unique needs. The situation may be external, as in an unhappy childhood, or internal, as in a counterproductive attitude. Regardless, individuation is achieved through active acceptance and adjustment.

As an analyst, Rank viewed each therapeutic hour as a microcosm of life, a time with its own beginning and end. In his therapy sessions, he emphasized the present, rather than the past or future. He encouraged patients to "experience" rather than to analyze the thoughts, feelings, and behaviors arising from the therapeutic process. He focused on recurring interactions and patterns instead of isolated events (Taft, 1958).

Rank is perhaps most famous for setting time limits. He used this strategy to help clients crystallize their conflicts regarding continuation or termination of therapy. Within this context, the conscious use of will becomes a therapeutic agent. For example, Rank noted that people must consciously choose to accept a course of action, even if there appears to be no other choice. By making ambivalence explicit, Rank enabled clients to mobilize their will. In the preface to his last book, *Beyond Psychology* (Rank, 1941), Rank explains, "Man is born beyond psychology and he dies beyond it but he can live beyond it only through vital experience of his own" (p. 16).

Relationship is the determining element in this therapeutic process. Rank rejected the stance of dynamic passivity. For him, the helping relationship is marked by mutuality, as in teaching and learning, but not by reciprocity, as in friendship. The therapist first establishes a setting in which the client can discover and use the strength that arises from vulnerability. Then the therapist becomes the tool that enables the client to explore and expand the will. Finally, the therapist precipitates termination by setting limits so that the client can achieve autonomy and avoid dependency.

Rank saw psychotherapy as an art as well as a science. Since every person is different, every therapeutic encounter will be different. The therapeutic alliance is characterized by spontaneity and creativity, for the analyst must fabricate conditions for growth in every session. It is this intense emotional process that produces change.

Rank frequently lectured in the United States. Although he scrupulously guarded the identity of his clients, it is known now that he worked with many famous individuals, including Henry Miller and Anaïs Nin. He led courses at the University of Pennsylvania School of Social Work, the New York School of Social Work, and the Graduate School for Jewish Social Work (Lieberman, 1985). Until his untimely death in 1939 at age 56, Rank continued to develop and revise his theories about the human condition.

Although he has had a major impact on the development of personality theory and psychotherapy, Rank's list of publications is not large, and his material is not widely read. There are several reasons for this. First, not all his books are available in any one language. Some, originally written in German, have not been translated into English; others, written in English, have not been translated into German. Second, Rank's complex, Germanic style has made translation difficult. Third, his lack of precision has frustrated many scholars.

The Emergence of Two Schools

In the field of psychology, the two great poles during the 1920s were psychoanalysis and behaviorism (Lieberman, 1985). In the field of social work, the primary focus was also on the internal problems of the individual (Kadushin, 1959), and there was relative indifference to behaviorism, social problems, or social reform (Meyer, 1970). Instead, the profession became deeply committed to the medical model, which in turn embraced psychoanalytic theory. The pace toward professionalism accelerated as the two factions, labeled the diagnostic and functional schools, endorsed and adapted psychoanalytic methods.

The Diagnostic School

Like the young Otto Rank, most social workers in the United States were enamored of the theories of Sigmund Freud. As the new theory swept through the profession, a major branch absorbed Freudian methods (Hollis, 1970). This group, first called the diagnostic and later the psychosocial school of social work, found in Freudian theory "the first great opportunity in history to break through to an understanding of the hitherto hidden mysteries" (Barlett and Saunders, 1970).

The diagnostic school evolved and expanded (Hollis & Woods, 1981), but in its early forms, diagnostic social work was based on scientific determinism, or the assumption that people are products of their past. The emphasis was on the past, for proponents maintained that only an understanding and acceptance of previous experiences can bring relief. The goal of treatment was to overcome blocks to normal, healthy functioning by bringing unconscious thoughts to mind (Hamilton, 1937a, 1937b). Research was conducted through the meticulous analysis of case materials (Hollis, 1939).

This approach assigned well-defined roles to social workers and clients. The client was presumed to be psychologically ill and in need of services. It was the worker's responsibility to collect information through the social history, to diagnosis the illness, and to provide treatment. Usually the presenting problem was viewed as a symptom of a deeper, all-pervading psychological problem (Hamilton, 1936).

The worker treated the client over an indefinite period of time, assuming sole responsibility for the goals and direction of treatment. As Hamilton (1937) explains, "Not everyone is equally capable of self-help, and the amount we must do for people is directly inverse to what they can do for themselves" (p. 171).

To avoid countertransference, the worker operated from a stance of dynamic passivity. The client was encouraged to expose deep-seated emotions that the worker subsequently interpreted. Hamilton (1940) explained that the effect of past influences was irreversible, so that the goal of treatment was not change, but adjustment or mitigation of "the crippling effects of deprivations or pathological exposures" (p. 168). She added, "Case work is less often able to free its clients than to help them live within their disabilities through social compensations" (p. 168).

Treatment rarely reached the termination stage in those early days. Hamilton (1940) recalled, "When social studies were being worked out, case workers carried on so much investigation that they scarcely got around to treatment. In the twenties, case workers became so interested in the psychogenetic causes of difficulty that long histories were a major activity and often the treatment did not progress, stagnating in a dead center of diagnosis" (p. 141).

The Great Schism

For many years, the diagnostic and functional schools competed for supremacy (Hamilton, 1941). Each group defended its stance with evangelistic fervor, for each believed it had found *the* way to end psychic pain and mental illness. The polemic was public and painful, and the subject of casework became a contentious one for social workers and others. (Kasius, 1950; Murphy, 1933).

In trying to integrate the two disparate schools of thought, Aptekar (1955) prepared a comparison of the primary tenets of each:

Summing up, we might say that the chief conceptions of Freud which have been taken over and widely used by caseworkers as follows:

1. Unconscious mind as a determinant of behavior.
2. Ambivalence in feeling and attitude.
3. Past experience as a determinant of present behavior.
4. The transference as essential to therapy.
5. Resistance as a factor to be dealt with in all helping.

The chief conceptions of Rankian thinking, taken over by the functional school and substituted for the above, are:

- The will as an organizing force in personality.
- The counter-will as a manifestation of the need of the individual to differentiate himself.
- Present experience as a source of therapeutic development.
- The significance of separation.
- The inherent creativity of man. (p. 35)

The principles and presuppositions of functional social work are explored more fully in the following sections.

Path into Social Work

While the majority of social workers espoused Freudian theory, a small group adopted the approach of Otto Rank. Led by Jessie Taft and the faculty of the School of Social Work at the University of Pennsylvania, this group came to be called the Rankians or functionalists, a term coined by Taft to describe the controls imposed by agency parameters. (The term "functional" in this context bears no relationship to the same term used in sociology.)

A child psychologist by training, Taft attained the doctorate from the University of Chicago in 1913. At the time she met Rank, she was a supervisor of the Foster Home Department of the Children's Aid Society of Pennsylvania. Their first contact occurred on June 3, 1924, at a meeting of the American Psychoanalytical Association where Rank discussed the ideas contained in *The Trauma of Birth*. Two years and many letters later, Taft began analysis with Rank in New York City (Robinson, 1962).

At first, Taft was ignorant of Rank's feud with Freud, but it was not long before she realized that she would have to "face Freudian difference, painful as it was, not merely through Rank but in my own thinking, reading, and use of the therapeutic relationship" (Robinson, 1962, p. 126). Taft immersed herself in Rank's philosophy and methods as she translated *Will Therapy* and *Truth and Reality* (1936). In addition to her agency employment, she concentrated on her psychoanalytic practice, studied the new theories, supervised others, and taught at the

University of Pennsylvania School of Social Work. It was through these activities that Taft introduced the ideas of Otto Rank to social work.

Evolution of Functional Theory

Rank was a catalyst. After his break with the established psychoanalytic community, he lectured at the University of Pennsylvania School of Social Work, but he never related his theory to the profession of social work. In his later years, he did not even recognize the term "functional" (Smalley, 1971). The evolution of Rankian theory into functional social work was fostered by others.

Virginia Robinson was one of its leaders. A lifelong colleague and companion of Taft, Robinson participated in therapy with Rank in 1927. At the time, Robinson was head of the casework department at the University of Pennsylvania School of Social Work. She was impressed by her brief experience with analysis. Like Taft, she adopted and applied Rank's ideas.

Colleagues of Taft and Robinson, and those who followed them—including Aptekar, Dawley, de Schweinitz, Faatz, Gilpin-Wells, Hofstein, Lewis, Phillips, Pray, Smalley, and Wessel—elaborated and expanded Rankian concepts into functional social work (Smalley, 1970). Taft (1937) added the pivotal concepts regarding agency function.

While functional theory was predicated on Rankian philosophy, it also incorporates material from George Herbert Mead, W. I. Thomas, James Tufts, and John Dewey—masters whom Taft and Robinson had encountered in Chicago (Robinson, 1978). Functionalism accepted the scientific changes of the time and embraced the proposition elucidated by Corner (1944) and Sinnott (1950), to wit: "human growth expresses *purpose* and constitutes a *process* (Smalley, 1971, p. 86).

The functionalists read widely in diverse fields, including philosophy, education, science, art, and literature, as a cursory perusal of the *Journal of the Otto Rank Society* attests. As Smalley (1967) reports, many assumptions were imported from psychology. From Gordon Allport (1955) came the confirmation that people have autonomy, the ability to reason, and the capacity to make choices in a free society. Kurt Lewin (1935) added an understanding of the dynamic nature of change and the importance of environment and context. Erik Erikson (1940) contributed his early notions predicating an epigenetic unfolding of the human life cycle replete with psychosocial crises, or challenges, and opportunities for revitalization. Helen Merrel Lynd (1961) posited a psychology of abundance to replace what she saw as the psychology of economic scarcity.

In addition, Maslow (1937) delineated the concept of self-actualization, and Karen Horney (1939) portrayed anxiety and inner strivings as the positive sign of a continuously maturing individual. Moustakas summarized the contributions of Lecky, Angyl, Goldstein, Rank, and others in *The Self: Explorations in Personal Growth* (1956). All of these theorists were expanding on the same themes: the capacity for positive growth and change, the uniqueness of the individual, and the ability of people to shape their own destinies.

Basic Assumptions of the Functional School

Increasingly dissatisfied with the restrictive, pessimistic Freudian view of people, the early functionalists eagerly endorsed the proposition that people are purposeful, change-oriented masters of their own fate. Biological and environmental forces were not ignored in Rankian thought, but these were relegated to a secondary position.

Optimistic Underpinnings. Robinson's milestone work, *A Changing Psychology in Social Casework* (1930), introduced Rankian philosophy to the broader social work community. Robinson presents a positive and hopeful view of individuals creatively using inner and outer experiences and resources to determine their own lives. The functionalists replace the psychology of illness with a belief in human growth, and they replace the obligation to treat with a mandate to serve (Lewis, 1966).

Ruth Elizabeth Smalley (1971), dean of the School of Social Work at the University of Pennsylvania, summarizes the optimistic underpinnings of the functional approach:

The functional school sees the push toward life, health, and fulfillment as primary in human beings, and the human as capable throughout his life of modifying both himself and his environment, in accordance with his own changing purposes with the limitations and opportunities of his own capacity and his own environment. (p. 90)

The individual is the "central, active figure" in the process (Faatz, 1953, p. 47). Functional caseworkers embraced the view that basic human nature is inherently good. Consequently, in a move considered revolutionary, they abandoned "judgmental standards of approval or condemnation of behavior" (Faatz, 1953, p. 22). Caseworkers presumed that change was not only possible, but inevitable, since each individual is endowed with an innate push toward psychological growth and a fuller, more integrated self. As Smalley (1960) suggests, the view sees people "as not only responsible for [their] own future evolution but capable of it" (p. 107).

Role of Will. The primary tenet of functional theory is Rank's revolutionary concept of will and self-determination. This new concept established the foundation on which all else rests. As Taft (1932) explains:

The anxious parent, the angry school teacher, the despairing wife or husband must bear their own burdens, solve their own problems. I can help them only in and for themselves, if they are able to use me. I cannot perform a magic on the bad child, the inattentive pupil, the faithless partner, because they want him made over in their own terms…. Here is a beloved child to be saved, a family unity to be preserved, an important teacher to be enlightened. Before all these problems in which one's reputation, one's pleasure in utilizing professional skill, as well as one's real feeling for the person in distress are perhaps painfully involved, one must accept one's final limitation and the right of the other—perhaps his necessity—to refuse help or to take help in his own terms, not as therapist, friends, or society might choose. My knowledge and my skill avail nothing unless they are accepted and used by the other. (p. 369)

Caseworkers realize that even when change is wanted, it comes with a price—the sacrifice of certainty and security. Accordingly, functionalists understand that people resist change even as they reach for growth. As Taft (1950) explains, "Only at points of growth crisis, where the pressure for further development becomes strong enough to overcome the fear of change and disruption, is the ordinary individual brought to the necessity of enlarging his hard-won integration" (p. 5).

The Value Base of Functionalism. As the preceding quotation illustrates, casework implies a collateral relationship marked by mutuality. Further, functionalists maintain that one person cannot change another, for the other is also endowed with will. Early writers did not specifically address issues related to sociocultural or ethnic sensitivity; they considered each person as a unique human being with distinct needs and particular gifts to contribute to the casework experience.

Putsch (1966), recounting her participation in the civil rights movement in Georgia, affirms this philosophy. Her agency had worked hard to develop an atmosphere in which people of many different colors and convictions could work out a more satisfying way of living together. Putsch reflects, "As I had learned from my own experience, when we know too surely what is right we are impatient of difference and miss the opportunity for attaining full understanding through considering different viewpoints" (p. 95).

Significant others and environmental pressures and resources are considered from Lewin's (1951) perspective; that is, they are elements in the topography of an individual's life space. They are part of the problem if they inhibit growth, and they are part of the solution is they allow or promote change. Although the functionalists accepted the common premise that people are subject to the physical laws of nature, their belief in growth suggests that a harmony with nature is possible and desirable. People were encouraged to use natural resources, but individual responsibility was stressed.

The functionalists always focus on the present time, and this "now" orientation is a hallmark of the functional theory. The past is explored only to the extent that it impinges on current concerns. The future is projected only as a guide for present activities. Aware that the future is always uncertain, caseworkers help people learn to live in the present, making the best of themselves with the resources that are currently available.

The overarching goal of casework is the exercise of free will moderated by responsibility; however, functional caseworkers never speculate on the type of change anticipated or desired, for setting goals is considered the prerogative of the client. The role of the caseworker is to help the client obtain and use whatever tools are needed to forge the future. Recognizing the limitations inherent in the situation, only the client can determine what that future can and should be.

Major Concepts of Functional Social Work Practice

Smalley (1971) summarizes three basic assumptions that, when combined with the concept of self-determination, describe functional social work practice. These three concepts, paraphrased below, were derived from Rankian methods, but they have been modified and expanded. They are applicable in private and public settings, with individuals, families, and communities.

Understanding the Nature of Humanity. The functional group works from a psychology of growth, which occurs in the context of relationship. The impetus for change lies with the client, not the worker. Taking social and cultural factors into account, the worker helps clients release their own potential for choice and growth through the power of the relationship. The functionalists use the term "helping" rather than "treatment" to describe this method.

Understanding the Purpose of Social Casework. The agency gives focus, direction, and content to the worker's practice. By so doing, the agency protects both the worker and the client. Casework is not a form of psychosocial treatment; it is a method for administering a specific social service.

Understanding the Concept of Process in Social Casework. Casework is a helping process through which agency services are made available. Workers take the lead in initiating, sustaining, and terminating the process; however, they enter the relationship without classifying the client, prescribing a particular treatment, or assuming responsibility for an anticipated outcome. Together, the work and client discover what can be done with the help offered (pp. 79–81).

Treatment Through Functional Social Work Methods

Functional social work is an insight-oriented therapy. Although its primary method is colloquy, proponents focus on the casework relationship, which offers an opportunity to reject old patterns in favor of new approaches that promote growth. In addition to the basic presuppositions listed above, Smalley (1967) captures the mature tenets of the functional school in the five generic principles, paraphrased here:

Diagnosis should be related to the use of agency services. It should be developed jointly, modified as needed, and shared with the client.

Time in the social work process—beginnings, middles, and endings—should be fully exploited for the use of the client.

Agency function gives focus, content, and direction to social work processes, ensures accountability by society, and engages the client in the process characterized by partialization, concreteness, and differentiation.

Conscious use of structure furthers the effectiveness of social work processes by using a myriad of elements such as application forms, agency policy, and the physical setting to define and delimit service.

All effective social work processes take place within *relationship*. The purpose of the relationship is to help clients make propitious choices.

Functional therapy flows directly from these key tenets. Because they are vital to the helping process, each is described and examined in greater detail.

Diagnosis. Functionalists eschew diagnosis as an objective of data collection (Austin, 1938). Diagnosis is considered important only when naming a condition helps a client to modify it. In the same vein, history is important only as it encroaches on the present, and early childhood experiences are analyzed only when the client and caseworker agree that they may be contributing to the current difficulty. The assessment process is a joint endeavor (Dawley, 1937), and it constitutes the first phase of therapy.

Relationship and the Process of Change. Instead of focusing on diagnosis, the functionalists stress relationship and the process of change. These two are considered to be inseparable, for all change takes place within the context of relationship. The act of giving and taking help is a dynamic process that occurs over time (Hofstein, 1964). Further, the process is "never static, never finished, always chiefly significant for its inner quality and movement, for its meaning to those it engages, rather than for its form or status or outcome at any instance of time" (Pray, 1949, p. 238).

Since every human being is unique, each person develops a distinct pattern for handling critical experiences. The pattern is initiated during the first separation, or beginning, which Rank called the birth trauma; it is reinforced through subsequent opportunities for change. The nature of the relationship with others determines whether an experience will produce or limit growth. For example, when early relationships with the mother are positive and constructive, the will learns to accept the inevitability of separation and to adapt to the limitations of reality. If early experiences with the mother are negative or destructive, the will develops a pattern of refusing to accept separation. This usually results in repeated and futile attempts to complete the self through the other person in the relationship.

To the functionalists, the concepts of will, counter-will, and resistance are not only inevitable but also necessary for "movement," a functional term connoting change or growth. Conflict is considered inherent in human growth as individual wants and needs clash with the wants and needs of other people and with society. The counter-will, or negative aspect of will, opposes the will of others and resists reality as presented by society. The counter-will carries with it a connotation of guilt. Resistance, a natural attempt to maintain the self, is inevitable in the beginning casework relationship. Resistance is not seen as a problem or deficit; rather, it is considered a sign of strength indispensable to new growth.

The term "transference" is rarely used in functional literature. Taft (1933/1962) explains,

"Transference, like resistance, is accepted for what it is, a stage in the growth process, in taking over of the own will into the self" (p. 97). Caseworkers assume that clients want to make themselves known and the only way they can do this is to project their desires, fears, and conflicts onto the worker (Robinson, 1942). A competent worker must be sensitive enough to identify with these projections without getting lost in them (Aptekar, 1941). Throughout the course of therapy, the caseworker establishes and maintains sufficient separateness from the client that neither confuses the self with the other. The worker's identification with agency function helps preserve this necessary separation.

Regardless of how negative previous experiences may have been, people have an opportunity to embrace growth and attain potential through the casework relationship. The therapeutic process consists of a beginning, a middle, and an ending phase. From the beginning, the caseworker displays a consistent attitude of respect and an unwavering belief that clients can change. The worker also creates an atmosphere in which clients feel safe and free to be themselves. The worker presents both reality and acceptance, creating for the client a "situation so safe, so reassuring that none of his defenses is needed and, therefore, fall away, leaving his underlying fears, loves and jealousies free to express themselves" (Robinson, 1962, p. 113).

During the middle phase of therapy, movement occurs as clients take increasing responsibility for their own actions. Caseworkers offer something new—either a new view of the situation or a new grip on it (Lewis, 1966), and relationships deepen as caseworkers continue to build on client strengths. Clients practice new behaviors with the caseworker and through this rehearsal gain a heightened sense of accomplishment and power.

Endings are feared and welcomed, for they embody both the emptiness of loss and the pride of accomplishment. During termination, the client and therapist recapitulate goals, assess movement, and summarize gains. When therapy has been successful, endings signal a rebirth of the client, now armed with courage, confidence, and a capacity for other healthy unions. Yet, termination also signals the end of the powerful alliance that gave the client this new life.

Thus, the ending is marked by sadness and joy, emptiness and fullness, security and challenge.

Some terminations are established by agency function, as when a patient leaves the hospital. More often, however, endings are introduced by the caseworker to help the client consolidate gains and move along independently. The technique of setting time limits is another hallmark of the functional approach.

Use of Time

Time is a critical element in functional casework, for it is the only medium through which help can be offered and received. Faatz (1953), who has written extensively about the nature of choice in casework, emphasizes the importance of the immediate present—the here and now—as the only setting in which change can actually occur. In this, Faatz anticipates systems theory, noting that emotions and events experienced during the therapeutic hour can influence and change the remainder of a client's life.

As Taft (1932) writes, "Time represents more vividly than any other category the necessity of accepting limitation as well as the inability to do so, and symbolizes therefore the whole problem of living" (p. 375). Taft elaborates on this precept with examples from therapy. She explains that the person who arrives very early bears responsibility for self and other, while the person who arrives very late is abdicating responsibility. By addressing these problems in the therapeutic hour, the therapist enables the client to live that one hour fully and thus conquer the secret of all hours.

There is no predetermined or ideal duration of treatment. For some people, a few sessions may suffice, while for others, therapy may continue for an extended period of time. Functional therapists frequently establish time limits in order to facilitate movement, a technique that has been misunderstood. Time limits may be derived from natural time periods, such as a school year or a season. The limits may be recommended by agency function, or they may evolve from therapeutic needs. Regardless of the origin, appropriate limits are never rigid or arbitrary; instead, they are derived from the situation. Appropriate time limits become an incentive to use the present productively and wisely.

Agency Function and the Conscious Use of Structure

The concept that may be the most relevant to social work involves the use of agency function and structure in the helping process. It was Taft (1937), not Rank, who first identified the importance of agency function. Taft viewed therapy as too unreal and public relief as too real. The concept of agency function enabled early caseworkers to find a productive place "between pure therapy and public therapy" (p. 11). Taft's introduction of agency function as the unifying theme in social work practice gave functional social work its moniker.

The principle is simple: the creative, positive acceptance of agency parameters can have significant philosophical and psychological benefits for both caseworker and client (Taft, 1937). In the conscious decision to work within the parameters of a specific agency, the worker accepts a circumscribed area of service. The caseworker's responsibility is mediated by what the agency can and cannot do. Worker attitude is important. The caseworker must not sink into resignation, chafe publically at limitations, revolt, or secretly resolve to overlook rules. When caseworkers recognize, accept, and use limitations, agency function becomes one of their most valuable tools.

Agency function is also a valuable tool for clients. When clients choose to accept agency limitations, they identify with the social purpose of the agency. Personal risk is minimized, for clients need not submit to an entire personality reconstruction. Rather, they can ask with help with specific concerns and know that their request will be respected. Through the casework relationship, clients learn to use limits to deal responsibility with reality in the pursuit of personal goals.

The structure and forms of service arise from the function of the agency. Agency policy is the primary authority that determines all other forms and structures. As we have seen, time is used deliberately. All forms and structures are consciously designed for the maximum effectiveness of all social work processes. Every item—from intake procedures, application forms, and assessment to termination rituals—is planned (Bellet, 1938). Even the setting—the structure of place—is considered important in defining and delimiting agency function. Because change is constant, forms and structures are reassessed regularly to ensure congruence with intent.

The relationship between freedom of choice and agency function is clear when a client voluntarily applies for service and then freely chooses to accept or reject the help that is offered. This relationship is less clear when the client participation is involuntary. Pray (1949), whose experience was primarily in the field of corrections, has written extensively about this apparent dilemma, and he argues that freedom and authority are not mutually exclusive. Pray identifies two conditions essential for success in an authoritarian setting. First, the authority must reflect the will of society, not the will of an individual. Second, within the setting, the captive client must be free to reject the service that is offered. Only by being free to reject can a client be free to accept and find fulfillment within the bounds (Yelaja, 1971).

Principal Applications of Functional Social Work

Functional methods were initially limited to work with individuals. In fact, when the University of Pennsylvania School of Social Work hired its first group worker, Helen Phillips, in the 1940s, the two areas were kept entirely separate (Robinson, 1960). Over time, their similarities became more apparent than their differences (Phillips, 1957). After Work War II, the number of opportunities for group work expanded dramatically (Eisen, 1960).

In her definitive summary, Smalley (1967) indicates that functional methods are effective with many types of groups and a wide variety of problems. Smalley cites case materials from a leisure-time group of adult women being served by a Jewish community center and from a therapy group of chronically mentally ill men in a psychiatric hospital. Although she acknowledges that specific knowledge and skill are required in these applications, she combines these dissimilar examples with case notes from a community organization to illustrate the five generic principles previously described.

Eisen (1960) reiterates the commonalities between group work and casework, adding that the group worker must also possess not only special knowledge about the impact of the group process on individuals, but also special skill in using group interaction. Eisen underscores the range of services that can be provided in functional groups, listing four types of groups that might be formed in an inpatient unit for the chronically mentally ill. These are special purpose groups, such as an orientation for new patients; a unit group for patient governance; peer groups for support and leisure activities; and community-focused programs.

The power in the group or community is essentially the same as the power in the individual (Smalley, 1967). Each is in process, striving toward self-fulfillment or purpose. Whether the goal is personal adjustment or social agitation, the worker facilitates the process through a helping relationship that is clearly delimited by agency controls. As Eisen (1960) explains, "Our service should be geared to helping patients overcome their disabilities, enhancing their capacity for group and self-direction. Toward this end, the group process becomes an individual experience" (p. 114).

The earliest writings acknowledge the importance of families (Taft, 1930) and address parent–child interactions, especially as related to abuse, neglect, and incompetence (Mayer, 1956). However, functional principles were not systematically applied to the family as a unit until the early 1960s. The process was initially called family casework.

Rappaport (1960) was an early proponent of family-focused service. Recognizing that family problems are often rooted in the problems of society, she calls for "more vibrant and vital ways of helping" families with multiple problems, and she recommends social action and coordination of resources as well as the application of functional principles to family practice (p. 86).

Berl (1964) also affirms the relationship between family and society and notes that the major challenges of family casework involve a dynamic balance between the elements necessary for successful functioning, the integration of knowledge and practice, and systematic progress toward health and growth. He recommends the application of functional methods to prevention and crisis intervention, to treatment settings and education institutions, and to society at large. The field of family casework evolved slowly, however, for in 1967 Smalley presents generic principles for functional casework, group work, and community organization, but she does not mention family work.

Whether practiced with individuals, dyads, families, groups, or communities, functional social work is most appropriate for client systems seeking solutions to problems they have identified and embraced. Functional casework is especially effective for people seeking personal growth. It provides an insight-oriented process appropriate for children and adults (Taft, 1930). Neither formal education nor high intelligence is a prerequisite, and individuals with cognitive limitations can benefit if they have the capacity for reflection. The only qualifications needed to benefit from this method are an ability and willingness to engage in the process of self-examination and change.

Because the worker and client explore the process of change together, functional methods are applicable whether the participants have similar or dissimilar backgrounds. The first tasks of the worker are to establish rapport and acquire a rich understanding of the situation from the perspective of the client. Through this exploration, the worker comes to appreciate and value both similarities and differences in racial/ethnic heritage, culture, background, tradition, and experience. The recognition and affirmation of difference is reinforced in supervision, a process that scrutinizes client–worker differences so that workers can maintain appropriate roles and separate their personal needs and goals from those of the client.

Proponents identify few limitations or contraindications; however, functional methods alone are not sufficient for clients who also require medical or pharmaceutical intervention. Functional practice is rarely effective with people who have psychotic disorders; dementia; or antisocial, paranoid, schizoid, or borderline personality disorders. With specific populations or problems, functional methods may require adaptations to be developed by the worker (Smalley, 1971).

Since participation is entirely voluntary, risks are few. When a client's problems lie outside the agency's function, workers are obliged to refer the client to a more appropriate venue where help can be obtained.

This method can be successfully applied to even the most complex problems, including psychosocial crises, introspective concerns, interpersonal conflicts, environmental issues, and social strife.

Administrative and Training Factors

The University of Pennsylvania School of Social Work developed the first master's program in this method around 1934 under the leadership of Taft (Robinson, 1960). From that point forward, caseworkers were expected to obtain the master's degree before they were allowed to provide therapy to clients. Educators assumed that these professional social workers would become leaders and administrators in their employing agencies (Pray, 1938), but no requisite knowledge or skill—other than the functional method—was identified.

Supervision is a critical element in training students and overseeing experienced workers (Faith, 1960), for before workers can help others, they must become aware of and manage their own inner and outer conflicts. Intrapersonal material, in addition to case content, constitutes the substance of supervision (Robinson, 1936).

The supervisory relationship is considered a special derivative of the therapeutic relationship, for it includes all the controls of the therapeutic alliance plus the needs of a third system. Sometimes the third entity is the agency and sometimes it is the client (Robinson, 1949). In either case, effective supervision is indispensable, for it binds people to agency function. It also prevents the condition often called burnout.

Hughes (1938) acknowledged that not all agency employees have professional training. In functional agencies, paraprofessional workers and volunteers are still required to uphold functional principles. As Hughes explained, "Lack of skill in knowing how to use our function helpfully is costly to the agency in time, in money, and in human misery" (p. 73).

Empirical Base

Single case studies have been conducted using agency records, but they often contain only idiosyncratic process recordings. These investigations focus more on product than process, since by definition goals are set by the client and can change during the course of therapy. They add little information about the overall effectiveness of functional methods.

Marcus (1966) maintained that functional principles are drawn from a substantive scientific base, and Smalley (1962, 1967) stressed the fact that casework students were consistently trained in research methods. De Schweinitz (1960) urged the university community to collaborate with practitioners. Lewis (1962) exhorted agencies to add the function or research analysis to agency services. Both Lewis and Smalley (1967) suggested engaging a research specialist, as Mencher (1959) recommended. Sprafkin (1964) accepted this challenge but reported on the process, not the outcome. Despite the attempt to embrace the scientific method, functional social work would not meet the rigorous inquiry standards or statistical analysis that has been developed during the past 20 years.

Prospectus

This chapter described the lively and dramatic debate that shaped social work practice during the first half of the 20th century. At its zenith, functional social work was practiced and taught at the Universities of Pennsylvania, North Carolina, and Southern California; the Graduate School for Jewish Social Work; and, briefly, at the New York School of Social Work (Robinson, 1978). The 16th edition of the *Encyclopedia of Social Work* devoted 12 pages to the functional method (Smalley, 1971), but by 1977, that number had already dropped to 11 pages (Smalley & Bloom, 1977). By the 19th edition in 1995, the topic had been dropped completely.

Currently, no graduate schools of social work in the United States teach the functional methods as a unitary approach, and few institutions explore the historical roots of this tradition; however, a few historians and psychoanalysts have rediscovered Otto Rank (Lieberman, 1985; Menaker, 1982; Rudnytsky, 1991; Timms, 1997). With passing reference to functional authors, a number of articles have encouraged a return to relationship as the context for helping and change (Ganzer, 2007; Reupert, 2006; Sudbery, 2002; Trevithick, 2003). Timms (1997) has recommended a reevaluation of functional social work.

In fact, the revolutionary concepts that engendered such controversy have been modified, adapted, and ultimately subsumed into the major theories of social work today. Theorists have incorporated once-heretical ideas—such as freedom of choice and self-determination, the human potential for change, and the use of time and agency constraints as treatment elements—without reference to their stormy origins in the functional school. In the 1950s, Helen Harris Perlman developed the "problem-solving casework model." For some, this approach represented a synthesis of the diagnostic and functional schools. This systematic approach appears today in the form of cognitive therapies and evidence-based practice (Pozzuto & Arnd-Caddigan, 2008).

Carl Rogers (1951), who studied Rank extensively, championed unconditional positive regard and an emphasis on the importance of the authentic relationship in which change or healing could occur. These concepts inform self-help groups, transactional analysis, Gestalt therapy, and group therapies (Berlin, 2005). Reality therapists regularly promote the functional limits of an agency (Glasser, 1965), and the empowerment movement was built on client strengths and capacities for change within the context of community (Saleebey, 1992). Today, few clinicians acknowledge the functional roots undergirding their modern methods.

Economic conditions today resemble those found in the 1920s and 1930s in the United States. As then, economic necessities compel agencies to maintain services strictly within budget realities. Communities wish to avert suffering, especially for children, but they do not have resources. To this end, elected officials are reviewing mandates, setting limits on allotments, and demanding personal responsibility. An understanding and intentional use of agency function can ensure accountability to society and the attainment of social work objectives (Smalley, 1967). A deeper awareness of historical antecedents can enable the profession to meet the needs of a changing environment with greater efficiency and increased effectiveness.

Acknowledgment

This chapter is dedicated to my teacher and mentor, Dr. Alan Keith-Lucas (Feb. 5, 1910–Aug. 5, 1995). A graduate of Western Reserve University in the diagnostic tradition, Dr. Keith-Lucas was brought to the University of North Carolina to "clean up that functional mess." Instead, he joined forces with the functionalists, and for more than 50 years his ideas and influence shaped social work services and group child care in North Carolina and the Southeast.

References

Allport, G. W. (1955). *Becoming*. New Haven: Yale University Press.

Aptekar, H. H. (1941). *Basic concepts in social case work*. Chapel Hill: University of North Carolina Press.

Aptekar, H. H. (1955). *The dynamics of casework and counseling*. Boston: Houghton Miflin.

Austin, L. N. (1938). Evolution of our case-work concepts. *Proceedings of the National Conference of Social Work*. Chicago: University of Chicago Press, 99–111.

Barlett, H. M., with Saunders, B. N. (1970). *The common base of social work practice*. Washington, DC: National Association of Social Workers.

Bellet, I. S. (1938). The application desk. *Journal of Social Work Process, 2*(1), 32–43.

Berl, F. (1964). Family casework—Dialectics of problem, process, and task. *Journal of Social Work Process, 14*, 55–76.

Berlin, S. B. (2005). The value of acceptance in social work direct practice: A historical and contemporary view. *Social Service Review, 79*(3), 482–510.

Corner, G. W. (1944). *Ourselves unborn*. New Haven: Yale University Press.

Dawley, A. (1937). Diagnosis—the dynamic of effective treatment. *Journal of Social Work Process 1*(1), 19–31.

De Schweinitz, K. (1960). The past as a guide to the function and pattern of social work. In W. W. Weaver (Ed.), *Frontiers for social work: A colloquium of the Fiftieth Anniversary of the School of Social Work of the University of Pennsylvania* (pp. 59–94). Philadelphia: University of Pennsylvania Press.

Drucker, P. (1959). *Landmarks of tomorrow*. New York: Harper & Row.

Eisen, A. (1960). Utilization of the group work method in the social service department of a mental hospital. *Journal of Social Process, 11*, 106–114.

Erikson, E. H. (1940). Problems of infancy and early childhood. In *Cyclopedia of medicine* (pp. 714–730). Philadelphia: Davis.

Faatz, A. J. (1953). *The nature of choice in casework process.* Chapel Hill: University of North Carolina Press.

Faith, G. B. (1960). Facing current questions in relation to supervision—How shall we value the uses of supervision. *Journal of Social Work Process,* 11, 122–129.

Ganzer, C. (2007). The use of self from a relational perspective. *Clinical Social Work Journal,* 35, 117–123.

Glasser, W. (1965). *Reality therapy: A new approach to psychiatry.* New York: Harper & Row.

Hamilton, G. (1936). *Social case recording.* New York: Columbia University Press.

Hamilton, G. (1937a). Basic concepts in social case work. *The Family,* 43(5), 147–156.

Hamilton, G. (1937b). Basic concepts in social case work. *Proceedings of the National Conference of Social Work* (pp. 1938–1949). Chicago: University of Chicago Press.

Hofstein, S. (1964). The nature of process: Its implications for social work. *Journal of Social Process,* 14, 13–53.

Hollis, F. (1939). *Social case work in practice: Six case studies.* New York: Family Welfare Association of America.

Hollis, F. (1970). The psychosocial approach to the practice of casework. In R. W. Roberts & R. H. Nee (Eds.), *Theories of social casework.* Chicago: University of Chicago Press.

Hollis, F., & Woods, M. E. (1981). *Casework: A psychosocial therapy* (3rd ed.). New York: Random House.

Horney, K. (1939). *New ways in psychoanalysis.* New York: W. W. Norton.

Hughes, S. S. (1938). Interpreting function to the visitor. *Journal of Social Work Process,* 2(1), 61–73.

Kadushin, A. (1959). The knowledge base of social work. In A. J. Kahn (Ed.), *Issues in American social work.* New York: Columbia University Press.

Karpf, F. B. (1953). *The psychology and psychotherapy of Otto Rank: An historical and comparative introduction.* Westport, CT: Greenwood Press, 1970.

Kasius, C. (Ed.) (1950). *A comparison of diagnostic and functional casework concepts.* New York: Family Service Association of America.

Klein, D. B. (1981). *Jewish origins of the psychoanalytic movement.* New York: Praeger.

Kuhn, T. S. (1970). *The structure of scientific revolutions* (2nd ed.). Chicago: University of Chicago Press.

Lewin, K. (1935). *A dynamic theory of personality* (D. K. Adams & K. E. Zener, Trans.). New York: McGraw-Hill.

Lewin, K. (1951). *Field theory in social science* (D. Cartwright, Ed.). New York: Harper & Row.

Lewis, H. (1962). Research analysis as an agency function. *Journal of Social Work Process,* 13, 71–85.

Lewis, H. (1966). The functional approach to social work practice—A restatement of assumptions and principles. *Journal of Social Work Process,* 15, 115–133.

Lieberman, E. J. (1985). *Act of will: The life and work of Otto Rank.* New York: Free Press.

Lynd, H. M. (1961). *On shame and the search for identify.* New York: Harcourt, Brace and World.

Marcus, G. (1966). The search for social work knowledge. *Journal of Social Work Process,* 15, 17–33.

Maslow, A. H. (1937). Personality and patterns of culture. In R. Stagner (Ed.), *Psychology of personality.* New York: McGraw-Hill.

Mayer, E. R. (1956). Some aspects of casework help young retarded adults and their families. *Journal of Social Work Process,* 7, 29–48.

Mead, G. H. (1936). *Movement of thought in the nineteenth century.* Chicago: University of Chicago Press.

Menaker, E. (1982). *Otto Rank: A rediscovered legacy.* New York: Columbia University Press.

Menaker, E. (1984). The ethical and the empathic in the thinking of Otto Rank. *American Imago,* 41(4), 343–351.

Mencher, S. (1959). *The research method in social work education: A project report of the Curriculum Study,* Vol. 9. New York: Council on Social Work Education.

Meyer, C. H. (1970). *Social work practice: A response to urban crisis.* New York: Free Press.

Moustakas, E. C. (Ed.) (1956). *The self-exploration in personal growth.* New York: Harper & Row.

Murphy, J. P. (1933). Certain philosophical contributions to children's case work. *Proceedings of the National Conference of Social Work* (pp. 75–90). Chicago: University of Chicago Press.

Phillips, H. U. (1957). *Essential of Social Group Work Skills.* New York: Association Press.

Pozzuto, R., & Arnd-Caddigan, M. (2008). Social work in the US: Sociohistorical context and contemporary issues. *Australian Social Work,* 61(1), 57–71.

Pray, K. L. M. (1938). New emphasis in education for public social work. *Journal of Social Work Process,* 2(1), 88–100.

Pray, K. L. M. (1949). *Social work in a revolutionary age.* Philadelphia: University of Pennsylvania Press.

Progoff, I. (1956). *The death and rebirth of psychology: An integrative evaluation of Freud, Adler, Jung and Rank and the impact of their insights on modern man.* New York: McGraw-Hill.

Putsch, L. (1966). The impact of racial demonstrations on a social agency in the Deep South. *Journal of Social Process,* 15, 81–100.

Rank, O. (1924/1973). *The trauma of birth*. New York: Harper & Row.

Rank, O. (1925). Der Kunstler (The Artist) (4th Ed.) (E. Solomon & E. J. Lieberman, Trans.). *Journal of the Otto Rank Association,* 15(1), 1–63.

Rank, O. (1928/1964). *Will therapy* (J. J. Taft, Trans.). New York: Alfred A. Knopf.

Rank, O. (1930). Literary autobiography. *Journal of the Otto Rank Society,* 16(1-2), 1–38.

Rank, O. (1932). *Art and artist: Creative urge and personality development* (C. E. Atkinson, Trans.). New York: Agathon Press.

Rank, O. (1936/1964). *Truth and reality* (J. J. Taft, Trans.). New York: Alfred A. Knopf.

Rank, O. (1941). *Beyond psychology*. Philadelphia: Privately published (Printed by Haddon Craftsmen, Camden, NJ).

Rappaport, M. F. (1960). Clarifying the service to families with many problems. *Journal of Social Work Process,* 11, 77–87.

Reupert, A. (2006). Social worker's use of self. *Clinical Social Work Journal,* 35, 107–116.

Roberts, R. W., & Nee, R. H. (Eds.) (1970). *Theories of social casework*. Chicago: University of Chicago Press.

Robinson, V. P. (1930). *A changing psychology in social casework*. Chapel Hill: University of North Carolina Press.

Robinson, V. P. (1936). *Supervision in social casework*. Chapel Hill: University of North Carolina Press.

Robinson, V. P. (1942). The meaning of skill. *Journal of Social Work Process,* 4, 7–31.

Robinson, V. P. (1949). *The dynamics of supervision under functional controls: A professional process in social casework*. Philadelphia: University of Pennsylvania Press.

Robinson, V. P. (1960). University of Pennsylvania school of Social Work in Perspective: 1909–1959. *Journal of Social Work Process,* 11, 10–29.

Robinson, V. P. (Ed.) (1962). *Jessie Taft: Therapist and social work educator*. Philadelphia: University of Pennsylvania Press.

Robinson, V. P. (1978). *The development of a professional self: Teaching and learning in professional helping processes, selected writings, 1930–1968*. New York: AMS Press.

Rogers, C. R. (1951). *Client-centered therapy: Its current practice, implications, and theory*. New York: Houghton Mifflin.

Rudnytsky, P. L. (Ed.) (1984). Otto Rank: A centennial tribute. *American Imago,* 1(4).

Rudnytsky, P. L. (1991). *Rank, Winnicott, and the legacy of Freud*. New Haven: Yale University Press.

Saleebey, D. (1992). *The strengths perspective in social work practice*. New York: Longman.

Sinnott, E. W. (1950). *Cell and psyche*. New York: Harper & Row.

Smalley, R. E. (1960). Today's frontiers in social work education. In W. W. Weaver (Ed.), *Frontiers for social work: A colloquium on the fiftieth anniversary of the School of Social Work on the University of Pennsylvania* (pp. 95–125). Philadelphia: University of Pennsylvania Press.

Smalley, R. E. (1962). The advanced curriculum in the University of Pennsylvania School of Social Work. *Journal of Social Work Process,* 7, 1–16.

Smalley, R. E. (1967). *Theory for social work practice*. New York: Columbia University Press.

Smalley, R. E. (1971). Social casework: The functional approach. In R. E. Morris (Ed.), *Encyclopedia of social work* (16th ed., Vol. 2, pp. 1195–1206). New York: National Association of Social Workers.

Smalley, R. E., & Bloom, R. (1977). Social casework: The functional approach. In J. B. Turner (Ed.), *Encyclopedia of social work* (17th ed., Vol. 2). Washington, DC: National Association of Social Workers.

Sprafkin, B. R. (1964). Introducing research into a family service agency. *Journal of Social Process,* 14, 117–132.

Sudbery, J. (2002). Key features of therapeutic social work: the use of relationship. *Journal of Social Work Practice* 16(2), 149–162.

Sward, K. (1980-1981). Self-actualization and women: Rank and Freud contrasted. *Journal of the Otto Rank Association,* 15(2), 49–63.

Taft, J. J. (1930). The "catch" in praise. *Child Study,* 7(8), 133–135, 150.

Taft, J. J. (1932). The time element in mental hygiene therapy as applied to social case work. *Proceedings of the National Conference of Social Work* (pp. 368–381). Chicago: University of Chicago Press.

Taft, J. J. (1933). *The dynamics of therapy in a controlled relationship*. New York: Macmillan.

Taft, J. J. (1937). The relation of function to process in social case work. *Journal of Social Work Process,* 1(1), 1–19.

Taft, J. J. (1950). A conception of the growth process underlying social casework practice. *Social Casework,* 31(8), 311–318.

Taft, J. J. (1958). *Otto Rank: A biographical study based on notebooks, letters, collected writings, therapeutic achievements, and personal associations*. New York: Julian Press.

Timms, N. (1997). Taking social work seriously: The contribution of the functional school. *British Journal of Social Work, 27,* 723–737.

Trevithick, P. (2003). Effective relationship-based practice: A theoretical exploration. *Journal of Social Work Practice,* 17(2), 163–176.

Yelaja, S. A. (1971). *Authority and social work: Concept and use.* Toronto: University of Toronto Press.

Yelaja, S. A. (1986). Functional theory for social work practice. In F. J. Turner (Ed.), *Social work treatment: Interlocking theoretical approaches* (3rd ed., pp. 46–67). New York: Free Press.

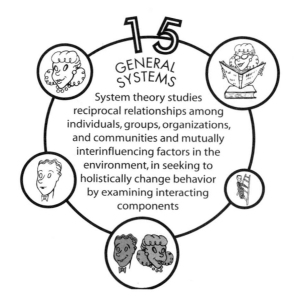

General Systems Theory: Contributions to Social Work Theory and Practice

Dan Andreae

The purpose of this chapter is to illustrate the relevance, applicability, and contributions of general systems theory (GST) to social work practice whether working with individuals, marital couples or other paired relationships, families, groups, organizations, and communities. By understanding the elements of GST, as well as its history, philosophy, principles, and techniques, social workers will be in a position to utilize this approach in a variety of settings and circumstances. The first section of this chapter will outline the concepts associated with GST and the second part will apply it specifically to family systems and interpersonal dynamics.

Social workers have a variety of treatment modalities at their disposal in order to effect change and promote optimal functioning. These could include such approaches as psychoanalytically oriented interventions, behavioral treatment models, client-centered therapy techniques or brief therapy procedures, to name but a few possibilities. Regardless of the particular methodology or combination of approaches employed, social workers possess an in-depth understanding of the relationship of the individual to various environments and the synergistic relationship that each entity has to the other. It is this contextual understanding of the holistic nature of human functioning that is unique to social work practice as opposed to most other helping professions, which tend to adopt a more individual-centered perspective to treatment. Social workers are taught to recognize that all parts of any system are interrelated, interconnected, and interdependent and therefore it is imperative to take into account the influence of various systems and subsystems on client functioning.

Definition

Of all the theoretical paradigms utilized by social workers, GST perhaps most clearly articulates this reality. Systems theories involve concepts that emphasize reciprocal relationships between the elements that constitute a whole. These concepts also focus on the relationships among individuals, groups, organizations, or communities and mutually influencing factors in the environment (National Association of Social Workers [NASW], 2003, p. 428). According to Gordon Hearn in *Social Work Treatment: Interlocking Theoretical Approaches*, edited by Dr. Frank Turner (Turner, 1974, p. 343), GST is "a series of related definitions, assumptions and postulates about all levels of systems from atomic particles through atoms, molecules, crystals, viruses, cells, organs, individuals, small groups, societies, plants, solar systems and galaxies. General Systems Behavior Theory is a sub-category of such theory dealing with living systems extending from viruses through societies." According to the fifth edition (NASW, 2003, p. 176) of the dictionary published by the NASW, GST is a conceptual orientation that attempts to emphasize holistically the behavior of people and societies by identifying the interacting components of the system and the controls that keep these components (subsystems) stable and in a state of equilibrium. It is concerned with the boundaries, roles, relationships, and flow of information between people. GST is a subset of systems theory that focuses on living entities from microorganisms to society. Perhaps the most significant fact about living systems is that they are open systems with important inputs and outputs. Laws that apply to them differ from those applying to relatively closed systems.

GST is intended to elaborate properties, principles, and laws that are characteristic of "systems" in general, irrespective of their particular kind, the nature of their elements, and the relations or "forces" between them. A "system" may also be defined as a complex of elements with interactions, these interactions being of an ordered (non-random) nature. Being concerned with formal characteristics or entities called systems, GST is interdisciplinary—that is, it can be employed for phenomena investigated in different traditional branches of scientific research. It is not limited to material systems but applies to any "whole" consisting of interrelating components. GST can be developed in various mathematical languages or vernacular language or can be computerized (von Bertalanffy, 1981, p. 109). According to systems theory the difference between a "collection" and a "system" is that in a collection, the parts remain individually unchanged, whether they be isolated or together—that is, they are simply a sum. In contrast, in a system the parts necessarily become more than the sum of the parts. Systems are not static but dynamic and in a constant state of flux. Not only are systems in constant movement, but also the interfaces between systems are constantly in the process of change (Turner, 1996, p. ix).

Historical Context of GST

GST represents a methodological approach to understanding the world. Since its earliest use in classical astronomy to its subsequent formalization in the metaphysics of Kant and Hegel, the utility of systems theory has been demonstrated in the conceptual breakthroughs of Darwin, Freud, Weber, and particularly Einstein. The wide use of the systems approach since the late 19th century by the physical sciences was fostered by the necessity to overcome the overpowering skepticism that was occurring with sciences whose principles were based upon the naïve conception of simple one-way cause-and-effect ideas. Early in the Enlightenment period, the philosopher David Hume demonstrated that to assume A causes B simply because A and B were in close proximity to each other in time and space was erroneous. He argued that there were no logical or empirical ways to prove that the supposed relationship between variable factors was not spurious (an artifact of our limited reasoning capabilities) (Jenson with Metcalfe, 1971, p. 132).

Certainly the world prior to systems theory was fundamentally mechanistic and reductionist. Complex phenomena were explained by breaking down and analyzing the separate, simpler parts. These increasingly smaller units were investigated in order to understand the cause of larger events. In this simple mechanistic view of the physical universe it made sense to think of linear causality; A causes B, which acts upon C, causing D to occur. Gregory Bateson, who was a cultural anthropologist by training but who had a profound interest in cybernetics (the study of methods of feedback control within a system), provided many of the theoretical underpinnings for the application of systems theory to human relationships. He labeled this stimulus–response paradigm as the billiard ball model: a model that describes a force moving in only one direction and affecting objects in its path, and that called instead for a focus on the ongoing process and development of a new descriptive language that emphasizes the relationship between parts and their effects on one another. Therefore, according to Bateson, A may evoke B—but it is also true that B evokes A. Shifting to a perspective that emphasizes circular causality helps to conceptualize, for example, a family's behavior in current transactional terms, as a network of circular loops in which every member's behavior affects everyone else. People mutually affect one another and there is no specific behavioral event (Goldenberg & Goldenberg, 1994, p. 40).

Indeed, an essential way in which a system, such as a family, maintains itself as a self-regulating system is through the constant exchange of information fed back into the system. This information automatically triggers necessary changes to keep the system fluid and functional. In systems theory, feedback loops (circles of response from which there is a return flow of information into the system) are operating, and information is being processed through the system. The concept of feedback loops was developed by Norbert Weiner, a mathematician and pioneer in the field of cybernetics who defined feedback as a method of controlling systems by reinserting into it the results of past performance. Stated another way, information about how a system is functioning is looped back (feedback) from the output to the input, thus modifying subsequent input signals. Feedback loops are the circular mechanisms whose purpose is to introduce information about a system's output back to its input in order to alter, correct, or ultimately govern the system's functioning (Goldenberg & Goldenberg, 1994, p. 41). The social work practitioner therefore needs to analyze the various repetitive links that keep the loop locked in place regardless of the system under study (and thus maintain the mutually defeating interaction patterns) that prevent individuals or units who make up the

particular system from moving on to more productive and fulfilling activities.

The importance of systems theory was originally grasped by Ludwig von Bertalanffy (1901–1972), who, as the putative founder of systems theory, understood the organismic connection early in his career. He recognized that a system, whether it be an atom, a cell, a Gestalt pattern, or an integrated universe of symbols, has holistic properties that are not found separately within the parts. Rather, these properties arise from the relations taken on by the parts forming the whole. In the late 1920s, he emphasized under the title of "organismic biology" the necessity of regarding the living organism as an "organized system" and defined the fundamental task of biology as the "discovery of the laws of biological systems at all levels of organization." This led von Bertalanffy in the 1930s and 1940s to develop the concept of GST, which to him represented a complex of component parts or interacting elements that may together form an entity. This new synthetic approach to understanding nature can be defined as "an interdisciplinary doctrine elaborating principles and models that apply to systems in general irrespective of their particular kind, elements and forces involved." Therefore, von Bertalanffy's goal was to achieve a general perspective, a coherent view of the "world as great organization," a framework in which all disciplines could be understood in their place. However, he recognized that such a worldview would not be completed if it did not provide a way of understanding and placing into context the most complex human system of all, the human being (von Bertalanffy, 1981, Introduction XV). According to Irma Stern, GST was conceived as a theory of interdisciplinary scope but it also hopes to develop something like a spectrum of theories—systems of systems (Stein, 1974, p. 7).

According to Stein, precursors of GST include the organismic viewpoint, which reflected the work of Cassirer's philosophy of symbolic form, Piaget (language of learning), and Goldstein (biology of neurophysiology). This emerging paradigm counteracted the mechanistic focus that emphasized parts and processes as opposed to wholes, and organizing relationships among the parts in holistic orientation. Von Bertalanffy postulated that living organisms are organized entities and that the biologist must deal with them as such. It believed that the analytic method of physics was inappropriate to explain the problems of a living organism or a social environment. Therefore, organismic theory introduced concepts that encompassed irreducible wholes in place of physically measurable variables (von Bertalanffy, 1981, p. xv). The second antecedent is the model of an open system, which focused on the idea of a system–environment exchange. Von Bertalanffy perceived this in relation to living animate systems in contrast to an inanimate or closed system. The open system is based on the hierarchical order of systems, the relationships between and within subsystems and their components, systems, and suprasystems and the utilization of intersystem generalization. Because open systems can incorporate and utilize matter, energy, and information from their environment, they have innate capacities for growth and elaboration that are capable of increasing differentiation and specialization (von Bertalanffy, 1981, p. 110).

Historically, the major focus in the behavioral sciences prior to GST had been on individual functioning as reflected in such approaches as psychoanalytic theory, classical behaviorism, and neobehaviorism as well as learning theories. Although each of these psychological paradigms is essentially different, they do share certain commonalities, one being the assumption that the psychological organism is essentially reactive—that is, behavior is to be considered as a response, innate, or learned, to a stimulus. From this perspective all current behavior was seen as a result of a series of outside forces that built upon one another in sequence, ultimately producing the behavior in question (von Bertalanffy, 1981, p. 109).

For the psychoanalyst, such forces are likely to result from early childhood experiences. For the behaviorally oriented social worker, the causes are more likely to be found in the past and present learning experiences and schedules of reinforcement. From the biological perspective, behavior is seen as determined by genetic inheritance. By attending exclusively to the individual, however, these viewpoints failed to examine the contexts in which, as well as the process by which, the current behavior occurs. They fail to understand fully the complexity of what transpires within a system in which the individual is involved. The systems view, by comparison, is more holistic and better attuned to targeted interpersonal relationships and stresses the reciprocity of behaviors between people. Circular causality emphasizes that forces do not simply move in one direction, each caused by the previous event, but rather become part of a causal chain, each event influenced by the other (von Bertalanffy, 1981, p. 110).

Also, the mechanistic view of linear causality was fundamental to the consideration of their goal of psychobiological behavioral phenomena as re-establishment of a disturbed equilibrium (homeostasis); a reduction to tensions arising from unsatisfied drives as postulated by Freud, the gratification of needs as described by the psychologist Hull, or to operant conditioning as hypothesized by B. F. Skinner. The needs, drives, and tensions in question were essentially biological, while the seemingly higher processes in humans were considered secondary and eventually reducible to primary biological factors such as hunger, sex, and survival. For a variety of reasons, this view of humans as automatons proved unsatisfactory to many theorists and practitioners. In the early 20th century an alternative view of human problems and their alleviation began to emerge. There was a growing dissatisfaction with the mechanistic or analytic explanation in various branches of science and mathematics that had a significant impact on psychology and social work. The departure from this paradigm of linear causality in the behavioral sciences is represented in the concepts of developmental psychology as reflected in Piaget's genetic epistemology as well as with neo-Freudian developments such as Carl Rogers' client-centered therapy, Abraham Maslow's self-actualization psychology, the personality theories of Murray Allport, as well as phenomenological and existential approaches. The common features to all of these emerging alternatives is that they did not treat human beings as reactive robots but rather as active personality systems, and recognized that systems are capable of dynamic change and growth as opposed to the homeostatic models of earlier times (Compton & Galaway, 1989, p. 123).

Social workers today, as helping professionals, incorporate several of these progressive modalities into their repertoire of intervention strategies and techniques. These new approaches proved compatible with social work practice, as social workers recognize the necessity of understanding the nature of the person–environment interrelatedness and person–situation transactions. GST provides social work practitioners with a conceptual framework that shifts attention from the cause-and-effect relationship between paired variables (does the environment cause the person to behave in a certain way, or does the person affect the environment in a certain way?) to a person/situation as an interrelated whole. The person is observed as part of his or her total life situation; personal situations are a whole in which each part is interrelated to all other parts in an intricate way through a complex process in which each element is both cause and effect. These dynamic interactions, transactions, and organizational patterns that are critical to the functioning of both the individual and situations are observable only when the entire system is studied. In attempting to understand a problem in social functioning, a social worker cannot achieve understanding simply by adding together as separate entities the assessment of the individual and the assessment of the environment. Rather, the social work practitioner must strive for a full understanding of the complex interactions between the client and all levels of the social and physical system as well as the meaning that the client assigns to each of these interactions (Teevan, 1993, p. 256).

Systems Theory Applied to the Family

Systems theory has been utilized as a model of social work treatment, especially involving a goal-oriented planning process. Pincus and Minchen (1973) developed a systems model and an organizing framework (Devore & Schlesinger, 1996, p. 141). It was intended for application in a diverse range of settings, with the objective being to avoid the often divergent dichotomies between person and environment, clinical practice and social action, and microsystem and macrosystem. According to their perspective, the profession's strength is a recognition of the connections among these factors. There are two basic foundational concepts framing their approach: (1) interaction between people and (2) the local environment. Resources include anything that assists in the achievement of goals, problem solving, alleviation of suffering, and the accomplishment of daily life tasks, as well as realizing and actualizing desires and values. Resources are often utilized in interaction with each other. There is therefore an interdependence among resources both with people and in the community. The former comprise family, neighbors, friends; the latter comprises societal, governmental, voluntary, health, educational, and social welfare services. This systems approach aids in highlighting five key concerns for social work: (1) the lack of resources; (2) the absence of linkages between people and resource systems or between resource systems; (3) problematic interactions between people within the same resource system; (4) problematic interaction between resource systems; and (5) problematic individual internal problem-solving involving corporate resources (Devore & Schlesinger, 1996, p. 131).

One of the major contributions of social work to furthering GST has been in the field of family systems and dynamics. A family traditionally has been defined as two or more people related by blood, marriage, or adoption and who reside together (Nye & Bernardo, 1973; Teevan, 1993; p. 259). However, in a 1990 survey by Seligmann (1992) that randomly selected 1,200 adults who were asked to define the word "family," only 22% selected this conventional definition. Almost three quarters of the people surveyed chose a more expansive definition that defined family as "a group of people who love and care for each other" (Nelson & Fleuras, 1993, p. 289). Social workers treat individuals, many of whom function in dyads and often within family units. Every client, even if living alone, originally grew up in a complex family system and was profoundly affected by his or her involvement.

The composition of the family has undergone significant change in recent decades and now encompasses many different constellations. These include the nuclear family, a family that encompasses only parents and unmarried children; single-parent families, a family consisting of one parent and one or more children; a common-law union—that is, a family including a man and a woman who are not legally married, with or without children; a reconstituted family, consisting of a husband and wife with children from a previous marriage/union of one of the spouses; a blended family, consisting of a husband and wife who are not necessarily married that includes children from one or more marriages/unions; an extended family, which includes more than parents and unmarried children (e.g., grandparents, married children or other relatives living in the same residence); consanguine family, consisting of a family organization in which the primary emphasis is upon the blood relationships of parents and children or brothers and sisters rather than upon the marital relationships of husband and wife; a conjugal family, in which the primary emphasis is placed upon the husband/wife relationship rather than blood relationships; and same-sex couples, consisting of two individuals of the same sex with or without children (Notes from social work lectures, 1995).

Regardless of the form taken by the family unit, it serves certain instrumental and expressive functions for family members, including providing for socialization, safety, certain resources, care, and protection; in most cases, it serves as a source for procreation. The family system represents a subsystem of the larger community, of which the following assumptions may be made:

1. The whole is greater than the sum of its parts.
2. Changing one part of the system will lead to changes in other parts of the system.
3. Families become organized and developed over time. Families are always changing and, over the lifespan, family members assume different roles.
4. Families are generally open systems in that they receive information and exchange it with each other and with people outside the family. Families vary in their degree of openness and closedness, which can vary over time and according to circumstances.
5. Individual dysfunction often reflects an active emotional system. A symptom in one family member is often a way of deflecting tension away from another part of the system and hence represents a relationship problem (Notes from social work lectures, 1995).

Andolfi (1979) notes that family members are studied in terms of their interactions and not merely in terms of their intrinsic personal characteristics. More than a sum of what each family member adds to the whole, it is the ongoing relationship between and among family members, their mutual impact, that requires the attention of a social work practitioner. From a systems perspective, every event within a family is multiply determined by all the various forces operating within that system. This global view, in which the fundamental unit of study is not the individual but rather the system itself, calls for the examination of the family's established behavioral sequences and patterns. Families form representative patterns over time, and it is this patterning over time that is the essence of the family system (Segel & Ben, 1983). As Constantine (1988) points out, the family is a good example of the complexity for the study of which systems theory is most appropriate (Goldenberg & Goldenberg, p. 1994, p. 39).

The family system consists of four major subsystems: (1) spousal in the broadest sense; (2) parent–child; (3) sibling; and (4) the smallest subsystem, the individual (Notes from social work lectures, 1995).

Environmental Influences

The individual as well as all members of the family unit must coexist within different environments, including work, school, church, government institutions, etc. For the purpose of social work practice, "environment" may be defined as "a continuation of people and their interactions and transactions in a particular geographic, socially-defined and constructed space over a particular period of time, both in the individual's and the family's life and in the life of the social and cultural systems" (Germain, 1979; Pincus & Minahen, 1973; Siporin, 1975). The environment, therefore, is us and we are the environment. From the moment of birth, it becomes an intimate part of each individual and presents each person with the material from which people construct their lives through the choices that are made and the social transactions that are engaged in response to the opportunities and deprivations presented to each person (Compton & Galaway, 1989, p. 201). This recognizes that in a stratified society, some people will be afforded better life chances than others due to such factors as a family's social status, level of income, education, geographical location, and access to resources.

The social environment deals with several layers, including that of the individual, group, family, community, institutions, class, and culture. In addition to the social environment, with its various range of systems, the environment also includes large divisions such as the physical. This is divided further into the natural physical environment (i.e., climate) and the constructed environment such as shelter to protect people from various natural phenomena of the environment and various unforeseen climatic events of nature. The environment is temporal, consisting of time and space. Because human life is finite and is lived in certain defined spaces, time and space are critical environmental dimensions. The individual's space can be divided into two subclasses: general and personal. Most human beings construct shelters to protect themselves from the environment but, in doing so, also construct personal and/or family space that gives them a certain privacy from the group. While this construction of shelter and marking of private space may be different from culture to culture, such effort is generally found in all cultures. Most Canadians and Americans see their shelter in relation to time and space. The shelter needs to be readily accessible to one's place of employment or education. Being the private world, it also needs to meet certain other criteria, such as having certain electrical appliances, heat, and perhaps air conditioning as well as a certain level of attractiveness, depending upon individual preference. In evaluation of our private space, we are able to create a demand (through money or other resources), which then intersects with feelings that an individual might have about himself or herself (Compton & Galaway, 1989, p. 101).

There are four key domains of environmental interactions for individuals and families: the situation, micro, meso, and macro levels. The "situation" is that part of the environment that is accessible to the individual's perception at any given moment. Situations play an important part because "it is in actual situations that we encounter and form our conceptions about the world and develop specific kinds of behaviours for dealing with it." Situations present the

information that individuals process and they offer the feedback necessary for building valid conceptions of the outer world. Knowledge about actual situations that an individual has encountered dealing with the accompanying physical, social, and cultural macro-environments will help the social worker to understand behavior at different stages of development (Compton & Galaway, 1989, p. 103).

The micro-level is defined by Magnusson and Allen (1983) as "that part of the total physical and social environment that an individual is in contact with and can interact with directly in daily life during a certain period of time." This level of the environment includes the individual's experience in his or her family and experiences at school, at work, in other social situations or during leisure time so that no other person experiences this environment in a similar way. The micro-environment is very important in the development of the individual and it determines the type of situations that an individual will encounter.

The meso-level is "that part of the environment that in some way or other influences and determines the character and functioning of the micro-environment" (Magnusson & Allen, 1983). It includes relationships between major groups, organizations, and institutions that touch the daily life of the individual, such as school, work, church, recreation, and community resources.

The macro-level is common to most members of groups living in it and involves the physical, social, cultural, economic, and political structures of the larger society in which individuals grow up, including technology, language, housing, laws, customs, and regulations. All of these levels impinge upon each other in a synergistic manner, the whole being reflected or contained in each of the parts and all parts being complementary aspects of the whole. The whole is thus indivisible without sacrificing its essence and context, no more than the human body is divisible into different organ systems without losing its unique essence.

For example, language is an element of the larger macro-system but is also a critical part of each individual. Some of the macro-level environment is part of each individual system. It is often easy for the social worker to overlook the meaning and influence of the macro-system to the smaller system. Some factors in the environment operate at all levels. Most important is the extent to which the environment sets limits on the behavior of individuals and offers opportunities for their development. The actual environment does have an impact on behavior and development, but it is the individual's perception and interaction of that environment that has the most influence. The three environments of which a social work practitioner should be aware of are (1) the actual environment, (2) the environment perceived by the client, and (3) the environment as perceived by the practitioner (Compton & Galaway, 1989, p. 104).

Rules and Roles of the Family

It is important for a social work practitioner to realize that family systems are also governed by rules, for the most part unstated, which have typically been developed and modified through trial and error over a period of time. Such rules (e.g., who has the right to say what to whom, what is expected of males and females, adults versus children) determine what is permitted and what is forbidden within the family, and this in turn serves the necessary function of regulating each member's behavior toward the others. The origin of such rules is embedded in years of explicit and implicit negotiation among family members. The rules themselves become so fine-tuned in most cases that they are taken for granted by all individuals and draw attention only when an effort is made by a member (an early adolescent in many cases) to change the longstanding regulations (Compton & Galaway, 1989, p. 104).

Each family member also engages in different roles within a family system that can change depending on the family dynamics, requirements at the time, and external circumstances. Roles are defined as "actual patterns of interaction with others" (Compton & Galaway, 1989, p. 104). Key concepts associated with roles of which a social worker should be aware include:

1. Role contiguity: whether A's expectations of A's behavior is the same as B's expectations of A's behavior
2. Role competency: whether a person has the skill and knowledge to meet the expectations that he or she or others have of that role (e.g., becoming a parent)
3. Role ambiguity: whether role expectations are explicit—do people have a clear understanding of what is expected of them (e.g., the role of a new stepparent)?
4. Role conflict: a person is in one role with certain expectations but that same person may also be in another role where there are different expectations, and sometimes the expectations of these roles are in conflict with each other (e.g., a mother as well as a full-time student) (Goldenberg & Goldenberg, 1994, p. 51)

Open and Closed Systems

Family systems are open or closed depending upon the degree to which they are organized and interact with the outside environment. An open system receives input such as matter, energy, and information from its surroundings and discharges output into the environment (Tepperman & Rosenberg, 1995, p. 15). Theoretically, closed systems are rarely if ever completely isolated or closed off from the outside. For a family to be truly operating in a closed system, all outside transactions and communications would have to cease to exist, which is highly improbable (Notes from social work lectures, 1995). As mentioned earlier in this chapter, systems of all levels seem to vary from time to time in terms of their openness and closedness. Family systems with which social workers work often seem to be too open or too closed for their own good or the welfare of others. Family systems go through cycles of opening and closing according to their perceptions of the potential security or threat in the impinging environment. Much of social work practice is dedicated to helping the client achieve an optimal degree of openness for the conditions of the moment and the capacity to change this state as conditions alter.

The operation of a closed system is described by Newton's Second Law of Thermodynamics, which holds that a certain quantity called entropy or degree of disorganization within the system tends to increase to a maximum until the process ends in a state of stable equilibrium. Entropy is present in all systems, but in open systems, the opposite process, which general systems theorists have called negentropy, is also present. This occurs because open systems have access to free energy upon which they can organize and build. That systems are open means that they engage in interchanges with the environment, and these exchanges represent an essential factor underlying the system's viability, reproductive capacity, or continuity and its ability to change. The typical response of natural closed systems to an intrusion of environmental events is a loss of organization, or a change in the direction or dissolution of the system (although depending on the nature and strength of the intrusion, the system may sometimes move to a new level of equilibrium). On the other hand, the typical response of open systems to environmental intrusion is elaboration or change of their structure to a higher or more complex plane. Both open and closed systems attain stationary states. In closed systems, it is a state of equilibrium or rest; in open systems, it is a dynamic interplay of forces that gives the appearance of rest but in reality is a steady state or a quasi-stationary equilibrium according to psychologist Kurt Lewin's concepts (Goldenberg & Goldenberg, 1994, p. 43).

Some families with whom social workers interact, such as recent immigrants, are members of insular ethnic groups existing in relative isolation, communicating only among themselves and suspicious of outsiders, thus fostering dependence on the family. Children may be instructed to trust only family members and no one else. Certain cultural groups engage in varying degrees of what is termed institutional completeness, whereby most if not all of their instrumental and expressive needs are met within their own peer group systems. As characterized by Constantine (1986), these familities are regulated predominantly by deviation of attenuating (negative) feedback loops and need to hold onto the traditions and conventions of the past and thus avoid change. Sauber (1983) describes such families as maintaining strict taboos regarding who and what should be admitted into the household, restricting the introduction of news and certain kinds of music, and screening visitors. New information and new outlooks are seen as threatening to the status quo in closed systems. As Kantor and Lehr (1975) describe them, closed family systems

enforce strict rules and a hierarchical and often patriarchal structure that causes individual members to subordinate their needs to the welfare of the group. Family loyalty is paramount; rules are absolute; traditions must be observed. Deviation in behavior can lead only to chaos from this perspective. As White (1978) describes closed family systems, parents see to it that doors are kept locked and family reading material and television programs are screened, children are expected to report their comings and goings scrupulously, and rigid daily schedules are adhered to as closely as possible. The stability of such arrangements is achieved through the maintenance of traditions (Goldenberg & Goldenberg, 1994, p. 44).

Open systems use both negative (attenuating) and positive (amplifying) feedback loops. They are considered to be operating on the systems principle of equifinality, meaning that the same end state may be reached from a variety of different starting points. Closed systems, in contrast, do not have the property of equifinality, and their final state is mainly determined by their initial conditions. Within open systems, not only may the same results be accomplished from different initial conditions, but the same initial state may produce different results. The major point here is that to appreciate family functioning, the social worker must study the organization of the family system (the group's interactive process) rather than searching for the origins or outcomes of these interactions. In open systems, when a variety of inputs is possible, the family feedback process is an overriding determinant of how it functions. Since a number of pathways lead to the same destination, there is no simple or correct way for families to raise children or to ensure a successful relationship. Uncertain beginnings do not necessarily mean that a relationship will fail; an unstable start may be compensated for by the introduction of corrective feedback as the relationship evolves. By the same token, a relationship that gets off to a positive start may later decline for a variety of reasons. The concept discussed earlier of causality, a linear description in which A inevitably leads to B, overlooks the central role played by the family's interactive process. The concept of equifinality means that the social work practitioner may intervene with a family at any of several points utilizing any of several therapeutic techniques to attain the same desired results.

In open systems, members are free to move in and out of interactions with one another, with extended family members (such as grandparents, aunts, uncles, or cousins), or with extrafamilial systems such as school, church, neighbors, or teachers. In contrast to the relatively closed family system, to which conformity and tradition are emphasized, open family systems tend to stress adaptability to unfamiliar situations, particularly if that serves a purpose or a goal that the family considers worthwhile. Because an open and honest dialogue both within and outside the family is encouraged most of the time, disagreement or dissent may be common and not viewed as a threat to the ongoing viability of the family unit. Negotiation, communication, flexibility in shifting roles, interdependence, and authenticity are hallmarks of an open system (Turner, 1974, p. 347). As previously noted, in systems theory, open systems are said to have negentropy in that they are organized to be adaptable, are open to new experiences, and can alter patterns that are inappropriate to the current situation. Through exchanges outside of their own boundaries, open systems increase the chance of becoming more highly organized and developing resources to repair minor or temporary breakdowns in efficiency (Nichols & Everett, 1986).

The lack of social exchanges in closed systems decreases their ability to deal with stress. Limited or perhaps nonexistent contact with others outside the family may lead to fearful, confused, and ineffective responses. In extreme cases of rigid systems and/or persistent stress, chaos and anarchy may follow within the family (Goldenberg & Goldenberg, 1994, p. 44).

Boundaries

Each family system has boundaries, which can be defined as invisible lines of demarcation that separate the family from the outside nonfamily environment (Goldenberg & Goldenberg, 1994, p. 45). Boundaries are useful if arbitrary metaphors for defining the overall system as a functioning unit or entity. They exist around the family as a whole, around its subsystems, and around individual family members. Without boundaries, there would be no progressive

differentiation of functions in individuals or in separate subsystems, and hence, as Umbarger (1983) contends, no system complexity. Without such complexity, a family's ability to create and maintain an adaptive stance in society is undermined. Adaptability is essential if the system is to avoid the forces of entropy and ultimate decay (Goldenberg & Goldenberg, 1994, p. 46). All members of a family participate in several subsystems simultaneously, and each subsystem stands in dynamic relationship with the others, both influencing and being influenced by others. Each subsystem with its own dynamic boundaries is organized to perform the functions necessary for the family as a whole to go about its tasks smoothly and effectively.

Boundaries circumscribe and protect the integrity of the system and thus determine who is regulated as inside and who remains outside the system. Within the family itself, boundaries differentiate subsystems and help to achieve and define the separate subunits of the total system. As Salvador Minuchin (1974) notes, they must be sufficiently well defined to allow subsystem members to carry out their functions without undue interference. At the same time, they must be open enough to permit contact between the members of a subsystem and others. The clarity of a subsystem's boundaries are more important than who performs what functions (Goldenberg & Goldenberg, 1994, p. 50). Boundaries may also represent nonphysical dividers that separate one system from another (family from family) or one part of a system from another part (one member of a family from another). They can represent physical boundaries such as walls separating one dwelling from other, or one room from another. Walls around a house may delineate territory, reality, space, and privacy (Goldenberg & Goldenberg, 1994, p. 52).

Of course, boundaries may also be emotional and psychological. Deviation from appropriate subsystem boundaries may occur in one of two ways, either through enmeshment or disengagement. In enmeshment the boundary is too permeable and thus family members become overly involved and intertwined with each other's lives. In disengagement, there are overly rigid boundaries, with family members sharing a house but operating as separate units, with little interaction or exchange of feelings or sense of connection with one another. Little support or concern for family loyalty is evident in disengaged families. At their extremes, enmeshed families run the risk of prohibiting separations by viewing them as acts of betrayal, thus making autonomy virtually impossible. As a result, disengaged families, whose members remain oblivious to the effects of their actions on one another, may thus preclude their members from ever developing caring relationships with one another (Goldenberg & Goldenberg, 1994, p. 51). According to eminent Toronto social worker and theorist Dr. Eva Philipp, "Families may be both enmeshed and disengaged to varying degrees at the same time. For example, a parent may be symbiotically involved with a child but at the same time may be rejecting and oblivious to the child's needs. It is therefore not a question of mutual exclusivity. Both may coexist within the same family unit" (Philipp interview, 1996).

Stability and Change

Dynamic systems, whether family or otherwise, must maintain their continuity while tolerating change. Evolution is a normal and necessary part of every system's experience, including the family system, as it progresses through the life cycle. However, as Nichols and Everett (1981) observe, a crucial question facing any system is how much change it can tolerate and still survive. Systems theorists have employed the terms "morphostasis" and "morphogenesis" to describe a system's ability to remain stable within the context of change, and conversely to change within the context of stability. To maintain a healthy balance, both processes are necessary. With any system, tensions inevitably exist between forces seeking constancy and the maintenance of the status quo, on the one hand, and opposing forces demanding change on the other. Morphostasis calls for a system to emphasize interactions involving negative or deviation attenuating feedback. It refers to the system's tendency towards stability or a state of dynamic equilibrium. Morphogenesis, on the other hand, demands positive or deviation amplifying feedback to encourage growth, innovation, and change (Goldenberg & Goldenberg, 1994, p. 51).

Systems theorists such as Maruyana (1968) and Hoffman (1981) pointed out that the survival

of any system depends on the interaction of these two key processes. Unlike homeostasis, which is the maintenance of behavioral constancy in a system, morphostatic mechanisms operate to maintain the system's structural constancy. Morphogenetic mechanisms, however, seek to push the system toward new levels of functioning, allowing it to adapt to changing conditions.

This view is reinforced by Umbarger (1983), who stresses that both stability and change are necessary for effective family functioning—that is, stability and change are necessary for the continuity of any family or system. Paradoxically, family stability is rooted in change. A family must maintain enough regularity and balance to maintain adaptability and preserve a sense of order and sameness. At the same time, it must subtly promote change and growth within members and the system as a whole.

Salvador Minuchin (1974), focusing on the family's structural components, notes that responding to these pressures calls for "a constant transformation of the position of the family members in relation to one another so they can grow while the family system maintains continuity." Minuchin argues that family dysfunction results from rigidity of its transactional patterns and boundaries when faced with stress and the corresponding resistance to exploring alternate solutions. Minuchin contends that families that function effectively adapt to life's inevitable stresses in ways that preserve continuity while facilitating family restructuring as required. It must be recognized that no family functions optimally in all circumstances over periods of time. There are great fluctuations in families' abilities to cope, and indeed families are both functional and at the same time dysfunctional, depending on the area under question (Goldenberg & Goldenberg, 1994, p. 51).

Minuchin developed his theories of intervention utilizing systems theory while working with delinquent youth in New York. The youngsters often lived in emotionally deprived families, headed by demoralized single mothers who fluctuated between excessive discipline on one hand and on the other delegating tasks to a child. Minuchin's structural family therapy involves a number of action-oriented strategies and techniques, including powerful verbal metaphors that allow the therapist to join the family and to reestablish an appropriate hierarchy and establish boundaries between family subsystems (e.g., marital, parent, child, and siblings) (Smelser & Baltes, 2001, p. 12488).

Murray Bowen, a key social work theorist who developed extended family system therapy, made a valuable contribution by extending GST beyond the nuclear family. He postulated that behavioral disorders are the result of multigenerational transmission processes in which progressively impeded levels of differentiation (for example, independence of self from others) occur as the family's lack of differentiation is transmitted from one generation to the following one. According to Bowen, the main goal of therapy is to facilitate the differentiation of family members. He visualized family relationships as triangles; therapy usually includes only two people—the spouses or partners—while the therapist becomes the third member of this therapeutic triangle. As long as the therapist remains neutral and objective and does not become entangled in the dysfunctional dynamics, his or her presence helps family members to deal with this fusion between them and to work toward higher levels of differentiation.

Both Minuchin and Bowen, among many others, built upon the foundations of systems theory to provide a practical theoretical framework to assist families to understand and work toward resolving complex interpersonal and family dynamics (Smelser & Baltes, 2001, p. 5403).

Summary

GST has provided social work theorists and practitioners with a unique and profound perspective on the complex functioning of individuals, groups, families, organizations, and communities in contemporary 21st-century Canadian and American society. This paradigm contributes to understanding the dynamic web and interconnections among component networks in which they are embedded. Systems theory is compatible with social work values and goals. It recognizes the interplay of various external factors on human functioning and offers hope that changes can occur at various points in

a system and may serve as a catalyst for subsequent changes in other areas. This theoretical model bridges the gap between micro and macro practice by providing an array of applied and practical treatment strategies and techniques, as outlined in this chapter.

When individual clients are being treated, direct access to other family members or relevant systems may not be possible. Yet being aware of the existence of important systems and subsystems and their potential impact on a client's functioning can provide for a more comprehensive and effective assessment and treatment plan.

In the past several years, concepts developed by GST have been incorporated into different practice models, from psychodynamically oriented to family therapy approaches. These concepts remain as relevant today as they were when originally developed in the latter half of the 20th century and need to be expanded upon and researched. Hearn noted in 1950 that "a very great deal remains to be done before the tangible contributions of generalized systems theory toward the illumination and refinement of social work practice are clearly demonstrated" (Strean, 1971, p. 146). This achievement, according to Hearn, is predicated upon three major tasks: it must become an objective study of the human realities of which we are already dealing with in social work practice; a model must be developed that is capable of conceptualizing these human realities; and the validity and utility of our models must be tested by determining whether their application leads to new insights for practice and ultimately to the rendering of better service (Strean, 1971, p. 146).

The advances made by GST in the past have enormously enhanced the repertoire of social workers in all areas of practice who wish to improve human functioning within systems and environments while championing the core social work value of social justice. Although in recent years GST may not have received the attention and focus in terms of research that it had previously enjoyed, its theoretical and practical contributions are indisputable and possibly in need of refinement. There indeed is a plethora of data upon which to build into the future.

References

Compton, B. R., & Galaway, B. (1989). *Social work processes*. Belmont, CA: Westworth Publishing Company.

Devore, W., & Schlesinger, E. (1996). *Ethnic sensitive social work practice* (4th ed.). Needham, MA: Allyn and Bacon.

Goldenberg, H. &, Goldenberg, I. (1994). *Counselling today's families* (2nd ed.). Pacific Grove, CA: Brooks/ Cole Publishing Company.

Hagendorn, R. (Ed.) (1981). *Essentials of sociology*. Toronto, Ontario: Holt, Rinehart and Winston of Canada Limited.

Jenson, A. F., with Metcalf, H. C (1971). *Sociology: Concepts and concerns*. Chicago: Rand McNally and Company.

Kuhn, A. (1974). *The logic of social systems*. San Francisco: Jossey-Bass Ltd.

Loomis, C. P. (1960). *Social systems. The Van Nostrand Series in Sociology*. Toronto, Ontario: D. Van Nostrand Company (Canada) Ltd..

National Association of Social Workers. Barke, R. L. (Ed.). (2003). *The social work dictionary* (5th ed.). Washington, DC: NASW Press.

Nelson, E. D., & Fleuras, A. (1993). *Social problems in Canada. Issues and challenges*. Scarborough, Ontario: Prentice Hall Canada, Inc.

Notes from social work lectures at McMaster University transcribed by Jennifer Krawczyk, February 1995.

Philipp, Eva. Interview, April 1996.

Smelser, N. J, & Baltes, P. B. (Editors in Chief). (2001). *Reference international encyclopaedia of the social and behavioural sciences*. Oxford, England: Elsevier Sciences Ltd.

Stein, I. (1974). *Systems theory, science and social work*. Metachan, NJ: Scarecrow Press.

Strean, H. (1971). *Social casework theories in practice*. Metachan, NJ: Scarecrow Press.

Teevan, J. J. (Ed.) (1993). *Basic sociology: A Canadian introduction* (4th ed.). Scarborough, Ontario: Prentice Hall Canada, Inc.

Tepperman, L., & Rosenberg, M. (1995). *Macro/micro: A brief introduction to sociology* (2nd ed.). Scarborough, Ontario: Prentice Hall Canada, Inc.

Travithick, P. (2005). *Social work skills: A practical handbook*. Berkshire, England: Open University Press.

Turner, F. J. (1974). *Social work treatment: Interlocking theoretical approaches*. New York: The Free Press.

Turner, F. J. (1996). *Social work treatment: Interlocking theoretical approaches* (4th ed.). New York: The Free Press.

Von Bertalanffy, L. (1981). *A systems view of men* (La Violette, P. A, ed.). Boulder, CO: Westview Press.

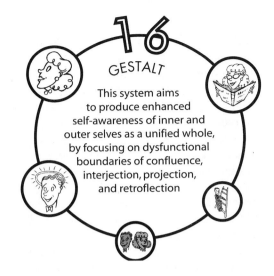

GESTALT

This system aims to produce enhanced self-awareness of inner and outer selves as a unified whole, by focusing on dysfunctional boundaries of confluence, interjection, projection, and retroflection

Gestalt Theory and Social Work Treatment

Elaine P. Congress

Contrary to popular belief, Gestalt theory is much more than a collection of techniques, as this model is firmly rooted in existential philosophy (Perls, 1992). Derived from a German word denoting wholeness, Gestalt refers to the holistic nature of human experience. A Gestalt is seen as much more than its collected parts. Although Gestalt therapy focuses on the "figure," the experience of the individual in current context, there is also consideration of the "ground," the present as well as past background of the individual. While the here and now is stressed, past experiences and relationships are examined in the present in order for the client to gain greater understanding about his or her current situation.

Overview

Historical Origins

First developed in the late 1940s, Gestalt theory introduced a new approach to understanding personality, human development, and therapy that differed from widely accepted psychoanalytic theory. The founder and principal proponent of Gestalt theory and therapy, Frederick (Fritz) Perls, disagreed with the Freudian lineal approach, which stressed the past, focused on individual pathology stemming from Oedipal conflicts, and promoted a treatment method that fostered dependency on the therapist.

Written over 60 years ago, *Ego, Hunger, and Aggression: A Revision of Freud's Theory and*

Method (Perls, 1947) presents the initial development of Gestalt theory. Perls disagreed with traditional psychoanalytic theory and instead embraced existential philosophy and Gestalt psychology. He was greatly influenced by the existential focus on individual responsibility for one's experience within the present. The Gestalt therapeutic relationship is likened to the I-thou relationship described by Buber in 1958 (Buber, 1958) in which the therapist unconditionally accepts the unique personality of the client. In the I-thou relationship the barrier between self and others is minimized and each person connects on a human level. From Gestalt psychology Perls derives his focus on the total person as an entity that is much more than a collection of component parts. In contrast to psychoanalytic theory, which presents sex and aggression as primary drives, Gestalt theory proposes that the basic human drive is that of self-actualization.

Gestalt therapy was most popular in the 1960s and Fritz Perls conducted many workshops and seminars to disseminate his theory during that time. Miller (1989) has suggested that Gestalt therapy, which focused on here-and-now experiential methods, was particularly suitable to the radical revolutionary nature of the sixties. Gestalt therapy, however, not only is a collection of dated dramatic techniques designed to bring about rapid personality change, but also presents a philosophical worldview and a therapeutic method that has continued to have relevance and a following into the 21st century.

Literature on Gestalt Theory and Therapy

Originally Frederick Perls was the principal author of literature on Gestalt theory. Important books by Perls that outline theoretical and treatment concepts of this model include *Gestalt Therapy Verbatim* (Perls, 1969a), *In and Out of the Garbage Pail* (Perls, 1969b), *The Gestalt Approach and Eye Witness to Therapy* (Perls, 1973), and *Gestalt Therapy* (Perls, Hefferline, & Goodman, 1951), written with R. F. Hefferline and P. Goodman. Other authors on Gestalt therapy include Polster (1992), Smith (1992a), Harman (1990), Korb, Gorrell, and VanDeRiet (1989), Clarkson (1989), Smith (1992a, 1992b), and Nevis (1992).

Gestalt therapy has been linked to psychoanalytic models in the work of Yontef (1987), to transactional analysis and redecision theory in Goulding (1989), to self psychology in Breshgold and Zahm (1992), to insight-oriented therapy in the work of Scanlon (1980), and to attachment theory (Sternek, 2007). Within the past decade Brownell (2008), Nevis (2000), Houston (2003), and Yontef (2005) have published books on Gestalt therapy. Many recent publications on Gestalt therapy have originated in Europe rather than in the United States, where Gestalt therapy began.

Recent literature on Gestalt therapy has focused on the use of body movement in psychotherapy (Klepner, 2001) and group supervision with supervisees (Melnick, 2008). *The International Journal of Gestalt Therapy* (renamed in 2002 from *Gestalt Therapy*) is a continual source of current work on Gestalt theory and practice. Applying Gestalt principles to increase understanding of child behavior has been a particular focus for current Gestalt therapists (Arfelli-Galli, 2006; Trombini, 2006, 2007). Trombini (2007) uses focal play therapy based on Gestalt principles to work with children with eating disorders. There is a focus on current client groups, such as Wedam's (2007) application of Gestalt principles to clinical work with traumatized refugees in which refugees who have experienced tortures must learn through therapeutic relations to develop new structures. In addition to clinical work Gestalt principles have also been used to understand communication patterns, including audience reactions to media. Members of the audience are not passive receivers of information, but instead actively seek out information they need (Umphrey, 2007).

Relationship to Social Work

Although Gestalt theory was originally developed by a psychiatrist, Fritz Perls, and his wife, a psychologist, Laura Perls, and the majority of literature has been written by psychologists, there are many tenets that seem particularly pertinent to the social work perspective. Both Gestalt and social work focus on beginning where the client is. What Gestalt therapists describe as the figure/ground experience is similar to the social work focus on the person-in-environment ecological perspective. Social work's concern about the total person, including the physical, cognitive, behavioral, and emotional, verbal and nonverbal, resembles the Gestalt therapy focus on wholeness. Both the Gestalt therapist and the social worker emphasize increasing self-awareness for client and therapist, as well as the positive use of self (Lammert, 1986).

Extent of Social Work Literature

Social work literature on Gestalt therapy has been limited. A review of *Social Work Abstracts* from 1968 to 2009 yields only 10 journal articles and three dissertations. Only half of the articles have been in social work journals. In Levenson (1979), differences between Gestalt therapy and psychoanalytic psychotherapy are considered. Other social work authors have focused on the application of Gestalt therapy to clinical practice (Lammert & Dolan, 1983), to groups for chronic schizophrenics (Potocky, 1993), to marriage counseling (Hale, 1978), and to training groups in Gestalt therapy (Napoli & Walk, 1989). In an earlier edition of this book Blugerman (1986) discussed the usefulness of Gestalt theory for social work practice and research. Although there has not been a recent article on Gestalt therapy in social work literature, the relevance of Gestalt principles to social work theory and practice is discussed in the Implications for Practice section later in this chapter.

Basic Concepts

Gestalt theory presupposes a belief in the wholeness of human experience and the value of each person. The six main concepts in Gestalt therapy are wholeness, awareness, contact, figure/ground, self-regulation, and here and now (Smith, 1992a, 1992b).

Wholeness: Gestalt theory stresses the wholeness of the person without separation between mind and body, thought, emotion, and action. The problems or symptoms presented by clients are viewed as integral parts of their experience.

Awareness: The Gestalt therapist seeks to help the client become more aware of internal feelings and processes as well as others in the external environment. As children, all human beings have the capacity for awareness and growth, but they are often encouraged to minimize certain thoughts and behaviors as inappropriate. For example, a young girl may be taught that girls should never be assertive and should always be passive and accepting. This may lead to conflicts as an adult when a boss places unreasonable demands on her. A Gestalt therapist would help this client become aware of her feelings of anger, which she had not been able to express as a child. By becoming more aware of both inner and outer experiences as a child and now as an adult, she can move toward developing more appropriate assertive behavior in the here and now.

Contact: The focus of Gestalt therapy is to expand the range and scope of contact between a person's inner and outer self and environment, as well as between client and environment. The Gestalt therapist views transference as a contact boundary disturbance and tries to increase the client's awareness of this distortion (Frew, 1990).

Figure/Ground: This concept, which stems from Gestalt psychology, alludes to the human person in relation to the environment (Perls, Hefferline, & Goodman, 1951). A Gestalt therapist helps the client to increase awareness of figure as a unified personality at the point of contact between the external and internal world, while the ground becomes everything that is not the focus of attention at the experienced moment.

Self-Regulation: Pursuant to the existentialist focus on personal responsibility, Gestalt therapists believe that each person has the capacity to regulate his or her own actions. Contrary to Freudian-determined drives of aggression and sexuality, Gestalt therapists believe that human beings can self-regulate their own needs, as well as self-support and self-actualize. This process is enhanced when clients increase self-awareness at contact points and view themselves in a more unified way.

Here and Now: The Gestalt therapist's focus on the here and now represents the most radical departure from psychoanalytic theory. While a Gestalt therapist is primarily concerned with increasing a client's self-awareness at the current contact point between client and external environment, it is assumed that the past does affect the present experience of the client. The Gestalt therapist, however, does not dwell on past experiences and instead is more likely to use exercises to help clients understand past experiences in the context of the here and now. When the client is able to assume new roles or become aware of previously unarticulated feelings, the client learns how past experiences impacted the here and now and can begin to work thorough "unfinished business" from the past.

Gestalt Definition of Personality

Gestalt theorists define personality as "the relatively stable or predictable ways in which one person will behave differently from another, under the same external conditions" (Wheeler, 1992, p. 115). This theory of personality departs markedly from psychoanalytic theory, which postulates that all people progress through certain well-defined developmental stages. The diversity of individual personality is stressed. Also in contrast to the Freudians, Gestalt therapists stress the unity, the total Gestalt of personality. Freudians emphasize the structural theory of personality, and psychodynamic therapy focuses on helping clients gain insight into different structural parts and making the ego dominate. While Perls in early Gestalt writings spoke of the ego, superego, and id and in *Gestalt Therapy Verbatim* (Perls, 1969a) even added an infraego, Gestalt therapists in general focus not on the divisions of personality structure but rather on the totality and integration of different parts of the personality.

Nature and Process of Change

Unlike most other psychotherapies, the focus of Gestalt theory is not to produce change in the client, but rather to produce increased awareness. Consistent with an existential approach, the Gestalt therapist accepts the client as a unified whole without judgment or criticism (Cole, 1994). The therapist does not seek to change the client according to the former's evaluation of the client's problems and/or pathology. Therapeutic change is defined as increased awareness of inner self and outer self as a unified whole. The client has the capacity to change, grow, and self-actualize, while the therapist serves only as a facilitator in this process.

Role of Significant Others

Gestalt therapists minimize the role of significant others in contributing to a client's move toward change and self-actualization. In fact, the Gestalt prayer, "I do my thing, and you do your thing. I am not in this world to live up to your expectations and you are not in this world to live up to mine," which Perls includes in the introduction to *Gestalt Therapy Verbatim* (Perls, 1969a), stresses the focus on the individual without regard for either support or hindrance of others. Other Gestalt therapists, however, have recognized the importance of significant others, and Gestalt techniques have been used in marital counseling (Hale, 1978). With Gestalt marital therapy each partner is encouraged to develop basic awareness of the other and of the effect of the partner on the self during each here-and-now moment.

Role of Resources

Similar to other psychological theories, Gestalt theory focuses primarily on the person of the client, rather than on environmental resources that may or may not be available to the client. Although Gestalt therapy may not concentrate on concrete resources in the client's environment or teach the client skills to access them, a Gestalt therapist does acknowledge the importance of the totality of a client's experience, which includes environmental resources as well as psychological resources.

Values Base of Theory

Time Orientation

The focus of Gestalt theory is most clearly on the present, the here and now, yet Gestalt therapists acknowledge that past experiences often influence the perception and behavior of clients in the present. Past relationships with significant others, especially parental figures, are often reenacted in the present to help clients develop greater understanding of how the perceptions and distortions of these relationships are impacting the here and now. Contrary to the Freudian deterministic belief that the past has inextricably influenced the present, Gestalt therapists believe that a client can revisit the past to reshape the present and future. The future, as well as the past, is not the primary focus of Gestalt therapy.

Unlike many current therapy models, such as cognitive behavioral theories, Gestalt therapy is not goal-directed. The existential moment is the most important, the way the client experiences the world with increasing self-awareness. The future in terms of client or therapist goals is unknown and not considered as important as the current process of Gestalt therapy.

Basic Human Nature

Gestalt theory presents an optimistic view of human nature. Each person is viewed as capable of self-actualization and increasing self-awareness. Each has the ability to see himself or herself as a unified whole. People are viewed neither as bad, vulnerable, nor sick. Consequently, focus on social problems and/or psychological dysfunction is minimized.

Relationship

A key relationship within Gestalt theory is the therapeutic relationship between therapist and client. This relationship resembles Buber's I-thou relationship in which power differentials do not exist. Other positive relationships within a person's here and now should follow a similar format. The nature of activity for Gestalt therapy is primarily emotional experience rather than behavioral change. The goal is to help the client understand his or her Gestalt rather than change behavior. Gestalt theory views people as existing in harmony with nature rather than in conflict or as dominant. By increasing self-awareness, a human being can become more aware of the impact of nature on the total Gestalt.

Social, Cultural, and Ethnic Sensitivity

Nowhere in Perls or other Gestalt theorists is there a focus on cultural and ethnic differences. Most of the early Gestalt clients were from white, middle-class, and American or Western European backgrounds. Gestalt therapy is thought to foster an American individualistic perspective (Saner, 1989). Yet the focus on self-actualization, acceptance of diverse perspectives, and concentration on the whole person seems particularly relevant for work with ethnically and culturally diverse people. It has been

suggested that the Gestalt focus on emotional experience may not be helpful for some culturally diverse clients (Corey, 1991).

Gestalt Therapy

Principal Therapeutic Goals

Although Gestalt therapists avoid specific goal setting with individual clients, the following general goals are relevant to Gestalt therapy:

1. Increase the variety of behaviors used by clients. Often clients have a very limited repertoire of behaviors. Gestalt therapy encourages them to expand their use of different behaviors.
2. Encourage clients to take more responsibility for their lives. While clients may initially blame others for their life situations, Gestalt therapy helps clients to accept their own roles in creating their current situation.
3. Maximize experiential learning. Gestalt therapy encourages clients to rely not only on cognition, but to integrate this type of thinking with their emotions.
4. Complete unfinished business from the past and integrate these experiences into their present. Gestalt clients with disturbing past experiences that detrimentally affect their current functioning are encouraged to bring these experiences into the here and now. By reliving and reworking through these experiences, clients become more receptive to new life experiences.
5. Increase opportunities for clients to feel and act stronger, more competent and self-supported, with conscious and responsible choices, thereby facilitating good contact (Korb, Gorrell, & VanDeRiet, 1989, p. 95).

Principal Therapeutic Concepts

These goals are achieved through the nature of the therapeutic relationship and the variety of techniques employed by the Gestalt therapist. In Gestalt therapy the focus is always on the client. It is assumed that clients have all the tools required to make any desired personal changes

(Korb, Gorrell, & VanDeRiet, 1989, p. 69). The therapist functions as a facilitator who aids in the client's discovery of what the client is doing and how the client is doing it, and explores the underlying processes that influence the behavior. The client is helped to accept responsibility for his or her behavior, not for the situation or other people's actions. The therapist enables the client to explore and take responsibility for his or her actions.

Nature of Therapeutic Relationship

The nature of the therapeutic relationship is crucial in Gestalt therapy. The most important quality for a Gestalt therapist is authenticity—that is, to have achieved good self-awareness and to be open and honest with the client. The therapist must be able to enter into the client's world. Gestalt therapists must develop a close, personal relationship with clients, rather than an "aloof, distant, or totally objective" interaction (Korb, Gorrell, & VanDeRiet, 1989, p. 110). The Gestalt therapist minimizes the power differential that occurs between therapist and client. The establishment of an authoritarian relationship between therapist and client (in which the therapist knows what is best for the client) is avoided, as the Gestalt therapist respects the client's desire to change as well as desire to remain the same (Cole, 1994). The client's reality is considered paramount, and the client is seen to possess the capacity to grow and change with minimal assistance from the therapist. The therapeutic relationship is likened to Buber's I-thou dialogue, which implies complete acceptance and respect for the other.

Unlike psychoanalytic approaches, the Gestalt therapist does not foster the development of a transference relationship. Yet Gestalt therapists acknowledge that clients come into therapy with expectations that the therapist will relate to them in ways similar to what they experienced in childhood. The I-thou position of the therapist, however, "chips away at the client's expectation of trauma in the client relationship" (Cole, 1994, p. 84). The Gestalt therapist may present himself or herself as the good parent, but only to facilitate the growth and change of the client. Transference in Gestalt therapy only functions as a means to an end, not as an end goal as in psychoanalytic treatment.

Perception of and Importance of History

Although the main focus of Gestalt therapy is on the here and now, it is a mistake to think of Gestalt therapy as ahistorical. A person's history is crucial, as all that is unfinished from the past manifests itself in the here and now (Huckabay, 1992). In contrast to the psychoanalytic model, which encourages clients to talk about past experiences, the Gestalt therapist uses exercises to help clients relive past events and relationships in the here and now.

Perception of and Importance of Assessment

A Gestalt therapist's assessment of a client differs significantly from a social worker's psychosocial assessment. Neither a discussion of the physical, psychological, intellectual, cognitive, and emotional characteristics of the client nor an analysis of familial, social, and environmental resources can be found in the Gestalt therapist's assessment of a client. In terms of diagnosis, Gestalt therapy does not focus on pathology. Diagnosis according to DSM-IV symptom description (American Psychiatric Association, 2000), defense mechanisms, and even client "problems" are not relevant to a Gestalt therapist's "assessment" of a client (Yontef, 1987). Statements such as, "This is a manic-depressive, single parent, or welfare recipient" are avoided. While psychoanalysts see the defense mechanism of resistance as a negative force to be eliminated, Gestalt therapists see the need "to enliven the resistances to awareness, so as to give them new flexibility and contact with the realities of the self and the social world" (Cole, 1994, p. 72).

While Gestalt therapy does not recognize assessment and diagnosis according to the psychoanalyst, psychiatric DSM-IV, social work psychosocial model, problems that occur at the point of contact, dysfunctional boundary disturbances, introjections, projection, and retroflection can be identified in clients and become the focus of treatment. Even the word "disturbances" has been considered too judgmental for

Gestalt therapists; it has been suggested that "processes" would be a better descriptive word (Swanson, 1988).

Specific Therapeutic Definitions

The four disturbances (processes) that occur between person and environment can be described as follows.

Confluence involves the denial of differences and an unrealistic focus on similarities. It is similar to the psychological phenomenon of accommodation and generalization. For example, if one places a hand on a wall, at first the person is very aware of temperature and tactile differences, but these differences blur within a short period. Similarly, in some marriages differences between the partners are denied and a false sense of togetherness ensues. Gestalt therapy helps couples to examine ambivalent feelings about each other, as well as the "shoulds" and expectations of their relationships (Hale, 1978). Couples become more aware of individual needs apart from their confluent relationship.

A second contact disturbance, **introjection**, refers to the inappropriate intake of information from others, especially significant historical figures. Often parental messages become internalized, with the result that the client is plagued by commands of "I should," "I ought to," or "I have to." When introjection is a client's disturbance, the Gestalt therapist may encourage the client to assume a voice apart from the introjected parent and carry on a dialogue in the here and now. The purpose of this exercise is to help clients differentiate themselves from the parental introject. While psychoanalysts would assess introjection as an ego defense against anxiety, Gestalt therapists perceive introjection as a disturbance between person and environment that can be readily be remedied in the here and now.

A third contact disturbance, **projection**, describes the process of disavowing parts of oneself and projecting these parts upon others. Ego psychologists consider this phenomenon a defense mechanism in which unacceptable parts of one's own personality are rejected and attributed to another. This defense mechanism is considered a lower-level type of ego defense that is used most frequently by the severely mentally ill. Gestalt therapists, on the other hand, do not

consider that clients who use this process are more mentally ill, but rather that these clients have lost a significant part of themselves. This behavior takes away power from them and gives the environment more control than warranted. Gestalt therapists would help clients reclaim lost parts of themselves. For example, a client who thought all men were angry at her might be helped to acknowledge her own feelings of anger toward significant men past and present.

A final disturbance of contact, **retroflection**, describes the process during which individuals do to themselves what they would like to do to someone else or to have someone else do to them. This behavior sometimes is a very healthy response, as when an angry mother very actively cleans the kitchen rather than abusing her child, or a woman rejected by a boyfriend buys herself a new suit (Polster & Polster, 1973). Retroflection can be overused, and a person may not be able to function in the current here and now because of powerful forces from the past. For example, clients rejected by their parents as children may not reach out to others as adults and may depend only on themselves for support. A Gestalt therapist would work with clients to help them understand that they no longer have to be the primary source of their support and that they can connect with others in their current environment.

The assessment of contact point disturbances occurs at the very beginning of treatment. Assessment is not viewed as a prerequisite to treatment. The integration of assessment and treatment from the very beginning serves to bring the Gestalt therapist and client together immediately, thus avoiding the professional distance created by a more formal, diagnostic assessment process.

Specific Techniques and Strategies

Gestalt therapists often use a variety of strategies or techniques in working with clients. Respect for the personhood of the client and flexibility are main principles that govern the choice of specific techniques to use with clients. The choice of techniques depends on the health and readiness of the client. Therapy often creates the safe emergency in which the client learns that it is acceptable to be angry, elated, or unhappy

(Stevens, 1975). Translating this safe emergency into action is often accomplished through the use of an experiment (Polster & Polster, 1973). A Gestalt experiment has been described as "an attempt to counter the absolutist deadlock by bringing the individual's action system right into the room" (Polster & Polster, 1973, p. 234). In general, experiments help clients to understand themselves better through acting out problems and feelings, rather than only talking about them.

While an important role for the Gestalt therapist is facilitator, the therapist often assumes the role of director in introducing and carrying through the following experiments. Some of the main classic experiments can be summarized as follows (Korb, Gorrell, & VanDeRiet, 1989).

Dialogue, the best-recognized of Gestalt therapy techniques, is commonly referred to as "the empty chair technique." Although this technique is often criticized as being overly dramatic, it should be remembered that it was originally designed to teach others about Gestalt therapy, as well as to facilitate growth in an individual client (Blugerman, 1986). When a client has conflict with another person past or present or with a part of his or her personality, the Gestalt therapist asks the client to imagine that this person or personality aspect is in the empty chair. By promoting this separation, the client is often able to achieve greater understanding of and insight into what is frequently an area of conflict. For example, a client who is very demanding and a perfectionist in his behavior may benefit from the experience of having his imagined father sit in the empty chair and having the opportunity of "talking" with his father about the latter's multiple demands for perfection.

Enactment of dreams often permits clients to become aware of issues and conflicts about which they are not aware. In contrast to psychoanalytic theorists, who encourage clients to discuss their dreams to provide greater understanding of the unconscious, Gestalt therapists see dreams as "existential messages" about the current situations in the client's life (Latner, 1992, p. 51). While psychoanalysts stress interpretation of dreams as most important, Gestalt therapists encourage clients to act out their dreams as an expression of their current Gestalt.

Exaggeration occurs when the Gestalt therapist asks the client to exaggerate some motion or speech pattern. This exercise may help the client get in touch with feelings about which there was no previous awareness. For example, a Gestalt therapist noted that a client frowned when she discussed an impending visit by her in-laws. After the client was encouraged to exaggerate her frown, she became more aware of her negative feelings about her in-laws' visit.

Reversal involves suggesting that a client reverse a statement that has been made. Polarities are common in human experience, and encouraging clients to state the opposite often leads to greater awareness and acceptance of integrated feelings toward significant others. For example, a mother who was having a difficult time separating from her latency-aged (about 6–12) son stated that she did not want her child to go to summer camp as he was too young to take care of himself away from home. When the client was asked to reverse the statement, she became more in touch with part of herself that really wanted to encourage her child to be more independent.

Rehearsal serves to prepare the client before seeking any change. Clients often lack a self-support system and fear there will be dire consequences if they try a new experience. Practicing words beforehand often gives the client confidence to approach a new situation. For example, the client who is fearful of asking the boss for a raise may benefit from the opportunity to rehearse this experience with the therapist. Many cognitive behavioral therapies also make use of this rehearsal technique.

Making the rounds is a Gestalt group work technique that provides an opportunity for the client to rehearse and receive feedback from other group members. By introducing the environment of other members, the client is helped to become clearer about his or her own experience. For example, a group member struggling with his plans to separate from his wife was asked to rehearse this discussion within the group and hear group members' reactions.

Exposing the obvious describes a technique in which Gestalt therapists are encouraged to follow up on a client's initial statements and movements, which are often indicative of deeper processes. This technique is familiar to social workers, who learn it to follow up on both verbal and nonverbal communication. An example of this occurred in Gestalt therapy when the therapist noted to the client that he had been yawning repeatedly since he came into the session.

Directed awareness experiments help clients establish contact with different inner and outer experiences. Gestalt therapists use these techniques to help clients gain a clearer picture of sensory as well as internal body sensations.

In *Creative Process in Psychotherapy*, Zinker (1977) outlines the following steps in a Gestalt therapy session:

1. Laying the groundwork
2. Negotiating a consensus between client and therapist
3. Grading (assessing that an experiment is challenging, not frustrating)
4. Surfacing the client's awareness
5. Locating the client's energy
6. Generating self-support for both client and therapist
7. Generating a theme
8. Choosing an experiment by mutual process
9. Enacting the experiment
10. Insight and completion

Reorientation is necessary after the use of a Gestalt experiment (Heikkinen, 1989).

Length of Treatment

Gestalt therapy, like other therapies, delineates the following four stages: (1) establishing a relationship, (2) exploring a problem in depth, (3) determining steps for the client to take, and (4) providing support and encouragement for growth (Egan, 1986).

Gestalt therapists believe that for some clients all four stages may occur in the first session, whereas with other clients the process may span several years. The average client often falls somewhere in between (Korb, Gorrell, & VanDeRiet, 1989). Flexibility in duration of treatment is consistent with Gestalt theory, which supports a client-centered focus on treatment. The client, not the therapist, makes decisions about the length of treatment. Allowing the client to make decisions about the length of treatment seems to contradict both the traditional psychoanalytic model, which favors long-term treatment, and

the current managed-care model of brief treatment. In general, however, Gestalt therapy is not usually considered a long-term model.

Because the focus is on flexibility and acceptance of each client, Gestalt therapy is often short term. This factor increases the usefulness of Gestalt therapy for those who practice in a managed-care environment.

Importance of Specific Methods

Work with Individuals and Groups

The founder of Gestalt therapy, Fritz Perls, was primarily an individual therapist. Even when he led groups, he worked primarily with one individual at a time, with little interaction from other group members (Nevis, 1992). Groups were seen to provide an excellent opportunity to demonstrate Gestalt theory and practice to others. An early Perls group would consist of placing one individual in the "hot seat" and exploring a particular topic, with the other group members as spectators. Other members might be asked to contribute in a structured way about the client in the hot seat. A client usually stayed in the hot seat about 10 to 30 minutes, and in a 2- to 3-hour session two to four participants took the hot seat (Korb, Gorrell, & VanDeRiet, 1989).

Currently the most frequently used Gestalt group therapy model is the Gestalt group process model (Huckabay, 1992; Zinker, 1977). With this model the therapist continues as the director of experimentation but is more receptive to interventions from other group members (Korb, Gorrell, & VanDeRiet, 1989). Group interaction and the development of cohesiveness are encouraged. With this model one group member may express awareness of a particular theme, which is shared by other group members. The group leader may lead the group in an activity related to this issue.

Although Gestalt therapy began as an individual model and is still used as an individual model, four features of Gestalt therapy are particularly suitable to work with groups: self-regulation, contact and the contact boundary, awareness, and an emphasis on the here and now (Frew, 1988). Groups, like individuals, demonstrate their own tendency to self-regulate and seek wholeness. The possibilities of contact between different group members, different subgroups, and the group leader are manifold in group process. Awareness or focused attention is even more important in group work than individual work. Finally, a focus on the here and now is paramount in group work. With this focus Gestalt group therapy is short term, which is particularly advantageous in the current managed-care mental health environment.

Work with Dyads

In addition to individual and group work, Gestalt therapy has also been applied to work with couples. Treatment of couples, however, may be difficult for the Gestalt therapist who has been trained to focus on the individual and his or her boundary in relation to the external world (Zinker, 1992). The Gestalt therapist must focus on the couple as a system, a Gestalt and the boundary of the couple as they relate to the outside world. Couple therapy consists of prescribing certain exercises for the couple to increase their awareness and interaction with each other (Hale, 1978; Zinker, 1992).

Work with Families

While not initially developed as a family therapy model, Gestalt theory has been used in family therapy. Kempler, a Gestalt family therapist, applied Gestalt theory and techniques in his work with troubled families (Kempler, 1974). Other family therapists, including Satir, adopted an experiential, existentialist approach in working with families and developed Gestalt-like family therapy techniques such as family posturing and family sculpture (Satir, 1983).

Work with Community

Gestalt therapy as it was originally developed was intended primarily for micro-practice with individuals and other small systems, including couples, groups, and families. Although not directing change efforts toward the community, Smith, a contemporary Gestalt therapist, writes, "My power to influence social change resides in my person and the effect of my person on others through intimate contacting" (Smith, 1992a, p. 294). Others have seen Gestalt therapy as being more

socially and community focused, in contrast to American individualism (Brown, Lichtenberg, Lukensmeyer & Miller, 1993). Gestalt therapy has been used to study macro organizational patterns (Critchley & Casey, 1989) and has also been used in therapeutic milieu settings such as psychiatric hospitals, group homes, day treatment centers, and sheltered workshops.

Principal Applications

Social Work Practice

Gestalt therapy was first developed for use with depressed, phobic, and obsessive clients with adjustment to neurotic disorders. Most clients are and have been from a white, middle-class background. Yet the existential focus of Gestalt therapy, which stresses the uniqueness and value of each client's experience, seems particularly well suited to the diverse economic, social, cultural, and racial clients with whom social workers work.

Gestalt therapy has been used primarily with young and middle-aged adults, but it has also been applied successfully in work with children (Oaklander, 1992) and older persons (Crouse, 1990). Other clients who have benefitted from Gestalt therapy include abused women (Little, 1990), abused children (Sluckin, Weller, & Highton, 1989), amputees (Grossman, 1990), people with AIDS (Klepner, 1992; Siemens, 1993), clients with family members who have committed suicide (Bengesser & Sokoloff, 1989), and alcoholics (Carlock, O' Halloran, Glaus, & Shaw, 1992; Shore, 1978).

Risks of Gestalt Therapy

A prevailing belief has been that Gestalt therapy is inappropriate for clients with severe personality disorders or psychoses (Shepard, 1970). Clients who have difficulty differentiating reality from fantasy may become more disoriented during guided fantasies, a frequent experiment used in Gestalt therapy. It has been suggested that Gestalt therapy can be modified for work with people who have been diagnosed as having borderline personalities (Greenberg, 1989), groups of people diagnosed as chronic schizophrenic (Potocky, 1993), and individuals hospitalized for psychoses (Harris, 1992). There is greater risk, however, in using Gestalt therapy with people who have a tenuous grasp of reality and sense of self, as they may not be able to return easily from fantasy to the real world.

Limitations of Gestalt Therapy

While Gestalt therapy presents risks for many clients with severe psychotic disorders, this model of therapy also may not be appropriate for poor clients for whom environmental advocacy and securing of resources is needed. Most successful with middle-class or working-class clients with neurotic or adjustment disorders, Gestalt therapy seems particularly to differ from case management, a current treatment model for work with the chronic mentally ill and others who require therapist activity in securing and coordinating community resources.

Administration and Training

Training for Gestalt Therapists

Gestalt therapy is often briefly covered in graduate social work or psychology programs, and most Gestalt therapists receive their training in postgraduate training centers located in many large cities. There are three major Gestalt therapy associations: the Association for the Advancement of Gestalt Therapy (AAGT), which is based in the United States; the European Association for Gestalt Therapy (EAGT), founded in 1985; and the Gestalt Australia and New Zealand (GANZ).

There are no universal guidelines for the extent of training, but most educators in the Gestalt therapy field believe that the three main areas to be covered in Gestalt training are (1) theoretical grounding, (2) intense personal Gestalt work, and (3) extended supervision (Korb, Gorrell, & VanDeRiet, 1989). Educators believe that beginning students must study extensively the theoretical orientation of Gestalt therapy in order to have an understanding of this method more than a collection of techniques. Because of the importance of the therapeutic relationship in Gestalt work, the therapist must have a good understanding of self as explored through his or her own Gestalt therapy.

Finally, ongoing supervision is considered essential for students studying the Gestalt method.

Importance and Function of Recording

Recording for Gestalt therapists focuses on the verbal and nonverbal process of the interview, similar to the process recordings of social work students. Diagnosis, history taking, and psychosocial assessment are usually absent from Gestalt recordings because these areas are not part of Gestalt therapist work with clients. Instead, Gestalt literature on practice with clients often focuses on the initial awareness contact phase with clients. What is stressed is the process that occurs between therapist and client.

Role of Setting

Although the agency context is certainly part of a client's total Gestalt, Gestalt therapists minimize the role of agency setting. Most Gestalt therapy occurs within Gestalt training institutes or in private practice, although many professionals may use some Gestalt techniques with their clients in a variety of mental health settings.

Individual Gestalt Therapy

Susan, a 25-year-old married woman, had been referred for therapy because of recurring symptoms of depression characterized by feelings of low self-esteem and crying spells. The therapist introduced herself as Jane Smith. Immediately the therapist noted that Susan seemed to sink into the chair and did not make any comments until asked. In this first session the therapist asked Susan to describe how she was feeling, to which Susan responded "terrible," but she did not understand why she felt this way as her husband was very supportive and she had a good job and a nice home. The therapist was careful to stay with the original feeling she had expressed and asked the client to describe in more detail the experience of feeling terrible. After some encouragement, the client indicated that she felt like a piece of garbage. The therapist asked the client to explore what being a piece of garbage felt like. The client described herself as feeling dirty, unclean, and rejected. She remembered that once as an adolescent she had cooked dinner and her mother had said the food tasted like garbage, and that her room had been compared to a garbage dump. It became apparent that Susan was very angry at her mother for such criticism but had turned this anger inward.

As a Gestalt therapist Jane saw that her client was suffering from retroflection, a process by which a client turns back on himself or herself what he or she would like to do to another, and Jane decided to use the Gestalt exercise of the empty chair to help Jane get in touch with and verbalize some of her previously unexpressed angry feelings toward her mother. (With Gestalt therapy, the past is not ignored, but brought into the present.) Susan was able to express angry feelings toward her mother (sitting in the empty chair) and after the exercise reported that she felt better than she had in a long time.

Group Gestalt Therapy

The second case vignette focuses on Gestalt work with a group whose members had recently been diagnosed as HIV-positive. This group follows a Gestalt group process model rather than the original Perls individual-in-group model. This group consisted of six homosexual men ranging in age from 20 to 35 who had learned of their HIV status within the past month. Group members were each asked to introduce themselves and tell what they expected to get out of the group. Most group members were in a state of denial as to their illness. Several made no reference to having HIV; one said he was sure he was misdiagnosed; another indicated that a cure was just around the corner. The Gestalt group leader was supportive of where each member was. When one member mentioned how hopeless and helpless he felt, the group leader again was able to support this member's awareness. The focus was on the here-and-now feelings of group members, not historical events.

In the beginning, the group leader related to each member individually, but was very encouraging when another group member reported that he too had felt powerless when he learned of his diagnosis. He reported that he had last felt this powerless when his mother died when he was 16. At this point the client started to cry; the other members were very supportive, as was the group leader.

The group leader tried to facilitate this interaction by asking if others had experienced losses. Reliving this loss in the here and now was an important experience because it allowed the client to work through issues of loss that had never been completely resolved. This interaction also served to promote group cohesiveness, as many group members reached out to this

client, while before they had all been quite isolated Also, this sadness over a past loss led to a discussion about current losses, health and impending disability, and fears of future losses (that is, death). Finally, this incident demonstrated a Gestalt therapist's concern about the whole person—that each person in the group is not only just a person who is HIV-positive but also has a history and current Gestalt, of which HIV is only one part.

After each member had the opportunity to express himself and some initial group cohesiveness was developed, the group leader introduced a Gestalt experiment. Group members were asked to imagine that they had a treasure box in which they could store all that was most precious to them. One member spoke very concretely that he would use this box to store T-cells for a time he might need them in fighting his illness. Another expressed concern about his younger brother and visualized that he would store him in this box to prevent him from being harmed. Another would store in his box all his successes in life, such as when he was selected to give the graduation address in college and when he was named director of his division at work. A group member saved sunsets and the first day of spring. This exercise served to create connection between the men and helped them begin to confront the present reality of their illness.

Empirical Base

Extent of Research Base

Because Gestalt theory focuses on the experiential rather the the empirical nature of treatment, single-subject case studies greatly outnumber large research studies on Gestalt therapy. Some of the many reports of clients who benefitted from Gestalt therapy can be found in Harman (1989), Smith (1992a, 1992b), and Nevis (1992). There has been clinical research on Gestalt methods (Clarke & Greenberg, 1988). "Good moments in psychotherapy," including extra-therapy behavior change, acceptance of problem, and increased general well-being, have been linked with specific Gestalt treatment methods (Mahrer, White, Howard, & Gagnon, 1992). Research on Gestalt therapy has demonstrated effectiveness in resolving decisional conflict (Greenberg & Webster, 1982), in groups (Anderson, 1978; O'Leary & Page, 1990), and in teaching (Napoli & Walk, 1989).

Gaps in Research

In general, empirical research on Gestalt therapy has been limited, and there is a need for more research to substantiate its effectiveness as a treatment method. There are difficulties, however, in conducting empirical research on an experiential, highly individualistic form of treatment, and most Gestalt therapists minimize the need for research of this type.

Present Status and Influence on Current Practice

In a different political and social climate than that of the 1960s, during which Perls developed and taught others about his model, Gestalt therapy has declined in popularity (Miller, 1989). Yet many Gestalt therapy institutions exist around the country, and the *International Gestalt Journal* continues to publish articles of current interest to Gestalt therapists. While Gestalt therapy has frequently been accused of relying too extensively on techniques, current Gestalt therapists have argued that Gestalt therapy is more philosophical than technical (Perls, 1992) and that creativity, not technical skill, is essential for Gestalt therapists (Zinker, 1991). Also, Gestalt therapy groups have changed over the years from the therapist's focus on individual clients in the group to the current emphasis on increasing client interactions with each other (Frew, 1988; Harman, 1989).

Contributions to the Profession

Many aspects of Gestalt therapy are particularly pertinent for the social work profession. First, the Gestalt focus on the point of contact between person and environment suggests social work's attention to person-in-situation. Also, the Gestalt figure/ground concept relates to the profession's use of the systems approach. While Gestalt stresses the I-thou relationship, social work speaks to the importance of developing an empathic helping relationship with the client. Both Gestalt therapist and social work professionals see much importance in increasing self-awareness and use of self.

Gestalt therapists, as well as social workers, focus on clients' strengths. Also, Gestalt therapists and social workers agree on self-actualiza-tion as a primary treatment goal. Finally, the Gestalt therapy's concern with the total Gestalt resembles the social work focus on the total person including physical, cognitive, behavioral, emotional, verbal, and nonverbal.

Implications for Practice

Current social work practice includes clients from very different social, economic, and cultural backgrounds. Gestalt therapy, which begins with the acceptance of the client and his or her Gestalt, would seem very useful for social workers in working with very diverse clients. Now more than ever, social workers work with clients from diverse cultural and socioeconomic backgrounds. A psychotherapeutic theory that speaks to the importance of accepting and valuing each person as he or she is seems particularly relevant to social workers.

Gestalt therapy, however, may not be an effective treatment modality for all social workers in all settings. Social workers who treat clients with severe psychiatric or socioeconomic problems may not be able to use this model. Also, the I-thou relationship of Gestalt therapist and client may be difficult for social workers who define their primary role as that of professional expert. Furthermore, the Gestalt therapist's lack of emphasis on history taking, diagnosis, psychosocial assessment, and goal setting may not be acceptable to social workers and their agencies who have been schooled in a more psychodynamic or psychosocial approach.

Connection to Other Models

In terms of treatment modalities, Gestalt therapy, which stresses the here and now, resembles current treatment modalities of brief treatment, problem solving, and crisis intervention, which are often used by social workers. Also, since most Gestalt therapy is brief, this treatment modality works within a short-term, financially mindful treatment environment that introduces many time constraints into treatment.

Future of Theory for the Profession

Currently a number of social workers are involved in Gestalt training institutes. Social workers often learn little about this treatment modality during their graduate education, and those who wish to develop their expertise in this area usually attend a Gestalt therapy institute for postgraduate training. For social workers interested in this model, Gestalt therapy will continue to be a significant practice method for use in social work treatment.

Gestalt therapy's focus on and acceptance of the individual person-in-environment points to its current, as well as future, value in social work treatment. The clients we serve are becoming increasingly diverse. The applicability of this model in working with clients from different cultural and socioeconomic backgrounds suggests that social workers can make greater use of Gestalt theory and therapy in their understanding and treatment of clients.

References

American Psychiatric Association (2000). *Diagnostic and statistical manual of mental disorders DSM-IV-TR* (4th ed.) Washington, DC: APA Press.

Anderson, J. (1978). Growth groups and alienation: A comparative study of Rogerian encounter, self-directed encounter, and Gestalt. *Group and Organization Studies,* 3(1), 85–107.

Arfelli-Galli, A. (2006). Field-theory and analysis of child behavior in Metzger's school. Development of self-consciousness and motivation for achievement. *Gestalt Theory,* 28(4), 389–402.

Bengesser, G., & Sokoloff, S. (1989). After suicide-postvention. *European Journal of Psychiatry,* 3(2), 116–118.

Blugerman, M. (1986). Contributions of Gestalt theory to social work treatment. In F. Turner (Ed.), *Social work treatment* (3rd ed.) (pp. 69–90). New York: Free Press.

Breshgold, E. (1989). Resistance in Gestalt therapy: An historical theoretical perspective. *Gestalt Journal,* 12(2), 73–102.

Breshgold, E., & Zahm, S. (1992). A case for the integration of self psychology developmental theory into the practice of Gestalt therapy. *Gestalt Journal,* 15(I), 61–93.

Brown, J., Lichtenberg, P., Lukensmeyer, C., & Miller, M. (1993). The implications of Gestalt therapy for social and political change. *Gestalt Journal,* 16(1), 7–54.

Brownell, P. (Ed.) (2008). *Handbook for theory, research, and practice in Gestalt therapy.* Newcastle upon Tyne, UK: Cambridge Scholars Publishing.

Buber, M. (1958). *I and thou* (2nd ed.). New York: Scribner and Sons.

Carlock, J., O'Halloran, Glaus, K., & Shaw, K. (1992). The alcoholic: A Gestalt view. In E. Nevis (Ed.), *Gestalt therapy: Perspectives and applications* (pp. 191–237). New York: Gardner Press.

Clarke, K., & Greenberg, L. (1988). Clinical research on Gestalt methods. In F. N. Watts. (Ed.), *New developments in clinical psychology* (pp. 5–19). New York: John Wiley and Sons.

Clarkson, P. (1989) *Gestalt counselling in action.* London: Sage Publications.

Cole, P. (1994). Resistance to awareness: A Gestalt therapy perspective. *Gestalt Journal,* 17(1), 71–94.

Corey, G. (1991). *Theory and practice of counseling and psychotherapy* (4th ed.). Pacific Grove, CA: Brooks/Cole.

Critchley, B., & Casey, D. (1989). Organizations get stuck too. *Leadership and Organization Development Journal,* 10(4), 3–12.

Crouse, R. (1990). Reviewing the past in the here and now: Using Gestalt therapy techniques with life review. *Journal of Mental Health Counseling,* 12(3), 279–2i.7.

Egan, G. (1986). *The skilled helper* (3rd ed.) Pacific Grove, CA: Brooks/Cole.

Frew, J. (1988). The practice of Gestalt therapy in groups. *Gestalt Journal,* 11(1), 77–96.

Frew, J. (1990). Analysis of transference in Gestalt group psychotherapy. *International Journal of Group Psychotherapy,* 40(2), 189–202.

Frew, J. (1992). From the perspective of the environment. *Gestalt Journal,* 15(1), 39–60.

Goulding, R. (1989). Teaching transactional anal ysis and redecision therapy. *Journal of Independent Social Work,* 3(4), 71–86.

Greenberg, E. (1989). Healing the borderline. *Gestalt Journal,* 12(2), 11–55.

Greenberg, L., & Webster, M. (1982). Resolving decisional conflict by Gestalt two-chair dialogues relating process to outcome. *Journal of Counseling Psychology,* 29(5), 468–477.

Grossman, E. (1990). The Gestalt approach to people with amputations. *Journal of AppliedRehabitation Counselling,* 21(1), 16–19.

Hale, B. (1978). Gestalt techniques in marriage counseling. *Social Casework,* 59(7), 428–433.

Harman, R. (1989). *Gestalt therapy with groups, couples, sexually dysfunctional men, and dreams.* Springfield, IL: Charles C. Thomas.

Harman, R. (1990). *Gestalt therapy: Discussions with the masters.* Springfield, IL: Charles C. Thomas.

Harris, C. (1992). Group work with psychotics. In E. Nevis (Ed.), *Gestalt therapy* (pp. 239–261). New York: Gardner Press.

Heikkinen, C. (1989). Reorientation from altered states: Please, move carefully. *Journal of Counseling and Development,* 67(9), 520–521.

Houston, G. (2003). *Brief Gestalt therapy.* London, UK: Sage Publications.

Huckabay, M. (1992). An overview of the theory and practice of Gestalt group process. In E. Nevis (Ed.), *Gestalt therapy* (pp. 303–330). New York: Gardner Press.

Jacobs, L. (1992). Insights from psychoanalytic self-psychology and intersubjectivity theory for Gestalt therapists. *Gestalt Journal,* 15(2), 25–60.

Kempler, W. (1974). *Principles of Gestalt family therapy.* Costa Mesa, CA: The Kempler Institute.

Klepner, J. (2001) *Body process: A Gestalt approach to working with the body in psychotherapy.* Cambridge: Gestalt Press, 2001

Klepner, P. (1992). AIDS/HIV and Gestalt therapy. *Gestalt Journal,* 15(2), 5–24.

Korb, M., Gorrell, J., & VanDeRiet, Y. (1989). *Gestalt therapy: Practice and theory.* New York: Pergamum Press.

Lammert, M. (1986). Experience as knowing: Utilizing therapist self-awareness. *Social Casework,* 23(1), 369–376.

Lammert, M., & Dolan, M. (1983). Active intervention in clinical practice: Contribution of Gestalt therapy. *Adolescence,* 18(69), 43–50.

Latner, J. (1992). *Theory of Gestalt therapy.* In E. Nevis (ed.), *Gestalt therapy* (pp. 13–56). New York: Gardner Press.

Levenson, J (1979). A comparison of Robert Lang's psychoanalytic c psychotherapy and Erving Polster's Gestalt therapy. *Smith College Studies in Social Work,* 49(2), 146–157.

Little, L. (1990). Gestalt therapy with females involved in intimate violence. In S. Smith, M. Williams, & K. Rosen (Eds.), *Violence hits home: Comprehensive approaches to domestic violence* (pp. 47–65). New York: Springer Publishing Company.

Mahrer, A., White. M., Howard, T., & Gagnon, R. (1992). How to bring some very good moments in psychotherapy sessions. *Psychotherapy Research,* 2(4), 252–265.

Melnick, J. (2008). Group supervision and Gestalt therapy. *Counselor Education and Supervision,* 48(1), 48–60.

Meyer, L. (1991). Using Gestalt therapy in the treatment of anorexia nervosa. *British Review of Bulimia and Anorexia Nervosa,* 5(1), 7–16.

Miller, M. (1989). Introduction to Gestalt therapy verbatim. *Gestalt Journal,* 12(1), 5–24.

Napoli, D., & Walk, C. (1989). Circular learning: Teaching and learning Gestalt therapy in groups. *Journal of Independent Social Work,* 27(1), 57–70.

Nevis, E. (Ed.). (1992). *Gestalt therapy.* New York: Gardner Press.

Nevis, E. (Ed.) (2000). *Gestalt therapy: Perspectives and applications.* Cambridge, MA: Gestalt Press.

Oaklander, Y. (1992). Gestalt work with children: Working with anger and introjects. In E. Nevis (Ed.), *Gestalt therapy* (pp. 263–284). New York: Gardner Press.

O' Leary, E., & Page, R. (1990). An evaluation of a person-centered Gestalt group using the semantic differential. *Counseling Psychology Quarterly,* 3(I), 13–20.

Perls, F. (1947). *Ego, hunger, and aggression: A revision of Freud's theory and method.* London: Allen & Unwin.

Perls, F. (1969a). *Gestalt therapy verbatim.* Moab, UT: Real Person Press.

Perls, F. (1969b). *In and out of the garbage pail.* Moab, UT: Real Person Press.

Perls, F. (1973). *The Gestalt approach and eye witness to therapy.* Palo Alto, CA: Science and Behavior Books.

Perls, F. S., Hefferline, R. F., & Goodman, P. (1951). *Gestalt therapy.* New York: Julian Press.

Perls, L. (1992). Concepts and misconceptions of Gestalt therapy. *Journal of Humanistic Psychology,* 32(3), 50–56.

Polster, E. (1992). The self in actjon: A Gestalt outlook. In J. Zeig (Ed.), *The evolution of psychotherapy: The second conference* (pp. 143–154). New York: Brunner/Mazel.

Polster, E., & Polster, M. (1973). *Gestalt therapy integrated: Contours of theory and practice.* New York: Brunner/Mazel.

Polster, E., Polster, M., & Smith. E. (1990). Gestalt approaches. In J. Zeig & M. Munion, (Eds.). *What is psychotherapy? Contemporary perspectives* (pp. 103–111). San Francisco: Jossey-Bass Publishers.

Potocky, M. (1993). An art therapy group for clients with chronic schizophrenia. *Social Work with Groups,* 16(3), 73–82.

Saner, R. (1989). Culture bias of Gestalt therapy: Made in USA. *Gestalt Journal,* 12(2), 57–71.

Satir, V. (1983). *Conjoint family therapy.* Palo Alto, CA: Science and Behavioral Books.

Scanlon, P. (1980). A Gestalt approach to insight-oriented trcatment. *Social Casework,* 61(7), 407–415.

Shepard, I. (1970). Limitations and cautions in Gestalt approach. In J. Fagan & I. L. Shepard (Eds.), *Gestalt therapy now.* Palo Alto, CA: Science and Behavioral Books.

Shore, J. (1978). The use of self-identity workshop with recovering alcoholics. *Social Work with Groups,* 1(3), 299–307.

Siemens, H. (1993). A Gestalt approach in the care of persons with HIV. *Gestalt Journal,* 16(1), 91–104.

Sluckin, A., Weller, A., & Highton, J. (1989). Recovering from trauma: Gestalt therapy with an abused child. *Maladjustment and Therapeutic Education,* 7(3), 147–157.

Smith, E. (1992a). *Gestalt voices.* Norwood, NJ: Ablex Publishing Company.

Smith, E. (1992b). Personal growth and social influence. In *Gestalt voices* (pp. 294–295). Norwood, NJ: Ablex Publishing Company.

Sternek, K. (2007). Attachment theory and Gestalt psychology. *Gestalt Theory,* 29(4), 310–318.

Stevens, L. (1975). *Gestalt is.* Moab, UT: Real People Press.

Swanson, J. (1988). Boundary processes and boundary states: A proposed revision of the Gestalt theory of boundary disturbances. *Gestalt Journal,* 11(2), 5–24.

Trombini, E. (2007). Focal play-therapy and eating behavior self-regulation in preschool children. *Gestalt Theory,* 29(4), 294–301.

Trombini, E., & Trombini, G. (2006). Focal play-therapy in the extended child-parents context: A clinical case. *Gestalt Theory,* 28(4), 375–388.

Umphrey, D. (2007), The contributions of Gestalt psychology to the active audience theory of communication. *Gestalt Theory,* 29(1), 74–86.

Wedam, U. (2007) Relations and structures: Psychotherapeutic care with traumatized refugees. *Gestalt Theory,* 29(4), 302–309.

Wheeler, G. (1992). Gestalt ethics. In E. Nevis (Ed.), *Gestal therapy* (pp. 113–128). New York: Gardner Press.

Yontef, G. (1987). Gestalt therapy 1986: A polemic. *Gestalt Journal,* 10(1), 41–68.

Yontef, G. (2005) Gestalt therapy theory of change. In A. Woldt & S. Toman (eds.), *Gestalt therapy, history, theory, and practice.* London, UK: Sage Publications.

Zinker, J. (1977). *Creative process in Gestalt therapy.* New York: Vintage Books.

Zinker, J. (1991). Creative process in Gestalt therapy: The therapist as artist. *Gestalt Journal,* 14(2), 7 1–88.

Zinker, J. (1992). The Gestalt approach to couple therapy. In E. Nevis (Ed.), *Gestalt therapy* (pp. 285–302). New York: Gardner Press.

HYPNOSIS

Hypnotic skills are used to tap the client's latent and actual potential to creatively cope with current problems by identifying abilities that might serve as useful problem-solving resources

Hypnosis and Social Work Practice: Incorporating New Perspectives from Neuroscience

Robert MacFadden

Social work has had a long history of embracing theories and interventions developed by other disciplines. Its biopsychosocial perspective makes approaches that bridge these three elements particularly attractive. Hypnosis is an altered state of consciousness that involves the brain, body, and mind in unique ways, and this state can be achieved naturally or through a therapeutic relationship. In certain situations, such as child abuse, victims may naturally develop dissociative self-hypnotic skills to cope with the trauma of abuse (Winsor, 1993). Details of the hypnotic state or trance are discussed further below.

The term "hypnosis" can also be used to imply an intervention where the state of hypnosis is achieved through various induction methods and suggestions are made to achieve particular goals. "Hypnotherapy" is another term for this deliberate type of intervention using hypnosis. The phrase "neutral hypnosis" is used to describe experiencing the hypnotic state but not incorporating any suggestions for change.

Hypnosis, however, has not generally been adopted by social workers. While some leaders in professional hypnosis associations are social workers, it is still very unusual for hypnosis to be part of the social work curriculum at any level. Without this kind of background knowledge, social workers may lack a fundamental understanding of what hypnosis is and how it can be helpful to their practice. There are still stereotypes that exist, fostered by the media and stage hypnosis, that depict the hypnotist in a controlling Svengali fashion, attempting to manipulate the audience. The negative publicity and issues concerning recovered memories through hypnosis may add to the concern.

Overview of Hypnosis

Three Approaches

There are many approaches to hypnosis, but authoritarian, indirect, and permissive are the most common. *Authoritarian* is the classic version of hypnotic approach, with the hypnotist as expert in a commanding position, with statements such as "you will." The *indirect* approach reflects the style developed by Milton Erickson (Erikson, Rossi, & Rossi, 1976; Knight, 1991; Lankton & Lankton, 2008; Rossi, 1980), which encourages the client to participate and suggests that the client "may or may not" experience certain feelings. This indirectness reduces resistance and keeps the conscious mind busy while the hypnotist works with the unconscious mind. An example is the use of metaphor during trance that has underlying messages. For instance, a client who is experiencing digestive problems that are largely psychological and fueled by excessive stress may be encouraged to imagine a free-flowing gentle and relaxing river, cooling the banks and cleaning the river bed (Miller & Whorwell, 2009). The *permissive* form of hypnosis is particularly popular and resonates with many social workers. It centers on the client, maximizing client choice and client self-involvement.

It is essential to understand that although hypnosis frequently involves a professional using techniques to help the client achieve a trance, all hypnosis is actually self-hypnosis. The hypnotic trance is achieved through the client's volition, actions, and resources. The social worker, using hypnosis, is essentially a guide or facilitator. This is a familiar role for social workers. In this sense, permissive hypnosis reflects a strengths and empowerment perspective. It also supports a client-centered, client-focused, and client-directed approach, as reflected in the Common Factors research (Duncan & Miller, 2000), which highlights the enormous significance of the client's contributions, including resources and situation, to therapeutic change.

In many cases, the skills and learnings through experiencing hypnosis can assist the client with other problems or can serve to strengthen the client's existing situation and resources. As an example, the social worker may use hypnosis to help the client develop skills in deep relaxation to reduce stress. Clients could also be taught self-hypnosis to achieve this state themselves. Detailed scripts or suggestions can be constructed to address a wide range of problems and goals. For a comprehensive reference text of professionally developed hypnotic suggestions and metaphors, see Hammond (1990). Frequently these self-hypnosis scripts and suggestions also include positive self-affirmations to strengthen the self-esteem or to achieve other goals.

Trance

Although the semantics of the word "trance" sound exotic, we all experience natural forms of trances regularly in our lives. This may occur when we are watching an engaging movie, reading a book, or staring at a fire, as examples. We are focusing so intently that time seems to fly by. In fact, time distortion is one of the primary characteristics of trance. We may check our watch after the movie and realize that 3 hours has just passed in what feels to be a very short period of time. Or we may be driving in a car and suddenly realize that we can't remember anything about the last 10 miles. Other characteristics of trance can involve focused attention, lowered blood pressure and pulse, dilated pupils, drawing inward and less-easy distraction by surroundings, reduced critical thinking, heightened receptivity to suggestion, possible heightening of imagination, and potential feelings of dissociation.

Acceptability and Effectiveness

Hypnosis has been accepted as a viable form of treatment for certain conditions by the American Medical Association and the British Medical Association since the mid-1950s. The National Institutes of Health, as one example, in 1996 declared there was "strong evidence for the use of hypnosis in alleviating pain associated with cancer" (NIH Technology Assessment Panel, 1996, pp. 313–318). Frederic Reamer (2006, p. 191) describes hypnosis as part of several "widely accepted clinical innovations" which are "based on solid research and theoretical foundations" (Reamer, 2006, p. 193).

Given that hypnosis has the power to directly influence the brain and to alter perceptions, cognitions, and behavior, its impact on a variety of conditions can be substantial. In a review of hypnosis in medicine, Stewart (2005) identifies improvement through hypnosis in areas such as allergies, pain from surgery and childbirth, skin conditions such as warts, irritable bowel syndrome, surgical healing, asthma, fibromyalgia, obesity, smoking, and sexual impotency, as examples. Stewart reports that hypnosis is generally considered a benign process, with few contraindications, with the caveat that pseudomemories may be created if leading questions are asked during a hypnotic investigation.

Hypnotizability and Contraindications

Individuals vary in their ability to be hypnotized, from those who have little or no ability (about 2% to 10% of the population) to the highly hypnotizable (about 10%) or virtuosos. Hilgard and Weitzenhoffer developed a standardized instrument called the Stanford Hypnotic Susceptibility Scales to assess the level of susceptibility of individuals to hypnosis (Hilgard, 1965). He and his colleagues found that suggestibility is relatively stable in individuals, although there is some peaking between the ages of 9 to 12, a slight decline in adolescence, a plateau in middle age, and a dropoff after that. According to Brown and Fromm (1986), 60% of the population are sufficiently hypnotizable to warrant the use of hypnosis. Others, such as Milton Erickson and many of his followers, believe that all people are hypnotizable if they trust the therapist, if they are motivated, if they understand what hypnosis is, and if the hypnotic induction is individualized to meet their needs and experiences. Contraindications for hypnosis can include hostile, suspicious, and highly rigid clients and those with borderline personalities, epilepsy, and schizophrenia.

Emerging Neuroscience Knowledge

Advances in neurosciences and allied fields and developments in imaging technologies have brought us much closer to understanding how our brains function (Damasio, 2000; Gazzaniga,

Ivry, & Mangun, 2002). Social workers have begun to address this new area (Applegate & Shapiro, 2005; Johnson, 1999, 2001), along with others (Badenoch, 2008; Grawe, 2007). Understanding the nature of hypnosis from a brain perspective promises to provide empirical insights into hypnosis, what it is and how it influences the mind, feelings, cognitions, and behaviors.

The key element in hypnotic change focuses on the unconscious, or what is sometimes called the subconscious. The unconscious is viewed as a powerful component of our mental processing, which is directly tied into our physical and mental functioning. Emerging neuroscience knowledge is supporting the primary nature of the unconscious in our mental life, with some authors estimating that well over 90% of our mental processing is unconscious (Jensen, 2008; Materna, 2007). Mental activity can be viewed in the context of two systems: explicit and implicit. Both systems are involved in perception, analysis, emotion, memory, and other functions. The explicit mental processing system involves conscious access and processing, including explicit or declarative memory. Explicit memory involves situational memories of events and facts that are available to our consciousness. This is the system that we sense as ourselves, and that we identify with. While it can be powerful, it operates through working memory, which can manage 5 to 9 bits of information at one time. Many approaches to therapy address the explicit system through rational exploration of problems, cognitions, affect, and behaviors. Identification of goals and the intervention are then consciously designed to achieve specific outcomes. Explicit memory processes are the easiest to access and impact from an intervention perspective.

The implicit processing system is generally unavailable to consciousness. It forms from birth and contains knowledge, memories, perceptions, biases, and other things that have been accumulated throughout life. It is powerful and can process many things in parallel. As examples, our implicit systems are always monitoring our bodily states to ensure that factors such as blood pressure, insulin levels, and heart rate stay within acceptable parameters. It is connected with these automatic control systems that maintain our health within normal conditions. Early learned skills such as how to stand, walk, and talk have been incorporated within the implicit system, and these activities occur automatically without conscious awareness.

The implicit system is more than just automatic responses and control. It contains ways to analyze information and develop knowledge, such as being able to identify relationships between things and to develop and use "rules of thumb" to help us make decisions. This implicit knowledge helps us make decisions quickly and automatically. We do not have the ability in our consciousness to handle all the decisions that life requires, so our implicit mental processing system has the capacity to do so much while our consciousness selects what's important to consider.

Most forms of therapy deliberately work at the explicit level, but forms of interventions such as psychodynamic models may target both the implicit and explicit levels.

Hypnosis, which provides access to the unconscious, can be used to foster change through helping to change perceptions, expectations, beliefs, feelings, and behaviors. Through trance, hypnosis assumes that the unconscious is accessed and the positive suggestions given while the conscious mind is distracted in some manner such as focusing on a task will have an impact on the unconscious. The unconscious is viewed as uncritical, accepting words regardless of issues of internal logic. Trance logic refers to a voluntary state of acceptance of suggestions without critical evaluation by the consciousness.

Hypnosis can also be used to influence what the person sees, hears, feels, and believes. Recent research in neuroscience indicates that hypnosis can change the top-down processing in the cortex that enables the brain to interpret sensory information. While in trance, people who are highly hypnotizable can respond to suggestions that overrule sensory data so that this data can be interpreted in unusual ways. For instance, through hypnosis people can temporarily lose the ability to see objects in color, or they can be encouraged to see color in gray-tone pictures. (Raz & Shapiro, 2002). Another example is the use of hypnosis to temporarily suppress the ability to recognize certain numbers. A classic hypnotic suggestion called "Missing Number Seven" can be employed so that subjects are unable to see the number seven in a list of numbers.

Oakley and Halligan (2009) describe how neuroscience has stimulated new research in hypnosis, especially in two areas: the cognitive and neural nature of hypnosis itself, and employing hypnosis to explore specific psychological conditions using targeted suggestions. These researchers can create symptoms of some neuropsychological disorders through hypnotic suggestion. These hypnotic analogues of psychological disorders may provide insights into how these disorders develop and function. Brain imaging is assisting with this discovery.

Neuroscience has shed some light on the state of hypnosis. Historically the nature of hypnosis has been controversial, with some critics viewing it not as a special state of altered consciousness, but merely an example of the subject being socially compliant or role playing. Neuroscience research has identified hypnosis as a special case of an altered state of consciousness with a distinct neural signature involving the anterior cingulate cortex and frontal cortical areas of the brain (Gruzelier, 2005; Oakley & Halligan, 2009; Raz & Shapiro, 2002).

It is increasingly being discovered that positive emotions are essential for both learning and change. Positive emotions, which bathe the brain in neurochemicals, generate changes in the brain that can improve memory retrieval and storage and enhance motivation and cognition, which enables clients to learn, solve problems, and make decisions. Hypnosis can assist in developing and maintaining positive emotions through fostering deep relaxation, positive visualization, and the use of scripts directed at enhancing optimism, hope, and positive self-image.

There are many approaches and variations possible for integrating hypnosis into social work practice. The following steps describe a process that incorporates hypnosis, elements of systematic desensitization, and social work practice methods.

Using Hypnosis

Steps for Incorporating into Practice

1. Develop a therapeutic alliance with the client to foster empathy and trust. Listen to the client's problems, how he or she thinks the problem developed, and things he or she thinks might work in reducing or

eliminating this problem. It is very important to acknowledge the client's view of the problem and the suffering that has been endured. Identify, articulate, and focus on the client's perceptions of positive goals as quickly as possible.

2. Explain the nature of hypnosis fully, including the fact that all hypnosis is self-hypnosis, and dispel any pre-existing myths. As examples, clients cannot be made to do things that they wouldn't normally do in a conscious state. If any danger occurs, the client will become fully conscious. Clients can never become "stuck" in a trance and can always become alert, and the client has control over the process.

3. Consider whether hypnosis might be a primary or adjunct approach to therapy for the client. Find out whether the use of hypnosis is acceptable to the client for work on this problem. Are any other better, evidence-based interventions for this type of difficulty?

4. Test for suggestibility. This might involve one of several approaches, such as the client standing upright with arms straight out and level with one hand flat and the other upright with the thumb sticking up. The client is asked to imagine a balloon filled with helium tied to one thumb while a heavy book rests in the palm of the other hand. The client is then asked to imagine the light balloon pulling up the one hand while the book weighs down the other. Eventually the client is asked to open his or her eyes, and the distance between the two arms is an approximate measure of suggestibility.

5. Use an induction procedure. One of the most common is deep relaxation with a focus on breathing, which can involve counting backwards from 10 to 1, relaxing key parts of the body from the head to the toes while focusing on breathing and the deep relaxation flowing throughout the body.

6. Use a deepening procedure after the induction to strengthen the depth of trance. This may involve helping the client to imagine stepping safely down a set of stairs and reaching the bottom and doubling the relaxation there.

7. Incorporate suggestions that are meant to help the client realize the goals. Suggestions for a client wishing to lose weight (in consultation with a physician) might be: "Pay attention to the size of each meal and eat only enough to keep you satisfied"; "A plate does not have to be cleared. Food can be left on it"; and "With each pound of weight lost, you are feeling lighter and enjoying how your clothes are starting to fit so much better." These are the kinds of images and suggestions that can be used. Like the goals, it is essential that these suggestions are the client's ideas, images, and things that are personally very meaningful. Wherever possible, use the exact words, phrases, and metaphors that the client uses. The early details shared about the problems, goals, and possible interventions should be used to deeply personalize the suggestions.

8. Sometimes a post-hypnotic suggestion is used to reinforce the goals and scripts (e.g., "Reaching for a snack and stopping yourself will remind you of the importance of waiting until mealtime").

9. Awakening. The client is gradually helped to become alert through methods such as the therapist counting backwards to 1, when the client will become alert, refreshed and having enjoyed the experience.

10. Debriefing. Discussing the experience with the client and any concerns or questions he or she might have is important. This information is used to refine the process and to connect this experience to the goals of therapy.

11. Consider assisting the client to develop a script for self-hypnosis and to learn how to conduct self-hypnosis at home. Working with the client, the social worker can develop a script that addresses the goals and may be a version of what is used in the face-to-face session, as reflected above. It is relatively easy for the therapist to record an audio version of this script on a CD, along with the other components that involve steps 5 through 9, that the client can use during the week. The client is advised to find a quiet place, to shut off all phones and devices, and to practice this in an uninterrupted way. The client may sit or lie down,

ensuring that hands and feet are not crossed, and then begin the recording. It is important not to fall asleep, so the posture and seating can be adjusted so that sleep is less likely. Repeated successful use of this process can lead to faster and deeper trances. Eventually the client will have learned this process so well that a recording may not be necessary. Having developed the skill of self-hypnosis, the client can use it in a variety of settings and for many different purposes. It can be especially useful to reduce stress at work through deep and quick relaxation. After the client gains experience in self-hypnosis, sometimes the social worker need only ask the client to go into trance using self-hypnosis, which can shorten the time needed for induction. This ability to influence their own thinking, feeling, and behavior builds a sense of self-control, moving clients away from feeling like victims to feelings of competency and control.

12. An interesting side benefit for the social worker is that this experience can be very relaxing as well. Indeed, the social worker has to learn to manage his or her own thinking while in a relaxed state to ensure that the words and instructions are carefully chosen and articulated. The worker also needs to stay alert enough to pay attention to the experience of the client, focusing on things such as signs of the depth of trance (e.g., eyelid movement, posture, delay in verbally responding) and any other client changes.

Case Example

Tom was about to be expelled from high school because he had developed a phobia for needles and was unable to tolerate the injections required by his school board. His mother attended the sessions with him and described how on a previous occasion he had to be physically held down for the injection, which had severely escalated his fear and panic about needles.

Tom was curious about hypnosis and enjoyed visualizing and imagining things. He was very motivated and interested in trying hypnosis to manage his anxiety over needles. A detailed discussion about hypnosis and trance was conducted with mother and son beforehand, with an emphasis on how all hypnosis is self-hypnosis and

that Tom would have to practice at home at least twice per week using an audio CD prepared by the author. The CD was created after the second week and contained a common relaxation induction and customized, positive self-statements related to needles and to positive well-being and enhancing self-esteem.

Tom created a scale from 1 to 10 with the least frightening thought (#1, seeing a needle at a large distance) to the most frightening thought (#10, having an injection and having the needle break off in the arm). All specific points on the scale were elaborated with descriptive details developed by Tom and were designed to create his graded experience of fear.

As part of the hypnotic experience, a virtual safe place was created by Tom that was comforting, soothing, relaxing, and beautiful. It contained pleasant and familiar sights, sounds, and common surroundings that invoked deep relaxation and feelings of comfort and safety in him. This safe place played a pivotal role in desensitizing Tom to needles. During hypnosis, with the therapist's help, Tom would move up each level in the graded hierarchy. At each level, when his anxiety reached a point that was uncomfortable, Tom would signal with his finger and he would then be verbally encouraged to return to his safe place and relax again until his anxiety had left. Once relaxed, he would signal with his finger and then proceed through the same level until he was able to tolerate his anxiety at that level without returning to the safe place. After each success, he would then return to his safe place, achieve deeper relaxation, and proceed to the next step.

After a few weeks Tom was able to tolerate his worst scenario (#10) and had developed an ability to relax quickly using the deep relaxation and visualization skills. At that point a real needle with a protective cap was brought into the room at a distance. Tom practiced his relaxation skills and was able to tolerate the needle being closer and removing the cap. An orange was added and Tom was able to watch the therapist inject the needle into the orange. Eventually Tom was able to handle the needle directly and use it himself to inject air into the orange. He actually was very interested in the mechanics and design of the needle and in understanding how it worked. Using his relaxation techniques, including moving in and out of his safe place, Tom was able to tolerate a mock injection where his sleeve was raised, water was dabbed on his arm, and the capped point of the needle was pressed into his arm. At that point Tom had the confidence to make an appointment for his injection.

The therapist was asked to attend the injection, and he assisted Tom with becoming relaxed. The nurse injected him without incident. Besides being successful with this critical requirement to attend school, Tom had developed important skills that he was able to apply in other situations when he felt anxious. Part of the hypnosis script or set of verbal messages to Tom was also directed at enhancing his self-esteem and confidence, as well as practicing deep relaxation, and positive visualizations. The homework involving the audio CD was essential and helped to deepen his abilities to relax and to visualize.

A key role for social workers is that of a teacher. Much social work involves helping clients to discover new learnings that are helpful in achieving their goals. Both successful therapy and successful learning involve neural changes. Research in neuroscience and allied fields highlights some of the conditions for this new learning to occur. Clients need to understand what is being taught or experienced. It needs to make sense to them, and most especially, it needs to be relevant. All goals need to be the clients' goals and have strong motivational meaning for them. It also helps immensely if the new knowledge can be connected to or built on the clients' existing knowledge. That's why using the clients' ideas, frameworks, and thinking is essential in developing successful scripts in hypnosis.

Additionally, the teaching and therapy have to occur within a situation of low threat yet with some challenge. And change occurs most when the clients' positive emotions are engaged, so it is important for them to be relaxed, hopeful, optimistic, and positive.

Training

As with any professional intervention, social workers require training in hypnosis to become competent. Reamer (2006) acknowledges the acceptability of hypnosis in social work practice but cautions that not obtaining formal training, certification, or supervision may exacerbate the clients' problems. Given that training in hypnosis is almost never incorporated into traditional social work curricula, professionals interested in acquiring this expertise need to seek training from other sources.

The National Guild of Hypnotists (NGH) (http://www.ngh.net/) offers certification in hypnosis and has local chapters throughout the United States and Canada. It offers several levels of training and publishes the magazine *Hypnosis*

Today. Students from a wide range of lay and professional backgrounds are accepted for training. For an example of an NGH-accredited school, see the Ontario Hypnosis Centre (http://www.ont-hypnosis-centre.com/).

The American Society of Clinical Hypnosis (ASCH) (http://www.asch.net/) is the largest U.S. organization for health and mental health care professionals using clinical hypnosis; it was founded by Milton Erickson. Members must be currently licensed, registered, or certified health care workers, with a minimum of a master's degree. Members include psychologists, clinical social workers, psychiatrists, medical doctors, dentists, master's-level nurses, and chiropractors. The ASCH offers training and certification and other resources to members.

Summary

The use of hypnosis offers social workers another important alternative in helping clients to achieve their goals. This approach is client-focused and strengths-based and uses the client's natural abilities to foster change. Knowledge and skills developed through this experience can be helpful to clients in many other ways through building self-esteem and self-efficacy and promoting positive well-being. The exciting and rich knowledge evolving from brain imaging, neuroscience, and allied fields promises to build an evidence-based understanding of how we think, learn, feel, and change and to uncover more about how hypnosis can be used effectively in professional social work practice.

References

Applegate, J., & Shapiro, J. (2005). *Neurobiology for clinical social work: Theory and practice*. New York: W. W. Norton & Company.

Badenoch, B. (2008). *Being a brain-wise therapist*. New York: W. W. Norton & Company.

Brown, D., & Fromm, E. (1986). *Hypnotherapy and hypnoanalysis*. Hillsdale, NJ: Lawrence Erlbaum Associates.

Damasio, A. (2000). *Descartes' error: Emotion, reason and the human brain*. New York: Quill.

Duncan, B. L., & Miller, S. D. (2000). *The heroic client: Doing client-directed, outcome informed therapy*. San Francisco, CA: Jossey-Bass Publishers, Inc.

Erickson, M. E., Rossi, E. L., & Rossi, S. I. (1976). *Hypnotic realities*. New York: Irvington.

Gazzaniga, M. S., Ivry, R. B., & Mangun, G. R. (2002). *Cognitive neuroscience: The biology of the mind* (2nd ed.). New York: W. W. Norton & Company.

Grawe, K. (2007). *Neropsychotherapy.* Hillsdale, NJ: Lawrence Erlbaum Associates.

Gruzelier, J. (2005). Altered states of consciousness and hypnosis in the twenty-first century. *Contemporary Hypnosis, 22*(1), 1–7.

Hammond, D. C. (1990). *Hypnotic suggestions and metaphors.* New York: W. W. Norton & Company.

Hilgard, E. R. (1965). *Hypnotic susceptibility.* New York: Harcourt Brace & World.

Jensen, E. (2008). *Brain-based learning: The new paradigm of teaching.* Thousand Oaks, CA: Corwin Press.

Johnson, H. C. (1999). *Psyche, synapse, and substance: The role of neurobiology in emotions, behavior, thinking, and addiction for non-scientists.* Greenfield, MA: Deerfield Valley Publishing.

Johnson, H. C. (2001). Neuroscience in social work practice and education. *Journal of Social Work Practice in the Addictions, 1*(3), 81–102.

Knight, B. M. (1991). Using hypnosis in private social work practice. *Journal of Independent Social Work, 5*(2), 43–46.

Lankton, S., & Lankton, C. H. (2008). *Answer within: A clinical framework for Ericksonian hypnotherapy.* Bethel, CT: Crown House Classics.

Materna, L. (2007). *Jump start the adult learner: How to engage and motivate adults using brain-compatible strategies.* Thousand Oaks, CA: Corwin Press.

Miller, V., & Whorwell, P. J. (2009). Hypnotherapy for functional gastrointestinal disorders: A review. *International Journal of Clinical and Experimental Hypnosis, 57*(3), 279–293.

Oakley, D. A., & Halligan, P. W. (2009). Hypnotic suggestion and cognitive neuroscience. *Trends in Cognitive Sciences, 13*(6), 264–270.

NIH Technology Assessment Panel (1996). Integration of behavioral and relaxation approaches into the treatment of chronic pain and insomnia. *Journal of the American Medical Association, 276,* 313–318.

Raz, A., & Shapiro, T. (2002). Hypnosis and neuroscience. *Archives of General Psychiatry, 59,* 85–90.

Reamer, F. (2006). Nontraditional and unorthodox interventions in social work: Ethical and legal implications. *Families in Society, 87*(2), 191–197.

Rossi, E. L. (1980). *The collected papers of Milton Erickson on hypnosis.* New York: Irvington.

Stewart, J. H. (2005). Hypnosis in contemporary medicine. *Mayo Clinic Proceedings, 80*(4), 511–524.

Winsor, R. M. (1993). Hypnosis: A neglected tool for client empowerment. *Social Work, 38*(5), 603–608.

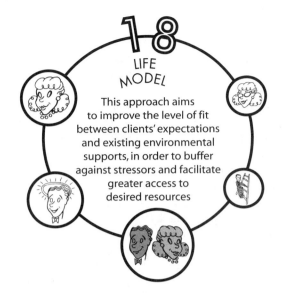

LIFE MODEL

This approach aims to improve the level of fit between clients' expectations and existing environmental supports, in order to buffer against stressors and facilitate greater access to desired resources

Advances in the Life Model of Social Work Practice

Alex Gitterman

Professor Carel Germain and I began our collaboration almost 40 years ago in the fall of 1972, when Dean Mitchell Ginsberg of Columbia formed a committee composed of Professors Germain, Funnye Goldson, and myself. The committee's charge was to reconceptualize the first-year practice courses of a two-year sequence in social work practice. We set out to develop an integrated social work practice curricula, a forerunner to foundations practice, in place of the traditional casework, group work, and community organization methods. We set out to identify the common concepts and methods in working with people, no matter what the size of the system. We shared a common belief that services should be based on the needs and preferences of clients rather than social workers' method specialization. Based on this experience, Professor Germain and I decided to conceptualize

a model of practice. This led to our first presentation of the Life Model (Gitterman & Germain, 1976). The first edition of our book followed, *The Life Model of Social Work Practice* (Germain & Gitterman, 1980).

The book represented a beginning effort to conceptualize and illustrate an integrated method of practice with individual, families, groups, organizations, and some aspects of neighborhoods and communities. We developed two conceptual mechanisms (degree of choice and problems in living) to describe and illustrate integrated practice. In conceptualizing an integrated method, we realized that there were also some distinctive knowledge and skills, such as those required to form groups or influence communities, organizations, and legislative processes. We also aimed to develop a method of practice that paid equal attention to practice with people and their social, physical, and natural environments. Ecological theory provided us with a conceptual framework that offers a dual, simultaneous focus on people and environments. In our first edition, we also attempted to differentiate the underlying theories and distinctive knowledge at various system levels—individuals, families, groups, communities, organizations, social networks—as well as the properties of social and physical environments. We also made a beginning effort to explicate the connections between "private troubles" and "organizational issues." These emerging ideas were placed within historical and philosophical perspectives.

During the next 16 years (1980–2006), dramatic changes took place in our society and profession. Social workers have been increasingly working with profoundly vulnerable clients, struggling to survive the economic and psychological consequences of poverty and discrimination. Practitioners were dealing with the devastating impact of AIDS, homelessness, substance abuse, chronic mental disorders, child abuse, and family and community violence. Clearly, the miseries and suffering in the 1990s were different in degree and substance from those encountered from the 1940s through the 1980s. With "safety net" resources being dismantled, for many clients it was difficult to endure.

Facing these bitter realities, social workers have been expected to do more in less time with decreasing resources. More than ever, professional courage, perseverance, creativity, and a widening repertoire of professional methods and skills are indispensable elements of contemporary practice. In response to these contemporary challenges, a revised and more fully expanded Life Model responded to these pervasive social changes through four major elaborations (Germain & Gitterman, 1996). First, to be responsive to oppression, social workers must develop competence in community, organizational, and legislative influence and change as well as in direct practice. The second edition of the Life Model specifies methods and skills to move back and forth from helping individuals, families, and groups, to influencing communities, organizations, and legislative bodies. Second, to effectively respond to people's varied needs, social workers must practice at whatever levels a particular situation begins and wherever

it may lead. The expanded Life Model conceptualizes and illustrates methods and skills distinct to various modalities as well as continues to describe and specify the common base of social work practice.

Third, people cope with oppression and scapegoating in many different ways. Practitioners must be careful about blaming oppressed people for their troubles. People's coping styles, strengths, and resilience must be understood and supported. In our early writing, the concept of "problems in living" organized ideas about professional assessment and interventions. Unwittingly, this formulation may have implied a deficit in the individual and collectivity. In our current writing, a more neutral stressor-stress-coping paradigm is substituted.

Finally, social workers must be sensitive to people's diverse backgrounds. Stage models of human development assume that social and emotional development follow in fixed, sequential, and universal stages. In our current presentation, a "life course" conception of human development replaces the traditional "life cycle" models.

In the 12 years since the publication of the second edition, dramatic changes have taken place in society and consequently in the profession. The third edition takes into account these pervasive changes and presents a more fully developed life-modeled practice. While retaining and refining the core of our previous work, we make use of new concepts and new content. We believe this book provides social work practitioners and students with the necessary knowledge base and practice guidelines to deal with the many professional, societal, theoretical, empirical, and ethical issues they face. In this edition, a new chapter traces social work practice and its historical traditions from its roots in the charity organization societies and the settlement house movement, to the development of professional methods, to the current social context that affects people's lives (global economy, immigration, role of federal government, new legislation, and cultural and technological changes). The chapter also explores current professional developments such as managed mental health care, practice outcomes, and evidence-based practice, and their respective influences on contemporary practice. Another new chapter, "Assessment, Practice Monitoring, and Practice

Evaluation," discusses assessment tasks common to all practice approaches and offers a few underlying distinctive ideas to life-modeled practice. The chapter also examines the tasks and skills of practice monitoring as well as the strengths and limitations of different research designs used to evaluate practice outcomes.

Ecological theory continues to provide concepts that illuminate the continuous exchanges between people and their environments. In this edition, we present new concepts from deep ecology and ecofeminism.

Human Ecology

In the revised Life Model, the ecological metaphor is broadened and deepened and continues to provide the lens for viewing the exchanges between people and their environments. Ecology, a biological science, examines the relation between living organisms and all the elements of the social and physical environments. How and why organisms achieve or fail to achieve an adaptive balance with their environments pose the major questions of ecological inquiry. Deep ecology and ecofeminism deepen and enhance our understanding that all phenomena are interconnected and interdependent as well as dependent on the cyclical processes of nature (Besthorn & Canda, 2002; Besthorn & McMillen, 2002; Gitterman & Germain, 2008; Mack-Canty, 2004; Ungar, 2002). Ecological theory, with its evolutionary, adaptive view, provides the theoretical foundation for life-modeled practice (Germain & Gitterman, 1987, 1995; Gitterman, 2008).

Person: Environment Fit

Over the life course people strive to improve the level of fit with their environments. When we feel positively about our own capacities and hopeful about having our needs and aspirations fulfilled, and when we view our environmental resources as responsive, our immediate environments and we are likely to achieve a reciprocally sustaining condition of adaptedness. Adaptive person:environment exchanges reciprocally support and release human and environmental potentials.

However, when perceived environmental and personal limitations are fueled and sustained by oppressive social and physical environments (e.g., racism, sexism, homophobism, ageism, unemployment, pollution), consequences range from heroic adaptation, to impaired functioning, to parasitic exploitation, and to individual and collective disintegration. In coping with toxic environments, some people mobilize inner strengths and resiliency to steel themselves against unnurturing environments—to be survivors rather than victims (Gitterman, 2001). Others internalize the oppression and turn it against themselves through such self-destructive behaviors as substance abuse and unprotected sex. Still others externalize the oppression, strike back, and vent their rage on those less powerful than they are through such behaviors as violence, crime, and property destruction. Readily accessible targets often include family members, neighbors, and community residents. Dysfunctional person:environment exchanges reciprocally frustrate and damage both human and environmental potentials.

In dealing with environmental demands, people appraise the adequacy of their environmental and personal resources. Stress is the outcome of a perceived imbalance between environmental demands and the capability to manage it with available internal and external resources. To relieve the stressful situation, the level of person:environment fit must be improved. This is accomplished by an active change in either—people's perceptions and behaviors, or in environmental responses, or in the quality of their exchanges.

The Environment

Person:environmental exchanges are dynamic rather than fixed processes. Ecological theory emphasizes the reciprocity of person:environmental transactions through which each influences and shapes the other over time. People need to receive from their environment the resources essential for development and survival. Reciprocally, the environment needs to receive the care necessary for its evolution.

The environment consists of social and physical layers. The former consists of the social world of other human beings, ranging from intimate social networks to bureaucratic institutions. The physical layer consists of the natural world inherited by human beings and the constructed built world of human structures, the space, which supports, contains, or arranges the structures, and the temporal rhythms, fluctuations, and periodicities of environments and of human biology (Gitterman, 2008a; Gitterman & Germain, 2008).

Complex bureaucratic organizations, a salient feature of the social environment, are prevalent forces in contemporary life. Health, education, and social service organizations profoundly affect most people's lives. In order to carry out its social assignment, an organization develops a mission and evolves structures (e.g., division of labor, chain of command, policies and procedures) to carry out its operations. While organizational mission and structures are essential to service delivery, they simultaneously create tensions and conflicts for professionals and service recipients. For example, an organization's division of labor integrates roles, minimizes duplication, and maintains accountability. At the same time, these differential role assignments create a vested interest in protecting one's own turf and other mischief. Organizational and client needs become held hostage to turf interest.

Political, economic, and cultural forces affect organizational mission and structures. Economic, social, and bureaucratic forces conspire to block access and quality services for vulnerable and oppressed people. Politicians redefine the failures of the economy as behavioral, the result of personality defects of public assistance recipients. Funding sources expect mental health agencies to diagnose and pathologize community residents rather than to view and assist them as residents experiencing life stressors.

Social networks, also a salient feature of the social environment, consist of kin, friends, neighbors, workmates, and acquaintances. Supportive linkages provide essential instrumental (goods and services), expressive (empathy, encouragement), and informational (advice, feedback) resources. They serve as essential buffers against life stressors and the stress they generate.

Not all people are able or willing to use available social supports. Some minimize, negate, or deny their difficulties or their need for assistance. Others, while aware of their life stressors, are unable to ask for assistance. Self-esteem issues and shame from negative social comparisons may account for their reluctance. Still others are inhibited by their needs for privacy.

Not all networks are able or willing to provide available social supports. Loosely knit networks may be unaware of members' difficulties. Lacking sufficient contact, a member's difficulties remain invisible. Some networks have insufficient resources to meet their members' varied needs; their resources are too stretched out to incur additional instrumental burdens. Still others withhold available resources for such reasons as selfishness and punishment (Gitterman & Germain, 2008).

Some networks provide resources but have a negative impact on recipients. Some reinforce deviance, such as drug and gang networks, by supporting dysfunctional behaviors and sabotaging more functional coping behaviors. Networks may also scapegoat and reinforce negative self-esteem. Exploitative and parasitic behaviors undermine a member's sense of well-being.

Life events such as sickness and death, job mobility and loss, marital separation and divorce, dissolve linkages to significant others. Social and emotional isolation are devastating experiences. Without viable networks, people are deprived of life-sustaining instrumental and expressive supports. Widowers who lose social ties maintained by their wives and people suffering from chronic mental illness suffer from impoverished networks.

The ecological concepts of habitat and niche are particularly relevant for understanding the environment's impact on us (Gitterman & Germain, 2008). *Habitat* refers to places where organisms are found, such as territories and nesting places. People's spatial behaviors are mediated by the texture of space, and by their age, gender, sexual orientation, culture, socioeconomic status, and experiences. The exchanges between people and their habitat take place within the context of personal space, semi-fixed space, and fixed space.

Personal space refers to an invisible spatial boundary that we maintain as a buffer against unwanted physical and social contact and to protect our privacy. Since the boundary is invisible, two or more people must negotiate a mutually comfortable distance. When less distance is transacted than desired, we experience crowding and intrusion and react with either subtle physical gestures, or with pronounced withdrawal, or with aggression. When more distance is transacted than desired, we feel the unpleasant state of disengagement and either withdraw or pursue greater intimacy. Since the amount of desired space is influenced by many individual and social factors, it carries the potential for misperception, misunderstanding, and stress.

Semi-fixed space refers to moveable objects and their arrangement in space. Furniture, floors, curtains, paint, decorative figurines, paintings, and lighting provide spatial meanings and boundaries. People rely on environmental props (doors, locks, gates, fences, signs) to regulate interactions with others and to protect their territory within the living dwelling and with the outside world. In families whose members share limited space, for example, the degree of interpersonal coordination required and the structural limits to privacy create stress. The close proximity, social overload, and spatial constraints are potential sources for interpersonal conflict.

The design of immovable objects and their arrangement in space, *fixed space,* have a profound impact on the quality of life. The high-density (i.e., limited space with a large number of people using it) structure and design of high-rise low-income housing, for example, creates unpredictable and indefensible spaces. With limited control over such public areas as elevators, hallways, and lobbies, these spaces represent dangerous threats to survival and are associated with feelings of withdrawal, alienation, and dissatisfaction.

Habitat also consists of the natural world of climate and landscape, water sources, quality of air, and animals and plants. The natural world provides the resources essential to the survival of all species. However, lack of attention to preservation of the natural world and careless, destructive abuse of our natural resources endanger us. Exploitative power by dominant groups creates technological pollution by corporations and government agencies of our air, water, soil, and food. Toxic materials are tolerated in disadvantaged neighborhoods, workplaces, and schools. Beyond supplying resources essential to survival, the natural world also lends special meaning to everyday life. Human beings have a need for a sense of kinship with nature, arising out of our evolutionary heritage. The kinship is expressed in our joy of pets and plants, our pleasures from walks in the park and swims in the ocean. Pets, for example, serve numerous functions, such as companionship and protection.

In ecology, *niche* refers to the status occupied in a community's social structure by its individuals and groups. Because dominant groups discriminate on the basis of personal or collective characteristics such as color, gender, sexual orientation, socioeconomic status, and physical or mental condition, many people are forced to occupy niches that limit their opportunities, rights, and aspirations. Dominant groups coercively use power to oppress and disempower vulnerable populations, creating and maintaining such social pollutions as poverty, chronic unemployment, lack of affordable housing, inadequate health care and schools, institutionalized racism and sexism, homophobia, and barriers to community participation by those with physical or mental disabilities. Communities of people are placed in marginalized, stigmatized, and destructive niches such as "welfare mother," "ex-addict," "ex-con," "the underclass," "homeless," "borderline," and so on.

Individuals, Families, and Groups

Over the life course, individuals, families, and groups experience unique developmental pathways.[2] Diverse human experiences create distinctive transactional processes that occur and recur at any point in the life course. These developmental processes take place within the context of historical, social, and individual time. People born at the same period of time (birth cohorts) experience common formative influences that have a profound effect on their opportunities and expectations. Because birth cohorts live through a different historical time and social forces, they undergo developmental processes of growing up and growing old differently from other birth cohorts. For example, the Great Depression of the 1930s, the civil rights movement and "war on poverty" of the 1960s, the Vietnam War of the 1970s, the terrorist acts of September 11, 2001, wars in Iraq and Afghanistan, and the dramatic economic changes of the 2000s differently shaped the experiences and expectations of the respective birth cohorts. Each birth cohort is deeply affected by its generational events.

The timing of collective life issues in a family, group, or community also influences individual biopsychosocial development (i.e., social time). For example, in contemporary society less predictable timetables exist for beginning and completing school, leaving home, remaining single or marrying, having a child, beginning a new career, retiring, etc. Similarly, family cultures may have different timetables for male and female developmental expectations. These collective experiences also affect people's experiences over the life course.

Within the context of historical and social time, people construct their respective meaning from life experiences. Personal constructions or narratives, individual time, also profoundly influence human development. Essentially, a life course view emphasizes understanding the impact of historical, social, and individual perspectives and sensitivity to the differences in human development.

Over the life course, individuals, families, and groups deal with external life stressors and their associated demands (Lazurus & Folkman, 1984). A life stressor (e.g., job change or loss, separation and divorce, death and dying, chronic and acute illness, interpersonal conflict) creates demands for the individual as well as the collectivity. When we appraise that a stressor(s) exceeds our external and/or internal resources to deal with it, we experience stress (manifested physiologically and/or emotionally). Stressful reactions and feelings range from unpleasant, to disquieting, to immobilizing. Intensity is determined by dimensions of the actual stressor(s), its meaning to the individual and collectivity, and the availability of environmental supports.

When confronting a life stressor, a process of conscious or unconscious primary appraisal takes place by which we ask ourselves, "What's going on here?" "Can I deal with it?" "Is this a challenge I can manage, or is it a current or future threat of serious harm or loss?" (Lazarus, 1984). We appraise a life stressor as a challenge rather than a threat when we believe we have sufficient personal and environmental resources to master it. Although a perceived challenge might be stressful, feelings of excitement make adrenaline flow and anticipated mastery prevails. In contrast, an appraised threat of harm and loss creates feelings of vulnerability and risk.

One person's threat is another person's challenge. The interplay of cultural, environmental, and personal factors and past experiences affect primary appraisal processes.

When a life stressor is perceived as a threat, a process of secondary appraisal takes place by which we ask ourselves, "What can I do about this situation?" At this moment, we launch our efforts to cope with the stressor. Coping measures primarily consist of efforts to manage our feelings and/or to use personal and environmental resources to manage the stressor(s). Personal resources include problem-solving skills, flexibility, motivation, belief systems, resilience, optimism, and self-esteem. Environmental resources include informal social supports such as family, friends, neighbors; public and private social agencies, and various institutions; and the built and natural dimensions of the physical environment. The two interrelated functions of coping, problem solving and management of feelings, have an interesting reciprocal relation to each other. In many coping responses to stressful person:environment encounters, the two functions may proceed together. However, in the early, acute phase of very severe stressors in particular, it may be difficult to proceed with problem solving until intense negative feelings are brought under some degree of control; otherwise the feelings are apt to immobilize problem-solving efforts. But such feelings may be difficult to control until the person has experienced some degree of progress in the beginning steps of problem solving. A saving grace in this seeming paradox is an ability to cope with the life stressor by unconsciously blocking out negative feelings temporarily so that some problem solving can begin. This is frequently seen in the unconscious denial (defense) of people who have suffered a grievous loss or harm.

When our coping efforts are effective, we experience a sense of relief. When coping efforts fail, physiological and emotional strains are intensified, which can lead to augmented coping efforts, immobilization, or dysfunctional physical, emotional, and social responses. Dysfunctional responses generate more stressors in a downward spiral toward deterioration and disintegration. For example, a terminated romance may trigger a reactive depression. To cope with feelings of abandonment and hopelessness, a person may turn to alcohol to numb the pain. The dependence on alcohol may then create additional stressors at the workplace and with other relationships.

The Life Model

Professional Function

Direct Practice Level: The professional function as defined by the Life Model is to improve the level of fit between people's (individual, family, group, community) perceived needs, capacities, and aspirations and their environmental supports and resources. Through processes of mutual assessment, the worker and the service recipient(s) determine practice focus, choosing to:

1. Improve a person's (collectivity's) ability to manage stressor(s) through more effective personal and situational appraisals and behavioral skills
2. Influence the social and physical environments to be more responsive to a person's (collectivity's) needs
3. Improve the quality of person:environment exchanges.

By helping people to change their perceptions, cognitions, feelings, or behaviors, their ability to manage a stressor(s) is improved, or its adverse impact may be reduced. By effectively influencing environmental responsiveness, people gain access to desired support and resources and, in turn, develop greater control over their lives. Finally, by improving the exchanges between people and their environments, both actively adapt to the needs and demands of the other. The latter provides the greatest opportunities for lasting improvement of the level of person:environment fit.

Community, Organizational and Political Levels: Social workers in practice today deal with profoundly vulnerable populations, overwhelmed by circumstances and events they feel powerless to control. On a daily basis, social workers are bombarded and reminded of the devastating assault on our clients and the dismantling of entitlements and services. The poor (particularly of color), the sick, the children, the immigrants are blamed for their plight and held to pay for the excesses of the affluent in our society. The anger, the alarm, and the despair intensify as we anticipate the suffering that lies ahead and the inhumanity that permits such injustices.

Corporate and other special interest lobbies ensure a widening gap between the poor and the wealthy; as the poor become poorer the wealthy become wealthier. The gun lobby and polluters reign supreme. While influential voting blocks receive government subsidies, the "safety net" established to mitigate and cushion economic forces is being brutally reduced. Martin Luther King, Jr. mordantly observed that our society preaches socialism for the rich and rugged individualism for the poor.

When community and family supports are weakened, social deterioration increases the risk of personal deterioration. The task of providing direct services to vulnerable and oppressed populations becomes progressively more difficult to fulfill. Within this social context, our professional function must include involvement at the community, organizational, and political levels. In life-modeled practice, professional function includes: mobilizing community resources to improve community life; influencing organizations to develop responsive policies and services; and politically influencing local, state, and federal legislation and regulations.

In this way, the historic polarity of cause versus function (Lee, 1929) is replaced with a contemporary melding of cause and function as an essential part of life-modeled practice (Schwartz, 1969). Historically, the profession experienced interpersonal and ideological conflicts between those who emphasized bringing about social change on behalf of social justice, the "cause," as the primary characteristic of social work, and those who emphasized "function" as the primary characteristic of social work practice—that is, the technologies used by practitioners to bring about individual change. In reality, however, a cause won requires a function (technology, services, and programs for individuals, families, and groups) to carry it out. A further and specific technology (organization and political advocacy) is required for winning a cause. Clearly, both cause and function must be hallmarks of practice and education for practice if social work is to ready itself for the new century.

Problem Definition
(Person: Environment Exchanges)

How a stressor is defined largely governs what will be done about it. If, for example, the source of a painful life issue is believed to be internal and defined in psychological terms, a disease model will psychologically guide social work interventions. Goals will refer to internal change through gaining psychological insight.

For example, Billy does not pay attention in school, and the school threatens to transfer him to a special school. Organic disability has been ruled out and the life issue is defined as an emotional disturbance. This emphasis on psychopathology leads to a linear dichotomized view of the child and his environment. He has an internal disorder that requires psychological "excision." He and his mother might be viewed as having symbiotic difficulties in separating, so his mother is added to the treatment program. Different therapists might treat the mother and child. Help exclusively focuses on psychological processes. Little or no attention is given to school, social networks, and neighborhood conditions that might contribute to the life stressor.

Similarly, if Billy is viewed through a cognitive behavioral lens, the emphases will be on teaching and rewarding more adaptive behaviors and extinguishing maladaptive behaviors. This view will also encourage a dichotomized child and environment association. The entire responsibility and burden for change is placed on the child.

If life issues are defined as rooted in social pathology, then intervention is likely to be conceived in social-institutional terms, on a social action. Goals will refer to external change and the practice method will be primarily case or class advocacy. In advocating for Billy, his right to stay in school may be won. He can stay in school, but the life issues that had kept him from learning in school may still remain. However, in life-modeled practice the social pathological definition does not preclude individual attention to Billy and his mother as well as to advocacy.

If life stressors are defined as disharmonious person:environment exchanges, then interventions are likely to be conceived as improving the level of fit between Billy and his environments. Goals will refer to reducing or eliminating the life stressor if possible, strengthening coping skills, and acquiring environmental instrumental and emotional resources.

Psychologically oriented skills will be directed to progressive forces in the personality or their development. These include sensory-perceptual capacities, positive emotions, and thinking and problem-solving abilities. Supports in the organizational and network fields and physical settings will be mobilized and used. If needed, the work will include increasing the responsiveness of the organization affecting the client, including the worker's own agency.

In Billy's situation, depending on the source(s) of the stressor(s), several separate or joint entry points into the person:environment field might be possible for effective help:

1. If the stressor arose from Billy's difficulty with the life transition of adapting to a nourishing school environment, help is directed to improving his coping skills through individual or group (other boys in a similar situation as Billy) modality (Gitterman & Shulman, 2005).

2. If the stressor arose from the family's dysfunctional patterns, help is directed to modifying those patterns with the family or a few families experiencing a similar stressor (Wise, 2005).

3. If the stressor arose from dysfunctional exchanges between Ricky and family and school, help is directed on an individual, family, or group basis toward removing barriers in their communication and stimulating mutual problem solving.

4. If the stressor emerged from the social structure and climate of Billy's classroom, the social worker and teacher could undertake classroom meetings. Such meetings are designed to help the children (and teacher) learn to express their feelings and ideas about their shared experiences. Such an approach would not only help Billy, but on a preventive level, it could be helpful to all the children and to the teacher by reducing scapegoating by the children, biased responses and expectations held by the teacher, or other dysfunctional exchanges.

5. If the stressor came from a lack of after-school resources, the worker could try to help the school obtain a grant and develop a program.

6. If the stressor converged from Billy's concerns about overcrowded classrooms, unsafe school bathrooms, or fears of walking past the neighborhood drug users and dealers or assaultive teenagers on his way to school, his parent(s) could be helped to join with other concerned neighborhood or community parents in approaching the school, police, and local legislators to improve school conditions and to gain safe routes to school.

This analysis is purposively oversimplified to highlight the varied practice options emerging from the Life Model's broad focus on person: environment exchanges. In reality, Billy's stress most likely arouse from multiple sources. Sometimes effective work on one stressor supports coping with others. Other times, work is directed to two or more stressors (guidelines for appropriate focus is discussed later).

The major point is that a social worker using a Life Model conceptual lens is more likely to "see" diverse points of entry into a complex situation and less likely to fit a client into a narrow theoretical construction. Our practice theories and models must be responsive to people and their situations rather than fitting their life issues into our own theoretical and practice preoccupations and biases. Similarly, a worker's specialization in individual, family, group, or community practice should not determine what service is provided, but rather the received service should be based on the applicant's or client's needs and preferences.

Life Stressors Schema

Over the life course, people must cope with three interrelated life issues: difficult life transitions and traumatic life events; environmental pressures; and dysfunctional interpersonal processes. Although these three life stressors are interrelated, each takes on its own force and magnitude and provides focus to practice with individuals, families, groups, communities, organizations, and politics.

Difficult Life Transitions and Traumatic Life Events: Life transitions include biological as well as social changes. The physical and biological changes of infancy, childhood, puberty, adolescence, adulthood, and advanced age are universal, but social expectations and patterns associated with the changes vary across cultures. For example, puberty is a biological condition; adolescence is a social status.[3] Biological factors associated with pubertal changes elicit changing responses and demands from the environment of family, school personnel, and peers.

People also experience stress from entering new experiences and relationships and leaving familiar ones. Beginnings (entrances) generate stress. Entering a new neighborhood, school, relationship(s), or job, having a baby, or acquiring a new diagnostic label are filled with ambiguity, new role expectations, and challenges. Leavings (endings) are usually more stressful than beginnings. Ending an intimate relationship through separation or death, losing a job, leaving a school, and separating from a child or parent are characterized by painful loss and change. Unexpected life transitions are more stressful than expected ones. Similarly, when life entrances and exits come too early or too late in the life course, they are likely to be stressful. For example, a young adolescent who becomes a parent, and an older grandparent who has primary responsibility for parenting, may find that the timing of the experience creates additional stress. The abruptness, enormity, and immediacy of traumatic life events cause personal crisis and long-lasting residue of pain. Unexpected death and illness, violence of rape, displacement caused by natural disasters, loss of a cherished home or job are overwhelming and immobilizing. Severe physical, psychological, and/or social loss is a primary characteristic of trauma.

Environmental Pressures: The social and physical environments provide essential instrumental resources and emotional support to the tasks of daily living. They also create significant troubles and distress. For some individuals and collectivities, organizational and informal network resources are available, but they are unable to access or use them. For others, organizational and network structures and functions are unresponsive to their personal styles and needs. And for still others, important organizational and network resources are unavailable and their basic needs remain unmet. Similarly, the physical environment's natural and built resources may be available, but some people are unable to use them. For others, available physical resources are unresponsive to their styles and needs.

And for others, basic natural and built resources are minimal.

Dysfunctional Interpersonal Processes: For conceptual clarity and consistency, interpersonal processes apply only when the social worker is involved with a family/group system or subsystem. If a social worker, for example, is working with an abused woman but not with the partner, the focus is on life transitional concerns (e.g., separation, grief) and/or environmental concerns (e.g., linkage with community resources, negotiating with her partner, securing a court order of protection). By contrast, a focus on dysfunctional interpersonal processes requires conjoint work with both partners and/or the children.

In responding to life transitional and environmental stressors, the family and group serve as a resource and buffer. However, problematic internal family or group relationships and communication patterns exacerbate existing stress and/or become yet another painful stressor in people's lives. Dysfunctional family and group processes are expressed in such behaviors as scapegoating, rigid alliances, withdrawal, and hostility. While dysfunctional for individual members and the collectivity, these behaviors may maintain an illusion of functioning and the collectivity's continued existence. For example, scapegoating may stave off disorganization in the family or group at the expense of the individual member. These behaviors become fixed and obstruct the potential for mutual support.

Similar dysfunctional processes arise between social workers and clients in the form of discrepant expectations, misunderstandings and misperceptions, value conflicts, and differences in backgrounds (Gitterman, 1983, 1989). These processes interfere with the helping process and create additional stress for clients.

A life stressor often generates associated stressors. When they are not managed or resolved, additional stressors erupt (the "spread phenomenon").

Case Example

Ms. Northern, the manager of a single mothers' residence, referred Marcia, a 23-year-old African-American single mother of a 2-month-old daughter, Denise, to Family Services. Marcia had been living in the residence for the past 6 months; remaining there was made conditional on her accepting the referral to the agency. In the first session, she expressed anger at Ms. Northern for forcing her to come to the agency and blaming her for all the arguments and fights in the residence. At the same time, she wanted help with the stress in her life, particularly being a single parent and her new role as a mother. She said that at times she is overwhelmed and even angry at Denise "for being so needy." We mutually agreed to focus on three interrelated stressors: (1) She had to deal with the life transition of living with a partner to living as a single parent; (2) She had to deal with problematic environmental transactions with the residence manager and the other residents; and (3) She had to secure permanent housing. A fourth stressor evolved from our work, namely her distrust and testing of me (and my reactions).

The life transitional stressor centers on Marcia's entry into motherhood and becoming the sole caretaker and responder to the unrelenting demands of an infant. Marcia's history feeds ambivalence about her single mother status and its associated roles. She was placed in foster care at age 7, moved from home to home, and lost contact with her mother at the age of 13. While she feels rage at her mother for not wanting her ("I'll probably forgive my mother someday, but right now I'd like to kill her even though she's already dead"), she is trying to forgive her because she recognizes that her mother was a "victim of the system." Soon after giving birth, she looked for a job and child care with minimal success. She states, "I feel stuck, isolated, like I have no life of my own…I can't get off welfare without a job; I can't get a job without child care; and I can't afford child care while on welfare." Marcia feels caught in a "vicious circle" that makes her want to "throw off all responsibility."

Marcia's ambivalence is evident in her vacillation between poignantly questioning whether Denise's needs exceed her ability to give and vehemently asserting that she will sell her body, if she must, to keep Denise happy, safe, well fed, and with her. When Marcia perceives herself to be a capable mother, she is responsive to Denise. However, when the urgency of Denise's needs conflicts with Marcia's needs, she becomes overwhelmed with the depth of her own unmet needs. Marcia's pain becomes more intense and intolerable. At these moments, she impulsively responds to Denise with anger and impatience. Incidents the worker observed during a couple of session illustrate life transitional stress:

1/11: Denise started to fret a little bit. Marcia responded by talking to her in a nonstop, repetitive manner. Denise tried to follow her mother's erratic cues, but looked helpless and confused. She began to cry and Marcia jammed a bottle in her mouth, which began to leak all over. Marcia swore and her anger became overt. Denise began to choke on the milk, and Marcia, trying to control her anger, set Denise on her lap, vigorously patting her back. When Denise regurgitated, Marcia scolded her. She seemed really furious and made a few half-hearted attempts to smooth her rage away by calling Denise by various pet names, and telling her that she was loved.

1/25: At the end of the session, Marcia yelled at Denise, "What the fuck?!…What did you do now?… I can't believe this!…Guess what, smarty pants: I brought another set of clothes—na! na!" Marcia continued to swear and became increasingly agitated, bordering on rage, that Denise had soiled her diaper. She was again talking to Denise nonstop, finally yelling, "And that fucking bastard of a father you have is a good for shit." She continued talking to Denise as she angrily unsnapped her clothes, saying, "stinky, stinky, stinky…"

Marcia feels that Denise, like the rest of the world, is unfair and taking advantage of her. With unresolved feelings of being abandoned by her family and by Denise's father, pressures of being a single parent ("I'm tired…I'm hungry…I hardly got to wash my face today"), and insufficient environmental supports and resources, Marcia is unable to be predictable and consistent with Denise. With so many of her own needs unmet, Marcia has difficulty viewing Denise as a separate human being with separate needs.

Severe environmental pressures exacerbate Marcia's difficult life transitions. Marcia lives well below the poverty line, receiving Aid to Families with Dependent Children, Medicaid, and food stamps benefits. She considers herself homeless, having a maximum of 6 months left at the residence before she must leave. She further states that Ms. Northern "keeps holding it over me that she can kick me out." She adds with bravado, "I am a survivor. I am not going to take shit from anybody," least of all Ms. Northern and the other "girls" in the residence. With neither sufficient income nor the necessary child care to support herself and Denise, Marcia is feeling increasingly hopeless about getting off welfare. Her relationship to her last foster parents represents the single most enduring relationship in Marcia's life. She describes them as "my friends when I need them." Outside of her ties to her foster family, her social network is negligible. She complains that she has no friends, that she pushes people away without realizing it. Finally, she has severed all ties with the remainder of her biological family, many of whom live nearby, because "I can't forgive them for refusing to take me and my sister and brothers in when my mom caved in."

Marcia's environment is fraught with severe limitations: chronic racial prejudice and discrimination; lack of affordable housing; limited employment opportunities; unavailability of child care services; Denise's father's heroin addiction; cohabitation with several other young women and their babies; demand for conformity to house rules; a limited social network; and finally, the unceasing and ever-present responsibility for being the sole caretaker of an infant. These environmental stressors combine together, and act independently, significantly to lessen Marcia's ability to tolerate the demands of new motherhood, which has radically changed her life. The social environment only serves to exacerbate Marcia's emotional and social neglect and profound sense of despair and worthlessness, which she probably has struggled with since childhood.

In working together, interpersonal stress also developed between Marcia and the worker. Marcia vacillated between viewing the worker as supportive listener and advisor, and as an authority figure not dissimilar from Ms. Northern who "sits in judgment" of her. In the second session, she commented, "I've got to do the political thing, and that's why I'm here—I've got the picture…" Beyond the obstacle posed by a mandated service, Marcia's and the worker's differences in race, social class, and level of education contributed tension in their communication.

Assessment

Throughout the helping process, social workers make decisions about such issues as points of entry in the person:environment field; goals and tasks; practice modality, methods time arrangements; and life stressor(s) focus. Professional judgments are made at any moment in time about which messages to explore (probe, chase) or when to respond with information and advice or when to point out contradictions between verbal and nonverbal communication. Similarly, during and after each session social workers make decisions about focus and next steps. These professional judgments must be based on disciplined reasoning and inferences within the context of sensitivity to differences related to values, beliefs, and perceptions derived from one's social class, race, ethnicity, religion, gender, sexual orientation, age, and mental and physical states.

Valid and reliable decisions rest on three assessment tasks: collecting, organizing, and interpreting data. First and foremost, professional judgments are based on collected data. To help an individual, family, or group with life stressors, the worker and applicant(s)/client(s) examine available salient information. Salient data include: the nature of the life stressors and their severity; the person(s)'s perceptions of and efforts to deal with the stressors; the person(s)'s perceptions of the role of family, networks, organizations, and features of the physical environment in cushioning and exacerbating the stressors; and expectations, if any, of the agency and social worker. Mutuality in stressor definition and collection of other relevant data actively engages applicants/clients in developing with the worker a common focus and direction. These data are collected from the person(s)'s verbal accounts, the worker's observations of nonverbal responses, significant others' verbal and nonverbal responses (obtained only with applicant's/client's informed consent), and written reports (also obtained only with the person(s)'s informed consent.)

Many applicants/clients are affected by overwhelming life stressors. Harsh environmental realities, multiple stressors, and the associated pain understandably overwhelm practitioners. A schema helps a practitioner to organize data. The life stressor formulation (i.e., difficult life transitions and traumatic life events, environmental pressures, and dysfunctional interpersonal processes) provides a tool for grouping and organizing data (see the above case situation of Marcia).

The life stressor schema also provides moment-to-moment assessment guidelines for professional interventions. For example, at an early moment in the third session, Marcia complains about her loneliness. At this moment, the social worker must assess whether Marcia is asking for help in exploring her grief associated with developmental transition and losses; or is she focusing on the lack of social connections in her life and asking for help with reaching out to organizations and social networks; or is she at this particular moment indirectly voicing some degree of dissatisfaction with the worker's pace or style

of helping. At each moment the worker has to assess with Marcia whether she is asking for help with life transitional, environmental, and/or interpersonal stressor(s). From moment to moment, Marcia may change her focus, and the social worker must skillfully follow her cues.

The final professional assessment task is to interpret the collected and organized data. To be valid, professional inferences must be rooted in disciplined inductive and deductive reasoning rather than in personal values and biases. Using inductive reasoning, social workers engage applicants/clients to pattern and to develop hypotheses about their person:environment exchanges, particularly the level of fit between personal strengths and limitations and environmental supports and obstacles. Deductive reasoning is more of a professional and less of a mutual process. The social worker applies relevant theory and research findings to the person(s)'s life situation(s). For example, knowledge about post-traumatic stress disorder may help a social worker better understand a person's reactions to an unexpected life stressor.

The assessment tasks of collecting relevant information, its systematic organization, and the analysis of data are common to most practice approaches. However, several beliefs are distinctive to the Life Model:

1. Engaging participation of applicant/client in the assessment process and developing mutual understanding
2. Understanding the nature of person(s): environment exchanges and the level of fit between human needs and environmental resources is the core assessment task.
3. Using the life stressor schema to organize and assess data.
4. Emphasizing moment-to-moment assessment.

Intervention (Modalities, Methods, and Skills)

In helping people with their life stressors, the social worker may be called on to intervene at the individual, family, group, community, social network, organization, physical environment, or political level(s). Social workers must competently work within all modalities, moving from one to another as situations require. In life-modeled practice, mutual assessment of life stressors and level of person:environment fit determines the selection of modality rather than professional specializations and preferences.

Based on a belief that many professional methods and skills are common to most modalities, the Life Model emphasizes an integrated perspective on practice. A few formulations are particularly helpful in presenting common practice methods and skills. Life-modeled practice is, like life itself, phasic. Its processes constitute three phases: the initial, ongoing, and ending. These phases provide a structure for conceptualizing and illustrating common professional methods and skills. However, in actual practice, these phases are not always distinct; they often appear, recede, and overlap. For example, in brief and episodic work, the temporal limits collapse the phases. Similarly, all beginnings are affected by past endings.

In the initial phase, the auspice of the service rather than the modality differentiates common professional methods and skills. Thus, a person(s)'s degree of choice (whether the service is sought, offered, or mandated) integrates practice modalities. For example, when a service is offered, the social worker begins by identifying her organizational auspice and role and presenting a clear offer of service, which takes into account the client's perceptions and definition of needs. The skills of offering a service are common to work with all modalities. Similarly, the life stressors schema supports an integrated practice related to assessment of and interventions in life transitional, environmental, and interpersonal issues.

While emphasizing the common base of social work assessment and interventions, the Life Model also examines the methods and skills specific to each practice modality. For example, in offering a group service the practitioner must have distinctive knowledge and skill in group formation. Forming a group requires achieving compositional balance; developing appropriate time arrangements related to number, frequency, and duration of sessions; deciding on group size; and developing organizational sanctions and supports. Distinctive knowledge and skill is identified for each respective modality.

While the Life Model presents practice principles, methods, and skills for integrative practice as well as for specific modalities, they are not prescriptive. This is because practitioner style and creativity are indispensable. A mechanical "professionalism" expressed by projecting an impression of neutrality and impersonality is not helpful. Professional skills must be integrated with a humanness, compassion, and spontaneity. The social worker's genuine empathy, commitment, and willingness to become involved speaks louder than assuming the "correct" body posture, saying the "right" words, or making the "appropriate" nonverbal gestures. Effective practitioners are "dependably real" rather than "rigidly consistent" (Rogers, 1961, p. 50).

Acknowledgment

This chapter is dedicated to Professor Carel Baily Germain. She died on Aug. 3, 1995, just when we were editing the final manuscript of our second edition. She had a profound impact on my intellectual development as well as that of many others. A brilliant, internationally acclaimed scholar, she left a lasting gift to the profession. A creative and intellectual explorer and discoverer, she roamed the globe of ideas and discovered their relevance for a profession she deeply loved. Never satisfied with the intellectual status quo, she leaped forward into uncharted theoretical territory, found new concepts from ecology, psychology, anthropology, and sociology, and made them available to us. Her ideas and words resonate throughout this chapter. More than a collaborator, she was a close personal friend whom I loved and miss.

Notes

1. Ecological theory perceives "adaptedness" and adaptation as action-oriented and change-oriented processes. Neither concept avoids issues of power, exploitation, and conflict that exist in the world of nature as well as in the social world of human beings. Adaptedness and adaptation are not to be confused with a passive "adjustment" to the status quo.
2. In the Life Model, "life course" replaces the traditional "life cycle" stage models of human development. Human beings do not experience universally fixed, sequential stages of development. Race, ethnicity, culture, religion, gender, sexual orientation, social class, and historical context have a profound influence on individual and collective development.

3. Among some groups or classes in our society, a fully independent adulthood may not be recognized until the twenties. Further, adolescence is not recognized in all societies. In some cultures, puberty alone marks the entry into the rights and responsibilities of adulthood, with no intervening state.

References

Besthorn, F. H., & Canda, E. R. (2002). Revisioning environment: deep ecology for education and teaching in social work. *Journal of Teaching in Social Work, 22*(1/2), 79–101.

Besthorn, F. R., & McMillen, D. P. (2002). The oppression of women and nature: Ecofeminism as a framework for an expanded ecological social work. *Families in Society, 83*(3), 221–232.

Germain, C. B. (1981). The ecological approach to people environment transactions. *Social Casework, 62*(June), 323–331.

Germain, C. B., & Gitterman, A. (1980). *The Life Model of social work practice.* New York: Columbia University Press.

Germain, C. B., & Gitterman, A. (1987). In A. Minahan (Ed.), Ecological perspective. *Encyclopedia of social work* (18th ed., pp. 488–499). Silver Spring, MD: NASW.

Germain, C. B., & Gitterman, A. (1995). Ecological perspective. In R. L. Edwards (Ed.), *Encyclopedia of social work* (19th ed., pp. 816–824). Silver Spring, MD: NASW.

Germain, C. B., & Gitterman, A. (1996). *The Life Model of social work practice* (2nd ed.). New York: Columbia University Press.

Gitterman, A., & Germain, C. B. (1976). Social work practice: A Life Model. *Social Service Review, 50*(December), 601–610.

Gitterman, A., & Germian, C. B. (2008). *The Life Model of social work practice: Advancement in theory and practice* (3rd ed.). New York: Columbia University Press.

Gitterman, A. (2008). Ecological framework. In Y. Mizrahi & L. Davis, (Eds.), *Encyclopedia of social work* (20th ed.). New York: Oxford University Press.

Gitterman, A. (2008a). The Life Model of social work practice. In A. Roberts & G. J. Greene (Eds.), *Social workers' desk reference* (2nd ed., pp. 231–241). New York: Oxford University Press.

Gitterman, A. (2001). *The handbook of social work practice with vulnerable and resilient populations* (2nd ed.). New York: Columbia University Press.

Gitterman, A. (1989). Testing professional authority and boundaries. *Social Casework, 70*(2), 165–171.

Gitterman, A. (1983). Uses of resistance: A transactional view. *Social Work, 28*(2), 127–131.

Gitterman, A., & Shulman, L. (2005). *Mutual aid groups, the life cycle and vulnerable and resilient populations* (3rd ed.). New York: Columbia University Press.

Lazurus, R., &. Folkman, S. (1984). *Stress, appraisal, and coping.* New York: Springer.

Lee, P. (1929). Social work: Cause and function. *Proceedings*, Nationak Conference of Social Work (pp. 3-20). New York: Columbia University Press.

Mack-Canty, C. (2004). Third-wave feminism and the need to reweave the nature/culture duality. *NWSA Journal, 16*(3), 154–179.

Rogers, C. (1961). The characteristics of a helping relationship. In C. Rogers (Ed.), O*n becoming a person* (pp. 333-347). New York: Aldine.

Schwartz, W. (1969). Private troubles and public issues: One job or two? In *Social welfare forum, proceedings of the national conference on social work* (pp. 22-43). New York: Columbia University Press.

Ungar, M. (2002). A deeper, more social ecological social work practice. *Social Service Review, 76*(3), 480–497.

Wise, J. (2005). *Empowering practice with families in distress.* New York: Columbia University Press.

MEDITATION

This centuries-old methodology aims to teach people the ability to observe interactions and responses, and to make compassionate choices; self-observation reveals problems past and present, and ways of dealing with them

Meditation and Social Work Practice

Thomas Keefe

Meditation is an ancient discipline wedded to several major psycho-philosophical systems arising from diverse cultures. Among others, American Indian, Central Asian Sufi, Hindu, Taoist, widespread Buddhist, and some Christian traditions have cultivated forms of meditation as a source of spiritual enrichment and personal growth.

Over 70 years ago, meditation began to attract Western psychotherapists and eventually the scrutiny of the rational-empirical tradition of Western science (for a brief history of mindfulness meditation, see Germer et al., 2005). In recent years it has been operationalized, stripped of its mystical trappings, tested in a variety of contexts, and enriched with empirical understanding. Currently, it is becoming clear that one form of meditation that enhances mindfulness or undifferentiated awareness is being adopted

by psychotherapists, including clinical social workers, and has been increasingly researched regarding its effectiveness and applications.

Meditation is a method that is adjunctive to social work practice. It is a mechanism for self-regulation and self-exploration. It can help reduce stress and aid coping. Its effectiveness in treating particular problems and persons is finding empirical support. It has the potential to be valuable in work with clients from diverse cultures. Yet meditation as a method continues to demand much from, and occasionally challenges, some theories underlying social work treatment for its full description and explanation. This chapter will track the origins, relevance, development, and application potential of meditation. Meditation, especially mindfulness meditation, has inspired a large and growing volume of needed research, and while a comprehensive review is beyond the scope of this chapter, reference will be made to founding and contemporary studies.

Description and Explanation: The Mind as an Open Hand

Meditation is a set of behaviors. Some of the consequences of meditation are directly observable; others can be indirectly inferred. For the purposes of this chapter, meditation does not refer to the mind's wandering and floating in fantasy or to the mind's laboring along a tight line of logic toward a solution. In contradistinction to these common notions, meditation is the deliberate cultivation of a state of mind exclusive of both fantasy and logic. While there are several varieties of meditation, they all share some common characteristics.

In essence, meditation is the development—or discovery, depending on one's orientation—of consciousness independent of visual and verbal thought. It is the deliberate cultivation of a mental state conducive to intuition. Meditation usually pairs a relaxed state of the body with either a concentrated or merely attentive focus of the mind. A brief description of this common process in meditation will help orient us to the method.

Method

One meditates by focusing attention upon a single thing while physically relaxed. This focus of attention may be a sound (mantra), a design (mandala) (Kapleau, 1967), an object, a part of the body, a mental image, the breath, or a prayer. This ostensibly simple task is seldom immediately mastered. Noises, bodily stimuli, internal dialogues, monologues, images, and emotions can constantly interrupt the task to break one's attention. Meditation then becomes a task of first, continually noticing or being mindful of a distraction; second, recognizing or naming the loss of attention—e.g., "thinking," "feeling," "remembering," etc.; and third, letting go of any resulting chain of associations to return to the meditation focus. Releasing attention to a distraction, easily refocusing attention, and cultivating an attitude of noninvolvement to the distracting chains of association constitute meditation for the beginner. A perhaps useful analogy

would be: The mind becomes like an open hand. Nothing is clung to. Nothing is pushed away.

Some theorists and practitioners distinguish two prominent forms of meditation. One is a concentrative form in which the meditator's attention is riveted to the meditation object to the exclusion of other stimuli. In contrast, insight or mindfulness meditation, described in more detail below, stresses the examination of these randomly occurring mental contents, often with a naming of each, e.g., memory, fantasy, fear, etc. There are many variations on these two themes. Interestingly, studies of electroencephalographic changes accompanying representative variations on these two themes indicate changes in brain activity that parallel the form of meditation underway (Anand, Cchhina, & Singh, 1984; Kasamatsu & Hirai, 1984). For advanced meditators, easy attention to the meditation object actually facilitates the examination of randomly occurring internal and external stimuli when they adopt the mental attitude of an open hand.

Mindfulness

In the past two decades one branch of meditation has been identified to be a salient and relatively easily accessed adjunct to various psychotherapeutic approaches (see, for example, Hick & Bien, 2008; Germer, Siegal, & Fulton, 2005; Roemer & Orsillo, 2009) and useful in coping on a daily basis (Germer, 2009; Williams, Teasdale, Segal, & Kabat-Zinn, 2007). The mindfulness meditation—described above and at the end of the chapter—is further subdivided into "formal" and "informal" activity, with the meditation being the formal endeavor and mindfulness being the informal application of mindfulness skills in daily life (Germer, et al., 2005; Roemer & Orsillo, 2009).

Hick (2008) describes the current interests in mindfulness: "Practitioners such as psychotherapists, social workers, psychiatrists, family therapists and other mental health professionals, as well as medical doctors, are showing extraordinary interest in mindfulness and how it affects practice, both for themselves and their clients. There is unparalleled interest in mindfulness-based interventions and approaches for a range of issues such as addictions, suicide, depression, trauma, and HIV/AIDS, to name a few" (p. 4).

Several definitions of mindfulness can help to triangulate the mental activity involved in mindfulness meditation. Undifferentiated or unconditioned awareness is certainly an aspect of mindfulness. Definitions by researchers, psychotherapists, and others provide a fuller picture. A succinct definition comes from Gunaratana (2002), who tells us that in meditation, "We train ourselves to see reality exactly as it is, and we call this special mode of perception mindfulness" (p. 33). While discussing mindfulness and psychotherapy, Germer et al. (2005) refine the definition of mindfulness as having three components: "All components of mindfulness–awareness, present-centeredness, and acceptance—are all required for a moment of full mindfulness" (p. 8). Under the influence of mindfulness, a particular attitude of mind and comportment is seen to develop over time. This was seen as the "approach" side of the hard-wired approach–avoidance construct by Williams, Teasdale, Segal, and Kabat-Zinn (2007): "Mindfulness embodies approach: interest, openness, curiosity (from the Latin *curare*, 'to care for'), goodwill, and compassion" (p. 67). Finally, Hick (2008) reports a definition from Lau and his associates, who combined definitions from multiple authors rendering mindfulness as "a nonelaborative, non-judgmental, present-centered awareness in which each thought, feeling, or sensation that arises in the attentional field is acknowledged and accepted as it is" (p. 5).

The Experience

A fuller understanding of meditation can be derived from a description of the experience. Most initially find that their attention is disrupted by a stream of thought. Distractions by the stream of thought may present themselves in a hierarchy of personal importance. Those incidents of the recent past evoking the most anxiety or anger intrude first. These are followed by memories or anticipations of decreasing concern. Thoughts, images, and feelings well up, momentarily distract the meditator, and if not clung to or elaborated upon, burn themselves out. When paired with the relaxed state of the body and followed

by refocusing upon the pleasantness of the meditation object, a global desensitization (Goleman, 1976) of cathected thoughts and images occurs. Increasing equanimity and objectivity secure the meditator in an attitude of observation of the thoughts and feelings that make up the symbolic self and its constituent concerns.

The meditation behaviors of focusing attention, recognizing when attention is interrupted, sometimes naming the nature of the interruption—e.g., "thinking," "feeling," "remembering," etc.—and deliberately refocusing attention are forms of discrimination learning (Hendricks, 1975). Perceptions, thoughts, and feelings are discriminated from the meditation focus. Slowly, the capacity to discriminate thoughts and feelings from any focus of attention is amplified. The meditator discriminates memory and anticipation, fear, and guilt from the immediate focus of attention. He or she cultivates a present centeredness. This is operationalized in research as time competence, a component of self-actualization (Brown & Robinson, 1993). As this learning to discriminate the ingredients of consciousness or contents of mind becomes easier, an observer self, also called watcher self (Deatherage, 1975) or witness (Goleman & Schwartz, 1984), emerges. The observer self is helpful in a variety of areas of functioning.

The observer self is not characterized as an alienated, depersonalized, or neurotic self-sustained by disassociation processes or suppression of thought and emotion. It is, instead, a secure subjectivity that, at its most refined level, allows mindfulness of internal experience without judgment, defense, or elaboration. In the cultivation of this observer self of meditation, several helpful capacities emerge that are taken up below and elaborated on as we examine meditation as a technique in personality change.

Capacities Learned in Meditation

For those of us involved in social work treatment, examining the postulated learnings transferred from meditation practice into the psychosocial functioning of the meditator may prove valuable. Some of the things learned from meditation can be termed "capacities," and there are several of them.

Focus and Inner Direction

The capacity to focus attention on a single thing or task in present time is enhanced. This is called "one-pointedness-of-mind" in some traditions. When carried over into everyday life, tasks undertaken with this state of mind are completed with less distraction and with the expenditure of less energy. The Buddhists call this state of mind, carried into everyday life, *right mindfulness* (Burt, 1955).

Consider the snow skier. Skiing requires concentration. As speed increases and the slope becomes steeper and the surface more varied, concentration must intensify. If the skier suddenly becomes preoccupied with a distant dropoff, a concern with his or her appearance or relative performance, or with an intruding and distracting fear of falling, his or her concentration is broken and the possibility of falling is more likely. The "clutched" athlete, the self-conscious speaker, the ego-involved attorney, and the overidentified social worker are all momentarily distracted from their intended focus, and this is experienced as loss of inner control. Brown and Robinson (1993), in a study of the relationship between meditation, exercise, and measures of self-actualization, found that meditation alone or in combination with exercise significantly increased subjects' inner direction beyond both subjects who only exercised and control subjects.

Discrimination Learning

The capacity to discriminate among internal stimuli, such as memories, fears, anger, etc., provides a measure of enhanced self-awareness that may be useful in empathic relating and communicating one's responses in social situations. Coupled with a present time focus, the capacity to view these internal processes with a degree of objectivity and non-attached concern allows enhanced performance in complex behaviors.

Receptive Perception

Finally, the capacity for an altered mode of perception is cultivated in meditation. The passive–receptive phase of perception, wherein one allows the senses to be stimulated, delaying cognitive structuring and allowing the things perceived to speak for themselves, is enhanced. Sidney Jourard (1966) and Abraham Maslow (Goble, 1970) both described this form of perception as necessary to supplement the more active, structured, need-oriented perception. Nyanaponika Thera described the Buddhist view of this perceptual mode generated in meditation as *bare attention*. Thera (1970) elaborated:

It cleans the object of investigation from the impurities of prejudice and passion; it frees it from alien admixtures and from points of view most pertaining to it; it holds it firmly before the eye of wisdom, by slowing down the transition from the receptive to the active phase of the perceptual or cognitive process, thus giving a vastly improved chance of close and dispassionate investigation. (pp. 34–35)

In sum, we see the results of meditation behaviors as including such global experiences and capacities as relaxation, desensitization of potentially charged stimuli, concentration of attention, inner direction, intentional present centeredness, enhanced discrimination, self-awareness, and augmented perceptual modes. Some of these theoretical and subjectively observed capacities have been addressed in clinical social work literature, such as Turner's review (2009), as a mindfulness skill set: attention, affect regulation, attunement–neurological activation related to interpersonal relationships, and empathy.

While the above capacities have implications for generally enhanced personal and interpersonal functioning, meditation is used to counter specific responses or behaviors seen as symptomatic or problematic for clients. As will be seen later, those supported by research include most prominently anxiety and stress, some forms of depression, substance abuse, phobic reactions, and interpersonal difficulties. Generally arising from traditions that are unhampered by notions of health and illness in relation to human behavior, meditation has been used in the personal growth and consciousness development of both the average lay person and the select initiates of particular religious orders. Used as a tool to extend the potential of its practitioners, meditation has been oriented toward the possible rather than the merely adequate or healthy in human functioning. Consequently, there are several ramifications for social work treatment. Meditation has, as shall be seen later, potential for the social work practitioner as well as for the client. It requires no predisposing diagnosis for its use, although there are empirically supported indications for its use and definite contraindicators. It has potential for use with individuals, families, groups and in community settings.

Origins and Paths into Social Work Treatment

As indicated earlier, meditation comes to us from diverse cultures and traditions. Yet the various forms, whatever their source, express a common origin in humankind's intuitive modes of thought. As an example, the *zazen* meditation of Zen Buddhism has its origin with the intuitive enlightenment of Siddhartha Gautama, Buddha, in about 544 B.C. (Burt, 1955). Siddhartha was said to have led a life of wealth and indulgence and then a life of asceticism in his quest to find the cause of suffering in the world. After relinquishing these extremes of self-preoccupation, his answer and enlightenment came. His Four Noble Truths together with his Eightfold Path served as vehicles for transmission of insight into his wisdom. The Buddha's Eightfold Path includes meditation as one of the routes to freedom from suffering (Beck, 1967). Thus it is a central practice in all branches of Buddhism, although characteristic variations have developed in each tradition. Buddhism is thought to have been carried from northern India of Siddhartha to China in A.D. 520 by Bodhidharma (Kennett, 1972). There the Indian *dhyana* became the Chinese *Ch'an*. Influenced by Taoism in China, meditation was transmitted to medieval Japan, where it is referred to as Zen, which literally means "meditation." Zen found its way to the West by several routes and has been popularized by D. T. Suzuki (1964), Allen Watts (1961), and others.

But Zen is only one form of meditation that has ancient and divergent cultural origins. In fact, meditation has been an important practice in the major world religions: Hinduism, Confucianism, Taoism, Buddhism, Judaism, Islam, and Christianity.

For centuries in India, meditation was taught in the oral traditions of the Hindu Vedas. Then, sometime before 300 B.C., some of these traditions of meditation were written in the Yoga Sutras of Patanjali (Wood, 1959). The techniques used in yoga include mantras, visualizations, breath control, and concentration on various postures or parts of the body. The purpose of yoga meditation is to unify the body, mind, and spirit, allowing an individual to become whole, integrated, and functioning as Atman, a godlike higher self (Prabhupada, 1972). Ultimately, union with Brahman, or God, is achieved. The Bhagavad Gita (200 B.C.) suggests meditation as one of the three main ways to achieve freedom from karma (Prabhupada. 1972), or the world of cause and effect.

In China, Confucius recommended meditation as a part of personal cultivation. Later it became the central feature of the Lu Chiu-Yuan school of Neo-Confucianism. Taoists during the same period in China also used meditation to facilitate mystical harmony with the Tao (Welwood, 1977).

Some types of Jewish mysticism incorporate meditation to achieve metaphysical insights. Philo of Alexandria (15 B.C.-A.D. 50) and other Jewish scholars in the Middle Ages used this type of meditation.

Since the 12th century A.D., Sufism, a popular folk Islam, has encouraged various types of meditation as well as other techniques such as whirling to induce trance. Meditation is considered to be an important remembrance of God. It is also used to facilitate perceptions of inner reality (Al-Ghazzali, 1971).

Christianity, too, is rich in traditions using a variety of meditative techniques, from the early Christian Gnostics to the medieval monasteries to 18th-century Greek Orthodox teachings. Some original training manuals include *The Philokalis* (Greek Orthodox) and *The Way of Perfection* by St. Theresa of Avila (Jourard, 1966). Recently, the origins of Western forms of meditation have been traced to early Christianity, including meditation's decline as a Western tradition in the 17th century (Schopen & Freeman, 1992). Driskill (1989) observed that the Christian tradition once recognized the therapeutic as well as the religious value of meditation.

The more recent work of clinicians and researchers such as Kabat-Zinn et al. (1992), with their Mindfulness-Based Stress Reduction used in pain management, and Huss and Baer (2007), with their integration of mindfulness and cognitive therapy, Mindfulness-Based Cognitive therapy, have helped inform the knowledge base for clinical social work. The work of Turner (2009) and Birnbaum (2008) on mindfulness meditation should contribute to the flow of theory and findings into social work.

Form Follows Philosophy

Interestingly, the philosophies of the Yogic and Buddhist meditators are reflected in their contrasting meditation behaviors. For example, most Yogic meditators seem to cultivate a habituation effect (Ornstein, 1977) to the object of meditation and experience a loss of perception of the object or a "blending" with it. This subjective experience of habituation corresponds with the brain's productivity of electromagnetic alpha waves that accompany relaxed awareness. These Yogic meditators reduce awareness of outside stimuli and experience a blissful indifference sometimes called *samadhi*. For the Yogi, samadhi is a high state of self-transcendent consciousness, a link with the godhead or universal consciousness to be attained through rigor and single-minded devotion.

Advanced Zen meditators undergo the habituation effect and record increased alpha wave productivity. However, when exposed to outside stimuli while meditating, they respond with sharp, momentary attention, as evidenced by corresponding short bursts of beta wave productivity. These meditators seem to be able to respond repeatedly to external stimuli without habituating to them. Psychologist Robert Ornstein (1977) suggests that they are responding without constructing a visual model or verbal label for the intruding stimulus, perceiving it clearly each time. For the Buddhist, the state of *nirvana*, analogous to *samadhi*, is attained but rejected by the protagonist in favor of an act of compassion. This act is to enter the world in a state of wisdom, or *prajna*, there to undertake the work of bringing other sentient beings—or aspects of the larger consciousness—to enlightenment. In interesting ways, then, the internal responses of meditators parallel the doctrines of their traditions. Given these parallels found in other traditions, it seems natural that meditation should become a part of Western therapeutic traditions. The reciprocal influences between meditation and social work should be exciting.

Relevance for Social Work

While meditation comes to the West by several ancient paths, it has far from penetrated to all parts of our industrial culture. Professional social work, a byproduct of the industrial market system, is itself relatively new in humankind's endeavors. Meditation is new to social work. It comes to the profession at a time when variety, diversity, and eclecticism are the norm. As the instability, contradictions, and stresses of socioeconomic change generate a search for relevant modes of treatment, meditation will perhaps be another technique to be taken up in the interest of more effective practice.

This vision of the reasons for the profession's potential interest in meditation rests on a common contemporary human experience: stress. Basically because of the contradictions and instability of the economic system, we live in an age of anxiety. Meditation may fill a symbolic and practical need in our personal and professional psyches. To face the fragmentation and contradictions of our lives, a safe and quiet place to recollect, sort out, and relax is a natural balm. Moreover, if meditation is not only a clinical adjunct technique but also a facilitator of other social work skills, and a precursor to action as well, it has relevance for the profession as a whole.

Meditation is used or discussed by various psychologists and psychiatrists. Engler (1984) notes that techniques from all the major meditative traditions have been incorporated or adopted for use in psychiatric treatment settings. Psychologists using biofeedback apparatus are naturally drawn to meditative techniques, and their work influences social work colleagues. Psychologists do the lion's share of research on meditation (Shapiro & Walsh, 1984).

Meditation as an aid for psychotherapists themselves (Keefe, 1975) and in the development of empathic and other therapeutic skills (Germer, Siegel, & Fulton, 2005; Hick & Bien 2008; Keefe, 1976, 1979; Roemer & Orsillo, 2009) has been proposed and examined clinically (see, for example, Sweet & Johnson, 1990) and by research, with mixed results (Pearl & Carlozzi, 1994). Both endeavors have generated interest among clinical social workers and social work educators. Other workers have had experience with meditation, especially Transcendental Meditation (TM) (Bloomfield & Kory, 1977), and have incorporated it into their work. Finally, integrating mindfulness with cognitive and dialectical therapy has been clinically developed in treatment of a person with borderline personality disorder (Huss & Baer, 2007). While a good fix upon the extent of its use is difficult without a study, one can assume that as more findings are reported in the literature, more interest will be generated in the social work profession.

Cross-Fertilization and Diversity

As noted in the historical origins of meditation, the technique has been refined for personal growth and positive behavior change in several cultural traditions (e.g., Shapiro, 1994). In each of these traditions, meditation is linked to conceptualizations that can help to explain for practitioners the subjective experiences of meditation and the behavioral and psychosocial outcomes. Each culture has placed meditation within its own context. To use meditation as an adjunct to psychotherapy and social work treatment is to place it within a rational, technological, cultural context. In so doing, we can refine and extend meditation technique and at the same time enrich our own traditions.

Because meditation has its origins in diversity, it has a naturally diverse appeal. In the author's experience, clients and practitioners whose cultures have longstanding meditative traditions have found the contemplative aspects of meditation compatible with their values and self-development. Others have ranged from very receptive to wary, depending on their particular backgrounds. While these observations are from limited clinical and teaching experience, a reasonable generalization is that persons from cultures and subcultures that value contemplation and intuitive modes of thought have good potential to be receptive to meditation as a treatment technique.

Meditation, the Personality, and the Conditioned Self

The experience and outcomes of meditation related to the organization and dynamics of the personality extend Western psychodynamic conceptualizations. They modify or extend psychodynamically and cognitively oriented social work treatment.

The ego or symbolic self in traditional Freudian theory develops out of the necessity to symbolically represent in thought the real objects that meet our needs. Our capacity to symbolize allows for deferred gratification in keeping with the physical and social reality. Thus, symbol formulation is seen as necessary to the creation of meaning and social interaction. Meditation experience does not refute these perspectives, but it does challenge certain assumptions underlying them.

Observing the Self

The symbolic self or ego is experienced as a network of verbal and visual symbols linked to emotional or physiological responses. However, as already described, the meditator can develop a capacity to observe the symbolic self as if from a vantage point of equanimity. In meditation, the emotions, internal verbalization, and visualization are recognized, accepted as they are without judgment, experienced vividly, and sometimes labeled, but they do not become a self-perpetuating stream of thought mistakenly taken as essential to our fundamental experience and awareness.

As suggested earlier, the advanced meditator generalizes certain capacities learned in meditation to daily functioning. These include the capacities to discriminate memory, fantasy, worry, the accompanying emotional content, and present time perceptions, and to decide to some degree which cognitive or emotional responses will become stimuli to further responses and which will not. In learning these two faculties, the meditator cultivates the observer self. In describing a form of Zen breath meditation useful in psychotherapy, psychologist Gary Deatherage (1975) suggests:

If a patient is taught over time to note interruptions in breath observation and to label each interruption with neutral terms such as "remembering," "fantasizing," "hearing," "thinking," or "touching," he will quickly discover a rather complicated, but comforting, situation where there is one aspect of his mental "self" which is calm and psychologically strong, and which can watch, label, and see the melodramas of other "selves" which get too involved in painful memories of the past or beautiful and escapist fantasies of the future. By helping the patient to identify for a time with a strong and neutral "watcher self" there begins to develop with him the strength, motivation, and ability to fully participate in, and benefit from, whatever other forms of psychotherapy are being provided to him. (p. 136)

For the meditator, then, the ego or symbolic self is not the basic locus of experience. There is an observer self or, in Deatherage's term a watcher self, undifferentiated or unconditioned awareness upon which the symbols and felt physiological responses play like a drama before a mirror.

Until more research is conducted to describe it, this aspect of the meditation process might be described as follows. The process of meditation occupies the focal attention of the rational, linear, verbal function of the personality. Meanwhile a diffuse, nonlinear awareness emerges as the observer self. The mediator experiences the larger linkages of his or her symbolically constructed self with the past, present, and future world. This experience of the "larger self" has again and again been described as ineffable, not communicable. This is because our verbal, logical self must focus on single components of what is a panorama of perception and experience undifferentiated in time—past, present, or future—and space—here, elsewhere, etc. Because only portions of our more diffuse, intuitive awareness can be the focus of the narrow beam of our focal attention, only portions of our larger consciousness are immediately accessible to our verbal-logical, verbal-conscious self. This notion of a larger self separate from what we have called our conscious self has provoked much interest.

In "Meditation and the Unconscious: A New Perspective," John Welwood (1977) hypothesized that the "unconscious" of traditional Freudian and Jungian theory limited our understanding of human functioning. In essence, Welwood postulated that the phenomena defined as evidence of an unconscious—forgetting, slips of the tongue, laughter, habit, neurotic symptoms, and dreams—are simply evidence that we function outside of our ordinary focal attention. Rather than postulate an internal, unknowable psychic region inhabited by instincts, Welwood

suggested that we might envision a focal attention that defines the figure in a universal ground of perception and awareness. For Welwood, the ground is not simply an internal structure. Instead, the ground comprises felt meanings, patterns of personal meanings, ways the organism is attuned to patterns and currents of the universe, and the immediate present.

Personality Change

While Welwood's particular definition of ground is very different from traditional concepts of the unconscious, the conceptualization is descriptive of the way in which the meditator experiences those aspects of awareness not labeled conscious in traditional psychodynamic terms. In meditation, the ego or symbolic self does not dissolve. The meditator does not become "ego-less."

Meditation, instead, facilitates the realization of the socially conditioned nature of the self. That each person has a history of conditioning by the interpersonal context of her world, that she can attend to or be conscious of only a small part of her own social programming at a given time, and that meditation is a means of discovering her potential apart from her social conditioning are realized in meditation. These are the sources of personality change in meditation.

From the perspective of meditation, then, the personality is not structured into static conscious-unconscious components. Rather, it is a web of interlacing symbolic meanings, each rooted in the changing social world. This symbolically constructed self is like an eddy in a stream. In a sense, it is illusory.

Conscious Control

In cultivating an observer self, the meditator grasps the illusory nature of the symbolically constructed self. Conflicts, anxiety-arousing ideas, rumination, and repetition compulsions are some of the experienced components of this symbolic self. Seen from the vantage of an observer self, their power and control seem less ominous. This is because the advanced meditator discriminates the sources of problems and decides, with a degree of neutrality, alternative lines of action. As the anxiety or anger related to particular incidents or situations is desensitized in the relaxed state of meditation, their power and control are further diminished as the capacity for intentional decision about such behaviors and responses is increased. This perspective can enhance treatment. As Deatherage (1975) puts it: "By becoming aware of the intentional process, one can then intercept and cancel unwanted words or deeds before they are manifested in behavior—something many patients find useful since it places control of their own behavior back at the conscious level" (p. 136). Not surprisingly, meditation is a component in the field of inquiry and treatment of behavioral self-control (Shapiro, 1994).

These experiences and outcomes of meditation, therefore, extend and modify traditional psychodynamic and cognitive perspectives, particularly with regard to the nature and function of the unconscious. They can also give rise to issues of spiritual and social perspectives.

Social Conditions

The traditional cultural contexts of meditation universally interjected myths to explain what exactly makes up the conditioning of the psychosocial self. Communication science, ego psychology, symbolic interactionism, and other Western perspectives augment traditional views of the processes that condition the self. However, even Western psychologists and therapists who have taken up the practice and systematic study of meditation sometimes fall back to philosophical musings when the parameters of the interpersonal ground are defined. Some use the language of mysticism and speak of the larger self or cosmic consciousness to which each small ego is linked and of which each person is a small manifestation. This language is very global and may fit with the beliefs of a given client or therapist. Such interpretation of the meditation experience has the potential for individuals to relinquish social responsibility and to retreat into a passive acceptance of social conditions that cause physical suffering and oppression. A more precise and critical view of the social realities should not be abandoned for a mystification of social realities. So, without disparaging the potential and wisdom in this view, we need not misuse it to gloss over social conditions. Indeed,

those concerned with spiritual development and compassion for those suffering may be among the first to acknowledge the inhibiting aspects of social conditions.

Social work, with its particularly broad orientation toward human behavior and the social environment, has a special contribution to make toward an understanding of this larger ground of the self. Social workers are cognizant of the extent to which social conditions interact with the individual psyche and condition its nature, prospects, and levels of awareness. Briefly extending this orientation, Marx and other materialists postulated that the economic organization or structure of society conditions or shapes the social and ideological life of a society (Marx, 1966). We might caution, then, that the global language of mystical traditions need not supplant critical analysis of the experiences of meditation, for these experiences are behaviors that may carry over into daily functioning with positive benefit to the meditator's personality and social functioning.

Personality and Specific Applications

Self-awareness, physical relaxation, stress reduction, desensitization of anxiety-arousing thoughts, self-regulation of problematic behaviors including substance abuse, discrimination of feelings and thoughts from other stimuli and self-exploration, and management of mild depression are specific applications of meditation in the treatment of problems. A thorough review of the bourgeoning literature, especially mindfulness meditation, is beyond the scope of this chapter, but some foundation studies will be noted.

Self-Awareness

First, learning to be more self-aware (aware of feelings and motivations) can inform one's responses to interpersonal situations. As we shall learn later, the self-awareness or mindfulness meditation facilitates sensing and then communicating one's responses to others, both behaviors conducive to empathy. Glueck and Stroebel (1975), in their study of the effects of meditation and biofeedback in the treatment of psychotherapy patients, made detailed observations of the physiological changes occurring during meditation. They found that TM generated recordable electroencephalographic changes in the brain that parallel relaxation. They think that the repeated sound, mantra, is the vehicle of relaxation that eventually involves both the dominant and nondominant hemispheres of the brain. This response is functional to self-understanding and psychotherapy by allowing repressed material to come into consciousness more quickly. This has the potential of permitting more rapid recovery of patients than standard therapeutic treatment would allow.

Relaxation and Stress

Second, learning to relax through meditation is conducive to managing anxiety-related problems. For example, Shapiro (1976) found Zen meditation combined with behavioral self-control techniques effective in reducing anxiety and stress in a client experiencing generalized anxiety and a feeling of being controlled by external forces. A 3-year follow-up study showed lasting benefit of mindfulness-based stress reduction in the treatment of anxiety (Miller, Fletcher, & Kabat-Zinn 1995). Several studies have now demonstrated significant results in the use of meditation or meditation as a supplement to reduce trait and state anxiety as well as physiological correlates of stress (e.g., Alexander, Swanson, Rainforth, & Carlisle, 1993; DeBerry, Davis, & Reinhard, 1989; Kabat-Zinn, Massion, Kristeller, & Peterson, 1992; Pearl & Carlozzi, 1994; Snaith, Owens, & Kennedy, 1992; Sudsuang, Chentanez, & Veluvan, 1991). In overcoming insomnia in patients, Woolfolk, Car-Kaffashan, McNulty, and Lehrer (1976), found meditation-derived attention-focusing techniques as effective as progressive relaxation exercises in reducing the onset of sleep. Both meditation and relaxation were effective in improving patients beyond controls on 6-month follow-up (Woolfolk et al., 1976).

Third, traditional therapy for anxiety-related problems has been broadened in recent years to the domain of ordinary stress. Stress, as a field of inquiry, promises to enrich our ability to prevent more serious symptoms and mental disorder. Stress is the physical and psychosocial response of a person who perceives external and/or internal demands as exceeding her capacity to adapt or cope (Fried, 1982). Some stress, of course, challenges us or piques our interests. Overstress, however, is a common problem in our industrial society.

Meditation and various forms of relaxation training have been studied for their potential in reducing the physical effects of stress and in helping people self-regulate aspects of their behavior or consciousness related to stress. In the early 1970s, research conducted by Robert Wallace, Herbert Benson, and Archie Wilson (1971) suggested that meditation might produce unique physiological and other changes. Later, other studies suggested that relaxation and various relaxation strategies and hypnosis may have effects similar to meditation (Beary & Benson, 1974; Fenwick, Donaldson, Gillis, Bushman, Fenton, Perry, Tilsley, & Serafinovicz, 1984; Morse, Martin, Furst, & Dubin, 1984; Walrath & Hamilton, 1984). Some studies are clear in indicating that meditation is at least as good as relaxation strategies in helping relieve stress and in lowering autonomic indicators of stress (Goleman & Schwartz, 1984; Marlatt, Pagano, Rose, & Marques, 1984). For example, in their study, Woolfolk, Lehrer, McCann, and Rooney (1982) compared meditation, progressive relaxation, and self-monitoring as treatments for stress. Meditation and progressive relaxation significantly reduced stress symptoms over time. More study is in order in this area.

Coping and Substance Abuse

The advantage of meditation as a strategy in helping clients deal with stress lies in the cognitive domain. What causes a person stress is determined in large part by the perceptions of an event or situation. Events viewed as threats are more stressful than those viewed as challenges in which one will grow. Meditation allows the individual to discover the symbolic meanings, the subtle fears, and other internal stimuli evoked by the event. Strategies, opportunities for coping, calm decisions, and previous successes can be distinguished in the mental contents and consciously enlisted in coping strategies. Moreover, one case study and some theorists support the aforementioned idea that meditation behavior may be transferred to other aspects of life and consciously enlisted to meet stressful events as they occur (Shapiro & Zifferblatt, 1976; Woolfolk, 1984). Maladaptive coping occurs when stress is responded to in ways that cause more problems for the stressed individual than they help. Meditation may help prevent these maladaptive responses, such as substance abuse, which relieve immediate stress but generate long-term physical, psychological, and even interpersonal problems.

Indeed, there is some evidence that meditation can help treat these maladaptive problems once they have developed. Several recent empirical studies indicate significant beneficial effects of meditation or meditation-assisted treatment in recovery and relapse prevention for substance abuse (Denney & Baugh, 1992; Gelderloos, Walton, Orme-Johnson, & Alexander, 1991; Royer, 1994; Taub, Steiner, Weingarten, & Walton, 1994). Finally, an analysis of mindfulness applications in relapse prevention with an information-processing orientation (Breslin, Zack, & McMain, 2002) should open new lines of inquiry in the substance abuse field.

A fourth outcome, combining self-awareness and the capacity to relax intentionally, permits an individual to transfer behaviors learned in meditation to other realms of life where there is stress or excessive stimulation that would hamper objective or reasoned functioning. The results of some studies suggested that meditation may be useful for alcohol and drug abusers to reduce anxiety, discriminate stimuli that evoke the problematic habits, and cultivate an "internal locus of control" (Benson & Wallace, 1984; Ferguson, 1978; Marlatt, et al., 1984). One might reason that anxiety-arousing stimuli are less likely to become self-perpetuating in the symbolic system if they are discriminated and desensitized in the meditative process. For example, some individuals have associated worry over coming events with positive outcomes of those events. Worry, intermittently rewarded, is likely to persist, complete with fantasized negative outcomes, anxiety, and preoccupation (Challman, 1975). Meditation enables the individual to discriminate worrisome fantasy and to observe its impact upon the body and overall functioning. Desensitization and a secure observer self enable the individual to recognize worry, limit the duration, and allow worrisome thoughts to burn themselves out, with lessened physiological consequences. As the observer self is cultivated, the not-uncommon state of consciousness of modern Westerners complete with split attention, worry, preoccupation, and anxiety can be sharpened to a mindfulness in which attention is voluntarily riveted to the action at hand. Preoccupation with oneself and how one is performing, worry over consequences, and wandering attention interfere less in the tasks one has decided to do. In a sense, the symbolic self is lost in the activity.

Fifth, observation and discrimination of one's thoughts in meditation enable the meditator to use thoughts and images more as tools to represent reality, to communicate, and to serve as intentional guides to action rather than as illusory and unintentional substitutes for real circumstances. Symbols and cognitive constructs interfere less with clear present time perceptions.

Depression

Finally, meditation as discrimination training may have specific usefulness in helping to manage depression. In her article "Learned Helplessness" social worker Carol Hooker (1976) reviewed literature suggesting that reactive depression is dynamically similar to experimentally induced states of learned helplessness in experimental animals. This stems from extrapolations to humans from the works of M. E. P. Seligman (1974, 1975) and others that suggest that subjects may learn, in effect, not to learn when repeatedly subjected to noxious circumstances over which subjects can find no mastery or control. Under such conditions, subjects learn that there is no escape, no solutions other than unresponsive withdrawal with little or no mobility, eye contact, or normal need-fulfilling behaviors. Hooker (1976), drawing on the work of Beck (1967), sees this learned helplessness as having cognitive components in humans wherein all known avenues of mastery and solution have been tried or rehearsed to no effect. Action and effort have no effect on circumstances. Beliefs about one's effectiveness sustain a depressive reaction. Loss of a loved one to death, for example, is an insoluble trauma. Repetition of guilt-evoking thoughts, self-deprecation, and beliefs that there is no future without the deceased may in some cases sustain a depressed mood for extended periods.

Meditation may help the depressed person regain a sense of self separate from the dilemma, partially sustained in the symbol system. In this scenario, traumatic thoughts associated with a traumatic event are desensitized and one learns increasing mastery over the contents of one's depression-sustaining ruminations. Eventually, thoughts that constitute new tasks and new opportunities for mastery and rehearsal of new roles to play can be sustained intentionally and used as guides for action and mastery. A groundbreaking study of the effects of a meditation-based stress-reduction program found that not only anxiety and panic symptoms but also depression were reduced, and results were maintained in 3-month follow-up (Kabat-Zinn et al., 1992). In another important study, "Prevention of Relapse in Major Depression by Mindfulness-Based Cognitive Therapy," patients with three or more episodes of depression were significantly less likely to relapse (Teasdale, Segal, Williams, Ridgeway, Soulsby, & Lau, 2000).

Similar processes, used with both caution and close, informed supervision, may be therapeutic for persons with thought disorders. In other words, observation of thinking, not building upon associations and becoming "lost in thought," is the intent of meditation for enhanced discrimination.

Combining the findings and expertise of four researchers and clinicians, Williams, Teasdale, Segal, and Kabat-Zinn, in their book *The Mindful Way Through Depression* (2007), have broadened and deepened our understanding of depression and our approach toward helping those beset with it. They formulate their approach on mindfulness and point out the nuances of mindfulness in everyday life that can liberate individuals from the attachment of depression.

In summary, research indicates that meditation is an effective adjunct to treatment of a potentially wide variety of problems. Shapiro (1994) summarized research on meditation in self-regulation and self-exploration, observing that the meditation has been stripped of the original cultural and religious contexts to avoid dilemmas and divisiveness. He makes a strong case for reintroducing the context of meditation, which fits the social work perspective of valuing cultural diversity and working with the whole person. With this idea in mind we must recognize that some clients and workers will find meditation an alien endeavor, even when it is isolated from its original context. Furthermore, there are certain problems that should not be approached with meditation except with close supervision by workers skilled in treatment of the problem and in meditation. While a preponderance of definitive studies show that direct contraindications for the use of meditation are few, some guidelines are emerging.

Cautions and Contraindications

Some people find meditation more suited to their temperament and culture or beliefs than others. Also, certain severe disorders make the correct practice of meditation difficult or impossible.

Attitude

Anxious but organized persons seem to take to meditation quickly. Relaxation and learning control over focal attention is rewarding and rather immediate. With very anxious, driven people, however, a caution is in order. Meditation of the Zen type, which requires a continued refocusing to the breath or another object of attention, or of those Yogic types that require strict postures and attention, can become a "do-or-die" endeavor for these persons. Individuals may incorrectly feel compelled to suppress thoughts and emotion or they may force their breath in an unnatural way rather than following their natural breathing rhythms. Often this response is not unlike their lifestyle, in which they constantly push themselves to perform or conform without attention to their own desires and physical needs. The attitude of wakeful awareness is misinterpreted as rigid attention where all interruptions are excluded before their full perception. Sometimes the body is not relaxed, but held rigid and tense. With such persons, the point must be made clear that they are to let go of interrupting thoughts, not push them away or compulsively follow them. The analogy of the mind as an open hand, neither pushing away nor grasping, helps in interpreting the correct mental attitude. In any case, the social worker/therapist must make sure that the client is in fact meditating and not magnifying anxiety, building anxiety-provoking images, or obsessing along an improbable chain of associations about hypothetical, destructive interpersonal events or outcomes.

Ensuring the above attitude may help to avoid some of the experiences discussed by Turner (2009), such as frustration, boredom, and irritability. Clinical profiles including dissociation or posttraumatic stress may indicate a need for gradual introduction and an emphasis on a nonjudgmental attitude and acceptance (Turner, 2009).

Severe Problems

Two authors have discussed use of meditation by persons who suffer severe mental problems or who are labeled psychotic or schizophrenic. Deatherage (1975), in discussing limitations on the use of Buddhist mindfulness meditation in psychotherapy, cautions, "While this psychotherapeutic approach is extremely effective when employed with patients suffering from depression, anxiety, and neurotic symptoms, a caution should be issued regarding its use with patients experiencing actively psychotic symptoms such as hallucinations, delusions, thinking disorders, and severe withdrawal..." (p. 142). He goes on to note that the particular meditation technique for self-observation requires "an intact and functional rational component of mind, as well as sufficient motivation on the part of the patient to cause him to put forth the effort to do that observation" (p. 142). Arnold Lazarus (1976), discussing psychiatric problems possibly precipitated by TM, cautions that his clinical observations have led him to hypothesize that TM does not seem to be effective with people classified with hysterical reactions or strong depressive reactions. He warns that some schizophrenic individuals might experience an increase in depersonalization and self-preoccupation (pp. 601-602).

As an activity derived from religious traditions, meditation is associated with notions of self-transcendence. This context may be culturally congruent or very alien for a client. Good judgment and sensitivity to the client's culture are very much in order when introducing meditation techniques for this reason alone.

Observation of the conditioned self or ego from a perspective of dispassionate neutrality can be confused with several problematic behaviors. Engler (1984), for example, cautions that borderline personalities and others without a well-developed self may be attracted to meditation. Also, persons in developmental stages struggling with identity may find meditation an unfortunate substitute for dealing with their developmental tasks or discovering who they are (Engler, 1984). Persons with very fragile identities, symptoms related to depersonalization, and inadequate ego development are not good candidates for meditation except under close supervision.

In general, therefore, clients or patients with fragile self-concepts or those with severe disorders, whose reality testing, perception, and logical thinking are such that they cannot fully understand meditation instructions or follow through with actual meditation under supervision, are poor candidates for its successful use in treatment. Just as the anxious client may build upon anxiety-arousing associations or the depressed client may ruminate on ineffectiveness and despair instead of actually meditating, clients with severe thought disorders and problems with reality testing may substitute hallucinations, delusions, withdrawal, depersonalization, and catatonic responses for meditation, thereby aggravating their problems.

Glueck and Stroebel (1975), however, found TM effective as adjunctive treatment with a sample of 96 psychiatric patients who would have been expected to have the kind of difficulties outlined here. Preliminary investigation indicated that the higher the level of psychopathology, the greater the difficulty patients had producing alpha waves. Testing TM against autogenic relaxation and electroencephalogram (EEG) alpha-wave biofeedback training, Glueck and Stroebel found TM to be the only one of the three experimental conditions that patients could persistently practice. Consequently, the authors match-paired their meditation sample with a comparison group and found their meditating patients to have higher levels of recovery than both their "twins" and the general patient population. Despite these findings, treatment of severely depressed and psychotic patients with meditation is experimental and without close supervision and immediate post-meditation checks is contraindicated until further research is done.

One phenomenon occurring in most forms of meditation is the intrusion of the memory of events in the meditator's life into the meditative state. Meditators employing concentration techniques experience mental images of significant and emotionally intense events replayed before their relaxed mind. Desensitization of these memories has been discussed. But intentional use of meditation to allow significant facts and events of the psychosocial history is possible. Requesting the client to record these memories following meditation, for use in the context of treatment and for rounding out a more complete psychosocial history, may be helpful to workers with psychodynamic and psychoanalytic orientations and those helping clients with family-of-origin work.

The diagnostic value of meditation, implicit in earlier discussions, lies in the nature of the difficulty that the client has in meditating correctly. Elsewhere, the author has discussed optimal psychosocial functioning based upon Eastern conceptualizations related to and developed from meditation (Keefe, 1978). Briefly stated, the capacity to attend to activities one is about without interference by irrelevant ideation and worry suggests a positive level of functioning. Meditation evokes memories and worries that intrude upon the meditation task. Repetitive anxiety or guilt-associated thoughts will indicate to the meditator and the worker or therapist those areas of conflict or "unfinished business" that hinder the client's functioning. Repetitive self-destructive images will indicate disturbed role rehearsal or depression. Conflicts from pushing or driving oneself will manifest themselves in forced breath or lack of relaxation in meditation.

The Therapeutic Relationship

There are several behaviors learned in mediation that would theoretically contribute to enhanced empathic functioning on the part of the social worker who meditates. First, learning increased voluntary control over one's attention permits one to shift from attending to the various verbal and nonverbal communications of the client to one's own emotional responses to the client. This ability to sense one's own emotional reactions from moment to moment facilitates sensing and verbalizing feelings that parallel those of the client. Accurate reflection of these feelings to the client, of course, is a major component in therapeutic empathy (Rogers, 1975), a worker skill conducive to positive behavior change for the client.

Second, learning to discriminate internal or cognitive stimuli from perceptual stimuli in meditation and enhancing voluntary control over cognitive processes can enhance empathic functioning in another way. The worker can hold complex cognitive elaboration in abeyance and allow herself to perceive the client as he is, without premature diagnosing or other cognitive elaboration coloring her bare attention to the client as he is. This intentional slowing of the perceptual process that allows the client to speak for himself holds the worker in the present time—where emotions are felt, where the worker can be fully with the client, and where behaviors are changed.

Third, the meditating worker is likely to have cultivated a strong centeredness or observer self not easily rattled by stresses or emotional interaction. Therefore, staying with the client in her deepest feelings, as Carl Rogers (1975) described high-level empathy, becomes more likely. And because such a worker has a perspective on his own reactions, countertransference responses may be more accessible.

Supervision would naturally include sharing of meditation experiences to help in refocusing. Dubin (1991) recommended meditative techniques in psychotherapy supervision to help learn theory and case management and to deal with countertransference. Meditation can assist the worker sharing about and dealing with countertransference or other issues of problematic attachment.

Meditation as an adjunctive technique to treatment has a virtue common to all profound and shared experiences. It is an experience a worker can teach and then share with the client that may serve as a basis for communication, trust, and mutual discovery when other bases for relationships are less productive. In this sense, meditation can be a common ground of mutual experience that can strengthen a therapeutic relationship.

Teaching Meditation: One Technique

There are several techniques for meditation useful as adjuncts for treatment. Among the more prominent are Yogic mantra techniques,

Benson's relaxation technique (Glueck & Stroebel 1975, p. 314), TM (Bloomfield & Kory, 1977), Zen techniques, and the commonly described mindfulness meditation (Birnbaum & Birnbaum, 2008; Kabat-Zinn, 1994; Turner, 2009). The technique to be briefly detailed here is derived from Zen.

The general instructions are readily found in a variety of texts. Expert instruction and a good period of time meditating are recommended for workers considering meditation as an addition to their repertoire of techniques.

The client is instructed to meditate half an hour each day in a quiet place where she is unlikely to be interrupted. The client is asked to record briefly in a log her meditation experiences for later discussion with the worker. The meditation posture, as suggested by Kapleau (1967), is as follows:

1. A sitting position with the back straight
2. Sitting cross-legged on a pillow is ideal for some.
3. If uncomfortable, sit in a straight chair without allowing the back to come to rest against the back of the chair.
4. The back must be straight for comfort since slumping causes cramping.
5. The hands should be folded in the lap.
6. The eyes may be open or closed; if open, they are not to focus on any particular thing.
7. Loose clothing around the waist is suggested.

The client is instructed to focus on the breath manifest in the rising and falling of the abdomen and to begin the first session by counting each exhalation up to 10 and beginning again. The attention should be focused on the surface of the center of the body about an inch below the navel. Thereafter, the client may simply follow the natural, unforced, uncontrolled breath for the duration of each session.

The client is told that there will be frequent intrusions of thoughts, feelings, sounds, and physical responses during her concentration. The response to these is in every case an easy recognition that attention has wandered and refocusing to the breath is necessary. Relaxing the muscles around the eyes and the tongue and throat is helpful in letting go of visual and verbal thoughts.

Repressed material will usually emerge as insights. These are automatically paired with a relaxed state. The client should be instructed that if the meditation becomes upsetting or frustrating, she should stop and resume the following day or wait until the next appointment with the therapist. Particular cautions with special clients were enumerated above. Generally, if the experience is not pleasant and rewarding, it may be evidence the client is pushing rather than allowing mental content to flow.

Settings and Levels of Intervention

Meditation is a worldwide phenomenon. It is practiced in settings as varied as Japanese corporate offices, quiet monasteries in all parts of the world, downtown apartments, and mental health centers. Most physical settings where social workers practice would be conducive to meditation. While each agency has its own major theoretical orientation or admixture of orientations, few would preclude meditation as an appropriate technique if thoughtfully and systematically introduced. While a psychodynamically oriented worker would define and describe meditation behavior and results differently than a behaviorist or an existentialist, the technique is not tied to a single system or culture. Therefore, agency acceptance hinges more upon tolerance for innovation, interest in research, and openness to new ideas. Meditation as a social work technique was thought to be well out of the mainstream and esoteric a few years ago, but it has gained wide acceptance in related disciplines and promises to become a more common technique in work with individuals, families, and groups.

Because meditation tends to be an individual activity, it is naturally thought of as a mode for individual treatment only. However, in addition to its use and ramifications for individual treatment, meditation can be of use for certain kinds of groups, including families.

Receptivity to meditation a few years ago was largely restricted to young people and the religiously or spiritually oriented. But over the years the various forms—TM (Bloomfield & Kory, 1977) and mindfulness-based meditation in particular—have crossed class and age barriers. Increasingly, meditation can be introduced into group work with a variety of people. In the author's experience, group meditation can enhance group processes. Beginning and ending a group with a meditation session can enhance group feeling and "mellow out" intense feelings enough to allow their sharing, analysis, and discussion. A group meditation sets the atmosphere for constructive interaction. Meditation to end a group meeting can have similar effects and can support solidarity and identity within the group. The author has used individual meditation to begin and group chants to end treatment groups for college-age youth and for sex-role consciousness-raising treatment groups for married persons ranging in age from 22 to 45. Meditation for family treatment may help to reduce conflict and give the family a positive, common experience to share and discuss.

The use of meditation to facilitate family-of-origin history-taking suggested above could be a part of an actual family treatment session. Sometimes the level of conflict and individual anxiety is such that constructive communication in a treatment session is hampered. Some minutes of meditation may allow sufficient calming to enhance communication. Except for young children and the contraindications already discussed, family members may be helped regardless of age. The particular phenomenon of enmeshment, or very dependent adult members without a secure sense of self apart from the family, may be helped through meditation. Just as with individual clients, sensitivity to the receptivity and experiences of each family member would be essential. While not a substitute for other techniques, meditation may be useful as an adjunct to family treatment, and systematic use and assessment may support its utility.

Claims of increased harmony and lower crime rates have been made as resulting from certain percentages of people engaged in meditation in given communities (Bloomfield & Kory, 1977, pp. 283-284). These findings require some critical assessment in the judgment of this author. But, obviously, if meditation contributes to personal functioning, certain aspects of community life will be enhanced.

Much research must be done to determine the long-term effects of the various forms of meditation on individuals, groups, families, and communities. Optimal personal and group functioning does not lead directly to more harmonious

community life if the social order is fundamentally exploitive and contradictory. As with many forms of treatment techniques, the gaps in our knowledge about meditation, as an adjunct to treatment at different levels of intervention, is growing, yet more research is still in order.

Implications for Research

Meditation is a widely studied behavior. Nevertheless, our understanding is incomplete. As a treatment technique, it has been found valuable in a variety of situations. Yet meditation is more than a technique. While review of the growing abundance of research is beyond the scope of a single chapter, some positive and some negative signposts are evident, especially in studies that discern patterns and provide guidance (Melbourne Academic Mindfulness Interest Group, 2006; Ospina et al., 2007). There is growing knowledge of the appropriate forms of meditation, contraindications, the relative value of meditation and other relaxation techniques, and even the effects of meditation upon stress and anxiety, substance abuse recovery and prevention, depression, the nervous system, psyche, and social life. Although there is much clinical evidence and intuitive exploration, more research concerning subset meditation phenomena is needed. This includes the desensitization, discrimination, and observer self mentioned earlier. Clinicians must begin to refine the appropriate use of meditation for particular kinds of clients and particular kinds of problems. Together with researchers, we must deduce where it helps and where it does not. The recent articles "Mindful Social Work: From Theory to Practice," (Birnbaum & Birnbaum, 2008) and "Mindfulness: The Present Moment in Clinical Social Work," (Turner, 2009), provide insightful discussions, suggest directions, and contribute to the theory base of clinical social work. Researchers also have rich opportunities to follow the differential effects of meditation used with various clinical problems and various personalities.

In a study that surveyed many available studies, "Meditation Practices for Health: State of the Research," Ospina et al. (2007) reported some health effects, such as lowering blood pressure; however, the overall conclusion ended with, "Scientific research on meditation practices does not appear to have a common theoretical perspective and is characterized by poor methodological quality. Firm conclusions on the effects of meditation practices must be more rigorous in the design and execution of studies and in the analysis and reporting of results" (p. v.). Their conclusion would possibly have been anticipated, given the rapid growth of interest and clinical application of meditation. Their conclusion can serve as a motivator to continue research that has a sound theoretical base and quality methodology.

Another study (Melbourne Academic Mindfulness Interest Group, 2006) surveying the research studies into mindfulness-based psychotherapies more optimistically concluded, "This group suggests, based on this review, that the combination of some well-developed conceptual models for the therapeutic action of mindfulness and a developing empirical base, justifies a degree of optimism that mindfulness-based approaches will become helpful strategies to offer in the care of patients with a wide range of mental and physical health problems" (p. 285).

The hope expressed in the earlier version of this chapter remains relevant. Being a technique of potentially great value for social work, meditation must continue to be examined empirically. Hopefully, it will not be picked up "whole hog" and incorporated into practice without continued critical evaluation. This would render it, like some other techniques, a passing fancy, soon discarded in favor of new approaches. Nor should meditation be disregarded as the esoteric product of some foreign and bygone cultures. Despite barriers that exclude the wisdom of other cultures and other lands from our consideration, a critical openness and valuing of diversity in the treatment domains is in order. We must try out, test, and incorporate meditation as an adjunct to treatment where it benefits our clients, our practice, and ourselves.

Conclusion

Meditation is, of course, more than just an adjunct to social work treatment. Meditation and its potential for better understanding ourselves and our functioning may flourish in our culture independent of the helping professions and their practice. If we in social work and others in related professions find it a powerful adjunct to treatment, we should not attempt to subsume it as ours alone. Indeed, Shapiro (1994) argues a strong case for reintroducing the cultural contexts of meditation where it is used. Such an endeavor would enrich the diversity of the cultural and philosophical basis of the treatment where meditation is used. It may even help us to reach clients from particular cultures with strong meditation traditions. It gives us new perspectives on the development of the self, amplifies our understanding of subjective experience, provides insights into what constitutes optimal psychosocial functioning, and is an empirically supported tool for dealing with stress, anxiety, and maladaptive coping such as substance abuse.

Meditation is at once a vehicle of consciousness and a portal to individual potential. It can be used to liberate, to extend individual functioning, and thereby to help to create social change in the democratic interest. It could also be used to mystify, to distract people from their social concerns related to their personal problems. How the technique will be used by social work is related to the conscience, wisdom, and position of the profession in the years of profound social change ahead.

This chapter began by identifying meditation as a set of behaviors. Meditation is, of course, the embodiment of a larger theory of self, coping, and change. For this reason it has begun to take interesting routes in the social work profession. It is a part of the field of stress management and finds frequent mention in that literature (e.g., Nucho, 1988). But it is also naturally linked to mainstream social work literature (Carroll, 1993; Cowley, 1993; Smith, 1995). As social workers openly discuss addressing the "whole person" or the spiritual aspects of client's experience, the understandings of that experience can be enhanced by familiarity with meditation-related phenomena such as global desensitization and an observer self. This perspective does not require adoption of a theological stance or the introduction of religion as a component of treatment. It does have the potential to help us understand our clients more fully. As long as social work is concerned with helping people secure themselves and make good choices, meditation and its body of related theory should have a role to play.

Finally, deep in the heart of meditation lies the insight that is the root of both compassion and social action: to help others is to help ourselves. Whether a clinician, a social activist, or both, this is a message every social worker can hear.

Case Example: The Use of Meditation in the Treatment of Functional Bowel Disease

A 36-year-old woman, married and the mother of three children—ages 3, 7, and 12—living in California was referred by her physician. She was suffering abdominal pain. Extensive physical examinations and tests had all been negative, although she had recently had an increase in pain when she was under stress. She wanted to understand why she was having these troubles and how she could control them.

She had been experiencing an increase in pain over the past year. She had gone on special diets, consulted several health care professionals, and taken many different medications, but there was no change in her distress, which was becoming overwhelming. She said she was becoming increasingly depressed, anxious, and overly self-critical as her symptoms continued and there seemed no hope for any change in them. Psychological tests completed at the time of the initial evaluation confirmed that she was indeed severely depressed, with little energy. There seemed to be an emotional overlay to her pains.

The client was quick to agree to short-term outpatient treatment of eight weekly sessions. The goals would include developing some understanding of her emotions, the stresses in her life, her coping skills and difficulties, and learning various types of relaxation techniques. It was also agreed that the results of the psychological tests would be fully reviewed with her in the third session. In addition, she was helped to work through some unresolved feelings from earlier years that were related to her parents' divorce and the death of her first husband. She explored how she could utilize some of her past coping skills with some of her present difficulties.

The client was experiencing many stressful and unstable living conditions at the present time while her husband was building their new home. This necessitated their living in a series of different friends' homes. Her husband had been so involved in building their dream home that he had not involved her in the process. He was included in one of the outpatient sessions

in order to increase communication between them and to help them to reinstitute their previous level of positive interactions, which had been present in the year previous to all of these changes.

In the second treatment session the client was taught a passive, modified hypnotic, relaxation technique that was tape-recorded for her daily use at home. She was quite pleased with her ability to immediately relax and experience a definite decrease in her abdominal pains. She was instructed to listen to the tape recording of the relaxation four times a day and to record her responses each time in a "Relaxation Log" that she was to bring with her to each session.

The following week the patient had several days without any pain until she would forget to use the technique because she felt "so good." The patient continued with the passive therapist-directed relaxation techniques by listening to the tape recording daily. The worker was very directive with this technique. The client was slowly encouraged to try the relaxation technique on her own, without using the tape. She quickly became able to do this.

After the fourth treatment session, the client was introduced to a new technique designed to help her relax on her own, to become more comfortable with her own body, and to learn how she could help herself on an ongoing basis. It was presented to her as a new coping skill that she could continue to utilize after the termination of treatment. Since the client was now feeling much better, she was eager to increase her skills in this area. She was therefore given oral and written instructions for meditation. She was asked to take the instructions home and read them and to try to implement them into her daily routine. Initially she had some difficulty in being totally comfortable with the technique, so she continued listening, once a day, to the relaxation tape. However, she found less need to rely on the tape recording as she increased her ability to relax with the meditation. After one week, the client found that she was able to relax just as fully as she had with the tape recording. Further, she felt quite proud of her ability to do it on her own. By the last session she was able to relax without any reliance on the tape. She found that if she meditated once a day, she had no pain, and could reduce any stresses that arose by short relaxation techniques, which she would go over in her mind. At that point she had been totally pain-free for three weeks. Follow-up contacts with the patient one month after formal termination of treatment showed that she continued to do her daily meditation, was pain-free, felt much more confident in her abilities and coping skills, and felt that all aspects of psychotherapy. relaxation, and finally meditation had been quite beneficial to her. She recognized the benefits of continuing to practice what she had learned, and her family was quite supportive.

Acknowledgment

The author wishes to thank graduate assistant Heather Sells for her help in gathering references for this edition of the chapter.

References

Alexander, C. N., Swanson, G., Rainforth, M. & Carlisle, T., et al. (1993). Effects of the Transcendental Meditation program on stress reduction, health, and employee development: A prospective study in two occupational settings. *Anxiety. Stress and Coping: An International Journal,* 6(3), 245–262.

Al-Ghazzali (B. Behan, Trans). (1971). *The revival of religious sciences.* Farnham, Surrey, England: Sufi.

Anand, B. K., Cchhina, G. S., & Singh, B. (1984). Some aspects of electroencephalographic studies in yogis. In D. H. Shapiro & R. N. Walsh (Eds.), *Meditation: Classic and contemporary perspectives* (pp. 475–479). New York: Aldine.

Beary, J. F., & Benson, H. (1974). A simple psychophysiologic technique which elicits the hypometabolic changes of the relaxation response. *Psychosomatic Medicine,* 36, 115-120.

Beck, A. T. (1967). *Depression: Clinical experimental and theoretical aspects.* New York: Harper and Row.

Benson, H., & Wallace, K, with technical assistance of E. C. Dahl, D. F. Cooke. (1984). Decreased drug abuse with Transcendental Meditation—A study of 1,862 subjects. In D. H. Shapiro & R. N. Walsh (Eds.), *Meditation: Classic and contemporary perspectives* (pp. 97-104). New York: Aldine.

Birnbaum, L., & Birnbaum, A. (2008). Mindful social work: From theory to practice. *Journal of Religion & Spirituality in Social Work: Social Thought,* 27(1–2), 87–104.

Bloomfield, H. H., & Kory, R. B. (1997). *Happiness.* New York: Pocket Books.

Breslin, F. C., Zack, M., & McMain, S. (2002). An information-processing analysis of mindfulness: Implications for relapse prevention in the treatment of substance abuse. *Clinical Psychology: Science and Practice,* 9(3), 275–299.

Brown, L., & Robinson, S. (1993). The relationship between meditation and/or exercise and three measures of self-actualization. *Journal of Mental Health Counseling,* 15(1), 85–93.

Burt, E. A. (Ed.) (1955). *The teachings of the compassionate Buddha.* New York: New American Library.

Carroll, M. (1993). Spiritual growth of recovering alcoholic adult children of alcoholics. Unpublished doctoral dissertation, University of Maryland, College Park.

Challman, A. (1975). The self-inflicted suffering of worry, cited in "Newsline." *Psychology Today,* 8(8), 94.

Cowley, A. D. (1993). Transpersonal social work: A theory for the 1990's. *Social Work,* 38(5), 527–534.

Deatherage, G. (1975). The clinical use of "mindfulness" meditation techniques in short-term psychotherapy. *Journal of Transpersonal Psychology,* 7(2), 133–143.

DeBerry, S., Davis, S., & Reinhard, K. (1989). A comparison of meditation-relaxation and cognitive/behavioral techniques for reducing anxiety and depression in a geriatric population. *Journal of Geriatric Psychiatry,* 22(2), 231–247.

Denney, M., & Baugh, J. (1992). Symptom reduction and sobriety in the male alcoholic. *International Journal of the Addictions,* 27(11), 1293-1300.

Driskill, J. D. (1989). Meditation as a therapeutic technique. *Pastoral Psychology,* 38(2), 83–103.

Dubin, W. (1991). The use of meditative techniques in psychotherapy supervision. *Journal of Transpersonal Psychology,* 23(1), 65–80.

Encyclopaedia Britannica, Macropaedia. (1974). Vol. 10, p. 183. London: Benton.

Engler, J. (1984). Therapeutic aims in psychotherapy and meditation: Developmental stages in the representation of self. *Journal of Transpersonal Psychology,* 16(1), 25–31.

Fenwick, P. B. C., Donaldson, S., Gillis, L., Bushman, J., Fenton, G. W., Perry, I., Tilsley, C., & Serafinovicz, H. (1984). Metabolic and EEG changes during Transcendental Meditation: An explanation. In D. H. Shapiro & R. N. Walsh (Eds.), *Meditation: Classic and contemporary perspectives* (pp. 447–484). New York: Aldine.

Ferguson, M. (Ed.) (February 1978). Valuable adjuncts to therapy: Meditation, relaxation help alcoholics cope. *Brain-Minded Bulletin,* 7, 2.

Fried, M. (1982). Endemic stress: The psychology of resignation and the politics of scarcity. *American Journal of Orthopsychiatry,* 52.

Gelderloos, A., Walton, K., Orme-Johnson, D., & Alexander, C. (1991). Effectiveness of the Transcendental Meditation program in preventing and treating substance misuse: A review. *International Journal of the Addictions,* 26(3), 293–325.

Germer, C., (2009). *The mindfulness path to self-compassion.* New York: The Guilford Press.

Germer, C., Siegel, R., & Fulton, R. (2005). Mindfulness and psychotherapy. New York: The Guilford Press.

Glueck, B. C., & Stroebel, C. F. (1975). Biofeedback and meditation in the treatment of psychiatric illness. *Comprehensive Psychiatry, 16*(4).

Goble, F. (1970). *The third force.* New York: Pocket Books.

Goleman, D. (1976). Meditation and consciousness: An Asian approach to mental health. *American Journal of Psychotherapy, 30*(1), 41–54.

Goleman, D., & Schwartz, G. E. (1984). Meditation as an intervention in stress reactivity. In D. H. Shapiro & R. N. Walsh (Eds.), Meditation: Classic and contemporary perspectives (pp. 77–88). New York: Aldine.

Gunaratana, B. (2002). *Mindfulness in plain English.* Boston: Wisdom Publications.

Hendricks, C. G. (1975). Meditation as discrimination training: A theoretical note.

Hick, S. (2008). Introduction. In Hick, S., & Bien, T. (Eds.), *Mindfulness and the therapeutic relationship.* New York: The Guilford Press.

Hick, S., & Bien, T. (2008). *Mindfulness and the therapeutic relationship.* New York: The Guilford Press.

Hooker, C. E. (1976). Learned helplessness. *Social Work, 21*(3), 194–198.

Huss, D., & Baer, R. (2007). Acceptance and change: The integration of mindfulness based cognitive therapy into ongoing dialectical behavior therapy in a case of borderline personality disorder with depression. *Clinical Case Studies, 6*(1), 17–33.

Jourard, S. (1966). Psychology of transcendent perception. In H. Otto (Ed.), *Exploration in human potential.* Springfield, IL: Charles C. Thomas.

Kabat-Zinn, J. (1994). *Wherever you go, there you are.* New York: Hyperion.

Kabat-Zinn, J., Massion, A., Kristeller, J., Peterson, L., et al. (1992). Effectiveness of meditation-based stress reduction program in the treatment of anxiety disorders. *American Journal of Psychiatry, 149*(7), 936–943.

Kapleau, P. (1967). *Three pillars of Zen.* Boston: Beacon Press.

Kasamatsu, A., & Hirai, T. (1984). An electroencephalographic study of the Zen meditation (Zagen). In D. H. Shapiro & R. N. Walsh (Eds.), *Meditation: Classic and contemporary perspectives* (pp. 480–492). New York: Aldine.

Keefe, T. W. (1975, April). Meditation and the psychotherapist. *American Journal of Orthopsychiatry, 45*(3), 484–489.

Keefe, T. W. (1976). Empathy: The critical skill. *Social Work, 21*(1), 10–15.

Keefe, T. W. (1978). Optimal functioning: The Eastern ideal in psychotherapy. *Journal of Contemporary Psychotherapy, 10*(1), 16–24.

Keefe, T. W. (1979). The development of empathic skill: A study. *Journal of Education for Social Work, 15*(2), 30–37.

Kennett, J. (1972). *Selling water by the river: A manual of Zen training* (p. 302). New York: Vintage Books.

Lazarus, A. (1976). Psychiatric problems precipitated by Transcendental Meditation. *Psychological Reports, 39,* 601–602.

Marlatt, A. C., Pagano, R. R., Rose, R., & Marques, J. K. (1984). Effects of meditation and relaxation training upon alcohol use in male social drinkers. In D. H. Shapiro & R. N. Walsh (Eds.), *Meditation: Classic and contemporary perspectives* (pp. 105–120). New York: Aldine.

Marx, K. (1966). Preface to "Contribution to the critique of political economy." In E. Allen, *From Plato to Nietzsche* (p. 159). New York: Fawcett.

Melbourne Academic Mindfulness Interest Group. (2006). Mindfulness-based psychotherapies: a review of conceptual foundations, empirical evidence and practical considerations. *Australian and New Zealand Journal of Psychiatry, 40,* 285–294.

Miller, J., Fletcher, K., & Kabat-Zinn, J. (1995). Three year followup and clinical implications of a mindfulness meditation-based stress reduction intervention in the treatment of anxiety disorders. *General Hospital Psychiatry, 17,* 192–200.

Morse, D. R., Martin, J. S., Furst, M. I., & Dubin, L. L. (1984). A physiological and subjective evaluation of meditation, hypnosis and relaxation. In D. H. Shapiro & R. N. Walsh (Eds.), *Meditation: Classic and contemporary perspectives* (pp. 645–665). New York: Aldine.

Nucho, A. (1988). *Stress management* (chapter 8). Springfield, IL: Charles C. Thomas.

Ospina, M., et al. (2007). Meditation practices for health: State of the research. Number 155. Edmonton, Alberta, Canada: University of Alberta Evidence-based Practice Center.

Ornstein, R. E. (1977). *The psychology of consciousness* (2nd ed.) New York: Harcourt, Brace, Jovanovich.

Pearl, J. H., & Carlozzi, A. (1994). Effect of meditation on empathy and anxiety. *Perceptual and Motor Skills, 78*(1), 297–298.

Prabhupada, Swami A.C.B. (1972). *Bhagavad Gita as it is.* New York: Bhaktivedanta Book Trust.

Roemer, L., & Orsillo, S. (2009). *Mindfulness & acceptance-based behavioral therapies in practice.* New York: The Guilford Press.

Rogers, C. R. (1975). The necessary and sufficient conditions for therapeutic personality change. *Journal of Consulting Psychology,* 21(2), 95–103.

Royer, A. (1994). The role of the Transcendental Meditation technique in promoting smoking cessation: A longitudinal study. *Alcoholism Treatment Quarterly,* 11(12), 221–239.

Schopen, A., & Freeman, B. (1992). Meditation: The forgotten Western tradition. *Counseling and Values,* 36(2), 123–134.

Seligman, M. E. P. (1974). Depression and learned helplessness. In R. J. Friedman & M. M. Katz (Eds.), *The psychology of depression: Contemporary theory and research* (pp. 83–107). New York: Halstead Press.

Seligman, M. E. P. (1975). *Helplessness: On depression, development and death.* San Francisco: Freeman.

Shapiro, D. H. (1976). Zen meditation and behavioral self-control strategies applied to a case of generalized anxiety. *Psychologia: An International Journal of Psychology in the Orient,* 19(3), 134–138.

Shapiro, D. H. (1994). Examining the content and context of meditation: A challenge for psychology in the areas of stress management, psychotherapy, and religion/values. *Journal of Humanistic Psychology,* 34(4), 101–135.

Shapiro, D. H., & Walsh, R. N. (Eds.) (1984). *Meditation: Classic and contemporary perspectives.* New York: Aldine.

Shapiro, D. H., & Zifferblatt, S. M. (1976). Zen meditation and behavioral self-control: Similarities, differences, and clinical applications. *American Psychologist,* 31(7), 519–532.

Smith, E. D. (1995). Addressing the psycho-spiritual distress of death as reality: A transpersonal approach. *Social Work,* 40(3), 402–413.

Snaith, P. R., Owens, D., & Kennedy, E. (1992). An outcome study of a brief anxiety management programme: Anxiety control training. *Irish Journal of Psychological Medicine,* 9(2), 111–114.

Sudsuang, R., Chentanez, V., & Veluvan, K. (1991). Effect of Buddhist meditation on serum cortisol and total protein levels, blood pressure, pulse rate, lung volume and reaction time. *Physiology and Behavior,* 50(3), 543–548.

Suzuki, D. T. (1964). *An introduction to Zen Buddhism.* New York: Grove Press.

Sweet, M., & Johnson, C. (1990). Enhancing empathy: The interpersonal implications of a Buddhist meditation technique. *Psychotherapy,* 27(1), 19–29.

Taub, E., Steiner, S., Weingarten, E., & Walton, K. (1994). Effectiveness of broad spectrum approaches to relapse prevention in severe alcoholism: A long term, randomized, controlled trial of Transcendental Meditation, EMG biofeedback and electronic neurotherapy. *Alcoholism Treatment Quarterly,* 11(1–2), 187–220.

Teasdale, J., Segal, Z., Williams, M., Ridgeway, V., Soulsby, J., & Lau, M. (2000). Prevention of relapse/recurrence in major depression by mindfulness-based cognitive therapy. *Journal of Clinical and Consulting Psychology,* 68(4), 615–623.

Thera, N. (1970). *The heart of Buddhist meditation.* New York: Weiser.

Turner, K. (2009). Mindfulness: The present moment in clinical social work. *Clinical Social Work Journal,* 37, 95–103.

Wallace, R. K., Benson, H., & Wilson, A. F. (1971). A wakeful hypometabolic state. *American Journal of Physiology,* 221(3), 795–799.

Walrath, L. C., & Hamilton, D. W. (1984). Autonomic correlates of meditation and hypnosis. In D. H. Shapiro & R. N. Walsh (Eds.), *Meditation: Classic and contemporary perspectives* (pp. 645–665). New York: Aldine.

Watts, A. (1961). *Psychotherapy East and West.* New York: Ballantine.

Welwood, J. (1977). Meditation and the unconscious: A new perspective. *Journal of Transpersonal Psychology,* 9(1), 1–26.

Williams, M., Teasdale, J., Segal, Z., & Kabat-Zinn, J. (2007). *The mindful way through depression.* New York: The Guilford Press.

Wood, E. (1959). *Yoga.* Baltimore, MD: Penguin.

Woolfolk, R. L, Car-Kaffashan, L., McNulty, T., & Lehrer, P. (1976). Meditation as a training for insomnia. *Behavior Therapy,* 7(3), 359–365.

Woolfolk, R. L., Lehrer, P. M., McCann, B. S., & Rooney, A. J. (1982). Effects of progressive relaxation and meditation on cognitive and somatic manifestations of daily stress. *Behavior Research and Therapy,* 20(5), 461–467.

Woolfolk, R. L. (1984). Self-control meditation and the treatment of chronic anger. In D. H. Shapiro & R. N. Walsh (Eds.), *Meditation: Classic and contemporary perspectives* (pp. 550–554). New York: Aldine.

Annotated Listing of Key References

Germer, C. K., Siegel, R. D., & Fulton, P. R. (2005). *Mindfulness and psychotherapy.* New York: The Guilford Press. This text begins with sound definitions and discussion of Buddhist and Western psychology. The therapeutic relationship and clinical applications are presented in readable style. Invaluable for practice.

Hick, S. F., & Bien, T. (2008). *Mindfulness and the therapeutic relationship*. New York: The Guilford Press. Integrates mindfulness into the therapeutic relationship with many insights into the connections.

Roemer, L., & Orsillo, S. M. (2009). *Mindfulness-based behavioral therapies in practice*. New York: The Guilford Press. Explores in depth the integration of acceptance-based behavioral therapies, theory, research, and application. Good for therapists seeking to enrich and extend their practice.

Williams, M., Teasdale, J., Segal, Z., and Kabat-Zinn, J. (2007). *The mindful way through depression*. New York: The Guilford Press. Grounded in research and clinical perspectives, this accessible and valuable book extends meditation and cognitive approaches, addressing a sound model of depression and ways to relieve it.

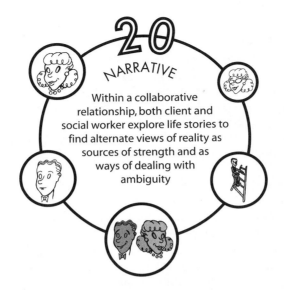

NARRATIVE

Within a collaborative relationship, both client and social worker explore life stories to find alternate views of reality as sources of strength and as ways of dealing with ambiguity

Narrative Theory and Social Work Treatment

Patricia Kelley

Narrative therapy was developed in the late 1980s and rose to prominence in the 1990s, especially in the fields of family therapy and social work with individuals, families, and communities. In this chapter narrative therapy is described, its historical and theoretical base explored, and how it fits into existing social work practice theory and values addressed.

Overview

The narrative approach described and discussed in this chapter will draw mainly on the works of White and Epston (1990), family therapists from Australia and New Zealand, respectively (both of whom were originally trained in social work; Epston had also studied community organization). They developed this approach in the 1980s, but it became popularized in North America

after their book *Narrative Means to Therapeutic Ends* was published on this continent in 1990. While some elements of their approach were unique at that time, their work emerged and co-developed in relation to theoretical and practice developments occurring in North America and Europe. Their approach falls under the general rubric of constructivist and social constructionist theories, from which several models emerged at about the same time, and which all developed in relationship to the postmodern culture, which crossed many academic disciplines (see Carpenter, Chapter 8, for further discussion of constructivism). In the 1980s, Anderson and Goolishian (1988) in Texas; Boscolo and Checchin of Milan, Italy; Penn and Hoffman of the United States, who worked with the Milan group (Boscolo, Checchin, Hoffman, & Penn, 1987); and Tomm (1987) of Alberta, Canada, who had studied with the Milan group, all wrote about these newer constructivist/constructionist approaches. White and Epston chose to place themselves in the social constructionist group. Freedman and Combs of Chicago (1996) further popularized the ideas by outlining the theory and practice of narrative therapy so clearly in their book, *The Social Construction of Preferred Realities*.

Hoffman, a social worker and prominent family therapist, described the earlier swing of family therapists away from the emphasis on intrapsychic focus to systems views with emphasis on interpersonal processes and behavior, as swinging back to more emphasis on ideas, meanings, beliefs, and myths (Hoffman, 1990). While systems approaches are based on cybernetic theory, a mechanistic theory of control that Hoffman declared had lost its usefulness, constructionist therapies are based on second-order cybernetics, which renders observations as dependent upon the observer. The systems theories, like some behavioral and cognitive approaches emerging in the same time period, were based on the modernist view of objectivity, rationality, and knowing through observation. On the other hand, the postmodern view, which has been embraced by scholars across many disciplines from art and literature to social sciences, recognizes the many realities and truths that coexist and sees reality as being socially constructed rather than a given (Neimeyer, 1993).

Relationships to Other Theories

Constructivism and social constructionism both fall under the postmodern movement. Narrative approaches borrow from the constructivists in the field of literary criticism, where narratives are taken apart and analyzed for meaning, and from the social constructionists in the field of social psychology, where reality is viewed as co-constructed in the minds of individuals in interaction with other people and with sociocultural beliefs. Neimeyer (1993) characterizes constructivism as a "meta-theory that emphasizes the self organizing and proactive features of human knowing" (p. 221) and as a view of humans as "meaning making agents" (p. 222). The roots of constructionist therapies can be traced to many sources, especially George Kelly's

personal construct theory, first articulated in the 1950s (Kelly, 1955). Kelly himself cited semanticist Korzybski (1933), who was also drawn upon by cognitive (Ellis, 1962) and systems (Watzlawick, Weakland, & Jackson, 1967) therapists, and by Moreno (1937), who developed psychodrama. Constructivist therapy has been compared and contrasted to cognitive therapy (Neimeyer, 1993) and to systems approaches (Kelley, 1994), and its emphasis on meaning connects it to the existential approaches (see Krill, Chapter 12). White and Epston (1990) state that they drew on the works of French philosopher and historian Michel Foucault (1980), as well as psychologist Jerome Bruner (1986) and anthropologist Gregory Bateson (1972), in the development of their narrative therapy. It is interesting to note that the systems thinkers also drew heavily on Bateson. Narrative therapy, then, is a new paradigm for viewing human change in some respects, but in other ways it can be seen as evolving out of existing practice theories.

The narrative, postmodern approaches to practice can be useful for social workers, who, as noted by Scott (1989), search for the meanings of events and behaviors as preconditions for action. The emphasis on understanding and meanings is useful as we work with the diverse clients of today's practice. White (2007) discusses narrative therapy as focusing on the expression of peoples' life experiences, noting that life, meaning, and experience are inseparable. The implications of postmodernism for practice have been discussed by social work scholars and others, who found these approaches useful for multicultural practice (Holland & Kilpatrick, 1993; Kelley, 1994; Waldegrave, Tamasese, Tuhaka, & Campbell, 2003), persons facing adversity (Borden, 1992), family violence (Jenkins, 1991; Rober, Eesback, & Elliot, 2006), feminist practice (Sands & Nuccio, 1992), adolescents (Kelley, Blankenburg, & McRoberts, 2002; Zimmerman & Dickerson, 1996), sexual abuse victims (O'Leary, 2004), and health care (Kelley & Clifford, 1997; Wynne, Shields, & Sirkin 1992). Narrative therapy has also been applied to group work (Laube, 2004) and community work (Epston, 2003; Kelley & Murty, 2003; Vodde & Gallant, 2003). International conferences on narrative therapy and community work, begun by White, are continuing with the 2009 conference held in Mexico (Dulwich Centre, 2009). The *International Journal of Narrative Therapy and Community Work* issued its second edition in November 2009 (Dulwich Centre, 2009).

Basic Assumptions

Knowledge is power, and self-knowledge can empower people. White and Epston (1990; White, 2007) believe that we all "story" our lives to make sense out of them. We cannot remember all of our lived experience; there is too much material and too many experiences unrelated to each other to retain it all, so our narrative structuring experience is a selective process. We arrange our lives into sequences and into dominant story lines to develop a sense of coherence and to ascribe meaning to our lives. As we develop our dominant story line, we remember events that support it and forget (White and Epston say "subjugate") other life experiences that do not fit into the dominant story line. The meanings we attribute to experience are influenced and shaped by cultural beliefs and practices. Certain events may be imagined or exaggerated to fill in the gaps of a story. White and Epston's concept of subjugated knowledge is similar to the psychodynamic concept of unconscious, in that both refer to forgotten material. They are different, however, in that "subjugated knowledge" refers to life experiences that are not remembered because they do not fit into the dominant story, whereas the psychodynamic idea of unconscious refers to memories that are repressed because they are painful.

Narrative therapy is similar to postmodern literary criticism, where the story line is deconstructed as the plot, characters, and time line are reassessed. Many times, presenting problems of clients fall within the dominant story line, and often clients have authored problem-saturated stories of their lives. These stories limit the clients' views of themselves and others and can immobilize them from action. Their problem-saturated stories have been co-constructed with others around them, including employers, social service workers, and other helpers, and are influenced by cultural norms. For example, social service agencies working to help families with multiple needs can do too much for them (Imber-Black, 1988), giving the message that they are incompetent, and their dominant narrative becomes that of a "multi-problem" or "dysfunctional" family. Similarly, Wynne, Shields, and Sirkin (1992) discuss how, for chronically ill people, the illness may become the dominant story line, as the family and professional helpers gradually become more involved with the patient, and the co-constructed reality is that the patient is the illness, as opposed to being afflicted with it. A goal of narrative therapy is to help clients see more realities, which offer more alternatives for them, and help them to self-empowerment. As Neimeyer has noted (1993), such therapy is more creative than corrective and is more reflective and elaborative than persuasive or instructive.

Role of Social Worker/Therapist

The role of the social worker is collegial. As narrative therapy helps clients re-author their lives through seeing other truths and other possible interpretations of events, the role of the therapist is to listen, wonder, and ask reflective questions. Clients are invited to assess other realities, which are not necessarily more true, but are also true. For narrative therapists, the harsh realities of many clients' lives, such as poverty, racism, or violence, are not denied as constructs of the mind, but the power given to these adverse events and the control they have over clients' lives are challenged. Clients are also challenged to question some "truths" accepted by family and the larger culture, which have affected their views and held them back. Questions are introduced that help clients assess other ways to view a situation, analyze for alternative meanings, and find other aspects of their lives, often involving strengths and coping, which may have been lost in the over-focus on problems. In this postmodern view, the therapist is not an outside objective observer but is part of the change system, and there is reciprocal influence between client and clinician. Thus, the therapist does not just hear the client's story, but co-creates it with the client, it is hoped with the client creating some new stories. History is not a collection of facts to be remembered, but is created in the telling. The therapist's role is non-hierarchical, especially compared to psychodynamic or systemic therapists. The therapist is not the expert on the problem or the client's life; the client is. The therapist takes a "not knowing" position (Anderson & Goolishian, 1988), which invites the client to do more exploring.

Cultural Sensitivity

Narrative therapy is culturally sensitive because it does not presume a way of being, but aims to understand the client's reality. The therapist listens for ways in which ethnicity, physical ability, gender, culture, and social and economic context may shape the client's worldview and view of self. Clients are encouraged to take action on their behalf. The "not knowing" position (Anderson & Goolishian, 1988) is useful in this respect, too, as the therapist learns from the client. Discussion of social justice, poverty, gender, and power are part of the social constructionist approaches. At the Family Centre in New Zealand, Waldegrave, and colleagues (2003) have developed "just therapy" (meaning socially just), where therapists and clients together weave webs of meaning where political as well as clinical responses are required, and where cross-cultural consultants are used on the therapy teams. Narrative therapists in general have taken on these social activist views and practices.

View of Human Nature

The view of humanity underlying this approach is that humans are complex and multi-faceted, not simply good or bad. Underlying pathology is not presumed. Rather than listening for underlying "root causes," the social worker listens for other aspects of the client's life that may also be true and that may involve strengths to be mobilized. These "unique outcomes" (White & Epston, 1990) cannot be explained by the client's problem story, and may have been subjugated. Here similarities to solution-focused therapy, which looks for exceptions and was developed by de Shazer and colleagues (de Shazer, Dolan, Korman, Trepper, McCollum, & Berg, 2007), can be seen. Differences between solution-focused and narrative therapy also need to be noted, however. In narrative work the clients are not asked for the "exceptions" to problems; instead, the therapist carefully listens for these times and brings them out, co-constructing new realities

with the client. In addition, instead of ignoring problems to focus on solutions only, problems are carefully listened to and deconstructed, and the past is not ignored. Borden (1992) discussed the importance of helping the clients assess the past, experience the present, and anticipate the future as specific life experiences are incorporated into the ongoing life story. While attention is paid to the past, the focus is on helping the client not to be stuck in the past but to develop a progressive, forward-looking narrative.

Narrative therapists see the clients in context—that is, part of a cultural whole, where views of self and the world are co-constructed in interaction with cultural and societal norms. Clients are invited to assess the truths they have assumed, and to challenge views that have not been useful. In this way, they may empower themselves to work on their own behalf or for social change. Further, as needs are assessed with client and clinician working together, the client may be made aware of resources available and the clinician may suggest a referral. Making lists of referrals to solve problems, however, is not part of this approach.

In a sense, then, the clients become their own case managers, assessing their own needs and monitoring the services they receive. In this view, a biological basis of some conditions is not denied, nor is the potential usefulness of psychotropic medications for some people. Diagnosis and treatment of medical conditions are not in the realm of social work treatment, however, and clients are encouraged to discuss such concerns with physicians. Clients on psychotropic medications are encouraged to develop a partnership relationship with the prescribing physicians, working together to fight the effects of the illness, rather than becoming passive recipients of treatment.

Social Work Treatment

The goal of narrative treatment approaches in social work practice is for clients first to understand, and then to broaden and change, the stories around which they have organized their lives, and to assess and challenge the sources, often sociocultural, that have influenced them. This work may involve helping the client to challenge the problem-saturated dominant story as the only truth, and to find other aspects of his or her life that may also be true. The discovery of more realities and more truths can free clients to see more alternatives and ways out of an impasse. It can also help clients recognize and mobilize the strengths they already possess and are using, but may have ignored in the focus on problems.

Through dialogue between social worker and client, these problem-saturated stories are gradually deconstructed as the worker introduces questions that challenge the client's narrow view of reality or draw out facets of the client's life that have previously been ignored. Some constructivist and constructionist approaches offer little guidance to the worker or client and little structure to the process. The "Down Under" therapists from New Zealand and Australia such as Jenkins (1991), Waldegrave and colleagues (2003), and White and Epston (1990) offer a bit more structure, and they challenge not-useful stories more than many of their North American counterparts. All stories are not seen as equally useful.

The narrative model offered by White and Epston (White & Epston, 1990; Epston, 2004; White, 2007) is helpful for teaching and for practice because it names specific practices and outlines stages of the process without being too prescriptive or technique-driven. Constructionist therapists in general do not distinguish between the "assessment" and "treatment" stages of practice, for they view assessment as an ongoing and ever-changing process, and hope that all sessions are therapeutic. All clinicians know, however, that some elements of the helping process are more appropriate in earlier stages and some are more useful later in the process. For this reason, White and Epston's (1990) discussion of the stages of their narrative approach as "deconstruction" and "reconstruction" is useful.

Deconstruction Stage

In the deconstruction stage, the clients' existing stories are heard and then deconstructed. Even here there are stages; it is important not to deconstruct the client's story too soon. Most people need to have their problem stories heard before they can move to other areas. First, the clinician carefully listens to the client's story: What does he or she define as the presenting problem? How does the client experience it? What meaning is ascribed to it, and how is it viewed in light of historical events and social context? This process is similar to the joining or relationship-building process of any good therapeutic endeavor. Asking questions to elicit the full meaning here is important: Who else is involved in this problem? What events in the past have contributed to its development? How did this problem evolve over time? What has been tried to fight the effects of the problem? How has this problem affected other aspects of the client's life? Again, as in any good therapeutic encounter, the development of an empathic relationship is important. This empathy is important not only for developing trust but also in helping the clinician understand the client's reality more fully. While the careful listening and reflecting is similar to most therapeutic approaches, the way the questions are worded is specific to the narrative approach.

Externalizing the problem, a key idea in narrative therapy, begins in the joining stage and continues throughout the treatment process. The purpose of this externalization is to separate the person from the problem, to view it as not intrinsic to the person but as something that has interfered with the person's life and needs to be challenged. Thus, at the early stages, where the client's story is being heard and understood, the nature of the reflective questions gradually shifts the view as to where the problem resides: "When did you first notice that depression began to interfere with your work?" "How did it happen that Andy's temper took over so much of his life? Who first noticed it? Who has been affected most by it?" It is important to distinguish between taking responsibility and viewing a problem as not intrinsic to the person. Clients are encouraged to take responsibility for fighting the effects of the problem and for their own behaviors, but to not see themselves as the problem.

Even the effects of physical illness can be externalized through questions about the effects of the illness on the person's life, and about the process by which it took on so much power over the person's life, and about how it has interfered with other aspects of the person's life, including relationships. As the client is able to separate from the problem, it becomes more manageable, and the problem, not the person, becomes the target for change. The client and therapist join together to fight the effects of the problem. At this early stage, even before deconstruction, the clinician listens carefully to the client's definition of the problem and begins to objectify the problem through the use of metaphors, through summary, and through the nature of the reflective questions.

The importance of language in sharing meaning has been discussed by many theorists and therapists over the years (Anderson & Goolishian, 1988; Bateson, 1972; Ellis, 1962; Watzlawick, Weakland, & Jackson, 1967), including narrative proponents (Epston, 2004; Freedman & Combs, 1996; White, 2007). The way questions are worded is an important aspect of this work. White (1989) has described the way in which he helped a family with a 12-year-old son with behavior problems to "escape from trouble." He asked family members to describe the ways in which John's problems had "plagued" his life and "influenced" their lives. White also asked the parents how they had coped with John's troubles and how they had become involved with them.

Narrative therapists, unlike those from some other schools, do not assume that clients "need" the problem or that it symbolizes a deeper problem, as do some psychodynamic therapists, nor do they believe that it "serves a function" for the family unit, as some systemic proponents believe. It is assumed that clients want the problem solved or remediated, but that they have gotten stuck in finding ways to do so. Thus, words like "unmotivated" or "resistant" are not considered useful. This belief in their clients and what they say is very respectful, and consistent with social work values. While it is not presumed that clients need problems, it is recognized that they and family members, friends, and helpers may have helped maintain the problems, possibly through their efforts to solve them. Thus the "influence" questions are useful in bringing about discussion on that matter. For example, family members may be asked how they were recruited into and influenced by the client's problem, and how cultural forces may have influenced them.

After the first part of the deconstruction stage, where the client's views are heard, understood, and acknowledged, the therapist gradually begins to help the client deconstruct the dominant story through continued summarizing and questioning. The client's view is not disputed or seen as not true, for that would not be respectful and the client would not feel validated. Instead, the story is fully discussed and analyzed for meaning, and other interpretations and other meanings can be assessed, bringing about alternative truths that are also valid. At this point, the "relative influence" of the problem's effects on the individual or family is mapped across time and across spheres. How has this problem affected the client in the past, present, and anticipated future across intellectual, personal, interpersonal, and social spheres?

For example, in White's case of helping the family "escape from trouble" mentioned above, it became clear through discussion that John's "trouble" had interfered with his life at school, academically and with classmates, and at home in his relationship with his parents. The degree to which the school come to view him as the problem and how he had taken on that view was examined. In addition, how the problems had "crept into" his parents' lives and affected their relationship with each other as well as their own work productivity was assessed. Ways in which "trouble" had caused guilt in John and feelings of helplessness in his parents were discussed. John was asked what would happen if he were to further "succumb" to trouble, and his parents were asked what might be the effects of their continued participation in the problem. Should they accept John's invitation to join him in participating in trouble, or should they renounce it and escape from it? This careful dissection of the effects of the problem across all spheres of life and the assessment of what might happen in the future if it is allowed to dominate challenged the family to find new ways to handle the problem. The family now could work with the clinician to explore ways to defend itself against the effects of trouble and to fight it when necessary. Since the problem was externalized, the family did not need to define John as the problem, but could join with John and the clinician to find ways to defend against this problem, which was interfering with his and their lives.

As the problem stories are gradually deconstructed through a dialogue between client and clinician, the clinician obtains a full history of the problem. The clients discuss events that they believe led up to the problem's formation. Not only the events but also the thoughts, beliefs, and social environment around the events are assessed for influence in the past, present, and possible future. Clients might be asked to ponder how the same events may have been viewed by others, or even how they might view it themselves if they were not involved. For example, a victim of childhood abuse may have blamed herself or himself, but may now begin to see that being a child in a helpless position, the choices were limited. Alternative futures are also discussed: How would it be if things were different, and who would do what? Who would first notice the difference? What would a better future look like? Here, again, similarities to de Shazer and colleagues' (2007) solution-focused therapy may be noted. This "visioning" of a desired future helps clients begin to think about ways in which they might get there. Different from solution-focused therapy, however, is the fact the narrative therapists also look at what would happen if things do not change.

Reconstruction Stage

In the second stage, the reconstruction stage, other truths are found that are also true but may have been subjugated because they did not fit into the dominant theme. It is a knowledge-expanding, more than knowledge-changing, experience. This subjugated knowledge is brought out through careful listening for "unique outcomes" or "sparkling events" (White, 2007) as clients tell their stories. These are events or outcomes that cannot be explained by the dominant story. For example, a man has described his problem as being a bully, stating that he has always been mean and has had a temper problem most of his life. He discusses how it has interfered with his relationships with peers and colleagues as a child and as an adult and how it has caused a breakup of his marriage (the precipitating problem) and interfered with his relationship with his children. He examines how it has also hurt himself, causing feelings of guilt and lowered self-esteem. Looking to the future, he sees a lonely existence if this problem continues to dominate his life. It is important to obtain his view of this situation, not to assume that he sees it as "bad" or that he wants to stop it. The purpose of helping

him to separate from the problem is not to alleviate him from responsibility for his actions, but to help him assess its effects on self and others, make a decision as to what he wants to do about it, and then develop ways to manage and control it (the problem). In fact, responsibility was implied here as the client was asked about how temper had taken over his life, and whether he wanted it to control his life.

Here the unique outcomes were not easy to find at first, but careful listening helped to uncover some. If he is such a "tough guy," where did he find the gentleness to visit his grandmother in a nursing home? How was he able to muster enough caring to take care of his dog so well? Again, the similarities to de Shazer and colleagues' (2007) solution-focused therapy can be seen, but instead of asking for "exceptions," which the client may not see, the therapist carefully sorts through the conversation in a detective-like manner to find the evidence. Just as the dominant story has been deconstructed to find who was involved in the construction of the tough-guy identity, now the client is asked to think about who may have helped him develop this gentler side. Gradually, a discussion of a relationship with a caring grandfather was brought out, and a gentle but manly teacher is also remembered. In addition, the cultural message in the media of needing to be tough to be a man is also compared to the conflicting social message about the honorable gentleman treating women and children well. Knowing there is another side to him helps the client find ways to fight the effects of his tough-guy side, allowing him to keep some aspects of that side while exploring and developing his other, gentler, side.

In another situation, a family that was viewed by others in the community, as well as themselves, as being a poor and "out-of-control" family, with "violent" adolescent boys, was challenged in this narrow definition of itself. They began to see they were also a resourceful family that has coped with poverty. They had found a way for mother to be home with the young children by day and earn money holding an evening job with the cooperation of the adolescent boys, who babysat after school. This discussion also challenged the "violent boys" idea, although the fact that they acted violently in school sometimes was not ignored. Seeing other aspects of themselves helped them to see that they had alternatives as to which side of themselves they wanted to develop and in which situations. Here, the social worker did not tell the boys what they must do, but helped them see options and potential outcomes of the options. Both the family and the school reported a marked decrease in violent behavior over the school year.

In another example, a social worker in a coping skills group for chronic pain patients helped the patients to find ways in which they were already coping with the illness and to see that there were times when they could fight the effects of the illness and when the pain was not as bad. At first, most of the patients believed the pain was always there and there was nothing they could ever do. Through careful listening by the worker and each other, they found that there were times when things were better, and they all found ways in which they were already coping (Kelley & Clifford, 1997). The illness was externalized by the social worker asking them, "If this illness were a member of the family, how would you treat it?" The group members began to discuss this question with great interest. Some found ways they would fight the illness and reject it, while others said that since it was there to stay they would look for ways to accommodate it and learn to live with it. The social worker did not teach them to cope, but instead, through careful listening, identified times when the patients were already coping, challenging the view that they were totally helpless. At the end, they reported feeling empowered.

At this reconstruction stage, then, clients are helped to reconstruct their views of reality by making it broader, not different. A depressed woman, who remembers her childhood as one deprived of maternal care because her mother was critically ill when she was a child and died when the client was 11, was asked if she remembered any times that her mother had the time and energy to give comfort to her. The client remembered her mother combing her hair every day and how good it felt. The tragedy of her mother being so sick that she only did basic tasks required of a mother was never minimized, but the client was also helped to remember other aspects of her childhood. She reported that she finds it comforting, when she feels depressed

now, to think about how good it felt when her mother combed her hair. Dolan (1991), in her work with sexual abuse survivors, has noted that having these clients tell their stories over and over can revictimize them if corrective experiences are not infused into the process. Helping clients broaden their life stories, rather than "polishing" their problem-saturated stories, is a corrective experience.

The last step under the reconstruction stage is what White and Epston (1990) called "spreading the news." After finding alternative views of self and others, it is important for people to notify others of their changes, to reinforce them. At the Dulwich Centre White and his colleagues often had groups where members shared experiences, singing songs and telling stories about their new selves. In another situation, a group of adolescent "girls in trouble" (Kelley et al., 2002), group members drew pictures of their new selves and shared the pictures and stories with other members.

Length of Treatment

Because of the philosophical nature of constructionist approaches to treatment, it is often assumed that the process is a long-term one, and questions have been raised about how such a long process can be applicable in today's social work practice arena. An interesting aspect of the narrative approach of White and Epston (1990) is that they use relatively few sessions, often as few as six or seven, although there is no set idea as to number. Clients are usually asked at the end of each session if they would like to return, and if so, how soon. Unlike some constructionist therapists, narrative therapists may ask the clients to do some activities between sessions. For example, in helping the family and boy "escape from trouble," White (1989) encouraged the family to plan escape meetings where all the family members reviewed the progress of their flight from escape. The meetings were formal in structure and even had minutes taken.

While the number of sessions is usually few, they are usually spread out over a longer time period than every week, to give the family time to think about and try new things. With families, especially, playful ideas and metaphors are used in asking them to try new things. In addition to asking members to try something different between sessions, White uses many forms of writing to expand the impact of each session. He often uses "therapeutic letters" to clients from the therapist between sessions that summarize his notes as to how he heard the client describe the problem and also record any solution knowledge obtained in the session. The therapist requests client corrections, deletions, and additions to make the statements more accurate. Clients report that each letter is worth about four sessions (White, 1992). While some might question the time involved in this process, these letters can also be used as case notes. White also finds taking notes in session helpful, not distracting, and he uses these notes to read statements back to clients to check for accuracy. Morgan (2002) even suggests copying notes taken in session to give to clients. Other forms of writing may also add to the value of sessions, too, such as client writing to himself or herself or the therapist, art or poetry, or charts and checklists (Kelley, 1990). White and Epston use certificates and documents, such as an "Escape from Guilt Certificate" (1990, p. 199) or a "Diploma of Special Knowledge" (1990, p. 201), which are especially useful with children.

White (1992) also reports other strategies he used to reduce the number of sessions but expand their power. In addition to the letters and documents, he may have "ceremonies of redefinition" (e.g., parties for children) where the victory over the problem is celebrated, or he may encourage the family to use "consultants," who are people in the clients' lives whom they can talk to for enlightenment about a problem or solution. Epston, early on, used the idea of supportive communities of people facing similar challenges to support clients in their change, such as his anti-anorexic/bulimic league. White also subscribed to this idea. At first, White used "reflecting teams" of trainees behind a one-way mirror who traded places with clients, and reflected back their ideas about what they heard. In more recent years, however, he has gone to having the team in the room, and often used former clients who had faced similar problems to reflect what they heard. Either way, clients report that these teams expanded the impact of each session and reduced the number of sessions.

Principal Applications in Social Work Practice

At first, a primary application of narrative work had been in family therapy and social work with individuals and families. However, its usefulness in group work has been explored also (Kelley & Clifford, 1997; Laube, 2004). White and others began to move into community work in the 1990s, and major efforts in the past decade of narrative work have been in communities (Dulwich Centre, 2009). Waldegrave and colleagues (2003) pioneered this work at the Family Therapy Centre in Auckland, New Zealand, where community work and social action went hand in hand with the family therapy in their "just therapy." Waldegrave is not a social worker, but his emphasis on social justice is very much in the tradition of social work. White, at his Dulwich Centre in Adelaide, Australia, also began to focus more on community action and social justice issues and developed the international conferences on narrative therapy and community work and the *Journal of Narrative Therapy and Community Work* noted previously. Epston edited an issue on the subject of narrative community work in the journal *Social Work Review* (of New Zealand) in 2003 (Epston, 2003).

Potential Problems and Counter-indications

While there is a wide range of applications of narrative-type approaches in social work, some questions have been raised regarding their use with specific populations. Some might fear that the de-emphasis on "reality" and the focus away from the problem story together could minimize clients' problems, especially in cases of sexual abuse, family violence, or severe mental illness. This is a real problem if the social worker deconstructs the story too quickly or denies the client's reality, but should not be problematic if the client is carefully listened to and attended, and if referrals are made for complementary services if needed. In a related concern, some might see this approach as superficial because it does not get at "root" causes or underlying pathology in deeply disturbed individuals. Since these ideas do not fall within the constructs of postmodern theory, narrative therapists would not see such concerns as relevant. Some social workers might fear that the process of externalization could reduce a perpetrator's responsibility for violence or other crimes, and its usefulness with mandatory clients could be questioned. White and Epston (1990, p. 65) spoke directly to this matter and noted that helping people separate from the problem and assessing it objectively can help them assume more responsibility for it. Social workers and other professionals express the idea that talking is not enough for some clients, that concrete services and possibly even medication may be required for the amelioration of some problems facing clients. Narrative therapists agree and believe that their approach can facilitate complementary services. Finally, there is a practical concern that without the use of labels, cross-disciplinary discussion may be impeded and that reimbursement for services may be denied. These are concerns to ponder and are not completely solvable. It should also be noted that labels may not have to be discarded in some situations, but the power given the labels can be challenged.

Because the narrative approaches are relatively new and there is little empirical research, it is difficult to say at this time which populations may or may not be well served by this approach. While narrative therapists report case studies with successful outcomes with a range of clients, future work needs to be aimed at isolating those clients best served by such approaches. Managed care companies, however, rely on evidence-based services, and using narrative therapy may require combining it with a more accepted approach, such as cognitive therapy, since narrative therapy deals with cognitions (Kelley, 1998). In addition, care needs to be taken in externalizing problems with persons experiencing serious emotional problems, who may already have trouble differentiating between themselves and outside forces.

Administrative and Training Factors

Narrative therapy is used mainly by clinical social workers, family therapists, and psychologists with graduate degrees. It involves more than story telling; it involves story *changing* through intensive listening and questioning in a specific manner, which is usually learned in special post-degree training. The "conscious use of self" and transference/countertransference issues discussed by psychodynamic social workers are also considered important by narrative social workers, although they do not use those terms. Narrative social workers need to be very clear about their own issues, views, and experiences to separate them from those of the clients. Since the client's history and reality are co-constructed through dialogue, the social worker cannot be an outside observer but is part of the change system through reciprocity. Great care must be taken to hear and understand the client's reality, and to individualize each client. Thus, there is no set of techniques or prescriptions; each client is viewed differently and treatment involves whatever fits his or her particular situation. A great deal of self-awareness and willingness to set aside one's own worldview is required to work in such a manner.

Although narrative approaches are infused into some academic social work programs (Kelley, 1995; Kelley & Murty, 2003; Vodde & Gallant, 2003), most training is conducted at family therapy training centers or at some social service agencies. In addition to the training centers already noted in Australia and New Zealand, there are several in North America, too. Freeman and Combs offer one in the Chicago area; Zimmerman and Dickerson in the Bay area, California; and Madigan and colleagues at Yaletown Family Therapy in Vancouver, British Columbia, Canada. In these centers, discussions and clinical work go hand in hand. As noted by Freedman and Combs (1996), narrative therapy is more a way of thinking about people and their situations than specific techniques.

Empirical Base

As noted, little empirical research has been conducted testing narrative approaches. Postmodernism, by definition, denies the possibility of objectivity, which is at the core of empiricism. For this reason, postmodern approaches have been criticized for keeping social work out of the scientific field where it should be placed (Epstein, 1995). While social constructionists are uncomfortable with the assumption of linear relationships among variables needed for most statistical procedures, Neimeyer (1993), a psychologist, has pointed out that there are several research methods that are appropriate to assess outcomes in constructionist therapy. He notes several examples, including the use of repertory grids, transcript analysis of developmental levels, task analysis of change events, stochastic modeling, and time series studies. He also notes, as have others, that more conversational ways of inquiry and of understanding personal meanings need to be explored, too. He stresses the need for diverse approaches to research for fuller understanding. Besa (1994) reported using single-subject design with some success. Ethnographic qualitative research approaches and transcript analysis have been found useful in studying constructionist approaches (Kelley, Blankenburg, & McRoberts, 2002; Kelley & Clifford, 1997), and White and Epston (1990) and others use the case study method in assessing outcome, noting symptom relief in clients. Finding new ways of measuring outcomes in narrative therapy and then conducting more research on these newer approaches are important directions for the future.

Prospectus

Narrative therapy fits into social work values and practices with its emphasis on respect, individualization, and collegial, client-centered approaches. Its focus on social and cultural forces as important in formation of problems and its emphasis on social action and political discourse increase this fit with the profession. In addition, narrative work bridges the gap between micro and macro practice, as it works with all levels. Because this theory is part of a cross-disciplinary trend, and because the approaches are useful with a wide variety of clients, it is appreciated by many social workers. There are problems using such approaches with clients in clinical practice, however, because of managed care setting parameters, and because of the demand for evidence-based practice in the field. More research needs to be conducted and new ways of conducting research will need to be found, however, before these approaches are fully accepted in the profession. Social worker and family therapist Hoffman (1990) has expressed the hope that this movement will facilitate a return of

therapy as an art of conversation as opposed to a pseudo-scientific activity. She also expressed beliefs that the aesthetic metaphors are closer to home than the biological or machine metaphors, as we work with our clients, and she expressed the hope that these metaphors will also create an "emancipator dialogue" (p. 11) that is socially and politically sensitive to our clients' needs. Indeed, the aim of narrative approaches of understanding and individualizing each client in his or her social context, and the emphasis on mobilizing strengths, is in the best tradition of the social work profession.

Dedication

This chapter is dedicated to Michael White, co-founder of narrative therapy, who died in 2008 at age 59 in California, where he had come to give a workshop. He was a dedicated teacher, scholar, innovator, and practitioner of individual, family, and community work.

References

Anderson, H., & Gollishian, H. A. (1988). Human systems as linguistic systems: Preliminary and evolving ideas about the implications for clinical theory. *Family Process, 27,* 371–393.

Bateson, G. (1972). *Steps to an ecology of mind.* New York: Ballantine.

Besa, D. (1994). Evaluating narrative family therapy using systems research designs. *Research in Social Work Practice,* 4(3), 309–325.

Borden, W. (1992). Narrative perspectives in psychological intervention following adverse life events. *Social Work,* 37(2), 135–141.

Boscolo, L., Cecchin, G., Hoffman, L., & Penn, P. (1987). *Milan systemic family therapy.* New York: Basic Books.

Bruner, J. (1986). *Actual minds, possible worlds.* Cambridge, MA: Harvard University Press.

deShazer, S., Dolan, Y., Korman, H., Trepper, T., McCollum, E., & Berg, I. (2007). *More than miracles: The state of art of solution-focused brief therapy.* New York: Haworth Press.

Dulwich Centre (2009). Dulwich Center Newsletter, Adelaide Australia. Retrieved August 24, 2009. from dulwichcentrenewsandconnections@dulwich center.com.au.

Dolan, Y. M. (1991). *Resolving sexual abuse: Solution-focused therapy and Ericksonian hypnosis for adult survivors.* New York: W. W. Norton.

Ellis, A. (1962). *Reason and emotion in psychotherapy.* New York: Stuart Press.

Epstein, W. M. (1995). Social work in the university. *Journal of Social Work Education, 31*(2), 281–293.

Epston, D. (2003). Guest editorial. *Social Work Review,* XV(4), 1–3.

Epston, D. (2004). Joel, can you help me train Amber to be a guard dog? *Journal of Brief Therapy, 3*(2), 97–107.

Foucault, M. (1980). *Power/knowledge: Selected interviews and other writings.* New York: Pantheon Books.

Freedman, J. and Combs, G. (1996) *Narrative therapy: The social construction of preferred realities.* New York: W. W. Norton.

Hoffman, L. (1990). Constructing realities: An art of lenses. *Family Process, 29,* 1–12.

Holland, T., & Kilpatrick, A. (1993). Using narrative techniques to enhance multicultural practice. *Journal of Social Work Education, 29*(3), 302–208.

Imber-Black, I. (1988). *Families and larger systems.* New York: Guilford Press.

Jenkins, A. (1991). *Invitation to responsibility: The therapeutic engagement of men who are violent and abusive.* Adelaide, S. A.: Dulwich Centre Publishing.

Kelley, P. (Ed.) (1990). *Uses of writing in psychotherapy.* New York: Haworth Press.

Kelley, P. (1994). Integrating systemic and post systemic approaches in social work with refugee families. *Families in Society, 75*(3), 541–549.

Kelley, P. (1995). Integrating narrative approaches into clinical curriculum: Addressing diversity through understanding. *Journal of Social Work Education, 31*(3), 337–346.

Kelley, P. (1998). Narrative therapy in a managed care world. *Crisis Intervention and Time-Limited Treatment, 4*(2-3), 113–123.

Kelley, P., & Clifford, P. (1997). Coping with chronic pain: Assessing narrative approaches. *Social Work, 42*(3), 266–277.

Kelley, P., Blankenburg, L., & McRoberts, J. (2002). Girls fighting trouble: Re-storying young lives. *Families in Society, 83*(5-6), 530–540.

Kelley, P., & Murty, S. (2003). Teaching narrative approaches in community practice. *Social Work Review,* XV(4), 14–20.

Kelly, G. A. (1955). *The psychology of personal constructs.* New York: W. W. Norton.

Korzybski, A. (1933). *Science and sanity* (4th ed.). Lakeville, CT: The International Non-Aristotelian Library Publishing Company.

Laube, J. (2004). Narrative group treatment for loss and trauma. *Journal of Brief Therapy, 3*(2) 125–138.

Moreno, J. L. (1937). Inter-personal therapy and the psychopathology of interpersonal relationships. *Sociometry, 1,* 9–76.

Morgan, A. (2002). Beginning to use a narrative approach in therapy. Retrieved September 13, 2009, from http://www.narrativetherapylibrary.com/img/ps/Morgan.pdf.

Neimeyer, R. A. (1993). An appraisal of constructivist psychotherapies. *Journal of Consulting and Clinical Psychology, 61*(2), 221–234.

O'Leary, P. (2004). Therapeutic relationships with men sexually abused in childhood—A narrative approach. *Journal of Brief Therapy, 3*(2), 153–169.

Rober, P., Eesbeek, D., & Elliot, R. (2006). Talking about violence: a microanalysis of narrative process in a family therapy session. *Journal of Marital and Family Therapy, 32*(3), 313–328.

Sands, R., & Nuccio, K. (1992). Postmodern feminist theory and social work. *Social Work, 37*(6), 489–494.

Scott, D. (1989). Meaning construction and social work practice. *Social Service Review, 63,* 39–51.

Tomm, K. (1987). Interventive interviewing: Part II, Reflective question as a means to enable self healing, *Family Process, 26,* 167–184.

Vodde, R., & Gallant, J.P. (2003). Bridging the gap between micro and macro practice: Large scale change and a unified model of narrative-deconstructive practice. *Social Work Review,* XV(4), 4–13.

Waldegrave, C., Tomasese, K, Tuhaka, F., & Campbell, W. (2003). *Just therapy: A journey.* Adelaide, S. A.: Dulwich Centre Publishing.

Watzlawick, P., Weakland, J. H., & Jackson, D. D. (1967). *Pragmatics of human communication.* New York: W. W. Norton.

White, M. (1989). Family escape from trouble. *Selected Papers,* 1(1), 59–63. Adelaide, S. A.: Dulwich Centre Publishing.

White, M. (1992). The re-authoring of lives and relationships. A workshop presentation, Iowa City, IA, Oct. 5–6, 1992.

White, M. (2007). An outline of narrative therapy. Retrieved September 14, 2009, from http://www.massey.au.nz/alock/virutal/white.htm.

White, M., & Epston, D. (1990). *Narrative means to therapeutic ends.* New York: W. W. Norton.

Wynne, L. C., Shields, C. G., & Sirkin, M. I. (1992). Illness, family theory, and family therapy: Conceptual issues. *Family Process, 31*(1), 3–18.

Zimmerman, J., & Dickerson, V. (1996). *If problems talked: Adventures in narrative therapy.* New York: Guilford Press.

NLP focuses on how people make sensible constructs of reality by encoding and decoding direct and physiological experiences to understand verbal and behavioral interaction

Neurolinguistic Programming Theory and Social Work Treatment

G. Brent Angell

Overview

Neurolinguistic Programming (NLP) is a practice approach founded on how people create sense-making constructs of reality by encoding and decoding direct and vicarious experience. Much like cartographers, humans are viewed as using physiological methods of perception (the senses) to generate neuropsychological "maps" of understanding that guide verbal communications and behavioral interactions with the physical and bio-psycho-social-spiritual environment. Accepting that individuals have unique relationships with their environment and, for that reason, form distinctive renderings of reality, practitioners of NLP focus on bringing about meaningful awareness and change in the here and now by working with clients to deconstruct their personal convoluted, unstable, and unworkable "maps." With this newfound knowledge, social workers use the therapeutic alliance to guide clients in the exploration and creation of alternative patterns of behaving and thinking. To achieve this, practitioners draw upon the distinctive conceptual framework and techniques of NLP, which evolved out of observing what preeminent psychotherapists did and do that works rather than out of what writers and researchers said and say works in treatment. In particular, the work of Gestalt's Fritz Perls, experiential family therapist Virginia Satir, metaphor-based hypnotherapist Milton Erikson, and cybernetic-anthropologist Gregory Bateson helped shape NLP. It is an approach that appeals to social workers because it provides clarity and direction on how to therapeutically intervene, while at the same time recognizing that clinical outcomes have much to do with the therapist's practice wisdom and differential use of self in engaging clients as collaborators in the treatment process. In saying this, NLP is also easily blended with other treatment modalities to enhance their synergistic effect making it one of the archetypal interlocking approaches (Angell, 1996, 2002; Field, 1990; Ignoffo, 1994; House, 1994; Mercier & Johnson, 1984).

Rooted in the disciplines of psychology, philosophy, transformational grammar, and cybernetics, NLP offers social workers a down-to-earth way of infusing themselves into the helping process when carrying out assessments, developing therapeutic rapport, and facilitating client development. Practitioners of this approach come to recognize that theoretical knowing and therapeutic doing are different, although interrelated, aspects of the helping process. Theory is viewed as an aggregation of experience that facilitates generalized understanding, explanation, and prediction of thought-based language and behaviour. Its utility lies in providing social workers with a common language to convey what they have observed and gives rise to specialized techniques for use in working with clients. In support of this, Ignoffo (1994) notes that NLP's concepts and techniques have been adopted by social workers and allied helping professionals who are interested in brief, empowering, cost-effective, client-centered, and technique-driven approaches. However, theory and techniques account for only a small percentage of the helping process. Lambert (1992) and Hubble, Duncan, and Miller (1999) note that psychotherapeutic techniques arising out of theory account for no more than 15% of the helping process, and relationship factors account for approximately 30% of the change process. Expectancy effects, being in treatment and having confidence that the approach being used will work, account for another 15% of getting better. All being said and done, 40% of improvement is attributable to extratherapeutic risk and protective factors related to resilience. In keeping with this knowledge of the helping process, NLP bridges the gap between theoretical knowing and practical doing by providing social workers with a clear and understandable, technique-rich treatment approach. The fundamental nature of NLP lies in developing a strong and effective therapeutic alliance founded on the belief that change is possible and will be positive. Not surprisingly, then, clients involved with NLP practitioners have a firm conviction that the approach will help them reach the goals they have set for themselves. Also not surprisingly, NLP has been shown to be helpful in dealing with a wide range of intrapsychic and interpersonal problems encountered in clinical treatment (Andreas, 1992; Field, 1990; House, 1994).

Origins

Since its beginning, NLP has added many practice techniques to the clinician's toolbox, but it remains deeply steeped in the avant-garde traditions forged in the early 1970s by its founders, Richard Bandler and John Grinder, that blend scientific inquiry with artistic interpretation (Dilts, 1976; Lankton, 1980). Thus, much to the chagrin of evidence-based researchers, NLP has defied standardization. Heavily influenced by Noam Chomsky's (1957) study of the shared principles of language, Bandler and Grinder developed their own typology, which contributed to the foundation of the approach (Bradley & Biedermann, 1985). To help complete their model, Bandler and Grinder drew upon phenomenologist Edmund Husserl's (Welton, 1999) concept of real versus perceived human experience and paired this with Wilhelm Wundt's (Rieber, 2001) psychological premise that the conscious expressive outer mind shapes and is shaped by the deeper unconscious inner mind. Together, the works of these three theorists helped Bandler and Grinder explore and explain how subjective experience is transformed into linguistic and behavioral expression.

As mentioned, Bandler and Grinder observed and analyzed the work of some of the finest and most revered psychotherapists of the time in an effort to bring their conceptual framework to life. The culmination of Bandler and Grinder's labors led them to discover the important and powerful role that communication plays in understanding and changing thinking and behavior. Building on their findings, Bandler and Grinder extracted the commonalities of how these great practitioners worked their "miracles" and went about constructing a language-based meta-model for clinical treatment. In essence, the meta-model facilitates understanding and intervening by providing therapists with a way to decipher details embedded in the client's communicated linguistic and behavioral patterns that cause impediment.

Applicability in Social Work

The alignment between NLP as a practice approach and social work's values and principles is evident. Vulnerability and oppression bring clients to treatment, and it is the social worker's main objective to assist them in finding ways to remove or overcome the barriers that encumber their ability to live productive and contented lives. Therefore, the ability to form a meaningful and trusting relationship is essential to bringing about desired change. NLP's focus on promoting client choice and providing person-centered strategies to strengthen decision making speaks to the approach's sensitivity to client diversity and empowerment. Indeed, practitioners using NLP understand the significance of being knowledgeable and skillful in the approach, recognizing both its strengths and limitations. They understand that psychotherapy is an intentional process aimed at deriving betterment and that the client has the right to determine what is needed and what is best. In keeping with this, NLP accepts that clients are collaborators in the helping process and that personal change can and does lead to multisystemic transformation.

NLP's brief approach focuses on solutions to personal challenges rather than endeavoring to understand the root causes of pathology, which can contribute to re-traumatizing clients. Narratives, shared by clients, serve as the seedbed for change as they contain pertinent information on what has occurred in their lives and how they have coped with living. As such, starting where the client is, long held as the aphorism for the profession of social work, is the beginning point of the helping process. Practitioners of NLP draw upon the approach's repertoire of techniques, which are aimed at enhancing understanding on how language construction, modification, and change reflect and shape thinking and behavior. Shared in a transparent and detailed way, the therapist's goal is to transfer this knowledge to clients using

evocative imagery and positive thinking so that they can take ownership of the process and outcome of the therapy and become personally empowered. As such, NLP is viewed as both therapeutic and psychoeducational.

Historically, NLP has been part of the lexicon of clinical practice approaches taught and used in social work (Angell, 1996, 2002; MacLean, 1986; Zastrow, 2009; Zastrow, Dotson, & Koch, 1987; Zastrow & Kirst, 1994). Most notably, NLP has played a central role in the communication and interviewing skills taught to social work students. The works of Ivey, Ivey, and Zalaquett (2009) and Cournoyer (2010) both draw upon NLP's framework and have had a significant impact on the professional education and training of interns preparing to enter their field placements. In particular, the work of Ivey et al. (2009) on intentional interviewing and counseling is the interdisciplinary standard text for skills and methods preparation. Similarly, Cournoyer's (2010) text is the benchmark book for social work education and draws on the conceptual framework of Bandler and Grinder (1979, 1982).

Presuppositions of Neurolinguistic Programming

Internal Resources

Deeming that everyone has the internal resources to deal with life's challenges, NLP guides clients in how to optimally use their personal capital to make constructive changes (Yapko, 1984). The approach also accepts that the worldview held by clients supplants that of others—and this includes that of the social worker. Existing limitations are seen as being related to the adequacy or relevancy of available thought-based linguistic and behavioral patterns previously used by clients to cope with challenges, which are now found to be insufficient and thus emotionally problematic. Rather than seeing this as somehow related to client inadequacy or personal deficiency, NLP views the situation as one of limited choices. The goal for the social work clinician, therefore, becomes one of helping clients locate effective patterns of communicating linguistically and behaviorally that they have used in the past to deal with similar challenges in the present. In situations where no direct link can be made, the therapist then guides clients through a process of locating connecting points between elements of the current narrative account and past challenges faced. In this process, narratives told by clients are deconstructed to pinpoint internal resources that can be reassembled to create new patterns of thinking and behaving that can bring about preferred change (Angell, 1996, 2002; Ivey, Ivey, & Zalaquett, 2009; MacLean, 1986; Pesut, 1991).

Sensitivity to Difference

The importance that NLP attaches to clients' taking ownership of the helping process speaks to the approach's anti-oppressive practice perspective. It is an experientially based treatment methodology that embraces the nuances of lived culture and linguistic idioms, which are central to the development of personae. As such, social workers using NLP embrace variability as the norm rather than the exception as they work with clients to discover new ways of addressing bio-psycho-social-spiritual challenges (Angell, 1996, 2002; Ivey et al., 2009; Ivey, D'Andrea, Ivey, & Simek-Morgan, 2006; Sandhu, Reeves, & Portes, 1993).

Deep and Surface Structure

NLP focuses on how information is received, processed, and sent. First, neurosensory data are collected and sorted. Next, the data are interpreted and assigned linguistic meaning. The final step entails programming the data into verbal and nonverbal patterns of communication, prioritized according to which ones have the greatest probability of securing preferred ends (Zastrow, 2009). NLP holds that the entirety of sensory experience gleaned from the environment is processed and stored at an unconscious level, which is referred to as the "deep structure" of experience. Edited aspects of sensory experience emerge or are extracted for day-to-day use in linguistic and behavioral needs at the conscious level, or "surface structure" (Bandler & Grinder, 1975).

Given the enormous amount of sensory data that individuals are exposed to on an ongoing basis, a three-stage filtering mechanism is posited by NLP. Deletion is one of these filters. It involves selectively removing segments of the deep structure, thereby making them unavailable for surface structure use. In so doing, attention is paid to specific aspects of experience while others are ruled out. Examples are the ability to focus on one conversation in a noisy and crowded room, to identify physical pain from other sensations after having stepped on a sharp shell on a warm, soft, and sandy beach, or to visually identify a hidden path when on a walk in the woods at dusk. Deletion allows individuals to reduce the range of possible choices to a more manageable level. The obvious hope is that the choices made prove advantageous; however, this is not always the case. Using the same examples, one can understand the folly of making the "wrong" choice: by focusing on one conversation, the pleas of a hurt child are ignored; continuing to walk with a hurt foot instead of stopping to attend to the injury; or missing the marked sign indicating that the path chosen was marked, "Danger: Do Not Enter".

Another filter is distortion, which entails modifying deep structure data to meet surface structure needs by reallocating the degree of importance assigned to experiences that have occurred or are anticipated. Portraying an event in a manner different than what actually occurred or fantasizing about what might happen are examples of distortion. It is creative and involves a purposeful misrepresentation of lived or vicariously experienced reality. The most famous of artists and writers use distortion to great effect. In everyday life, distortion is beneficial in downplaying or exaggerating experience—for example, minimizing thoughtless words expressed by a detractor, smiling when in physical or emotional pain, or dressing well when financially destitute. Once again, this can prove double-edged, as each scenario is embedded with misinformation that may push away important support or draw unwanted attention.

Generalization is an essential filter that requires an extrapolation of explicit experience, which is reconfigured in such a way as to represent an entire grouping. As such, one identifiable deep structure incident is made to represent all similar surface structure phenomena. Representing experience this way can be quite functional. Loud music causes hearing loss, shaking hands spreads disease, and looking in people's eyes is rude. This may be well and good unless one has been invited to a rock concert by a new love interest, a hand to shake is extended by a banker about to lend a loan, or poor eye contact is quietly questioned by a potential employer during a job interview.

Distortions, deletions, and generalizations are essential filters used in protecting clients from disagreeable deep structure experiences while at the same time allowing satisfying ones to permeate to the surface structure. However clear the purpose of these filters seems to be, they are not foolproof in repressing unpleasant experiences or in providing pathways for ones that can help in times of duress. Yet both "positive" and "negative" experiences contain elements that can be reconfigured, assigned new meaning, and used to create fresh patterns of communicating thoughts and behavior.

Treatment

Principal Therapeutic Goal

Focused on the ins and outs of client communication in the here and now, NLP provides social workers with tangible clinical explanations and distinct techniques to bring about desired change. Practitioners of the approach hold the following principles as basic to successful treatment:

- Clients are motivated to change and come into therapy expecting to get help. Even involuntary clients have chosen to enter treatment rather than face the consequences of not seeking help.
- Clients possess the internal resources needed for change to occur. Retrieving and effectively using them becomes the challenge.
- Clients are in control of the helping process. Through modeling, guidance, and education, the social worker helps clients to find or create patterns of communicating thoughts and behavior to meet their needs.

Treatment Concepts and Strategies

Preferred Representational System. The "representational system" of NLP includes sight (visual), sound (auditory), touch (kinesthetic), smell (olfactory), and taste (gustatory). Together these

senses provide crucial data used in the formation and communication of thoughts and behaviors at both the deep and surface structure levels. Typically, resilient people draw upon all components of the representational system when interfacing with the world; however, when stressed there is a tendency to revert to using fewer parts of the system. In extremely demanding or traumatic situations, individuals withdraw to their one preferred representational system (PRS). Being able to identify a person's PRS is beneficial at all times in communicating effectively and is of crucial importance when someone is distressed. In the case of clients, knowing which PRS is favored has clinical significance in being able to rapidly establish rapport, make precise psychosocial assessments, and provide targeted clinical interventions. Helm (2000) discusses the use of a standardized questionnaire to determine the PRS of visually impaired clients and has noted a growing trend to use NLP techniques in law enforcement when conducting interviews with victims and perpetrators (Helm, 2003).

The most common way of identifying the PRSs of clients is through their use of spoken language predicates (adverbs, adjectives, and verbs). Being able to discern client PRSs through the predicates they use and matching them in response provides social workers with the ability to relate accurately and directly with clients. Typically, predicates relate to visual, auditory, and kinesthetic representational systems. Although gustatory and olfactory predicates do appear at times in everyday speech, and may be more present in the language of some cultures than others, they are not seen as common when it comes to identifying the PRSs of clients. In keeping with this, social workers using NLP must be skillful at detecting and using predicates in their practice. What follows is a series of sample PRS exchanges between a client and therapist using predicates and matching:

Visual PRS Predicate Matching

Client: I thought I could *see* myself doing it, but I just *blanked out*. It was just a bad *scene*.

Worker: It *looks* to me like you *painted* yourself out of the *picture* and you can't *imagine* what you're going to do. *Observing* what you've *portrayed*, perhaps I can help you *look* at it another way so that you can gain a different *perspective*.

Auditory PRS Predicate Matching

Client: I just *told* it like it was and for my effort I got *screamed* at. I was only *stating* my opinion.

Worker: What I *hear* you *saying* is that you are not being *listened* to. Your disappointment *rings loud and clear*. It *sounds* to me like you would like others to be more *in tune* with you. You want to be *paid attention to* and I'd like to help you be *heard*.

Kinesthetic PRS Predicate Matching

Client: I've been *wrestling* with this for a long time. It just *grates* on my nerves that I can't *handle* this better. Sometimes I get so upset I can't even *catch* my breath and my heart starts *racing*. You know, I get this *cold chill* all over and just come to a *standstill*.

Worker: I get the *feeling* that you're *struggling* to *move forward*, but keep getting *stuck*. The important thing is that you *keep working* to *uncover* what's causing you to *feel* this way. I have an idea that if you stop *backing away* from what's upsetting you you'll get a *better grasp* of what your *next step* should be. I'm here to *lend a hand*.

An elevated degree of attending is required to pinpoint the PRSs of clients through their use of predicates. On the other hand, it would be clinically reckless to simply rely on the standard response of "So, how does that make you feel (kinesthetic)?" and listening to the client respond "I am not sure what you are looking for (visual)" when it is understood that clients might well be using a different representational system.

As mentioned, clients often embrace a number of PRSs unless extremely clinically compromised. In these instances an overlapping approach may be justified and allows the social worker to cover the breadth of predicates used by clients. At the same time, the therapist can model different patterns of communication that clients might want to adopt (Ivey et al., 2009; Lankton, 1980). The following illustration depicts the use of PRS predicate overlapping:

Overlapping Preferred Representational Systems

Client: I *felt* awful having to *speak* so harshly to him, but he just refused to *see* my *point of view*. Now, here I *sit* trying to *picture* the *words* I'd *say* to make both of us *feel* better.

Worker: It is always *hard* to *retract* what we've *said*. This is especially true when we *feel* we've *hurt* someone we *look* to for support. If you could *see* yourself *doing* this again, what *words* would you use, and do you think the outcome would *look* any different?

Eye Accessing Cues. An alternative way to identify client PRSs involves observing the direction in which the client's eyes move. Referred to as "eye accessing cues," it is a shortcut way of determining the favored representational system of clients that does not require them to verbally respond. To make use of this technique, the social worker asks a sensory nonspecific question and observes the direction in which the client's eyes move. The requirement of using sensory unspecified language lies in the need to allow clients to at random access sensory data from their deep and surface structures in response to the question asked. In so doing, clients invariably use their PRS in framing their thoughts and replies. Following are a series of examples of sensory neutral phrases that could be used by therapists in determining client PRSs using the eye accessing cue method:

> *Sense* how you might do this in your own way.
> *Think* about your most cherished experience.
> *Mull over* what you *remember* about that experience.
> *Consider* where you are most relaxed.
> *Deliberate* when you might have done things differently.
> *Be aware of* your most pleasant time.

In terms of deciphering a client's PRS using eye accessing cues, if looking up and to the left or right the person is visual. Looking straight forward with defocused eyes is also indicative of a client whose PRS is visual. If the client looks either to the left, right, or down and to the left, then the PRS is auditory. A client who looks down and to the right has a kinesthetic PRS. If the client's eyes keep shifting back and forth, the social worker should consider this much like a computer hard drive accessing information. Patience is needed: the PRS will soon become evident as the client fixes his or her gaze in one direction or the other. If the client is left-handed, the eye accessing cues schemata is reversed, with down and to the left becoming a kinesthetic PRS and down and to the right becoming an auditory PRS.

The Four-tuple. As mentioned, clients naturally and normally use all representational system components in their linguistic and behavioral communication patterns. This being said, people cascade their preferences from most to least called upon and assign an internal (remembered experience) or external (here-and-now experience) value to them. In clinical practice this "what works" hierarchy is a helpful way of understanding how clients frame and make sense of their experiences. Called the "four-tuple," social workers reviewing client communication use the nomenclature of V for visual, A for auditory, K for kinesthetic, and O to represent both olfactory and gustatory senses. In addition, each of the representational system used by clients is assigned a locus of either internal $^{(i)}$ or external $^{(e)}$. Used to initially assess clients, the four-tuple can also be used to mark client progress during therapy and to set treatment goals. For example, clients with an internal locus four-tuple would be consumed with reminiscing about the past and seemingly unaware of what is happening around them. Their four-tuples would be represented as V^i, A^i, K^i, O^i. On the contrary, clients with external locus four-tuples would present as detached from their inward selves, while obsessed with what is going on around them. Four-tuples for these clients appear as V^e, A^e, K^e, O^e. Most clients display a blended internal (remembered) and external (here-and-now) four-tuple, which might present as A^e, K^i, V^e, O^e. From a practice perspective, social workers can use the four-tuple to assist clients in achieving a better balance between their various representational systems and explore with them ways to increase their range of rewarding experiences, which in turn contribute to their internal and external loci formation.

Metaphors. NLP's focus on client communication patterns to understand thought and behavior makes using metaphors in the helping process a logical segue. Through metaphors, wanted changes can be achieved by drawing narrative parallels with the presenting problem. This is done by having clients express what is currently causing them concern and linking this with other experiences to figure out how thinking and behavior have influenced the development of communication patterns. Using clients' experiences in this way, the social worker can help them create alternative empowering endings to existing personal narratives using metaphorical inference. If the building blocks for change are not readily available, metaphors can be used to generate new narratives wherein clients overcome adversity by thinking and behaving differently when confronted with crisis.

Anchoring. Sensory stimuli continually inundate people. The resulting imprinting can be positive or negative. With repeated exposure, the initial impression made can be reinforced and can have an effect on future thinking and behavior. Whether a one-time event or repeated exposure to certain or similar stimulus lasting responses associated with the stimulus can occur and become collapsed together. In NLP these predictable spontaneous sensory reactions are called *anchors* and provide individuals with templates of awareness on how information is to be received and responded to. For example, positive anchors can provide validation and are generally empowering, whereas negative anchors are more often than not demeaning and impart feelings of powerlessness.

In treatment, clients frequently present narrative-packed anchors that are either negative or incongruent with positive past experience. Overwhelming the ability to function, negative anchors can disrupt the ability to accurately interpret received messages and jumble linguistic and behavioral responses. Sooner or later, this skewed processing of information leads to a reduction in the number of choices made available to clients as data are distorted, deleted, and generalized at the deep and surface structures. However, NLP holds that what is done can be undone. By changing the attributes of anchors, clients can improve the quality of their anchors and even replace them. This, then, requires a rescripting of the client's narrative accounts of experience and imbedding in them more satisfying thought and behavior patterns; this, it is anticipated, will bring about advantageous changes in the filtering of content held in the deep and surface structure.

Anchors run the gamut of the senses. Most common are physical or kinesthetic anchors such as a touch on the arm, elbow, or shoulder,

which are associated with greetings or expressing condolences. However, contact involving
handshakes, pats on the back, hugs, or caresses
are also kinesthetic anchors. These types of physical encounters occur quite frequently in daily
dealings with others. In clinical settings, social
workers selectively use many of them as well and
often do not always appreciate the importance
and impact of their actions. Understanding that
therapy is an intentional process, practitioners
using NLP are ever vigilant of when and how
best to use kinesthetic anchors. They are normally applied in conjunction with talk therapy
but can be used as nonverbal standalone interventions, and are applied to form a suggestive
sublevel narrative such as, "You're *feeling* that
you're not *in control*, but you are and you will
carry on" wherein the bolded and italicized
words are stated by the social worker with a corresponding kinesthetic anchor. Body language,
physical proximity, and movement also play
an important part in kinesthetic anchoring.
Obviously, physical contact with clients can be
open to discussion and as such other modes of
anchoring may prove preferable; however, they
may not match the client's PRS and as such will
have diminished or no influence.

An auditory approach involves the use of
voice modulation and directing one's speech
either by looking at or away from the client to fix
the anchor. The conversation base of most therapies and the emphasis of NLP on language make
using auditory anchors a natural fit for practitioners. Determining what words and which
phrases to use and emphasize is important; they
need to match the client's PRS. As an example of
a therapist using an auditory anchor with an
auditory client would be, "I *hear you* are saying
`No one wants to *listen to me*'" wherein the
bolded and italicized words denote the sublevel
communication, the words of which are stated
in a strong and clear tone. Written and read
communication is also auditory, and important
anchors can be imparted to clients via letters,
assigned readings, text messages, and web-based
means such as e-mail and chat.

Visual anchors include facial expression,
dress, gestures, and even room décor, all of which
can shape the course of treatment. It is not surprising, then, that clients often have a strong
transference reaction with their therapists and

have been known to start dressing in the same
way and decorating their homes in a similar way.
As with the kinesthetic anchor, visual anchors
are regularly used in conjunction with talk therapy, but they can be used separately in their own
right to fix positive change. Indeed, clients with a
visual PRS are often hypersensitive to how things
appear rather than to what is said or how things
feel. In keeping with this, the worker meets the
client's PRS needs to include both words and
visual cues. Visual anchoring in treatment might
appear thusly, "As you *picture* your options, can
you *see yourself* in that *new role* at work? You
look like *you can*." Here the bolded and italicized
words of the sublevel communication present a
series of visual words that could be accompanied
by a corresponding change in facial expression to
create even greater emphasis. Photographs, films,
and visual arts can also be used to accentuate the
treatment and further anchor desired changes.

Olfactory and gustatory anchors are less commonly used in the therapeutic process, but that is
not to say that they could not or will not be.
Certainly, it is not uncommon to find social workers and clients with their favorite hot or soft drink
in hand during the therapeutic session. Providing
aromatic beverages and flavorful foods can provide important anchors for clients, leading to
positive growth. Many self-help groups do this as
a matter of course—case in point, Alcoholics
Anonymous. As further evidence of progress in
this regard, Abramowitz and Lichtenberg (2009)
cite work using hypnotherapy in the olfactory
conditioning of clients to create positive anchors
in the treatment of posttraumatic stress disorder
(PTSD), needlephobia, and panic attacks.

The same anchors can have different meanings for different people and can include things
seemingly extraneous to the therapeutic relationship. For instance, the clinician's office can
anchor either negative or positive emotions
depending on the link clients make between the
setting and the help they perceive they are getting. When clients retell the story that led them
to enter treatment, thoughts and emotions
associated with the event or events are rekindled,
as are the anchors attached to them. In many
ways, the very act of retelling what happened
causes clients to be re-victimized. Social workers
understanding this potentiality use their skills in
NLP to bring these recollections into the here

and now so that the connotations can be altered and new anchors set. To illustrate how this can be done effectively and ineffectively, the following excerpt from a simulated therapeutic session is offered wherein the range of PRS anchors are used:

Negative anchor:

Worker: So, what has been happening since the last time we were together?

Client: (Looking down and to the right) I'm really feeling bad. I feel like the life has been sucked out of me. The plant where I work, or should I say worked, closed and I am now laid off for good.

Worker: (In a concerned voice, looking at the client and firmly touching his shoulder) I'm sorry that this happened to you. (Loosening and removing hand, looking away, and stating softly) Things will turn around and I'm sure you'll find something.

Client: (Continuing to look down, shaking head from side to side and beginning to snivel)

Positive anchor:

Worker: So, what has been happening since the last time we were together?

Client: (Looking down and to the right) I'm really feeling bad. I feel like the life has been sucked out of me. The plant where I work, or should I say worked, closed and I am now laid off for good.

Worker: (Speaking in a soft monotone, looking down and away from the client) I'm sorry that this happened to you. (Looking at the client, touching his shoulder with intensifying firmness, and speaking in a convincing reassuring voice) Things will turn around and I'm sure you'll find something.

Client: (Nodding head up and down and offering a faint smile)

Change Personal History. During the course of life, people continue to expand their personal narratives founded on their experiences with the bio-psycho-social-spiritual and physical environment. The resulting narratives are multistoried and contain countless subplots filled with linguistic and behavioral patterns that help in both goal attainment and avoidance of threats to well-being. However, they can also have the opposite effect and hinder individuals from reaching their objectives and place them at risk. These unhelpful experience-based narrative subplots and imbedded patterns are not set in stone, but rather are fluid and malleable.

Knowing this clinically makes it feasible to consider ways of deconstructing existing narratives and creating new ones. In NLP, the intervention called Change Personal History (CPH) provides social workers with a straightforward intervention to help clients generate preferred alternative narratives that are resistant to problem saturation.

The CPH helps clients retrieve disturbing parts of personal narratives, rooted in stimuli overload and riddled with negative linguistic and behavioral patterns and anchors, into the here and now for examination, deconstruction, and reconfiguration. Methodically, these limited ways of communication are transformed into revised sensory sequences of events that are woven using metaphors and suggestion to become integral parts of the client's re-authored personal history. Using mental imagery, clients participating in this treatment procedure can select not to verbalize their unpleasant experiences, which can expedite recovery, increase their control over the therapeutic process, and reduce the chances of re-traumatizing them. Conducting a CPH requires that the social worker systematically follow these steps:

1. Invite the client to recount an unpleasant past experience. Looking for negative linguistic and behavioral patterns, have the client imagine reliving the feelings, sights, sounds, smells, and tastes associated with the experience. Look for physical cues such as a shifting of the body, nodding or shaking of the head, tensing of the muscles, skin flushing or perspiration, accelerated breathing, eye movement, changes in pupil dilation, fist clenching, muscle tone, breathing pattern, eye flutter, etc., which indicate that the client has in fact connected with the experience. Anchor the unpleasant pattern or patterns and have the client refocus on the here and now.

2. Using the unpleasant pattern as a starting point, encourage the client to think about other times when he or she had a similar experience or feeling. Once more looking for behavioral cues, request the client to use his or her senses to relive the experience and anchor the pattern or patterns that emerge.

3. Repeat step 2 several times to amass a body of related experiential patterns.

4. Next, have the client describe how he or she coped with the situation. As each experience is recounted, reframe the narrative by identifying each strategy used as a positive linguistic or behavioral resource. Again, look for the client to display physical cues indicating that he or she has accepted the suggestion as beneficial and anchor the change. If the client is having difficulty identifying a helpful strategy, assist him or her in creating one, look for the physical cue, and anchor the change.

5. With the client, merge the anchored resources and create a new potent super-resource and anchor it. Using the super-resource, have the client recount each of his or her past experiences, including the original unpleasant experience, and sequentially apply and anchor the super-resource. The objective is to change all negative linguistic or behavioral patterns associated with the experience to contribute to the creation of a new positive narrative. With each anchoring of the super-resource, be sure to check for physical cues that the change has occurred and the positive resource has been accepted by the client and is sufficient.

6. To ensure that the needed changes have occurred, request the client go over each experience before and after the new super-resource was anchored. Look for physical assurances of positive change, which will confirm that the super-resource has done what was hoped. If the desired change is not physically confirmed, repeat step 5 to help the client locate or create supplementary resources that can be added to the super-resource.

7. The last step in the Change Personal History technique involves having the client imagine a similarly unpleasant experience taking place in the future and suggesting to him or her that the super-resource be used to overcome the adversity. Observe the client's physical response to confirm that the hoped-for change is now embedded in the personal narrative and can be accessed for use in other situations. If it has not, than steps 4, 5, and 6 will need to be repeated (Bandler & Grinder, 1979).

Swish Visualization. In NLP, imagery and suggestion play an important role and form the foundation of the Swish Visualization intervention. Using visualization, clients cleanse themselves of negative thoughts and behaviors and, using positive visual metaphors, replace them with positive ones. Used mostly in work with individuals, Juhnke, Coll, Sunich, and Kent (2008) have found success using a version of the approach in working with couples and families as well. In particular, the authors found the Swish Visualization helpful with couples who survive a child's parasuicide or suicide, though they warn that therapists need to ensure that the intervention matches the couple's presenting problem. They also recommend that the technique not be used with clients whose mental illness is characterized by panic attacks, suicidal ideation, delusions, or hallucinations. Below are outlined the five steps in the Swish Visualization with individuals:

1. Identify with the client an unwanted or negative episodic event or condition.
2. Have the client describe the sensory triggers that signal the beginning of the unwanted or negative episode.
3. Ask the client to describe a pleasing memory that can be used to replace the negative episode later.
4. Consider any potentiality for adverse consequences that might arise from replacing the negative episode with the positive recollection.
5. Have the client visualize being in a theater watching a movie of the negative memory through reversed binoculars. Request the client to now imagine the picture getting blurry and shrinking into the bottom right corner of the screen. Next ask the client to picture the positive memory in the top right corner of the screen, making the image get larger, louder, and more colorful. Then, using the "Swish Visualization anchor," direct the client to imagine the negative memory being pushed off the screen by the positive memory. Once this happens, ask the client to view the positive memory through binoculars while the negative memory is eliminated from the screen (Juhnke et al., 2008).

Reframing. Personal narratives are animated by way of linguistic and behavioral patterns connected to positive intention. From the perspective of NLP, no matter how dysfunctional the parts of the narrative are and how problematic the patterns seem to be, the intention of the individual's thoughts and actions are geared towards reaching positive outcomes. Indeed, the approach assumes that with unlimited choices, clients will consistently pick the most rewarding means to arrive at their desired ends even if they are negative. The challenge therapeutically, then, is to help clients find the most rewarding linguistic and behavioral ways of framing or reframing internal experience to achieve external goals and thereby achieve congruence. In turn, this will cause clients to amend their personal narratives in ways that are constructive and empowering. In NLP, this is achieved using the reframing technique to transform questionable and challenging thoughts, feelings, and behaviors into goal-fulfilling positive resources and empowering narratives using metaphors, anecdotes, and imagery.

Bandler and Grinder (1982) note that there are many ways to reframe how the internal experience of clients or their external perceptions of the environment can be changed. Using this technique, as it is systematically presented, allows the social worker to assist clients in redefining experience by creating alternative responses.

In the following reframing example, a six-step intervention is posited:

1. Invite the client to choose a linguistic or behavioral pattern that is problematic and that he or she wants to change. Assign a number, letter, or color to the pattern to partition the pattern from the client's overall personal narrative.

2. Providing the client with the option to close his or her eyes, make contact with the encrypted pattern by asking permission to communicate with the "part" of the person responsible for the renamed pattern. Suggest to the client that he or she increase the part's brightness, volume, or intensity and look for verbal or physical "yes or no" cues that verify that permission has been granted. Remember that the "yes or no" responses serve as anchors.

3. Ask the client to separate the positive intention from the problematic part and request that he or she confirm when this task is completed by providing a verbal or physical "yes or no" answer. Follow this by asking the client, "If you had a means of reaching your positive intention that worked as well as or better than the 'renamed pattern,' would you be willing to

test it out?" Make sure to confirm the client's response with a verbal or physical "yes or no" answer.

4. Together with the client, use creativity to construct several alternative patterns to reach the positive intention. Suggest that the client generate at least three choices and have them confirmed each time with a "yes" verbal or physical response.

5. Ask the client, "Are you willing to replace your old part with the three new patterns to reach your positive intention?" A "yes" verbal or physical response confirms that the reframe has occurred.

6. Finally, ask the problematic part to remain calm, blank, and quiet while asking if there are any other parts that object to the new patterns being used. If a verbal or physical "yes" answer is received, circle back to step 2 and work your way back through the ensuing steps. If the answer is "no," then thank the part for staying calm, blank, and quiet (Bandler & Grinder, 1982).

Implications and Applications for Social Work Practice

The robustness of a clinical approach is its ability to provide a broad spectrum of treatment options that can be used with clients. In the case of NLP, it has been found highly effective in working with individuals, and a number of intervention strategies have been outlined above. What is perhaps less known about the approach is that its scope includes an array of direct and indirect practice applications (Angell, 1996, 2002; Dilts, 1983). A further attribute of NLP lies in the ease with which it can be combined with other treatment models to create a powerful and operable interlocking theoretical perspective.

Interventions with Dyads, Families, and Small Groups

NLP is deeply steeped in the experiential dyadic and family and Gestalt small therapy traditions forged by pioneers such as social worker Virginia Satir and psychiatrist Fritz Perls (Andreas, 1991; Bandler, Grinder, & Satir, 1976; Davis & Davis, 1983; Grinder & Bandler, 1976; Nichols, 2007). In particular, a main tenet of the experiential approach is to evoke change as a way of helping clients find congruence between their intentions and patterns of linguistic and behavioral communication. In the process, clients come to understand how the complexity of interpersonal messaging affects their interactions with significant others. Consequently, communicating intrapersonal changes in thinking and behaving will affect and transform interpersonal dyadic and family member relationships—it is unavoidable. In small group work, NLP builds between-member rapport throughout the stages of the group. Client members also find the approach valuable in their own development and ability to relate to and help other group members (Chiders & Saltmarsh, 1986; Shelden & Shelden, 1989). It is therefore essential that clients involved in interpersonal treatment become aware of their internal resources and learn how to access them in ways that bring about advantageous personal growth and positive systemic change.

For clients, discovering their "front-stage" and "backstage" presentation of self is a key starting point in therapy using NLP. The incongruence between how outer and inner communication is perceived can be profound and leads to many of the difficulties experienced by clients. As such, assisting clients in determining their PRS and communication category is of the utmost importance. As noted earlier, PRSs are displayed both verbally and nonverbally and are rooted in linguistic and behavioral patterns arising out of experience, so they lead clients to take on predictable character roles when interacting with others. Depending on the value attached to the relationship, these character roles will modulate according to the presentation of self to and perception of self by others.

The four basic character roles of NLP are placater, blamer, computer, and distracter. The placater's role in the system is one of incessantly trying to please others at the expense of self. The blamer, on the other hand, is consumed with self-interest and is preoccupied with having power and control of others whatever the cost. The character role of the computer exudes correctness. This type of person presents as logical, reasonable, and intellectual on the surface but upon closer inspection is found to be emotionally lacking and focused entirely on being politically and socially correct. The distracter is an anarchistic

and spontaneous character role, whose disrespectful and inappropriate actions are communicated in total disregard for one's self, others, or circumstances (Bandler et al., 1976; Grinder & Bandler, 1976).

Using each client's PRSs and character roles, the therapist works to disentangle the unhelpful distortions, deletions, and generalizations that unfavorably impact interpersonal communication and relationships. Hence, the process of change involves helping clients gain an understanding of the effect that their personal intentions, as presented linguistically and behaviorally, have on others. In so doing, the assumed character roles of clients are explored, deconstructed, and reconfigured in ways that bring about interpersonal congruity between the internal meaning and external intent of the communication. To do this, the issues presented by clients as needing to be changed or reframed are looked upon as either content or context-based.

Reframing a client's content requires that linguistic and behavioral patterns be reworked and anchored to positively connect with internalized "front-stage" intentions. For instance, a tearful daughter who is upset because her unwavering mother won't allow her to go on a road trip vacation with a boyfriend who just got his driver's license may have the situation reframed as one of love and concern for her well-being. On the other hand, a context reframe has to do with positively connecting and anchoring patterns of communication with the "front-stage" intentions of others. For example, a father who gets angry for being called to the school because of his son's acting-out behavior may find solace if the problem is reframed as a strength that he taught the child as an effective coping strategy in dealing with bullying classmates.

Additional Applications in Social Work Practice

Many clinical social workers encounter clients presenting with primary or dual diagnosis substance abuse issues. Numerous authors have reported positive outcomes from using NLP to treat clients with addiction problems (Davis, 1990; Doorn, 1990; Hennman & Hennman, 1990; Isaacson, 1990; Sterman, 1990a, 1990b, 1990c, 1990d, 1990e; Tierney, 1990). Particularly,

Davis (1990) has found that using NLP in working with alcoholics and codependent family members improves interpersonal communication and self-reliance, leading to a positive and supportive relationship.

Clients with PTSD report that NLP provides helpful strategies to reduce and eliminate symptoms by locating and disabling the triggers that lead to traumatic re-experience and associated heightened levels of anxiety (Gregory, 1984). An imaginary scrapbook technique, drawing on the positive life experiences of clients, has also been found to be effective in reducing anxiety and depression diagnostically linked to PTSD and many other mental health disorders (Hossach & Standidge, 1983). NLP has also been used in treatment with adult survivors of childhood sexual abuse to help victims talk about their traumatization and the impact it has had on them as adults by looking at and helping them reframe their patterns of communication and personal histories (Shelden & Shelden, 1989). Apart from the treatment foci already mentioned, NLP has also been used in treating a variety of psychosocial and psychosomatic clinical concerns (Bandler, 1984; Einspruch & Forman, 1988).

Empirical Base

From the outset, NLP has presented itself as an art wherein the therapist is the artist using described and prescribed techniques in working with clients to create personal and interpersonal change. Understanding that researching the work of an artist is difficult at best, practitioners of NLP have been resistant to engage in scientific inquiry. This reluctance has not curtailed research on the approach and, not surprisingly, the findings have been mixed in terms of empirical evidence to support the assertions made for NLP's consistent clinical effectiveness. A great deal of the research on NLP is centered on the validity of the approach's deduction that people have PRSs and that they can be determined via predicate usage and eye movement. While a number of studies purport that the NLP's premises and techniques are ill founded and unreliable at best (Elich, Thompson, & Miller, 1985; Fromme & Daniell, 1984; Gumm, Walker, & Day, 1982; Krugman et al., 1985; Sharpley, 1984, 1987) still others have

deduced the approach to be illuminating and its methods to be effective (Davis, 1990; Dilts, 1983; Einspruch & Forman, 1988; Graunke & Roberts, 1985; Gregory, 1984; Hossach & Standidge, 1983; Shelden & Shelden, 1989). However, more than three decades since its foundation, many of the tenets of NLP have yet to be tested.

The foundational premise of NLP, "starting where the client is," has been challenged by authors such as Zastrow (2009) as being much too focused on building rapport rather than on the psychopathology of the client. Needless to say, this flies in the face of much research and practice wisdom, which attributes a significant, empirically supported role for the therapeutic relationship in achieving positive treatment outcomes (Goldstein, 1990; Hubble, Duncan, & Miller, 1999; Meredith, 1986; Turner, 1986)—not to mention NLP's conviction that clients have the necessary resources to achieve positive change and schooling them in the approach's methodology builds expectancy that they will receive the help they need.

The main limitations of the approach lie in the need for clients to have a level of cognition that allows them to fully participate in and thereby benefit from the approach's interventions. Clearly, clients who are on psychotropic medications, abusing substances, or seriously mentally ill and exhibiting delusions and hallucinations will not be able to take full advantage of what NLP has to offer. The here-and-now orientation of NLP will also not appeal to clients interested in exploring their pasts, who would be better suited by seeking therapists using insight-oriented approaches.

Prospectus

The founders of NLP set out to demystify the helping process and did so effectively. Subsequent writers have taken steps to remystify therapeutic helping using NLP as a scaffold. In this chapter, the value of the approach's concepts and methods are revisited in a way that offers the clarity that was originally intended. NLP continues to be broadly used by colleagues in allied professions including psychiatry, psychology, nursing, and education. The approach has also become increasingly popular in other professional fields, including business, law, and criminal justice.

In large part, NLP's appeal lies in its understandable clinical rubric and interventions, which have applicability in helping clients with a continuum of challenges. Given NLP's experiential basis, social work practitioners interested in gaining proficiency in the model should seek specialized training and supervision to master what the approach has to offer. This being said, NLP evolved out of the interview room, not the classroom, and so doing is believing.

References

Abramowitz, E. G., & Lichtenberg, P. (2009). Hypnotherapeutic Olfactory Conditioning (HOC): Case studies of needle phobia, panic disorder, and combat-induced PTSD. *International Journal of Clinical and Experimental Hypnosis*, 57(2), 184–197.

Andreas, S. (1992). *Neuro-linguistic programming*. New York: Guilford Press.

Angell, G. B. (1996). Neurolinguistic programming theory and social work treatment. In F. J. Turner (Ed.), *Social work treatment: Interlocking theoretical perspectives* (4th ed.) (pp. 480–502). New York: The Free Press.

Angell, G. B. (2002). Neurolinguistic programming. In A. R. Roberts & G. J. Green (Eds.), *Social workers' desk reference* (pp. 421–428). New York: Oxford University Press.

Bandler, R., & Grinder, J. (1975). *The structure of magic* (Vol. 1). Palo Alto: Science & Behavior Books Inc.

Bandler, R., & Grinder, J. (1979). *Frogs into princes: Neurolinguistic programming*. Moab, UT: Real People Press.

Bandler, R., & Grinder, J. (1982). *Reframing: Neuro-linguistic programming and the transformation of meaning*. Moab, UT: Real People Press.

Bandler, R. (1984). *Magic in Action*. Cupetino, CA: Meta Publications.

Bandler, R., Grinder, J., & Satir, V. (1976). *Changing with families*. Santa Clara, CA: Science and Behavior Books, Inc.

Bradley, E. J., & Biedermann, H. J. (1985). *Bandler and Grinder's NLP: Its historical context and contribution*. *Psychotherapy*, 22 (1), 59–62.

Chiders, J. H., & Saltmarsh, R. E. (1986). Neurolinguistic programming in the context of group counseling. *Journal for Specialists in Group Work*, 11(4), 221–227.

Chomsky, N. (1957). *Syntactic Structures*. The Hague-Paris: Mounton.

Cournoyer, B. R. (2010). *The social work skills workbook*. Belmont, CA: Brooks/Cole Publishers Company.

Davis, D. I. (1990). Neuro-linguistic programming and the family in alcoholism treatment. In C. M. Sterman (Ed.), *Neuro-linguistic programming in alcoholism treatment* (pp. 63–77). Binghamton, NY: Hawthorn Press.

Davis, S. L. R., & Davis, D. I. (1983). Neuro-linguistic programming and family therapy. *Journal of Marital and Family Therapy*, 9(3), 283–291.

Dilts, R. (1976). *Roots of neurolinguistic programming*. Cupertino, CA: Meta Publications.

Dilts, R. (1983). *Applications of neurolinguistic programming*. Cupertino, CA: Meta Publications.

Doorn, J. M. (1990). An application of hypnotic communication to the treatment of addictions. In C. M. Sterman (Ed.), *Neuro-linguistic programming in alcoholism treatment* (pp. 79–89). Binghamton, NY: Hawthorn Press.

Einspruch, E. L., & Forman, B. D. (1988). Neurolinguistic programming in the treatment of phobias. *Psychotherapy in Private Practice*, 6(1), 91–100.

Elich, M., Thompson, W., & Miller, L. (1985). Mental imagery as revealed by eye movements and spoken predicates: A test of neurolinguistic programming. *Journal of Counseling Psychology*, 32(4), 622–625.

Field, E. S. (1990). Neurolinguistic programming as an adjunct to other psychotherapeutic/hypnotherapeutic interventions. *American Journal of Clinical Hypnosis*, 32(3), 174–182.

Fromme, D. K., & Daniell, J. (1984). Neurolinguistic programming examined: Imagery, sensory mode, and communication. *Journal of Counseling Psychology*, 31(3), 387–390.

Goldstein, H. (1990). The knowledge base of social work practice: Theory, wisdom, analogue, or art? *Families in Society: The Journal of Contemporary Human Services*, 71(1), 32–43.

Graunke, B., & Roberts, T. K. (1985). Neurolinguistic programming: The impact of imagery tasks on sensory predicate usage. *Journal of Counseling Psychology*, 32(4), 525–530.

Gregory, P. B. (1984). Treating symptoms of post-traumatic stress disorder with neuro-linguistic programming. In R. Bandler, *Magic in action*. Cupertino, CA: Meta Publications.

Grinder, J., & Bandler, R. (1976). *The structure of magic* (Vol. 2). Palo Alto: Science & Behavior Books Inc.

Gumm, W. B., Walker, M. K., & Day, H. D. (1982). Neurolinguistics programming: Method or myth? *Journal of Counseling Psychology*, 29(3), 327–330.

Helm, D. J. (2003). Neuro-linguistic programming: Deciphering truth in the criminal mind. *Education,* 124(2), 257–260.

Helm, D. J. (2000). Neuro-linguistic programming: Enhancing learning for the visually impaired. *Education,* 120(4), 790–794.

Hennman, J. O., & Hennman, S. M. (1990). Cognitive-perceptual reconstruction in the treatment of alcoholism. In C. M. Sterman (Ed.), *Neuro-linguistic programming in alcoholism treatment* (pp. 105–123). Binghamton, NY: Hawthorn Press.

Hossach, A., & Standidge, K. (1983). Using an imaginary scrapbook for neurolinguistic programming in the aftermath of a clinical depression: A case history. *The Gerontologist,* 33(2), 265–268.

House, S. (1994). Blending neurolinguistic programming representational systems with the RT counseling environment. *Journal of Reality Therapy,* 14(1), 61–65.

Hubble, M. A., Duncan, B. L., & Miller, S. D. (1999). *The heart and soul of change: What works in therapy.* Washington, DC: American Psychological Association.

Ignoffo, M. (1994). Two compatible methods of empowerment: Neurolinguistic hypnosis and reality therapy. *Journal of Reality Therapy,* 13(2), 20–25.

Isaacson, E. B. (1990). Neuro-linguistic programming: A model for behavioral change in alcohol and other drug addiction. In C. M. Sterman (Ed.), *Neuro-linguistic programming in alcoholism treatment* (pp. 22–47). Binghamton, NY: Hawthorn Press.

Ivey, A. E., Ivey, M. B., & Zalaquett, C. P. (2009). *Intentional interviewing and counseling: Facilitating client development in a multicultural society* (7th ed.). Belmont, CA: Brooks/Cole Publishing Company.

Ivey, A. E., D'Andrea, M., Ivey, M. B., & Simek-Morgan, L. (2006). *Theories of counseling and psychotherapy: A multicultural perspective* (6th ed.). Columbus, OH: Allyn and Bacon.

Juhnke, G. A., Coll, K. M., Sunich, M. F., & Kent, R. R. (2008). Using a modified neurolinguistic programming swish pattern with couple parasuicide and suicide survivors. *The Family Journal: Counselling and Therapy for Couples and Families,* 16(4), 391–396.

Krugman, M., Kirsch, I., Wichless, C., Milling, L., Golicz, H., & Toth, A. (1985). Neuro-linguistic programming treatment for anxiety: Magic or myth? *Journal of Counseling Psychology,* 53(4), 526–530.

Lambert, M. J. (1992). Implications of outcome research for psychotherapy integration. In J. C. Norcross & M. R. Goldfried (Eds.), *Handbook of psychotherapy integration* (pp. 94–129). New York: Basic Books.

Lankton, S. (1980). *Practical magic: A translation of basic neuro-linguistic programming into clinical psychotherapy.* Cupertino, CA: Meta Publications.

MacLean, M. (1986). *The neurolinguistic programming model.* In F. J. Turner (Ed.), *Social work treatment.* New York: The Free Press.

Mercier, M. A., & Johnson, M. (1984). Representational system predicate use and convergence in counseling: Gloria revisited. *Journal of Counseling Psychology,* 31(2), 161–169.

Meredith, N. (1986). Testing the talking cure. *Science 86,* 7(5), 30–37.

Nichols, M.P. (2007). *Family therapy: Concepts and methods* (8th ed.). Columbus, OH: Allyn and Bacon.

Pesut, D. J. (1991). The art, science, and techniques of reframing in psychiatric mental health nursing. *Issues in Mental Health Nursing,* 12(1), 9–18.

Rieber, R. W. (2001). *Wilhelm Wundt in history: The making of a scientific psychology (Path in Psychology).* New York: Springer.

Sandhu, D. S., Reeves, T. G., & Portes, P. R. (1993). Cross-cultural counseling and neurolinguistic mirroring with Native American adolescents. *Journal of Multicultural Counseling and Development,* 21(2), 106–118.

Sharpley, C. F. (1984). Predicate matching in neurolinguistic programming: A review of research on the preferred representational system. *Journal of Counseling Psychology,* 31(2), 338–348.

Sharpley, C. F. (1987). Research findings on neurolinguistic programming: Nonsupportive data or an untestable theory? *Journal of Counseling Psychology,* 34(2), 103–107.

Shelden, V. E., & Shelden, R. G. (1989). Sexual abuse of males by females: The problem, treatment modality, and case example. *Family Therapy,* 16(3), 249–258.

Sterman, C. M. (1990a). A specific neuro-linguistic programming technique effective in the treatment of alcoholism. In C. M. Sterman (Ed.), *Neuro-linguistic programming in alcoholism treatment* (pp. 91–103). Binghamton, NY: Hawthorn Press.

Sterman, C. M. (1990b). Are you the product of my misunderstanding? or The role of sorting mechanisms and basic human programs in the treatment of alcoholism. In C. M. Sterman (Ed.), *Neuro-linguistic programming in alcoholism treatment* (pp. 125–140). Binghamton, NY: Hawthorn Press.

Sterman, C. M. (1990c). Neuro-linguistic programming as a conceptual base for the treatment of alcoholism. In C. M. Sterman (Ed.), *Neuro-linguistic programming in alcoholism treatment* (pp. 11–25). Binghamton, NY: Hawthorn Press.

Sterman, C. M. (1990d). Neuro-linguistic programming rapport skills and alcoholism treatment. In C. M. Sterman (Ed.), *Neuro-linguistic programming in alcoholism treatment* (pp. 49–61). Binghamton, NY: Hawthorn Press.

Sterman, C. M. (1990e). Neuro-linguistic programming as psychotherapeutic treatment in working with alcohol and other drug addicted families. *Journal of Chemical Dependency,* 4(1), 73–85.

Tierney, M. J. (1990). Neuro-linguistics as a treatment modality for alcoholism and substance abuse. In C. M. Sterman (Ed.), *Neuro-linguistic programming in alcoholism treatment* (pp. 141–154). Binghamton, NY: Hawthorn Press.

Turner, P. (1986). The shrinking of George. *Science 86,* 7(5), 38–44.

Welton, D. (Ed.). (1999). *The essential Husserl: Basic writings in transcendental phenomenology (Studies in Continental Thought)*. Bloomington, IN: Indiana University Press.

Yapko, M. D. (1984). Implications of the Ericksonian and neurolinguistic programming approaches for responsibility of therapeutic outcomes. *American Journal of Clinical Hypnosis,* 27(2), 137–143.

Zastrow, C. (2009). *The practice of social work: A comprehensive worktext* (9th ed.). Belmont, CA: Brooks/ Cole.

Zastrow, C., Dotson, V., & Koch, M., (1987). The neurolinguistic programming treatment approach. *Journal of Independent Social Work,* 1(1), 29–38.

Zastrow, C., & Kirst, K. K. (1994). *Understanding human behavior and the social environment* (3rd ed.). Chicago, IL: Nelson Hall Publishers.

OPPRESSION

This approach views social work as a social institution with the potential to transform oppressive social relations that govern the lives of many people by supporting transformational potential

Oppression Theory and Social Work Treatment

Susan P. Robbins

Oppression theory is derived from several different disciplines and theoretical traditions and encompasses a broad array of concerns related to power, privilege, domination, stratification, structural inequality, and discrimination. However, due to oppression theory's varied foundations, it is probably more accurate to speak about oppression *theories,* because the primary concern of each theory generally focuses on different aspects of oppression or specific oppressed groups, often to the exclusion of others. To a large degree, oppression theory shares similar conceptual frameworks with sociological conflict theory, critical social theory, feminist theory, and the empowerment approach to social work practice, based on their overlapping interests in power and inequality. Drawing on these theories, anti-oppressive social work practice is primarily concerned with the

social, political, and economic structures as well as social and psychological processes that initiate, maintain, and enforce oppression.

Historical Context

The current use of oppression theory and the newly emerging field of anti-oppressive social work practice are based on the profession's long-standing commitment to social justice. According to Heinonen and Spearman (2001), social justice is "an abstract and strongly held social work ideal that all people should have equal rights to the resources of a society and should expect and receive fair and equal treatment" (p. 352). Although the development and articulation of anti-oppressive practice is relatively new, concern for social justice has been prominent in both earlier and contemporary radical, progressive, structural, feminist, and liberatory frameworks (Campbell, 2003).

The ideal of social justice can be traced to the work of the Settlement House Movement and its corresponding advocacy for progressive social reforms at the beginning of the 20th century. Social workers during this era were actively involved in social policy initiatives to improve the conditions of the immigrant poor, women, and children. Spurred by collapse of the economy and the ensuing Great Depression, the Rank-and-File Movement of the 1930s brought with it an awakening of political activism that had all but vanished in the 1920s. This movement's affiliated journal, *Social Work Today*, advocated progressive legislation, labor organizing, and other measures that would be seen today as radical or anti-oppressive practice (Gil, 1998; Reisch & Andrews, 2001; Wenocur & Reisch, 2001). Progressive social work did not re-emerge again for several decades, despite the fact that professional social work organizations continued to espouse official rhetoric that reflected anti-oppressive sentiments. However, Reisch and Andrews (2001) note that while advocating social justice ideals, they also promoted practices that reinforced the status quo. This is not surprising, because the ideals of progressive social work have never been held by the majority of those in the profession (Mullaly, 2006). Thus, conventional social work, which seeks to preserve the prevailing social order, has been the mainstay of social work practice through much of the profession's history.

The social movements of the 1960s brought about a renewed awareness and interest in structural factors that influenced people's lives, and the radical social work movement of the 1970s embraced a neo-Marxist class analysis with a focus on reducing poverty and inequality, effecting structural change, and influencing social policy. Specific concern about social class and economic forces can be seen in the materialist approach to social work practice (Burghardt, 1996). Embracing the radical social work heritage, but critical of its narrow focus on class analysis, structural social work theory proposed a broader framework that examined all forms of oppression, including inequality based on race, class, gender, sexual orientation, ability, and age

(Campbell, 2003; Mullaly, 2006; Rose 1990). Campbell credits structural social work as a key development in articulating an anti-oppression stance. However, subsequent feminist, antiracist, cross-cultural, and postmodern theorists voiced concerns that anti-oppressive theory failed to adequately address issues related to their specific interests. In response to this critique, oppression theory today more clearly incorporates the multiple dimensions and expressions of oppression.

Basic Assumptions and Concepts

Although theorists have proposed varying definitions of oppression and its dimensions, Marsiglia and Kulis (2009) have noted that two basic ingredients are necessary for oppression to exist: "a group that is being oppressed and an oppressor who benefits from such oppression" (p. 33). For one group to oppress another, there must also be differential power between the two that results in inequality and injustice. There are many ways to define and conceptualize power, and there is variation and disagreement within and among oppression theorists. Some portray power as relational, as something that people "use and create" (Fook, 2002), while others define it as the ability to control collective actions and decisions (Robbins, Chatterjee, & Canda, 2006). The element of control does not necessarily depend on physical coercion, but may be accomplished through unjust policies and practices that lead to and enforce discrimination, exploitation, and marginalization of devalued groups of people. These variations of definition will be discussed in more detail below in relation to specific theories.

Privilege, domination, and exploitation are central features of oppression, and theorists have started to examine multiple levels of oppression and, in particular, the ways in which oppression is linked to interlocking systems of privilege or domination. Privilege can be understood as the flip side of oppression and is an unearned structural advantage that allows those with power to dominate and exploit the powerless. In essence, oppression cannot exist in the absence of privilege, as they are interdependent on one another. Further, domination is not necessarily a conscious act, and those with privilege need not be aware of their relative privilege in order to be part of an oppressive system. Importantly, oppression takes place within specific historical contexts, and oppression theorists typically include this in their analysis.

Social stratification plays an important role in oppression as well because it places entire groups of people into categories and, based on these categories, systematically allows or denies them access to social and economic rewards. Oppression theory proposes that the way in which these categories are created and maintained is based on power, privilege, and domination. Those in power have the ability not only to define these categories, but also to control which groups have access to the rewards. Due to this, inequality is seen as a structural feature of society because those in power arrange economic and social relations and rewards to benefit themselves. Thus, power and privilege are structurally rooted in the economic and political system.

An important mechanism by which structural inequality is maintained is discrimination. Discrimination involves actions on the part of dominant groups that have a differential and negative effect on people who are devalued and marginalized due to their group membership. Like domination, discrimination may not always be intentional or overt but is a necessary prerequisite for exploitation. Concomitant with discrimination are the processes of stereotyping and prejudice, which are used to justify the exploitation of others.

Oppression, domination, and exploitation exist on multiple levels of social interaction, and contemporary oppression theory examines the ways in which social and cultural categories of differentiation interact or intersect to create a system of oppression. The term *intersectionality* is used in oppression theory to address the experiences of people who are subjected to multiple forms of oppression and domination.

Oppression Theory

As noted above, authors in diverse academic fields have written about oppression, and there is an extensive literature on various aspects of power, privilege, domination, discrimination, and inequality. Oppression can be based on a variety of factors, including social class, race,

gender, ethnicity, sexual orientation, disability, or other categories by which people are defined as "lesser than." This, in turn, provides justification to treat them as objects of discrimination, exclusion, and domination. Oppression occurs not only at the institutional level, but at the intergroup and individual levels as well. This chapter reviews some of the theories that have been most prominently used in anti-oppressive social work practice.

Theories of Class Oppression

Theories of class oppression examine the ways in which social class is used to oppress and marginalize people based on their class status. These theories most typically emphasize the institutional nature of oppression and see power as the ability to dominate other groups or individuals, often referred to as "power over."

All contemporary versions of oppression theory have their roots in the work of Karl Marx, a 19th-century German philosopher, revolutionary, and theorist who integrated works from a variety of disciplines, including economics, political science, history, and sociology. Although best known for *The Communist Manifesto* (Beer, 1955; Marx & Engels, 1848/1955), he was a prolific writer who was profoundly concerned about the transition of Europe to an industrial, manufacturing economy. This transformation irrevocably changed the nature of labor, products, consumption, as well as the economic and social structure of society. Such changes, according to Marx, created a polarization between two dominant classes—workers (the proletariat) and capitalists (the bourgeoisie)—and led to exploitation, inevitable class conflict and struggle, and alienation.

Although class antagonism and struggle over resources had existed in previous eras, industrialization created a new class system as well as new forms of oppression. Because the machinery necessary for mass production was now concentrated in the hands of a very few, workers were forced to sell their labor for wages that were set by the owners whose primary interest was in maximizing their own profits. According to Marx, this created an inherent form of exploitation because the wages paid to the laborers did not reflect the true value of the wealth created by their labor. This was compounded when items they produced were later sold back to them at inflated prices (Perdue, 1986). Capitalist exploitation also led to the pauperization of the working class and created hostility between owners and laborers, who struggled against their exploitation. In turn, owners further consolidated their interests and developed an awareness of their class position, which Marx termed *class consciousness.*

The exploitation of workers also created alienation in three interrelated spheres of social life: political, religious, and economic. According to Marx, when people become alienated, they become estranged, demeaned, depersonalized, and powerless. The economic monopoly of the bourgeoisie was evident in the political arena and, by consolidating their interests, they transformed their economic power into political power and dominated the political institutions as well (Abraham, 1983).

The bourgeoisie also controlled the dominant ideologies and, in this manner, controlled the ideas by which workers came to understand themselves and the world around them. According to Marx, the religious, political, and economic ideologies of the wealthy legitimized and reinforced the status quo, which favored their interests. Further, ideology was used as a form of social control to disguise and subdue class conflict. He believed that exploitation, alienation, and ideological domination were intricately interwoven with one another. Ideological domination by the ruling class could be seen in common and pervasive aspects of people's lives such as religion and nationalism.

Calling religion the *"opium of the people,"* Marx argued that the emphasis on rewards in the afterlife focused people's attention away from the inequality and oppression they experienced in their lives here. When people believe that their lot in life is preordained, religion becomes a form of social control that thwarts attempts at rebellion. This, according to Marx, was a central feature of religious alienation. Political ideology and political alienation function in a similar manner because the ideology of "nationalism" disguises the inequalities inherent in a capitalist system.

Marx believed that the struggle for both the proletariat and bourgeoisie was to free themselves from false consciousness, an unquestioning acceptance of a prevailing social order that

supported an inherently oppressive system. In Marx's utopian vision, he believed that workers worldwide would eventually unite, become politicized, and organize to overthrow capitalistic exploitation by means of a violent revolution. The political and economic order that he predicted would emerge would be socialism, followed by communism, the hallmark of which was the end of private property and social classes. Although Marx's prediction of worldwide revolution did not come to fruition, his theory represents an important sociological and economic analysis of society that provided the conceptual basis for subsequent theories of oppression. Importantly, Marx laid the groundwork for an examination of both the structural features of oppression as well as the social and psychological processes by which people come to accept their own domination and subjugation.

Drawing on Marxist theory and Catholic liberation theology, Paulo Freire, a Brazilian educator and theorist, sought to liberate people from the domination of the ruling class through a critical pedagogy that would prepare students to challenge and break the prevailing cycles of injustice, exploitation, and oppression. Freire, like Marx, believed that the ruling class imposed its values and culture on others and that knowledge was used by dominant groups to oppress and subjugate the masses. He proposed that oppressed people experience life as "objects" being acted upon, rather than as "subjects" who are in control of their own lives. Due to this, they lack skills that are essential for influencing the institutions that have control over their lives. Freire proposed that one of the primary institutions used as a tool of subjugation is standardized education.

Best known for his criticism of "banking" education, Freire held that through repetition and memorization, teachers deposit knowledge into students, who are treated as empty accounts, or receptacles. According to Freire (1993), banking education indoctrinates students to adapt to oppression, subverts their creative abilities, and reduces them to manageable beings who adopt the oppressive view of reality deposited in them. The more the oppressed adapt to their situation, the more easily they can be dominated. In addition, banking education fosters ideological control that serves the interests of the oppressors by diverting the attention of the oppressed away from the situation that oppresses them. In essence, the insidious nature of oppression prevents the oppressed from recognizing the reality of their circumstance. According to Freire, their perception of themselves is impaired by their submersion in the reality of oppression (p. 45). Many of Marx's themes are apparent in Freire's work and, like Marx, Freire also believed that the problem is not only with the oppressed, but the oppressors as well, who subvert their own humanity by turning everything around them into objects to be dominated.

Another characteristic of the oppressed is self-depreciation, which results from internalizing the opinion the oppressors hold of them. Through this process the oppressed become convinced of their own unfitness and suffer from a duality that becomes established in their innermost selves: "They are at one and the same time themselves and the oppressor whose consciousness they have internalized" (Freire, 1993, p. 49). This consciousness becomes so ingrained that people come to identify with and imitate their oppressors. Freire believed that in order to free themselves from oppression, people must first recognize that they have been destroyed, eject negative images of themselves, replace such images with those of autonomy and responsibility, and begin to transform themselves from objects to subjects.

To combat the fatalism experienced by the oppressed and to actively involve them in their own liberation from object to subject, Freire proposed a dialogical method that consisted of identifying problems, analyzing the root causes, and initiating action plans. This represented a significant change from traditional banking education and required that educators and learners be equal participants in order to engage in continuous dialogue with each other. Through mutual dialogue, the oppressed become better able to analyze their conditions, develop a critical consciousness or *conscientização*, and subsequently engage in action to become liberated from their external and internal oppression. According to Freire, this requires collective strategies that include the liberation of the oppressors as well as the oppressed. Goldenberg (1978) aptly sums up the condition of the oppressed: "Oppression, in short, is a condition of being in which one's past and future meet in the present—and go no further" (p. 3).

Theories of Racial Oppression

In contrast to class oppression theories, theories that examine racial oppression emphasize both the institutional nature of oppression as well as the intergroup dynamics that sustain it. Thus, the focus is on both the oppressive structures as well as the intergroup processes of prejudice and discrimination. Much of the literature on racial oppression in the United States emerged in response to the history of black slavery and, due to this, examines the history and contemporary experiences of black Americans, the system of racial oppression in America, and the oppressive dynamic of white privilege (Blauner, 2001).

Blauner suggests that Marxist theory and the dominance of European social thought that guided many successive generations of American theorists diverted attention from race and race relations. This was due to the incorrect assumption that race and ethnicity would become irrelevant as societies matured. Contrary to this stance, Blauner believes that race, racism, and racial oppression occupy a central and independent role in American economics, politics, and culture, and white privilege and domination are critical components of the dynamics that give rise to pervasive inequality. Relying of the framework of colonialism, as seen in the broad context of the expansion of white European control, he proposes that racial oppression and conflict today are based on white Western dominance over non-Western people of color (p. 22). Thus, contemporary ethnic and racial divisions are, in part, a product of our colonial past. This alone, however, is insufficient to understand the complexity of racial oppression, and he proposes that racial oppression theory must include the "combined existence" and "mutual interpenetration of both colonial-racial and capitalist class realities" (Blauner, 2001, p. 23). Even though white privilege is pervasive in all social institutions, he sees its expression in the labor market as the primary factor that determines people's lifestyle and social status.

In their examination of the history of the oppression of black Americans, Jonathan H. Turner, Royce Singleton, Jr., and David Musick (1986) propose that oppression can be defined as "a situation in which one, or more, identifiable segments of the population in a social system systematically and successfully act over a pro-longed period of time to prevent another identifi-able segment, or segments, of the population from attaining access to the scarce and valued resources of that system" (pp. 1–2). This definition under-scores several important dimensions of oppres-sion and proposes that it requires more than one group simply exerting "power over" another group. In their formulation, oppression must not only prevent access to resources, it must also be systematic, it must be prolonged, it must target an identifiable group, and it must be successful. According to Turner et al., oppression is "both a process and a structure" (p. 2). As a process it involves attitudes and acts, such as prejudice, ster-eotyping, and discrimination, that place and keep others in the lower ranks of the social structure. At the structural level, a hierarchical system is cre-ated by this process, and identifiable groups are placed at the bottom of this structure. These groups then organize their lives and identities around their place in the social structure.

Importantly, Turner et al. point out that oppression varies by degree and does not always lead to people being placed in the lowest ranks. Drawing on Max Weber's three dimensions of stratification (power, property, and prestige), the authors stress that some groups may be allowed access to material well-being (property) but denied access to power and prestige. Thus, oppression can be selective and differentially applied. However, when groups, such as black Americans, are systematically and successfully denied access to all three resources, they become trapped in a caste-like structure and experience greater oppression than those who are allowed to occupy the middle ranks.

Other racial oppression theorists and authors have examined the structural and behavioral manifestations of racism and internalized oppres-sion, and their work adds to an important body of literature that informs antiracist and diversity practice in social work (Batts, 1998; Dominelli, 2008; Williams, 1999).

Theories of Gender Inequality and Oppression

The fields of women's studies and feminist theory have provided an extensive literature related to women's inequality and oppression, and the theories briefly summarized here examine the social and psychological processes that lead to the power disparities that undergird oppression. The primary focus of feminist theories is on the subordination of women and, due to this, draws less from Marxism than do other oppression theories. However, feminist theory has made a significant contribution to oppression theory by expanding the scope of analysis to include an examination of the intersectionality of sexism with other forms of subordination, such as racism, heterosexism, and class oppression.

Feminist theory has also expanded the defi-nition of power to include four forms of power that many contemporary feminist authors use in their understanding and analysis of oppression: power over, power from within, power with, and power to do (see Townsend, Zapata, Rowlands, Alberti, & Mercado, 1999). As dis-cussed above, *power over* refers to institutional-ized power that allows people to dominate others. *Power within* is a form of personal power that develops when oppressed people join together to share their struggles. *Power with* emerges in work with others, as people collec-tively and cooperatively organize to change their conditions, and *power to do* (also called *power to*) refers to the capacity to act and the concrete actions that people take to effect change (Finn & Jacobson, 2008). Many see this as a more nuanced approach to power, but the shift to seeing power as relational rather than a struc-tural feature of society has significant implica-tions. Lukes (2005) has suggested that the way in which power is conceptualized is, itself, shaped by power relations: "how we think about power may serve to reproduce and reinforce power structures and relations, or alternatively it may challenge and subvert them" (p. 63). In fact, some feminist scholars contend that the concept of *power over* is a product of a male worldview of domination. Many believe that redefining power from a relational perspective provides a sounder theoretical base for practice with transformational possibilities.

Writing from a feminist perspective and influenced by Foucault's (1980) concept of power, Iris Marion Young (1990), rejected the static concept of *power over* as being the primary force in oppression and proposed five forms, or "faces," of oppression that she believed better explained the interactional nature of oppression: exploitation, marginalization, powerlessness, cultural imperialism, and violence. She also held that racism, sexism, ageism, and homophobia can operate separately from the dynamics of class and, therefore, are distinct forms of oppression.

Exploitation is "a steady process of the transfer of results of the labor of one social group to benefit another" (Young, 1990, p. 49). Accordingly, the two aspects of gender exploitation include the transfer of the fruits of labor to men as well as the transfer of sexual satisfaction and emotional nurturing (p. 50). Although this is exploitive, it is not necessarily coercive because it arises from, and is supported by, ongoing social relations and processes. Marginalization, which Young saw as the most dangerous form of oppression, is the process by which categories of people are excluded from participation in social life and may also be severely, materially deprived or exterminated (p. 53). Powerlessness, according to Young, is a relative phenomenon for most people, in that they may have some degree of power in relation to others, even if they do not have the power to decide policies that affect their lives. People who are truly powerless have no power at all. Cultural imperialism establishes the dominant group's experience and culture as universal norms, and those who do not conform to these norms are labeled as the "Other." Violence, the fifth face of oppression, includes not only unprovoked physical attacks, but also harassment, intimidation, and ridicule, when used intentionally to stigmatize others. Young sees violence as a social process that is systematic.

Although these five types of oppression, or combinations of these, may be experienced by a specific oppressed group, Young does not believe that any of these is a necessary condition of oppression for any specific group. Nonetheless, the presence of any one of these is sufficient to determine that a group has been oppressed. She believes that by examining these systems of oppression separately, it is possible to compare the specific types of oppression that are experienced by each oppressed group.

In a feminist, phenomenological examination of the psychological dimensions of oppression, Sandra Lee Bartky (1990) incorporates insights from Freire and Young, and, more directly, from Frantz Fanon's (1967) study of the psychic alienation of black men. While recognizing the fact that economic and political oppression can be psychologically oppressive, she proposes that psychological oppression has its own distinct modes that operate to produce internalized messages of inferiority. She examines three social processes, as set forth by Fanon, which are used to deliver messages of inferiority to women: stereotyping, cultural domination, and sexual objectification. In describing these processes she is particularly concerned about the ways in which fragmentation and mystification are present in all three. *Fragmentation* is the splitting of the person into parts, while *mystification* obscures the reality of psychological oppression and produces a depreciated self and corresponding guilt or neuroses.

Stereotypes are used to sustain both racism and sexism and prevent people from achieving an authentic choice of self. Female stereotypes also limit women's independence and autonomy by portraying then as beings that cannot and should not be as autonomous as men. Cultural domination and depreciation also robs women of an authentic sense of self because male characteristics are portrayed as the norm for personhood. Finally, sexual objectification reduces women to their sexual parts and also distorts their ability to see themselves as whole persons. As these negative messages become internalized, women are placed in a double bind, in that it is "psychologically oppressive both to believe and at the same time not to believe that one is inferior" (Bartky, 1990, p. 30). Bartky sees a strong similarity between psychic alienation and Marx's alienation of labor: in both, human functions are split from the person and prevent people from engaging in activities that are essential to leading a full human existence.

As noted above, extensive feminist literature has addressed many of the concepts that are central to oppression theory. Given the differences in the way that power is conceptualized, one of the challenges for future research and scholarship in this area will be achieving a better theoretical integration regarding the nature of power.

Social Work Contributions to Theories of Oppression

Over the past several decades there has been an emerging literature in social work on anti-oppressive practice (see, for example, Appleby,

Colon, & Hamilton, 2007; Baines, 2008; Clifford & Burke, 2009; Dominelli, 1996, 1998, 2002; Fook, 2002; Gil, 1998; Marsiglia & Kulis, 2009; Mclaughlin, 2005; Mullaly, 2002, 2006; Sinclair & Albert, 2008; van Wormer, 2004). However, no social work authors have developed unique theories of oppression, and most have relied on frameworks related to feminist, antiracist, critical, conflict, empowerment, or social justice theories.

David Gil (1998), for example, provides an in-depth analysis of the evolution of thought related to exploitation and oppression, strategies to overcome injustice, the importance of radical policy analysis, strategies for social change practice, and the dilemmas faced by the social work profession in fully embracing a social justice stance toward practice. Katherine van Wormer (2004) reviewed a range of social, political, and psychological theories and concepts that undergird anti-oppressive practice and proposes an excellent model for anti-oppressive policy analysis. She also delineates various methods for achieving restorative justice. Bob Mullaly (2006) offers a conceptual framework for structural social work that incorporates many of the elements of theories discussed in this chapter, and his work is often cited as a useful theoretical base for anti-oppressive practice.

One of the leading proponents and authors advocating anti-oppressive social work practice is Lena Dominelli (1996, 1998, 2002, 2008). Her classic book on theory and practice for anti-oppressive social work draws heavily on feminist and antiracist theory and provides a contextual framework for effecting change at the intergroup and structural levels. Her work in this area reflects theoretical sources that also can be seen in her earlier writing on feminist and antiracist practice.

Anti-Oppressive Social Work Practice

Anti-oppressive social work practice includes a variety of approaches and theories related to social work's commitment to social justice. The tenet that social workers engage in anti-oppressive practice can be found in the *Code of Ethics* of both the National Association of Social Workers (NASW) and the International Federation of Social Workers (IFSW). Concomitant with professional values and principles related to the

concepts of social justice and political action, social workers are expected to address social injustice by pursuing "social change, particularly with and on behalf of vulnerable and oppressed individuals and groups of people" as well as prevent and eliminate domination, exploitation, and discrimination (NASW, 2008). Similarly, a basic principle of the IFSW (2004) is that social workers challenge unjust practices and policies that are "oppressive, unfair or harmful."

Due to the fact that anti-oppressive practice is an "umbrella term" for diverse approaches, it is best seen as a stance, or perspective, toward practice rather than a particular method (Campbell, 2003). Despite variations, Campbell lists core values and principles embodied in anti-oppressive practice to include:

- Shared values of equity, inclusion, empowerment, and community
- An understanding that the thoughts, feelings, and behaviors of individuals are linked to material, social, and political conditions
- Recognition of the link between personal troubles and public issues
- Recognition that an unequal distribution of power and resources leads to personal and institutional relationships of oppression and domination
- The necessity of promoting critical analysis
- The importance of encouraging, supporting, and "centering" the knowledge and perspectives of those who have been marginalized and incorporating these perspectives into policy and practice
- The importance of articulating the multiple and intersecting bases of oppression and domination while not denying the unique impact of various oppressive constructs
- Conceiving of social work as a social institution with the potential to either contribute to, or to transform, the oppressive social relations that govern the lives of many people
- Supporting the transformative potential of social work through work with diverse individuals, groups, and communities
- Having a vision of an egalitarian future.

These values and principles can be seen in a variety of practice approaches, all of which seek to challenge oppressive conditions and redress social injustice. Approaches that are most commonly associated with anti-oppressive practice include structural social work, critical social work, feminist practice, antiracist practice, Africentric practice, practice with Aboriginal and indigenous peoples, and disability practice. Campbell has noted the one factor preventing the adoption of a generic, anti-oppressive model of practice is concern that unique and specific expressions of oppression will be minimized or lost in such an approach. Thus, some have deliberately retained, for example, a feminist or antiracist approach to practice to ensure that their specific concerns are fully addressed.

This trend can also be seen in the abundant literature on feminist, antiracist, diversity, and radical social work practice in the United States. Although this is true in other countries as well, much of the emerging scholarship on anti-oppressive practice has come from Canada, England, and Australia (Dominelli, 1996, 1998, 2002; Fook, 2002; Mclaughlin, 2005; Mullaly, 2002, 2006; Sinclair & Albert, 2008).

Anti-oppressive practice addresses the eradication of oppression at the multiple levels in which it occurs: the personal, interpersonal, structural, and cultural. Because oppression involves attitudes, behaviors, intergroup relations, as well as institutional and cultural norms and policies, associated practice techniques and methods are similar to activist approaches used in the structural and empowerment approaches. These include, but are not limited to, education, participation, community and neighborhood organizing, consciousness raising, advocacy, policy practice, and practice aimed at eradicating structural inequities. At its core, anti-oppressive social work is social justice-oriented practice (Finn & Jacobson, 2008).

Research Challenges

Due to the fact that oppression theory is based on a series of assumptions and premises that do not lend themselves to empirical verification, quantitative research on oppression theory is difficult, if not impossible, to conduct. One can readily examine, for example, the degree of inequality by examining a variety of concrete conditions such as income, health, or educational attainment through census data and studies on mobility.

The sheer existence of inequality, however, cannot explain why or how it occurs, and it is this very explanation that is at the heart of all theories of oppression. Not surprisingly, oppression theories most typically rely on qualitative methods, due to their ability to provide a rich description of the lives and realities of the oppressed. Qualitative methods can also be used to examine the way in which policies can create unequal or unjust situations or examine the ways in which policies are differentially applied to create injustice. Katherine van Wormer (2004), for example, contends that policy analysis is inherently political and discusses the necessity for conducting historical, international, economic, and political analysis of policies that affect people's lives. She also outlines a specific process for examining policies that is consistent with anti-oppressive practice and discusses how emphasis on structural barriers differentiates it from traditional policy analysis.

A central tenet of oppression theory is that there are multiple truths about society, social relationships, and the nature of reality and, thus, it is important to embrace research methods that accurately describe these multiple truths. Although this stance is philosophically consistent with the theory itself, it presents challenges in a profession that increasingly calls for evidence based on quantitative methods and. Due to this, it is unlikely that this tension will be resolved. This is unfortunate, because qualitative methods may ultimately provide the most appropriate form of research for these theories.

Conclusions and Future Prospects

Anti-oppressive practice encompasses a variety of practice approaches that are concerned with social justice. The unique and particular interests of those who embrace a model of practice based on a social justice perspective have prevented the broad adoption of a more general anti-oppressive framework. This is likely to continue due to the specialized interests that people bring to the practice of social work. Finally, as Gil (1998) has so aptly pointed out, despite the profession's commitment to social justice, most social workers see their practice as apolitical and rarely challenge systemic sources of oppression. Not surprisingly, those invested in the system are the least likely to engage in its liberation.

References

Abraham, M. F. (1983). *Modern sociological theory.* New York: Oxford University Press.

Appleby, Colon, & Hamilton, (2007). *Diversity, oppression and social functioning: Person in environment assessment and intervention.* Boston: Allyn & Bacon.

Baines, D. (2008) *Doing anti-oppressive practice building transformative, politicized social work.* Black Point, Nova Scotia: Fernwood Publishing.

Bartky, S. L. (1990). *Femininity and domination: Studies in the phenomenology of oppression.* New York: Routledge.

Batts, V. (1998). *Modern racism: New melody for the same old tunes.* Cambridge, MA: Episcopal Divinity School.

Beer, S. H. (Ed.) (1955). *Marx and Engels: The communist manifesto.* New York: Appleton- Century-Crofts.

Blauner, B. (2001). *Still the big news: Racial oppression in America.* Philadelphia: Temple University Press.

Burghardt, S. (1996). A materialist framework for social work theory and practice. In F. J. Turner (Ed.), *Social work treatment: Interlocking theoretical approaches* (3rd ed., pp. 409–433). New York: The Free Press.

Campbell, C. (2003). Anti-oppressive social work: Promoting equity and social justice. Halifax. Author. Retrieved August 27, 2009, from http://aosw.socialwork.dal.ca/

Clifford, D., & Burke, B. (2009). *Anti-oppressive ethics and values in social work.* Hampshire, England: Palgrave Macmillan.

Dominelli, L. (1996). Deprofessionalizing social work: Anti-oppressive practice, competencies, postmodernism. *British Journal of Social Work, 26,* 153–175.

Dominelli, L. (1998). Anti-oppressive practice in context. In R. Adams, L. Dominelli, & M. Payne (Eds.), *Social work: Themes, issues and critical debates* (pp. 3–22). Houndmills: MacMillan Press Ltd.

Dominelli, L. (2002). *Anti-oppressive social work theory and practice.* Hampshire, England: Palgrave Macmillan.

Dominelli, L. (2008). *Anti-racist social work* (3rd ed.) Hampshire: Palgrave Macmillan.

Fanon, F. (1967). *Black skins, white masks.* New York: Grove Press.

Finn, J. L., & Jacobson, M. (2008). *Just practice: A social justice approach to social work* (2nd ed.). Peosta, IA: Eddie Bowers Publishing.

Fook, J. (2002). *Social work: Critical theory and practice.* London: Sage Publications.

Foucault, M. (1980). Two lectures. In C. Gordon (Ed.), *Power/knowledge: Selected interviews and other writings, 1972–1977.* New York: Pantheon.

Freire, P. (1993). *Pedagogy of the oppressed.* New York: Continuum Books.

Gil, D. G. (1998). *Confronting injustice and oppression: Concepts and strategies for social workers.* New York: Columbia University Press.

Goldenberg, I. (1978). *Oppression and social intervention.* Chicago: Nelson-Hall.

Heinonen, T., & Spearman, L. (2001). (Eds). *Social work practice: Problem solving and beyond.* Toronto: Irwin Publishing.

International Federation of Social Workers (2004). *Ethics in Social Work, Statement of Principles.* Bern, Switzerland. Retrieved August 27, 2009, from http://www.ifsw.org/f38000032.html

National Association of Social Workers (2008). *Code of Ethics of the National Association of Social Workers (Approved by the 1996 NASW Delegate Assembly and revised by the 2008 NASW Delegate Assembly).* Washington, DC, Retrieved August 27, 2009, from http://www.socialworkers.org/pubs/Code/code.asp

Lukes, S. (2005). *Power: A radical view* (2nd ed.) London: Macmillan.

Marsiglia, F. F., & Kulis, S. (2009). *Diversity, oppression and change.* Chicago: Lyceum.

Marx, K., & Engels, F. (1848/1955). *The Communist manifesto* (S. H. Beer, Ed.). New York: Appleton-Century-Crofts.

Mclaughlin, K. (2005). From ridicule to institutionalization: Anti-oppression, the state and social work. *Critical Social Policy, 25*(3), 283–305.

Mullaly, B. (2002). *Challenging oppression: A critical approach to social work.* New York: Oxford University Press.

Mullaly, B. (2006). *The new structural social work: Ideology, theory, practice.* New York: Oxford University Press.

Perdue, W. D. (1986). *Sociological theory: Explanation, paradigm, and ideology.* Palo Alto, CA: Mayfield Publishing Company.

Reisch, M., & Andrews, J. (2001). *The road not taken: A history of radical social work in the United States.* Philadelphia: Brunner-Routledge.

Robbins, S. P., Chatterjee, P., & Canda, E. R. (2006). *Contemporary social work theory: A critical perspective for practice.* Boston: Allyn & Bacon.

Rose, S. (1990). Advocacy/empowerment: An approach to clinical practice for social work. *Journal of Sociology and Social Welfare, 17*(2), 41–51.

Sinclair, R., & Albert, J. (2008). Social work and the anti-oppressive stance: Does the emperor really have new clothes? *Critical Social Work, 9*(1).

Turner, J. H., Singleton, Jr., R., & Musick, D. (1986). *Oppression: A socio-history of black-white relations in America.* Chicago: Nelson-Hall.

van Wormer, K. (2004). *Confronting oppression, restoring justice: From policy analysis to social action.* Alexandria, VA: Council on Social Work Education.

Wenocur, S., & Reisch, M. (2001). *From charity to enterprise: The development of American social work in a market economy.* Champaign, IL: University of Illinois Press.

Williams, C. (1999). Connecting anti-racist and anti-oppressive theory and practice: Retrenchment or reappraisal? *British Journal of Social Work, 29*(2), 211–230.

Young, I. M. (1990). *Justice and the politics of difference.* Princeton, NJ: Princeton University Press.

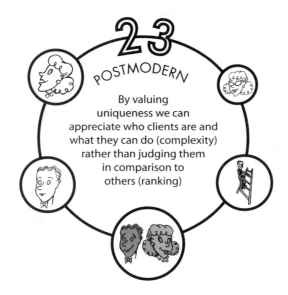

By valuing uniqueness we can appreciate who clients are and what they can do (complexity) rather than judging them in comparison to others (ranking)

Postmodern Social Work

Dan Wulff

Postmodernism is a word that in recent times has attracted a great deal of attention in society and in the helping fields in particular. This word has accrued many diverse meanings and has come to represent a variety of viewpoints that attract both friendly associations and prickly responses. Conversations about postmodernism and its influence often invite heated exchanges that, upon close examination, seem to touch the conversants in ways that go beyond what a straightforward consideration of an idea would merit. These conversations seem to activate strong emotional reactions. An idea or viewpoint that becomes a sort of personal and/or interpersonal lightning rod can become difficult to critically examine with a clear-eyed approach. Bohm (1996) reminds us that "[t]he thing that mostly gets in the way of dialogue is

holding to assumptions and opinions, and defending them" (p. ix).

In this chapter I would like to invite the reader to consider some of the points of intersection between postmodernism and social work from a vantage point outside the "dueling dichotomy" of either proselytizing or attacking. I will discuss some opportunities for how postmodernism can be a generative influence in the field of social work (Chambon & Irving, 1994; Gorman, 1993; Mullaly, 1997; Payne, 2005; Witkin & Saleebey, 2007) while also mentioning some of the aspects of postmodernism that seem to be unhelpful or benign with respect to social work. The ideas presented herein are not true in an ultimate sense, but I think they can highlight some useful constructions and practices while stimulating thinking.

Modernism and Postmodernism

The theoretical debates between modernism and postmodernism (often oversimplified as One Truth vs. "anything goes") seem to be academic squabbles that are not relevant or useful for practitioners. Modernism and postmodernism each illuminate ways of thinking that can provide constructive guidance for social workers. The fit between these idea regimes and the social workers who choose to embrace either of them may be the more critical distinction rather than focusing on the effort to impose one set of ideas over the other in some all-encompassing sense.

Other fields of study (e.g., art, architecture, and literature) have incorporated postmodernism into their thinking. In the art field, a postmodern point of view eschews the modernist alignment with a single stable ideology or absolute and "undermines the manipulative aspect of ideologies by exposing the artificiality of style" (Berry, 2006). As an alternative, "postmodern works of art elicit individual interpretations, personal stories of responsive consciousness" (Berry, 2006). Postmodernism in art loosens the grip of the standard form and style and invites the marginal, the new, and unexpected.

Postmodernism partakes of uncertainty, insecurity, doubt, and accepts ambiguity. Whereas Modernism seeks closure in form and is concerned with conclusions, postmodernism is open, unbounded, and concerned with process and 'becoming.' (Witcombe, 1997)

The Emperor's New Suit

Hans Christian Andersen's children's story, "The Emperor's New Suit" (Andersen, n.d.), provides an apt framework to review the modernist/postmodernist debates. This is a story about an extravagantly dressed emperor who was led to believe by some clever would-be weavers that they possessed a cloth of the highest quality that also had the particular quality of "being invisible to any man who was unfit for his office or unpardonably stupid." The emperor commissioned a suit to be made for him that would serve the double function of being made of exquisite material as well as being able to reveal those in his office or kingdom who were unworthy. When the emperor donned the "suit," many noticed the emperor's nakedness but dared not speak for fear of being harshly judged. It was a child who one day noticed the emperor's actual nakedness (the "naked truth") and said so, voicing what so many had noticed but denied.

Those involved in the mostly academic modernist/postmodernist debates have struggled to claim the true or accurate view, with each coming out of these debates claiming victory. They each claim a ground from which to base the credibility of their arguments (but those groundings are not shared); therefore, no resolution is forthcoming and the stage is set for another debate. Within the metaphor of Andersen's story, both modernists and postmodernists may attempt to claim the position of the knowing child, and seeing the other side as the adults who were deluded.

A postmodernist could relate to Andersen's story in many other ways than as a character within the story. Other postmodernist takes on this story would be to wonder about Andersen's aims in writing this tale, by "putting him back into the picture," what readers take away from this story, what children like about this story, how this story today reads differently (or not) from when it was written in 1837, and how this story is understood differently in Andersen's home country of Denmark and elsewhere in the world. Rather than join in the storyline to attempt to become the knowledgeable one within the story's overt narrative, the larger story of Andersen could become the focus of the postmodernist.

A postmodern approach looks for the "absent but implicit" (White, 2003, p. 30), the not visible but nonetheless present, the story within or beyond the story. Postmodernism does not try to establish Truth within the bounds of a story; rather, it examines the bounds set by the story and the implications of those bounds. The options in relating to the story are noticeably expanded.

Definitions of Postmodernism and Social Constructionism

Postmodernism is defined as "of, relating to, or being a theory that involves a radical reappraisal of modern assumptions about culture, identity, history, or language" (Postmodernism, *Merriam-Webster's Online Dictionary*, 11th ed., n.d.). From a social constructionism lens, one sees the social world as a network of interpretive relationships actively and creatively produced by human beings. As persons, we are constituted by all our relationships and allegiances, now and in the past. We are composites of many influences.

Postmodernism's philosophical roots and intellectual pyrotechnics with modernists have led some to worry about the over-academization of the ideas of postmodernism, rendering it relatively useless to the common man, the rank-and-file (Esteva & Prakash, 1998). Esteva and Prakash propose a grassroots postmodernism that hopes to "identify and give a name to a wide collection of culturally diverse initiatives and struggles of the so-called illiterate and uneducated non-modern 'masses,' pioneering radical post-modern paths out of the morass of modern life" (p. 3). A grassroots postmodern world offers initiatives that are autonomously organized by "the people" themselves, for their own survival, flourishing and enduring; both independent from and antagonistic to the state and its formal and corporative structures; hospitable to "the Other" and thus open to diversity; mainly expressed in reclaimed or regenerated commons, in both urban and rural settings, and clearly concerned with the common good, both natural and social (p. 13). They highlight the postmodern emphasis on the local experience, situation, or decision, with no desire to generalize, replicate, or standardize.

In particular, a postmodernist appreciates working from a position that openly acknowledges and values that "the realities we live in are outcomes of the conversations in which we are engaged" (Gergen, 2009, p. 4). This quote represents some key ideas that my work centers around, namely that realities are plural (not singular), language is crucial, relationships are central to our lives, and life and our understandings of it are fluid. Our understandings of the world have verisimilitude—they have the appearance of truth more than capturing some universal called Truth itself. These imperfect understandings are the maps with which we navigate our lives.

Social work itself has been referred to as a vague profession, filled with uncertainty, ambiguity, and changeability (Schön, 1983). Perhaps

it makes useful sense to see social work as an attitude or stance in the world—an epistemology or way of knowing that offers us general guidance while not being over-specified.

Generative Possibilities with Postmodern Social Work

The following stances or approaches of a postmodern social work highlight some of the specific opportunities available to the social worker.

Legitimacy of Alternatives

In a diverse world of people, opinions, and social structures, the breadth of possibilities is hard to refute, but we often temper this appreciation by privileging some while simultaneously marginalizing others. It is extremely difficult to valorize a wide range of possible understandings, particularly when we have a strong or vested interest in one or two of those possibilities. The social work value of self-determination is difficult to live up to when some viewpoints are considered more legitimate than others (in particular, the social worker's understanding over the client's understanding).

Social work practice deliberately focuses on the complex situations of persons in their environments, a strategy that stands against simple or circumscribed understandings and interventions. Given the inherent complexity of human situations and the various ways to construct them, a single preferred way of understanding any given human situation is automatically limited.

From a postmodern social work perspective, alternative viewpoints (particularly when they are held by clients) are considered to be legitimate viewpoints, regardless of whether or not the social worker holds or values those particular views. This does not suggest that all viewpoints will be enacted or have the same value and potential in a given circumstance. However, this does suggest that all viewpoints are legitimate *as viewpoints* and the holders of those viewpoints are credited with being legitimate viewpoint-holders. First and foremost, the client is respected as a legitimate participant in a social work interaction, a relevant conversational partner.

Evidence-based practices (EBP) can be useful if their "claims to fame" are explicitly grounded in the criteria that made them. A problem can arise when the criteria of their selection for promotion are hidden or assumed. They represent legitimate and often useful practices, but can override alternative practices only when hegemonic influences embrace them. In other words, it is not the EBP themselves that establish credibility; rather, it is the criteria or power brokers who do that.

Absence of Universals

One of the criticisms of postmodernism in social work is its failure to incorporate a vision of a better society, or a universal understanding of social justice and human rights. As such an understanding is fundamental to social work, it is clear that postmodernism, while it has important contributions to make to an alternative social work, is not sufficient to form a basis for practice (Ife, 1997, p. 92).

Perhaps it is precisely this aversion to developing universal understandings or standards that allows postmodernist practitioners to contribute to social work at its definitional level. Could social workers envision their work minus the specification of a preferred state or world? The mission of developing a "universal understanding of social justice and human rights" may lead us directly into the wheelhouse of divisions and tensions that prevent any substantive improvement in the lives of the millions who exist in poverty and disenfranchisement. Could social workers provide a significant humanistic presence without establishing what a preferred world would look like? This desire to locate a definitive position on what fairness, justice, or health is may be limiting our abilities to envision alternative ways, and these alternative ways may be sources of generative ideas and actions.

Non-impositional

Postmodern social workers deliberately avoid imposing ideas or behavioral mandates on clients. This becomes very challenging with respect to the social work function of enforcing statutes and court orders and could seem to be an impossible issue to reconcile. As with so many social work issues and dilemmas, if they are approached as a choice to between two (and only two) possibilities, the situation seems deadlocked. When one can imagine more than two choices, then the deadlock dissipates. The possibility of a third choice opens space for the two competitive choices to find places of agreement or cooperation. Note, too, that the feasibility of a third choice is often initially questioned—but to act *as if* a third choice exists allows the participants to at least think imaginatively of another way.

This issue of imposition is addressed as a centerpiece of approaching social work practice from an Aboriginal perspective. We can take guidance here from Aboriginal social work scholars who have justifiably focused their attentions on the social work practices that resemble domination (Hart, 2001) and have advocated for other practice pathways (Aitkin, 1990). "The position taken here explicitly avoids imposing specific treatments and cultural values—including professional social work values and beliefs—on clients" (Hart, 2001, p. 232). If a preferred way is pervasive and/or mandated by persons or institutions of power, it can itself be (or become) the source of oppression and hardship, the very thing that social work may need to challenge. Attending to the ways that social work values and beliefs can themselves serve to dominate and oppress illustrates the postmodern attention to reflexivity and the need to consistently deconstruct all thought and behavioral sets. Deconstruction here refers to a process whereby an idea or practice is taken apart in order to examine its component parts, and then recomposed, but now with an enhanced understanding of what it is and how it works. Only by engaging in a process of deconstruction can we carefully evaluate the size and shape of the impact of an idea or practice.

Privileging the Uniquenesses of Individuals and Communities

From a postmodern stance, a social worker prefers the uniquenesses available rather than the generalities. This runs counter to the emphasis on creating large-scale understandings that can be implemented broadly, often under the label of efficiency. The large-scale initiatives provide services or products to masses of people, but in a more impersonal way and with many individual casualties. The efficiency angle benefits the stakeholders and administrators at the organizational level, not the consumer. Often the promises of improved services or shorter wait times attract the consumer, but these claims are usually overstated and become under-realized.

Valuing the unique allows us to appreciate what people can do and who they are. We are able to accentuate their abilities and perspectives, rather than judge them harshly through comparisons with others. We focus on coming to know the person in their complexity rather than finding ways to rank them, thereby focusing on their comparative characteristics.

The focus on the individual case (a forte of qualitative research) allows a more complex view of people—understanding people as composites of many influences and infinitely changeable (an important principle of social work practice). A postmodern stance allows us to see people as always in motion, always changing, which provides the grounding for social workers to approach their clients as moving, changing, and reinventing themselves (a critical element if you are hoping to help people make changes).

Larger and Longer View

Helping as a Part of Healing

A construct in the Aboriginal approach called *pimatasiwin* is a theme that refers to "a good life and the lifelong journey of healing" (Hart, 2001, p. 253), a more encompassing idea than problem solving. From this perspective, social workers help "another in her or his process of healing" (p. 253), a more modest endeavor than social workers often envision for themselves. This contextualizes the social worker's role in the client's life that maintains the focus on the client as the director of her/his life and envisions the social worker as a significant assistant along the bigger path.

Works in Progress

The persistent effort to understand and act effectively keeps any final comprehension or best practice elusive. Language that suggests completion or total inclusiveness is absent in postmodern applications to social work. Rather than being a point of frustration, this keeps the effort going to do better. In support of this ever-evolving notion, Brand (1994) describes this process in terms of building construction:

The point is to make adjustments to a building in a way that is always future-responsible—open to the emerging whole, hastening a richly mature intricacy. The process embraces error; it is eager to find things that don't work and to try things that might not work. By failing small, early, and often, it can succeed long and large. And it turns occupants into active learners and shapers rather than passive victims…. A successful building has to be periodically challenged and refreshed, or it will turn into a beautiful corpse. The scaffolding was never taken completely down around Europe's medieval cathedrals because that would imply that they were finished and perfect, and that would be an insult to God. (p. 209)

Person in Context

The "performance" of a client is intimately connected to all efforts to help. Just as the performance of a quarterback on a football team is entwined with the performance of all of his on-the-field teammates, and a student's performance in a course is connected to the instructor, the materials, and his/her classmates, a client (or protagonist)'s performance cannot be understood outside of those who interact with him/her, including the helpers (inclusive of social workers).

Languaging

Client Labeling

The whole notion of calling those persons who social workers work with *clients* falls under the scrutiny of postmodernism, which wonders how that label inscribes those persons in ways that may freeze them into behavior patterns and reputations that are limiting.

According to Powell and Geoghegan (2005), "for postmodern social work the challenge is to break out of the mould of clientisation and discover a more inclusive practice based upon civic engagement, in which clients are reconstituted as citizens—civic social work" (p. 130). The medicalization of clients has tended to lower expectations, relegating clients to sick persons from whom little can be realistically expected other than cooperation with the treatments presented to them by experts.

Asking Generative Questions

Social workers use questions to gather much of the information they need in order to develop ways to be most helpful. There are various types of questions—for example, questions that gather facts or data and questions that stimulate reflective or new thinking. Both types are important but they serve quite different purposes. In postmodern social work, the questions that generate new insights or understandings have the ability to serve both functions, to gather information or knowledge and to stimulate the client and the social worker to imagine new understandings (Dean & Rhodes, 1998).

Story Rather Than Case

Seeing clients and their lives as "unfolding novels" or stories allows the worker to actively appreciate their lives and futures. The case metaphor tends to separate the social worker from the client and helps him or her to see the client as an illustration of a problematic situation or illness. Instead, seeing the client as the protagonist in an evolving story with other actors, with movement from earlier "chapters" in his or her life, and seeing the present moment as a step in the development of the subsequent chapters provides the social worker with another metaphorical understanding that avoids writing in a case genre that might be termed a *literature of despair*.

Postmodern Social Work Practices

The following examples represent some ways that postmodernist ideas can be seen within social work practices. Some of these illustrations may seem ordinary and some may seem radical. The ideas now being grouped under the label *postmodern* have been influential in social work for many years, but not necessarily described in this way. The following examples illustrate the possibilities when the boundaries of previously discrete ideas or practices are blurred or bridged. The process of looking for similarities or commonalities rather than differences opens up the possibilities of new practices to address social work issues or dilemmas.

Macro Micro

A longstanding tradition in social work and social work education dividing social work practices into *macro* or *micro* (in other words, emphasizing a distinction between working on a large level versus working on an individual or smaller level) has limited social work practice as much as it has facilitated it. This commonsensical distinction has reached a level of acceptance such that it is largely invisible; few even question it.

Such an established assumed position seems ripe for reconsideration or deconstruction—to examine it for what opportunities are opened as well as for what it renders invisible or "undoable." (The macro micro notion is not being singled out here unfairly; any distinction in the world opens some doors and simultaneously closes others. Focusing attention in one direction precludes attentions in other directions.)

Just Therapy

The Just Therapy Team from New Zealand has developed the Family Therapy Centre in Wellington. They understand frontline practice as simultaneously operative at the largest macro levels. While there are differing job definitions, all activities of the Centre are embedded in all levels of agency practice (direct assistance, policy development, research, information dissemination):

> …we are as committed to the preventive work through community development projects, the research, and advocacy, as we are to the casework. We no longer address the symptoms of poverty and racism, for example, while ignoring the causes. We have developed a congruence between our casework and the rest of our work at the Centre. Each informs the other. (Waldegrave, 2000, p. 161)

The Just Therapy team has conceptualized their work as occurring on all levels simultaneously—the frontline casework is connected to their advocacy efforts on behalf of their clients, their research stems from the data they gather by working with clients in their therapeutic and educational programs, and their administrative structure and processes are informed by the same principles of cultural and gender fairness that inform their programs for clients. This congruence of practices at all levels creates a Centre that simultaneously addresses poverty and marginalization on all levels in which it appears.

Families as Subsystems

Family therapy provides a way of conceptualizing individual behavior as contextual to family dynamics, derivative of interpersonal family relationships. This was a major contribution to understanding human behavior in ways that are not limited to individual characterological qualities. Rather than seeing individuals as rather freestanding entities who occasionally are impacted by outside forces, the individual is understood as a subsystem within a family. This was a major shift in understanding individual behaviors (Becvar & Becvar, 2008).

In a similar fashion, families could be understood as subsystems of larger systems. Families would not be understood as relatively freestanding entities in the world, but rather, active interactants in larger configurations of people. This nesting of persons within relationships at many different levels does not mean to suggest an orderly well-defined and predictable set of relationships. This is not a mechanical or even organic metaphor. Rather, it is an appreciative and linguistic view that provides space for relationships to ebb and flow in ways specific to those interactions. Predictability is not available. In place of predictability, we insert a sort of poised attentiveness (Shotter, 2008). Instead of planning for future events, we develop a readiness to respond to situations as they present themselves.

Nonviolence Resistance in Family Therapy

I have been working on an idea that large social problems (e.g., violence) can be impacted by the collective influence of practitioners who do their jobs in ways that deliberately and specifically contravene those problematic behaviors. This is built upon the grassroots belief that the cumulative effect of individual actors can affect large social forces. These grassroots efforts gather energy and momentum to stimulate change and, perhaps even more importantly, stimulate individuals' and groups' senses of self-agency. It is this belief that one can impact the world in significant ways that may possess the more lasting and durable effects.

In my work as a family therapist, I work often with families in which domination and violence are pronounced themes. This may emanate from the parents and/or the children, and their strategies to improve their lives may revolve tightly around this notion. Often they see no remedies to their problems other than to (a) become tougher, (b) become softer, or (c) vacillate between the two. This overarching metaphor takes the shape of dominate or be dominated, control or be controlled, use violence or be a victim.

If the therapist accepts this framing of the issue, he/she may be inadvertently reinscribing this metaphor. If a family therapist in this situation chose to build his/her work around another metaphor, perhaps this might in a small way weaken the hold of this guiding metaphor on us as a society. If violence insinuates itself in our lives in a myriad of small and omnipresent ways, perhaps its undoing might be similarly achieved—by small and incessant acts of resistance.

The alternative metaphor I am using to further these aims is the metaphor of nonviolent resistance, à la Mahatma Gandhi and Martin Luther King, Jr. I am using strategies borrowed from the nonviolent resistance movements historically and worldwide to help families resolve their conflicts. The work of Haim Omer (2004) has stimulated my thinking in this direction. Finding ways for families to resolve their problems without using "power-over" tactics may help families remove violence from their home lives and, if it is successful, may expand the resistance to violence more broadly throughout their lives.

This idea is a formative one, not one that seeks to deny the pernicious effects of real and present violence in the lives of families. Social work practitioners ethically and responsibly attend to issues of safety and security of their clients. But efforts to produce safety do not address the circular nature of violence in our world, the ready dedication to use violent means in response to violent means. If we were able to curtail the amount of violent responses in our intimate relationships, I believe we might be able to intrude on the all-too-automatic tendencies to reinscribe violent behavior in our everyday lives.

Women Helping Women

Another developing project challenging conventional therapeutic discourses is one where mothers and daughters in violent disagreement with one another are invited to speak not as mother and daughter, but rather as one woman to another (admittedly one is older than the other, but the framing of their conversation is as two women speaking) (Wulff & St. George, 2009). The aim is to fracture the well-worn generational argument format that locks mothers and daughters into conversational patterns that are hierarchical and often ineffective. While this style of speaking is at significant variance with traditional expectations of family therapy, it offers the possibility of fresh dialogue.

These types of conversations are instigated by questions like the following:

- "What aspects of how you understand what it means to be a woman do you see your daughter accepting? Which ones does she seem to reject?"
- "How does your belief about what it means to be a woman help you to be true to the kind of mother you most want to be, regardless of what your daughter says or does?"
- "How does your belief about what it takes to be a woman in today's world help you to act as a woman who is supporting a young woman?"

These conversation starters invite a mother to engage with her daughter in types of dialogue that offer the possibility of outcomes other than arguing. They deemphasize the hierarchical nature of family life and present a more collaborative alternative that may be more generative than the customary parent–child discourse of "power-over and defend."

Research + Practice

Another distinction that social work and social work education has maintained has been the areas of research and of practice. This distinction has assigned research to a more detached position within social work practice than needs to be the case. Students in social work programs often fear or resent research classes as being painful and irrelevant to their desires to help people. It may be seen as a necessary evil to survive in one's curriculum. But a closer look at the two initiatives can reveal many similarities that lead one to wonder why they have been split in two (Table 23.1).

Based on this chart, the processes of conducting research or practice are remarkably similar. The language used to describe each vary somewhat, but not substantively (Wulff, 2008). Each process involves critical thinking and leads to an outcome. In research, it is common to produce some new or verified knowledge and to disseminate it. In practice, a behavioral change is the usual goal. But they each identify a focus, do something to study it, and then distribute the knowledge or attempt to produce a behavior change.

Clarke (2005) makes the comparability of research and practice explicit: "How can we develop data-gathering strategies that will enable us analytically to better get at silences, at tacit knowledges and practices, at sites of the heretofore inchoate?" (p. 75)

The enterprise of getting at tacit knowledges and practices is shared by both researchers and practitioners. Once again, Clarke: "the major means of avoiding the present as 'a necessary outcome' is problematizing how we have arrived

Table 23-1. Comparison of the Steps of Research and Practice

Research	Practice
Research question	Practice concern/problem
Literature review	Collect information/history
Develop a hypothesis	Write an assessment
Design a study	Write a treatment plan
Collect data	Carry out the plan
Analysis	Evaluate the effectiveness of the plan
Publish the results	Write up the results in a report or in case notes

at the present moment, seeking out those elements that each and all had to be in place for this present to 'happen,' and 'how things could have been otherwise.'" (p. 263)

Conclusion

Social workers have always practiced in ways that we might now label as *postmodern*. Understanding the premises underlying these postmodern practices can sensitize us to how we might make best use of them in current practices and in the envisioning of new ones. The abstract debates about modernist/postmodernist ideas can reveal new areas to explore, but they are not necessary for social workers who are positioned on the frontlines of social work. Postmodern ideas are ready, willing, and able to press our practices into new places of possibility.

"The survival of social work in postmodern society is about a search for new paradigms, designed to empower the socially excluded, in a discursive shift that reconstructs practice as civic engagement and the client as citizen" (Powell & Geoghegan, 2005, p. 141). Postmodern social work reminds us of our mission to improve the lives of those who are poor, shunned, and disenfranchised by continuously looking for more effective ways to reach that goal, leaving no stone unturned.

References

Aitkin, L. P. (1990). The cultural basis for Indian medicine. In L. P. Aitkin & E. W. Haller (Eds.), *Two cultures meet: Pathways for American Indians to medicine* (pp. 15–40). Garrett Park, MD: Garrett Park Press.

Andersen, H. C. (n.d.). *The emperor's new suit.* Retrieved on November 21, 2009, from http://hca.gilead.org.il/emperor.html (Original 1837)

Becvar, D. S., & Becvar, R. J. (2008). *Family therapy: A systemic integration* (7th ed.). New York, NY: Allen & Bacon.

Berry, F. (2006, June). *Role of ideology in modern art versus postmodern art.* Retrieved November 26, 2009, from http://www.postmodern-art.com/

Bohm, D. (1996). *On dialogue.* London, UK: Routledge.

Brand, S. (1994). *How buildings learn: What happens after they're built.* New York: Viking Penguin.

Chambon, A. S., & Irving, A. (1994). (Eds.). *Essays on postmodernism and social work.* Toronto, Canada: Canadian Scholars' Press.

Clarke, A. E. (2005). *Situational analysis: Grounded theory after the postmodern turn.* Thousand Oaks, CA: Sage.

Dean, R. G., & Rhodes, M. L. (1998). Social constructionism and ethics: What makes a "better" story? *Families in Society, 79*(3), 254–262.

Esteva, G., & Prakash, M. S. (1998). *Grassroots postmodernism: Remaking the soil of cultures.* London, UK: Zed Books.

Gergen, K. J. (2009). *An invitation to social construction* (2nd ed.). Los Angeles, CA: Sage.

Gorman, J. (1993). Postmodernism and the conduct of inquiry in social work. *Affilia, 8*(3), 247–264.

Hart, M. (2001). An Aboriginal approach to social work practice. In T. Heinonen & L. Spearman (Eds.), *Social work practice: Problem solving and beyond* (pp. 231–256). Toronto, Canada: Irwin.

Ife, J. (1997). *Rethinking social work: Towards critical practice.* Melbourne, Australia: Longman.

Mullaly, B. (1997). *Structural social work: Ideology, theory, and practice* (2nd ed.). New York: Oxford University Press.

Omer, H. (2004). *Nonviolent resistance: A new approach to violent and self-destructive children.* New York: Cambridge University Press.

O'Nan, S. (1999). *A prayer for the dying: A novel.* New York: Henry Holt.

Payne, M. (2005). *Modern social work theory* (3rd ed.). Chicago, IL: Lyceum.

Postmodernism. (n.d.). In *Merriam-Webster's online dictionary* (11th ed.). Retrieved from http://www.merriam-webster.com/dictionary/postmodernism

Powell, F., & Geoghegan, M. (2005). Reclaiming civil society: The future of global social work? *European Journal of Social Work, 8*(2), 129–144.

Schön, D. A. (1983). *The reflective practitioner: How professionals think in action.* New York: Basic Books.

Shotter, J. (2008). *Conversational realities revisited: Life, language, body and world.* Chagrin Falls, OH: Taos Institute.

Waldegrave, C. (2000). "Just Therapy" with families and communities. In G. Burford & J. Hudson (Eds.), *Family group conferencing: New directions in community-centered child & family practice* (pp. 153–163). New York: Aldine de Gruyter.

White, M. (2003). Narrative practice and community assignments. *International Journal of Narrative Therapy and Community Work, 2,* 17–55.

Witcombe, C. (1997). *Art & artists: Modernism and postmodernism.* Retrieved November 26, 2009, from http://www.arthistory.sbc.edu/artartists/modpostmod.html

Witkin, S. L., & Saleebey, D. (Eds.). (2007). *Social work dialogues: Transforming the canon in inquiry, practice, and education*. Alexandria, VA: Council on Social Work Education.

Wulff, D. (2008, November). "Research/Therapy": A review of Adele Clarke's *Situational Analysis: Grounded Theory after the Postmodern Turn. The Weekly Qualitative Report,* 1(6), 31–34. Retrieved on December 3, 2009, from http://www.nova.edu/ssss/QR/WQR/clarke.pdf

Wulff, D., & St. George, S. (2009). *Family therapy with a larger aim.* Manuscript submitted for publication.

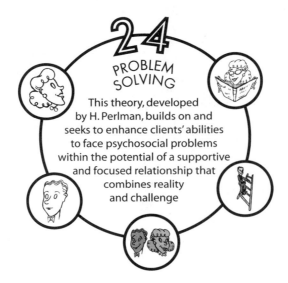

PROBLEM SOLVING

This theory, developed by H. Perlman, builds on and seeks to enhance clients' abilities to face psychosocial problems within the potential of a supportive and focused relationship that combines reality and challenge

Problem Solving and Social Work

Michael L. Shier

Overview

Perlman's (1957) problem-solving method was a critical and timely alternative for understanding the help-seeking process. Her foundational points—person, problem, place, and process—together provide a holistic model or framework for understanding social work practice in general. While this seminal work to problem solving within social work practice is instrumental in understanding present methods of client/worker interaction, it does not say enough about treatment beyond a general application of psychosocial methods of intervention with a moderate focus on educating and improving the coping capabilities of clients to the problems that develop within life. In recent years, problem solving has been little explored in relation to therapeutic intervention and prevention within

the social work profession or other more general approaches to practice, such as community-based work. The alternative has been increasing focus on the strengths and solution-focused approaches; fundamental to both, though, is problem solving.

Social science and social work have both contributed a growing body of literature recently on the therapeutic aspects of problem solving. Foundational points similar to Perlman's person and process appear in many of these discussions. Such work might have significant impact on social work practice with clients who need therapeutic intervention and could help clarify generalist practice for new social workers. Here the premises of problem solving within the counseling psychology literature are discussed, particularly those points related to problem orientation, as they apply to social work practice and education, to examine how these two streams of literature intersect.

Problem Solving

Within clinical psychology literature, solving problems that occur in day-to-day living has been referred to as "social problem solving" (D'Zurilla & Nezu, 1982). The concept of social problem solving, like the problem-solving process in social work, was a critical development in the literature. Until the 1960s, problem solving was investigated only in relation to the physical and physiological aspects of the problem-solving act, and, as a result, was an area of investigation primarily for the discipline of neuropsychology. Some writers began to ask what purpose problem solving had for human functioning. From that question developed a trajectory of research that investigated the implications of problem solving for psychological and social functioning.

The term "social problem solving" highlights the social context of problem solving. Many writers of problem-solving methods of interaction and intervention have stressed the importance of the social environment on human problems (D'Zurilla & Goldfried, 1971; Haley, 1987; Perlman, 1957). The social context refers to the place where the real-life problems take place and considers the impact of factors within the social realm (i.e., beyond the individual) on these problems. Nezu, Nezu, and Perri (1989) have defined social problem solving as "the process by which people both understand and react to problems in living" (p. 27).

The process of problem solving involves both cognitive and behavioral aspects. D'Zurilla and Nezu (2007) suggest three aspects in particular. The first is the metacognitive level, where a particular orientation to problems (the cognitive-emotional responses a person has when faced with a particular problem or problems in general) exists, which they refer to as the motivating function. The second level is the performance level, where there is a set of problem-solving skills. Underlying this performance level is the third level, which comprises the cognitive abilities that determine an individual's capability to solve any given problem.

In this framework, a solution to a problem is any coping response a person has to alter the problematic experience (D'Zurilla, 1986; Nezu, 1987). Such a response may be positive or negative; that is, it may or may not create the desired change or outcome. Thus, as noted in earlier work of D'Zurilla and Goldfried (1971), an effective problem-solving intervention must consider the adequacy and effectiveness of people in resolving problems. Problem solving is considered an important aspect of social competence (D'Zurilla, 1986), and it calls for the establishment of specific problem-solving skills. A process for effective problem solving, known as problem-solving therapy, has been developed by clinical psychologists over the past several decades. Problem-solving therapy includes (1) problem orientation (how people perceive problems); (2) problem definition and formulation (clarifying and understanding the specific nature of the problem); (3) generation of alternatives (identifying as many solutions as possible); (4) decision making (evaluating the available solutions); and (5) solution implementation and verification (self-monitoring and evaluation of outcome), along with specific abilities required of a person to solve problems (D'Zurilla, 1986; D'Zurilla & Goldfried, 1971; D'Zurilla & Nezu, 1982, 1999, 2007). Problem orientation is the motivational component, which refers directly to people's perception of problems in general and their own ability to find an effective solution to a specific problem, while points 2 through 5 refer to the specific skills that a person needs to be taught to solve a problem effectively (Nezu, Nezu, & Perri, 1989).

When taken together, the skills necessary to help solve problems resemble the process of problem solving identified by Perlman (1957) and others. For example, Compton and Galaway (1994) suggest that "problem solving is a rational process including actions to define the problem, actions to collect information on which to base decisions, actions to engage the client in goal setting and decision making, actions to produce change, and actions to produce progress" (p. 10). A difference between the two streams of literature, however, is the emphasis placed on the problem orientation of the client and its subsequent implications for the process of problem solving.

Problem-Solving Theory in Social Work

The problem-solving process in social work theory was founded on principles associated with functionalist theory. According to Perlman (1986), the process assumes, as the functionalist theorists argued, (1) that clients seek help at a point when they are in crisis (or facing a particular problem that they are unable to resolve on their own with their present abilities), (2) that the agency in which a client seeks services can affect both the help-seeking process and the client's problem itself, (3) that the impact of the relationship between the social worker and client needs to be considered in order to help with the problems being presented, (4) that the length of time of the therapeutic process impacts outcomes with clients (i.e., the therapeutic process must have a beginning, middle, and end), and (5) that it is often possible to break down a problem into manageable parts (partialization). Together with Perlman's years of experience in social casework, these principles formed the basis of her problem-solving process.

As a caseworker, Perlman began to recognize that the process itself was primarily about the social caseworker helping individual clients to cope more effectively with their problems. This realization contrasted with the primary focus of social work education at the time, which was diagnostic and treatment. In her initial work on the subject, Perlman (1957) described social casework as follows: "A person with a problem comes to a place where a professional representative helps him [or her] by a given process" (p. 4). In other words, a person who experiences some challenges or barriers in personal functioning (whether individually or socially based) seeks help from a professional who works in an agency that specializes in a particular type of help. While at this place, the person forms a helping relationship with the professional, who then helps the person to develop coping responses to the problems he or she is facing. Compton and Galaway (1994) describe this problem-solving process as the underlying framework for generalist social work practice. They also argue that the problem-solving process itself is not a method of treatment; instead, the method of treatment is to be determined on the basis of client goals and presenting problems while engaged in this process. As a result of this distinction, emphasis within the social work literature has been placed primarily on highlighting the *process* of problem solving.

Following Perlman (1957), others have attempted to define the stages or steps of problem solving in social work (Compton & Galaway, 1994; Sheafor, Horejsi, & Horejsi, 1988). Perlman (1957) initially postulated three primary components of the problem-solving process: collecting information about the problem, explaining the problem and setting a particular goal, and implementing a plan of action to resolve the problem. The relationship between the therapist and the client was the defining feature that made this process significantly different from the process of diagnosis (Woehle, 1994). Compton and Galaway (1994) similarly describe a contact phase, a contract phase, and an action phase. Likewise, Turner and Jaco (1996) in the fourth edition of this chapter provided a succinct overview of these phases. For each phase, Compton and Galway (1994) suggest how social workers can proceed with clients and monitor their own reflection and desires in the helping process. This process includes an assessment of the client's motivation, capacities, and opportunities to work through the problem (Compton & Galloway, 1994; Perlman, 1986). Compton and Galaway (1994) describe motivation as the level of hope or discomfort with achieving the desired goal (i.e., the solution to the problem); capacity as the skills and knowledge needed to work on the problem; and opportunity as the resources and supports required to engage in the problem-solving process.

These steps and stages are important and have already been largely incorporated into generalist social work practice and the values and ethics of the profession (Heinonen & Spearman, 2006; Turner & Jaco, 1996). However, this framework does not provide enough empirical evidence on why solving problems is important, how some people can solve problems effectively and others cannot, what the long-term psychosocial implications are for people to be able to effectively solve problems, and how coping capabilities differ for each person. Also, this literature focuses primarily on the process of problem solving and the stages to move through to resolve a particular problem (or set of problems). Instead, if we were using problem solving as an intervention in practice, greater emphasis would likely be placed on the motivational aspects that both Perlman (1957) and Compton and Galaway (1994) describe as instrumental in the assessment phase. While these authors view motivation in terms of hope or discomfort about solving the problem, in most cases motivation is more complicated. It might include the social environment or cultural, psychological, and emotional factors, as shown in the counseling psychology literature on problem-solving therapy. In particular, the description of problem orientation in problem-solving therapy suggests an alternative understanding of motivation.

Problem-Solving Therapy

Various forms of problem-solving therapy have emerged over the years, but D'Zurilla and Goldfried (1971) are generally credited with creating this method of therapeutic intervention. Problem-solving therapy was developed from the recent tradition within psychosocial intervention scholarship that focuses on teaching clients a particular skill set (D'Zurilla & Goldfried, 1971)—specifically, teaching clients a process for solving the problems that they experience. Within this therapeutic orientation are assumptions about problems themselves and the implications of solving problems for psychological, emotional, and physical well-being (Nezu, 2004). The primary focus of this approach is to improve individual-specific "coping" with problematic life situations. Like most psychosocial interventions, it attempts to achieve outcomes by teaching individuals different ways of responding to their problems that will improve their psychological and social functioning and overall well-being (D'Zurilla & Nezu, 2007).

Recent research has evaluated this approach and applied it in multiple settings with a variety of demographic subpopulations (Arean et al., 2008; Barrett et al., 1999; Bender, Springer, & Kim, 2006; Catalan et al., 1991; Chen, Jordan, & Thompson, 2006; Gellis et al., 2008; Hegel, Barrett, & Oxman, 2000; Hegel, Dietrich, Seville, & Jordan, 2004; Rath et al., 2003; Slonim-Nevo & Vosler, 1991; Sternberg & Bry, 1994). Most of this literature finds problem-solving therapy to

be an effective method of clinical intervention, although the long-term implications of the intervention have yet to be determined. It is likely that the same factors that affect psychotherapies in general—voluntariness of the client, the issues or problems being presented, the individual or group therapeutic context, the duration of treatment, and the assignment of homework—also affect the outcome of problem-solving therapy (Malouff et al., 2007). It is important to recognize also that I used the word "intervention" because problem-solving therapy in theory could also help to prevent problems or side effects of poor coping skills. However, further research is needed to explore the preventive potential of this method.

A fundamental distinction between problem-solving therapy and a process of problem-solving needs to be recognized. While many treatment methods might focus on solving a particular problem, problem-solving therapy attempts to teach people how to solve problems in general. Compared to other treatment methods, it may be less concerned with solving a specific presenting problem (D'Zurilla & Nezu, 2007). Scholars of problem-solving therapy have not yet determined which elements of the intervention are shared with other therapeutic types and which aspects are unique. The absence of these comparisons limits our ability to determine whether problem-solving therapy leads to solving more real-life problems over time, which is one of the primary intentions of the intervention (Mynors-Wallis, 2002).

Problem-Solving Therapy and Social Work

Within social work education, problem solving is taught in relation to generalist social work more as a theoretical framework of practice and less as the foundation of a specific therapeutic intervention. While problem solving has historical roots in social work, this intervention style has not been explored enough within clinical social work settings. In fact, applying problem-solving therapy to the practice of social work may seem problematic—especially in relation to other theoretical paradigms of social work, such as structural social work theory or even person-in-environment theory. Social workers who work from other theoretical models might not support the wholehearted focus of problem-solving therapy on an individual's present coping abilities, given the types of problems that develop in their clients' lives. Such a therapeutic approach would likely need to be tailored to social work ethics and practice guidelines and social work theoretical principles of working with clients.

However, the focus on problem orientation within problem-solving therapy has useful implications for social work practice and our present discipline-specific understanding of problem-solving theory. Problem orientation describes how people perceive or evaluate social problems and their own ability to cope with the problems that develop (Nezu, 2004). The other aspect of problem-solving therapy, problem-solving style, refers to those cognitive behavioral activities that people engage in to solve their problems. Thus Perlman's (1957) approach, an example of problem-solving style, does not fully take into account the fact that problem orientation will have a direct impact on problem solving. Problem orientation is about changing one's perception of the problem, while problem-solving style is about solving the problem (with or without the intended outcome). This latter aspect has been more closely aligned with social work practice. Incorporating the problem orientation principles from counseling psychology might usefully expand our understanding of problem solving in social work to include its role as a specific intervention within practice, rather than a structured process that defines practice in general.

Indeed, social work practitioners are engaged with clients in a way that seeks to link clients' personal experiences with their social environment. How we interact, as individuals, with our social environment, or how our lives are shaped by the social milieu that surrounds us, is of great importance for social work. As we all know, social problems such as poverty or oppression have a negative impact on people and their overall functioning. Incorporating a problem-solving intervention approach might help people to realize the implications of their social environment for their present situation and individual problems, such as homelessness or substance abuse. People who realize that certain interactions with the social realm have resulted in or maintained their present problems might be able to challenge

future negative interactions and resolve an issue before it creates further problems. Recent research on labor market attachment supports this point. While people may recognize that barriers within their social environment are affecting their employment status, they associate these issues with their own unemployment experiences only minimally, in many cases identifying things that they need to change within themselves to solve their problems (Graham, Jones, & Shier, 2010; Shier, Graham, & Jones, 2009). It would seem that these people have negative problem orientations that have likely contributed to maintaining a cyclical pattern of underemployment or unemployment.

At present, problem-solving therapy focuses primarily on the individual and his or her capabilities to cope with life problems. Social work could add a further layer—a stage where people recognize that some of their problems are socially rooted or have a social environment component. This recognition might also contribute to the preventive component of the problem-solving therapy intervention.

By recognizing as we interact with clients that their problem orientation affects their present situation, we can expand our understanding of the problem-solving process. Building on the contributions of Perlman and cognitive behavioral psychologists, we can use the idea of problem orientation to provide a more structured approach within teaching generalist social work practice. How people respond to problems would seem to be a useful place to start, rather than just going ahead with the process of solving the problem through a mix of intervention techniques. What is missing in the formulations about problem solving is an understanding of how clients perceive problems and how social workers perceive them, both in practice and in social work education and training programs. Including problem orientation changes the problem-solving approach from a simple procedure for working with clients to a determined and defined method of intervention.

In no way is it being suggested here that practitioners should wholeheartedly take this problem-solving therapy model and apply it to generalist social work practice, but it would be useful to begin to take pieces of it to understand better how people respond to problems and the reasons for seeking help that underlie any specific presenting problem of a client. What this clinical psychology research has shown is that just helping people to develop skills to solve a particular problem is not effective for producing long-term competency in problem solving (Nezu, 2004). When working with people in community-based practice, we offer immediate, short-term relief. This is a problem-solving process, although it is just immediate and reactive to a presenting problem. Addressing the problem orientation of the person first and then working through the process of problem solving (using whichever therapeutic method of intervention is necessary) redirects the thinking of practitioners from the here and now to the long term. It means using a method of interaction that could be preventive and offering a structured process that new graduates of BSW programs can implement when working with clients, especially in settings that are not traditional clinical settings offering counseling therapies. Problem solving as a process of practice has not been redefined in recent years to reflect the changing nature of social work within the many diverse areas and settings of practice that are now available.

Problem Orientation and Social Work Practice

By assessing the later models of the problem-solving process in social work, we find that many people have moved away from understanding the sociological aspects of problem solving, which Perlman was seemingly describing by emphasizing the person, the place, and later the provisions (resources) and the profession (Perlman, 1986). There is too much emphasis on the process and too little training of new practitioners in how to engage effectively with clients through problem solving. For example, the motivational aspects of problem assessment are missing from these models of the problem-solving process. It is within this motivation that we begin to understand how a particular person is adapting to the external environment and how the individual's internal processes are influenced (positively or negatively) by the problems he or she is facing. I have discussed the possible link of problem orientation to a direct clinical setting of practice, but what about other areas of social

work practice? Two examples here are provided that have relevance beyond the clinical setting and suggest alternative methods of interaction within practice when problem orientation is considered within the assessment. Considering problem orientation within the problem-solving process might have an impact on the overall process that is undertaken by the practitioner. The first example is a case of culturally sensitive practice, and the second relates to mezzo social work practice—specifically, that of third-sector (non-profit) organizations—and the related structures and service delivery models.

Applications to Practice

Recent studies (Al-Krenawi & Graham, 2001, 2009; Graham, Brownlee, Shier, & Doucette, 2008) have found that the social work knowledge base needs adaptation to ensure effective practice with groups of differing cultures or in particular geographic or local contexts. Recognizing the problem orientation of the client helps to define intervention that is appropriate for differing cultural groups. It would be reasonable to suppose that a mix of factors (e.g., cultural, social, psychological) must be considered to understand the particular problem orientation of a client and the client's perception of the helping relationship as it relates to this specific problem orientation.

Studies by Graham, Bradshaw, and Trew (2008, 2009) of one distinct cultural group, Muslims living in North America, found that some Muslim-Canadians have different expectations from the helping relationship for resolving their problems—that is, their view differs from what students in general social work education programs are taught to expect. Graham, Bradshaw, and Trew (2009) also found discrepancies between formal social work education and training and the methods of practice adapted for assessment and clinical intervention with some Muslim-Canadian clients, as well as challenges to professional boundaries and termination of treatment.

An expanded understanding of the problem-solving process that includes problem orientation could offer a solution to these discrepancies in practice. The way these particular clients perceive the helping relationship and their expectations of specific solutions to issues and more direct approaches to intervention when receiving services are a direct result of their problem orientation. Culture clearly plays a role in developing problem orientation, not only in this group but in any distinct group.

Failure to recognize a client's problem orientation affects the practitioner's responses to that person, and in the case of a distinct group, has direct implications for effective, culturally appropriate social work practice. In other cases, not recognizing the particular problem orientation of clients might act to maintain cyclical patterns of help-seeking. For example, if clients have a negative perception of problems and their own ability to solve them, they may be able to resolve the current presenting problem but will not develop the necessary perspective to solve future problems.

Until now, I have discussed the implications of including problem orientation at the micro level of practice. The next example considers how problem orientation affects practice at the mezzo level, specifically in third-sector (non-profit) organizations. In the present political and economic climate, a process of social welfare retrenchment and decreasing resources for social service provision at the macro level is affecting such organizations (Chappell, 2006), limiting their overall ability to function and meet their service mandate. The solution (or specific coping response) to this problematic situation has been identified as seeking philanthropic donations for services and volunteers to run programs—as is characteristic in a neoliberal ideology of social welfare development (Anheier, 2005; Hasenfeld, 2000; Powell, 2007).

If they followed the traditional problem-solving process, these organizations would likely focus primarily on the problem (the lack of resources) and seek to develop the skills needed to relieve the problem (although these actions do not necessarily make things better). For example, some organizations may choose to undertake social justice campaigns, seek opposition political-party support, contact private foundations for monetary support, or quietly make cuts to their present programming structure. The alternative approach of focusing first on problem orientation helps these organizations to recognize that they have a negative problem orientation, which is probably a direct result of their interactions with the social environment. At the root of this negative problem orientation is the fact that many organizations see themselves as an outlier in relationships with government and the private sector. This perception changes their view of the problem of social welfare cutbacks, their role within the system of social welfare provision, and, more importantly, possible solutions. In this instance, focusing first on problem orientation would allow the organization to consider its positive role in the present situation of social welfare provision, as well as alternative ways to relieve the immediate problems. These solutions might be more aligned with forming collaborative relationships (Graham & Barter, 1999) with similar organizations and with government sectors, or might include activities such as research, practice evaluations, and local community forums to discuss service delivery. Both negative and positive problem orientations may lead an organization to act in direct response to changes in its social environment in order to maintain services and meet intended goals. However, the responses or solutions to those problems are likely to differ depending on whether the problem orientation is positive or negative.

Problem Orientation and Social Work Education

Incorporating the concept of problem orientation into the problem-solving theory of Perlman (1957) and later writers has direct implications for social work education, and in particular for training generalist social work practitioners in undergraduate programs. Recognizing the problem orientation of the client could allow us to create a revised model of problem solving within social work that practitioners could apply in their direct work with clients. Further investigation of how practitioners could assess a client's problem orientation would be needed.

Problem orientation can also usefully inform discussions about social action and social justice. How people make the link (as suggested in structural social work theory) between their personal problems and the inequalities that exist within the wider social realm has not been explored within the literature. Practitioners could help clients make these links by incorporating problem orientation into the intervention process, first by illustrating how the social environment affects their present situation and then by helping clients to achieve the change that is desired.

Teaching people how to take part in social action could also be considered an exercise in teaching problem orientation. The way people respond to a particular social issue that affects their lives (whether directly or indirectly) and the way they view their ability to solve structurally based problems or participate in social action are direct considerations of problem orientation. As a result, teaching social work students about social action and social justice, focusing specifically on how they can create change or contribute to rectifying the many structural inequalities within society, might be useful in developing positive problem orientations.

Considering problem orientation can also help improve practitioners' understanding of the effectiveness of problem-solving skills within practice. The process outlined by Perlman and others taught clients to identify a problem, articulate their goals, create a plan of action, and follow through on that plan in order to develop their problem-solving skills. Perlman (1986) highlighted the assumption that if people are taught how to solve one problem, they will apply the skills to other settings as well. However, the research on this subject is inconsistent and inconclusive. Some people may not be able to maintain their problem-solving skills for more than a limited time after treatment. If the practitioner does not recognize the problem orientation of the client, developing and applying these skills may not help the client to achieve the desired outcome, especially if the client's problem orientation is negative.

Conclusion

In the previous edition of this book, Turner and Jaco (1996) concluded that there was a need for more empirical research on how the problem-solving method could be applied in a more precise manner for social workers to incorporate in their clinical work with clients. This latest edition began the discussion from where they left off. Problem solving is an underlying aspect of social work practice, but it has received less attention in recent years as a foundational concept—or even assumption—of contemporary social work practice. Why do social workers spend so much time solving problems? While Perlman explained why a problem-solving process might be useful in social casework, her reasoning was largely premised on her own experiences in working effectively with clients through direct practice. While this form of knowledge transfer (from the practice realm to the academic community) is commendable, the problem-solving process has not been the subject of extensive empirical inquiry and analysis in recent years. Here we have examined problem solving in two contemporary social work contexts, communities that include diverse cultural groups and third-sector organizations. The interdisciplinary nature of human problem solving allows us to learn from another helping profession—clinical psychology—to reevaluate our own practice in problem solving. The essential difference is to include problem orientation in our assessment.

I wish I could provide for the reader a client/ social worker case example outlining a process of intervention where problem orientation is assessed. Unfortunately the literature is at a bit of a crossroads with regard to problem-solving theory, and there is less certainty about the future of this method of intervention. Problem solving, though, acts as a theoretical foundation to the social work profession, and therefore this crossroads gives opportunity for practitioners, educators, and students to think about how problem solving intersects with their work and to explore this concept of problem orientation within the multiple domains and mix of methods of intervention of our practice.

This leads to a final point. A topic missing from this discussion that warrants future investigation is how to work with clients who have negative problem orientations. For example, we might ask: What practices were useful in helping clients to establish more positive problem orientations? Is problem orientation improved with increases in self-esteem or recognition of personal experiences in solving problems, or are there other factors to consider? The focus on problem orientation is important to producing longer-term solutions for clients, groups, or communities, but we are left with limited answers about how to engage with them in a way that helps develop our capabilities as practitioners faced with challenging negative problem orientations.

References

Al-Krenawi, A., & Graham, J.R. (2001). The cultural mediator: Bridging the gap between a non-Western community and professional social work practice. *British Journal of Social Work,* 31(4), 665–686.

Al-Krenawi, A., & Graham, J. R. (2009). *Helping professional practice with indigenous peoples: The Bedouin-Arab case.* Lanham, MD: University Press of America.

Anheier, H. K. (2005). *Nonprofit organizations: Theory, management, and policy.* New York: Routledge.

Arean, P., Hegel, M., Vannoy, S., Fan, M. Y., & Unutzer, J. (2008). Effectiveness of problem solving therapy for older, primary care patients with depression: Results from the IMPACT project. *The Gerontologist,* 48(3), 311–323.

Barrett, J. B., Williams, J. W., Oxman, T. E., Katon, W., Frank, E., Hegel, M. T., Sullivan, M., & Schulberg, H. C. (1999). The Treatment Effectiveness Project: A comparison of paroxetine, problem-solving therapy, and placebo in the treatment of minor depression and dysthymia in primary care patients. *General Hospital Psychiatry,* 21, 260–273.

Bender, L., Springer, D. W., & Kim, J. S. (2006). Treatment effectiveness with dually diagnosed adolescents: A systematic review. *Brief Treatment and Crisis Intervention,* 6(3), 177–205.

Catalan, J., Gath, D. H., Anastasiades, P., Bond, S. A. K., Day, A., & Hall, L. (1991). Evaluation of a brief psychological treatment for emotional disorders in primary care. *Psychological Medicine,* 21, 1013–1018.

Chappell, R. (2006). *Social welfare in Canadian society* (3rd ed.). Toronto: Nelson-Thomson.

Chen, S. Y., Jordan, C., & Thompson, S. (2006). The effect of cognitive behavioral therapy (CBT) on depression: The role of problem-solving appraisal. *Research on Social Work Practice,* 16(5), 500–510.

Compton, B. R., & Galaway, B. (1994). *Social work processes* (5th ed.). Pacific Grove, CA: Brooks/Cole Publishing.

D'Zurilla, T. J. (1986). *Problem solving therapy: A social competence approach to clinical intervention.* New York: Springer Publishing Company.

D'Zurilla, T. J., & Goldfried, M. R. (1971). Problem solving and behavior modification. *Journal of Abnormal Psychology,* 78(1), 107–126.

D'Zurilla, T. J., & Nezu, A. M. (2007). *Problem solving therapy: A positive approach to clinical intervention* (3rd ed.). New York: Springer Publishing Company.

D'Zurilla, T. J., & Nezu, A. M. (1999). *Problem-solving therapy: A social competence approach to clinical intervention* (2nd ed.). New York: Springer Publishing Company.

D'Zurilla, T. J., & Nezu, A. (1982). Social problem solving in adults. In P. C. Kendall (Ed.), *Advances in cognitive-behavioral research and therapy* (pp. 201–274). New York: Academic Press.

Gellis, Z. D., McGinty, J., Tierney, L., Jordan, C., Burton, J., & Misener, E. (2008). Randomized controlled trial of problem-solving therapy for minor depression in home care. *Research on Social Work Practice,* 18(6), 596–606.

Graham, J. R., & Barter, K. (1999). Collaboration: A social work practice method. *Families in Society: The Journal of Contemporary Human Services,* 80(1), 6–13.

Graham, J. R., Bradshaw, C., & Trew, J. (2008). Social workers' understanding of the Muslim client's perspective. *Journal of Muslim Mental Health,* 3, 125–144.

Graham, J. R., Bradshaw, C., & Trew, J. L. (2009). Adapting social work in working with Muslim clients. *Social Work Education: The International Journal,* 28(5), 544–561.

Graham, J. R., Brownlee, K., Shier, M., & Doucette, E. (2008). Localization of social work knowledge in Canada's geographic norths: An exploratory qualitative analysis of practitioner adaptations to social work knowledge in northern Ontario and Northwest Territories. *Arctic,* 61(4), 399–406.

Graham, J. R., Jones, M. E., & Shier, M. (2010). Tipping Points: What participants found valuable in labour market training programs for vulnerable groups. *International Journal of Social Welfare,* 19(1), 63–72.

Haley, J. (1987). *Problem-solving therapy* (2nd ed.). San Francisco: Jossey-Bass Publishers.

Hasenfeld, Y. (2000). Social welfare administration and organizational theory. In R. Patti (Ed.), *The handbook of social welfare management* (pp. 89–112). Thousand Oaks, CA: Sage Publications.

Hegel, M. T., Barrett, J. E., & Oxman, T. E. (2000). Training therapists in problem-solving treatment of depressive disorders in primary care. *Families, Systems, and Health,* 18(4), 423–435.

Hegel, M. T., Dietrich, A. J., Seville, J. L., & Jordan, C. B. (2004). Training residents in problem-solving treatment of depression: A pilot feasibility and impact study. *Family Medicine,* 36, 204–208.

Heinonen, T., & Spearman, L. (2006). *Social work practice: Problem solving and beyond* (2nd ed.). Toronto: Nelson–Thomson.

Malouf, J. M., Thorsteinsson, E. B., & Schutte, N. S. (2007). The efficacy of problem solving therapy in reducing mental and physical health problems: A meta-analysis. *Clinical Psychology Review,* 27, 46–57.

Mynors-Wallis, L. M. (2002). Does problem-solving treatment work through resolving problems? *Psychological Medicine,* 32, 1315–1319.

Nezu, A. M. (1987). A problem solving formulation of depression: A literature review and proposal of a pluralistic model. *Clinical Psychology Review,* 7, 121–144.

Nezu, A. M. (2004). Problem-solving and behavior therapy revisited. *Behavior Therapy,* 35, 1–33.

Nezu, A. M., Nezu, C. M., & Perri, M. G. (1989). *Problem solving therapy for depression: Theory, research, and clinical guidelines.* New York: John Wiley & Sons.

Perlman, H. H. (1957). *Social casework: A problem-solving process.* Chicago: The University of Chicago Press.

Perlman, H. H. (1986). The problem solving model. In F. J. Turner (Ed.), *Social work treatment: Interlocking theoretical approaches* (3rd ed., pp. 245–266). New York: The Free Press.

Powell, F. P. (2007). *The politics of civil society: Neoliberalism or social left?* Bristol: The Policy Press.

Rath, J. F., Simon, D., Langenbahn, D. M., Sherr, R. L., & Diller, L. (2003). Group treatment of problem-solving deficits in outpatients with traumatic brain injury: A randomized outcome study. *Neuropsychological Rehabilitation,* 13(4), 461–488.

Sheafor, B. W., Horejsi, C. R., & Horejsi, G. A. (1988). *Techniques and guidelines for social work practice.* Boston: Allyn & Bacon.

Shier, M., Graham, J. R., & Jones, M. (2009). Barriers to employment as experienced by disabled people: a qualitative analysis in Calgary and Regina, Canada. *Disability and Society,* 24(1), 63–75.

Slonim-Nevo, V., & Vosler, N. R. (1991). The use of single-system design with systemic brief problem-solving therapy. *Families in Society,* 72, 38–44.

Sternberg, J. A., & Bry, B. H. (1994). Solution generation and family conflict over time in problem-solving therapy with families of adolescents: The impact of therapist behavior. *Child and Family Behavior Therapy,* 16(4), 1–23.

Turner, J., & Jaco, R. M. (1996). Problem-solving theory and social work treatment. In F. J. Turner (ed.), *Social work treatment: Interlocking theoretical approaches* (4th ed., pp. 503–522). New York: The Free Press.

Woehle, R. (1994). Variations on a theme: Implications for the problem-solving model. In B. R. Compton & B. Galaway, *Social work processes* (5th ed., pp. 69–76). Pacific Grove, CA: Brooks/Cole Publishing.

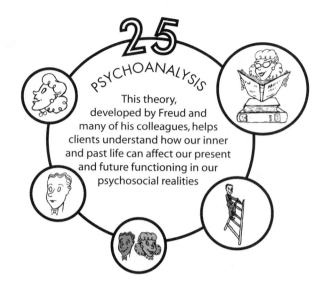

This theory, developed by Freud and many of his colleagues, helps clients understand how our inner and past life can affect our present and future functioning in our psychosocial realities

Psychoanalysis and Social Work: A Practice Partnership

Elizabeth Ann Danto

When we associate social work with the history of psychoanalysis, we may perhaps envision a circle of intellectuals at odds with the reality of human suffering. The following chapter aims to shift this erroneous narrative from psychoanalysis as Sigmund Freud's lone clinical construction, to psychoanalysis as a modernist social welfare ideology, born of *début de siècle* Vienna and bred as a flow of ideas and practices across time and geographies. As psychoanalysis spread, American social workers incorporated these theories or used them as cautionary signposts. Anna Freud, who worked with many of them, said that psychoanalysis was seen after the First World War and in the early 1920s as the embodiment of the spirit of change, the contempt for the convention, freedom of thought and, in the minds of many, the eagerly looked-for prospect of release from sexual restrictions.

A Practice Partnership

Telling the story of psychoanalysis and Sigmund Freud is sure to trigger the same controversy among social workers as it does among all critical thinkers. Yet this particular model of the mind that processes all of human experience from pleasure to trauma has earned a historical place that cannot be ignored. Freud was a gifted writer—relaxed, often funny, sometimes self-deprecating—and he began his career in neurology without the benefit of technology that, one hundred years later, largely confirms his discoveries. Perhaps because of its resonance in Western culture, Freud's work exerts as great an influence today as it did in the early part of the 20th century. Psychoanalysis comes into perspective when set against a backdrop that includes the Enlightenment philosophies of Europe, the

French surrealists, anti-Semitism, monarchy, modernism, fascism, and ultimately democracy. Richard Sterba (1982, p. 81), who wrote lyrically about life in the Vienna Psychoanalytic Society and was just a medical student at the time, evoked the sheer power of these ideas: "The closeness to Freud's work *in statu nascendi*," he said, "gave us the feeling of participating in a major, future-shaping scientific and cultural process." Virtually all the "talk" therapies we use today derive from that same process, whether the client is a whole organization or an individual adult, a child, a family, a group, or a community.

When Sigmund Freud decided to unite the psychoanalysts in 1918, he settled on two principles that have largely disappeared from the story and that are critical to social workers. The first was to standardize all psychoanalytic training programs scattered throughout Europe (though still lacking in America); he would convince the psychoanalysts of the need for a systematic method by appealing to their Enlightenment sensibility and beliefs in social progress. This was the original generation of psychoanalysts—the pioneers of the early 20th century's radically new kind of mental health treatment. The setting was Vienna, a city about to launch a massive social welfare system that included vast housing projects, public health and mental health agencies, early childhood education programs, clean streets, and local gardens. Post-war "Red Vienna," as it has come to be known, produced the social justice core of psychoanalysis.

The second principle was more significant. Freud was puzzled by physicians' class-based approach to psychiatry. In truth, he believed, "the poor man should have just as much right to assistance for his mind as he now has to the life-saving help offered by surgery" (Freud, 1918, p. 167). Freud grew up in a liberal family and, though a Jew, had had access to a humanist education at the University of Vienna. World War I had shown him that many soldiers were affected by "war neurosis" (or shell-shock, a cluster of psychiatric symptoms resembling what we call posttraumatic stress disorder today), but they were relegated to crude and punitive hospitals. Freud thought their treatment was mindless and that, as his colleague Ernst Simmel said, society could not afford to ignore "whatever in a person's experience is too powerful or horrible for his conscious mind to grasp and work through" (Simmel, 1994, p. 7). He felt that this social ignorance had the effect of widening the gap between poor soldiers and those from affluent families. Freud's second principle, then, was that the psychoanalysts should start free community-based clinics, first for the soldiers, then for anyone who was unable—for any reason—to pay for their treatment. Regardless of the level of intervention, the client's unconscious does not have a social class; class is a social arrangement that may resonate with a client's subjectivity, but is no more innate than the clothes we wear. This subjectivity or class consciousness and social justice would become pervasive themes in psychoanalysis.

By the time Freud had crystallized these ideas, two major changes were underway in American psychology and social work. The psychologists had adopted behaviorism and adhered to John B. Watson's definition of their field as "a purely objective experimental branch of natural science. Its theoretical goal is the prediction and control of behavior" (Watson, 1913). Dispensing with the introspective methods that James Jackson Putnam and Morton Prince were introducing to psychology, the behaviorists applied animal research to study the human mind. Meanwhile, professional social work was gaining strength and founding schools in New York, Chicago, and Boston.[1] If 1909 was a watershed year for psychoanalysis, social work saw President Theodore Roosevelt initiate the legislation establishing a Federal Children's Bureau, the first White House Conference on the Care of Dependent Children, and Sigmund Freud lecture on the assessment and treatment of childhood trauma at Clark University.

In this series of landmark lectures, Sigmund Freud repudiated the Victorian era's attempts to disdain psychopathology, refute the effects of trauma on children, repress desire, and ignore sexuality—all in the name of "civilization" (Freud, 1910a/1909). The Clark lectures, later published as a series of modernist essays, outlined the fundamental elements of psychoanalytic theory and technique, and became the foundation of a system for developing psychotherapies that respected human experience and individual disposition. Thus, beyond the theory came Freud's attempt to describe how he would resolve psychological problems that proved well beyond the technical and theoretical capabilities of his predecessors.

Like the professor he was, Freud divided the essence of his findings into five distinct categories. The first, and the least controversial, explained the often unacknowledged distress of people whose depression or anxiety interfered with everyday functioning, and who could simply be treated in the analyst's office or at the clinic. Too few clinicians were able to handle recurring psycho-physiological symptoms (manifestations of conflict between the conscious and the unconscious) without medication or hypnosis, a technique Freud disliked. Later Freud and his colleagues would devise a formula for allocating such outpatient services. For the second lecture, Freud focused on obstructions in child development—the unnerving traumatic effects of family or institutional abuse (often sexual) that had been noted by many others but described in a way that placed the blame on children themselves. This account led to a third category, in which Freud urged his audience to lend meaning to those cryptic wishes (for the return of the dead, for sex with a parent) so distressing to society that we disguise them even in dreams. And with this, he moved into a fourth pillar of psychoanalytic theory, the delicate subject of infantile sexuality. He even broached the idea that we are all born bisexual, and that this undercurrent not only stays with us all our lives regardless of sexual orientation, but also should not be subjected to any moral charge. "One may attribute to every child," Freud said, "without wronging him, a bit of the homosexual disposition." Perhaps because he refused to idealize culture or human nature, Freud knew that the fear of liberating sexual repression was deeply threatening.

So, in the last lecture, Freud took up the question of people who truly need help yet who reject it because of the fear of cultural stigma. Why is mental illness experienced as such a profound disgrace? Even surgeons are allowed to excise a tumor without dishonor to themselves or their patients. In contrast, a therapist might be "afraid of doing harm by psychoanalysis; anxious about calling up into consciousness the repressed sexual impulses of the patient, as though there were danger that they could overpower the higher ethical strivings and rob him of his cultural acquisitions." This was a sobering venture into cultural criticism: that Freud could consider the long-term consequences not of psychic pain, but of the harm done by culture that prevents people from getting the help they need to ameliorate the pain. Even today, it remains to be seen how much evidence is required to justify a truly comprehensive public mental health system of the kind the psychoanalysts were proposing in the 1920s.

Freud's lectures gave social workers a way of understanding the troubled children with whom they (and few others) worked daily. Disturbances of childhood were neither personality defects nor biological inheritances, Freud claimed, but rather the result of brutal environmental forces such as rape and poverty. He showed that "civilization" demands repression and applies a particularly stringent moral code to the "cultured classes." America's ethic of Puritan morality exemplified, for Freud, the repression inherent in civilization's moral codes; he had seen the symptoms disable his adult patients. The influential anthropologist Franz Boaz attended Freud's 1909 lectures. And years later, members of that audience from Emma Goldman to the American psychiatrist Adolf Meyer (who joined the rotating faculty of the Smith School for Social Work) still talked about psychoanalysis with enthusiasm not of a professor or a critic, but the enthusiasm of a humanist. "For the first time I grasped the full significance of sex repression and its effect on human thought and action," Emma Goldman recalled (Goldman, 1977, p. 173). "[Freud] helped me to understand myself, my own needs; and I also realized that only people of depraved minds could impugn [his] motives." Bringing all of this together was formidable and involved sophisticated and intelligent leadership—the kind of intellectual leadership for which social work is rarely given credit, and that the Nobel Prize-winner Jane Addams, among others, proved it possessed.

Freud called his therapy "psychoanalysis." He believed that psychoanalysis would both revolutionize our understanding of the human mind and also result in a large-scale regrouping of modern life. Eventually, Freud thought, "the conscience of society [would] awake" (1918, p. 167) and the psychoanalysts' urban activism would encourage governments to engineer deliberately new forms of social welfare planning. From 1920 to 1933, arguably the most generative period in the history of psychoanalysis, members of the International Psychoanalytic Association formally refuted Europe's monarchist traditions, not only with their belief in the dynamics of the individual unconscious, but also by pooling their creativity toward the greater good: they joined municipal governments, mounted lecture programs in the public schools, advocated for reforms in health and mental health, and planned free outpatient clinics (some brought about and some not) for indigent citizens of Vienna, Berlin, London, Budapest, Zagreb, Moscow, Frankfurt, Trieste, and Paris. "Whatever fosters the growth of culture," Freud wrote to Albert Einstein in 1932, "works at the same time against war" (Freud, 1932).

While the theories and therapies have been amended and transformed by psychoanalysts over the past hundred years, Freud's own impact on Western culture and society has been virtually incalculable. The name has become synonymous with the practice. But almost since its inception, and certainly since its arrival in America, anti-clinical clichés have surrounded psychoanalysis from across the political spectrum.[2] Psychoanalysts themselves have, at times, alleged that clinical objectivity requires distance from politics, social policy, and social thought. As Wilhelm Reich, one of the field's most biting theoreticians, observed as early as 1936, "the conflict within psychoanalysis in regard to its social function was immense long before anyone involved noticed it" (Reich, 1936, p. 75). Almost every new interpretation of the history of psychoanalysis claims from the outset that none of its predecessors have placed the subject within its accurate social, political, and cultural context. Yet each one of these histories, from Freud's own (1914) through Carl Schorske (1981) to Elisabeth Roudinesco (1990), has crafted a distinct way of traversing precisely this arena, as well as the seemingly irreconcilable contradictions between individual human behavior and the larger social environment. According to Eli Zaretsky (2004), no one has been able to grasp psychoanalysis in its entirety because we lack an explicit sociocultural framework in which to understand its

opposite—that is, ourselves as individuals distinct from family and society. To fill this gap, Zaretsky proposes, we should see that psychoanalysis was "the first great theory and practice of 'personal life'" (Zaretsky, 2004, p. 5). This definition reframes psychoanalysis and offers us a postindustrial, dawning of modernism (1880s–1920s), deep sense of identity so distinct from the family and so totally individual that each person carries his or her own unconscious system of symbols and narratives "apparently devoid of socially shared meaning" (Zaretsky, 2004, p. 6). Social work is no exception, and social work critics have long suggested that individual psychological investigation precludes anti-oppression advocacy, and that psychoanalytic studies place the individual person at a remove from culture.

"I discovered some new and important facts about the unconscious in psychic life," Freud said simply at the end of his life, in 1938. "Out of these findings grew a new science, Psycho-Analysis" (Freud, 1938). Like Freud, many clinicians have found that what may seem paradoxical—a deliberate use of two implicitly contradictory words "unconscious" and "science" within one thought—accurately represents the challenge of understanding the human mind. To others, psychoanalysis is simply another dimension of Western hegemony wrought of capitalism and undifferentiated reverence for the individual. But to most, psychoanalysis has survived as a system of thought, richer today in its variety of applications than ever before. In 1918, when Freud took up the task of rebuilding the psychoanalytic movement eroded by World War I, he did so within the Social Democratic framework that would soon remake post-monarchy Vienna. Psychoanalysis expanded in the context of *début de siècle* Vienna's humanist and vigorous social welfare ideologies, and repositioned the analysts from their social margins (as intellectuals and Jews) to a newfound political nucleus predicated on "otherness."

The history of psychoanalysis is also, in many ways, the history of social work. With the advent of modernism at the turn of the 20th century in both Europe and America, the psychoanalysts were joined by conscientious social service agencies that sent, at different times and places, a vast range of patients into their offices: children, adolescents, alcoholics and substance overusers, men suffering with sexual dysfunction and women who were accused of the same, people of all ages with diseases aggravated by depression. Runaway and misbehaving children were sent to analytic group homes in Vienna long before 1938 and in Detroit after the war. Adults with schizophrenia or psychoses were treated in psychoanalytic sanatoria outside of Berlin until 1933, and later in their American equivalents in Massachusetts, Maryland, and Kansas. Psychiatry brought in new diagnoses every decade. Neurosis was the original mode, then borderline personality disorder, and today "bipolar" is in fashion. In the narrative of culture wars closely fought since the early 1940s, two rival concepts of psychoanalysis—as nefariously liberal to conservatives, as elite to class-conscious liberals—have played out in politics, in the arts, and in society at large. American psychoanalysts themselves (social workers included) have struggled with choices between orthodoxy and revisionism, between individual treatment and public advocacy, and between two models of service delivery, the medical and the social. And not all social workers chose to affiliate with Sigmund Freud. "We read all about [Alfred] Adler. We formed two gangs, one pro-Freud and one pro-Adler," said Gisela Konopka in 1984 during the taping of an oral history session with the National Association of Social Workers Vida Grayson (Grayson, 1984, p. 35). "I chose Adler because [of his] concept of the fight against authoritarianism. … Adler was part of the Socialist movement in Vienna, and I felt identified with that. I thought he knew more about the environment. When social work said 'inner' versus 'outer' I can't see any of those things in terms of 'versus.' It's not the way I grew up." In fact, Freud and Adler were quite compatible politically; they differed on the impact of sexuality in human development.

Selected Psychoanalytic Treatment Modalities

One of Freud's earliest interventions was a radical reshaping of the clinical environment. The setting was the therapist's private office, replete with personal icons—books, antiques, paintings—and the patient used a couch instead of a chair.[3] This unusual design, with the therapist's own seat placed outside the patient's sight line,

precluded superficial exchanges between patient and analyst. Instead the patients, perhaps just short of dozing off, could let their memories float into present consciousness, and the analyst could organize these thoughts into more or less logical insights concerning the painful consequences of repressing horrible childhood experiences. In Vienna, where this reconfiguration was introduced in 1896, the medical and academic communities first ignored the new method, then rejected it, and then finally embraced it as their native contribution to world science and culture.

As we have seen in this brief historical overview, most of the psychoanalytic treatment techniques that social workers apply today, and effectively so, originated in the early 20th century. Clinical methodologies still used—and still debated—today were pioneered in the psychoanalysts' first free outpatient clinic, the Berlin Poliklinik. Anna Freud, Melanie Klein, and Hermione Hug-Hellmuth forged child analysis there. Karen Horney introduced the female perspective and cultural relativity in psychoanalysis. Sandor Ferenczi's fractionary (or time-limited) analysis was put into practice there, as was Wilhelm Reich's in-depth case conference, and a range of protocols such as free treatment eligibility and length of treatment guidelines. The underlying theories—the childhood roots of psychological disorders in adulthood, the dream-like logic of the most rigid yet unexplainable symptoms, the powerful pressures of ambivalence toward family, and the deeply subversive acknowledgment of human sexuality—worked well.

When turning our attention to early 20th century psychoanalysis, we can see the extent to which the era's health and mental health endeavors enriched each other and were animated by common ideals. We begin with Sigmund Freud, the paradoxically bourgeois yet revolutionary neurologist whose unrelenting clinical investigations and lyrical case studies of mental disorders made him, then as now, a scientific celebrity. Freud championed, among others, Sándor Ferenczi, a modernist Hungarian intellectual who alternated lengths of treatment and varied the psychotherapist's level of activity; Ernst Simmel, a German doctor who brought about inpatient psychoanalytic treatment; and Wilhelm Reich, whose journey through Marxism and psychoanalysis remains a controversial narrative of possibility. The impact of their discoveries, added to those of Melanie Klein, Anna Freud, and Karen Horney, helped to create a mythology of discovery that is still with us today. What follows is a selective overview of psychoanalytic theory and technique that continue to thrive in today's social work milieu.

Child Psychoanalysis

In the spring of 1928, Margaret Powers, a State Charities Aid Association child welfare worker who would later set "the highest standards of casework" (Davies, 1928) at Cornell University Hospital's department of psychiatry, set out to find a new treatment method suited to the mental health needs of urban adolescents. Powers interviewed Mary Jarrett, associate director of the Smith College School for Psychiatric Social Work, before turning her search to Berlin and its extraordinarily dynamic Psychoanalytic Poliklinik. As Powers spoke with the Institute's resident psychoanalysts—child analysts, educators, political activists, specialists in psychiatric disorders—she learned that many had been pursuing highly innovative clinical paths. The most important advances in the understanding of infant and child development have emerged primarily from these psychoanalytic studies of children and adolescents. As Erika Schmidt (2009, p. 56) wrote in her recent integrative paper, "both clinical social work and child psychoanalysis borrow from psychoanalytic theory for explanations of motivation, development, and technique." But exactly who "discovered" child analysis is a matter of debate.

Variously attributed to Anna Freud, Melanie Klein, or Hermine von Hug-Helmuth, the practice of child analysis really took root in Vienna and Berlin in the mid-1920s. Freud had derived his own theory of infantile and childhood sexuality from the retrospective analysis of adult patients, and ambiguously corroborated his conceptual framework with observations of his own children, grandchildren, and "Little Hans" (Freud, 1909). Later, while all three analysts (Klein, Hug-Helmuth, and Anna Freud each claimed to the truest adherence to Freud) sought to understand the psychic life and mental development of children, the women took significantly different positions on technique. In

Vienna, von Hug-Hellmuth played with the children in their home environments but stayed away from interpretation (Hug-Hellmuth, 1921). In contrast, Klein in Berlin (who also used little wooden toys for play therapy) valued in-depth interpretation that emphasized her belief that children had a capacity for transference similar to that of adults.[4] "She absolutely insists on keeping parental and educative influences apart from analysis," Alix Strachey reported to her husband and co-translator James (Meisel & Kendrick, 1990). One can see the value of this highly individualized approach when working with traumatized children, for whom protective fantasy may override painful reality. Meanwhile Anna Freud, also in Berlin at the time, disavowed transference in children and took up the ego-psychological supportive stance to which social workers largely still adhere (Freud, 1927/1975). Avoiding suggestion, she sought to accurately understand and then clarify the meaning of the child's self-directed play.

Anna Freud's position and her emphasis on ego-supportive treatment is echoed today in numerous American child therapy centers. Among her most influential adherents were Erna Furman, Rudolf Ekstein, Yonata Feldman, Thesi Bergman, and countless more child analysts who spread out across the United States after fleeing fascism in Austria and Germany (Hosley, 1998). Erik Erikson worked with Anna Freud and Dorothy Burlingham at their innovative school in Vienna. Others, like Esther Menaker, George Mohr, Helen Ross, and Margaret Gerard, were among the Americans who had traveled to Europe before 1933 (or the United Kingdom after 1938) and who brought home a new understanding of child development, along with a unique set of therapeutic skills. These analysts articulated the method of child psychoanalysis but also, in a sense, a license to listen to children's speech, to value and respect it with a mind newly alive to the pain implicit in their narratives of trauma. The method found its way into residential treatment facilities, outpatient clinics, private offices, and group homes for adolescents like Fritz Redl's Pioneer House in Detroit. In their unconstrained play, children can (consciously or not) express the underlying meaning of feelings and problems unacceptable to parents and teachers. The fundamental premises of social work theory such as the psychosocial perspective, when combined with the centrality of relationship as a medium of change and a commitment to social justice, inform the work of today's child therapist. Dr. Furman, when interviewed by Theresa Aiello in the 1980s, told her that they "analyze the very rich and the very poor and we all agree that they are very much alike in the tragedy of their early childhood. It's the in-betweens who do a bit better" (Aiello, 2009, p. 12).

Brief Psychoanalytic Treatment

"Is there such a thing as a natural end to an analysis?" Freud asked in *Analysis Terminable and Interminable* (Freud, 1937, p. 299). Written in 1937, with the Nazis at Vienna's doorstep and World War II starting to take shape, Freud's short book took on one the great puzzles of psychotherapy. Two streams of thought—not in themselves inherently incompatible—converge in the debate on length of treatment. If the goal of psychoanalysis is to know oneself by making what is unconscious conscious, the answer is "no" because the human mind evolves incessantly in response to psychological impulses and environmental pressures. If, however, the goal is the relief of symptoms, then the answer is "yes"—as in, for example, the treatment ends once the anxiety is reduced. The answers are as variable as the therapies themselves. But the real challenge in the book's title, as Gilda de Simone (1997) points out, is not to select which analyses can be terminated and which not; instead one looks for which *elements* of an analysis can be concluded and which others should be continued. "Terminability" and "interminability" are not fixed points but coexist on a dialectic continuum. And most important, this dialectic exists for both therapist and patient. Given the forces of transference and countertransference, the therapist is as liable to wrap up a therapy prematurely as the client.

Common American wisdom would have it that psychoanalysis is endless. In a society predicated on individual independence, the ongoing need for psychological or social support implies a kind of vulnerability that violates our Calvinist cultural values. Largely because of this, as Robert Emde (1988) says, the question of termination is really "a fundamental challenge concerning our thinking about developmental continuity and change." The first and second generations of analysts, however, seemed to have fewer qualms. Psychoanalytic practice unfolded in plain offices, case by case, on couches where theory hovered invisibly over clinical encounters. At least between 1918 and 1938, psychoanalysis was neither impractical for working people, nor rigidly structured, nor luxurious in length. And by 1937, Freud had concluded that "whatever our theoretical view may be, I believe that in practice analyses do come to an end" (Freud, 1937, p. 353).

The early psychoanalysts exercised nearly all variations of clinical flexibility. They adapted alternative solutions to bewildering dilemmas: appropriate duration of treatment, for example, was subjected to as much debate, or perhaps more, in the 1920s as today. Influenced by Ferenczi, the Berlin version of brief therapy became an official curative technique called "fractionary" analysis. In Vienna the clinicians asked whether they "should endeavor to achieve quick successes in order to shorten the duration of the treatment." Paul Federn questioned the wisdom of discharging patients at their own request. Then again, lengthy treatment was just as debatable as the interrupted analysis because, after all, nobody is ever truly symptom-free. Who (therapist or patient) is served best by what (long or short treatment)? These were the kinds of problems thrashed out in the basement conference room of the Ambulatorium, the psychoanalyst's free clinic in Vienna where Erik Erikson worked in the 1920s; the case conference was initiated by Wilhelm Reich and remains today the standard format for discussing clinical practice (including the therapist's own errors) in mental health settings.

Treatment plans had to be carefully worded (for example, designating an analysand "symptom-free" instead of "cured"), especially given the imperative for confidentiality and the psychoanalysts' relationship to public social services. Prospective patients had to be made to feel welcome, and it was important that former patients who had interrupted or ended analysis prematurely (or who had been intended for fractionary analysis) should feel comfortable enough to resume treatment.

How many days each week are necessary for effective analysis? Just how many months should an analysis last to be complete? Are such decisions best made by the patient or by the clinician?

Most analysts refused to implement a priori time limits on treatment regardless of diagnosis. Daily sessions were ideal, but since so many of the patients were employed, analysis three times a week was more widespread. By 1926, the 3-hour weekly treatment schedule was found generally adequate and was retained as standard practice in Berlin. Just as Freud had compared therapy for neuroses to the treatment of other chronic illnesses like tuberculosis: "the fuller and the deeper the success, the longer does the treatment take" (Report, 1928, p. 148). Shorter-term treatment was one of those "hyper-ingenious, forcible interventions" whose outcomes vary according to pathology"; nevertheless, analysts were urged to investigate fractionary (that is, time-limited or intermittent) regimens (Report, 1928, pp. 148–149). They "liked to experiment with interruptions," Franz Alexander recalled, "and the expression 'fractioned analysis' was frequently used" (Alexander, 1928). Eitingon viewed length of treatment as patient-driven, or failing that, as a mutual decision between therapist and patient. He enjoyed developing advantageous "fraktionäre" schedules devised for patients like schoolteachers who needed "a month at Xmas, 3 weeks at Easter, etc., beginning in December" (Meisel & Kendrick, 1990, p. 134). Activity in treatment was an innovation, an extension of psychoanalysis perhaps, but not a replacement.

The question of length of treatment has confounded psychoanalysts ever since Ferenczi came up with the idea of flexibility. Can individual treatment be shortened or speeded up? Is the analytic hour 60 minutes or 45, or can it vary? In the history of clinical practice, psychoanalysts have alternately embraced and repudiated short-term treatment, but they never sought to deny anyone the basic right to treatment based on the mere ability to pay. In doing so, they gave today's therapists a roadmap of sorts. Jeremy Safran (2002), for one, brilliantly followed this map into relational treatment, pointing out the influence of the brief timeframe on the uses of countertransference, disclosure, and the ongoing process of therapeutic enactment. But the basic idea is perhaps best summarized by Charles Socarides (1954): "By using the insights gained through a thorough knowledge of psychodynamics and the rapid application of these concepts… an important tool is added to the armamentarium of the therapist."

Psychoanalytic Treatment of Severe Disorders

"Psychoanalytic Therapy Wins Backing" proclaimed the *New York Times* in 2008, as though fish could speak or corn grew on Mars (Carey, 2008). "Intensive psychoanalytic therapy, the 'talking cure' rooted in the ideas of Freud, has all but disappeared in the age of drug treatments and managed care," the reporter alleged. "But now researchers are reporting that the therapy can be effective against some chronic mental problems, including anxiety and borderline personality disorder." The core of this statement is an attempt to describe how psychoanalysis can, even in today's apparently rapid-fire world, gain on mental health problems that seem beyond the capabilities—moral as well as physiological—of medication. Paradoxically, the tempting myth that analysis is intended only for the "worried well" persists (in social work as elsewhere), though the subject has always been more of a clinical challenge than a mystery to psychoanalysts themselves. As Otto Kernberg, arguably the dean of psychodynamic treatment today, said in 2004, psychoanalysts are well equipped because they have both the theoretical and clinical tools to diagnose and treat severe cases of personality disorder, including borderline and narcissistic structures.[5] And in the summer of 2008, Glenn Gabbard, Peter Fonagy, and Stephen Sonnenberg joined Kernberg in Belfast to present the contemporary psychoanalytic conceptualization of severe disorders, including the treatment of psychotic states, trauma, addictions, violence, and the nature and function of suicidal ideation. Known for his empirically grounded frameworks, Gabbard consistently refutes the cynics. "Psychoanalytic treatments," he says, "may be necessary when other treatments are ineffective" (Gabbard et al., 2002).

The *New York Times* notwithstanding, the effectiveness of psychoanalytic treatment for severe disorders is neither new nor unknown. In the mid-1920s, Ernst Simmel, a colleague of Freud's and co-director of the Berlin Poliklinik, created the Schloss Tegel sanitarium, just outside

Berlin, for indigent people with severe psychiatric disorders to be treated psychoanalytically. Simmel believed that impinging social and economic forces are as great a challenge to patients' recovery as are their internal disorders. "This was a pioneering enterprise," said his colleague David Brunswick (1947), "in which [Simmel] not only introduced psychoanalytic treatment of somatic illness, addictions, sexual offenders, schizophrenic borderline cases and other psychoses, but also saw to it that nursing and occupation therapy were carried out with psychoanalytic insight and aims." Harry Stack Sullivan, Adolf Meyer, William Alanson White, and Edward Kempf applied psychoanalysis to their work with psychotic patients in American state hospitals (Engel, 1990). They thought of psychoanalysis as a way of enhancing what the psychiatrists had started: by developing a therapeutic relationship based on transference and countertransference, or using the structural model of the mind to restore the functioning of a weakened ego, or tolerating a schizophrenic person's compromised representation of reality. The "basic concept," emphasized Sullivan, "is neither *mind* nor *society* but *person*" (italics original; Sullivan, 1939, p. 62). The analyst's own sensibility was, for Sullivan, what had to be studied, and the questions he posed on anxiety, schizophrenia, and human loneliness had to be pondered before they could work with patients.

Neuroscience and Empirical Studies of Psychoanalysis

The systematic exploration of irrational behavior, the domain of the unconscious, is the predominant theme in psychoanalytic theory and therapy. Despite a century of exploring the nature of unconscious processes, however, empirical investigations have lagged behind clinical inquiry. Fortunately today's exciting research in neuroscience and brain physiology is confirming the biological basis for virtually all unconscious emotional processing, and also providing major insight into the link between behavior and biology. Certain social workers may be concerned that biological investigations—and even biologically based interventions like psychotropic medications—may compromise psychoanalytic sensibility, blame the victim, or unduly stigmatize

mental illness. In contrast, neuroscience actually completes the "bio" component in the biopsychosocial model. "Underenthusiasm for the neuroscientific revolution," summarizes the social worker Rosemary Farmer (2009, p. 40), "is as unwarranted and as harmful as overenthusiasm." And basic knowledge of neuroscience is indispensable when working psychoanalytically with people with severe "biologically based" disorders, emphasizes Glen Gabbard (1992), who studied the intimate and reciprocal connection between psychosocial and neurophysiological factors.

American culture's present-oriented appetite for tangible results seems to feed everything from risky mortgages to managed care. While psychoanalysis is hardly immune to this imperative, the demand for confirmation of treatment efficacy and effectiveness may not be misplaced. Of course the question "does it work?" needs to be contextualized with responses such as "for whom?" and "what is the definition of 'successful treatment'?" In view of these large questions, the research has been divided into several categories: studies of the psychoanalytic process itself, and empirical studies of psychoanalytic concepts.

Launched in the 1970s, psychoanalytic process studies seek to measure, in a very precise way, the relationship between therapeutic technique and the outcome of treatment by quantifying selected micro interventions or, occasionally, whole sessions. The studies first caught on among clinicians eager to acquire the cachet promised by empirical validation, the "gold standard" of the randomized controlled trial, making psychoanalysis as valuable as competing treatments. The politics of the medical market looms as large in psychoanalysis as elsewhere. Nevertheless the studies move in surprising directions, and for those who still hold to the traditional case report for evaluation, the ambiguity of clinical practice is well reflected in their often incomplete conclusions. One of the most comprehensive comparisons of treatment outcomes and related factors (Blomberg et al., 2000) studied more than 400 subjects before, during, and up to three years after subsidized psychoanalysis or long-term psychodynamic psychotherapy. The longer patients were in treatment, the study showed, the more they improved—impressively so among patients in psychoanalysis—on self-rating measures of symptom distress and morale. In contrast, improvement was weak in both groups on a self-rating measure of social relations. As to brief treatment (defined as less than 20 sessions), Peter Fonagy and his colleagues (2005) recently updated their exhaustive survey of the therapy outcomes literature to answer key questions frequently asked by their colleagues: (a) Are there any disorders for which short-term psychodynamic psychotherapy can be considered evidence-based? (b) Is short-term psychodynamic psychotherapy uniquely effective for certain disorders, as either the only evidence-based treatment or as a treatment that is more effective than alternatives? (c) Is there any evidence base for long-term psychodynamic psychotherapy, either in terms of achieving effects not normally associated with short-term treatment or addressing problems that have not been addressed by short-term psychodynamic psychotherapy? In an interesting critique of quantification, Drew Westen and Joel Weinberger (2004) reconsider a contemporary "chicken-and-egg" phenomenon, namely the predictive (or not) correlation between expert clinical assessment and statistical prediction. In fact, they conclude, standard psychometric procedures can be so utilized that quantified clinical description becomes statistical prediction.

Freud called off his *Project for a Scientific Psychology* because he was hampered by the limited technology available in 1895, not because he thought that biology was irrelevant. Given today's vast improvements in medicine and specifically neuroscience, biological theories of mental health have entered public awareness in the way psychoanalysis did 100 years ago. The latest technology in neuroscience, together with today's more stringent research methods in psychotherapy, is allowing us to understand more clearly how the brain and the (unconscious) mind intersect (Gabbard, 2000).

In a whole new field of investigation called "neuro-psychoanalysis" Mark Solms and Oliver Sachs have gone a long way in demonstrating the biological basis for unconscious emotional processing within the human brain, perhaps the same process Wilhelm Reich attempted to isolate over 40 years ago. With the advent of functional brain imaging technology and the emergence of a molecular neurobiology, Solms has tried to connect the psychoanalytic study of the mind (thoughts, dreams, emotions, associations) with the anatomical structure of the brain. His method enables us to identify the neurological organization of almost any mental function without contradicting essential psychoanalytic hypotheses (Solms & Turnbull, 2002). Interestingly, this laboratory-based neuroscientific work confirms many of Freud's original observations, not least the pervasive influence of nonconscious processes and the organizing function of emotions. And finally, the neuropsychological structures and processes associated with the human unconscious are beginning to be understood.

Macro Psychoanalysis

Just as psychoanalysis has never been limited to clinical work with adults, so too it goes beyond the scope of individual treatment. "The replacement of the power of the individual by the power of a community," Freud (1930) wrote, "constitutes the decisive step of civilization." On this macro level, psychoanalysts believe that social systems (from work organizations to local and national communities) are amenable to self-reflection, and that psychodynamically oriented social workers who are organizational consultants can help them become more democratic and tolerant of internal conflict. The treatment relationship is, itself, a social process. The progenitors of contemporary sociology, the "founding fathers" of the discipline—Talcott Parsons, Clyde Kluckholn, Paul Lazarsfeld, Marie Jahoda—knew this well, and their work was informed by psychoanalytic theory and method. Parsons joined the Boston analysts Grete and Edward Bibring to study the ambiguous development of self-control in response to collapsing external authority. The social psychologist Erich Fromm incorporated psychoanalysis into his writings on critical theory developed at the famously Marxist Frankfurt Institute for Social Research. Like Wilhelm Reich and Ernst Simmel, Fromm tried to account for the paradoxical tolerance for fascism he saw in Germany of the early 1930s. Similar to an individual who unconsciously internalizes oppression, subjugated social groups seem to conform subjectively to situations that are objectively against their best interests. And like individuals, social groups can best resist by pursuing insight or critical consciousness. This too was Freud's premise in *Civilization and Its Discontents* of

1930, his habitually misinterpreted call for collective resistance to oppression.

The key factor in macro psychoanalysis, as Ernst Simmel and Otto Fenichel's work suggests, is to think of treatment as a unified clinical and political discourse, a praxis based not on the strictures of establishment standards but on an ideology of dialectical materialism. Simmel had served as an army doctor and director of a hospital for shell-shocked soldiers during World War I, and because he had witnessed "the waste of human life during the war years," Simmel urged his colleagues to participate in "the human economy... for the preservation of all nations" (Simmel et al., 1921). Simmel was, in the 1930s, director of both the Schloss Tegel inpatient psychoanalytic facility and the Socialist Physicians Union, where he was joined by Albert Einstein in Berlin. The Union's study groups explored legalizing the eight-hour workday (along with its health implications and cultural meaning), occupational health and safety, maternity leave for pregnant and nursing mothers, child labor laws, and socialized medicine. They fought for birth control and against the criminalization of abortion. Simmel's colleague Otto Fenichel, author of the classical textbook of psychoanalytic orthodoxy while, at the same time, heading a left-wing opposition group in Europe and later—in hiding—in America, argued that the importance of psychoanalysis lay precisely in its social, even Marxist, dimension. "We are all convinced," Fenichel wrote from Oslo in March 1934 (Fenichel, 1934), "that we recognize in Freud's Psychoanalysis the germ of the dialectical-materialist psychology of the future, and therefore we desperately need to protect and extend this knowledge."

If we think of psychoanalysis as a comprehensive theory of mind, and of the mind as a system, then we can expand the scope of clinical investigations to look at the nature of unconscious processes in macro systems such as work organizations. Work organizations can benefit particularly from drive and object relations theory to explain, for example, employees' reluctance to form attachments to a corporation that fails to provide a holding environment; drive theory explores patterns of aggression and gratification.[6] Social work consultants, who are highly attuned to the psychodynamics of the consultation process itself, can develop strategic interventions for agencies questioning their mission as well as "the impact of unconscious motives on group and organizational membership" (Eisold, 1995). One of these unconscious motives is described in Freud's original concept of "signal anxiety." This self-protective ("defensive" is the more classical word) function of the ego is used to anticipate dangers, both real and imagined. While the neurophysiological structures and processes related to unconscious anticipation in humans are just beginning to be understood (Wong, 1999), work organizations have named this same function "strategic planning" or "forecasting."

Psychoanalysis brings tensions to light and locates them within historical, political, economic, scientific, and international systems at play within the organization's unconscious processes. For example, white-on-black racism can be explained psychoanalytically as a defense (fear of the unknown) or a projection (their fault, not our guilt). Of course, no explanation excuses misbehavior, and this does not in itself relieve the organization of its responsibility to handle the conflict democratically. As with other systems, however, coupling insight with appropriate organizational or social policy can reduce intergroup (in this case, interracial) tension. And release of tension is, after all, a key purpose of psychoanalytic treatment.

In Sum

The acclaimed Viennese writer Sigmund Freud presented, over 100 years ago, a way of imparting logic to our tempestuous minds and societies. When we first read Freud's essays on psychoanalytic theory and practice, they seem more a collection of scabrous anecdotes than a rigorous consideration of clinical technique. They involve attacks of frantic crying, overwhelming parents, violent traditions, nasty jokes, spurned lovers, and the intransigent push of sexual desire from infancy onward. Psychoanalysis would help us, if not make sense of all this, at least gain a measure of stability and learn to live with it.

Psychoanalysis blends a theory and a practice that, taken together, straddles human physiology, social justice, and psychology to resolve an interminable succession of possible conflicts: between mind and body, person and culture, imposed norms and instinctual desire, the unconscious and consciousness. How important is it today? Because psychoanalytic terms are now so entrenched in Western language, arguments for and against have become fairly trite. True, psychoanalysis can serve as a reminder that mental anguish makes for social discomfort—and vice versa. Nevertheless, as we have seen in this chapter, the overall discourse remains breathtaking in its scope and possibilities.

Notes

1. For a good summary, see *Comprehensive Handbook of Social Work and Social Welfare*, edited by Barbara White (Wiley, 2008). However, I believe that Abraham Flexner's celebrated 1915 critique in "Is Social Work a Profession?" has been given undue credit.
2. See Hale, N. G. (1971). *Freud and the Americans—The Beginnings of Psychoanalysis in the United States, 1876–1917* (Oxford and New York: Oxford University Press).
3. For a comprehensive overview of the psychoanalytic couch and its meanings, see Marinelli, L. (2006). *Die Couch—Vom Denken im Liegen* (Munich and New York: Prestel).
4. See Klein, M. (1932). *The Psychoanalysis of Children* (London: The Hogarth Press).
5. See Kernberg, O. (2004). *Aggressivity, Narcissism, and Self-Destructiveness in the Psychotherapeutic Relationship: New Developments in the Psychopathology and Psychotherapy of Severe Personality Disorders* (New Haven, CT: Yale University Press).
6. See Czander, W. (1993). *The Psychodynamics of Work and Organizations* (New York: Guilford Press).

References

Aiello, T. (2009). Psychoanalysts in exile. *Psychoanalytic Perspectives*, p. 12.

Alexander, J. Psychoanalytic training.

Blomberg, J., et al. (2000). Varieties of long-term outcome among patients in psychoanalysis and long-term psychotherapy: A review of findings in the Stockholm Outcome of Psychoanalysis and Psychotherapy Project. *International Journal of Psycho-Analysis*, 82, 205–210.

Brunswick, D. (1947). *Recollections of Ernst Simmel* (unpublished speech from the Simmel Memorial Meeting). Archives of the Los Angeles Psychoanalytic Society.

Carey, B. (Oct. 1, 2008). Psychoanalytic therapy wins backing. *New York Times*.

Davies, S. Letter dated March 12, 1928, and addressed to "Training Committee," Archives of the Berlin Poliklinik, Koblenz, Germany, by permission.

De Simone, G. (1997). *Ending analysis: Theory & technique*. London: Karnac Books.

Eisold, K. (1995). *Psychoanalysis today: Implications for organizational applications*. Paper presented at ISPSO International Symposium, London.

Emde, R. N. (1988). Development terminable and interminable, II. Recent psychoanalytic theory. *International Journal of Psychoanalysis*, 69, 283–296.

Engel, M. (1990). Psychoanalysis and psychosis: the contribution of Edward Kempf. *Journal of the American Academy of Psychoanalysis*, 18, 167–184.

Farmer, R. L. (2009). *Neuroscience and social work practice—The missing link*. Thousand Oaks, CA: Sage.

Fenichel, O. (1934). Letter to Edith Jacobson, Annie Reich, Barbara Lantos, Edyth Gyomroi, George Gero, and Frances Deri, Runbrief #March 1, 1934, Box 1, Folder 1, archives of the Austen Riggs Library, Stockbridge, MA.

Fonagy, P., Higgitt, A., & Roth, A. (2005) Psychodynamic psychotherapies: Evidence-based practice and clinical wisdom. *Bulletin of the Menninger Clinic*, 69(1), 1–58.

Freud, A. (1927/1975). *Introduction to the technique of child analysis*. London: Ayer.

Freud, S. (1909). Analysis of phobia in a five-year-old boy. In J. Strachey (ed. and trans.), The standard edition of the complete psychological works of Sigmund Freud (Vol. 10, pp. 3–149). London: The Hogarth Press.

Freud, S. (1910a [1909]). Five lectures on psychoanalysis. In J. Strachey (ed. and trans.), The standard edition of the complete psychological works of Sigmund Freud (Vol. 11, pp. 7–55). London: The Hogarth Press.

Freud, S. (1914). On the history of the psychoanalytic movement. In J. Strachey (ed. and trans.), The standard edition of the complete psychological works of Sigmund Freud (Vol. 14, pp. 7–66). London: The Hogarth Press.

Freud, S. (1918). Lines of advance in psychoanalytic psychotherapy. In J. Strachey (ed. and trans.), The standard edition of the complete psychological works of Sigmund Freud (Vol. 17, p. 167). London: The Hogarth Press.

Freud, S. (1930). Civilization and its discontents. In J. Strachey (ed. and trans.), The standard edition of the complete psychological works of Sigmund Freud (Vol. 21, pp. 64–141). London: The Hogarth Press

Freud, S. (1932). Why war?

Freud, S. (1937). Analysis terminable and interminable. In J. Strachey (ed. and trans.), The standard edition of the complete psychological works of Sigmund Freud (Vol. 23, pp. 209–253, 353). London: The Hogarth Press.

Freud, S. (1938). From a 40-second excerpt of Freud speaking in English and recorded in London in December 1938, less than a year before his death. Available at: http://web.utk.edu/~wmorgan/psy470/freudvoi.htm.

Gabbard, G. O. (1992). Psychodynamic psychiatry in the "decade of the brain." *American Journal of Psychiatry*, 149, 991–998.

Gabbard, G. O. (2000). A neurobiologically informed perspective on psychotherapy. *British Journal of Psychiatry*, 177, 117–122.

Gabbard, G. O., Gunderson, J. G., & Fonagy, P. (2002). The place of psychoanalytic treatments within psychiatry. *Archives of General Psychiatry*, 59, 505–510.

Goldmann, E. (1977). *Living my life*. New York: New American Library.

Grayson, V. (1984). Interview with Gisella Konopka. Oral History Collection, Columbia University Libraries, New York.

Hosley, E. M. (1998). *A century for children—A history of the Day Nursery Association of Cleveland*. Cleveland, OH: The Hannah Perkins Center, pp. 103–104.

Hug-Hellmuth, H. von (1921). On the technique of child analysis. *International Journal of Psychoanalysis*, 2, 287–305.

Meisel, P., & Kendrick, W. (Eds.) (1990). *Bloomsbury/Freud: The letters of James and Alix Strachey 1924–1925*. New York: Norton.

Reich, W. (1936). The living productive power, 'Work-Power,' of Karl Marx. In *People in trouble* (P. Schmitz, trans.). New York: Farrar, Strauss and Giroux, 1976, p. 75.

Report (1928). *International Journal of Psychoanalysis*, 9, 148–149.

Roudinesco, E. (J. Mehlman, trans.) (1990). *Jacques Lacan & Co: A history of psychoanalysis in France, 1925–1985*. Chicago: University Of Chicago Press.

Safran, J. (2002). Brief relational psychoanalytic treatment. *Psychoanalytic Dialogues*, 12, 171–195.

Schmidt, E. (2009). Social work and child psychoanalysis: where the twain shall meet. *Clinical Social Work Journal*, 37(1), 55–66.

Schorske, C. (1981). *Fin de Siecle Vienna: Politics and culture*. New York: Vintage Books.

Simmel, E. (1994). War neuroses and "psychic trauma." In A. Kaes et al. (eds.), *The Weimar Republic sourcebook*. Berkeley, CA: University of California Press.

Simmel, E., Ferenczi, S., Abraham, K., & Jones, (1921) *Psycho-analysis and the war Neuroses*, intro. S. Freud. London: International Psycho-Analytical Press. First published as *Kriegs-Neurosen und Psychisches Trauma* (Munich: Otto Nemnich, 1918).

Socarides, C. W. (1954). On the usefulness of extremely brief Psychoanalytic Contacts. *Psychoanalytic Review*, 41, 340–346.

Solms, M. and Turnbull, O. (2002). *The Brain and the Inner World: An Introduction to the Neuroscience of Subjective Experience*. New York: Other Press.

Sterba, R., (1982) *Reminiscences of a Viennese psychoanalyst*. Detroit: Wayne State University Press, p. 81.

Sullivan, H. S. (1939) "Intuition, Reason and Faith in Science" in *The Fusion of Psychiatry and Social Science* (Helen S. Perry, ed 1964) New York: W.W. Norton, p. 62.

Watson, J. B. (1913) "Psychology as the Behaviorist Views It" in *The Psychological Review*, 20:158–177.

Westen, D. and Weinberger, J. (2004) When Clinical Description Becomes Statistical Prediction. *American Psychologist*, 59(7): 595–613.

Wong, P.S. (1999) Anxiety, Signal Anxiety, and Unconscious Anticipation: Neuroscientist Evidence for an Unconscious Signal Function in Humans. *Journal of the American Psychoanalytic Association*. 47 (3): 817–841.

Zaretsky, E. (2004) *Secrets of the Soul—A Social and Cultural History of Psychoanalysis*. New York: Alfred A. Knopf.

26

PSYCHOSOCIAL

This theory, strongly influenced by Hollis and Woods, formulates a multi-method intervention based on a diagnostic assessment of significant persons and relevant social systems in a client's life

Psychosocial Theory and Social Work Treatment

Howard Robinson and Carol Kaplan

Psychosocial treatment is a discrete practice model developed from the writings of Mary Richmond at the turn of the 20th century, transformed through the integration of new and evolving knowledge in the human sciences, and accompanied by a set of empirically derived treatment procedures that have become standard techniques of both generalist and advanced social work practice today. In fact, what many social workers understand as fundamental to professional practice—techniques of engagement, the importance of empathy and relationship, factual exploration and differential assessment, understanding of personality dynamics, worker–client transferences, and ecosystemic intervention, including concrete service provision—are all central components of psychosocial treatment.

The psychosocial perspective, based on ecosystemic thinking, provides social workers with a comprehensive way to intervene within multiple social systems, using multiple modalities of treatment and a blend of treatment techniques. Treatment is tailored to the particular needs and unique circumstances of the client who, in a mutual collaboration with the social worker, defines the goals of their work together. Motivating and facilitating clients to be self-directed and active in the change process is one of the basic principles of psychosocial treatment. Generally speaking, this highly adaptable and integrative treatment aims to create a better fit between people and their social environments: to restore and improve individual and family well-being, to facilitate social adaptations of people interpersonally, and to strengthen the capacity of individuals and families to recover from adversity.

At the same time that social factors are taken into account when understanding a client's difficulties, psychosocial treatment attends to personality characteristics and intrapsychic dynamics, integrating the situational factors of clients with their innate capacity to strengthen adaptive functioning. In assessment and treatment planning, psychosocial treatment looks "outward" toward the client's physical and social environment as well as "inward" to the client's biology, cultural and spiritual beliefs, developmental history, ego functions (including the ego defenses), and psychodynamics. Of course "environment" and "person" interact and transform each other so that changes in one set of factors modify, to a lesser or greater degree, other factors. The art and science of psychosocial treatment lies in the practitioner's ability, with the help of the client, to assess the nature of the environment–person transactional system and determine, again in collaboration with the client, a systemic intervention.

A defining feature of the psychosocial approach is its open, flexible system of thought drawn from many sources of knowledge. As new information and ideas emerge from social work experience and from related fields, additional light is shed on our understanding of personality, social forces, and the interplay between them. Because psychosocial treatment has succeeded in the incorporation of new knowledge with its sturdy principles of practice, even as historical and social forces have shifted the emphasis given to particular treatments and procedures, psychosocial treatment continues to play an important and enduring role today in social work practice. Psychosocial treatment not only provides the foundation for social casework, but it also becomes richer and deeper as practitioners learn from their clinical experiences and integrate new knowledge and skills with psychosocial principles.

Historical Background

Although social work in the United States has roots in the 19th-century charity organization society movements of North America and Great Britain (Katz, 1983), it was Mary Richmond who actually set the stage for the development of modern casework theory and practice. For more than a quarter-century, from 1899 to 1930, she and her associates formulated and evaluated

practice concepts and techniques, constantly examining, modifying, and elaborating their ideas as new evidence appeared, always trying to respond to concerns and questions raised by the growing number of social workers.

From the outset, Richmond's dual focus on people and their environments marked the beginning of the person-in-situation orientation of psychosocial practice. She also promoted the idea that caseworkers' actual experiences should be measured by the best standards available, thus introducing a scientific approach. She developed the processes of social study, diagnosis, and treatment planning, which are still central to psychosocial treatment. She learned from the study of case histories that diagnosis and treatment must be individualized, just as contemporary psychosocial practitioners recognize that they cannot make assumptions about clients on the basis of their backgrounds (ethnicity, sexual orientation, etc.), their specific problems (addiction, child abuse, etc.), or their clinical diagnosis (borderline, passive-aggressive, etc.). Relying on a broad empirical base of many cases, Richmond sought to define procedures for intervening in the client's environment, for locating resources, and for cooperating with all possible sources of assistance and influence ("indirect treatment"). She also stressed the importance of a trusting worker–client relationship. In short, she was a pioneer in the process of standardizing and defining psychosocial casework procedures, which would be further refined in future years.

After World War I and through the 1920s, social work was influenced by new theories of psychology and psychiatry, especially those of Freud. At times this led to family and socioeconomic factors being downplayed. In the 1930s, a dispute developed between the "functional" school and the Freudian, or diagnostic, school. The functional school deemphasized the unconscious, history taking, and diagnostic inquiry, basing treatment on agency function and time limitations in order to foster clients' ability to find solutions to problems. The diagnostic, or psychosocial, approach ultimately prevailed, but it gradually incorporated some ideas of the functionalists, including more selective gathering of history, a problem-solving approach, and the recognition that treatment begins immediately, even before all the evidence is in. At the same time, the concept of self-determination became popular. Some of Freud's ideas were incorporated into psychosocial practice, but social workers explored how they could be used and how social work and psychoanalysis differed.

During the 1950s, theories of ego psychology made a significant impact on psychosocial practice. Although based on Freud's ideas, ego psychology assisted individuals in adapting to external realities by focusing on improving ego functioning, without the necessity of uncovering unconscious material. Ego-supportive treatment, sometimes misunderstood as simple warmth or reassurance, focused on restoring, maintaining, or enhancing the functions of the ego (Goldstein, 1995). Adaptive defenses, mastery-competence, intellectual processes, reality testing and judgment, and impulse regulation, among other qualities, were nurtured. Thus, individuals were assisted to cope creatively with life circumstances, rather than being totally ruled by them. Perlman's problem-solving therapy (1957), as well as brief, task-centered, and crisis-oriented therapies, among others, all resulted from social work's appreciation of the need to utilize ego strengths in helping people to grapple with life dilemmas.

By the time Florence Hollis published the first edition of *Casework: A Psychosocial Therapy* (1964), many ideas from the social sciences had been incorporated into the psychosocial framework. The Great Depression had made social workers aware of how economic hardship can devastate individuals and families. They also recognized the frequent bias of mental health professionals in their diagnosis and treatment of poor and minority clients. The family therapy movement had been launched, and social workers began treating families. Practitioners had begun to be attuned to the influence of culture on the personalities and attitudes of clients, the impact on diagnosis and treatment of cultural differences between worker and client, and the need to engage in open, mutual discussion of this issue. Knowledge in many areas began to snowball. However, Hollis's framework, which insisted upon the inseparability of the psychodynamic and social components in individual and family functioning, permitted the psychosocial

approach to incorporate new ideas without automatically discarding old ones that have held up over time.

Principles of Psychosocial Treatment

Psychosocial Understanding is Ecosystemic

The psychosocial approach is solidly grounded in the idea that people's behaviors develop within the context of many open systems interacting in mutually causative ways. Human adaptation is based upon the dynamic interplay between person and situation in which new and shifting equilibriums are continually established to make a better "fit" between individual needs and environmental resources. Change in any one system inevitably creates change in others. When a parent is laid off from work, for example, stress is placed on the whole family, a stress that may be acted out by a child misbehaving in school; or the recovery of a spouse from alcohol addiction will shift the marital system, usually requiring new definitions of the relationship. In many cases, family systems provide the most significant context for personality growth and development where even a relatively small shift in support patterns can create significant, long-lasting change.

Families, as we know, are also subject to stress from larger systems and macro-level forces, including dehumanizing bureaucracies, poverty, racism, political persecution, and war. Psychosocial caseworkers are trained to link families with community and social resources and to advocate for fair and just access to services that promote individual and family well-being. In all of these efforts to aid individual and family coping, the worker mobilizes and helps to amplify the inherent strengths of clients, their families, and their communities, with the goal of nurturing the resilience needed to weather the most adverse circumstances.

At the level of the individual system, psychosocial theory incorporates Freud's model of the dynamic unconscious as well as concepts from ego psychology, object relations, self-psychology, and intersubjectivity. These models of intrapsychic functioning are also systemic; not only do the id, ego, and superego-ego ideal proposed by Freud, for example, interact within the individual, but the emerging ego, and later the superego-ego ideal, are shaped through social interaction with the client's external world. Ego psychology underscores the individual's capacity to cope with stress, master challenges, and develop greater strength and competency in the face of unpredictable life events and changing social conditions.

Relationship is Essential to Treatment and a Significant Source of Change in Itself

Years of experience and research have demonstrated that successful psychosocial casework depends heavily on the quality of the relationship between client and worker (Norcross, 2002). The social worker's demonstrated ability to engage clients empathically and with authenticity is central to the establishment of a constructive working alliance. The worker–client relationship may serve as a reparative or corrective emotional experience different from patterns of interactions with original caretakers. When, for example, a worker encourages independence and self-direction in a client who historically had controlling caretakers, the new interpersonal experience can promote client growth. Other clients, in contrast, who were neglected or received too little guidance may need a worker to provide firm, caring limits that help to contain anxiety or acting-out; self-esteem can thereby be nurtured. Still others may need repeated demonstrations of reliability and empathy by a worker who is neither judgmental nor punitive. These new interpersonal experiences can help clients to consolidate developmental tasks by repairing some of the past gaps, delays, or trauma that hindered healthy maturation; ideally, the more benign relationship model is internalized (Hartman & Zimberoff, 2004).

Client Reflections are Central to Psychosocial Study, Assessment, and Intervention

Psychosocial workers are keenly aware that people ascribe individual and collective meanings to events and situations. Based on a lifetime of family and social experience, each person represents a subjective universe of perception. How people view their lives and define their purposes are in great part culturally constructed through belief systems of the family, community, and ethnic group. Because we view clients as the experts on their own lives, we use reflective procedures that facilitate the expression of our clients' thoughts and feelings. Through client reflections, meaningful patterns of experience emerge that become a source of deeper understanding and a basis for change.

Psychosocial Treatment is Based on Study and Assessment of the Person–Situation Gestalt

Treatment planning in psychosocial work flows from careful thinking about the facts of a case. In an effort to understand the multisystemic dynamic of the person-in-situation configuration, practitioners explore the relevant contexts of a person's life and organize their study into a coherent and explanatory assessment. Although psychosocial study and assessment often dovetail in practice, we need to be able to distinguish the facts of a case from the inferences we draw and the interpretation of the facts that we make. Careful psychosocial study and assessment underpin the psychosocial method and provide workers with a professional framework for practice.

The Value Base

An essential and enduring value of psychosocial treatment is the abiding respect for the innate worth of every individual. We sustain an attitude of warmth and goodwill, recognizing that social stigma, poverty, bigotry, and oppression afflict the dignity, capacity, and well-being of all people. Empathy, the capacity to enter into and grasp the inner feelings or subjective state of another, is a critical component of acceptance and is key, in our view, to engaging clients in a constructive, collaborative partnership.

We believe that each person has the right to choose his or her style of life, and we promote the right of individuals to make their own decisions and to determine how they want to conduct their lives. The client's right to act in self-directing ways guides us as we work with clients to mobilize their own competencies and autonomy in service of the choices they make, a concept referred to as self-determination.

Clients have a right to privacy and confidentiality that requires meticulous effort and thoughtfulness to guard. Threat to life or suspicions of abuse and neglect, particularly to minors and the elderly, are circumstances, however, that limit client confidentiality. Yet even in these difficult situations, we do our best to communicate directly and openly with clients about the reasons for sharing information and, when possible, use these circumstances as opportunities to promote client change and personal growth.

Psychosocial Study: The Search for Relevant Facts

Fact-gathering commences as the worker elicits from clients their perception of the problem, what they think led up to it, how they have attempted to remedy it, what they believe might help now, and what other people, agencies, or systems are involved. Not only do the worker's inquiries help clients feel understood, but the importance of their participation in thinking through the current difficulties is underscored. Furthermore, the very act of recounting their impressions may enable them to view their difficulties in a new light. Meanwhile the worker searches for what, in systemic terms, may contribute to the problem. In the words of Florence Hollis (1970), the "person-in-interaction-with-situation" is the "minimum unit of attention" (pp. 46–47), for a set of interacting forces is always at play, be it the individual personality system, a parent–child system, a marital or family system, or health, school, or work system.

Most data about the client are obtained in early interviews; however, selective collection of facts usually continues as long as the contact lasts and as new understandings and treatment emphases emerge. Although study and assessment may proceed simultaneously, the psychosocial study is separate from diagnostic understanding, which represents the thinking of the worker about the facts. Keeping facts and their interpretation as distinct as possible helps steer the worker away from skewing facts to fit theory.

To develop a psychosocial study, the client's own statements and reflections are essential; however, other sources of information, including observations of the client's nonverbal behaviors and demeanor, as well as the dynamic of the client–worker relationship, usually prove useful. Body posture, eye contact, and gestures may all provide clues to client-feeling states or attitudes toward the worker. Accurate decoding of these nonverbal cues, however, requires sensitivity to cultural patterns and to individual meanings assigned by the client. In the end, of course, the client is the best source of information about what nonverbal messages actually signify.

Conjoint interviews provide the worker with in vivo information about interpersonal transactions that are otherwise difficult to capture from client report alone. A husband may complain that his wife is distant and unfeeling but, upon seeing the couple in action together, the worker can discern that the husband is also pushing the wife away, preventing opportunities for closeness. Dynamics between parents and children become apparent in conjoint sessions where communication styles, relationship patterns, emotional responses, distortions, and discrepancies in perception are open to view and discussion.

Psychosocial study of children often requires collateral interviews with parents, teachers, and helping professionals; influential participants in the child's world often become primary sources for significant psychosocial information. Because children tend to be especially sensitive to milieu, direct observation of the parent–child or child–family relationships (sometimes in the home) can throw important light on the dynamics among family members that may be relevant to the child's situation. Observations at school can provide a picture of the child in interaction with other children and with school personnel.

How extensively or deeply early life history is explored depends on the concerns presented by the client. Psychosocial casework focuses on conscious and preconscious material, in contrast to psychoanalysis, and the uncovering of repressed early feelings or memories is *not* the aim of the study. However, family-of-origin issues and early developmental information that seem directly pertinent to either the client or worker are often pursued or clarified. Such explorations may naturally follow a theme that is unfolding in the course of discussions about the origins of the difficulty. Clients themselves often wonder or notice how current behavior patterns relate to childhood relationships or early developmental phases. One woman declared, "Everything changed when I was twelve and my father left home, just as I was going into adolescence; from an outgoing, confident child, I turned into a withdrawn teenager who was deathly afraid of the opposite sex."

Many problems in living emerge during developmental phases of the individual and family life cycle, requiring shifts in personal adjustment and in the family equilibrium. A child's maturation into adolescence, for example, brings with it tasks, challenges, and anxieties for the teenager, the family, and the community. Attention given to expectable stages and transitions of family life broadens the focus of study while normalizing situations clients may label as unusual or pathological. Anxiety often accompanies shifts in parental roles and tasks. Limit-setting with toddlers, for example, challenges mothers in ways that nursing an infant does not; learning to respond to rebellious teenagers' calls for negotiating skills that are usually different from those needed to communicate with younger children; becoming a caretaker to frail elderly parents sometimes means that roles are radically reversed from what they were just a few years ago. Clients often feel relief when they realize that their confusion or frustration is experienced by many others in the same situation.

The effects of life-stage transitions—marriage, parenthood, divorce, retirement—may require careful scrutiny (McKenry & Price, 2005). Expectations people carry into new life phases influence their capacity to cope and make adjustments. When elderly grandparents, for example, suddenly become guardians of their grandchildren orphaned by AIDS, we need to understand what the role shift means to them. Have their dreams for leisure - at long last - been shattered? Do the burdens of the new roles feel overwhelming? Is taking on the responsibility consonant with cultural expectations and viewed stoically as "rightful duty"? Or does having children in the home again invigorate the grandparents, bringing a new sense of purpose to their lives? Psychosocial study is enhanced when we listen carefully to clients for the meanings that only they can specify.

Psychosocial Assessment and Intervention

Psychosocial assessment begins by thinking critically about the facts gathered in the psychosocial study. Now, the worker's task is to conceptualize how the multiple systems at play within the person–situation configuration are mutually interacting. In most cases, even in brief contacts, the worker analyzes how situational stresses, life events, personality functioning, family context, and other relevant forces are working together to create the particular dilemma facing the client.

More specifically, assessment simultaneously addresses and formulates hypotheses about two major matters: (1) how and why a problem exists and (2) who and what within the person–situation Gestalt is accessible to change. Only after determining where we can enter the constellation of multiple systems, and which system or systems are probably most amenable to change, can effective treatment strategies be designed. Assessment, therefore, must identify points of access and evaluate the capacity, motivation and opportunity (Ripple, Alexander, & Polemis, 1964) for change—of individuals, the family, social networks, and communities.

There are common questions the worker considers: What individual strengths can be tapped? What family members are most accessible or most motivated? What community systems and resources can be located or mobilized? If, for example, a husband seeks marital counseling to save his marriage but his wife is absolutely determined to pursue divorce, no amount of intervention will reunite the couple. However, the divorcing parents may then contract for help in working as a team to support their young son rather than allowing him to be caught in the crossfire of anger between them. The worker's knowledge of a support group for children of parents who are separating may provide the youngster with an opportunity to feel less alone in his plight. In another case, the housing shortage may not be remedied to help a family made homeless by fire, but extended family and/or community networks might be mobilized to provide emergency relief. Even in the face of terminal illness, when it might seem little can be done, hospice care can be located, family caretakers can be supported, and the ill person's participation in decision making or in sharing feelings with loved ones may be facilitated.

As should be clear by now, from the psychosocial perspective, individual personality functioning is part of assessment, not the whole. Certainly, the strengths and limitations of a client's ego functioning are important to evaluate, but "individual" performance is always mediated by situational factors: as we all know, the same person can feel and behave very differently in different contexts. For example, at work, where she is valued and successful, a woman may feel comfortable, cheerful, and competent. On the other hand, at home as a single mother living with a belligerent teenage son, she may feel hopeless and depressed.

Psychosocial workers believe that descriptive categories of psychiatry refer to conditions, not to the people themselves. Thus, people with characteristics of borderline personality disorder are not "borderlines." We are concerned with how conditions, psychiatric or otherwise, may affect the achievement of goals desired by a client. Most relevant is the assessment of how the individual's capacities, support systems, and social resources can be mobilized to surmount obstacles. Current research focusing on protective factors, risk factors, and resilience (Corcoran & Nichols-Casebolt, 2004) enriches the psychosocial perspective and provides a new conceptual tool for assessing the balance of forces within a client's situation.

Case Example

Joseph, a 16-year-old Irish-Italian boy from a blue-collar, lower-middle-class family, was initially referred by his mother for individual treatment. She complained of his "angry outbursts at home," frequent and violent fights with peers, and verbal abuse of his younger brother. Psychosocial study revealed, however, that the entire family system was in crisis. The father, years ago diagnosed with multiple sclerosis, was becoming increasingly disabled and fearful of losing his job and health benefits; he was depressed, argumentative, and frequently critical of Joseph. The mother, overloaded with worry and responsibility yet trying to pacify the father, was making rigid demands on her son. She reported that she was frightened of the future and admitted that she tried to "over-control everything" in

the family. Conflicts between Joseph and his parents were heightened by the boy's need to individuate and emancipate himself from the family. Yet the parents' cultural ethic that the children should "love and obey" them placed Joseph in a bind: he felt restrained from taking the next developmental step—that is, making age-appropriate decisions and pursuing his own interests. "They never allow me out of their sight," he complained. Furthermore, the boy—whom, the worker surmised, longed for a strong male in his life—could not seem to muster respect for his physically weak, albeit forceful and judgmental, father.

As it turned out, after the first family meeting, Joseph announced to the worker that he would not return; he had explained how his parents were treating him, he said, and it was up to them to change. With a little support from the worker, the mother, who seemed to be the most self-aware and engageable family member, decided to continue treatment; she saw the need to make changes in her own behavior. Spontaneously, she connected her current fear of loss to a history of loss in her family-of-origin. Soon, she was able to encourage her reluctant husband to join in sessions with her; for the first time, they spoke openly with each other about the future and the impact of the father's illness on all of them. When it was revealed that the younger son, previously described as the "easy" one, was becoming increasingly withdrawn, the parents prepared together for an upcoming conference with the child's teacher. With the worker's help, both parents were able to see how Joseph had been scapegoated by the family process, so weighed down by sorrow and fear. Above all, the parents themselves were no longer arguing with each other or with their children because each was less alone in the crisis.

The worker introduced the parents to the local MS organization, which offered a group for spouses. That organization also steered the father to a consultant on medical insurance and benefits as well as to a physical therapy program. Before termination, at the urging of the parents, the boys agreed to a family meeting. Tensions in the household had diminished considerably. The parents' new ability to talk openly about difficult issues, and to listen to each other, allowed the boys to feel less burdened by the gloomy, angry, and anxious family climate. Now that the illness could be discussed, and Joseph no longer felt criticized and controlled by his parents, he was able to share sadness with his father—about the illness and about some of his own previous behavior.

The Nature of Psychosocial Interventions

As the case example demonstrates, psychosocial treatment often uses a blend of individual, couple, family, and environmental modalities. When indicated by the assessment, collateral meetings with significant others and group work expand the range of direct practice. Whether arranging for a home health attendant to assist an ill parent, or advocating for a client's right to receive a housing allowance, when the joint assessment of worker and client indicates it, psychosocial workers intervene directly within a client's social and community milieu.

Psychosocial workers frequently engage collaboratively with other helping professionals on treatment teams or community task forces. Assessment of young children at risk almost always requires expertise that only a team approach provides. Along the same lines, social workers often spearhead meetings with other providers to develop coordinated treatment plans for families utilizing multiple services; without such collaboration, families and individuals can "fall through the cracks" and may end up with inadequate service or no service at all.

The growing need for coordinated and integrated community services has spawned community-based practices that are family-centered, strengths-based, multisystemic, and collaborative (Lightburn & Sessions, 2006). By using comprehensive psychosocial assessments, social workers, in collaboration with other helping professionals and non-professional community care providers alike, provide "wrap-around" community-based services that empower families in the care and recovery of family members with complex psychosocial needs (Walker, Bruns, & Penn, 2008). This "system of care" model for the delivery of psychosocial treatment (Stroul & Blau, 2008) amplifies Mary Richmond's original idea of "indirect" treatment by focusing on the organization and delivery of community services as the treatment itself.

Psychosocial workers play many roles when using the "environmental procedures" categorized by Hollis (Woods & Hollis, 2000): provider and locator of resources, interpreter and mediator with collaterals, and aggressive intervener (or client advocate). All of these are integral to the dual focus of person and situation that defines psychosocial practice. Turner adds the role of broker, highlighting how social workers may function as the "coordinator and manager of various services and resources in which the client is involved" (Turner, 1986, p. 496). The emergent "system of care" places a critical responsibility on psychosocial workers to communicate and teach specialized clinical knowledge to the non-professionals with whom they collaborate; in addition, social workers need to develop new clinical skills to collaborate effectively with treatment teams (Lightburn & Sessions, 2006; Waldrop, 2006).

As we see, psychosocial practitioners employ many modalities other than individual treatment. Treating children and adolescents in the context of the family is an established part of psychosocial work and can help young and old enhance family relationships (Cunningham & Booth Jr., 2008). Multi-family groups combined with family psychoeducation are used to help family members taking care of loved ones with schizophrenia (Drapalski, Leith, & Dixon, 2009; McFarlane, 1983). Many evidence-based practices are "bundled" with psychosocial intervention, as with multisystemic therapy, where workers engage clients directly in their homes and provide family treatment and group work with peers at school (Henggeler, Schoenwald, Borduin, Rowland, & Cunningham, 1998). Psychosocial treatment in social work practice frequently takes place in a diversity of settings beyond the clinical social worker's office: in schools, hospitals, group homes and residential settings, nursing homes, courts and juvenile justice, prisons, and military bases, among others.

The Psychosocial Typology of Worker–Client Communication

Based on systematic research of hundreds of case records, Florence Hollis and colleagues categorized worker–client communications that have become fundamental to all modalities of direct psychosocial practice (Hollis, 1968; Woods & Hollis, 2000). The six major categories of treatment procedures are used differentially by the worker (in different ways at different times, in the service of mutually determined goals) to build rapport; to offer suggestions; to help clients discharge pent-up feelings; to gather information; and to encourage reflective consideration of present circumstances, of their own patterns of behavior, and of the influence of early life experiences on their present attitudes and actions. Sometimes the worker takes a great deal of initiative in these communications; in other instances, the client leads the explorations and reflections. A brief summary of these procedures follows.

1. *Sustainment* refers to verbal and nonverbal communications that demonstrate interest, acceptance, empathic understanding, reassurance, and encouragement. An understanding nod or smile and statements such as, "Those feelings are natural" or "Say more" help reduce clients' anxieties and encourage them to trust the worker enough to share their concerns.

2. *Direct influence* consists of various degrees of carefully considered suggestion or advice: "Would it help to ___?" "It might be better to ___" "I think you ought to ___." Parent guidance and crisis intervention can require direct influence, with workers sometimes expressing strong opinions, even urging the client to follow a particular course of action. Preferably, of course, clients arrive at decisions by way of their own thinking, but there are times when some degree of direction is clearly indicated.

3. *Exploration, description, and ventilation* describe communications between client and worker that elicit knowledge of the facts of the client's situation and that bring out feelings about it. A worker might say, for example, "Please tell me a little more about the problem at work," or "Just what is it that happens when you and your family get together?" When the feelings are ventilated, clients often experience immediate emotional relief.

4. *Reflection of person–situation configuration* helps clients become more aware of perceptions, thoughts, and feelings concerning their current circumstances and interactions with others. A father, angered and confused by his daughter's disobedience, might be asked, "Can you think of anything upsetting your daughter right now that could make her so defiant?" and "What is it that makes her behavior so difficult for you?" Invitations to explore the client–worker relationship are also part of person–situation reflection: "I was wondering if you thought I was judgmental (indifferent or angry)?"

5. *Pattern dynamic reflection* helps to identify behavioral tendencies of clients, or patterns of thinking and feeling that lead them to particular actions or ways of thinking about events. Patterns of behavior can be clarified: "Do you think you tend to seek closeness with people who are not available?" or "Does it seem to you that you sometimes argue with your son when you are really annoyed with your husband?" These procedures also encourage clients to explore their intrapsychic functioning: "Have you noticed how you criticize yourself and devalue your own ideas?" or "I wonder if you wish others would take care of you the way you devote yourself to them."

6. *Developmental reflection* moves clients to consider family-of-origin or early life experiences that contribute to current personality and functioning. "Have you had feelings like this before?" can help people connect feelings of the present with situations in the past; sometimes just one such question prompts the client to recognize relationships between specific early experiences and current actions or attitudes. Parents of teenagers can be helped to reflect on their own earlier stages: "What was adolescence like for you?" Sensitively phrased inquiries may promote developmental insight: "Do you think you withdraw from your boss, expecting him to be critical the way your father was?" Questions, rather than interpretations, are usually preferable; then the client can feel free to disagree, or correct the worker's opinion.

Illustration

A client complains about a stormy relationship with his wife (**ventilation**), carefully watching the worker for signs of disapproval. The worker nods his head as if to say "I understand" (**sustainment**), and encourages the client to "tell me more so I can really understand what your marriage is like for you." The worker's nonjudgmental, concerned attitude aids the client in further probing about the situation (**sustainment and exploration**). As the client gives more details, he expresses feelings of inadequacy and self-doubt (**ventilation**), but is reassured by the worker's comment that "close relationships are often confusing and filled with intense feelings" (**sustainment**). This reassurance leads the client to describe frequent and "verbally abusive" fights. He shares feelings of shame and remorse (**ventilation**). While acknowledging the client's feelings, the worker encourages him to discuss exactly what transpires (**sustainment and exploration**). As the client continues, the worker gently asks, "How does it feel to you when you find yourself calling your wife those names?" With the aid of the worker, he speaks of his anger when his wife pushes him away (**person–situation reflection**). When the worker asks what being pushed away means to him, the client responds, "I always feel like I don't matter when someone turns away from me" (**pattern dynamic reflection**). In future sessions, the client initiates comments about his childhood—his father's frequent absence and his mother's preoccupation with a chronically ill sister. With little help from the worker at this point, he sees the link between his strong reaction to his wife and the feelings he had so many years ago (**developmental reflection**).

Psychosocial Treatment for the 21st Century

Post-Freudian Relational Theories

As psychosocial treatment enters the 21st century, the spotlight turns to the influence of relational theories on social work practice (Borden, 2000; Goldstein, Miehls, & Ringel, 2009; Saari, 2005; Tosone, 2004), especially attachment theory (Sable, 1992, 1995, 2008; Schore & Schore, 2008), object relations theory (Berzoff, Flanagan, & Hertz, 2007) and self psychology (Goldstein, 2002). In essence, these theories posit the critical importance of relationships for human development as well as for treatment. All the relational theories assume that infants and young children internalize interactions with the important people in their lives, a process that determines their perceptions of themselves and others as they go through life. Post-Freudian relational theories propose that the therapist, using empathy, warmth, and genuineness, prepares the groundwork for change by providing a safe holding environment and a facilitating relationship (Applegate, 1993; Applegate & Bonovitz, 1995; Winnicott, 1965). Transference is now understood as resulting not only from drives and defenses, but also from very early insecure attachment patterns as well as problems in separation–individuation (Mahler, Pine, & Bergman, 1975) and primitive self-object needs (Kohut, 1971). Clients are given opportunities for new and more positive interactions, which, it is assumed, will eventually become internalized (Goldstein, Miehls, & Ringel, 2009).

The notion of a reparative worker–client relationship characterized by empathy, authenticity, and mutual problem solving in the here and now is not new to psychosocial treatment. However, relational theory amplifies and extends these ideas to include new understandings of such concepts as countertransference and resistance, as well as the concept of the therapeutic relationship as an "intersubjective" field (Goldstein et al., 2009; Kahn, 1997; Ornstein & Ganzer, 2005; Stolorow, Brandchaft, & Atwood, 1987).

Expansion of the "Bio-Psycho-Social" in Contemporary Psychosocial Treatment

Greater attention is being given to the role of culture, spirituality, client strengths, and resilience as well as to neuroscience and trauma in psychosocial assessment and intervention. The commonly used rubric of "Bio-Psycho-Social" no longer captures the full extent of the psychosocial perspective (Dean & Poorvu, 2008). Accurate assessments of cultural beliefs and practices are essential to work effectively and competently with our increasingly diverse populations and changing immigrant groups (Congress & Gonzalez, 2005; Congress & Kung, 2005; Fong, 2004; Kung, 2001; McGoldrick, Giordano, & Garcia-Preto, 2003; McGoldrick & Hardy, 2008; Sue, 2006; Webb, 2001; Yan & Wong, 2005). The role of spirituality in well-being, family strength, and resilience are being highlighted in social work practice by numerous authors (Canda & Furman, 1999; Evans, Boustead, & Owens, 2008; Greeff & Fillis, 2009; Hodge, 2005; Limb & Hodge, 2008; Suarez & Lewis, 2005; Walsh, 1998; Walsh & Pryce, 2003) and the strengths perspective, so important in understanding human resilience, is taking greater prominence in our psychosocial thinking (Norman, 2000; Probst, 2009; Rawana & Brownlee, 2009; Saleeby, 2006).

Advances in neurobiology and neuropsychology have revolutionized our knowledge of the relationship between biology and social behavior (Cozolino, 2006; Farmer, 2009; Garland & Howard, 2009; Shonkoff & Phillips, 2000). The importance for infants and young children of their relationship with a primary caregiver has long been recognized (Ainsworth, 1969, 1973; Bowlby, 1969, 1973). Among other things, we have understood that attachment, secure or insecure, plays a crucial role in the child's sense of security, ability to explore the environment, and capacity to regulate affect (Bowlby, 1988). Now, as a result of recent research in neuroscience, we understand that the attachment process is a biological as well as a psychological one and directly affects brain development (Perry, 2002, 2006). The "internal working model" posited by Bowlby has been shown to concretely exist, since a young child's social experience becomes encoded and determines the structure and function of the brain. Thus, there is no dichotomy between nature and nurture. The first 3 years of life constitute a "sensitive period" for brain development, but brain "plasticity" exists and change can occur throughout life (Shapiro & Applegate, 2000). Progress in neuroscience research informs infant mental health, a prevention approach utilizing a multidisciplinary team, including social workers (Lillas & Turnbull, 2009). Brain research also helps us to understand the way in which many types of therapeutic intervention utilize the worker–client relationship to assist clients in re-regulating dysregulated affects (Applegate & Shapiro, 2005).

Advances in neuroscience have also revolutionized the treatment of children, teens, and adults who have experienced trauma. Many of these treatments employ evidence-based practices that are delivered psychosocially to improve the parent–child relationships disrupted by trauma (Lieberman & Van Horn, 2008) and use combinations of psychoeducation, relaxation, affect modulation, and cognitive reprocessing with children, teens, and their parents (Cohen, Mannarino, & Deblinger, 2006). The trauma systems therapy approach developed by Saxe, Ellis, and Kaplow (2007) is a collaborative, multisystem

approach to treat traumatized children within their communities. It recognizes that effective treatment of the child requires that the systems of care within the child's social environment be engaged and organized in a trauma-sensitive way. Psychosocial interventions with organizations and communities are also being developed to treat larger populations exposed to trauma (Webb, 2003), and Sandra Bloom's "sanctuary model," an intervention gaining widespread acceptance, exhorts institutions to create a trauma-sensitive system of care that infuses our understanding of trauma treatment into organizational policies and the day-to-day practices of child care staff, teachers, and social workers (Bloom, 1997).

The Future of Psychosocial Treatment

Community-based mental health services are revolutionizing the concept of psychosocial treatment by focusing on recovery through family empowerment and community systems of care (Lightburn & Sessions, 2006; Stroul & Blau, 2008). Psychosocial practitioners have always known that relationship is a key factor in positive treatment outcomes, but research on trauma demonstrates how increasing the web of positive social relationships promotes recovery and mental well-being (Perry, 2006). The system of care model identifies the community itself as the focus of intervention, where the multiple needs of children and adults are served by fortifying the family and engaging the community in the provision of care to maintain even seriously disturbed children and adults in least-restrictive settings within their communities. For this to happen, social workers must continue to make comprehensive psychosocial assessments and further their skills in working collaboratively with social networks within the community as well as with fellow professionals (Lightburn & Sessions, 2006).

By the same token, direct practice with individuals, as previously discussed, is becoming more relational, fitting well with our profound conviction—derived from the history of psychosocial treatment—that relationship is the keystone to professional helping and central to the psychosocial method. Even as we bolster our community systems of care and extend psychosocial treatment into the natural environments of our clients, the need for sensitive and skillful direct practice will remain. Mary Richmond's dual focus on people and their environments continues to be a vital and necessary component of psychosocial practice as we enter the 21st century.

Acknowledgment

Mary E. Woods, a mentor, colleague, and friend, passed away on May 24, 2005. She was the co-author of the original chapter (Woods & Robinson, 1996) and her words, spirit, and influence have taken root in this revision.

References

Ainsworth, M. S. (1969). Object relations, dependency and attachment: A theoretical review of the infant–mother relationship. *Child Development, 40,* 969–1025.

Ainsworth, M. S. (1973). The development of mother-infant attachment. In B. Caldwell & H. Ricciuti (Eds.), *Review of Child Development Research, 3,* 1–94. Chicago: University of Chicago Press.

Applegate, J. S. (1993). Winnicott and clinical social work: A facilitating partnership. *Child and Adolescent Social Work Journal, 10*(1), 3–19.

Applegate, J. S., & Bonovitz. (1995). *The facilitating partnership: A Winnicottian approach for social workers and other helping professionals.* Lanham, MD: Jason Aronson.

Applegate, J. S., & Shapiro, J. R. (2005). *Neurobiology for clinical social work: Theory and practice.* New York: W. W. Norton.

Berzoff, J., Flanagan, L., & Hertz, P. (2007). *Inside out and outside in: Psychodynamic clinical theory, practice, and psychopathology in contemporary multicultural contexts* (2nd ed.). Lanham, MD: Jason Aronson Publishers.

Bloom, S. (1997). *Creating sanctuary: Toward the evolution of sane societies.* New York: Routledge.

Borden, W. (2000). The relational paradigm in contemporary psychoanalysis: Toward a psychodynamically informed social work perspective. *Social Science Review, 74*(3), 352–379.

Bowlby, J. (1969). *Attachment and loss. Vol. 1: Attachment.* New York: Basic Books.

Bowlby, J. (1973). *Attachment and loss. Vol. 2: Separation anxiety and anger.* New York: Basic Books.

Bowlby, J. (1988). *A secure base.* New York: Basic Books.

Canda, E., & Furman, L. D. (1999). *Spiritual diversity in social work practice: The heart of helping.* New York: Free Press.

Cohen, J. A., Mannarino, A. P., & Deblinger, E. (2006). *Treating trauma and traumatic grief in children and adolescents.* New York: Guilford.

Congress, E., & Gonzalez, M. (Eds.) (2005). *Multicultural perspectives in working with families* (2nd ed.). New York: Springer.

Congress, E., & Kung, W. (2005). Using the culturagram to assess and empower culturally diverse families. In E. Congress & M. Gonzalez, (Eds.), *Multicultural perspectives in working with families* (2nd ed., pp. 3–21). New York: Springer.

Corcoran, J., & Nichols-Casebolt, A. (2004). Risk and resilience ecological framework for assessment and goal formulation. *Child and Adolescent Social Work Journal, 21*(3), 211–235.

Cozolino, L. (2006). *The neuroscience of human relationships: Attachment and the developing social brain.* New York: W. W. Norton.

Cunningham, J. M., & Booth Jr., R. A. (2008). Practice with children and their families: A specialty of clinical social work. *Child & Adolescent Social Work Journal, 25,* 347–365.

Dean, R.G., & Poorvu, N.L. (2008). Assessment and formulation: A contemporary social work perspective. *Families in Society: The Journal of Contemporary Social Services, 89*(4), 596–604.

Drapalski, A. L., Leith, J., & Dixon, L. (2009, April). Involving families in the care of persons with schizophrenia and other serious mental illnesses: History, evidence, and recommendations. *Clinical Schizophrenia & Related Psychoses, 3,* 39–49.

Evans, C. J., Boustead, R. S., & Owens, C. (2008). Expressions of spirituality in parents with at-risk children. *Families in Society: The Journal of Contemporary Social Services, 89*(2), 245–252.

Farmer, R. L. (2009). *Neuroscience and social work practice: The missing link.* Thousand Oaks, CA: Sage.

Fong, R. (Ed.) (2004). *Culturally competent practice with immigrant and refugee children and families.* New York: Guilford.

Garland, E. L., & Howard, O. H. (2009). Neuroplasticity, psychosocial genomics, and the biopsychosocial paradigm in the 21st century. *Health & Social Work, 34*(3), 191–199.

Goldstein, E. G. (1995). *Ego psychology and social work practice* (2nd ed.). New York: Free Press.

Goldstein, E. G. (2002). *Object relations theory and self psychology in social work practice.* New York: Free Press.

Goldstein, E., Miehls, D., & Ringel, S. (2009). *Advanced clinical social work: Relational principles and techniques.* New York: Columbia University Press.

Greeff, A. P., & Fillis, A. J. (2009). Resiliency in poor single-parent families. *Families in Society: The Journal of Contemporary Social Services, 90*(3), 279–285.

Hartman, D., & Zimberoff, D. (2004). Corrective emotional experience in the therapeutic process. *Journal of Heart-Centered Therapies, 7*(2), 3–84.

Henggeler, S. W., Schoenwald, S. K., Borduin, C. M. Rowland, M. D., & Cunningham, P. B. (1998). *Multisystemic treatment of antisocial behavior in children and adolescents*. New York: Guilford.

Hodge, D. R. (2005). Spiritual ecograms: A new assessment instrument for identifying clients' strengths in space and across time. *Families in Society: The Journal of Contemporary Social Services, 86*(2), 287–296.

Hollis, F. (1964). *Casework: A psychosocial therapy*. New York: Random House.

Hollis, F. (1968). *A typology of casework treatment*. New York: Family Service Association of America.

Hollis, F. (1970). The psychosocial approach to the practice of casework. In R. Roberts & R. Nee (Eds.), *Theories of social casework* (pp. 33–75). Chicago: University of Chicago Press.

Kahn, M. (1997). *Between therapist and client: The new relationship*. New York: Holt.

Katz, M. (1983). *Poverty and policy in American history*. New York: Academic Press.

Kohut, H. (1971). *The analysis of the self*. New York: International University Press.

Kung, W. W. (2001). Consideration of cultural factors of working with families with a mentally ill patient. *Families in Society: The Journal of Contemporary Social Services, 82*(1), 97–107.

Lieberman, A. R., & Van Horn, P. (2008). *Psychotherapy with infants and young children: Repairing the effects of stress and trauma on early attachment*. New York: Guilford.

Lightburn, A., & Sessions, P. (Eds.) (2006). *Handbook of community-based clinical practice*. New York: Oxford University Press.

Lillas, C., & Turnbull, J. (2009). *Infant/child mental health, early intervention, and relationship-based therapies: A neurorelational framework for interdisciplinary practice*. New York: W. W. Norton.

Limb, G. E., & Hodge, R. (2008). Developing spiritual competency with Native Americans: Promoting wellness through balance and harmony. *Families in Society: The Journal of Contemporary Social Services, 89*(4), 615–622.

Mahler, M., Pine, F., & Bergman, A. (1975). *The psychological birth of the human infant*. New York: Basic Books.

McFarlane, W. (Ed.) (1983). *Family therapy in schizophrenia*. New York: Guilford Press.

McGoldrick, M., Giordano, J., & Garcia-Preto, N. (Eds.) (2003). *Ethnicity and family therapy* (3rd ed.). New York: The Guilford Press.

McGoldrick, M., & Hardy, K. V. (Eds.) (2008). *Re-visioning family therapy: Race, culture, and gender in clinical practice* (2nd ed.). New York: Guilford Press.

McKenry, P., & Price, J. (Eds.) (2005). *Families & change: Coping with stressful events and transitions* (3rd ed.). Thousand Oaks, CA: Sage Publications, Inc.

Norcross, J. C. (Ed.) (2002). *Psychotherapy relationships that work: Therapist contributions and responsiveness to patients*. New York: Oxford University Press.

Norman, E. (Ed.) (2000). *Resiliency enhancement: Putting the strengths perspective into social work practice*. New York: Columbia University Press.

Ornstein, E. D., & Ganzer, C. (2005). Relational social work: A model for the future. *Families in Society: The Journal of Contemporary Social Services, 86*(4), 565–572.

Perlman, H. (1957). *Social casework: A problem-solving process*. Chicago: University of Chicago Press.

Perry, B. D. (2002). Childhood experience and the expression of genetic potential: What childhood neglect tells us about nature and nurture. *Brain and Mind, 3*, 79–100.

Perry, B. D. (2006). Applying principles of neurodevelopment to clinical work with maltreated and traumatized children: The neurosequential model of therapeutics. In N. B. Webb (Ed.), *Working with traumatized youth in child welfare* (pp. 27–52). New York: Guilford.

Probst, B. (2009). Contextual meanings of the strengths perspective for social work practice in mental health. *Families in Society: The Journal of Contemporary Social Services, 90*(2), 162–166.

Rawana, E., & Brownlee, K. (2009). Making the possible probable: A strength-based assessment and intervention framework for clinical work with parents, children, and adolescents. *Families in Society: The Journal of Contemporary Social Services, 90*(3), 255–260.

Ripple, L., Alexander, E., & Polemis, B. (1964). *Motivation, capacity and opportunity*. Chicago: University of Chicago Press.

Saari, C. (2005). The contribution of relational theory to social work practice. *Smith College Studies in Social Work, 75*(3), 3–14.

Sable, P. (1992). Attachment theory: Application to clinical practice with adults. *Clinical Social Work Journal, 20*(3), 71–283.

Sable, P. (1995). Attachment theory and post-traumatic stress disorder. *Journal of Analytic Social Work, 2*, 89–109.

Sable, P. (2008). What is adult attachment? *Clinical Social Work Journal, 36*(1), 21–30.

Saleeby, D. (Ed.) (2006). *The strengths perspective in social work practice* (4th ed.). New York: Pearson.

Saxe, G. N., Ellis, B. H., & Kaplow, J. B. (2007). *Collaborative treatment of traumatized children and teens: The trauma systems therapy approach.* New York: Guilford.

Schore, J. R., & Schore, A. N. (2008). Modern attachment theory: The central role of affect regulation in development and treatment. *Clinical Social Work Journal, 36*(1), 9–20.

Shapiro, J. R., & Applegate, J. S. (2000). Cognitive neuroscience, neurobiology and affect regulation: Implications for clinical social work. *Clinical Social Work Journal, 28*(1), 9–21.

Shonkoff, J. P., & Phillips, D. A. (Eds.) (2000). *From neurons to neighborhoods: The science of early childhood development.* Washington, DC: National Academy Press.

Stolorow, R. D., Brandchaft, B., & Atwood, G. E. (1987). *Psychoanalytic treatment: an intersubjective approach.* Hillsdale, NJ: The Analytic Press.

Stroul, B. A., & Blau, G. M. (Eds.). (2008). *The system of care handbook: Transforming mental health services for children, youth, and families.* Baltimore: Paul H. Brookes.

Suarez, Z. E., & Lewis, E. A. (2005). Spirituality and culturally diverse families: The intersection of culture, religion and spirituality In E. Congress & M. Gonzalez (Eds.), *Multicultural perspectives in working with families* (2nd ed., pp. 425–441). New York: Springer.

Sue, D. W. (2006). *Multicultural social work practice.* Hoboken, NJ: Wiley.

Tosone, C. (2004). Relational social work: Honoring the tradition. *Smith College Studies in Social Work, 74*(4), 475–487.

Turner, F. J. (1986). Psychosocial theory. In F. J. Turner (Ed.), *Social work treatment: interlocking theoretical approaches* (3rd ed., pp. 484–513). New York: Free Press.

Waldrop, D. P. (2006). Caregiving systems at the end of life: How informal caregivers and formal providers collaborate. *Families in Society: The Journal of Contemporary Social Services, 87*(3), 427–437.

Walker, J. S., Bruns, E. J., & Penn, M. (2008). Individualized services in systems of care: The wraparound process. In B. A. Stroul & G. M. Blau (Eds.), *The system of care handbook: Transforming mental health services for children, youth, and families* (pp. 127–153). Baltimore: Paul H. Brookes.

Walsh, F. (1998). *Strengthening family resilience.* New York: Guilford.

Walsh, F., & Pryce, J. (2003). The spiritual dimension of family life. In F. Walsh (Ed.), *Normal family processes: Growing diversity and complexity* (3rd ed., pp. 337–372). New York: Guilford.

Webb, N. B. (Ed.) (2001). *Culturally diverse parent-child and family relationships: A guide for social workers and other practitioners.* New York: Columbia University Press.

Webb, N. B. (Ed.) (2003). *Mass trauma and violence: Helping families and children cope.* New York: Guilford.

Webb, N. B. (Ed.). (2005). *Working with traumatized youth in child welfare.* New York: Guilford.

Winnicott, D. W. (1965). *Maturational processes and the facilitating environment.* New York: International Universities Press.

Woods, M. E., & Hollis, F. (2000). *Casework: A psychosocial therapy* (5th ed.). New York: McGraw-Hill.

Woods, M. E., & Robinson, H. (1996). Psychosocial theory and social work treatment. In F. Turner (Ed.), *Social work treatment: Interlocking theoretical approaches* (4th ed., pp. 555–580). New York: The Free Press.

Yan, M. C., & Wong, Y. R. (2005). Rethinking self-awareness in cultural competence: Toward a dialogic self in cross-cultural social work. *Families in Society: The Journal of Contemporary Social Services, 86*(2), 181–188.

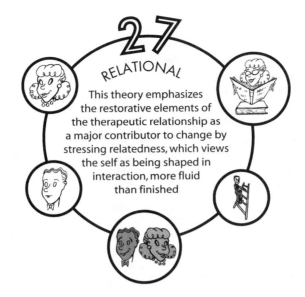

RELATIONAL

This theory emphasizes the restorative elements of the therapeutic relationship as a major contributor to change by stressing relatedness, which views the self as being shaped in interaction, more fluid than finished

Relational Theory and Social Work Treatment

Dennis Miehls

In this chapter, relational theory is considered to be a framework of ideas that have grown out of a number of clinical and psychodynamic theories of the past 50 years. Psychoanalytic thinkers who moved away from a classical Freudian theory began to offer alternative ways of understanding the relationship between clinicians and their clients. There are two distinct phases in the development of relational theory. This progression moved from what were termed theories that are one-person psychologies to two-person psychologies (Goldstein, Miehls, & Ringel, 2009). Broadly speaking, relational theory has evolved into a way of understanding client–worker interactions that emphasizes the mutuality of the interaction. Relational theorists recognize that clients and social workers co-create the clinical relationship in such a way

that empowers clients to maximize their strengths and potential. Clinicians who utilize relational principles in their professional relationships emphasize the restorative elements of the therapeutic relationship as a major contributor to change processes. Furthermore, relational theory "focuses on studying relatedness in context and makes this integral to a theory of practice. It views the self as more fluid than fixed, and as shaped in interaction relative to social or interpersonal settings and backgrounds" (Hadley, 2008, pp. 205–206). Relational theory is particularly suited to working with oppressed populations as the social identities of clients are honored and understood to be a major contributor to one's identity. Feminist scholars who wrote about the social construction of gender (Benjamin, 1988, 1998; Dimen, 2003) and authors who theorize about race and class (Altman, 1995, 2000; Leary, 1997) have made major contributions to relational theory.

Recognizing the influence of culture on one's development furthers the fundamental social work construct of working with "person-in-environment." Social workers have a long history of applying relational theory principles in their work with clients. The social work profession, with its emphasis historically on the benefits of the therapeutic relationship (Richmond, 1917, 1922; Hamilton, 1940), foreshadowed the relational theory movement in the psychotherapy literature (Sheppard, 2001). Ironically, other mental health disciplines have not traditionally credited social workers for their contributions. Horowitz (1998) comments, "Like Moliere's Bourgeois Gentlemen who didn't realize that he'd been speaking prose for more than forty years without knowing it, perhaps social workers should consider that we've been relational, postmodern, and cutting-edge for eighty years without knowing it" (p. 378).

Historical Origins of the Theory

As noted above, there are two distinct periods of relational theory development. Though moving away from some of Freud's classical "drive-structural model" of understanding human behavior, the formulations of early relational theorists "still referred to what has been termed a 'one-person' psychology that views development as an 'individual' activity that is aided by the presence of a caregiving other. A second group of more contemporary theorists have put forth concepts that are broadly referred to as 'two-person' psychologies that emphasize mutuality and interaction" (Goldstein, Miehls, & Ringel, 2009, p. 18). As noted above, there were numerous contributors to the shift in psychoanalytic thinking that began to emphasize the idea that relationships with other people shape the structure of the mind (internal world) of individuals and that these important attachment relationships shape the personality of individuals. Again, this is in contrast to the Freudian understanding of what shapes the nature of the mind and personality structure.

Contributors to the one-person psychology of relational thinking originated from both the United States and England. Much of the earlier thinking about relational theory was formulated by authors who have been grouped together, as a result of the similarities of their theories. These are:

- British object relations (Bowlby, 1958, 1988; Klein, 1932, 1952; Fairbairn, 1940, 1952; Winnicott, 1965, 1975)
- The American interpersonal school (Harry Stack Sullivan, 1953, 1954)
- American object relations (Jacobson, 1964; Kernberg, 1975, 1976, 1980; Mahler, Pine, & Bergman, 1975)
- Self psychology (Kohut, 1971, 1977, 1984)
- Self-in-relation theory (Jordan, 1995, 1997; Miller, 1973)

Common tenets of this range of theorists include the fundamental notion that humans are relational by intent and that attachment to caregivers is necessary for species survival. In other words, one's libidinal energy is object seeking, not pleasure seeking (as suggested by Freud). An important concept of all of the above theories is that infants/children develop an internal world of object relations that has been shaped by the interpersonal interactions with significant others, such as parents or grandparents. The internal world of object relations shapes the individual's interpersonal interactions with others. Many of these interactions are unconscious, and thus individuals who have unsatisfying or troubled relationships as adults are often not aware of their interpersonal style. Often, one-person relational therapy would assist clients to become aware of their relationship patterns and to also use the clinical/therapy relationship as a holding environment that helps reshape the client's earlier object relations impairments.

The more contemporary two-person intersubjective and relational theorists emphasize the mutual and interactional process that occurs between infants and significant objects. These theorists support and elaborate the findings of infant researchers and developmental psychologists who have been studying the attachment and interactive styles of infants and their parents (Beebe & Lachmann, 1988; Stern, 1985). Following this research, relational theorists understand that the clinical relationship is shaped by the mutual interaction of client and clinician. Both shape the interaction in a recursive and reciprocal manner. In two-person relational theory, the clinician interacts with clients with authenticity and transparency. As such, relational theorists are mindful of their subjective reactions to clients and use these reactions, when appropriate, with self-disclosure of feelings and genuine responses to clients.

Goldstein, Miehls, and Ringel (2009) note that three different streams of thought contributed to the development of two-person psychology:

- New York University postdoctoral program in psychoanalysis (Mitchell, 1998, 2000; Mitchell & Aron, 1999; Mitchell & Black, 1995)
- Intersubjective theorists (Atwood & Stolorow, 1984; Stolorow & Atwood, 1992; Stolorow, Brandchaft, & Atwood, 1994)
- Infant researchers (Beebe & Lachmann, 1988; Stern, 1985)

Relevance for the Social Work Profession

Contemporary relational theory is particularly relevant to the social work profession, considering its mandate to work with and provide services to oppressed populations. As noted, social work is relational at its core, and the added dimensions of empowerment, mutuality, and authenticity of the clinical relationship underscore and emphasize the National Association of Social Workers Code of Ethics (2008). For example, three values and their corollary principles are directly relevant to relational social work: the principles of respecting the inherent dignity and worth of the person, the importance of human relationships, and social workers behaving in a trustworthy manner, with integrity (NASW Code of Ethics, 2008, p. 5–6). Beyond these clear links to the Code of Ethics, Goldstein, Miehls, and Ringel (2009) note that "The relational model's emphasis on the client's and clinician's subjectivities and the co-construction of new relational patterns based on a mutually created therapeutic space add new dimensions to clinical social work practice with vulnerable and oppressed populations" (p. 148).

The compatibility of feminist thought to relational theory further complements the underlying tenets of the social work profession. Relational theory continuously contextualizes one's identity, and thus the interface of clinical work with social advocacy work is another important link for social work practitioners. In other words, relational theory offers an opportunity to critique social practices that marginalize vulnerable populations and to assist clients to reconsider their own internalized oppression, if it is present. For example, many gay or lesbian clients have internalized a negative sense of themselves based upon the social construction of queer identity in society. A relational theorist assists the client to update his or her own sense of self by critiquing the social construction of the dominant culture's view of homosexuality. Other social identity factors are deconstructed in similar ways by the social work relational practitioner. Further, relational social workers encourage discussion between themselves and their clients in terms of their differences in social identity. Again, the recognition that the client and clinician are equal participants in the clinical process, with equal authority and agency, is often a very liberating and empowering experience for the generally marginalized client. Goldstein, Miehls, and Ringel (2009) suggest that relational theories initiate new questions in the process: "These questions concern the therapist's, as well as the client's subjectivities, their mutual perceptions of one another, and the ways in which both influence each other through the racial, social, economic, and cultural contexts they are embedded in" (p. 149).

The Conceptual Frame of Relational Theory

Basic tenets of the conceptual frame of relational theory have been introduced in the previous sections of the chapter. One of the most important concepts in relational theory underscores that the subjectivities of both client and social worker shape the helping relationship in a complex and dynamic manner. The social worker certainly has a level of experience, expertise, and a knowledge base. However, the social worker does not necessarily act as an "expert" in the interaction; the clinician is not a neutral observer in the process of the client. Relational theory suggests that both "construct this dynamic together, influenced by what each brings to the dyad, including the influences of their experiences in the contexts in which each has lived" (Hadley, 2008, p. 211). So, the traditional views of transference and countertransference are significantly extended in a relational model. Following the lead of intersubjective theorists (Atwood & Stolorow, 1984; Mitchell, 2000; Natterson & Friedman, 1995), relational theorists suggest that every feeling response of the client is explicitly related to the real interpersonal interaction with the clinician. Traditional views of transference would suggest that the client is attributing characteristics to the clinician in a way that is a repetition of relationship patterns that were established in one's past interactions. In this model, transference is thought of as being something that the clinician understands as a conflict within the client alone. Not so in relational theory; rather, relational theory suggests that any reaction of the client is embedded in a real experience with the clinician. Relational theory recognizes that transference does exist, but it also suggests that both conscious and unconscious reactions of the client and social worker are stimulated as a result of the interpersonal exchange between the two. Similarly, countertransference responses are not considered idiosyncratic responses of the clinician towards the client (that traditionally would have been thought to originate from some conflict within the clinician or would have been understood as a response to some dynamic within the client). Rather, relational theory suggests that the countertransference response has been co-created in the unique interactions of the dyad and that an understanding of this response is firmly rooted in the subjectivities of both participants.

The conceptual frame of the mutuality and co-creation of the relationship then leads to a more nuanced and complex view of the treatment relationship. Certainly, the goals of the clinical process are formulated around the client's particular needs and circumstances. However, the social worker does not only offer "technical" observations but offers an authentic relationship with the client. At times, this may involve social workers disclosing aspects of their own feelings and/or uncertainties to the client. This does not imply that an "anything goes" approach is endorsed by relational theory; self-disclosure is used to understand the rich dynamic between the two so that clients can better understand the complexity of their inner world and/or to facilitate change. At times, the clinical relationship becomes the focus of the work in a direct and continuous manner. This process leads to the possibility that some relationship rupture between the two and the successful repair of the rupture can yield significant growth for the client in terms of relationship patterns and offers an opportunity to update one's sense of self. Relational theory terms this sort of relationship rupture an "enactment," and this concept will be elaborated later in the chapter.

De Young (2003) suggests that relational therapy is essentially performative in nature. She suggests that insight (alone) about one's family history or relationship patterns does not contribute to a change process for the client. She says, "particular insights… have no power to change anything for a client unless they are performative insights, or insights that are intimately connected to interactive, emotional experience" (p. 4). Again, read the importance of the treatment relationship. She elaborates, saying, "The essence of therapy…is in everything that you and your client do together—how you interact to construct ideas, how those meanings move both of you, and how your interactions change over time, especially when you reflect on what goes on between you" (p. 4). Rather than trying to avoid conflict between the client and the clinician, the relational social worker fully anticipates that he or she will become fully immersed in the client's life narrative in an intimate way and that if the treatment is to be effective, then there inevitably will be relational issues and enactments between the client and the social worker. As noted before, the relational worker does not see the site of the "problem" within the client but with the client's interactions within the social context of one's life and within the social context of the clinician's life. The motivations of the actions of the clinician should always be transparent to the client; De Young (2002) comments on Owen Renik's metaphor about the therapist process, citing that he suggested that the therapist's engagement is *playing with your cards face-up*. According to De Young, Renik (1966) suggests that the patient can engage with the clinician's transparent feelings and intentions as fallible opinions, not as scientific or moral pronouncements.

One further conceptual framework is important to note in relational theory. It is clear that relational theory discusses the interactions of the self (client) and other (clinician and/or context) as being fundamental in shaping the client's view of self. Relational theorists suggest, though, that there is a third construct to consider in understanding relationships. This is referred to as the third space. Mitchell (1988) comments:

> Relational theory focuses on three aspects: the self, the other, and the space between the two. There is no "object" in a psychologically meaningful sense without some particular sense of oneself in relation to it. There is no "self," in a psychologically meaningful sense, in isolation, outside a matrix of relations with others. Neither the self nor the object (other) are meaningful dynamic concepts without presupposing some sense of psychic space in which they interact, in which they do things with or to each other (p. 33).

This concept underscores the essence of relational theory—that is, that there is no such thing as a linear interaction in which a message or communication is a one-way street. Rather, relational theory suggests that communication of any sort happens in this third space that is neither wholly self or other. This concept is very similar to contemporary neurobiological theory as well. There, theorists are suggesting that there is no such thing as a single brain. For example, Cozolino (2006), suggests that all brain development happens only in interaction with another person. Of relevance for this chapter, Cozolino (2006) suggests that there is a space between two people called a social synapse. It is in this intermediary space that brain development happens in a recursive fashion.

The concept of third space in relational theory is "utilized to understand how culture, race, and ethnicity that both client and therapist bring with them influence the treatment, and how the interaction between client and therapist is transformed into a new, third dimension" (Goldstein, Miehls, & Ringel, 2009, p. 157). Mattei (2008) refers to this as the "ethnic third"; she emphasizes that this is a crucial (although often unverbalized) dimension of any treatment process. With these core conceptual frameworks in mind, the chapter

now turns to the practice implications of relational theory.

Implications for Assessment and Treatment

Assessment

As the reader might expect, the treatment relationship is a key component to understanding the client's concerns and presenting issues. Regardless of the presenting concerns, relational theory suggests that aspects of relationship history and the social context in which one grew up and the client's understanding of his or her relationship narratives will be intrinsically involved in the assessment and treatment process. Keeping a focus on the context of the individual's history is crucial in completing an assessment based on relational theory. De Young (2003) comments, "what's wrong is neither entirely inside the client, in his psychological makeup or dysfunction patterns, nor entirely outside in the world, in forces that impinge upon him. Instead, according to a relational model of psychotherapy, the problem exists in those spaces or activities where outside influences and inside responses interact to create the shape and feel of a 'self'" (p. x). Here, too, relational theory is compatible with the social work profession's view of assessment, which is biopsychosocial in nature and thus more holistic than that of some other professions.

A key aspect of assessment is to determine the immediacy or "crisis" elements of the client's presentation. Clearly, relational practitioners assist in initial problem solving around the crisis components of the client's presenting concerns. An active, collaborative approach is essential, and the clinician recognizes that a premature focus on "relationship" issues might be detrimental to a client who is experiencing an acute situational crisis. That said, the relational clinician does listen attentively for relationship and contextual themes in the assessment of any crisis situation. The relational clinician understands that most presenting concerns will have some connection to attachment relationships; however, the timing of when this concept is introduced is important.

Clients in crisis often require some ego-supportive work in order to restore some equilibrium to their world. And, as appropriate, the relational clinician begins to educate clients about the interface of current feelings with one's past relationships with others, while considering the social context and identities of the client. Goldstein, Miehls, and Ringel (2009) suggest, "It is useful for the clinician to explore the meaningful relationships in a client's current life situation and whether there are any changes, stresses, disruptions, disappointments, rejections, conflicts, or losses that are affecting the client" (p. 94).

The relational clinician certainly engages in empathic listening during the assessment phase of the work. And the clinician will gently guide the process so as to help the client fill in missing pieces of information. The clinician will assist clients to expand their understanding of their life narratives. Relational theory understands the benefit of "making meaning" out of the complexity of one's history as a key aspect of feeling more cohesive in terms of one's sense of self. It is important that the clinician fully understand that his or her own attitudes, belief systems, and actions will be continuously be scrutinized by the client, even during the assessment phase of the work. Thus, it is important for the worker to be self-monitoring and to be in tune to any subtle shift that the client demonstrates. The beginning interactions of the dyad are particularly telling in terms of the client's internal world, and how the client positions himself or herself with the clinician is a very important source of assessment data.

During the assessment, the clinician gleans some understanding of what motivates the client generally, and the client's typical way of engaging and interacting with the world. It is useful to consider how adaptive or maladaptive these patterns have become for the client. Much of the client's usual way of presenting in the world will be somewhat unknown to him or her, and thus the assessment process begins to ascertain what the client is consciously aware of, in terms of his or her interpersonal patterns. Here, too, it is important to have some assessment of how the client understands the influence of the social construction of his or her identity. Most clients do not appreciate how powerful societal messages are and how these messages shape their sense of self; the clinician begins to introduce these ideas to the client during the assessment

process. As noted previously, messages about gender, race, ethnicity, sexual orientation, as examples, profoundly shape the client's view of himself or herself.

The relational clinician will appraise the degree of traumatic events in the client's earlier life. It is an unfortunate reality that many of our clients who seek social work services have experienced some sort form of trauma during their childhood. Understandably, this reality will complicate the assessment and the treatment process. Commenting specifically on the process with traumatized individuals, De Young (2003) suggests, "As clients share themselves with you more deeply, they hope that you will understand them ever more deeply, they hope that you will understand them ever more deeply and completely. But at the same time, their painful relational history leads them to expect that you will fail them, judge them, and abandon them. And inevitably, in small ways at least, you do fail them" (p. xi). In some instances, clinicians fail their clients in large ways as well and enactments happen in the treatment process. The chapter now turns to the treatment process and will elaborate on the concepts of enactments and self-disclosure in relationally based practice.

Treatment

Treatment principles of relational theory draw from both the earlier relational theorists (one-person psychologies) and more contemporary relational theorists (two-person psychologies). Earlier relational theorists emphasized the holding functions of the treatment process, which include empathic attunement to the client and the minimization of any countertransference responses that might interfere with the development of empathy with the client. Early relational theorists focused on understanding the client's past, including developmental arrests and relational patterns, and this focus led to treatment interventions that aimed to strengthen the sense of self, which would lead to the development of more satisfying relationships with others. The clinical relationship offered an opportunity for some corrective experiences for the client. In earlier models, client transference was thought of as a combination of what the client brought to the treatment and what might be triggered within the client as a reaction to the clinician's personality and actions. Earlier theorists tended to think that clients could induce certain countertransference responses within the clinician and these could be used to understand the client's internal world.

Contemporary relational theorists stress the interaction between the therapeutic dyad rather than seeing the main function of the clinician as providing a holding environment. More space is given to the expression of the clinician's responses, including countertransference responses. Contemporary relational theorists promote a more spontaneous and authentic stance for the clinician. The deconstruction of the therapeutic relationship is emphasized, and these theorists see transference and countertransference as co-created by the dyad; understanding and working through conflict (enactments) between the two offers great opportunity for change when managed correctly by the clinician. In reality, most clinicians who consider themselves relational likely practice with components of each of these models influencing the treatment. The following treatment principles may be used somewhat differentially by different workers, but these comprise the essence of relational treatment principles.

The treatment is framed as a highly collaborative process, and relational clinicians educate their clients that both members of the therapeutic dyad will be intricately involved in the treatment process. This is often relieving to clients, who may have a stereotypical view that the clinician will be the prototype of a worker who is neutral, objective, and expert. Some clients will have had previous therapeutic experience in which perhaps the therapist listened attentively but reflected back their questions to them in a routine and nonspecific manner. A relational clinician is more apt to offer genuine responses, at times, when clients ask questions about the clinician's identity and/or treatment approach. Goldstein, Miehls, and Ringel suggest, "A collaborative approach communicates respect and validates clients' own experience and goes a long way in preventing a nontherapeutic interaction in which clients are placed in a diminished position in relationship to clinician's authority" (p. 107). As clients tell their life narrative, relational clinicians actively ask questions so as to fill in missing pieces of crucial information. Relational clinicians might share their own feelings of confusion and/or uncertainty about parts of the client's presenting concerns. This open, not-knowing stance is a key component to the treatment process as it empowers the client, often resulting in enhanced self-esteem and a sense of efficacy within the client.

As noted, a treatment goal is the establishment of a therapeutic holding environment. However, relational clinicians take a more nuanced view of this and do not approach every client with a cookie-cutter approach. Rather, the therapist's stance is determined by the particular and specific needs of each client. Some clients may require a great deal of reassurance; some may require contact in between sessions and some may like more autonomy, for example. Likewise, it may be very important for certain clients to have some information about the background of the clinician, and at times the clinician may need to self-disclose certain aspects of himself or herself to firmly establish a strong holding environment. Likewise, a clinician needs to take a very active protective stance towards clients who are somewhat impulsive and/or self-destructive. At times, the relational clinician will perform a number of case management functions for particularly vulnerable and/or distressed clients. Ensuring that the client has a strong network of health and mental health providers is crucial to doing the clinical work, and the relational clinician actively helps the client to become as grounded as possible by supporting the client's ego functions and helping the client to build a broad network of support.

Similar to the nuances of the holding environment, another treatment principle of relational theory is to recognize the complexity of empathic attunement with a range of clients. Some clients need more distance in order to feel safe, while others need a great deal of confirmation that their feelings and life situations are exquisitely understood by the clinician. Beyond empathy, the relational clinician may need to set limits on problematic behavior. Again, it is best to work collaboratively with clients to assist them to manage anxiety, to deal with any addictive behavior, and/or to prevent any form of self-harm, including suicidal behaviors. Goldstein, Miehls, and Ringel (2009) note, "The unilateral establishment of strict rules should be avoided.

For example, some clients who abuse drugs, alcohol, or food or who engage in self-mutilation and other forms of destructive behavior may not be able to maintain total abstinence or refrain from their usual behavior as a prerequisite to treatment" (p. 117). A relational clinician will certainly address self-destructive behaviors, but the timing of such interventions is important, and working with clients to set reasonable goals about the change process of self-destructive behavior often yields more treatment compliance and changed behavior over the long term.

As noted before, the relational clinician exercises spontaneity and genuineness while interacting with clients. The treatment approach in relational theory implies a more frequent use of self-disclosure by the clinician. Self-disclosures generally take one of three forms during the treatment. First, clinicians may disclose some aspects of their own feelings, attitudes, values, life experiences, and factual information about themselves or others in their life. Second, clinicians may disclose their feelings about what is going on in the treatment. They may share the rationale for certain interventions or comments. Or, they may share some dilemmas that they are experiencing in the work with the client. For example, a clinician may suggest to a client that she is confused about how to raise a sensitive issue with the client. The clinician may suggest that she wants to ask the client about her sexual acting-out behavior but doesn't want the client to perceive the clinician as judgmental. Pointing out the dilemma to the client often encourages the client to be more forthcoming about the details of the dynamic issue, and it certainly offers opportunities to deepen the treatment relationship. The third type of self-disclosure involves the clinician's sharing some countertransference reactions. This is particularly important in dealing with ruptures in the treatment relationship (which will be elaborated shortly).

Therapist self-disclosure often leads to many positive outcomes. A client who often feels a sense of shame about her own feelings and actions may feel a great deal of relief when she hears that the clinician had struggled with a similar feeling or circumstance in the past. Usually a client does not want to hear explicit detail of a clinician's experience but does feel some sense of mutual connection when the clinician is honest in response to a difficult question or questions that are present within the client. As the reader might anticipate, however, some self-disclosure by the clinician may lead to unexpected and problematic results. This author was working with a woman who was a parentified child and who often had to take care of her mother's emotional world. Her mother was often depressed and the client had to often prop her mother up emotionally. In order to attend the funeral services of his brother, who had died precipitously, the author canceled two sessions with the client on short notice. This was at a particularly difficult time for the client. Likely arising from guilt, the author disclosed the reason for the cancellations. The author assumed that this explanation would offer some rationale for the client, but while it certainly explained the cancellation, the client seemed to become more distracted and sullen during the session. The author listened for some minutes and then commented, "It seems to me that your demeanor shifted when I told you of my brother's death." The client replied, "What do you expect? I guess I will have to take care of you, too." The author quickly said that she didn't need to do that and that he had his own support system. This further statement only aggravated the hurt feelings of the client and she seemed to feel chastised. The author went on to say, "I am sorry, I should have realized that my saying what I did might have felt like a burden." The client replied, "Maybe I'm being a selfish bitch. Of course I'm sorry about your brother, but I just want my therapy to be for me. I don't want to have to worry about you." Further dialogue revealed the extent of the client's caretaking activities with a range of others. This led to a deeper understanding of this dynamic within her, which had been activated by the clinician's self-disclosure (also reported in Goldstein, Miehls, & Ringel, 2009, pp. 121–122).

One final treatment principle is how the relational clinician manages disruptions and/or enactments in the treatment relationship. As noted, relational theorists understand that the here-and-now interpersonal interaction between the therapeutic dyad leads to transference responses of the client that are co-created between the two. The relational clinician expects that there will be disruptions in almost all treatment relationships. These are viewed as opportunities to facilitate change for the client (and perhaps the clinician). The clinician may become aware of disruptions in the treatment relationship when the client begins to show a subtle or more apparent shift in his or her behavior in sessions. The client may become more quiet in sessions; he or she may become detached or aloof or perhaps angry as well. The repair of disruptions offers a potentially powerful therapeutic moment. Dealing with disruptions is a multistep process. First the clinician needs to directly acknowledge that there has been some sort of impasse between the two. It is important that both client and clinician explore the clinician's role in causing the disruption. The clinician needs to encourage the client to verbalize feelings of anger and/or disappointment and to certainly empathize with and legitimize these feelings. Often the clinician needs to give the client "permission" to express these feelings of anger, sadness, or rejection. It is also important for the clinician to acknowledge that he or she has played a role in the disruption. Further, the dyad needs to fully unearth the client's meaning and perceptions of the rupture. The clinician may or may not offer some explanation for the empathic failure. In addition, the clinician needs to ask the client how this rupture can be repaired. If appropriate, the clinician eventually may link the feelings generated by the rupture to the client's past experiences with significant others. Clearly, this needs to be conveyed in a nonjudgmental manner, and the timing of this is crucial. It is very important that the clinician does acknowledge his or her real part of the interaction that contributed to the impasse, and it is often useful if the clinician apologizes to the client. Making the link to the client's earlier relationship experiences offers a powerful opportunity that leads to change and enhanced self-esteem within the client. Last, the clinician may make observations that their interaction is prototypical of conflict that the client might be experiencing in current relationships. Self-reflection for clinicians is important, and they may discuss the impasse with their supervisor or their own therapist.

Relational theorists also understand that a more troubling sort of treatment rupture happens when there is an enactment between the client and clinician. Enactments refer to actual exchanges between the dyad that are often potentially destructive and have been experienced previously by the client in harmful and/or traumatic relationships. Individuals who are survivors of childhood trauma often do stimulate strong feelings within clinicians, and work with trauma survivors can be particularly prone to enactments. Trauma theory suggests that there is a "triadic self" that is internalized by survivors of childhood trauma. Basham and Miehls (2004) discuss this triadic self and understand that trauma survivors all internalize some aspect of identity that is described as victim-victimizer-bystander (rescuer). In other words, survivors of trauma often play out the role of the victim in the treatment relationship. At times, the clinician plays the corollary role to this and actually becomes somewhat victimizing in the relationship. At other times, the client victimizes the clinician, or the clinician might either arduously adopt a rescuer stance with the client or may ignore the real pain of the client, which is an enactment of the bystander role (many survivors of trauma describe that others in their family stood by and did not intervene in the abusive dynamics between them and the perpetrator).

While it is true that clients who are not survivors of trauma may also experience enactments in the treatment, this dynamic happens with some regularity with trauma survivors. The client and clinician unconsciously create a dynamic that actually replays the original relationship that was destructive. Trauma theory suggests that these enactments are an inevitable part of the treatment process. The clinician often is caught unaware of the enactment until the exchange has happened. Clinicians need to be particularly self-scrutinizing of their responses to clients and must be particularly alert to the possibility of enactments when they are behaving in ways that seem to contribute to affect escalation or dysregulation within the client. The steps outlined above in terms of dealing with ruptures and impasses have relevance here as well when the clinician recognizes that an enactment has occurred.

The preceding are the key components to assessment and treatment from a relational model. Of importance, and as mentioned, relational clinicians will modify their stance on a case-by-case basis, but it is certainly true that a relational clinician will definitely be actively involved in co-creating the treatment relationship. Effective relational clinicians need to have a very well-examined sense of self, and often one's own therapy furthers this process.

Limitations and Cautionary Notes

An oversimplification of relational theory may lead to some misuses of the concepts that have been put forward in this chapter. Practicing from a relational perspective certainly requires a great deal of experience and supervision. While the tenets of mutuality and equality in a clinical relationship have appeal to many practitioners and student practitioners, these concepts are complex and require a great deal of thoughtfulness in their application to social work treatment. Rather than suggesting an "anything goes" approach to treatment, relational practitioners use self-disclosure in a judicious and planned manner. It takes a highly skilled assessment to know when and how to use self-disclosure effectively in treatment. In addition, while relational theory suggests that practicing from a relational perspective can lead to growth for both the client and the clinician, relational theorists also emphasize that the focus of the growth process needs to be centered on the client's needs and goals. Relational therapists are sometimes criticized as being "self-indulgent," but of course the opposite is true; effective relational clinicians are anything but self-indulgent, and they do recognize that the work is not for the faint-hearted. Practicing relationally demands a particular type of self-awareness and self-monitoring. For this reason, it is this author's belief that social work students should be exposed to principles of relational treatment only after they have learned how to practice social work with more traditional boundaries and parameters.

Implications of Relational Theory for the Future

Relational theory has captured the attention of many psychodynamic thinkers and academics. The author imagines that relational theory will continue to be influential in the development of treatment models in social work and beyond. As noted, this theory is a natural fit with social

work, as it is particularly suited to working with oppressed populations. The theory contextualizes identity and deconstructs the social construction of identity. This is an encouraging shift in our understanding of the human condition and grows increasingly relevant as our North American society grows more and more diverse in terms of cultures and ethnicity.

This chapter has focused on the application of relational theory to clinical work with individuals. Goldstein, Miehls, and Ringel (2009) demonstrate the application of relational theory to couples, families, groups, and oppressed populations in their text, and readers are encouraged to look there for further application of the theory. In addition, relational theory is starting to be integrated into classroom teaching in schools of social work and other mental health professionals. Many are now integrating relational principles into their supervisory relationships (Miehls, in press).

Last, the author also recognizes the links between relational theory and contemporary attachment theory and also the burgeoning field of neurobiology. All three of these theory bases are converging in a manner that emphasizes the crucial importance of sound relationships that aid healthy psychological and brain development. As we embark on the second decade of the "new millennium" it is an exciting time to be practicing social work, and relational theory adds to the ever-changing and increasingly sophisticated theory bases that contribute to our effectiveness as practitioners.

References

Altman, N. (1995). *The analyst in the inner city. Race, class and culture through a psychoanalytic lens.* Hillsdale, NJ: The Analytic Press.

Altman, N. (2000). Black and white thinking: A psychoanalyst considers race. *Psychoanalytic Dialogues*, 10, 589–604.

Applegate, J., & Shapiro, J. (2005). *Neurobiology for clinical social work: Theory and practice.* New York: W. W. Norton & Co.

Atwood, G. E., & Stolorow, R.D. (1984). *Structures of subjectivity: Explorations in psychoanalytic phenomenology.* Hillsdale, NJ: Analytic Press.

Basham, K., & Miehls, D. (2004). *Transforming the legacy: Couple therapy with survivors of childhood trauma.* New York: Columbia University Press.

Beebe, B., & Lachmann, F. M. (1988). Mother-infant mutual influence and precursors of psychic structure. In A. Goldberg. (Ed.), *Progress in self psychology* (vol. 3, pp. 3–25). Hillsdale, NJ: Analytic Press.

Benjamin, J. (1988). *The bonds of love: Psychoanalysis, feminism, and the problem of domination.* New York: Pantheon.

Benjamin, J. (1998). *The shadow of the object: Intersubjectivity and gender in psychoanalysis.* New York: Routledge.

Bowlby, J. (1958). The nature of the child's tie to the mother. *International Journal of Psychoanalysis, 39,* 350–373.

Bowlby, J. (1988). *A secure base.* New York: Basic Books.

Cozolino, L. (2006). *The neuroscience of human relationships: Attachment and the developing social brain.* New York: W. W. Norton & Co.

De Young, P. (2003). *Relational psychotherapy: A primer.* New York: Brunner-Routledge.

Dimen, M. (2003). *Sexuality, intimacy and power.* Hillsdale, NJ: Analytic Press.

Fairbairn, W. R. D. (1940). Schizoid factors in the personality. In W. R. D. Fairbairn, *Psychoanalytic studies of the personality* (pp. 2–27). London: Routledge.

Fairbairn, W. R. D. (1952). *Psychoanalytic studies of the personality.* London: Routledge.

Goldstein, E., Miehls, D., & Ringel, S. (2009). *Advanced clinical social work practice: Relational principles and techniques.* New York: Columbia University Press.

Hadley, M. (2008). Relational theory. In J. Berzoff, L. Melano Flanagan, & P. Hertz (Eds.), *Inside out and outside in: Psychodynamic clinical theory and psychopathology in contemporary multicultural contexts* (pp. 205–227). New York: Jason Aronson.

Hamilton, G. (1940). *Theory and practice of casework.* New York: Columbia University Press.

Horowitz, J. (1998). Contemporary psychoanalysis and social work theory. *Clinical Social Work Journal, 26,* 369–383.

Jacobson, E. (1964). *The self and the object world.* New York: International Universities Press.

Jordan, J. V. (1995). *Relational awareness: Transforming disconnection: Work in progress, No. 76.* Wellesley, MA: Stone Center Working Paper Series.

Jordan, J. V. (1997). The meaning of mutuality. In J. V. Jordan, A. Kaplan, J. Baker Miller, I. Stiver, & J. Surrey (Eds.), *Women's growth in connection: Writings from the Stone Center* (pp. 81–96). New York: Guilford Press.

Kernberg, O. (1975). *Borderline conditions and pathological narcissism.* New York: Jason Aronson.

Kernberg, O. (1976). *Object relations theory and clinical psychoanalysis.* New York: Jason Aronson.

Kernberg, O. (1980). *Internal world and external reality.* New York: Jason Aronson.

Klein, M. (1932). *The psychoanalysis of children.* London: Hogarth Press.

Klein, M. (1952). The origins of transference. In *Envy and gratitude and other works, 1946–1963.* New York: Delacorte Press.

Kohut, H. (1971). *The analysis of the self.* New York: International Universities Press.

Kohut, H. (1977). *The restoration of the self.* New York: International Universities Press.

Kohut, H. (1984). *How does analysis cure?* Chicago: University of Chicago Press.

Leary, K. (1997). Race, self-disclosure, and "forbidden talk": Race and ethnicity in contemporary psychoanalytic practice. *Psychoanalytic Inquiry, 66,* 163–189.

Mahler, M., Pine, F., & Bergman, A. (1975). *The psychological birth of the human infant: Symbiosis and individuation.* New York: Basic Books.

Mattei, L. (2008). Coloring development. Race and culture in psychodynamic theories. In J. Berzoff, L. Melano Flanagan, & P. Hertz (Eds.), *Inside out and outside in* (2nd ed., pp. 245–270). New York: Jason Aronson.

Miehls, D. (in press). Contemporary trends in supervision theory: A shift from parallel process to relational and trauma theory. *Clinical Social Work Journal.*

Miller, J. B. (Ed.) (1973). *Psychoanalysis and women: Contributions to new theory and therapy.* New York: Brunner/Mazel.

Mitchell, S. (1998). *Relational concepts in psychoanalysis: An integration.* Cambridge: Harvard University Press.

Mitchell, S. (2000). *Relationality from attachment to intersubjectivity.* Hillsdale, NJ: Analytic Press.

Mitchell, S., & Aron, L. (1999). *Relational psychoanalysis: The emergence of a tradition.* Hillsdale, NJ: Analytic Press.

Mitchell, S., & Black, M. (1995). *Freud and beyond.* New York: Basic Books.

National Association of Social Workers. (2008). *Code of ethics of the National Association of Social Workers.* Washington, DC: Author.

Natterson, J., & Friedman, R. (1995). *A primer of clinical intersubjectivity.* Northvale, NJ: Jason Aronson.

Renik, O. (1966). The perils of neutrality. *Psychoanalytic Quarterly, 65,* 495–517.

Richmond, M. (1917). *Social diagnosis.* New York: Russell Sage Foundation.

Richmond, M. (1922). *What is social casework?* New York: Russell Sage Foundation.

Sheppard, D. (2001). *Clinical social work, 1880–1940 and American relational psychoanalysis: An historical-integrative analysis of relational concepts in practice.*

Ph.D. Dissertation, New York University School of Social Work.

Siegel, D. (2007). *The mindful brain.* New York: W. W. Norton & Co.

Stern, D. (1985). *The interpersonal world of the infant.* New York: Basic Books.

Stolorow, R. D., & Atwood, G. (1992). *Contexts of being: The intersubjective foundations of psychological life.* Hillsdale, NJ: Analytic Press.

Stolorow, R. D., Brandchaft, B., & Atwood, G. (1994). *The intersubjective perspective.* Northvale, NJ: Analytic Press.

Sullivan, H. S. (1953). *The interpersonal theory of psychiatry.* New York: Norton.

Sullivan, H. S. (1954). *The psychiatric interview.* New York: Norton.

Winnicott, D. (1965). *The maturational processes and the facilitating environment.* Madison, CT: International Universities Press.

Winnicott, D. (1975). *From pediatrics to psychoanalysis.* New York: Basic Books.

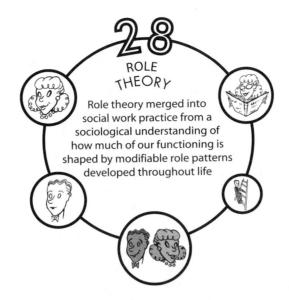

28
ROLE THEORY

Role theory merged into social work practice from a sociological understanding of how much of our functioning is shaped by modifiable role patterns developed throughout life

Role Theory and Concepts Applied to Personal and Social Change in Social Work Treatment

Dennis Kimberley and Louise Osmond

Role theories and related concepts, largely adopted from theater, have been used metaphorically as a heuristic in social psychology, as developed or interpreted by sociologists (e.g., Goffman, 1963; Mead, 1934), psychologists (e.g., Moreno and Zeleny, 1958), anthropologists (e.g., Mead, 1949), social workers (e.g., Grinker, MacGregor, Selan, Klein, & Kohrman, 1961), and psychiatrists (e.g. Ackerman, 1958). Role theories have provided sensitizing concepts, paths for analysis, and dynamic understandings about how people and collectives view, construct, and express themselves, as well as meet social expectations, especially in social interaction. Some social workers have used role concepts, and theories about roles as developed and as acted out, explicitly to address problems, risks,

needs, harm, strengths, and human potential that people and collectives experience or exhibit within the context of personal and social functioning. Most have had a special interest in assessing and supporting needed, desired, or required changes in social role functioning (e.g., Karls & O'Keefe, 2008; Karls & Wandrei, 1994; Kestenbaum & Wahl, 1994). In addition, many social work concepts, theories, and practices (e.g., feminist theory and gender analysis, as well as interactional theory) and those from cognate disciplines applied by social workers (e.g., deviance theory, labeling theory [Scheff, 1975] as well as stigma theory [Goffman, 1963]) make implicit assumptions about role expectations and related social positions. The latter is referred to in some postmodern thought as "social location." For example, social justice and oppression theories describe how some people take on identities (e.g., "survivor" role after an experience of rape) and related life scripts (role scripts, such as volunteers in rape crisis counseling). They also analyze how role expectations and development may be associated with identification of people and collectives as marginalized, stigmatized, victimized, traumatized, exploited, over-responsible, and disadvantaged, all while being resilient, evidencing strengths, and demonstrating abilities. Fundamentally, role theory and related concepts help social workers analyze client systems in dynamic interaction with their environments based, in part, on role expectations, social role functioning, and associated personal and social responsibilities. The empirical indicators of social role functioning[1] are typically found in actions, beliefs, attitudes, values, and expectations as expressed, as well as patterns of interaction that people have with their social and physical environments.

Social role theory may sensitize social workers who provide social work treatment to attend to potential, and actual, problems, risks, harm, and injustices associated with role functioning and role expectations, as part of a social work assessment and social diagnosis. Social functioning may be expressed in terms of normative, deviant, or pathological role performances. For example, workers may challenge how some roles in society may be stereotypically ghettoized or associated with one group (e.g., women more often provide personal care to infirm parents of both sexes). Other roles may be inherently unjust (e.g., the scapegoated child or youth; Pillari, 1991) or may be expressed in unjust family dynamics (e.g., the parentified child; De Young, 2003). Also, role adaptations to cope with life situations may appear functional at one level but may also create problematic relational dynamics at another (e.g., the over-responsible partner of an alcoholic; Bepko, 1985). In addition, social workers are aware of how anticipated and unanticipated life transitions may be associated with personal and collective distress; role theory points to assessment opportunities within the context of role-related distress associated with complexities of role functioning as well as transitions in role expectations (Karls & Wandrei,

(1994). Just as people may experience intrapsychic conflicts (e.g., to follow basic instincts or to self-regulate), they also may experience social role conflicts (e.g., parental caregiver and disciplinarian, or female parent and male parent roles). "Sick role" dynamics may be normative (e.g., reduction of social expectations after heart surgery) or may be judged as representing pathological dynamics (e.g., in Munchausen's by proxy syndrome). Other roles may be defined as primarily deviant (e.g., pedophile who distributes child porn), or as reflecting a self-fulfilling prophecy based on the unjust application of a deviance label (e.g., mentally disordered [Denzin, 1968], physically disabled [Goffman, 1963]). Notions of role, ambiguity, confusion, complexity, conflict, rigidity, incongruence, strain, progression, and regression, role modeling, and overwhelming social expectations, may also inform social work assessments.[2] Questions for the social worker and the client system include: What are the problems, risks, needs, strengths, and potentials in terms of role functioning within a set of roles? To what extent are role expectations of a person or collective, contextually, just or unjust? What are the implications of role expectations, and privileges, ascribed, or internalized, within the context of imperatives associated with culture, color, sex and gender, sexual orientation, ability status, or age?

Social work, as a change- and action-oriented vocation and profession (Goldstein, 1984; Kimberley & Osmond, 2009), enables personal and social change, including reducing injustice, in part by helping people and collectives understand the roles they play and related psychosocial dynamics (e.g., victim of bullying in interaction with a bully). Also, patients/clients/consumers may wish explore how they might change their roles in a social context; social workers may then apply various intervention theories (e.g., empowerment theory) and concepts (e.g., self-actualization) to support the desired change. Professionals may help the person or collective sustain the change in role identity (e.g., from victim to social-emotional leader), in social role functioning (e.g., presenting self as confident and assertive, and acting congruently), and in acting on role responsibilities. In this analysis, the authors focus on how role theory, concepts, and related practice wisdom may be applied directly and indirectly in assessment and treatment in diverse social work contexts in the interest of enabling personal and social change.[3]

Role: Concepts and Theories for Social Work Practice

Role as Determined and Role as Constructed

The concept of role (sometimes referred to as social role) implies a societally determined set of social expectations, associated with the boundaries of status and identity (e.g., foster child) and patterns of conduct internalized in social interaction, and undertaken, or placed on, the person by himself or herself, by significant others, and/or by the community or society. People in roles and associated social positions typically internalize and assume role expectations (e.g., becoming socially bonded with a surrogate parent). Role also implies sets of interactive, interdependent, and interrelated responsibilities, rights, and opportunities for individual and collective agency. The latter is evident in terms of conscious and willful acts to construct personal realities and meanings associated with role conduct, and to more consciously process biopsychosocial determinates of role performance. Individual or collective commitments to needed changes in role expectations, role functioning, and/or role responsibilities are implied in much of social work intervention. While roles may be socially determined, people and collectives also have opportunities for a degree of agency in how they manage, modify, interpret, and act out a role, relative to their social position, social situation, and social context. Another implication is that roles are determining some boundaries of self-identities but that people and collectives also actively construct their identities within role boundaries. Important questions for social workers include: To what degree is best interest served by meeting social role expectations (e.g., parent, student, employee)? To what degree is best interest served by empowering client systems to be agents in changing expectations, related role responsibilities, and related social identities?

Social Position and Role

If the role has elevated social position and related status assigned to it (e.g., professional social worker) within a given social context (e.g., protection of children and youth), then associated rights (privileges) and responsibilities may have significant social value and high performance expectations associated with that role (e.g., to assess a child as in need of protection and to apprehend a child exploited for child porn). Others may have deviant, marginalized, or otherwise contextually "lower" social positions (e.g., sex trade worker). Important questions for the social worker are: To what extent are role expectations and related social responsibilities, for me or potential clients/consumers/patients, clear, confusing, ambiguous, double-binding, overwhelming, or contributing to "role strain" (e.g., when role expectations and identity demands are not sufficiently congruent)? To what extent are the social requirements of a role inconsistent with the respect given to the person or collective in the related social positions?[4]

Roles Sanctioned and Required

The term "role" may be used to give direction to the analysis of responsibilities that a person or people undertook in acts of omission or commission, which might be interpreted as warranted or not, in a given social situation, in a broader social context. Such roles may be sanctioned before or after the fact (e.g., expecting that an abusive male leave the family home) or may be challenged after the fact (e.g., failure to take a male's complaint about partner abuse seriously). Or, the social worker may ask: "What role did this parent have in protecting, or failing to protect, the child?" In assessing role functioning there is an implication that people in a given culture or society are reasonably familiar with the boundaries of role expectations (e.g., child caregiver), social role functioning (e.g., caring for a child), and how related responsibilities are typically expressed in actions required of individuals (e.g., parent) or collectives (e.g., school personnel). A person, or people, within a role set may be judged to be overly or underly responsible within the context of their age, stage, and a given social situation in a social context, or as an adequate or less-than-adequate role model.

Roles in Interaction and Social Organization

A major assumption in role theory is that social organization and social order of a society, community, social organization, social group, or family is, in part, created by the individual and collective socialization, internalization, acceptance and congruent actions, converging and integrating in a relatively coherent whole (Mead, 1934). In the majority of social contexts, to not have an internalized working understanding of interdependent and interacting sets of social role expectations and related responsibilities would likely result in family chaos, broader social disorder, or deviant or pathological coping patterns.[5] The expectations for the conduct of one set of social actors (e.g., social worker) typically implies reciprocal expectations for an associated social actor (e.g., client/consumer). Similarly, some mutual patterns of conduct may be expected of people within a group of social actors with a common identity or purpose (e.g., members of a support group for Aboriginal people who had been abused in residential schools). Other role transactions may represent complementary patterns of conduct (e.g., one foster parent may be very able as a caregiver and the other as a disciplinarian). From an interactional perspective, the social group affects the person, and the person affects the social group, including in terms of role functioning and modification of social functioning (Shulman, 2009). General questions for the social worker and the client system are: In whose best interests are the expectations and related responsibilities of social roles set or changed? In whose interests are role expectations met or not? Who defines and applies the criteria associated with roles that are judged to be personally, collectively, and/or socially functional or not—with due consideration to social context and situation? To what extent are role scripts acted out, in a more or less unconscious fashion, or more or less habitual, without much conscious thought?

A Paradox of Flexible Fixed Roles

Notwithstanding that common expectations of a role within a social context may be relatively fixed in definition and recognizable patterns, role expectations, role function, and related responsibilities are not as likely to be fixed or immutable. The boundaries of role functioning may include a wide array of related expectations, not all of which need to be performed in any given situation in order to sustain a role position or to act out the role with efficacy. The boundaries of role expectations and function may change over time with the social development of the collective (e.g., women's roles and men's roles; Tranter, 2004). The roles of members of a therapy group may change developmentally as the social group coheres (Shulman, 2009). A person may change role performance or roles based on a multitude of reasons (e.g., role transitions during developmental and life transition changes; Hick, 2006). Also, role function or roles may change through conscious, willful, and planned effort (e.g., personal agency, advocacy, counseling, therapy, or policy) or through relatively unconscious processes (e.g., assuming traditional aspects of role in an aging Aboriginal who is gradually treated more and more as a community "elder"). Some roles may have relative stability and continuity for a period of time (e.g., parent, or child protection social worker) or may be temporary and transitory (e.g., person undertaking "unexpected crisis intervention" or a "bingeing party animal"). Assessment of a person's life experiences and presenting concerns may explore relatively stable roles, changing roles, temporary roles, potential roles, desired roles, required roles, and the ability to modify roles and self-identities while still being in a role. Increased awareness may help the client/consumer to set goals for role function changes, to modify role expectations, to negotiate changes in related responsibilities, or to assume new roles.[6]

Assessment of Role, Function, Responsibilities, and Expectations:

Biopsychosocial Assessment of Personal and Social Functioning: PIE

Based on biopsychosocial and person-in-environment (P-I-E) assumptions, the PIE system for classifying social function, within the context of typical ranges of social roles and contexts of the expression of those roles, was designed by social workers who wished to move away from a dominantly medicalized model of assessment and diagnosis. They wished to integrate valid concerns with personal and social functioning problems and strengths, as well as social environmental, mental health, and physical health considerations, which might act as associated risks or supportive factors for individuals (Karls & O'Keefe, 2008; Karls & Wandrei, 1994). The P-I-E classification system enables the social worker to make quantified estimates of problem levels[7] and to integrate social functioning assessments with mental health assessments while applying DSM or ICD criteria (Diagnostic and Statistical Manual of Mental Disorders, International Statistical Classification of Diseases and Related Health Problems). The model supports the social worker and client in assessing problems with social role functioning (Factor I)[8] and related difficulties along a number of dimensions, any of which may change over time.[9] Considerations in social work assessment include:

- Identifying the range and scope of the roles that are problematic (e.g., parent role: child care, parenting, providing for the children's basic needs)
- Evaluating problems directly associated with role functioning (e.g., responsibility: current parental capacity is not congruent with the parents' evidenced knowledge and skills)
- Judging the severity of the problem (e.g., there is a high risk of child removal)
- Describing the duration of the problem (e.g., over 12 months)
- Evaluating the range and scope of client coping as evidenced by social role functioning (e.g., "The parents have taken a recommended parenting course and have done well in learning parenting knowledge and skills but have yet to implement their learning in the interests of the children, even with supplementary in vivo parent coaching.")

The process is often one of assessment with the client, at times using collaterals, as well as formulation and articulation in terms that the client/consumer/patient is able to comprehend.

Integrating Systemic and Situational Factors in Assessment of Role Function

The P-I-E assessment model then supports the social worker and the client in considering environmental problems (Factor II), with special reference to those that typically are associated with creating, aggravating, sustaining, or blocking resolution of concerns in role functioning. For example, parents may have added stress because their child may have a problem with bullying at school, which affects his academic and social role at school as well as his social functioning in his family; also, parental complaints to school authorities have resulted in no effective action. The dimensions of social factors included in the P-I-E system are broad enough to enable relatively unlimited options regarding social situations and social structures that may compromise needed, desired, or required social role functioning or related change.[10] The question for the social worker is: What are the social factors, social structural factors, social situational factors, or contextual realities in the client's environment that may support role functioning, impair role functioning, or impose unfair role expectations? An additional layer of assessment complexity may be added to the assessment and related service plan if the client desires to assume or retain a social role (e.g., sex trade worker), especially a role set that conflicts with community norms for another role (e.g., being an active caregiver and parent and acceptable role model). Role theory predicts that there are likely conflicts and strain within a role (e.g., caregiver and disciplinarian) and between or among roles (e.g., sex trade worker and parental child care), and that the resolution of conflicts between the desired and the required role performance may be imperfect, thus contributing to role strain (Tranter, 2004).[11] Simple, ideologically based resolutions of role conflicts such as client empowerment, client strengths, and client self-determination may not be highly achievable; in social work interventions, in client/consumer/patient actions, or through expressed social expectations, one "best interest" may be purchased at the expense of another.

Integrating Health and Mental Health Factors in Assessment of Role Function

The P-I-E assessment model supports the social worker and the client in considering mental health problems (Factor III) that may interact with the client's problems in meeting desired and/or required role expectations. For example, if a parent's capacity is compromised by mental health and addiction problems, then problems in personal and social functioning may present risks and harm for children and the family (Kimberley, 2008). The mental health considerations may intersect with environmental considerations (e.g., people with concurrent disorders are more likely, within a group of people needing mental health services, not to be provided with, or not to use, needed services). The general questions for the social worker are: What range of social role functioning is efficacious, even under conditions of being compromised or at risk due to mental health and/or addiction problems? What are the likely impacts, or interactions, of mental health problems on compromised, desired, and expected role functioning? How do improvements in mental health affect the prognosis for verifiable, sustained, and meaningful gains in social role functioning?

The P-I-E classification system similarly supports the social worker and the client in considering physical health problems (Factor IV) that may interact with social role functioning and related personal, social, and environmental problems.[12] For example, if the capacity of a person who has been effective in multiple social roles is seriously decreased by a stroke, then what implications might that have for role expectations, responsibilities, and self-identity associated with employee roles, spouse/partner roles, parent/child care roles, community/citizenship roles, and instrumental roles, such as driving a vehicle? In some situations return to some desired social role functioning, such as driving, may not be permitted. Return to required expectations of employment, such as operating a vehicle, may never be able to be met again. The client's social environment (e.g., employer) may or may not be willing to make supportive accommodations. The progress of the client in resuming desired and expected role functioning and related self-identity, with due respect to age

and stage, may be slow, even with needed treatment, with regressions. Also, improvements are likely to be imperfect, though often demonstrating genuine strengths, compromised by medical realities. Similar to mental health, general questions for the social worker are: What range of social role functioning is efficacious even under conditions of being at risk, compromised, or otherwise constrained due to health problems or related social responses? What are the likely impacts, or interactions, of health problems with compromised, desired, and expected role functioning? How do improvements in health status affect the likelihood of sustained and relevant improvements in role functioning?

In general, the application of role concepts may help the social worker and the client/consumer/patient formulate a social work assessment, modify an assessment, and plan for person-centered personal and social change. The change process may include systemic change and monitoring of progress, which includes changes in role functioning and social expectations or responsibilities associated with ascribed and assumed social positions, related roles, and self-identities. At times new roles may be needed and the client/consumer/patient may have to cope with a transition to new responsibilities and changes in social position.

A Synthesis for Informed Action[13]

A Biopsychosocial Interactional Perspective

In reflecting on treatment options and service planning that promote and enable personal and social change, including systemic changes, with the general goals of optimizing the best interests of the client, the authors propose a biopsychosocial interactional (BPSI) model. This model is change-oriented and supports an integrative approach to treatment.[14] What follows is an integration of some role theory, role concepts, and selected practices as well as overlaying role theory concepts within existing practices from other models. The orientation is towards changing role expectations by self and others, and in changing role functioning in the interests of modifying problems, risks, needs, and harm, as well as actualizing strengths and potential, including changing self-identities associated with roles. Some change-oriented interventions may be in the interest of supporting a client's self-determination, where the changes might be in the direction of reducing internal and external pressures for changes in role expectations, role functioning, or related responsibilities that may be unjust and/or unwarranted. While many role dynamics may determine patterns of thought, affect, and expression, the client/consumer/patient is defined as having agency in changing role functioning as it interacts with changeable biopsychosocial dimensions. Taking on roles and constructing parts of roles or new roles fits with an interactional model, without adopting the non sequitur that all the person's or collective's psychosocial realities are socially constructed.

Social workers may apply one or more interventions, with varied practices, applying varied concepts, and with logically intersecting theories, converging to support a coherent and integrated approach to personal and social change, desired by (e.g., improved parenting) or required of (e.g., no longer acting with the rights and powers of a custodial parent) the client. In applying integrated interventions from a BPSI perspective, social workers may apply role theory (e.g., role expectations desired or required), concepts (e.g., inter-role and intra-role conflicts), explicit role application practices (e.g., psychodrama [Emunah, 1994; Landy, 1993]; play therapy [Webb, 1993]; family therapy [Hanna & Brown, 1999; Waters & Lawrence, 1993]) and practices that implicitly apply social role-like notions (e.g., strengths-based practices [Berg & Reuss, 1998]; social justice practices [Csiernik & Rowe, 2010]).

In promoting a change orientation, the social worker may explore a set of personal and social change opportunities, embedded with role-oriented analysis, with herself or himself, the client, significant others in the social environment, and social systems and structures. The following dimensions may be applied to guide interventions to enable relevant, verifiable, and sustained change, with due respect to social role expectations, role functioning, and role responsibilities, and with due consideration of specific social situations, within a broader social context, where role responsibilities are actualized or where they are compromised.

A Biological Self, in Psychosocial Context

What changes in biophysical, biochemical, biomedical, and neuropsychological realities would support improved social role functioning by the person or collective (e.g., being a supportive group citizen in a therapy group)? Are there role expectations that might be changed, and by whom, to give just recognition to biological realities of the person or collective (e.g., living with AIDS)? For example, social workers with family support and child protection roles were faced with parents who expected too much in terms of family, school, and community role functioning of their 12-year-old son, who had to manage severe symptoms related to attention-deficit/hyperactivity disorder, cognitive functioning limitations associated with Klinefelter's syndrome, and social marginalization, in part due to physical features and problems with self-regulation, even after treatment with multiple medications. The boy's school was less than supportive and contributed to further marginalization. School personnel defined his not meeting role expectations as "willful" and a "sign of resistance." Interventions included working with the school system to acknowledge the boy's potential, as well as coaching selected school personnel to provide support, to help build strengths and capacity, and to apply just expectations in academic and social role functioning. In vivo family therapy included modifying the role expectations of the parents (e.g., eliminating unnecessary negative consequences, including blaming the child for his mother's depression) and the boy (e.g., accepting that he could not follow the parents' agenda and obtain a college diploma). The social environment was further modified for him in what the therapists called a "two-family system." This included the child going into a foster home that was integrated therapeutically with the child's parent's home to create a seamless therapeutic effect so that the boy could gradually assume more age stage, and situationally fair, role functioning. The therapists advocated for improved medical treatment of confounding biomedical conditions. With the support of in vivo individual and dual family therapy, simulating therapeutic foster care, and a long-term case plan, the youth completed high school when he was at risk to leave school prematurely, and he obtained gainful employment, when he was at risk to be unemployed. He maintained relationships with his social supports, who learned not to be unreasonably demanding in terms of role expectations and responsibility taking. The social work therapists saw their roles as actualizing personal and social functioning potential by building needed supports, controlling risks, ameliorating harm, and removing unwarranted barriers.

Self in Social-Historical and Developmental Context

What changes in personal and social developmental needs and experiences would support improved social role functioning by the person or collective? Are there role expectations that might be changed, and by whom, to give just recognition to common and unique developmental needs and experiences? For example, a social worker with a women's services role was faced with a young professional woman who was very apprehensive about losing her professional license because she "slept with 150 different men a year," abused drugs and alcohol, and was observed by others in multiple compromising situations. Her developmental history was one of severe sexual abuse, including exploitation for the production of child pornography. She had severe problems with attachment, bonding, and trust and "would not sleep with the same man twice." She wished to be able to be a partner in a committed relationship, to reinforce her professional identity, and to leave her role as a "one-night-stand barfly" behind her. In-depth dynamic therapy, applying some developmental and trauma theory, included work on posttraumatic stress disorder and attachment disorder. A rational emotive behavioral therapy model was also applied to reduce fears of healthy social bonds, to increase her ability to enter into social roles that could develop into mutual social bonds, without rushing to sexualize emotional, intellectual, and social intimacy. The therapist also worked with her at breaking patterns of accepting advances from men who were likely a

risk, and increasing her understanding of healthier expectations in female–male relations. When she did give up her "street life" and connected with a man who was able to bond at a healthier level, he took part in a few of her therapy sessions. There he could learn to moderate his expectations of her as a woman with unique developmental damage in a committed relationship, a new role for her linked with "self-reformation." A subtext of her progress was controlling her substance use so it did not compromise her progress in personal and social functioning, including professional role functioning; she stopped showing up at her professional office with symptoms of withdrawal. The social worker saw the fundamental strategy as overcoming developmental damage that compromised the client's present personal and social functioning.

An Emotive Self, in Interaction

What changes in affect and the experience of related sensations, or expression of feelings and emotions would support improved social role functioning? Are there role expectations that might be changed, and by whom, that respect the person's or collective's preferences for experiencing and expressing sensations, feelings, and emotions? For example, a social worker with family and battered woman support roles was faced with a young mother with a 5-year-old child who felt ambivalent about returning to her seriously abusive and very dangerous husband. She loved her son and typically was very good as a caretaker and parent. On the other hand, she felt lonely, alone, and sad and grieved for the multiple losses in her life. She and the protection workers were both uncertain about her resolve to protect herself and her son. The social work counselor explored how the client's social supports from extended family could be activated and how neighborhood supports might be built and sustained. The client was supported to the role transition of a single mother, through counseling, including plans for increasing self-confidence and self-esteem, in part through a gradual program for academic progress, correlated with expected increases in positive affect. The social worker saw herself as applying trauma theory and strengths-based theory to enable improved personal and social functioning and social support, and thus sustained changes in stability and affect and its expression.

An Aware Self and Cognition, in Interaction

What changes in cognitive functioning, cognitive content, and cognitive-neurological factors would support improved social role functioning? Are there role expectations that might be changed, and by whom, that respect the person's or collective's cognitive change ability? For example, a social worker with addictions assessment, counseling, and case management roles was faced with a boy aged 19, with an IQ of 140, who was near death due to use of multiple mind-altering chemicals. The client had used methamphetamine, which is associated with changes in neurological structures that decrease memory. He had also used "crack" cocaine, which can speed up mental processes (e.g., a flight of ideas) and at the same time decrease the ability to sustain focus and attention. The drugs he used were associated with paranoid thinking that compromised much reasoning and decision making. The other drugs he used, such as Ecstasy and alcohol, impaired his judgment and disinhibited his sexual expression. His life, as conceived and lived, included pro-drug and pro-street lifestyle beliefs, attitudes, and values, which increased his imminent risks. The client expected the street drugs to make him feel better without considering the negative consequences.

The social worker suggested beginning with a harm reduction program to enable clearer self-directed thinking about changes that were needed to reduce the likelihood of his death, as well as to increase his motivation to commit to an inpatient program. The social worker challenged the client's plan for a premature return to his role as a student at a community college because his performance would likely be compromised by his impaired cognitive abilities at the time. The social worker saw his role as balancing the need for safety with timely problem solving, and a need for insight (e.g., making the unconscious more conscious as associated with personal and social functioning). Strategies included empowerment while challenging premature solutions, with harm reduction commitments expected to enable improved cognitive

functioning to support deeper, self-directed and lasting gains.

Behaviors Determined and Actions Willed, in Interaction

What changes in patterns of behavior, willful action, and self-regulation in social interaction would support improved social role functioning? Are there role expectations that might be changed, and by whom, that respect the person's or collective's preferences for behavior, consciously willful actions, and/or self-control? For example, a social worker with a family services role was faced with patterns of habitual behavior by a father of not assuming care and parenting responsibilities for his 8-year-old stepdaughter. The stepfather claimed that he had made conscious attempts to take on a parental role earlier, when he moved in, but that it "did not work" for him and the girl. The stepfather said he avoided discussing the parenting and child care issue because there is a risk of conflict that he did not know how to resolve, so "doing nothing was better than doing something that would likely go wrong." The social worker recommended that she interview all the family members in terms of their needs and wishes and then hold joint sessions with the mother and child, followed by a family session. She noted that at some point there would likely be, among other plans, work on role complementarity, shared parenting and child care, avoiding conflicts and role strain, and stepfather role boundaries and reality constraints, which might work for all three. She recommended knowledge and skills development particular to a step-parenting role with a daughter. The social worker saw her role as supporting verifiable and sustained change in interrelated role exchanges through the coherent application of cognitive behavioral theory, social learning theory, and family dynamics theories.

Self, Social Bonds, and Intimate Relationships

What changes in intimacy, attachments, and sexual expression would support improved social role functioning? Are there role expectations that might be changed, and by whom, that respect the person's or collective's needs and preferences for attachments, intimacy, and/or sexual expression that might be expected in marriages, families, and other close or life-long partnerships? For example, a social worker with health counseling, psychosocial assessment, and case management roles was faced with a woman who had had a mastectomy and who, as part of coping, had distanced herself from her husband. The male believed that his partner of 15 years had detached, had become more superficial in terms of emotional and verbal intimacy, and had expressed a wish, "going forward, to avoid anything sexual… at all costs," even though he was sensitive and made no such expectations. The social worker focused on a message of normalization ("to be expected") in terms of short-term critical responses by the woman, hope for the future based on other couples who had been through a similar crisis, support for needed patience, and reaching for past strengths and solutions that might provide the basis for a return to, or building anew, relationship- and marriage-sustaining joint expectations. The social worker saw her role as helping with crisis management, relationship solutions, couple strengths building, and individual and couple's counseling.

Self, Social Bonds, and Social Relationships

What changes in relationship needs, social bonds, and/or interpersonal relationship patterns would support improved social role functioning? Are there role expectations that might be changed, and by whom, that respect the person's or collective's needs and preferences for relationship, social bonds, and efficacious interpersonal relationship patterns? For example, two social workers co-led a group for advanced treatment of sex offenders. The social workers interpreted their roles as helping the group and each member to progress towards reducing and consciously controlling re-offense risks as well as increasing pro-social functioning. As part of two group sessions the social workers used psychodrama techniques: half of the group assumed victim roles (based on their real-life experiences as victims, or as perpetrators to their victims) and the other half were "getting in touch with

their perpetrator roles and identities." These psychodrama experiences were followed by group debriefing about what each drama experience meant emotionally and cognitively, especially in relation to feeling and building accurate victim-centered empathy. The social workers saw themselves as applying integrated group dynamics theories, psychodynamic theories associated with accurate empathy building, social bonding without eroticization, and dramaturgy, as well as capacity building with respect to increasing social responsibility, and replacing perpetrator roles with genuine protective roles.

Role Performance in Social Situational Context

What changes in structural, systemic, contextual, and situational determinants could support improved social role functioning? Are there role expectations that might be changed, and by whom, that respect the person's or collective's needs and preferences for social systemic change? For example, a social worker working with victim assessment, support, case management, and referral roles was faced with a female client who was a victim of partner violence; the partner was charged and convicted. When the young woman returned to live with her former partner, her children were removed as children exposed to violence and were facing long-term placements. The woman was battered again and made a complaint; this time she was "determined" not to live with the male batterer "ever again." The victim's services worker advocated to children's protection and the court for "another chance" as the mother was effective in terms of independent child care and parenting, and had agreed to stronger supervision and safety measures than in the past. The victim services social worker saw her roles as offering support for strengths building and systems change, within the context of feminist-based advocacy, with due respect for relevant child safety needs. She supported the mother's role transition to more self-confidence and motivation in sustaining self-protection, as well as increasing child-centered parenting, care, and safety, through counseling and psychosocial education (e.g., impacts on children with respect to exposure to violence).

Motivation for Role Compliance or Role Change

What changes in personal and collective motivation, including intrinsic and extrinsic factors and self-direction, would support improved social role functioning? Are there role expectations that might be changed, and by whom, that respect the person's or collective's needs for self-direction and preferences for change in motivation? For example, a children's protection social worker was faced with a family with four children, one a newborn, where both parents had adequate knowledge and skills for child care and parenting but did not evidence an ability to sustain competent and safe parenting, even under conditions of supervised access, where the motivation to demonstrate motivational change might be expected to be the highest. The children had to be removed for their safety, as the parents spent most family resources on alcohol, drugs, and themselves and devoted little quality time or resources to the needs of the children. The children evidenced many significant indicators of physical and emotional neglect, even though the father had a good-paying job. The parents expressed a high wish for self-directed parenting, without intrusion, as they defined their care and parenting knowledge and skills as being "above average." Neither parent had insight into intrinsic factors that might compromise sustained motivation in the best interest of their children. Both had some insight into extrinsic factors, which they summarized as: "If we don't get our act together, then we are going to lose our kids for good." The protection worker commissioned an independent assessment of parenting capacity that included an evaluation of the dynamics compromising intrinsic child-centered motivation and related personal and social functioning, especially as related to parental capacity. The independent assessor uncovered multiple developmental dynamics, maternal mental health and addictions, and paternal developmental dynamics and substance use concerns that had to be addressed before sustained gains in child-centered parenting, based on intrinsic motivation, could be expected. In short, protection services could not expect timely gains in sustained parental role functioning until the parents resolved and stabilized some of their developmental, mental health, and addictions issues. Inpatient addiction counseling was expected to have the added benefit for the mother of offering a model for role and identity transition to being "a person in recovery." A goal was to make sufficient substantive and sustained parent-centered changes to enable movement towards genuine and sustained child-centered motivation.

Identity Formation as Biopsychosocial Interaction and Convergence

What changes in the interaction of biopsychosocial factors and convergence of personal and social factors, in identity formation, and in self-concept, self-esteem, and self-worth would support improved social role functioning? Are there role expectations that might be changed, and by whom, that respect the person's or collective's needs and preferences for experiencing and expressing themselves in social contexts? For example, a social worker with responsibility for children's mental health, especially children who had been maltreated, had been involved with the family in a case noted above, where the eldest daughter, aged 6, was rejected by her stepfather, even though she was adopted by him. The girl was then systematically and relentlessly scapegoated and took on the role of scapegoat in that she began to "look for" and expect negative attention and blame. She was parentified, and in acting out this role, such as monitoring the needs of her newborn brother and cuing her mother to provide needed care and attention, she was further scapegoated for being "too big for her britches" and, alternatively, for "not helping her mother" (a double-bind communication that contributes to role strain). Her stepfather blamed the child for supervised visits not working and for not "letting her mother to show what she could do." He gave the child the clear responsibility for making supervised visits work; the child would even cue the supervising social worker that her mother would "not last much longer"—a metaphor for the beginning deterioration of a supervised visit. The child would ask to leave early, to return to her foster placement, as if to protect herself from being blamed for parental "failures." The child could not count on her mother to protect her or to care for her; the stepfather provided more adequate care. The social worker examined how biopsychosocial factors in the child's development and her family life and community life supported negative identity and related role function, as well as positive identity (e.g., a teacher saw her as a sweet and helpful child). The social worker put integrated therapeutic foster care plans and supports in place to enable the child to assume the role of a dependent child and to build self-esteem based on child role expectations and responsibilities, so that she no longer felt the need to reinforce self-esteem and identity as a "little adult" who takes age- and stage-inappropriate initiatives and is very wise, very able, stable, and very helpful to adults.[15] Part of the goal was to reduce role conflicts and role strain and to differentiate an age- and stage-appropriate role set for the child, thus supporting transition to a more stable, integrated, and healthy identity and related role expectations.

An Existential Self

What changes in existential meaning, existential realities, and spiritual paths would support improved social role functioning? Are there role expectations that might be changed, and by whom, that respect the person's or collective's needs and preferences for meaning, spiritual paths, and processing existential shifts? For example, social workers who have a role in helping with grief, loss, mourning, complex grief, or other sources of loss of meaning in life are faced with many complexities and uncertainties. Among the challenges are supporting a return to role functioning (e.g., widowed, but still a mother and employee) or significant existential shifts based on life's new realities (e.g., a change in meaning, position, role expectations, and identity after having a stroke and related job loss). Social workers also help people process existential shifts based on insight into new meaning in life (e.g., happiness associated with having a child and being a father, rather than accumulating material goods) or with fundamental spiritual existential shifts, sometimes associated with cancer (e.g., sometimes through new mindfulness).[16] Some social workers may also approach change from a human potential movement perspective that is not so much based on

problems, risks, harm, pathology, oppression, solutions, or "dysfunction," but rather on a path to future-oriented self-actualization, self-discovery, and personal growth, versus only socially predetermined objectives.[17]

This BPSI model recommends the integration of the above dimensions with due respect to all relevant biospsychosocial dimensions in interaction, each with the others. The net result respects the complexity and uncertainties in the phenomena and situations where social workers undertake assessment and treatment responsibilities. The shift in the biopsychosocial realities may appear as if they fit chaos theory more so than any well planned treatment intervention with presumed predictive validity. On the other hand, if the treatment objectives and outcomes are framed, at least in part, in terms of desired, required, expected, and needed changes in role functioning, related responsibilities, and expectations, then there will be empirical referents to verify change and sustained changes that are directly relevant to personal and social functioning, in given social situations, in given social contexts. The paradox is that while social roles are socially constructed, they also have empirical referents that provide clear, relatively repeated, relatively patterned, and partially integrated indicators that the socially constructed role is being expressed in predictable patterns of personal and social functioning. These patterns of role functioning both create and determine predictable patterns of social interaction and social order. An advantage of the BPSI model, applied with due respect to personal and social functioning of individuals and collectives, is that it does not expect the social worker to become fixated on any ideology or theory, or to become obsessed with any narrow and rigid concept, in providing service. Fixation on narrow boundaries of practice is seldom in the best interest of the client/consumer/patient but may well be in the interest of proselytizing an ideology and theory. The BPSI model, integrated with role functioning theory, may be applied in traditional service methods such as individual, family, couple, group, organization, community, policy, or societal change, or in nontraditional service contexts such as a virtual community, with virtual roles (e.g., exhibitionism online, or counseling online).[18] Role theory enables informed assessment and intervention throughout the life cycle, including with newly constructed roles that reflect the ongoing transitions and evolution of social systems (e.g., role concepts may be applied in traditional service contexts such as child, youth, and family services, or in nontraditional services, such as secret services, where counseling service records may not be kept). In short, role theory may help guide assessment and treatment under conditions where complex role functioning is interactive with complex social situations, in uncertain social contexts, and where social integration of roles is expected, or needed, often in the interest of social order or the sense of an integrated and stable self.[19]

Notes

1. By applying the concept of social role and social functioning in a synthesis, the social worker may help assess "normative" (e.g., parent as caregiver and provider), "deviant" (e.g., parent as sex trade worker) and "pathological" (e.g., parent as sexually addicted adult) role executions, within the context of what is functional for each role, as well as evaluate the broader implications for personal and social functioning.

2. A common example from social work is where the professional has a helping role and a social control role; these roles often conflict and contribute to role strain or incongruence between one set of expectations and another.

3. The cases used in this analysis are all based on the realities of social work practice, especially in the Western world, and are in no way intended to further marginalize, disadvantage, stigmatize, or oppress any social group.

4. For example, in the role of parentified child, it is not unusual that the child is given a metaphorical double message, such as "Take responsibility" and "Back off, who elected you boss?"

5. Depending on the depth of theorizing and conceptualizing, there are cognitive theory assumptions that people internalize sets of beliefs, attitudes, values, and expectations that guide their actions relative to a role and associated position (e.g., cognitive scripts). Also there are dynamic theory assumptions that some aspects of role are expressed with little conscious awareness (e.g., unconscious motivation to create family stability by the parentified child). There are also behavioral theory assumptions that some sets of role behaviors become habitual and that a social stimulus sets off a predictable pattern of behavior (e.g., disinhibited actions

of the impaired alcoholic). Also, there are interactional or transactional assumptions that people assume, change, and govern their roles based in part on how the "other" is playing, or not, his or her role (e.g., the over-responsible partner of the alcoholic).

6. Besides those references noted in our analysis of the concept of role and related concepts, the authors benefited from a review of the sections on role in the *Blackwell International Encyclopedia of Sociology* (Ritzer, 2007).

7. Quantification is based on a severity index that ranges from "no problem" to a 5-point scale from "low" to "severe"; a duration index that ranges from "more than 5 years" to "2 years or less" on a 6-point scale; and a coping index expressed on a 6-point scale ranging from "outstanding" to "no coping skills" (Karls, & Wandrei, 1994, 35–37).

8. Factor I: Social role functioning and problems are conceptualized and articulated under broad headings such as family roles, occupational roles (which includes a student role), and "life situation roles" (e.g., client roles). Each broad category has multiple subcategories and includes a subcategory of "other." The categories schema also includes a set of role problem types, each extensively developed, that reflect common social work treatment dynamics; among these are power, ambivalence, responsibility, dependency, loss, isolation, victimization, and mixed (Karls, & Wandrei, 1994, 18).

9. While medical and psychiatric diagnoses may change over time, they are often presented as more substantially stable than are changes in problematic social role functioning and related social factors.

10. The environmental systems classifications schema articulates broad categories, each more fully developed, such as economic/basic needs, education and training, justice and legal processes, health, safety and social services needs, voluntary supports, and "affectional" support systems. The schema addresses issues of injustice, discrimination, lack of support, unjust expectations, and unexpected crises (Kestenbaum, & Wahl, 1994, 23–34).

11. The P-I-E classification system would explore the environmental factors as potentially being unjustly discriminating (e.g., "lifestyle" discrimination; Kestenbaum, & Wahl, 1994, 34) against a sex trade worker-parent unless there were other social role functioning issues associated with the sex trade occupational role that significantly compromised the parenting role or child care.

12. To be clear, the notions are that mental health or health problems may exacerbate problems in role

functioning, but mental health or health services may also ameliorate some problems and support the person, or significant others, in enabling more efficacious role performance, or in assuming new, possibly less demanding and more efficacious roles.

13. This applied role functioning model is derived from the theoretical and conceptual analysis and synthesis by Kimberley and Bohm (1999) and Kimberley and Osmond (2009).

14. An integrative approach differs from an eclectic approach in that the goal is to have situation-relevant logical consistency and coherence in the application of concepts and practices that are derived from selected multiple theoretical-conceptual schemas.

15. The paradox with roles such as the parentified child and the scapegoated child is that they may be very functional in terms of some family dynamics and family homeostasis, and may even serve a family preservation agenda, though they are also developmentally damaging, at best, and pathological, at worst.

16. The reader is referred to the application of mindfulness therapy in social work such as Hick and Bien (2008).

17. See for example, Satir, Banmen, Gerber, and Gomori (1991).

18. Goffman (1963) analyzed virtual identities.

19. It was not the primary purpose of this analysis to focus on social worker roles in treatment. For a more in-depth analysis the reader is referred to Dorfman (1996).

References

Ackerman, N. (1958). *The psychodynamics of family life*. New York: Basic Books.

Bepko, C., with J. A. Krestan (1985). *The responsibility trap: a blueprint for treating the alcoholic family*. New York: The Free Press.

Berg, I. K., & Reuss, N. H. (1998). *Solutions step-by-step: a substance abuse treatment manual*. New York: W. W. Norton & Company.

Csiernick, R., & Rowe, W.S. (Eds.) (2010). *Responding to the oppression of addictions: Canadian social work perspectives* (2nd ed.). Toronto: Canadian Scholars Press Inc.

Dandaneau, S. P. (2007). Role taking. In G. Ritzer (Ed.), *Blackwell encyclopedia of sociology*. U.K.: Blackwell Publishing. Blackwell Reference Online. November 6, 2009.

Denzin, N. (1968). The self-fulfilling prophecy and patient-therapist interaction. In S. Spitzer &

N. Denzin, *The mental patient: studies in the sociology of deviance* (pp. 349–357). New York: McGraw-Hill.

De Young, P. A. (2003). *Relational psychotherapy: a primer* (pp. 82–83). New York and Hove: Brunner/Routledge.

Dorfman, R. (1996). *Clinical social work: definition, practice and vision* (chapter 3). New York: Brunner/Mazel.

Emunah, R. (1994). *Acting for real: drama therapy, process, technique, and performance*. New York: Brunner/Mazel.

Franks, D. D. (2007). Role. In G. Ritzer (Ed.), *Blackwell encyclopedia of sociology*. U.K.: Blackwell Publishing. Blackwell Reference Online. November 6, 2009.

Goffman, E. (1963). *Stigma: notes on the management of spoiled identity*. London: Penguin.

Goldstein, H. (1984). *Creative change: a cognitive-humanistic approach to social work practice*. New York: Tavistock Publications.

Grinker, R. S., MacGregor, H., Selan, K., Klein, A., & Kohrman, J. (1961). *Psychiatric social work: a transactional case book*. New York: Basic Books.

Hanna, S. M., & Brown, J. H. (1999). *The practice of family therapy: key elements across models*. Belmont, CA: Brookes/Cole Wadsworth.

Hick, S. (2006). *Social work in Canada: an introduction* (2nd ed.). Toronto: Thompson Educational Publishing.

Hick, S. F., & Bien, T. (Eds.) (2008). *Mindfulness and the therapeutic relationship*. New York: Guilford Press.

Hindin, M. J. (2007). Role theory. In G. Ritzer (Ed.), *Blackwell encyclopedia of sociology*. U.K.: Blackwell Publishing. Blackwell Reference Online. November 6, 2009.

Kadushin, A. (1972). *The social work interview*. New York: Columbia University Press.

Karls, J. M., & Wandrei, K. E. (1994). *PIE Manual: Person-in-Environment System: The PIE classification system for social functioning problems*. Washington, DC: National Association of Social Workers.

Karls, J. M., & O'Keefe, M. (2008). *Person-in-Environment System Manual*. Washington, DC: National Association of Social Workers.

Kestenbaum, J. D., & Wahl, M. K. (1994). Applications of the PIE system in family services agencies. In Karls, J. M. & Wandrei, K. E. (Eds.), *Person-in-Environment System: The PIE Classfication System for Social Functioning Problems* (pp. 59–66). Washington, DC: NASW Press.

Kimberley, D. (2008). *Assessing the consequences for children and families when a parent has a problem with substance use and abuse: Considerations for* social workers and other helping professionals. Presented in Oxford, England, at the Oxford Round Table.

Kimberley, D., & Osmond, L. (2009). Social workers. In J. C. Turner & F.J. Turner (Eds.), *Canadian social welfare* (6th ed., pp. 353–374). Toronto: Pearson Canada.

Kimberley, M. D., & Bohm, P. (1999). Drug addiction: a BPSI model. In F. Turner (Ed.), *Adult psychopathology: A social work perspective* (2nd ed.). New York: The Free Press.

Landy, R. J. (1993). *Persona and performance: The meaning of role in drama, therapy, and everyday life.* New York: The Guilford Press.

Mead, G. H. (1934). *Mind, self and society.* Chicago: University of Chicago Press.

Mead, M. (1949). *Male and female: a study of sexes in a changing world.* New York: Morrow. [Re-issued in 2001 by Harper Collins, with an introduction by Helen Fisher and Mary Catherine Bateson.]

Moreno, J. L., & Zeleny (1958). Role theory and sociodrama. In J. S. Roucek (Ed.), *Contemporary sociology* (pp. 642–653). New York: Philosophical Library.

Pillari, V. (1991). *Scapegoating in families: intergenerational patterns of physical and emotional abuse.* New York: Brunner/Mazel.

Ritzer, G. (Ed.) (2007). *Blackwell encyclopedia of sociology.* U.K.: Blackwell Publishing. Blackwell Reference Online. November 6, 2009.

Satir, V., Banmen, J., Gerber, J., & Gomori, M. (1991). *The Satir model: family therapy and beyond* (Chapters 1, 10, and 11). Palo Alto, CA: Science and Behavior Books, Inc.

Scheff, T. J. (Ed.) (1975). *Labeling madness.* Englewood Cliffs, NJ: Prentice Hall.

Shulman, L. (2009). The skills of helping individuals, families, groups, and communities (6th ed.). Florence, KY: Cengage Learning Inc..

Tranter, D. (2004). Different than dad: a phenomenological exploration of masculine gender role strain. St. John's, Newfoundland: Ph.D. Thesis, Faculty of Social Work Memorial University.

Waters, D. B., & Lawrence, E. C. (1993). *Competence, courage, and change: an approach to family therapy.* New York: W. W. Norton & Company.

Webb, N. B. (Ed.) (1993). *Helping bereaved children: a handbook for practitioners.* New York: The Guilford Press.

29

SELF-EFFICACY

This highly useful theory emerged from the tradition of learning theory, and builds on the belief in one's capacity to organize and execute action patterns required to produce given attainments

Self-Efficacy Theory

Kathleen J. Farkas

Among the bedrock values of the profession of social work are the client's right to self-determination and client empowerment. Social workers are quick to highlight the unique value of the individual and to encourage self-enhancement and self-improvement. The National Association of Social Workers Code of Ethics prominently features the idea of clients right to self-determination. Identification and clarification of the client's goals are key components of a social worker's ethical responsibility (National Association of Social Workers, 2006). Self-efficacy theory, with its focus on an individual's capacity to act and to exercise control, is compatible with the profession of social work's mission and goals and provides an underpinning for social work practice with individuals, families, and groups.

Self-efficacy is defined as "beliefs in one's capabilities to organize and execute the courses of action required to produce given attainments" (Bandura, 1997, p. 3). This core belief in the individual's right to choice and the effect of choice on action underlines the importance of self-efficacy to social work practice. Because self-efficacy theory easily flows to guidelines to assist people to gain control over various problems in life, it is widely used in social work practice. Self-efficacy theory is evident across many fields of social work practice: child welfare (Jackson, 2000); child development (Bandura, Barbaranelli, Caprara, & Pastorelli, 2001); gerontology (Levy, Hausdorff, Hencke, & Wei, 2008; McAuley & Blissmer, 2000), and health (Burditt, Robbins, Paiva, Velicer, Koblin, & Kessler, 2008; Luszczynska, Benight, & Cieslak, 2009). Petrovich (2004) makes the case that self-efficacy theory is useful in training social work students for practice. Social researchers also have made good use of the concept. The Cochrane Reviews show nine entries for systematic reviews focusing on self-efficacy across a variety of problems and age groups (*Cochrane Database of Systematic Reviews*. Retrieved on September 15, 2009, from http://www.cochrane.org). On another front, social work education has focused on the use of self-efficacy as an outcome measure for professional training (Holden, Anastas, & Meenaghan, 2003) and for curriculum structure (Wilson, 2006).

Self-efficacy has been linked to other important ideas in the development of individual change, including motivation for change, intention to act, and empowerment. Despite the wide use of the ideas about self-efficacy, there is confusion between the *concept* of self-efficacy and the *theory* of self-efficacy. As a concept, self-efficacy can be used in clinical practice to discuss client traits, goal, and outcomes. However, it is the theory of self-efficacy—the process and relationships among concepts—that provides a powerful tool to develop knowledge and to foster personal and social change.

Social Cognitive Theory

One cannot understand the concept of self-efficacy or a theory of self-efficacy without understanding the basic ideas of social cognitive theory (Bandura, 1977, 1986, 1997, 2001). Bandura's social cognitive theory developed out of the context of formal learning theory. Formal learning theory emerged primarily from animal studies and rigorously controlled experiments with humans. Learning theorists rejected the psychodynamic stance that humans were motivated by internal drives and were troubled by the lack of empirical investigation of psychodynamic principles. Learning theorists approached human behavior from a strictly empirical stance and focused solely on how humans respond to external stimuli. Bandura's objection to formal learning theory was that it was too narrowly focused; it did not take into account the broader role of the environment and human interactions with the environment to explain human behavior and human learning. Bandura's social cognitive theory posits that humans learn through both interaction with the environment and internal processes rather than solely according to the principles of operant or classical conditioning. Bandura and Walters (1963) introduced the idea that humans learn by imitating and observing others and by paying attention to the outcomes of behaviors in the context of the social environment. Bandura further developed those ideas to posit, in social cognitive theory, that humans can learn by modeling the behaviors of others and by testing the outcomes of those behaviors in their own lives. Humans, according to Bandura, can learn in a vicarious manner using a cognitive processing of the observations of others.

Central to Bandura's thinking is the assumption that humans desire to control their life circumstances, and this desire for personal control is at the root of most human action. Control is not important solely for control's sake. Control is important because it either fosters an intended, desired outcome or minimizes an unintended, unpleasant outcome. Control assists in pushing back negative outcomes and in pulling toward positive ones. Bandura also assumes that humans have the capacity to change and will act in ways that enhance control over events in their lives. Through attempts to control life circumstances, humans learn about the relationships between their actions and outcomes. When actions produce intended outcomes, humans learn and benefit from the cause-and-effect knowledge, leading to predictability and certainty. When actions do not produce intended outcomes, humans experience feelings of uncertainty, upset, and anxiety. Bandura theorized that humans will act in ways that increase certainty and decrease uncertainty and, in doing so, will increase their abilities to exert personal control. In the attempt to increase certainty and to decrease uncertainty, humans will also learn to manipulate and influence their social environments. Humans will attempt not only to change themselves to increase certainty of particular outcomes, but will also attempt to change those around them and their social conditions to foster intended outcomes and to increase predictability. Bandura wrestled with the notion that an individual's need for control and predictability could have individual gain but diffuse loss. "The capacity for human control," he wrote, "can be exercised for good or for ill" (1997, p. 2), but he reasoned that humans can, and do, work towards common purposes to balance self-interest with social good.

Bandura's theory on the causes of human behavior involves the relationship between internal personal factors of cognitive, affective, and biological events and the external environmental factors. Bandura's "sociocognitive analysis of reciprocal causation" has much in common with the social work concepts of the biopsychosocial perspective and the person–environment fit. Humans are change agents, but they also are changed by others and by the social environment. The social environment and social structures are similarly changed through human action. The transactions of events and the ways people learn from these events and their outcomes are the base for individual and social adaptability and interdependence.

Self-Efficacy Theory

In theorizing about personal agency and control, Bandura introduced the role of human belief to explanations of the concepts of motivation, affective states, and actions. Bandura reasoned that the objective facts of reality are less important in a person's motivations, feelings, and actions than are his or her beliefs about them. One's beliefs about one's ability to influence life are seen as the single most important aspect of human action. In fact, without that belief in effectiveness, Bandura argued there was very little incentive or motivation to act. The idea of personal efficacy, then, takes center stage in explanations of how people behave in all aspects of life. Stated simply, "Perceived self-efficacy refers to beliefs in one's capabilities to organize and execute the courses of action required to produce given attainments" (1997, p. 3).

Bandura theorizes that self-efficacy is developed through four specific learning strategies that (1) capture personal experiences of success and achievement; (2) draw upon the successful experiences of others; (3) provide supportive yet realistic feedback on success and failure; and (4) identify physiological and emotional arousal, especially in stressful situations (1997). Using self-efficacy theory, social workers engage with clients to change emotions, motivation, actions, and/or thoughts. However, the target of the work

begins with a focus on the perceptions or beliefs about the client's capability to influence or affect change because "beliefs of personal efficacy constitute the key factor of human agency" (1997, p. 3). According to self-efficacy theory, it is the confidence or belief in one's abilities that determines success rather than the actual ability itself. Bandura, however, was careful to state that "self as agent" and "self as object" are integrated, and this requires a shift in perspective rather than a duality of self (1997, p. 3).

Self-Concept, Self-Esteem, and Self-Efficacy

The terms "self-concept," "self-esteem," and "self-efficacy" are all common to social work practitioners. Especially in work with individuals, social workers often use interventions to identify, build, and sustain a person's sense of self. Bandura, however, clearly points out the distinctions among these three concepts and the increased utility of the self-efficacy theory to explain and predict human behavior and change. Definition and use of the concept of self-efficacy required Bandura to define and describe similar yet distinct concepts of self-concept and self-esteem—all familiar concepts to social workers but often used without much clarity. For Bandura, self-influence refers to the use of cognitive self-regulation to use one's self to influence a particular outcome. Self-influence requires using the knowledge and opportunities available, making decisions, and taking actions that result in advantageous outcomes. Making "good" choices based upon reflective thought and acting upon those choices sums up the idea of self-influence. Self-influence encompasses the ability to refrain from action when reflective thought warrants it. Self-concept and the process of self-development are related to, but not synonymous with, the ideas of self-efficacy theory. Self-concept is "the composite view of oneself formed through direct experience and evaluations adopted from significant others" (1997, p. 11). Bandura argues that theories using self-concept are not successful in predicting human behavior because self-concept is too global an idea and not well related to specific actions. Because the idea of self-concept is a composite, it cannot address specific behaviors in specific settings and fails to explain why people, with uniform self-concepts, can behave in different ways at different times. Self-esteem, according to Bandura, is also a distinctly different concept from self-efficacy. Self-esteem is primarily and singularly concerned with self-worth and not at all related to perceptions of ability or capability. Self-esteem and self-efficacy are not necessarily related; a person's estimation of his or her value can remain unaffected by the same person's estimation of his or her abilities. However, self-esteem or self-valuation does bear a relationship to self-efficacy in the empirical world in that "people tend to cultivate their abilities in activities that give them a sense of self-worth" (1997, p. 11). Self-efficacy is not a trait, but rather a perception of capability that is developed through both observations of others as well as personal experiences. Self-efficacy is not static but varies by setting and situation. Self-efficacy, in the context of social cognitive theory, explains how people perceive specific tasks, why they pursue specific goals, and how hard they try to reach those goals.

Criticism of Bandura's Theory

Bandura's theory of self-efficacy is not without criticism. Researchers questioned Bandura's assertion that perceived self-efficacy is an effective predictor of future action (Eastman & Marzillier, 1984; Marzillier & Eastman, 1984). The leading criticism was that Bandura was not specific or clear in the definition of the concepts of efficacy explanations and efficacy outcomes. Critics charged that perceptions of self-efficacy are interrelated and inseparable from expectations of outcome and, therefore, are not a valid theory to predict or control human behaviors. Eastman and Marzillier also questioned whether a person's belief in competency determined actual behavior. Earlier critics had focused on the theory's inability to distinguish both motor and emotional coping responses to specific aversive stimuli (Wolpe, 1978). Bandura responded to these criticisms on theoretical and methodological levels and refined the theory over the next 20 years (Bandura, 1997, 2001). Social science researchers and clinical practitioners continue to draw on Bandura's self-efficacy theory to explain and predict human behavior.

Social Work Practice

For social workers, who are interested in ways to foster positive change at various levels of intervention, self-efficacy is an appealing theory. Self-efficacy theory is tied to change and provides a clear, predictive path tying thoughts and attitudes with actions. While not all social work outcomes are behavioral in nature, social workers often see behavioral change as a desired and measurable outcome. The theory is compatible with social work's focus on person-in-environment. Not only do clients learn from their own experiences, but also they benefit from observing others—models or peers—and their experiences in particular situations. It is a theory that can be used on various intervention levels—self-efficacy can be influenced by individuals, families, groups, and environmental settings. Self-efficacy theory is compatible with a strengths approach (Saleeby, 2002), but also allows for recognition of problems and barriers in setting and attaining goals. The fact that perceived self-efficacy changes with time and situation means that it can and must be modified as a person goes through life. Many of the problems social workers address are chronic in nature; substance abuse problems, mental and physical health conditions, and relationship difficulties are among them. Self-efficacy theory's flexibility allows social workers to address multiple problems, but also in multiple situations throughout the lifespan.

Self-efficacy, as a theory, has not received uniform recognition in social work texts or references (Roberts & Greene, 2002; Walsh, 2006), but the ideas implicit in self-efficacy theory are a solid aspect of the social work helping process (Hepworth, Rooney, Rooney, Strom-Gottfried, & Larson, 2006) and are often included in social work's use of specific approaches such as motivational interviewing (Walsh, 2010).

Assessment, and Goal Setting

According to self-efficacy theory, the social work helping process should begin with a focus on a person's evaluation of his or her personal abilities to attempt and achieve a particular change behavior. A strength-based assessment will help clients identify ways in which they may have successfully addressed particular needs or barriers in the past. Active listening and reflective questioning are other techniques that can help clients develop a self-awareness of a pattern of particular thoughts and actions. Perceived success in one arena of life can be used to develop an awareness of the possibility of success in another, unrelated area. Within a trusting therapeutic relationship, clients can rely on the social worker to provide supportive, yet very objective and realistic feedback.

The social-cognitive learning context of self-efficacy theory provides social workers with many opportunities to draw upon models from not only the client's life, but also from media, literature, and history. The popular children's story *The Little Engine That Could* provides a simplistic yet effective example of how perceived self-efficacy can result in goal attainment. The little engine, with no special skills or specialized training, is able to pull the load to the top of the mountain. The factor that set the little engine apart was the perception of "I think I can" and the subsequent belief "I knew I could." Social work treatment often provides emotional support and objective evidence to assist in the development of positive perceptions of self-efficacy. Self-efficacy theory provides a clear paradigm for the relationships among beliefs, thought processes, goal-seeking behaviors, and goal achievement. Self-efficacy is not a set of skills or sub-skills, but the perception or belief that one has the ability to marshal one's skills—social, emotional, and behavioral—and to apply those skills effectively to address specific goals. Perceived self-efficacy, according to Bandura, allows people to tackle difficult problems and to persevere long and hard enough to obtain success (1997). If the level of perceived self-efficacy is low, a person will doubt his or her ability for success and not attempt or not stick with the problem. Individual levels of perceived self-efficacy are not uniform, but are situation-specific. The social work tasks of reframing, reflective support, and collaborative goal setting, in the context of Bandura's theory, are seen as tailoring perceptions of ability and focusing on the relationship between cognition, effort, and success in support of change. People with low levels of perceived self-efficacy interpret failures or setbacks differently than those with

higher levels of perceived self-efficacy. Social workers can also help clients understand and interpret past efforts for change in the context of self-efficacy theory. The idea that one learns from one's past efforts, successful or not, and incorporates that learning into the next attempt for change is consistent with the theory. Objective, supportive information and feedback on self-performance and from the performances of others is useful in helping clients understand the role of perceived self-efficacy in initiating and maintaining personal change. Bandura and Adams (1977) demonstrated that avoidance behaviors could be decreased through interventions to increase perceptions of personal efficacy. Many people seeking help use avoidance to deal with painful and stigmatizing problems. Social workers can effectively use the concepts of modeling to confront and help change avoidance behaviors into more active, positive steps.

High levels of perceived self-efficacy are not desirable in all situations with all clients, however. Some clients demonstrate an inflated sense of self-efficacy that is not supported by an objective review of achievement or personal efforts. Clients may perceive themselves as being able to achieve too lofty goals or may not realize their own agency in negative outcomes. By the same token, healthy perceptions of self-efficacy may be tied with desired yet deviant behaviors. Again, the social work tasks of reframing and supportive reflection can assist the client to realign faulty self-efficacy perceptions without harming his or her self-concept or self-esteem. The context of a supportive, therapeutic relationship allows a social worker to structure a mastery experience, but also to provide truthful, objective feedback. Social workers often provide models of specific behaviors or attitudes and make those models explicit in client discussions. When social work activities are focused upon a client's perception of his or her "capabilities to organize and execute the courses of action required to produce given attainments" in a specific arena or specific situation, there is a direct tie with self-efficacy theory.

Self-efficacy theory calls for the "continuous improvisation of multiple subskills to manage ever-changing situations, most of which contain ambiguous, unpredictable and often stressful elements" (Bandura, 1997, p. 37). Using the ideas of contextual assessment, social workers work with their clients to understand the personal perceptions of "cause and effect." Social work assessment, using both a personal and an environmental lens, is well suited to gather information about a client's views of his or her abilities, the difficulties of the tasks, and the amount of effort and energy necessary to tackle those changes. Social work's principles of client self-determination guide the use of such assessment information into a collaborative goal-setting process. Skill identification, skill building, and skill rehearsal are tools social workers commonly use to help clients prepare for change actions. These activities are used to develop particular abilities, but also to build perceptions of self-efficacy in relationship to particular action steps. Social work practitioners may be more likely to use the terms "motivation," "optimism," or "confidence," but Bandura's theory and his concept of perceived self-efficacy, whether acknowledged directly or not, are central to assessment and change strategies in social work practice.

The social worker's beliefs about the client's self-efficacy are also important. Torrey and Wyzik (2000) parallel the concepts of self-efficacy theory in their discussion of how social workers in mental health practice should relate to clients. Their advice includes communicating optimism about the client's prospect of recovery and assisting in the development of knowledge and skills necessarily to support accountable behaviors in recovery processes. Seligman's concept of learned optimism touches on the idea that people can learn to interpret information from their experiences in a positive, productive way (1990).

Substance Abuse Treatment

One area of social work practice that has directly incorporated principles of self-efficacy theory is in the assessment and treatment of substance use disorders. Prochaska, DiClemente, and Norcross (1992) and their trans-theoretical stages of change and Miller and Rollnick (2002) and their development of motivational interviewing incorporate many aspects of Bandura's self-efficacy theory. Prochaska et al.'s trans-theoretical stages of change provides a continuum of motivational levels for change and specific strategies used at each level to support and encourage success.

Not all the stages involve action, but they successively build upon self-perceived assessment of specific ideas and actions in relationship to substance use (Velicer, DiClemente, Rossi, & Prochaska, 1990). The trans-theoretical model presents a spiral rather than a linear approach to change, so people can learn from their experiences and incorporate those experiences into future behaviors. Rather than equate relapse as a failure, the trans-theoretical model acknowledges that there is a setback, but similar to self-efficacy-based interventions it encourages use of information, experience, and emotions to develop a more effective strategy for future actions. The mastery principle of self-efficacy theory would support assessment questions that link past successes in abstinence with current experiences. In talking with a client who recently relapsed, the social worker might ask, "Think about the times you have not used alcohol or drugs. How were those times different than the recent past?" The question implicitly supports past successes—times the client was sober—and conveys the idea that he or she has the ability to gain sobriety. The trans-theoretical model sets up a decisional balance and asks people to evaluate the costs of changing against the costs of staying the same. The trans-theoretical model also normalizes relapse as part of the spiral of recovery and assumes people will learn additional skills and adopt different attitudes because of their experiences, consistent with self-efficacy ideas.

Motivational interviewing (MI) more specifically uses the concept of self-efficacy in its approach to assessment and treatment options for the treatment of substance use disorders. It emphasizes the client's role in change and espouses an empathic and nonconfrontational approach (Miller & Rollnick, 2002; Noonan & Moyers, 1997). Miller and Rollnick set forth four general principles to guide motivational interviewing: Express Empathy; Support Self-Efficacy; Roll with Resistance; and Develop Discrepancy. In assessment and treatment with substance-abusing clients, social workers communicate a sense of hopefulness that change can happen and that people do change. Decision and accountability for change rest with the client; motivational interviewing techniques help instill and reinforce perceptions of self-efficacy for change in drinking and drug-using behaviors.

Assessment techniques move away from measures of quantity and frequency and away from the use of labels to discussions about how the client sees the role of alcohol or drugs in his or her life. The social worker provides information in response to topics the client brings up and promotes reflection rather than confrontation or diagnostic labels.

A consistent problem in substance abuse treatment is the client's false perception of self-efficacy in the ability to control his or her use of alcohol or other drugs. Known as "denial" in some contexts, the over-reliance on self-control mechanisms is a common cause of relapsing behaviors. In this situation, the social worker must assist the client in developing a more objective view of his or her relationship with the substance and to evaluate the risks and benefits of continued use. Self-efficacy theory adds a dimension of capacity: does the client perceive that he or she can survive without the use of the substance? Assessment might include a discussion of how equipped the client thinks he or she is to live without the substance. How does the client view his or her situation as similar or different from others who have stopped using alcohol or drugs? What fears or anxieties stand between use and abstinence? Does the client perceive alcohol and drug use as a behavior that can be changed, and how capable does he or she feel about making that change? All of these questions spring from self-efficacy theory and have direct implications for social work practice in the addictions.

Research on perceived self-efficacy in the treatment of substance use disorders have yielded mixed results. Project Match, a large randomized study of alcohol treatment, emphasized the importance of pre-treatment levels of motivation and self-efficacy on positive post-treatment outcomes (Project MATCH Research Group, 1998). However, a meta-analysis of 11 studies (Forcehime &Tonigan, 2008) found the beneficial effects of self-efficacy on abstinence behaviors were not supported across all studies. The authors countered that the findings may be due to differences in measurement, sample, and length of follow-up intervals. All 11 studies involved research participants who had been introduced to 12-step programs such as Alcoholics Anonymous. McQueen, Howe, Allan, and Mains (2009) conducted a meta-analysis of brief interventions that used self-efficacy with hospitalized heavy drinkers and found inconclusive evidence of success at follow-up. Self-efficacy interventions were only one part of the multifaceted, brief interventions examined in this review.

Prevention of substance use and substance abuse provides a useful venue for self-efficacy theory. The belief that one's ability to refuse alcohol, theoretically, would be related to lower alcohol consumption. Theory would also promote modeling behaviors of others who do not use alcohol. Supportive and objective feedback on positive decisions and behaviors would also support abstinence behaviors. Faggiano, Vigna-Taglianti, Versino, Zambon, Borraccino, and Lemma's (2005) systematic review of school-based prevention studies for alcohol and other drug use supported skill-based interventions, but not affective, self-efficacy–based prevention techniques. All of the research participants for these reviews were adolescents.

Conclusion

Social workers may not consciously operate from the perspective of self-efficacy theory, but many use concepts drawn directly from it. Bandura's theory provides an explanatory framework, but gives rise to many questions about human behavior and social work interventions. Cognitive behavioral methods, now so popular in treatment of mental health and substance abuse problems, owe a debt to self-efficacy theory. The application of motivational interviewing to a wide array of behavioral problems provides opportunities for social workers to think more critically about the concept of self-efficacy and its fit with Bandura's theory. Bandura argues that the perception of self-efficacy is formulated by mastery experiences, vicarious learning, accurate feedback, and affective states—all part of the social work helping process. Earlier criticisms about the relationship of attribution and outcome may also prove useful to social workers who are interested in how a client's self-attribution may create avenues to behavioral changes. What are the actual causal paths clients travel en route to behavioral changes? How is perceived self-efficacy translated from one area of clinical concern to others? To what extent do gains in perceived self-efficacy remain after treatment? What might be the specific balance among Bandura's four developmental elements of self-efficacy? Other related questions may be fruitful, yet vexing. What is the role of stigma or guilt in the formation of perceived self-efficacy? Does the perceived self-efficacy of the social worker affect the client's behavioral outcomes? What are the environmental barriers to development of perceived self-efficacy? In his semi-autobiographical account of the process of recovery, Dr. Drew Pinsky (2003) talks about clients who are able to change their behaviors and live their lives without alcohol or other drugs. He quotes them as saying, "I just got it. I don't know how else to explain it" (p. 44). What does it mean to "get it" in terms of those behavior changes? Does "getting it" refer to that crucible of perceived self-efficacy, when mastery, vicarious modeling, feedback, and emotional control all merge to transform our ways of being in the world? Drew Pinsky admits he does not know, but perhaps we can solicit teams of social work practitioners and social work researchers, who both bring useful knowledge, and enhance both self-efficacy theory and its application to social work practice.

References

Bandura, A. (1977). Self-efficacy: Toward a unifying theory of behavioral change. *Psychological Review*, 84, 191–215.

Bandura, A. (1986). *Social foundations of thought and action: A social cognitive theory.* Englewood Cliffs, NJ: Prentice-Hall.

Bandura, A. (1997). *Self-efficacy: The exercise of control.* New York: W. H. Freeman and Company.

Bandura, A. (2001). Social cognitive theory: An agentic perspective. *Annual Review of Psychology, 52,* 1–26.

Bandura, A., & Adams, N. (1977). Analysis of self-efficacy theory of behavioral change. *Cognitive Therapy and Research, 1*(4), 287–310.

Bandura, A., Barbaranelli, C., Caprara, G., & Pastorelli, C. (2001). Self-efficacy beliefs as shapers of children's aspirations and career trajectories. *Child Development, 72*(1), 187–206.

Bandura, A., & Walters, R. H. (1963). *Social learning and personality development.* New York: Hold, Rinehart & Winston.

Burditt, C., Robbins, M., Paiva, A., Velicer, W. F., Kiblin, B., & Kessler, D. (2008). Motivations for blood donation among African Americans: developing measures for stage of change, decisional balance and self-efficacy constructs. *Journal of Behavioral Medicine,* 32, 429–422.

Eastman, C., & Marzillier, J. S. (1984). Theoretical and methodological difficulties in Bandura's self-efficacy theory. *Cognitive Therapy and Research,* 8(3), 213–229.

Faggiano, F., Vigna-Taglianti, F., Versino, E., Zambon, A., Borraccino, A., & Lemma, P. (2005). School-based prevention for illicit drugs' use. *Cochrane Database of Systematic Reviews,* Issue 2. Art. No.: CD003020. DOI: 10.1002/14651858.CD003020. pub2. Retrieved on October 5, 2009, at http:/www. cochrane.org.

Forchimes, A. A., & Tonigan, J. S. (2008). Self-efficacy as a factor in abstinence from alcohol/other drug abuse: A meta-analysis. *Alcoholism Treatment Quarterly,* 26(4), 480–489.

Foster, G., Tayler, S. J. C., Eldridge, S., Ramsay, J., & Griffiths, C. J. (2007). Self-management education programs by lay leaders for people with chronic conditions. *Cochrane Database of Systematic Reviews,* Issue 4. Art. No. CD005108, DOI: 10.1002/14651858.CD005108.pub2. Retrieved on September 15, 2009, from http:www.cochrane.org/

Hepworth, D. H., Rooney, R. H., Rooney, G. D., Strom-Gottfried, K., & Larsen, J. (2006). *Direct social work practice; Theory and skills* (7th ed.). Belmont, CA: Thomson Higher Education.

Holden, G., Anastas, J., & Meenaghan, T. (2003). Determining attainment of the EPAS Foundation Program objectives: Evidence for the use of self-efficacy as an outcome. *Journal of Social Work Education,* 39(3), 425–440.

Jackson, A. P. (2000). Maternal self-efficacy and children's influence on stress and parenting among single black mothers in poverty. *Journal of Family Issues,* 21(1), 3–16.

Levy, B., Hausdorff, J., Hencke, R., & Wei, J. (2008). Reducing cardiovascular stress with positive self-stereotypes of aging. *Educational Gerontology,* 34(6), 520–530.

Luszczynska, A., Benight, C. C., & Cieslak, R. (2009) Self-efficacy and health-related outcomes of collective trauma. *European Psychologist,* 14(1), 51–62.

Marzillier, J., & Eastman, C. (1984). Continuing problems with self-efficacy theory: A reply to Bandura. *Cognitive Therapy and Research,* 8(3), 257–262.

McAuley, E., & Blissmer, B. (2000). Self-efficacy determinants and consequences of physical activity. *Exercise and Sport Sciences Review,* 28(2), 85–88.

McQueen, J., Howe, T. E., Allan, L., & Mains, D. (2009). Brief interventions for heavy alcohol users admitted to general hospital wards. *Cochrane Database of Systematic Reviews,* Issue 3. Art. No.: CD005191.

DOI: 10.1002/14651858.CD005191.pub2. Retrieved on September 15, 2009, from http://www.cochrane.org/

Miller, W. R., & Rollnick, S. (2002). *Motivational Interviewing: Preparing people for change*. (2nd ed.). New York: The Guilford Press.

National Association of Social Workers (2006). *Code of Ethics of the National Association of Social Workers*. Washington, DC: Author.

Noonan, W. C., & Moyers, T. C. (1997). Motivational interviewing. *Journal of Substance Abuse*, 2(1), 8–16.

Petrovich, A. (2004). Teaching notes: Using self-efficacy theory in social work teaching. *Journal of Social Work Education*, 40(3), 429–443.

Pinsky, D. (2003). *Cracked: Putting broken lives together again, A doctor's story*. New York: Regan Books/HarperCollins Publishers.

Prochaska, J. O., DiClemente, C. C., & Norcross, J. C. (1992). In search of how people change: Applications to addictive behaviors. *American Psychologist*, 1102–1114.

Project MATCH Research Group (1998). Matching alcoholism treatments to client heterogeneity: treatment main effects and matching effects on drinking during treatment. *Journal of Studies on Alcohol*, 59, 631–639.

Roberts, A. R., & Greene, G. J. (2002) (Eds.). *Social workers' desk reference*. New York: Oxford University Press.

Saleeby, D. (2002). *Strengths perspective in social work practice* (4th ed.). Boston: Allyn & Bacon.

Seligman, M. E. (1990). *Learned optimism*. New York: Alfred A. Knopf.

Torrey, W. C., & Wyzik, P. (2000). The recovery vision as a service improvement guide for community mental health center providers. *Community Mental Health Journal*, 36(2), 209–216.

Velicer, W. F., DiClemente, C. C., Rossi, J. D., & Prochaska, J. O. (1990). Relapse situations and self-efficacy: An integrative model. *Addictive Behaviors*, 15, 271–283.

Walsh, J. (2006). *Theories for direct social work practice*. Belmont, CA: Wadsworth Cengage Learning.

Walsh, J. (2010). *Theories for direct social work practice* (2nd ed.). Belmont, CA: Wadsworth Cengage Learning.

Wilson, S. Z. (2006). Field education: Linking self-efficacy theory and the strengths perspective. *Journal of Baccalaureate Social Work*, 12(1), 261–275.

Wolpe, J. (1978). Self-efficacy theory and psychotherapeutic change: A square peg for a round hole. *Advances in Behavior Research and Therapy*, 1, 231–239.

30

SOCIAL LEARNING

Based on the premise that behavior is malleable, knowledge of operant, respondent, and observational learning is used to beneficially modify client behavior through the use of tested, ethical procedures

Social Learning Theory and Social Work Treatment

Bruce A. Thyer

The purpose of the practice of social work is to change behavior. Whether one engages in clinical work with individuals, couples, families, small groups, or organizations, or provides supervision, administration, community organization, or policy practice, the eventual bottom line is to effectively change the behavior of people. Towards this end our discipline has adopted and developed a plethora of approaches, some of which are firmly grounded in a well-crafted theoretical orientation, others less so. A very widely used approach to practice is known as behavioral social work, which has been defined as:

...the informed use by professional social workers of assessments and interventions based on empirically derived learning theories. These theories include, but are not limited to, respondent learning, operant

learning, and observational learning. Behavioral social workers may or may not subscribe to the philosophy of science known as behaviorism. (Thyer & Hudson, 1987, p. 1)

These learning theories were developed largely outside of social work but have been incorporated into our field almost from its inception. Box 30.1 includes some selected quotations dating back to the 1920s reflecting the positive contributions that the behavioral orientation was seen to have for social work practice. Discipline-specific reviews, those addressing a social work audience, of operant (Reid, 2004; Schwartz & Goldiamond, 1975; Wong, 2008), respondent (Thyer, 2008), and observational learning theories (Fischer & Gochros, 1975; Wodarski & Bagarozzi, 1979) help translate these principles into the unique aspects of what social

Box 30.1 Early Statements on the Importance of Behaviorism to Social Work

"Sooner or later, too, I believe, every conscientious physician, as every earnest educator, *social worker*, econo-mist, sociologist, every attorney and judge, every artist and craftsman, every laborer for human welfare, every man or woman hurt or seeking to avoid being hurt, striving to understand intelligently themselves and their fellow creatures, must come to grips and to terms with its [behaviorism's] strange doctrines that possess a power and a fascination."

(Berman, 1927, pp. 26–27, emphasis added)

"Two dominant schools of thought may be recognized as differentiating case work approach and treatment at the present time; behaviorist psychology and psychiatric interpretation. The former emphasizes habit training, conditioning and reconditioning in treatment... Illustrations of a partial use of this psychology in treatment are abundant in any case work area."

(Robinson, 1934, pp. 83–84)

"Behaviorism may be described as the theory that learning is the association of a new impression with the circumstances present at the time of receiving it. It has several obvious merits. It integrates emotion and intellect in a manner which realistically reproduces actual experience. It is socially acceptable, in the main, as it places such large faith upon capacity to learn, given the right conditions for association... behaviorism affords a first-class technic, without specializing in the abnormal.... It is invaluable for the social worker in his efforts to understand the conduct of his clients, because it refers him back to the past experiences in which are to be found the particular circumstances which have determined the attitude or the habitual responses for each individual. Thus behaviorism opens up endless possibilities for social work.... It is also of value in treatment, for some of the most interesting work of the behaviorists has been in the field of what is called reconditioning."

(Bruno, 1934, pp. 197–198)

"...the socio-behavioral approach provides a viable and potentially durable framework within which to prac-tice. Contained within it are important empirical bases lacking in many more traditional approaches."

(Thomas, 1967, p. 15)

"...social learning theory holds a rather optimistic view of man's ability to change his behavior. Since all behav-ior is malleable, and if the conditions maintaining behavior can be controlled, and the proper reinforcers found, then change is possible...the promise of social learning theory for the treatment field appears to be great."

(Whittaker, 1974, pp. 86–87)

workers do. As noted in the definition provided above, behavioral social work is a strongly theo-retically based orientation, and any social worker proposing to make use of behavioral methods should have a thorough grounding in the scien-tific theories underlying its approaches to assess-ment, intervention, and the evaluation of practice. Sundel and Sundel (2005) is one excel-lent general introduction to social learning theory focusing on a social work audience, as is Kilpatrick and Holland (2006).

Behavioral social work can be seen as three related but distinguishable components: a wide-ranging theory, numerous specific practice methods, and a comprehensive philosophy of science. It is important to keep these three ele-ments distinct because the merits and limitations

of each should not be confused with the approach as a whole. For example, the philosophy of sci-ence called behaviorism is a well-developed approach to addressing the major elements that are the focus of philosophy, issues such as episte-mology, ontology, language, free will versus determinism, values and ethics, etc. (see Thyer, 1999). However, one need not subscribe to the philosophy of behaviorism to make use of the interventive methods based upon social learning theory, and objections to the philosophy may have little bearing on the validity of the approach's underlying theory or practice utility. Similarly, one can subscribe to the principles of social learning theory yet not be a philosophical behav-iorist. Or one can use behavior practice tech-niques even if you believe the underlying theory is incorrect. Individuals whose conceptual framework embraces all three elements—the theory, the practice methods, and the philosophy—generally call themselves behavior analysts or radical behaviorists, with radical meaning "complete" (not referring to political extremism).

However, most social workers who make use of behavioral methods do so as a part of a more eclectic approach to practice. A large-scale survey of clinical social workers conducted by Timberlake, Sabatino, and Martin (1997) found that 43% reported using behavioral methods "frequently." A more recent but smaller-scale survey (Pignotti & Thyer, 2009) of licensed clinical social workers found that the most common theoretical *orientation* they reported using was eclectic (31%), with cognitive behavioral the next most common (24%). However, in terms of the most frequent *interventions* used during the past year, cognitive behavioral methods topped the list, being used by 73% of the clinicians. Conveniently, behavioral social work enjoys the strongest level of empirical support, in terms of outcome studies with positive results, of any approach to practice (Gorey, Thyer, & Pawluck, 1998; MacDonald, Sheldon, & Gillespie, 1992; Reid & Fortune, 2003; Reid & Hanrahan, 1982; Rubin, 1985).

What is Behavior?

In behavioral social work, as is true for behaviorism in general, behavior refers to what the person does. It makes no difference whether or not an outside observer can view what is occurring; if it something a person is doing, it is behavior. I stress this point because behaviorism is commonly construed as focusing only on the overt actions of people and not on their inner, lived experiences. Given the importance of these latter elements in our lives (e.g., the love I feel for my family), if it is seen (erroneously) that behavioral methods ignore these issues, then the approach may be discarded as somehow incomplete or limited. Although it was the psychologist John B. Watson in the early part of the last century who claimed that the sole legitimate subject matter of psychology was overt behavior, this limitation was never really adhered to, and several decades later B. F. Skinner asserted that the proper subject matter of behaviorism was both public

behavior and our inner lives. It is in this sense that behavioral social work is currently interpreted, and this is reflected in the definition of behavior contained in *The Social Work Dictionary*: "Any action or response by an individual, including observable activity, measurable physiological changes, cognitive images, fantasies, and emotions" (Barker, 2003, p. 40).

Thus, the focus of behavioral social work is not only on changing overt behavior, but also on any private events experienced by clients as problematic. This would include attitudes (e.g., racism, see Lillis & Hayes, 2007; Hayes, Niccolls, Masuda, & Rye, 2002), fear, opinions, dreams, obsessions, anxiety, hallucinations, depression, delusions, etc., as well as an interest in enhancing positive inner qualities, such as self-esteem, optimism, and hope. Some of the earliest behavior therapies were focused on helping clients with affective problems such as severe anxiety, and were found to be very helpful in this regard.

What is the Relationship Between Inner and Outer Behavior?

In much of lay and professional psychology it is contended that our inner lives drive our outer actions. For example, to eliminate racist actions the first step often is said to be to change an individual's attitudes, since one's attitudes are said to cause one's actions. Or to alleviate the lethargic behavior, weeping, and expression of hopelessness associated with depression, it is claimed to be crucial to alleviate the inner state of depression (the feeling), and then the overt symptoms will improve. Behaviorism does not subscribe to the theory that attitudes (or other inner mental events) cause overt actions. Rather, the behaviorist puts forth the more credible hypothesis that both overt actions and attitudes (or feelings, opinions, etc.) are similarly brought about largely by one's learning history. How one has experienced reinforcement and punishment for past actions helps shape both future overt activity and our inner lives related to those activities. Therefore, to change attitudes and behavior, one will likely need to experience changes in the reinforcers and punishers one is exposed to.

Social worker Harris Chaiklin (in press) has recently prepared an overview on research on the relationships between attitudes and behavior, and contends that our disciplinary preoccupation with changing attitudes in order to bring about changes in comportment is unsupported by the available scientific research. Chaiklin concludes, "It is not necessary to change attitudes to change behavior" (p. x). Are attitudes and feelings important, in a behavioral analysis? Very much so. However, they are not seen as causal; they are more behaviors to be explained.

Basic Propositions of Behavioral Social Work

Behavioral social work is based on a limited number of deceptively simple but fundamental propositions (Fischer & Gochros, 1975). These include the following:

1. Human behavior consists of what we do—both observable behavior and unobservable behavior: overt acts, covert speech, thoughts and cognition, feelings, and dreams. All those phenomena that people engage in are considered behavior.
2. To a large extent, much (but not all) of human behavior is learned through life experiences. This learning occurs throughout the lifespan.
3. It seems very likely that similar fundamental learning processes give rise to individual human behavior across cultures and life circumstances and account for both normative and many so-called dysfunctional actions, feelings, and thoughts.
4. Interpersonal behavior is also a function (to some extent) of these learning processes, giving rise to dyadic, group, organizational, community, and societal phenomena. These larger-scale activities are, to a great extent, a more complex operation of fundamental learning mechanisms.
5. There are at least three major empirically supported learning processes that collectively make up social learning theory: respondent learning, operant learning, and observational learning.
6. To the degree that the learning processes responsible for developing and maintaining behavior can be identified and altered, it may be possible to effectively change behavior toward desired ends.

Each of the above propositions is well supported and difficult to argue against, particularly given the qualifiers used (e.g., "to some extent," "but not all"). This is not persiflage. Behaviorists recognize the importance of other factors giving rise to human activity, factors such as one's genetic endowment, life *in utero*, and other biological factors such as health, disease states, exposure to toxins, radiation, pollution, etc. Our lived environments are both physical and behavioral, and consist in part of the extent to which our actions result in various consequences. Behaviorists make no claim that their orientation provides a sufficient accounting to explain *all* human activity. Theirs is the more modest claim that the factors they focus on are very likely salient in most situations and deserve careful consideration as to their potential role in a given circumstance.

Learning Theory

The three major learning processes which behavioral social work is based upon are called operant learning, respondent learning, and observational learning. Each of these will be briefly reviewed.

Operant Learning

This type of learning is simplistically defined as "A type of learning defined by B. F. Skinner (1904–1990) in which behaviors are strengthened or weakened by altering the consequences that following them" (Barker, 2003, p. 306). It is called operant learning because it refers to the extent to which the behavior "operates" on the environment, which in turn produces consequences for the behaving person. Consequences that strengthen subsequent behavior are called reinforcers. If a stimulus is presented, and behavior is later strengthened, this stimulus (colloquially, something good) is called a *positive reinforcer*. If a stimulus is removed, and behavior is later strengthened, this stimulus is called a *negative reinforcer* (think of the term *relief*). The corresponding processes are called positive and negative reinforcement, respectively. Consequences that have the effect of weakening behavior are called punishers. If a stimulus follows a behavior and that behavior later is subsequently weakened, this type of consequence is called punishment. If the consequence involves the presentation of a stimulus (something bad), the stimulus is called a *positive punisher*, and a stimulus that, if removed (something good), subsequently weakens behavior is called a *negative punisher* (think of being fined). The corresponding operations are called positive and negative punishment. Any behavior that produces consequences is liable to be affected, either strengthened or weakened, by those consequences.

Other operant processes include that of extinction, which occurs when the consequences that are maintaining a given behavior are discontinued, and the behavior subsequently weakens. Shaping occurs when "new patterns of behavior are fashioned by reinforcing progressively closer approximations of the desired behaviors and not reinforcing others" (Barker, 2003, p. 395). In this way, simple actions (hitting a piano key) can be systematically refined to yield more complex activities (e.g., playing a sonata). Operant processes are crucially involved in much of human learning, including both normal development across the lifespan (Bijou, 1993; Schlinger, 1995), as well as in the etiology of so-called abnormal behavior and psychosocial problems. Contingencies of reinforcement affect not only individuals, but also the functioning of larger groups of people, including organizations, communities, and society as a whole. The entire field of social welfare policy can be construed as the governmental imposition of artificial contingencies of punishment (usually) and reinforcement (less often) related to behaviors that politicians deem important to change (Thyer, 1996).

Here are some everyday examples to make these processes a bit clearer. You place coins in a soda machine and a few moments later receive a can of cold soda. The act of putting the coins in the machine was positively reinforced: positive (because something was presented), and reinforced because you are more likely to do the same actions in a similar situation. Drinking the soda refreshes your thirst. The act of drinking is negatively reinforcing: negative because something aversive was taken away (thirst), reinforced because you are more likely to drink that beverage in the future (as opposed to chugging down

highly salted water). During dinner you reach across your mother to grab the salt. Your elderly mother slaps your hand, saying "Mind your manners." In the future you are less likely to reach across your mother. This is positive punishment: positive because something unpleasant was presented contingent on your behavior, and punishment because this behavior is weakened (at least around Mom). You are speeding home from class. You are stopped by the police for speeding and have to pay a substantial fine. In the future, you speed less (for a while, at least). Speeding has been negatively punished: negative because something pleasant or desirable was taken away, and punishment because the behavior in question is weakened. Keep in mind that negative reinforcement and punishment are not synonymous. The former always strengthens behavior and the latter weakens it. We usually like to be negatively reinforced (think of relief) and we dislike being punished.

Respondent Learning

Another fundamental way in which people learn is via respondent conditioning, also known as Pavlovian conditioning. Respondent learning is quite distinct from operant learning, although it is common (and a mistake) for the two approaches not to be separated. Most social workers will have learned something of the fundamentals of respondent learning, which occurs when a neutral stimulus is paired with a unconditioned stimulus (UCS), something that automatically elicits a simple reflexive form of behavior. Some example of UCSs in everyday life include sharp pain and loud noises, each of which usually causes the listener to flinch or withdraw quickly. If some neutral stimulus occurs just before a UCS, after one such (or several) pairing(s), the previously neutral stimulus can come to evoke a similar reaction. Many readers will have fearful reactions to the sound of the dentist's drill, a reaction which is a conditioned response to the sound of the previously neutral noise of the drill, because in the reader's past the drill sounds immediately preceded a sharp pain. After only a few such experiences, the sound of the drill alone may be sufficient to make one flinch, to feel fearful, or to have an elevated heart rate. A more complex example occurs when cancer patients initially receive chemotherapy, medications with toxic effects often administered in clinic settings via an intravenous drip. The clinic surroundings and the IV apparatus are initially neutral stimuli. After one or more episodes when the medication is administered (neutral stimuli), the person may experience nausea and vomiting as a side effect of the medication. Soon, many chemotherapy patients come to experience nausea and even vomiting upon entering the clinic environs. The medication is a UCS; the naturally occurring nauseating side effects are unconditioned responses. The neutral clinic setting becomes a conditioned stimulus (CS) resulting in anticipatory nausea (a conditioned response) even before the medication is administered.

There are many subtle variations of natural and contrived respondent learning processes, including *respondent extinction*, wherein a conditioned stimulus is repeatedly presented, absent the UCS, so that the conditioned response is gradually weakened. One need not personally experience respondent learning processes in order to be affected by it; observing others is another way, known as *vicarious conditioning*. Few of us have personally been attacked by a vampire, but if we saw a fanged Bela Lugosi outside our window most people would be seriously frightened. Why? None of us have been injured by a vampire, but we have certainly seen plenty of movie depictions of people being killed by them. This is vicarious respondent learning. *Higher-order respondent conditioning* occurs when a neutral stimulus immediately precedes an established CS (or CS_1). In this way the neutral stimulus can come to evoke reactions similar to those elicited by the original CS, leading to the development of a CS_2, then perhaps a CS_3, and so forth. By the time one has developed a CS_n^{th} the links may be so subtle as to elude discovery, leading to conditioned reactions that seem inexplicable or nonsensical.

Respondent learning is responsible for many of our emotional reactions and is implicated in the establishment of emotions and attitudes. It is intimately involved in much of normal human development as well as in the emergence of problematic behavior such as anxiety disorders. Many therapeutic approaches make use of respondent learning principles, and one of the earliest books on this topic appeared in 1949, a text called *Conditioned Reflex Therapy* (Salter, 1949). Thyer (2008) provides a good overview of the application of respondent learning principles to social work theory and practice.

Observational Learning

Observational learning is also known as modeling, defined as "a form of learning in which an individual acquires behaviors by imitating the actions of one or more other people" (Barker, 2003, p. 276). Much behavior acquired by operant learning can also be acquired by observation. Observing others can help one develop an entirely new behavior, may inhibit certain activities, or may have the effect of reducing any reluctance to try something. For example, at an amusement park I was recently confronted with a terrifying roller coaster my kids wanted me to ride with them. I was able to calm myself to the point of getting on and riding the thing by observing the reactions of the prior riders as they coasted to a halt at the end of their ride. Most were laughing and happy. This relieved my anxiousness (somewhat!).

Although one need not receive immediate reinforcement for imitating the successful behavior of others, this does not mean that observational learning is unrelated to reinforcement. In fact, modeled behavior that is never subsequently reinforced will probably undergo operant extinction. It is more likely that the capacity to acquire new behavior by observing others is another form of learning present from infancy throughout one's life, but that to the extent that modeled behavior is followed by reinforcement, even sporatically, we develop a strengthened repertoire for imitating others. Simply put, if you do as Mommy demonstrates and the new behavior is immediately reinforced by naturally occurring consequences, two things in reality get strengthened: the first is the modeled behavior directly, and the second is the likelihood of imitating Mommy (and then of course others). With many repetitions of this process, first perhaps with parents, then siblings, others family members or caregivers, and ultimately strangers, the human being develops a strong generalized capacity for imitation. This is a highly efficient form of learning that shortcuts the need to directly and immediately experience the effects of contingency shaping. Baer and Deguchi (1985) provide a very good exposition of how modeling may well be a highly developed form of operant learning. Fischer and Gochros (1975, pp. 101–102) provide a list of conditions that appear to facilitate learning via modeling, including, among others:

- Use models who are important to the observer.
- Show the model being reinforced.
- Reinforce the observer for imitating the model's behavior.
- Use multiple models.
- Use repeated modeling experiences.
- Graduate practice exercises (from less to more difficult).
- Arrange for reinforcement from the natural environment as soon as possible, etc.

These three learning theories have been combined to develop a viable alternative to the traditional stage-based theories of human development across the lifespan (see Bijou, 1993; Schlinger, 1995), a perspective that remains oddly excluded from most social work textbooks on human development in the social environment. Similarly ignored are behavioral perspectives on what has been labeled personality theory (Lundin, 1974; Staats, 2003). This is difficult to fathom, since social work theorists of every persuasion are in accord that these principles are to some degree valid and important. The processes of operant, respondent, and observational learning are well supported in terms of empirical research as to their legitimacy, and they have led to the development of some very effective methods of interpersonal helping.

Learning Theory and the Person-in-Environment Perspective of Social Work

If social work has anything akin to a unique perspective that distinguishes it from related human service disciplines, it is said to be the person-in-environment (PIE) point of view. Here are some representative quotes illustrating the perceived centrality of this perspective:

- "Behavior is the result of the effort of the person to establish himself in his environment in such a way as to give satisfaction to himself." (Bruno, 1934, p. 45)

- "Flexibility, change, and movement are of the very nature of social interaction. It is no wonder that social workers give close attention to behavior, which is the pulse of the human organism's attempts at adaptation." (Hamilton, 1940, p. 305)

- "A basic assumption…is that human behavior is the product of the interactions between the individual and his environment." (Northen, 1982, p. 63)

- "The human being and the environment reciprocally shape each other. People mold their environments in many ways and, in turn, they must then adapt to the changes they created." (Germain, in Bloom, 1992, p. 407)

- "The ecosystems perspective is about building more supportive, helpful and nurturing environments for clients through environmental helping, and increasing their competence in dealing with the environment by teaching basic life skills." (Whittaker & Garbarino, 1983, p. 34)

- "The ecological perspective makes clear the need to view people and environments as a unitary system within a particular cultural and historic context. Both person and environment can be fully understood in terms of their relationship, in which each continually influences the other within a particular context… . Ecological thinking examines exchanges between A and B, for example, that shape, influence, or change both over time. A acts, which leads to a change in B, whereupon the change in B elicits a change in A that in turn changes B, which then changes or otherwise influences A, and so on." (Germain & Gitterman, 1995, p. 816)

- "Person-in-environment perspective…an orientation that views the client as part of an environmental system. This perspective encompasses the reciprocal relationships and other influences between an individual, the *relevant other* or others, and the physical and social environment." (Barker, 2003, p. 323, emphasis in original)

Here are some selected quotes illustrating how this same perspective is central to social learning theory and behavioral analysis and therapy:

- "Men act upon the world and change it, and are changed in turn by the consequences of their action. Certain processes which the human organism shares with other species, alter behavior so that it achieves a safer and more useful interchange with a particular environment. When appropriate behavior has been established, its consequences work through similar processes to keep it in force. If by chance the environment changes, new forms of behavior disappear, while new consequences build new forms." (Skinner, 1957, p. 1)

- "Most behavioral science emphasizes the power of the environment; it sees environment as constantly controlling behavior, and it sees behavior as constantly affecting the environment. Indeed, the point of most behavior is to affect the environment." (Baer & Pinkston, 1997, p. 1)

- "Behaviorism's environmentalism does not imply that the organism passively reacts to the environment. The relationship between the organism and the environment is interdependent and reciprocal... That is, although the organism interacts with its environment, its reaction also changes the environment. The organism is then influenced by an environment changed by its own behavior, behaves again, changes the environment again, and so on. Thus the organism's relationship to its environment is one of mutual influence." (O'Donohue & Ferguson, 2001, p. 57)

- "Behavior analysis is essentially the study, definition, and characterization of effective environments as arrayed over time, with 'effective' defined by the dynamics of behavior... Psychological process is construed as behavior-environment interaction. It does not consist in phenomena that underlie that interaction." (Hineline, 1990, p. 305)

The apparent congruence between social work's PIE and behavior is both obvious and compelling. Behavioral approaches are a largely environmentally based perspective on understanding, predicting, and controlling human behavior, as opposed to the mentally oriented theories common to most other approaches to social work. An example of this behavioral perspective on PIE is called functional analysis, and an illustration of this process was narratively described by one social worker over 40 years ago:

> During the initial phases of a project integrating orthopedically handicapped children into groups of nonhandicapped children, no specific instructions were given to the group leaders regarding the degree of "special attention" they were to provide the handicapped children. After a few sessions, it was noticed that one leader appeared especially overprotective: Every time the handicapped child approached this leader, he was treated with excessive warmth and openness. At the direction of his supervisor, the leader observed the results of this interaction carefully. It became apparent that the leader was, in effect, rewarding passive, dependent behavior and that this was detrimental to the integrative attempts. On the basis of this observation, the leader predicted that if he were to respond more critically to this behavior, that is, to redirect the handicapped child whenever feasible and realistic, the child would become less passive and more independent and would interact more with his peers (at this point, a hypothesis has been developed and a "prediction" made wherewith to test the hypothesis). The leader adopted this approach, and his prediction was borne out, namely, that a more objective response did affect the specific elements of behavior under consideration in a desirable fashion. (Holmes, 1967, pp. 95–96)

In effect, when a target behavior is identified, the social worker observes the client in his or her natural environment to ascertain the antecedent circumstances and consequences surrounding this behavior. From these qualitative observations specific hypotheses are generated regarding potential etiological and maintaining contingencies. These hypotheses are then tested by deliberately changing the presumptive causal consequences via environmental manipulation. If the behavior reliably changes as the consequences are changed, then one has, in effect, isolated at least some of the variables causally responsible for the behavior in question. One is thus examining the functions that the behavior has for the individual concerned—hence the term functional analysis.

Ethical Issues

Behavioral approaches represent perhaps one of the most ethical approaches to the delivery of the human services compared to other theoretical orientations. This is because they enjoy a generally sound empirical foundation and are thus consistent with our ethical standards that mandate social workers base their practice, in part, on empirical research. Indeed, it can be reasonably contended that clients have a right to be offered effective interventions—that is, those supported by sound outcome studies yielding positive results with individuals who are similar to one's client, and who experienced similar problems (Myers & Thyer, 1997). Like all approaches to social work intervention, behavioral methods are governed by our professional codes of ethics and legal regulations. Clients can be abused by all forms of therapy, and no approach is exempt from this potential for misuse. Social workers attempting to make use of behavioral methods should do so with a sound understanding of social learning theory so that these approaches are applied in an informed and professional manner, and not as a rote-like technical skill. Social workers choosing to focus their professional life through providing behavior analysis and therapy may wish to join any of a number of behaviorally oriented professional organizations such as the Association for Behavior Analysis (http://www.abainternational.org/) for purposes of professional development, training, and continuing education. Many states offer an advanced practice credential called Board Certified Behavior Analyst (see http://www.bacb.com/) that clinical social workers may qualify for. This is a credential that can be earned in addition to, or in lieu of, licensure as a clinical social worker.

References

Berman, L. (1927). *The religion called behaviorism.* New York: Boni & Liveright.

Baer, D. M., & Deguchi, H. (1985). Generalized imitation from a radical-behavioral viewpoint. In S. Reiss & R. R. Bootzin (Eds.), *Theoretical issues in behavior therapy* (pp. 179–217). New York: Academic Press.

Baer, D. M., & Pinkston, E. M. (Eds.) (1997). *Environment and behavior.* Boulder, CO: Westview Press.

Barker, R. L. (2003). *The social work dictionary* (5th ed.). Washington, DC: NASW Press.

Bijou, S. W. (1993). *Behavior analysis of child development* (2nd ed.). Reno, NV: Context Press.

Bloom, M. (1992). A conversation with Carel Germain. In M. Bloom (Ed.), *Changing lives: Studies in human development and professional helping* (pp. 406–409). Columbia: University of South Carolina Press.

Bruno, F. (1934). *The theory of social work.* New York: D. C. Heath.

Chaiklin, H. (in press). Attitudes, behavior, and social practice. *Journal of Sociology and Social Welfare.*

Fischer, J., & Gochros, H. L. (1975). *Planned behavior change: Behavior modification in social work.* New York: Free Press.

Germain, C. B., & Gitterman, A. (1995). Ecological perspective. In R. L. Edwards (Ed.), *Encyclopedia of social work* (pp. 816–824). Washington, DC: NASW Press.

Gorey, K. J., Thyer, B. A., & Pawluck, D. E. (1998). Differential effectiveness of social work practice models. *Social Work, 43,* 269–278.

Hamilton, G. (1940). *Theory and practice of social casework.* New York: Columbia University Press.

Hayes, S. C., Niccolls, R., Masuda, A., & Rye, A. K. (2002). Prejudice, terrorism and behavior therapy. *Cognitive and Behavioral Practice, 9,* 296–301.

Holmes, D. (1967). Bridging the gap between research and practice in social work. In National Conference on Social Welfare (Ed.), *Social work practice, 1967* (pp. 94–108). New York: Columbia University Press.

Kilpatrick, A. C., & Holland, T. P. (2006). *Working with families: An intergrative model by level of need.* Boston: Pearson.

Lillis, J., & Hayes, S. C. (2007). Applying acceptance, mindfulness, and values to the reduction of prejudice: A pilot study. *Behavior Modification, 31,* 389–411.

Linn, J. W. (1935). *Jane Addams: A biography.* New York: Appleton-Century-Crofts.

Lundin, R. W. (1974). *Personality: A behavioral analysis.* New York: Macmillan.

MacDonald, G., Sheldon, B., & Gillespie, J. (1992). Contemporary studies of the effectiveness of social work. *British Journal of Social Work, 22,* 615–643.

Myers, L. L., & Thyer, B. A. (1997). Should clients have a right to effective treatment? *Social Work, 42,* 288–298.

Northen, H. (1982). *Clinical social work.* New York: Columbia University Press.

O'Donohue, W., & Ferguson, K. (2001). *The psychology of B. F. Skinner.* Thousand Oaks, CA: Sage.

Pignotti, M., & Thyer, B. A. (2009). Use of novel unsupported and empirically supported therapies by licensed clinical social worker: An exploratory study. *Social Work Research, 33,* 5–17.

Reid, W. J. (2004). The contribution of operant theory to social work practice and research. In H. E. Briggs & T. L. Rzepnicki (Eds.), *Using evidence in social work practice: Behavioral perspectives* (pp. 36–54). Chicago: Lyceum Press.

Reid, W. J., & Fortune, A. E. (2003). Empirical foundations for practice guidelines in current social work knowledge. In A. Rosen & E. Proctor (Eds.), *Developing practice guidelines for social work intervention: Issues, methods, and research agenda* (pp. 59–79). New York: Columbia University Press.

Reid, W. J., & Hanrahan, P. (1982). Recent evaluations of social work practice: Grounds for optimism. *Social Work, 27,* 328–340.

Robinson, V. R. (1930). *A changing psychology in social casework.* Durham: University of North Carolina Press.

Rubin, A. (1985). Practice effectiveness: More grounds for optimism. *Social Work, 30,* 469–476.

Salter, A. (1949). *Conditioned reflex therapy: The direct approach to the reconstruction of personality.* New York: Creative Age Press.

Schlinger, H. D. (1995). *A behavior analytic view of child development.* New York: Plenum Press.

Schwartz, A., & Goldaimond, I. (1975). *Social casework: A behavioral approach.* New York: Columbia University Press.

Skinner, B. F. (1957). *Verbal behavior.* Englewood Cliffs, NJ: Prentice Hall.

Staats, A. W. (2003). A psychological behaviorism theory of personality. In T. Millon & M. J. Lerner (Eds.), *Handbook of psychology: Personality and social psychology* (Vol. 5, pp. 135–158). Hoboken, NJ: Wiley.

Sundel, M., & Sundel, S. (2005). *Behavior change in the human services* (5th ed.). Thousand Oaks, CA: Sage.

Thomas, E. J. (1967). *The socio-behavioral approach and applications to social work.* New York: Council on Social Work Education.

Thyer, B. A. (1996). Behavior analysis and social welfare policy. In M. A. Mattaini & B. A. Thyer (Eds.), *Finding solutions to social problems: Behavioral strategies for change* (pp. 41–60). Washington, DC: American Psychological Association.

Thyer, B. A. (Ed.). (1999). *The philosophical legacy of behaviorism.* Dordrecht, The Netherlands: Kluwer.

Thyer, B. A. (2008). Respondent learning theory. In B. A. Thyer (Ed.), *Comprehensive handbook of social work and social welfare: Vol. 2. Human behavior in the social environment* (pp. 39–67). New York: Wiley.

Thyer, B. A., & Hudson, W. W. (1987). Progress in behavioral social work: An introduction. *Journal of Social Service Research, 10*(2/3/4), 1–6.

Timberlake, E. M., Sabatino, C. A., & Martin, J. A. (1997). Advanced practitioners in clinical social work: A profile. *Social Work, 42,* 374–386.

Whittaker, J. (1974). *Social treatment: An approach to interpersonal helping.* New York: Aldine.

Whittaker, J., & Garbarino, J. (1983). *Social support networks: Informal helping in the human services.* New York: Aldine.

Wodarski, J. S., & Bagarozzi, D. A. (1979). *Behavioral social work.* New York: Human Sciences Press.

Wong, S. W. (2008). Operant theory. In B. A. Thyer (Ed.), *Comprehensive handbook of social work and social welfare: Vol. 2. Human behavior in the social environment* (pp. 69–99). New York: Wiley.

SOCIAL NETWORKS

This theory, with strong sociological origins, aims to understand clients' social and personal networks in order to mobilize them in ways useful for both macro and micro practice

Social Networks and Social Work Practice

Elizabeth M. Tracy and Suzanne Brown

Practitioners recognize that clients are surrounded by social networks that may either support or weaken the efforts of professional helping. This chapter will trace the significance of social networks, and the related concept of social support, to the social work profession and the corresponding development of social network assessment and intervention within contemporary social work practice. We believe that knowledge and skills in assessing and mobilizing social networks are important for every social work practitioner, micro and macro practice alike. We begin by defining basic terms and concepts. We next examine how the concept of social networks is closely linked to the origins and mission of social work practice. The development of social network analysis and the entrance of social network assessment and intervention into the

profession of social work are described, followed by a presentation of program examples illustrating the range and types of applications of social networks. The chapter ends with a discussion of current issues and challenges for the future.

Central Terms and Definitions

The term *social network* refers to the ties that exist among a set of individuals (Wasserman & Faust, 1994). There are two broad sub-fields within the study of social networks (Scott, 2000). One is the study of whole networks, examining the pattern of relations within a defined group, such as all the clients in a treatment program. The second approach, the focus of this chapter, studies personal social networks, examining the relationships surrounding a specific focal person, such as a client in a treatment program. A personal network approach considers the individuals in the context of other people with whom they directly interact. Personal network variables can be conceptualized as either *compositional* or *structural*. Compositional network qualities include, among others: (a) size (the total number of people in the network); (b) relationships of network members (friends, family, professionals, etc.); (c) frequency of contact (how often people in the network interact with one another); (d) duration (how long people in the network have known one another); and (e) reciprocity (the amount of give and take between network members). Examples of structural network qualities include: (a) density (the percent of ties that exist out of all possible ties); (b) components (network members who are connected to one another directly or indirectly); (c) multiplexity (network relationships that serve more than one function); and (d) centrality measures (measures of network activity and information flow). Sometimes composition and structure can be combined, such as identifying who is the most structurally central person who provides support.

It is important to distinguish the structural links of the social network from the resources or "supports" exchanged within the network. *Social support* refers to the many different ways in which people assist one another. According to Gottlieb's (1983) empirically derived definition, "social support consists of verbal and/or nonverbal information or advice, tangible aid or action that is proffered by social intimates or inferred by their presence and has beneficial emotional or behavioral effects on the recipient" (pp. 28–29). Social support, then, consists of a number of different ways of helping, including offering and/or providing advice and guidance, companionship, emotional support and encouragement, and concrete assistance (Barrera & Ainley, 1983; House & Kahn, 1985; Wood, 1984). Social support can occur through natural or informal helping networks of family and friends or can be mobilized through formal professional intervention.

A *social support network* refers to that set of relationships that nurtures and reinforces coping with day-to-day life tasks (Whittaker & Garbarino, 1983). It is possible to have a social network that is not a social support network, in that some social networks or members of the network may not provide positive forms of support. Likewise, larger social networks do not always provide more or better types of social support. Supportive and nonsupportive ties frequently coexist within networks (Wellman, 1981). In addition to the actual support received, the perception that others would be available to help is a factor in the experience of supportive relationships (see Hobfall, 2009, for a recent discussion of received versus perceived support). Due to such complexities, social support provided through personal social networks is viewed as a multidimensional construct consisting of social network resources, types of supportive exchanges, perceptions of support availability, attitudes toward help seeking, and skills in accessing and maintaining supportive relationships (Heller & Swindle, 1983; Marsella & Snyder, 1981). Pierce, Sarason, and Sarason (1996) posit three overlapping and mutually influencing components of social support: support schemata, supportive relationships, and supportive transactions. Sarason and Sarason (2009) point out the bidirectional nature of social support in that support occurs in the context of a relationship between the receiver and the provider of support.

Historical Significance to Social Work

Almost by definition, social work has recognized the importance of social networks in clients' lives. Social work's traditional focus on the person-in-environment has repeatedly focused the profession on natural helping networks. The early social workers took naturally occurring social resources into consideration as they worked with clients (Becker, 1963). In essence, the friendly visiting of the Charitable Organization Society workers *was* a social network intervention, in that the social network of the client was expanded with the addition of a formal helping resource. The friendly visitor arranged services through personal and professional social network contacts. For example, friendly visitors asked their friends and acquaintances about possible job openings for their clients and arranged summer holidays for children in the homes of their personal friends. Friendly visitors were to

(a) establish "friendly relations," (b) offer practical advice and training, and (c) arrange or procure concrete services (Richmond, 1918). Friendly visiting could never fully overcome the social class and ethnic differences between the visitor and the family, and while neighborly, friendly visiting never approached the mutuality typically associated with informal helping.

One of the basic principles of friendly visiting was to seek the most natural and least official sources of relief from kin, friends, and neighbors (Richmond, 1918). Mobilizing natural sources of help was considered an important aspect of coordinated, organized welfare services. The overall purpose of charity work was to develop resources internal to the family, rendering material help from the outside unnecessary. Each potential resource was to be contacted regarding "some definite promise as to what they themselves will do" (Richmond, 1918, p. 188), following the lines of the client's social network. Indiscriminate charity was avoided since it was thought to destroy such natural social network resources.

Richmond was aware that prior to "social work," people had natural systems of helping. She stated in *What is Social Casework?* (1922, p. 5):

Almost as soon as human beings discovered that their relations to one another had ceased to be primitive and simple, they must have found among their fellows a few who had a special gift for smoothing out tangles in such relations; they must have sought, however informally, the aid of these 'straighteners'.

Richmond (1917) outlined a number of practical strategies to enlist cooperation and support, and principles to guide the choice and use of social network resources. In this way the linking and mobilizing of resources differed from the personal influence of the friendly visitor. Work with the social network was beginning to be viewed as an adjunct to treatment. The worker's task was to identify, mobilize, and organize resources. Relatives, for example, were asked to supply family history and to support and cooperate with treatment plans (see Tracy, 1988).

Origins of Social Network Analysis

The development of social network theory and analysis drew from a variety of disciplines, including sociology, anthropology, and psychology. Scott (2000) describes the study of social networks as stemming from three main traditions. One tradition from which contemporary social networks theory draws is the sociometric analysts who, informed by Gestalt theory, sought to depict group dynamics, structure, and the flow of information among group members. For example, Moreno (1934) examined friendship patterns and how psychological well-being was related to what he termed social configurations. His innovative use of the sociogram was a way to depict the properties of these social configurations; by using points to represent people and lines to represent social relationships, the sociogram could visually display how one person influences another, who had multiple connections and who was isolated within a group.

Another theoretical foundation of social network theory derives from the work of anthropologists and sociologists in the 1930s and 1940s who investigated informal relations and structures within larger systems. For example, Hawthorne's classic study of the Western Electric Company used anthropological fieldwork techniques to construct sociograms to depict the informal organization as opposed to the formal organization of the company (Scott, 2000). Anthropologists began to apply field work methods to study urban communities, subgroups, and cliques.

The third tradition undergirding social network analysis stems from the work of British anthropologists. Barnes's (1954) analysis of a Norwegian fishing village and Bott's (1959) study of London families are generally thought to be the precursors to social network analysis. Mitchell's (1969) set of sociological concepts sought to explain the structural properties of ego or person centered networks; concepts such as reciprocity, density, and reachability, among others, were posited to describe relationships within social networks. Granovetter's work (1973) on the strength of weak ties extended these concepts in his research on how people acquire information about jobs through personal social networks.

Theoretical and Conceptual Background/Frameworks

A number of different theoretical frameworks inform the study and application of social networks within social work practice. Stress and coping theory posits that the ability to cope with stress is a function of personal and social resources (Lazarus & Folkman, 1984). Social support has been viewed as a coping resource or social "fund" (Thoits, 1995, p. 64) from which to draw upon in responding to stressful life events. Social network resources may enable people to change the situation, change the meaning attributed to the situation, and/or change their emotional reaction to the situation—all aspects of coping responses. Two models have been proposed to explain the process through which being embedded in a social network has a beneficial effect on well-being: the main or direct effects and the buffering hypothesis. The direct effects model argues that social support has a beneficial effect irrespective of stress level. Large social networks may provide many direct beneficial effects (e.g., Berkman & Syme, 1979). Belonging to a social network may also help people avoid situations that would otherwise result in physical or psychological distress. The buffering model states that people who are facing life stress, but who have strong social support, will be protected from symptoms associated with stress. In this model social networks are important in the stress appraisal process, emotional reactions, and coping behaviors (Cassel, 1974; Cobb, 1976). For example, as applied to the field of substance abuse, research by Longabaugh, Wirtz, Zweben, and Stout (1998) supports both direct positive effects of networks supportive of abstinence as well as buffering effects of abstinent supporters within substance-using networks.

Additional alternative models have been proposed, including the stress deterioration model, in which stressful life events are thought to impair or perhaps overburden social support resources, in turn resulting in more stress (Dean & Ensel, 1982). For example, divorce may result in substantial changes in social network composition, which may in turn impact the availability of social support (Wilcox, 1981). Particular life events, such as cancer, may lead to stigma, with resulting loss of social network contact and social support. Another alternative model is the stress prevention model (Gore, 1981; Gottlieb, 1983), in which the availability of social networks is thought to prevent the occurrence of stressful life events in the first place, or to prevent the labeling of events as stressful when they do occur.

Social network analysis at this point in time consists of an approach and set of methods more than a full body of social theory per se (Scott, 2000). There continue to be discipline-specific diverse approaches to social network analysis, the distinction between whole and ego-centered networks being the most obvious division. In addition to the stress and coping theoretical approach outlined above and the ecological perspective detailed below, which have received the most attention within social work, social networks have been viewed within the context of exchange theory (Wellman, 1981), rational choice theory (Lin, 1982), and attachment theory (Mikulincer & Shaver, 2009). More recently, the importance of social networks as a form of social capital has been explored (Bottrell, 2009).

Social Networks' Entry into Social Work

Ecological Perspective

Social work's interest in social networks is firmly rooted in the ecological perspective (Bronfenbrenner, 1979), which focuses on the interface between people and their environments. This approach recognizes that social ecologies—the people, places, times, and contexts in which social interaction occurs—offer both the cause of and solution to problems (Barth, 1986). The implications of the ecological approach have been conceptualized as (1) building more supportive nurturing environments through various forms of environmental helping and (2) improving client's competencies through the teaching of specific life skills (Whittaker, Schinke, & Gilchrist, 1986). Social network assessment and interventions share with the ecological perspective an understanding of the potential for growth and stress within the client's social network, the functions of network resources, and obstacles to using network resources as essential parts of an environmental assessment (Gitterman & Germain, 1981).

Drawing from the ecological perspective and following the social network tradition of visual displays of social relationships, Hartman's ecomap (Hartman, 1994; see also Mattaini, 1993) is perhaps the most widely used means to visually document the social context of a client's life. First, names of people, groups, and organizations are identified and encircled. The distance between circles indicates closeness of relationships, while lines drawn between the circles represent the quality of the relationship (e.g., stressful, tenuous, positive). The ecomap has been adapted to a variety of social service settings and helps the worker and client jointly determine available resources, gaps in resources, and goals for intervention.

Linking Formal and Informal Helping

The ecological perspective also drew attention to the fundamental importance of neighborhood and extended family resources. Consequently, the linking of formal and informal helping networks was seen as an important function of social work practice and supported the entrance of social networks into social work. The incorporation of social networks into practice and policy was prominent from the 1980s on. This was evident in Great Britain. The Barclay Report (see Olsen, 1983, for a discussion of social support networks from a British perspective) on the roles and tasks of social workers stressed utilizing and developing close working relationships with informal caregivers and community networks. The term "community social work," as defined in the report, referred to enhancing informal support networks as well as coordinating the interface between formal and informal care. In the United States, there was interest in informal helping resources across a variety of social work practice fields. The 1981 White House Conference on Families took up the issue of informal support networks, and how support systems could be strengthened by government policies (Wingspread Report, 1979). Enhancement of social support networks—strengthening existing ties, enhancing family ties, and building new ties—became an important thrust of case management services for persons with severe mental illness (NIMH, 1987). Child welfare policies following the passage of PL 96-272, The Adoption Assistance and Child Welfare Act of 1980, required that supportive services be provided to families as a means to prevent family disruption, to reunite families where separation had been

necessary, and to place children in alternative permanent settings.

During this period, there were several key social work educators and researchers who were largely responsible for introducing and articulating the role of informal community helpers in relation to more formal service delivery systems. Maguire (1983) published a concise guide *Understanding Social Networks,* which presented networking approaches as a means to "maximize the use of natural helping networks and use professionals more efficiently" (p. 7). Whittaker and Garbino (1983) published *Social Support Networks: Informal Helping in the Human Services,* a compilation of informal helping strategies across a wide range of client populations and service delivery systems; the preface to this volume states that the book addresses a "quiet revolution" taking place in human services and identified that the purpose of the volume was to suggest ways in which "formal and informal caregivers can join together in new and creative alliances to offer a more effective and compassionate response to people in need of help" (p. xi). Their volume was the first work to compile the growing research evidence of the role of social networks across many fields of practice within social work, and to draw upon the ecological perspective to present social workers with compelling ways to complement rather than compete with informal social support networks.

In a similar vein, Naparstek, Biegel, and Spiro (1982) described a community empowerment model in *Neighborhood Networks for Humane Mental Health Care* that utilized strengths of city neighborhoods to mobilize support systems and create linkages between professional and informal service systems; in particular, collaborative linkages with friends, neighbors, natural helpers, and clergy were encouraged in order to empower and build upon community strengths. In *Community Support Systems and Mental Health: Practice, Policy and Research,* Biegel and Naparstek (1982) examined the roles of self-help groups, neighborhood networks, and informal helpers in a variety of contexts as a supplement to professional services; in addition, the ways in which professional services might weaken these natural support systems was also examined. Biegel, Shore, and Gordon (1984), in *Building*

Support Networks for the Elderly, presented a practitioner-friendly introduction to social networks and social network interventions based upon their extensive experience training and preparing resource materials for human service workers; strategies for neighborhood helping, volunteer linking, mutual aid, and community empowerment were outlined. Whittaker (1986) presented a well-developed conceptual framework for integrating formal and informal social care and introduced the social work role of "network/system consultant," who works "through a preexisting or contrived support systems to aid an individual client or group of clients" (p. 46). Whittaker also examined management and practice implications for formal and informal helping in child welfare services as part of a "paradigm shift" in human services. Taking the then-current social work landscape into consideration, Meyer (1985, p. 291) concluded:

The research evidence is in: There is a strong relationship between individual physical-social-psychological health and social supports and between social isolation and the breakdown in these areas or functioning. In view of the importance of natural support networks, social workers can do no less than explore the linkages between them and professional intervention.

Contemporary Applications of Social Networks within Social Work

A social network approach can be useful to both micro- and macro-oriented social workers alike, providing us with a useful lens through which to view the social environment of our clients and helpful aids in social work assessment and intervention planning. Social workers have made use of social network mapping techniques as an adjunct to social work assessment and intervention (Antonucci, 1986). Hill (2002) offers a useful description of both social network features and methods for assessing social networks. Important features to assess within social networks include the network structure or shape, interactions between network members, social support functions provided by network members, network composition, and diversity (Hill, 2002). Hill (2002) also outlines the following six types of diagrams commonly used to assess personal social networks:

1. *Ecomap*: identifies important individuals and visually represents their connections to a central person with lines
2. *Concentric circles*: visually represents the emotional or geographic distance between individuals and a central person
3. *Genogram*: visual tree that represents relationships between family members
4. *Life-space representations*: uses the important locations in the individual's life to represent the individuals and activities central to that person
5. *Life-course changes*: uses visual representations of households and houses in which the individual has lived
6. *Matrices*: uses tables to list the individuals and their importance to a central person.

For graphic illustrations of diagrams, see Mattaini, 1993.

A number of tools are currently available for measuring social support and social networks (see Streeter & Franklin, 1992). Tracy and Whittaker (1990) developed a social network map, drawing on the work of Fraser and Hawkins (1984) and Lovell and Hawkins (1988), which enabled the collection of information on the size and composition of the social network and the nature of relationships within the network. Several pilot studies were conducted across a variety of practice settings in which use of the social network map enabled practitioners to identify and assess strains and resources within the social environment, to understand culturally specific patterns of help giving, and to identify others who could participate in network interventions (Whittaker, Tracy, Overstreet, Mooradian, & Kapp, 1994).

Current Policy

The importance of both formal and informal social support and personal social networks has been acknowledged in recent public policy as well as practice. The President's New Freedom Commission report (2003) highlights multiple areas where improving social network support and linkages could improve the provision of mental health services to adults and children. The report recommends the involvement of the consumer's family members and social supports in care coordination and planning. It also calls for the strengthening of linkages between service systems such as medical service systems, mental health service systems, and schools. The commission also advocated the provision of mental health services within the community and schools, where children spend the majority of their time. Internationally, in the area of child civil rights, the United Nations Convention on the Rights of the Child (1990) also acknowledges the importance of informal social and kinship networks in child development. The convention recommends that decisions regarding the adoption and foster care of children prioritize placements that allow the child to maintain established familial, community, and cultural networks over those that necessitate the dissolution of those networks. This priority is further evidenced in child welfare practices that serve to strengthen the social networks of families at risk (Vonk & Yoo, 2009).

Types of Network-Related Interventions

While interventions with social networks are not as fully developed as person-oriented interventions, Kemp, Whittaker, and Tracy (1997) describe four general approaches to social network interventions. Each of these approaches share a number of social work roles and values. Linking is an essential practice skill underlying social network interventions; this is similar to the resource and referrals skills used by many social workers to locate needed resources, establish a linkage between the client and the resource, and ensure that the linkage will be maintained as planned. Linkages capitalize on the strengths between clients and their social networks, so a basic value undergirding social network interventions is the strengths perspective. Finally, collaborative worker–client relationships are typically a hallmark of social network interventions, with the client fully involved in decision making and action steps. With these shared foundations, descriptions of approaches to social network intervention follow.

Natural Helping Networks. People often turn to "natural helpers" for advice and support, as these are people who have been successful in coping with life challenges and transitions (Pancoast,

Parker, & Froland, 1983). Natural helper interventions focus on developing consultative relationships with key helpers, or gatekeepers, in a community in order to extend the agency's services, to reach out to hard-to-reach clients, and to offer prevention and early intervention services. The classic form of this intervention is described by Collins and Pancoast (1976). Some examples of natural helper interventions include (1) help from hairdressers, barbers, apartment managers, and postal workers to elderly people living in the community (Hooyman & Lustbader, 1986) and (2) natural mentoring relationships for youth transitioning out of foster care (Munson & McMillan, 2008).

Network Facilitation. Network facilitation mobilizes the social network to provide support for a targeted individual or family, either to supplement an existing network or to add new network members through recruitment and matching of volunteer helpers. Network meetings are a basic component of intervention (Morin & Seidman, 1986); during such meetings all participants discuss the client's situation and develop a plan of coordinated action. In this way, some network members may be reconnected in meaningful ways, while other network members may learn to take on new helping roles. In this form of intervention, it is important for personal social network members to be connected to one another, both to communicate and support one another and to avoid duplication of effort. Some examples of network facilitation include:

1. Family group decision making, in which network members are identified and network meetings are convened to plan for meeting child and family safety. This intervention has been used in child protection (Crampton, 2007) and in juvenile justice and domestic violence services (Pennell & Anderson, 2005).
2. Volunteer linking programs, in which new network members and community connections are added (Dunn, 1995; German & Gittermain, 1996). For example, Compeer (Skirboll & Pavelsky, 1984) matches community volunteers with persons with mental illness for support and modeling of coping skills. Other variants match consumers with one another, as in peer support programs.

Mutual Aid/Self-Help Groups. Self-help groups mobilize relationships among people who share common tasks or problems (Gitterman & Shulman 1986; Silverman, 1980). This approach provides an ongoing source of support as well as advocacy and empowerment (Mehr, 1988). Self-help groups allow people to learn from one another and to realize that they are not alone; such groups allow people to see the political aspects of personal problems. While there are hundreds of self-help organizations nationwide, some examples include:

1. People First is a self-advocacy rights organization for people with mental retardation (Shapiro, 1993).
2. Cox (1991) describes a self-help advocacy group for women receiving public assistance.
3. Lewis and Ford (1991) and Weil (1996) describe the use of social support networks to address problems in impoverished communities.

Social Network Skills Training. Based on life and social skills training models and cognitive behavioral treatment, social network skills training teaches people how to initiate and sustain positive social relationships (Richey, 1994). Some examples include:

1. friendship group for families referred from child protective services that taught key interpersonal skills for supportive relationships through demonstration and guided practice (Lovell & Richey, 1991).
2. Pinto (2006) describes the importance of engaging natural supports such as family members by improving their interpersonal skills, and mobilizing community members as part of support networks in order for clients with mental illness to maintain their functioning within the community.

Examples of Social Network Assessment and Intervention

Integrated Dual Disorders Treatment (IDDT)

An evidence-based treatment model for intervention with individuals with co-occurring disorders of substance abuse and mental illness, IDDT utilizes interventions focused on enhancing social supports within families and communities. Viewing all areas of an individual's life as important to maintaining recovery, IDDT interventions engage consumers' family members in psychoeducation and skills building. In this way social workers enhance the capacity of the family to engage with and support the consumer. Furthermore, IDDT encourages intervention within the consumer's community as workers establish linkages between individual consumers and community self-help groups or community activities. In these ways, the natural personal social networks of consumers are enhanced by increasing both density and functions within the consumer's network (Ohio SAMI CCOE, 2008).

Multisystemic Therapy (MST)

MST is a home-based treatment model designed to assist adolescents and their families within their natural settings, also incorporates interventions at the level of the family's social network. MST social workers intervene in part by identifying the resources and supports already present in the adolescent's life, including extended family members, neighbors, school personnel, church members, and community members (Borduin et al., 1995). Once network resources are identified, MST workers help adolescents and families strengthen their connections to these individuals or create linkages between these families and potential network members. The goal in this model is to strengthen linkages between parents and social network members who will reinforce parenting efforts and goals.

Future Directions

Overcoming Barriers to Social Network Interventions

In 1986, Whittaker identified a number of barriers to policy and practice implementation in the area of social networks; unfortunately many of these barriers remain to this day.

> *Institutional barriers*: organizational and administrative complexities of introducing informal helpers into formal service plans

(e.g., agency liability, client's rights to privacy, and administrative accountability)

Economic: a diminishing pool of potential informal caregivers and difficulty funding support services for caregivers

Professional: resistance and unwillingness to share roles, power, and authority with informal helpers

Conceptual: multiple and imprecise definitions of social networks and social support, making it difficult to communicate

In an exploratory study of barriers to social network interventions, Biegel, Tracy, and Song (1995) identified paperwork, high caseload size, community stigma, and lack of community resources as the barriers most frequently reported by mental health case managers. A training strategy (e.g., training practitioners in social network intervention techniques) may not be sufficient to overcome such barriers; administrative system changes as well as community organization strategies to develop new programs and resources may be needed to promote an environment more conducive to social network interventions (Tracy & Biegel, 1994).

A challenge for the future is that there are limitations inherent in social network strategies, and a need to weigh costs and benefits of reliance on social networks. Not everyone has a caring social network or is able to utilize social resources. In fact, those most in need of informal helping may lack social resources, may lack networks with the skills and capabilities to help, or may live in communities with inadequate or strained helping resources (Garbarino & Sherman, 1980). The same stressors or conditions that create the need for increased social support may also negatively impact the time and resources of those available to provide informal care.

There is also stress associated with the provision of informal care. The financial and personal costs of caregiving are already high, and it is important that policies promoting the use of informal care from social networks not burden informal helpers even further. A critique of family caregiving strategies also points out that relying on informal helpers has led to increased stress and strain primarily on women, who provide a disproportionate amount of informal care

and already assume multiple caregiving roles, and the lack of supportive services for care providers, such as financial reimbursements and respite care (Graycar, 1983).

Research Implications for Social Work

Recent research on social networks has examined the role of social networks for diverse groups dealing with a myriad of health, mental health, and life stage issues. White and Cant (2003) used social network analysis to explore the role of instrumental and emotional social support in the lives of HIV-positive gay men. Lewandowski and Hill (2009) used the Scale of Perceived Social Support (MacDonald, 1998) to examine the relationship between perceived social support and drug treatment completion for women in a residential drug treatment program. The role of perceived social network support in the well-being of same-sex and opposite-sex couples was examined by Blair and Holmberg (2008). Findings indicated the importance of social support as predictive of relationship well-being for both same-sex and opposite-sex couples.

Most researchers and practitioners in the area of social support agree that much more research is needed in experimental manipulations of social networks in order to better understand the mechanism or process by which social support "works" and at what point in the stage of treatment network interventions might be more useful. In a review of social network interventions, Ertel, Glymour, and Berkman (2009) point out the following limitations of social network intervention research: a focus on method of delivery versus timing of delivery, patient samples versus community samples, and failure to measure changes in social networks over time. In spite of many research studies on social support, Sarason and Sarason (2009) concluded that a clear consensus has not been reached on "the definition of social support, how to assess it, select and implement effective research strategies, and interpret the empirical evidence" (p. 114). In addition to research that examines factors moderating the effectiveness of social network interventions, research is needed to examine the requisite organizational structure for social network service delivery, the role of community resources, and the larger impacts of social networks on organizations and communities.

Concluding Thoughts

Social network approaches are consistent with social work values and practice approaches and are increasingly recognized and incorporated as active components of current treatment packages and practice models. Social network approaches have been applied broadly across a variety of client populations and service delivery systems and have a longstanding tradition within social work. A social network approach allows practitioners to assess and intervene in multiple levels of the client's environment and thus may play a role in supporting and maintaining change efforts. As such, these approaches help bridge the unhelpful division between micro and macro practice within social work and offer strategies to fulfill the social work profession's primary mission: to intervene at multiple system levels in order to improve the quality of life for all persons.

Acknowledgment

The authors thank MSASS doctoral student Min-Kyoung Jun for her assistance in the preparation of the reference list for this chapter.

References

Antonucci, T. C. (1986). Hierarchical mapping technique. *Generations: Journal of the American Society on Aging*, 10, 10.

Barnes, J. A. (1954). Class and communities in a Norwegian island parish. *Human Relations*, 7(1), 39–58.

Barrera, M., & Ainlay, S. L. (1983). The structure of social support: A conceptual and empirical analysis. *Journal of Community Psychology*, 11, 133–144.

Barth, R. P. (1986). *Social and cognitive treatment of children and adolescents*. San Francisco: Jossey-Bass Publishers.

Becker, D. G. (1963). Early adventures in social casework: The charity agent, 1880–1910. *Social Casework*, 44(5), 255–261.

Berkman, L. F., & Syme, S. (1979). Social networks, host resistance, and mortality: a nine-year follow-up study of Alameda County residents. *American Journal of Epidemiology*, 109, 186.

Biegel, D. E., & Naparstek, A. J. (Eds.) (1982). *Community support systems and mental health: Practice, policy, and research*. New York: Springer Publishing Company.

Biegel, D. E., Shore, B. K., & Gordon, E. (1984). *Building support networks of the elderly: Theory and applications*. Newbury Park, CA: Sage.

Biegel, D. E., Tracy, E. M., & Song, L. (1995). Barriers to social network interventions with persons with severe and persistent mental illness: A survey of mental health case managers. *Community Mental Health Journal*, 31, 335–349.

Blair, K. L., & Holmberg, D. (2008). Perceived social network support and well-being in same-sex versus mixed-sex romantic relationships. *Journal of Social and Personal Relationships*, 25(5), 669–791.

Borduin, C. M., Mann, B. J., Cone, L. T., Henggeler, S. W., Fucci, B. R., Blaske, D. M., & Williams, R. A. (1995). Multisystemic treatment of serious juvenile offenders: Long-term prevention of criminality and violence. *Journal of Consulting and Clinical Psychology*, 63, 569–578.

Bott, E. (1959). *Family and social network*. London: Tavistock.

Bottrell, D. (2009). Dealing with disadvantage: Resilience and the social capital of young people's networks. *Youth & Society*, 40(4), 476–501.

Bronfenbrenner, U. (1979). *The ecology of human development*. Cambridge: Harvard University Press.

Cassel, J. (1974). Psychosocial processes and "stress": Theoretical formulation. *International Journal of Health Services*, 4, 471–482.

Cobb, S. (1976). Social support as a moderator of life stress. *Psychosomatic Medicine*, 38, 300–314.

Collins, A., & Pancoast, D. (1976). *Natural helping networks: a strategy for prevention*. Washington, DC: National Association of Social Workers.

Convention on the Rights of the Child (1990). Retrieved October 12, 2009 from www.unicef.org/cre/.

Cox, E. O. (1991). The critical role of social action in empowerment-oriented groups. *Social Work with Groups*, 14, 77–107.

Crampton, D. (2007). Research review: Family group decision making: A promising practice in need of more programme theory and research. *Child & Family Social Work*, 12(2), 202–209.

Dean, A., & Ensel, W. M. (1982). Modelling social support, life events, competence, and depression in the context of age and sex. *Journal of Community Psychology*, 10, 392–408.

Dunn, P. L. (1995). Volunteer management. In *Encyclopedia of social work* (19th ed., Vol. 3, pp. 2483–2490). Washington, DC: National Association of Social Workers.

Ertel, K. A., Glymour, M. M., & Berkman, L. F. (2009). Social networks and health: A life course perspective integrating observational and experimental evidence. *Journal of Social and Personal Relationships, 26,* 73–92.

Fraser, M., & Hawkins, J. D. (1984). Social network analysis and drug misuse. *Social Service Review,* March, 81–97.

Garbarino, J., & Sherman, D. (1980). High-risk neighborhoods and high risk families: The human ecology of child maltreatment. *Child Development, 51,* 188–198.

Germain, C. B., & Gitterman, A. (1996) *The life model of social work practice: Advances in theory and practice* (2nd ed.). New York: Columbia University Press.

Gitterman, A., & Germain, C. B. (1981). Education for practice: Teaching about the environment. *Journal of Education for Social Work, 17*(3), 44–51.

Gitterman, A., & Shulman, L. (Eds.) (1986). *Mutual aid groups and the life cycle.* Itasca, IL: Peacock.

Gore, S. (1981). Stress-buffering functions of social supports: An appraisal and clarification of research models. In B. S. Dohrenwend & B. P. Dohrenwend (Eds.), *Stressful life events and their contexts.* New York: Prodist.

Gottlieb, B. H. (1983). *Social support strategies.* Beverly Hills, CA: Sage.

Granovetter, M. S. (1973). The strength of weak ties. *American Journal of Sociology, 78,* 13–60.

Graycar, A. (1983). Informal, voluntary and statutory services: The complex relationship. *British Journal of Social Work, 13,* 379–393.

Hartman, A. (1994). Diagrammatic assessment of family relationships. In B. R. Compton & B. Galaway (Eds.), *Social work processes* (pp. 154–165). Pacific Grove, CA: Brooks/Cole.

Heller, K., & Swindle, R.W. (1983). Social networks, perceived social support and coping with stress. In R. D. Felner, L.A. Jason, J. Moritsugu, & S. S. Farber (Eds.), *Preventive psychology: Theory, research and practice* (pp. 87–103). New York: Pergamon.

Hill, M. (2002). Network assessments and diagrams: A flexible friend for social work practice and education. *Journal of Social Work, 2*(2), 233–254.

Hobfoll, S. E. (2009). Social support: The movie. *Journal of Social and Personal Relationships, 26,* 93–101.

Hooyman, N. R., & Lustbader, W. (1986). *Taking care: Supporting older people and their families.* New York: Free Press.

House, J. S., & Kahn, R. L. (1985). Measures and concepts of social support. In S. Cohen & S.L. Syme (Eds.), *Social support and health* (pp. 83–108). Orlando, FL: Academic Press.

Ohio Substance Abuse and Mental Illness Coordinating Center of Excellence. (2008). *Integrated dual disorder treatment: An overview of the evidence-based practice.* www.ohiosamiccoe.case.edu, Retrieved October 12, 2009.

Kemp, S., Whittaker, J. K., & Tracy, E. (1997). *Person-environment practice: The social ecology of interpersonal helping.* New York: Aldine de Gruyter.

Lazarus, R. S., & Folkman, S. (1984). *Stress, appraisal and coping.* New York: Springer Publishing Co.

Lewandowski, C. A., & Hill, T.J. (2009). The impact of emotional and material social support on women's drug treatment completion. *Health and Social Work, 34*(3), 213–221.

Lewis, E. A., & Ford, B. (1991). The network utilization project: Incorporating traditional strengths of African-American families into group work practice. *Social Work with Groups, 13,* 7–22.

Lin, N. (1982). Social resources and instrumental action. In P. Marsden & N. Lin (Eds.), *Social structure and network analysis.* Beverly Hills, CA: Sage Publications.

Longabaugh, R., Wirtz, P., Zweben, A., & Stout, R. (1998). Network support for drinking, Alcoholics Anonymous and long-term matching effects. *Addiction, 93,* 1313.

Lovell, M. L., & Hawkins, J. D. (1988). An evaluation of a group intervention to increase the personal social networks of abusive mothers. *Children and Youth Service Review, 10,* 175–188.

Lovell, M. L., & Richey, C.A. (1991). Implementing agency-based social support skill training. *Families in Society, 72,* 563–571.

MacDonald, G. (1998). Development of a social support scale: An evaluation of psychometric properties. *Research on Social Work Practice, 8,* 564–576.

Maguire, L. (1983). *Understanding social networks.* Beverly Hills, CA: Sage Publications.

Marsella, A. J., & Snyder, K. K. (1981). Stress, social supports, and schizophrenia: Toward an international model. *Schizophrenia Bulletin, 7,* 152–163.

Mattaini, M. A. (1993). *More than a thousand words: Graphics for clinical practice.* Washington, DC: National Association of Social Workers.

Mehr, J. (1988). Human services: Concepts and intervention strategies (4th ed.). Boston: Allyn and Bacon.

Meyer, C. (1985). Social supports and social workers: collaborators or conflict. *Social Work, 26,* 5–7.

Mikulincer, M., & Shaver, P. R. (2009). An attachment and behavioral systems perspective on social support. *Journal of Social and Personal Relationships, 26,* 7–19.

Mitchell, J. C. (1969). The concept and use of social networks. In J. C. Mitchell (Ed.), *Social networks in urban situations.* Manchester: Manchester University Press.

Moreno, J. (1934). *Who shall survive?* New York: Beacon Press.

Morin, R. C., & Seidman, E. (1986). A social network approach and the revolving door patient. *Schizophrenia Bulletin, 12,* 262–273.

Munson, M. R., & McMillan, J. C. (2008). Nonkin natural mentors in the lives of older youths in foster care. *Journal of Behavioral Health Services, 35*(4), 454–468.

Naparstek, A. J., Beigel, D. E., & Spiro, H. R. (1982). *Neighborhood networks for human mental health care.* New York: Plenum.

National Institute of Mental Health. (1987). *Toward a model plan for a comprehensive community-based mental health system.* Rockville, MD: U.S. Department of Health and Human Services, Public Health Service, Alcohol, Drug, and Mental Health Administration.

Olsen, M. R. (1983). Social support networks from a British perspective. In J. K.Whittaker & J. Garbarino (Eds.), *Social support networks: Informal helping in the human services* (pp. xv–xx). New York: Aldine Publishing Company.

Pancoast, D. L., Parker, P., & Froland, C. (1983). *Rediscovering self-help: Its role in social care.* Beverly Hills, CA: Sage.

Pennell, J., & Anderson, G. (Eds.) (2005). *Widening the circle: The practice and evaluation of family group conferencing with children, youths and their families.* Washington, DC: NASW Press.

Pierce, G. R., Sarason, B. R., & Sarason, I. G. (Eds.) (1996). *Handbook of social support and the family.* New York: Plenum.

Pinto, R. M. (2006). Using social network interventions to improve mentally ill clients' well-being. *Clinical Social Work Journal, 34,* 1, 83–100.

President's New Freedom Commission Report. (2003) Retrieved October 12, 2009 from www.mental healthcommission.gov.

Richey, C. A. (1994). Social support skill training. In D. K. Granvold (Ed.), *Cognitive and behavior treatment: Methods and applications* (pp. 299–338). Belmont, CA: Brooks/Cole.

Richmond, M. E. (1917). *Social diagnosis.* New York: Russell Sage Foundation.

Richmond, M. (1918). *What is social casework?* New York: Russell Sage Foundation.

Richmond, M. E. (1922). *What is social casework?* New York: Russell Sage Foundation.

Sarason, I. G., & Sarason, B. R. (2009). Social support: Mapping the construct. *Journal of Social & Personal Relationships, 26,* 113–120.

Scott, J. (2000). *Social network analysis: a handbook* (2nd ed.) London: Sage Publications.

Shapiro, J. P. (1993). No pity: People with disabilities forging a new civil right movement. *New York Times.*

Silverman, P. R. (1980). *Mutual help groups.* London: Sage Publications.

Skirboll, B. W., & Pavelsky, P. K. (1984). The Compeer program volunteers as friends of the mentally ill. *Hospital and Community Psychiatry, 35,* 938–939.

Streeter, C. L., & Franklin, C. (1992). Defining and measuring social support: Guidelines for social work practitioners. *Research on Social Work Practice, 2,* 81–98.

Thoits, P. A. (1995). Stress, coping, and social support processes: where are we? What next? *Journal of Health & Social Behavior, Spec No. 53.*

Tracy, E.M . (1988). Social support resources of at risk families: Implementation of social support assessments in an intensive family preservation program. (Doctoral dissertation, University of Washington, 1988). *Dissertation Abstracts International, 49,* 09.

Tracy, E., & Biegel, D. E.. (1994). Preparing social workers for social network interventions in mental health practice. *Journal of Teaching in Social Work, 10,* 19–41.

Tracy, E. M., & Whittaker, J. K. (1990). The social network map: Assessing social support in clinical practice. *Families in Society: The Journal of Contemporary Human Services,* 461–470.

Tracy, E., & Whittaker, J. K. (1991). Social network assessment and goal setting in intensive family preservation services practice. In E. M. Tracy, J. Kinney, D. Haapala, & P. Pecora (Eds.), *Intensive family preservation services: An instructional sourcebook.* Cleveland: Mandel School of Applied Social Sciences.

Vonk, M. E., & Yoo, S. Y. (2009). The family in the community. In A. C. Kilpatrick & T. P. Holland (Eds.), *Working with families* (5th ed.). Boston: Pearson Publishers.

Wasserman, S., & Faust, K. (1994). *Social network analysis methods and applications.* New York: Cambridge University Press.

Weil, M. (1996). Community building: Building community practice. *Social Work, 41,* 481–501.

Wellman, B. (1981). Applying network analysis to the study of support In. B. H. Gottlieb (Ed.), *Social networks and social support* (pp. 171–200). Beverly Hills, CA: Sage.

White, L., & Cant, B. (2003). Social networks, social support, health and HIV-positive gay men. *Health and Social Care in the Community, 11*(4), 329–334.

Whittaker, J. K. (1986). Integrating formal and informal social care: A conceptual framework. *British Journal of Social Work*, 16, Supplement, 39–62.

Whittaker, J. K., & Garbarino, J. (1983). *Social support networks: Informal helping in the human services.* New York: Aldine Publishing Company.

Whittaker, J. K., Schinke, S. P., & Gilchrist, L. D. (1986). The ecological paradigm in child, youth, and family services: Implications for policy and practice. *Social Service Review*, 60, 483–503.

Whittaker, J. K., Tracy, E. M., Overstreet, E., Mooradian, J., & Kapp, S. (1994). Intervention design for practice: English social support for high-risk youth and families. In J. Rothman & E. J. Thomas (Eds.), *Intervention research: Designing and developing human service interventions* (pp. 195–212). New York: Haworth.

Wilcox, B. L. (1981). Social support, life stress, and psychological adjustment: A test of the buffering hypothesis. *American Journal of Community Psychology*, 9, 371–386.

Wingspread Report (1979). *Strengthening families through informal support systems.* Racine, WI: The Johnson Foundation.

Wood, Y. R. (1984). Social support and social networks: Nature and measurement. In P. McReynolds & G. J. Chelvne (Eds.), *Advances in psychology assessment* (Vol. 6, pp. 312–353). San Francisco: Jossey-Bass.

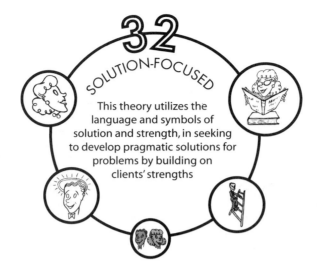

32

SOLUTION-FOCUSED

This theory utilizes the language and symbols of solution and strength, in seeking to develop pragmatic solutions for problems by building on clients' strengths

Solution-Focused Theory

Mo Yee Lee

Solution-focused brief therapy holds clients accountable for solutions rather than responsible for problems. Building on a strengths perspective and using a time-limited approach, solution-focused brief therapy postulates that positive and long-lasting change can occur in a relatively brief period of time by focusing on "solution talk" instead of "problem talk" (Berg, 1994; de Jong & Berg, 2007; de Shazer, 1994; Lee, Sebold, & Uken, 2003). Focusing on and emphasizing solutions, competencies, and strengths in clients must never be equated with a naïve belief in positive thinking. The choice of solution-focused approach in using the language and symbols of "solution and strengths" in treatment is influenced by a systemic perspective (Bateson, 1979), social constructivism (Berg & Luckmann, 1966; Neimeyer & Mahoney, 1993; Rosen & Kuehlwein, 1996), and the work of the

psychiatrist Milton Erickson (1985a, 1985b). Despite its relatively recent development, this practice model is now widely adopted in diverse social work practice settings, which is partly accounted for by the fact that the assumptions and practice orientation of solution-focused therapy are consistent with social work values as well as the strengths-based and empowerment-based practice in social work treatment.

History

The development of solution-focused brief therapy was inspired by the work of Insoo Kim Berg, Steve de Shazer, and their associates at the Brief Family Therapy Center in Milwaukee, which was established in 1978 and formally became the home of solution-focused therapy in 1982. Solution-focused therapy began as an atheoretical practice with a focus on finding "what works in therapy." Trying to not be influenced or limited by the assumptions or the presumptions of many theory-based practice approaches pertaining to clients, problems, and diagnoses, the pioneers of solution-focused brief therapy took a new approach in exploring the therapy process by only asking one simple question: "What works in treatment?" The original team regularly got together and observed therapy sessions using a one-way mirror. While focusing on observing the therapeutic dialogues and process, the team behind the mirror diligently attempted to observe, discover, and converse about what brought positive changes in clients and families. In other words, the early development of solution-focused therapy was antithetical to the modernist epistemology of understanding human behavior and change based on a presumed understanding of the observed phenomena. Instead of taking a positivistic, hierarchal, or expert stance, the understanding is accomplished by a bottom-up and grounded approach, which strives for a contextual, local understanding of what works in therapy.

Another major historical root of solution-focused therapy was related to the brief therapy tradition at the Mental Research Institute (MRI) of Palo Alto, CA. The late Steve de Shazer, co-founder of solution-focused therapy, was well trained in brief therapy at MRI. Brief therapy, as based on MRI, is based on a systems perspective (Bateson, 1979), social constructivism (e.g., Berg & Luckmann, 1966; Neimeyer & Mahoney, 1993; Rosen & Kuehlwein, 1996), and the work of the psychiatrist Milton Erickson, who was a genius in using what clients brought in to solve their presenting problems and a firm believer that individuals have the strengths and resources to solve their problems (Erickson, 1985a, 1985b). These theoretical assumptions clearly had a strong impact on the beliefs, assumptions, and practice of solution-focused therapy. The major difference between MRI and solution-focused therapy is that while the brief therapy approach developed at MRI focuses on disrupting the problem-maintaining pattern, solution-focused therapy emphasizes the solution-building process. The choice of a focus on the solution-building process, however, has to be understood in view of the power of language on human experience (de Shazer, 1994).

Assumptions and Basic Premises of Solution-Focused Therapy

Insoo Kim Berg and Steve de Shazer strongly emphasized that solution-focused therapy was not just a set of techniques but a way of thinking (de Shazer, 1985). Knowing the set of techniques is lifeless without a deep appreciation of the underlying assumptions and beliefs of solution-focused therapy toward clients and change, which is strongly influenced by a systems perspective, social constructivism, and the work of Erickson. These theoretical influences lead to the following practice assumptions of solution-focused therapy.

A Focus on Solutions, Strengths, and Health: Clients have the Answer

Solution-focused therapy focuses on what clients can do versus what clients cannot do. Instead of discussing or exploring clients' problems or deficiencies, the focus is on the successes of clients in dealing with their problems, and how to notice and use them more often (Berg & Kelly, 2000; de Shazer, 1985). Focusing on solutions is neither a consequence of "naïve" beliefs regarding strengths in clients nor simplistic "positive thinking." This approach is supported by repeated clinical observation about how clients discover solutions in a much quicker manner if the focus is on what they can do, what strengths they have, and what they have accomplished (Berg & Dolan, 2001; Berg & Reuss, 1998). The focus on solution talk to achieve change is also supported by a systems perspective (Bateson, 1979) and the role of language in creating reality (de Shazer, 1994).

A Systems Perspective. One basic assumption of a systems perspective is that change is constant. As such, every problem pattern includes some sort of exception to the rule (de Shazer, 1985). Such a view underlies our beliefs in the strengths and potentials of clients (De Jong & Berg, 2007). Despite the multiple deficiencies and/or problems clients may perceive that they have, there are always times when they handle their life situations in a more satisfying way or in a different manner. These exceptions provide the clues for solutions (de Shazer, 1985, 1988) and represent the client's "unnoticed" strengths and resources.

The task for the therapist is to assist clients in noticing, amplifying, sustaining, and reinforcing these exceptions regardless of how small and/or infrequent they may be (Berg & Kelly, 2000). Once clients are engaged in non-problem behavior, they are on the way to a solution-building process (Berg & Steiner, 2003).

A systems perspective also does not assume a one-to-one direct relationship between the problem and the solution to the problem. Another major assumption of a systems perspective is the interrelatedness of all parts of a system: everything is connected and change in one part of a system leads to change in other parts of the system (Bateson, 1972; Becvar & Becvar, 2003; Keeney & Thomas, 1986). The focus is on circular rather than linear relationships among different parts of a system. As such, solutions to a problem can happen in multiple pathways and do not have to be directly related to the presenting problem. In other words, insight into the problem's origin is not necessary to initiate a process of change in clients.

The choice of not drilling on the history and patterns of problems but focusing on what clients do well is further influenced by the power of language on shaping clients' experience of their reality.

Language and Reality. Solution-focused therapy strongly believes that it is ethical and more effective to focus on the therapeutic solution dialogues than on problem dialogues. There is a conscious effort to stay focused on solution talk and to deemphasize problem talk. Such a conscious effort grows out of a concern about the role of language in creating or sustaining reality. Such a belief is influenced by social constructivism, which suggests that reality is constructed socially through language (Gergen, 1999). Solution-focused therapy views language as the medium through which personal meaning and understanding are expressed and socially constructed in conversation (de Shazer, 1991, 1994). Furthermore, the meaning of things is always contingent on the contexts and the language within which it is described, categorized, and constructed by clients (Wittgenstein, 1958). Because the limits of reality that can be known and experienced by an individual are framed by the language available to him or her to describe

it, and these meanings are inherently unstable and shifting (Wittgenstein, 1958), a major question for the therapist to consider is how to use language in treatment to assist clients in describing and constructing a "beneficial" reality.

Because language is inherently powerful in creating and sustaining realities, the preferred language is the "conversation of change"— conversation that facilitates clients' efforts to create and sustain a solution reality (de Shazer, 1991; Walter & Peller, 1992). Solution-focused therapy prefers to use language that assists clients to "get to the surface of their problems" (de Shazer, 1991). "Get to the surface of problems" should never be equated with being superficial in the solution-finding process, however; this dialogue avoids going "deep" into the problem, but rather aims to construct meanings and solutions by describing goals, observable behaviors, and progressive lives in new, more beneficial ways that are attainable, in the present, and "on the surface" (De Shazer, 1994; Miller, 1997). Pathology/problem talk sustains a problem reality through self-fulfilling prophecies and distracts clients' and our attention from developing solutions (Miller, 1997). Solution-focused therapy similarly resists diagnoses or language that labels the client's problem as stable and unchanging (de Jong & Berg, 2007; de Shazer, 1994). Pathologizing clients' claims of their problems and drilling on the "deep" causes of problems may serve to further disempower clients. A pathological or deficit approach also focuses therapeutic effort on the problem rather than on what a life free from the problem would be like. The concern about language plays a decisive role in the shift from disrupting the problem-maintaining pattern (as espoused by MRI) to a focus on the solution-building process in solution-focused therapy.

Accountability for Solutions

A de-emphasis on problems/deficits and a focus on health and strengths do not mean that solution-focused therapy is easy. Solution-focused therapy holds the client responsible for solutions instead of problems. Not focusing on clients' responsibility for problems and/or deficits is a decisive way for the therapist and client to direct all therapeutic energy toward supporting client's responsibility for building solutions.

Change requires hard work (Berg & Kelly, 2000). Solutions neither come easily nor effortlessly. De Jong and Berg (2007) describe the process as a solution-building process that requires discipline and effort. Clients would not need treatment if they had a clear vision of the solution to their complaints and how to realize it. The "solution" as described by solution-focused therapy is established in the form of a goal that is to be determined and attained by the client (Lee, Uken, & Sebold, 2007). Berg and Miller (1992) described the characteristics of solutions/goals as personally meaningful and important to the clients; small enough to be achieved; concrete, specific, and behavioral so that indicators of success can be established and observed; positively stated so that the goal represents the presence rather than the absence of something; realistic and achievable within the context of the client's life; and being perceived as involving hard work.

Present and Future Orientation

While the problems belong to something in the past, solutions and goals exist in the present and future. Without minimizing the importance of the client's experience and perception of the history of the problem, solution-focused therapists view what is going on in the present and in the future as more important than what caused the problem at the very beginning. The focus of treatment is on assisting clients in their present and future adjustment. The minimization of "problem talk" or drilling on the history and patterns of problems is based on a systems perspective and also the power of language in creating and sustaining reality. Since a complex, interrelated, circular relationship of different parts of systems renders the effort to establish a causal understanding of problems essentially futile, it is almost impossible to precisely ascertain why a problem occurs in the first place. In addition, solution-focused brief therapy assumes that the meanings of a problem are only artifacts of the context (de Shazer, 1991). Since one can never know exactly why a problem exists, and problem perceptions are not objective "realities," insight into the problem's origin is not necessary to initiate a process of change in clients.

Influenced by social constructivism, solution-focused brief family therapy assumes that "the future exists in our anticipation of how it will be" (Cade & O'Hanlon, 1993, p. 109). Instead of delving into the past that will easily lend itself to discussing the history of the problem, and thereby problem talk, the therapist asks questions that will help clients to describe a future that does not contain the problem. The task of therapy, therefore, is to help clients to do something different by changing their interactive behaviors and/or their interpretations of behaviors and situations so that a solution can be achieved (de Shazer, 1991). Treatment helps clients to identify the first small step they can take to attain a future without the problem. Such descriptions help clients to be hopeful about their future as well as to help them discover for themselves specific directions for achieving positive changes in their lives.

Clients Define Their Goals: Solutions as Clients' Constructions

Influenced by social constructivism (Berg & Luckmann, 1966; Neimeyer & Mahoney, 1993; Rosen & Kuehlwein, 1996), solution-focused therapy assumes that solutions are not objective "realities" but are private, local, meaning-making activities by an individual (Miller, 1997). The importance of and the meaning attached to a goal or solution is individually constructed in a collaborative process. Clients' orientations to and definition of their goals clearly have significant implications for their actions and how they experience life. Because the client is the only "knower" of personal experiences and the sole "creator" of solutions, he or she defines the goals for their treatment and remains the main instigator of change (Berg, 1994). Externally imposed therapeutic goals are often inappropriate or irrelevant to the needs of clients. In addition, clients are willing to work harder if the goal of therapy is defined by them and is perceived as personally meaningful (Lee et al., 2007).

A Collaborative Therapeutic Relationship

A social constructivist view of solutions has significant implications for the client–therapist relationship. Because clients are the "knower" and the "expert" regarding their individual experiences, realities, and aspirations (Cantwell &

Holmes, 1994), their stories, explanations, and narrations become the only valid data to work with in the treatment process. Their stories are no longer data to be filtered through formal treatment theories to help the therapist arrive at a diagnosis and treatment plan. Similarly, the therapists are no longer experts who know the right answer to clients' problems. The therapist provides a therapeutic context for clients to construct and develop a personally meaningful goal. She enters into their perspective, adopts their frame of mind, listens to and understands their goals, and looks for strengths instead of weaknesses or labels. In place of a hierarchical therapist–client relationship is a more egalitarian and collaborative relationship (de Jong & Berg, 2007). The client takes the role of expert in determining and achieving goals that will lead to a more satisfying life. The therapist takes the role of expert in constructing a dialogue with the client that focuses on change and solution (Lee et al., 2003). A collaborative approach that respects the expertise and the knowledge of clients about themselves and their strengths helps to enhance their motivation to accomplish positive changes in their lives through treatment (Berg, 1994; Lee et al., 2003). Such an approach also aids the process of engagement in treatment because clients feel listened to and of value.

Utilization: A Non-instructional/ Educational Approach

Erickson believed that individuals have the strengths and resources to solve their problems and that the main therapeutic task is to uncover and activate these resources in clients (Haley, 1973). Influenced by the work of Erickson, solution-focused therapists utilize whatever resources clients bring with them to uncover the solution (de Shazer, 1985). The principle is one of utilizing clients' existing resources, skills, knowledge, beliefs, motivation, behavior, symptoms, social network, circumstances, and personal idiosyncrasies to lead them to their desired outcomes (O'Hanlon & Wilk, 1987). Such a practice orientation is related to our belief in the presence of exceptions in every problem situation (de Shazer, 1985). Instead of attempting to teach clients something new and foreign-based on our presumed notions of what is best for them, solution-focused therapists focus on when clients are already engaged in non-problem behaviors. Utilizing and building on these exceptions is a more efficient and effective way for clients to develop solutions that are relevant to and viable in their unique life circumstances. Clients are most invested in solutions that they discover or identify themselves, so the task for the therapist is to elicit, trigger, reinforce, expand, and consolidate exceptions the client generates. Therapists stay away from teaching clients skills or intervening in their lives in ways that may fit our "model" of what is good, but may not be appropriate or viable in their lives.

Tipping the First Domino: A Small Change

Consistent with the old saying "A journey of a thousand miles begins with one step," solution-focused approach suggests that the therapist must assist clients in describing the first, small step that they need to take if they were to accomplish their goal (Berg & Dolan, 2001). Having a vision of the ultimate solution without a clear idea of the first small step to achieve it may prove to be too distant and too vague. In other words, it is of foremost importance to assist clients in making the first small step that will show them that they are moving in the right direction—the right direction as defined by them. Small change is more possible and manageable, while consuming less energy. Clients are usually encouraged when they experience successes, even small ones.

A focus on small change is also consistent with a "minimalist" approach to therapy as suggested by brief therapists at MRI, including Bateson (1972) and Watzlawick, Weakland, and Fisch (1974). Based on a systems perspective, they are concerned about introducing any change that may disturb a person's equilibrium in unpredictable ways as a result of reiterating feedback. Repetitive attempts at the same unsuccessful solution are precisely what creates problems in the first place (Watzlawick et al., 1974). Following such a concern, solution-focused therapy believes that the best responses to client's problems involve minimal, but personally meaningful, intervention by the therapist into the client's life. Clients should determine what constitutes acceptable solutions. The most important thing is for us to help clients identify the first small behavioral step toward desirable change.

Solution-Focused Assessment

Solution-focused therapy views assessment as a significant part of treatment that contributes to positive outcomes in clients. The content and process of solution-focused assessment, however, is distinctively different from conventional social work assessment. Briefly stated, conventional models of assessment focused on the presenting problem that constitutes the primary content of assessment. In terms of the process, social work practitioners assume an expert position in conducting assessment with the purpose of determining a comprehensive treatment plan for each particular client. In addition, assessment is based on expert knowledge and is viewed as notably different and separate from the treatment process.

Solution-oriented assessment involves a different set of assumptions and, as a result, different content and process in conducting assessment (Lee et al., 2003). Solution-oriented social work assumes: (1) There are exceptions to every problem pattern; (2) Language is powerful in creating and sustaining reality, so the preferred language is the "language of solution and change"; (3) It is more helpful to focus on what clients can do and their strengths than what is lacking and the problems in the change process; (4) Problems and solutions are the client's construction, and therefore the client determines goals of treatment; (5) Everything is connected, and therefore it is not necessary for the solutions to be directly related to the problems, or vice versa (De Shazer, 1985). These assumptions and beliefs strongly influence how solution-oriented social workers approach the content and process of assessment; such a process is designed to draw out clients' strengths and unique personal features rather than classifying clients based on formal knowledge of problems and diagnoses.

A Focus on What Clients Can Do and Their Strengths

The content of solution-oriented assessment is on what clients can do and the strengths and resources in them or their environment as opposed to the history of problems, what is lacking, deficits in clients and/or their environment, or the diagnosis. Such a focus is supported by a systems perspective that postulates that everything is connected. Therefore, the solution needs not be directly related to the problem. As solution talk is more likely to sustain a solution reality, the preferred content of assessment is on developing an explicit, clear, specific description of a desirable future or a solution picture determined by the client.

Contextualized Understanding: Staying on the Surface

Instead of going deep in search of the history and complexities presented by the problem scenario, solution-oriented social workers prefer to stay on the surface in conducting assessment. The "surface" issues include the immediate presentation of the clients, their intention, and situational variables and resources that are squarely rooted in clients' current context. Such "surface" information is far more helpful than diagnoses or an elaborate history of the problem for clients and practitioners, as these are factors that exist in the presence and are readily available for clients and practitioners to utilize in the process of change (Lee et al., 2003). A contextualized understanding, therefore, brings forth the unique features of individual clients and their context as opposed to a homogeneous or generalized view of the client as someone with a certain diagnosis or problem. Staying on the surface also has the benefits of not limiting clients to their past histories, which are usually not changeable. In addition, because contextual and surface factors are more flexible and unstable than historical factors, clients and practitioners have more opportunities to make a shift in describing and constructing a "beneficial" reality.

The Client as Assessor

A distinctive characteristic of solution-oriented assessment is its focus on the client as the assessor (Lee et al., 2003). Influenced by an ecosystems perspective, conventional social work assessment involves a joint effort between the social work practitioner and the client (Karls, 2009). Still, the social work practitioner possesses expert knowledge and is an outsider who has the knowledge to conduct an objective assessment of client's problem. Solution-oriented assessment, as influenced by social constructivism, fundamentally shifts the position of the client to be the center of change. The client is the assessor who constantly self-evaluates what the problem is, what may be feasible solutions to the problem, what the desirable future is, what the goals of treatment are, what strengths and resources she has, what may be helpful in the process of change, how committed or motivated she is to make change a reality, how quickly she wants to proceed with the change, etc. (Lee et al., 2003). Solution-oriented social work practitioners are experts on the "conversation of change"; they keep the dialogues going in search of a description of alternative, beneficial, reality (de Shazer, 1994). Such a view fundamentally shifts the relationship between the client and the social work practitioner, which is no longer a hierarchal relationship but a collaborative one, with the client as the assessor and the social work practitioner as an expert of the conversation of change.

Assessment as an Open Process of Self-Evaluations and Choice Making

More importantly, there is no longer an objective problem or reality to be assessed that exists independently outside the client. In solution-oriented social work, assessment is essentially an ongoing and open process that the client and the social work practitioner actively engage in, describing an inherently unstable reality that is different from the problem reality. Assessment is no longer an alienated procedure operated on the client by an expert. It becomes an open process in which the client continuously makes evaluations and choices. Ownership, options, and choices become an integral part of the assessment (Lee et al., 2003).

Solution-Focused Interventions

The purpose of solution-focused interventions is to engage the client in a therapeutic conversation that is conducive to a solution-building process. In this conversation, the therapist invites the client to be the "expert" by listening and

exploring the meaning of the client's perception of his or her situation. The therapist uses solution-oriented questions, including exception questions, outcome questions, coping questions, scaling questions, and relationship questions, to assist clients in constructing a reality that does not contain the problem. These questioning techniques were developed by de Shazer, Berg, and their colleagues to fully utilize the resources and potential of clients (e.g., Berg & Kelly, 2000; de Shazer, 1985). Questions are perceived as better ways to create open space for clients to think about and self-evaluate their situation and solutions.

In terms of the therapy process, clients are first oriented to a solution-focus frame in which the focus of therapy is to assist clients in finding solutions to their problems with as few sessions as needed. Clients are immediately encouraged to give a clear and explicit statement of their presenting complaint. Without focusing on the history of the problems, the therapist uses solution-building questions to assist clients in identifying solutions for their problems:

- *Exception questions* inquire about times when the problem is absent, is less intense, or is dealt with in a manner that is acceptable to the client (de Shazer, 1985). The therapist presupposes that change is happening in the client's problem situation. Such an effort shakes the rigid frames constructed by many clients with respect to the pervasiveness and permanency of their complaints. Examples of exception questions include: When don't you have this problem? When is the problem less bad? What is different about these times?

- *Miracle question* provide a space for clients to separate themselves from their problem-saturated context and construct a future vision of life without the presenting complaint or with acceptable improvements in the problem. Miracle question fosters a sense of hopefulness and offers an opportunity for clients to develop a beneficial direction for improving their lives. The focus is on identifying small, observable, and concrete behaviors that are indicators of small changes, which make a difference in the client's situation (de Shazer, 1985). A widely used format of miracle question is: Suppose that after our meeting today, you go home, do your things, and go to bed. While you are sleeping, a miracle happens and the problem that brought you here is suddenly solved, like magic. The problem is gone. Because you were sleeping, you don't know that a miracle happened, but when you wake up tomorrow morning, you will be different. How will you know a miracle has happened? What will be the first small sign that tells you that the problem is resolved? (Berg & Miller, 1992). A variation of the miracle question is the dream question (Greene, Lee, Mentzer, Pinnell, & Niles, 1998) and the nightmare question (Reuss, 1997).

- *Coping questions* help clients to notice times when they are coping with their problems and what it is they are doing at those times when they are successfully coping. The purpose of asking coping questions is to indirectly reframe the meaning frames of clients who have assumed that they are entirely helpless and have no control over the problem situation (Berg, 1994; Berg & Steiner, 2003). Examples of coping questions include: How have you been able to keep going despite all the difficulties you've encountered? How are you able to get around despite not being able to walk?

- *Scaling questions* ask clients to rank their situation and/or goal on a one-to-ten scale (de Jong & Berg, 2007). Usually one represents the worst scenario that could possibly be and ten is the most desirable outcome. Scaling questions provide a simple tool for clients to quantify and evaluate their situation and progress so that they establish a clear indicator of progress for themselves. For example, a scaling question may be phrased, as "On a one-to-ten scale, with one being the worst the problem could possibly be and ten as the most desirable outcome, how would you put yourself on the scale?"

- *Relationship questions* ask clients to imagine how significant others in their environment might react to their problem/situation and any changes they make (Berg, 1994; de Jong & Berg, 2007). Relationship questions not only contextualize problem definition but also the client's desired goals and changes. Establishing multiple indicators of change helps clients to develop a clearer vision of a desired future appropriate to their real-life context. Examples of relationship questions include: What would

your mother (or spouse, sister, etc.) notice that is different about you if you are more comfortable with the new environment? How would your wife (or other significant others) rank your motivation to change on a one-to-ten scale?

A solution-focused approach also uses task assignments to assist clients in noticing solutions in their natural life context (de Shazer & Molnar, 1984). If clients are able to identify exception behaviors to the problem, clients are asked to "do more of what works." For clients who focus on the perceived stability of their problematic pattern and fail to identify any exceptions, an observation task is given: "Between now and next time we meet, we (I) want you to observe, so that you can tell us (me) next time, what happens in your (life, marriage, family, or relationship) that you want to continue to have happen" (Molnar & de Shazer, 1987). Another observation task directs clients to notice what they do when they overcome the temptation or urge to take part in the problem behavior. Other tasks that assist clients in interrupting their problem patterns and developing new solutions include "do something different" ("Between now and next time we meet, do something different and tell me what happened") and the prediction task, which asks the client to predict his or her behavior by tossing a coin ("If it is a head, do what you normally do; if it is a tail, pretend that the miracle day has happened") (Berg, 1994).

The purpose of solution-focused questions and tasks is to assist clients to "notice a difference that can make a difference in their lives" in their natural environment. The therapist cautiously refrains from providing/suggesting any predetermined solutions. The therapist is responsible for creating a therapeutic dialogue in which clients experience a solution-building process that is initiated from within and grounded in clients' cultural strengths as well as a personal construction of the solution reality (Lee, 2003). It is for clients to discover what works for them in their unique life context.

Case Example

Tom was a 32-year-old man who came in for treatment because of his depressive mood. Tom was an accountant with a stable job. He came from a violent family background and witnessed his alcoholic father beating his mother to a point that she was hospitalized for severe injury and could not take care of him and his younger sister. The parents were divorced afterward and the children were placed in foster homes. Tom described all these losses as "baggage in life that he can't get over with." His recent depressive episode was triggered by relational problems with his girlfriend, and they were currently in a "cooling down" period. Tom shared that he has been depressed since the death of his mother five years ago. This is the first time he sought mental health treatment.

First Session

Solution-focused assessment views clients as the assessors. The assessment offers an opportunity for clients to self-evaluate what are the issues troubling them and what might be the solutions to their problems. In the first session, clients are encouraged to give a clear and explicit description of their presenting complaint. While it is important to empathetically listen to clients' description of their problem, the focus of treatment is not on exploring the history of the problems. The therapist always looks for an opportunity to make a shift from problem talk to solution talk without rushing the process.

Therapist: Why don't you just tell me a little bit about what brings you in here today? What can we work on today that'll be helpful for you?

Tom: Depression.

Therapist: How long can you, could you say you can trace your depression back?

Tom: It's been going on for a while but really, really, really hit me hard when my mother died five years ago.

Therapist: I'm sorry to hear that. That's a real difficult thing to deal with. What made you decide to come in now?

Tom: A relationship.

Therapist: OK.

Tom: It was the straw that broke the camel's back.

Therapist: When did you start to notice problems in the relationship?

Tom: Three months ago. It's not really a breakup. It's just like slowing down.

Therapist: Ok. So the two of you are kind of backing off?

Tom: Yeah.

Therapist: What do you notice about your depression? What tells you that it's depression?

Tom: I am an accountant and I have trouble concentrating, which is really bad for my job.

Therapist: OK.

Tom: Feeling like crap all the time; dizziness, lightheadedness, loss of appetite. Just on the verge of crying.

Therapist: Kind of tough on you, right.

Tom: We just have a fight, I mean, my girlfriend and me. I'm not sure whether this is a relationship that I should hang on.

Therapist: So you are somewhat confused about where should you go with this relationship?

Tom: Yeah.

Tom: What have you been doing to try to cope with the depression?

(Coping question uses pre-suppositional language that assumes Tom has already been doing something helpful to deal with his depression.)

Tom: Work.

Therapist: OK.

Tom: Just grinding through it, just grinding through it. Just trying to forget. It's constantly there so I can't get rid of. I feel like I'm spinning my wheels.

(While Tom has mentioned work being helpful to cope, he still feels like spinning the wheels.)

Tom: And it's like all my life I've been able to handle my own problems. You know, I come from a violent family. My dad hit my mom so badly that she was hurt all the time. They finally divorced and my sister and I ended up in foster care. I've just had to stand up and take care of myself. I haven't had to ask for any help from anybody. And I've come to the point where I can't do it anymore.

Therapist: This is tough. Are you proud of being able to stand up against bad experience and take care of yourself, even as a child?

(Solution-focused therapist tries not to make assumptions of what is helpful or not. Instead, the therapist uses questions that allow Tom to self-assess whether any behavior is helpful or not. It is more important for Tom to come up with the answers.)

Tom: I mean, I've always been the type of tough guy who can handle a lot of problems.

Therapist: Very independent.

Tom: Well, as far as working out problems, yeah.

Therapist: It sounds like it's taken a lot of courage to come in today.

(Reinforcing the motivation to seek help is important for Tom perceives himself as an independent guy.)

Tom: This definitely makes me feel weak.

Therapist: I think a lot of people sort of feel that way in the beginning, so I think that is pretty normal. I mean especially for anyone who's had that history of toughing it out.

(At this point, more conversation about the problem might just reinforce depression and Tom's feeling of being weak. This is a time to make a shift and introduce the miracle question to begin helping Tom to visualize the time when he is able to get over with his depression.)

Therapist: Let me ask you. It's kind of a hypothetical question. Suppose after you leave this session today and you go about your daily routine and tonight you go to sleep. When you are sleeping, a miracle happens. This depression that you have been experiencing is no longer a problem for you. You get up tomorrow morning and things are just better. But because you are asleep you are not aware that this miracle has actually taken place.

Tom: OK.

Therapist: What will you notice that's different about yourself? What would be the first small thing that you would be doing tomorrow morning that tells you that you are in a good mood?

Tom: Probably gets up, feels good.

Therapist: Suppose that you get up and feel good.

(It is important to use Tom's language.)

Tom: Perhaps sing in the shower.

Therapist: You like singing in the shower?

Tom: Yeah. Feed my dog. Take off for work.

Therapist: OK. What would be the first small thing you'd do differently at work if you were feeling just a little bit better that you are feeling now? This miracle is happening.

(The therapist continues to use solution-focused questions to help Tom visualize those things that he would do differently when he is no longer depressed. He identifies a list that includes dress well, able to concentrate and perform well at work, reconnect with friends, stop drinking, etc. Tom however, mentioned that, "It's like right now I feel like I'm buried. I feel like I'm just muck." While not focusing on the problem, it is important to help Tom to find a solution to his feeling of buried and muck.)

Therapist: What would be the first thing that you would maybe do to get yourself unburied? What would be your first thing?

Tom: Figure out why I'm feeling this way. What just happened is just the tip of the iceberg. There's been a lot other garbage that I'm carrying around, you know, and I've got to get rid of it.

Therapist: Looking at it from tomorrow, what would be the first thing that you would do to take away this sack of garbage that you're carrying around on your shoulders? What's that first piece of garbage that you would just sort of take out of there?

Tom: Losses.

Therapist: What do you think is the first loss that you are dealing with most that you need to pull out of that bag?

Tom: I would say loss of friends and family.

Therapist: What's one piece of it that you can take out of that bag? What would be the smallest piece that would make that load a little lighter?

(This is an illustration of how to process negative experience in a solution-focused way. Tom began sharing his story of coming from a violent family and ending up in foster care. He felt abandoned and alone.)

Tom: As a child, I felt being left alone.

Therapist: How long have you been carrying this whole feeling of alone on your shoulders?

Tom: A long while. I think sometimes when these things happened in life when you're young, it makes you feel alone. There are times even when we get older and these things happened, that feeling of being alone comes back.

Therapist: Again this miracle happens. What would happen tomorrow, which would help you feel a little less alone? What could you do to help yourself feel a little less alone?

Tom: I would say having more friends over.

Therapist: OK. What would be different for you tomorrow? How could you have a friend or a few friends come over tomorrow?

(The conversation moves on around ways that Tom can be more connected with his friends. Tom also mentions his desire to reconnect with his sister to process these losses together.)

Bridging Statement and Solution-Focused Task

Solution-focused therapy utilizes assignments as a way to engage clients in solution-building process in a real-life context. Prior to sharing the solution-focused assignment with Tom, the therapist summarizes her clinical observation as a bridging statement to the solution-focused assignment.

Therapist: I wish to share with you that I think you exhibit a lot of courage by coming in today. You have certainly touched on some issues which are obviously very close to your heart. There are some things that you need to conclude yourself, which have obviously been difficult for you. You have dealt with a number of losses. When things like that happen, they can heighten our sense of aloneness, especially when you have been struggling with some depression. But you obviously have a lot of successes. You have a good career. You've always been independent. You also strike me as being a person with great determination; someone who seeks to solve the problems that you face.

(Compliments have an important place in solution-focused therapy because they bring out the strengths of the client and help clients build solutions upon their strengths. However, it is imperative that compliments are authentic and built upon the conversation that happens in the session.)

Tom: There's something that I've noticed too. However, for this time, it's like I've let them build up until there are too many and I couldn't handle them all at once. Maybe I've just got to handle them one at a time.

Therapist: It sounds like you are aware of what might be helpful. You know as much as you can, as much as you've been able to do. I sometimes find it helpful to encourage people to act as if it's a miracle day and do things when they are having a miracle day. I would invite you to each morning flip a coin before you get up. If the coin comes up heads, I want you to pretend having the miracle day that we have discussed. Like singing in the shower, feeding the dog, going to work, making an effort to be around your coworkers, talking to people and finding times to have fun with friends, etc. If this is a tail, just do whatever you wish to do that day.

Tom: OK.

Therapist: While you are doing so, just notice any differences about what you are doing on those days so that we can talk about it next time.

(This is a combined pretending and predicting task. This is especially helpful for clients who believe that they have little control over the situation or get stuck in a situation. The client just pretends to have a good day when s/he gets a head when flipping a coin.)

Second Session

Therapist: So, what's better?

Tom: It is like I am looking at things a little bit differently now. Instead of flipping the coin, like you told me to, I just mentally flipped it and it just always comes up heads.

Therapist: Mentally flipped it. How did you do that?

(The "How did you do it?" is a great solution-focused question that allows Tom to recognize he is the one who is actively making a decision for the positive changes in his life.)

Tom: I just did it.

Therapist: OK, and what did you do as a result of that?

Tom: So, I had a good day.

Tom: I have also talked to a few friends about the situation itself. They gave me a few clues on what to do. You know, as far as the girlfriend goes.

Therapist: What else is better when you mentally flipped the coin?

Tom: Well, basically the fear of being alone. You know. I don't have any fear of being alone at all yet. I just got together with friends when I wish to be with somebody.

Therapist: Wow! What else?

(The therapist continues to help Tom further elaborate what he's done on the miracle day. It is very important to invite Tom to describe his success in great detail so that he notices his successes and registers his successes.

Therapist: That's great. But how did you decide to have a miracle day instead of staying depressed and lonely?

(This is a "choice" question that helps Tom to take ownership of the change.)

Tom: I just decided to quit screwing around. I was almost feeling sorry for myself about the situation I was in. And it was like, wait a minute. You are supposed to be live to the fullest. It is like, life is too short not to be happy.

Therapist: Yeah.

Tom: You know, you are supposed to live life to the fullest. And here I am sitting in this muck. Saying, well, shit, what am I going to do now?

Therapist: It sounds like you have kind of adopted a new perspective on some things. You have changed your way of thinking a little bit in the last couple of weeks too.

Therapist: And I think it fits right into with what you said last time when you said that you are very independent and that you are an independent problem solver. You are very independent and autonomous and have always relied on yourself. Once you made that decision and you said to yourself, you indeed did that.

(Solution-focused therapy focuses on utilizing client's strengths and resources. It is important therefore to recognize and utilize Tom's frame of himself as an independent solver in the treatment process. It also allows space for Tom to begin thinking what he'll need to do next.)

Therapist: Let me ask you on the same scale we used last time, 10 being that you just feel good about the way your life is going now and 1 is where you were just before you called in here, feeling depressed and muck. Where would you say you are now?

Tom: I would say at about a 7.

Therapist: A 7. Wow! OK. If I ask your best friend, what would he say you are on that scale right now?

Tom: He would probably put it at the same place, a 7.

(This is a scaling question that solution-focused therapy uses for clients to self-evaluate their progress, problem state, confidence of change, motivation to change, etc. Oftentimes it is used in conjunction with the relationship question that allows clients to see things from the perspective of other significant people in their lives.)

Therapist: Fantastic. Let me ask you this. What would you need to do that would tell you have moved from a 7 to an 8?

Tom: Taking care of myself a little bit better and watching what I am doing, watching my stuff.

Therapist: How exactly will you be taking better care of yourself that you are not doing now?

Tom: Getting to bed on time, eating right.

Therapist: What time will you be going to bed at night?

Tom: 11 pm. I usually go to bed about 1:00 am.

Therapist: That helps you to get going the next morning a little bit.

Tom: Oh, yeah.

Therapist: What else? You said eating right. How so, how will you be eating?

Tom: Eating regularly. Instead of just Coke, cookies, or choke down a sandwich. Lately, I have been eating a couple of meals, big meals.

Therapist: What else would you like to do differently when you are at an 8 that you are not doing now?

(The "different question" allows Tom to compare and contrast things that he will do when he is better that he is not doing now. The different question helps people to develop "creative perception" that allows them to make better decisions and responses to the situation [Lee, 2008]).

Tom: Watching situations a lot more and looking into them instead of looking at the surface of them. I didn't look much into the big picture before I've made my decision. Instead of looking at the whole thing, and that is where I have really screwed myself.

Therapist: What have you done here recently to help yourself look at the big picture instead of just focusing on the small picture or just looking at the surface?

Tom: For instance, the problem I had with my girlfriend. She'll come up and accuse me of something that I should be blamed for. I couldn't think. I couldn't react.

I can't say, fire back. I was just upset and let my emotions take over.

Therapist: In other words, you kind of just stopped and looked things over?

Tom: Yes. The more I thought about it, the more I analyzed the situation and all the stuff that happened and all the blame that was being thrown on me. Then I started seeing the other side of the coin. It is like, wait a minute. Maybe I am going to slow down and pull back for a while. I am not going to take that crap, and no one is going to step on me for being good.

Therapist: It sounds that it's more helpful not taking action right away, but pulling back and giving you an opportunity to think things through. Do you notice anything different about yourself when you are able to pull back and give yourself time to think through?

Tom: Oh yeah. I'm not being impulsive. I am not flying off the handle as much. I don't get upset as much as before. Someone may say something really smart or just jokingly and I don't snap back.

Therapist: This is big. How does that change your relationship with others when you are able to think before react?

Tom: You know, my friends said that I'm calmer.

Therapist: Anything else?

Tom: I've noticed something else too: I quit drinking.

Therapist: Is that what you want and good for you?

(Again, the therapist does not make any assumptions about the effect of quitting drinking on Tom, but lets Tom elaborate on his desired future and successes.)

At the end of the session, the therapist complimented Tom as a man of action who was already taking helpful steps in a direction that got things better, which was sort of like a domino effect. The therapist also commented Tom as a creative person who mentally flipped the coin in doing the solution-focused homework assignment. As Tom is already on the right track to get over his depression, the solution-focused task is, "Do it more often"—continue to do the same things that you have been doing and pay close attention to all the things you have done so that we can talk about them next time when you come back.

Applications and Current Status of Solution-Focused Therapy in the Social Work Profession

Solution-focused therapy is relatively recent compared to other established practice approaches in social work treatment such as cognitive behavioral approaches, humanistic approaches, task-centered approaches, psychodynamic approaches, etc. Even so, solution-focused therapy does have an increasing influence on social work treatment, primarily for two reasons. First, compared to many psychotherapy approaches, which are primarily developed by psychologists, social work professionals actively participate in the development and dissemination of solution-focused therapy. The late Insoo Kim Berg and Steve de Shazer, founders of solution-focused therapy, were social work professionals. Peter de Jong, Michelle Weiner-Davis, and Eve Lipchik, who all belonged to the original group at the Brief Family Therapy Center, were social work professionals. Cynthia Franklin and her social work colleagues have applied solution-focused therapy to family practice and school social work (Franklin & Jordan, 1998; Kelly, Kim, & Franklin, 2008). Mo Yee Lee, Adriana Uken, and John Sebold are social work professionals using solution-focused therapy to work with domestic violence offenders (Lee et al., 2003). Wally Gingerich, who did the first meta-analysis of solution-focused therapy outcome studies, is a social work professional (Gingerich & Eisengart, 2000). The list is long, as there are many other social work professionals actively applying solution-focused therapy with their client populations in creative and beneficial manners. Because the founders of solution-focused therapy were social work professionals, it is no accident that the practice orientation of solution-focused therapy is consistent with social work's overarching framework of person-in-environment as well as the social work values of respecting clients' dignity and self-determination (NASW, 1999). The historical roots of solution-focused therapy in social work give rise to its systems-based, collaborative, strengths-based, respectful, pragmatic, and focused style of treatment. To a certain extent, the similarities and consistencies between social work values and the assumptions of solution-focused therapy toward treatment and human change facilitate the adoption of this model by social work professionals.

Second, the focus of the solution-focused approach on solutions, strengths, and health is consistent with the empowerment-based and strengths-based approaches in human services, approaches that have gained increased prominence in the past decade (Rees, 1998; Saleebey, 2008). While the development of empowerment-based and strengths-based approaches in human services is independent of the development of solution-focused therapy, the increasing recognition of the importance of empowerment-based and strengths-based practice in social work treatment does promote the adoption of this practice model. Solution-focused therapy provides a specific set of treatment skills and techniques that operationalizes empowerment-based practice and informs the practice of social work treatment. In other words, solution-focused therapy translates the concept of strengths and empowerment to everyday practice of using the "language of empowerment" (Rappaport, 1985; Rees, 1998) and the "lexicons of strengths" (Saleebey, 2008) in social work treatment.

Currently, solution-focused therapy is increasingly being adopted in different practice settings in which social work professionals practice (Nelson & Thomas, 2007). The fields include, but are not limited to, the following:

- Child welfare (Berg & Kelly, 2000; Turner, 2007)
- Family practice (Berg, 1994; Franklin & Jordan, 1998)
- Child and adolescent practice (Berg & Steiner, 2003; Selekman, 1993, 1997)
- Schools (Franklin & Gerlach, 2007; Kelly, Kim, & Franklin, 2008; Metcalf, 2008)
- Substance use (Berg & Reuss, 1998; Smock et al., 2008)
- Mental health (Knekt et al., 2008a, 2008b; Macdonald, 2007)
- Domestic violence (Lee et al., 2003, 2007)
- Health (O'Connell & Palmer, 2003)
- Administration and management (Lueger & Korn, 2006)
- Culturally competent practice (Lee, 2003)
- Supervision (Triantafillou, 1997; Wheeler, 2007)

Relevant Research and Challenges

With the advent of evidence-based practice movement, the effectiveness of social work treatment approaches will need to be empirically supported and verified. While solution-focused therapy has gained increasing prominence in the practice world, the evidence is slowly accumulating. The challenges encountered by research pertaining to solution-focused therapy have to be understood in its historical development. Solution-focused therapy was developed by social work professionals in practice and not by academics at universities or research institutes. Nonetheless, the founders of solution-focused therapy, the late Insoo Kim Berg and Steve de Shazer, had a clear vision and support for advancing research in solution-focused therapy (de Shazer & Berg, 1997). The Solution-Focused Brief Therapy Association (SFBTA), which is the professional organization promoting solution-focused therapy in North America since 2002, continues to have a strong vision for developing evidence for solution-focused therapy. Currently, the Research Committee of SBFTA is charged with the mission to promote, strengthen, and disseminate research pertaining to solution-focused therapy. Nonetheless, while the development of research is gaining momentum, the challenges cannot be underestimated.

Outcome Research

Numerous intervention studies have been conducted for solution-focused therapy in diverse practice settings. The first meta-analysis of solution-focused therapy outcome study was conducted by Gingerich and Eisengart (2000). Their systematic review of 15 outcome studies on solution-focused therapy did not provide adequate empirical support for the efficacy of solution-focused therapy. The primary limitations included limited research design, small samples, and lack of a systematic intervention protocol (Gingerich & Eisengart, 2000). More recently, Johnny Kim conducted another meta-analysis that consisted of outcome studies between 1988 to 2005 (Kim, 2008). This review included 22 studies that used a control or comparison group in their study design. In addition, this meta-analysis focused on external behavioral outcomes, internal behavioral outcomes, and family/relationship problem outcomes. Findings showed that solution-focused therapy demonstrated small but positive solution-focused therapy treatment effects on all three measured outcomes. However, only internalizing behavior problems showed a significant difference in treatment effects of the solution-focused

therapy group compared to the control group. In addition, while the overall mean effect size estimates were small for solution-focused therapy treatment (.13 for externalizing problem outcomes, .26 for internalizing problem outcomes, and .26 for family/relationship problem outcomes), the mean effect size was comparable to outcome studies of psychotherapy conducted in real-life settings, which is .24 (Weisz, McCarty, & Valeri, 2006).

While there is increasing empirical evidence of the effectiveness of solution-focused therapy, the rigor of these studies is limited by numerous issues in research design. These limitations, however, are not unusual in intervention studies conducted in real-life practice settings. The identified problems include small and nonrepresentative samples, lack of randomized controlled procedures, lack of a specific manualized protocol, problems with treatment fidelity, measurement problems, etc. (Gingerich & Eisengart, 2000; Kim, 2008; Lee, Uken, & Sebold, 2007). To further develop and strengthen evidence for the efficacy of solution-focused therapy, future studies should consider a more rigorous research design that (1) uses larger and more representative samples; (2) includes control or comparison groups using randomized assignment procedures; (3) uses standardized measures that are sensitive enough to measure treatment changes; (4) uses observation-based rating systems in data collection when possible and appropriate; (5) refines and develops the treatment manual for training purposes and fidelity analyses; (6) increases the rigor of the fidelity procedures by using observation-based approaches with a refined, specific, and rigorous fidelity measurement protocol; (7) carefully monitors the data collection process to reduce problems in measurement attrition; and (8) includes research sites that serve ethnically and/or racially diverse populations.

Process Research

In addition to studies that focus on measuring outcomes and effectiveness, another major research question pertains to the mechanism of change—that is, what treatment components or process contribute to positive outcomes in clients and families. A group of researchers led by Janet Bevalas that includes Peter de Jong, Harry Korman, Sara Smock, Christine Tomori, Sara Healing, and others are currently using microanalysis to study therapeutic communication as a mechanism of change in solution-focused therapy. Their work includes three types of research: (1) process research (e.g., microanalysis of communication within therapy sessions) that assesses congruence between theory and practice and also reveals similarities and differences in therapeutic approaches (de Jong & Bavelas, 2009; Froerer & Smock, 2009; Tomori & Bavelas, 2007); (2) basic experiments in a laboratory setting that provide evidence supporting fundamental assumptions such as co-construction in the treatment process (e.g., Bavelas, Coates, & Johnson, 2000, 2002); and (3) experiments on therapeutic techniques, which test key techniques such as the miracle question in the laboratory using nontherapeutic tasks and populations (Healing & Bavelas, 2009). This line of research will illuminate important mechanisms of change and other process issues involved in the treatment process. In addition, such an approach also introduces novel research methodologies in understanding the therapeutic processes of other types of social work treatment approaches.

Conclusion

There is much diversity and great differences in how the problems of living should be approached. A solution-focused approach uses the language and symbols of "solution and strengths" in the treatment process. It is part of a pluralistic, professional effort to develop pragmatic solutions to address a wide range of problems of living in clients and families. The use of the language and symbols of "solution and strengths" in treatment is not without controversy. Not focusing on the problem is somewhat unfamiliar to most social work professionals, who are usually trained in the conventional problem-focused or problem-solving models of treatment. On the other hand, solution-focused therapists are well aware of the power of therapeutic dialogues and the potential harmful effects of a pathology-based and deficits-based perspective in sustaining the problem and disempowering clients. Solution-focused therapists prefer to include clients' voices as well as their strengths and resources in the search for effective solutions. While doing so, it is important to evaluate the effectiveness of solution-focused therapy and carefully examine the associated mechanisms and processes that contribute to its effectiveness so that treatment is based on an informed position in addition to ethical choices or theoretical preferences.

References

Bateson, G. (1979). *Mind and nature: A necessary unity.* New York: Dutton.

Bateson, C. (1972). *Steps to an ecology of mind.* New York: Ballantine Books.

Bavelas, J. B., Coates, L., & Johnson, T. (2000). Listeners as co-narrators. *Journal of Personality and Social Psychology, 79,* 941–952.

Bavelas, J. B., Coates, L., & Johnson, T. (2002). Listener responses as a collaborative process: The role of gaze. *Journal of Communication, 52,* 566–580.

Becvar, D. S., & Becvar, R. J. (2003). *Family therapy, a systematic integration* (5th ed.). Allyn and Bacon.

Berg, I. K. (1994). *Family-based services: A solution-focused approach.* New York: W. W. Norton.

Berg, I. K., & Dolan, Y. M. (2001). *Tales of solutions: A collection of hope-inspiring stories.* New York: W. W. Norton.

Berg, I. K., & Kelly, S. (2000). *Building solutions in child protective services.* New York: W. W. Norton.

Berg, I. K., & Miller, S. (1992). *Working with the problem drinker: A solution-focused approach.* New York: W. W. Norton & Co.

Berg, I. K., & Reuss, N. (1998). *Solutions step by step: A substance abuse treatment manual.* New York: W. W. Norton.

Berg, I. K., & Steiner, T. (2003). *Children's solution work.* New York: W. W. Norton.

Berger, P. L., & Luckmann, T. (1966). *The social construction of reality: A treatise in the sociology of knowledge.* New York: Doubleday.

Cade, B., & O'Hanlon, W. (1993). *A brief guide to brief therapy.* New York: W. W. Norton.

Cantwell, P., & Holmes, S. (1994). Social construction: A paradigm shift for systemic therapy and training. *Australian and New Zealand Journal of Family Therapy, 15,* 17–26.

de Jong, P., & Bavelas, J. (2009). *The role of formulations in co-constructing meanings in cognitive-behavioral therapy, motivational interviewing, and solution-focused brief therapy.* Presentation at 2009 Conference on Solution-Focused Practice, November 4–9, Albany, New York.

de Jong, P., & Berg, I. K. (2007). *Interviewing for solutions* (3rd ed.). Pacific Grove, CA: Brooks/Cole.

de Shazer, S (1985). *Keys to solutions in brief therapy.* New York: W. W. Norton.

de Shazer, S. (1988). *Clues: Investigating solutions in brief therapy.* New York: W. W. Norton.

de Shazer, S. (1991). *Putting difference to work.* New York: W. W. Norton.

de Shazer, S. (1994). *Words were originally magic.* New York: W. W. Norton.

de Shazer, S., & Berg, I. K. (1997). What works? Remarks on research aspects of solution focused brief therapy. *Journal of Family Therapy, 19,* 121–124.

de Shazer, S., & Molnar, A. (1984). Four useful interventions in brief family therapy. *Journal of Marital and Family Therapy, 10,* 297–304.

Erickson, M. (1985a). *Conversations with Milton H. Erickson, Volume I: Changing individuals* (J. Haley, ed.). New York: W. W. Norton.

Erickson, M. (1985b). *Conversations with Milton H. Erickson, Volume I: Changing couples* (J. Haley, ed.). New York: W. W. Norton.

Franklin, C., & Gerlach, B. (2007). Clinical applications of solution-focused brief therapy in public schools. In T. S. Nelson & F.N. Thomas (Eds.), *Handbook of solution-focused brief therapy: Clinical applications* (pp. 168–169). Philadelphia, PA: Haworth Press.

Franklin, C., & Jordan, C. (1998). *Family practice: Brief systems methods for social work.* Pacific Cove, CA: Brooks/Cole.

Froerer, A., & Smock, S. (2009). *Microanalysis of solution-focused formulations.* Presentation at 2009 Conference on Solution-Focused Practice, November 4–9, Albany, New York.

Gergen, K.J. (1999). *An invitation to social construction.* Thousand Oaks, CA: Sage Publications.

Gingerich, W., & Eisengart, S. (2000). Solution-focused brief therapy: A review of outcome research. *Family Process, 39,* 477–496.

Greene, G. J., Lee, M. Y., Mentzer, R., Pinnell, S., & Niles, D. (1998). Miracles, dreams, and empowerment: A brief practice note. *Families in Society, 79,* 395–399.

Haley, J. (1973). *Uncommon therapy: The psychiatric techniques of Milton H. Erickson, M.D.* New York: W. W. Norton.

Healing, S., & Bavelas, J. (2009). *An experimental study of mechanisms of change: Effects of questioning on attributions and performance.* Unpublished manuscript.

Karls, J. M. (2009). Person-in-environment system. In A. R. Roberts (Eds.), *Social workers' desk reference* (2nd ed., pp. 371–375). New York: Oxford University Press.

Keeney, B. P., & Thomas, F. N. (1986). Cybernetic foundations of family therapy. In F. P. Piercy & D. H. Sprenkle (Eds.), *Family therapy sourcebook* (pp. 262–287). New York: Guilford Press.

Kelly, M. S., Kim, J. S., & Franklin, C. (2008). *Solution-focused brief therapy in schools: A 360-degree view of the research and practice principles.* New York: Oxford University Press.

Kim, J. S. (2008). Examining the effectiveness of solution-focused brief therapy: A meta-analysis. *Research on Social Work Practice, 18,* 107–116.

Knekt, P., et al. (2008a). Randomized trial on the effectiveness of long-term and short-term psychodynamic psychotherapy and solution-focused therapy on psychiatric symptoms during a 3-year follow-up. *Psychological Medicine, 38,* 689–703.

Knekt, P., et al. (2008b). Effectiveness of short-term and long-term psychotherapy on work ability and functional capacity–A randomized clinical trial on depressive and anxiety disorders. *Journal of Affective Disorders, 107,* 95–106.

Lee, M. Y. (2003). A solution-focused approach to cross-cultural clinical social work practice: Utilizing cultural strengths, *Families in Society, 84,* 385–395.

Lee, M. Y. (2007). Discovering strengths and competencies in female domestic violence survivors: An application of Roberts' continuum of the duration and severity of woman battering. *Brief Treatment and Crisis Intervention, 7,* 102–114.

Lee, M. Y. (2008). A small act of creativity: Fostering creativity in clinical social work practice. *Families in Society, 89,* 19–32.

Lee, M. Y., Sebold, J., & Uken, A. (2003). *Solution-focused treatment with domestic violence offenders: Accountability for change.* New York: Oxford University Press.

Lee, M. Y., Uken, A., & Sebold, J. (2007). Role of self-determined goals in predicting recidivism in domestic violence offenders. *Research on Social Work Practice, 17,* 30–41.

Lueger, G., & Korn, H-P. (Eds.) (2006). *Solution focused management.* München, Mering: Rainer Hampp Verlag.

Macdonald, A. J. (2007). Applying solution-focused brief therapy to mental health practice. In T. S. Nelson & F.N. Thomas (Eds.), *Handbook of solution-focused brief therapy: Clinical applications* (pp. 267–294). Philadelphia, PA: Haworth Press.

Metcalf, L. (2008). *A field guide to counseling toward solutions.* San Francisco, CA: Jossey-Bass.

Molnar, A., & de Shazer, S. (1987). Solution focused therapy: Toward the identification of therapeutic tasks. *Journal of Marital and Family Therapy*, 13(4), 349–358.

Miller, G. (1997). *Becoming miracle workers: Language and meaning in brief therapy*. New York: Aldine de Gruyter.

National Association of Social Workers (1999). *The NASW Code of Ethics*. Washington, DC: NASW.

Neimeyer, R. A., & Mahoney, M. J. (1993). *Constructivism in psychotherapy*. Washington, DC: American Psychological Association.

Nelson, T. S., & Thomas, F. N. (Eds.) (2007). *Handbook of solution-focused brief therapy: Clinical applications*. Philadelphia, PA: Haworth Press.

O'Connell, B., & Palmer, S. (2003). *Solution focused therapy: A handbook for health care professionals*. London: Sage.

O'Hanlon, W., & Wilk, J. (1987). *Shifting contexts: The generation of effective psychotherapy*. New York: Guilford.

Rappaport, J. (1985). The power of empowerment language. *Social Policy, Fall*, 15–21.

Rees, S. (1998). Empowerment of youth. In L. M. Gutierrez, R. J. Parsons, & E. O. Cox (Eds.), *Empowerment in social work practice: A sourcebook* (pp. 130–145). Pacific Grove, CA: Brooks/Cole.

Rosen, H., & Kuehlwein, K. T. (Eds.) (1996). *Constructing realities: Meaning-making perspectives for psychotherapists*. San Francisco: Jossey-Bass Publishers.

Reuss, N. H. (1997). The nightmare question: Problem-talk in solution-focused brief therapy with alcoholics and their families. *Journal of Family Pyschotherapy*, 8(4), 71–76.

Saleebey, D. (2008). *Strengths perspective in social work practice* (5th ed.). NJ: Allyn & Bacon.

Selekman, M. (1997). *Solution-focused therapy with children*. New York: Guilford Press.

Selekman, M. (1993). *Pathways to change: Brief therapy solutions with difficult adolescents*. New York: Guilford Press.

Smock, S. A., et al. (2008). Solution-focused group therapy for level 1 substance abusers. *Journal of Marital & Family Therapy*, 34, 107–120.

Tomori, C., & Bavelas, J. B. (2007). Using micro-analysis of communication to compare solution-focused and client-centered therapies. *Journal of Family Psychotherapy*, 18, 25–43.

Triantafillou, N. (1997). A solution-focused approach to mental health supervision. *Journal of Systemic Therapies*, 16, 305–328.

Turner, A. (2007). Thinking and practicing beyond the therapy room: solution-focused brief therapy, trauma, and child protection. In T. S. Nelson & F.N. Thomas (Eds.), *Handbook of solution-focused brief therapy: Clinical applications* (pp. 295–314). Philadelphia, PA: Haworth Press.

Walter, J., & Peller, J. (1992). *Becoming solution-focused in brief therapy*. New York: Brunner/Mazel.

Watzlawick, P., Weakland, J. H., & Fisch, R. (1974). *Change, principles of problem formulation and problem resolution*. New York: W. W. Norton.

Weisz, J. R., McCarty, C. A., & Valeri, S. M. (2006). Effects of psychotherapy for depression in children and adolescents: A meta-analysis. *Psychotherapy Bulletin*, 132, 132–149.

Wheeler, J. (2007). Solution-focused supervision. In T. S. Nelson & F.N. Thomas (Eds.), *Handbook of solution-focused brief therapy: Clinical applications* (pp. 343–370). Philadelphia, PA: Haworth Press.

Wittgenstein, L. (1958). *Philosophical investigation* (translated by G. E. M. Anscombe). New York: Macmillan.

STRENGTHS PERSPECTIVE

This positive view of clients seeks to identify and build strengths by helping clients to first appreciate their inherent resources and aptitudes before acting

Some Basic Ideas About the Strengths Perspective

Dennis Saleebey

The Core Conditions of Change

One way to understand the orientation of those who adhere to a strengths-based approach to practice is to ask, "What are the factors in life and in helping that make things go well?" It is odd, when you think of it, that even though we know in some intuitive way that most people, in the midst of significant challenges and stresses, do better than we might expect and do not completely succumb to the pressures and nerve-racking surges of their lives, that we know so little about how they do that. On the other hand, we do have a prodigious lore about those who, at least initially, fall or fail under these stresses and ordeals. Our knowledge about those people who change naturally and spontaneously everyday is trifling by comparison.

So what do we know about discovering and building upon strengths? There are ideas, hints, and data everywhere, but let's look at one perspective that I find rich in implication. In their review of the studies done over many years of the efficacy of psychotherapy, Michael Lambert and Ted Asay (1999) say that there appear to be four factors that account for most of the positive change in individuals and families. These factors also have significant empirical support behind them. They are also plump with inferences for strengths-based approaches.

The largest share of the benefit experienced by individuals can be attributed to their personal, social, and spiritual resources as well as contingent factors (luck) that intercede in their lives (Lambert and Asay call them extra-therapeutic change factors that aid in positive change, whether or not an individual ever experiences psychotherapy; that is to say, many people who make an initial appointment with a therapist but don't keep that appointment because they seem to sense that they are better for having made the initial move toward help). This sociocultural, institutional matrix of clients' daily lives goes a long way toward explaining how they might react to sudden stress or slowly mounting challenges: their external strengths and assets, their social supports and burdens, and the contingent factors that move inexplicably in and out of their lives. This means being mindful of things in a person's world—relationships, culture, traditions, opportunities—those conditions and people that might be positive, supportive, helpful, or even therapeutic. Being mindful means listening and looking for evidence of the resources and aptitudes of clients as they tell their stories and recount their hardships. Regardless of circumstance, clients always provide evidence an array of capacities, traits, interests, and motivations, even if unintentional. These speak to the power of context as well—those micro-environments, the intimate spaces and places where people live and work, that have a powerful impact on how they act, think, and feel. Most of us are exquisitely sensitive to changes in context (Gladwell, 2000).

In the view of Asay and Lambert (1999) the second most powerful force for salubrious change is the character and tenor of the helping relationship. The quality of the rapport between social worker, helper, physician, and client or patient has always been understood (and in some cases undervalued) as a powerful tool for healing. Hans Strupp (1995), who studied the effectiveness of psychotherapy for decades, claims that the relationship is the heart of all forms of therapy. It is the medium of change, a dynamic not to be underestimated. The important elements of that kind of relationship are well known thanks, in large part, to the pioneering work of Carl Rogers (1951): respect, genuineness, concern, collaboration, and empathy. In addition, release of tension, reassurance, the alliance forged with the client, and direct activity play a role here. If healers are seen as nonjudgmental, trustworthy, caring, and expert, they have some influential tools at hand whether they are addressing the depths of a serious depression or the disappointments, anguish, and pains of unemployment or sexual abuse. A relationship of this sort provides a special milieu and context

for confronting the grueling and considering the imaginable.

The third and fourth factors, roughly equal in their impact, are the technical operations and methods of the theory employed by the helper (for example, family systems, empowerment, cognitive, or behavior therapy) and expectancies of the client, and the placebo effect. We will examine more closely the power of the placebo below. The methods derived from theory often, but not always, carry with them assumptions about cause (the nature of the problem) as well as guidelines about what to do. We know that some theories and their methods work well in certain instances: cognitive behavior therapy, or interpersonal therapy, occasionally with antidepressant medication, are generally effective with mild to moderately severe depression; certain behavioral techniques have been successful in treating specific kinds of anxiety and phobias; medication, psychosocial intervention, psychoeducation, and the strengths model of case management have found some modicum of success in helping people suffering from serious psychiatric disabilities. But my guess is that these, to an uncertain extent, succeed or fail because of the presence (or not) of these other, possibly more salient, factors: environmental resources, the helping relationship, and the power of positive expectations.

Of great interest to those who subscribe to a strengths-based orientation is the aforementioned influence of expectancy, hope, positive expectations, and the placebo effect. Consider the following: Michael Fisher (2000) reported that in the 1950s at the University of Kansas Medical Center, in order to test a new medical procedure for the treatment of angina, the design required some surgeons to perform real operations on one group of male patients with angina, and others to do a "placebo operation" on another group of men with angina. Members of both groups were randomly assigned. The placebo group was told that they were going to have heart surgery; they were given a local anesthetic, and superficial incisions were made in their chests, but no real operation was done. The "fake incisions" were sewn up so that postoperatively the patients had the sutures and some pain to indicate that they actually had surgery (the ethics of this may be distressing, but the fact is there have been hundreds of such studies, which we will discuss below). Seventy percent of the people who had the real surgery reported long-term improvement in their angina, but *all* of the placebo group did. In another venue, it is not at all uncommon, in tests of psychoactive drugs, for the placebo groups to show an improvement rate of 25% to 60%. In these studies, it is important to remember that the extent that the real drug is better than the placebo is thought to be the extent that the drug is effective. But even then we cannot be sure, for instance, just how much of the effect of the actual drug is also a placebo phenomenon.

Joseph Arpala (2000) reports that a study by Fisher and Greenberg revealed that in 30% to 40% of all the studies they reviewed of antidepressant drugs and placebos, the placebo was as powerful or therapeutic as the drug. A recent study of heretofore classified Food & Drug Administration data (Kirsch et al., 2003.) revealed that in the clinical trials of six major antidepressants done over 15 years by drug companies, the placebos were virtually equal in their clinical effect to the drugs. In discussing the hundreds of studies of successful sham surgeries done on knees, shoulders, and backs, the physician Jerome Groopman (2005) observes:

Patients are awash in a sea of statements about the link between their emotions and maladies. For years I diverted or dismissed their inquiries because I did not know how to answer. Now my response is formed by the lessons taught to me by my patients and the stirrings of serious science. I…say we are just beginning to appreciate hope's reach and have not defined its limits. I see hope as the very heart of healing. For those who have hope, it may help some to live longer, and it will help all to live better. (p. 212)

So what are we to make of all this? Perhaps when people are sick, because of the sway of the medical model, they have a belief, because of a procedure or pill, that they will get better. Thanks to such a conviction, there may be an "unconscious" mobilization of the healing systems within, whether it is the immune system, endorphins (endogenous morphine produced by the body), or a parasympathetic nervous system relaxation response that lowers, among other things, cortisol, the production of which is related to stress. Maybe it is just some unknown process about which we have no clue. But surely

what may be important here is the expectation of the healer that you will get well, as Groopman suggests above, and, as he and others suggest, that seems to involve the harvesting of hope and possibility. Helpers sometimes squander much of their possible goodwill and power to positively and ethically influence people by suggesting or implying that the clients' situations are not likely to improve much; that once stuck or hurt or disappointed or abused or ill they will always bear scars, and the remembrance and the consequences of these will continue to echo throughout contours of their lives. So, in the case of positive influence, it is probably not just people's expectation that they will recover, rebound, do better; it is likely the unmistakable belief of the social worker, physician, healer, minister, teacher, coach, relative, friend, or parent that it can be done; that the will and the resources to leap the hurdle, climb the wall, escape the burden can be summoned. People may waver, it may take some time, but if belief in them is constant and resolute, we can come to see them, as they can come to see themselves, not as someone "at risk," but as Beth Blue Swadener (1995) suggests, as someone "at promise."

There has been a lot of conceptual work and actual application of ideas related to hope—more than you might think. The late C. R. Snyder at the University of Kansas has done considerable work in this area. Hope is also very much a part of the strengths perspective, and the recovery and resilience movements. I cannot "hope" to reflect the depth of work that Snyder and others have done, but I begin with a quote from the late Paulo Freire, who was one of the most eloquent spokespersons for the oppressed all over the world, whose book *The Pedagogy of the Oppressed* should be required reading for all social workers. He wrote in the *Pedagogy of Hope*: "There is no change without the dream, as there is no dream without hope" (Freire, 1996, p. 91).

Hope is about imagining the possible, the "untested feasible" as Freire would have it. But more specifically, it is about thinking of one's self as an *agent*, to be able to effect some change in one's life, to have *goals* that not only have promise but that have *pathways* to their accomplishment—pathways that may be short or long, full of ruts or smooth, well lit or darkened (Snyder, 2000). We, as social workers, consort with the possible and we help to assure the agency of others, working on fashioning their hopes into goals and finding, as partners with them, those pathways to promise. In one sense, it matters not so much whether you reach the end of the journey but that you begin the journey and reach some of the stops along the way.

So, to reiterate: the expectation that you will get better; that there is a chance that you can beat the odds; that you have within you the power to transform or at least fight the disease process; my expectation, as your friend, intimate partner, or social worker, that you will do as well as possible confronted with whatever difficulties you have, are all extremely important elements in recovery or at least in stemming the advance of the effects of the adversities you face. At the very least, the strengths perspective and the resilience literature obligate us to understand that, however downtrodden, beaten up, sick, or disheartened and demoralized, individuals have survived and in some cases even flourished. They have taken steps, summoned up resources, coped, or maybe just raged at the darkness. For some, even getting to the place where they can get help is a major step. In order to provide consequential assistance, we need to know what they have done to mitigate their difficulties, how they did it, and what inner and outer resources provided ballast in the storms of their struggles. People are always engaged in their situations, working on them, even if they just decide to resign themselves to their fate. In some cases, work goes on at some level of consciousness even though the person may not be fully aware of that effort.

Circumstances can overwhelm and debilitate. We do know a lot about that. But facing dire conditions can also bring a surge in resolve and resilience. We must know more about that and how to make an alliance with those forces for positive growth.

Elements of Strengths-Based Practice

What follows is a loose representation of some of the stages and phases of practice. In truth, they may occur in a different sequence; they even might occur simultaneously; and there may be more of them than are represented here. Practice of all kinds is a discursive kind of experience, not necessarily a well-staged and predictable stroll through a set of certainties toward an inevitable destination. What follows is a way to look at the process, knowing that it will be in some ways different every time you engage in helping an individual, family, or community.

Individuals, families, and communities come to you voluntarily because they sense or have been told that things are not right in their lives; because they perceive, and/or experience discontent, stress, pain, and/or loss. They may be profoundly dissatisfied with their condition; they may be put upon by all sorts of environmental challenges—from abusive relationships, to poverty, to deleterious work conditions, to unemployment, to social disorganization in their neighborhood and the like. Clients must speak to these, and they want you to listen, honor, and understand their stories and narratives about these miseries and disruptions.

As a social worker you are ethically bound to "begin where the client is." This can mean many things, but, at the least, it means that you encourage the client to set the pace, to frame the situations they are in using the language with which they are most comfortable. So far, so good. But in practicing from the standpoint of strengths you listen as well for what every strengths-based practitioner believes is surely there—maybe as a leitmotif, or perhaps shrouded in the language of agony—and those are signs of capacity, resolve, determination, promise, and faith, however muted and modest they might be. I don't think it is unusual for individuals and families, even as they dutifully make an accounting of their problems and dilemmas, to mention, often in passing and without any fanfare, decisions they have made, actions that they have taken that have been purposeful, positive, and growth-promoting, although what they are experiencing most intensely is the pain of the moment. Marshall, troubled by intermittent heavy drinking and the consequences of that (one DUI some time ago, and some fractured relationships), said in passing to his social worker that he was careful not to drink during those weeks that his son (in the custody of his wife after a recent divorce and very important to Marshall) visited. Marshall did not mention this to illustrate a strength but rather as part of an exploration of some deeply disturbing elements of his current life. So, at some point, it is incumbent on you, as a strengths-oriented practitioner, to reflect this exemplar of strength back to Marshall so that he can see he does have some power to, at least momentarily, right himself, to deflect problems, to alter the beat and tempo of his life. You are always looking for evidence of the seeds of resilience and rebound. And it may be incumbent upon you to bear witness to this for the client, who may not see it for himself or herself.

Energizing the Dialogue and Narratives of Resilience and Strength

There is often great reluctance to acknowledge one's gifts, talents, and abilities. This also seems to be a sometime theme of the larger, dominant culture—it is *de rigueur* never to brag about yourself (although a lot of celebrities and professional athletes seem to have gotten past that prohibition!). In addition, many traits and capacities that are signs of strength can obscured by years of self-doubt, the blame of others, and the wearing of diagnostic labels. Or they can be reinterpreted by others as something negative (patience seen as passivity, humor seen as a defense, for example). Sometimes the difficulty in talking about resilience and competence is having no words for, or experience in, doing that. Sometimes it is lack of faith and trust in the self. So if a person has no experience in talking this way about the self, and it is contradicted by the understanding of his or her personal situation, and perhaps a deeply skeptical view about the powers and possibilities that lie within and around the self, the social worker may have to begin to provide the language, to look for, address, and give name to those resiliencies that people have demonstrated in the past and in the present. The daily struggles and triumphs of one's life as revealed in stories and narratives are useful (e.g., what they have done, how they survived, what they want, what they want to avoid) in suggesting what strengths might be at play in sectors of an individual's life. At some point in this process, people do have to acknowledge their strengths, play them out, see them in the past and the present, feel them, and have them affirmed by the worker and others. What is happening, often slowly, is the writing of a better life text. The stimulation of a strengths discourse involves at least three acts on the part of the worker: (1) providing a vocabulary of strengths (as nearly as possible in the language of the client); (2) mirroring—providing a positive reflection of the client's abilities and accomplishments, and helping the client to find other positive mirrors in the environment; and (3) keeping alive the awareness of what is actually possible in a person's life so that, at some level, the social worker is the keeper of the dream. In that role, the social worker acknowledges, affirms, articulates, and helps individuals act on their strengths.

Setting Goals, Developing a Project, and Realizing It in Context

Goal setting and the creation of a collaborative project between worker and client is important here. It can be described in many ways, but it is the manifestation of one's dreams and hopes: the result of linking hopes and individual and environmental strengths together in a mutually crafted scheme. While this is difficult for people who have not experienced much success in their worlds, and who currently are bent under the weight of their pain, it is essential for the development and realization of a better quality of life. In the long run, it is only by acting in context (with whatever moral and psychological supports that are needed) that changes in feeling, thinking, and affiliation will become more congruent with and buoyed by their capacities and hopes. So it is through action with the worker (by the way, it could also be a mentor, minister, teacher, friend, or relative)—collaborative and continuous—that individuals really begin to employ their strengths as they move toward well-formed, achievable goals. It is extremely important that the goals that are initially shaped through dialogue be framed in terms that are positive and verifiable and require specific and doable changes in behavior, knowledge, thinking, and/or feeling. As individuals decide and act, as they identify multiple strategies for achieving outcomes, they are encouraged to put their assets, resources, strengths, and resiliencies to work toward achieving these goals. But, in the end, it is deciding and acting, the recruitment of resources within and without, that lead to changes in their life world that are more congruent with their goals and reflective of their strengths.

It is the belief of strengths-oriented practitioners that resources and assets are available in all environments, even those that seem to the outsider to be impoverished. Also important here is that these resources be, as far as possible, naturally occurring: local organizations, associations, institutions; individuals, neighbors, relatives, and friends. For the worker this means practicing advocacy: discovering what natural or formal resources are available and accessible, and to what extent they are adequate and acceptable to the client (Kisthardt, 1993). Any environment is full of people, families, institutions, and associations who are willing to and can provide instruction, succor, relief, resources, time, and support. For example, in three public housing communities where, under the auspices of the local Housing Authority and the School of Social Welfare at the University of Kansas, we had community-building projects, we quickly discovered that there were a number of individuals who wanted to contribute in a consequential way to improving their neighborhood—making it safer, more appealing to the eye, more convivial, and less marginalized. We learned over the life of these projects that when people begin the work of achieving their goals and of exercising and realizing their strengths in action, the effect is sometimes synergistic: they can do more personally and are more energized; they find themselves in a tighter bond with the community; and, in the end, the community benefits. In this spirit, student interns (MSW) and some residents developed a mini-grant program (fashioned, to a degree, after that begun at Clark University in Atlanta under Dean Lou Beasley). Residents were encouraged to submit written proposals for modest programs that they thought would benefit some aspect of communal life and/or the physical environment of the community. The proposals were evaluated by a group of students and residents. Those who submitted proposals were given whatever help they needed in developing a compelling case for their proposed projects (no one was ultimately denied). Grants up to $200 (thus, mini) were available, thanks to a private donor. The array of proposals was remarkable; their ingenuity and sincerity were unmistakable. They included, among other things, planting a communal vegetable garden, developing community celebrations and get-togethers (breaking bread together turned out to be extremely important for communal spirit), street fairs (with games, readings, fashion and talent shows, and food), clean-up projects, enlisting the help of local institutions (grocery stores, churches, for example) in various ventures, such as ensuring that a pastor from a local church would come at least once a week to hold services for those who could not travel. Because of the turnover in residents and students, these were sometimes hard to sustain. But they did survive for the life of the projects themselves, and, in a couple of instances, are still alive.

Toward Normalizing and Capitalizing upon One's Strengths

Over a period of time, often a short period, the worker and the individual or family together will begin to consolidate the strengths that have emerged, reinforce the new vocabulary of strengths and resilience, and bolster the capacity to discover resources within and around. Furthermore, the worker and the family should periodically make an accounting of, and celebrate, the goals and successes that have been realized. The purpose is to cement the foundation of strengths and to nourish the energy of the continuing development and articulation of strengths. One important avenue to normalization for many who have been helped through a strengths-based approach is teaching others what one has learned in the process, a kind of mentorship. This is also the beginning of the process of letting go for both workers and clients. Disengagement is the ritual transition to normalization and is done with the assurance that the personal strengths and the communal resources are in place.

Root Principles of Strengths-Based Practice

There are some root principles of strengths-based practice that we should not ignore. They are disarmingly simple but difficult to put into practice because they do run counter to some of the thinking that characterizes some practices and agency mandates today.

Believe the Client and Believe in the Client

We are sometimes encouraged, by our own experience or by the expectations of others, to disbelieve clients. We are leery of being trumped or duped by the artful manipulator or the deft sociopath. But, until proven otherwise, believing the client and believing in the client are two of the most powerful tools for engaging clients in what is a most difficult and arduous task—making life better.

Affirm and Show Interest in the Client's View of Things

It is the narratives and stories that clients bring to us and share with us that allow us to discover who they are, what they know, what virtues they possess, what troubles they have faced, and what dreams they have (Hoyt, 1996).

A focus on the dreams, hopes, and visions of people encourages them to begin thinking subjunctively about what might be and how it might come about. Troubles may trump the ability to do this, but at some point it is the possible and the promise that drive the engine of change (Snyder, 2000).

Central, of course, to the strengths approach to practice is to begin to make an extensive and detailed accounting of the assets, resources, reserves, and capacities within the client and in the environment—family, extended family, neighborhood, and institutions (like churches, schools, informal associations). This inventory of strengths should be every bit as detailed, descriptive, and refined as the diagnostic categories of the *DSM-IV-TR* (American Psychiatric Association, 2000). The point, I suppose, is that we need to develop as fully as we can a dictionary, an encyclopedia of strengths, so that we have a language and imagery as compelling and captivating as that found in the *DSM-IV-TR*.

A core belief for strengths-oriented practitioners is that within and around individuals and families there are resources and assets, and these should be searched for, nursed, and employed in the service of achieving goals on the way to the dream. Many observers, some clinicians, and researchers have begun to realize just how potent natural forces for recovery and transformation can really be (Deegan, 2006). This is true of all people, at least potentially if not actually.

In summary, to enlist participation and involvement and to engage individuals, families, and/or communities: (1) assume a positive, collaborative demeanor; (2) radiate the resilience attitude (deeply believing in people's capacity for transformation); (3) rely on indigenous wisdom, resources, and natural assets, capitalizing on what people know, what they can do, and where they want to go; (4) convey positive expectations, and claim affirmations of the possible; (5) be engaging, likable, credible, and responsive, as you work shoulder to shoulder with individuals, families, and community members; and (6) be flexible and willing to assume many perspectives and to take many roles.

To discover the strengths and health within, it is imperative to work with people in developing a distinctive and enriched inventory and accounting of resources, assets, and possible solutions or pathways to goals for individuals, families, and communities. Discovering and rediscovering, drawing lessons from, and celebrating the times when the individual, family, or community has surmounted adverse conditions and bad luck provides an enriched history of possibility rather than problems. The Wolins (1997) encourage us to seek out "survivors' pride" in individuals, families, and communities—that spark of recognition and self-regard that comes from having successfully and often courageously met challenges. And the other side of this coin is to, as much as you can, discuss and imagine with people how things could be otherwise, what a dream fulfilled would feel, taste, smell, and look like, and how it would change daily life. Employ, as much as possible, clients' own ideas about what the problems and obstacles are and how they think they might change in order to realize a better life. When developing goals, think small but always think success. When success comes, celebrate it in a way that has meaning for the client. Encourage the client to look around and look ahead but not to spend too much time looking back. Finally, remember that change does happen. It happens in many different ways—both subtle and remarkable—and that the client, with your help, can be the author of that change.

Bringing the Strengths Perspective to Your Work: Quick Takes

1. Hear the voice, the story, the theory, and the ideas of the client and take them seriously; the clients probably have the most intimation about how life could be different.

2. Adopt the resilience attitude—that is, a belief in the client, the family, and the community—and that they can become what they hope and can move in the direction that they want to or must.

3. The Four A's. You have to believe in the client's capacities and strengths—which means, as stated earlier, you have to account for, appreciate, affirm, and act on them in as many ways as you can. Everything that I have said about the strengths of clients applies to you as a helper as well. And, in my experience, this is essential for respecting and realizing client strengths. In other words, this is a double feedback loop: from you to client from client to you.

4. Represent clients' views, narratives, and perspectives wherever possible—staffings, in-service trainings, rounds, newsletters, bulletin boards, board meetings, etc.

5. Always challenge views of clients, families, and the community, no matter where they originate, and how forceful, that demean or diminish their humanity or simply make them a case, a label, or a jumble of neediness and problems.

6. Celebrate, ritually and officially, personally and publicly, the accomplishments and successes of clients and the work that you do with them.

7. Invite clients to participate, to the extent feasible, in the workings of the agency—to be liaisons, advisors, mentors, participants, tutors, and outreach workers, for example.

8. Create organizational narratives that document both client and worker heroics, capacities, leadership, ingenuity, accomplishments, and strengths. In our community projects, we sometimes created a photo album on walls and windows of the central office of people doing good things, of their engagement in community projects, of their accomplishments and successes.

9. Help foster an organizational culture where conversation in the coffee room is not always about how awful it is but usually about how awesome it is—especially with respect to what the clients and you have accomplished together.

10. Write records in such a way that you would not mind clients' reading them; better yet, invite clients to read them; even better, invite clients to amend the record as they see fit.

Conclusion

Of the strengths perspective, Stan Witkin (2002), editor of *Social Work*, has written:

Do not be fooled by the simplicity of the strengths perspective; it has transformational potential. Indeed, if all of its tenets were adopted and put into practice, we would be living in a different world. ... The strengths perspective has been quietly fostering a small revolution in which the hegemony of deficit explanations is beginning to weaken, belief in resilience is rebounding, and collaborative practice is growing.

And Howard Zinn (1999) has written:

What we choose to emphasize in this complex history will determine our lives. If we see only the worst, it destroys our capacity to do something. If we remember those times and places—and there are so many—where people have behaved magnificently, this gives us the energy to act, and at least the possibility of sending this spinning top of a world in a different direction.

I believe that the work that we do, however modest in compass, is the work that, when added up, will be a critical mass in spinning this world on a different axis.

References

American Psychiatric Association. (2000). *Diagnostic and statistical manual of mental disorders (DSM-IV-TR)*. Washington, DC: American Psychiatric Association.

Asay, T. P., & Lambert, M. J. (1999). The empirical case for the common factors on therapy: Qualittative findings. In M. A. Hubble, B. L. Duncan, & S. D. Miller (Eds.), *The heart and soul of change: What works in therapy* (pp. 33–56). Washington, DC: American Psychological Association.

Deegan, P. (2006). Foreword. In C. A. Rapp & R. J. Goscha (Eds.), *The strengths model: Case management with people with psychiatric disabilities* (2nd ed.). Oxford University Press.

Freire, P. (1996). *Pedagogy of hope: Reliving pedagogy of the oppressed*. New York: Continuum.

Gladwell, M. (2000). *The tipping point: How little things can make a big difference*. Boston: Little, Brown, & Company.

Groopman, J. (2005). *The anatomy of hope: How people prevail in the face of illness*. New York: Random House.

Kirsch, I., Moore, T. J., Scoboria, A., & Nicholls, S. (2003). The emperor's new drugs An analysis of anti-depressant medication data submitted to the U. S. Food and Drug Administration. *Prevention & Treatment*, 5, 5–23. http://journals.apa.org/prevention/volume 5/pre0050023a.html.

Kisthardt, W. E. (1993). A strengths model of case management: The principles and functions of a helping partnership with persons with persistent mental illness. In M. Harris & H. Bergman (Eds.), *Case management for mentally ill patients: Theory and practice*. Langhorne, PA: Harwood Academic Publishers.

Rogers, C. (1951). *Client centered therapy: Its current practice, theory, and implications*. Chicago: Houghton Mifflin.

Snyder, C. R. (2000). There is hope. In C. R. Snyder (Ed.), *Handbook of hope: Theory, measures, and applications*. San Diego: Academic Press.

Strupp, H. H. (1995). The therapist's skills revisited. *Clinical Psychology*, 2, 70–74.

Swadener, B. B. (1995). Children and families "at promise": Deconstructing the discourse of risk. In B. B. Swadener & S. Lubeck (Eds.), *Children and families "at promise": Deconstructing the discourse of risk*. Albany: State University of New York Press.

Witkin, S. (2002). Foreword. In D. Saleebey (Ed.), *The strengths perspective in social work practice* (3rd ed., pp. xiii–xv). Boston: Allyn & Bacon.

Wolin, S., & Wolin, S. J. (1997). Shifting paradigms: Taking a paradoxical approach. *Resiliency in Action*, 2, 23–28.

Zinn, H. (1999). *A people's history of the United States: 1492 to the present*. New York: HarperCollins.

STRATEGIC THERAPY

By focusing on defining problems and goals, clients are encouraged to cooperatively carry out behavioral tasks and directives between sessions

Strategic Therapy and Social Work Intervention

Gilbert J. Greene

Social workers provide professional services to clients with problems that the clients have not been able to overcome on their own. In strategic therapy, according to Haley (1973), "the clinician initiates what happens during therapy and designs a particular approach for each problem (p. 17)." A clinician using strategic therapy identifies solvable problems, defines goals, and designs and implements interventions for achieving those goals. After implementing an intervention a strategic therapist closely observes how the client responds and when necessary makes adjustments and modifies or uses different interventions depending on the client's response to the interventions (feedback to the clinician) (Haley, 1973, p. 17). The theoretical underpinnings of strategic therapy are communications theory and systems theory. Systems theory will not be discussed in this chapter

because it is presented elsewhere in this book (see Chapter 15, "General Systems Theory: Contributions to Social Work Theory and Practice").

Communication Theory and Strategic Therapy

In social work practice success depends on our ability to communicate effectively with clients. It is a basic tenet in social work practice that clients need to feel comfortable enough with the worker in order to communicate openly with her or him. The social worker must know how to communicate skillfully with the client in order for the type of relationship to develop in which open client communication can occur. In addition, a common dynamic operating in clients' lives involves communication problems with significant others.

Often a desired outcome of social work practice is the improvement of clients' communication in their everyday lives. Human communication, however, is complex and multifaceted and social workers must go beyond focusing only on their ability to develop a "helping relationship" and facilitating improved client communications skills with significant others.

Communications theory focuses on identifying the redundant communicational patterns that are involved when the client's presenting problem is present. These redundant patterns are the rules governing interactions. Since these problematic patterns integrally involve the client's communications, the social worker must know how to skillfully communicate with the client in a way that interrupts these patterns, which then allows the client to develop and/or rediscover more effective ways of feeling/thinking/behaving, especially in relation to other people.

The communications theory underpinning of strategic therapy was developed by the Mental Research Institute (MRI) in Palo Alto, California (Watzlawick, Beavin & Jackson, 1967; Watzlawick & Weakland, 1977). The communications theory of the MRI grew out of the work of the anthropologist Gregory Bateson and his team of researchers based at the Veterans Administration (VA) Hospital in Palo Alto, California, beginning in 1952. The original team consisted of John Weakland, a chemical engineer and anthropologist; Jay Haley, a communications specialist; and William Fry, a psychiatrist. Don D. Jackson, a psychiatrist, joined them in 1954, followed by Jules Riskin, also a psychiatrist, in 1957.

Bateson's work in Palo Alto began as a result of a grant from the Rockefeller Foundation for a project titled "The Significance of the Paradoxes of Abstraction in Communication." Initially, the project involved anthropological research on paradoxes of abstraction in communication with non-clinical subjects and situations, including communication between animals and animals and humans (Weakland, Walzlawick, & Riskin, 1995). It was only after a couple of years of the project that Bateson and his research team started observing, filming, and studying the interactions of schizophrenics and their family members at the Palo Alto Veterans Hospital and focusing entirely on human communication,

especially in regard to problematic behavior and its treatment. One of the first published papers by the members of the Bateson project (1956), "Toward a Theory of Schizophrenia," was also probably their most influential one because it introduced the concept of the double-bind theory as a significant factor in human relationships (this will be discussed in more detail later in this chapter). Many other publications followed over the next several years as the Bateson project continued until 1962.

A number of social workers have contributed to the development and practice of strategic therapy, often publishing in the family therapy literature rather than the social work literature (Bross, 1982; Cade, 1980; Grove & Haley, 1993; Hoffman, 1981; Papp, 1983; Segal, 1980). In fact Braverman (1986) has pointed out how some of the original developers of social casework used techniques and approaches that are consistent with the present-day practice of strategic therapy.

The primary versions of strategic therapy include what has become known as the MRI approach (Segal, 1991), also referred to as the interactional view (Ray & Watzlawick, 2005; Watzlawick & Weakland, 1977) or the Palo Alto Model (Rohrbaugh & Varda, 2001; Schlanger & Anger-Diaz, 1999); the Haley/Madanes approach (1987, 1984), also referred to as the Washington School (Keim, 2000); and the approach of the group in Milan, Italy (the Milan Approach) (Selvini Palazzoli, Boscolo, Cecchin, & Prata, 1978a, 1978b). The MRI approach and the Haley/Madanes approach are the most widely used and best known. Because of space limitations only these first two approaches will be discussed in this chapter.

The MRI Approach to Strategic Therapy

In 1959 Don D. Jackson left the Bateson project and started the MRI along with Jules Riskin and Virginia Satir, a social worker; the MRI staff and members of the Bateson project continued to collaborate for several more years. Paul Watzlawick came to MRI in 1960 and Jay Haley and John Weakland in 1961 as the Bateson project was winding down (Weakland et al., 1995). After a few years at MRI, Haley and Satir left and eventually set up clinical training programs of their own. Watzlawick and Weakland continued their association with MRI. In addition, Lynn Segal, a social worker, has been closely associated with the MRI for many years.

Basic Assumptions

Pragmatics of Human Communication. The early work of the MRI (Segal & Bavelas, 1983; Watzlawick, Beavin, & Jackson, 1967; Weakland, 1976) focused on the pragmatics of human communication; that is, how communication affects behavior. Watzlawick et al. posited that "all behavior, not only speech, is communication, and all communication—even the communicational clues in an impersonal context—affects behavior" (Watzlawick, Beavin, & Jackson, 1967, p. 22). These authors were especially concerned with how interactants mutually affect each other and not just that of a sender of a message on its receiver.

Information. According to Bateson (1979), information is "a difference that makes a difference" (p. 99). Information is a result of contrasting phenomena and noticing distinctions between them. This view distinguishes information from new facts. A new fact may not be information if it fits one's existing assumptions about himself or herself and the world. Information occurs when a communication is different from any of one's current assumptive categories. Such a communication is truly "news of difference" or "a difference that makes a difference"; it is considered to be novelty in view of one's current assumptive categories.

Information affects how social systems behave. Social systems and their environment mutually affect each other through feedback. Feedback involves part of a system's output being reintroduced into the system as information about the output (Watzlawick et al., 1967, p. 31). According to Watzlawick et al. (1967), a single unit of communication is a message, and an interaction is the exchange of a series of messages between two people. Over time, communicational feedback processes become redundant and patterned, and these patterns of interactions become the rules (assumptions) of the system. According to Bateson (1979), systems cannot

change without information; that is, new or *novel* input acts as a catalyst for systems to go beyond their current rules or assumptions.

The Axioms of Human Communication. At the heart of the interactional view of the MRI are their five axioms of communication. The first of these is "one cannot not communicate" (Watzlawick et al., 1967, p. 51). In the presence of another person, one cannot *not* behave nor can one not *not* communicate. Even when one is silent in the presence of another person, she or he may be communicating to the other that she or he is not interested in having a conversation at that time. The other person may give additional meaning to the situation such as deciding that the silent person may be arrogant, socially inept, or mentally ill. Problems can occur in relationships when people do not commit to making their communications clearly understood to others. One can reject, accept, or disqualify another's communication. Communications must be clear for there to be a mutual understanding of rejection or acceptance. Disqualifying a communication, however, leaves the situation ambiguous. Disqualifying communications invalidates one's own or other's communications, and this can be done in a variety of ways, such as "self-contradictions, inconsistencies, subject switches, tangentializations, incomplete sentences, misunderstandings, obscure style or mannerisms of speech, the literal interpretations of metaphor and the metaphorical interpretation of literal remarks, etc." (Watzlawick et al., 1967, p. 76). One can also avoid committing to clear communication by means of symptomatic behavior, which gives the responsibility to the symptom rather than the individual for not committing to clearly communicating.

The second axiom of human communication is: "Every communication has a content and a relationship aspect such that the latter classifies the former and is therefore a meta-communication" (Watzlawick et al., 1967, p. 54). When people communicate with each other, they are not only conveying a substantive message but they are also making a statement about the definition of the relationship (Haley, 1963); this involves communicating about the communication (Watzlawick et al., 1967). According to Haley (1963), people not only communicate substantive messages to each other, but they also communicate about their communication. Communicating about one's communication is referred to as meta-communication (Haley, 1963). Meta-communication involves the qualifying of messages. Communication is qualified by other verbal messages, the nonverbal communication of bodily movements, paralinguistic patterns, or the context of the communication (Haley, 1963). Problems can develop in relationships when the individuals disagree at the relationship level but they try to resolve their differences at the content level; this may result only in temporary peace in the relationship because the real differences still have not been resolved.

The third axiom of communication states: "The nature of a relationship is contingent upon the punctuation of the communicational sequences between the communicants" (Watzlawick et al., 1967, p. 59). This axiom involves the issue of cause and effect, or blame, in relationships. Just as punctuation marks are used to break up a series of written words on a page to make sense of them, for example, by indicating the beginning and ending of sentences, people break up the ongoing stream of communicating between them in order to make sense of their meaning. For instance, when a couple has an argument, they often put considerable energy into attributing blame to each other for having started it. Each person is truly convinced about the correctness of his or her view of reality. This situation occurs because each person is punctuating the sequence of events in his or her relationship differently. They each have different but equally valid ways of "chopping up" the communicational stream in their relationship and giving meaning to them, finding a beginning (who started it) and ending to interactions.

The fourth axiom of communication holds that people communicate both digitally and analogically. Digital communication consists of words, which are "arbitrary signs that are manipulated according to the logical syntax of language" (Watzlawick et al., 1967, p. 61). Analogical communication, on the other hand, involves all nonverbal communication in the broadest sense, such as "posture, gesture, facial expression, voice inflection, the sequence, rhythm, and cadence of the words themselves" (Watzlawick et al., 1967, p. 62) as well as the context in which the communication takes place. This axiom is related to axiom two in that the content of messages is usually conveyed digitally and the relationship aspect of messages is conveyed analogically.

Axiom number five states: "All communicational interchanges are either symmetrical or complementary, depending on whether they are based on equality or difference" (Watzlawick et al., 1967, p. 70). In symmetrical communication people interact in ways that define their relationship as one between equals. In complementary communication, on the other hand, individuals interact in ways that define one person in the "one-up" position and the other in the "one-down" position. Difficulties in communications and relationships can occur when the individuals interact in ways that reflect disagreement in how the relationship is to be defined but lack rules for successfully meta-communicating and, thus, effectively negotiating the definition of the relationship (Watzlawick et al., 1967).

From these five axioms, it is evident that human communication occurs at different levels. Given that there are different levels, it is quite easy for confusion and ambiguity to exist in human communication and interpersonal relationships. People in relationships need to be willing and able (to be committed) to openly and directly communicate with each other (to meta-communicate) when such confusion and ambiguity inevitably arises. Failure to do so can lead to difficulties for the interactants and their relationship.

The Double Bind. Difficulties in relationships arise in the case of the double-bind situation. According to Abeles (1976), "double bind theory is about relationships, and what happens when important basic relationships are chronically subjected to invalidation through paradoxical interaction" (pp. 115–116). Watzlawick et al. (1967) define *paradox* as a "contradiction that follows correct deduction from consistent premises" (p. 188). The classic example of this is the liar's paradox, where, for example, in response to the social worker's question as to the presenting problem a man replies: "I am a liar." In this case the man is telling the truth if he is lying and lying if he is telling the truth. It is a "no-win situation" for the social worker in trying to definitively decide which is true.

The double-bind situation becomes especially problematic when it characterizes the nature of the ongoing relationship between a child and his or her parents. Child development occurs in a learning context in which individuals come to answer important questions such as "who am I," "what is expected and acceptable behavior," or even "what is real." In a double-bind learning context the child can never get straight answers from the parents to these all-important questions. Bateson et al. (1956) presented the "essential ingredients" of the double bind, and others later elaborated on them (Sluzki, Beavin, Tarnopolsky, & Veron; 1967; Sluzki & Veron, 1971). The common elements (essential ingredients) of the double bind are the following:

1. An intense relationship involving two or more persons with one person being in a one-up position and the other person in the one-down position. Because it is an intense relationship, it is necessary for the person in the one-down position to be able to accurately interpret the messages the one-up person is giving her or him. The usual context for a person to learn a double-bind view of the world is the family of origin, with a child in the one-down position and at least one parent in the one-up position. The double-binding situation may involve others, such as the other parent, siblings, or a grandparent. If only one parent and a child are involved, then for the double bind to have lasting impact, it requires that no one else regularly intervene to neutralize the impact of the double-binding situation.

2. Double-binding dynamics involve the person in the one-up position (the parent) giving the child in the one-down position messages (injunctions), usually verbal, about how to feel, think, or behave appropriately (what to do or not do). In order to "motivate" the child, the parent consistently uses punishment or threats of punishment and never rewards, thus creating a learning context based on avoidance of punishment rather than reward seeking. In regard to this, Bateson et al. (1956) state "that the punishment may be either the withdrawal of love or the expression of hate

or anger—or most devastating—the kind of abandonment that results from the parent's expression of extreme helplessness" (p. 253).

3. At the same time the parent is giving the child verbal messages, he or she is also sending another message, usually nonverbal, that conflicts with the verbal message. The non-verbal message may be communicated by means of "posture, gesture, tone of voice, meaningful action, and the implications concealed in verbal comment" (Bateson et al., 1956, p. 254).

4. All parents sometimes give conflicting messages and are inconsistent. What makes a situation a double bind is the inability of the child to escape the situation or get clarity about the conflicting messages by meta-communicating. A very young child may not be able to escape because of dependency on the parent for survival. For someone older the escape may be made impossible "by certain devices which are not purely negative, e.g., capricious promises of love, and the like" (Bateson et al., 1956, p. 254). Also in the double-bind situation, if the child comments on the conflicting messages and/or tries to gets clarification from the parent about his or her communications (he or she meta-communicates), the parent will deny he or she is giving conflicting messages and/or will verbally attack the child for even raising the question. Because the child can never get a straight answer, he or she is in an impossible, paradoxical, no-win situation—"damned if you do and damned if you don't."

5. For the child to learn to perceive the world through a double-bind lens in a lasting way, double-bind experiences must be repeated and pervasive.

The double-binding situation is confusing and disorienting for the person, resulting in him or her being very prone to experiencing anxiety, panic, and rage (Bateson et al., 1956). After a person learns to experience the world in double-bind communicational patterns, he or she is then hypersensitive to experiencing double-binding communications from others even when such messages are not present. Consequently, the person comes to distrust most communication from other people, even when it is direct, clear, and consistent. A result of the person in the one-down position developing such a double-bind view of the world is that now the person in the one-up position will get double-bind messages from the person in the one-down position. Consequently, a pattern of reciprocal double-bind messages between the two or more people is now set. No longer is one person in the one-up position and the other in the one-down position—they are now stuck in this pattern together (Elkaim, 1990).

In illustrating the double bind, Bateson et al. (1956, pp. 256–258) provide an example of a parent having strong feelings, such as hostility or affection, toward a child and also feeling a strong need to withdraw from the child. But instead of the parent saying something like, "Go away, I need some alone time," he or she says, "Go to bed, you're tired and I want you to get your sleep." This loving statement may disguise the parent's true feeling of "Get out of my sight because I'm sick of you." If the child is able to accurately perceive the parent's true feelings, then he or she would have to accept the fact that his or her parent does not want him or her around and is using a loving statement to deceive him or her. If the child takes the parent's "loving" statement at face value he or she might seek more closeness with the parent, and this in turn might provoke the parent to withdraw even more. If the child withdraws, the parent might interpret this as the child seeing the parent as unloving, which is unacceptable to the parent, who then might get angry with the child. If the child were to comment on what is going on or ask for clarification from the parent as to what he or she really means, the parent might accuse the child of being unloving or bad or somehow deficient for even questioning the parent. The child, then, might find it easier to just accept the parent's definition of how the child is feeling. The child, therefore, is punished for accurately discriminating what the parent is expressing but also punished for inaccurately discriminating and, thus, is in a double bind (Bateson et al., 1956, pp. 256–258).

Problems and Symptoms. A usual result of a child growing up in an ongoing double-bind situation is symptomatic behavior of various forms. Though originally conceptualized as significantly

contributing to the etiology of schizophrenia, Sluzki and Veron (1971) see the double-bind situation as a significant contributing factor in the etiology of all clinical disorders. According to Haley (1963), problematic symptoms are likely to develop when a person's behavior has extreme influence on another person and the symptomatic person indicates that he or she cannot help it; that is, the person exhibits the symptomatic behavior "involuntarily." From the communications theory perspective, symptomatic behavior involves incongruence between levels of messages. In this situation the symptomatic person "does something extreme, or avoids doing something, and indicates that he is not doing it because he cannot help himself" (Haley, 1963, p. 5). Symptomatic behavior, therefore, is very likely to occur in relationships in which the individuals are not able to establish a mutual definition of their relationship through direct communication (Haley, 1963). Developing symptoms is a way for one person to control the definition of the relationship while at the same time denying that he or she is doing so (Haley, 1963).

A by-product of symptomatic behavior is that it makes the social world of the symptom-bearer and his or her significant others more predictable (Haley, 1963). Another significant byproduct of symptomatic behavior is it "protects" significant others of the symptombearer from having to face their own issues, such as depression, anxiety, insecurity, incompetence, low self-esteem, and so on (Haley, 1963). This situation is not something the symptom-bearer has consciously decided or openly discussed with his or her significant others but is an unspoken *quid pro quo* (Haley, 1963; Jackson, 1965). At the same time, however, having symptoms is usually very unpleasant not only for the person with the symptoms but for the significant people in their social world.

First- and Second-Order Change. Because of the unpleasantness of the situation, the person with the problem usually will make various efforts to solve the problem and get rid of their symptoms; his or her significant others, out of caring and concern, or a need for relief themselves, will do likewise. However, the attempts by the person with the problem and/or the significant others often do not result in the desired changes. In an effort to bring about change in the situation, the problematic person and/or the significant others often will increase their efforts to make changes. Often these increased attempts to solve the problem still do not result in the desired changes. When such a situation occurs, many people will try even harder to make change using even more of the same ineffective solutions, still resulting in no change (Fisch, 1999). After a while, those involved in the problematic situation find themselves stuck in a "vicious cycle" whereby, unknown to them, the attempts to solve the problem are maintaining the problem such that now "the solution is the problem." The MRI approach refers to this repetitive pattern of using even "more of the same" ineffective solutions to a problem as *first-order change* (Watzlawick, Weakland, & Fisch, 1974).

First-order change is change that is attempted according to the rules and structure (organization) of a client system. These attempts at change are logical and commonsensical to the client system because they are in keeping with their assumptions and structure. Consequently, the problematic person and/or the significant others assume that if a little of an attempted solution does not get results, then "more of the same" needs to be applied to the problem, and if this does not get results, then one should try even harder at making change but by using even more of the same attempted solutions. Usually, first-order change involves applying the opposite of the problem. For example, a person experiencing insomnia may consciously and willfully try to make himself or herself go to sleep, or parents will use rational appeals to teenagers to change when they think the teenagers are thinking irrationally and behaving irresponsibly. Some other common attempts that result in first-order change are giving advice, nagging, punishing, appealing to another logically and rationally, lecturing and teaching, and so on. The result is that "things change but everything remains the same" (Watzlawick et al., 1974, p. 1).

First-order change attempts introduce no novelty into the client system and, thus, they are assimilated according to one's assumptions about the world, usually resulting in no change occurring in the client system, be it an individual, couple, family, organization, or community (Dowd & Pace, 1989; Hoffman, 2007). Client systems get stuck in the vicious cycle of

first-order change when they do not have enough flexibility to allow themselves to step outside their situation to look at it from a new perspective. What they are lacking is a rule for changing the rules (a meta-rule) regarding problem solving. In order to change the rules, those within the problematic situation must be able to communicate about their communication (meta-communicate) and, thus, the rules. Without a meta-rule (the ability to meta-communicate), change cannot be generated by those operating within the assumptive world (the rules) of that system. To break such an impasse, the client system needs to experience *second-order change* (Dowd & Pace, 1989; Watzlawick, et al., 1974).

Second-order change is change that is outside the client system's current rules (assumptions); it results in an expansion and increasing complexity in the rules (assumptions). In first-order change, attempts are made to solve the problem according to the rules and structure (organization) of the client system. However, in second-order change the rules and structure themselves are permanently changed; it changes the operating premises of the entire client system (Hoffman, 2007). The catalyst for such change is the introduction of novelty (a difference that makes a difference) to the client from his or her environment to which the client has to accommodate (Dowd & Pace, 1989; Hoffman, 2007). Second-order interventions focus on making changes in the problem-maintaining patterns of the attempted solutions rather than the presenting problem (Fisch & Schlanger, 1999). Of course, if the client, his or her significant others, or the social worker use very different types of solutions to the problem, then resolution of the problem should result.

Changing the patterns of first-order change by intervening to bring about the completely new patterns of second-order change results in a change in the context in which the problem had previously occurred. Changing the context thus changes the meaning the client system had previously attributed to the problem because behavior makes sense only within a specific context(s); all behavior is contextual. Because second-order change is beyond the client system's current assumptions about the world, it involves a logical jump, and thus the client will usually initially experience the effect of the intervention as illogical, uncommonsensical, perhaps even weird and/or radical. This results in some degree of disequilibrium, disorientation, shock, and/or confusion, at least temporarily until a new homeostasis is established. Clients can experience this transitional state as a crisis, or this transitional state can be the result of clients first experiencing a crisis in their life. Once the client accommodates to the novelty, he or she will experience permanent growth, development, and change (Dowd & Pace, 1989). Whereas first-order change results in a system being unchanged, second-order change results in changing the rules, structure, and organization of a client system. In therapy second-order change is promoted not by trying to persuade clients to change but rather providing them with novel experiences in which change is possible and often experienced as spontaneously occurring like an epiphany (Hoffman, 2007). In strategic therapy insight is not viewed as a necessary precursor to change but rather is something clients experience, if at all, after change has occurred.

The MRI Approach to Intervention

The various approaches to strategic therapy focus on resolving the presenting problem as defined by the client. A more important focus for intervention is the pattern of attempted solutions that are maintaining the problem. Therefore, the clinician needs to develop and implement interventions that will interrupt these rigid problem-maintaining patterns, and this in turn opens the door for clients to try something new and different. The pragmatic orientation of the MRI approach posits that if what one is doing is not getting results, then one should stop doing it and try something different (Fisch et al., 1982). This pragmatic position holds very true for the social worker using a strategic approach to practice and is quite different from most other theoretical approaches (Dowd & Pace, 1989). According to Dowd and Pace (1989), most theoretical approaches to treatment use first-order change interventions in attempting to bring about client change. These interventions are first-order in that they are logical and commonsensical, try to bring about the opposite of the problem, focus primarily on making change in the problem, and tend to utilize more of the same ineffective interventions when clients do not respond to or are noncompliant with (resist)

treatment. What is needed, according to Dowd and Pace (1989) is the use of interventions that will result in second-order change.

The Stages of Treatment

In keeping with its pragmatic orientation, MRI strategic therapy organizes treatment in a stepwise approach. The following is an adaptation of the MRI stages of treatment (Nardone & Watzlawick, 1993): (1) Develop a positive therapeutic relationship; (2) Define the problem from the client's perspective; (3) Identify the unsuccessful attempts to solve the problem that are maintaining the problem; (4) Define the outcome goal from the client's perspective; (5) Develop and implement intervention strategies to bring about second-order change; (6) Termination. Much of each session involves the clinician asking questions. The purpose of such questions is not just to provide the clinician with useful information but also to increase clients' openness and readiness to change. Thus, how we conduct sessions is very important to the success of treatment (Nardone & Salvini, 2007).

1. In *developing a positive therapeutic relationship,* a social worker must know how to communicate so that the client feels comfortable with the social worker and experiences him or her as trustworthy. The development of a positive therapeutic relationship is facilitated when the social worker demonstrates empathy, acceptance, support, and genuineness and maintains a focus on the problems and goals defined by the client. This process is enhanced when the social worker "matches" the client nonverbally and "uses the client's language" (Nardone & Watzlawick, 1993); this involves initially adopting the client's verbal and nonverbal styles of communicating. In using the client's language the social worker must observe and listen carefully for the client's metaphors, figures of speech, and concepts of reality. This approach to practice is quite different from most others, which usually require the client to learn to speak the language of whatever theoretical approach the clinician is using. According to Nardone and Watzlawick (1993), research has consistently found that people feel most comfortable by things familiar and/or similar to

them. Initially adopting the client's verbal and nonverbal communication style communicates such familiarity and similarity.

2. *Defining the problem* involves getting a concrete and specific definition and description from the client. Problems can fall within three general categories: (1) a person's relationship with herself or himself, (2) a person's relationship with others, and (3) a person's relationship with the world, which involves "the social environment, the values and norms of the social context within which the person lives" (Nardone & Walzlawick, 1993, p. 49). Eliciting a concrete and specific definition of the problem involves the social worker obtaining the following information from the client: (1) How does the client define the problem? (2) How is the problem manifested? (3) Who is involved when the problem appears, worsens, or does not appear? (4) Where does the problem usually appear? (5) In what situations does the problem occur? (6) How and how often does the problem manifest itself? (7) Whom or what does the problem benefit? (8) What would be the negative consequences if the problem disappeared? (Nardone & Watzlawick, 1993, p. 50). In other words, the problem needs to be defined from the client's perspective as concretely and specifically as possible in terms of who, what, where, when, how, and how often.

3. *Identifying unsuccessful attempted solutions* indicates how the client and/or significant others are caught up in a vicious cycle of first-order change. At this point the social worker wants to know what the client and significant others have been doing in attempting to solve the presenting problem and reach the desired goal. By identifying the unsuccessful attempted solutions of first-order change, the clinician initially learns what types of interventions to avoid using; Fisch et al. (1982) refer to this as the "mine field" (p. 114). After eliciting from the client in as much detail as possible the unsuccessful attempts to solve the problem, it is usually helpful to ask the client if any of these have been helpful. The client's usual response is "no," or else he or she would not be there in the session with the clinician. Having this conversation with clients usually is helpful in increasing their motivation to try doing something different because what they have tried so far has not worked for them. The MRI approach assumes that the problem-maintaining patterns of the vicious cycle may have nothing to do with what got the entire process going in the first place. Therefore, it is not necessary to investigate a client's intrapsychic world or past history (Nardone & Watlawick, 1993, p. 52).

4. *Defining the outcome goal* also needs to be done as concretely and specifically as possible and from the client's perspective. In defining the goal the social worker is asking the client to describe a future in which the problem no longer exists or at least has been significantly reduced to the client's satisfaction. In addition, outcome goals should be defined in the positive rather than in terms of the absence of something. The goal provides a specific focus for treatment and provides a basis for evaluating practice (Greene, 1989; Nardone & Waltzlawick, 1993). Setting a specific outcome goal also is an indirect use of visualization in that the client, in describing a future without the problem, must imagine what this will be like for him or her and significant others (*unguided imagery*). In addition, the worker and client mutually discussing and agreeing upon the focus of treatment can increase the client's cooperation in and commitment to achieving the outcome goal (Nardone & Watzlawick, 1993). To achieve as much specificity and concreteness as possible in defining an outcome goal, the MRI approach advocates asking the client what he or she would consider to be the first minimal indicator of change. To obtain this the worker could ask the client: "What, if it were to happen, would you see as a first sign that a significant, though maybe small, change had occurred?" (Fisch et al., 1982, p. 79) or "What would be the first minimal change to occur that would indicate you were starting to turn the corner towards some meaningful change?" Such a question breaks down the problem and goal further and increases the likelihood of the client achieving and experiencing some success early in the treatment.

5. The *development and implementation of change strategies* follows from the assessed problem, goal, and attempted solutions. For a

client system stuck in a vicious cycle, the change strategies usually must be of a second-order nature to bring about lasting positive change. Second-order change strategies tend to be the opposite of the problem-maintaining attempted solutions involved in the vicious cycle; consequently, interventions focus primarily on interrupting the attempted solution(s) (Fisch et al., 1982). Strategic therapy assumes that clients have the resources to make desired changes once the vicious cycle is disrupted. As a general rule, the clinician's initial intervention(s) should seek only small change (Fisch et al., 1982). Clients are much more likely to comply with requests for small change, and this can set change processes in motion, which gets the momentum going toward larger change (Fisch et al., 1982). Some specific second-order change interventions will be discussed below.

6. In strategic therapy *termination of treatment* is not as much of a significant issue as it is in many other therapeutic approaches (Fisch et al., 1982). A strategic approach to treatment tends to be briefer than most other approaches because it is problem- and goal-focused and the primary interventions are tasks clients carry out in their everyday lives. The treatment relationship, therefore, is viewed as important in facilitating the client's completing the tasks rather than being the primary vehicle for client change. Given that the clinician and client keep a focus on resolving the presenting problem and achieving the outcome goal throughout treatment, the stage is set for terminating treatment when this has been accomplished (Fisch et al., 1982). When a presenting problem and an outcome goal are concretely and specifically defined by the client, then both the clinician and client will more likely be aware of when this has been achieved and treatment is no longer necessary.

The Interventions and Strategies

A strategic approach to treatment is a way of thinking and, thus, provides more than just a list of interventions. In this section of the chapter, however, some commonly used strategic interventions will be reviewed. A strategic approach to treatment has generated numerous interventions over the years. The interventions of a strategic approach to treatment can be grouped into four categories: (1) reframing, (2) restraint from change, (3) positioning, and (4) between-session tasks (behavioral prescriptions) (Dowd & Pace, 1989).

Reframing. Reframing involves the clinician offering a plausible, alternative meaning to some aspect of the "facts" of the client's presenting problematic situation. Therefore, the "facts" of the situation do not change; rather, the meaning attributed to them by the client and/or significant others changes (Watzlawick et al., 1974). Most of the time reframing involves the clinician taking the "facts" of the presenting situation the client and/or significant others have defined negatively and providing a positive meaning to them; this has also been referred to as positive connotation (Selvini Palazzoli et al., 1978a). It is important that the clinician offer the plausible, alternative meaning in a tentative manner in order to avoid an unnecessary power struggle with the client over its rightness or wrongness. When reframing is successful, clients cannot return to their previous narrow view of reality that contributed to the problem-maintaining vicious cycles (Watzlawick et al., 1974). The suggested positive reframe may introduce enough novelty to the client's assumptive world that it will start to put a small "chink" in the client's habitual problem-maintaining patterns (Nardone & Watzlawick, 1993).

An example of reframing used in family therapy would be suggesting that a 6-year-old child's acting out could be a result of caring for and protecting a depressed parent. When the child acts out the parent gets angry at him or her and, thus, the child's misbehavior mobilizes the parent out of his or her depression. The parent being angry is also reassuring to the child, since usually children would rather have their parents angry at them rather than seeing them depressed.

Restraint from Change. Restraining clients from changing can be useful in the initial sessions and later when positive change is beginning to occur. Restraint from change interventions can take several forms, with some of the more commonly used ones involving the clinician suggesting to the client that he or she "for now, should probably go slowly in trying to make any changes" or "it might not be a good idea to try to make too many changes too quickly." Restraining interventions can be helpful with compliant clients who present problems that are at least partially maintained by the attempts to keep them from happening, such as obsessive thinking, anxiety, and insomnia (Tennen, Eron, & Rohrbaugh, 1991, p. 197); complying with such restraints will short-circuit the problem-maintaining patterns.

Restraining interventions are also useful with clients who tend to be oppositional and noncompliant (resistant), in that one way the client can oppose the clinician is by taking some steps in the direction from which the clinician is restraining him or her. For clients who have not complied with homework tasks and/or are ambivalent about changing, it might be helpful for the clinician to restrain change by discussing with the client "the possible dangers of improvement" and/or the "possible benefits of not changing." An intervention such as this is the opposite of the client's significant others, who have been trying to get the client to change by focusing only on the benefits of the client changing.

Restraint from change is helpful when clients have high expectations from themselves or others for change. Frequently clients respond with relief when the clinician uses a restraint from change intervention. Clients can experience the clinician as accepting and nonjudgmental when the clinician, unlike themselves and others, will not be putting high expectations on them for immediate change; this can also facilitate the joining process and client cooperation with treatment. Clinicians often tend to have expectations of even more change once clients start to make some positive changes. Sometimes change, even small change, needs time to stabilize; restraint from change allows such stabilization to occur. In addition, if the client tends to be oppositional, then he or she may make even more positive changes, which is what one wants to occur in treatment in the first place.

Predicting a Relapse. Many people, including clinicians, tend to have expectations of even more change once clients start to make some positive changes. Sometimes change, even small change,

needs time to stabilize before clients attempt to make even more change; predicting a relapse allows such stabilization to occur. In addition, if the client tends to be oppositional, then he or she may make even more positive change, which is what one wants to occur in treatment in the first place. The clinician predicting a relapse can also be helpful when clients are starting to make positive changes in treatment. Such an intervention might involve suggesting to the client that he or she might be changing too much too fast, and thus it might be a good idea for him or her to slow down for the time being. Often when clients start making positive changes clinicians will become excited and start encouraging clients to make even more changes. However, the client may start regressing if he or she has not yet consolidated and stabilized the changes made thus far and/or tends to take an oppositional position toward outside influence; use of predicting a relapse can prevent this from happening.

Sometimes when clients relapse after making some positive changes, they try too hard to get themselves (or their partner or child) to go back to where they were in terms of their progress. This overcorrecting can sometimes make matters worse. Another possible response for some people might be getting so discouraged that permanent positive change can happen that they give up hope and stop working on change. Normalizing and warning them about a possible relapse increases the likelihood of their being able to relax and ride out the relapse and let nature take its course. In an end-of-session message that contains predicting a relapse, the practitioner might say the following:

Now I don't want to "rain on your parade" (or "be the skunk at the picnic") but I feel I should warn you to not be surprised if between now and our next meeting you experience some backsliding. Of course, I hope you don't, but it is not uncommon that in the process of change we take three steps forward and two steps backward, at least temporarily. If you don't experience any backsliding, then that's great. However, if you do some backsliding, then don't freak out, but just realize that it is a normal part of the change process and that the backsliding is usually only temporary.

Positioning. According to Parrott (2004), positioning is "the dynamic construction of personal identities relative to those of others and is an essential feature of social interaction" (p. 29). In social interactions people take positions or stances on different ideas, issues, themselves, or other people, especially those with whom they are in active conversation, based on their values and beliefs as to what is good or bad, right or wrong, desirable or undesirable, and so on (Harre & Moghaddam, 2004). People can take positions or counter-positions in an attempt to position themselves or other people in ways that can result in various positions, such as competent/incompetent, leader/follower, powerful/powerless (victim), and so on. Whenever we are taking a position in a conversation, we are also implicitly or explicitly inviting or offering "the other person(s) we are addressing a position (or choice of positions) from which to respond" (Winslade, 2005, p. 353). People tend to interpret their interactions from a position once they have taken "that strategic position" (Tirado & Galvez, 2008, p. 230). At the same time, the positioning process is very dynamic and subject to change. Positions are negotiable and people can question and resist the positions into which other people invite or try to maneuver (Tirado & Galvez, 2008).

Often problem-maintaining patterns involve the client's friends, family members, and others consistently communicating their position of optimism that the client can and will get better. The client's response to such optimism is a position of pessimism. However, the more optimistic (competent) the significant others are, the more the client responds with pessimism (incompetence), resulting in an ongoing, spiraling vicious cycle of first-order change. One way to begin to disrupt this vicious cycle is for the clinician to take an even more pessimistic position than the client. The clinician can do this after listening to the client's story about his or her interactions with the significant others around the problem and then responding with something like, "Instead of being all that optimistic about your situation, Mr. Jones, actually I'm surprised that things aren't really worse than you say they are." If the client has experienced a number of "treatment failures," the clinician might want to add, "perhaps all we might realistically be able to accomplish in our work together is for you to learn to live with your situation." The clinician's communication of pessimism greater than the client's then invites the client to challenge (take a counter-position) the clinician's

pessimism with optimism. Positioning can be especially helpful with oppositional clients who are "help-rejecting complainers"—those who play the "Why Don't You/Yes But" game with professionals (Berne, 1972).

Between-Session Tasks. The previous interventions involve how the clinician responds to clients during sessions; the ones presented here involve tasks the client is to engage in between sessions. Many approaches to practice believe that clients will make desired changes if they understand "why" they currently behave as they do (develop insight). Strategic therapy, on the other hand, believes that insight is not necessary for change to occur, and if the client does develop insight, he or she will do so after having made some desired behavioral changes (Nardone & Watzlawick, 1993). To bring about these changes, the strategic approach advocates using behavioral prescriptions (Nardone & Watzlawick, 1993), also referred to as directives (Haley, 1987).

Direct Tasks. Clinicians can use tasks directly by giving the client good advice and information in order to try to bring about desired change. Offering advice to clients about how to change usually will be ineffective because by the time they enter treatment other people have already given them a lot of advice, which the clients have not followed (Haley, 1987). Giving advice usually involves telling clients how they can stop having the problem and symptoms. Such advice and information are first-order change interventions, which most theoretical approaches emphasize in one form or another (Dowd & Pace, 1989). Though the advice and information may be correct, many clients do not comply because they experience it as being critical and judgmental of them. Clients may not comply with such advice and information as a way to maintain some dignity and self-esteem (Greene, 1996). In addition, clients may not comply with such direct interventions as a result of the double-binding communications they received during their developmental years in the family of origin. They have learned to perceive the world through double-binding lenses and thus tend not to trust direct communications; they tend to be on guard against the "hidden message."

Indirect Tasks (Therapeutic Paradox). In strategic therapy, interventions are designed to bring about second-order change and are also usually considered to be paradoxical. A therapeutic paradox (double bind) is the mirror image of the pathological paradox (double bind) (Hoffman, 1981; Watzlawick et al., 1967). In the pathological paradox the client, when growing up, was given prescriptions in the family of origin about how to feel, think, and behave appropriately. However, when the client did what was appropriate he or she was ignored, criticized, or punished for not performing in the right way or not having the right motivations. Therefore, in the family of origin, the child was told verbally to "change" but the nonverbal context said "don't change." In the therapeutic paradox, the client, in so many words, receives the message of "don't change" in a context for change (Hoffman, 1981; Watzlawick et al., 1967).

Therapeutic paradox involves prescribing a change in either the usual pattern and/or sequence around the exhibition of the presenting problem or the frequency or intensity of the problem itself. The clinician does not explicitly focus on trying to improve the presenting problem but rather just changing some small aspect of the Gestalt of the problematic situation. In doing so, the clinician asks the client to go ahead and have the problem/symptom but to modify its performance in some way. Therefore, instead of directly trying to get the client to stop having the problem, the clinician "goes with the resistance" and utilizes the problem (symptom) in the service of the changes the client desires. A properly designed therapeutic paradox (double bind) results in the following: if the client complies with the prescription, the problem-maintaining pattern will be interrupted and thus change will begin occurring (compliance-based paradox); however, if the client does not follow the clinician's prescription, then the only way he or she can resist is by making some changes in the desired direction (defiance-based paradox). In the therapeutic paradox (double bind) the client is "changed if she or he does or changed if she or he doesn't" which is contrary to the pathological paradox (double bind) in which the client is "damned if she or he does or damned if she or he doesn't." Such a prescription can also contribute to change because the client is now asked to

voluntarily perform an aspect of the presenting problem, which previously had been defined as being entirely "involuntary" (Haley, 1987; Nardone & Watzlawick, 1993; Watzlawick et al, 1967).

Cade and O'Hanlon (1993), in discussing designing paradoxical prescriptions, listed several general ways to do so (taken from O'Hanlon, 1987, pp. 36–37):

- Changing the frequency/rate of the symptom/symptom pattern
- Changing the duration of the symptom/symptom pattern
- Changing the time (of day/week/month/year) of the symptom/symptom pattern
- Changing the location (in the body or geographically) of the symptom/symptom pattern
- Changing the intensity of the symptom/symptom pattern
- Changing some other quality or circumstance of the symptom
- Changing the sequence (order) of events around the symptom
- Creating a short circuit in the sequence (i.e., a jump from the beginning of the sequence to the end)
- Interrupting or otherwise preventing all or part of the sequence from occurring ("derailing")
- Adding or subtracting at least one element to or from the sequence
- Breaking up any previously whole element into smaller elements
- Having the symptom performed without the symptom pattern
- Having the symptom pattern performed minus the symptom
- Reversing the pattern
- Linking the occurrence of the symptom pattern to another pattern—usually an undesired experience, an avoided activity, or a desirable but difficult-to-attain goal ("symptom-contingent task").

Most therapeutic paradoxes involve prescribing some change in the patterns and sequence around the problem. Such second-order change interventions are considered to be indirect since change in the presenting problem occurs because of first focusing on making some change in the problem-maintaining patterns (Nardone & Watzlawick, 1993). There is no limit to the types of indirect prescriptions. The indirect prescriptions that can be used are limited to the nature of clients' presenting problems, problem-maintaining patterns, and the creativity of clinicians. Additional indirect prescriptions have been developed, and some are briefly described below.

Advertising Instead of Concealing. Some problems are made worse by individuals trying to conceal them. For instance, it is not unusual for someone with an anxiety or phobia to try to conceal and control it when in the presence of other people. However, one can become more anxious worrying about whether the anxiety will become evident. In other words, the person gets anxious about being anxious (anticipatory anxiety). Consequently, such a person can become so anxious that the feared event happens anyway. One way to deal with this situation is for the person to announce the existence of the anxiety and the fears he or she has about it right off to others—to deliberately perform the very thing the client fears. One example given by Watzlawick et al. (1974) is anxiety about public speaking. The more one tries to relax and conceal anxiety about speaking publicly, the more tense and anxious one becomes and the less effective the speaking becomes. An opposite tactic would be for the person to say something (very calm and straight-faced) like the following: "Before I start my speech there is one thing I would like to tell the group. I get very anxious when I give a speech. I just want to forewarn you that I could get so anxious that I might faint and pass out. But don't worry, I usually recover quickly and give an even better speech from that point on." The audience is very likely to laugh at this, and so will the speaker thus becoming more relaxed. By performing this prescription, the client is able to make voluntary what previously had been considered involuntary, thus allowing the client to gain some control over the "uncontrollable." Even if a person does not follow through on this prescription, just suggesting it to a client can be therapeutic because he or she most likely will be thinking of this suggestion and chuckling inside and feeling more relaxed when preparing for and giving a speech.

The Great Effects of Small Causes. Another way a person can escalate his or her anxiety is by being "perfectionistic." This can be problematic on the job; people may constantly worry that they will make a mistake, will be considered incompetent, and will be fired from the job. The more they worry about this, the more tense and anxious they become, and the less they like their jobs. Eventually, worry and anxiety about job performance can occupy most of their nonworking time as well. One way of helping the client deal with this "no-win" situation is to suggest that he or she purposely make one small, inconsequential mistake every day on the job. Again, the client deliberately performs voluntarily what heretofore had been defined as being involuntary; thus, the client is able to have some control over the "uncontrollable" (Watzlawick et al., 1974).

A version of this intervention can be applied to clients who are underachieving academically. A dynamic in this situation is a perfectionistic client who procrastinates in studying and doing course assignments. Students such as this often have exceptionally high standards and pressure themselves for nothing less than "A" work. Because of the pressure and fear of doing less than "A" work, the student puts off doing the schoolwork until the last possible minute and ends up doing mediocre work. In this situation, the clinician can instruct the student for his or her next assignment to deliberately try to do only "C" work. Aiming for a grade of only a "C" takes the pressure off the student and allows her or him to actually enjoy doing the assignment. Following this prescription usually results in the student decreasing procrastination and increasing his or her academic performance.

The Devil's Pact. An underlying issue involved in clients' staying stuck is their unwillingness to take risks necessary for change to occur. It could be said that always playing it safe is the attempted solution maintaining the problem. This dynamic is often seen in clients who are "help-rejecting complainers." Nothing a clinician suggests seems appropriate for them. Sometimes they may have agreed to a homework assignment but did not follow through on it. Despite their resistance, they are still reporting unhappiness with the status quo and a strong desire for relief. In the devil's pact, clients are asked to agree to carry out a task that is guaranteed to bring about change, but they must agree to do it before the clinician will tell them what it is. If the client makes such an agreement, then some change has already occurred, since he or she has now taken the risk of agreeing to an intervention before knowing what it is. In this instance he or she did not play it safe. After the client makes this agreement, the task the clinician asks him or her to do can be any number of possibilities. It is best to use the devil's pact toward the end of a session, thus not telling clients what the sure-fire intervention is, and to suggest clients think about it between sessions to ensure they are making the right decision; this heightens their anticipation and, thus, willingness to change.

Odd-day/Even-day Ritual In this prescription, the client is asked to perform one behavior on one day and another behavior, usually the opposite, on another day. With an individual client, the clinician asks him or her to perform the problematic behavior on odd-numbered days and the desired outcome behavior on even-numbered days. This prescription helps to reduce client resistance and increase risk-taking in that he or she is asked to make desired changes in half-steps rather than full steps (Bergman, 1983). In addition, clients are more likely to comply, since change is requested to last for no more than one day (Bergman, 1983).

A version of this prescription can be used in family therapy if a child is getting contradictory (double-binding) messages from parents and the parents are making no efforts to reconcile their inconsistencies (Selvini Palazzoli, Boscolo, Cecchin, & Prata, 1978a). In this case one parent is instructed that on even days of the week (Tuesdays, Thursdays, and Saturdays) he or she is to be completely in charge of parenting and the other parent is to behave as if he or she were not there. On odd days of the week the other parent is then to be completely in charge of parenting and the first parent is to behave as if he or she is not there. On Sundays, everyone in the family must spontaneously do what they usually do. This prescription can be adapted for use with single-parent families when a grandparent is giving the child messages that contradict the parent. Another adaptation of this can be used when a single parent is giving the child

inconsistent messages. For example, the single parent can be asked to be strict and firm with the child on even days and lenient on odd days.

Two other skills the clinician can use throughout working with clients are "taking a one-down position" and "using qualifying language" (Fisch et al., 1982). In the treatment situation the clinician is inherently in a one-up, authority position and the client feels in a one-down position by the very nature of having a problem(s) necessitating professional help. Such an arrangement may increase client resistance and decrease cooperation, since people often resent experts and authorities (Fisch et al., 1982), especially while feeling one-down. To counter this barrier, it is helpful for the clinician to take a one-down position. The one-down position is often subtly conveyed and can be expressed in a variety of ways. An example of taking a one-down position is, "I'm sorry, but I'm a fairly concrete kind of person in my thinking, so will you bear with me while I ask some questions which may seem to be nitpicky." The one-down position can also be used if the client asks the clinician early in treatment what he or she should do in particular situation; the clinician can respond, "I really can't say right now. I am still getting to know you, and you are the expert on you. You know more about yourself than anyone else, so I need your help in getting to know you better."

In using qualifying language the clinician refrains from taking a definitive position, thus preventing an unnecessary power struggle with the client (Fisch et al., 1982). In making qualifying comments and suggestions, the clinician uses such words as "may," "depends upon," "if," and so on. By using such qualifying words, the clinician can introduce novel ideas or behaviors so that the client cannot reject them outright just because they came from the clinician. Clients are much more likely to consider the ideas or try the suggestions if they feel they have the freedom to reject them. An example of using qualifying language is, "I have some ideas about your situation which may or may not be true or helpful. I have found what I am about to say and suggest to be true and helpful for some clients I have worked with who have had problems similar to yours, but this may not be the case in your situation; it is just food for thought at this time." Another example is, "I have a suggestion to make, but I'm not sure how much it will accomplish. It will depend on your ability to use your imagination and, perhaps, on your readiness to take a step toward improvement" (Fisch et al., 1982, p. 31).

The Washington School Approach (Haley/Madanes)

The Washington School was developed by Jay Haley (Haley & Richeport-Haley, 2003), who later collaborated extensively with Chloe Madanes; for the sake of brevity their approach will be referred to as the Washington School (Keim, 2000). As a result of Haley's time at MRI and at the Philadelphia Child Guidance Clinic, where he spent several years working after he left MRI, the Washington School combines elements of both the structural and strategic approaches. Like MRI the Washington School emphasizes using between-session tasks not only to change patterns but also to restructure how a family is organized. The Washington School approach has been developed to be used primarily with couples and families. An acronym this approach uses for thinking about and organizing therapy is PUSH:

Protection. By the time a family seeks professional services, they have often come to view the person with the presenting problem as being malevolently motivated, as if he or she is trying to hurt the other family members. In the Washington School, family members are viewed as usually trying to protect each other, but sometimes they may do that in ways that are not helpful. Thus, in the Washington School approach the person with the presenting problem is viewed as trying to somehow protect the other family members, especially parents or the other spouse, by means of having the problem.

Unit. The basic unit for working with couples and families involves at least three people (a triad/triangle). A unit of three allows for a sufficient variety of interventions to interrupt problem patterns and restructure the family organization.

Sequence. Presenting problems triggered by, occur in, and are maintained by a sequence of interactional patterns. According to Keim (2000),

"[the] goal of strategic therapy is to replace the maladaptive sequences of behavior with healthier ones" (p. 178).

Hierarchy. In families the parents are the ones with power, authority, and responsibility; thus, there are appropriate generational differences in families. A family member can develop a presenting problem when there is confusion and breaching of generational boundaries. "Attempting to change hierarchy is one of the most commonly used interventions in the Washington School. Marital difficulties are often mapped as having power imbalances in the marital hierarchy" (Keim, 2000, p. 179).

According to Haley (1987) the Washington School approach structures the clinical work with clients by following five stages:

1. *Social engagement of the family.* The therapist should address each family member in an effort to help him or her feel less anxious about being there. This step helps to set the stage for establishing the importance of each family member being involved and for beginning to redefine the problem as belonging to the family system and not just the individual. The clinician engages the family as if he or she were hosting the family in his or her own home.

2. *Definition of the problem.* Initially the clinician should introduce himself or herself to the family and explain his or her role. During this step the clinician shares with the family what he or she already knows about them and the presenting problem and explains why he or she asked all family members to attend. In explaining this the clinician usually describes the family members as having valuable knowledge and insight about the problem because they know the client and their family a lot better than the clinician does or ever will, and thus the clinician needs their help. Next the clinician asks the family members for their views on the problem and how they define it. At this point each family member addresses his or her responses directly to the clinician; discussions between family members are avoided. During this process the clinician listens carefully and validates each family member's perspective. After listening carefully, the clinician redefines the

individual's problem as one shared by the other family members.

3. *Interaction stage.* The clinician next asks the family members to discuss the presenting problem among themselves. It is very important that the clinician not get pulled into the discussion; this should be a relatively open discussion among the family members. During this discussion the clinician should look for and be able to observe interpersonal patterns and the structure and organization of the family (coalitions, triangles, hierarchy, etc.).

4. *Definition of desired changes.* The goal should be defined in terms of what the family members will see differently when the presenting problem is resolved. Like the problem, the family should define the changes concretely, specifically, and with as many behavioral indicators as possible.

5. *Ending the interview with directives and scheduling the next appointment.* The clinician develops a between-session task based on his or her hypotheses about the family dynamics and organization; this task is given in the form of a message delivered at the end of the session. The purpose of the task is to change the way the family members interact with each other, especially the person with the presenting problem, and thus changing their patterns of interacting and the structure and organization of the family. For the family members to buy into performing the task, it is usually necessary for the clinician to provide them a plausible rationale that is consistent with their values and beliefs, using their language and figures of speech.

The Washington School uses all the interventions used in the MRI approach to change patterns and sequences of interactions. However, because the Washington School approach also focuses on restructuring the couple or family system, it has developed other interventions for this purpose (Haley, 1984; Haley & Richeport-Haley, 2007; Madanes, 1981, 1984). Some of these interventions include:

1. Asking the parents to direct their symptomatic child to have the problem
2. Asking the parents to direct their symptomatic child to pretend to have the problem

3. Prescribing the pretending of the function of the symptom
4. Prescribing a reversal of the family hierarchy
5. Prescribing who will have the presenting problem
6. Prescribing the presenting problem with a small modification of the context
7. Paradoxical ordeals
8. The illusion of alternatives.

Task Frames (Rationales for Tasks)

Clients need to make sense of the therapeutic tasks for them to be willing to perform the tasks and/or continue in treatment. The clinician therefore needs to provide the client a plausible rationale for the task that makes sense to the client. In strategic therapy the most effective way to do this is for the clinician to frame the task using the client's position on the cause of the problem, his or her motivations, or the motivations of other people (Fisch, Weakland, & Segal, 1982). In other words, task frames (rationales) are constructed using the client's values, beliefs, and language (metaphors and figures of speech). For example, the parents of an acting-out teenage son may unintentionally be engaged in a pattern of over-functioning for the teenager, with the rationale that they must do things for their son because he is so incompetent. They further describe themselves as being devoted to their son and self-sacrificing for his benefit. Thus, they are involved in a repetitive pattern of first-order change in that the more they over-function for him to try to make him more competent, the more incompetent he perceives himself and the more he continues to under-function. Because second-order change involves doing the opposite of the problem-maintaining pattern, then one way for them to make a pattern shift resulting in second-order change is for them to start behaving incompetently relative to their son. One way to frame the rationale for this task is for the clinician to emphasize how much of a "sacrifice" this will require them to make. Presenting this example, however, does not do justice to the time, skill, and nuance required by the clinician in order to be successful in getting the parents to accept this frame and to make the necessary pattern change in parenting their son.

Principal Applications in Social Work Practice

Strategic therapy provides a way of viewing problem formation and problem resolution involving both clinical and non-clinical situations. In regard to use with various client configurations, strategic therapy has been used extensively in clinical practice with individuals (Fisch, Weakland, & Segal, 1982), couples (Coyne, 1986; Ray, 2003; Shoham, Rohrbaugh, & Cleary, 2008; Sutton, Ray, & Cole, 2003), families in general (Segal, 1991; Segal & Bavelas, 1983), and single-parent families in particular (Bray & Anderson, 1984; Morawetz & Walker, 1984).

The strategic approach has been used successfully with a variety of presenting problems and types of clients who social workers often treat in a variety of practice settings: depression (Chubb, 1982), post-stroke depression (Watzlawick & Coyne, 1980), suicidal behavior (Aldridge & Rossiter, 1983), anxiety-related somatic complaints (Greene & Sattin, 1985), chronic pain (Shutty & Sheras, 1991), chronic physical illness (Norfleet, 1983), phobias (Nardone, 1995; Nardone & Portelli, 2005), obsessive-compulsiveness (Nardone, 1995; Nardone & Portelli, 2005), alcoholism (Lewis & Allen-Byrd, 2007; Potter-Efron & Potter-Efron, 1986), chemical dependency (McGarty, 1986), adolescent substance abuse (Heath & Ayers, 1991), different cultural groups (Anger-Diaz, Schlanger, Rincon, & Mendoza, 2004; Appasamy, 1995; Richeport-Haley, 1998; Soo-Hoo, 1999), acting-out adolescents (Cecchin, Lane, & Ray, 2003), school problems (Littrel & Peterson, 2001; Nelson, 2006), vague medical problems (Weakland & Fisch, 1984), child protective services (Weakland & Jordan, 1992), primary medical care (Fraser, Morris, Smith, & Solovey, 2001, 2002), severe mental disability (Bergman, 1982; Haley, 1980; Soo-Hoo, 1995), children (Chubb, 1983; Efron, 1981; Zimmerman & Protinsky, 1990), older adults (Herr & Weakland, 1979), crisis intervention (Fraser, 1986), eating disorders (Moley, 1983), marital problems (Madanes, 1984), domestic violence (Madanes, 1995; McCloskey & Fraser, 1997), and psychosis (Haley & Schiff, 1993). Because strategic therapy focuses on interrupting problem-maintaining patterns and family structure rather than treating diagnoses, it has wide application. Therefore, if used properly, the strategic approach is not contraindicated for use with any type of client problem. With some presenting problems, such as suicidal ideation or substance abuse, however, one needs to be careful to not prescribe the symptom but rather a change in some aspect of the problem-maintaining pattern or context. Changing some aspect of the pattern/context might introduce enough novelty to the client that small, positive change occurs.

In two early books, the members of MRI used a number of organizational and community examples to explain and illustrate various concepts (Watzlawick, Beavin, & Jackson, 1967; Watzlawick, Weakland, & Fisch, 1974). Some specific strategic therapy concepts and interventions have been used in assessing and intervening in organizations and communities. Reframing has been systematically applied as a skill in leading and managing organizations (Bolman & Deal, 1991; Fairhurst & Sarr, 1996). The double-bind concept has been used to examine intra- and interorganizational dynamics (Markowitz & Nitzberg, 1982) and the dynamics of community change (Andelson, 1981). The concept of second-order change is increasingly being used to analyze and change organizations and communities (Beitler, 2006; Crawford & Stein, 2005; Gharajedaghi, 2007; Marzano & Waters, 2009; Meynell, 2005; Perkins, Bess, Cooper, Jones, Armstead, & Speer, 2007; Sartorius, 2006; Sun & Scott, 2005; Wilson, 2006). Some scholars have also added the notion of third-order change to first- and second-order change in facilitating organizational development (Bartunek & Moch, 1987, 1994; Tsoukas & Papoulias, 2005). In addition, second-order change and strategic therapy has been used to analyze how individuals change within organizations (Brandon, 1985; George & Jones, 2001; Morrissette, 1989; Schinder-Zimmerman, Washle, & Protinsky, 1990; Woodruff & Engle, 1985).

The concepts of first- and second-order change have been adapted and applied in discussions of first-, second-, and third-order reality (Greene, 1996; Keeney, 1987; Keeney & Silverstein, 1986). First-order reality deals with discrete behaviors of individuals, second-order reality is the interactional pattern in which discrete behaviors are a part, and third-order reality is the larger social ecology in which the interactional pattern is one of several patterns. What is involved here are levels of reality that are increasingly more complex; the communicational patterns at the higher levels can override what takes place at the lower levels. The implication for social work treatment is that if interventions at a lower level are not effective, then interventions at the next higher level may be necessary. Therefore, first-order reality involves intervening with individuals, second-order reality involves treatment of couples and the nuclear family, and third-order reality involves intervening with the extended family and/or the parts of the larger community impinging upon the client system. Keeney's model and strategic therapy have considerable potential for macro-level social work practice. For instance, Allen (1987) has pointed out how a strategic perspective can be used in viewing and bringing about large-scale change.

Administrative and Training Issues in Strategic Therapy

One must be able to use a number of skills and techniques with a high degree of competence and finesse in order to do strategic therapy competently. To develop such competence, one needs specific training in and supervision on strategic therapy. The MRI approach (Anger-Diaz & Schlanger, 2005; Eubanks, 2002) and the Washington School (Haley, 1996; Mazza, 1988) have been providing systematic training and supervision in their approaches to strategic therapy for many years. Many graduates of these programs have gone on and established training and supervision programs of their own. Though these three training programs differ in various ways, they all have the following in common: (1) required reading; (2) role play; (3) watching videotapes of the clinical work of others; (4) observing the clinical work of others from behind a one-way mirror; (5) having their own clinical work observed by others from behind a one-way mirror; (6) interrupting sessions to give the trainee suggestions and corrective feedback; and (7) having videotapes of one's own clinical work viewed and critiqued.

Other learning activities can be used if one does not have the time or money to receive training and supervision at one of these strategic therapy training programs. A person can receive training and supervision at his or her place of employment if there is a supervisor who is competent in strategic therapy. Also, one can do co-therapy and/or form a peer supervision group with other social workers who want to learn strategic therapy and are at a similar level of competence (Rabi, Lehr, & Hayner, 1984). This peer supervision group can view and critique videotapes of each other's clinical work and/or once or twice a month take turns observing from behind a one-way mirror. In addition, one can attend workshops on strategic therapy as well as rent or purchase videotapes developed by the experts. Finally, of course, one should read as much as possible on the topic of strategic therapy.

A social worker who is the only one using strategic therapy in an agency can expect some fallout and reaction from coworkers, supervisors, and administrators (Bobrow, Batchelor, & Harris, 2008). A strategic approach is such a different paradigm than other theoretical approaches that other professionals in the agency may have no idea what you are doing and, thus, may criticize your work. You can feel isolated and frustrated if you are the only strategic therapist in an agency. This is one reason that being in a strategic therapy training program or having a peer supervision group is important. Keeping in mind the basic tenet of the MRI approach of "doing what works" is helpful, as well as consistently having good results with difficult clients. Others in the agency are then likely to leave you alone, and some might even start asking questions about what it is you are doing.

Empirical Base

The MRI group frequently makes 3-month follow-up calls to clients to obtain their self-evaluation of the success of treatment. In one report on 148 cases, Segal (1991b) stated that 38% experienced no improvement, 26% had significant improvement, and 36% had complete success in that they achieved all their treatment goals; however, there was no control or comparison group. Similar results have been found in other evaluation studies (Geyerhofer & Komori, 2005; Nardone, 1995).

Chubb (1990) compared the efficiency of an HMO that used only the MRI approach to an HMO that used a traditional eclectic-psychodynamic approach. The MRI HMO had no waiting list, whereas the comparison HMO had an average waiting period of 22 weeks. In addition, the MRI HMO clients had many fewer sessions than the comparison HMO and, thus, the MRI therapists were able to see considerably more clients over a 2-year period than the therapists at the comparison HMO. Also, the MRI HMO had many fewer hospital admissions and much shorter average lengths of stay than the comparison condition. Well over 90% of the clients of the MRI HMO reported satisfaction with the services and, according to Chubb (1990), this is quite comparable to client satisfaction ratings reported in other studies. The findings of this study are supportive of the efficiency of the MRI approach in an HMO setting, but the findings were not statistically analyzed, nor were results on effectiveness reported.

Throughout the history and development of strategic therapy, its use in marital and family therapy has been emphasized. Analyses of marital and family therapy research have generally found all the various theoretical approaches, including strategic, to be effective, with no one approach being more effective than any other (Shadish, Montgomery, Wilson, Wilson, Bright, & Okwumabua, 1993; Sprenkle, Davis, & Lebow, 2009). A therapeutic approach combining the techniques of MRI and the strategic therapy of Haley/Madanes was found to be effective in a family approach to psychiatric crises (Langsley, Machotka, & Flomenhaft, 1971). In addition, strategic therapy has been found effective when integrated with other approaches for specific problems such as with structural family therapy in treating substance abuse (Stanton et al., 1982) and behavioral family therapy in treating delinquents (Alexander, Barton, Schiavo, & Parsons, 1976).

The effectiveness of some of the key interventions of strategic therapy has also been examined. In a review of research on the use of paradox with various symptoms and problems, Kim, Poling, and Ascher (1991) found it to be effective with insomnia, agoraphobia, obsessive disorders, and disorders of elimination (urinary frequency/retention and encopresis). The studies reviewed by Kim et al. used single-subject or group designs. In the group designs, paradoxical interventions were consistently found to be more effective than no-treatment control conditions and equally effective to and sometimes more effective than various comparison treatments. These findings are consistent with a meta-analysis of studies on the effectiveness of paradoxical interventions with such problems as insomnia, depression, agoraphobia, procrastination, and stress (Hill, 1987; Shoham-Salomon & Rosenthal, 1987). In addition, Shoham-Salomon and Rosenthal concluded that paradoxical interventions resulted in more durable positive outcomes and were more effective with clients presenting with more severe problems and resistance to treatment than non-paradoxical interventions. Positive reframing and the restraint-from-change intervention of discussing "the dangers of improvement" were both found to be effective in the treatment of depression, with reframing being more effective than restraining (Swoboda, Dowd, & Wise, 1990). Other studies have also found positive reframing to be very effective in the treatment of depression (Shoham-Salom & Rosenthal, 1987).

The research on the effectiveness of using strategic therapy with couples and families is mounting. Strategic therapy is the basis of brief strategic family therapy, a well-established evidence-based approach (Horigian, Suarez-Morales, Robbins, Zarate, Mayora, Mitrani, & Szapocnik, 2005; Szapocnik, Robbins, Mitrani, Santisteban, Hervis, & Williams, 2002), and integrative family and systems treatment, a newer evidence-informed approach (Lee, Greene, Hsu, Solovey, Grove, Fraser, Washburn, & Teater, 2009). Elements of strategic therapy are integral parts of the other established evidence-based approaches to couple and family therapy, such as multidimensional family therapy (Liddle, Rodriguez, Dakof, Kanzki, & Marvel, 2005), functional family therapy (Sexton & Alexander, 2005), and multisystemic therapy (Schoenwald & Henggeler, 2005).

Conclusions

Over the years strategic therapy has been criticized for being manipulative, primarily because of its indirectness and use of paradox (Hoffman, 1985). Therapist manipulation and being in a one-up position are seen as being disrespectful and disempowering to clients. It is true that early in its development, the proponents of strategic therapy placed considerable emphasis on the therapist being in control of treatment and "tricking" clients out of their symptoms. A basic tenet in the use of paradox has been that it works best when concealed from clients. However, it has been pointed out (Haley, 1987; Strupp, 1977) that regardless of theoretical orientation, a clinician must use some concealment in that he or she cannot completely reveal all of his or her thoughts to the client, and, therefore, all therapy involves some manipulation.

In recent years, however, strategic therapy has been modified in ways that minimize its manipulative qualities (Greene, 2006; Greene, Jones, Frappier, Klein, & Culton, 1996). These modifications include: (1) Designing indirect, paradoxical techniques that are plausible explanations for the client's situation. For instance, when restraining change by suggesting that "the client should go slowly and not change too much too quickly," it may very well be that doing so is in the client's best interest in the short run; the decision for making any changes resides with the client (Greene, 2006; Greene et al., 1996); (2) The clinician suggesting, not prescribing, to the client both direct and indirect interventions (sometimes three or more interventions) to clients but prescribing none (Greene, 2006; Greene et al., 1996). This introduces novel ideas to clients but still leaves it up to the client to accept or reject any of them; (3) Discussing and designing paradox openly with clients (Hill, 1992). In this way, the client is an active participant in the construction and implementation of paradoxical interventions. This is consistent with some research that suggests that openly discussing paradox with clients does not hinder its effectiveness (Kim, Poling, & Ascher, 1991). In addition, research evidence indicates that therapeutic paradox, even when concealed, is not deleterious to the clinician–client relationship (Kim et al., 1991).

A basic assumption of strategic therapy is that clients already have the strengths and resources they need in order to make the changes they want. This position of the clinician lends itself to a positive therapeutic relationship and client empowerment (Coyne, 1987; Jacobson, 1983). Coyne (1987) and Jacobson (1983) both discuss how major strategic therapy interventions allow clients to discover solutions to their problems on their own and, thus, clients are able to give themselves credit and not the clinician for positive change (Stanton, 1980). An empowering approach such as this also lends itself for use with diverse client populations such as women (Terry, 1992) and minorities (Boyd-Franklin, 1987; Ho, 1989; Kim, 1985; Lemon, Newfield, & Dobbins, 1993) who have been denied power in this country. In addition, the use of strategic therapy has not been restricted to the United States; it has been effectively used in India (Appasamy, 1995), Argentina (Weyland, 1995), Sweden (Pothoff, 1995), and, of course, Italy (Nardone & Portelli, 2005).

Several approaches to practice have evolved out of the communications theory/strategic therapy tradition in recent years that place major emphasis on the clinician–client relationship being nonhierarchical and collaborative, such as solution-focused therapy (de Shazer, 1985), narrative therapy (White & Epston, 1990), and constructivist therapy (Hoffman, 1988). These approaches also deemphasize the use of indirectness, concealment, and paradox. The primary originators of these approaches are all social workers.

Another trend is the integration of strategic therapy and its various techniques with other approaches (Case & Robinson, 1990; Held, 1984; Seaburn, Landau-Stanton, & Horwitz, 1995). The integration of strategic therapy with structural family therapy and with behavioral therapy was referred to earlier in this chapter. In addition, reframing is used in cognitive therapy (Schuyler, 1991), and paradox is used in both cognitive therapy (Dattilio & Freeman, 1992) and task-centered treatment (Reid, 1990). The integration of strategic therapy, solution-focused therapy, narrative therapy, and constructivist therapy in various combinations with each other has also been discussed in the literature (Dagirmanjian, Eron, & Lund, 2007; Duncan, Miller, & Sparks, 2003; Lee et al., 2009; Murphy & Duncan, 2007; Quick, 2008; Selekman, 2005). Such integrations are natural for these approaches since they come out of the communications theory tradition, which emphasizes "using what works." Because of this emphasis, strategic therapy and its newer adaptations of solution-focused therapy, narrative therapy, and constructivist therapy lend themselves to brief treatment.

References

Abeles, G. (1976). Researching the unresearchable: Experimentation on the double bind. In C. E. Sluzki & D. C. Ransom (Eds.), *Double bind: The foundation of the communicational approach to the family* (pp. 113–149). New York: Grune & Stratton.

Aldridge, D., & Rossiter, J. (1983). A strategic approach to suicidal behavior. *Journal of Strategic and Systemic Therapies*, 2, 49–62.

Alexander, J. F., Barton, C., Schiavo, R. S., & Parsons, B. V. (1976). Systems-behavioral intervention with families of delinquents: Therapists' characteristics, family behavior, and outcome. *Journal of Consulting and Clinical Psychology*, 44, 656–664.

Allen, J. R. (1987). The use of strategic techniques in large systems: Mohandas K. Gandhi and the Indian independence movement. *Journal of Strategic and Systemic Therapies*, 6, 57–64.

Andelson, J. G. (1981). The double bind and social change in communal Amana. *Human Relations*, 34, 111–125.

Anger-Diaz, B., Schlanger, K., Rincon, C., & Mendoza, A. B. (2004). Problem-solving across cultures: Our Latino experience. *Journal of Systemic Therapies*, 23, 11–27.

Anger-Diaz, B., & Schlanger, K. (2005). Problem-focused supervision: Consultations with John Weakland. *Journal of Brief Therapy*, 4, 47–52.

Appasamy, P. (1995). Doing brief therapy in India. In J. H. Weakland & W. A. Ray (Eds.), *Propagations: Thirty years of influence from the Mental Research Institute* (pp. 157–173). New York: The Haworth Press.

Bartunek, J. M., & Moch, M. K. (1987). First-order, second-order, and third-order change and organization development interventions: A cognitive approach. *Journal of Applied Behavioral Science*, 23, 483–500.

Bartunek, J. M., & Moch, M. K. (1994). Third-order organizational change and the Western mystical tradition. *Journal of Organizational Change Management*, 7, 24–41.

Bateson, G. (1979). *Mind and nature: A necessary unity*. New York: E. P. Dutton.

Bateson, G., Jackson, D. D., Haley, J., & Weakland, J. (1956). Toward a theory of schizophrenia. *Behavioral Science*, 1, 251–264.

Beitler, M. A. (2006). *Strategic organizational change: A practitioner's guide for managers and consultants*. Practitioner Press International.

Bergman, J. S. (1982). Paradoxical interventions with people who insist on acting crazy. *American Journal of Psychotherapy*, XXXVI, 214–222.

Bergman, J. S. (1983). On odd days and even days: Rituals used in strategic therapy. In L. Wolberg & M. Aronson (Eds.), *Group and family therapy 1983* (pp. 273–281). New York: Brunner/Mazel.

Bern, E. (1972). *What do you say after you say hello?* New York: Grove Press.

Blotcky, A. D., Tittler, B. I., & Friedman, S. (1982). The double-bind situation in families of disturbed children. *Journal of Genetic Psychology*, 141, 129–142.

Bobrow, B., Batchelor, J., & Harris, J. (2008). Maintaining the integrity of strategic therapy in an agency setting. *Journal of Brief, Strategic & Systemic Therapies*, 2, 93–116.

Bolman, L. G., & Deal, T. E. (1991). *Reframing organizations: Artistry, choice, and leadership*. San Francisco: Jossey-Bass Publishers.

Boyd-Franklin, N. (1987). The contribution of family therapy models to the treatment of Black families. *Psychotherapy*, 24, 621–629.

Brandon, J. (1985). Some applications of a strategic family therapy perspective in the practice of OD. *Journal of Strategic and Systemic Therapies*, 4, 15–24.

Braveman, L. (1986). Social casework and strategic therapy. *Social Casework*, April, 234-239.

Bray, J. H., & Anderson, H. (1984). Strategic interventions with single-parent families. *Psychotherapy*, 21, 101–109.

Bross, A. (Ed.) (1982). *Family therapy: Principles of strategic practice*. New York: The Guilford Press.

Cade, B. (1980). Strategic therapy. *Journal of Family Therapy*, 2, 89–99.

Cade, B., & O'Hanlon, W. H. (1993). *A brief guide to brief therapy*. New York: W. W. Norton.

Carr, A. (1991). Milan systemic family therapy: A review of ten empirical investigations. *Journal of Family Therapy*, 13, 237–263.

Case, E. M., & Robinson, N. S. (1990). Toward integration: The changing world of family therapy. *American Journal of Family Therapy*, 18, 153–160.

Checchin, G., Lane, G., & Ray, W. A. (2003). Prejudice and position: Fostering the symptoms of happiness in brief therapy. *Journal of Brief Therapy*, 2, 101–108.

Chubb, H. (1982). Strategic brief therapy in a clinic setting. *Psychotherapy: Theory, Research and Practice*, 19, 160–165.

Chubb, H. (1983). Interactional brief therapy: Child problems in an HMO clinic. *Journal of Strategic and Systemic Therapies*, 2, 70–76.

Chubb, H., & Evans, E. L. (1990). Therapist efficiency and clinic accessibility with the Mental Health

Research Institute brief therapy model. *Community Mental Health Journal*, 26, 139–149.

Coyne, J. C. (1986). Strategic marital therapy for depression. In N. S. Jacobson & A. S. Gurman (Eds.), *Clinical handbook of marital therapy* (pp. 495–512). New York: The Guilford Press.

Coyne, J. C. (1987). The concept of empowerment in strategic therapy. *Psychotherapy*, 24, 539–545.

Crawford, M., & Stein, W. (2005). "Second-order" change in UK local government: the case of risk management. *International Journal of Public Sector Management*, 18, 414–423.

Dagirmanjian, S., Eron, J., & Lund, T. (2007). Narrative solutions: An integration of self and systems perspectives in motivating change. *Journal of Psychotherapy Integration*, 17, 70–92.

Dattilio, F. M., & Freeman, A. (1992). Introduction to cognitive therapy. In A. Freeman & F. M. Dattilio (Eds.), *Comprehensive casebook of cognitive therapy* (pp. 3–11). New York: Plenum Press.

de Shazer, S. (1985). *Keys to solution in brief therapy*. New York: W. W. Norton.

Dowd, E. T., & Pace, T. M. (1989). The relativity of reality: Second-order change in psychotherapy. In A. Freeman, et al. (Eds.), *Comprehensive handbook of cognitive therapy* (pp. 213–226). New York: Plenum Press.

Duncan, B. L., Miller, S. D., & Sparks, J. A. (2003). Interactional and solution-focused brief therapies: Evolving concepts of change. In T. L. Sexton, G. R. Weeks, & M. S. Robbins (Eds.), *Handbook of family therapy: The science and practice of working with families and couples* (pp. 101–123). New York: Brunner-Routledge.

Duncan, B. L., Hubble, M. A., Miller, S. D., & Coleman, S. T. (1998). Escaping the lost world of impossibility: Honoring clients' language, motivation, and theories of change. In M. F. Hoyt (Ed.), *The handbook of constructive therapies: Innovative approaches from leading practitioners* (pp. 293–313). San Francisco: Jossey-Bass.

Efron, D. E. (1981). Strategic therapy interventions with latency-age children. *Social Casework*, November, 543–550.

Elkaim, M. (1990). *If you love me, don't love me: Constructions of reality and change in family therapy*. New York: Basic Books.

Eubanks, R. A. (2002). The MRI reflecting team: An integrated approach. *Journal of Systemic Therapies*, 21, 10–19.

Fairhurst, G. T., & Sarr, R. A. (1996). *The art of framing: Managing the language of leadership*. San Francisco: Jossey-Bass Publishers.

Ferreira, A. (1960). The double bind and delinquent behavior. *Archives of General Psychiatry*, 3, 359–367.

Fisch, R., & Schlanger, K. (1999). *Brief therapy with intimidating cases: Changing the unchangeable*. San Francisco: Jossey-Bass Publishers.

Fisch, R., Weakland, J. H., & Segal, L. (1982). *The tactics of change: Doing therapy briefly*. San Francisco: Jossey-Bass Publishers.

Fraser, J. S. (1986). The crisis interview: Strategic rapid intervention. *Journal of Strategic and Systemic Therapies*, 5, 71–87.

Fraser, J. S., Morris, M., Smith, D., & Solovey, A. (2001). Brief therapy in primary care settings: A catalyst model. *Journal of Brief Therapy*, 1, 7–16.

Fraser, J. S., Morris, M., Smith, D., & Solovey, A. (2002). Applications of a catalyst model in primary care settings. *Journal of Brief Therapy*, 1, 131–140.

George, J. M., & Jones, G. R. (2001). Towards a process model of individual change in organizations. *Human Relations*, 54, 419–444.

Gharajedaghi, J. (2007). Systems thinking: a case for second-order-learning. *The Learning Organization*, 14, 473–479.

Geyerhofer, S., & Komori, Y. (2005). Integrating post-structuralist models of brief therapy. *Journal of Brief Therapy*, 4, 103–122.

Greene, G. J. (1989). Using the written contract for evaluating and enhancing practice effectiveness. *Journal of Independent Social Work*, 4, 135–155.

Greene, G. J. (2002). The Mental Research Institute approach to strategic therapy. In A. R. Roberts & G. J. Greene (Eds.), *Social workers' desk reference* (pp. 125–130). New York: Oxford University Press.

Greene, G. J. (2006). Dialectical-pragmatic therapy (DPT): An integrative approach to brief treatment. *Journal of Brief Therapy*, 5, 117–145.

Greene, G. J., Jones, D. H., Frappier, C., Klein, M. & Culton, B. (1996). School social workers as family therapists: A dialectical-systemic-constructivist model. *Social Work in Education*, 18, 222–236.

Greene, G. J., & Sattin, D. B. (1985). A paradoxical treatment format for anxiety-related somatic complaints: Four case studies. *Family Systems Medicine*, 3, 197–204.

Grove, D., & Haley, J. (1993). *Conversations on therapy: Popular problems and uncommon solutions*. New York: W. W. Norton.

Haley, J. (1963). *Strategies of psychotherapy*. New York: Grune & Stratton.

Haley, J. (1973). *Uncommon therapy: The psychiatric techniques of Milton H. Erickson, MD*. New York: W. W. Norton.

Haley, J. (1980). *Leaving home: The therapy of disturbed young people*. New York: McGraw-Hill.

Haley, J. (1984). *Ordeal therapy*. San Francisco: Jossey-Bass.

Haley, J. (1987). *Problem-solving therapy* (2nd ed.). San Francisco: Jossey-Bass.

Haley, J. (1996). *Learning & teaching therapy*. New York: Guilford Press.

Haley, J., & Richeport-Haley, M. (2003). *The art of strategic therapy*. New York: Brunner-Routledge.

Haley, J., & Richeport-Haley, M. (2007). *Directive family therapy*. New York: Haworth Press.

Haley, J., & Schiff, N.P. (1993). A model therapy for psychotic young people. *Journal of Systemic Therapies, 12,* 74–87.

Harre, R., & Moghaddam, F. (2004). Introduction: The self and others in traditional psychology and in positioning theory. In R. Harre & F. Moghaddam (Eds.), *The self and others: Positioning individuals and groups in personal, political, and cultural contexts* (pp. 1–11). Praeger.

Heath, A. W., & Ayers, T. C. (1991). MRI brief therapy with adolescent substance abusers. In T. C. Todd & M. D. Selekman (Eds.), *Family therapy approaches with adolescent substance abusers* (pp. 49–69). Boston: Allyn & Bacon.

Held, B. S. (1984). Toward a strategic eclecticism: A proposal. *Psychotherapy, 21,* 232–240.

Herr, J. J., & Weakland, J. H. (1979). *Counseling elders and their families: Practical techniques for applied gerontology*. New York: Springer Publishing Co.

Hill, K. A. (1987). Meta-analysis of paradoxical interventions. *Psychotherapy, 24,* 266–270.

Hill, M. (1992). A feminist model for the use of paradoxical techniques in psychotherapy. *Professional Psychology, 23,* 287–292.

Ho, M. K. (1989). Applying family therapy theories to Asian/Pacific Americans. *Contemporary Family Therapy, 11,* 61–70.

Hoffman, I. R. (2007). *Changing perspective-changing solutions: Activating internal images for change in systemic brief therapy*. Heidelberg, Germany: Carl-Auer Verlag.

Hoffman, L. (1981). *Foundations of family therapy*. New York: Basic Books.

Hoffman, L. (1985). Beyond power and control: Toward a second-order family systems therapy. *Family Systems Medicine, 3,* 381–396.

Hoffman, L. (1988). A constructivist position for family therapy. *Irish Journal of Psychology, 9,* 110–129.

Horigian, V. E., Suarez-Morales, L., Robbins, M. S., Zarate, M., Mayorga, C. C., Mitrani, V. B., & Szapocznik, J. (2005). Brief strategic family therapy for adolescents with behavior problems. In J. L. Lebow (Ed.), *Handbook of clinical family therapy* (pp.73–102). Hoboken, NJ: John Wiley & Sons.

Jackson, D. D. (1965). Family rules: Marital *quid pro quo*. *Archives of General Psychiatry, 12,* 589–594.

Jacobson, A. (1983). Empowering the client in strategic therapy. *Journal of Strategic and Systemic Therapies, 2,* 77–87.

Keeney, B. P. (1983). *Aesthetics of change*. New York: The Guilford Press.

Keeney, B. P. (1987). The construction of therapeutic realities. *Psychotherapy, 24,* 469–476.

Keeney, B. P., & Silverstein, O. (1986). *The therapeutic voice of Olga Silverstein*. New York: The Guilford Press.

Keim, J. (2000). Strategic family therapy: The Washington School (pp. 170–207). In A. M. Horne (Ed.), *Family counseling and therapy* (3rd ed.). Itasca, IL: F. E. Peacock Publishers.

Kim, R. S., Poling, J., & Ascher, L. M. (1991). An introduction to research on the clinical efficacy of paradoxical intention. In G. R. Weeks (Ed.), *Promoting change through paradoxical therapy* (revised ed., pp. 216–250). New York: Brunner/Mazel Publishers.

Kim, S. C. (1985). Family therapy for Asian Americans: A strategic-structural framework. *Psychotherapy, 22,* 342–348.

Kleckner, T., Frank, L., Bland, C., Amendt, J. H., & Bryant, R. (1992). The myth of the unfeeling strategic therapist. *Journal of Marital and Family Therapy, 18,* 41–51.

Koss, M. P., & Shiang, J. (1993). Research on brief psychotherapy. In A. E. Bergin & S. L. Garfield (Eds.), *Handbook of psychotherapy and behavior change* (pp. 664–700). New York: John Wiley & Sons.

Langsley, D. G., Machotka, P., & Flomenhaft, K. (1971). Avoiding mental hospital admissions: A follow-up study. *American Journal of Psychiatry, 127,* 1391–1394.

Lee, M. Y., Greene, G. J., Hsu, K. S. Y., Solovey, A., Grove, D., Fraser, J. S., Washburn, P., Teater, B., 2009. Utilizing Family Strengths and Resilience: Integrative Family and Systems Treatment with Children and Adolescents with Severe Emotional and Behavioral Problems. *Family Process, 48* (3), pp. 395-416.

Lemon, S. D., Newfield, N. A., & Dobbins, J. E. (1993). Culturally sensitive family therapy in Appalachia. *Journal of Systemic Therapies, 12,* 8–26.

Lewis, V., & Allen-Byrd, L. (2007). Coping strategies for the stages of family recovery. *Alcoholism Treatment Quarterly, 25,* 105–124.

Liddle, H. A., Rodriguez, R. A., Dakof, G. A., Kanzki, E. & Marvel, F. A. (2005). Multidimensional family therapy: A science-based treatment for adolescent drug abuse. In J. L. Lebow (Ed.), *Handbook of clinical family therapy* (pp. 128–163). Hoboken, NJ: John Wiley & Sons.

Littrell, J. M., & Peterson, J. S. (2001). Facilitating systemic change using the MRI problem-solving approach: One school's experience. *Professional School Counseling, 5,* 27–33.

Madanes, C. (198). Marital therapy when a symptom is presented by a spouse. *International Journal of Family Therapy*, 2, 120–136.

Madanes, C. (1981). *Strategic family therapy*. San Francisco: Jossey-Bass.

Madanes, C. (1984). *Behind the one-way mirror: Advances in the practice of strategic therapy*. San Franciso: Jossey-Bass.

Madanes, C. (1995). *The violence of men: New techniques for working with abusive families: A therapy of social action*. San Francisco: Jossey-Bass.

Markowitz, M. A., & Nitzberg, M. L. (1982). Communication in the psychiatric halfway house and the double bind. *Clinical Social Work Journal*, 10, 176–189.

Marzano, R. J., & Waters, T. (2009). *District leadership that works: Striking the right balance*. Solution Tree Press.

Mazza, J. (1988). Training strategic therapists: The use of indirect techniques. In H. A. Liddle, D. C. Breunlin, & R. C. Schwartz (Eds.), *Handbook of family therapy training and supervision* (pp. 93–109). New York: The Guilford Press.

McCloskey, K. A., & Fraser, J. S. (1997). Using feminist MRI brief therapy during initial contact with victims of domestic violence. *Psychotherapy*, 34, 433–446.

McGarty, R. (1986). Use of strategic and brief techniques in the treatment of chemical dependency. *Journal of Strategic and Systemic Therapies*, 5, 13–19.

Meynell, F. (2005). A second-order approach to evaluating and facilitating organizational change. *Action Research*, 3, 211–231.

Moley, V. (1983). Interactional treatment of eating disorders. *Journal of Strategic and Systemic Therapies*, 2, 10–28.

Morawetz, A., & Walker, G. (1984). *Brief therapy with single-parent families*. New York: Brunner/Mazel.

Morrissette, P. J. (1989). Benevolent restraining: A strategy for interrupting vicious cycles in residential care. *Journal of Strategic and Systemic Therapies*, 8, 31–35.

Murphy, J. J., & Duncan, B. L. (2007). *Brief intervention for school problems*. New York: Guilford Press.

Nardone, G. (1995). Brief strategic therapy of phobic disorders: A model of therapy and evaluation research. In J. H. Weakland & W. A. Ray (Eds.), *Propagations: Thirty years of influence from the Mental Research Institute*. New York: Haworth Press.

Nardone, G., & Portelli, C. (2005). *Knowing through changing: The evolution of brief strategic therapy*. Crown House Publishing.

Nardone, G. & Salvini, A. (2007). *The strategic dialogue: Rendering the diagnostic interview a real therapeutic intervention*. London: Karnac.

Nardone, G., & Watzlawick, P. (1993). *The art of change: Strategic therapy and hypnotherapy without trance*. San Francisco: Jossey-Bass Publishers.

Nardone, G., & Watzlawick, P. (2005). *Brief strategic therapy: Philosophy, techniques, and research*. New York: Jason Aronson.

Nelson, J. (2006). For parents only: A strategic family therapy approach to school counseling. *Family Journal*, 14, 180–183.

Norfleet, M. A. (1983). Paradoxical interventions in the treatment of chronic physical illness. *Journal of Strategic and Systemic Therapies*, 2, 63–69.

O'Hanlon, W. H. (1987). *Taproots: Underlying principles of Milton H. Erickson's therapy and hypnosis*. New York: W. W. Norton.

Papp, P. (1983). *The process of change*. New York: Guilford Press.

Parrott, W. G. (2004). Positioning and the emotions. In R. Harre & F. Moghaddam (Eds.), *The self and others: Positioning individuals and groups in personal, political, and cultural contexts* (pp. 29–43). Praeger.

Perkins, D. D., Bess, K. D., Cooper, D. G., Jones, D. L., Armstead, T., & Speer, P. W. (2007). Community organizational learning: Case studies illustrating a three-dimensional model of levels and orders of change. *Journal of Community Psychology*, 35, 303–328.

Pirrota, S., & Cecchin, G. (1988). The Milan training program. In H. A. Liddle, D. C. Breulin, & R. C. Schwartz (Eds.), *Handbook of family therapy training and supervision* (pp. 38–61). New York: The Guilford Press.

Pothoff, K. (1995). A Swedish experience. In J. H. Weakland & W. A. Ray (Eds.), *Propagations: Thirty years of influence from the Mental Research Institute* (pp. 197–198). New York: The Haworth Press.

Potter-Efron, P. S., & Potter-Efron, R. T. (1986). Promoting second-order change in alcoholic systems. *Journal of Strategic and Systemic Therapies*, 5, 20–29.

Quick, E. K. (2008). *Doing what works in brief therapy: A strategic solution focused approach* (2nd ed.). New York: Academic Press.

Rabi, J. S., Lehr, M. L., & Hayner, M. L. (1984). The peer consultation team: An alternative. *Journal of Strategic and Systemic Therapies*, 3, 66–71.

Ray, W. A. (2003). Brief therapy with a couple in "alcoholic transaction": The Don Jackson way. *Journal of Brief Therapy*, 3, 13–26.

Ray, W. A., & Watzlawick, P. (2005). The interactional view: Enduring conceptions from the Mental

Research Institute (MRI). *Journal of Brief Therapy*, 5, 9–31.

Reid, W. J. (1990). An integrative model for short-term treatment. In R. A. Wells & V. J. Giannetti (Eds.), *Handbook of the brief psychotherapies* (pp. 55–77). New York: Plenum Press.

Richeport-Haley, M. (1998). Approaches to madness shared by cross-cultural healing systems and strategic family therapy. *Journal of Family Psychotherapy*, 9, 61–75.

Rohrbaugh, M. J., & Varda, S. (2001). Brief therapy based on interrupting ironic processes: The Palo Alto Model. *Clinical Psychology*, 8, 66–81.

Sartorius, C. (2006). Second-order sustainability—conditions for the development of sustainable innovations in a dynamic environment. *Ecological Economics*, 58, 268–286.

Schindler-Zimmerman, T., Washle, W., & Protinsky, H. (1990). Strategic intervention in an athletic system. *Journal of Strategic and Systemic Therapies*, 9, 1–7.

Schlanger, K., & Anger-Diaz, B. (1999). The brief therapy approach of the Palo Alto group. In D. M. Lawson & F. F. Prevatt (Eds.), *Casebook in family therapy* (pp. 146–168). Brooks/Cole Wadsworth.

Schuyler, D. (1991). *A practical guide to cognitive therapy*. New York: W. W. Norton.

Schoenwald, S. K., & Henggeler, S. W. (2005). Multisystemic therapy for adolescents with serious externalizing problems. In J. L. Lebow (Ed.), *Handbook of clinical family therapy* (pp. 164–194). Hoboken, NJ: John Wiley & Sons.

Seaburn, D., Landau-Stanton, J., & Horwitz, S. (1995). Core techniques in family therapy. In R. H. Mikesell, D. D. Lusterman, & S. H. McDaniel (Eds.), *Integrating family therapy: Handbook of family psychology and systems theory* (pp. 5–26). Washington, DC: American Psychological Association.

Segal, L (1980). Focused problem resolution. In E.R. Tolson & W.J. Reid b(Eds.), *Models of family therapy* (pp.199–223). New York: Columbia University Press.

Segal, L., & Bavelas, J. B. (1983). Human systems and communication theory. In B. B. Wolman & G. Stricker (Eds.), *Handbook of family and marital therapy* (pp. 61–76). New York: Plenum Press.

Segal, L. (1991). Brief therapy: The MRI approach. In A. S. Gurman & D. P. Kniskern (Eds.), *Handbook of family therapy*, Vol. II. New York: Brunner/Mazel Publishers.

Selekman, M. D. (2005). *Pathways to change: Brief therapy with difficult adolescents* (2nd ed.). New York: W. W. Norton.

Selvini Palazzoli, M., Boscolo, L., Cecchin, G., & Prata, G. (1978a). A ritualized prescription in family therapy: Odd days and even days. *Journal of Marriage and Family Counseling*, 4, 3–9.

Selvini Palazzoli, M., Boscolo, L., Cecchin, G. F., & Prata, G. (1978b). *Paradox and counterparadox: A new model in the therapy of the family in schizophrenic transaction*. New York: Jason Aronson.

Sexton, T. L., & Alexander, J. F. (2005). Functional family therapy for externalizing disorder in adolescents. In LJ. L. Lebow (Ed.), *Handbook of clinical family therapy* (pp. 164–194). Hoboken, NJ: John Wiley & Sons.

Shadish, W. R., Montgomery, L. M., Wilson, P., Wilson, M. R., Bright, I., & Okwumabua, T. (1993). The effects of family and marital psychotherapies: A meta-analysis. *Journal of Consulting and Clinical Psychology*, 61, 992–1002.

Shoham, V., Rohrbaugh, M. J., & Cleary, A. A. (2008). Brief strategic couple therapy. In A. S. Gurman (Ed.), *Clinical handbook of couple therapy* (4th ed., pp. 299–322). New York: Guilford Press.

Shoham-Salomon, V., & Rosenthal, R. (1987). Paradoxical interventions: A meta-analysis. *Journal of Consulting and Clinical Psychology*, 55, 22–28.

Shutty, M. S., & Sheras, P. (1991). Brief strategic psychotherapy with chronic pain patients: Reframing and problem resolution. *Psychotherapy*, 28, 636–642.

Sluzki, C. E., Beavin, J., Tarnopolsky, A., & Veron, E. (1967). Transactional disqualification: Research on the double bind. *Archives of General Psychiatry*, 16, 494–504.

Sluzki, C. E., & Veron, E. (1971). The double bind as a universal pathogenic situation. *Family Process*, 10, 397–410.

Soo-Hoo, T. (1995). Implementing brief strategic therapy within a psychiatric residential/daytreatment center. In J. H. Weakland & W. A. Ray (Eds.), *Propagations: Thirty years of influence from the Mental Research Institute* (pp. 107–128). New York: The Haworth Press.

Soo-Hoo, T. (1999). Brief strategic family therapy with Chinese Americans. *American Journal of Family Therapy*, 27, 163–173.

Sprenkle, D. H., Davis, S. D., & Lebow, J. L. (2009). *Common factors in couple and family therapy: The overlooked foundation for effective practice*. New York: Guilford Press.

Stanton, M. D. (1980). Who should get credit for change which occurs in therapy? In A. S. Gurman (Ed.), *Questions and answers in the practice of family therapy*. New York: Brunner/Mazel.

Stanton, M. D., et al. (1982). *The family therapy of drug abuse and addiction*. New York: The Guilford Press.

Strupp, H. H. (1977). A reformulation of the dynamics of the therapist's contribution. In A. S. Gurman & A. M. Razin (Eds.), *Effective psychotherapy: A handbook of research* (pp. 3–22). New York: Pergamon Press.

Sun, P. Y. T., & Scott, J. (2005). Sustaining second-order change initiation: structured complexity and interface management. *Journal of Management Development*, 24, 879–895.

Sutton, J., Ray, W. A., & Cole, C. L. (2003). Breaking the ties that b[l]ind: An interactional approach to brief therapy with premarital couples in a relational impasse. *Journal of Brief Therapy*, 2, 109–118.

Swoboda, J. S., Dowd, E. T., & Wise, S. L. (1990). Reframing and restraining directives in the treatment of clinical depression. *Journal of Counseling Psychology*, 37, 254–260.

Szapocznik, J., Robbins, M. S., Mitrani, V. B., Santisteban, D., Hervis, O., & Williams, R.A. (2002). Brief strategic family therapy with behavior problem Hispanic youth (pp. 83-109). In J. Lebow (Ed.), *Integrative and Eclectic Psychotherapies* (Vol. 4). In F. Kaslow (Ed.), *Comprehensive Handbook of Psychotherapy*, New York: Wiley & Sons.

Tennen, H., Eron, J. B., & Rohrbaugh, M. (1991). Paradox in context. In G. R. Weeks (Ed.), *Promoting change through paradoxical therapy* (rev. ed., pp. 187–215). New York: Brunner/Mazel, Inc.

Terry, L. L. (1992). I want my old wife back: A case illustration of a four-stage approach to a feminist-informed strategic/systemic therapy. *Journal of Strategic and Systemic Therapies*, 11, 27–41.

Tirado, F., & Galvez, A. (2008). Positioning theory and discourse analysis: Some tools for social interaction analysis. *Historical Social Research*, 33, 224–251.

Tsoukas, H., & Papoulias, D. B. (2005). Managing third-order change: The case of the public power corporation in Greece. *Long Range Planning*, 38, 79–95.

Watzlawick, P., & Coyne, J. C. (1980). Depression following stroke: Brief, problem-focused family treatment. *Family Process*, 19, 13–18.

Watzlawick, P., Beavin, J. H., & Jackson, D. D. (1967). *Pragmatics of human communication: A study of interactional patterns, pathologies, and paradoxes.* New York: W. W. Norton.

Watzlawick, P., & Weakland, J. H. (1977). *The interactional view: Studies at the Mental Research Institute Palo Alto 1965–1974.* New York: W. W. Norton & Co.

Watzlawick, P., Weakland, J. H., & Fisch, R. (1974). *Change: Principles of problem formation and problem resolution.* New York: W. W. Norton & Co.

Weakland, J. H. (1976). Communication theory and clinical change. In P. J. Guerin (Ed.), *Family therapy: Theory and practice* (pp. 111–128). New York: Gardner Press, Inc.

Weakland, J. H., & Fisch, R. (1984). Cases that "Don't make sense": Brief strategic treatment in medical practice. *Family Systems Medicine*, 2, 125–136.

Weakland, J. H., & Jordan, L. (1992). Working briefly with reluctant clients: Child protective services as an example. *Journal of Family Therapy*, 14, 231–254.

Weakland, J. H., Watzlawick, P., & Riskin, J. (1995). Introduction: MRI—a little background music. In Weakland, J. H., & Ray, W. A. (1995). *Propagations: Thirty years of influence from the Mental Research Institute.* New York: The Haworth Press.

Weyland, D. (1995). From the dictatorship of Lacan to the democracy of short-term therapies. In J.H. Weakland & W.A. Ray (Eds.), *Propagations: Thirty years of influence from the Mental Research Institute* (pp. 189–195). New York: The Haworth Press.

White, M., & Epston, D. (1990). *Narrative means to therapeutic ends.* New York: W. W. Norton.

Wilson, S. R. (2006). First- and second-order changes in a community's response to a child abuse fatality. *Communications Monograph*, 73, 481–487.

Winslade, J. M. (2005). Utilising discursive positioning in counseling. *British Journal of Guidance & Counselling*, 33, 351–364.

Woodruff, A. F., & Engle, T. (1985). Strategic therapy and agency development: Using circular thinking to turn the corner. *Journal of Strategic and Systemic Therapies*, 4, 25–29.

Zimmerman, T., & Protinsky, H. (1990). Strategic parenting: The tactics of changing children's behavior. *Journal of Strategic and Systemic Therapies*, 9, 6–13.

TASK CENTERED

This theory, developed by William J. Reid, is based on observations that clients benefit from time-limited therapy involvement where social workers support, challenge, and aid in carrying out tasks useful to address present and future changes

Task-Centered Social Work

Anne E. Fortune and William J. Reid

Overview

Task-centered social work evolved from a model of casework tested in the mid-1960s (Reid & Shyne, 1969). The results suggested that brief psychosocial casework might provide a more efficient means of helping individuals and families with problems in family relations than conventional, long-term forms of psychosocial practice. Using that brief service approach as a starting point, William J. Reid and Laura Epstein attempted to develop a more comprehensive, systematic, and effective model of short-term treatment (Reid & Epstein, 1972). The task-centered approach uses the time-limited structure and techniques of short-term psychosocial casework as a means to help clients devise and carry out actions or tasks to alleviate their problems. Its initial formulation relied heavily on

Hollis' (1964) psychosocial techniques, Perlman's (1957) view of casework as a problem-solving process, and Studt's (1968) notion of the client's task as a focus of service.

At its inception, Reid and Epstein designed the task-centered model to be an open, pluralistic practice system that could incorporate theoretical and technical contributions from diverse sources. The model is not wedded to any particular theory of human functioning; instead, it provides a core of characteristics, including value premises of theory and of intervention methods that can be augmented by compatible approaches. This chapter summarizes the basic characteristics, theory, and intervention methods for work with individuals, families, treatment groups, and case management situations. It includes a case example, a summary of research on the model, and limitations on the use of the model.

Basic Characteristics

Empirical Orientation

The task-centered model is based in an empirical orientation. Preference is given to methods and theories supported by empirical evidence, and interventions are selected based on the best available evidence and the clients' desires. Data from clients guide the treatment plan: all hypotheses and concepts about client systems need to be grounded in case data at relatively low levels of inference. Outcome data are collected systematically and the effects of intervention are monitored regularly through task-accomplishment and goal-attainment ratings. Finally, the model is improved through a sustained program of developmental research (design and development [D&D]).

Integrative Stance

The model draws selectively on empirically based theories and methods from compatible approaches (e.g., problem-solving, cognitive behavioral, cognitive, and family structural approaches). Within the model's basic structure, practitioners may draw on eclectic theories to fashion sequences of tasks to resolve problems.

Focus on Client-Acknowledged Problems

The focus of service is on resolving specific problems that clients explicitly acknowledge as being of concern to them (problems-in-living). This focus contrasts with personality change, attributed problems, or social justice, but it can include environmental contexts.

Systems and Contexts

Problems occur in a context of multiple systems, and contextual change may be needed to resolve the problem or to prevent it from recurring. Conversely, resolution of a problem may have beneficial effects on its context, and the context may provide resources for problem alleviation.

Planned Brevity

Service is generally planned short term by design (6 to 12 weekly sessions within a 4-month period).

Collaborative Relationship

Relationships with clients emphasize a caring but collaborative effort. The practitioner shares information about assessment and progress and avoids hidden goals and agendas. Client and practitioner contract explicitly about the target problems to be worked on, goals, and duration. Extensive use is made of clients' input in developing treatment strategies not only to devise more effective interventions, but also to develop the clients' problem-solving abilities. The practitioner's role includes structuring sessions for collaborative problem-solving work and occasionally carrying out tasks on behalf of clients.

Structure

The intervention program, including treatment sessions, is structured into well-defined sequences of activities that focus on resolving target problems. In addition to clear steps in beginning, middle, and end phases, middle phases include systematic task planning and implementation activities.

Problem-Solving Actions (Tasks)

Change occurs primarily through problem-solving actions (tasks) undertaken by clients during and outside of the session. Emphasis is placed on mobilizing clients' actions in their own environments. The primary function of the treatment session is to lay the groundwork for such actions. In addition, practitioner tasks provide a means of effecting environmental change in the clients' interest.

These core characteristics are the building blocks on which the task-centered model evolved. Reid and Epstein and their colleagues continued systematic development of the task-centered model. Reid emphasized a D&D research approach to model development (Thomas & Rothman, 1994), collaborating with MSW students in field practica, with doctoral students, and with community practitioners to test new developments (Fortune, in press). He was also an eclectic reader of theory and research about how people change and continued to add new ideas from these sources. Epstein concentrated on placing the task-centered approach in the context of social work and social work education and developed skills-based models of teaching social work (Epstein, 1988; Epstein & Brown, 2001).

Over time, the core was augmented by innovations in task-centered theory base, intervention methods, and adaptations for particular settings and populations. Among major sources were theories of learning and cognition as well as problem solving, behavioral, cognitive behavioral, and structural family therapy approaches. Based on D&D, task planning as a core of middle-session interventions was elaborated into the task planning and implementation sequence (Fortune, in press). Task planning was augmented by task strategies as guidelines to sequential or incremental tasks (Reid, 1992, 2000).

The task-centered approach was widely adopted (and adapted) in the United States, Europe, and Asia, and continues to develop through systematic research. Task-centered practice is the basis of social services in three countries (England, Netherlands, and Norway) (Eriksen, 2010; Marsh, 2010; Trotter, 2010) and is used as a standalone or component of social work intervention in 12 other countries in Europe, Africa, Australia, and Asia. By 2010, there were over 200 publications in at least 9 languages, including original textbooks in Great Britain, Netherlands, and Norway (Doel & Marsh, 1993; Eriksen, 1999; Eriksen & Norstrand, 1995; Jagt & Jagt, 1990; Jagt, 2001, 2008; Marsh & Doel, 2005). The task-centered model was adapted for work with groups (Alley & Brown, 2002; Fortune, 1985; Harris & Franklin, 2003; Lo, 2005; Pomeroy, Rubin, & Walker, 1995; Rooney, 1977), family units (Caspi, 2008; Reid, 1985, 1987; Reid & Donovan, 1990), as a method of case management (Naleppa & Reid, 2003; Colvin, Lee, Magnano, & Smith 2008a, 2008b), as a system of agency management (Parihar, 1983, 1994), as a model for clinical supervision (Caspi & Reid, 2002), and as an approach to community work (Ramakrishnan, Balgopal, & Pettys, 1994). It was also been integrated into generalist practice–multilevel, multisystems intervention (Hepworth, Rooney, Dewberry-Rooney, Strom-Gottfried, & Larsen, 2010; Tolson, Reid, & Garvin, 1994).

Specific adaptations were developed for most settings in which social workers practice, including child welfare (Rooney, 1981; Rzepnicki, 1985; Trotter, 2010), public social services (Eriksen, 2010; Marsh & Doel, 2005; Rooney, 1988; Sinclair & Walker, 1985), schools (Colvin et al., 2008a, 2008b; Epstein, 1977; Magnano, 2009; Reid & Bailey-Dempsey, 1995; Reid, Bailey-Dempsey, Cain, Cook, & Burchard, 1994; Viggiani, Reid, & Bailey-Dempsey, 2002); corrections (Bass, 1977; Goldberg & Stanley, 1985; Huh & Koh, 2010; Larsen & Mitchell, 1980), medical (Abramson, 1992; Alley & Brown, 2002; Pomeroy, Rubin & Walker, 1995), industrial (Taylor, 1977; Weissman, 1977, geriatric (Dierking, Brown, & Fortune, 1980; Naleppa & Reid, 2003; Rathbone-McCuan, 1985), and mental health (Eriksen, 2010; Ewalt, 1977; Gibbons, Bow, & Butler, 1985; Newcome, 1985).

Problems and populations with which the task-centered model has been used include suicide and depression, AIDS, addictions, sexual abuse, child neglect, frail elderly, sex offenders, juvenile delinquents, maladaptive youth in treatment centers, homeless persons with psychiatric difficulties, immigrants, loss and grief, parent–child conflict, pregnant adolescents, families of children with developmental disabilities, and aggressive siblings. This is not a comprehensive list but is meant to demonstrate the breadth of application of the model.

The basic principles and methods of the model can be found in a series of volumes that have appeared since the early 1970s. Recent volumes in English include works by Caspi and Reid (2002); Doel and Marsh (1993); Epstein (1988); Epstein and Brown (2001); Marsh and Doel (2005); Naleppa and Reid (2003); Rooney (2009); Reid (1992; 2000); Tolson, Reid, and Garvin (1994); and Trotter (2006).

This chapter reviews the current task-centered system of clinical practice—that is, task-centered practice with individuals, families, and groups and in case management on behalf of clients. The review includes the major theoretical assumptions that underlie the practice model; the model itself (that is, the problem-solving strategies and task-planning methods that guide work with clients); the range of application; and research evidence relating to the efficacy of the model.

Theoretical Assumptions

The essential function of task-centered practice is to help clients move forward with solutions to psychosocial problems that they define and hope to solve. The primary agents of change are not social workers but clients. The practitioners' role is to help clients bring about changes they desire and are willing to work for.

Psychosocial Problems

The theoretical base of the model consists largely of formulations concerning the nature, origins, and dynamics of psychosocial problems. A problem classification defines the types and range of difficulties considered to be targets of the model. Included are problems in family and interpersonal relations, in carrying out social roles, in decision making, and in securing resources and emotional distress reactive to situational factors. At the same time, target problems are part of a larger context that must be taken into account. The context of a problem is a configuration of factors that interact with the problem. The context includes obstacles to solving the problem and resources that can be applied to work on it. These obstacles and resources in turn can reflect almost any aspect of the multiple systems of which clients are a part.

The task-centered model assumes that problems generally reflect temporary breakdowns in problem coping that set in motion forces for change. These forces, which include clients' own motivations to alleviate distress and the resources in the clients' environments, operate rapidly in most cases to reduce the problem to a level of tolerance, at which point the possibility of further change lessens. Thus, clients may benefit as much from short-term treatment as from more extended periods of service. Placing time limits on service may enhance effectiveness by mobilizing the efforts of both practitioners and clients. Concentrated attention on delimited problems further augments effectiveness.

Opportunity for Change

The planned brevity of the model is thus based on the proposition that the most benefit clients will derive from interpersonal treatment will be derived within a relatively few sessions and a relatively brief period of time. This proposition is supported by research evidence that suggests the following: (1) recipients of brief, time-limited treatment show at least as much durable improvement as recipients of long-term, open-ended treatment (Bloom, 2002; Bloom, Yeager, & Roberts, 2006a, 2006b; Johnson & Gelso, 1982; Moyer, Fenney, Swearengen, & Vergun, 2002; Reid & Shyne, 1969); (2) most of the improvement associated with long-term treatment occurs relatively soon after treatment has begun (Bloom, Yeager, & Roberts, 2006b; Orlinsky & Howard, 1986); (3) regardless of their intended length, most courses of voluntary treatment turn out to be relatively brief—the great majority of such treatment courses probably last no longer than a dozen sessions or a 3-month time span. This generalization suggests that most people may exhaust the benefits of treatment rather quickly (Fahs-Beck & Jones, 1973; Garfield, 1994).

Action as a Strategy for Change

The psychosocial problems that make up targets of intervention are the expression of something that clients want that they do not have. The usual and most effective way to obtain what one wants is to take action to get it. Because clients are human beings, their actions are guided by sophisticated sets of beliefs about themselves and their worlds, beliefs that help them form and implement plans about what they should do and how they should do it. Their plans and actions usually involve others—the individuals, groups, and organizations that make up their social systems. Clients' perceptions of the social system response in turn shape their actions. Task-centered practice thus does not deal with remote or historical origins of a problem, but rather with current obstacles that may be blocking the resolution or with resources that may facilitate it.

The theoretical assumption about action for change stresses people's autonomous problem-solving capacities—their ability to initiate and carry through intelligent action to obtain what they want (Goldman, 1970). In this conception, the person is less a prisoner of unconscious drives than in the theories of the psychoanalyst and less a prisoner of environmental contingencies than in the theories of the behaviorist. Instead, people are viewed as having minds and wills of their own that are reactive but not subordinate to internal and external influences.

Their human problem-solving capacities are complex, ingenious, and, in the main, quite effective.

Change is effected primarily through problem-solving actions or tasks that clients and practitioners undertake outside the interview. The central and distinctive strategy of the task-centered system is its reliance on tasks as a means of problem resolution. The success of these tasks largely determines whatever benefit results from the application of the model. The stress on tasks builds on the considerable capacity of human beings to take constructive action in response to difficulty. In effect, the intervention strategy is modeled after the way most people resolve most of their problems—by doing something about them.

The reliance on client action leads to a parsimonious form of intervention that respects clients' rights to manage their own affairs. If clients are clear about what is troubling them and how to resolve the difficulty, the practitioners' role may be limited to providing encouragement and structure for their problem-solving efforts. If more is needed, more is supplied. Even when practitioners' involvement is great, its purpose is to develop and augment the clients' own actions. Practitioners help clients determine what they want (and in the process may need to challenge wants that are unrealizable). Practitioners help clients identify and modify action and interaction sequences contributing to the difficulty, provide corrective feedback on their actions, teach necessary skills, work to alter beliefs that are interfering with problem solving, bring about changes in the social system, and secure resources from it. Practitioners even suggest specific tasks. But whatever is done is done collaboratively and leads to actions that must be agreed to by clients. The decisive actions in most cases are those that clients themselves perform in their own way and on their own behalf.

Enabling clients to take constructive and responsible action in their own interests has an important corollary: the action is more likely to be incorporated as part of their strategies for future coping with their problems. Because clients participated in planning, understood the rationale for tasks, agreed to carry them out, actually implemented them, and reviewed their results, the action is more a part of them and, thus more likely to be used again, than if clients were simply following the practitioners' instructions.

Despite the problem-focused terminology, task-centered intervention is an optimistic, strengths-oriented approach. It stresses self-determination and supports clients' empowerment (Rooney, 2010). It assumes that clients have the ability and capacity to improve their situations, and it draws on their problem-solving ideas and resources.

Practitioner–Client Relationship

In the task-centered approach, the relationship between the practitioner and client by itself is not the medium of treatment. Instead, the relationship provides a means of stimulating and promoting problem-solving action. Therapeutic sessions set in motion and guide actions through which change will be effected. Nevertheless, problem solving is facilitated by relationships in which clients feel accepted, respected, liked, and understood.

A good treatment relationship contains both support and expectancy (Perlman, 1957). Within the task-centered system, the expectations are a therapeutic force at least equal in importance to support. Practitioners expect clients to work on agreed-upon problems and tasks and communicate these expectations to clients both explicitly and implicitly. Clients may reject help, but once contracts are established, they are held accountable for following through. Thus, clients are viewed as persons who can make responsible decisions.

Notions of the working alliance support this approach to relationship. The working alliance includes an agreement between clinicians and clients on goals and on therapeutic strategies, and the client–clinician bond (Bordin, 1994; Horvath & Greenberg, 1989, 1994). Research evidence suggests that a strong working alliance is related to engagement, continuation in treatment, and outcome (Horvath & Greenberg, 1989). The working alliance is not curative in and of itself but interacts with technical aspects of the therapy (such as insight, cognitive methods, or, in the task-centered model, tasks and task planning) (Horvath & Greenberg, 1994). Client involvement is critical. Bordin (1994, pp. 13–14) suggests that the first part of the working alliance, agreement on goals, "can result in increased client capacity to collaborate and even to cope independently."

Contextual Change

The immediate purpose of the task-centered model is to help clients resolve problems-in-living. However, effort is made to help clients alleviate target problems in ways that will exert a positive influence on the context of the problem. Clients are usually embedded in intertwined systems including family, work or school, acquaintances, etc., which may aid or inhibit problem resolution. Contextual change may facilitate solutions, prevent recurrences and side effects, and strengthen clients' problem-solving abilities. Contextual change is defined and limited by the nature of the target problem. It is not just any change that would help clients. Practitioners move from the agreed-upon problem outward by degrees, considering contextual change only when it is directly relevant to the problem at hand.

Two major ways of achieving contextual change have been identified. First, contextual change can occur as a direct consequence of alleviation of a target problem—"ripple effects," so to speak. Improvement in Shawn's grades may lead to a more positive attitude from his teachers, which, in turn, may result in more cooperative behavior from Shawn. Second, contextual change may occur in the process of working through obstacles that prevent resolution of target problems. For example, to help a withdrawn adolescent make friends, the practitioner may deal with the youngster's poor self-image. Despite the importance of contextual change, in the task-centered approach, the manifest problem is not seen as a point of entry to the "real difficulties" underneath. The focus of attention is on the target problem even if its resolution requires considerable change in its context.

Interventions: Client and Practitioner Problem-Solving Activities

The basic problem-solving strategy and practitioner–client activities of the task-centered model will be presented as they are used in work with individual clients. Variations for practice with families and groups and in case management contexts will then be taken up.

It is assumed that, in general, clients can be helped best if they are provided with an orderly, facilitative structure in which to work out immediate problems and to develop problem-solving skills, with practitioners in the roles of guides and consultants.

The central structure of the model is a series of problem-solving activities carried out collaboratively during sessions by practitioners and clients. The aim is to develop effective actions or tasks that clients may use between sessions to resolve the target problems. Early research studies showed that task accomplishment was associated with problem resolution and overall situation (Reid, 1978; Sinclair & Walker, 1985). Thereafter, developmental research concentrated on testing and refining one part of the problem-solving structure, task planning (Fortune, in press). The task-planning process was expanded to include both task planning and task implementation—that is, more attention to how the tasks would be done rather than just what the tasks were to be (Reid, 1978). More emphasis was put on anticipating and overcoming obstacles, thus developing a technology for assessing "what goes wrong when well-planned goals go awry" (Rooney, 2010). Multilevel or multipurpose tasks were introduced to effect change in the family systems context (Reid, 1985)—for example, tasks designed to resolve a problem while also strengthening parental or sibling bonds. Tasks were reconceptualized as occurring during the session as well as in the environment—for example, the family problem-solving sequence, which paired tasks, one completed in the session (e.g., a discussion of conflict resolution between parent and child) and one completed at home after the session (implementing the resolution method) (Reid, 1987). The problem-solving structure and task-planning and implementation sequence are outlined in Table 35.1, organized by phase of intervention.

Initial-Phase Activities

In the initial phase, practitioners and clients explore and agree on the problems to be worked

Table 35-1. The Task-Centered Model in Clinical Practice: Outline for Complete Cases

I. Initial Phase (sessions 1 and 2)
1. Discussion of reasons for referral, especially with nonvoluntary client(s)
2. Exploration and assessment of client-acknowledged target problems and their contexts
3. Formation of the service contract, including problems and goals to be addressed, explanation of treatment methods, agreement on durational limits
4. Development and implementation of initial external tasks (see II-5 and 6 below).
II. Middle Phase
Each session follows the format below:
1. Problem and task review
2. Identifying and resolving (actual) obstacles
3. Contextual analysis
4. Session tasks (if two or more clients in session)
5. Planning external tasks
a. Generating task possibilities
b. Establishing motivation
c. Planning implementation of task(s)
d. Identifying and resolving (anticipated) obstacles
e. Guided practice, simulation
f. Task agreement
g. Summarizing task plans
6. Implementation of task(s) (between sessions)
III. Terminal Phase (final session)
1. Review of target problems and overall problem situation
2. Identification of successful problem-solving strategies used by client(s)
3. Discussion of what can be done about remaining problems, making use of strategies identified in II above
4. Acknowledgment of reactions to termination

Adapted from W. J. Reid (1992). *Task strategies: An empirical approach to clinical social work.* New York: Columbia University Press, Table 1.2, p. 6.

on, form a contract about the focus and duration, and select initial tasks or task strategies.

Problem Exploration, Specification, and Assessment. In the initial interview, the social worker and clients explore and clarify problems. The focus is on what clients want, not on what the practitioner thinks the clients need. However, the practitioner may point out potential difficulties that clients have not acknowledged or the consequences that may result if these difficulties go unattended. In short, the target problem is not necessarily defined by what the clients say they want initially, but rather by what they want after a process of deliberation to which practitioners contribute their own knowledge and point of view.

At the end of the exploration process, at the close of the first or second interview, the practitioner and clients come to an explicit agreement on the problems to be dealt with. These problems are defined as discrete entities—usually in a single sentence—and are specified in terms of specific conditions to be changed.

As an example, Mrs. N, who had difficulties in caring for her 2-year-old daughter, Ann, produced the following problem statement and specification. Problem: Mrs. N constantly loses her temper with Ann, frequently shouting at her and slapping or shaking her. Mrs. N becomes quickly irritated whenever Ann won't obey. Mrs. N generally starts shouting at her when these things happen. If Ann then persists in the behavior or starts to cry, Mrs. N usually will scream at her and then slap her or shake her. During the past week, Mrs. N lost her temper with Ann an average of five times a day and slapped or shook her at least once a day.

As the example of Mrs. N illustrates, problems are spelled out in concrete terms and in language that clients understand. Estimated frequencies of problem occurrence over a specified period add additional precision and provide a baseline against which change in the problem can be measured. Normally, the problem of most concern to clients becomes the primary focus in treatment, although several problems may be defined and worked on. Exploration of the context of the problem concentrates on identifying causes that can be changed and on client resources that may help change. What are the immediate aggravating factors in clients' beliefs, actions, or environment that practitioners or clients can do something about? What strengths can clients bring to bear on the situation? What are resources that can help solve the problem? Exploration may also include pertinent history and general contextual factors involving health, family, work, school, and other relevant aspects of the clients' situation.

Problem exploration is the data-gathering tool for assessment activities, which involve efforts to understand the dynamics of the problem and its contextual features. Assessment is problem-focused, a dialogue that includes practitioners' professional knowledge and clients' unique personal knowledge of the problem and its context. Assessment starts with the problems to be dealt with and incorporates whatever information about clients' situations—such as history or personality—might be relevant to those problems.

In making assessments, practitioners may use a variety of diagnostic theories, but problems are derived empirically from clients' views of their difficulties. Practitioners do not use theory to formulate problems but rather start with a description of the problem ("Mrs. N loses her temper with her child") and then scan relevant knowledge, including theories, to locate possible explanations. Certain guidelines are offered for this eclectic use of theory: (1) Whatever hypotheses are selected to explain the problem should be evaluated through case data to see if the hypothesis appears to be correct in the particular case. (2) Preference is given to theories that have been supported by empirical research. (3) The practitioners do not fix on a single explanation but consider alternative explanations in a search for the theory that provides the best fit with the problem and case at hand.

Contracting. Practitioners and clients develop oral or written contracts in which clients agree to work on one or more explicitly stated, acknowledged problems. The contract also includes a statement of clients' goals in relation to the problem—that is, what kind of solution to the problem do clients want to achieve? Marsh and Doel (2005, p. 36) recommend SMART goals: Specific, Measurable, Achievable, Realistic, and Timely. Specificity of goals and problems aids the choice of treatment strategy and makes it easier to measure progress.

The contract also includes an estimation of the limits of treatment, usually expressed in number of sessions and length of time—for example, 8 sessions over 2 months. Typically contracts are set between 6 and 12 interviews, weekly or twice weekly, within a 1- to 3-month time span. The contract is open to renegotiation at any point, to include new problems or longer periods of service. Setting a time limit enhances motivation and accountability and for that reason should be done even when the duration is uncertain.

Initial Task Planning. Once agreement is reached on the target problems and duration of treatment, tasks are formulated and selected and their implementation is planned. A task defines what client are to do to alleviate their problems. In order for a proposed course of action to be considered a task, clients must agree to try to carry it out.

General tasks are broad, giving clients a direction for action but no specific programs of behavior to follow—for example, Mr. and Mrs. C are to develop a plan for the care of their developmentally delayed daughter. Or a task may be very specific or "operational." Operational tasks call for specific actions clients will undertake: Mr. A is to apply for a job at the local employment agency within the next week, or Johnny is to volunteer to recite in class on Monday. Task specificity is preferred, so there is little ambiguity about who should do what.

Middle-Phase Activities

Middle-phase interviews, where the bulk of the work occurs, each follow similar patterns of activities focused on reviewing tasks and their effects and generating new tasks to further effect change. These activities may, of course, be done at other phases (for example, generating initial tasks at the beginning or discussing alternatives after the contract ends). But in the middle phase, these activities provide the structure for conduct of an interview.

Problem and Task Review. Clients' progress on problems and tasks is routinely reviewed at the beginning of each middle-phase session. The review covers developments in the problem, client and practitioner task accomplishment (or not), and the effects of the tasks on problems. What happens next depends on the results of the review. If the tasks have been substantially accomplished or completed, practitioners and clients may formulate new tasks to address the same problems or may move to a different problem. If the task has not been carried out or has not had the desired effect, practitioners and clients discuss obstacles, devise a different plan for carrying out the task, or apply other task implementation activities. The task may be revised or replaced by another task or the problem itself may be reformulated.

Identifying and Resolving Obstacles. An important procedure in task planning is to identify potential obstacles to the task and to shape plans so as to avoid or minimize these obstacles. Obstacles may be identified when practitioners press for specificity in the task plan, or practitioners may ask clients to think of ways that tasks might fail (Birchler & Spinks, 1981). For example, a wife might identify her husband's irritability at homecoming as an obstacle to intimate conversation. To avoid that obstacle, she might plan to wait until her husband has finished complaining about his day before broaching a sensitive topic.

If substantial obstacles appear, techniques of contextual analysis (discussed below) can be used to plan how to avoid them, or the task may be modified or replaced with a more feasible task. Although analyzing obstacles may appear to emphasize difficulties, if presented to clients as a routine part of problem solving, it helps clients make more realistic assessments of their situations and teaches useful analytic skills.

Contextual Analysis. During the course of the review of tasks and problems, obstacles to task achievement and problem change are usually encountered. The difference between a target problem and an obstacle is that a problem is a difficulty that clients and practitioners have contracted to change, and an obstacle is a difficulty standing in the way of progress toward resolution of a target problem.

Whereas obstacles block progress, resources facilitate it. Resources are usually found in strengths and competencies of individual clients, in the ties of loyalty and affection that hold families together, and in the intangible and tangible supports provided by external systems. Any given characteristic may be an obstacle or a resource, depending on its function in relation to the problem. In contextual analysis, practitioners and clients identify obstacles in the larger social system and then develop tasks to avoid them or engage resources to assist. For example, school policies about tardiness may block parents' attempt to get their teen to school even if late.

Planning External Tasks: Task Planning and Implementation Sequence. The activities related to selecting tasks and planning their implementation are the core problem-solving activities in the middle phase of the task-centered model. Evidence suggests that the more time spent doing task planning, the more likely it is that tasks are successful and that problems are improved (Blizinsky & Reid, 1980; Reid, 1978). The core activities are outlined in logical order in Table 35.1; the logical order is sometimes the temporal order, but in any given session, activities may be intertwined.

Generating Task Possibilities. The process of task planning works best if both practitioners and clients freely suggest alternatives as they come to mind, without too much consideration initially as to their appropriateness. Research on problem solving indicates that this kind of "brainstorming" is an effective means of devising solutions, perhaps because it stimulates imaginative thinking about a wide range of approaches to a difficulty (Osborn, 1963). The best alternatives can then be selected for more serious consideration. In addition to suggesting alternatives, practitioners encourage clients to generate their own ideas. What has or has not worked for the client before? What other ways might the goal be achieved? Not only do clients know their situations well, but generating ideas aids motivation and sense of mastery. At this stage, practitioner criticism of particular client proposals is kept to a minimum.

Often practitioners are the primary generators of alternatives. Practitioners may have special knowledge about the kinds of tasks that generally work well for particular problems. An important source of ideas is task strategies: clusters of tasks or sequences of tasks designed to alleviate particular problems, as much as possible based on evidence of effectiveness (Reid, 1992, 2000). However, even when a well-validated task strategy is proposed, it should be part of a collaborative discussion with the clients. Practitioners' suggestions are *ideas* for tasks; practitioners do not "assign" tasks to clients. Client commitment to do a task is a critical predictor of success, and commitment is enhanced by engagement in the task-planning process (Reid, 1997).

Establishing Motivation. Practitioners and clients develop a rationale or purpose for carrying out the task (if it is not already clear). What is the potential benefit to be gained from completing the task? What good will come of it? How will it affect the problem? Will it take care of an obstacle? Or will it set clients up for future tasks? Practitioners reinforce clients' perceptions of realistic benefits or point out positive consequences that clients may not have perceived.

Planning Impl.ementation of Tasks and Identifying and Resolving Obstacles. The middle-phase procedures for planning implementation of tasks and identifying obstacles are the same as those discussed earlier under the initial phase. If practitioners have been diligent about using a problem-solving process, planning should get easier and clients should be more able to generate their own ideas and predict realistic obstacles. Practitioners may direct more of their efforts to addressing obstacles, either contextual or internal. For example, practitioners may attempt to increase the clients' understanding using focused exploration, explanation, and other methods designed for insight. They may help clients modify distorted perceptions or unrealistic expectations, or may point out dysfunctional patterns of behavior or interactions. They might consciously reinforce adolescents' pro-social skills (Trotter, 2010). Or they might use narrative approaches to finding and constructing alternative views of their competence and strengths (Freeman & Couchonnal, 2006).

Simulation and Guided Practice. In preparation for clients implementing a task, practitioners may model possible task behavior or ask clients to rehearse what they are going to say or do. Modeling and rehearsal may be carried out through role playing, especially with children. For example, if a shy pupil's task is to speak up in class, a practitioner might take the role of the teacher and the child could rehearse what to say in response to being called on. Or the roles could be reversed, with the practitioner modeling what the child might say.

Guided practice is the performance of the actual (as opposed to simulated) task behavior. Thus, a child may practice reading or spouses may practice constructive interactions. If two or more clients are in the session, guided practice may take the form of a session task, where the clients conduct tasks with the practitioners facilitating and coaching (Reid, 1985). For example, families may develop generic problem-solving skills, plan out-of-session tasks that family members may enjoy, or address obstacles.

Task Agreement. Once alternatives have been sorted out and the best have been selected, clients and practitioners agree on the clients' tasks—that is, on what clients will do between sessions. An agreement at this point may concern the global nature of the proposed action and not the detail, which is developed subsequently. However, in some cases practitioners may explore in some depth the tactics of carrying out a possible task before reaching agreement on it with clients. Such exploration may be necessary before a judgment can be made about a task's usefulness. In any event, the final plan may consist chiefly of a general task (to look for an apartment) together with one or more operational tasks that can be carried out in the short term (to contact a rental agency).

Summarizing Task Plans. For the plan to work, it is essential that clients have a clear notion of what they are to do. To this end, at the end of the interview, the plan is summarized. Summarizing the plan gives practitioners the opportunity to convey expectations that the tasks will be carried out and then reviewed. "So you will try to do this and so…. We'll see how it worked out next time we meet."

The same principles apply to planning practitioner tasks or actions practitioners will take outside the session in an attempt to bring about desired changes in the clients' social systems. Practitioner tasks need not be discussed in detail, but some discussion enables clients to understand and shape the practitioners' environmental interventions and makes practitioners accountable, as are clients, for task performance.

Terminal Phase

Termination lasts one or two sessions. The process of terminating begins in the initial phase when the duration of treatment is set. In the middle sessions, practitioners reinforce the passage of time (and the need to work actively) by mentioning the session—for instance, "This is the fifth of our eight planned meetings." In the final interview, practitioners and clients review progress on target problems, using the problem specification from the first phase to gauge progress. They review successful problem-solving

strategies to solidify newly learned skills. The clients' achievements and efforts are stressed to help clients gain a sense of control over change. If appropriate, practitioners and clients plan how the clients will continue work on tasks or develop new ones. They may also develop general plans for what to do if the problem recurs or obstacles are encountered, which is sometimes called "fail-safe planning" (Fishman & Lubetkin, 1980).

The intent of activities in the final interview is not only assessment of gains but also improving clients' abilities to continue the gains and use problem-solving or other new skills in different environments. Thus, interventions include activities believed to prolong gains: giving clients a sense of mastery and control over successful action, reinforcing skills, and applying problem solving to the future (Fortune, 1985, 2009).

The final interview also includes acknowledgment of reactions to ending. Because ending is expected and treatment is time-limited, strong reactions to termination are rare. Still, both practitioners and clients may feel ambivalent: pride, satisfaction, anxiety about the future, sadness at ending a relationship, regret for missed opportunities, etc. Such feelings should be acknowledged as normal, healthy reactions, but not as reasons to prolong treatment.

Extensions beyond agreed-upon limits are normally made if clients request additional service and have a particular goal in mind. Extensions, which usually involve a small number of additional sessions, occur in only a minority of cases in most settings.

Task Strategies

Reid and Epstein (1972, p. 8) initially conceptualized task-centered practice as a general model in which "certain fundamental principles can be successfully applied to a broad range of situations…. A practitioner need not master a large assortment of approaches…but rather can rely on variations of a single approach." The general model included the basic principles of the task-centered model and the task implementation and planning sequence. Once these interchangeable approaches received some empirical support (Reid, 1975, 1978; Reid & Epstein, 1972), development turned from the practitioners' and clients' in-session activities to the broader context of which strategies (clusters or sequences of tasks) were more effective with particular problems. Several task-centered volumes present strategies that are specific to particular problems: sequences of tasks to deal with target problems such as family problems, coping with stress, increasing social involvement, depression, problem drinking, chronic mental illness, health problems, and so on (Naleppa & Reid, 2003; Reid, 1992, 2000). They also include task strategies for resolving obstacles such as poor motivation, distorted beliefs, and lack of skill to complete a task. These compendiums, like other menus of evidence-supported practice, are useful references for practitioners, but they are supplements for generating ideas about tasks, not prescriptions or protocols for intervention. As with all good evidence-based practice, and especially with task-centered practice, clients' desires and engagement in task strategies are paramount.

Work with Families and Formed Groups and in Case Management

The task-centered approach outlined for the treatment of individual clients can be applied to work with clients in families and in groups formed to resolve individual problems. This section reviews selected modifications for these multiple-client situations.

Families

Treatment of a family unit, like treatment of the individual client, focuses on resolution of specific client-acknowledged problems and associated contextual change. Problems are viewed in a multiple-systems context in which the family is a major, though not always the most critical, system. Research and theory on family interaction, as well as specific contributions from behavioral, structural, strategic, and communications schools of family therapy, are used to understand problems and their contexts.

In most cases family members are seen together, and to the extent possible problems are defined in interactional terms. Tasks may be carried out by individual family members, the practitioner, and jointly by family members, either in the session or at home. Tasks within the session (session tasks) generally involve family members in face-to-face problem-solving efforts, structured and facilitated by the practitioner, who may in addition help family members improve their skills in problem-solving communication. Session tasks such as enactments of family interactions or solutions devised by family members during sessions are used as a basis for tasks to be carried out at home. The theme of collaborative effort is continued in these home tasks. Shared tasks, which family members do together, continue the problem solving at home, enabling family members to work together on practical projects such as home improvements, and affecting relationships between family members. Reciprocal tasks are exchanges between family members. All participants must be willing to cooperate and must regard the exchange as equitable. In real life, this means that participants must be prepared to accept reasonable approximations of expected behavior rather than perfect performance and must be willing to adjust in the light of unanticipated circumstances. These complications of reciprocal tasks suggest that work in the session should clarify and negotiate conflicts before the task is tried at home. Reciprocal tasks that are "tacked on" at the end of a session without sufficient preparatory work are likely to fail.

Frequently, contextual change is necessary to resolve obstacles in family interaction that may be blocking solutions to problems. For example, a coalition between mother and son may be undermining the father's attempts at discipline. Session and home tasks might be designed to weaken the mother–son coalition and to strengthen the parental alliance. In this way, the model draws on the strategies of systems-based, especially structural, family therapy.

A fundamental principle, however, is to concentrate on alleviating target problems through relatively simple, straightforward tasks. Although tasks may be designed to effect contextual change, the target problems are the first priority. Structural dysfunctions, underlying pathologies, and so on are left alone unless they intrude as obstacles. If they do, practitioners can shift to tasks directed at contextual change. This progression from the simple to the not-so-simple makes the task-centered approach appropriate for a wide range of family types, from normal to highly disturbed, across a wide variety of problems and settings.

Groups

Unlike families, where the target of change includes interaction of group members outside the session, in a treatment group, the ultimate change target is resolution of the separate problems of each member.

In task-centered group treatment, the group process—norms, interaction patterns, social control, etc.—is used to further the basic activities of the model. Group members, guided by the leader, help one another to specify problems, plan tasks, rehearse and practice behavior, analyze obstacles to task achievement, review task progress, and so on. A major role for the social worker is to use group dynamics to focus and enhance the problem-solving efforts of the individuals.

Members of task-centered groups should be relatively similar with respect to target problems, such as problems of academic achievement, post-hospitalization adjustment, or depression. The homogeneity increases members' ability to contribute to the group. Because they have firsthand knowledge of the kind of problems others are experiencing, they are in a good position to provide support and guidance. Moreover, they can more readily apply lessons learned from the task work of others to their own situations. While work in groups does not permit the kind of sustained, focused attention on individual problems and tasks possible in one-to-one treatment, the group mode has certain distinct advantages. Group members in the aggregate may possess more detailed knowledge than the leader about intricacies of the target problems. Thus, group members can often suggest task possibilities that may not have occurred to either the social worker or the member being helped at the moment. Gaining recognition from a group provides an incentive for task accomplishment not available in individual treatment; in particular, a member who carries out a task successfully can serve as a model to others.

These advantages of group work are not always realized, however. Groups may become unfocused and discordant. Members may become competitive and overly critical. Certain participants may become objects of group hostility (the scapegoating phenomenon). To avoid its pitfalls, the group leader needs to exert a constructive influence on the dynamics of the group so that its purpose—to help individual members with their target problems—is kept in view.

Thus, practitioners channel communications of the participants in relation to the purpose. Beliefs that members have about one another and about appropriate behavior in the group influence the sociometric and normative structures of the group, so they should be functional for the group's purpose: for example, that all participants are worthwhile persons who deserve help in working out their problems; that each has to find a solution that is right for him or her; that each has a right to a fair share of attention and assistance from the leader and the group members. Shared beliefs about how the group should conduct itself become the basis for group control of the behavior of its members. Positive control efforts will maintain focus on problems and tasks; will facilitate sharing of relevant information (but discourage prying into aspects of the members' lives not germane to work on their problems); and will stress constructive reactions to task accomplishment over despondency at task failure. The practitioner also must encourage member leadership roles that enhance group functioning—for example, reducing tension in the group or redirecting members to the business at hand.

The group may use a "hot seat" model where each person in turn is the center of problem-solving focus, or it may use a "buddy system" where members pair off simultaneously to review tasks and develop new ones. Rooney has developed a series of structural aids such as problem- and task-review posters and instructions for buddies that help keep group dynamics positive and solution-focused.

While procedures for forming and conducting groups vary, the following format is typical. Preliminary individual interviews with prospective group members are used to determine if applicants have problems that would fall within the prospective focus of the group and to orient the applicants to the general structure and purpose of the group treatment model. In the initial group meeting, clients state the problems they wish to work on and assist one another in problem exploration and specification. A contractual agreement is reached on the purpose of the group and its duration (which is planned to be short term, as in individual treatment). In subsequent sessions each member formulates, plans, practices, and reviews tasks using a "hot seat" or buddy model. Practitioners may undertake tasks outside the session on behalf of a single client or the group as a whole, or group members may perform extra session tasks to help one another with their problems.

Case Management

A third variation of the task-centered model is its use for case management when a case involves multiple service providers. For example, work with a troubled child and family may involve a school social worker, one or more teachers, a school psychologist, a school nurse, a probation officer, and a case worker from a county child protection unit. In a mental health setting the "cast of characters" might include a social worker, a psychiatrist, a clinical psychologist, a mental health aide, a sheltered workshop supervisor, an occupational therapist, and the director of a group home. In such multiple-provider cases, a task-centered case management structure provides a useful device for monitoring and facilitating coordination among different actors (Colvin, Lee, Magnano, & Smith 2008a, 2008b; Naleppa & Reid, 2000; Viggiani, Reid, & Bailey-Dempsey, 2002). In task-centered case management, social workers function as case managers or coordinators. Usually case management team meetings bring clients and participants together to discuss aspects of the clients' problems that involve coordination among participants. There needs to be some common agreement on problems, but the strategies and tasks to resolve the problems usually differ by disciplines. Tasks for relevant participants, including clients, are developed. In addition to helping develop tasks, practitioners record the tasks on a sheet that is distributed to all participants. Social workers may take responsibility for monitoring and recording task progress and for serving as facilitators and coordinators (e.g., giving reminders). Practitioners usually also work directly with the client system, using individual- or family-oriented task-centered methods, as appropriate.

Range of Application

A question inevitably asked of any treatment system, in one form or another, is "For what kind of case is, and is not, the system applicable?" In answering this question, it is important to distinguish between the task-centered model as a whole and use of its structured activities for task planning, implementation, and review. The latter have, of course, a much wider range of application than the model as a whole. Task strategies or sequences of task-centered activities can be used in almost any form of treatment to enable clients to define and carry through particular courses of action. Thus, practitioners might use task-centered methods during the course of long-term psychosocial treatment to help clients translate into action insight into their problems.

When the task-centered model as a whole is used as the sole or primary method of treatment, its range of application, while narrower, is still broad enough to serve as a basic approach for the majority of clients seen by social workers. As mentioned, it is the default mode of intervention in social services in some European countries. With its emphasis on clients' definitions of problems and on clients' actions to resolve them, the model appears robust to cultural differences. It has been used successfully with persons from different social classes and from many cultural groups in the United States and Great Britain as well as with local persons in the Middle East, Africa, and Asia.

However, clients for whom the task-centered model may not be optimal include (1) clients who are not interested in taking action to solve specific problems in their life situations, but who rather want help in exploring existential issues—concerns about life goals or identity—or who wish to talk about stressful experiences, such as the loss of a loved one; (2) clients who are unwilling or unable to utilize the structure of the model—for example, clients who prefer a more casual, informal mode of helping or clients faced with highly turbulent situations in which it is not possible to isolate and follow through on specific problems; (3) clients who wish to alter conditions, such as psychogenic or motor difficulties, for which it is not possible to identify problem-solving tasks that the client is able to carry out; (4) clients who wish no help but may need to be seen for "protective reasons." The last category deserves additional comment because of frequent misunderstandings about the use of the model with involuntary clients. The task-centered approach can be used with many persons who may not have sought social workers' help or who may be initially reluctant to accept it. Many of these situations involve "mandated" problems—problems that are defined not by clients but by the community and its representatives, including practitioners. A reasonable approach is to work with the client and relevant community agencies to negotiate problem definitions that are acceptable to those involved. Such problem definitions can usually be found, even if no more than that the problem is the practitioner's presence in the client's lives; the client and practitioner can then work collaboratively to accomplish what is needed to eliminate the intrusion. Several authors have elaborated such work with involuntary clients, including techniques for collaborative problem definition (Jagt, 2001; Rooney, 2009; Trotter, 2006).

Effectiveness

At least 11 controlled group experiments have suggested the effectiveness of individual, family, and group forms of the task-centered model to alleviate specific problems of living (Gibbons, Bow, & Butler, 1985; Gibbons, Butler, Urwin, & Gibbons, 1978; Harris & Franklin, 2003; Larsen & Mitchell, 1980; Lee, 2005, as cited in Huh & Koh, 2010; Magnano, 2009; Newcome, 1985; Reid, 1975, 1978; Reid & Bailey-Dempsey, 1995; Reid, Bailey-Dempsey, Cain, Cook, & Burchard, 1994; Reid, Epstein, Brown, Tolson, & Rooney, 1980). All but one of these studies found improvements in target problems and, in some cases, improvements in more general measures such as self-efficacy, social problem-solving, or grades. Sample sizes ranged from 18 to 400. Populations in these studies included psychiatric patients, distressed marital couples, sick elderly patients, pregnant adolescents, families seeking to regain their children from foster care, schoolchildren with academic and behavioral problems, and delinquents in a residential center. The one study without effects showed no improvement in behavior in either the experimental or control students; it involved task-centered case management with teachers and parents of severely disturbed children in special classrooms (Magnano, 2009).

Less rigorous research designs also suggest positive outcomes for those receiving task-centered services. These include quasi-experimental designs, where comparison groups were formed without random assignment (Colvin et al., 2008a [comparable school district]; Pomeroy, Rubin, & Walker, 1995 [wait list]; Viggiani, Reid, & Bailey-Dempsey, 2002 [comparable classrooms]) and a variety of uncontrolled (pre-test/post-test only) group evaluations (Colvin et al., 2008b; Goldberg & Stanley, 1985; Huh & Koh, 2010; Sinclair & Walker, 1985; Trotter, 2010). Much of the literature describing adaptations of the model to particular populations also used either controlled single-case experiments or systematic D&D research to formulate and validate the adaptations.

Thus, there is reasonable support for the effectiveness of the task-centered model in alleviating problems-in-living and modest evidence that directly related characteristics such as coping, stress, or self-control can be improved. However, problem alleviation is not problem resolution. Frequently, the effects of the model are confined to the reduction in clients' difficulties or improving their ability to cope with them. Moreover, knowledge of the long-term impact of the model is still limited. Only four studies followed clients after treatment. Three of these found that gains were sustained for between 30 days and 18 months. For example, the target problems of schoolchildren and psychiatric outpatients remained the same or showed continued improvement (Reid, 1978); self-poisoning clients held gains in depression, social relations, and problems with significant others, but not with changes in social problems (neither task-centered nor service-as-usual had an effect on practical difficulties like employment or housing) (Gibbons, Bow, & Butler, 1985); and pregnant adolescents maintained gains on school attendance and social problem solving (Harris & Franklin, 2003). However, Reid and Bailey-Dempsey (1995) found that middle-school girls' gains in attendance and grades did not carry over to the following year; the authors were not able to follow up measures of problem reduction, self-esteem, or family functioning. Quite possibly, the durability of effects of the model varies with the kind of population or problem to which it is applied. This issue is among many to be addressed in future research.

Case Example

The following case illustrates basic features of the model as well as application to work with families.

Mrs. Johnson contacted a family agency because of problems concerning her 16-year-old daughter, Nancy, and the resulting fighting in her family. In an initial interview with the parents, Nancy, and her 14-year-old brother, Mark, the family members presented their views of their problems. Mr. Johnson began the session with a stream of complaints about Nancy. Her "attitude" toward him and his wife was "hostile." She did not accept his beliefs or standards. Any attempt to communicate with her was futile. He then turned to the problem that precipitated their contact with the agency: Nancy's insistence that her boyfriend, Mike (age 19), be allowed to visit in their home over the weekend.

Mr. Johnson had objected to Nancy's relationship with Mike ever since Nancy's pregnancy and abortion about 6 months previously, but had accepted it because Nancy was determined to see Mike anyway. Mr. Johnson even tolerated Mike's coming to their home, but he did not want him there all weekend. Mr. Johnson saw Mike as an unwelcome intruder whose presence deprived Mr. Johnson of his privacy.

Joining in, Mrs. Johnson complained of Nancy's nagging her to get permission to do things her father might not allow. If Mrs. Johnson refused, Nancy would become belligerent and insulting. On top of this, Mrs. Johnson would usually be the one to patch things up between Nancy and her father. Nancy said little but expressed bitterness that her parents were trying to disrupt her relationship with Mike. When asked about his views of the problem by the practitioner, brother Mark commented in a somewhat detached way that the fighting between his mother and Nancy was the main difficulty.

From the family's presentation of the problems and their interactions in the session, the practitioner was impressed with the father's lack of real control and Nancy's efforts to get what she wanted through her mother, who was put in the middle. Further exploration made clearer the mother's "peacekeeping" role and her discontent with it. The practitioner presented this picture as an additional problem to be considered. In ranking the problems that had been brought up, the family agreed that the issue of greatest priority concerned the conflict over Mike's visiting. They accepted the practitioner's formulation of "mother's being in the middle" as a second problem.

The family was seen for seven additional sessions. The main interventions were structured around problem-solving tasks in the session and at home. These tasks were designed to achieve a compromise about Mike's visiting and, in the process, to work on the dysfunctional interaction patterns that had been identified. Initially, these tasks were designed to bring about more direct communication between Nancy and her father as well as more cooperation between the two parents. It became apparent, however, that the interaction pattern was more complex than originally thought. Mrs. Johnson was not the only peacemaker; Mr. Johnson frequently assumed this role with Nancy and her mother. The parents were then coming to each other's rescue without taking responsibility either individually or jointly for dealing with Nancy's behavior. In subsequent family problem solving, the parents jointly developed rules that each could apply consistently in dealing with Nancy.

Midway in treatment, a compromise was reached on Nancy's relationship with Mike: Mike could spend one night a week at the Johnsons' home but would not be there on the weekend. Interestingly enough, the solution was suggested by Mark, who had remained somewhat on the sidelines in the family discussions. The plan was implemented and, perhaps to everyone's surprise, held up. The case ended on a positive note: the immediate problem had been worked through and the family members, in their evaluation of treatment, indicated that their situation as a whole was better. In the final session, the family discussed how to remember the consistent discipline for Nancy, and what to do if Mike started coming over more often. In her consumer questionnaire, Mrs. Johnson commented that the experience had been a "good lesson in problem working."

The case illustrates several features of the model. Focus was on the specific problem the family wanted most to solve. The major intervention strategy was based on tasks in which family members struggled toward a solution in their own way. At the same time, contextual analysis identified dysfunctional patterns that might underlie this and other problems. The family helped identify these and worked on the patterns as a part of the problem-solving tasks. Not all cases present such opportunities to achieve contextual change within the context of family problem solving, but in this case they were present and were well utilized by the family and practitioner.

Summary

Task-centered social work treatment is a system of brief, time-limited practice that emphasizes helping clients with specific problems of their own choosing through discrete client and practitioner actions or tasks. Treatment interviews are devoted largely to the specification of problems, and to the identification and planning of appropriate tasks, which are then carried out between sessions. Sessions are structured by problem-solving activities. The middle sessions are devoted to task planning and implementation activities, which were elaborated through developmental research. Although there are limits on its range of application, the task-centered model can be—and is—offered as a basic service for the majority of clients dealt with by clinical social workers. The core methods of the approach—problem-solving and task planning and implementation—can be used within most long- or short-term practice frameworks. The model has a better base of research support than most social work intervention models and is appropriate for many cultures.

References

Abramson, J. (1992). Health-related problems. In W. J. Reid (Ed.), *Task strategies: An empirical approach to social work practice* (pp. 225–249). New York: Columbia University Press.

Alley, G. R., & Brown, L.B. (2002). A diabetes problem solving support group: Issues, process and preliminary outcomes. *Social Work in Health Care, 36*(1), 1–9.

Bass, M. (1977). Toward a model of treatment for runaway girls in detention. In W. J. Reid & L. Epstein (Eds.), *Task-centered practice.* New York: Columbia University Press.

Birchler, G. R., & Spinks, S. H. (1981). Behavioral-systems marital and family therapy: Integration and clinical application. *American Journal of Family Therapy, 8,* 6–28.

Blizinsky, M. J., & Reid, W. J. (1980). Problem focus and change in a brief treatment model. *Social Work, 25,* 89–98.

Bloom, B. L. (2002). Brief interventions for anxiety disorders: Clinical outcome studies. *Brief Treatment and Crisis Intervention, 2*(4), 325–340.

Bloom, B. L., Yeager, K. R, & Roberts, A. R. (2006a). Evidence-based practice with anxiety disorders: Guidelines based on 59 outcome studies. In A. R. Roberts & K.R. Yeager (Eds.), *Foundations of evidence-based social work practice* (pp. 275–290). New York: Oxford University Press.

Bloom, B. L., Yeager, K. R, & Roberts, A. R. (2006b). The implications of controlled outcome studies on planned short-term psychotherapy with depressive

disorders. I. In A. R. Roberts & K. R. Yeager (Eds.), *Foundations of evidence-based social work practice* (pp. 258–274). New York: Oxford University Press.

Bordin, E. S. (1994). Theory and research in the therapeutic working alliance. In A. O. Horvath & L. S. Greenberg (Eds.), *The working alliance: theory, research, and practice* (pp. 13–37). New York: John Wiley & Sons.

Caspi, J. (2008). Building a sibling aggression treatment model: Design & development research in action. *Research on Social Work Practice, 16*(6), 575–585.

Caspi, J., & Reid, W. J. (2002). *Educational supervision in social work.* New York: Columbia University Press.

Colvin, J., Lee, M., Magnano, J., & Smith, V. (2008a). The Partners in Prevention Program: The evaluation and evolution of the task-centered case management model. *Research on Social Work Practice, 18,* 607–615.

Colvin, J., Lee, M., Magnano, J., & Smith, V. (2008b). The Partners in Prevention Program: Further development of the task-centered case management model. *Research on Social Work Practice, 18,* 586–595.

Dierking, B., Brown, M., & Fortune, A. E. (1980). Task-centered treatment in a residential facility for the elderly: A clinical trial. *Journal of Gerontological Social Work, 2,* 225–240.

Doel, M., & Marsh, P. (1993). *Task-centered social work.* London: Wildwood House.

Epstein, L. (1977). A project in school social work. In W. J. Reid & L. Epstein (Eds.), *Task-centered practice.* New York: Columbia University Press.

Epstein, L. (1988). *Helping people: The task-centered approach.* Columbus, OH: Merrill Publishing Company.

Epstein, L., & Brown, L. B. (2001). *Brief treatment and a new look at the task-centered approach* (4th ed.). Boston: Allyn & Bacon.

Eriksen, R. E. (1999). *Arbeidshefte i innføring i oppgaveorientert tilnærming.* Oslo: Diakonhjemmet høgskole.

Eriksen, R.E. (2010). Task-centred practice in Norway. In A. E. Fortune, P. McCallion, & K. Briar-Lawson (Eds.), *Social work practice research for the 21st century.* New York: Columbia University Press.

Eriksen, R. E., & Nordstrand, M. (1995). *Innføring i oppgaveorientert tilnærming (OOT).* Oslo: Diakonhjemmet høgskole, Høgskolen i Sør Trøndelag og Sosial og helsedepartementet.

Ewalt, P. L. (1977). A psychoanalytically oriented child guidance setting. In W. J. Reid & L. Epstein (Eds.), *Task-centered practice.* New York: Columbia University Press.

Fahs-Beck, D., & Jones, M. A. (1973). *Progress on family problems: A nationwide study of clients' and counselors' views on family agency services.* New York: Family Service Agency of America.

Fishman, S. F., & Lubetkin, B. S. (1980). Maintenance and generalization of individual behavior therapy programs: Clinical observations. In P. Karoly & J. J. Steffen (Eds.), *Improving the long-terms effects of psychotherapy: Models of durable outcome.* New York: Gardner.

Fortune, A. E. (1985). *Task-centered practice with families and groups.* New York: Springer.

Fortune, A. E. (2009). Terminating with clients. In A. R. Roberts (Ed.), *Social workers' desk reference* (2nd ed., pp. 627–631). New York: Oxford University Press.

Fortune, A. E. (in press). Development of the task-centered model. in T. Rzepnicki, S. McCracken, & H. Briggs, *From the task-centered approach to evidence-based and integrative practice.* Lyceum Books.

Freeman, E. M., & Couchonnal, G. (2006). Narrative and culturally based approach in practice with families. *Families in Society,* 87(2), 198–208.

Garfield, S. L. (1994). Research on client variables in psychotherapy. In A. E. Bergin & S. L. Garfield (Eds.), *Handbook of psychotherapy and behavior change* (4th ed., pp. 190–228). New York: Wiley.

Garvin, C. D. (1994). Task-centered group work. *Social Service Review,* 48, 494–507.

Gibbons, J., Bow, I., & Butler, J. (1985). Task-centred social work after parasuicide. In E. M. Goldberg, J. Gibbons, & I. Sinclair (Eds.), *Problems, tasks and outcomes: The evaluation of task-centred casework* (pp. 169–247). London: Allen and Unwin.

Gibbons, J. S., Butler, J., Urwin, P., & Gibbons, J. L. (1978). Evaluation of a social work service for self-poisoning parents. *British Journal of Psychiatry,* 133, 111–118.

Goldberg, E. M., & Stanley, S. J. (with Kenrick, J.) (1985). Task-centred casework in a probation setting. In E. M. Goldberg, J. Gibbons, & I. Sinclair (Eds.), *Problems, tasks and outcomes: The evaluation of task-centred casework* (pp. 87–168). London: Allen and Unwin.

Goldman, A. I. (1970). *A theory of human action.* Englewood Cliffs, NJ: Prentice-Hall.

Harris, M. B., & Franklin, C. G. (2003). Effects of a cognitive-behavioral, school-based, group intervention with Mexican American pregnant and parenting adolescents. *Social Work Research,* 27(2), 74–84.

Hepworth, D. H., Rooney, R. H., Rooney, G. D., Strom-Gottfried, K., & Larsen, J. A. (2010). *Direct social work practice: Theory and skills* (8th ed.). Brooks-Cole/Cengage.

Hollis, F. (1964). *Casework: A psychosocial therapy.* New York: Random House.

Horvath, A. O., & Greenberg, L. S. (1989). Development of the Working Alliance Inventory. *Journal of Consulting and Clinical Psychiatry,* 36, 223–233.

Horvath, A. O. & Greenberg, L. S. (1994). Introduction. In A. O. Horvath & L. S. Greenberg (Eds.), *The working alliance: theory, research, and practice* (pp. 1–12). New York: John Wiley & Sons.

Huh, N. S., & Koh, Y. S. (2010). Task-centered practice in South Korea. In A. E. Fortune, P. McCallion, & K. Briar-Lawson (Eds.), *Social work practice research for the 21st century.* New York: Columbia University Press.

Jagt, L. (2001). *Moet dat nou? Helpverlening aan onvrijwillige clienten.* Houten/Zaventem: Bohn Stafleu Van Loghum.

Jagt, L. J. (2008). *Van Richmond naar Reid: Bronnen en ontwikkeling van taakgerichte* Houten/Zaventem: Bohn Stafleu Van Loghum.

Jagt, L., & Jagt, N. (1990). *Taakgerichte hulpverlening in het maatschappelijk werk.* Houten/Zaventem: Bohn Stafleu Van Loghum.

Johnson, D. H., & Gelso, C. J. (1982). The effectiveness of time limits in counseling and psychotherapy: A critical review. *Counseling Psychologist,* 9, 70–83.

Larsen, J., & Mitchell, C. (1980). Task-centered strength oriented group work with delinquents. *Social Casework,* 61, 154–163.

Lee, J. H. (2005). *A study on the effectiveness of an integrated program for potential school dropouts to improve school adjustment.* MSW thesis, Graduate School of Hallym University.

Lo, T. W. (2005). Task-centered group work: Reflections on practice. *International Social Work,* 48(4), 455–465.

Magnano, J. (2009). *Partners in success: An evaluation of an intervention for children with severe emotional disturbance.* Doctoral dissertation, University at Albany, State University of New York, Albany.

Marsh, P. (2010). Task-centred practice in Great Britain. In A. E. Fortune, P. McCallion, & K. Briar-Lawson (Eds.), *Social work practice research for the 21st century.* New York: Columbia University Press.

Marsh, P., & Doel, M. (2005). *The task-centred book.* Abingdon & New York: Routledge.

Moyer, A., Finney, J. W., Swearingen, C. E., & Vergun, P. (2002). Brief interventions for alcohol problems: A meta-analytic review of controlled investigations in treatment-seeking and non-treatment-seeking populations. *Addiction,* 97(3), 279–292.

Naleppa, M., & Reid, W. J. (2003). *Gerontological social work: A task-centered approach*. New York: Columbia University Press.

Newcome, K. (1985). Task-centered group work with the chronic mentally ill in day treatment. In A. E. Fortune (Ed.), *Task-centered practice with families and groups*. New York: Springer.

Orlinsky, D. E., & Howard, K. I. (1986). Process outcome in psychotherapy. In S. L. Garfield & A. E. Bergin (Eds.), *Handbook of psychotherapy and behavior change*. New York: John Wiley and Sons.

Osborn, A. F. (1963). *Applied imagination: Principles and procedures of creative problem-solving* (3rd ed.). New York: Scribner's.

Parihar, B. (1983). *Task-centered management in human services*. Springfield, IL: Charles C. Thomas.

Parihar, B. (1994). Task-centered work in human service organizations. In E. R. Tolson, W. J. Reid, & C. D. Garvin (Eds.), *Generalist practice: A task-centered approach*. New York: Columbia University Press.

Perlman, H. H. (1957). *Social casework: A problem-solving process*. Chicago: University of Chicago Press.

Pomeroy, E., Rubin, A., & Walker, R. J. (1995). Effectiveness of a psychoeducational and task-centered group intervention for family members of people with AIDS. *Social Work Research*, 19, 142–152.

Ramakrishnan, K. R., Balgopal, P. R., & Pettys, G. L. (1994). Task-centered work with communities. In E. R. Tolson, W. J. Reid, & C. D. Garvin (Eds.), *Generalist practice: A task centered approach*. New York: Columbia University Press.

Rathbone-McCuan, E. (1985). Intergenerational family practice with older families. In A. E. Fortune (Ed.), *Task-centered practice with families and groups*. New York: Springer.

Reid, W. J. (1975). A test of a task-centered approach. *Social Work*, 20, 3–9.

Reid, W. J. (1978). *The task-centered system*. New York: Columbia University Press.

Reid, W. J. (1985). *Family problem solving*. New York: Columbia University Press.

Reid, W. J. (1987). The family problem solving sequence. *American Journal of Family Therapy*, 14, 135–146.

Reid, W. J. (1992). *Task strategies: An empirical approach to social work practice*. New York: Columbia University Press.

Reid, W. J. (1997). Research on task-centered practice. *Social Work Research*, 21(3), 132–137.

Reid, W. J. (2000). *The task planner: An intervention resource for human service professionals*. New York: Columbia University Press.

Reid, W. J., & Bailey-Dempsey, C. (1995). The effects of monetary incentives on school performance. *Families in Society*, 76, 331–340.

Reid, W. J., Bailey-Dempsey, C. A., Cain, E., Cook, T. V., & Burchard, J. D. (1994). *Cash incentives versus case management: Can money replace services in preventing school failure? Social Work Research*, 18(4), 227–236.

Reid, W. J., & Donovan, T. (1990). Treating sibling violence. *Family Therapy*, 71, 49–59.

Reid, W. J., & Epstein, L. (1972). *Task-centered casework*. New York: Columbia University Press.

Reid, W. J., Epstein, L., Brown, L. B., Tolson, E., & Rooney, R. H. (1980). Task-centered school social work. *Social Work in Education*, 2, 7–24.

Reid, W. J., & Shyne, A. (1969). *Brief and extended casework*. New York: Columbia University Press.

Rooney, R. H. (1977). Adolescent groups in public schools. In W. J. Reid & L. Epstein (Eds.), *Task-centered practice*. New York: Columbia University Press.

Rooney, R. H. (1981). Task centered reunification model for foster care. In A. A. Malluccio & P. Sinanoglue (Eds.), *Working with biological parents of children in foster care*. New York: Child Welfare League of America.

Rooney, R. H. (1988). Measuring task-centered training effects on practice: Results of an audiotape study in a public agency. *Journal of Continuing Social Work Education*, 4, 2–7.

Rooney, R. H. (Ed.). (2009). *Strategies for work with involuntary clients*. New York: Columbia University Press.

Rooney, R. H. (2010). Task-centered practice in the United States. In A. E. Fortune, P. McCallion, & K. Briar-Lawson (Eds.), *Social work practice research for the 21st century*. New York: Columbia University Press.

Rzepnicki, T. L. (1985). Centered intervention in foster care services: Working with families who have children in placement. In A. E. Fortune (Ed.), *Task-centered practice with families and groups*. New York: Springer.

Sinclair, I., & Walker, D. (1985). Task-centred casework in two intake teams. In E. M. Goldberg, J. Gibbons, & I. Sinclair (Eds.), *Problems, tasks and outcomes: The evaluation of task-centred casework* (pp. 13–73). London: Allen and Unwin.

Studt, E. (1968). Social work theory and implication for the practice of methods. *Social Work Education Reporter*, 16, 22–46.

Taylor, C. (1977). Counseling in a service industry. In W. J. Reid & L. Epstein (Eds.), *Task-centered practice*. New York: Columbia University Press.

Thomas, E. J., & Rothman, J. (1994). An integrative perspective on intervention research. In E. J. Thomas & J. Rothman (Eds.), *Intervention research: Design and development for human service* (pp. 3–23). New York: Haworth Press.

Tolson, E. R., Reid, W. J., & Garvin, C. D. (1994). *Generalist practice: A task-centered approach.* New York: Columbia University Press.

Trotter, C. (2006). *Working with involuntary clients* (2nd ed.). Crows Nest, NSW: Allen & Unwin.

Trotter, C. (2010). Task-centred practice in Australia. In A. E. Fortune, P. McCallion, & K. Briar-Lawson (Eds.), *Social work practice research for the 21st century*. New York: Columbia University Press.

Viggiani, P. A., Reid, W. J., & Bailey-Dempsey, C. (2002). Social worker-teacher collaboration in the classroom: Help for elementary students at risk of failure. *Research on Social Work Practice,* 12(5), 604–620.

Weissman, A. (1977). In the steel industry. In W. J. Reid & L. Epstein (Eds.), *Task-centered practice.* New York: Columbia University Press.

36

TRANSACTIONAL ANALYSIS

Developed by Eric Berne, this theory stresses the essential roles of the structure and function of ego states, and how their transactions can be modified to achieve full autonomy and intimacy

Transactional Analysis Theory and Social Work Treatment

Annie E. Wenger-Nabigon

Transactional Analysis (TA) developed through the work of Eric Berne, MD, and the early work of psychiatric clinicians who participated in his clinical seminars. Berne's original conceptualizations of TA as both a theory and treatment model grew from his training in traditional Freudian psychoanalysis and his work as an army psychiatrist during and after World War II. Berne considered TA to be part of social psychiatry, and game analysis to be only a "special aspect of TA" (Berne, 1964, p. 51). The understanding of interpersonal transactions is central in importance in the application of theory to treatment (Turner, 2005) and is applicable in a wide range of settings.

TA is currently defined as "a theory of personality and a systematic psychotherapy for personal growth and personal change"

(Stewart & Joines, 1987, p. 3). TA is psychodynamically oriented but is also solidly cognitive (Gitterman, 1991; Prochaska & Norcross, 1994). It has grown into a full-fledged profession regulated by organizations that confer accreditation and advance the growth and development of TA. Research, education, and practice of TA flourish worldwide, and it is used by educators, organizational specialists, social workers, counselors, and psychotherapists. While it is not widely taught in Canadian schools of social work, TA is compatible with the goals and values of the social work profession (Turner, 2005). The International Transactional Analysis Association (ITAA) welcomes membership from social workers and provides an educational and certification process for those who aspire to become Transactional Analysts. Certification and regulation as analysts is not required to be a member of the organization at an introductory level.

Berne's definitive statement of TA was given with the publication of his book *Transactional Analysis in Psychotherapy* (1961); it was developed first as a specific theory of personality and secondly as a treatment approach for psychotherapy. His book *Principles of Group Treatment* (1966), based on 20 years of experience with group psychotherapy, had significant input from the California TA seminars. While he never completely abandoned psychoanalytic theory, he had deep disagreements with Freudian methodology.

TA theory holds a basic assumption that an individual's personality is composed of three ego states known as Parent, Adult, and Child, and that the basic units of social interaction, called "social intercourse" (Berne, 1961), occur between people operating from internal ego states formed from decisions made as very young children (Berne, 1966; Goulding, 1978). In TA terminology, "strokes" are exchanged to create social intercourse, which is weighted by "games" (Berne, 1964; Cooper & Turner, 1996). These "transactions" can be positive or negative and express pathology, or autonomy and intimacy. The goal of TA therapy is to promote autonomy, which Berne presented as "manifested by the release or recovery of three capacities: awareness, spontaneity and intimacy" (p. 178). Berne believed that script analysis, designed to "cure the patient" and promote autonomy, was "Freudian, but it is not psychoanalytic" (Berne, 1972, p. 58).

While this chapter provides a basic understanding of the fundamentals of TA theory and therapy, a full understanding of the concepts and methods can only come through study of the TA literature, workshops, training, and supervision. Practitioners interested in using TA should obtain more thorough instruction in TA than this chapter provides.

History

Eric Berne, MD, was born Eric Lennard Bernstein in Montreal, Quebec, Canada, on May 10, 1910. He graduated with a medical degree from McGill University and moved to the U.S. in 1935, where he began a psychiatry residency in 1936. In 1939, he became an American citizen, and he changed his name to Eric Berne around 1943 when he entered the U.S. Army as a psychiatrist. In 1941, he began his psychoanalytic training under Paul Federn, who had been a student of Sigmund Freud. Berne later studied at the San Francisco Psychoanalytic Institute (SFPI), where Eric Erikson was his analyst. In 1956 his application for entrance into the SFPI was denied with a recommendation that he reapply after 3 or 4 more years of training and personal analysis, at which point he turned away from psychoanalysis to develop his own theories further (Forman & Ramsburg, 1978; Steiner, 1974). His TA theory integrated social psychiatry with Freud's explanation of intrapsychic development, and was primarily a "relational system of behavior analysis" (Forman & Ramsburg, 1978, p. 23). Freud's focus was on instincts, drives, and internal processes, while Berne's focus was on interpersonal relationships and a psychosocial approach to people problems; however, Berne never completely rejected Freudian theory (Berne, 1972).

Berne was 46 years old when he abandoned his goal of admittance to professional status as a Freudian-school psychoanalyst, and he was to live only another 14 years (Steiner, 1974, pp. 10–11). His unexpected death of coronary disease on July 15, 1970, came as a shock to his colleagues and the TA community. His close friend, Dr. Claude Steiner, believed Berne had a "limited life-expectancy script" that he lived out by dying at the age of 60, just as his mother had done. His "loving relationships were short lived" (p. 17) and he believed that people were lucky if they had even 15 minutes of true intimacy in a lifetime (p. 18). Others who knew him well and saw his life as fundamentally work-oriented, with barriers to close relationships, echoed this sad and somewhat cynical view of Berne's life (p. 16). Several children, who had also provided input into his writing (Berne, 1972), survived him.

Berne began his seminars in the 1950s, where he presented his views on transactional and structural analysis. He viewed his patients as equals and believed therapists and patients simply had different roles and responsibilities. His equality stance led him to insist that patients be part of clinical staffings, and he wrote, "Anything that's not worth saying in front of a patient is not worth saying at all" (Berne, quoted in Steiner, 1974, p. 5). Out of these seminars rose the foundations of the ITAA, which currently has branches in over 64 countries. The ITAA publishes the *Transactional Analysis Journal* quarterly, and *The Script* newsletter nine times a year. It provides training, conferences, publications, awards, scholarships, supervision, and certification for its members at four levels. The formal certification process takes up to 7 years. The European Association of Transactional Analysis, founded in 1976, has member bodies in 27 different European countries, with over 7,000 members. The worldwide growth of TA has moved to specialization in psychotherapy, organizational and educational settings, and counseling areas. Modern Transactional Analysts incorporate techniques from other schools of therapy as well, such as psychoanalytic, brief-therapy models, neurolinguistic programming, systems theory, Eriksonian theory, dialectical behavioral therapy, family therapy, and others, yet always use the ego-state model and life-script theory as an organizing principle (Stewart & Joines, 1987, p. 277).

Transactional Analysis Theory

TA theory revolves around its assumptions regarding autonomy, communication, intimacy, and the relationship between structure and function of ego states. Stewart and Joines (1987) classify the four major aspects of TA theory into the following categories: personality theory (ego-state model), communication theory (a method of analyzing systems), child and human development theory (life position and life-script formation), and a theory of psychopathology. These assumptions are viewed differently by different schools of TA, categorized as the classical school (Berne), the redecision school (Goulding & Goulding, 1979; Sills, 2007), and the cathexis school, or re-parenting, a controversial approach first developed in the 1970s (Childs-Gowell & Schiff, 2000).

TA systematizes and analyzes the information arising from transactions (Harris, 1967). Understanding the life positions taken by individuals allows for the analysis of the ego-state (structure) and the transactional (function) processes. A functional model of the ego states will classify behaviors, and a structural model will classify memories and strategies, or the content of the ego states in transactions (Stewart & Joines, 1987). The terminology used by Berne, Harris, and others has entered the vernacular, becoming trivialized as it gained popularity. Steiner (1974) was very concerned that the popularity of TA was manipulated by the mass market for profit, not for integrity in healing (p. 8). Berne's reason for using simple, straightforward language was that people could clearly understand what is happening and why, and could be empowered to act effectively in making necessary changes. He developed the colloquial terms "Parent," "Adult," and "Child" to represent internal ego states activated and fixated in early childhood that are, in technical psychoanalytical language, known as "exteropsychic, neopsychic, and archaeopsychic ego states" (Berne, 1964, p. 23).

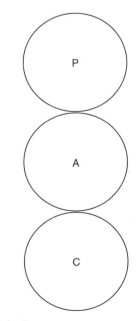

Figure 36-1. Ego states.

The structural analysis of ego states (normal physiological phenomena) provides for a full understanding of human personality development and functioning. These states (Fig. 36.1) exist in all people, and the relationships between people are understood by knowing the rules of communication and transactional patterns between these states. The source of people's problems can be found by analyzing the "life position," the "games" people engage in with each other, and the "life-scripts" they act out for themselves. Relationship diagrams can be used with clients in helping them understand what is happening within them and with other people (refer to the section on Structural Analysis of Ego States later in this chapter). People can increase their capacity for full autonomy and intimacy as they practice clear communication and understand the structure and function of their own, and others', ego states and transactions. TA as a theory, while having much in common with traditional psychoanalytic theory, is closely aligned with systems theory framework in its analysis of communication (Pitman, 1984).

TA Basic Assumptions

TA begins with the first premise that people are "OK." They are born with a pure ability to fully sense the world, and begin life making decisions and engaging in behaviors that are oriented toward survival, growth, and meaning making. Humans are not born with an inherently flawed self, but have an innate capacity for making decisions in either positive or negative directions. Within the environment surrounding the growing human there are forces (from caretakers, culture, and society) that support growth and health, or become destructive. As the developing human being responds to the surrounding forces, he or she makes decisions about himself or herself, and others, that can interfere with healthy development, prevent the emergence of a fully autonomous "grown-up," or Adult self, and lead to pathologies (problems). The child becomes confused and mystified and unconsciously internalizes destructive messages as part of the creation of a life position and life-script. Self-awareness, creativity, and spontaneity decrease as a result, and the human being must

make changes in order to become fully conscious again and achieve autonomy and intimacy. This self-awareness is the crucial component in the journey toward full autonomy (Novellino, 2005). TA theorist and analyst Claude M. Steiner (1974) referred to this assumption as a basic "positive life tendency," with life problems and lack of autonomy arising from a tendency to go "dormant" for whatever reason.

The second premise of TA is that people actively participate in problem-solving processes (Berne, 1961; Cooper & Turner, 1996). If they seek the help of a TA therapist, the therapist's job is to engage with them as a full partner in the work. Making "contracts" with the client is a crucial part of the work together. TA assumes that clients will be fully capable of this work, a stance that is empowering and motivating and encourages self-mastery. The ability to separate behaviors and feelings and bring an observing, fully functioning Adult ego state to the work is something that anyone can accomplish. Even young children can learn these basic approaches (Bry, 1973; Freed, 1973/1991).

The third premise of TA assumes that people's problems result from a lack of autonomy, knowledge, awareness, and understanding rather than from innate pathologies. While people may not know why they have the problems they have, they are fully capable of gaining crucial self-awareness and demonstrating responsibility to lead productive lives, no matter how serious their problems. TA holds that this can be achieved no matter what the impairment— developmental disability, addiction, psychosis, or poor relationships (Harris, 1967). With the appropriate amount and type of support, people are capable of overcoming even the most severe difficulties and achieving full autonomy and intimacy. The individual's willingness and choice to make different decisions and be fully responsible for his or her life is the source of autonomy, which arises from redecision work (Goulding, 1978, p. 11). Change is the result of both the client's work (redecision) and the relational social transactions with the therapist (Hargaden & Sills, 2002). Fritz Perls (1969) had a great impact on TA in developing the empathic and relational aspects of TA that encompass affective change (Hargaden & Sills, 2002, p. 4). Berne's more cognitive and psychodynamic focus places greater reliance on the role of the analyst in helping the client achieve autonomy.

Four Life Positions

Harris (1967), in *I'm OK–You're OK,* brought much of the theory and practice of TA into public consciousness and made the claim that TA provided the knowledge necessary for people to understand the laws and "secrets" of human behavior (p. 36). He emphasized that TA had its own "language" and was a "tool" that, if based on instruction on proper use, would allow people to function as fully autonomous, free individuals able to have intimate relationships. He popularized Berne's following four basic life positions: "I'm not OK–You're OK"; "I'm not OK–You're not OK"; "I'm OK–You're not OK"; "I'm OK–You're OK."

As Berne (1966) stated, "Every game, script, and destiny is based on one of these four basic positions" (p. 270) that arise early in life from the psychobiological experiences of the growing human organism. Deficient sensory stimulation (or lack of strokes) in early life has an endocrinological effect (p. 281) as well as a psychological and social effect. The developing human being takes a position toward life from one of the first three basic stances depending upon the nature of the stimulus exposure and the support of the environment. Scripts and games arising from childhood experience are largely unconscious, and serve to protect from threat or meet a need (Cornell, 2008, p. 97). The fourth position arises from conscious thoughts that allow for autonomous function.

An "I'm not OK–you're OK" stance is conceived of as the earliest position the infant takes as a result of total dependence, helplessness, and reliance on caregivers who may or may not be consistently nurturing. When nurturance, or stroking, is given inconsistently or inadequately to the infant, affective states of "I'm not OK" will theoretically build up within the unconscious or preconscious ego state, and the developing human being will respond in ways designed to elicit attention to needs, even if it is negative attention. The individual with a "You're not OK" position has had to learn to survive with a

minimum of stroking, and has come to believe that other people are responsible for their OK or not OK feelings. People operating from the "I'm OK–You're not OK" position were usually emotionally and/or physically abused in some manner as young children and learned to rely solely on themselves for survival and strokes, taking a blaming stance toward others (Cooper & Turner, 1996, p. 644). Only when a person has fully confronted the childhood affective experience and made a conscious redecision from a combined cognitive-emotional approach will he or she be able to operate from an "I'm OK–You're OK" stance as a fully autonomous human being (Goulding & Goulding, 1979).

Structural Analysis of Ego States

TA provides a method by which the structure of an individual's personality, or internal ego state, can be understood in a systemic fashion. Berne (1964) considered the structure of the internal ego to be a "set of coherent behavior patterns" (p. 23) as well as affective psychological realities. What he came to call the "Parent," "Adult," and "Child" (or PAC) was an abbreviated way of saying that individuals carry around within themselves representations of the internalized messages and identifications gained throughout childhood development. He outlined these three states as being present at a very young age and further developing into adulthood (p. 24), and expressed them colloquially in the following phrases:

- "Everyone carries his parents around inside of him." (P)
- "Everyone has an Adult." (A)
- "Everyone carries a little boy or girl around inside of him." (C)

These representations were never used in a negative or judgmental way (e.g., "Child" does not imply undesirability), and he was clear that he made no distinctions in the system as "mature" or "immature." He was concerned primarily with what was appropriate behavioral adaptation and believed that only when one or the other of the ego states upset the balance in the structural system was analysis required for reorganization

(p. 28). Both P and C have two forms, expressed in P as "direct" and "indirect," and expressed in C as "natural" and "adapted" (p. 26). Berne viewed the "natural Child" as the ego state from which one could access spontaneous expression that was free of any "Parent" influence. Later developments in TA theory have expanded and changed some of the original understanding of these states (Sills, 2007, pp. 16–17).

A structural and functional analysis of the individual's ego states will elucidate at what level communication is occurring—where the stimulus and response pattern originates. These transactions can be duplex, with one occurring on a social level (e.g., Adult to Adult) and another on a psychological level (e.g., Parent to Child, or Child to Adult). The transactions determine which ego states are active in the stimulus/response set (Berne, 1966, pp. 220–232) and are not just simple interactions. The multiplicity within each individual as represented by the PAC model (Joseph, 2008, p. 222) means that individuals choose transactions with other people from a variety of possible positions. Understanding not only where one is "coming from" but also where the other is "coming from" will help people have clear communication that is congruent and complementary. TA addresses covert or ulterior messages and the power they effect (Steiner, 1974, p. 64).

Rowan (2007) describes the "dialogic self" as an expansion of the TA concept of PAC. The process of structural and functional analysis is augmented by understanding how the individual conducts an inner dialogue among the "parts." This dialogue allows for assimilation of conscious and unconscious material arising from the varying inner ego states (pp. 35–36). Hargaden and Sills (2002) note that TA developed in the social context of rigid social "shoulds" that needed to be discarded, but the social context has changed to a contemporary situation where societies face a world that cannot provide a safe "holding environment" for the inner self. TA techniques help provide a treatment environment structured to help people understand the structural and functional aspects of their inner functioning and relationships, and develop strategies to adapt or change. Schmid (2008) approaches the classical TA concepts from the stance of role analysis by which he integrates a systemic analysis of multiple organizational levels with TA concepts (p. 17). These applications of structural and functional analysis of the various ego states facilitate a broader and deeper understanding of interpersonal transactions.

Time Structure

Berne (1966) described the importance of time structuring in the functioning of the personality. He delineated six different behavior types that humans use to create meaningful use of their time.

- *Withdrawal*: extraneous fantasies or transactions that are adapted or unadapted
- *Rituals*: either stereotyped or predictable
- *Pastimes*: similar to rituals but less stereotyped
- *Activities*: a matrix for structuring time, such as work or hobbies
- *Games*: structured forms of social contact
- *Intimacies*: only possible in a game-free transaction or exchange (pp. 230–232)

Time structuring allows for behaviors and transactions aimed toward either "tactile" or "stimulus" hunger fulfillment, and the management of "privileges, restrictions, responsibilities, and demands" (p. 283). He saw true intimacy as being only a very small part of human experience, with autonomy of behavior and time structuring as being the source of happiness (Berne, 1972).

In *Games People Play: The Psychology of Human Relationships,* Berne (1964) described in detail his structural and transactional analysis of games, but also went beyond games to a discussion of the historical matrix. He postulated that game patterns stretched throughout a period of 100 years into the past to 50 years into the future, at minimum. This systemic analysis is described in TA terminology rather than critical historical analysis terminology. He distinguished "mathematical" game analysis from "transactional" game analysis, which he considered "more real" due to the "non-rational" character of transactions between people (p. 172). The co-created relational dynamics of Berne's game theory is compatible with other psychodynamic models of personality development and functioning (Cornell & Hargaden, 2005, pp. 245–246).

Transactional Analysis of Behavior

TA terminology uses easily understood language to describe its concepts of strokes, rackets, scripts, and games that explain transactions between people and ego states within individuals. While Berne acknowledged the role of external socioeconomic and cultural forces on script development, he focused very little on the structural role of these forces in script development. Most contemporary TA work remains focused on the micro level rather than on a critical analysis of the macro level of human functioning in wider social contexts. Hargaden and Sills (2002) look at social and political contexts of therapy, emphasizing increased use of the therapist's self in the therapeutic relationship. They take the position that the relational implies the social transactional; thus, the relationship of the therapist and the client is the key to effective therapy (p. 1), more so than any particular technique. Petriglieri (2007) considers the social context of the day-to-day lives of clients who are stuck at an impasse in their change process and uses TA to assist clients in their developmental process as they attempt to move towards change as opposed to "away from" the impasses in their psychosocial contexts. Barr's (2005) Therapeutic Relationship model, based on Berne's ego-state model, emphasizes the relevance of the client's "holding environment," including culture.

Berne (1972) credited Alfred Adler in some of his work on script analysis, but he also acknowledged the influence on his work of the ancient "script analysts" of India who based their work on astrology (p. 59), and suggested that myths provided basic "templates" for understanding "psychological phenomena." He gave credit to the Freudian roots of script analysis, which he asserted was not psychoanalytic (p. 58). Game analysis and script analysis are the major route to understanding the problem patterns keeping people locked in unhealthy functioning, although Berne did not consider scripts or defenses "inherently irrational or pathological" (Cornell, 2008, p. 96).

As Berne's work progressed, he increasingly came to focus on helping patients through strengthening their Adult ego state and developing their insights, helping them to use the models of scripts, games, etc., as modes for adaptation and creativity (Cornell & Hargaden, 2005, p. 239). Similar to Gestalt therapists (Perls, 1969), TA analysts use humor, forthrightness, and even bluntness in their work with clients, and use techniques such as the empty chair and "the hot seat." A sense of respectful partnership in the work is necessary for effectiveness in using TA tools. The following definitions of terms used in TA are keys to understanding TA terminology.

- *Stroke*: a sensory acknowledgement, approval, or recognition that can be physical or nonphysical, verbal or nonverbal, positive or negative; recognition by the "other," which is essential for human development, growth, and sustenance at all ages or levels of functioning. Ethics prohibit TA therapists from sexual involvement with clients and indicate caution regarding physical touch of clients.
- *Transaction*: an "exchange of strokes"; "a unit of social intercourse" (Berne, 1964, p. 15); a simple transaction analysis consists of "diagnosing which ego state implemented the transactional stimulus, and which one executed the transactional response" (p. 29); may be "complementary or crossed, simple or ulterior, and ulterior transactions may be sub-divided into angular and duplex types" (p. 34).
- *Racket*: a persistent archaic childhood feeling left as residue in the behavior patterns of scripts; a feeling or behavior used or expressed when the "real" feeling is unacceptable; supports the life-script function; almost always not in conscious awareness of the individual enacting the racket. For instance, depression or anger is a racket used to gain attention when playing a Martyr Game, in place of conscious acknowledgment of feelings of helplessness, or desire for attention.
- *Ritual*: "stereotyped series of simple complementary transactions programmed by external social forces" (p. 36); can be formal or informal (e.g., greetings).

- *Game:* game theory was originally developed by Potter (1947); is not used in a mathematical sense in TA; has a significant survival function because it can meet structure-hunger, stimulus-hunger, or recognition-hunger in order to avoid boredom, or sensory and emotional deprivation (p. 18); "the most gratifying forms of social contact" (p. 19); most game outcomes are determined by the Child ego state (p. 34); looks like a set of operations but the payoff reveals a game to be a certain sequence of maneuvers designed to obtain a specific outcome (Berne, 1964, pp. 48–49); unconscious unless it is a "con" (p. 49), a form of ulterior transaction (Fig. 36.2).
- *Script:* a life script is formed within the Adult ego state of the developing child (each child has a PAC that forms throughout early childhood); each script grows from responses chosen, either overtly or by default, in the developing person as he or she encounters environmental influences, which includes messages from parents, siblings, teachers, friends, society, etc.; scripts direct people's choices but are largely unconscious until brought into awareness (Goulding, 1978; Steiner, 1974).
- *Egogram:* an egogram, represented in bargraph format, was developed to explain the TA theory that different ego states contain a

certain amount of energy, accounting for the sum of psychological energy available to each person; there are actually five distinct ego states represented in this model (Dusay, 1972, 1977). "Because each person's personality is unique, these five psychological forces are aligned differently in each individual" (Cooper & Turner, 1996, p. 649) (Fig. 36.3).

Transactional Analysis Therapy

This section will describe therapy with a TA approach and will look at some of the aspects of therapy that are central to TA, such as group therapy, contracts, script analysis, and therapy applications to specific populations. When conducted in a TA framework, therapy does not look like classical psychoanalysis. It developed out of Berne's desire to create a "model of functional adaptation and creativity in addition to awareness of psychological defenses and psychopathology" (Cornell, 2008, p. 96), along with his desire to make psychological help more accessible to people. It has continued to move away from the medical model within which Berne worked, and is increasingly diverse in its application. TA therapy has been proven effective in providing treatment in areas such as schizophrenia treatment (Paley & Shapiro, 2001); health promotion (Murakami, Matsuno, Koike, Ebana,

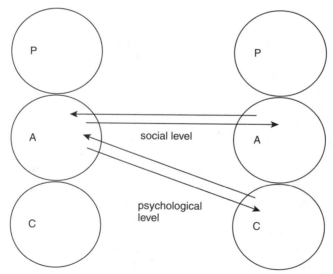

Figure 36-2. Ulterior transactions.

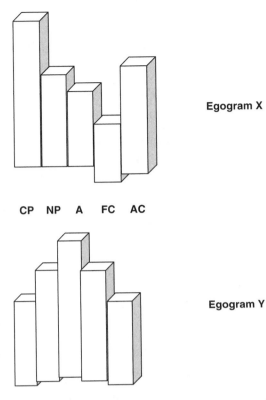

Egogram X

CP   NP   A   FC   AC

Egogram Y

Egogram X and Y represent the amounts of energy invested in each ego state of an individual. In Egogram X, The Critical Parent ego state contains the largest amount of psychological energy. The Adapted Child state has the second largest amount of energy, leaving the Nurturing Parent, the Adult, and the Free Child ego states with the least amounts of energy. By working together on this descriptive representation, a therapist and client can see which ego states need more energy for the individual to experience greater balance in functioning.

Egogram Y depicts a "Bell Shape" configuration showing the Adult ego state of the individual as having the greatest available energy. Egograms are not static or rigid but can fluctuate over time and in varying conditions, and are useful in assisting people in understanding which aspects of their personality need rebalancing. Egograms represent the "...intensity and frequency of use of several ego states of a given individual" (Forman & Ramsburg, 1978, p. 43).

Figure 36-3. Egograms (adapted from Dusay, 1972, 1977).

Hanaoka, & Katsura, 2006); care of terminally ill people (Shirai, 2006); a variety of clinical therapy situations (Noma, 2006; Wilson, 2006); and as part of an approach to professional creativity in a range of fields (Schmid, 2008). TA not only affirms a strengths-based approach in working with clients, but it also provides techniques that help people solve their problems relatively rapidly, which is of increasing concern due to pressures from managed care delivery systems, and increased need for mental health services.

Group Therapy

Principles of Group Treatment (Berne, 1966) was one of the first systematic treatises on group use of TA. Berne laid out not only his theory of personality but also his approach to treatment as it had emerged through his experience in U.S. Army hospitals during World War II. His work was solidly in the medical model, where the physician held the primary responsibility for the correct diagnosis, treatment, and welfare of the patient (p. xvii). Berne emphasized the need for therapists to be professional, ethical, authentic, dignified, courteous, and enthusiastic (p. 71), and was very thorough in laying out the necessary format of the group from structure, to contract, to membership, to supervision, and was specific right down to the first 3 minutes of the group meeting. He considered the role of the therapist as a strong leader to be a core part of the success of a group. He insisted that therapists bring their whole self to the process and be fully present sensorily, mentally, and spiritually. His thoughts on the role of spirituality in the treatment process is evidenced in his statement "we treat them, but it is God who cures them" (p. 63).

Berne was an early proponent of marital group treatment, described as the "contractual work of comprehending the nature of their transactions with each other and the games and scripts upon which those were based" (p. 90). He believed that treatment of marital problems in group settings was not only efficient but also highly effective as the couples helped each other through the process of their work on change. In *Principles of Group Treatment,* he devoted a chapter to examining TA's relationship to other therapies, and addressed Gestalt therapy, psychodrama, and existential analysis. His review of the group treatment literature from pre-1945 to after 1951 highlighted TA's unique approach to group processes.

Contracts

Making "contracts" with the client is a crucial part of the work together in TA. While Berne functioned solidly in his role as medical doctor with full responsibility for his patient, he insisted on detailed contracts with his clients that targeted the changes they wanted to make. In TA therapy, clients formally contract for their behavioral, emotional, and relationship changes in specific, measurable, attainable, and realistic terms that have a time frame (SMART) for completion. These contracts develop in the work between the client and the therapist, who has an attendant responsibility of maintaining rigorous self-awareness. Berne considered those therapists who were unwilling to undertake such rigorous self-examination to be "amateurs" (p. 23).

Prior to entering a formal contract with a TA analyst, it is common for clients to take an introductory class in TA principles. Stewart and Joines (1987) emphasize that while it is necessary that the language and ideas specific to TA be familiar to clients, it is important not to trivialize the concepts in a "pop psychology" manner. Berne never intended for TA to become a "cookbook" approach to the process of change. TA contracts are applicable in individual, group, and family therapy, as well as in educational settings (Gaft & El, 2004), management and organizational analysis (Claringbull, 2006; Neath, 1995), community trauma work (Allen, 2006), correctional settings (Inciardi, Martin, & Sarratt, 2001), and others. Using an oversimplified model that does not utilize the full range of TA concepts and language will be helpful only to a point, as contracts need to be fully descriptive of each ego state and take into account the time factor that Berne emphasized.

Contracts provide a tool for therapists to avoid the myths of therapy that place a therapist on a pedestal, or in a "one-up" position in relationships with clients. Common problems faced are the game of rescuer, the drama triangle, and overall burnout problems. Having clear, direct, and openly negotiated contracts keeps the work focused appropriately where it needs to remain—on the client process of change. Moreover, contracts help to avoid transference and countertransference difficulties.

Analysis of Scripts

Accurate script analysis depends on having a firm grasp of TA concepts, language, and techniques. It is also important to integrate a solid cultural analysis, which requires an ability to think critically, an understanding of clients' cultural contexts, and an understanding of systems theory. Steiner (1974) removed Berne's terms "patient" and "cure" from his work in a move to distance himself from mainstream medical psychiatry and to augment Berne's view of clients as equals in the therapy relationship. Client and therapist simply have different roles and responsibilities in analyzing the script, which can also be thought of as the manifestation of a lifelong "repetition compulsion." Steiner's approach to script analysis defines it as "a decision theory rather than a disease theory of emotional disturbance" (p. 23) and "the blueprint for a life course" (p. 51). The analysis of a script helps the client consciously alter his or her life course through identifying injunctions, attributions, games, beliefs, ego positions, and transaction patterns. Script analysis makes it possible to alter the internalized system that is keeping a dissatisfactory life-script locked in place. The ultimate goal of script analysis in TA is to promote the development of basic trust and the growth of autonomy in the individual, thus create a fulfilling life capable of intimacy.

Berne (1972) developed catchy little phrases to describe some common scripts. "Waiting for Santa Claus," "The Little Fascist," and "The Ventriloquist Dummy" are examples of phrases he used to describe certain patterns of transactions that did not serve people well. His desire to encourage people to "live happily in a brave new world [and not to] live bravely in an old unhappy world" (p. 272) motivated him to find ways to quickly describe to people what they were doing that was the source of so much pain in their lives. His approach to script analysis was to apply it like a map that looked "at the ground first, and then at the map, and not vice versa" (p. 409). While some of the names he used for scripts may be outdated, the theory behind it remains the same.

The Future of TA Therapy

The decades spanning the transition from the 20th century into the 21st century have seen the development and growth of forms of psychotherapy unknown during the "age of Freud." TA was one of the early forms of psychotherapy that emerged in distinct opposition to classical Freudian psychoanalysis, but recent observers predict that TA will decline, along with classical psychoanalysis and solution-focused theories (Norcross, Hedges, & Prochaska, 2002). The panel for their Delphi study was composed only of United States therapists, while the Jacobs (2000) study on future development of psychotherapy was composed solely of programs in the United Kingdom, which also found the future of psychotherapy moving away from classical

psychoanalysis. The Jacobs study condensed together all humanistic/integrative therapy approaches (which includes TA) and found that they had results that seemed equally good to the psychoanalytic approach and were especially cost-effective (p. 460). A third study, measuring the effectiveness of TA, composed of 27 international certified transactional analysts from eight different countries (Novey, 2002), found that TA therapists were more effective than psychologists, psychiatrists, social workers, marriage counselors, and physicians in four different domains as measured by client self-report. They postulated that some of the difference in results could be attributed to the lengthier training and certification process of TA therapists, and to the ability of TA therapists to be eclectic and integrative in their use of therapeutic modalities (pp. 21–23). It is important to note that the social work profession is represented among trained TA analysts, as are other professions (Pitman, 1984).

Prochaska and Norcross (1994), in *Systems of Psychotherapy*, criticize TA and its relevance in psychotherapy in general due to the limitations in depth of analysis that comes from its commonsense and individualistic approach. They describe it as failing to allow for a critical analysis of social and political structures, or cultural scripts that reinforce disparities, inequities, and power differentials among people (p. 221). They believe that Berne and his followers approached script theory as if it were fully verified while acknowledging it as not verifiable scientifically (p. 219), and that Berne's time structure theory failed to address the human need to live in the "eternal now." Nonetheless, they do credit TA for reducing client confusion, accurately diagnosing troubles, structuring the work, and examining potential solutions with the client in a rational way. The work of TA therapy relies primarily on clients doing their own work by engaging with the therapist in a complementary transaction, analyzing their problems from their Adult ego state, and accurately and honestly reporting information to their therapist. Clients grow to understand that safety, like happiness, is an inside job, yet the TA therapist is responsible for providing a safe holding environment and structuring the work. "If therapists want clients to act as Adults, then they should themselves be Adults in their communication" (p. 202).

Conclusion

Application of TA theory and therapy principles can enrich social work practice in many settings, yet it is important to understand that TA is much more than an adjunct methodology for social work. The uniqueness of the profession of social work can enhance, and be enhanced by, TA, which has emerged as a profession with its own standing, requirements, and regulations. Some would debate the viability of TA as a therapy model in the 21st century, yet it is clear that TA has contributed important concepts to our understandings of human development, social interaction, and personal well-being, and that it is compatible with many different approaches to helping solve "people problems." Early in its development, TA transformed the work of psychiatric healing from a Freudian model to a holistic model, and made psychotherapeutic help available to the general public.

The three basic assumptions of TA are now more widely accepted in society and psychotherapy than in Eric Berne's time. His belief that parental environment either promotes or hampers the development of the inherently "OK" human being is now tempered by new findings in the neurobiological sciences regarding the role of prenatal development, genetic influence, and environmental impact on human development (Bronfenbrenner, 2005). The affective perspectives of the relational in TA work (Cornell & Hargaden, 2005) have adapted the cognitive concepts of the four basic life positions. While many of the key TA concepts, such as the PAC model and the life-script model, have gained common usage in many fields, there continues to be much misunderstanding of the depth of analysis offered by TA concepts. The effectiveness of TA as a model for human change, growth, and development is illustrated by research, yet this research is not widely available to the general population (Norcross, Hedges, & Prochaska, 2002; Novey, 2002).

Some of the most exciting work on the horizon for TA lies in its capacity for transcultural application. TA has the potential to expand human societies' abilities to build shared frames of references as common problem-identification and solution-identification processes are negotiated (Schmid, 2008). TA's power for co-creative relationships (p. 23) is a model for transformation in a world rapidly evolving into a global village. As communities build capacity in problem solving and peaceful interaction, TA has much to offer in understanding the motivations of human behavior, and promoting choices for collective approaches to the serious problems encountered in the 21st century. TA has moved from the individualistic to the macro level, addressing issues in large social structures and organizations, yet has not lost its deeply personal and relational treatment principles. Teaching TA concepts in social work education offers benefit in expanding student and practitioner "tool kits" for responsible and ethical social work practice.

References

Allen, J. R. (2006). Oklahoma City ten years later: Positive psychology, transactional analysis, and the transformation of trauma from a terrorist attack. *Transactional Analysis Journal, 36*(2), 120–133.

Barr, J. (2005). The therapeutic relationship model: Perspective on the core of the healing process. In W. F. Cornell & H. Hargaden (Eds.), *From transactions to relations: The emergence of a relational tradition in transactional analysis* (pp. 41–52). Oxfordshire: Haddon Press Ltd.

Berne, E. (1961). *Transactional analysis in psychotherapy.* New York: Grove Press.

Berne, E. (1964). *Games people play: The psychology of human relationships.* New York: Grove Press, Inc.

Berne, E. (1966). *Principles of group treatment.* New York: Oxford University Press.

Berne, E. (1972). *What do you say after you say hello?* New York: Grove Press, Inc.

Bronfenbrenner, U. (2005). *On making human beings human: Bioecological perspectives of human development.* Thousand Oaks, CA: SAGE Publications.

Bry, A. (1973). *The TA primer: Transactional analysis in everyday life.* New York: Perennial Library/Harper & Row, Publishers, Inc.

Childs-Gowell, E., & Schiff, J. (2000). *Reparenting schizophrenics: The Cathexis experience.* New York: Backinprint.com.

Claringbull, N. (2006). Workplace counselling: New models for new times. *Counseling at Work,* Autumn, 17–21.

Cooper, M., & Turner, S. (1996). Transactional analysis theory and social work treatment. In F. J. Turner

(Ed.), *Social work treatment: Interlocking theoretical approaches* (4th ed., pp. 641–662). New York: The Free Press.

Cornell, W. F. (2008). What do you say if you don't say "unconscious"? Dilemmas created for transactional analysts by Berne's shift away from the language of unconscious experience. *Transactional Analysis Journal, 38*(2), 93–100.

Cornell, W. F., & Hargaden, H. (Eds.). (2005). *From transactions to relations: The emergence of a relational tradition in transactional analysis.* Oxfordshire: Haddon Press Ltd.

Cornell, W. F., & Hargaden, H. (2005). Reflections: Dialogue and dialectic. In W. F. Cornell & H. Hargaden (Eds.), *From transactions to relations: The emergence of a relational tradition in transactional analysis* (pp. 239–249). Oxfordshire: Haddon Press Ltd.

Dusay, J. M. (1972). Egograms and the "constancy hypothesis." *Transactional Analysis Journal, 2*(3), 37–41.

Dusay, J. M. (1977). *Egograms: How I see you and you see me.* New York: Harper & Row, Publishers.

Forman, L. H., & Ramsburg, J. S. (1978). *Hello Sigmund, this is Eric: Psychoanalysis and TA in dialogue.* Kansas City: Sheed Andrews and McMeel, Inc.

Freed, A. M. (1973/1991). *T.A. for tots (and other prinzes)* (Revised ed.). Rolling Hills Estates, CA: Jalmar Press, Inc.

Gaft, S., & El, C. M. B. (2004). Transactional analysis in the college classroom. *Transactional Analysis Journal, 34*(3), 243–248.

Gitterman, A. (Ed.). (1991). *Handbook of social work practice with vulnerable populations.* New York: Columbia University Press.

Goulding, M. M., & Goulding, R. L. (1979). *Changing lives through redecision therapy.* New York: Brunner/Mazel, Publishers.

Goulding, R. L. (1978). *The power is in the patient: A TA/Gestalt approach to psychotherapy.* San Francisco: TA Press.

Hargaden, H., & Sills, C. (2002). *Transactional analysis: A relational perspective.* New York: Brunner-Routledge/Taylor & Francis Group.

Harris, T. A. (1967). *I'm OK—you're OK: A practical guide to transactional analysis.* New York and Evanston: Harper & Row, Publishers.

Inciardi, J. A., Martin, S. S., & Sarratt, H. L. (2001). Therapeutic communities in prisons and work release: Effective modalities for drug-involved offenders. In B. Rawlings & R. Yates (Eds.), *Therapeutic communities for the treatment of drug users* (pp. 241–256). Philadelphia: Jessica Kingsley Publishers.

Jacobs, M. (2000). Psychotherapy in the United Kingdom: Past, present and future. *British Journal of Guidance & Counselling, 28*(4), 451–466. doi:10.1080/03069880020004686

Joseph, S. (2008). Humanistic and integrative therapies: The state of the art. *Psychiatry, 7*(5), 221–224.

Murakami, M., Matsuno, T., Koike, K., Ebana, S., Hanaoka, K., & Katsura, T. (2006). Transactional analysis and health promotion. *International Congress Series 1287,* 164–167.

Neath, M. (1995). Evaluating transactional analysis as a change strategy for organizations. *Leadership & Organization Development Journal, 16*(1), 13–17. Retrieved from http://proquest.umi.om/pqdink?did=5377778&Fmt=3&clientid=2

Noma, K. (2006). How TA is applied in clinical psychiatry. *International Congress Series 1287,* 168–172.

Norcross, J. C., Hedges, M., & Prochaska, J. O. (2002). The face of 2010: A Delphi poll on the future of psychotherapy. *Professional Psychology: Research and Practice, 33*(3), 316–322. doi:10.1037//0735-7028.33.3.316

Novellino, M. (2005). Unconscious communication and interpretation in transactional analysis. In W. F. Cornell & H. Hargaden (Eds.), *From transactions to relations: The emergence of a relational tradition in transactional analysis* (pp. 53–60). Oxfordshire: Haddon Press Ltd.

Novey, T. B. (2002). Measuring the effectiveness of transactional analysis: An international study. *Transactional Analysis Journal, 32*(1), 8–24.

Paley, G., & Shapiro, D. (2001). Transactional analysis functional ego states in people with schizophrenia and their immediate relatives. *International Journal of Psychiatric Nursing Research, 6*(3), 737–744.

Perls, F. S. (1969). In J. O. Stevens (Ed.), *Gestalt therapy verbatim.* Moab, UT: Real People Press.

Petriglieri, G. (2007). Stuck in a moment: A developmental perspective on impasses. *Transactional Analysis Journal, 37*(3), 185–194.

Pitman, E. (1984). *Transactional analysis for social workers and counsellors: An introduction.* London: Routledge & Kegan Paul.

Potter, S. (1947). *The theory & practice of gamesmanship, or, the art of winning games without actually cheating.* London: Rupert Hart-Davis.

Prochaska, J. O., & Norcross, J. C. (1994). *Systems of psychotherapy: A transtheoretical analysis* (3rd ed.). Pacific Grove, CA: Brooks/Cole Publishing Company.

Rowan, J. (2007). The dialogical self. *Therapy Today, 18*(8), 35–36.

Schmid, B. (2008). The role concept of transactional analysis and other approaches to personality, encounter, and cocreativity for all professional fields. *Transactional Analysis Journal, 38*(1), 17–30.

Shirai, S. (2006). How transactional analysis can be used in terminal care. *International Congress Series 1287,* 179–184.

Sills, C. (2007). Transactional analysis—a relational psychotherapy. *Therapy Today,* 18(1), 15–17.

Steiner, C. M. (1974). *Scripts people live: Transactional analysis of life scripts.* New York: Grove Press, Inc.

Stewart, I., & Joines, V. S. (1987). *TA today: A new introduction to transactional analysis.* Nottingham and Chapel Hill: Lifespace Publishing.

Turner, F. J. (Ed.). (1996). *Social work treatment: Interlocking theoretical approaches* (4th ed.). New York: The Free Press.

Turner, F. J. (Ed.). (2005). *Encyclopedia of Canadian social work.* Waterloo, ON, Canada: Wilfrid Laurier University Press.

Wilson, S. (2006). Using transactional analysis as a psychotherapist: How to use TA in clinical situations. *International Congress Series 1287,* 173–178.

This holistic approach assesses and intervenes in issues related to clients' spiritual dimensions, spiritual malaise, emergencies, and moral development beyond one's ego potential

Transpersonal Social Work: An Integrative Model

Au-Deane Shepherd Cowley and David S. Derezotes

Historical Context

Clinical social work developed out of philanthropy, settlement movements, community service organizations, and charity work. By 1829 social work had begun to carve out its own special place in the helping professions, and the Milford Conference affirmed that there was a distinctive approach that could be called generic social casework. In the late 19th century the thrust of social work interventions shifted toward a psychosocial approach with an emphasis on internal as well as environmental factors. According to Dorfman (1988), Florence Hollis (1964) deserves the most credit for making the psychosocial approach a distinct theoretical system within social work practice (p. 108). As the profession expanded its scope of practice, a split between the diagnostic (clinical) and functional (environmental)

approaches developed that lasted for about 25 years. In the late 1950s Perlman's *Social Casework* attempted to heal the rift by positing a problem-solving approach (Dorfman, 1988). Task-centered, client-centered, and other psychological perspectives, in turn, influenced social work practice as it continued to evolve. Currently, clinical practice is based on a broad assessment process across multiple systems (Hepworth, Rooney, Rooney, Strom-Gottfried, Larsen, 2009) and utilizes interventions best described as multimodal or pluralistic.

Even though the momentum of social work practice has moved consistently toward a more inclusive and comprehensive stance, one aspect of the client system has too often been ignored or avoided: the spiritual dimension. In 1967 an article in *Social Casework* by Solomon observed that what was needed by social work practitioners was an increased understanding of the moral and spiritual aspects of our clients. Over the years, social work literature included other pleas for the integration of the spiritual dimension into clinical social work practice (Canda, 1988a, 1988b; Cowley, 1993; Cowley & Derezotes, 1994; Cox, 1985; Derezotes, 1995; Spencer, 1957; Stroup, 1962; Vincentia, 1987). In 2001, as social work educators sought to honor diversity, CSWE accreditation guidelines were expanded to include spiritual development across the lifespan.

The Four Forces of Psychology

The methods of clinical social work have been influenced by the development of various psychological theories throughout the Western world. According to London (1974) therapy has always been "a reactive trade" whose theories and models have operated as social indexes by evolving "to serve the social ills of the day." As each of the four major psychological theories emerged out of its own unique place in history, each offered important insights into human growth and development as well as distinctive perspectives on issues like what the primary concern of therapy should be, what constitutes health and pathology, what constitutes change, and what role the therapist should play in the helping process. Although London only described three "phases" or "stages" of psychotherapy (now referred to as the First, Second and Third Forces), the views he expressed then are equally applicable to the rise of the Fourth Force or transpersonal psychology. (Table 37.1).

First Force: Dynamic Theory

Around the turn of the century, Freud's psychoanalytic theory grew out of an Age of Repression as experienced by the traditional or inner-directed man (London, 1974). From the beginning psychoanalysis was essentially a theory of intrapsychic functioning (Pine, 1985, p. 11). Dynamic theory began to take human behavior out of the realm of mystery. However, it also made it clear that unconscious drives and impulses, left undiscovered, could sabotage consciously chosen goals. Even though Freud wrote about a process of intense introspection he called "soul-making" (Bettelheim, 1983), the body of his work focused on pathology and the basement of human nature. For example, the index to Freud's complete works

contains over 400 references to neurosis and none to health (Walsh & Shapiro, 1983, p. 5).

Freud's model of man as an organism seeking relief from tension, forced to negotiate compromise between instinct, reason, and society, leaves even the most successful negotiator in a position of impoverishment as pathological, in its own way, as any illness listed in the diagnostic manual (p. 38).

Historically, First Force theory has viewed therapy as a process whereby the patient replaced neurotic conflict by learning how to live with everyday unhappiness. According to Brown (1988), this view was essentially pessimistic.

Pine (1985) divided the evolution of First Force theory into three great waves or models. Freud's drive psychology was the first wave. Ego psychology, with a view that focused on the ego, its development, and its functions, was the second. The third wave, object relations, added key understandings about the importance of early relationships, the potentially serious effects of developmental deficits in early childhood, and the role of defense mechanisms. Object relations' focus on the observation of child development and the progressive differentiation of self from other gave birth to a body of literature on self-esteem and self-psychology.

Generally speaking, all of the models of dynamic theory did a better job of theorizing about pathology and offering developmental explanations about how it came to be than they did in providing guidelines for specific clinical interventions. Having uncovered repressed psychological issues, many practitioners were left unclear as to what to do about them. How could such mysterious, unconscious forces ever be tamed? Another problem limited the use of this approach as time went on. Its concepts were not readily amenable to empirical research.

The Second Force: Behavioral Theory

Over time, criticism accumulated about the exclusive hold dynamic theory had on psychotherapy prior to World War II. Its methods were too deterministic, expensive, and slow to suit the other-directed man in the Age of Anxiety (London, 1974). As society began to expect quick and mechanistic responses to life challenges, both clients and therapists became more interested in

Table 37-1. The Four Forces

Theory	Dynamic	Behavioral	Humanistic Experiential Existential	Transpersonal
Focus	Pathology	Specific behaviors	Awareness	Spiritual development
	Dynamics/past	Specific symptoms	Experience	Self-transcendence
			Self-responsibility	
Level Of	"it"	"I"	"I"	"Above I"
Individuation Focused On	Prepersonal	Personal	Personal	Transpersonal "Beyond ego"
View Of Pathology	Unconscious conflicts	Faulty learning	Alienation from feelings	Spiritual malaise
	Sexual repression	Maladaptive behavior	Reduced potential	Dis-spiritation
	Disorganization of ego	Neurotic anxiety	Ennui	Morbid preservation
	Repetition compulsion	Negative patterns	Meaninglessness	Egoitis
	Deficits of development	Irrational ideas	Lacking purpose	Dark night of the soul
View Of Health	Ego over id	Symptoms controlled	Self-actualized	Wholeness
	A personal self	Appropriate behavior	Authentic	"Beyond" ego
	Firm ego boundaries	Self-management	Purpose of life	Accepting "what is"
	Ability to love/ work	Anxieties in check	Open to goodness	Transcendent
Curative Process	Insight	Action	Eclectic	Healing is wholing
	Long-term/ intense	Short-term/ structured	Here & now focus	Meditation
	Interpretation	Education	Use of relationship	Integration
	Introspection	Diagnostic tests	Removing blocks	Dis-identification
	Reveal unconscious	Behavioral contracts	Heart-to-heart	Connecting to all
	Structure-building	Skills training	Making meaning	Mystical experience
Nature Of The Helping Relationship	Vertical	Vertical	Horizontal	Reciprocal
	Medical model	Education model	Person-to-person	Servant/co-voyager
	Interpretive	Modeling	Process-oriented	Mutuality
	Developmental	Coaching	Phenomenological	Guide
	Partnering	Goal-oriented	Remove blocks to growth	Midwife
			Facilitator	Evocateur
Models	Drive psychology	Behavior modification	Humanistic	Psychosynthesis
	Ego psychology	CBT	Person-centered	Self-creation
	Object relations	RET	Experiential	Holotropic

Continued...

Table 37-1. Contd.

Theory	Dynamic	Behavioral	Humanistic Experiential Existential	Transpersonal
	Self-psychology	Reality therapy	Gestalt	Full spectrum
	Jungian	Task-centered casework	Existential	Jungian
	Adlerian	Redecision therapy	Logotherapy	Process-oriented
	Eriksonian			Transpersonal social work
Interventions	History taking	Anchoring	Therapeutic love	Mediation
(Skills/Techniques)	L.S.I.G.	Reinforcement	Visualization	Spiritual practice
	Early recollections	Desensitization	Creative imagery	I AM affirmations
	Uncovering	Behavioral contracts	Stream of awareness	Dreamwork
	Free association	Shaping/ substitution	Experiential exercises	Breathwork
	Sentence stems	Aversion therapy	Being present	Use of seed thoughts
	Interpretation	Perturbation	Gestalting dreams	Listening within
	Use of transference	Role play	Top-dog/ bottom-dog	Detached observer
	Catharsis	Education	Empty-chair work	Interpreting up
	Analyses of dreams	Homework	Psychodrama	Interpreting down
	Freudian slips	Bibliotherapy	Choreography	Socratic dialogue
	Working through	Skills training	Mind journeys	Wisdom circles
	Spitting in the soup	Self-monitoring	Journaling	Community building
	Script analysis	Stress management	Strength bombardment	Shamanic journey
	Ego-gram	Relaxation training	De-repressing	Study with guide
	Ego-state analysis	Cognitive restructuring	Clearing exercises	Contemplation
	Play therapy	Thought-stopping	Burning bowl	Path of the yogis
	Re-parenting	Positive self-talk	De-reflexion	Path of the saints
	Corrective experience	Rehearsal	Philosophizing	Path of the sages

finding relief from specific symptoms than they were in a seemingly endless search for insight into some unconscious, underlying "cause." This led to a search for more practical and precise conceptualizations. Psychoanalytic premises related to repression weren't a good fit for the symptoms of the day in a time characterized by free love, sexual revolution, and value deficits (Schnall, 1981). As psychotherapy reacted to the need for more direct, action-oriented methods, Second Force (behavioral theory) came to the fore.

The behavioral approach sought to create empirical order out of phenomenological chaos.

By focusing on the importance of social learning and the process of socialization, it hoped to demonstrate that much of human behavior could be objectified, operationalized, tested, and shaped with proper reinforcement. Specificity and concreteness in understanding human behavior provided not only concepts and interventions that could be quantified, but also more predictable relief for specific behavioral symptoms. Structural, strategic, and cognitive models of behavioral theory delivered observable results. This more empirical focus brought confidence to the scientific-minded research/practitioner in an age of accountability.

The Third Force: Experiential Theories

In the middle to late 1940s, again reflecting changes in the social context, the longing for a more holistic view of human possibilities and a more humanistic connection between the healer and the client called forth a new approach. Virginia Satir described it like this:

At the end of World War II, we all heaved a sigh of relief and had hope of building a more just world. The United Nations was a manifestation of that dream. These hopes were also translated into a new psychological construct—the human potential movement. In 1946 we heard the voices of Abraham Maslow, Rollo May, Carl Rogers and others who believed that human beings are and can be more than what their behavior led us to believe. We set on a journey to find out what else there was to the human being that had not yet been discovered and assessed (Satir, 1987, p. 60).

That journey of discovery emerged out of an Age of Existential Alienation to serve psychological man in his efforts to combat ennui through embarking on a search for self-fulfillment (London, 1974). It resulted in the development of three Third Force theories: 1) humanistic theory, to help individuals who felt isolated and bored to reconnect to life and become more fully human and self-actualized; 2) experiential theory, to work with clients who knew so much but felt so little, to bring back sensation, feeling, and the phenomenological; and 3) existential theory, to deal with crises that occur when life loses its meaning and purpose. Third Force theories dared to suggest that a person didn't need to be sick in order to get better. According to London (1974), the idea of undergoing a therapeutic process for the purpose of growth rather than cure represented a dramatic change in focus:

Until now, psychotherapy has been mainly reactive to feeling bad, that is to having symptoms. Now it is reacting to not feeling good—that is, to a faulty lifestyle … Men want to be healthy, wealthy and wise in that order. As each is gained, the next gets wanted more (p. 68).

And so it was: as individuals in an affluent society became healthier, many of their contemporary ailments began to express in existential symptoms that required remedies more experiential and philosophical in nature.

The rise of Third Force psychology during the 1970s and 1980s reflected a culture-wide shift away from the Newtonian-Cartesian worldview. Nontraditional therapists began to move out of the mainstream of Western psychology to explore the contemplative practices and psychological traditions of the Far East. When they began to include alternative views and report data that were trans-rational and extrasensory in nature, reactions from other professionals ran the gamut from horrified to celebratory. However, neither reaction altered the determination of Third Force pioneers to expand psychology to transcend the limits of the observable and the measurable (Grof, 1985).

Ultimately, it took the courage of an intellectual loner like Maslow (1968, 1971) to challenge mainstream psychological research to pursue the search for the farther reaches of human nature:

Abraham Maslow was convinced that the value-life of human beings is biologically rooted. There seemed to him to be a species-wide need (comparable to the need for basic food elements and vitamins) for what he called "B" (for being) values, e.g., truth, goodness, beauty, wholeness, justice, playfulness, meaningfulness, etc. These values are biological necessities for avoiding illness and for achieving one's full potential. The epidemic of spiritual illnesses ("metapathologies") resulting from deprivation of these values include anomie, alienation, meaninglessness, loss of zest for life, hopelessness, boredom, and axiological depression. (Clinebell, 1995, p. 92)

Maslow's early work radically revised our picture of the human species and created a vastly expanded map of human possibilities (Leonard, 1983). In his later work, Maslow's view of human potential continued to expand, and his explorations of human potential delineated three groups of optimally healthy people: self-actualizers, transcenders, and transcending self-actualizers. Eventually, Maslow came to believe that even his definition of self-actualized transcenders was not expansive enough to encompass the highest levels of human potential:

Maslow has found that the self that was actualized could still be isolated in an alien world. Building on the theory of Erich Fromm (and resonating with Carl Jung and William James before him), Maslow postulated that we long to transcend our aloneness and belong to the cosmos. Even when we have fulfilled every secular need, the hunger for transcendence is not satisfied. So it was a short step, from actualization to transcendence and from plateau experiences to the "cosmic connection." (Bradshaw, 1988, p. 228)

Maslow, who read extensively in Eastern literature, is considered the philosophical father of both humanistic and transpersonal theories. Near the end of his life, Maslow was still seeking more. He made yet another call for a fourth psychology that would be "transpersonal, trans-human, centered in the cosmos rather than in human needs and interests, going beyond humanness, identity, self-actualization, and the like" (Wittine, 1987, p. 53).

The Fourth Force: Transpersonal Theory

By 1969 this fourth psychology had not only come into being, but had established some common parameters. The professional *Journal of Transpersonal Psychology* was introduced, and in the frontispiece of its first issue Anthony Sutich made history when he defined the transpersonal domain as:

concerned specifically with ultimate values, unitive consciousness, peak experiences, ecstasy, mystical experience, awe, transcendence of the self, spirit, one-ness, cosmic awareness, and related concepts, experiences and activities.

Transpersonal theory evolved out of a cultural context exacerbated by not only an existential vacuum, but a spiritual one as well. It arose to serve the dis-spirited man or woman in an age characterized by spiritual poverty and a lack of what Schnall (1981) called "limits" or traditional values. In 1988, when Bradshaw described this pain as "a hole in the soul," his words resonated with those whose suffering was

spiritual in origin. In 1980, Goldberg labeled this postmodern crisis in consciousness "a malaise of the soul":

In a word, we live in an era in which men find it oner-ous to accept responsibility for their own actions and for the embittered and hollow course their existence has taken … Much of our agony is in the soul (p. 1).

In a post-Sept. 11 world, much of our indi-vidual and societal pain is lodged in the spiritual dimension. Transpersonal theory is particularly suited to treat postmodern maladies character-ized by economic insecurity, addiction, violence, and a religious extremism that can result in mass casualty terrorism. The most prominent present-ing symptom of the day (often oversimplified as clinical depression) is a sense of demoralization or dis-spiritation (Bugental & Bugental, 1984). Hence, practitioners are increasingly being chal-lenged by the people they serve to take their spiritual concerns, value conflicts, and existen-tial angst (Park, 2000) into account. Excellent resources to aid the social worker are readily available (but too seldom tapped) in the transper-sonal literature (see Cowley, 1993, 1996a).

Of particular interest to social workers utiliz-ing the transpersonal approach is a body of lit-erature that includes work by a growing number of authors: Canda, 2006; Cowley, 1993, 1996a, 1996b, 1999, 2001; Cowley and Derezotes, 1994, Derezotes, 2001; Moxley and Washington, 2001; and Smith, 1995. References that link social work practice and spirituality include Banerjee and Pyles, 2004; Canda, 1988a, 1988b, 1995, 1998, 2006; Canda, Nakashima, & Furman, 2004; Derezotes, 2006, 2009a, 2009b; Furman et al., 2004; Hodge, 2004, 2005; Hodge and Williams, 2002; Limb, Hodge, and Panos, 2008; Martin and Martin, 2003; Moody, 2005; Nelson-Becker, 2005; Nelson-Becker et al., 2007; Russel, 2006; Scales et al., 2002; Tullis, 1996; Van Hook, Hagen, and Aquillar, 2002; and Weinstein-Moser, 2008.

Social work practitioners with a transper-sonal perspective have a new vision to offer their clients about who they might become:

Typically the journey in our culture stops with reach-ing adulthood. It ends once a strong ego and a strong sense of reality is developed. From this perspective there is no need for a further journey. The transpersonal view is that the ultimate meaning of life is encountered when one moves beyond this preoccupation with self-identity. (Keen, 1983, pp. 7–8)

While offering a more expansive view of human potential, the transpersonal approach does not attempt to supplant other psychological theories, but rather to complement and enrich them. It challenges clinical minds that are steeped in the first three forces to transcend traditional boundaries to include the spiritual dimension, to honor the intuitive and trans-rational elements of practice. However, a plea for openness and creativity is not the same as encouraging ungrounded theory and irresponsible practice: transpersonalists recognize the importance of assessing potential risks and benefits of interventions and value both the scientific and artistic elements of practice.

Just as any theory can be used or abused, spiritual practices, concepts, and theories can be applied in both adaptive and unhealthy ways (Keen, 1983). Of special concern are charlatans who prey on the spiritually hungry and seek to induce dependence on a cult-like, external authority. In a world where many of our clients shop in what amounts to a "psychospiritual supermarket," social work practitioners need to be knowledgeable enough to help clients distinguish between authentic paths to inner transformation, as opposed to shallow pseudomystical psychopathology masquerading under the guise of higher development (Anthony, Ecker, & Wilber, 1987).

Spiritual quackery not only operates as a psychological detour, it can also be potentially dangerous to mental health. Experimenting with altered states of consciousness may compromise or damage a weak ego structure, or even induce a "spiritual emergency" (Grof & Grof, 1989). Spontaneous rising of kundalini energy, egoitis, ego-inflation (the saint that ain't), Trungpa's (1973) spiritual materialism, and what Ferrucci (1982) called "going about in psychic smog" are just a few of the possible negative outcomes that may await an unsuspecting or ill-prepared spiritual seeker. People who expose themselves to various kinds of psychic experiences without first developing the prerequisite ego strengths may even collapse into regressive or psychotic states requiring hospitalization (Aurobindo, 1971; Crittenden, 1980).

Although the ego or personal level of consciousness is viewed by transpersonal psychology as a necessary prerequisite to further development up the Ladder of Being, Wilber cautions about the danger inherent in making an exclusive identification with any specific idea of self. Like Freud's concept of fixation or developmental arrest, "morbid preservation" is a term Wilber has coined to describe an unwillingness to release one's current level of growth or sense of identity in order to access a higher level of functioning (Wilber, 1986, p. 82). For example, morbid preservation at the personal level describes a situation wherein the ego changes from a structure that protects into one that becomes a "trap" that incarcerates. However, this call to go "beyond ego" is not to be misunderstood as an invitation to wage an aggressive war against the ego:

Trying to induce change by waging an assault on the ego structure is a common mistake that various spiritual and therapeutic approaches make. Sometimes this kind of "therapeutic aggression" is quite blatant … and sometimes it takes more subtle forms of persuasion and confrontation which imply that one would be a better person if one were different from the way one is. Unfortunately, such attacks on the personality structure rob people of what it is they have to work with. This can leave them in a state of helplessness and dependency. (Welwood, 1986, p. 132)

Far from this kind of iatrogenic or misguided attempt to undermine ego strengths and induce dependency, the transpersonal approach seeks to empower those whose quest is for spiritual health and well-being. M. Scott Peck has posited: "Spiritual healing is a process of becoming whole or holy. Most specifically, I would define it as an ongoing process of becoming increasingly conscious" (Peck, 1987, p. 33). Whether this healing or wholing is called making the unconscious conscious (First Force dynamic theory), taking more effective control over behavior (Second Force behavioral theory), becoming more fully human (Third Force theories), or accessing a higher consciousness to go beyond ego (Fourth Force transpersonal theory), psychological theories have always sought to help client systems become more conscious and mature, and more skilled in the important tasks of loving and working.

Three Levels of Consciousness

Talk of consciousness and consciousness raising did not begin with the New Age or the women's liberation movement. Robert Ornstein (1972) observed that psychology is and always has been primarily the science of consciousness. Bugental (1978) expanded on Ornstein's definition by calling psychotherapy the art, science, and practice of studying the nature of consciousness and of what may reduce or facilitate it. In the West, attempts to facilitate the development of consciousness (or increased structuralization of ego) were augmented by Freud's insights. However, according to Bruno Bettelheim, key concepts of Freud's work were mistranslated and sometimes even totally misunderstood. For instance, the terms Freud used when he divided the structure of consciousness into three levels have remained largely misrepresented to this day. Freud wrote about the chaotic "it," not id; the "I," not ego; and the "above I" rather than the superego (Bettelheim, (1983).

Jung was another pioneer to call attention to the centrality of consciousness in human development. Like Freud, Jung's conceptualization of consciousness was three-tiered: shadow, ego, and Self (Campbell, 1971). In a like manner, Roberto Assagioli (1965), an Italian contemporary of Freud, designated three levels or structures of consciousness: lower consciousness, middle consciousness, and superconsciousness. When Freud's, Jung's, and Assagioli's paradigms are compared to Ken Wilber's three general levels of consciousness, prepersonal, personal, and transpersonal, similarities are apparent (Table 37.2).

Although Freud, Jung, and Assagioli all acknowledged a level of consciousness beyond ego, only Wilber (1986) has divided transpersonal states of consciousness into three layers (psychic, subtle, and causal), described what pathologies exist at different levels of the full

spectrum of consciousness, and made further suggestions about which interventions are best suited for treatment in nine different levels of consciousness.

Models of Transpersonal Theory

It is important to keep in mind that the transpersonal approach is not unidimentional, but composed of many strands. Like First, Second, and Third Force theories before it, several models have already emerged under the broad umbrella of Fourth Force theory. Undoubtedly, more will continue to be developed in the future. Each new model offers an opinion about what it means to be fully human, and its own distinctive view about how to deal with issues related to religion and spirituality. Some address the topic of self-transcendence and the facilitation of spiritual development toward higher states of consciousness. Historically some theorists, such as Jung, Washburn, and Levin, envisioned the transpersonal in the "depths" or "dynamic ground" (Washburn, 1994). Others, like Assagioli, Grof, Small, Wilber, and Cowley, referred to transpersonal states as being "up" the Ladder of Being. Table 37.3 offers a comparative view of five transpersonal models whose hierarchical or developmental levels are especially applicable to practice with different levels of consciousness.

Psychosynthesis Model

Even though Jung's work is sometimes considered transpersonal in nature because he took into account trans-rational or psychic-level aspects of being, probably the first modern clinical model that had spiritual development as its main focus was Roberto Assagioli's (1965) model of psychosynthesis. Assagioli began disseminating his ideas about lower, middle, and superconsciousness in Italy around 1910.

Table 37-2. Three Levels of Consciousness

Freud	Jung	Assagioli	Wilber
"Above I" (not superego)	self	superconsciousness	transpersonal level
"I" (not ego)	ego	middle consciousness	personal level
"It" (not id)	shadow	lower consciousness	prepersonal level

Table 37-3. Transpersonal Models

Psychosynthesis	Self-Creation	Holotropic Breathwork	Full-Spectrum Model	Transpersonal Social Work
Robert Assagioli (1965) Superconsciousness	Jacquelyn Small (1982) Self-mastery Basic urge: Unity	Stanislav Grof (1985) Transpersonal domain	Ken Wilber (1986) *Transpersonal* Nondual Causal Subtle Psychic	Au-Deane Cowley (1996) Spiritual maturation
	Intuition/Altruism Basic urge: Compassion	Level of birth and death		Moral maturation
Middle Consciousness	Comprehension/ Authenticity Basic urge: Understanding	Individual consciousness	*Personal* Existential Formal-reflexive Rule/role mind	Psychosocial maturation
	Harmonizing bridge Basic urge: Awakening			Cognitive maturation
Lower Consciousness	Self-definition Basic urge: Identity-seeking	Sensory level	*Prepersonal* Representational mind	Affective maturation
	Self-gratification Basic urge: Passion		Phantasmic-emotional Sensoriphysical	Physical maturation
	Self-preservation Basic urge: Fear			

He wanted to find the common boundaries of medicine, education, and religion, as well as to provide a corrective view of human psychology to balance Freud's emphasis on pathology. His position was not that psychoanalysis was an incorrect approach, but rather that it was incomplete (Kramer, 1995, p. 22). The process of psychosynthesis is a subjective one of balancing, harmonizing, and integrating the various aspects of human experience:

In Psychosynthesis there is no "chart on the wall" which tells the counselor what a Self-realized human being should be like. There are no ultimate Truths, no recipes to follow, only the incredible wisdom of the unfolding Self and its aspirations for meaning and purpose. (Whitmore, 1991, p. ix)

Assagioli introduced the idea of "subpersonalities," and saw the integration of all of one's parts as a process essential to reaching the goal of psychic wholeness. He introduced disidentification exercises intended to help one to view the self impartially, and to give up false identifications, distorted attitudes, and unfounded beliefs. Assagioli wanted to help people get in touch with the core (or real) self. Taking the psyche's inherent thrust towards mature self-realization as a basic premise, psychosynthesis recognizes values, meaning, peak experience, and the unquantifiable, ineffable essence of human life as integral elements in the counseling process (Whitmore, 1991). Assagioli was probably one of the first to point out that:

not all serious psychological disturbances were to be understood as symptoms of pathology, but rather some are to be understood as crises of spiritual awakening. (Washburn, 1994, p. 2)

Self-Creation Model

Out of her 12-step work with addictions and recovery, Jacquelyn Small (1982) developed a transpersonal model with seven hierarchical levels. In Small's self-creation model therapists serve as guides in facilitating the processes of inner work and personal evolution. Through breath work, karmic balancing, seed-thoughts, imagery, meditation, centering, processing, developing an observer self, transmutation of emotions, dis-identification, work-on-oneself, and other techniques and exercises, individuals are helped to access and redefine their soul. Small holds that the work of the therapist of the future (the transformer) is to "re-mind" us of our essence, the self we were intended to be before we lost our way.

Holotrophic Breathwork Model

In 1985 Stanislav Grof developed a cartography of the human psyche that included four distinct levels or realms: 1) the sensory barrier; 2) individual consciousness (or the biographical realm); 3) the level of birth and death (which includes the perinatal realm, with four basic perinatal matrices); and 4) the transpersonal domain (which taps sources of information clearly outside of the conventionally defined range of individual consciousness). The word "holotropic" is derived from the Greek *holos* (whole) and *trepein* (aim for, or more in the direction of). Therefore, holotropic literally means aiming for wholeness or moving in the direction of totality. A basic premise of this approach is that healing results when experiential exercises help one overcome inner fragmentation and a sense of isolation.

Full Spectrum Model

Wilber's full spectrum model (1986) is developmental, structural, hierarchical, and systems oriented. It is in complete agreement with Western theories—as far as they go—which is up to and including the personal level of development. Wilber had to draw on Eastern contemplative practices for theory related to the transpersonal or spiritual domain. From this synthesis of East and West, Wilber developed a master template of nine most central and functionally dominant structures of consciousness. Arising out of an undifferentiated matrix, consciousness evolves into three prepersonal levels (sensoriphysical, phantasmic-emotional, representational-mind); three personal levels (rule-role, formal-reflexive, existential); and three transpersonal levels (psychic, subtle, causal). Sometimes optimal spiritual

development or the nondual/unitive consciousness level is included.

These structures of consciousness are not discrete but infinitely shade into one another. A person is not confined to one level, but usually spends most of waking life within a very narrow range of the spectrum or within a dominant mode. A key concept of Wilber's model is that the more developed, mature, or conscious the person is, the more freedom of choice is possible. The well-integrated psyche will be able to access and utilize all levels of consciousness appropriately, while the person operating at lower levels will not have access to "higher" structures. Wilber posits that the overall level of self-structuralization is what determines the particular types of needs, motivations, cognitions, object relations, defense mechanisms, and pathologies the individual will exhibit. Interventions that are appropriate and effective at one level of development may be contraindicated and ineffective for symptoms or problems at another level of consciousness. Therefore, accurate assessments and effective interventions depend on the practitioner's understanding of the entire spectrum of consciousness.

For example, in working with prepersonal psychoses, Wilber proposes interventions that are meditation or pacification oriented. For the narcissistic/borderline patient, the therapeutic emphasis is on structure building. For cases involving psychoneuroses, Wilber suggests using uncovering techniques. At the personal or ego level, script pathology is ameliorated with script analysis. The remedy proposed for identity neuroses is introspection. Problems that occur at the existential level are best served by existential therapy. Unlike Maslow's "metapathologies," Wilber points out that real pathology exists at all levels of consciousness, and that pathology occurring at the transpersonal level can be "serious" or "profound." His suggested interventions at the transpersonal level are couched in language that may need to be translated into more culturally friendly terms. For instance, for pathology at the psychic level Wilber recommends the "path of yogis"; for intervention at the subtle level, the "path of the saints"; and for causal level issues, the "path of the sages." In addition, the following caveats are offered to those utilizing Wilber's full spectrum of consciousness model:

> Needless to say, the standard cautions and qualifications about using such hierarchical models of pathology should be kept in mind; i.e., no pure cases, the influence of cultural differences, genetic predispositions, genetic and traumatic arrest, and blended cases. (Wilber, 1986, pp. 107–108)

Wilber's transpersonal model was followed by *Integral Psychology* (2000) and *Integral Spirituality* (2003). While both of these latter works are most enlightening and monumental in their scope, neither is as well suited for application to clinical practice as is his full spectrum model.

Transpersonal Social Work Model

The social work model of transpersonal practice first proposed by Cowley in 1996 is a comprehensive, inclusive approach. It offers clinicians concrete matrixes to aid decision-making about which theories, models, and interventions will best serve the individual needs of each client-system they serve. Since it includes the other three forces of psychology, it provides guidelines for clinical practice whether the treatment goal is oriented toward structure building, cognitive behavioral change, symptom relief, existential angst, or issues related to the spiritual dimension. Developmentally oriented, it is in agreement with the position articulated by Basch (1988):

> Psychology as I see it is applied developmental psychology. The therapist uses his or her knowledge of normal development to reach some conclusions about the reasons for a patient's malfunctioning and how one may enter the developmental spiral either to foster or to reinstitute a more productive, or at least less destructive, developmental process. (p. 29)

Building on Wilber's full spectrum of consciousness model, Cowley's transpersonal model is based on the following six premises: (1) All psychological theories arise out of a specific cultural context to treat the social ills of the day; (2) The dominant malaise of our time is spiritual in nature and requires a Fourth Force approach for its amelioration; (3) To be thorough, clinical assessments need to be multidimensional in

scope and include the physical, affective/emotional, cognitive, psychosocial, moral, and spiritual dimensions; (4) In addition to other knowledge of developmental theory, clinicians need to understand the developmental line within each of the dimensions assessed; (5) Understanding the dominant level of the client's structuralization of ego (i.e., prepersonal, personal, or transpersonal) is of key importance; and (6) An overarching commitment must be made to individualize and affirm each person's culturally diverse and spiritually unique quest for meaning and purpose.

The transpersonal social work model meets many of the criteria called for by Lazarus (1987), when he wrote: "Psychotherapy is in dire need of broader integrative theoretical bases" (p. 166). Lazarus also postulated:

> We need a clinical thesaurus that would cross-reference an objective body of actual operations of patient/therapist interactions across many conditions. We need to operationalize and concretize therapist decision-making processes … Eventually, a super-organizing theory may emerge, a superstructure under whose umbrella present-day differences can be subsumed and reconnected. (p. 166)

Cowley's (1996a) model is a beginning attempt to provide the kind of broad umbrella called for by Lazarus. It does not seek to supplant traditional approaches, but holds that all of the Four Forces (theories and models) can be selectively utilized for ameliorating problems of living and pathologies that occur in different dimensions and at different levels of consciousness. When interventions are designed according to a multimodal rationale, each theory and model can be utilized in a way that is complementary rather than competitive (Ingram, 1987).

Multidimensional Assessments

Effective practice is dependent on the quality and comprehensiveness of the assessment process. It is difficult to even get a partial glimpse of all the complex factors that impinge on an individual's functioning at any given moment over a lifespan: genetic and biochemical factors, faulty learning, deficits in opportunities, risks and traumas of various kinds, sociocultural and environmental events, and so on. The challenge to find a comprehensive way to guide a multidimensional assessment has been well articulated by Gazda (1989):

We need a coherent model of human functioning that generates efficient and effective treatment strategies, one that considers the whole person and yet provides precision without sacrificing comprehensiveness. (p. 403)

In making an initial assessment, the transpersonal social work practitioner is looking for clues that will help to ascertain which of at least six dimensions of being are manifesting the most distress: the physical, the affective/emotional, cognitive, psychosocial, moral, or spiritual:

Actually ego psychologists no longer think in terms of stages of development in the global sense, but in terms of different "developmental lines" for different psychological functions with the relationship between them constituting the organization of the psyche at any point in time. (Wilber, 1986)

By pinpointing where the client is within each developmental line of each dimension assessed, the transpersonal practitioner is able to get a more accurate view of the person-in-situation. In the following description (although he uses the term "unit" or "system" instead of "dimension"), Wolberg makes a strong case for why a multidimensional approach to clinical intervention is essential:

A systems approach recognizes that no unit of psychopathology exists in isolation, but rather it is part of an aggregate of interrelated units. These consist of interacting, biochemical, neurophysiologic, developmental-conditioning, intrapsychic, interpersonal, and spiritual-philosophic systems that determine how a person thinks, feels, and behaves … The most immediate help (to the client-system) will be rendered by diagnosing and targeting initial treatment on the system area most importantly implicated. (Wolberg, 1987, p. 256)

By assessing the developmental strengths and deficits of the client across multiple dimensions, the transpersonal practitioner can target interventions to the developmental lines most salient to the client's presenting problems. In this way the clinician shows respect for the autonomy of the growing person, while at the same time offering a vision of "what ought to be" for optimal functioning (Rosen, 1988, p. 317). Multiple

dimensions are assessed and reassessed as the processes of establishing a relationship, negotiating goals and contracts, and the formulation of interventions proceed. Although the various dimensions are artificially separated for purposes of assessment and intervention, experientially they are all part of one information system (Rossi, 1987). As Capra (1990) has reminded us, distinction is not the same as separation.

Assessing the Physical Dimension

The body provides many surface clues that are easy to assess: appearance, energy level, and general state of health. Less visible but crucial to assessment of physical functioning are things like belief systems related to the body, nutrition, exercise, etc. Since the physical body is the instrument through which human becoming is experienced, each individual has a unique history and relationship to the organism he or she inhabits. Often, observation of body language gives us an accurate understanding of another person, since it can reveal much that is left unsaid. If practitioners do less than a thorough assessment of the physical dimension, they risk missing data important to understanding biophysical problems like brain tissue damage, neurological disorders, thyroid or blood sugar imbalances, circulatory issues, concerns associated with aging, or effects of toxic substances, malnutrition, and other forms of chemical imbalance (Lantz, 1978). Developing the capacity to "listen to" one's body and to practice self-soothing is a hallmark of physical maturation. Enlightened self-care requires the ability to balance a consistent regimen of nutritious diet, exercise, rest, and proper attitude.

Kreuger's developmental line (Table 37.4) is seldom addressed during assessment. However, it can be a very helpful way to understand a person's relationship to his or her body. According to Kreuger (1989), the formation of a healthy body self is prerequisite to further expansion and cohesiveness of the total sense of self (p. 15). Kreuger's five levels of physical development include: (1) a sense of being undifferentiated or symbiotic; (2) an awareness of physical boundaries or having a sense of a separate self (the idea of "I"); (3) an ability to form mental images or representations of things or people not physically present;

Table 37-4. Multi-dimensional Development

Krueger (1989) Physical Development	Basch (1988) Affective Development	Ivey (1986) Cognitive Development	Erikson (1950) Psychosocial Development	Kohlber/Woolf (1984) Moral Development	Wilber (1986) Spiritual Development
6. Self-Mastery Self-Empathy Self-Soothing	5. Attunement	6. Deconstruction Paradox	8. Ego Integration vs. Despair Accrued ego strength = Wisdom (60 yr. +)	6. Universal Mind Harmony Congruence	9. Causal Level 8. Subtle Level 7. Psychic Level
					6 Existential Level Vision-Logic
	4. Empathetic Understanding Going beyond self-reference	5. Dialectic Thesis/antithesis/synthesis	7. Generativity vs. Self-absorption Accrued ego strength = Caring (34 yr – 60 yr)	5. Principled Reciprocity "Spirit of the law"	
5. Self-as-a-whole Integration of bodymind (36 mo – 6 yr)		4. Formal Operations Identifying patterns (12 yr.)	6. Intimacy vs. Isolation Accrued ego strength = Love (22 yr – 34 yr)		5. Formal-reflexive
		3. Concrete Operations Logical, objective reality (7 yr – 12 yr)	5. Identity vs. Identity diffusion Accrued ego strength = Fidelity (12 yr – 22 yr)	4. Law-Oriented Cares about self, other, context "Letter of the Law"	4. Rule/role mind
	3. Emotion Feeling states are joined with experience (24 mo)		4. Industry vs. Inferiority Accrued ego strength = Competence (6 yr -11 yr)	3. Pleaser Cares about: self and other	

Continued...

Table 37-4. Contd.

Krueger (1989) Physical Development	Basch (1988) Affective Development	Ivey (1986) Cognitive Development	Erikson (1950) Psychosocial Development	Kohlber/Woolf (1984) Moral Development	Wilber (1986) Spiritual Development
4. Body/Mind Mental representation of one's body (18 mo – 36 mo)	2. Feeling Sensations are abstracted, objectified (18 mo – 24 mo)	2. Preoperational Magical, scattered thinking (2 yr – 7 yr)	3. Initiative vs. Guilt Accrued ego strength = Purpose (4 yr – 6 yr)		3. Representational Mind
3. Body Self Physical boundaries (15 mo – 18 mo)			2. Autonomy vs. Shame and doubt Accrued ego strength = Will (18 mo – 4 yr)	2. Self Centered Cares about self	2. Phantasmic-emotional Image mind
2. Symbiotic (1 mo – 15 mo)	1. Affect Automatic responses (0 – 18 mo)	1. Sensorimotor Relies on sensory experience (0 – 24 mo)	1. Trust vs. Mistrust Accrued ego strength = Hope (0 - 18 mo.)	1. Premoral Doesn't know how to care	1. Sensori-physical
1. Undifferentiated (0 – 1 mo)					0. Undifferentiated Matrix

(4) a capacity to make mental representations, but still working on healing the mind/body split; and (5) optimal development for the physical dimension; at this level the person has healed the mind/body split and developed a capacity for self-empathy, self-soothing, and self-mastery. Not everyone will achieve these gifts of maturation, but with the help of a developmental therapist, it is at least a possibility.

Assessing the Affective Dimension

Assessing IQ (intelligence quotient) is widely accepted as an important element of clinical practice. However, it is equally likely that an accurate assessment of EQ (emotional quotient) may actually hold the key to successful interventions. Tomkins (1977) identified affectivity as the primary innate biological motivating mechanism. Kaufman (1989) agreed:

It is affect that gives texture to experience, urgency to drives, satisfaction to relationships, and motivating power to purposes envisioned in the future. The affect system and drive system are distinct, interrelated motivators. They empower and direct both behavior and personality, but drives must borrow their power from affect. (p. 11)

Often the prime factors in a case point to disturbances in affective development (Basch, 1988). Emotional distress or "dis-ease" can manifest in a variety of ways: emotional discomfort, depression, mania, inappropriate or erratic affect, being "over-emotional" or "under-emotional," an inability to connect feelings with situations or experiences, or as a lack of capacity to understand what self or other is feeling. Often the biggest challenge of therapy is that of helping the client to become more emotionally mature. This involves learning how to access and appropriately express the full range of emotions. Therefore, a key aspect of assessment of the emotional line of development lies in ascertaining the level on Basch's scale at which the client is currently operating (see Table 37.4).

Level 1 on Basch's scale represents a primitive level of unconscious and automatic reactivity. Unfortunately, many clients much older than 18 months are still prone to react in an automatic and reactive way. When working with a client who behaves in emotionally immature ways, the therapist is challenged to facilitate a move up Basch's developmental line. For example, the first step in an intervention to mature the affective dimension might be to teach the client to become aware of various sensations and feelings. The next task might be to demonstrate how to recognize and distinguish between different feeling states by giving them a name. Next, the therapist must teach the skill of linking affects or feelings with the people or situations that evoke them. Through the use of coaching, modeling, and corrective experiences, the client may develop a capacity not only to understand his or her own emotions, but also to begin to exhibit an ability to extend emotional empathy to others (Basch's level 4). Optimal affective maturation (level 5) is relatively rare. It is not attained until (or unless) an individual is in touch with his or her own deepest emotions, able to be in tune (attuned) to the emotional states of others, and capable of consciously choosing healthy emotional responses. Judith Orloff calls this kind of affective development "emotional freedom."

Assessing the Cognitive Dimension

Cognition has long been recognized as a key aspect of well-being, hence the term "mental health." As long ago as 400 B.C. Buddha declared that all suffering comes from wrong beliefs. Cognitive therapists would agree. Assessing what is mentally healthy or intellectually competent requires a consideration of multiple factors besides IQ. Attitudes and beliefs play an integral part in an individual's perception of what constitutes personal and interpersonal pleasure or pain. In addition, sometimes the determinants of behavior are unconscious and must be recognized. Ultimately, however, the developmental capacity of one's cognition is a prime determinant of a person's quality of life.

The research of Piaget (1952) demonstrated that development of cognitive capabilities occurs across predictable, hierarchical stages: sensorimotor, preoperational (magical), concrete, and formal. Expanding on Kegan's (1982) suggestion of a post-formal possibility, Ivey (1986) expanded this developmental line by proposing two "higher" modes of cognition than Piaget: the dialectic and deconstruction levels (see Table 37.4). According to Ivey, most people never learn how to think at these two top more mature and complex levels (levels 5 and 6).

The post-formal or dialectic stage is one that many adults do not reach, because it requires an ability to abstract and think about thinking that exceeds the intellectual capacities of many individuals and because it is not a characteristic of what is necessary for survival in this culture (Ivey, 1986, p. 204).

Ivey further opines:

the assumption at the dialectic level is that contradictions, incongruity, and discrepancies are facts of life and must be sought actively and lived with. Although resolution may be sought after, contradiction must be recognized as a very real part of the life experience. (p. 151)

A "tolerance for ambiguity" is an accepted byproduct of maturation. Ivey has proposed a definition of cognitive health that includes an "awareness of, and a capacity to live with incongruency and contradiction" (p. 154). In fact, one of the goals of his developmental therapy is to make people aware of the contradictions and discrepancies in their thinking and behavior through the use of a process called "perturbation." Basch (1988) also values this artful technique and considers it an efficient way to provoke growth:

Psychotherapy could be defined as the art of effective perturbation—the act of confronting client discrepancies and contradictions wisely and accurately and in a timely fashion. Effective confrontation of client behavior is a major precursor to growth, development, and later integration of new knowledge and skills. (pp. 191–192)

Only the most cognitively developed reach Ivey's level 6, or the capacity to think deconstructively. At this level of consciousness a person begins:

to encounter Platonic *noesis* (intelligence) that each hard-won knowledge has inherent flaws ... This may require a willingness to live with the unknowable and to accept the logic of our illogic. (Ivey, 1986, p. 110)

Understanding the cognitive line of development gives the therapist not only vital information about the mental capacity of a given client but also an effective rationale for choosing therapeutic interventions. When a therapist is able to "match" his or her level of input to the dominant cognitive mode used by a client to process the world, it maximizes the likelihood that the interventions chosen will be understandable or will "make sense" to the client. Ivey has provided examples to illustrate how to teach a client to think in more complex and mature ways through a process of asking specific "transformational questions" (pp. 107–111).

Despite the most effective interventions, some clients may remain stuck in nonproductive and ineffective thinking patterns. Others may be able to "move up" the cognitive developmental line to more mature and complex levels. For interventions in the transpersonal or trans-rational domain to succeed, both the client and the practitioner must have the capacity to process cognitively at the formal and post-formal levels (Ivey's levels 4, 5, and 6).

Assessing the Psychosocial Dimension

Assessing the way a client handles relationships with self, others, and the world benefits from ascertaining how the individual has balanced each of Erikson's (1950) eight stages of psychosocial development (see Table 37.4). Each age or stage of development (from womb to tomb) presents what Erikson called a "developmental crisis." Each crisis has a specific task that must be negotiated or balanced in a positive direction in order to accrue syntonic ego strengths and avoid dystonic or maladaptive orientations to life. An important part of the psychosocial assessment process is to determine if the client is proceeding in a healthy trajectory or if developmental arrests or deficits are blocking growth. Ascertaining which stage or stages require a remedy allows the practitioner to function as a "developmental partner" (Krueger, 1989). By designing specific structure-building or corrective experiences, the therapist is able to help the client heal or balance developmental lesions that may have occurred at any age or stage.

For example, if a person's development suffers deficits at stage 1 (trust versus mistrust), that is where the worker must begin. Without a sense of basic trust, the accrued ego strength of hope is not added to character structure. Erikson called trust the cornerstone of personality because without it, a person is developmentally disabled psychosocially. Until imbalances in this first crisis of development are mitigated or healed, all subsequent stages of psychosocial development are compromised. Imbalances at stage 2 (autonomy versus shame and self-doubt) can freeze the individual in a "shame-based" life position, unable to exert a healthy sense of will. Developmental blocks at stage 3 (initiative versus guilt) may prevent a person from being decisive or achieving a sense of purpose in life. Unresolved issues at stage 4 (industry versus inferiority) can leave one unable to risk being productive without experiencing painful feelings of inferiority instead of the ego strength of competence. To the extent that one exits childhood feeling mistrustful, self-doubting, guilty, and inferior, as opposed to having developed the ego strengths to feel hopeful, able to act, purposeful, and competent, the developmental tasks of adolescence and adulthood are put in jeopardy.

Just as Erikson considered a sense of basic trust to be the cornerstone for optimal child development, developing a firm sense of identity (knowing and internalizing who one is and what one believes) was posited as a prerequisite for optimal adult development. Failing to balance the key developmental task at stage 5 (identity versus identity diffusion or role confusion) leaves the person prone to suggestibility and vulnerable to external manipulation. Most importantly, without a firm sense of personal identity, one does not accrue the ego strength of fidelity. When a person is unable to be true to self, and lacks the capacity to be faithful to another, balancing the developmental task of stage 6 (intimacy versus isolation) in a positive direction is highly unlikely. Erikson maintained that identity *must* precede intimacy. Consequently, if stages 5 and 6 aren't balanced in a positive direction, one does not accrue the ego strengths required for mature love.

The developmental crisis of stage 7 demands a positive balance between generativity versus self-absorption. If one approaches mid-life with identity diffused, dependent on external authority, and with a crippled ability to love, the chance of balancing this developmental crisis becomes a mission improbable if not impossible. A collapse into self-centeredness or self-absorption is likely to be the result. On the other hand, if one approaches this stage of life with a healthy sense of self (self-esteem), a capacity for intimacy, and a mature ability to care about others, it is likely that the ego strength of generative caring will be added to character.

In old age, the last developmental task, stage 8 (ego-integration versus despair) is a psychological moment of truth time. Optimal psychosocial maturation occurs when the individual has managed to accrue enough ego strengths to give a sense of integrity, wisdom, and wholeness to his or her life. Such a person is then developmentally equipped to provide the next generation with the kind of basic trust that is so essential when a new life is just beginning. Erikson alluded to this circular quality of life when he wrote: "Healthy children will not fear life if their elders have integrity enough not to fear death" (Erikson, 1950, p. 269).

Assessing the Moral Dimension

London has posited that the therapist is often called upon to function as a moral agent or secular priest (1986, p. xiii). Be that as it may, each complete assessment requires an evaluation of the client's level of moral development (Woolf, 1973). Kohlberg/Woolf's paradigm can be of assistance to the practitioner (see Table 37.4). Some adult clients are still operating at level 1 ("premoral" or "amoral" level). Since these clients have never learned to care about self, other, or the social context, we often encounter them in conjunction with the legal system. The continuum of behavior for sociopaths and character disorders runs the gamut from blatant to so subtle they can "pass" undiagnosed. Confrontation and perturbation, along with massive reality checks, may provide some relative success, but the prognoses for work with this level of moral development are guarded if not pessimistic.

A client whose moral development is at level 2 ("self-centered") is challenging because the developmental capacity for including the other or the social context is very limited or nonexistent. Helping a person to develop more empathy and compassion is one way to move him or her toward a more mature stance morally. At level 3 ("pleaser") an individual knows how to care about the other and the social context, but often placates at the expense of selfhood. Working to develop self-esteem and a stronger sense of personal identity must become a part of the pleaser's evolutionary journey. At level 4 ("law-oriented") one knows how to care about self, others, and the social context, but a rigid adherence to the "letter of the law" and a general lack of flexibility can make life difficult, not only for the person, but for everyone else as well. Kohlberg (1981) wrote that none of the problems we face (individually or globally) are solvable as long as we operate at these first four levels of moral development.

It represents nothing less than a quantum leap in consciousness to reach level 5 (principled level of moral development). This is where people begin to understand how to go beyond ego, operate according to the "spirit of the law," and implement principles like fairness and reciprocity, etc. Working with a principled person can be a very rewarding experience for a therapist. Occasionally, the morally mature, universal-minded (level 6) walk among us and demonstrate the moral attributes of a harmonizer/peace-maker. Their issues are likely to be existential or transpersonal in nature and may require a referral to a practitioner prepared to intervene at those levels. It is necessary to make the important distinction between working out of a transpersonal perspective and being qualified to utilize transpersonal interventions. The former level of practice is open to clinicians who approach practice with an attitude that respects and embraces the spiritual dimension. To intervene at the transpersonal level, one must be well versed in transpersonal psychology and to have concluded that it is appropriate to focus on the spiritual dimension.

Assessing Values and Worldviews

As an adjunct to assessing moral development, spiral dynamics is a model that holds great promise for augmenting our understanding about the values individuals hold as well as the cultural milieu in which they are embedded. Based on decades of research, Graves (1970) built an "emergent, cyclical, double-helix model of adult biopsychosocial systems development." A color-code was added to the model in the 1970s to give each meme or value structure its own distinctive hue. Then, building on Graves' work, Beck and Cowan (1995) further refined

spiral dynamics' view of the journey taken by the individual or entire cultures across eight fluid waves of the values dimension. Each of the eight waves or value memes has both a healthy or unhealthy adaptation.

First-tier levels (1–6) are considered "subsistence levels." They are exclusive in nature since each believes it has the only true worldview. First-tier memes are (1) Beige = Archaic/Instinctual values; (2) Purple = Magical/Tribal values; (3) Red = Egocentric/Power God values; (4) Blue = Mythic/Traditional values; (5) Orange = Modern/Individualistic values; (6) Green = Postmodern/Pluralistic values. Levels 7 and 8 are considered second-tier value orientations. According to Graves, it is at this level that there is "a momentous leap of meaning" and values and worldviews become more integrative and inclusive. Moving beyond egocentric and ethnocentric perspectives, second-tier thinkers recognize the valuable contribution each wave and each culture has contributed, historically, to prepare the human family for membership in a global village where an inclusive worldcentric perspective prevails. Second-tier MEMES are (7) yellow = Integrative/Systematic values and (8) Turquoise = Holistic/Universal Mindedness values.

According to Wilber (2003), even though each individual starts at square one and less than 2% of the world's population is at second-tier levels, "it is an elitism to which all are invited." Wilber posits that an increase in second-tier consciousness is on the way, with the expectation that even higher MEMES or value orientations may be in the offing. So, in contrast to secular voices, the lure of spiral dynamics is that the spiral of development is not headed away from Spirit, but toward it.

Assessing the Spiritual Dimension

Assessing a client's spiritual developmental line may not become a focal point. Until Maslow's hierarchy of needs for food, shelter, belonging, self-esteem, and self-actualization are met, self-transcendence may not be an appropriate focus for intervention. Spiritual maturation often becomes targeted when, for example, the client is experiencing spiritual malaise or a deprivation of nonmaterial resources, suffers a traumatic event, and/or desires to strengthen his or her connection to Spirit. However, issues related to the spiritual dimension can emerge at any time in the therapeutic process. When they do, it is crucial that the worker is conceptually prepared to recognize and honor them.

Wilber's (1986) full spectrum model specifically describes and delineates nine hierarchical levels of spiritual development (Table 37.4). Levels 1 through 6 originated in the West (the first Three Forces of psychology), and levels 7 through 9 (Fourth Force) are primarily based in Eastern psychology and other traditions of spiritual practice. For the purposes of clinical assessment, it is useful to break Wilber's nine general levels of consciousness into three general levels of ego structuralization: prepersonal, personal, and transpersonal. When intervening in the spiritual dimension (or transpersonal level of consciousness), the practitioner will need to make distinctions between levels 7 through 9 in Wilber's model: the psychic, subtle, and causal levels.

At the psychic level of consciousness, the individual begins to open up to the trans-rational or transpersonal domain. If the lure of psychic experiences becomes too seductive, this level can function as a spiritual detour and preclude a further advance to higher levels of consciousness. If a seeker is able to access the subtle level of consciousness, a beginning capacity for self-transcendence evolves. Sometimes mystical or cosmic experiences, near-death experiences, and the like may trigger an actual change in the structure of consciousness, and sometimes they merely induce temporary "states" of expanded or peak experiencing. It is important for the worker to be able to help the client make those kinds of distinctions. According to Wilber, optimal spiritual maturation (Wilber's causal or non-dual levels) may involve years of study and spiritual practice under the tutelage of a guide or teacher. Mastering Wilber's full spectrum of consciousness model requires a return to its original source. For the most comprehensive (and possibly the only "integral") discussion of spirituality (and religion's role in the future), one must turn to Wilber's book *Integral Spirituality* (2003).

The transpersonal models presented in this chapter are offered to "show the strong possibilities [more] than the final conclusions" (Wilber,

1986, p. 159). Few in our culture profess the goal of achieving cosmic consciousness; more seem to be searching for an alternative way to find a purpose in life and a sense of meaning that transcends the personal or social level (Derezotes, 2009b). The quest for a healthy sense of spiritual connection that offers a worldcentric thrust was expressed succinctly by Frances Vaughn in her description of healthy spirituality:

As a subjective experience of the sacred, authentic, healthy spirituality does not hinge on a particular concept of God or religious observance. It depends, rather, on how we relate to ourselves, to each other, to the earth, and to the cosmos. (Vaughn, 1996, p. 51)

Sometimes a complete assessment of the spiritual dimension requires us to look at the myriad of ways there are to participate in the many worlds of religion.

Assessing Religious Maturation

Even though the tide toward a heightened interest in the spiritual dimension has been rising for several decades, fewer people are choosing to conform to the theologies of traditional religious institutions. Sometimes the very religious institutions people rely on for support become instead a major part of their psychological or spiritual distress. As social workers are called to intervene in areas of ultimate concern, or deal with religious practices that may be spiritually abusive to their adherents (Derezotes, 2009a), the practitioner must develop a knowledge base broad enough to help client-systems differentiate between religions that are legitimate and authentic (Anthony, Ecker, & Wilber, 1987).

Categories in the DSM-IV legitimate mental health support for religious or spiritual problems. Several other helpful guides are available to aid the practitioner when the client's level of religious development becomes the focal point. For example, James Fowler's (1981) six stages of faith describe an evolutionary process that begins at birth. According to Fowler's research, faith may proceed through six stages during one's lifetime, or it may lodge itself at any stage along the way. Fowler's first stage of faith (0) begins at birth. It is described as primal or undifferentiated. Faith at stage 1 is intuitive-projective in nature. Stage 2 faith has a mythic-literal quality.

At stage 3 faith becomes more synthetic or conventional. Stage 4 is a level of individuated or reflective faith. Fowler called stage 5 faith "conjunctive." An individual at stage 6 has developed an inclusive or "universalizing" faith. For some clients, being helped to view their religious development along Fowler's continuum may normalize the discomfort experienced during periods of doubt or when making a transition from one stage of faith to another.

M. Scott Peck (1987) offered another view of stages or levels of spiritual growth that may be helpful when discerning if religious maturation is stalled at an unhealthy or unproductive level. Peck's four levels of spiritual development are (1) chaotic and antisocial; (2) formal and institutional; (3) skeptic and individual, and (4) mystic and communal. A more recent exploratory study (Derezotes, Cowley, Thompson, Shields, & Morgan, 2008) documents a beginning effort to delineate levels of religious maturity based in part on acceptance of spiritual and religious diversity and a desire for connection and service to others.

Multimodal Interventions

Transpersonal social work takes Nelson's (1994) insightful observation into account: "only when people engage in treatment specific to their level of consciousness can they resume growth" (p. 375). Since each of the four broad umbrella theories has a different focus, view of pathology, premise about what constitutes health or pathology, the curative process, and the nature of the helping relationship, etc., the practitioner must make at least four conceptual distinctions when designing a person-specific, multimodal intervention: (1) which dimension(s) will be focused on initially; (2) which of the Four Force theories will best serve each dimension chosen; (3) which model or models will fit with each theory selected; and (4) which clinical skills or interventions match or complement each theory and model. Making these kinds of conceptual distinctions may distinguish a professional helper from a layperson who is inherently helpful. Cowley (1996b) has offered a beginning effort to provide a clinical thesaurus for each of the Four Forces, their models, and their most popular interventions or techniques (see Table 37.1).

This matrix has proven to be an effective guide for students and beginning practitioners as they sort through the plethora of theories, models, and skills available for their use.

Lazarus (1987) distinguished clearly between choosing a theory (or theories) to guide the therapeutic process, and choosing specific techniques to accomplish designated goals by pointing out that in choosing a theory one must be theoretically "pure" while acknowledging that, at the some time, one could be technically "eclectic" (p. 166):

By underscoring the virtues of technical eclecticism and the dangers of theoretical eclecticism, I hope to pave the way for a sincere appreciation of the scientific method, the significance of breadth versus depth approaches, and the overriding need for specificity. (Lazarus, 1987, p. 165)

When a practitioner is able to intentionally pick which theory, model, and intervention is the best match for intervening in a specific dimension of development for a specific client-system at each given moment in the therapeutic process, he or she gets close to answering the classic question posed by Paul in 1967: "What treatment, by whom, is most effective for this individual with that specific problem, under which set of circumstances, and how does it come about?"

The Importance of a Premise

Whether an evolution of consciousness takes place within individuals or societies in the years ahead will depend to a large degree on the belief systems that shape and guide us personally and professionally. The premises we hold about the possible human and the boundaries of exceptional heath and well-being will not only shape our practice choices, but also help to determine our future as a species. As Walsh and Vaughn opined (1980): "Our premises about human potential shape our perceptions and influence our areas of inquiry and therefore act in self-validating ways" (p. 17). Allport underscored this observation when he declared:

By their own theories of human nature, psychologists have the power of elevating or degrading that same nature. Debasing assumptions debase human beings; generous assumptions exalt them. (Walsh & Shapiro, 1983, p. 31)

Walsh and Shapiro (1983) expanded on this theme to conclude:

If our prevailing cultural and psychological models have underestimated what we are and what we can become then perhaps we have set up a self-fulfilling prophecy. In such a case, the exploration of extreme psychological well-being, and the permeation of that knowledge into psychology and the larger culture, becomes a particularly important undertaking. Indeed, it may even be that shifting our self-concept may be one of the most strategic interventions for personal and cultural transformation. What is envisaged as possible may become a compelling vision and attraction. (p. 10)

One of Maslow's major premises was succinctly expressed in what later became known as "Maslow's metaphor": "Freud supplied to us the sick half of psychology, and we must now fill it out with the healthy half" (Wittine, 1987, p. 54). In the 21st century Maslow's exhortation to study the farther reaches of human nature was honored when the social work profession's accrediting body (CSWE) added the spiritual dimension to its definition of diversity. In the United States electives that include spirituality content have increased significantly over the past 10 to 12 years (Russel, 2006). Also, the Society for Spirituality and Social Work (SSSW), founded by Edward Canda in 1990, has now become international in scope. For instance, a center has been established in Dubrovnik, and there are active groups in Canada, the United Kingdom, Europe, Scandinavia, Africa, Asia, as well as New Zealand and Australia.

Healing Splits

Traditional Western psychologies (First, Second, and Third Forces) have been challenged to deal with the concerns that reside in the spiritual dimension, and they have been found lacking. They have failed to provide the lure to being so desperately needed in a time when we are still "in a race between consciousness and catastrophe" (Walsh, 1993, p. 134). In a world splintered by religious differences and competing value systems, the transpersonal approach (Fourth Force) claims no monopoly on practice with the spiritual dimension. Perhaps, however, it can be instrumental to help heal the effects of ideological and political splits that seek to divide the human family into competing factions. According to Rossi (1987):

We can view the entire history of psychotherapy as a series of efforts to heal the artificial divisions in man's nature … the basic problem is always dissociation or split that needs to be healed. (p. 370)

Social work has long been committed to the goal of helping to bring about the good person in a good society. It seems that, paradoxically, each step toward individuation and optimal spiritual health ultimately leads back to a healthier connection with the Whole. Bee expressed this sage observation when she wrote: "Each decentering takes the individual further from identification with the individual self, and toward identification with the All" (Bee, 1986, p. 341).

The transpersonal social work model offers a practice model theoretically comprehensive enough to honor our most generous premises about spiritual potential. It also serves to reconnect the profession to its origins in philanthropy, theology, and moralism (Weick, 1992). By including the spiritual dimension, it can also offer hope to a secular society that has been artificially divorced from its source.

As the profession prepares to move forward in the 21st century, much remains to be accomplished. As is, the transpersonal social work model has much to offer to clinical practice. However, its culturally specific perspective may appeal or be applicable to only a small percentage of the population of the Western world. To serve a global population, all of the helping professions must become more sensitive to and more knowledgeable about the many different ways there are to experience the numinous and to serve the domain of spirit. Remaining relevant in a postmodern world will challenge us all to go beyond our individual and cultural comfort zones to access and honor the rich diversity of wisdom traditions, ancient and modern, East and West. Anything less will not suffice.

References

Anthony, D., Ecker, B., & Wilber, K. (1987). *Spiritual choices: The problem of recognizing authentic paths to inner transformation*. New York: Paragon Press.

Assagioli, R. (1965). *Psychosenthesis*. New York: Viking Press.

Aurobindo, S. (1971). *Letters on yoga*. Pondicherry, India: Sri Aurobindo International University Center.

Banerjee, M. M., & Pyles, L. (2004). Spirituality: A source of resilience for African American women in the era of welfare reform. *Journal of Ethnic and Cultural Diversity in Social Work, 13*(2), 45–70.

Basch, M. (1988). *Understanding psychotherapy: The science behind the art*. New York: Basic Books, Inc.

Bee, H. (1986/Fall). Psychology's journey toward spirituality. *The American Theosophist, 74*(9), 338–342.

Beck, D., & Cowan, C. (1995). *Spiral dynamics: Mastering values, leadership, and change*. Cambridge, MA: Blackwell Publishers.

Bettelheim, B. (1983). *Freud and man's soul*. New York: Alfred A. Knoff.

Bradshaw, J. (1988). *Bradshaw on: The family*. Deerbeach, FL: Health Communications, Inc.

Brown, D. (1988/Spring). The transformation of consciousness in meditation. *Noetic Sciences Review*, (6), 14.

Bugental, J. (1978). *Psychotherapy and process*. Reading, MA: Addison Wesley.

Bugental, J., & Bugental, I. (1984/Winter). Dispiritedness: A new perspective on a familiar state. *Journal of Humanistic Psychology, 24*(1), 49–67.

Campbell, J. (1971). *The portable Jung*. New York: Viking Press.

Canda, E. (1988a). Conceptualizing spirituality for social work: Insights from diverse perspectives. *Social Thought, 13*(1), 30–46.

Canda, E. (1988b). Spirituality, religious diversity, and social work practice. *Social Casework, 69*(4), 238–247.

Canda, E. (1995/Fall). Retrieving the soul of social work. *Society for Spirituality and Social Work Newsletter, 2*(2), 5–8.

Canda, E. (1998). *Spirituality in social work: New directions*. New York: Haworth Press.

Canda, E. (2006). The future of spirituality in social work: The further reaches of human nature. *Advances in Social Work, 6*(7), 97–108.

Canda, E., & Furman, L. (1999). *Spiritual diversity in social work practice: The heart of helping*. New York: The Free Press.

Canda, E., Nakashima, W. & Furman, L. (2004). Ethical considerations about spirituality in social work: Insights from a national qualitative survey. *Families in Society, 85*(1). 27.

Canda, E., & Smith, E. (Eds.) (2001). *Transpersonal perspectives on spirituality in social work*. New York: The Haworth Press.

Capra, F. (1990). Life as mental process. *The Quest, 3*(2), 7–11.

Clinebell, H. (1995). *Counseling for spiritually empowered wholeness: A hope-centered approach*. New York: The Haworth Press, Inc.

Cowley, A. (1993/September). Transpersonal social work: A theory for the 1990s. *Social Work, 38*(5), 527–534.

Cowley, A. (1996a). Transpersonal social work. In F. J. Turner (Ed.), *Social work treatment* (4th ed). New York: The Free Press.

Cowley, A. (1996b/Fall). Expressing the soul of social work. *Society for Spirituality and Social Work Newsletter, 3*(2), 1, 6–8.

Cowley, A. (1999). Transpersonal theory and social work practice with couples and families. *Journal of Family Social Work, 3*(2), 5–21.

Cowley, A. (2001). Cosmic consciousness: Path or pathology? In E. Canda & E. Smith (Eds.), *Transpersonal perspectives on spirituality in social work*. New York: The Haworth Press. (Published simultaneously in *Social Thought: Journal of Religion in the Social Services, 20*(1/2), 77–94).

Cowley, A., & Derezotes, D. S. (1994/Winter). Transpersonal psychology and social work education. *Journal of Social Work Education, 30*(4), 32–41.

Cox, D. (1985). The missing dimension in social work practice. *Australian Social Work, 38*(4), 5–11.

Crittenden, E. (1980). A Jungian view of transpersonal psychology. In S. Boorstein (Ed.), *Transpersonal psychotherapy*. Palo Alto, CA: Science and Behavior Books.

Derezotes, D. S. (1995). Spiritual and religious factors in practice: Empirically-based recommendations for social work education. *Arête, 20*(1), 1–15.

Derezotes, D. S. (2001). Transpersonal social work with couples: A compatibility-intimacy model. *Social Thought: Journal of Religion in Social Services, 20*(1), 163–174.

Derezotes, D. S. (2006). *Spiritually-oriented social work practice*. Boston: Pearson/Allyn & Bacon.

Derezotes, D. S. (2009a). Spirituality and mental health. In V. Vandiver (Ed.), *Social work desk reference II - Special section: mental health*. New York: Oxford University Press.

Derezotes, D. S. (2009b). Religious resurgence, human survival, and global religious social work. *Journal of Religion & Spirituality in Social Work: Social Thought, 28*(1), 63–81.

Derezotes, D. S., Cowley, A., Thompson, J., Shields, E. & Morgan, A. (2008). Spiritual maturity: An exploratory study and model for social work practice. *Currents: New Scholarship in the Human Services, 7*(1), 1–18.

Dorfman, R. (Ed.) (1988). *Paradigms of clinical social work*. New York: Brunner/Mazel.

Erikson, E. (1950). *Childhood and society.* New York: W. W. Norton & Co., Inc,

Ferrucci, P. (1982). *What we may be.* Los Angeles: J. P. Tarcher.

Fowler, J. (1981). *Stages of faith: The psychology of human development and the quest for meaning.* San Francisco: Harper & Row.

Furman, L., Benson, P., Greenwood, C., & Canda, E. (2004). Religion and spirituality in social work education and direct practice at the millennium: A survey of UK students. *British Journal of Social Work,* 34(8), 767.

Gazda, G. (1989). *Group counseling: A developmental approach.* New York: Simon & Schuster.

Goldberg, C. (1980). *In defense of narcissism.* New York: Gardner Press.

Graves, C. (1970/November). Levels of existence: An open systems theory of values. *Journal of Humanistic Psychology,* 10(2), 131–155.

Grof, S. (1985). *Beyond the brain.* Albany: State University of New York Press.

Grof, S., & Grof, C. (Eds.) (1989). *Spiritual emergency: When personal transformation becomes a crisis.* Los Angeles: J. P. Tarcher.

Hepworth, D., Rooney, R., Rooney, G., Strom-Gottfried, K., Larsen, J. (2009). *Direct social work practice: Theory and skills.* Florence, KY: Cengage Publishing Company.

Hodge, D., & Williams, T. (2002). Assessing African American spirituality eco-maps. *Families in Society,* 83(5/6), 585–595.

Hodge, D. (2004). Spirituality and people with mental illness: Developing spiritual competency in assessment and intervention. *Families in Society,* 86(1), 36–44.

Hodge, D. (2005). Spiritual assessment in marital and family therapy: A methodological framework for selecting between six qualitative assessment tools. *Journal of Marital and Family Therapy,* 31(4), 341–356.

Hollis, F. (1964). *Casework: A psychosocial therapy* (1st ed.) New York: Random House.

Ingram, C, (1987/September/October). Ken Wilber: The pundit of transpersonal psychology. *Yoga Journal,* 40–49.

Ivey, A. (1986). *Developmental therapy.* San Francisco: Jossey-Bass.

Kaufman, G. (1989). *The psychology of shame: Theory and treatment of shamed-based syndromes.* New York: Springer.

Keen, S. (1983). Uses and abuses of "spirituality technology" in therapy. *The Common Boundary,* 1(5), 7–8.

Kegan, R. (1982). *The evolving self: Problem and process in human development.* Cambridge, Mass.: Harvard University Press.

Kohlberg, L. (1981), *The philosophy of moral development.* San Francisco: Harper & Row.

Kramer, S. (1995). *Transforming the inner and outer family: Humanistic and spiritual approaches to mind-body systems theory.* New York: The Haworth Press.

Krueger, D. (1989). *Body self & psychological self.* New York: Brunner/Mazel.

Lantz, J. (1978). Cognitive theory and social casework. *Social Work,* 23, 361–366.

Lazarus, A. (1987). The need for technical eclecticism: Science, breadth, depth and specificity. In J. Zeig (Ed.), *The evolution of psychotherapy.* New York: Brunner/Mazel.

Leonard, G. (1983). Abraham Maslow and the new self. *Esquire* (December), p. 376.

Limb, G., Hodge, D., & Panos, P. (2008). Social work with native people: Orienting child welfare workers to the beliefs, values and practices of Native American families and children. *Public Child Welfare,* 2(3), 383–397.

London, P. (1974/June). From the long couch for the sick to the push button for the bored. *Psychology Today,* 8(1), 63–68.

London, P. (1986). *The modes and morals of psychotherapy.* New York: Hemisphere Publishing Company.

Martin, C. P., & Martin, J.M. (2003). *Spirituality and the black helping tradition in social work.* Washington, DC: NASW Press.

Maslow, A. (1968). *Toward a new psychology of being.* Princeton: Van Nostrand.

Maslow, A. (1971). *The farther reaches of human nature.* New York: Viking/ Compass.

Moody, H. (2005). *Religion, spirituality, and aging: A social work perspective.* New York: The Haworth Press.

Moxley, D., & Washington, O. (2001). Strengths-based recovery practice in chemical dependency: A transpersonal perspective. *Families in Society,* 82(3), 251.

Nelson-Becker, H. (2005) Development of a spiritual support scale for use with older adults. *Journal of Human Behavior in the Social Environment,* 11(3-4), 195–212.

Nelson-Becker, H., Nakashima, M., & Canda, E. (2007). Spiritual assessment in aging: A framework for clinicians. *Journal of Gerontological Social Work,* 48(3/4), 331.

Nelson, J. (1994). *Healing the split: Integrating spirit into our understanding of the mentally ill.* New York: State University of New York Press.

Ornstein, R. (1972). *The psychology of consciousness.* New York: Penguin Books.

Park, J. (2000). *Our existential predicament: Loneliness, depression, anxiety and death.* New York: Existential Books.

Paul, G. (1967). Strategy of outcome research in psychotherapy. Journal of Consulting Psychology. 31, 109-118.

Peck, M. S. (1987/May/June). A new American revolution. New Age Journal, 32-37, 50–51.

Perlman, H. (1957). Social casework: A problem-solving process. Chicago: University of Chicago Press.

Piaget, J. (1952). The origins of intelligence in children. New York: Humanities Press.

Pine, F. (1985). Developmental theory and clinical practice. New Haven: Yale University Press.

Rosen, H. (1988). The constructivist-developmental paradigm. In R. Dorfman (Ed.), Paradigms of clinical social work. New York: Brunner/Mazel.

Rossi, E. (1987). Mind/body communication and the new language of human facilitation. In J. Zeig (Ed.), The evolution of psychotherapy. New York: Brunner/Mazel.

Russel, R. (2006). Spirituality and social work: Current trends and future directions. Arête, 30(1), 42–52.

Satir, V. (1987). Going beyond the obvious: The psychotherapeutic journey. In J. Zeig (Ed.), The evolution of psychotherapy. New York: Brunner/Mazel.

Scales, T., Wolfer, T., Sherwood, D., Garfield, D., Hugen, B., & Pittman, S. (Eds.) (2002). Spirituality and religion in social work practice: Decision cases with teaching notes. Washington DC: CSWE.

Schnall, M. (1981). Limits: A search for new values. New York: Crown Publishers.

Small, J. (1982). Transformers: Therapists of the future. Marina del Rey, CA: DeVores & Co.

Smith, E. (1995/May). Addressing the psychospiritual distress of death as reality: a transpersonal approach. Social Work, 40(3), 402–413.

Solomon, E. (1967). Humanistic values and social casework. Social Casework, 48(1), 26–32.

Spencer, S. (1957). Religious and spiritual values in social casework practice. Social Casework, 38(10), 519–525.

Stroup, H. (1962/March/April). The common predicament of religion and social work. Social Work, 7(2), 89–93.

Sutich, A. (1969). Some considerations regarding transpersonal psychology. Journal of Transpersonal Psychology, 1(1), 11–20.

Tomkins, S. (1977). The quest for primary motives: Biography and autobiography of an idea. Journal of Personality and Social Psychology, 41, 306–329.

Trungpa, R. (1973). Cutting through spiritual materialism. Boston: Shambhala.

Tullis, R. (1996). Spirituality in social work practice. Washington, DC: Taylor & Francis.

Van Hook, M., Hagen, B., & Aquilar, M. (Eds.) (2002). Spirituality within religious traditions in social work practice. Pacific Grove, CA: Brooks/Cole.

Vaughn, F. (1996/Winter). Spiritual freedom. The Quest, 8(4), 48–55.

Vincentia, J. (1987/Winter). The religious and spiritual aspects of clinical practice: A neglected dimension of social work. Social Thought, 12–23.

Walsh, R., & Vaughn, F. (Eds.) (1980). Beyond ego: Transpersonal dimensions in psychology. Los Angeles: J. P. Tarcher.

Walsh, R., & Shapiro, E. (Eds.) (1983). Beyond health and normality: Explorations of exceptional psychological well-being. New York: Van Nostrand Reinhold.

Walsh, R. (1993). The transpersonal movement: A history and state of the art. Journal of Transpersonal Psychology, 25(2), 123–139.

Washburn, M. (1994). Transpersonal psychology in psychoanalytic perspective. New York: State University of New York Press.

Weick, A. (1992/Spring/Summer). Publishing and perishing in social work education. Journal of Social Work Education, 28(2), 129–130.

Weinstein-Moser, E. (2008). Spirituality and social work: The journey from fringe to mainstream. Social Work Today, 8(2), 32.

Welwood, J. (1986). Personality structure: Path or pathology? Journal of Transpersonal Psychology, 18(2), 131–142.

Whitmore, D. (1991). Psychosynthesis counseling in action. Newbury Park, CA: Sage Publications.

Wilber, K. (1986). The spectrum of development, The spectrum of psychopathology, and Treatment modalities. In K. Wilber, J. Engler, & D. Brown (Eds.), Transformation of consciousness: Conventional and contemplative perspectives on development. Boston: New Science Library/Shambhala.

Wilber, K. (2000). Integral psychology. Boston: Shambhala.

Wilber, K. (2003). Integral spirituality: A startling new role for religion in the modern and postmodern world. Boston: Shambhala.

Wittine, B. (1987/September/October). Beyond ego. Yoga Journal, 51–57.

Wolberg, L. (1987). The evolution of psychotherapy: Future trends. In J. Zeig (Ed.), The evolution of psychotherapy. New York: Brunner/Mazel.

Woolf, V. (1973). The relationship between peer involvement in a drug rehabilitation group and judgment of moral maturity on the Kohlberg moral maturity stages. Provo, UT: Brigham Young University.

38

An Interlocking Theoretical Perspective for Treatment

Francis J. Turner

Once again we have concluded our set task of presenting a discussion of the principal theories, each of which plays a positive influencing role in contemporary social work practice. We now need to pause and ask: What have we learned from this ongoing odyssey? Unlike what was expected when this process began some 40 years ago, the emergence of new practice theories has not diminished. Then, we considered 14 systems; now we have 36, and no doubt this number will increase.

For some this is a sign of professional weakness, for others a strength. I welcome it! This expansion of diversity reminds us, indeed compels us, to consider how complex is our scope of practice and how naïve we are to attempt to include this scope into any one theoretical framework. This awareness helps us to become more open to new ideas, concepts, strategies,

methodologies, techniques, and technologies, all of which greatly enrich our practice and expand the bases of our theory (Lewis, 1982).

Apart from the occasional wish for more theoretical simplicity, there has been little movement to a unifying mega-theory, although the development of the "Fourth Force" in theory development, as discussed by Dr. Cowley and Derezotes in Chapter 37, raises the possibility. Also in some other fields there is speculation that a theory such as "string theory" is going to be a unifying theory for many bodies of knowledge (Kiritsis, 2007).

Our theoretical richness helps us to appreciate the enormity of our task as we seek to understand our clients in a biopsychosocial framework, and the complex range of systems and subsystems this entails. A part of this challenge requires us to strengthen our understanding of the biological dimension of clients and expand our awareness of our environmental issues. Dr. Gitterman's discussion of the Life Model in Chapter 18 gives us a way of looking at and dealing with this complexity.

Our profession probably cuts the broadest swath of necessary knowledge of any of the human professions. In spite of this some suggest that at times theory can be dangerous (Thyer, 2008). However, this viewpoint cannot lead to an abandonment of theory unless we view practice only as a random application of a range of techniques and strategies using as a measuring stick which interventions bring about sought-for change and which do not, without attempting to ask why.

Overall there is much less faddism about new theories than before, although that very human tendency of seeking to be fashionable can still be seen. More positively and maturely, though, is the strong commitment of our theory builders to seek cutting-edge theoretical formulations (Thyer, 1994).

Also, there is an overall growing tolerance of differences among theories and theorists. There is more acceptance of the idea that a great unifying panacea is not going to emerge, nor will a major theoretical breakthrough occur that will make everything clear and precise. This awareness makes us more cautious, humble, critical, outward-looking, and curious about both the process of building theory and the use of theories as they emerge (Caspi, 1992).

There is also a growing interest and comfort in comparing theories and examining their conceptual bases—not in an argumentative, self-validating way, but in an exploratory manner, seeking a broadening of purview and areas of commonality. In doing so, however, there is still a tendency, at least in this part of the world, to prefer the new to the old, even though, as the authors who address our more traditional theories demonstrate in their respective chapters, there is still much to be learned from them. The chapters on Functional, Psychosocial, and Problem-Solving are good examples of this.

Our growing comfort with the need, wish, and possibility to be multi-theoretical continues. This is the reality of most other professions. Such a position is accompanied by the understanding that systems are helped, not threatened, when

they seek and incorporate interconnections with other systems. The "holy wars" of earlier days between adherents of various theories have all but disappeared as the profession's awareness grows that each system has something to teach us.

This does not mean that all theories are the same or of equal importance and utility. As a group our theories give us a differential pool from which to draw and, as such, all deserve some degree of recognition. The tests are: Does it work? When is it efficacious? Is it safe and ethical? Even when our efforts are turned to disproving or challenging a theory, we must expand our knowledge of the theory we are challenging and in so doing expand our knowledge of our own theory as well as the one we are challenging (Imre Wells, 1984).

As Freud told us many years ago, there are many ways of dealing with a client or a social issue. The challenge is for us to know what we are doing, why we are doing it, and how we are doing it. Theory helps us to sort our what is most effective and when. As for a physician or pharmacist there are often many ways for us to address the same presenting problem or same issues. Of course, there are some situations and issues that can be addressed in only one way. If this be so, we have a responsibility to be acquainted with all theories. The belief that a strong theory base enhances practice seems evident but is not universal; thus, there exists an equally strong awareness of our challenge to demonstrate this (Thyer, 1994).

Throughout these presentations there is an understanding that within the differences there are almost always some common threads that contribute to unification with other theories. With this growing comfort in looking over one another's theoretical shoulders in a collegial manner comes an appreciation of the need to look not only at differences among theories but also similarities. Perhaps when a new theory first emerges there is a tendency to maintain closed boundaries, a tendency that passes as a theory wins more credibility, renown, and maturity.

There is, as well, an increased comfort in finding knowledge from sources outside of social work. Even if a theory is adapted from other sources or disciplines than social work it becomes a social work theory when it is adapted to our needs and shows how it fits our "person-in-situation" reality, the cornerstone of our profession.

Although we may not have developed the original theory, it becomes a social work theory if it assists our practice and we take responsibility for what we are dong in using it. To reinforce this, we ensured that each chapter was written by social workers, either alone or with a colleague. Each author has examined the tenets of a particular system and its origins and has demonstrated its relevance and utility to contemporary social work practice theory.

What is New?

But much of what has been said above was identified in earlier editions of this book. Have there been any observable changes in our addressing theoretical plurality? Certainly the fact that in the 15 years since the previous edition we have added nine new theories marks the march to increasing complexity. Also, the range of writing about various theories and the place of theory in practice has expanded (Mishne, 1993). This reflects a growing interest in the differential application of theories as well an expanding commitment to explore the specific application of each theory, either through practice or more formal research.

Although not addressed in a formal way by the various authors, one of the ways in which theories are developed is through the interaction of graduate students, especially doctoral students, with a professor particularly interested in a particular theory. Such students, impressed with the leadership of the professor, often choose to pursue their doctoral dissertations based on the advancement of some component of the theory, with the academic support of the theory guru. This is the way much theory is developed and tested in other disciplines, where doctoral students and postdoctoral fellows are able to take some theoretical component further or in a different direction, thus expanding its relevance.

Within these chapters, a lessening on the focus on pathology, as circumscribed by the APA's *Diagnostic and Statistical Manual* through its various editions, as the primary target of intervention can be noted. Instead, we are observing a thrust to build our diagnosis and plan our treatment on the client's goals and aspirations within the parameters of his or her strengths and available resources. In so doing, with enrichment from our spectrum of theories, increased understanding and attention is given to the client's social reality and his or her or their perception of it within the broad base from which it is composed. More and more this includes the need to address many forms of oppression. Pathology is not denied or excluded from the purview of the clinical social worker, but it is seen in a much more comprehensive and multisystemic way, so that when present it must be viewed in context and as only one part of the client's reality with which we deal.

Diagnosis is still an unpopular word for some, principally because of its perceived labeling and pathologizing perception, rather than viewing it as a responsibility to be clear as to the professional judgments we make in every case as the basis for our intervention. However, we are learning that a social work understanding of the concept restores it to the forefront of our profession. Clearly what is meant by "diagnosis" is still highly varied. However defined, rejected, praised, or vilified, it relates to the need to take responsibility for what we do, knowing and stating what in our view is appropriate and what is inappropriate and why.

Each author has identified the limitations and counterindications for the application of the theoretical system that he or she addressed. The implications of this are that we need to know these limitations and their implications for each client that we meet—the true role of diagnosis.

Although not as prominent a development as expected, with the increasing permeability between theoretical systems and their application, the need for an expanded understanding of the physical and biological components of our client's reality is emerging and expanding. This growing awareness of the effects of our biological and environmental reality on our psychosocial functioning increases our responsibility to give these aspects of our clients more attention. Gestalt and its awareness of the way our body and its functioning can convey messages about our psychological status helps in this area. Meditation's interest in body and mind connections has helped bring into clearer focus the relevance of this material to our practice, as have the chapters on Cognitive theory and

Neurolinguistics. Perhaps the most important theme that continues in this expanded collection of theories is the greater understanding and appreciation of the fact that theories need be open, dynamic systems that grow, change, and develop as they interact with other systems and are variously applied and assessed by the practitioners. The earlier tendency in the helping professions of seeing various theories as virtually closed systems whose ramparts needed to be protected against contamination and assault from other systems has all but disappeared

Much of the growing comfort with the dynamic growth and development of the theories and a move away from cultism and dogmatism has resulted from the expansion of the research base of each system. As more research on various uses and outcomes of such use for each theory is carried out, with the predominance of findings that support the effectiveness of each system in various situations, there is a lessening of the need to preach and seek to win converts (Rubin, 1985; Thomlison, 1984). This has been supplanted by a growing comfort with explorations and experimentation resulting in changes and modifications of systems as data emerge.

Throughout, however, there continues to be an emphasis on the client's reality: the inherent thrust to growth, health, and strength, the ability to reason, to take responsibility, to change both self and situation, to adjust, to plan reflectively for both the present and future, and to be accountable within the realities in which lives are lived. This theme is not a naïve one that holds that a client can change all aspects of his or her reality; the crushing impact of poverty, racism, oppression, and lack of the basic necessities of life for so many is understood and decried. But within there is a theme that is less pessimistic than before of the extent to which change can take place.

Undoubtedly there are differences in the relative weighting of the various components of the client's reality within and among the spectrum of theories. There are also differences in the perception of the potential for change of individuals, groups, and systems. But again there is more consensus than disagreement on the importance of the components of the significant environments and their mixture as well as the client's inner life. An inherent theme here is to view the client more as an equal, a fellow human being in search for meaning, rather than as an interesting object for study (Saleebey, 1993).

What is Still to Be Done?

We have come far in our quest for the optimal method of tapping the richness of our theoretical diversity for the clients and the various systems and subsystems of reality. But just as certainly we have far to go. Clearly we have advanced in incorporating a concept of a pluralistic methods approach to practice and need to do so with theories. All of the theories presented speak about their application or work with individuals, families, and groups and systems, although differentially ranking their order of importance.

A further methodological challenge for all theories relates to the macro components of practice. Especially here in North America, we are still a long way from putting behind us longstanding intra-familial micro/micro tensions. We have long hoped that as we became more comfortable with theoretic and methodological plurality we would move toward a resolution of this issue.

As mentioned in Chapter 1, for a theory to be relevant to social work, it must speak to the "person-in-situation" paradigm and how change is brought about in each factor of this paradigm, including, of course, "the situation." Thus, even the most individualistic-based therapy must understand and address the larger systems that impinge on the lives of our clients to be truly a social work theory. This is relevant for understanding systems and situations in themselves as well as in their potential to make an impact on individuals, dyads, families, groups and systems.

Thus, each of our theories needs to examine its potential and relevance for macro practice. For example, meditation, a system one would consider to be far away from macro practice, does address the potential impact of its methods on community life and social change. Others do so differentially. It is hoped that as we move forward in this task of boundary opening and crossing, more attention will be given to the application of all of our theories to large systems practice.

All of the articles in this volume were written by colleagues practicing in North America, but the focus of the writing is much broader. In this way the extent to which each theory is applicable to a multicultural clientele is addressed, much more intensively than in earlier editions. Whether we have fully examined the extent to which each system has culture-wide application needs to be left as an open question. As the profession becomes more and more worldwide, with a commonality of values, knowledge, skills, and comfort with theoretical plurality, much work remains to be done in examining the relative efficacy of each system in relation to the culture or cultures in which it is practiced.

It is gratifying to note the extent to which the research base of most of our theories has expanded. All of the references are much richer than before, not only from the perspective of being updated since the last edition, but also reflecting the amount of research that has been conducted to test out various aspects of a theory or the application of a theory to a particular setting, problem, or client group. As mentioned earlier, with an increased number of doctoral graduates, each of whom has completed a theory-based dissertation, we have a rich store of theory-based research available to us.

What we still need, of course, is more work that focuses precisely on the differential use of theories in similar situations. In other words, can we begin to demonstrate that there are different outcomes when differential theories are used in similar situations?

Interesting as such questions are from a conceptual perspective, of perhaps even more importance is the responsibility to continue to expand our knowledge as to when the use of a particular theory is counterindicated. Accompanying the earlier-mentioned growing comfort with openness to change in theories is an expanded readiness to understand that not all theories are useful for all clients all of the time. This is aided by a minimalization of viewing theories as belief systems.

The authors of the various chapters have addressed this question well. Often the comments about counterindications are speculative, stemming from a rich experience with a particular theory's use. We need to continue our efforts to expand our knowledge through rigorous testing with regard to when the use of a particular system is counterindicated. This is particularly important in view of the North American tendency to adulate fashion and thus to have some theories "in style" over others at different times and in different situations.

There appears to be much less effort in trying to develop only our own theories. Rather, there is a comfort that we need to accept knowledge wherever it is found and in working with others to comfortably seek to find ways of drawing on our own strength from our own practices. With the tendency to have theories change in style and timeliness, their popularity frequently changes, with some coming back into style from time to time; role theory is a good example of this.

Research Challenges

From the perspective of theory and social work practice, there are a number of research challenges. One important component of this relates to the earlier-mentioned question of fashion (Shulman, 1993). This question of why some theories are more popular in some parts of the profession and at different times and places is an interesting one. Apart from the sociological impact, the effect on practice of these undulating periods needs to be examined. Related to this is the concomitant question of why some systems have become mainstream and others remain on the periphery of practice. If there were evidence that this was related to specific utility, the question would not be of much importance.

But few such data exist. It appears that the critical variables have not yet been identified. The reality of having some theories differentially in fashion over others means that some clients are deprived of various approaches to therapy based on reasons extraneous to the needs of the presenting situation. In this way clients can be harmed; this factor then makes the issue a question of ethics.

A second research challenge facing us relates to the critical importance of theory in practice. As discussed in Chapter 1, an essential premise of this volume, and one that is a major tenet of the profession, is that responsible practice needs to be founded on sound theory. We have long proclaimed this but have not always acted as if it were so. The task we now face is to demonstrate that this is true—or better still, as researchers to ask if it is true.

One still meets colleagues in practice who proclaim that they do not need theory nor do they use it. However, in these instances I think that these persons are theory-rich, as is evidenced when they talk about a client. However, it appears their theory has become so intuitive to them that it is difficult for them to explicate it. As a researcher I have to accept that they may be right, and that my explanations may be only a rationalization to soothe my being challenged in this way.

I have thought about this and have speculated on the question of how one goes about testing either of these hypotheses as to whether the quality of outcome is related to soundness of theory or skill at empathy or some other factor. This conundrum raises a series of possible questions for examination. For the most part these are the same questions I raised before in earlier editions:

1. What theories do people say drives their practice?
2. How much do clinicians know about the theories they follow?
3. Does one have to have a strong theory base, or is it enough to believe in one?
4. Is it possible to observe differences in outcomes when clinicians do not profess to practice from theory or use theory as a basis for diagnosis?
5. Can we see differences in outcomes in cases where different theoretical bases are used?
6. How much difference is there in outcomes of persons who do not profess to practice from theory or use theory as a basis for diagnosis?
7. Rather than theory, do we need to give more attention to technique—that is, to what we do for, with, and to a client rather than what we think our theory tells us to do?

Of course, these are highly generic questions, each of which lends itself to a multitude of diverse specific research projects. However, until we begin to address the general question of the relationship of theory to practice, we need to humbly accept that we do not know.

We must then live with the reality that much of what we do in practice rests on the accumulation of practice wisdom, skills, technique, and ethical commitment. However daunting the task, we ought not fear it. There is abundant evidence that what we do helps people. Clients are better off as a result of our interventions with them and

our ability to help understand and alter their significant environments. But we need to do much more to make precise a further question asked some years ago by Kendell and Butcher (1982): "What intervention, conducted by what therapist, with what clients to resolve their psychosocial dysfunction, produces what effects?"

The answers to challenges such as these will not come from one or two breakthrough kinds of studies, but through a myriad of small, well-designed, carefully conducted projects that together, in a step-by-step manner, will help us to build this needed further body of tested knowledge. As mentioned earlier, one place where we can look for help in this area is the population of our doctoral students and their dissertations. In this arena many areas of theory are tested but often overlooked in the need for our social work doctors to become immersed in the realities of practice. In so doing they often lose the opportunity to pursue their theoretical research interests further (Harrison & Thyer, 1988).

The Comparison of Theories

One of the premises of this book is that we should increase our efforts to use our various theories in a differential manner. In other words, we need to enhance our efforts to match theory to clients and situation rather than theory to therapist. Since theories have different value bases and alternate views of what constitutes helping, so too do clients. By having our range of theories analyzed from the perspective of clients, it may well be that more efforts at matching a client's profile to a theory profile would foster the formulation of a "client-friendly" strategy of helping (Souflee, 1993).

However, one of the challenges facing anyone interested in the therapeutic applications of our theoretical plurality is how to find a way to compare theories that appear to be so divergent. If we really wish to implement an interlocking perspective, we need to find a way that helps us see where theories are similar and where they are different (Corey, 1995).

Implications for Practice

As the above comments indicate, the premise of this work is that in spite of apparent differences there is a high degree of consensus between and among the various theories, and more importantly the theoreticians and the factors that combine to make up a practice theory. The differences emerge when we put specificity to each factor. If we accept this premise of a higher level of consensus among different thought systems than is usually considered, important questions emerge related to the nature of practice from an interlocking theoretical perspective. Perhaps the most important one is the extent to which a practitioner can and should be knowledgeable about and comfortable with the range of theoretical systems here presented and others that may emerge (Shaw & Compton, 2003).

To answer this, an essential question that remains to be tested further is how strongly practice is linked to theory. We have taken the position that they are very strongly linked but are aware that others do not agree.

But much of this is speculation. It would be cynical in the extreme to suggest that these theories have no influence on practice, but I think it would it would be equally naïve to imply that practitioners, consciously, deliberately, and consistently formulate their interventive strategies from a specific conceptual base (Reid, 1984).

Until proven otherwise, our position is that all of the various theories are important. If so, it is our responsibility as a profession to be aware of each, to strive to understand each, and to deliberately attempt to utilize aspects of each system in our practice when appropriate (Hawkins & Fraser, 1981). Only if we identify particular theoretical orientations from an ideological perspective can we avoid a commitment to look for the utility in each system.

I believe we are now past an impression or conviction that adherence to one approach to practice by definition excluded others, or, in looking more broadly, that there was some component of disloyalty or some quality of Machiavellian manipulation to attempt to move from one approach to another depending on the situation, the setting, the resources, the persons, or the request. One could support a mono-theory approach if it were held that the various theories are mutually exclusive and contradictory. This is much less true if one is committed to the concept of a large element of interconnectedness and inter-influences (Meyer, 1983).

Does this position mean that we need to know something of all the theories here discussed? I believe it does. We need to be acquainted with at least the basic parameters of each and, most important, their potential to help and to hurt. In many aspects of our lives we deal with a high degree of diversity. We are able to absorb large amounts of information about many topics and issues—so too with theories. It is possible to address this diversity in a knowing and responsible way.

Since every theory does address many of the same questions, once we understand the profile of a theory and how it addresses a range of these specifics, we can incorporate the profiles of many theories into our armamentarium of interventive resources. Colleagues in other disciplines deal with an even greater profile of diversity; so too can we. Our colleagues in medicine do it, philosophers do it, as do English scholars, and indeed all disciplines, as knowledge is tested and advanced (Scriven, 1998).

I am not suggesting that we need to be fully proficient in each system, but we do need to know the dimensions, potentials, and limitations of each. If not, as mentioned elsewhere, we may be depriving a client of access to a form of help that might be of particular benefit because of a goodness of fit between the theory and the client (Smid & Van Kreeken, 1984).

There is a second reason why we need to be informed about all systems: because clients expect that we will be resources for them when they are seeking help. For example, a client may be considering a particular type of therapy that has been found to be inappropriate for the kind of person he or she is. With the understanding that we need to respect a client's decision, we also know that our opinions are frequently viewed as all-knowing and all-powerful by many of our clients, and our viewpoints about particular systems will be of considerable import to them (Siporin, 1975).

The Way Ahead

It is difficult to predict with certainty where we are going as a profession from the perspective of theoretical plurality. Clearly we are beyond the point where we have to advocate for it. It is no longer a concept that appears to be "off the wall." Rather there is an appreciation, awe, and wonderment regarding the immense yet exciting challenge that this reality presents. This in turn is accompanied by an understanding and acceptance that to translate these convictions to evidenced material will be a long, slow process. But it is one that is worth the prize.

There are many directions in which we can and ought to go, and each of us must find our own way. We began this volume with some help from Alice (Carroll, 1891), and we end in the same vein: "Alice asked, `Would you tell me, please, which way I ought to go from here?' `That depends a good deal on where you want to get to,' said the Cheshire Cat."

References

Carrol, L. (1891). Through the looking glass. London: Collier-McMillan, 1963.

Caspi, Y. (1992). A continuum theory for social work knowledge. *Journal of Sociology and Social Welfare*, 19(3) 105–120.

Corey, G. (1995). *Theory and practice of group counseling* (4th ed.) Pacific Grove, CA: Brooks Cole Publishing.

Curnock, K., & Hardicker, P. (1979). *Towards practice theory*. London: Routlidge and Keegan Paul.

Harrison, D. F., & Thyer, B. A. (1988). Doctoral research on social work practice. *Journal of Social Work Education*, 24, 107–114.

Hawkins, J. D., & Fraser, M. W. (1981). Theory and practice in delinquency prevention. *Social Work Research and Abstracts*, 17(4), 3–13.

Imre-Wells, R. (1984). The nature of knowledge in social work. *Social Work*, 29(1) 51–56.

Kendell, P. C., & Butcher, J. N. (Eds.) (1982). *Handbook of research methods in clinical psychology*. New York: J. Wiley.

Kiritsis, E. (2007). *String theory in a nutshell. Introduction to modern string theory*. Princeton/New York: Princeton University Press.

Lewis, H. (1982). *The intellectual base of social work practice*. New York: Haworth Press,

Meyer, C. M. (1983). Selecting appropriate practice models. In A. Rosenblatt & D. Waldfogel (Eds.), *Handbook of clinical social work* (pp. 731–749). San Francisco: Jossey Bass.

Mishne, J. M. (1993). *The evolution and application of clinical theory*. New York: Free Press.

Morris, T. (1997). Is it possible to know when theories are obsolete? In M. Bloom & W. C. Klein (Eds.), *Controversial issues in human behavior in the social environment* (pp. 71–78). Boston: Allyn & Bacon.

Reid, W. J. (1984). Treatment of choice of choice of treatments: an essay review. *Social Work Research and Abstracts*, 20(2), 33–38.

Rubin, A. (1985). Practice effectiveness: More grounds for optimism. *Social Work*, 30, 469–476.

Saleebey, D. (1993). Theory and the generation and subversion of knowledge. *Journal of Sociology and Social Welfare*, 20(1), 5–25.

Scriven, M. (1998). Minimalist theory: the least that practice requires. *American Journal of Evaluation*, 19, 57–70.

Shaw, I., & Compton, A. (2003). Theory, like mist on spectacles, obscures vision. *Evaluation*, 9(9), 192–204.

Shulman, L. (1993). Developing and testing a practice theory: An interactional perspective. *Social Work*, 38(1.Jan.), 91–93.

Siporin, M. (1975). *Introduction to social work practice* (chapters 4 and 5). New York: Macmillan.

Smid, G., & Van Kreeken, R. (1984). Notes on theory and practice of social work: A comparative view. *British Journal of Social Work*, 14(1), 11–22.

Souflee, J. F. (1993). A metatheoretical framework for social work practice. *Social Work*, 38(3 May), 317–333.

Thomlison, R. J. (1984). Something works. Evidence from practice effectiveness studies. *Social Work*, 29(Jan-Feb), 51–56.

Thyer, B. A. (1993). Social work theory and practice research: The approach of logical positivism. *Social Work and Social Science Review*, 4(1) 5–26.

Thyer, B. A. (1994). Are theories for practice necessary? No! *Journal of Social Work Education*, 30, 147–151.

Thyer, B. A. (2008). The potentially harmful effects of theory in social work. In B. A. Thyer (Ed.), *Comprehensive handbook of social work and social welfare: Volume II–Human behavior in the social environment* (pp. 519–541). New York: Wiley.

Index